Queensland

& The Great Barrier Reef

Justine Vaisutis

Lindsay Brown, Simone Egger, Miriam Raphael

Contents

Far North Queensland p365
Cairns, Islands & Highlands p327
Cape York Peninsula & Gulf Savannah p394
Townsville & North Coast p287
Whitsunday Coast p250
Outback Queensland p416
Capricorn Coast p222
Fraser Coast p195
Darling Downs p151
Sunshine Coast p171
Brisbane p75
Around Brisbane p115
Gold Coast p127

Destination Queensland

Take a dip in the Queensland sunshine, mill about in its intoxicating glow and bask in its luscious heat. Adjust the temperature gauge and slide the pace down to a blissful, languid state.

This is the holiday state – the Sunshine State – where people head to ward off the ailments of urban decay and winter chills. Get your medicinal fix on the sandy white beaches, but don't dally – there's a whole lot more to this mighty swathe of Australia to keep you captivated.

A sunburnt outback dominates the interior, terra firma untouched for centuries, with miles of red-sand wilds and humbling horizons. The bronzed hues switch to azure blues peppered with all the colours of the rainbow in the depths of the Great Barrier Reef. For deep rich greens, immerse yourself in one of the many rainforests; marvel at the wealth of wildlife dwelling beneath the exquisite Daintree Rainforest's lush canopy.

Stock up on city culture in Brisbane or Cairns and overindulge on the heady Gold Coast. Then test your mettle with white-water rafting, scuba diving and snorkelling, bushwalking, horse riding, surfing, bungee jumping, skydiving or rock climbing…

When you've absorbed enough culture, cuisine and fun, slip into the calm of a national park. Whether you're after stark oases, dense Australian bush or subtropical forests, Queensland's smorgasbord of conservation areas has a flavour to suit your palate.

Lastly, don't forget to exploit one of the state's greatest assets – the genuine hospitality of Queenslanders, whose affable humour permeates all the varied cultural and visual landscapes to be found here.

JOHN BANAGAN

Highlights

Walk through lush tropical rainforest and swim in sparkling waters at Mossman Gorge (p375)

Set sail for a secluded anchorage in the Whitsunday Islands (p266)

Aborigines from Tjapukai Cultural Park (p333), Cairns, making fire

OTHER HIGHLIGHTS

- Partake in a tipple at one of the wineries of the Granite Belt (p157)
- Take a wild ride at a Gold Coast theme park (p135) or watch wildlife at Australia Zoo (p174)
- Visit the eerie rock tunnels created by ancient volcanic activity in remote Undara National Park (p408)
- Surf by day and dine at some of Queensland's best restaurants by night at Noosa (p181)

JOHN BANAGAN

Venture to the beautiful Wet Tropics World Heritage Area at Cape Tribulation (p381), the end of the road for conventional vehicles

Live it up with the locals at the Birdsville Races (p434)

RUSSELL MOUNTFORD

MICHAEL AW

Snorkel the reefs encircling Heron Island (p232)

RICHARD I'ANSON

Take a sand safari to the wreck of the *Maheno* on Fraser Island (p210)

LEONARD DOUGLAS ZELL

Dive one of the natural wonders of the world, the Great Barrier Reef (p57)

Cycle or walk along the river city's waterfront in Brisbane (p84)

CHRIS MELLOR

Sandblows shelter Lake Wabby (p212) from the eastern beach of Fraser Island

A humpback whale breaches off Harvey Bay (p204)

Take a unique journey through the Gulf Savannah on the *Gulflander* (p410)

Follow the twists and turns of sandstone cliffs at Carnarvon Gorge (p247)

Revel in the nightlife in Cairns (p342), the
party capital of north Queensland

PAUL DYMOND

MARTIN COHEN

Discover the diverse ecology of World Heritage–
listed Fraser Island (p209) on a rainforest walk

Savour ethereal views while bushwalking in the Glass House Mountains (p173)

RICHARD I'ANSON

Getting Started

Queensland has been a permanent fixture on the itineraries of foreign and domestic holiday-makers for generations. Friendly and welcoming to travellers of any ilk, the well-trodden path here accommodates backpackers, families, couples and retirees living it up.

In the vast majority of the state finely tuned infrastructure and tourism services make life easy for visitors. This is particularly so in the southeast, where transport, accommodation and attractions are served up on a platter. For the majority of the year, they can be booked at the last minute.

Queensland is immense though, and the further north you travel the more convenient it is to drive, particularly if you're not in the state for very long, as distances between towns lengthen. The same applies to Queensland's outback, where you will need to be prepared for the harsher conditions. The good news is that transport, whether private or public, can be arranged very easily throughout the state, and comes in budget-friendly and creature-comfort varieties. Unless you've got all the time in the world up your sleeve, an itinerary of some sort, even if it's vague, is highly recommended; you'll benefit most from focussing on one area for short trips.

WHEN TO GO

Australia's winter months are typically Queensland's busiest time for tourism – it's the place the Mexicans (the Queensland term for anyone from south of the border) head to escape the cold southern winters. The main tourist season stretches from April to November, and the official high season is from June to September. As with elsewhere in the country, the Easter (April), winter (June and July) and Christmas (December and January) breaks are also considered to be high season. Australian families swarm into the Sunshine State on school holidays and *everything* is booked out.

Now you know when everyone else goes, but when should *you* go? Queensland's climate isn't really broken up into summer and winter; it's a tropical state so it has wet and dry seasons. Loosely, the dry season runs from April to December (the main tourist season). In the far north (anything north of Cairns) and outback Queensland, however, January to March (December to April in Cape York) is the wet season and the heat and humidity can make life pretty uncomfortable. Once the monsoonal rains of the Wet arrive, which usually occurs in January and February, most parts of Cape York Peninsula and the Gulf of Carpentaria, and

See Climate Charts (p440) for more information.

DON'T LEAVE HOME WITHOUT...

- Plenty of light summer gear such as shorts, cotton dresses and flip-flops
- An umbrella or lightweight raincoat for tropical downpours
- Sunscreen, sunglasses and a hat to deflect fierce UV radiation (see p469)
- Travel insurance (p445) for any adrenalin-charged activities, ie bungee jumping, white-water rafting or rock climbing
- Double checking the visa situation (p450)
- Your favourite hangover, seasickness and motion-sickness cures (if you need them)

much of the outback, are often inaccessible except by light aircraft. The Daintree region virtually shuts down and the Bloomfield Track is often impassable. Cooktown too only has limited services between November and May. Deadly 'stingers' (box jellyfish) also frequent the waters at this time (see the boxed text on p226).

The further south you head the less are the effects of the wet season. For the vast majority of the state, anytime between June and October is the perfect time to visit – the extreme heat and stifling humidity of summer have been replaced by warm sunny days and refreshingly cool nights.

COSTS & MONEY

The Australian dollar has experienced roller-coaster exchange rates over the last three years, but despite its increasing value against the US dollar, British pound and Euro at the time of writing, Australia remains an inexpensive destination. Generally the cost of living is cheaper than in the USA, Canada and European countries. An exception is manufactured goods, which are often marked up to cover the cost of import.

Budget travellers and backpackers who plan to stay at hostels or camp, travel by bus, cook their own meals (with the odd splurge) and take in the sights can get by on a budget of around $60 per day. A traveller who plans to hire a car, see the sights, stay in midrange hotels, motels and B&Bs and eat out should budget for around $150 per day; two people travelling together could do it for $200 to $250 per day.

Many accommodation options increase their tariffs only slightly for family rooms as opposed to doubles, and Queensland is littered with museums and galleries that offer free or very cheap entry for kids. Even the expensive child-magnets, such as theme parks, often discount their entry fees for children by up to 50%, but virtually anywhere that has an admission charge offers a family ticket covering two adults and at least two children. Queensland's biggest benefit for families is its climate, which is perfectly suited to outdoor activities. The beach and playgrounds are free, and a day's bike ride in any of the cities is relatively cheap.

The biggest cost in any trip to Queensland will be transport, simply because the state is so big. Car rental is relatively cheap, but fuel costs can quickly chew through your wallet, particularly if you're travelling long distances.

TRAVEL LITERATURE

For a taste of things to come amid Queensland's varied flavours, pick up some predeparture reading to imbue a sense of place.

Thea Astley's *It's Raining in Mango* (1987) is an almost tangible taste of Queensland's history. It follows a Sydney family's relocation to Cooktown, and their exposure to the tragic and murderous clash of indigenous and European cultures.

The White Earth (2004) by Andrew McGahan is a cross-generational saga encompassing the 150-year history of white settlement of the Darling Downs, with an insight into Native Title and the growing alienation of rural white Australia.

Zigzag Street (2000) by Nick Earls is the humourous, engaging story of a 20-something bachelor coming to terms with social pressure, life and love in contemporary Brisbane.

Discovery Guide to Outback Queensland (2003), published by Queensland Museum Publishing, is a vivid travel book about life, history and culture in the Queensland outback, with useful travel information as well.

LONELY PLANET INDEX

One litre of petrol: 90c to $1

One litre of bottled water: $3

Glass of XXXX beer: $2.50

Souvenir T-shirt: $20

Fresh fruit juice: $5 to $6

TOP FIVES

Must-see Movies
One of the best predeparture and planning aids is a dose of visual stimulation, which is best done on a comfy couch with a bowl of popcorn in one hand and a remote in the other. The following flicks provide sumptuous insights to Aussie culture. See p30 for full reviews.

- *Muriel's Wedding* (1994) Director: PJ Hogan
- *Praise* (1998) Director: John Curran
- *Blurred* (2002) Director: Evan Clarry
- *Gettin' Square* (2003) Director: Jonathan Teplitzky
- *Swimming Upstream* (2003) Director: Russell Mulcahy

Top Reads
If you want to digest a sense of Queensland's culture, history, contemporary issues and people on a much deeper level, then the following top reads will fill your head with a genuine depiction. Many have won critical acclaim. See p31 for full reviews.

- *On Our Selection* (1899) Steele Rudd
- *Fly Away Peter* (1982) David Malouf
- *It's Raining in Mango* (1987) Thea Astley
- *Praise* (1992) Andrew McGahan
- *Heart Country* (2002) Kerry McGinnis

Festivals & Events
Australians certainly know how to celebrate, and Queenslanders are no exception. There's almost always something interesting going on around the state. The following is our Top Five, but for a comprehensive list flick to p443 and see the Festivals & Events headings in individual chapters.

- Easter in the Country, Roma (p166) Easter.
- Ten Days in the Towers, Charters Towers (p309) Late April to early May.
- Cairns Festival, Cairns (p337) September.
- Brisbane Riverfestival, Brisbane (p97) September.
- Woodford Folk Festival, Maleny (p193) December.

Rae Wear's *Johannes Bjelke-Petersen: The Lord's Premier* (2002) provides readers with an understanding of the conservative side of Queensland's culture, and the prevalence of the Aussie battler ethos in this state.

INTERNET RESOURCES

Courier Mail (www.couriermail.news.com.au) Website for Brisbane's daily newspaper, with current affairs, weather information and features.

Lonely Planet (www.lonelyplanet.com) Great destination summaries, links to related sites and the Thorn Tree.

Queensland Holidays (www.queenslandholidays.com.au) Official tourism site, providing comprehensive information on destinations, accommodation, attractions, tours and more.

Queensland Parks and Wildlife Service (www.epa.qld.gov.au) Official site with extensive information about Queensland's national parks and conservation areas.

Tourism Tropical North Queensland (www.tropicalaustralia.com.au) Official tourism site of the far north, with excellent information on the Great Barrier Reef and destinations from Cairns north.

Itineraries
CLASSIC ROUTES

THE SENSATIONAL SOUTH
Two weeks/Gold Coast to Sunshine Coast & Fraser Island

Start in **Coolangatta** (p144) and warm your toes in the sea lapping the fine beaches. Try your hand at surfing, but save some energy for further north. Head up the Gold Coast Hwy through the meandering resort towns and plant yourself in the eternal party that is **Surfers Paradise** (p133). Let loose your inhibitions (and your tummy) at the **Gold Coast Theme Parks** (p135).

When you've thoroughly exhausted yourself, hit the Pacific Hwy and head north to **Brisbane** (p75). Take in the sights before continuing your trek north. On the way, veer onto Glass House Mountains Rd and snake your way through the **Glass House Mountains** (p173). Soak up the languid Sunshine Coast with its wide beaches at **Maroochy** (p177) or **Coolum** (p181). Another half-hour north and you can slip into **Noosa's** (p181) classy milieu and drink in the sublime beaches and first-class cuisine.

Then journey north to **Hervey Bay** (p202). If you're here in season, go whale-watching, then head to enigmatic **Fraser Island** (p209) and bask in its endless beach, ethereal lakes and dense rainforest.

You can cover the distance of this 390km road trip in two weeks, but a month or more would be better. Three days on Fraser Island and four days in Noosa alone are recommended, and then you'll need a few days to recover from the fun of the Gold Coast with a good stretch on the Sunshine Coast.

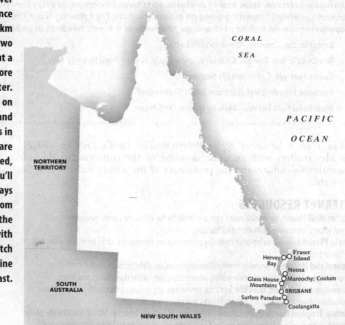

RAINFORESTS, ISLANDS & REEF   Two weeks/Mackay to Whitsunday Islands & Cairns

Begin your rainforest and reef adventure in **Mackay** (p254), where you can mill about the Art Deco downtown. Then head west on the Peak Downs Hwy and Mackay-Eungella Rd to course through the lush **Pioneer Valley** (p260). An hour's drive will place you in mountainous and magnificent **Eungella National Park** (p262). Go platypus spotting or paddle in the swimming pools beneath the tumbling Araluen Falls at **Finch Hatton Gorge** (p262).

Head back east to the Bruce Hwy and then trek north for around two hours to sizzling **Airlie Beach** (p270). Immerse yourself in the heady haze before choosing which way to see the **Whitsunday Islands** (p265). Spend a couple of days drifting around verdant islands, snorkelling in azure waters and sunbaking on heavenly Whitehaven Beach.

Pack yourself up and continue the northern adventure along the Bruce Hwy, journeying for around three hours before hitting **Townsville** (p289). Mingle with the locals, scale Castle Hill and head out to **Magnetic Island** (p300) for a two-day retreat.

From Townsville, continue north on the Bruce Hwy for two or three hours and detour east from Tully to **Mission Beach** (p318). Chill out in the isolated settlements and meddle in the tropical surrounds. Another two hours north takes you to **Cairns** (p328) with its global village ambience, multicultural cuisine and access to the **Great Barrier Reef** (p57). Snorkel, dive, sail or fly over the biggest reef system in the world, and marvel at its colours and the myriad marine life.

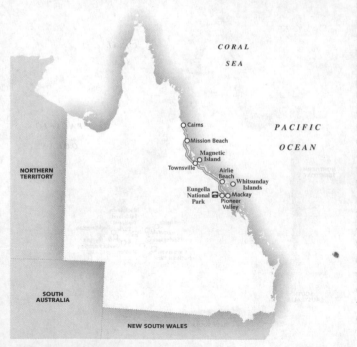

With two weeks you can cover the highlights of this 880km journey, but why not indulge in a long Whitsundays sail, a couple of days on the Reef and a full exploration of Townsville, Mackay, Magnetic Island and Mission Beach? Three to five weeks would lessen the tempo and enhance your experience of this strip of the Queensland coast.

ROADS LESS TRAVELLED

CAPRICORN FLING

One week/Rockhampton to Emerald
& Carnarvon National Park

Start off in **Rockhampton** (p232), the 'beef capital of Australia'. Potter through the gracious architecture, learn about Aboriginal culture at the Dreamtime Cultural Centre, tuck into an outstanding steak and yeeehaaa with the cowboys at a Great Western Hotel rodeo.

Hit the Burnett Hwy and head southwest for 40km to historic **Mt Morgan** (p237) with its heritage buildings. Continue your expedition south, following the Burnett and Leichhardt Hwys southwest for a taste of life on the land; go a drovin' at **Myella Farm Stay** (p238).

Turn yourself north again and head up Fitzroy Rd to connect with the Capricorn Hwy, which cuts a route through the Queensland outback. Spend some time in the **Blackdown Tableland National Park** (p243) and ogle at the infinite views, Aboriginal rock art and beautiful waterfalls.

Head west to **Emerald** (p243), the entry to the Capricorn hinterland. Just west of here are the **gemfields** (p245), where you can fossick in one of the world's richest sapphire deposits. From Emerald, drive south to **Springsure** (p246), with its sea of sunflowers, and on to **Rolleston** (p247), the northern gateway to **Carnarvon National Park** (p247). The highlight of this rugged conservation area is the stunning **Carnarvon Gorge** (p247), where you can explore the towering sandstone cliffs, waterfalls and Aboriginal art.

Bushwalkers and nature lovers could spend close to a week alone in Blackdown Tableland National Park. But you can exploit this rugged 600km Capricorn trip in seven to 10 days and get your money's worth. If you strike it lucky in the gemfields you could easily extend your journey to two weeks.

THE NORTHERN TREK   Two weeks/Cooktown to Cape York

To cover the magnificent, untouched ground from Cooktown to Cape York you'll need a 4WD to get you off the beaten track, and back on it again.

Begin your northern adventure in **Cooktown** (p387), where you can peek into the town's history and culture at Nature's Powerhouse and James Cook Historical Museum. Then head northwest on McIver Rd into isolated, wild **Lakefield National Park** (p399), Queensland's second largest. Camp a while and explore the diverse environments and wildlife – the barramundi fishing and croc spotting are unparalleled here.

From the north of the park head west to hook up with the Peninsula Development Rd. A drive of 100km north will put you in **Coen** (p401), the Cape's 'capital' and gateway to the Rokeby section of **Mungkan Kandju National Park** (p401). Push on for another 100km or so and turn east onto Archer River Rd to delve into **Iron Range National Park** (p401), Australia's largest conservation area of lowland tropical forest, with spectacular birdlife and flora.

From here you can backtrack to the Peninsula Development Rd and head north for around 120km to enjoy some creature comforts in the mining town of **Weipa** (p401), on the cape's western coast. But to reach the top of the Cape you need to drive the 200km or so extent of Telegraph Rd, which skirts Jardine River National Park. Here you can swim in the gorgeous natural pools at Twin Falls. Once you cross the **Jardine River** (p403) you're only 70km or so from a smattering of communities and the tip of Oz.

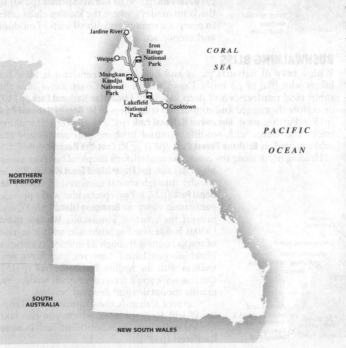

You'll need at least two weeks to cover the ground of this rugged 900km trek. This is frontier country, but your efforts will be rewarded with scenery and landscape few travellers witness. If getting away from it all is your idea of paradise, go nuts and take anywhere from three to five weeks.

TAILORED TRIPS

QUEENSLAND FOR KIDS

Queensland is a playground for kids of all ages, offering a host of treats to keep inquisitive minds and unyielding staminas entertained. The **Gold Coast Theme Parks** (p135) provide days of fun with immense water slides, Hollywood heroes and heart-stopping rides. In Brisbane the bends and turns of **Streets Beach** (p85) take on the form of an outdoor beach, surrounded by parkland and playgrounds. BBQs and picnic spots make it an all-day affair. Nearby, the **Sciencentre** (p85) inside the Queensland Museum keeps inquisitive young minds in a suspended state of fascination with interactive displays that make physics and chemistry downright fun.

Get the kids in touch with nature at **Australia Zoo** (p174) on the Sunshine Coast, where crocodile shows and koala cuddles will have them oohing for more. In Townsville they can spot Nemo and touch sea cucumbers and starfish at the giant **Reef HQ** (p293) aquarium. In Cairns, kids love a good splash in the saltwater **lagoon** (p333).

Sea kayaking (p136) in the gentle waters of the Gold Coast Broadwater is good fun for water babies, while bush babies will love **horse rides** (p136) through the Gold Coast hinterland.

Do some island-hopping and head to tropical **Daydream** (p279) or **Hamilton Islands** (p280) in the Whitsundays, where the kiddies clubs cater to energetic youngsters with all sorts of outdoor and indoor activities.

Cairns
Townsville
Daydream & Hamilton Islands
Sunshine Coast
Brisbane
Gold Coast

BUSHWALKING BLISS

With a bevy of national parks and bushland, Queensland is ideal for hikers who like to go bush. Down on the Gold Coast, delve into the subtropical rainforests and deep valleys of **Lamington National Park** (p149) or explore the rugged and untouched wilderness of **Mt Barney National Park** (p150). Further west, **Girraween National Park** (p158) has 17km of walking tracks and teems with wildlife. Around Brisbane you can escape the urban spread in **Brisbane Forest Park** (p87) or **Mt Coot-tha Reserve** (p86).

Heading north along the coast, you can trek for a couple of hours or a couple of days on the **Fraser Island Great Walk** (p208) or wander through coastal rainforest in **Conway National Park** (p277). Two spectacular walks provide panoramic views on **Brampton Island** (p263), and just off the coast of Townsville, **Magnetic Island** (p300) is like one big bushwalk, with a myriad of tracks running through its interior. It's nearby Hinchinbrook Island, however, that lures avid walkers with the mighty **Thorsborne Trail** (p315). On this walk you'll traverse unspoilt wilderness, granite mountains and deserted beaches.

North of Cairns is the exquisite Wet Tropics World Heritage Area, where you can take guided walks into the magnificent, lush **Daintree Rainforest** (p377).

Daintree Rainforest
Hinchinbrook Island
Magnetic Island
Conway National Park
Brampton Island
Fraser Island
Brisbane Forest Park & Mt Coot-tha Reserve
Mt Barney National Park
Lamington National Park
Girraween National Park

The Authors

JUSTINE VAISUTIS   Coordinating Author

Justine became a nomad as a child, living in South Africa and South Korea, then in Canberra, where she cultivated a love of warm places. As a teenager she experienced a Queensland winter and confused it with Utopia. She was happy to relive the fabrication for 'work'.

This is Justine's second Queensland title for Lonely Planet, having doused herself in the Queensland sun, dipped in its tepid waters and ogled at the Reef for *Australia & New Zealand on a Shoestring*. She accidentally left a snippet of her soul there, so she's looking forward to heading back soon.

My Queensland

If I had to choose favourites from Queensland's deep well of seductions, I'd start with a bohemian breakfast in Brisbane's West End (p105) to think it over. Then I'd ignore the task at hand and drive through the Sunshine Coast's Glass House Mountains (p173) and abscond to Fraser Island (p209) for some downtime in a freshwater lake. From here I'd have to skip up to Airlie Beach (p270) and weigh anchor somewhere unreachable in the waters of the Whitsunday Islands (p266) to gather my thoughts. After snorkelling on the Great Barrier Reef (p335), bushwalking on the islands and soaking up the sun, I'm sure I'd be ready to come up with a list of favourites.

Great Barrier Reef

Whitsunday Islands

Airlie Beach

Fraser Island

Glass House Mountains

Brisbane

LINDSAY BROWN

After completing a PhD in evolutionary genetics and spending a short period as a marine scientist and science editor, Lindsay started editing at Lonely Planet. There followed stints as a senior editor and series publishing manager of outdoor-activity guidebooks, where he was responsible for the Walking, Cycling, Diving & Snorkeling and Watching Wildlife series. As a Lonely Planet author Lindsay has contributed to several titles, including *Australia*. For this guide, he wrote the Capricorn Coast, Whitsunday Coast, Cape York Peninsula & Gulf Savannah and Outback Queensland chapters.

SIMONE EGGER

Simone works from Melbourne as a freelance photojournalist. Before authoring for Lonely Planet, Simone also had a stint as an editor. Travel has always been in her bio. For Simone, a road trip along Queensland's north coast and hinterland is bliss. Sure, it's about amazing beaches, lush rainforests, history and local people. But it's also about getting photos in front of as many 'big things' as roadside businesses can build. Simone wrote the Townsville & North Coast; Cairns, Islands & Highlands; and Far North Queensland chapters of this guide.

MIRIAM RAPHAEL

Miriam's first experience with the Sunshine State was a school project on cane toads when she was 10. Since then she has spent some of the best summers of her life in southeast Queensland. While Miriam has no complaints about sand, sea and over-ripe mangoes, it's the hinterland with its stunning national parks, great wineries, welcoming towns and a refreshing lack of Speedos that takes her back every time. Miriam wrote the Darling Downs chapter.

CONTRIBUTING AUTHORS

Michael Cathcart wrote the History chapter (p20). Michael lectures in Australian history at the Australian Centre, University of Melbourne. His published work includes an acclaimed abridgement of Manning Clark's six-volume classic *A History of Australia* (1993). He is the coeditor of *Stirring Australian Speeches* (2004) and is currently writing a history of water in Australia. Michael is well known as a former presenter on ABC Radio National and as the host of the ABC TV history series *Rewind*. He lives in Melbourne and is married to the playwright Hannie Rayson.

Professor Tim Flannery wrote the Environment chapter (p35). Tim's a naturalist and explorer and the author of a number of award-winning books, including *The Future Eaters, Throwim Way Leg* (an account of his adventures as a biologist working in New Guinea) and the landmark ecological history of North America, *The Eternal Frontier*. His latest book, written about Australia, is *Country*. Tim lives in Adelaide, where he is director of the South Australian Museum and a professor at the University of Adelaide.

Dr David Millar wrote the Health chapter (p466). David is a travel medicine specialist, diving doctor and lecturer in wilderness medicine who graduated in Hobart, Tasmania. He has worked as an expedition doctor with the Maritime Museum of Western Australia, accompanying a variety of expeditions around Australia. David is currently a medical director with the Travel Doctor in Auckland.

Thanks also for the contributions from **Steve Irwin**, who wrote the 'Crikey – Quarantine Matters!' boxed text on p441, and **David Kramer**, who wrote the 'Andrew McGahan' boxed text on p165.

Snapshot

After leading the charge as Australia's most conservative state for generations, Queensland and its population have spent the better part of a decade undergoing a mature evolution to reinvent the state's identity. Progressive leadership from the Queensland Labor Party has heralded an era of growth, not just in the physical sense (although relentless development, particularly in the densely populated southeast, continues on a healthy scale), but also in the areas of arts and culture. Some Queenslanders may grumble about the increasing price of property, but they are also happy to inhabit one of the fastest-growing areas of Australia.

The state has cemented itself as an accommodating location for film production. Alongside commercial projects, independent flicks reflecting contemporary and gritty themes are being nurtured as Queenslanders embrace their colourful character without apology (see p30). Festivals too, which once focussed on American-style country fairs, are now breeding grounds for innovative and multicultural expression – Brisbane's Pride Festival and Riverfestival (p96) and the Cairns Festival (p337) celebrate those cities' global flavours.

Some things remain constant, however. In local pubs outside of the cities you're likely to be engaged in a conversation about politics and the state of the environment. A growing awareness of Australia's role in global politics seeps into conversations and Queenslanders present opinionated and often polarised views about which allies the country should align itself with, or whether this should be a period of forging an independent approach. Controversial domestic issues, including the future of indigenous development and the state of immigration, or more pointedly, asylum seekers, also provide fodder for animated conversation, and regardless of which side of the fence you sit, there's a good chance you'll exit the conversation with information and viewpoints you may not have considered.

Queensland's landscape is constantly battered by the elements; bushfires can ravage the south for months at a time and the continual presence of drought, in either moderate or extreme degrees, incites talk about the future of the state's agricultural industry, as well as the pressing need to address a steady water shortage. In the far north a recurring topic of conversation is whether or not the state's crocodile numbers are too high. It seems an unsuspecting (or careless) visitor is attacked once a year, and the age-old question of controlled culling arises. The recent zoning changes to the Great Barrier Reef, implemented by the federal government, also get a healthy verbal workout. Locals are protective of this World Heritage Site, but they are also acutely aware of the impact that rezoning is likely to have on commercial fishing.

Most visitors will be encouraged at some stage to remark upon Queensland's magical climate. Queenslanders take genuine pride in inhabiting a corner of the country so well endowed with sunshine and warmth, and they love to hear of its medicinal qualities for visitors from 'temperature-challenged' quarters. Fortunately, the weather generally allows you to oblige, provoking genuine and affable smiles from the locals.

FAST FACTS

Population: 3.86 million

Cattle raised in Queensland: around 10.5 million

Percentage of Queenslanders who live in cities: 52%

Sporting colours: maroon and gold

Average number of babies born every year: 48,000

Average weekly family income: $800 to $1000

Unemployment rate: 5% to 7%

Percentage of homes with at least one bicycle in good working order: around 47%

Length of Queensland's coastline: 7400km

Inflation rate: 2.9%

History Michael Cathcart

INTRUDERS

In April 1770, Aborigines standing on a beach in southeastern Australia saw an astonishing spectacle out at sea. It was an English ship, the *Endeavour,* under the command of Lieutenant James Cook. His gentleman-passengers were English scientists visiting the Pacific to make astronomical observations and to investigate 'new worlds'. As they sailed north along the edge of this new-found land, Cook began drawing the first British chart of Australia's eastern coast. His map heralded the end of Aboriginal supremacy.

Michael Cathcart presented the ABC TV history series *Rewind.* He is a lecturer in history at the Australian Centre, the University of Melbourne.

A few days after that first sighting, Cook led a party of men ashore at a place whose name was Kurnell. Though the Kurnell Aborigines were far from welcoming, the *Endeavour*'s botanists were delighted to discover that the woods were teeming with unfamiliar plants. To celebrate this profusion, Cook renamed the place Botany Bay.

As his voyage northwards continued, Cook strewed English names the entire length of the coastline. In Queensland, these included Hervey Bay (after an English admiral), Dunk Island (after an English Duke), Cape Upstart, the Glass House Mountains and Wide Bay.

One night, off the great rainforests of the Kuku Yalanji Aborigines, in what is now known as Far North Queensland, the *Endeavour* was inching gingerly through the Great Barrier Reef when the crew heard the sickening sound of ripping timbers. They had run aground near a cape which today is a tourist paradise. But Cook was in a glowering mood: he named it Cape Tribulation 'because here began all our troubles'. Seven days later Cook managed to beach the wounded ship in an Aboriginal harbour named Charco (Cook renamed it Endeavour) where his carpenters patched the hull.

A brilliant, classic biography is *The Life of Captain James Cook* (1974) by JC Beaglehole. There are several Cook biographies online.

Back at sea, the *Endeavour* finally reached the northern tip of Cape York. On a small, hilly island (Possession Island), Cook raised the Union Jack and claimed the eastern half of the continent for King George III. His intention was not to dispossess the Aborigines, but to warn off other European powers – notably the Dutch, who had already charted much of the Aboriginal coast.

SETTLEMENT

In 1788, the English were back. On 26 January, 11 ships sailed into a harbour just north of Botany Bay. The First Fleet was under the command of a humane and diligent officer named Arthur Phillip. Under his leadership, the intruders cut down trees, built shelters and laid out roadways. They were building a prison settlement in the idyllic lands of the Eora people. Phillip called the place Sydney.

In the early years of the settlement, both the convicts and the free people of Sydney struggled to survive. Their early attempts to grow crops failed and the settlement relied on supplies brought in by ship. Fortunate or canny prisoners were soon issued with 'tickets of leave', which gave them the right to live and work as free men and women

TIMELINE

60,000 BC	1770
According to most experts, Aborigines settled in Australia.	English captain James Cook maps Australia's east coast in the scientific ship *Endeavour*. Runs aground on Great Barrier Reef.

on the condition that they did not attempt to return home before their sentences expired.

The convict system could also be savage, however. Women (who were outnumbered five to one) lived under constant threat of sexual exploitation. Female convicts who offended their jailers languished in the depressing 'female factories'. Male offenders were cruelly flogged and could be hanged even for such crimes as stealing. In 1803, English officers established a settlement to punish reoffenders at Port Arthur on the wild south coast of Tasmania.

The impact of these settlements on the Aborigines was devastating. Multitudes were killed by unfamiliar diseases such as smallpox; and in the years that followed many others succumbed to alcoholism and despair as they felt their traditional lands and life being wrenched away.

CONVICTS TO QUEENSLAND

By the 1820s, Sydney was a busy port, bustling with soldiers, merchants, children, schoolmistresses, criminals, preachers and drunks. The farms prospered, and in the streets, the children were chatting in a new accent which we would probably recognise today as 'Australian'.

The authorities now looked north to the lands of the Yuggera people, where they established another lonely penal colony at Moreton Bay. Here men, labouring under the command of the merciless Captain Logan, built their own prison cells and sweated on the farms they had cleared from the bush. These prisoners suffered such tortures that some welcomed death, even by hanging, as a blessed release.

Logan himself met a brutal end when he was bashed and speared while he was riding in the bush. Shortly after his murder, a group of soldiers reported that they had seen him on the far bank of a river screaming to be rescued. But as they rowed across to investigate, his tormented ghost melted into the heat.

Logan's miserable prison spawned the town of Brisbane, which soon became the administrative and supply centre for the farmers, graziers, loggers and miners who had occupied the region. But the great hinterland of Queensland remained remote and mysterious – in the firm control of its Aboriginal owners.

Robert Hughes' bestseller *The Fatal Shore* (1987) is a provocative read about convict history.

EXPLORERS & SETTLERS

That frontier was crossed in 1844, when an eccentric Prussian explorer named Ludwig Leichhardt led a gruelling 15-month trek from Brisbane to Port Essington (near today's Darwin). His journal – the first European travel guide to Australia's top end – would have secured his place in Australian history. But today he is remembered for the manner of his death. In 1848, his entire party vanished in the desert during an attempt to cross the continent. Journalists and poets wrote as if Leichhardt had been received into a Silent Mystery which lay at the heart of Australia. It might seem strange that Australians should sanctify a failed explorer, but Leichhardt – like two other dead explorers, Burke and Wills – satisfied a Victorian belief that a nation did not come of age until it was baptised in blood.

As Queensland formally separated from New South Wales in 1859, graziers, miners and small farmers were pushing further west and north.

Leichhardt's story inspired Patrick White's *Voss* (1957), revered by some as the great Australian novel.

1823	1840
Government explorer John Oxley surveys Moreton Bay (Brisbane) for a convict settlement. It is established the next year.	Squatters from New South Wales establish sheep runs on the Darling Downs.

Tom Petrie's *Reminiscences of Early Queensland* (1904) is a bushman's story of life with Aborigines. A Queensland classic.

Some whites established cooperative relations with local tribes, sharing the land and using Aborigines as stockmen or domestics. But others saw settlement as a tough Darwinian struggle between the British race and a primitive Stone Age people – a battle which it was the white's destiny to win. Indeed, squatters who ran sheep on the vast grasslands of the Darling Downs sometimes spoke as if they had taken possession of a great park where no other humans had ever lived. Today, Aborigines across the country tell stories of how white settlers shot whole groups of their people or killed them with poisoned food. Some Aboriginal tribes fought back, but the weapons of the white man were formidable – including the notorious Native Police, a government-backed death squad made up of Aborigines recruited from distant tribes.

Meanwhile, on the tropical coast, growers were developing a prosperous sugar-cane industry which relied on the sweat of thousands of labourers from the Solomons, Vanuatu and other Pacific islands. Known as the Kanakas, these workers endured harsh and sometimes cruel conditions that were considered intolerable for white workers (see the boxed text on p291).

GOLD & REVOLUTION

In 1871 an Aboriginal stockman named Jupiter spotted gold glinting in a waterhole near Charters Towers. His find triggered a gold rush which attracted thousands of prospectors, publicans, traders, prostitutes and quacks to the diggings. For a few exhilarating years, any determined miner, regardless of his class, had a real chance of striking it rich, and by the 1880s, Brisbane itself had grown prosperous on wool and gold. But by then life on the goldfields was changing radically. The easy gold was gone. The free-for-all had given way to an industry in which the company boss called the shots.

River of Gold (1994) by Hector Holthouse is a high-spirited novel set in the wild days of the Palmer River gold rush.

As displaced prospectors searched for work, the overheated economy of eastern Australia collapsed, throwing thousands of labouring families into the miseries of unemployment and hunger. The depression of the 1890s exposed stark inequalities as barefoot children scavenged in the streets. But this was Australia, 'the working man's paradise' – the land where the principle of 'a fair day's pay for a fair day's work' was a sacred text. As employers tried to drive down wages, a tough Queensland working class began to assert itself. Seamen, factory workers, miners, loggers and shearers organised themselves into trade unions to take on Queensland's equally tough bosses and shareholders.

'Banjo' Paterson's famous song 'Waltzing Matilda' was inspired by this strike.

The result was a series of violent strikes. The most famous erupted in 1891 after angry shearers proclaimed their socialist credo under a great gum tree, known as the 'Tree of Knowledge', at Barcaldine in central Queensland. As the strike spread, troopers, right-wing vigilantes and union militants clashed in bitter class warfare. The great radical poet Henry Lawson expected revolution: 'We'll make the tyrants feel the sting / O' those that they would throttle; / They needn't say the fault is ours / If blood should stain the wattle!'

The striking shearers were defeated, and their leaders jailed, by a government determined to suppress the unrest. But trade unions remained a powerful force in Australia for the next hundred years, and that strike

1872	1891
The gold rush sweeps into Charters Towers. Queensland is connected to Europe by telegraph.	A violent shearers' strike around Barcaldine establishes a labour legend.

contributed to the formation of a potent new force in Australian politics – the Australian Labor Party.

NATIONALISM

Whatever their politics, many Queenslanders still embody the gritty, independent but solidly white outlook that was so potent in colonial thinking. At end of the 19th century, Australian nationalist writers and artists idealised the people of 'the bush' and their code of 'mateship'. The most popular forum for this 'bush nationalism' was the *Bulletin* magazine, whose pages were filled with humour and sentiment about daily life, written by a swag of writers, most notably Henry Lawson and 'Banjo' Paterson.

But while writers were creating national legends, the politicians of Australia were forging a national constitution…

For more on the nationalist painters and writers, visit www.cultureandrecreation .gov.au/articles/bush/.

FEDERATION & WAR

On 1 January 1901, Australia became a federation. When the bewhiskered members of the new national parliament met in Melbourne, their first aim was to protect the identity and values of a European Australia from an influx of Asians and Pacific Islanders. Their solution was the White Australia Policy. Its bar to nonwhite immigrants remained a core Australian value for the next 70 years.

For whites, this was to be a model society, nestled in the skirts of the British Empire. Just one year later, in 1902, white women won the right to vote in federal elections. In a series of radical innovations, the government introduced a broad social welfare scheme and protected Australian wage levels with import tariffs. Its mixture of capitalist dynamism and socialist compassion became known as 'the Australian settlement'.

The Stockman's Hall of Fame at Longreach shamelessly celebrates the bush legend. See www.outbackheritage .com.au or p426.

When war broke out in Europe in 1914, thousands of Australian men rallied to the Empire's call. They had their first taste of death on 25 April 1915, when the Anzacs (the Australian and New Zealand Army Corps) joined an Allied assault on the Gallipoli Peninsula in Turkey. Eight months later, the British commanders acknowledged that the tactic had failed. By then, 8141 young Australians were dead. Soon, Australians were fighting in the killing fields of Europe. When the war ended, 60,000 Australian men had been slaughtered. Ever since, on 25 April, Australians have gathered at the country's many war memorials for the sad and solemn services of Anzac Day.

TURBULENT TWENTIES

Australia careered wildly into the 1920s, continuing to invest in immigration and growth. In Queensland, breathtakingly rich copper, lead, silver and zinc deposits were discovered at Mt Isa, setting in motion a prosperous new chapter in the history of Queensland mining.

This was also the decade in which intrepid aviators became international celebrities. For a state that felt its isolation so profoundly, the aeroplane was a revolutionary invention. The famous airline Qantas (an acronym for Queensland and Northern Territory Aerial Services) was founded at Longreach in the centre of the state in 1920. Eight years later, veteran Queensland aviator Bert Hinkler flew solo from England to Darwin in just 16 days.

See Peter Weir's epic film *Gallipoli* (1981). The cast includes the young Mel Gibson.

1901	1915
The new federal government removes Kanakas from Queensland in line with the White Australia Policy.	Australian and New Zealand troops (the Anzacs) join the Allied invasion of Turkey.

For more, see Ross Fitzgerald's two-volume *A History of Queensland*.

It was not just aeroplanes that linked Australia to the rest of the world. Economics too was a global force. In 1929, the Wall St crash and high foreign debt caused the Australian economy to collapse into the abyss of the Great Depression. Once again, unemployment brought its shame and misery to one in three houses. But for those who were wealthy – or who had jobs – the depression was hardly noticed.

In the midst of the hardship, sport diverted a people in love with games and gambling. Down south, the champion racehorse Phar Lap won an effortless and graceful victory in the 1930 Melbourne Cup ('the race that stops a nation'). In 1932, the great horse travelled to the racetracks of America where he mysteriously died. Back in Australia, the gossips insisted that the horse had been poisoned by envious Americans. And the legend of a sporting hero cut down in his prime grew.

WAR & GROWTH

As the economy began to recover, the whirl of daily life was hardly dampened when Australian servicemen sailed off to Europe for a new war in 1939. Though Japan was menacing, Australians took it for granted that the British navy would keep them safe. In December 1941, Japan bombed the US Fleet at Pearl Harbor. Weeks later, the 'impregnable' British naval base in Singapore crumbled, and soon thousands of Australians and other Allied troops were enduring the savagery of Japan's prisoner of war camps.

The new MacArthur Museum is at 201 Edward St, Brisbane.

As the Japanese swept through Southeast Asia and into Papua New Guinea, the British announced that they could not spare any resources to defend Australia. But the legendary US general, Douglas MacArthur, saw that Australia was the perfect base for American operations in the Pacific, and established his headquarters in Brisbane. As the fighting intensified, thousands of US troops were garrisoned in bases the length of Queensland – and Australians and Americans got to know each other as never before. In a series of savage battles on sea and land, Australian and American forces gradually turned back the Japanese advance. The days of the British alliance were numbered.

As the war ended, a new slogan rang through the land: 'Populate or Perish!' The Australian government embarked on an ambitious scheme to attract thousands of immigrants. With government assistance, people flocked from Britain and from non-English speaking countries. They included Greeks, Italians, Slavs, Serbs, Croatians, Dutch and Poles, followed by Turks, Lebanese and others.

David Malouf's wonderful novel *Johnno* (1975) recalls his childhood in wartime Brisbane.

This was the era when Australian families basked in the prosperity of a 'Long Boom' created by skilful government management of the economy. Manufacturing companies such as General Motors and Ford operated with generous tariff support. The social welfare system became more extensive, and now included generous unemployment benefits. The government owned many key services, including Qantas, which it bought in 1947. This, essentially, was the high point of the 'Australian settlement' – a partnership of government and private enterprise designed to share prosperity as widely as possible.

At the same time, there was growing world demand for the type of primary products produced in Queensland: metals, coal, wool, meat and wheat. By the 1960s mining dominated the state's economy. Coal was

1928	1929
Reverand John Flynn starts the Royal Flying Doctor Service in Cluncurry.	The Great Depression: thousands go hungry. Irene Longman becomes the first woman elected to Queensland Parliament.

the major export, while the great underground mine at Mt Isa produced massive quantities of copper, zinc, silver and lead. That same decade, the world's largest bauxite mine roared into life at Weipa on Cape York.

This era of postwar growth and prosperity was dominated by Robert Menzies, the founder of the modern Liberal Party and Australia's longest-serving prime minister. Menzies had an avuncular charm, but he was also a vigilant opponent of communism. As the Cold War intensified, Australia and New Zealand entered a formal military alliance with the USA – the 1951 Anzus security pact. And when the USA hurled its righteous fury into a civil war in Vietnam more than a decade later, Menzies committed Australian forces to the conflict. In 1966, Menzies retired, leaving his successors a bitter legacy. The antiwar movement split Australia.

For a gallop through Australian history, try Stuart Macintyre's A Concise History of Australia *or Geoffrey Blainey's* A Shorter History of Australia.

A QUESTION OF TOLERANCE

At the same time, increasing numbers of white Australians saw that Aborigines had endured a great wrong which needed to be put right. From 1976 until 1992 Aborigines won major victories in their struggle for land rights. As Australia's imports with China and Japan increased, the White Australia Policy became an embarrassment. It was officially abolished in the early 1970s, and soon Australia was a little astonished to find itself leading the campaign against the racist apartheid policies of white South Africa.

By the 1970s, more than one million migrants had arrived from non-English speaking countries, filling Australia with new languages, cultures, foods and ideas. At the same time, China and Japan far outstripped Europe as major Australian trading partners. As Asian immigration increased, Vietnamese communities became prominent in Sydney and Melbourne. In both those cities a new spirit of tolerance known as 'multiculturalism' became a particular source of pride. But the impact of postwar immigration was never as great in Queensland, and the values of multiculturalism made fewer inroads into the state's robustly old-time sense of what it meant to be Australian.

This Aussie insularity was cannily exploited by the rough-hewn and irascible Joh Bjelke-Petersen, premier of Queensland for 21 years from 1968. Kept in office by a blatant gerrymander (he never won more than 39 per cent of the vote), he was able to impose his policy of development at any price on the state. Forests were felled. Heritage buildings were demolished. Aborigines were cast aside. Protesters were bashed and jailed. But in the late 1980s, a series of investigations revealed that Bjelke-Petersen presided over a system that was rotten. His police commissioner was jailed for graft and it became clear that many police officers, whom the premier had used as a political hit squad, were racist, violent and corrupt.

Read all about the corruption in Hugh Lunn's The Life and Political Adventures of Johannes Bjelke-Petersen *(from secondhand bookshops).*

Today Australia faces new challenges. Since the 1970s, the country has been dismantling the protectionist scaffolding which allowed its economy to develop. Wages and working conditions, which used to be fixed by an independent authority, are now much more uncertain. And two centuries of development have placed great strains on the environment – on water supplies, forests, soil, air quality and the oceans. The country is closer than ever to the USA. Some say that this alliance

1941	1962
The Japanese bomb Townsville.	Indigenous Australians gain the right to vote in federal elections – and receive full citizenship in 1967.

protects Australia's independence. Others insist that it reduces Australia to a fawning 'client state'.

In Queensland, old fears and prejudices continue to struggle with tolerance and an acceptance of Asia. In Cape York, Aboriginal leaders, white land-owners and mining companies displayed a new willingness to work with each other when they signed the Cape York Agreement in 2001. But Aboriginal leaders acknowledge that poverty, violence and welfare dependency continue to blight the lives of too many Aboriginal communities. The degradation of the Great Barrier Reef has slowed – and parts of the Reef are even recovering from earlier abuse. But environmentalists warn that global warning may yet kill the fragile coral, reducing the Reef to an ocean desert. In short, the struggle for life, prosperity and social justice goes on – in a state were the sun shines all year round, and the locals believe they live in the best damn place on earth.

Find out more about Cape York Aborigines at www .balkanu.com.au.

1969	1979
Joh Bjelke-Petersen becomes premier.	The Great Barrier Reef Marine Park is proclaimed.

The Culture

REGIONAL IDENTITY

On the surface, Queenslanders epitomise the Australian lifestyle of sun, surf and smiles perhaps more than the people of any other state or territory. The laconic Australian drawl grows thicker once the highway heads north of Brisbane, and life takes on a more languid tick virtually everywhere outside the capital city. Inhabitants of the Sunshine State cherish their climate and wealth of natural beauty to the point of being smug. It's not uncommon to detect a note of pity or bewilderment in a Queenslander's tone when visitors talk of winter days buffeted by rain or snow – with an alleged 300 days of sunshine a year, who can blame them?

Beneath these contented aesthetics, though, lies a general feeling that these folk have earned their place in the sun through generations of effort. Australia's national identity is rooted in its past. The seminal times of the colony were characterised by extreme hardship, resentment at being sent so far with so little, and an incalculable sense of loss of loved ones and homes left behind. To cope with this struggle against nature and tyranny, Australians forged a culture based on the principles of a 'fair go' and back-slaps for challenges to authority, and told stories of the 'Aussie battler' that were passed down from generation to generation.

Extreme stereotypes of tamings of the bush are rife; the films *Crocodile Dundee* and *Crocodile Hunter*, for example, both depict dinky-di Aussies mud-wrestling crocodiles in the 'wilds' of the Queensland bush. These stereotypes celebrate a nostalgia and romanticism for the 'heroism' of the early white settlers.

But times have changed. Immigration has had a huge effect on Australian culture, as migrants have brought their own stories, cultures and myths to meld with those of the colonial 'battler'. Many migrants have arrived in Australia with a huge sense of hope and expectancy, to start life afresh. The iconic white 'Aussie battler' is becoming less relevant. And there's a long-overdue acknowledgment that the original inhabitants of this country are fundamental to a true definition of Australian culture today.

The immense prosperity the landscape has given has forged the title 'lucky country', the land of opportunity, and for most Queenslanders this rings true. As part of the wider Australian community, they enjoy a sophisticated, modern society with immense variety, a global focus, if not a regional one, and a relentless sense of optimism tempered by world events.

'The laconic Australian drawl grows thicker once the highway heads north of Brisbane'

LIFESTYLE

Despite the state's vast and diverse expanse, most Queenslanders inhabit the suburban smear occupying the fertile coastal strip between Coolangatta and Cairns. An understandable dependency on infrastructure is a key ingredient of this recipe, of course, but at heart, Queenslanders are urban folk. The 'Great Australian Dream' of owning a house on a chunk of suburban land with a car, a mutt and some kids is a high priority, and plays a large part in the state's psyche. Queensland's building industry is booming, with some 10,000 new houses being built in the state every three months.

Inside the average middle-class home it's likely that you'll find a married, heterosexual couple, though it's becoming increasingly likely that they will be in a de facto relationship or in their second marriage. Mum and Dad will have an average of 1.4 children, probably named Joshua and Chloe (and yes, Kylie is still popular). They'll cart the whole family, probably with a caravan attached, to the beach every summer, and on weekends they'll barrack for the Lions, Cowboys or Broncos (see p30 for a translation).

During the era of the National Party (see p25), Queensland considered itself to be one of Australia's great bastions of conservatism. The leader of the National Party, Sir Joh Bjelke-Petersen, was almost obsessive in his rejection of anything outside the 'hard-working white family' mould. The notorious 1976 raid on the 'hippie commune' at Cedar Bay, in the rainforests north of Cape Tribulation, was one of many examples of Joh's refusal to accept anyone or anything beyond the mainstream.

Queensland still toes a very conservative line and gender roles and stereotypes lag behind much of the country. This said, attitudes have changed substantially. Artistic communities speckle the Gold and Sunshine Coast hinterlands, and several of Brisbane's inner suburbs have a distinctly alternative flavour. The far north has to make do with Kuranda in the mountains north of Cairns, which has deteriorated into a commercial circus. The rainforests of Far North Queensland are still home to a few members of the state's best-known alternative lifestylers, the Ferals, though the movement is fading quietly into the background.

POPULATION

Australia has been strongly influenced by immigration, and its ethnic mix is among the most diverse in the world. At one time Queensland was the most multicultural place in Australia, with huge numbers of Indian and Chinese coolies, Pacific Islanders (known as Kanakas) and German contract workers, but the White Australia Policy brought in at Federation (see p23) marked the end of this comparatively enlightened period.

At last count 900,000 Aussies were setting up home abroad.

Queensland's current population is estimated at around 3,860,000, making up about 18% of the total Australian population. Of this figure approximately 112,8000 people are of Indigenous origin: Aborigines and Torres Strait Islanders, most of whom live in the north of the state or on the islands of Torres Strait, between Cape York and Papua New Guinea.

Queensland is notable for being the Australian mainland state with the largest proportion of its people living outside its capital city. Still, the southeastern corner of the state is Queensland's most crowded region, with more than 60% of the total population living within 150km of Brisbane. The majority of the population's remainder inhabits the fertile coastal strip between Brisbane and Cairns. The other parts of the state are sparsely populated.

INDIGENOUS AUSTRALIANS

Indigenous people of many tribes inhabited the area encompassing Queensland for tens of thousands of years before European settlement. Like many precolonial countries, the cultural and geographic boundaries of Indigenous Australians bore little resemblance to the state's borders as they are today. By the turn of the 19th century, the

ABORIGINAL SPIRITUALITY

Traditional Aboriginal religious beliefs centre on the continuing existence of spirit beings that lived on earth during creation time (or Dreamtime), which occurred before the arrival of humans. These beings created all the features of the natural world and were the ancestors of all living things. They took different forms but behaved as people do, and as they travelled about they left signs to show where they had passed.

Despite being supernatural, the ancestors were subject to ageing and eventually returned to the sleep from which they'd awoken at the dawn of time. Here their spirits remain as eternal forces that breathe life into the newborn and influence natural events. Each ancestor's spiritual energy flows along the path it travelled during the Dreamtime and is strongest at the points where it left physical evidence of its activities, such as a tree, hill or claypan. These features are called 'sacred sites'. These days the importance of sacred sites is more widely recognised among non-Aboriginal communities, and most state governments have legislated to give these sites a measure of protection.

Every person, animal and plant is believed to have two souls – one mortal and one immortal. The latter is part of a particular ancestral spirit and returns to the sacred sites of that ancestor after death, while the mortal soul simply fades into oblivion. Each person is spiritually bound to the sacred sites that mark the land associated with his or her spirit ancestor. It is the individual's obligation to help care for these sites by performing the necessary rituals and singing the songs that tell of the ancestor's deeds. By doing this, the order created by that ancestor is maintained.

The links between the Aboriginal people and their spirit ancestors are totems (or Dreaming); each person has his or her own totem. These totems can take many forms, including trees, caterpillars, snakes, fish and magpies. Songs explain how the landscape contains these powerful creator ancestors, who can exert either a benign or a malevolent influence. They also have a practical meaning: they tell of the best places and the best times to hunt, and where to find water in drought years. They can also specify kinship relations and identify correct marriage partners.

Aborigines who had survived the bloody settlement of Queensland, which saw some of the most brutal massacres in Australia, had been comprehensively run off their lands, and the white authorities had set up ever-shrinking reserves to contain the survivors. A few of the reserves were run according to well-meaning, if misguided, missionary ideals, but the majority of them were strife-ridden places where people from different areas and cultures were thrown unhappily together and treated as virtual prisoners.

Today, 'Murri' is the generic term used to refer to the indigenous people of Queensland. Torres Strait Islander people come from the islands of the Torres Strait, located off the coast of Cape York. They are culturally distinct from Aboriginal tribes that originated on Australia's mainland, having been influenced by the indigenous people of Papua New Guinea and the Pacific islands. Traditionally they were seafaring people, engaging in trade with people of the surrounding islands and Papua New Guinea and with Australian Aboriginals. Some 6800 Torres Strait Islanders remain on the islands in the Strait and an estimated 42,000 live in north Queensland.

Queensland athletes made up around 18% of the Australian Olympic and Paralympic teams that competed in Athens in 2004.

SPORT

If you're an armchair – or wooden bench – sports fan, Queensland has plenty to offer. Rugby is the main game in Queensland – that's rugby league, the 13-a-side working-class version of the game – that attracts the crowds. The most awaited event in the calendar is the State of Origin series every June/July, where the mighty Maroons take on their arch rivals, New South Wales (the Blues).

Queensland has two teams in the National Rugby League (NRL; www .nrl.com.au) – the Brisbane Broncos, who you can catch in Brisbane (see p109) and the North Queensland Cowboys, whose home ground is in Townsville.

Fast catching up to rugby league in popularity, due in no small part to the mighty Brisbane Lions, is Australian Rules Football (AFL or Aussie Rules; www.afl.com.au). The Lions are Queensland's only side in the national league and have proved themselves a force to be reckoned with, winning back-to-back-to-back premierships in 2001, 2002 and 2003. In 2004 they were finally knocked off their mantle, losing to Port Adelaide in the final. You can watch the Lions play a home game at the Gabba (p109). Both the NRL and AFL seasons run from March to September.

During the other (nonfootball) half of the year there's plenty of cricket to watch (see www.cricket.com.au). International test and one-day matches are played at the Gabba every summer. There is also an interstate competition (the Pura Cup) and numerous local grades. The Australian cricket team has dominated the sport for the better half of a decade, topping the international ladders in both test and one-day competitions. The team hasn't lost the Ashes to England since 1987, and in 2004 they won a test series in India (an *almost* impossible feat) for the first time in 22 years.

Rodeos are held at dozens of places throughout the state, and are often large community events. Some of the biggest rodeos are held at Mareeba in the far north, Warwick in the Darling Downs, and Mt Isa and Longreach in the outback.

The autobiography *Cathy Freeman* gives great insight into the national and Aboriginal icon who was a gold-medal runner at the Sydney Olympics. She was born in Mackay on Queensland's Whitsunday Coast.

Australia's state funding of professional sports is among the highest proportionally in the world.

ARTS

In the epilogue to his 1982 *A History of Queensland*, local historian Ross Fitzgerald lamented 'the cultural wasteland that is Queensland'. Fitzgerald thought the blame for the state's cultural malaise lay with a range of factors, including the authoritarianism and anti-intellectualism of the then National/Liberal Party government, the historically low value that had been placed on education in Queensland and the low levels of immigration.

Fortunately for the arts, the fall of the National Party marked the beginning of a cultural renaissance in Queensland. The new Labor government restored the civil liberties that were taken away by Bjelke-Petersen, such as the right to assembly, and did much to stimulate and encourage artistic and cultural development. Brisbane in particular has been gripped by a new spirit of creative endeavour, with theatre, opera, alternative cinema, poetry, music and other artistic activities going on every night of the week.

This said, the artistic spirit fades pretty quickly once you leave the capital and travel up the coast or into the outback. There are some interesting regional art galleries, with very 'pioneer' artwork, but for the most part the arts in rural Queensland are restricted to pub bands and Aboriginal souvenirs.

One of Australia's most acclaimed thespians, Geoffrey Rush, is a Toowoomba native. His performance as David Helfgott in *Shine* earned him an Oscar.

Cinema

Although Australia's film industry has been firmly lodged in Victoria and New South Wales, Queensland has spent the last decade making significant inroads. Annual film production has increased almost tenfold in financial terms since the early 1990s, which in turn has fostered new growth in the artistic wing of the industry.

The commercial industry is based around the Warner Roadshow studios at Movie World on the Gold Coast (see the boxed text on p135), which has produced a number of successful films targeted at the family market, including *Scooby Doo* (2002) and *Peter Pan* (2003). Other commercial films produced here include the horror/thriller *Ghost Ship* (2002) and *The Great Raid* (2002), which tells the story of a rescue mission in WWII of American prisoners in a Japanese prisoner of war camp in the Philippines. If you're a fan of horror, don't miss *Undead* (2002), filmed in southeast Queensland, about a town that becomes infected with a zombie virus.

Other international titles filmed in the state include: *The Thin Red Line* (1998), Terrence Malick's critically acclaimed tale of soldiers in the Pacific in WWII; Jackie Chan's *First Strike* (1997), a kung-fu romp partially filmed on the Gold Coast; and, of course, *Crocodile Dundee in LA* (2001), the latest instalment of the record-breaking Aussie series (parts one and two were also partly filmed in Queensland).

Queensland has also been either the setting or location for some excellent local productions. One of the most successful was the hit independent movie *Muriel's Wedding* (1994) which strips the lino off the suburban dream and chases Muriel's misadventurous efforts to escape the boredom and monotony of her life.

Gettin' Square (2003), directed by Jonathan Teplitzky, is an exquisitely funny and dark story of two low-grade criminals trying to extricate themselves from their illegal past and former employers. Every performance in this film is superb, but Gary Sweet's formidably foul Gold Coast gangster and David Wenham's portrayal of a tragically hapless junkie are stand outs. Wenham won an Australian Film Industry (AFI) award for his efforts.

Swimming Upstream (2002), is the autobiographical story of Anthony Fingleton, a Queensland state swimmer in the 1960s. His success was embittered by the tragic impact his damaged and alcoholic father (played by Geoffrey Rush) had on him and his family. Utterly gritty and raw, you can almost taste the hardship faced by families on the breadline in 1960s Queensland.

He Died with a Felafel in His Hand (2000) is based on the top-selling novel of the same name by John Birmingham, and delves into the humorous, sticky and often quite appalling experience of perennial share-house living.

Blurred (2002) follows the story of five teenagers indulging in schoolies week. This is a great flick for teenagers past and present, who will be able to relate to the dramas and lifetime bonds of puberty.

Praise (1998), adapted from the novel by Andrew McGahan (p33), is a gritty and honest tale of mismatched love in down-and-out Brisbane.

Literature

Two of the most widely acclaimed early Australian writers were AB 'Banjo' Paterson (1864–1941) and Henry Lawson (1867–1922). Paterson's classic works include the much-recited poems *Clancy of the Overflow* (1889) and *The Man from Snowy River* (1890). Henry Lawson's greatest contributions were his short stories of life in the bush, published in collections such as *While the Billy Boils* (1896) and *Joe Wilson and His Mates* (1901).

The Pacific Film and Television Commission (PFTC) website www.pftc.com.au provides a good insight into Queensland's burgeoning film industry.

The *Oxford Companion to Australian Literature* (1994) edited by William H Wilde, Joy Hooton and Barry Andrews is a comprehensive guide to Australian authors and writing from European settlement to the 1990s.

The annual Queensland Premier's Literary Awards celebrate the state's professional and budding authors. There are 14 awards in total with recipients sharing in a $225,000 prize pool.

Steele Rudd (1868–1935), a contemporary of Paterson and Lawson, was born in Toowoomba. With his classic sketches of the hardships of early Queensland life and the enduring characters he created such as 'Dad and Dave' and 'Mother and Sal', Rudd became one of the country's best-loved comic writers. His work *On Our Selection* (1899) is a humourous insight into the Australian bush myth of life on a plot of land in the Darling Downs.

Rolf Boldrewood's classic *Robbery Under Arms* (1889) tells the adventurous tale of Captain Starlight, Queensland's most notorious bushranger and cattle thief. Nevile Shute's famous novel *A Town Like Alice* (1950) is set partly in Burketown, in the Gulf Savannah. Many of Ion Idriess' outback romps were set in Queensland, including *Flynn of the Inland* (1932), the story of the man who created the Royal Flying Doctor Service.

In 1938 Xavier Herbert produced his classic *Capricornia*, an epic tale of the settler existence in the Gulf country. In a similar vein, Kerry McGinnis' *Heart Country* (2001) is an evocative autobiography about her life as a cattle drover in the Gulf – McGinnis still raises cattle at Bowthorn Station near Burketown. An interesting play (now also a film) set in Queensland is *Radiance* (1993) by esteemed Aussie playwright Louis Nowra.

Queensland has produced plenty of outstanding writers of its own. In particular, Brisbane's University of Queensland has for many years been one of Australia's richest literary breeding grounds.

Lebanese-Australian author David Malouf (1934–) is one of Queensland's most internationally recognised writers, having been nominated for the Booker Prize. He is well known for his evocative tales of an Australian boyhood in Brisbane – *Johnno* (1975) and *12 Edmondstone Street* (1985) – and *The Great World* (1990) among other titles. His 1982 novel *Fly Away Peter* tells the poignant story of a returned soldier struggling to come to terms with ordinary life and the unjust nature of hierarchy, and is set on the Gold Coast.

Australia's best-known Aboriginal poet and writer, Oodgeroo Noonuccal (Kath Walker), was born on North Stradbroke Island in 1920, and buried there in September 1993. See the boxed text on p122 for a closer look at her life and work. Herb Wharton (1936–), an Aboriginal author from Cunnamulla, has written a series of novels and short stories about the lives of the Murri stockmen, including *Unbranded* (1992) and *Cattle Camp* (1994).

Thea Astley (1925–2004) published 11 novels including *Hunting the Wild Pineapple* (1979), set in the rainforests of northern Queensland, and *The Multiple Effects of Rainshadow* (1996). *It's Raining in Mango* (1987) is a historical saga that traces the fortunes and failures of one pioneer family from the 1860s to the 1980s.

Expatriate writer Janet Turner Hospital (1942–) was educated in Melbourne and has used the rainforests of Queensland for many of her books, including the wonderful *The Last Magician* (1992).

Ipswich-born Thomas Shapcott (1935–) is an editor and one of Australia's most prolific writers. His recent books include *The White Stag of Exile* (1984), set in Brisbane and Budapest around the turn of the century.

Brisbane-born journalist Hugh Lunn (1941–) has written a number of popular books on and about Queensland. They include his humorous two-part autobiography *Over the Top with Jim* (1995) and *Head Over Heels* (1992).

Queensland artist Bill Robinson won the 1995 Archibald Prize for portraiture with his quirky *Portrait of the Artist with Stunned Mullet*.

For a dose of 100% Australian music talent, tune in to the national radio station Triple J (www .triplej.net.au/listen/) for 'Home and Hosed', 9pm to 11pm weeknights.

In recent years Brisbane has produced a wave of promising young writers. Andrew McGahan (1956–), a university dropout, used the seedy underbelly of the Fortitude Valley scene as the setting for his controversial first novel *Praise* (1992), which was later made into a film. See the boxed text on p165 for a better insight into his work. Verano Armanno's (1959–) *Romeo of the Underworld* (1994) is another contemporary novel set in the Valley.

Another prominent young writer is Matthew Condon (1962–), whose novels include *The Motorcycle Cafe* (1988) and *Usher* (1991). Helen Darville (1971–) gained notoriety for her novel *The Hand That Signed the Paper* (1995), which won the Miles Franklin Award in 1995 amid controversy over plagiarism and the author's claim that she had a Ukranian background. Another prominent Brisbane talent is children's author James Moloney (1954–), who has picked up many awards for his books *Swashbuckler* (1995) and *A Bridge to Wiseman's Cove* (1996).

Painting

Charles Archer (1813–62), the founder of Rockhampton, produced some interesting settler paintings in the 1850s. Lloyd Rees (1895–1998) is probably the best-known artist to have come out of Queensland and has an international reputation. Others include abstract impressionist John Coburn (1925–), Ian Fairweather (1891–1974), Godfrey Rivers (1859–1925) and Davida Allen (1951–), famous for her obsessive portraits of the actor Sam Neill.

Queensland is a rich centre of traditional and contemporary Aboriginal art. Judy Watson (1959–) and Gordon Bennett (1955–) have both won the Moët & Chandon Prize for contemporary artists.

Recently, a number of outback artists have come to prominence, including figurative painter Matthew McCord from Mundubbera in the Darling Downs.

Although Tracey Moffatt is now based in Sydney, her work is also worth looking out for. See p86 for details of galleries featuring Australian art.

Music

Indigenous music is one of the Australian music industry's great success stories of recent years. Yothu Yindi, with its land-rights anthem 'Treaty' (1991), is the country's best-known Aboriginal band, but Queensland has produced some outstanding indigenous musicians of its own. Christine Anu is a Torres Strait Islander who was born in Cairns. Her debut album *Stylin' Up* (1995) blends Creole-style rap, Islander chants and traditional languages with English, and was followed by the interesting *Come My Way* (2000) – highly recommended listening. Other regional artists include Torres Strait Islander Rita Mills and Maroochy Barambah of the Sunshine Coast.

Brisbane's pub-rock scene has produced a couple of Australia's all-time greatest bands. The Saints, considered by many to be one of the seminal punk bands, started out performing in Brisbane in the mid-1970s before moving on to bigger things in Sydney and, later, London.

Queensland's musicians have given their counterparts elsewhere a run for their money in recent years. Powderfinger has played a dominant role in the music industry for more than a decade and continue their pursuit of the perfect harmonic rock tune. Their albums make for excellent driving soundtracks – get your hands on *Vulture Street*

Finely tuned to the backpacker market, *Great Southern Land* (2003) selects Oz classics from Cold Chisel's 'Khe Sanh', The Angels' 'Am I Ever Gonna See Your Face Again' (response: no way, get fucked, fuck off!) to Men at Work's 'Down Under'– it's the perfect accompaniment to full-volume sing-alongs.

'Banjo' Paterson wrote the lyrics to 'Waltzing Matilda', Australia's un-official national anthem, in 1895 while visiting his fiancée near Winton in central Queensland.

(2003), *Odyssey Number Five* (2000) or *Fingerprints* (2004), their best-of album.

The debut and Australian Record Industry Association (ARIA) Award–winning album *Polyserena* (2002), by Queensland band George, is deliciously haunting and well worth a listen. It went platinum in just three weeks. Another rising star hailing from the Sunshine State is Pete Murray. His acoustic licks and chocolate-smooth voice have earned him national and international acclaim. Give his debut *Feeler* (2003) a burl.

Alternative Queensland bands that have made a name for themselves include Custard and Regurgitator.

Environment

Tim Flannery & Justine Vaisutis

Australia's plants and animals are just about the closest things to alien life you are likely to encounter on Earth. That's because Australia has been isolated from the other continents for a very long time – estimated to be at least 45 million years. The other habitable continents have been able to exchange various species at different times because they've been linked by land bridges. Just 15,000 years ago it was possible to walk from the southern tip of Africa right through Asia and the Americas to Terra del Fuego. Not Australia, however. Australia's birds, mammals, reptiles and plants have taken their own separate and very different evolutionary journey, and the result today is the world's most distinct – and one of its most diverse – natural realms.

The first naturalists to investigate Australia were astonished by what they found. Here the swans were black – to Europeans this was a metaphor for the impossible – while certain mammals (called monotremes) such as the platypus and echidna were discovered to lay eggs. To the eyes of the European naturalists, Australia really was an upside-down world, where many of the larger animals hopped and each year the trees shed their bark rather than their leaves.

You might need to go out of your way to experience some of the richness of Australia's natural environment. If you are planning to visit Queensland for only a short time and cannot escape the city environs, it is worthwhile visiting some of the zoos and wildlife parks that are found throughout the state. That's because Australia is a subtle place, and some of the natural environment – especially around the cities – has been damaged or replaced by trees and creatures from Europe.

Before you enjoy Australia's environment, though, it's worthwhile understanding the basics about how nature operates on this continent. This is important because there's nowhere like Australia, and once you have an insight into its origins and natural rhythms, you will appreciate the place, and its unique inhabitants, so much more.

THE LAND

There are two really big factors that go a long way towards explaining nature in Australia: its soils and its climate. Each is unique. Australian soils are the more subtle and difficult to notice of the two, but they have been fundamental in shaping life here. On the other continents, in recent geological times, processes including volcanism, mountain building and glacial activity have been busy creating new, fertile soil. Just think of the glacial-derived soils of North America, north Asia and Europe. Those soils feed the world today, and were made by glaciers grinding up rock of differing chemical composition over the last two million years. The rich soils of India and parts of South America were made by rivers eroding mountains, while the soils of Java in Indonesia owe their extraordinary richness to volcanic activity.

All of these soil-forming processes have been almost absent from Australia in recent times. Only volcanoes have made a contribution, and they cover less than 2% of the continent's land area. In fact, for the last 90 million years, beginning deep in the age of dinosaurs, Australia has been geologically comatose. The continent was too flat, warm and dry to attract glaciers, its crust too ancient and thick to be punctured by volcanoes or folded into mountains.

Tim Flannery is a naturalist, explorer and prolific writer. His latest book, about Australia, is *Country*. Tim Flannery lives in Adelaide where he is director of the South Australian Museum and a professor at the University of Adelaide.

Tim Flannery's *The Future Eaters* is a 'big picture' overview of evolution in Australasia, covering the last 120 million years of history, with thoughts on how the environment has shaped Australasia's human cultures.

Under such conditions, no new soil is created and the old soil is leached of all its goodness, and is blown and washed away. The leaching, or washing away of nutrients, is done by rain. Even if just 30cm of rain falls each year, that adds up to a column of water 30 million kilometres high passing through the soil over 100 million years, and that can do a great deal of leaching! Almost all of Australia's mountain ranges are more than 90 million years old, so you will see a lot of sand here, and a lot of country where the rocky 'bones' of the land are sticking up through the thin topsoil. It is an old, infertile landscape, and plant and animal life in Australia has been adapting to these conditions for aeons.

Australia's misfortune in respect to soils is echoed in its climate. In most parts of the world outside the wet tropics, life responds to the rhythm of the seasons – summer to winter, or wet to dry. Most of Australia experiences seasons – sometimes very severe ones – yet life does not respond solely to them. This can clearly be seen by the fact that although there's plenty of snow and cold country in Australia, there are almost no trees that shed their leaves in winter, nor do any Australian animals hibernate. Instead there is a far more potent climatic force that Australian life must obey: El Niño.

El Niño is a disruption in ocean currents and temperatures in the tropical Pacific that effects weather around the globe. The cycle of flood and drought that El Niño brings to Australia is profound. Our rivers – even the mighty Murray River, the nation's largest, which runs through the continent's southeast – can have plentiful water and be miles wide one year, while you can literally step over its flow the next. This is the power of El Niño, and its effect, when combined with Australia's poor soils, manifests itself compellingly. As you might expect from this, relatively few of Australia's birds are seasonal breeders, and few migrate. Instead, they breed whenever the rain comes, and a large percentage are nomads, following the rain across the breadth of the continent.

So challenging are conditions in Australia that the continent's birds have developed some extraordinary habits. The kookaburras, magpies and blue wrens you are likely to see – to name just a few – have developed a breeding system referred to as 'helpers at the nest'. The helpers are the young adult birds of previous breedings, which stay with their parents to help bring up the newly hatched chicks. Just why they should do this was a mystery until it was realised that conditions in Australia can be so harsh that more than two adult birds are needed to feed the nestlings. This pattern of breeding is very rare in places such as Asia, Europe and North America, but it is common in a wide array of Australian birds.

WILDLIFE

For those intrigued by the diversity of tropical rainforests, Queensland's world heritage is well worth visiting. Birds of paradise, cassowaries and a huge variety of other birds can be seen by day, while at night you can search for tree kangaroos (yes, some kinds of kangaroos do live in the treetops). In your nocturnal wanderings you are highly likely to see curious possums, some of which look similar to skunks, and other marsupials that today are restricted to a small area of northeast Queensland. Fossils from as far afield as western Queensland and southern Victoria indicate that such creatures were once common and widespread throughout much of the continent.

B Beale and P Fray's *The Vanishing Continent* gives an excellent overview of soil erosion across Australia. Fine colour photographs make the issue more graphic.

H Cogger's *Reptiles and Amphibians of Australia* is a bible to those interested in Australia's reptiles. You can use it to identify the species, and wield it as a defensive weapon if necessary.

ANTECHINUS ANTICS *Justine Vaisutis*

You may be able to spot yellow-footed antechinuses (before they combust as a result of their strange sexual exploits; see p39) around Lake Eacham (p364) and Lake Barrine (p363) on the Atherton Tableland in Far North Queensland. The antechinuses' mating season runs from July to August, and this is a good time of year to catch a glimpse of the creatures, as the usually nocturnal marsupials become daring in their unstoppable and ultimately deadly urge to procreate. During this brief period of time, the antechinuses can become bold enough to loiter in urban settings.

Although difficult to see during the rest of the year due to their speed and aversion to humans, members of this particular species have been known to build nests in TV sets and lounge chairs – while they're still in use!

A cousin of the yellow-footed breed is the brown antechinus, found in northern and southern Queensland.

Australia's deserts are a real hit-and-miss affair as far as wildlife is concerned. If you are visiting in a drought year, all you might see are red, dusty plains, the odd mob of kangaroos and emus and a few struggling, forlorn-looking trees. Return after big rains, however, and you're likely to encounter something resembling a Garden of Eden. Fields of wildflowers, such as white and gold daisies, stretch endlessly into the distance, perfuming the air with their fragrance. The salt lakes fill with fresh water, and millions of water birds – pelicans, stilts, shags and gulls – can be seen feeding on the super-abundant fish and insect life of the waters. It all seems like a mirage, and like a mirage it will quickly vanish as the land dries out, only to spring to life again in a few years or a decade's time.

The birdwing butterfly, found in the Queensland tropics, has a wingspan of 20cm.

The fantastic diversity of Queensland's Great Barrier Reef is legendary, and a boat trip out to the Reef from Cairns or Port Douglas is unforgettable. See p57 for more information.

Animals

Australia is, of course, famous for being the home of the kangaroo and other marsupials only found on this continent. Unless you visit a wildlife park, such creatures are not easy to see because most of them are nocturnal. Their lifestyles, however, are exquisitely attuned to Australia's harsh environmental conditions. Have you ever wondered why kangaroos, alone among the world's larger mammals, hop? It turns out that hopping is the most efficient way of getting about at medium speeds. This is because the energy of the kangaroo's bounce is stored in the tendons of the legs – much like in a pogo stick – while the intestines bounce up and down like a piston, emptying and filling the lungs without the animal needing to activate the chest muscles. When kangaroos travel long distances in search of meagre feed, such efficiency is a must.

The Great Barrier Reef is the most extensive reef system in the world.

Marsupials are so efficient that they need to eat a fifth less food than placental mammals of equivalent size (everything from bats to rats, whales and ourselves). But some marsupials have taken energy efficiency much further. If you get to visit a wildlife park or zoo to see koalas, you might notice that far-away look in their sleepy eyes. It seems as if nobody is home – and this in fact is near to the truth. Several years ago, biologists announced that koalas are the only living creatures that have brains that don't fit their skulls. Inside their large heads they have a shrivelled walnut of a brain that rattles around in

QUEENSLAND'S FURRED & FEATHERED *Justine Vaisutis*

Birds

Queensland is positively teeming with birds, with more species found here than in any other Australian state or territory. Two huge flightless birds found in Queensland are unusual because only the males incubate the eggs and care for the young: the emu, found in woodlands and grasslands west of the Great Dividing Range; and the endangered and elusive cassowary, found in dense rainforests in Far North Queensland. A great variety of waterbirds, such as ducks and geese, herons, egrets and smaller species, can be seen in the tropical lagoons of the far north, especially as the dry season wears on and wildlife starts to congregate near permanent water.

Other birds that can be found in Queensland include the jabiru, a striking iridescent black and white bird that grows up to 1.2m tall, and all bar 53 species of noisy, garrulous, colourful parrots. The gorgeous rainbow lorikeet is particularly common along the east coast, and the pink and grey galah can be seen in any rural area.

The kookaburra's raucous laughter is one of the most distinctive sounds of the bush, and it can be heard in many places throughout the state. Smaller but more colourful kingfishers include the sacred and forest kingfishers and the blue and orange azure kingfisher, which is always found near water. During the wet season, Julatten (p376) is a good place to see magnificent buff-breasted paradise-kingfishers.

Dingoes

Australia's wild dog, the dingo, first came to Australia and Asia around 4000 years ago and was domesticated by Aborigines. Dingoes can appear quite tame around camping grounds, but they *are* wild animals and their interest in people and the places they inhabit lies solely in scavenging food, a practice that can be harmful to both campers and the dingoes themselves. In April 2001 Fraser Island was the setting for a controversial dingo cull, following the killing of a nine-year-old boy (see the boxed text on p213). This tragedy was twofold: dingoes are highly sensitive and intelligent creatures, and had they not been fed and encouraged to visit camping grounds by tourists, neither event would have occurred.

---

a fluid-filled cranium. Other researchers have contested this finding, however, pointing out that the brains of the koalas examined for the study may have shrunk because these organs are so soft. Whether soft-brained or empty-headed, there is no doubt that the koala is not the Einstein of the animal world, and we now believe that it has sacrificed its brain for energy efficiency. Brains cost a lot to run – in humans, our brains typically weigh 2% of our body weight, but use 20% of the energy we consume. Koalas eat eucalypt (gum) leaves, which are so toxic that koalas use about 20% of their energy simply detoxifying this food. This leaves little energy for their brains, and living in the treetops where there are so few predators means that koalas can get by with few wits at all.

The peculiar constraints of the Australian environment have not made every creature dumb. The koala's nearest relative, the wombat (of which there are three species), has a comparatively large brain for a marsupial. Wombats live in complex burrows and can weigh up to 35kg, making them the largest herbivorous burrowers on Earth. Because the creatures' burrows are effectively air-conditioned, wombats have the neat trick of turning down their metabolic activity when they are in residence. One physiologist who studied wombats' thyroid hormones found that biological activity ceased to such an extent in sleeping wombats that, from a hormonal point of view, they appeared

Queensland has the greatest diversity of wildlife in Australia. Lonely Planet's *Watching Wildlife Australia* is a great companion to any wildlife-watching expedition.

Kangaroos
Kangaroos are perhaps the most famous inhabitants of the bush, and the eastern grey kangaroo is commonly encountered in Queensland woodlands. The family of about 50 species also includes many smaller species such as wallabies and the adorable pademelon – smaller than a wallaby again.

Koalas
Common along Australia's entire eastern seaboard, this endearing creature is adapted to life in trees, where it feeds exclusively on eucalyptus leaves. The female carries her young in her pouch until it is old enough to cling to her back. Their cuddly appearance belies an irritable nature, and koalas will scratch and bite if provoked.

The best places to spot these animals in the wild are Magnetic Island (p300) and the Daisy Hill Koala Sanctuary (p89) in Brisbane.

Platypuses & Echidnas
The platypus and the echidna are monotremes, a group containing only three species (the third lives in New Guinea). Both animals lay eggs, as reptiles do, but suckle their young on milk secreted directly through the skin from mammary glands. The shy and elusive platypus lives in freshwater streams and is rarely seen by the casual observer. One of the best places to look for it is in Eungella National Park (p262).

The echidna, or spiny anteater, eats only ants and protects itself by digging into the ground or by rolling itself into a bristling ball.

Possums & Gliders
Brush-tailed and ring-tailed possums are commonly found in big cities scavenging for household scraps. Much rarer, the striped possum is unique to the wet tropics and has an elongated finger for digging into rotten wood for grubs.

Gliders have a membrane stretching between their front and hind legs that acts as a parachute as they jump between trees. Several species are common in woodlands and forests.

to be dead! Wombats can remain underground for a week at a time, and can get by on just one-third of the food that is needed by a sheep of equivalent size. One day, perhaps, efficiency-minded farmers will keep wombats instead of sheep. At the moment, however, that isn't possible, because the largest of the wombat species, the endangered northern hairy-nose wombat, is one of the world's rarest creatures, with only around 100 of the animals surviving on a remote nature reserve in central Queensland.

One of the more common marsupials you might catch a glimpse of in Queensland are the species of antechinus. These nocturnal, rat-sized creatures lead quite an extraordinary life. The males live for just 11 months, the first 10 of which are taken up with a concentrated burst of eating and growing. Like human teenage males, the day comes when the antechinuses' minds turn to sex, and in the male antechinus this becomes an absolute obsession. As the males embark on their quest for females they forget to eat and sleep. Instead, they gather in logs and woo passing females by serenading them with squeaks. By the end of August – just two weeks after the male antechinuses reach 'puberty' – every single male is dead, exhausted by sex and burdened with carrying around swollen testes. Like many aspects of animal behaviour in Australia, this extraordinary life history may have evolved in response to the continent's trying environmental conditions. It seems likely that

The stately brolga – a member of the crane family – performs graceful courtship displays that have been absorbed into Aboriginal legends and ceremonies.

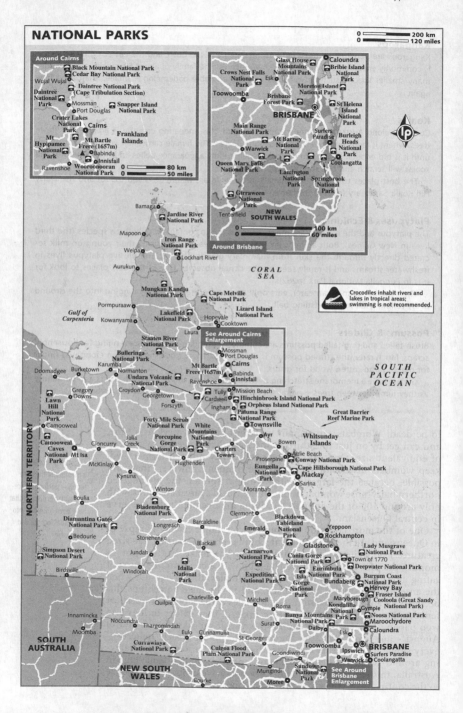

NATIONAL PARKS

QUEENSLAND'S NATIONAL PARKS   *Justine Vaisutis*

Queensland has 506 areas of environmental or natural importance, making up just over 4% of the state's 1,727,200 sq km. Of these areas, 219 are national parks, some of which comprise only a single hill or lake, while others are vast expanses of wilderness. The remainder are a mix of state parks, resources reserves and nature refuges.

Queensland is also home to five of Australia's 16 Unesco World Heritage Sites. The Wet Tropics World Heritage Area, which spans 450km of Queensland's northern coast, and the Great Barrier Reef are acknowledged as two of the world's most diverse ecosystems. In Queensland's northwest, the Australian Fossil Mammal site of Riversleigh is among the world's 10 best fossil sites. Spanning sections of southern Queensland and northern New South Wales, the Central Eastern Rainforests Reserves shelter temperate and unique rainforests. Then there's Fraser Island, the world's largest sand island and home to a diversity of fragile and complex ecosystems, including lush rainforests and crystal-clear lakes.

You can get information about these areas directly from park rangers, or from the **Queensland Parks & Wildlife Service** (QPWS; ☎ 13 13 04; www.epa.qld.gov.au), a wing of the Environmental Protection Agency. There are QPWS offices in most major towns, or you can access and download a wealth of information and make camping bookings for many of the parks on the website. The main visitors centres:

Central Region Office (p233; ☎ 4936 0511; 61 Yeppoon St, North Rockhampton)
Naturally Queensland (p79; ☎ 3227 7111; 160 Ann St, Brisbane)
Northern Region Office (p291; ☎ 4722 5211; Marlow St, Townsville)
Southern Region Office (☎ 3225 8723; 288 Edward St, Brisbane)

Exploring the national parks is an excellent way to immerse yourself in the environment and witness Australia's native landscape. Many parks have camping grounds with toilets and showers. See p438 for more information. Big parks usually have a network of walking tracks.

Our Favourite National Parks

Park	Features	Activities	Best Time	Page
Carnarvon	Ancient Aboriginal paintings, rich birdlife, gaping Ward's Canyon, spectacular views	Overnight bushwalks, bird-watching	Cooler months, Apr-Oct	p247
Eungella	Unique wildlife including platypuses, tumbling Araluen Falls	Wildlife watching, bushwalking, swimming, scenic drives	Apr-Nov, Aug for platypuses	p262
Great Sandy	Vast tracts of beach, freshwater lakes, rainforests, mangrove forests	Bushwalking, swimming, 4WD driving, fishing	Drier months, from Apr-Dec	p210
Hinchinbrook Island	Unspoiled wilderness, towering mountains, dense rainforest, idyllic beaches, the Thorsborne Trail	Bushwalking, bird-watching, swimming, bush camping	Cooler months, Apr-Sep	p315
Lakefield	Mighty rivers, wetlands, freshwater crocodiles, immense grasslands	Barramundi fishing, wildlife watching, bush camping	Dry months, Apr-Oct	p399
Lamington	Rugged mountains, cascading waterfalls, gorges, subtropical rainforest, wildlife	Bushwalking, wildlife watching, bush camping, abseiling	Year-round; Nov-Mar are the hottest months	p149
Lizard Island	Stark, sandy terrain, sublime and remote beaches, diverse wildlife	Swimming, snorkelling, scuba diving, bushwalking, wildlife watching	Cooler, dry months, May-Oct	p392

if the males survived mating, they would then have to compete with the females as they tried to find enough food to feed their growing young. Essentially, antechinus dads are disposable. They do better for the survival of antechinuses as a species if they go down in a testosterone-fuelled blaze of glory.

One thing you will see lots of in Australia are reptiles. Snakes are abundant, and they include some of the most venomous species known. Of Australia's 155 species of land snakes, 93 are venomous, and Australia is home to something like 10 of the world's 15 most venomous snakes. Where the opportunities to feed are few and far between, it's best not to give prey a second chance, hence their potent venom. However, you are far more likely to encounter a harmless python than a dangerously venomous species. Snakes will usually leave you alone if you don't fool with them. If you see a snake, observe, back quietly away and don't panic, and most of the time you'll be OK. For information about snake bites, see p471.

Another reptile you may see, either in a wildlife park or, if travelling in northern Queensland, in the wild, is crocodiles. Both of Australia's crocodile species are found in Queensland: saltwater or estuarine crocs (called 'salties'), which can grow up to 7m in length and are the more dangerous of the two, and smaller, freshwater crocs (or 'freshies'). There are several crocodile farms in Queensland where you can see crocs being fed, or you can take a tour, such as those on the Daintree River (see p377).

Queensland has more than 600 species of birds, boasting a greater variety than any other Australia state. Most can be seen in the rainforests within 100km of Cairns, including the endangered cassowary (see the boxed text on p383).

Pizzey and Knight's *Field Guide to Birds of Australia* is an indispensable guide for bird-watchers and anyone else even peripherally interested in Australia's feathered tribes. Knight's illustrations are both beautiful and helpful in identification.

CANE TOADS   Joe Bindloss

One of Queensland's most notorious citizens, the cane toad *(Bufo marinus)* was introduced from Argentina by way of Hawaii in 1935 to wipe out the sugar cane beetles that were devastating Australia's sugar cane plantations. Unfortunately, while the Hawaiian cane beetle was a ground dweller and easy prey for the toads, the Aussie variety lived at the top of the cane, far beyond the toads' reach.

Sugar cane beetles turned out to be about the only Australian species that wasn't at some kind of risk from the cane toad. Predators that try to eat the toads are killed by the poison glands on the toads' backs, and the amphibians breed prolifically, devastating populations of native insects. There are even reports of saltwater crocodiles being found dead with stomachs full of toads.

With no real predators to speak of, cane toads have spread across Queensland and into other states and territories like a plague. In recent years they have been found as far afield as northern New South Wales, Cape York Peninsula and in much of the Northern Territory. Aided by the warmer climates predicted by global warming models, the toads could reach Sydney by 2050.

The noisome toad is now public enemy number one and Queenslanders have come up with all sorts of bizarre ways to reduce the toad population. Among the more obscure are cane toad races, a popular gambling game where the toads race for their lives, and cane toad golf, with the hapless toads as balls. By far the most humane way to kill a cane toad is to catch it in a plastic bag and place it in the freezer, where it will die quite painlessly – just remember to take it out before your next dinner party. If you see a car swerving in front of you on a Queensland road, the driver might just be doing their bit for the environment and squashing a cane toad.

BATTLE FOR THE BILBIES *Justine Vaisutis*

A member of the bandicoot family, bilbies are about the size of rabbits. Like most nocturnal marsupials they have oversized ears that enable them to hear at night. This feature, along with their long snouts and black and white tails, gives them the appearance of a mouselike kangaroo; aesthetics that have earned them many an adoring fan among the Australian public and that have seen them depicted in chocolate as an Australian version of the Easter bunny. But the bilbies' survival has become increasingly dependent on a group of dedicated and tireless conservationists and volunteers.

Once inhabiting more than 70% of mainland Australia, bilbies have no natural predators. However European settlement and the ensuing introduction of rabbits (who compete for food), feral cats and foxes has had a devastating effect on their population. Having disappeared altogether from three states, bilby populations are now limited to the Tanami Desert in the Northern Territory, the Great Sandy Desert in Western Australia, and an area of some 100,000 sq km between Birdsville and Boulia in southwestern Queensland. Their numbers in the state are estimated to have dropped to as little as six or seven hundred and bilbies are now listed as endangered.

In an effort to prevent their extinction, the Queensland government has contributed more than $1 million towards a coordinated recovery programme run in conjunction with the Federal Government. One of the most effective implementations of the plan has been to purchase tracts of the bilbies' remaining habitat and fence it off to exclude predators such as feral cats. In addition, the Queensland Parks and Wildlife Service (QPWS) is embarking on a plan to reintroduce a colony of bilbies, bred in captivity, to Currawinya National Park, which lies on the Queensland/New South Wales border.

There is a great deal of hope surrounding these efforts. To find more information on the bilbies' progress and ways in which you can help, contact the **Save the Bilby Appeal** (☎ 07-4654 1255; bilby@epa.qld.gov.au).

Plants

Australia's plants can be irresistibly fascinating to observers. The diversity of prolific flowering plants found on the continent has long puzzled botanists. Again, Australia's poor soils seem to be the cause. The sand plain is about the poorest soil in Australia – it's made up of almost pure quartz with few nutrients. This prevents any one fast-growing species from dominating the environment. Instead, thousands of specialist plant species have learned to find narrow niches of their own, and so many species coexist. Some live at the foot of metre-high sand dunes, some on top, some on an east-facing slope, some on the west, and so on. The plant's flowers need to be striking in order to attract pollinators, because nutrients are so lacking in this sandy world that even insects such as bees are rare.

ENVIRONMENTAL ISSUES

The European colonisation of Australia, commencing in 1788, heralded a period of catastrophic upheaval, leaving Australians today with some of the most severe environmental problems to be found anywhere on Earth. It may seem strange that a population of just 20 million people, living on a continent the size of the USA minus Alaska, could inflict such damage on its environment. But Australia's long isolation, fragile soils and difficult climate have made it particularly vulnerable to human-induced change.

Damage to Australia's environment has been inflicted in several ways, the most important being the introduction of pest species, the destruction of forests, overstocking rangelands, inappropriate agriculture

Despite anything an Australian tells you about koalas (or dropbears), there is no risk of one falling onto your head as you walk beneath the trees.

and interference with natural waterflows. Beginning with the escape of feral cats into the Australian bush shortly after 1788, a plethora of vermin, from foxes to wild camels and cane toads (see the boxed text on p42), have run wild in Australia, causing the extinction of native fauna. One out of every 10 native mammals living in Australia prior to European colonisation is now extinct, and many more are highly endangered. Extinctions have also affected native plants, birds and amphibians.

The destruction of forests has also had a profound effect. Most of Australia's rainforests have been subject to clearing, while conservationists fight with loggers over the fate of the last unprotected stands of 'old growth'. Much of Australia's grazing lands have been chronically overstocked for more than a century, the result being the extreme vulnerability of both scarce soils and rural economies to Australia's drought and flood cycle, as well as the extinction of many native species. The development of agriculture has involved land clearance and the provision of irrigation, and here again the effect has been profound. Clearing of the diverse and spectacular plant communities of the Western Australian wheatbelt began just a century ago, yet today up to one-third of that country is degraded by salination of the soils. Between 70kg and 120kg of salt lies below every square metre of the region, and the clearing of native vegetation has allowed water to penetrate deep into the soil, dissolving the salt crystals and carrying brine towards the surface.

In terms of financial value, just 1.5% of Australia's land surface provides more than 95% of agricultural yield, and much of this land lies in the irrigated regions of the Murray-Darling basin. This is Australia's agricultural heartland, yet it too is under severe threat from salting of soils and rivers. Irrigation water penetrates into the sediments laid down in an ancient sea, carrying salt into the catchment fields. If nothing is done, the lower Murray River will become too salty to drink in a decade or two, threatening the water supply of Adelaide, a city of more than a million people.

Despite the enormity of the biological crisis engulfing Australia, governments and the community have been slow to respond. It was in the 1980s that coordinated action began to take place, but not until the '90s that major steps were taken. The establishment of Landcare (an organisation enabling people to effectively address local environmental issues; www.landcareaustralia.com.au) and the expenditure of $2.5 billion through the National Heritage Trust Fund have been important national initiatives. Yet so difficult are some of the issues the nation faces that, as yet, little has been achieved in terms of halting the destructive processes.

Individuals are also banding together to help in conservation efforts. Groups such as the Australian Bush Heritage Fund (www.bushheritage.asn.au) and the Australian Wildlife Conservancy (AWC; www.australianwildlife.org) allow people to donate funds and time to the conservation of native species. Some of these groups have been spectacularly successful; the AWC, for example, already manages endangered species over its 1.3 million-acre holdings.

In Queensland, land clearing, sustainable development within the rainforests of Far North Queensland and the protection of the Great Barrier Reef are recognised as major environmental issues. See the boxed text on p380 to learn about coordinated conservation efforts in the Wet Tropics World Heritage Area, and the boxed text on p68

The Australian Conservation Foundation (ACF; www.acfonline.org.au) is the largest nongovernment organisation involved in protecting the environment.

Almost all of the remnants of the tropical rainforest that once covered the Australian continent are found in north Queensland.

for information about environmental threats to the Great Barrier Reef caused by tourism, fishing, global warming and natural predators.

So severe are Australia's problems that it will take a revolution before they can be overcome. This is because sustainable practices need to be implemented in every arena of the life of every Australian – from farms to suburbs and city centres. Renewable energy, sustainable agriculture and sustainable water use lie at the heart of these changes, and Australians are only now developing the road map to sustainability that they so desperately need if they are to have a long-term future on the continent.

Queensland Outdoors

Queensland is Australia's natural adventure playground, and the sheer size of the state's coastline alone means there is an incredible range of activities available to visitors. Scuba diving and snorkelling are extremely popular in the vivid waters of the Great Barrier Reef, and surfing is almost in the genes for locals from Coolangatta up to the Whitsunday Coast. Throughout the state you can also go bushwalking in rainforests and the bush, camping on isolated tropical islands, horse riding along coastal beaches, and wildlife spotting in the plethora of national parks and reserves.

During the 2004 federal election campaign senator Andrew Bartlett took his campaign to new heights by bungee jumping at Surfers Paradise to advocate public liability insurance reforms. After the jump he said 'It's something every 40-year-old should do – that and get a prostate check'.

BUNGEE JUMPING & SKYDIVING

There are plenty of opportunities for adrenaline junkies to get a hit in Queensland. Surfers Paradise (p136) is something of a bungee Mecca, offering brave participants a host of creative spins on the original bungee concept. Another hot spot is Cairns (p335). A jump generally costs around $100.

Tandem skydiving is also a popular activity and is one of the most spectacular ways to get an eyeful of Queensland's palette. Prices depend on the heights of your jump. Most folk start with a jump of 10,000ft, which provides 35 to 40 seconds of freefall and costs around $200 to $250. You can go up to 14,000ft, which affords considerably more freefall and costs around $300. Caloundra (p175) is one of the most popular spots in Queensland to skydive, and the set-up there allows you to land right on the golden sands of the beach. Readers regularly write in singing accolades. Other popular locations include Surfers Paradise (p135), Brisbane (p92), Airlie Beach (p272), Mission Beach (p320) and Cairns (p335). Operators at all of these places offer tandem jumps that are suitable for beginners.

BUSHWALKING

Bushwalking is a popular activity in Queensland year-round. There are a number of bushwalking clubs and several useful guidebooks that provide local information. Lonely Planet's *Walking in Australia* describes 23 walks of different lengths and difficulty in various parts of the country, including three in Queensland.

The Queensland Environmental Protection Agency has published *National Parks Bushwalks of the Great South East* ($25), which details more than 160 walks in 25 of southeast Queensland's national parks.

Look for Tyrone Thomas' *50 Walks in North Queensland* (for walks on the beach or through the rainforest areas of the Wet Tropics World Heritage Area, from Cape Hillsborough near Mackay up to Cape Tribulation and inland as far as Chillagoe) and his *50 Walks: Coffs Harbour & Gold Coast Hinterland* (covering Tamborine Mountain, Springbrook and Lamington National Park). *Take a Walk in Queensland's National Parks Southern Zone* by John and Lyn Daly provides a comprehensive guide to walks across the southern stretch of the state. There's also *The Bushpeople's Guide to Bushwalking in South-East Queensland*, with colour photos and comprehensive walking-track notes.

One of the best ways to find out about bushwalking areas is to contact a local bushwalking club, such as the **Brisbane Bushwalkers Club** (☎ 07-3856 4050; www.bbw.org.au) or look in the *Yellow Pages* under 'Clubs – Bushwalking'.

National parks and state forests are some of the best places for walking. See p41 for contact details and more information. National parks on the

RESPONSIBLE BUSHWALKING

■ Don't urinate or defecate within 100m of any water sources. Doing so pollutes precious water supplies and can lead to the transmission of serious diseases.

■ Use biodegradable detergents and wash at least 50m from any water sources.

■ Avoid cutting wood for fires in popular bushwalking areas as this can cause rapid deforestation. Use a stove that runs on kerosene, methylated spirits or some other liquid fuel, rather than stoves powered by disposable butane gas canisters.

■ Hillsides and mountain slopes are prone to erosion; it's important to stick to existing tracks.

mainland favoured by bushwalkers include Lamington (p149), Mt Barney (p150) and Springbrook (p147) in the Gold Coast hinterland, and Brisbane Forest Park (p87), which is a popular escape for urban critters. More good parks for bushwalking include Girraween (p158) on the Darling Downs, the Cooloola Section of Great Sandy National Park (p190) just north of the Sunshine Coast, Carnarvon Gorge (p247) in central Queensland, and Wooroonooran National Park (p345) south of Cairns, which contains Queensland's highest peak, Mt Bartle Frere (1657m).

The Queensland Federation of Bushwalking Clubs website is useful for tracking down local bushwalking clubs throughout the state. Click onto www.geocities .com/qfbwc/.

A recent initiative of the state government is the creation of the Great Walks of Queensland. The six walking tracks are in the Whitsundays, Sunshine Coast hinterland, Mackay highlands, Fraser Island, Gold Coast hinterland and the Wet Tropics World Heritage Area (in tropical North Queensland). The Whitsunday Great Walk (p272) and Fraser Island Great Walk (p208) are already completed and the remaining four walks should be up and running by mid-2006. The walks are designed to allow bushwalkers to experience rainforests and bushlands without disturbing the ecosystems.

There are some celebrated tracks for experienced walkers in Queensland. Bear in mind that these can be difficult grades and the conditions for some require substantial bushwalking smarts. In northern Queensland the 32km ungraded Thorsborne Trail (p315) on Hinchinbrook Island is a spectacular bushwalking retreat. Walker numbers are limited for this trail at any one time and it traverses a gamut of environments, including remote beaches, rainforests and creeks amid spectacular mountain scenery.

Less experience is needed for the myriad trails throughout Magnetic Island (p302), where koalas and birdlife are prolific.

Walking in the southern half of the state is feasible and pleasant all year round due to the accommodating climate. Regardless of the time of year, however, you should always take plenty of drinking water with you. From the Capricorn Coast north, things can get pretty hot and sticky over summer, particularly in the wet season between December and February. If you're planning to walk at these times you must take into account the harsher conditions. Summer is also the most prolific period for bushfires, which are a constant threat throughout Queensland. **Queensland Parks & Wildlife Service** (QPWS; ☎ 13 13 04; www.epa.qld.gov.au) can advise you on current alerts, or see p441 for more information.

Click onto Bicycling Queensland's website (www.bq.org.au) for information about bike shops and rentals, cycling events and more.

CYCLING

There are possibilities for some great rides in Queensland. For information on long-distance cycling, see p456. Available from most bookshops, *Pedalling Around Southern Queensland* by Julia Thorn has tour notes and mud maps for numerous bike rides in the south of the state. For longer trips, Lonely Planet's authoritative *Cycling Australia* covers the epic east coast trip and other rides in Queensland.

There are companies that offer cycling tours in various places, including Cairns (p336) and Brisbane (p89). The Redcliffe foreshore (p116) is skirted by a lovely bike path, which is popular with families. You can also do some excellent mountain biking in and around Noosa; see p183 for more information.

As with bushwalking, the best time for lengthy bike rides is outside Queensland's hottest months. Most experienced riders will have had practice in similar, hot conditions and will be able to cope, but it's perhaps not a great idea to embark on your first 40km ride in the middle of a January heatwave! Similarly, basic safety precautions including taking plenty of water with you apply to cycling in the same way they do to bushwalking.

It might also be worth contacting one of the local cycling clubs such as the **Brisbane Bicycle Touring Association** (http://bbta-au.org/index.php). The **Bicycling Federation of Australia** (www.bfa.asn.au) is an excellent online resource, with links to cycling clubs and organisations throughout Queensland. Alternatively you can look under 'Clubs – Bicycle' in the *Yellow Pages*.

> Queensland Transport has a useful website (www.transport.qld .gov.au/cycling) that provides information on road rules, route maps, resources and cycling safety throughout Queensland.

DIVING & SNORKELLING

The Queensland coast is littered with enough spectacular dive sites to make you giddy. The Great Barrier Reef provides some of the world's best diving and snorkelling, and there are dozens of operators vying to teach you to scuba dive or provide you with the ultimate dive safari. There are also some 1600 shipwrecks along the Queensland coast, providing vivid and densely populated marine metropolises for you to explore.

Learning to dive here is fairly inexpensive by world standards, and a four- or five-day **Professional Association of Diving Instructors** (PADI; www.padi.com)

SAFETY GUIDELINES FOR DIVING

Before embarking on a scuba-diving, skin-diving or snorkelling trip, carefully consider the following points to ensure a safe and enjoyable experience:

- Possess a current diving certification card from a recognised scuba diving instructional agency (if scuba diving).
- Be sure you are healthy and feel comfortable diving.
- Obtain reliable information about the physical and environmental conditions at the dive site (from a reputable local dive operation), such as water temperature, visibility and tidal movements.
- Be aware of local laws, regulations and etiquette about marine life and the environment.
- Dive only at sites within your realm of experience; if available, engage the services of a competent, professionally trained dive instructor or dive master.
- Be aware that underwater conditions vary significantly from one region, or even site, to another. Seasonal changes can significantly alter any site and dive conditions. These differences influence the way divers dress for a dive and what diving techniques they use.
- Ask about the environmental characteristics that can affect your diving and how local divers deal with these considerations.

course leading to a recognised open-water certificate costs anything from $170 to $500 – and you can usually choose to do a good part of your learning in the warm waters of the Great Barrier Reef.

Every major town along the coast has one or more diving schools, but standards can vary, so it's worthwhile doing some research before you sign up. Diving professionals are notoriously fickle and good instructors move around from company to company – ask around to see which one is currently well regarded.

When choosing a course, look carefully at how much of your open-water experience will be out on the Reef. Many of the budget courses only offer shore dives, which are often less interesting than open-water dives. At the other end of the price scale, the most expensive courses tend to let you live aboard a boat or yacht for several days, with all your meals included in the price. Normally you have to show that you can tread water for 10 minutes and swim 200m before you can start a course. Most schools also require a medical, which will usually cost extra (around $50).

For certified divers, trips and equipment hire are available just about everywhere. You'll need evidence of your qualifications, and some places may also ask to see your log book. Renting gear or going for a day dive generally costs $60 to $100.

Popular diving locations are utterly prolific. Cairns (p334) and Port Douglas (p369) have plenty of dive companies that operate in the waters of the Great Barrier Reef. Further south, the SS *Yongala* shipwreck (p294), just off Townsville's coast, has been sitting beneath the water for more than 90 years and is now home to teeming marine communities. From Airlie Beach (p267) you can organise dives in the azure waters of the Whitsundays. Possibly the cheapest spot in all in Australia, if not the southern hemisphere, is the hamlet of Bagara, near Bundaberg. See p221 for more information.

If you're in Queensland for a while and you're really serious about your scuba diving you can join other addicts at a club, such as **All-Ways Diving** (☎ 07-38489100; 149 Beaudesert Rd, Moorooka; www.allwaysdiving.com.au) in Brisbane, or the **North Queensland Underwater Explorers Club** (www.vk4tub .org/nquec/index.html).

You can snorkel just about everywhere in Queensland; it requires minimum effort and anyone can do it. All the locations mentioned above are relevant and popular snorkelling sites. There are also coral reefs off some of the mainland beaches and around several of the islands, and not far from Brisbane the brilliant Tangalooma Wrecks lie off the west coast of Moreton Island (p124). Most cruises to the Great Barrier Reef and through the Whitsunday Islands include use of snorkel gear for free (although you may have to pay extra to hire a wetsuit if you want one) and these are some of the loveliest waters to float atop. Backpacker hostels along the coast also provide the use of snorkel gear for free.

During the wet season, usually January to March, floods can wash a lot of mud out into the ocean and visibility for divers and snorkellers is sometimes affected.

All water activities, including diving and snorkelling, are affected by the box jellyfish, or stingers, which are found on the Queensland coast from Rockhampton north. See the boxed text on p226 for more information.

Whether you're snorkelling or diving on the Great Barrier Reef it's important to remember how vulnerable the ecology is. Ensuring you

An excellent resource for diving schools and locations in the state is Dive Queensland (www .dive-queensland .com.au).

'Extreme Underwater Ironing' is a new fad whereby you literally iron a shirt (minus the electricity) underwater and take photos to prove you did it. Fair dinkum! Click onto www.diveoz.com .au/aeui to take a look.

leave no indelible impact is quite easy. Most coral damage occurs when divers accidentally cut or break it with their fins. Be aware of where your feet are (this can be surprisingly hard when they're attached to odd flippers and you're carrying a hefty tank on your back!). Never stand on the coral – if you need to rest, find sand to stand on or use a rest station.

FISHING

As you'll soon realise, fishing in all its forms is incredibly popular in Queensland, especially in coastal areas. You will see people surf fishing all the way up the coast, and more than a few Queensland families spend entire summers living out of the back of their 4WDs while trying their luck in the surf breaks. There are also plenty of dams and freshwater bodies that provide good fishing haunts.

The barramundi (or 'barra') is Australia's premier native sport fish, partly because of its tremendous fighting qualities and partly because it's delicious! Note that the minimum size for barramundi is 50cm in Queensland – there are also bag limits, and the barra season is closed in most places from 1 November to 31 January. There are quite a few commercial operators offering sports-fishing trips focussing on barra in the far north.

The Great Barrier Reef has traditionally been a popular fishing ground, but new zoning laws introduced in July 2004 have tightened the area of reef that can be fished in response to concerns about environmental damage and over-fishing. See p68 for more information. There are also limitations on the number of fish you catch and their size, and restrictions on the type of gear you can use. You also need to be aware of which fish are protected entirely from fishing. While this may sound like bad news for fisher folk, it's great news for the Reef and there are still plenty of sites where you can cast a line in search of the elusive coral trout and other tasty reef fish. The easiest way to find out what you can catch, where and how is to contact the nearest QPWS office wherever you are on the mainland. The QPWS rangers will be able to provide you with a zoning map and let you know of any restrictions. For QPWS offices in Cairns and Airlie Beach, see p332 and p272. Alternatively, contact the **Great Barrier Reef Marine Park Authority** (☎ 07-4750 0700; www.gbrmpa.gov.au).

To find weekly fishing reports for popular fishing spots along the Queensland coast, click to www.fishingmonthly .com.au

On the two sand islands of North Stradbroke (p119) and Fraser (p209), surf fishing is extremely popular and at times the 4WD traffic on the eastern surf beaches resemble peak hour. Not far from Fraser Island, Rainbow Beach (p198) is another popular spot and is easily accessed. On the Gold Coast, fishing tours operate out of Main Beach (p131) and on the Sunshine Coast, Caloundra (p175) and Maroochy (p177) are inundated with holiday-makers catching their own dinner. In these areas plenty of fishing shops provide good advice, bait and equipment.

If you want a unique fishing experience away from the maddening crowds, the Wellesley Islands (p415) offer beautiful fishing spots with abundant fish in the waters of the gulf.

Barramundi fishing is excellent in the coastal and estuarine waters of Far North Queensland. One of the best places to throw in a line is Lake Tinaroo (p358), and the season there is open year-round. On Cape York Peninsula, Lakefield National Park (p399) is one of the few national parks in which you can fish and it's renowned for its barramundi haul. Note that the season in Lakefield is closed between 1 November and

31 January and you should check with park rangers to be certain of bag limits outside this period. A number of reef-, river- and land-based fishing charters operate out of Port Douglas (p369). Hamilton Island (p280) in the Whitsundays and Dingo Beach (p284) are also good for big game.

The heavy-tackle season runs from September to December, and the annual Black Marlin Classic on Halloween night (31 October) is a major attraction. Hamilton Island also hosts the Billfish Bonanza each December.

To find information on weather and tide conditions and what's biting, tune into local radio stations. An excellent resource is the *Queensland Fishing Monthly* magazine ($4.40), which you can pick up at any newsagency; it provides comprehensive information on where the best fishing spots are, how to get to them and how to capitalise on your haul. The magazine's website, www.fishingmonthly.com.au, has up-to-the-minute information on conditions from locals as well as general trends so you can plan ahead.

In 1979, 13-year-old Sarli Nelson found a 2019.50-carat sapphire in Queensland's gemfields. Her father sold it for less than $60,000; in 1991 it went for $5 million.

FOSSICKING

There are lots of good fossicking areas in Queensland – see the *Gem Fields* brochure, published by Tourism Queensland, for information about this novel pastime. The brochure tells you the places where you have a fair chance of finding gems and the types of gems you're (hopefully) likely to find. You'll need a miners right or 'fossickers licence' before you hit the gemfields; most caravan parks in the fossicking areas can sort you out with a licence or you can visit any office of the **Department of Natural Resources and Mines** (☎ 07-3896 3111; www.nrm.qld.gov.au; 1-month licence adult/family $5.55/7.80). Note that fossicking is strictly a no-go in national parks.

Most of Queensland's gemfields are in relatively remote areas. Visits to these areas can be adventurous, great fun and possibly even profitable. Even if you don't strike it lucky with rubies, opals or sapphires you're bound to meet some fascinating characters while you're trying your luck in the gemfields. Queensland's main fossicking areas are the gemfields around Sapphire and Rubyvale (about 300km inland from Rockhampton; p245), the Yowah Opal Fields (deep in the southern outback, 150km west of Cunnamulla; p436) and the topaz fields around Mt Surprise and Georgetown (about 300km southwest of Cairns; p409 and p409).

Click onto www.gemfields.com, a virtual meeting place for avid fossickers, with loads of information and advice on fossicking in the Capricorn hinterland.

HORSE RIDING & TREKKING

Horse riding is another activity available all along the Queensland coast and in the outback, and it always a hit with kids. You can choose from one-hour strolls to gallops along the beach and overnight (or longer) treks, and find treks suited to your level of experience. Some of the most pleasant spots to ride include the Gold Coast hinterland (p136) and the Cooloola Section of Great Sandy National Park (p189), where you can do a four-day pub trek on horseback, which should solve all issues of drink driving. Two- or three-hour treks generally cost $50 to $60 per adult and $30 to $50 per child.

Homesteads and farmstays are another great way to experience horse riding, and Queensland has a few gems up its sleeve. You can spend several days getting to know your steeds near Hervey Bay (p205) on the temperate Fraser Coast and also en route between Mackay and Eungella National Park (p261).

PARAGLIDING & PARASAILING

Paragliding is a popular activity at many locations along the Queensland coast, but the best place of all is above the Carlo Sandblow at Rainbow Beach (p199), where championship competitions are held every January. Other good spots for paragliding include the Gold Coast hinterland (p149) and Eungella National Park (p262), near Mackay. Tandem flights generally cost around $130 to $165 and two-day lessons cost approximately $550.

Parasailing is another exhilarating way to view the coast from above. Outfits operate out of the Gold Coast (see p131) and many other beach resorts along the coast.

ROCK CLIMBING & ABSEILING

Believe it or not, Brisbane is a good place to learn rock climbing; activity is centred on the cliffs (p89), a series of 18m rock faces along the southern banks of the Brisbane River. The cliffs are floodlit at night to allow climbing in the cooler evening hours, and they offer great city and river views from the top. A number of operators offer climbing and abseiling instruction in Brisbane and other popular climbing areas around the city, including in national parks and the Glass House Mountains – climbing and outdoor shops are also good sources of information. Look under 'Outdoor Adventure Activities and Horse Riding' in the *Yellow Pages* to find climbing clubs and courses.

SAILING & OTHER WATER SPORTS

Queensland's waters are pure Utopia for seafarers of all skill, with some of the most spectacular sailing locations in the world. The hands-down winner of all of the state's picture-postcard possies is the Whitsunday Islands (see the boxed text on p266). Around these 74 idyllic gems is a massive smear of translucent blue sea that, at times, has a seamless and uninterrupted horizon. There are countless charters and boat operators based at Airlie Beach, the gateway to the islands.

There are plenty of day tours which hop between two or three islands, but the three-day/two-night all-inclusive cruises are much better value and provide a greater appreciation of just how beautiful the area is. You can also choose between tours that sleep their passengers onboard or ones that dock at an island resort for the night. The greatest benefit of a tour is that you don't require any sailing experience – some outfits will get you to join in under guidance, but you can have no skills and still enjoy a true sailing experience. The range is huge and as with most activities, the smaller the number of passengers the greater the price. As a general guide, day tours cost $60 to $100 for adults and $40 to $60 for children.

It's also fairly easy to charter your own boat at Airlie Beach, but be warned: that glassy sea has the potential to turn nasty, and regardless of what operators say, this should only be attempted by sailors with some experience. If you're lacking the skills but still want a far more intimate experience than a tour, consider chartering your own boat and hiring a skipper to do all the hard work for you. The cost of a 'bareboat' (unskippered) charter will set you back somewhere between $500 and $800 per day, depending on the size of the boat.

There's also a sizable local sailing scene around Manly (p117), just south of Brisbane, or you can explore some of the islands off the Far North Queensland coast on board a chartered boat or cruise from Port Douglas (p369).

An excellent online charter guide for those wanting to do the Robinson Crusoe thing is www.charterguide.com.au. It's nationwide, but you can just select 'Queensland' as a region and Rob's your uncle.

TOP FIVE WATER FUN SPOTS FOR KIDS

■ Cairns' foreshore (p333) Make a splash in the saltwater lagoon or Muddy's playground.

■ Streets Beach, Brisbane (p85) Cool off in a safe man-made lagoon in the heart of the city.

■ Wet 'n' Wild theme park (p135) Get your adrenaline pumping with wild slides, pools and rapids.

■ Chermside Aquatic Centre (p92) Explore the slides and tube rides at this suburban waterpark.

■ Settlement Cove Lagoon (p116) Keep the little ones happy at Redcliffe's colourful lagoon.

Water-skiing is often available too. There are water-sports hire places in all the coastal resorts and on most of the islands where you can hire catamarans, sailboards, jet skis, canoes, paddle boats and snorkelling gear by the day or hour.

SURFING

From a surfer's point of view, Queensland's Great Barrier Reef is one of nature's most tragic mistakes – it's effectively a 2000km-long breakwater! Mercifully, there are some great surf beaches along the coast in southern Queensland. Starting right at state's border with New South Wales, Coolangatta (p144), particularly at Kirra Beach, is a popular surfing haunt for Gold Coast locals. Nearby Burleigh Heads (p143) has some serious waves, which require some experience, but if you've got it you'll be in seventh heaven.

Virtually the entire shoreline of the Sunshine Coast is surfie stomping ground. The area from Caloundra (p175) to Mooloolaba (p177) is a good strip with popular breaks. Further north, the swanky resort of Noosa (p184) started life as a humble surfie hangout before it became trendy. It's still a popular hangout for longboarders, with good wave action at Sunshine Beach and the point breaks around the national park, especially during the cyclone swells of summer (December to February). Caloundra and Noosa are also increasingly popular venues for kite-surfing.

Near Brisbane, North Stradbroke Island (p121) also has good surf beaches, as does Moreton Island (p124). Because they take a little effort to get to, these areas tend to be less crowded than the Gold and Sunshine Coast beaches. Despite its exposed coast, Fraser Island has a few too many rips and sharks to appeal to surfers; see p210 for greater detail.

Queensland's most northerly surf beaches are at Agnes Water and the Town of 1770 (p225), just south of Gladstone. Here you can actually surf off the Great Barrier Reef, which at this point of its stretch does create some excellent breaks. This spot is strictly for old hands, though; the walls can get pretty hairy, you have to swim well out from shore and you may be sharing your personal space with the odd reef shark.

You can hire secondhand boards from almost any surf shop along the coast, and op shops in surf resorts are usually full of used boards. Unless you're taking lessons, it's probably best to start off with boogie boarding and work your way up, as surfing isn't as easy as it looks. Always ask locals and life savers about the severity of breaks – broken boards and limbs are not uncommon, particularly among inexperienced surfers with high ambitions.

If you're new to the sport, the best way to find your feet (literally!) is with a few lessons, and there are dozens of surf schools in southeast

For up-to-date surf reports tune into local radio stations or click onto www.coastalwatch .com and check out the latest conditions at various locations throughout southern Queensland.

Queensland. Two of the best spots to learn, mostly because the waves are kind to beginners, are Surfers Paradise (p136) and Noosa. Two-hour lessons cost between $40 and $50 and five-day courses for the really keen go for around $180.

Surfing enthusiasts will be glad to hear that Mark Warren's definitive *Atlas of Australian Surfing* is now available in a more portable size, as well as the previously published large coffee-table book. You may also find copies of the slim surf guide *Surfing Australia's East Coast* by Aussie surf star Nat Young.

Surfing competitions are held at several locations in Queensland, including North Stradbroke Island and Burleigh Heads on the Gold Coast; there are also numerous surf life-saving carnivals that take place on the beaches of southern Queensland from December, culminating in the championships in March/April. While these carnivals don't usually involved surfing, they are a good way to see other surf skills such as surf-skiing, board paddling and swimming demonstrated. Agnes Water, at the southern tip of the Great Barrier Reef, plays host to a longboard classic competition in March.

For definitive surfing information, events and tuition in Queensland, click onto www .surfingaustralia.com, go to 'state websites' and click on 'Queensland'.

SWIMMING

The very word 'Queensland' conjures up visions of endless stretches of sun-bleached sand with tepid, turquoise-blue waters lapping at the shore, backed by palm trees swaying gently in the breeze. Swimming in Queensland is one of life's great pleasures – and it's free and accessible to everyone.

You certainly won't be disappointed in the south of the state. Some of the most pleasant beaches with gentle surf conditions are at Coolum and Peregian (p181) on the Sunshine Coast, where smaller crowds give you plenty of room to splash about.

For a completely different swimming experience, head out to Queensland's islands, which range from sandbars to mountainous continental groups. They should provide all the white sand, blue skies and azure ocean you can take. The exquisite lakes on Fraser Island (p212) and North Stradbroke Island (p119) are some of the most beautiful swimming holes in the state, and the lack of surf generally means they're safe for everyone. Some of them reach significant depths though, so general safety, particularly with little tackers, is essential, and their waters can be quite cold.

The Sunshine State's sultry climate ensures an average water temperature of around 22° in winter and 26° to 29° in summer…yum!

Once you get north of Gladstone, the allure of many of the mainland beaches is spoiled by mudflats and mangroves. Further damaging the illusion of tropical paradise are the lethal box jellyfish that swarm along the north coast of Queensland every summer (see the boxed text on p226 for more information on stingers). You can protect yourself by wearing a stinger suit and swimming within the stinger enclosures found on many beaches, but many coastal towns have produced their own solution to the problem in the way of artificial lagoons. Generally built close to the water's edge to provide as authentic an experience (once you've disregarded the concrete) as possible, these are lovely antidotes to the heat. Two of the best are at Airlie Beach (p272) and in Cairns (p333). In a similar vein, Streets Beach (p85) in Brisbane is a sizable artificial beach set in parklands by the Brisbane River, which services the city's population, especially it's kids, when the mercury rises.

Once you start climbing to the very top of the state or heading inland you need to be wary of a different hazard altogether. You'll find a smor-

COOL KAYAKING

Great Sandy National Park

The base of the Cooloola Section of the Great Sandy National Park is dominated by the vast (but surprisingly shallow) Lake Cootharaba, which interrupts the Noosa River as it heads from Tewantin north into the depths of the park. Following the river's banks are 15 camping grounds, many accessible only by paddlers and bushwalkers. The protected conditions of the waterways and the surrounding landscape of high-backed dunes, vivid wildflowers, mangroves and thick rainforests make it an ideal kayaking destination. Best of all there are few roads through it and the only way to really explore the park is with a paddle.

- Nearest town: Elanda Point (p190)
- Tours: three-hour tours per adult/child $60/50, kayak hire per person $25 to $45
- Information: ☎ 07-5449 7792
- Website: www.epa.qld.gov.au (search parks and enter 'Cooloola Section Great Sandy National Park')

North Stradbroke Island

One of the world's largest sand islands, 'Straddie' is circumnavigated by long stretches of stunning white beach that skirt the Moreton Bay Marine Park on the island's west coast. The abundance of coastline and the opportunity to see wildlife including dolphins makes it an excellent and popular kayaking destination. At the north of the island, Cylinder Beach, near Point Lookout, generally has quiet conditions suitable for paddlers. There's a good distance of shallow water close to the point itself, so you can head east around the point to North Gorge – a popular stomping ground for turtles and dolphins.

- Nearest town: Point Lookout (p119)
- Tours: 2½-hour tours per person $35 to $40, kayak hire per hour/day around $20/50
- Information: ☎ 07-3409 9555
- Website: www.stradbroketourism.com

gasbord of magnificent lakes and rivers where you can cool off, but they tend to be inhabited by crocodiles. Take notice of warning signs around water holes and beaches, ask the locals for advice, and never swim in areas frequented by crocodiles at night.

Lastly, if the beaches, lakes and rivers are all a tad too far away, almost every country town has its own Olympic-sized swimming pool where you can cool off.

WHITE-WATER RAFTING, KAYAKING & CANOEING

The mighty Tully, North Johnstone and Russell Rivers between Townsville and Cairns are renowned white-water rafting locations, benefitting from the very high rainfall in the area. The Tully is the most popular of the three and has grade three to four rapids. This means the rapids are moderate, but require continuous manipulation of the raft to stay upright. Most of the guides operating tours here have internationally recognised qualifications and safety is fairly high on their list of priorities. This said, you don't need any experience, just a desire for a rush. You also need to be older than 13 (sorry kids).

You can do rafting day trips for about $150, including transfers, or longer expeditions. See the Cairns (p334) and Tully (p317) sections for more details.

The Tully River has 44 rapids with names such as Double D Cup, Jabba the Hut, Doors of Deception, and Wet and Moisty.

Sea kayaking is also popular in Queensland, and there are numerous operations along the coast that offer paddling expeditions through the calm Barrier Reef waters, often from the mainland out to offshore islands. There are also plenty of companies that operate guided tours of the waters of the Gold and Sunshine Coasts. For more information see the boxed text on p55.

Coastal Queensland is full of waterways and lakes, so there's no shortage of territory suitable for canoeing. You can rent canoes or join canoe tours in several places – among them Noosa (p183), Magnetic Island (p303), Mission Beach (p320) and around the Whitsunday Islands (p267).

Great Barrier Reef

When the sun beats a brilliant beam across the kaleidoscopic corals and teeming marine life of the Great Barrier Reef, it appears that Mother Nature has summoned all the colours of her vast palette and applied them in exquisite and liberal detail. Quite simply, exploring this unique environment is the closest we mere mortals can get to visiting another world, and even the briefest of visits will endow you with enough vivid memories to last a lifetime.

The Reef is one of Australia's World Heritage areas and one of the seven wonders of the natural world. It's also one of nature's richest realms. Stretching 2000km from just south of the tropic of Capricorn (near Gladstone) to just south of Papua New Guinea, it is the most extensive reef system in the world, and one made entirely by living organisms.

The southern and fragmented end of the Reef smears itself as far as 300km from the mainland, but at the northern end the Reef sits close to the coast in continuous stretches up to 80km wide. The lagoon between the outer reef and the mainland is dotted with smaller reefs, cays and islands. Drilling has indicated that the coral is more than 500m thick in places and it's estimated that most of the Reef is around two million years old, with some sections dating back 18 million years.

The Great Barrier Reef is longer than the Great Wall of China, bigger than England and about half the size of Texas.

NATURE'S THEME PARK

The Great Barrier Reef is made up of about 2900 separate fringing reefs (which form an outer ribbon parallel to the coast and dot the lagoons around the islands and the mainland) and barrier reefs (which are further out to sea). The 'real' Great Barrier Reef, or outer reef, is at the edge of the Australian continental shelf. All of these reefs exist because of one teeny tiny organism called a polyp.

Divers observe a Hawksbill turtle at the wreck of the *Yongala* (p295) off Townsville
ROBERT HALSTEAD

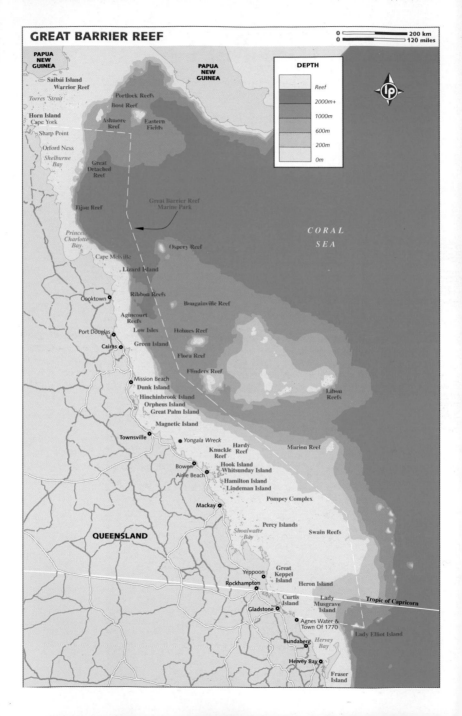

GREAT BARRIER REEF

DEPTH	
	Reef
	2000m+
	1000m
	600m
	200m
	0m

0 ▭▭ 200 km
0 ▬▬ 120 miles

PAPUA
NEW
GUINEA

Saibai Island
Warrior Reef

Torres Strait

Portlock Reefs

Boot Reef

PAPUA
NEW
GUINEA

Horn Island
Cape York

Ashmore
Reef

Eastern
Fields

Sharp Point

Orford Ness

*Shelburne
Bay*

Great
Detached
Reef

Tijou Reef

Great Barrier Reef
Marine Park

*Princess
Charlotte
Bay*

C O R A L

S E A

Cape Melville

Osprey Reef

Lizard Island

Cooktown

Ribbon Reefs

Bougainville Reef

Agincourt
Reefs

Port Douglas

Low Isles

Holmes Reef

Cairns

Green Island

Flora Reef

Mission Beach

Flinders Reef

Dunk Island

Hinchinbrook Island

Orpheus Island

Great Palm Island

Lihou
Reefs

Magnetic Island

Townsville

Yongala Wreck

Hardy
Reef

Marion Reef

Knuckle
Reef

Bowen

Hook Island

Airlie Beach

Whitsunday Island

Hamilton Island

Lindeman Island

Pompey Complex

Mackay

QUEENSLAND

*Shoalwater
Bay*

Percy Islands

Swain Reefs

Great
Keppel
Island

Yeppoon

Rockhampton

Heron Island

Curtis
Island

Lady
Musgrave
Island

Tropic of Capricorn

Gladstone

Agnes Water &
Town Of 1770

Lady Elliot Island

Bundaberg

*Hervey
Bay*

Hervey Bay

Fraser
Island

BEST OF THE REEF

- Watching protected sea turtles hatch and make their first daring dash on **Lady Elliot Island** (p231) or **Heron Island** (p232), then watching their older relatives glide gracefully through the ocean while you're on a cruise.

- Taking a fast cat from Airlie Beach out to **Knuckle Reef** (p268) or **Hardy Reef** (p268) and immersing yourself in some of the best snorkelling spots in the world.

- Soaring above the reef on a **scenic flight** (p336) and watching its huge and vivid mass carpet the sea beneath you.

- Exploring pristine and protected **Fitzroy Reef** (p225) – one of the least-touristed areas of the Great Barrier Reef.

- Going on an underwater 'forest' **tour** (p335), taking advantage of a guided dive and discovering the reef with experts.

- Catching a **day tour** (p335) and snorkelling amid hundreds of iridescent fish in the middle of the ocean, or watching their hustle and bustle from a glass-bottomed boat.

- Embarking on a sailing adventure from Airlie Beach through the **Whitsunday Islands** (p266) and exploring exquisite fringing reefs on the islands' perimeters.

The Building Blocks

There are two types of coral – hard and soft – but it's the hard corals that are the architects and builders of the Reef. Hard corals begin life as industrious little animals known as polyps, which look a little like tiny cucumbers with a mouth leading to their stomach. Polyps are soft and vulnerable, so they create an outer 'skeleton' to protect and support their bodies by excreting a small amount of hard limestone. This skeleton, with the polyp inside, is what we refer to as coral. When polyps die, their 'skeleton' remains as the architecture of the Reef, gradually building it up. Like a city in a state of constant renovation, new polyps grow on top of deceased corals, their billions of skeletons cementing together into an ever-growing natural bulwark. It's the new and living polyps that provide the reefs with their multitude of colour; when corals die they turn white. Different

The Great Barrier Reef is the only living thing visible from space. Astronauts call it the 'white scar on the face of the Pacific Ocean'.

Sea-whips and other types of coral

MICHAEL AW

Left to right:

Tubastrae hard coral
MICHAEL AW

A Clarks anemone fish
MICHAEL AW

polyps form varying structures, from staghorn and brain patterns to flat plate or table corals.

Coral is dependent on sunlight, which is why it's so visible – it can grow no deeper than 30m below the water's surface for sufficient light to filter through. It also needs clear and salty water to survive and consequently does not grow around river mouths – the Barrier Reef ends near Papua New Guinea because the Fly River's enormous water flow is both fresh and muddy.

Polyps, the animals that form coral, are close relatives of the jellyfish.

One of the most spectacular sights of the Barrier Reef occurs for a few nights after a full moon in late spring or early summer each year, when vast numbers of corals spawn at the same time. The tiny bundles of sperm and eggs are visible to the naked eye, and together they look like a gigantic underwater snowstorm. Many other reef organisms reproduce around this time, giving their spawn a greater chance of surviving predators.

Sorting the Reef from the Cays

Reefs fall into three categories: barrier or ribbon reefs, platform reefs and fringing reefs. The barrier reef proper lies on the outer, seaward edge of the reef system, lining the edge of the continental shelf in an often-unbroken formation. Platform reefs grow on the land side of these barrier reefs and often support coral cay islands. These occur when the reef grows to be above sea level, even at high tide; dead coral is ground down by water action to form sand, and sometimes vegetation takes root. Many famous Great Barrier Reef islands – such as Green Island near Cairns, the Low Isles near Port Douglas, Heron Island off Gladstone and Lady Musgrave Island north of Bundaberg – are coral cays. Closer to shore fringing reefs surround the hillier, continental islands. Great Keppel Island, most of the Whitsundays, Hinchinbrook and Dunk Islands, for example, were once the peaks of mainland coastal ranges, but rising sea levels submerged most of these mountains, leaving only the tips exposed. Today these are good places to spot coral close to the beach.

A school of Hussar Emperor fish
MICHAEL AW

Marine Communities

So what exactly lives in these vast coral cities? A lot! Marine environments demonstrate the greatest biodiversity of any ecosystem on Earth – much more so than rainforests. There are thousands of species within this complex ecosystem, all contributing to a perfectly symbiotic balance. To give you an idea of the quantities we're talking about, the Great Barrier Reef is home to:

- 1500 species of fish
- 400 types of coral
- 4000 breeds of clams and other molluscs
- 800 echinoderms, including sea cucumbers
- 500 varieties of seaweed
- 200 bird species
- 1500 different sponges
- 30-plus species of marine mammals
- 118 species of butterflies

Among the common species of fish you're likely to encounter are dusky butterfly fish, rich navy blue in colour with sulphur-yellow noses and back fins; large and lumbering graphic turkfish with luminescent pastel coats; teeny neon damsels darting flecks of electric blue; and six-banded angelfish, with blue tails, yellow bodies and tiger stripes.

The Reef is also a haven to many marine mammals such as whales, dolphins and dugongs (sea cows). Dugongs are listed as vulnerable and a significant percentage of their global numbers live in Australia's northern waters. The Great Barrier Reef is home to around 15% of the population. Humpback whales migrate to the Reef's warm waters from Antarctica to breed between May and October, and minke whales can be seen off the coast from Cairns to Lizard Island in June and July. Porpoises and killer and pilot whales also make their home on the Great Barrier Reef.

One of the Great Barrier Reef's most-loved inhabitants is the sea turtle. Six of the world's seven species live on the Reef and lay eggs on the islands' sandy beaches in spring or summer. All are endangered, but spying their huge, graceful bodies glide through the water is fairly common and enough to make any animal lover melt.

Sharks are also prevalent and play a pivotal role in the Great Barrier Reef's fragile balance. Like diligent cleaners they free the reefs of ailing,

The Reef near Cairns (p335)
PETER HENDRIE

Roberto Rinaldi's *Great Barrier Reef Dive Guide* provides a good insight into what you'll see diving on the reef, as well as some of the best spots to go.

Each of the 2900-odd reefs that make up the Great Barrier Reef contain around the same number of fish species as the entire Atlantic Ocean.

injured or overproducing species. Reef sharks are a common sight throughout, but if you're under the water don't bother running – their generally timid nature will often have them swimming from you! Rays in all shapes and sizes also dwell here, sailing languidly through the water while feeding on fish and plankton.

Butterflies are among the more unusual residents, with the Reef claiming 118 species and a total of 30% of all Australian butterflies. While some fit the stereotype of fragile little creatures, vulnerable to their environment and the wind's whimsy, others have the vigour and yen to travel several kilometres across open water – 'just island-hopping dahling'.

There are several species you need to be wary of, but common sense will usually prevent any unpleasant encounters or injuries. See p470 for more information.

Invertebrates outnumber vertebrates by around 20:1 on the Great Barrier Reef, with new species being discovered on a monthly basis.

HOW SHOULD I SEE IT?

The Reef's size is mammoth, as is its popularity. On average, the Great Barrier Reef's tourism industry contributes around $4.2 billion to the Australian economy every year. At the time of writing, there are some 730 certified tourism operators visiting the Reef, which accommodates crowds of close to two million visitors annually. All these numbers boil down to the fact that there is a multitude of ways to see this magnificent spectacle.

By far and away the best way to get up close and personal with the menagerie of marine life and dazzling coral is by diving or snorkelling. Immersing yourself underwater – even if you're just snorkelling – furnishes you with the most exhilarating appreciation of just how wonderful and rich this community is. Above a bed of undulating coral, tiny, iridescent schools swim in Olympic-standard synchronicity about sea turtles, anemones resembling aliens, scurrying reef sharks and fish the size of your Esky. The unremarkable surface of the water belies the colourful congestion less than a metre or so beneath. If you're lucky, you might also glimpse whales, manta rays, squid and dugongs.

Many places where the Reef grows today were land before the last ice age.

Almost all the diving and snorkelling in the Great Barrier Reef is boat-based, although there are a few good reefs surrounding some of the islands (see opposite). Free use of snorkelling gear is usually part of any cruise to the Reef and typically you can fit in around three hours of underwater wandering. Overnight or 'live-aboard' trips obviously provide a more in-depth experience and greater coverage of the reefs. If you want to do more than snorkel but don't have your diving certificate, many operators offer the option of doing an introductory dive. Basically, this is a guided dive where an experienced diver conducts an underwater tour. A solid safety and procedure lesson is given so you don't require a five-day PADI course or a 'buddy'.

You can surround yourself with the fabulous fishies without getting your feet wet on a semisubmersible or glass-bottomed boat, which provide windows to the underwater world. Alternatively, you can descend below the ocean's surface inside an underwater observatory or take a reef walk. Another spectacular way to see the Reef while staying dry is on a scenic flight. Soaring high above gives you a macro perspective of the Reef's beauty and size and allows you to see the veins and networks of coral connecting and ribboning out from one another.

If you are so strapped for time you can't do any of this, the excellent Reef HQ (p293) in Townsville has a myriad of the Reef's inhabitants, including corals and a massive, teeming aquarium.

Trip costs depend on the distance travelled, the type of boat and extras such as lunch and use of dive equipment.

WHERE SHOULD I SEE IT?

It's said you could dive here every day of your life and still not see the entire Great Barrier Reef. Consequently, choosing where to see it from can be quite perplexing. Individual chapters in this book provide in-depth information, but the following are some of the most popular and remarkable spots from which to see the Reef. Bear in mind that individual areas vary from time to time, depending on the weather or any recent damage.

Islands

Speckled throughout the Great Barrier Reef is a profusion of islands and cays. They offer some of the most stunning access to the Reef, and the job

Dive Sites of the Great Barrier Reef by Neville Coleman is a great, comprehensive guide to diving and snorkelling on the reef.

The water surrounding the Great Barrier Reef encompasses about 210,000 sq km.

Lady Elliot Island (p231)
BOB CHARLTON

DIVING ON THE REEF

The Great Barrier Reef is home to some of the world's best diving sites. Here are a few to get you started:

- The SS *Yongala* (p295) – a sunken shipwreck that has been cultivating a vivid marine community for more than 90 years.
- Spectacular Cod Hole (p393) on Lizard Island, where you can get nose to nose with a potato cod – the friendly giants of the reef.
- Beautiful Heron Island (p232), where you can step straight off the beach and join a crowd of colourful fish.
- Lady Elliot Island (p231) – with 19 highly regarded dive sites it's hard to know where to begin.
- Pixie Bommie (p393) on Lizard Island – delve into the after-five world of the reef by taking a night dive.

---

of choosing between them can be perplexing. All offer different activities and attractions, and each has its own aesthetic identity. The following is a list of some of the best islands, travelling from south to north.

You can learn a whole lot more about the Reef during an informative lecture at Reef Teach in Cairns; see p334.

For more information on individual islands, see the Whitsunday Coast (p250), Capricorn Coast (p222), Townsville & North Coast (p287), Cairns, Islands & Highlands (p327) and Far North Queensland (p365) chapters.

LADY ELLIOT ISLAND

The coral cay of Lady Elliot Island (p231) is the most southerly of the Great Barrier Reef islands. It's awe-inspiring for bird-watchers, with some 57 species living on the island. Sea turtles also nest here and it's possibly the best location on the Reef to see manta rays. It's also a famed div-

Hook Island (p278) in the Whitsundays

LEONARD DOUGLAS ZELL

ing location. There's a simple and pricey camping resort here, but you can also visit Lady Elliot on a day trip from Bundaberg.

Inside a semisubmersible
PAUL DYMOND

HERON ISLAND
Tiny Heron Island (p232) is another coral cay, sitting amid a huge spread of reef and a diving Mecca. The snorkelling is also good and it's possible to do a reef walk from here.

Heron is a nesting ground for green and loggerhead turtles and home to some 30 species of birds. It's an exclusive, utterly tranquil place and the single resort on the island charges accordingly.

HAMILTON ISLAND
The daddy of the Whitsundays, Hamilton Island (p280) is a sprawling resort laden with infrastructure. While this doesn't create the most intimate atmosphere, it does provide a wealth of tours going to the outer reef. It's a good place to see patches of the Reef unexplored from the mainland and families are extremely well catered for.

Green Island (p350)
CHRISTOPHER GROENHOUT

HOOK ISLAND
One for budget travellers, Hook Island (p278) is an outer Whitsunday Island surrounded by fringing reefs. There is excellent swimming and snorkelling here, and the island's sizable bulk provides plenty of good bushwalking. There's good and affordable accommodation on Hook and it's easily accessed from Airlie Beach, making it a good choice for those on a modest budget who want to experience a slice of the Reef from an island.

ORPHEUS ISLAND
This national park island is one of the Great Barrier Reef's most exclusive, tranquil and romantic hideaways. Orpheus (p313) is particularly good for snorkellers – you can step right off the beach and be surrounded by a glut of the Reef's colourful marine life. Clusters of fringing reefs also provide plenty of diving opportunities.

Operated by a private company, www.great -barrier-reef.au.com is a handy online resource to help figure out which tours and sections of the Reef are best suited to your holiday.

GREEN ISLAND
Another of the Great Barrier Reef's true coral cays, the entirety of Green Island (p350) is national park made up of dense rainforest. The fringing reefs surrounding Green Island are considered to be among the most beautiful of any island and the diving and snorkelling are quite spectacular. The birdlife is also a lure here: there are around 60 species on the island. The resort on Green Island is well set up for reef activities

Sunset on Flinders Reef
LEONARD DOUGLAS ZELL

and several tour operators offer diving and snorkelling cruises. There's also an underwater observatory here. You can also access Green Island as a day trip from Cairns.

LIZARD ISLAND

Remote and rugged, Lizard Island (p392) is the place to head to escape civilisation. It has a ring of talcum-white beaches, remarkably blue water and few visitors. It's also world-renowned as a superb scuba-diving location, with what is arguably Australia's best-known dive site at Cod Hole (p393). Here you can swim with the resident giant and docile potato cod, which can grow to weigh as much as 60kg. Pixie Bommie is another highly regarded dive site on the island.

Snorkellers will also get an eyeful of marine life here, with giant clams, manta rays, barracudas and dense schools of fish filling the waters just off shore.

If you're staying overnight you need to have deep pockets or no requirements whatsoever – it's bush camping or five-star luxury.

Mainland Gateways

There are several mainland gateways to the Reef, all offering a slightly different experience or activity. Deciding which to choose can be difficult, so the following, in order from south to north, is a brief breakdown.

International studies have highlighted Australia as the world leader in managing reef ecosystems. The Great Barrier Reef is among the healthiest in the world.

AGNES WATER & TOWN OF 1770

The tiny beach hamlet of 1770 and Agnes Water (p225) is good if you want to escape the crowds. Tours head to Fitzroy Reef Lagoon, one of the most pristine sections of the Reef, where numbers are still limited. It's excellent for snorkelling but also quite spectacular just aboard the boat.

GLADSTONE

Slightly bigger, but still a relatively small gateway, Gladstone (p228) is an excellent choice for avid divers and snorkellers, being the closest access point to the southern or Capricorn reef islands and innumerable cays. Among these is Lady Elliot Island (see p64). A number of islands near Gladstone are also great for a bout of isolated bush camping.

AIRLIE BEACH

'Airlie' (p270) is a small town with a wallop of sailing outfits. The big attraction here is spending two or more days aboard a boat and seeing some of the fringing coral reefs amid the Whitsunday Islands. The surrounding scenery is sublime, but you'll only touch at the edges of the Reef. There are, however, a number of fast catamaran operators that zoom out the 60km required for visitors to immerse themselves in some spectacular reefs, which provide outstanding snorkelling, swimming and diving.

Airlie is also friendly to all wallets, so whether you're a five-star or no-star traveller, there'll be a tour to match your budget.

> For information on the Great Barrier Reef, including how to protect it and where to fish, contact the Great Barrier Reef Marine Park Authority, based at Reef HQ (p293) in Townsville.

TOWNSVILLE

Townsville (p289) is renowned among divers. Whether you're learning or experienced, a four- or five-night onboard diving safari around the numerous islands and pockets of the Reef is a great choice. Kelso Reef and the *Yongala* shipwreck in particular are teeming with marine life. There are also one or two day-trip options on glass-bottomed boats, but you're better off heading to Cairns for greater choice.

The Reef HQ (p293) aquarium, which is basically a version of the Great Barrier Reef in a nutshell, is also here.

> Most of the Great Barrier Reef's living corals are 'young'. They've developed over the last 18,000 years; basically sometime since the last ice age.

MISSION BEACH

Closer to the Reef than any other gateway destination, Mission Beach (p318) is small and quiet and has a few boat and diving tours to sections of the outer reef. Although the choice isn't huge, neither are the crowds, and you won't be sharing the experience with a fleet of other vessels.

CAIRNS

Undeniably the main launching pad for Great Barrier Reef tours, there is a bewildering number of operators in Cairns (p328). Subsequently the choice is huge – you can do anything from relatively inexpensive day trips on large boats to intimate five-day luxury charters. The variety of tours covers a wide section of the Reef, with some operators going as far north as Lizard Island. Inexpensive tours are likely to travel to inner reefs, ie those close to the mainland, which tend to be more damaged than outer reefs. Scenic flights also operate out of Cairns. Bear in mind, though, that this is the most popular destination, so unless you've got the pockets for a private charter you'll be sharing the experience with many others, year-round.

> A diver explores the diverse array of coral found on the Reef
>
> NIGEL MARSH

PORT DOUGLAS

The swanky resort town of Port Douglas (p367) is the gateway to the Low Isles and Agincourt Reef, an outer ribbon reef featuring crystal-clear water and particularly

THREATS TO THE REEF

The sheer size of the Great Barrier Reef makes it difficult to fathom how this ecosystem could be in danger of survival, but three main threats (land-based pollutants, overfishing and the big one, global warming) jeopardise the Reef's future. Coral polyps need a water temperature of 17.5°C to 28°C to grow and cannot tolerate too much sediment. Global warming (aided by regular El Niño events) is overheating sections of the world's oceans. This rise in temperature literally bleaches the coral – the brightly coloured algae living alongside living polyps is expelled, leaving 'bleached' white coral that soon dies if temperatures do not return to normal.

Pollutants in the form of sewage and agricultural phosphate runoff also damage the Reef by promoting algal growth and blocking sunlight to the coral, as do the high impact of development from increased tourist activity, damage from boat anchors, and trawling (which can accidentally trap animals such as sea turtles and birds). Shipping in the area adds the possibility of oil spills, and in 2000 a section of the Reef was blasted to release a ship that had become stuck.

Infestations of the crown-of-thorns sea star are notorious because the animals appear to chew through large areas of coral and occur when the reef ecology is disturbed.

Some environmentalists and scientists predict that under the current conditions, coral cover within the Reef may be reduced to less than 5% by the year 2050. Because all the living organisms in the Reef are symbiotic, the colourful and diverse ecosystem we see today may be gone forever.

Fortunately, it's not all doom and gloom. In July 2004 the Australian Government introduced new laws that increased 'no-take' zones, where it is forbidden to remove animal or plant life (ie no fishing), to 33% of the Reef (it was previously only 4.5%). The Queensland Government also unveiled the Great Barrier Reef Coast Marine Park, a state park encompassing the actual coastline from just north of Bundaberg to the tip of Cape York – a total of 3600km. Although it will be several years before the success of these plans can be measured, they are certainly a huge step towards tackling the human-induced threats to the Reef.

Responsible tourism also plays an important role. Take all litter with you, even biodegradable material such as apple cores. Admire, but don't touch or harass, marine animals and be aware that if you touch or walk on coral you'll damage it (and it can also cause some very nasty cuts).

Many visitors will take at least a one-day cruise to the Reef and most operators are conscientious and responsible, but if you see staff dumping dodgy substances, question them. Even the simple act of feeding fish can be highly detrimental. Aside from the environmental impact of this kind of behaviour, there is a multibillion-dollar tourism industry based on the Great Barrier Reef, and its sustainability relies on the Reef remaining healthy.

stunning coral. Although Port Douglas is smaller than Cairns, it's still very popular and has a wealth of tour operators. Diving, snorkelling and cruising trips tend to be classier, pricier and less crowded than in Cairns. You can also do a scenic flight from here.

COOKTOWN

Another one for divers, Cooktown's (p387) lure is its close proximity to Lizard Island (see p392). Although you can access the island from Cairns,

The Reef is a great place to learn to dive

LEONARD DOUGLAS ZELL

you'll spend far less time travelling on the boat if you go from here. Cooktown's relatively remote location means there are only a handful of tour operators and small tourist numbers, so your experience is not likely to be rushed or brief. The only drawback is that Cooktown, and its tour operators, shuts down between November and May due to the wet season.

Food & Drink Matthew Evans & Justine Vaisutis

Queensland's culinary beginnings relied heavily on a diet influenced by Britain. The legacy of steak and three veg spanned many lifetimes and was only interspersed with seafood. Invention was reserved for the potato, which was the only thing that was cut, boiled, mashed, fried, roasted and cooked in every way imaginable. But Queensland is now home to some of the most dynamic places in the world to have a feed, thanks to immigration and a dining public willing to give anything new, and better, a go. Anything another country does, Queensland does too. Vietnamese, Indian, Thai, Italian – it doesn't matter where it's from, there's an expatriate community and interested locals desperate to cook and eat it.

Noosa on the Sunshine Coast is renowned for its fine cuisine, and has been the subject of cookbooks and food guides. Brisbane is fast becoming a culinary hero to rival the feats of Sydney and Melbourne, and can claim to be a destination worthy of touring gourmands. Tourist numbers on the Gold and Sunshine Coasts have demanded a higher calibre of eatery, and the regions have responded by coming up with the goods. Cairns too has a global palate, satiated by eclectic offerings to suit all budgets. Outside of these foodies' wonderlands you should expect simpler fare. But whereas 'pub grub' once meant a lamb roast, bangers and mash or chicken parmigiana, it now encompasses everything from a laksa to a Madras curry. The bangers and mash are still on the menu, but they're likely to be of the sundried tomato, smoked cheddar and beef variety.

We've coined our own phrase, Modern Australian, to describe our cuisine. If it's a melange of East and West, it's Modern Australian. If it's not authentically French or Italian, it's Modern Australian – our attempt to classify the unclassifiable. Dishes aren't usually too fussy and the flavours are often bold and interesting. Spicing ranges from gentle to extreme, coffee is great (though it still reaches its greatest heights in Brisbane, Noosa, Townsville and Cairns), and the meats are tender, full-flavoured and usually bargain-priced.

STAPLES & SPECIALITIES

Australia's best food comes from the sea. Nothing compares to this continent's seafood, harnessed from some of the purest waters you'll find. Right along the Queensland coast, even a simple dish of fish and chips (and that includes the takeaway variety) is super fresh and cooked with care.

Connoisseurs prize Queensland's sea scallops and blue swimmer crabs. One of the state's iconic delicacies is the Moreton Bay bug – like a shovel-nosed lobster without a lobster's price tag. The prawns and calamari here are also incredible. Add to that countless wild fish species and Queensland has one of the greatest bounties on earth.

Queenslanders love their seafood, but they've not lost their yen for a hefty chunk of steak. As the rest of the country draws increasingly from that meat and three veg legacy, Queensland has kept a firm grip on it, but spun it up with a fat dose of creativity. Rockhampton is the beef capital of Australia and visiting carnivores would be crazy not to cut into a steak sizzling on a stone slab so you can cook it to your liking. Elsewhere beef and lamb remain staples, but they are now done with tandoori, Greek or provinçal flavourings…as well as just chops or steak.

Queenslanders also embrace 'bush' foods, and in the restaurants of Cairns, Noosa and Brisbane you may find emu pâté, gum leaf–smoked

Matthew Evans was a chef before he crossed to the 'dark side' as a food writer and restaurant critic. Matthew is the award-winning author of four food books, and there is little that he wouldn't eat (that isn't endangered).

A Good Plain Cook: an Edible History of Queensland by S Addison & J McKay is a collection of recipes spanning Queensland's history, with newspaper snippets and photos from different eras.

venison or wattle-seed ice cream. Kangaroo, once regarded as exotic game, is now so common on restaurant, café and pub menus it's almost passé.

Queensland's size and diverse climate, from the humid, tropical north to the mild, balmy south, means there's an enormous variety of produce on offer. If you're embarking on a road trip throughout the state, you're bound to encounter rolling banana, sugar or mango plantations or quilted orchards. In summer, mangoes are so plentiful that Queenslanders actually get sick of them. But this is not the case with macadamias. This native nut with its smooth, buttery flavour grows throughout southeastern Queensland and fetches prices of $40 per kilo and up. Queenslanders use it in everything – you'll find it tossed in salads, crushed and frozen in ice cream and stickily petrified in gooey cakes and sweets.

> Witchetty grubs are considered a delicious snack in the Australian outback. These fat white grubs are nutritious and said to have a nutty flavour.

There's a small but brilliant farmhouse cheese movement, hampered by the fact that all the milk must be pasteurised (unlike in Italy and France, the home of the world's best cheeses). Despite that, the results can be great. Keep an eye out for the goat's cheese from Gympie (p196) and anything from the boutique Kenilworth Country Foods (p194).

Australians' taste for the unusual generally kicks in at dinner only. Most people eat cereal for breakfast, or perhaps eggs and bacon on weekends. They devour sandwiches for lunch and then eat anything and everything in the evening. Yum cha (the classic southern Chinese dumpling feast), however, has found huge popularity with urban locals in recent years, particularly on weekends. Some non-Chinese even have it at the traditional time, first thing in the morning.

DRINKS

You're in the right country if you're after a drink. Once a nation of tea and beer swillers, Oz is now turning its attention to coffee and wine.

> 'Shouting' is a revered custom where people rotate paying for a round of drinks. Just don't leave before it's your turn to buy!

Queensland's climate is generally too warm to produce good wines, but the Granite Belt (p157) in the Darling Downs is a blossoming and excellent wine-growing district. Other small wine areas include the Atherton Tableland, the Sunshine and Gold Coast hinterlands and around Kingaroy.

Australian wine is mostly a product of the southern states. If you're buying a bottle or scrutinising a wine list you can't go wrong with a Cabernet Sauvignon from Coonawarra, Riesling from Tassie or the Clare Valley, Chardonnay from Margaret River or Shiraz from the Barossa Valley.

Other notable regions to keep an eye out for include the Hunter Valley in New South Wales and the Mornington and Bellarine Peninsulas, Mount Macedon and the Yarra Valley in Victoria.

There's a bewildering array of beer available in bottle shops, pubs, bars and restaurants. The Queensland staple is XXXX. It's much maligned elsewhere in the country, but the locals swear by it. On tap in every pub and bar in the state you'll find domestic lagers, but the appearance of imported ales, pilseners and stouts in city pubs and bars is increasing.

TALKING STRINE

The opening dish in a three-course meal is called the entrée, the second course (what North Americans call an entrée) is called the main course and the sweet bit at the end is called dessert, sweets, afters or pud. In lesser restaurants, of course, it's called dessert.

When an Australian invites you over for a baked dinner it might mean a roast lunch. Use the time as a guide – dinner is normally served after 6pm. By 'tea' they could be talking dinner or they could be talking tea. A coffee definitely means coffee, unless it's after a hot date when you're invited up to a prospect's flat.

Most beers have an alcohol content between 3.5% and 5%. That's less than many European beers but stronger than most of the stuff in North America. Light beers come in under 3% alcohol and are finding favour with people observing the superstringent drink-driving laws.

A local speciality in Queensland, which has found its way to the rest of the country in varying degrees of popularity, is 'Bundy and Coke'. The self-explanatory mix of Bundaberg Rum (distilled in…Bundaberg), and Coke can be found on tap in most parts of the state. It's pretty sweet and obviously alcoholic, but if spirits are your poison you'll be accommodated well.

In terms of coffee, Australia is leaping ahead, with Italian-style espresso machines in virtually every café, boutique roasters all the rage and, in urban areas, the qualified barista (coffee maker) just about the norm.

Fresh fruit juice is a popular and healthy way to beat the heat. Juice bars that specialise in all sorts of yummy concoctions are common, but you can also get good versions at cafés and ice-cream stores.

In Queensland, when ordering a beer you can order a five or small (140mL), a pot, 10 or middy (all 285mL), a schooner (425mL), a pint (568mL) or a jug (1125mL).

CELEBRATIONS

Celebrating in the Australian manner often includes equal amounts of food and alcohol. A birthday could well be a BBQ (barbie) of steak (or prawns) washed down with a beverage or two. Weddings are usually a big slap-up dinner, though the food is often far from memorable. Christenings are more sober, mostly offering home-baked biscuits and a cup of tea.

For many an event, especially in summer, Australians fill the car with an Esky (an ice chest or cooler), tables, chairs and a cricket set or footy, and head for a barbie by the lake/river/beach. If there's a total fire ban (which occurs increasingly each summer), the food is precooked and the barbie becomes more of a picnic, but the essence remains the same.

Christmas in Australia often finds the more traditional (in a European sense) baked dinner being replaced by a BBQ, full of seafood and quality steak. It's a response to the warm weather. Prawn prices skyrocket, chicken may be eaten with champagne at breakfast, and the meal is usually in the afternoon, after a swim and before a really good, long siesta.

Various ethnic minorities have their own celebrations. The Tongans love an *umu* or *hangi*, where fish and vegetables are buried in an earthen pit and covered with coals; Greeks may hold a spit BBQ; and the Chinese go off during Chinese New Year every January or February.

Tim Tam bombs, exploding Tim Tams or Tim Tam slams are a delicious Aussie ritual. Take a Tim Tam biscuit, nibble off the two diagonally opposite corners, dunk it into a hot drink (tea, coffee or hot chocolate) and suck through the fast-melting biscuit like a straw. Ugly but good.

WHERE TO EAT & DRINK

Typically, a restaurant meal in Australia is a relaxed affair. It may take 15 minutes to order, another 15 before the food arrives and half an hour between courses. The upside is that your table is yours for the night, unless you're told otherwise. So sit, linger and live life in the slow lane.

Competitively priced places to eat are clubs or pubs that offers counter meals. Returned & Services League (RSL) clubs are prolific in Queensland, and while the décor can be outdated – plastic palm trees and portraits of Queen Elizabeth II are still all the rage – the tucker is normally excellent. Generally you order staples such as a fisherman's basket, steak or chicken cordon bleu at the kitchen, take a number and wait until it's called out. You collect the meal yourself, saving on staff and on your total bill, which comes in at around $10 to $15 for a slap-up meal.

The other type of club you're bound to come cross is the surf life-saving club (SLSC). Most coastal towns have at least one, sometimes up to three. They're similar to RSL clubs, but many now compete with finer restaurants and their bistros stock inventive fare. Additionally, they're almost always perched on the beachfront so the views alone tend to be worth a visit.

Queensland produces an estimated 256,000 tonnes of bananas a year.

Other clubs to keep an eye out for are bowls clubs, Irish clubs and sports clubs. In all cases, you'll have to sign in as a temporary member and you may be asked to prove you're a bone fide visitor.

Some of the best value food in Brisbane can be found in its diminutive but excellent Chinatown (p101).

Solo diners find that cafés and noodle bars are welcoming. Good fine-dining restaurants often treat you like a star but, sadly, some midrange places may still make you feel a little ill at ease.

One of the most interesting features of the Australian dining scene is the Bring Your Own (BYO), a restaurant that allows you to bring your own alcohol. If the restaurant sells alcohol, the BYO bit is usually limited to bottled wine and a corkage charge is added to your bill. The charge is either per person or per bottle, and ranges from nothing to $15 per bottle. BYO is a dying custom, however, and most licensed restaurants don't like you bringing your own wine, so ask when you book.

Most restaurants open around 11am for lunch and from 5.30pm or 6pm for dinner. Australians usually eat lunch shortly after noon, and dinner bookings are usually made for 7.30pm or 8pm, though in Brisbane and other major cities some restaurants stay open past 10pm.

> The *Courier Mail* publishes the *Goodlife Restaurant Guide*, which reviews some 250 restaurants, mostly in southern Queensland. It's an excellent resource for good eats.

Quick Eats

There's not a huge culture of street vending in Australia, though you may find a pie or coffee cart in some places. Most quick eats traditionally come from takeaways, which serve burgers (with bacon, egg, pineapple and beetroot if you want) and other takeaway foods. The humble sandwich is perennially popular and gone are the days when you were served two pieces of bread with a slice of cheese and meat in the middle. Paninis, focaccias and toasted Turkish rolls with a smorgasbord of ingredients offer a healthy, filling lunch. Fish and chips is still popular, with the fish most usually being shark (often called flake) dipped in batter and eaten at the beach on Friday night. Sushi is another popular quick eat and a healthy alternative. Virtually every regional centre has a small sushi shack, and they seem to appear on every corner in Brisbane and Cairns.

American-style fast food has taken over in recent times, though many Aussies still love a meat pie or dinky-di sausage roll, often from a milk bar, but also from bakeries, kiosks and some cafés. If you're at an Aussie Rules football or rugby league match, a beer, a meat pie and a bag of hot chips are as compulsory as wearing your team's colours to the game.

Pizza is one of the most popular fast foods; most pizzas that are home-delivered are American style (thick with lots of toppings) rather than Italian style. That said, more and more wood-fired, thin Neapolitan-style pizza can be found, even in country towns. In the city, Roman-style pizza (buy it by the slice) is becoming more popular.

> The cuisine in Noosa is so good it prompted its own cookbook – *Noosa the Cookbook* by Madonna Duffy.

Middle Eastern kebabs are another staple in Australia's multicultural takeaways. Served with chicken, lamb, beef or felafel, they now rival hot dogs as the standard after-pub feed.

There are some really dodgy mass-produced takeaway foods, bought mostly by famished teenage boys, including the dim sim (a kind of deep-fried Chinese dumpling) and Chiko Roll (for translations, see p74).

VEGETARIANS & VEGANS

In Queensland's regional centres and big cities, vegetarians are catered for as well as carnivores. Most restaurants and pubs put as much effort into their vegetarian dishes as they do their meat ones. In the cities you're likely to find excellent vegetarian restaurants, while other places may have

---

AUTHORS' RECOMMENDATIONS

Need a quick reference of Queensland's best eateries? The team of authors who put this book together reckon the following options are worth skipping breakfast for:

- Oskars (p143), Burleigh Heads, has sweeping views and sassy seafood.
- Circa (p103), Brisbane, has elegant surrounds and an award-winning menu.
- Berardo's (p187), Noosa, is a highly acclaimed restaurant with heavenly ambience and inventive cuisine.
- Pier Restaurant (p207), Hervey Bay, serves exquisite seafood with first-class seafood.
- Angelo's on the Marina (p258), Mackay, has a lively atmosphere and Mediterranean treats.
- Deja Vue (p275), Airlie Beach, is an unpretentious restaurant with multicultural creations and decadent deserts.
- Harold's Seafood (p298), Townsville, has excellent takeaway fish and chips and a glass cabinet full of prawns.
- Fusion Organics (p341), Cairns, has inspiring organic juices and deli fare for budget wallets and enlightened palates.
- On the Inlet (p373), Port Douglas, has outstanding seafood, outstanding service and understated surrounds.
- North Gregory Hotel (p426), Winton, offers local hospitality and slap-up pub meals the size of your table.

---

vegetarian menus. Cafés also have vegetarian options. Take care with risotto and soups, though, as meat stock is often used. The more remote the region, the fewer vegetarian options you're likely to find on the menu.

Vegans will find the going much tougher, but local Hare Krishna restaurants or Buddhist temples often provide relief, and there are usually dishes that are vegan-adaptable at restaurants.

EATING WITH KIDS

Queensland is an incredibly family-friendly state and dining with children is relatively easy. Avoid the flashest places and children are generally welcomed. Kids are usually more than welcome at cafés and bistros and clubs often see families dining early. Many fine-dining restaurants don't welcome small children (they just assume that *all* children are ill-behaved).

Most places that welcome children don't have separate kids' menus, and those that do usually offer food straight from the deep fryer, such as crumbed chicken and chips. It can be better to find something on the main menu and have the kitchen adapt it to your children's needs.

The best news for travelling families is that there are plenty of free or coin-operated BBQs in parks. Beware of weekends and public holidays when fierce battles can erupt over who is next in line for the BBQ.

HABITS & CUSTOMS

It's good manners to use British knife and fork skills, with the fork in the left hand and the knife in the right, though Americans may be forgiven for using a fork like a shovel. Talking with your mouth full is considered rude, and fingers should only be used for food such as sandwiches.

If you're invited to dinner at someone's house, always take a gift. You may offer to bring something for the meal, but even if the host refuses – insisting you just bring your scintillating conversation – you should still take a bottle of wine. Flowers or a box of chocolates are also acceptable.

When you order fish and chips from a takeaway there's a good chance you'll be eating shark – known as flake – it's delicious!

BILLS & TIPPING

The total at the bottom of a restaurant bill is all you really need to pay. It should include GST (as should menu prices) and there is no 'optional' service charge added. Waiters are paid a reasonable salary, so they don't rely on tips to survive. Often, though, especially in urban Australia, people tip a few coins in a café, while the tip for excellent service can go as high as 15% in whiz-bang establishments. The incidence of add-ons (bread, water, surcharges on weekends etc) is increasing.

Australians like to linger a bit over coffee. They like to linger a really long time while drinking beer. And they tend to take quite a bit of time if they're out to dinner (as opposed to having takeaway).

Smoking is banned in most eateries in Queensland, so sit outside if you love to puff. And never smoke in someone's house unless you ask first. Even then it's usual to smoke outside.

COOKING COURSES

The food store **Black Pearl Epicure** (☎ 07-3257 2144; 36 Baxter St, Fortitude Valley, Brisbane), and **Mondo Organics** (☎ 07-3844 1132; 166 Hardgrave Rd, West End, Brisbane), a food store and restaurant, both offer excellent and highly regarded cooking classes.

Also in Brisbane is the **James St Cooking School** (☎ 07-3252 8850; Level 1, 22 James St, Fortitude Valley, Brisbane), which uses produce from the popular James St Market (p106) in its classes.

EAT YOUR WORDS

The Australian Vegetarian Society has a useful website (www.veg-soc.org) that lists a number of vegetarian and vegetarian-friendly places to eat.

Australians love to shorten everything, including peoples' names, so expect many food-related words to be abbreviated.

Food Glossary

barbie/BBQ	A barbecue, where (traditionally) smoke and overcooked meat are matched with lashings of coleslaw, potato salad and beer.
bugs	Not the earthy sort, but an abbreviation for Moreton Bay bugs, a Queensland shellfish speciality.
Chiko Roll	A fascinating large, spring roll–like pastry for sale in takeaway shops. Best used as an item of self-defence rather than eaten.
dim sim	A Chinese dumpling served either steamed or fried as fast food.
Esky	An insulated ice chest to hold your tinnies, before you hold them in your tinny holder. May be carried onto your tinny, too.
pav	Pavlova, the meringue dessert topped with cream, passionfruit and kiwi fruit or other fresh fruit.
pot	A medium glass of beer (285mL, same size as a middy or 10).
reef 'n' beef	A main course, usually of gargantuan proportions, consisting of a steak and seafood combination.
sanger/sarni/sambo	A sandwich.
schooner	A big glass of beer (425mL) but not as big as a pint (568mL).
snags	Sausages (aka surprise bags).
stubby holder/tinny holder	Insulating material that you use to keep the tinny ice cold, and nothing to do with a boat.
Tim Tam	A commercial chocolate biscuit that lies close to the heart of most Australians.
tinny	Usually refers to a can of beer, but could also be the small boat you go fishing for mud crabs in (and you'd take a few tinnies in your tinny, in that case).
Vegemite	Salty, dark brown breakfast spread, popular on toast, adored by Aussie masses, much maligned by visitors.

Brisbane

CONTENTS

HIGHLIGHTS

- Beating the heat at Streets Beach in the **South Bank Parklands** (p85), then picnicking with river views
- Delving into some Sunshine State culture at the **Queensland Museum**, **Art Gallery** and **Sciencentre** (p84)
- Supping Saturday morning lattes with sassy scrambled eggs in **Fortitude Valley's** (p103) cosmopolitan village
- Going bush in the city: exploring wilderness, botanical gardens and the planetarium at **Mt Coot-tha** (p86)
- **Cycling** (p89) through Brisbane's parks and meandering along the riverbank on two wheels
- Discovering what's behind every bend of the Brisbane River on a scenic **river cruise** (p96)
- Lunching lazily in **West End** (p105) with a side of jazz and bohemia
- **Market hopping** (p110) on a sunny Sunday morning and scooping up some bargains and atmosphere

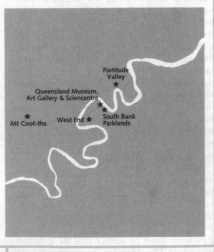

Fortitude Valley ★

Queensland Museum, Art Gallery & Sciencentre ★

Mt Coot-tha ★   West End ★   South Bank Parklands ★

- www.ourbrisbane.com
- www.brisbane.citysearch.com.au

Brisbane seems to acquire more nicknames than any other city in Australia – BrisVegas and Brisneyland have been the flavour of the last decade. 'Southerners' like to perpetuate the labels, but listen carefully and you'll hear the locals bandy them about with a nudge and a wink. That's because they know Brisbane's glitz is but a paltry component of its guts. The city is a smorgasbord of flavours simmering in cosmopolitan cafés, lazy picnics in vast, subtropical gardens, and panoramic views from lookouts up high and river vessels down low. Blow your tastebuds with some world-class cuisine and celebrate the city's heart and soul during the multitude of festivals that cram its annual calendar.

Reclining languidly over a tropical landscape and blessed with a temperate climate, Brisbane is now recognised as one of the most desirable places to live in Australia. It lacks the pretensions of a big city, but scores the perks. The undisputed arts capital of Queensland, Brisbane enjoys dozens of theatres, art-house cinemas, opera and concert halls, galleries, museums and live-music venues. The contemporary culture on offer is in a constant state of reinvention. And then there's the landscape. It's easy to forget you're in Australia's third-largest city when the high-rises still compete with a leafy spread of trees. The Brisbane River ambles through the city, keeping the concrete and steel in check, and adding its bulk to the changing character of the suburbs that line its banks.

Venture an hour or two from the city in the car and you'll hit some of Queensland's major tourist destinations, including the Gold and Sunshine Coasts with their mountainous hinterlands, and the islands of Moreton Bay.

HISTORY

The first settlement in the Brisbane area was established at Redcliffe on Moreton Bay in 1824 as a penal colony for Sydney's more recalcitrant convicts. After struggling with inadequate water supplies and hostile Aborigines, the colony was relocated to the banks of the Brisbane River, the site of the city centre today, but suffered at the hands of numerous crooked warders and was abandoned in 1839. The Moreton Bay area was thrown open to free settlers in 1842, marking the beginning of Brisbane's rise to prominence, and the beginning of trouble for the region's Aborigines.

By the time of Queensland's separation from New South Wales in 1859, Brisbane had a population of around 6000. Huge wealth flowed into the city from the new pastoral and gold-mining enterprises in the Darling Downs, and grandiose buildings were built to reflect this new-found affluence. The frontier-town image was hard to shake off, however, and it wasn't until the 1982 Commonwealth Games and Expo '88 that Brisbane's reputation as a cultural centre became recognised. Brisbane has now cemented its place as Australia's third-largest city, with a population of 1½ million.

ORIENTATION

Brisbane's **central business district** (CBD) is bound by a U-shaped loop of the Brisbane River, about 25km upstream from the river's mouth. The centre is small in size (just over 1 sq km) and laid out in a grid pattern. Most of the CBD's action buzzes around the pedestrianised Queen St Mall. At the southern end of Queen St is Victoria Bridge, which connects the centre to South Brisbane and the cultural development known as **South Bank**. Further south is the bohemian **West End**.

Fortitude Valley ('The Valley' in BrisVegas speak) lies northeast of the CBD as a continuation of Ann St. To the southeast of the Valley is **New Farm**, another trendy sub-

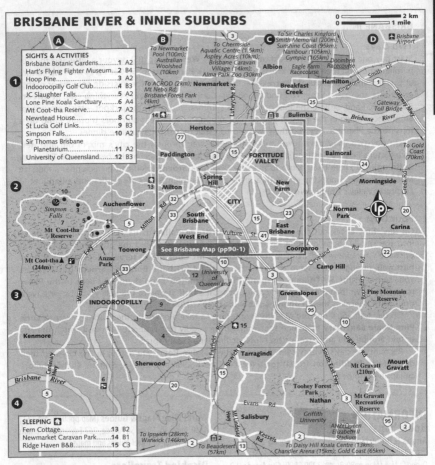

BRISBANE RIVER & INNER SUBURBS

0 —————— 2 km
0 —————— 1 mile

SIGHTS & ACTIVITIES
Brisbane Botanic Gardens...........1 A2
Hart's Flying Fighter Museum....2 B4
Hoop Pine.................................3 A2
Indooroopilly Golf Club............4 B3
JC Slaughter Falls....................5 A2
Lone Pine Koala Sanctuary......6 A4
Mt Coot-tha Reserve...............7 A2
Newstead House......................8 C1
St Lucia Golf Links...................9 B3
Simpson Falls........................10 A2
Sir Thomas Brisbane
Planetarium.....................11 A2
University of Queensland.......12 B3

SLEEPING
Fern Cottage.........................13 B2
Newmarket Caravan Park.......14 B1
Ridge Haven B&B..................15 C3

urb close to the action. The Story Bridge (Brisbane's answer to the Sydney Harbour Bridge) connects Fortitude Valley with **Kangaroo Point**, a pleasant spot to stay and handy for access to the Gold Coast.

The Roma St Transit Centre, where you'll arrive if you're coming by bus, train or airport shuttle, is on Roma St, about 500m west of the city centre. Heading east, Roma St meets the CBD at Ann St, near King George Sq, the large open area in front of Brisbane's City Hall. Central Station is about 200m north of Queen St, at the corner of Ann and Edward Sts.

Brisbane Airport is about 15km northeast of the city. There are shuttles to/from the city (see p112).

Maps
You can pick up free copies of *The Brisbane Map*, *i on Brisbane* and *Brisbane Map – a Backpackers Guide* from the Brisbane Visitors Information Centre in the Queen St Mall. All of these include maps of the CBD. For more comprehensive detail, pick up a copy of Lonely Planet's *Brisbane and Gold Coast City Map* ($6). Alternatively, *Brisbane Suburban Map* by UBD ($7.25), *Brisbane and Region* by Hema Maps ($5.95) or Gregory's *Brisbane Street Directory* ($24.50) are all good.

The definitive guide to Brisbane's streets is UBD's *Brisbane Street Directory* (known locally as 'Refidex'; $39), which includes maps of the Gold and Sunshine Coasts.

BRISBANE

BRISBANE IN...

Two Days
Start day one with a cruisey breakfast in Brisbane's **West End** (p105), savour a latte and the bohemian vibes and then saunter across to **South Bank Parklands** (p85). Get savvy with the culture at the **Queensland Cultural Centre** (p84), then head into one of the riverside eateries or grab a quick bite and bask in the river and city views. Cool your heels, and everything else, at **Streets Beach** (p85) and explore the parklands. If it's summer, you've hit the jackpot – stick around for an alfresco movie in the park. If you've had enough of the great outdoors though, jump on a ferry to the Riverside Pier and then walk up to **Circa** (p103) for a sublime dinner.

On day two head downtown and snake your way through the city's mix of old and new architecture. Explore Brisbane's history at **City Hall** (p83) and gape at the beautiful old **Treasury Building** (p83), then head south to the **City Botanic Gardens** (p84) and picnic under a massive Moreton Bay fig. Finish the day with a brew at the **Belgian Beer Cafe** (p106) and a banquet in Fortitude Valley's **Chinatown** (p103).

Four Days
On day three check out the café culture in **Fortitude Valley** (p103). Fuel up and then delve into the trendy shops or linger in the numerous galleries. Spend the afternoon seeking out Brisbane's best view and head to the lookout at **Mt Coot-tha Reserve** (p86). Take in a short bushwalk through the reserve and visit the beautiful **Brisbane Botanic Gardens** (p87). Dazzle your senses at the **Sir Thomas Brisbane Planetarium** (p87) and then head back to the Valley for a Chinatown banquet or a chic dinner. Work it all off at one of the Valley's clubs, or have a drink with a local at the **Elephant & Wheelbarrow** (p107).

On day four you'll need to give the feet a rest, so take a cruise up the Brisbane River to **Lone Pine Koala Sanctuary** (p88) and see what all the cuddly fuss is about. In transit watch the city unfold around you and take a closer look at Brisbane's leafy sprawl.

Recount the day's events over a beer at the **Belgian Beer Cafe** (p106) in the city and then gravitate to **Paddington** (p104) for a feast at the Kookaburra Café or Sultans Kitchen before collapsing into bed.

INFORMATION
Bookshops
Angus & Robertson Post Office Sq (Map pp80-2; ☎ 3229 0717; Shop 1-4, Post Office Sq, Adelaide St) Queen St Mall (Map pp80-2; ☎ 3229 8899; City Arcade, 52 Queen St) Generic chain selling books of all genres.
Archives Fine Books (Map pp80-2; ☎ 3221 0491; 40 Charlotte St; ☒ 9am-9pm Mon-Sat, 10am-4pm Sun) Fantastic range of secondhand books, boasting one million titles.
Avid Reader (Map pp90-1; ☎ 3846 3422; www.avid reader.com.au; 193 Boundary St, West End; ☒ 8.30am-6pm Mon, Tue & Sat, to 8.30pm Wed-Fri, to 5pm Sun) Diverse range; great for pottering.
Book Nook (Map pp80-2; ☎ 3221 3707, 3221 6055; Lower Ground fl, 51 Edward St) This bookshop primarily sells top-quality performing arts and poetry books, as well as travel guides.
Borders Bookstore (Map pp80-2; ☎ 3210 1220; 162 Albert St) Sizable branch of this reliable chain.
Folio Books (Map pp80-2; ☎ 3221 1368; 80 Albert St) Small bookshop with eclectic offerings.

World Wide Maps & Guides (Map pp80-2; ☎ 3221 4330; Shop 30, Anzac Sq Arcade, 267 Edward St) Comprehensive range of travel guides and maps.

Disabled Travellers
The city centre is commendably wheelchair friendly and Brisbane City Council (BCC) produces the *Brisbane Mobility Map*. These are usually available from the **BCC Customer Services Centre** (Map pp80-2; ☎ 3403 8888, TTY 3403 8422; www.brisbane.qld.gov.au; Lower Ground fl, City Plaza, 69 Ann St; ☒ 8.15am-4.45pm Mon-Fri).

The **Disability Information Awareness Line** (DIAL; ☎ 1800 177 120, 3224 8444, TTY 3224 8021; www .disability.qld.gov.au) provides information on disability services and support throughout Queensland. Its phone lines are open from 9am to 5pm Monday to Friday. DIAL also publishes the quarterly *Connect* magazine.

Information about disabled access on public transport can be obtained from **Trans-Info** (☎ 13 12 30; www.transinfo.qld.gov.au).

Emergency
Ambulance (☎ 000, 1300 369 003)
Brisbane Rape Crisis Centre (☎ 3844 4008)
Fire (☎ 000, 3247 5539)
Lifeline (☎ 13 11 14)
Police (☎ 000) City (Map pp80-2; ☎ 3224 4444;
67 Adelaide St); Headquarters (Map pp80-2; ☎ 3364 6464;
100 Roma St); Fortitude Valley (Map pp80-2; ☎ 3131 1200;
Brunswick St Mall)
RACQ (☎ 13 19 05, breakdown 13 11 11) City (Map
pp80-2; GPO Building, 261 Queen St); St Pauls Tce (Map
pp80-2; 300 St Pauls Tce) Roadside service.

Internet Access
Internet cafés are fairly prolific in Brisbane, particularly in the CBD. Rates range from $3 per hour in the CBD to $6 in the 'burbs.
Central City Library (Map pp80-2; ☎ 3403 8888;
Lower Ground fl, City Plaza, 69 Ann St; ☺ 9am-6pm
Mon-Fri, 10am-3pm Sat & Sun) Free, but there's a two-hour limit and bookings are essential.
Dialup Cyber Lounge (Map pp80-2; ☎ 3211 9095;
128 Adelaide St; ☺ 9.30am-7pm Mon-Thu, to 8pm Fri,
10am-6pm Sat)
Global Gossip City (Map pp80-2; ☎ 3229 4033; 290
Edward St; ☺ 8am-midnight); Fortitude Valley (Map pp80-2;
☎ 3666 0900; 312 Brunswick St; ☺ 8am-midnight) Plenty
of terminals and cheap-call phone booths.
Internet City (Map pp80-2; ☎ 3003 1221; Level 4,
132 Albert St; ☺ 24hr) Cheap broadband access.
State Library of Queensland (Map pp80-2; ☎ 3840
7666; South Bank; ☺ 10am-8pm Mon-Thu, 10am-5pm
Fri-Sun) Free, but advance bookings required.

Internet Resources
www.ourbrisbane.com Extensive online city guide.
www.brisbane.citysearch.com.au Good for up-to-the-minute information about entertainment, restaurants and drinking holes.
www.brisbane-australia.com

Medical Services
Brisbane Sexual Health Clinic (Map pp90-1;
☎ 3227 8666; 270 Roma St)
Day & Night Pharmacy (Map pp80-2; ☎ 3221 4585;
141 Queen St; ☺ 7am-9pm Mon-Thu, 7am-9.30pm Fri,
8am-9pm Sat, 8.30am-5.30pm Sun)
Queensland Statewide Sexual Assault Helpline
(☎ 1800 010 120)
Royal Brisbane Hospital (Map pp90-1; ☎ 3253 8111;
Herston Rd, Herston; ☺ 24hr casualty ward)
Travel Clinic (Map pp80-2; ☎ 1300 369 359, 3211
3611; 1st fl, 245 Albert St; ☺ 7.30am-7pm Mon-Thu,
7.30am-6pm Fri, 8.30am-5pm Sat, 9.30am-5pm Sun)

Travellers' Medical & Vaccination Centre (Map
pp80-2; TMVC; ☎ 3221 9066; 5th fl, 247 Adelaide St;
☺ 8am-5pm Mon & Fri, 10am-7pm Tue, 8am-9pm Wed,
8am-2am Thu, 8.30am-2pm Sat)

Money
There are foreign-exchange bureaus at Brisbane Airport's domestic and international terminals, as well as ATMs that take most international credit cards. For after-hours foreign exchange, the tellers in the Treasury Casino are there 24 hours a day. ATMs are prolific throughout Brisbane.
American Express (Map pp80-2; ☎ 1300 139 060;
131 Elizabeth St)
Interforex Brisbane (Map pp80-2; ☎ 3221 3562;
Shop Q255, Wintergarden Centre, 171-209 Queen St)
Travelex Edward St (Map pp80-2; ☎ 3221 9422; 276
Edward St); Queen St Mall (Map pp80-2; ☎ 3210 6325;
Shop 149F Queen St Mall)

Post
Australia Post (☎ 13 13 18) GPO (Map pp80-2; 261
Queen St; ☺ 7am-6pm Mon-Fri); Wintergarden (Map
pp80-2; 2nd fl, Wintergarden Centre, Queen St, ☺ 8.30am-
5.30pm Mon-Fri, 9am-4pm Sat) The GPO has poste restante.

Tourist Information
Brisbane Visitor Information Centre (Map pp80-2;
☎ 3006 6290; cnr Albert & Queen Sts; ☺ 9am-5.30pm
Mon-Thu, 9am-7pm Fri, 9am-5pm Sat, 9.30am-4.30pm
Sun) Great one-stop info counter for all things Brisbane.
Brisbane Visitors Accommodation Service (Map
pp80-2; ☎ 3236 2020; 3rd fl, Roma St Transit Centre,
Roma St; ☺ 7am-6pm Mon-Fri, 8am-5pm Sat & Sun) Privately run outfit specialising in backpacker travel, tours and accommodation in Brisbane and elsewhere in Queensland.
Naturally Queensland (Map pp80-2; ☎ 3227 7111;
160 Ann St; ☺ 8.30am-5pm Mon-Fri) The Queensland Parks & Wildlife Service (QPWS) runs this excellent information centre. You can get maps, brochures and books on national parks and state forests, as well as camping information and Fraser Island permits.
South Bank visitors centre (Map pp80-2; ☎ 3867
2051; Stanley St Plaza, South Bank Parklands;
☺ 9am-6pm, to 9pm Fri).

Travel Agencies
Flight Centre (Map pp80-2; ☎ 3221 8900; 170 Adelaide St; ☺ 9am-5.30pm Mon-Fri, 10am-4pm Sat)
STA Travel (www.statravel.com; ☺ 9am-5.30pm
Mon-Fri, 9am-3pm Sat); Brisbane Arcade (Map pp80-2;
☎ 3221 3722; Brisbane Arcade, 111 Adelaide St); City
(Map pp80-2; ☎ 3229 2499; Shop G11, Queen Adelaide
Bldg, 59 Adelaide St)

BRISBANE

CENTRAL BRISBANE

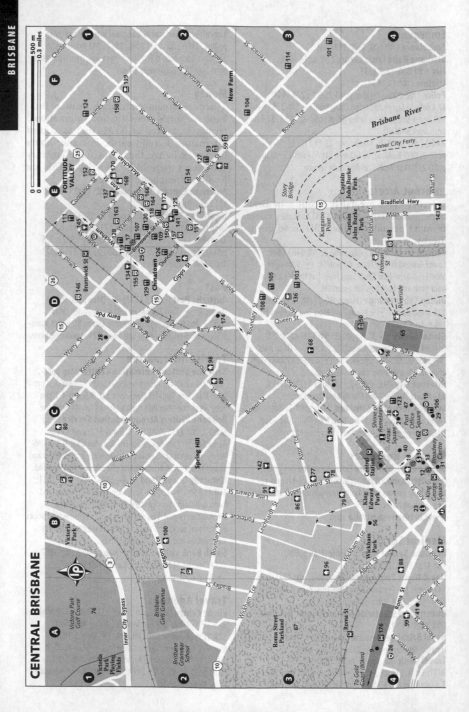

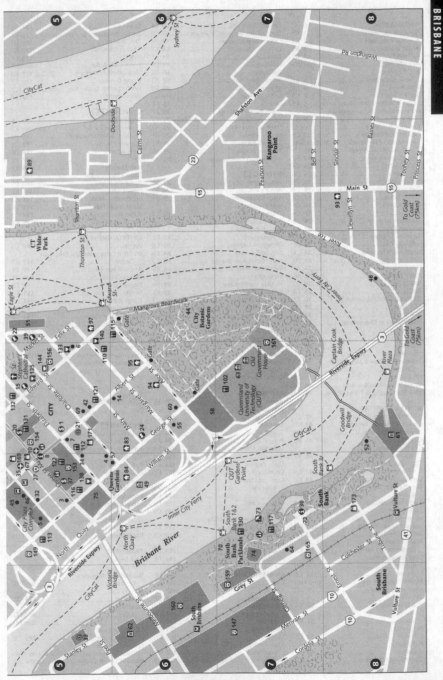

BRISBANE

Trailfinders (Map pp80-2; ☎ 1300 780 212, 3229 0887; 91 Elizabeth St; ☺ 9am-6pm Mon-Fri, 9am-4pm Sat, 10am-3pm Sun)
YHA Membership & Travel office (Map pp80-2; ☎ 3236 1680; 450 George St; ☺ 8.30am-6pm Mon, Tue, Thu & Fri, 9am-6pm Wed, 9am-3pm Sat) Tours, YHA membership and YHA hostel bookings.

SIGHTS

Most of Brisbane's major sights are in the CBD or inner-city suburbs. A walk through the city will reveal Brisbane's colonial history and architecture, and a ferry ride across the river lands you in the glut of attractions and activities at South Bank. Chinatown and Brunswick St, both in Fortitude Valley, provide a healthy injection of culture, shopping and food to keep you busy.

Further afield is Mt Coot-tha Reserve, where spectacular views from the lookout are easily accessed by bus. The free *Brisbane's Living Heritage* brochure, available from the visitors centre and at www.brisbane livingheritage.com, highlights many of the sights Brisbane has to offer.

City Centre

CITY HALL

Brisbane's **City Hall** (Map pp80-2; ☎ 3403 6586; btwn Ann & Adelaide Sts; admission free; ☺ lift & viewing tower 10am-3pm Mon-Fri, 10am-2.30pm Sat) is a gracious sandstone edifice overlooking the sculptures and fountains of King George Sq. Built in 1930, its splendour is not only skin deep; when you enter be sure to draw your eyes from the marble staircase upwards to the kaleidoscope roof and gothic Art Deco light fittings. There's an observation platform up in the bell tower, which affords brilliant views across the city. A delightful, old-fashioned elevator runs up to the top, but a word of warning – beware the bells. It's a terrifying, deafening experience if you are up here at noon when the bells start tolling.

On the ground floor is the **Museum of Brisbane** (Map pp80-2; admission free; ☺ 10am-5pm), which is broken into two wings. One half follows the city's historical journey with interactive exhibits. The Memory Theatre here shows a continuous film featuring Brisbanites of various backgrounds, each giving their historical, creative and social spin on the city. The other half of the museum has a more creative bent, showcasing artworks, crafts and photography by local

and international artists. There are free guided tours of the museum on Tuesday, Thursday and Saturday at 11am.

ROMA ST PARKLAND

This **park** (Map pp80-2; ☎ 3006 4545; www.romastreet parkland.com; 1 Parkland Blvd; admission free; ☺ 24hr, free guided tours 10am & 2pm Thu-Sun Sep-May, 11am & 2pm Thu-Sun Jun-Aug) is a veritable feast of flora inhabiting 16 hectares of the northern edge of the city. Apparently it's the biggest urban subtropical garden in the world. Broken into 16 precincts, the park offers visitors the opportunity to explore lily gardens, an Indian-inspired tea and coffee plantation, a rockery, native gardens and much more. Scattered throughout the park are works by local artists. There's also an outdoor theatre and plenty of public BBQs so you can do the very Australian picnic thing.

Southeast of the Parkland, on Wickham Tce, is the **Old Windmill & Observatory** (1828; Map pp80-2), one of the oldest buildings in Brisbane. Due to a design flaw, the sails were too heavy for the wind to turn, and a convict-powered treadmill was briefly employed before the mill was abandoned. The building was converted to a signal post and later a meteorological observatory.

TREASURY CASINO TO QUEENSLAND UNIVERSITY OF TECHNOLOGY

At the western end of the Queen St Mall, overlooking the river, is Brisbane's magnificent Italian Renaissance–style **Treasury Building** (Map pp80-2). It has a lavish façade, with commanding balconies and columns. The treasury now contains an entirely different kind of money spinner: Conrad's 24-hour casino. Casino junkies are sure to love the generic interior, but for everyone else, a circumnavigation of the exterior will reveal the building's best features.

In the block southeast of the casino, Conrad also occupies the equally gorgeous former **Land Administration Building**. Here, however, it's been converted to a five-star hotel (see p101).

Closer to the water is another of Brisbane's historic gems: the **Commissariat Stores Building** (Map pp80-2; ☎ 3221 4198; 115 William St; adult/child $4/2; ☺ 10am-4pm Tue-Fri & Sun). Built by convicts in 1829, it was used as a government store until 1962. Today it houses a museum that follows the development of the Moreton Bay settlement, which eventually became Brisbane. The ground floor delves into the history of the Moreton Bay penal colony, which incarcerated repeat offenders from all over the country during the 1820s.

Continuing south along George St, on the right immediately after the junction with Margaret St, is the **Mansions** (Map pp80–2), a beautiful and unusual three-storey terrace built in 1890. Look out for the cats on top of the parapet at each end of the building. Opposite is the imposing Greek-revival façade of the **Queensland Club** (Map pp80–2).

One block south of the Mansions, **Parliament House** (Map pp80-2; ☎ 3406 7562; cnr Alice & George Sts; admission free) occupies a suitably regal position overlooking the City Botanic Gardens (below). Set against a tropical backdrop, its grand, sandy façade is quite magnificent and arguably Brisbane's most stunning historical piece of architecture. The structure dates from 1868 and was built in French Renaissance style with a roof clad in Mt Isa copper. Free guided tours are available on demand between 9am and 4pm Monday to Friday, and 10am to 2pm weekends, unless parliament is sitting, in which case you can hang out in the public gallery and watch the politicians strut their stuff. If you're lucky you may strike a hot topic; otherwise the bureaucratic banter can be as thrilling as watching the carpet grow.

Virtually next door, within the Queensland University of Technology (QUT) campus, is the **QUT Art Museum** (Map pp80-2; ☎ 3864 2797; 2 George St; admission free; ✆ 10am-4pm Tue-Fri, noon-4pm Sat & Sun). Modest in size but not in talent, this excellent gallery showcases contemporary art in all its mediums and 'isms'. There's a definite lean towards Australian works, but temporary exhibits by international artists are also displayed. Best of all are the frequent displays of work by students at the university, demonstrating future directions of art in Australia.

CITY BOTANIC GARDENS
These expansive **gardens** (Map pp80-2; ☎ 3403 0666; Albert St; ✆ 24hr, free guided tours 11am & 1pm Mon-Sat) are a mass of green lawns, towering Moreton Bay figs, bunya pines, macadamia trees and other tropical flora, descending gently from the QUT campus. A network of paths throughout enables strollers, joggers, picnickers, cyclists and in-line skaters

to make their way to quiet spots for respites, or to nowhere in particular. The pretty **Mangrove Boardwalk**, a wooden walkway skirting the riverbank on the eastern rim, is lit until midnight. The glow provides good opportunities to spot tame possums in the trees.

Between October and March, the alfresco **Moonlight Cinemas** (☎ 1300 551 908; www .moonlight.com.au; adult/child $12.50/8; ✆ 6pm Tue-Sun) screens movies in the gardens.

RIVERFRONT
The former docks area northeast of the CBD is one of the most attractive and lively areas in the city. The striking, domed **Customs House** (1886-89; Map pp80-2; ☎ 3365 8909; 399 Queen St; admission free; ✆ 10am-4pm) is so aesthetically pleasing it's hard to imagine it was used as a functional building. However, as the name suggests, for almost a century this was where all ships heading into Brisbane's port were required to pay duties. The University of Queensland now leases the building and uses it as a swank venue for fundraisers and private gatherings. On the lower level, a free gallery under excellent curatorship displays diverse, temporary exhibits ranging from classical landscapes to printed broadsheets packing a political wallop. There's also a very good brasserie here (see p102).

Further south are the **Riverside Centre** and **Eagle St Pier** (Map pp80–2) complexes. Despite some awful plastic kit-architecture this is an attractive riverside site and home to some very fine restaurants. A good time to come here is on Sunday morning, when the area becomes a busy craft market. There are ferry terminals at both complexes.

Queensland Cultural Centre
On South Bank, just over Victoria Bridge from the CBD, the Queensland Cultural Centre is the epicentre of Brisbane's cultural confluence. It's a huge compound that includes a concert and theatre venue, an enormous conference and convention centre and a modern concrete edifice containing the city's main art gallery, museum and the Queensland State Library (a lot of culture to cram into one building!).

At the back of the complex, the **Queensland Museum** (Map pp80-2; ☎ 3840 7555; www.qmuseum.qld .gov.au; Grey St, South Brisbane; admission free; ✆ 9am-5pm) occupies imaginations with all manner of curiosities. Queensland's history is given a once over with an interesting collection of exhibits, including a skeleton of the state's own dinosaur *Muttaburrasaurus* and the *Avian Cirrus*, the tiny plane in which Queensland's Bert Hinkler made the first England-to-Australia solo flight in 1928. Upstairs there's an enlightening, if not distressing, display on Queensland's endangered species, as well as a reconstruction of the host of mammoth marsupials that roamed these shores more than 100,000 years ago. There are also good temporary exhibits on the likes of bug, beetle and butterfly parades, or dinosaur skeletons from around the globe.

Within the museum is the excellent **Sciencentre** (Map pp80-2; www.sciencentre.qld.gov.au; per adult/child/family $9/7/28), a hands-on exhibit that has interactive displays, optical illusions, a perception tunnel and regular film shows.

Inside an austere chunk of concrete, the **Queensland Art Gallery** (Map pp80-2; ☎ 3840 7303; www.qag.qld.gov.au; Melbourne St, South Brisbane; admission free; ☒ 10am-5pm Mon-Fri, 9am-5pm Sat & Sun, free guided tours at 11am, 1pm & 2pm Mon-Fri, 11.30am, 1pm & 2.30pm Sat & Sun) houses a fine permanent collection, mostly of domestic and European artists. The first floor is devoted to celebrated Australian artists, and you can view works by masters including Sir Sydney Nolan, Arthur Boyd, William Dobell, George Lambert, Margaret Preston and Brett Whitely. The gallery also features some excellent temporary exhibits and you may catch anything from a Clifford Possum exhibition to the cutting edge of international art.

At the time of writing the Queensland Art Gallery was constructing the new **Queensland Gallery of Modern Art** (Map pp90-1) at Kurilpa Point, 200m north of the existing gallery. It's due to open in 2006 and will be the second biggest public art museum in Australia. Its focus will be contemporary Australian, Indigenous Australian, Asian, Pacific and international art. It also promises multimedia works and programmes for art enthusiasts of all ages.

South Bank Parklands

This beautiful smear of green **park** (Map pp80-2; admission free; ☒ dawn-dusk), skirting the western side of the Brisbane River, is home to cultural attractions, fine eateries, small rainforests, hidden lawns and gorgeous flora. Scattered throughout are BBQs and climbing gyms where youngsters swarm like bees

to honey. A scenic esplanade offers spectacular views of the city and the whole area is laden with atmosphere and character.

The two stand-out attractions are **Stanley St Plaza** (Map pp80-2), a renovated section of historic Stanley St lined with cafés, shops and restaurants, and **Streets Beach** (Map pp80-2). On hot days people converge on this artificial swimming hole, which wraps around trees, bridges and rockeries before opening up to resemble a tropical lagoon. The beach even has its own lifeguards, but the lack of rips, undertows and sharks tends to keep the drama to a minimum.

On Friday evening and all day Saturday and Sunday, there's a large and popular **craft and clothing market** in the plaza.

The **Suncorp Piazza** (Map pp80-2) is an outdoor theatre that screens international sporting events regularly and movies during school holidays, both for free. It's also a venue for concerts and performances.

The Parklands are within easy walking distance of the CBD. You can also get there by CityCat or City Ferry (there are three jetties along the river bank) or by bus or train from the transit centre or Central Station.

Queensland Maritime Museum

This **museum** (Map pp80-2; ☎ 3844 5361; Sidon St, South Brisbane; adult/child $6/3; ☒ 9.30am-4.30pm), at the western end of the South Bank promenade, has a wide range of displays on maritime adventures (and misadventures) along the state's coast. A daunting highlight is the sizable map showing the location of more

---

BRISBANE'S TOP FIVE PICNIC SPOTS

■ **Mt Coot-tha Reserve** (p86) Choose from a host of pretty picnic spots.

■ **City Botanic Gardens** (opposite) Munch on lunch beneath fig and macadamia nut trees.

■ **Brisbane Forest Park** (p87) Take your BBQ out bush.

■ **Roma St Parkland** (p83) Explore these global gardens then pull up a patch of grass for lunch.

■ **South Bank Parklands** (left) Sizzle some snags in-between swims and soaking up the sun.

than 1500 shipwrecks (mostly victims of the Reef) in Queensland's waters since 1791. You can indulge your naval-battle fantasies by clambering about the HMAS *Diamantina*, a restored 1945 navy frigate, and there's also a good display on the tragic sinking of the *Pandora*, the ship sent to retrieve the mutineers from Captain Cook's *Bounty*.

Inner North

For over a decade the alternative neighbourhoods of Fortitude Valley and nearby New Farm have been the hub of all things contemporary and cool, thanks to a confluence of artists, restaurateurs and various fringe types flooding the area. Recently a whiff of café culture with yuppie overtones has seeped in, but the edge remains.

During the day the action is concentrated on **Brunswick St Mall** (Map pp80–2), a pedestrianised arcade full of pavement cafés, bars and shops. This strip buzzes on Friday and Saturday nights, when it becomes the nerve centre for Brisbane's nightlife. On Saturday mornings the scent of cigarettes and beer is replaced by lattes and incense as weekend brunchers join the bustle of the **Brunswick St Markets**. This is a good spot to pick up art and craft wares or handmade clothing from budding designers.

McWhirter's Markets (Map pp80–2) at the Wickham St end of the mall is a Brisbane landmark with an impressive Art Deco corner façade.

Alongside the funky restaurants and bars, Brisbane's very own **Chinatown** occupies one street (Duncan St) but exhibits the same flamboyance and flavour of its counterparts in Sydney and Melbourne. The Ann St end is guarded by an exquisite Tang dynasty archway and oriental lions. The mall itself is populated by Chinese restaurants, herbalists, massage therapists and acupuncture businesses. Chinese landscaping throughout includes pagodas and a waterfall.

Just west of the Valley, **St John's Cathedral** (Map pp80-2; ☎ 3835 2248; 373 Ann St; admission free; ☯ 9.30am-4.30pm Mon-Sat, 11am-4.30pm Sun; tours 10am & 2pm Mon-Sat, 2pm Sun) is a beautiful piece of 19th-century Gothic Revival architecture. Inside the church is a magnificent fusion of carved timber and stained glass. The building is a true labour of love – construction began in 1906 and is still going! A small donation is appreciated for the guided tours.

New Farm, just east of the Valley along Brunswick St, became 'desirable' among young professionals a few years ago and is now chock-a-block with wine bars and restaurants. At the eastern end of Brunswick St, **New Farm Park** (Map pp90–1) is a large, open parkland with playgrounds, picnic areas and gas BBQs, jacaranda trees and beautiful rose gardens.

The inner north is renowned for its profusion of private galleries and exhibition spaces, mostly showing paintings and ceramic works for sale. The best and biggest is the **Institute of Modern Art** (Map pp80-2; ☎ 3252 5750; www.ima.org.au; ☯ 11am-5pm Tue-Fri, 11am-4pm Sat), a noncommercial gallery with an industrial exhibition space and regular showings by local names. It's housed inside the **Judith Wright Centre for Contemporary Arts** (Map pp80-2; ☎ 3872 9000; www.judithwrightcentre.com; 420 Brunswick St, Fortitude Valley), which is another excellent venue for live performance of all genres.

Other galleries in the area:
Jan Murphy Gallery (Map pp80–2; ☎ 3254 1855; 486 Brunswick St; ☯ 10am-5pm Tue-Sat)
Philip Bacon Gallery (Map pp80–2; ☎ 3358 3555; 2 Arthur St; ☯ 10am-5pm Tue-Sat)

Newstead House

North of the centre, on the Brisbane River, is Brisbane's best-known heritage site, the lovely old **Newstead House** (Map p77; ☎ 3216 1846; Breakfast Creek Rd, Newstead; adult/child/family $4.40/2.20/11; ☯ 10am-4pm Mon-Fri, 2-4pm Sun). Set in attractive forested grounds, the historic homestead dates from 1846 and is beautifully fitted out with Victorian furnishings and antiques, clothing and period displays.

Mt Coot-tha Reserve

About 7km west of the city centre, **Mt Coot-tha Reserve** (Map p77) is a 220-hectare bush reserve that's teeming with wildlife (mostly of the possum and bush-turkey variety). Aside from the chunk of wilderness, the big attractions here are a massive planetarium and the spectacular lookout. The latter affords panoramic daytime views of Brisbane and a few bits beyond, and at night, a sea of twinkling lights blanketing the terrain for miles. The lookout is accessed via Samuel Griffith Dr and has wheelchair access.

There are picnic spots with tables and BBQs scattered throughout the park. One of the nicest is **Simpson Falls** (Map p77), set in a gentle valley and surrounded by scrub. In less of a bush enclave but with a thick carpet of lawn is **Hoop Pine** (Map p77). Bigger than both is **JC Slaughter Falls** (Map p77), where you can create an alfresco banquet amid oodles of trees and grass. The turn-off to JC Slaughter Falls is just north of Sir Samuel Griffith Dr. At the end of the road you can access the circuitous, 1.8km **Aboriginal Art Trail**, which takes you past eight art sites with work by local Aboriginal artists. Also here is the **JC Slaughter Falls Track** (3.4km return), which leads through the reserve to the lookout. It's quite steep in several sections; decent walking shoes are recommended.

The very beautiful **Brisbane Botanic Gardens** (Map p77; ☎ 3403 8888; admission free; ⏰ 8.30am-5.30pm Sep-Mar, 8am-5pm Apr-Aug; free guided walks 11am & 1pm Mon-Sat) cover 0.5 sq km and include over 20,000 species of plants. The plethora of mini ecologies, which include cactus, Japanese and herb gardens, rainforests, and arid zones, make you feel like you're traversing the globe's landscape in all its vegetated splendour. There is also a compact tropical dome in which exotic palms soar above you like science-fiction props.

Also within the gardens, the **Sir Thomas Brisbane Planetarium** (Map p77; ☎ 3403 2578; adult/child/family $2/1/5; ⏰ 2.30-4.30pm Tue-Fri, from 10am during school holidays, 11am-8.30pm Sat, 11am-4.30pm Sun) is Australia's largest planetarium with a series of mind-boggling astronomical displays. There's a great observatory here and the shows inside the **Cosmic Skydome** (adult/child/family $11.50/6.80/31) will make you feel like you've stepped on board the *Enterprise*.

To get here via public transport, take bus No 471 from Adelaide St, opposite King George Sq ($2.60, 30 minutes, hourly Monday to Friday, six services Saturday and Sunday). The bus drops you off in the lookout car park and stops outside the Brisbane Botanic Gardens en route. The last trip to the city leaves at around 4pm on weekdays and 5pm at weekends.

Brisbane Forest Park

Brisbanites suffering from suburban malaise satiate their wilderness cravings at this 28,500-hectare park in the D'Aguilar Range, 10km north of the city centre. It's a great area for bushwalking, cycling, horse riding, camping and scenic drives. At the park entrance the Brisbane Forest Park **visi-**

tors centre (☎ 3300 4855; www.brisbaneforestpark.qld .gov.au; 60 Mt Nebo Rd; ⏰ 8.30am-4.30pm Mon-Fri, from 9am Sat & Sun) has information about **camping** (per person $4) and maps of the park. If you plan to camp, keep in mind that it is bush camping, without any facilities, and you must contact the visitors centre for permits and access.

The birdlife is a big lure here and it's a beautiful spot for a BBQ. There are **walking trails** ranging from a few hundred metres to 8km, including the 6km Morelia Track at the Manorina Bush Camp and the 5km Greene's Falls Track at Maiala National Park.

Beside the visitors centre is **Walk-About Creek** (adult/child/family $5/2.50/12.50; ⏰ 9am-4.30pm), a freshwater study centre where you can see a resident platypus up close, as well as turtles, green tree frogs, lizards, pythons and canoodling gliders. There's also a small but wonderful walk-through aviary. It's an outstanding alternative to a zoo.

To get here catch bus No 385 ($3.40, 30 minutes), which departs from the corner of Albert and Adelaide Sts hourly from 8.20am to 3.20pm. The bus stops outside the visitors centre and the last departure back to the city is at 4.55pm. The actual park walks are a fair distance from the visitors centre so if you're planning on attacking them, it's best to have your own transport.

University of Queensland

The **university** (Map p77) occupies a 1.1-sq-km site in a loop of the Brisbane River

---

BRISBANE'S TOP FIVE FOR A RAINY DAY

- Dose up on art, culture, science and history at the **Queensland Cultural Centre** (p84).

- Find out what the XXXX fuss is all about – take a **brewery tour** (p96).

- Catch an art-house flick at the Dendy or kid-pleasers at South Bank **cinemas** (p109).

- Test your mettle and go **indoor rock climbing** (p89).

- Slip into an astronaut's skin and explore the universe at the **Sir Thomas Brisbane Planetarium** (left).

7km south of the city. It's an attractive and interesting place to visit, with several museums, good sporting facilities, an excellent bookshop and a cinema. You can ride a bike all the way here from the city along the Bicentennial Bikeway, which follows the western bank of the Brisbane River out of the centre (see opposite).

The helpful **information office**, in a small building beside the main entrance, has a map of the grounds and information about the facilities.

The university is centred around the lovely **Great Court**, a spacious area of lawns and trees surrounded by a semicircle of impressive cloistered sandstone buildings. There are several museums open to the general public by appointment, including the **Anthropology** (☎ 3365 2674; admission free; ⏱ 11am-3pm Tue-Thu during semester), **Antiquities** (☎ 3365 2191; admission free; ⏱ 9am-5pm Mon-Fri), and **Zoology** (☎ 3365 4856; admission free; ⏱ 9am-4pm Mon-Fri) museums.

The best way to get here is by CityCat (see p113).

Greater Brisbane
LONE PINE KOALA SANCTUARY
About 11km southwest of Brisbane's CBD, this **wildlife sanctuary** (Map p77; ☎ 3378 1366; Jesmond Rd, Fig Tree Pocket; adult/child/family $16/11/39; ⏱ 8.30am-5pm) is an easy half-day trip. It's the world's largest koala sanctuary and with more than 130 of the cute and cuddly bears you won't be lacking photo opportunities. A cuddle costs an extra, but irresistible, $15, and you can hand feed the tame kangaroos for around $1 per bag of pellets. Keeping the koalas and roos company are wombats, possums, dingoes, Tasmanian Devils and other native animals. The sanctuary is set in attractive parklands beside the river and there are plenty of BBQ facilities. Talks are given on the animals at set times throughout the day.

To get here catch the No 430 express bus ($3.40, 35 minutes, hourly), which leaves from the Queen St Mall bus station (under the Myer Centre) between around 8.30am to 3.45pm daily.

Alternatively, **Mirimar Cruises** (☎ 1300 729 742; incl park entry per adult/child/family $44/25/120) cruises to the sanctuary along the Brisbane River from North Quay, next to Victoria Bridge. It departs daily at 10am, returning from Lone Pine at 1.30pm.

HART'S FLYING FIGHTER MUSEUM
This **Museum** (Map p77; ☎ 3272 9484; Archerfield Aerodrome, Wirraway Ave, Archerfield; admission free; ⏱ 7.30am-4pm Mon-Fri, 10am-2pm Sat), about 12km south of the city centre, has a collection of beautifully restored fighter planes all in flying order. Still on the aeronautical theme, beside the Brisbane Airport freeway is the **Sir Charles Kingsford Smith Memorial**, a hangar holding the famous *Southern Cross*, in which Sir Charles made the first trans-Pacific flight in 1928.

AUSTRALIAN WOOLSHED
For an impressive setup celebrating the 'outback experience', visit the **Australian Woolshed** (☎ 3872 1100; 148 Samford Rd, Ferny Hills; adult/child $15/10; ⏱ 8.30am-4.30pm Mon-Fri, 8.30am-5pm Sat & Sun). Beyond a large souvenir shop specialising in Australiana, the Woolshed is a spacious and attractive park with free picnic and BBQ facilities, a small fauna park with koalas (available for hugging) and kangaroos (up for feeding). Other attractions include sheep-shearing and wool-spinning demonstrations, and a one-hour 'ram show', starring eight trained rams and several sheepdogs.

There are also waterslides here, open from 9.30am to 4.30pm on weekends only. Entry fees per 1-/2-/4-hours/day are $6.50/8/10/12.

The Woolshed is 15km northwest of the centre. You can drive or come by train – it's 800m from Ferny Grove station to the Woolshed. Some of the commercial bus-tour operators also have day trips here (see p95 for more information).

ALMA PARK ZOO
You can bond with a multicultural mix of furred and feathered brethren at this **zoo** (☎ 3204 6566; Alma Rd, Dakabin; adult/child/family $23/15/55; ⏱ 9am-5pm, last entry 4pm), 28km north of the city centre. Inhabiting 8 hectares of subtropical gardens is a large collection of native birds and mammals, including koalas, kangaroos, emus and dingoes. Among the impressive representation of beautiful exotics are Malaysian sun bears, Tamarin and squirrel monkeys and leopards. You can touch many of the animals, and feeding times are all between 11am and 2.30pm.

To get here via public transport catch the Zoo Train (on the Caboolture line), which leaves from Roma St Transit Centre daily at 9am ($4, 45 minutes) and connects with the free zoo bus at Dakabin station. The zoo bus departs the zoo at 1.30pm daily to connect with the 1.47pm service from Dakabin back to the city.

DAISY HILL KOALA CENTRE
Located about 25km southwest of the city, this **centre** (☎ 3299 1032; Daisy Hill Rd, Daisy Hill Forest Reserve; admission free; ☘ 10am-4pm) has informative displays and a number of fat and happy looking koalas, but it's no zoo. The surrounding area is an important koala habitat and several bodies have banded together to establish the centre as a coordinated conservation area, which is essentially an amalgamation of national park bushland, state forests and reserves. The centre is designed to acquaint visitors with koalas on a much more comprehensive level than just a cuddle and photo encounter. Once you've delved into their world you can head out into the reserve and spot them in the wild. There are also lovely picnic and bushwalking spots, plus plenty of opportunities to see birdlife and other furry natives.

ACTIVITIES
Brisbane's climate and geography are perfect for outdoor activities and the city's relatively flat incline and numerous parks and gardens enable you to walk, cycle, skate, swim and scale walls to your heart's content.

Cycling
Brisbane has some 500km of cycleways, all of which are detailed in the *Brisbane Bicycle Experience Guide* booklet, available from visitors centres. The most scenic routes follow the Brisbane River and range from 5km to 20km. A good starter takes you from the City Botanic Gardens, across the Goodwill Bridge and out to the University of Queensland. It's about 7km one way and you can stop for a beer at the Regatta pub in Toowong.

Bicycles are allowed on Citytrains, except on weekdays during peak hours. You can also take bikes on CityCats and ferries for free, but cycling in malls is a no-no.

Brisbane bike rentals:

Brisbane Bicycle Sales (Map pp80-2; ☎ 3229 2433; www.brizbike.com; 87 Albert St; per hr/day $12/20; ☘ 8.30am-5.30pm Mon-Fri, 8.30am-4pm Sat, 10am-4pm Sun)

Riders (Map pp80-2; ☎ 3846 6200; Shop 9, Little Stanley St, South Bank; per hr/day $12/30; ☘ 8am-5pm Mon-Sat, 10am-4pm Sun)

Valet Cycle Hire (☎ 0408-003 198; www.valetcyclehire .com; per half-day/day $30/40). Bikes delivered to your door. Also a daily afternoon guided tour ($38) with small numbers.

In-Line Skating
You can also traverse all those cycleways on two legs. **Skatebiz** (Map pp80-2; ☎ 3220 0157; 101 Albert St; per 2/24hr $13/20; ☘ 9am-5.30pm Mon-Thu, 9am-4pm Sat, 10am-4pm Sun) rents out in-line skates and the necessary safety equipment. Some of the best skating areas are the South Bank Parklands, the City Botanic Gardens and the bike paths by the Brisbane River.

Experienced skaters can see Brisbane on a tour, which can be great fun. Both **Sk8tours** (☎ www.sk8tours.com; ☘ 7.30pm) and **Planet In-line** (☎ 3255 0033; www.planetinline.com) organise Wednesday night tours ($10) starting from the top of the Goodwill Bridge. The latter also runs a Saturday morning breakfast club tour ($15), and Sunday afternoon tours that differ each week and last about three hours ($15).

Rock Climbing
Rock climbing is a very popular pastime in Brisbane, and you can do the Spiderman dance in spectacular fashion at the **cliffs rock-climbing area** (Map pp80–2), on the southern banks of the Brisbane River at Kangaroo Point. These pink volcanic cliffs are allegedly 200 million years old and, regardless of your level of expertise, joining the other scrambling figures is good (and exhilarating!) fun. The cliffs are floodlit until midnight or later. Several operators offer climbing and abseiling instruction here:

K2 Extreme (☎ 3257 3310; k2extreme@k2basecamp .com.au; per person $30) Saturday morning sessions including safety procedures and a climb.

Torre Outdoor Adventures (☎ 3870 3223; climbing $15) This rock-climbing club meets on Wednesday night at 5.45pm; just make your way to the base of the cliffs.

Worth Wild Rock Climbing (☎ 3395 6450; www .worthwild.com.au; group instruction per person $75)

You can also climb indoors at **Urban Climb** (Map pp90-1; ☎ 3844 2544; www.urbanclimb.com.au; 2/220 Montague Rd, West End; ☘ noon-10pm Mon-Fri, 8am-6pm Sat, 10am-6pm Sun), or **Rocksports** (Map pp80-2; ☎ 3216 0462; 224 Barry Pde, Fortitude Valley; ☘ 10am-9.30pm Mon-Fri, 10am-6pm Sat & Sun). Casual climbs cost around $14.

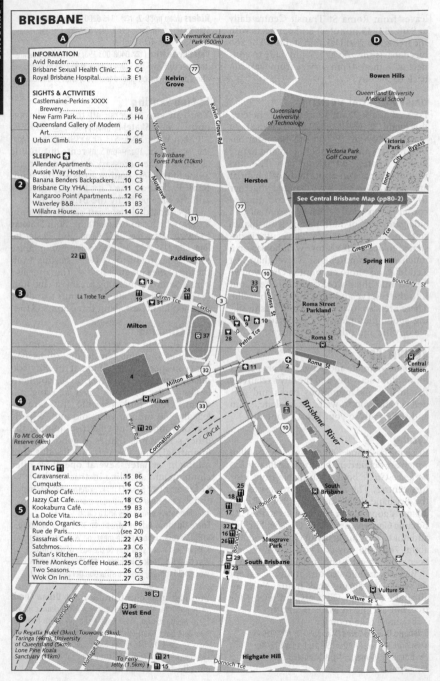

BRISBANE

INFORMATION
Avid Reader.................................1 C6
Brisbane Sexual Health Clinic......2 C4
Royal Brisbane Hospital..............3 E1

SIGHTS & ACTIVITIES
Castlemaine-Perkins XXXX
  Brewery................................4 B4
New Farm Park...........................5 H4
Queensland Gallery of Modern
  Art......................................6 C4
Urban Climb...............................7 B5

SLEEPING
Allender Apartments....................8 G4
Aussie Way Hostel.......................9 C3
Banana Benders Backpackers....10 C3
Brisbane City YHA.......................11 C4
Kangaroo Point Apartments.......12 F6
Waverley B&B............................13 B3
Willahra House..........................14 G2

EATING
Caravanserai.............................15 B6
Cumquats.................................16 C5
Gunshop Café............................17 C5
Jazzy Cat Cafe...........................18 C5
Kookaburra Café........................19 B3
La Dolce Vita.............................20 B4
Mondo Organics.........................21 B6
Rue de Paris.....................(see 20)
Sassafras Café...........................22 A3
Satchmos.................................23 C6
Sultan's Kitchen........................24 B3
Three Monkeys Coffee House....25 C5
Two Seasons.............................26 C5
Wok On Inn..............................27 G3

Newmarket Caravan
Park (500m)

Kelvin
Grove

Bowen Hills

Queensland University
Medical School

Queensland
University
of Technology

Victoria
Park

To Brisbane
Forest Park (10km)

Herston

Victoria Park
Golf Course

See Central Brisbane Map (pp80-2)

Spring Hill

Gregory

Boundary St

Paddington

Roma Street
Parkland

La Trobe Tce

Given Tce

Caxton

Milton

Roma St

Central
Station

Milton Rd

Milton

Roma St

Coronation Dr

CityCat

Brisbane River

To Mt Coot-tha
Reserve (4km)

Park Rd

South
Brisbane

South Bank

Melbourne St

Musgrave
Park

South Brisbane

Merivale St

Boundary St

Vulture St

Vulture St

West End

To Regatta Hotel (3km), Toowong (3km),
Taringa (4km); University
of Queensland (5km);
Lone Pine Koala
Sanctuary (11km)

Montague Rd

Riverside Dve

To Ferry
Jetty (1.5km)

Dornoch Tce

Highgate Hill

Stephens Rd

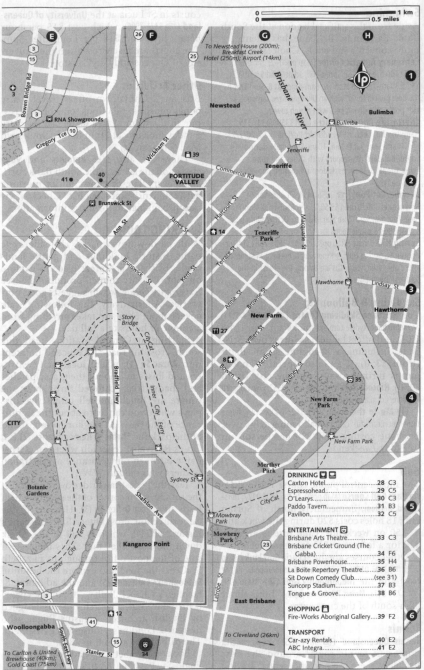

Swimming

Aside from the artificial lagoon at the South Bank Parklands, Brisbane has plenty of more conventional pools. Choices include:
Centenary Aquatic Centre (Map pp80–2; ☎ 3831 7665; 400 Gregory Tce, Spring Hill; adult/child $4.30/3.30; ☯ 5.30am-7.30pm Mon-Fri, 6am-6pm Sat & Sun) This is the best pool in town, with an Olympic-sized lap pool, a kids pool and a diving pool with a high tower.
Chermside Aquatic Centre (☎ 3359 6134; 375 Hamilton Rd, Chermside; adult/child/family $7.70/7/23; ☯ 10am-3pm Sat & Sun, 10am-5pm daily during school holidays) Waterpark with slides and tube rides. Great for families. Indoor swimming pool also open daily.
Newmarket Pool (☎ 3356 8434; 71 Alderson St, Newmarket; adult/child $3.50/2; ☯ 6am-7pm Mon-Fri, 8am-7pm Sat, 9am-7pm Sun mid-Apr–Oct) Wading pools, slides, BBQs & picnic spots.
Spring Hill Baths (Map pp80–2; ☎ 3831 7881; 14 Torrington St, Spring Hill; ☯ morning & evening in summer) These old-fashioned baths are among the oldest in the southern hemisphere.

Skydiving & Ballooning

The **Brisbane Skydiving Centre** (☎ 07-5464 6111; www.brisbaneskydive.com.au) picks up from the CBD and offers tandem skydives over Brisbane, including a 30-minute scenic flight (from $350). They also operate tandem jumps further away from the city (from $250). **Ripcord Skydivers** (☎ 3399 3552; www.ripcord-skydivers.com.au) does the same.

Fly Me to the Moon (☎ 3423 0400; www.flymetothemoon.com.au) offers ballooning trips over Brisbane costing $250/290 per person on weekdays/weekends.

Golf

The most central public course is the **Victoria Park Golf Course** (Map pp80-2; ☎ 3403 0177; Herston Rd, Herston), immediately north of Spring Hill; 18 holes costs $20 during the week and $24.50 on weekends. Club hire is another $20 for a full set or $11 for a half set.

Other courses are the **St Lucia Golf Links** (Map p77; ☎ 3403 0177; cnr Carawa St & Indooroopilly Rd, St Lucia) and the **Indooroopilly Golf Club** (Map p77; ☎ 3721 2173; Meiers Rd, Indooroopilly), both about 8km south of the city centre.

Tennis

Tennis Queensland (☎ 3871 8555) represents numerous tennis courts around the city; probably the closest to the centre are the courts in St Lucia at the **University of Queensland** (☎ 3371 7906), which cost $15 per hour before 5pm and $18 per hour after 5pm. The courts are just across from the University of Queensland CityCat stop.

Other Activities

Brisbane's Chinatown offers travel-weary bones, muscles and minds some blissful respite in the form of free **tai chi** classes every Sunday morning at 11am in the Chinatown Mall (Duncan St).

There are also free **aerobics** and **yoga** classes on the lawns at the South Bank Parklands every Tuesday and Sunday morning between April and August. Check www.south-bank.net.au for more information.

WALKING TOUR

With its downtown parks, riverside cycle paths, historic buildings and gentle landscape, Brisbane is a great place to explore on foot. The city council produces the free *Experience Guide*, which suggests good itineraries. Alternatively, the following walk covers about 5km and takes anything from a couple of hours to a full day.

Starting at Central Station, head due south, cross the road and descend the steps into **Anzac Sq (1)**, where locals, city workers and ibises mill about the grassy patches and shady trees. Scattered throughout the square are touch-and-tell interactive displays where you can learn about the significance of the park. At the northwestern end of the park the **Shrine of Remembrance (2)** is a Greek Revivalist cenotaph where an eternal flame burns in remembrance of Australian soldiers who died in WWI.

Take the pedestrian bridge over the road at the southeastern corner of the square, which leads into **Post Office Sq (3)**. Heading in the same direction, cross Queen St to Brisbane's historic **GPO (4)**, which is still in use. Walk down the small alley that skirts the eastern side of the post office through to Elizabeth St. Cross the road and explore the beautiful **St Stephen's Cathedral (5)** and the adjoining St Stephen's Chapel. Built in 1850, the chapel is Brisbane's oldest church and was designed by English architect Augustus Pugin, who designed London's Houses of Parliament. The cathedral was built in 1874.

Back on Elizabeth St, head northeast onto Eagle St. Pass the **Riverside Centre (6; p84)**

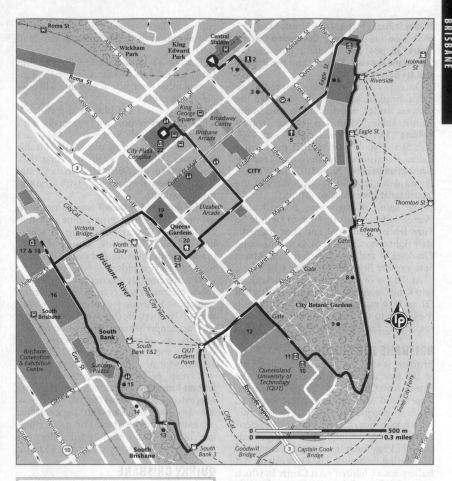

WALK FACTS

Start: Central Station
Finish: City Hall
Distance: 5km
Time: two hours to a day

and enter the gracious **Customs House** (7; p84). From the back of the building you can access a riverfront boardwalk. Head south again and take in the city views to your right and the river views to your left.

When you get to Edward St Pier take the **Mangrove Boardwalk** (8; p84), which cuts southwest into the **City Botanic Gardens** (9; p84). Follow the Mangrove Boardwalk

along the riverbank and then take the sign-posted walking track through the gardens to the campus of Queensland University of Technology (QUT). Check out the columned foyer of **Old Government House (10)**, built in 1860, and pop into the **QUT Art Museum (11**; p84).

By now you'll be heading northwest. Continue past the museum and pause to take in the splendour of Queensland's regal, copper-topped **Parliament House (12**; p84). Turn left at Parliament House and head down to the QUT Gardens Point ferry terminal. Catch a southbound ferry to South Bank 3 terminal.

Meander north through the pleasant and pretty **South Bank Parklands (13**; p85), past

Stanley St Plaza (**14**; p85) and **Streets Beach** (**15**; p85). Continue past the **Queensland Cultural Centre** (**16**; p84) and be sure to pop into the **Queensland Museum** (**17**; p84) and the **Queensland Art Gallery** (**18**; p85).

Once you've thoroughly explored these sights, head back towards the CBD on the Victoria Bridge, which will take you to the unmistakable Italian-Renaissance **Treasury Building** (**19**; p83). Turn right onto William St and you'll pass another spectacular Italian-Renaissance building, the **Land Administration Building** (**20**; p83). Cross William St and delve into Brisbane's history at the **Commissariat Stores Building** (**21**; p83).

Just south of the stores a small alley (Stephens Lane) cuts through to George St. Turn left on George St and then immediately right onto Charlotte St. Continue along Charlotte St and then turn left onto Albert St to explore Brisbane's modern CBD.

At the top of Albert St, cross Adelaide St into King George Sq. On your left is **City Hall** (**22**; p83). Wrap up your tour here by taking the lift up to the top of the bell tower and soaking up the views over the CBD.

BRISBANE FOR CHILDREN

Brisbane is tops for kids and families. One of the best attractions for children is the Queensland Cultural Centre (p84). Here the Queensland Museum runs some fantastic, hands-on programmes for little tackers during school holidays. The incorporated Sciencentre is made for inquisitive young minds and will keep them inventing, creating and discovering for hours. The Queensland Art Gallery has a Children's Art Centre in which it runs regular programmes throughout the year and a bunch of excellent ones during holidays.

Hands On Art (Map pp80–2; ☎ 3844 4589; www.handsonart.org.au; South Bank; per child $6; ☒ 10am-5pm Wed-Fri, 10am-5pm Mon-Fri during school holidays) is an art workshop where kids get to unleash their inner Picasso with clay moulding, printing, painting, dancing, puppet-making and more. Bookings are essential for this one. Budding thespians can unfurl some creative vigour of another genre at dance and theatre workshops at the Brisbane Powerhouse (p109).

The South Bank Parklands (p85) has the safe and child-friendly Streets Beach and a scattering of jungle gym playgrounds with rubber surfaces. There are more imaginative playgrounds in the Roma St Parkland (p83).

The Sir Thomas Brisbane Planetarium (p87) has exhibits and shows on stars, planets and other intergalactic goo that will boggle young minds.

The river is a big plus; many children will enjoy a river-boat trip, especially if it's to Lone Pine Koala Sanctuary (p88) where they can cuddle up to one of the lovable creatures. Similarly, a trip to Alma Park Zoo (p88) or the Daisy Hill Koala Centre (p89) will keep them engaged with local and foreign wildlife.

The **Brisbane City Council** (www.brisbane.qld.gov.au) runs Chill Out, a programme of activities for 10 to 17 year olds during the school holidays, and Visible Ink, an ongoing programme with activities and events designed for 12 to 16 year olds.

The free monthly booklet *Brisbane's Child* (www.brisbaneschild.com.au) has information about Brisbane for parents. Click onto the *Bub Hub* website (www.qld.bubhub.com.au) for comprehensive information for new parents, including everything from clinic contacts and locations, prenatal care and activities for newborns to toddlers.

Daycare or babysitting options include **Anytime Babysitting** (☎ 3882 3455; anytimebabysitting@bigpond.com), **Dial an Angel** (☎ 1300 721 111; www.dialanangel.com) and **Care4Kidz** (www.careforkidz.com.au/brisbane/babysitting.htm). For more childcare listings click onto http://directory.ourbrisbane.com/directory/categories/63.html.

QUIRKY BRISBANE

Brisbane has many a cultural festival event on its annual calendar, but perhaps none quite as close to Australians' hearts as the **National Festival of Beers** (www.nfb.com.au; RNA Showgrounds, Gregory Tce, Bowen Hills; per person $20) held at the RNA Showgrounds over three days in mid-September. Beer lovers gather to pay homage to the amber ale and are indulged with brews from around 45 Australian breweries – both macro and micro. There's also a fairly impressive entertainment line-up to enhance the mood, and the University of Beer, where you can receive invaluable tuition from the top brewers.

Many Australians mistakenly believe the Melbourne Cup is the 'race that stops a nation', but any self-respecting Brisbanite can tell you this tag really belongs to the annual Australia Day Cockroach Races held at the Story Bridge Hotel (p107) every 26 January. The heart-stopping line-up includes no fewer than 14 races plus additional competitions such as Miss Cocky and the Cocky Day Costume Competition.

If races do keep you on the edge of your seat, then you'll also be in the front row for the annual Great Brisbane Duck Race. No, the locals have not figured out a way to train waddling water birds into becoming elite athletes. This is a *rubber* duckie race, an annual event on the Brisbane Riverfestival calendar (see the boxed text on p97). You get to 'adopt a duck' for $5 and spur it down the river (strictly a vocal affair), willing it to defeat its competitors and become the first to cross the line. The competition is fierce – an estimated 20,000 ducks fight for the winner's crown each year. If you happen to be the lucky caretaker of the victor, you'll be rewarded for your efforts with a new car! If your duck performed at a substandard level, you get to go home knowing you helped raise invaluable funds for the Surf Life Saving Foundation, which benefits from all the proceeds.

Another annual event that has drawn Brisbanites for more than 21 years is the Australian National Marble Championships, hosted by the Caxton Hotel (p106) in early October. Teams enter the all-day competition, which goes through a series of heats, semifinals and finals. Bribes for losers are warmly welcomed, so if the team you're barracking for (or in!) slips down the rankings, a bit of cold, hard cash will put them back in the running. All proceeds go to charity.

Every Wednesday night, the Brisbane Go Club meets at the **Pancake Manor** (Map pp80-2; ☎ 3221 6433; 18 Charlotte St) for several hours of tuition and competition of the Chinese board game...plus pancakes. You can go along to watch the masters in action ($1) or even participate and give some of them a run for their money.

If you came to Brisbane looking for a little love, the Port Office Hotel (p106) regularly holds Blink Speed Dating nights, where you can attempt to find your perfect match by spending seven minutes one-on-one with a fleet of suitors. It costs $55, which includes two drinks, finger food and possibly the love of your life, so it's a pretty good deal.

TOURS

There are all sorts of organised tours of Brisbane and the surrounding areas on offer – ask at any of the visitors centres for brochures and details. Most of the tour-bus companies have offices in the Roma St Transit Centre.

City Tours

The **City Sights tour** (day tickets per adult/child $20/15) is a hop-on-hop-off shuttle bus taking in 19 of Brisbane's major landmarks. Tours depart every 45 minutes between 9am and 3.45pm from Post Office Sq on Queen St (Map pp80–2). Day tickets can be bought on the bus and allow you to get off and on whenever and wherever you want. The same ticket covers you for unlimited use of conventional city bus and ferry services. Its **City Nights tour** (Map pp80-2; adult/child $20/15; ☒ 6pm Mar-Oct & 6.30pm Nov-Feb), departing from the City Hall, goes a little further afield and includes Mt Coot-tha Lookout and a cruise on a CityCat. Tickets for both can be bought on the bus or at the visitor information kiosk in the Queen St Mall.

Several private companies also offer interesting tours, including **Artours** (☎ 3899 3686; www.artours.coaus.com; adult/child $45/15; ☒ 9.15am & 1.15pm Tue-Sat), which focuses on Brisbane's art scene around New Farm. Typical half-day tours take in five to six galleries and last 3½ hours.

Ghost Tours (☎ 3844 6606; www.ghost-tours.com .au; adult/child from $30/15.50) offers something a little different: guided tours of Brisbane's haunted heritage, murder scenes, cemeteries and the infamous Boggo Rd Gaol. Most tours are on Saturday nights and bookings are essential.

Tours and Detours (☎ 1300 300 242, 3847 3666; www.toursanddetours.com.au; adult/child $50/30; ☒ 9am) runs a Brisbane highlights tour, which takes in many of the city's historical buildings, sights and gardens, as well as a river cruise. The tour lasts four hours and includes hotel pick-up.

Brisbane Walking Tours (☎ 0410-425 762; adult/ child $16/10) is a small outfit running two-hour walking tours of the city or Fortitude Valley. The accompanying commentary is interesting and insightful, and the itinerary contains a mix of old and new Brisbane.

Mr Day Tours (☎ 3269 3913; www.mrdaytours.com .au; adult/child $135/65; ☒ 9am) specialises in small group tours and offers a good 'Brisbane and Outback' tour. This full-day tour takes you to the Australian Woolshed (p88) and Brisbane Forest Park (p87). Tours include entry fees to the Woolshed plus a BBQ lunch, and morning and afternoon tea.

Brewery Tours

If you're a fan of the amber ale, you'll enjoy touring the **Castlemaine-Perkins XXXX Brewery** (Map pp90-1; ☎ 3361 7597; www.xxxx.com.au; cnr Black & Paton Sts; adult/child $18/10; ☾ hourly 10am-4pm Mon-Fri & 6pm Wed). Adult entry includes four ales to quench your thirst at the end of the tour, so leave the car at home. The brewery is a 20-minute walk west from the transit centre, or you can take the Citytrain to Milton station. Wear enclosed shoes.

You can also tour the **Carlton & United Brewhouse** (☎ 3826 5858; cnr Mulles Rd & Pacific Hwy, Yatala; entry with/without transfer bus $30/15; ☾ 10am, noon & 2pm Mon-Fri). Apparently this is one of the most technologically advanced breweries in the world, pumping out three million bottles of the good stuff a day. Just to see this much liquid gold in one spot is awesome enough – Homer eat your heart out. This tour also includes free beer at the end.

River Cruises

Coasting up and down the Brisbane River is a great way to see the pretty peaks and troughs of the city. **Kookaburra River Queens** (☎ 3221 1300; www.kookaburrariverqueens.com; 2-hr lunch cruises per person $45, 2½-hr dinner cruises per person $60) chug up and down the river in restored wooden paddle steamers. The effect is nice and the cruises include a buffet meal or seafood platter. Lunch cruises depart from South Bank at 11.30am and from Eagle St Pier at noon daily. Dinner cruises depart from South Bank at 6.30pm and Eagle St Pier at 7.30pm, except for Sunday when they depart at 6pm and 7pm respectively.

If you just want the sights without the fancy fuss, **River City Cruises** (☎ 0428-278 473; www.rivercitycruises.com; South Bank 1 Ferry Terminal; adult/child/family $20/15/55) has 1½-hour cruises with commentary, departing South Bank at 10.30am and 12.30pm (plus 2.30pm during summer).

Another popular option is **Mirimar Cruises** (☎ 1300 729 742; Queens Wharf Rd, North Quay; 1½-hr cruises per adult/child/pensioner $18/10/16, day tours

$88/49/85). This company also operates cruises to Lone Pine Koala Sanctuary (see p88).

Hinterland Tours

Run by a former backpacking globetrotter, **Rob's Rainforest Tours** (☎ 0409-496 607, 3357 7061; http://homepage.powerup.com.au/~frogbus7/index.html; per person $65) offers several day trips out of Brisbane, taking travellers to the rainforests at Mt Glorious, Kondalilla Falls and the Glass House Mountains (Monday and Thursday), Lamington National Park (Tuesday and Friday) and Springwood National Park (Wednesday and Saturday). Readers consistently write in with high praise for the tours, which include morning tea, pick-up and return to inner-city Brisbane accommodation, and insightful commentary.

Araucaria Ecotours (☎ 5544 1283; www.learnabout wildlife.com), 18km east of Rathdowney in the Gold Coast hinterland, offers three-day naturalist-led wilderness tours in the Mt Barney National Park area. The tour picks up in Brisbane every Wednesday morning and calls in at the Daisy Hill Koala Centre and the Karawatha Wetlands on the way down to Mt Barney. The cost is $275 per person, including accommodation (self-catering, with stops to buy food), or $330 with meals. This company also operates day tours including Bushwalking in Brisbane ($55) and Coochiemudlo Island ($80), which both include lunch.

For information on more hinterland tours see p192 and p146.

FESTIVALS & EVENTS

Information on festivals and events in Brisbane can be found at visitors centres or at www.ourbrisbane.com/whatson.

Chinese New Year Always a popular event in the Valley in January/February.

Tropfest (www.tropfest.com) Nationwide short film festival telecast live at South Bank in late February.

St Patrick's Day On March 17 Brisbane's Irish and not-so-Irish pubs celebrate heavily. There's also a parade through the city.

Queensland Winter Racing Carnival (www.queens landracing.com.au) From late April to late July there are major horse-race meetings each weekend at both Doomben and Eagle Farm Racecourses, including the Brisbane Cup in mid-May.

Paniyiri Festival (paniyiri@thegreekclub.com.au) Greek cultural festival with dancing, food and music. Held in late May at Musgrave Park in West End.

REVELLING IN THE RIVERFESTIVAL

Brisbane's streets become a hurly-burly of colour, flair, flavour and fireworks during the city's biggest arts event of the year – the Riverfestival. Running over 10 days, from late August to early September, the festival celebrates Brisbane's relationship with its river, highlighting the city's diverse and eclectic communities and showcasing the best it has to offer. The common thread between the performances, artistic displays, mini food festivals and cultural celebrations is that they are as intrinsic to Brisbane as its undulating river: continuously shaping and adding to the city's evolving character.

Several events are constants and highlights. The festival is opened each year with a bang – literally. Staged over the Brisbane River, with vantage points from South Bank, the city and West End, Riverfire is a massive fireworks show with dazzling visual choreography, air force jets and a synchronised soundtrack. Also a staple is the Riversymposium, an international conference on best practice for river management, with more than 400 delegates attending to develop new approaches and methods to preserve the world's waterways. Over its seven-year lifespan it has attracted some of the world's leading scientists and experts on the topic, and been the confluence of invaluable innovation.

Other events combine Indigenous culture with contemporary performance to pay homage to the river and celebrate cultural collaboration. Leading restaurants come together to engage in outstanding culinary events, such as the Seafood Festival, where you can chow down on your favourite dish from the deep, or try your hand at prawn-peeling and oyster-opening contests.

Music plays the role of a constant backdrop throughout the festival, either as an accompaniment to a main event, or an event on its own. The Riverconcert, held in the City Botanic Gardens, features live acts performing everything from jazz to hip-hop to electronic soundscapes. The city's live-music venues also fill their playlist on a nightly basis.

Among the other events are live debates, dramatic performances, dance and fun runs. Most of the events are free and family friendly and there's a smorgasbord of activities for the kids.

For more information click onto www.riverfestival.com.au.

Brisbane Pride Festival (www.pridebrisbane.org.au) Brisbane's fabulously flamboyant gay and lesbian celebration, held in June.

Queensland Music Festival Outstanding celebration of the world of music, held over 15 days in July in odd-numbered years.

Brisbane International Film Festival (www.biff.com .au) Ten days of quality films in July.

Valley Fiesta Food and music festival held in Chinatown and Brunswick St Mall in mid-July.

'Ekka' Royal National Agricultural (RNA) Show (www.ekka.com.au) The country comes to town in early August with competitions, wood-chopping and rides.

Brisbane Riverfestival (www.riverfestival.com.au) Brisbane's major festival of the arts, with buskers, performances, music and concerts held in September. See the boxed text above for more information.

Livid (www.livid.com.au) Annual one-day alternative rock festival in October.

Christmas Festival (www.south-bank.net.au) Massive Chrissy celebrations held during the week before Christmas at South Bank.

Woodford Folk Festival Over New Year's Eve, 78km north of Brisbane in Woodford (see p193).

SLEEPING

Brisbane, like any large city, has an excellent selection of accommodation options that will suit any budget. Most are outside the CBD, but more often than not they're within walking distance or have good public transport connections.

The inner suburbs have their own distinct flavours. Spring Hill, just north of the CBD, is quiet and within easy striking distance of downtown and Fortitude Valley. Petrie Tce and Paddington, just west of the city centre, combine trendy restaurants and rowdy bars. Staying in the alternative neighbourhood of Fortitude Valley and nearby New Farm places you next door to Chinatown, Brunswick St's café strip and the city's most concentrated night-life scene. West End, south of the river, has a decidedly chilled-out atmosphere and some great cafés and restaurants.

The main motel drags are Wickham Tce and Gregory Tce, on the northern edge of the city, and Main St in Kangaroo Point, which is also the link road to the southern

BRISBANE

GAY & LESBIAN BRISBANE

While Brisbane can't compete with the pro-lific gay and lesbian scenes in Sydney and Melbourne, what you'll find here is quality rather than quantity.

Most action, centred in Fortitude Valley, is covered by the fortnightly *Q News* (www .qnews.com.au). Queensland Pride, another gay publication, takes in the whole of the state. **Dykes on Mykes** (www.queerradio.org), a radio show on Wednesday from 9pm to 11pm on FM102.1, is another source of in-formation on the city.

Major events on the year's calendar in-clude the Queer Film Festival held in late March, which showcases gay, lesbian, bi-sexual and transgender films and videos, and the Brisbane Pride Festival in June (see p97). Pride attracts up to 25,000 people every year, and peaks during the parade held midfestival.

Brisbane's most popular gay and lesbian venue is the **Wickham Hotel** (Map pp80-2; ☎ 3852 1301; cnr Wickham & Alden Sts, Forti-tude Valley), a classic old Victorian pub with good dance music, drag shows and danc-ers. The Wickham celebrates the Sydney Mardi Gras and the Pride Festival in style and grandeur.

Other good options:

GPO (p107)
Family (p108) Brisbane's best nightclub.
Sportsman's Hotel (Map pp80-2; ☎ 3831 2892; 130 Leichhardt St, Spring Hill) Another fan-tastically popular gay venue, with a different theme or show for each night of the week.

The **Gay & Lesbian Welfare Association** (GLWA; ☎ 1800 184 527; www.glwa.org.au) of Brisbane can offer information on groups and venues and also provides counselling.

Gold Coast Hwy. North Kangaroo Point is a nice place to be. Although the Story Bridge and its associated highway soar above the streets, it's quiet and leafy and there are frequent ferries across to the city centre.

The Brisbane Visitors Accommodation Service (p79) has a free booking service, and brochures and information on hostels and other budget options in Brisbane and up and down the coast.

If you decide to stay longer, there is rental accommodation advertised in the *Courier-Mail* – Wednesday and Saturday are the best days to look – or on the no-tice boards at hostels and cafés, and at the universities.

Budget

B&BS

Annie's Inn (Map pp80-2; ☎ 3831 8684; www.anniesinn .net; 405 Upper Edward St; s/d $50/60, d with bathroom $70; **P**) In a central location within walk-ing distance of the CBD, this modest B&B is awash with lace and frills and feels a little like a large doll house. The owners are in-credibly helpful and friendly and the whole place is spick and span.

Acacia Inner-City Inn (Map pp80-2; ☎ 3832 1663; fax 3832 2591; 413 Upper Edward St; s/d with bath incl breakfast $55/75; **P**) This reasonable B&B has small, motel-style rooms in a functional en-vironment. The singles are fairly snug, but the doubles have more space and there's not a speck of dirt to be found. All rooms come with TVs and bar fridges.

HOSTELS

Brisbane's hostels are generally of a high standard and will almost always have laun-dry facilities, a TV lounge and plenty of information on sights, activities and hostels up and down the coast.

Bunk Backpackers (Map pp80-2; ☎ 1800 682 865; www.bunkbrisbane.com.au; cnr Ann & Gipps St, Fortitude Val-ley; dm $23-26, s $40, d & tw $70; **P**) More like a snazzy hotel than a backpackers, this excellent hostel has generous dorms with bathrooms, luscious mattresses, gleaming kitchens and bathrooms, and funky décor. It's extremely secure and the faaaabulous bar and swimming pool belong on a CD cover. It's also wheelchair friendly.

Tinbilly (Map pp80-2; ☎ 1800 446 646, 3238 5888; www .tinbilly.com; 462 George St; 13-/7-/4-bed dm $22/25/27, tw & d $85;) This sleek hostel flaunts its youth with a modern interior, excellent facil-ities and clinical cleanliness. Each room has air-con, a bathroom and individual lockers, and it's wheelchair-accessible. Downstairs a happy, helpful buzz swims around the job centre, travel agency and very popular bar.

Palace Backpackers (Map pp80-2; ☎ 1800 676 340, 3211 2433; www.palacebackpackers.com.au; cnr Ann & Ed-ward Sts; dm/s/d $22/36/60;) This colossal backpacker institution caters to loners, partygoers and everyone in-between in an ageing, multistorey labyrinth. The rooms are a little cramped but there are comfy TV rooms, a huge kitchen, a tour-information desk, a job club and a great rooftop sundeck.

Tourist Guesthouse (Map pp80-2; ☎ 1800 800 589; 3252 4171; www.touristguesthouse.com.au; 555 Gregory Tce, Spring Hill; dm $20, s/d/tr with bathroom $60/75/85; P 🔀 🖳) A short walk from Brunswick St, this hotel-hostel is scrubbed-up rustic: plenty of faded pine but mod cons too. All rooms have a TV and a fridge, and the doubles are excellent value.

Brisbane City YHA (Map pp90-1; ☎ 3236 1004; brisbanecity@yhaqld.org; 392 Upper Roma St, Petrie Tce; dm $23, tw & d $55-70; P 🔀 🖳) You can't miss the Legoland exterior of this hostel, but inside it's classy, spacious and comfortable. There's a great café here as well as a tour desk and provisions for the disabled. It's very popular, attracting all ages and groups.

Banana Benders Backpackers (Map pp90-1; ☎ 1800 241 157, 3367 1157; www.bananabenders.com; 118 Petrie Tce, Petrie Tce; dm $21-23, tw & d $50; 🖳) This small and comfy hostel is a great spot if you're planning to hang your hat for a while. Rooms are spacious and functional, and the corridors are dressed up with Mambo prints. There's also an outdoor patio and BBQ area. The friendly owners can also help you find work.

Aussie Way Hostel (Map pp90-1; ☎ 3369 0711; 34 Cricket St, Petrie Tce; dm/s/d $22/36/50; 🔀) Another small hostel, this one's housed in a picturesque, two-storey timber Queenslander and feels more like a guesthouse than a hostel. Dorms are a tad more spacious than most and come with fridges and televisions. The friendly hosts are knowledgeable and can organise just about anything for you.

CAMPING

Most of the camping options are a long way from the centre, so any money you save on accommodation may quickly be eaten up by public transport. All rates are for two people.

Newmarket Gardens Caravan Park (Map p77; ☎ 3356 1458; www.newmarketgardens.com.au; 199 Ashgrove Ave, Ashgrove; powered/unpowered sites $23/21, caravans $38, cabins $70-90; P 🔀 🖳) This clean site is just 4km north of the city centre, and is connected to town by several bus routes and the Citytrain (Newmarket station). There aren't too many trees, but the bathrooms are spotless and there are good

laundries and BBQs on site. Some cabins are wheelchair friendly.

Other recommendations:

Aspley Acres (☎ 3263 2668; www.aspleyacres.com.au; 1420 Gympie Rd, Aspley; unpowered/powered sites from $22/24, cabins $55-95; P 🔀 🖳) Spacious park with BBQs, a playground and plenty of trees. Good range of cabins with disabled access.

Brisbane Caravan Village (☎ 1800 060797, 3263 4040; www.caravanvillage.com.au; 763 Zillmere Rd, Aspley; unpowered/powered sites $21/25, cabins $80-90; P 🔀 🖳 🐾) A tidy park with excellent facilities.

Midrange

Most midrange hotels cater predominantly to corporate clients and usually have lots of empty beds on weekends. You'll find that most offer good weekend deals.

HOTELS & MOTELS

Inchcolm Hotel (Map pp80-2; ☎ 3226 8888; www.inchcolmhotel.com.au; 73 Wickham Tce; s/d $140; P 🔀 🐾) This small and personable hotel is inside a converted block of medical offices. Much of the heritage structure and charm of its former life remains, but the rooms have been renovated extensively and are supercomfortable. All come with kitchenettes and cable TV. There are good standby deals during slow periods.

Holiday Inn Brisbane (Map pp80-2; ☎ 3238 2222; reserve@holidayinnbrisbane.com.au; Roma St Transit Centre, Roma St; r from $120; P 🔀 🐾) Right beside

---

THE AUTHOR'S CHOICE

Dahrl Court Apartments (Map pp80-2; ☎ 3830 3400; www.dahrlcourt.com.au; 45 Phillips St, Spring Hill; r per night/week $90/560; P 🔀) Tucked into a quiet, leafy pocket of Spring Hill, this boutique complex offers outstanding value. The sizable apartments are fully self-contained with stylish bathrooms (including baths), kitchens and heritage aesthetics throughout. Large timber wardrobes grace the bedrooms and there are fat, spacious couches in the living rooms from where you can watch cable TV. There are also phones in each room and laundry facilities on site. The commodious townhouses are a step up in style and go for $120/770 per night/week. They come with a courtyard or numerous balconies and one or two bedrooms.

the transit centre, this four-star hotel offers all the services and comforts you would expect of the Holiday Inn chain. Rooms are inconspicuous and accommodating and the hotel's facilities include foreign exchange, babysitting, a tour desk and laundry facilities. Look out for Internet and weekend deals.

Allender Apartments (Map pp90-1; ☎ 3358 5832; www.allenderapartments; 3 Moreton St, New Farm; r $100-135; ⊠) The yellow-brick façade may not grab you but Allender's studios and one-bedroom apartments are tasteful and immaculate. The cool, shaded interiors are a fusion of funky décor and homely amenities and there's plenty of room to spread out.

Central Brunswick Apartments (Map pp80-2; ☎ 3852 1411; www.centralbrunswickhotel.com.au; 455 Brunswick St, Fortitude Valley; r $120-140; P ⊠) The studios and apartments in this modern complex have a fairly generic, business-traveller manner about them but are still very comfortable. Some have balconies and spas, and week-long stays attract excellent discounts. All guests have access to the sauna and gym, and babysitting can be arranged.

Kangaroo Point Apartments (Map pp90-1; ☎ 1800 676 855, 3391 6855; www.kangaroopoint.com; 819 Main St, Kangaroo Point; apt per night/week from $80/390; P ⊠ ⬛) These contemporary, serviced apartments are excellent if you're staying a week or more. The 3½-star units are fitted with appealing furnishings and fully-equipped kitchens. A step up in style are the 4½-star units (from $145 per night), which are sleek, spacious and indulgent, with large balconies. Good disabled access.

Il Mondo (Map pp80-2; ☎ 3392 0111; www.ilmondo .com.au; 25 Rotherham St, Kangaroo Point; r $100-165; P ⊠ ⬛) This postmodern boutique hotel has contemporary rooms that are reminiscent of an Ikea showroom. There's plenty of block colours, minimalist design and space, and the bathrooms are quite blissful. The cheaper options are standard hotel rooms while the more expensive are self-contained apartments.

Royal on the Park (Map pp80-2; ☎ 1800 773 337, 3221 3411; www.royalonthepark.com.au; cnr Alice & Albert Sts; r $140-175; P ⊠ ⬛) With wonderful views of the City Botanic Gardens, this four-star hotel has attractive rooms with stylish furnishings, a spa, a gym and two restaurants. It's very popular with business travellers due to the excellent facilities and accom-

modating staff, so the cheaper rates are for Friday, Saturday and Sunday nights.

Astor Metropole (Map pp80-2; ☎ 3144 4000; www .astorhotel.com.au; 193 Wickham Tce; d $100-110, ste from $120; P ⊠) This central complex has a good range of rooms. The standard rooms feel like small apartments and it's worth paying a few dollars more to get one with a balcony and a view. The suites are self-contained, but they're a little dated.

Dorchester Inn (Map pp80-2; ☎ 3831 2967; www .dorchesterinn.com.au; 484 Upper Edward St, Spring Hill; 1-/2-/3-person units $70/80/90; P ⊠) The self-contained units in this renovated, two-storey block may be a little dated in the décor department, but they're spotless and for space, amenities and service the Dorchester is virtually unbeatable. There are also laundry facilities and if the hosts were any friendlier, you'd take them home.

Metropolitan Motor Inn (Map pp80-2; ☎ 3831 6000; www.metropolitanmotorinn.com; 106 Leichhardt St, Spring Hill; r $100; P ⊠ ⬛) This business hotel has decent rooms still dressed in soft and friendly '80s décor, but they're comfortable and a tad roomier than your average motor inn. Each has a fridge, a TV and a balcony.

Best Western Gregory Terrace (Map pp80-2; ☎ 3832 1769; ggtmotel@bigpond.net.au; 397 Gregory Tce, Spring Hill; r $98-130, f $110-145; P ⊠ ⬛) Out on Spring Hill's northern edge, this four-star establishment overlooks Victoria Park and has respectable rooms that have been well maintained. The décor is fairly plain, but some rooms have balconies and the family rooms are extremely accommodating. The price range reflects the quality of the views.

Paramount Motel (Map pp80-2; ☎ 1800 636 772, 3393 1444; www.paramountmotel.com.au; 649 Main St, Kangaroo Point; s/d/f $70/75/105; P ⊠ ⬛) This clean and comfy complex has terrifically cheerful and impeccably clean rooms. Mod cons and extras include TVs, fully-equipped kitchens and hairdryers. There's also a BBQ by the pool and the staff are friendly and helpful.

Chifley on George (Map pp80-2; ☎ 3221 6044; reservations.george@chifleyhotels.com; 103 George St; r from $150; P ⊠ ⬛) The Chifley has pleasant and straightforward hotel rooms, a spa and a restaurant. Most of the rooms are standard doubles and suites, which are accommodating if not a little snug. There is also a handful of commodious and swank spa suites.

Also recommended:

Explorers Inn (Map pp80-2; ☎ 1800 623 288, 3211 3488; stay@explorers.com.au; 63 Turbot St; s/d/tr $85/90/120; ⓟ ✖) Modern hotel with snug rooms.

Soho Motel (Map pp80-2; ☎ 3831 7722; www.soho motel.com.au; 333 Wickham Tce; s/d $70/85; ⓟ ✖ ⌨) Smart, compact rooms.

B&BS

Thornbury House B&B (Map pp80-2; ☎ 3839 5334; thorn-b@bigpond.net.au; 1 Thornbury St, Spring Hill; d $90-100) Behind a trellised frontage lies this beautifully maintained two-storey Queenslander built in 1886, with cool, crisp rooms and warm hosts. The polished timber throughout is spotless, but there's nothing clinical about the ambience. Extras such as TVs in each room and bathrobes come free of charge and breakfast is served in a lovely courtyard.

Waverley B&B (Map pp90-1; ☎ 3369 8973; fax 3876 6655; http://babs.com.au/waverley; 5 La Trobe Tce, Paddington; s/d incl breakfast $90/110; ⓟ ✖) This stylish B&B has cool rooms decorated with period furniture and with beds so plump you could pop them. Each room also has a small sitting area and little trimmings such as pamper products in the exquisite bathrooms. There is also a self-contained unit which is excellent value at $440 per week.

Fern Cottage (Map p77; ☎ 3541 6685; 89 Fernberg Rd, Paddington; s/d $90/120; ✖) Another good B&B choice, Fern Cottage is a beautifully renovated Queenslander with a splash of Mediterranean ambience. The rooms are utterly cushy and there's a lush garden retreat out the back with a shady balcony. The hosts here go to great lengths to make sure your stay is comfy.

Also recommended:

Ridge Haven B&B (Map p77; ☎ 3391 7702; http://uq connect.net/ridgehaven; 374 Annerley Rd, Annerley; s $110-125, d $120-135; ⓟ ✖) Historic Victorian home with atmospheric rooms.

Willahra House (Map pp90-1; ☎ 3254 3485; willahrahouse@mhpm.com.au; 268 Harcourt St, New Farm; s $75-100, d $95-125; ⓟ ✖) Beautiful homestead-style house with plush rooms.

Top End

Conrad Treasury (Map pp80-2; ☎ 3306 8888; www .conradtreasury.com.au; 130 William St; r $230-350, ste $330-1075; ⓟ ✖) Brisbane's classiest hotel is in the beautifully preserved former Land Administration Building. Every room is unique and awash with heritage features, polished

wood, elegant furnishings and marble. Rates start with standard rooms, but a step up takes you to the voluminous Parlour Rooms; those on the 4th floor have balcony access. The suites will make you giddy.

Quay West Suites Brisbane (Map pp80-2; ☎ 1800 672 726, 3853 6000; reservations@qwsb.mirvac.com.au; 132 Alice St; 1-/2-bedroom ste $250/320; ⓟ ✖ ✖) This sophisticated hotel has opulent self-contained units with modern kitchens, fully equipped laundries, numerous TVs, stereos, modem ports and spectacular views. Recently refurbished, the refined interiors are worth the price tag and the staff are utterly gracious.

Stamford Plaza Brisbane (Map pp80-2; ☎ 3221 1999; sales@spb.stamford.com.au; cnr Edward & Margaret Sts; r from $280; ⓟ ✖ ✖) At the southern end of the city, the Stamford has a historic façade in front of a modern tower. The indulgent rooms have antique touches, large beds and plenty of atmosphere. On site is a gym, a sauna, a spa and several restaurants. There are often good package deals up for grabs.

EATING

Brisbane's CBD has a number of fine, pricey eating options, but there is also an extensive array of culinary offerings outside the city centre. Most cafés in the CBD are closed on weekends.

In the Valley you'll find inexpensive cafés and a smorgasbord of Asian flavours on offer, thanks to Chinatown. In nearby New Farm the area around the junction of Annie and Brunswick Sts is a good spot to head. West End is a distinctly cosmopolitan corner, with trendy cafés and eclectic cuisine. In every pocket of town, eateries take advantage of Brisbane's perfect winter climate with open-air courtyards or tables out on the street.

For cheap eats, there are surprisingly varied options in the food courts in Brisbane's shopping malls. Breezy outdoor food courts can also be found at the Riverside Centre and Eagle St Pier on the riverfront, northeast of the city, and at South Bank Parklands.

City Centre

RESTAURANTS

E'cco (Map pp80-2; ☎ 3831 8344; 100 Boundary St; mains around $30; ⏰ lunch Tue-Fri, dinner Tue-Sat) One of the finest restaurants in the state, award-winning E'cco is a must for any culinary aficionado. Masterpieces on the menu include slow-cooked duck with a cassoulet of white beans, Lyonnaise sausage and tomato. The interior is suitably swish and you'll need to book well in advance.

FIX (Map pp80-2; ☎ 3210 6016; cnr Edward & Margaret Sts; mains $15-25; ⏰ lunch Mon-Fri, dinner Mon-Sat) This bustling brasserie delights office workers and social diners with a varied menu. You don't have to splurge to enjoy prawns with *wakami* (Asian seaweed) and ginger in crisp wontons or sticky duck shanks, and although vegie options are limited to pastas and salads, they're all good. Service is superb and the attached bar dolls out spiffy cocktails.

II (Map pp80-2; ☎ 3210 0600; cnr Edward & Alice Sts; mains $33-40; ⏰ lunch Mon-Fri, dinner Mon-Sat) This classy restaurant is agreeable without making too much of a statement – that mission is saved for the food. Dishes including seared scallops with seaweed and lemon risotto or veal with porcini risotto and artichoke chips attract business crowds and refined foodies.

Grosvenor on George (Map pp80-2; ☎ 3236 2288; 320 George St; mains $17-25; ⏰ lunch & dinner) Sassy suits love this classy bar during the week, when they tumble in for creative fusions like *hoi sin* duck pizza, or vanilla-bean-and-sweet-pea risotto. The menu is in a constant state of flux and the walls carry work by local artists. Friday nights are for drinkers.

Govinda's (Map pp80-2; ☎ 3210 0255; Upstairs, 99 Elizabeth St; Sun feast $6.50, all you can eat $8.50; ⏰ lunch Mon-Sat, dinner Fri, Sun feast from 5pm) This Hari Krishna eatery is perfect if you like a little enlightenment with your lentils. You can still enjoy the vegetarian curries, snacks, salads and stews without the philosophy though, and the divine smells and tranquil interior is inviting to all.

Customs House Brasserie (Map pp80-2; ☎ 3365 8921; 399 Queen St; mains $20-27; ⏰ lunch daily, dinner Tue-Sat) Wedged at the base of Customs House (p84) and conveniently shielded from the city's high-rises by a glass office tower, this brasserie has an impressive menu. Prawn-and-green-papaya salad, or beef mignons wrapped in pancetta taste oh so much better with the uninterrupted views of the river.

CAFÉS

Verve Cafe & Bar (Map pp80-2; ☎ 3221 5691; 109 Edward St; mains $10-20; ⏰ lunch Mon-Fri, dinner Mon-Sat)

This funky subterranean venue is a bar-café-restaurant fusion with muted tunes and tones, and excellent service. The menu includes a spread of imaginative café fare with plenty of good salads and pastas, but the portions are restaurant size. The crowd is arty and relaxed.

Jorge (Map pp80-2; ☎ 3012 9121; 183 George St; mains $15-25; ⏰ 11am-late Mon-Fri, 3pm-late Sat & Sun) Jorge's catch phrase is 'Groove, Lounge, Dine' and this spunky bar snags style cats of all ages by fulfilling all three. The open kitchen sizzles up smoked kangaroo salads, grilled prawn burgers and roast pumpkin, rocket and pesto pastas. See p106 for Jorge's after-dark activities.

Artisans on the Yard (Map pp80-2; QUT campus, George St; lunch $5-10; ⏰ lunch Mon-Fri) This relaxed alfresco café caters to students, academics and garden-faring folk. All dig into cheap and spectacular burgers, Turkish pizzas, paninis and a smattering of Thai and Japanese dishes.

Rush Lounge (Map pp80-2; ☎ 3211 9511; Post Office Sq; mains $10-20; ⏰ breakfast, lunch & dinner Mon-Fri) A luscious injection of suede, oriental-style cut velvet and ambient tunes makes this one of the most atmospheric spots in the city. Deli-standard quiches and sambos are served in sanguine surrounds and the humble steak sanga is turned into a work of art.

Bubbles and Beans (Map pp80-2; ☎ 3832 0322; Admiralty Towers, 35 Howard St; mains $14-20; ⏰ breakfast daily, lunch & dinner Wed-Sun) Ignore the fact that it's beneath a high-rise – this café has one of the best views in the city. Shielded by the glass tower above it, Bubbles and Beans sits in a sheltered pocket right on the Brisbane River. The atmosphere is classy, but the food and prices are midrange – stir fries, pasta and salads.

QUICK EATS

Metro Cafe (Map pp80-2; ☎ 3221 3181; cnr Albert & Mary Sts; dishes $4-8; ⏰ breakfast & lunch Mon-Fri) Deservedly popular with the suit brigade, this petite diner dishes up mountainous breakfasts, sizzling burgers and kebabs, and dozens of fresh and tasty sandwiches. Devoid of the lunch-hour deadline you can munch slowly at the great window seating.

There are food courts in the major shopping malls offering multicultural quick eats. The best are between Queen and Elizabeth Sts on the ground floor of the **Wintergarden**

Centre (Map pp80–2) and on Level E (the ground floor) of the **Myer Centre** (Map pp80–2). Both places have hugely popular sushi bars and kiosks selling noodles, curries and kebabs, as well as more familiar Aussie standards such as fish and chips, roast meats and gourmet sandwiches. You can eat well for less than $8 in any of these places and the malls are open seven days.

Fortitude Valley

RESTAURANTS

Vietnamese Restaurant (Map pp80–2; ☎ 3252 4112; 194 Wickham St; mains $10-13; ☒ lunch & dinner) This authentic Vietnamese restaurant serves exquisite food in no-nonsense surrounds. Dishes come in every carnivorous, seafood and vegetarian version imaginable, but the real delights are to be found on the 'Authentic Menu'. The shredded beef in spinach rolls is divine, as is any dish containing the word sizzling.

Garuva Hidden Tranquillity Restaurant & Bar (Map pp80–2; ☎ 3216 0124; 324 Wickham St; mains around $20; ☒ dinner) This is no restaurant, it's a dining experience! Garuva's rainforested foyer leads to tables with cushioned seating concealed by walls of fluttering white silk. Options such as Turkish shark and Chinese roast beef, along with dim lighting, smooth soundtracks and lulled voices, create a debaucherous air. Fantastic!

Monsoon (Map pp80–2; ☎ 3852 6988; 455 Brunswick St; mains $20-30; ☒ lunch & dinner Tue-Sat) This trendy restaurant serves a fusion of modern Asian and Australian cuisine. Mains include baked kangaroo rump with mint and turnip pudding, and Moreton Bay bugs in a red curry. The staff are knowledgeable and professional, but the vegie options are limited.

Sunbar Restaurant and Lounge (Map pp80–2; ☎ 3257 4999; 367 Brunswick St; mains $28; ☒ lunch Tue-Fri, dinner Tue-Sat) Super slick and chic, Sunbar dazzles its customers with a sophisticated menu. Only a perfectionist could come up with a dish consisting of vanilla and sea salt–encrusted reef fish, sword fish, carpaccio of tuna, scallop, foi gras and sea urchin roe emulsion. See p106 for lounge activities.

Also recommended:

Mellino's (Map pp80–2; ☎ 3252 3551; 330 Brunswick St Mall, Fortitude Valley; mains $7.50-17.50; ☒ 24hr) Good pizza and pasta.

Tibetan Kitchen (Map pp80–2; ☎ 3358 5906; 454 Brunswick St; dishes $8-16; ☒ dinner) Tasty Tibetan fare.

THE AUTHOR'S CHOICE

Circa (Map pp80–2; ☎ 3832 4722; 483 Adelaide St; mains around $35; ☒ lunch Mon-Fri, dinner Mon-Sat) In a sun-drenched interior of block white and polished wood, Circa perfects the art of elegant eating. The outstanding menu has earned more than a couple of awards and you can expect to see meals along the lines of lamb rump with a warm salad of artichoke and beans served with grilled goats cheese, or a warm croustade of sand crab with sweet corn puree. Ingredients such as Iranian caviar, saffron gnocchi and foi gras parfait pepper the entrees and mains, and the wine list is pure class. Seating is arranged to exploit the extensive views of the river and the service will make you feel like royalty.

CAFÉS

Spoon Deli & Café (Map pp80–2; ☎ 3257 1750; 22 James St; dishes $8-18; ☒ 11am-3pm Mon-Fri, 11.20am-4pm Sat & Sun) This upmarket deli serves deliciously rich pasta, salads and soup and colossal paninis and focaccias. The fresh juices are a liquid meal unto themselves. Diners munch their goodies at oversized square tables or low benches skirting the windows, which flood the place with sunlight.

Main Squeeze (Map pp80–2; ☎ 3257 4429; 350 Brunswick St; mains $12-18; ☒ breakfast & lunch Mon-Sat) Fashionistas head to this groovy café-bar and fill up on chick pea burgers, chargrilled, grain-fed sirloin and Asian dishes. You don't have to be wearing the latest kit to enjoy the atmosphere; the environment is unpretentious and the service amicable.

Fatboys Cafe (Map pp80–2; ☎ 3252 3789; 323 Brunswick St; dishes around $15; ☒ breakfast, lunch & dinner Mon-Wed, 24hr Thu-Sun) This popular spot fills its crevices with coffee-sipping 20-somethings without being overly sceney. The menu boasts fairly standard café fare (pasta, paninis and salads) but it's the ambience that most come to ingest. On weekend mornings you can vacuum up a huge brekkie while the markets hum behind you.

Cosmopolitan Coffee (Map pp80–2; ☎ 3252 4179; 322 Brunswick St; mains around $15; ☒ breakfast, lunch & dinner) Pizza, pasta and calzone are the specialty at this elongated café and they're good, particularly in the wee hours. Copious choices suit all palates and the

---

BRISBANE'S TOP FIVE BREKKIE SPOTS

■ **Gunshop Café** (opposite) Breakfast is pure art and the coffee is good.

■ **Fatboys Cafe** (p103) Fat portions and trendy weekend ambience.

■ **Sassafras Cafe** (opposite) Hip food and funky surrounds – great window seating.

■ **Satchmos** (opposite) All-day breakfasts for pocket change.

■ **Bubbles and Beans** (p102) Oh for views like this all the time. Don't forget to eat!

Cosmopolitan also serves fresh salads and designer breads…oh and coffee.

QUICK EATS

Veg Out (Map pp80-2; ☎ 3852 2668; cnr Brunswick & Wickham Sts, McWhirters Arcade; dishes $7-14; ⏰ 7.30am-9pm Mon-Thu, 7.30am-10pm Fri & Sat, 10am-8pm Sun) This teeny canteen-style café cooks up super-healthy organic and vegetarian nosh with Asian, Middle Eastern and Mediterranean overtones. Even avid carnivores won't go hungry here.

Thai Wi-Rat (Map pp80-2; ☎ 3257 0884; Beirne Bldg, Chinatown Mall; dishes $7-10; ⏰ 10am-9pm) This hole-in-the-wall joint cooks up good Thai and Laotian takeaway, including tom yum, salads, and curries.

Chinatown is sprinkled with more nooky eateries serving Thai, Chinese and Korean dishes for around $10.

New Farm

RESTAURANTS

Himalayan Cafe (Map pp80-2; ☎ 3358 4015; 460-2 Brunswick St; dishes $9-15; ⏰ dinner Tue-Sun) Amid a sea of prayer flags and colourful cushions, this unfussy restaurant serves authentic Tibetan and Nepali fare such as Sherpa chicken, momos and filling dahls. It's extremely popular and kids are welcome.

Anise (Map pp80-2; ☎ 3358 1558; 697 Brunswick St; tapas $10, mains $20-30; ⏰ breakfast Sat & Sun, lunch Wed-Sun, dinner daily) In the am this stylish nook is a coffee bar for cool cats. As the morning fades it snaps into its main role as a fashionable wine bar for lunch and dinner. The menu is a work of French art, with dishes such as smoked duck on Paris mash, and

gorgonzola and mascarpone soufflé tart. See p106 for more information.

QUICK EATS

BurgerUrge (Map pp80-2; ☎ 3254 1655; 542 Brunswick St; dishes $8-11; ⏰ lunch Fri-Sun, dinner Tue-Sun) These have to be the city's best burgers, and even though the menu is one dimensional, the shapes, flavours and sizes include Portabella mushroom burgers, marinated free-range chicken burgers, and lamb and mint-chutney burgers – as well as the standard beef sort.

Wok on Inn (Map pp90-1; ☎ 3254 2546; 728 Brunswick St; dishes around $8; ⏰ lunch & dinner) This industrious and popular noodle bar cooks up hot and tasty noodle mains and soups and has a regular $6.50 lunch special.

South Bank

If all the cultural offerings at South Bank have given you an appetite, there are some good dining choices in the parklands.

RESTAURANTS

Cafe San Marco (Map pp80-2; ☎ 3846 4334; South Bank Parklands; mains $16-25; ⏰ breakfast, lunch & dinner) Swimming in a blithe, balmy atmosphere, this waterfront bistro is the perfect spot for a relaxed feed in photogenic surrounds. The subdued menu offers chargrilled steaks, Asian curries, salads and good seafood dishes: just the ticket for picky palates and the patter of little feet. Good for families.

Also recommended:

Kapsali (Map pp80-2; ☎ 3846 1803; South Bank Parklands; mains $17-28; ⏰ lunch & dinner) Bustling taverna serving Greek and Turkish food. Good for families and groups.

Wang Dynasty (Map pp80-2; ☎ 3844 8318; South Bank Parklands; mains $18-24; ⏰ lunch & dinner) Authentic Chinese cuisine and excellent views.

QUICK EATS

There's a small outdoor **food court** (Map pp80-2) located in South Bank Parklands, where it's particularly pleasant to indulge in a cheap lunch ($8 and under) in the sun.

Petrie Terrace & Paddington

RESTAURANTS

Sultans Kitchen (Map pp90-1; ☎ 3368 2194; 163 Given Tce, Paddington; dishes $15-20; ⏰ dinner) If Indian food is your weakness, then this award winner will make you wobble. The service is impeccable and flavours from all corners of the subcontinent are represented on the menu. The nine types of naan are a meal unto themselves, and you can grab your vino from the Paddo Tavern's bottle shop down the road.

Kookaburra Café (Map pp90-1; ☎ 3369 2400; 280 Given Tce, Paddington; meals $10-25; ✆ lunch & dinner) Dressed down in timber and tin, this popular eatery serves good grills with a distinctly Aussie twist. Tourists and locals vacuum up the perfect steaks, fancy fish and chips, and lamb shanks, but be warned, the pizza has won awards, so bring an empty tum.

The bistros at the **Caxton Hotel** (p106; mains $10-25; ✆ lunch & dinner) and the **Paddo Tavern** (p107; mains $8-15; ✆ lunch & dinner) serve good pub grub.

CAFÉS

Sassafras Cafe (Map pp90-1; ☎ 3369 0600; 88 La Trobe Tce, Paddington; dishes $7-18; ✆ 7.30am-7pm Mon-Sat, 7.30am-3pm Sun) This small café with a hippy edge churns out smart, fresh deli lunches and scrumptious cooked breakfasts. A modest dinner menu includes goodies such as salt-crusted roast lamb studded with sundried tomatoes or lentil, potato and spinach curry. The interior is full of chunky wood and happy vibes.

Milton

Rue de Paris (Map pp90-1; ☎ 3368 2600; Shop 16, 30 Park Rd; mains $15-25; ✆ breakfast, lunch & dinner) Amid Milton's flashy alfresco strip, this ambient spot has the wicker chairs and marble of a Parisienne café but the menu is an extensive list of Mediterranean, Middle Eastern, Mod Oz and Asian flavours. There's a wealth of breezy outdoor seating and the service is snappy.

La Dolce Vita (Map pp90-1; ☎ 3368 1191; 20 Park Rd; mains $16-26; ✆ breakfast, lunch & dinner) The tacky décor of this restaurant – Italian statues and fountains beneath a giant model of the Eiffel Tower – can be forgiven due to its fine food. The menu is pure Italian.

West End

RESTAURANTS

Cumquats (Map pp90-1; ☎ 3846 6333; 145 Boundary St; dishes $15-25; ✆ lunch & dinner Tue-Sat) The menu at this multi-award winning restaurant reads like a who's who of Australian game: seared wallaby, braised Tasmanian possum and emu fillets to name a few. The talented

chef fuses flavours and ingredients perfectly and the accompanying wine list is excellent. There are also vegie dishes for the timid.

Mondo Organics (Map pp90-1; ☎ 3844 1132; 166 Hardgrave Rd; mains $16-30; ✆ breakfast Sat & Sun, lunch daily, dinner Tue-Sat) Blow your tastebuds, not your arteries, at this exquisite organic restaurant. In urban timber surrounds diners savour dishes such as roast vegetable, pine nut and lemon terrine, and crispy squid stuffed with seafood, pistachios and rice. It's not food, it's a culinary epiphany.

Jazzy Cat Cafe (Map pp90-1; ☎ 3864 2544; 56 Mollison St; mains $15-20; ✆ breakfast, lunch & dinner) Set in a beautifully restored Queenslander, this restaurant-cum-café is a wee warren of dining nooks, bohemian vibes and friendly staff. The menu is imaginative, and amid the risotto, Asian salads and pasta are tofu and beef steaks.

Also recommended:

Caravanserai (Map pp90-1; ☎ 3217 2617; 1-3 Dornoch Tce; mains $10-18; ✆ lunch Thu-Sun, dinner Tue-Sun) Lovely Turkish restaurant with an open kitchen in the centre.

Two Seasons (Map pp90-1; ☎ 3217 2622; 151 Boundary St; mains $14-20; ✆ lunch & dinner Tue-Sun) Northern Chinese cuisine in a cool, crisp setting.

CAFÉS

Gunshop Café (Map pp90-1; ☎ 3844 2241; 53 Mollison St; mains $15-20; ✆ breakfast, lunch & dinner Tue-Sat, 8am-3pm Sun) Lovers of faaabulous breakfasts, languid brunches and delectable dinners cram into this popular institution. Organic eggs and bread start the day and make way for mains such as beef spare ribs with sticky plum sauce and potato mash. You can wash it all down with great coffee, microbrewery beers and good wines.

Three Monkeys Coffee House (Map pp90-1; ☎ 3844 6045; 58 Mollison St; dishes $8-18; ✆ breakfast, lunch & dinner) A far departure from the profusion of minimalist cafés, this laid-back alternative is steeped in pseudo-Moroccan décor and ambience. You can munch away on focaccias, paninis, pizza, salads, nachos…the menu is long, so the list goes on. Three Monkeys also serves wicked cakes and good coffee.

Satchmos (Map pp90-1; ☎ 3846 7746; 185 Boundary St; meals $5-12; ✆ breakfast, lunch & dinner) True to its namesake, Satchmos oozes blues and jazz, and dining here is like a long, lazy Sunday breakfast. There's a good all-day $6 big breakfast on the contemporary menu and live music from Thursday to Sunday.

Breakfast Creek

North of the CBD, near the junction of Breakfast Creek and the Brisbane River, this area is famous for its historic pub.

Breakfast Creek Hotel (☎ 3262 5988; 2 Kingsford Smith Dr; mains $15-25; ☺ lunch & dinner) In a great rambling building dating from 1889, this is a Brisbane institution. The pub's open-air Spanish Garden Steak House serves incredible steak, including the behemoth 450g rump.

Self-Catering

There's a **Coles Express** (Map pp80-2) on Queen St, just west of the mall, and a **Woolworths** (Map pp80-2) on Edward St in the city. In Fortitude Valley there's a great produce market inside **McWhirters Marketplace** (Map pp80-2; cnr Brunswick & Wickham Sts). The Asian supermarkets in Chinatown mall also have an excellent range of fresh vegies, Asian groceries and exotic fruit.

Not a potato, asparagus spear or Lisbon lemon sits out of place at the upmarket **James St Market** (Map pp80-2; James St, Fortitude Valley). It's pricey, but the quality is excellent and there's a good seafood shop here.

DRINKING

The drinking establishments of Brisbane are generally situated around the CBD, Fortitude Valley, Petrie Tce and West End. The CBD, however, is often dead on weekends, when most punters head for the more lively inner suburbs. Wine and style bars have very much taken over as *the* places to drink, especially in the more fashionable parts of town such as the Valley and West End, but a few good pubs and bars remain.

Press Club (Map pp80-2; ☎ 3852 4000; 339 Brunswick St, Fortitude Valley) The underworld setting is a mixture of minimal lighting, stylish Goth décor, comfy couches and plenty of dark corners. Heavenly beats throb, courtesy of live DJs, from Wednesday to Sunday and the atmosphere is more one of chilled-out drinking rather than beer guzzling.

Anise (Map pp80-2; ☎ 3358 1558; 697 Brunswick St, New Farm) Bring your fancy threads and palates to this trendy wine bar and restaurant (see p104) in the heart of New Farm. Patrons plant themselves at high-backed chairs along the long, narrow bar and nibble on tapas ($10), while plunging into the extensive, excellent range of wines.

Port Office Hotel (Map pp80-2; ☎ 3221 0072; 40 Edward St) The industrial edge of this renovated city pub is spruced up with swathes of dark wood and jungle prints. Pull up a stool, find a bench early and settle in for the evening. When things get hectic (Thursday to Saturday nights) the crowd fills the upstairs balcony and seating.

Jorge (Map pp80-2; ☎ 3012 9121; 183 George St) After sunset, from Wednesday to Sunday, the permanent decks at this city café-cum-bar (see p102) get a good workout when DJs spin funk into the wee hours. More lounge bar than dance venue, the funky punters sip boutique beers and cocktails in-between buzzy conversations.

Sunbar Restaurant and Lounge (Map pp80-2; ☎ 3257 4999; 367 Brunswick St, Fortitude Valley) The drinking quarters at this chic eatery (see p103) could have been lifted out of a music video: muted soft vinyl and a luminescent orange bar around which you can perch your designer-clad tush. If your tush is generically clad, you're just as welcome, but the emphasis is still on sophisticated fun.

Caxton Hotel (Map pp90-1; ☎ 3369 5544; 38 Caxton St, Petrie Tce) This unpretentious but stylish pub is hugely popular on Friday and Saturday nights, when the buzz of the heaving crowd wafts out the wide-open bay windows onto the street. Mambo meets Picasso in the wall prints, and you'll need to adhere to the dress code to enjoy the fun. Expect mainstream music in the background and sports on the telly.

Pavilion (Map pp90-1; ☎ 3844 6172; cnr Boundary & Wilson Sts, West End) A Jack of all drinking trades,

---

THE AUTHOR'S CHOICE

Belgian Beer Cafe (Map pp80-2; ☎ 3221 0199; cnr Edward & Mary Sts) Oh yea lovers of the fine liquid gold, fear not if the XXXX blues have you by the short and curlies. With no fewer than 26 Belgian nectars available here even the fussiest connoisseur will be tickled tiddly. It's not all about the beer though; convivial socialising is a mainstay in the sunny courtyard and inside the big, brassy bar. Any night of the week you could be entertained by mariachi musos or acoustic folk, and regardless of the hour the city outside falls miles away. Oh yes, local boutique beers and good wines are also served.

the Pavilion contains a café and bistro, but the pub dominates. Drink specials are on offer most weeknights and there's live entertainment on Friday and Saturday nights. The crowd of 20- and 30-somethings come for frenzied socialising and fierce pool.

Paddo Tavern (Map pp90-1; ☎ 3369 0044; 186 Given Tce, Paddington) The clientele is local but the décor in this huge pub is kitschy Wild West saloon bar. An odd marriage, sure, but the punters lap it up along with icy beers, footy telecasts and pool tables. Great beer balcony and Sunday sessions.

Irish Murphy's (Map pp80-2; ☎ 3221 4377; cnr George & Elizabeth Sts) Recently swanked up with a lick of fine paint, this big, old-fashioned public house is a popular choice for an after-work drink and down to earth surrounds. A cool warren of booths, open streetside windows and a modicum of ales on tap add to the atmosphere.

GPO (Map pp80-2; ☎ 3252 1322; 740 Ann St, Fortitude Valley) The dressed up old post office in the Valley is the location of this fashionable bar. Downstairs you'll find strappy heels and trendy haircuts, while upstairs offers chilled tunes and the occasional live band.

O'Learys (Map pp90-1; ☎ 3368 1933; 25 Caxton St, Petrie Tce) This atmospheric pub is like a big, brassy drinking barn with kegs for tables and lots of polished timber beneath the cavernous roof. There's a great beer garden and live music throughout the week.

Story Bridge Hotel (Map pp80-2; ☎ 3391 2266; 196 Main St, Kangaroo Point) This beautiful old pub beneath the bridge at Kangaroo Point is a perfect place for a pint after a long day spent sightseeing. You can mingle with the fashionable in the back bar with its floor to ceiling glass or hunker down in the casual beer garden.

Elephant & Wheelbarrow (Map pp80-2; ☎ 1800 225 005, 3257 2252; 230 Wickham St, Fortitude Valley; 🖳) This cavernous English theme pub may not mirror a Putney local, but the ales are good and the atmosphere positively festive. There are plenty of snugs and tables, which fill to bursting on weekends.

Also recommended:

Down Under Bar & Grill (Map pp80-2; ☎ 3211 9277; cnr Ann & Edward Sts) Backpackers haunt, which heaves on a nightly basis.

Exchange Hotel (Map pp80-2; ☎ 3229 3522; 131 Edward St) Spacious city pub popular with a big cross-section of drinking socialisers.

TOP FIVE COFFEE JOINTS

- **Jamie's Espresso Bar** (Map pp80-2; ☎ 3257 1010; cnr James & Robertson Sts, Fortitude Valley; ☯ 7am-2pm & 4-6pm Mon-Fri, 9am-4pm Sat & Sun) Teeny-tiny café serving outstanding coffee.

- **Sugar and Spice** (Map pp80-2; ☎ 3210 1007; 79 Albert St; ☯ 7am-4pm) Clinic for city-bound coffee addicts.

- **Espressohead** (Map pp90-1; ☎ 3844 8324; 69 Boundary St, West End; ☯ breakfast & lunch) Chilled cube of a café.

- **Tongue & Groove** (p108) Bohemian latte culture.

- **Fude & Drinc** (Map pp80-2; ☎ 3839 4666; Shop 402, 471 Adelaide St; ☯ breakfast & lunch) Great coffee, delectable hot chocs, naughty cakes and river views.

Regatta Hotel (☎ 3871 9595; 543 Coronation Dr, Toowong) Ambient riverside pub serving microbrewery beers.

ENTERTAINMENT

Brisbane pulls all the international bands heading to Oz and the city's clubs have become nationally renowned. There's also plenty of theatre. Pick up copies of the free entertainment papers *Time Off* (www.timeoff.com.au), *Rave* (www.ravemag.com.au) and *Scene* (www.sceneonline.com.au) from any café in the Valley. Another good source of information is the website www.brisbane247.com.

The *Courier-Mail* also has daily arts and entertainment listings, and a comprehensive 'What's On In Town' section each Thursday.

Ticketek (☎ 13 19 31; http://premier.ticketek.com.au) is an agency that handles phone bookings for many major events, sports and performances. You can pick up tickets from the Ticketek booth on Elizabeth St, at the back of the Myer Centre.

To ensure you can get into Brisbane's nightspots, carry proof of age and (especially if you're male) avoid wearing tank-tops, shorts or thongs (flip-flops).

Nightclubs

Brisbane is proud of its nightclub scene and offers more than a couple of venues to dance until you drop. Most are open Thursday to Sunday nights, are adamant about ID and charge between $5 and $15 cover. The alternative scene is centred on the Valley, and attracts a mixed straight and gay crowd.

Family (Map pp80-2; ☎ 3852 5000; 8 McLachlan St, Fortitude Valley) Voted Australia's best nightclub *two* years in a row, Family exhilarates dance junkies every weekend on four levels with two dance floors, four bars, four funky themed booths and a top-notch sound system. Elite DJs from home and away frequently grace the decks, including Ministry of Sound residents and the likes of Fergie and Don Diablo.

Empire (Map pp80-2; ☎ 3852 1216; 339 Brunswick St, Fortitude Valley) Things get going at this huge converted hotel after 9pm on weekends, when DJs upstairs in the Moon Bar serve drum 'n' bass and swanky lithe things mingle in the sceney Corner Bar downstairs.

Monastery (Map pp80-2; ☎ 3257 7081; 621 Ann St, Fortitude Valley) From the outside this club resembles a generic office block, but there's nothing suit-and-tie about the dim interior with soft suede couches and lucid soundscapes. Big domestic acts such as Endorphin intermittently play live, but it's the resident DJs that keep the fans coming back.

R-Bar (Map pp80-2; ☎ 3220 1477; 235 Edward St) Extensive renovations have lifted the atmosphere and interest of this dance club. Dance tunes get a workout from Wednesday to Sunday, but Satellite Saturdays are the main event. Punters head here to listen to progressive house and lounge by resident DJs.

Fringe Bar (Map pp80-2; ☎ 3252 9833; cnr Ann & Constance Sts, Fortitude Valley) Too cool for skool, this bar is the kind of place where the next afro will be invented. The '70s décor slapped up with style lends itself to swaying punters. Live DJs get their groove on from Wednesday to Sunday nights and long lines are standard on the weekends.

Source (Map pp80-2; 697 Ann St, Fortitude Valley) A little more generic, this spot club keeps clubbers of all ages and genres happy with live DJS from Thursday to Saturday nights playing R&B, hip-hop and drum 'n' bass. On Sunday there's an open-mic session so you can rap to your heart's content.

Live Music

Brisbane's love affair with live music began long before three lanky lads sang harmonic

ditties and called themselves the Bee Gees. In recent years successful acts, including Regurgitator, Powderfinger, Pete Murray and the soulful George, have illustrated Brisbane's musical diversity and evolution. You can get in early to see history in the making at any number of venues. Cover charges start at around $6.

Zoo (Map pp80-2; ☎ 3854 1381; 711 Ann St, Fortitude Valley) The long queues here start early for a good reason: whether you're into hard rock or electronic soundscapes, Zoo has a gig for you. Musos rate this as an excellent venue and it's one of your best chances to hear some raw, local talent.

Brisbane Jazz Club (Map pp80-2; ☎ 3391 2006; 1 Annie St, Kangaroo Point) A Brizzie institution for addicts of the swinging and soulful, this club lures jazz purists aplenty on Saturday and Sunday nights. There's usually a cover charge of $8 to $12, and anyone who's anyone in the jazz scene plays here when they're in town.

Indie Temple (Map pp80-2; ☎ 3852 2851; 210 Wickham St) Good and grungy, the emphasis is on alternative music and rock at this student stomping ground. Metal nights and live music alternate with theme nights. It's also becoming the fashionable small venue for big international acts, so keep an eye out.

Tongue & Groove (Map pp90-1; ☎ 3846 0334; 63 Hardgrave Rd, West End) This funky little venue in West End hosts everything from reggae and blues to dance beats from Tuesday to Sunday. Jazz also features in the line-up, and all nightlife takes place in the subterranean bar.

Rev (Map pp80-2; 25 Warner St, Fortitude Valley) Another promoter of home-grown talent, this smallish venue presents live rock, punk and electronic music from around Brisbane. You can blow your mind next to the speakers inside or listen from the modest beer garden out front.

Brisbane Convention and Exhibition Centre (Map pp80-2; ☎ 3308 3000; Glenelg St, South Bank) When the big guns are in town they do their thang at this multifunctional entertainment complex. It's more about size and capacity than atmosphere, but you'll catch anyone from PJ Harvey to the Wiggles!

Arena (Map pp80-2; ☎ 3252 5690; 210 Brunswick St, Fortitude Valley) Another huge industrial venue, Arena attracts lots of local and international rock acts but more for the under 30s (or for those with the same tastes).

More live music venues:

O'Leary's (Map pp90-1; ☎ 3368 1933; 25 Caxton St, Petrie Tce) Popular acoustic sessions to help the drinking along throughout the week.

Satchmos (Map pp90-1; ☎ 3846 7746; 185 Boundary St, West End) Acoustic jazz, folk and rock on the weekends.

Cinemas

There are several mainstream cinemas along the Queen St Mall, and Brisbane has excellent art-house cinemas. For details of what's showing see the daily *Courier-Mail* or the freebie paper *Scene*.

There are also free open-air movies screened over summer in the South Bank Parklands (p85) and City Botanic Gardens (p84).

The **Dendy Cinema** (Map pp80-2; ☎ 3211 3244; 346 George St) shows good art-house films. In the Valley, **Palace Centro** (Map pp80-2; ☎ 3852 4488; 39 James St, Fortitude Valley) also screens good art-house films.

South Bank Cinema (Map pp80-2; ☎ 3846 5188; cnr Grey & Ernest Sts, South Bank) is the cheapest cinema for mainstream flicks; tickets cost about a third less than at other places.

Cinemas on Queen St Mall:

Greater Union (Map pp80-2; ☎ 3027 9999; Level A, Myer Centre) Mainstream blockbusters.

Hoyts Regent Theatre (Map pp80-2; ☎ 3027 9999; 107 Queen St Mall) A lovely old cinema worth visiting for the building alone.

Theatre

Brisbane is well stocked with theatre venues, most of them located at South Bank. The Queensland Cultural Centre has a dedicated **phone line** (☎ 13 62 46) that handles bookings for all the South Bank theatres. Also keep an eye out for *Centre Stage*, the events diary for the complex, available from tourist offices.

Queensland Performing Arts Centre (QPAC; Map pp80-2; ☎ 3840 7444; www.qpac.com.au; Queensland Cultural Centre, Stanley St, South Bank) This centre consists of three venues and features concerts, plays, dance and performances of all genres. Catch anything from international comedy acts to *Alice in Wonderland*.

Queensland Conservatorium (Map pp80-2; ☎ 3875 6375; 16 Russell St, South Bank) South of the Queensland Performing Arts Centre, the Conservatorium showcases the talents of attending students.

Brisbane Powerhouse (Map pp90-1; ☎ 3358 8622, box office ☎ 3358 8600; 119 Lamington St, New Farm) A one-stop venue for contemporary arts and performance in the inner north. The Powerhouse presents an evolving schedule of theatre, dance, music and workshops.

Metro Arts Centre (Map pp80-2; ☎ 3221 1527; 109 Edward St) This progressive venue hosts community theatre, local dramatic pieces, dance and art shows. It's a good spot to head for a taste of Brisbane's creative performance talent.

QUT Gardens Theatre (Map pp80-2; ☎ 3864 4213; QUT, George St) This university theatre plays host to touring national and international productions as well as performances from the university's dramatic, musical and dance companies.

Brisbane Arts Theatre (Map pp90-1; ☎ 3369 2344; 210 Petrie Tce, Petrie Tce) Amateur theatre performances along the lines of Shakespeare and Dickens are held here.

La Boite Repertory Theatre (Map pp90-1; ☎ 3010 2611; 424 Montague Rd, West End) This small theatre presents an interesting range of art-house theatre in intimate surroundings.

Sit Down Comedy Club (Map pp90-1; ☎ 3369 4466; Paddo Tavern, Given Tce, Paddington) There are a few comedy venues in town, the most prominent being this one. Thursday is stand-up night, with a good programme of touring acts, and Wednesday is given over to improvisation.

Sport

Like other Australians, Brisbanites are sports-mad. You can see interstate cricket matches and international test cricket at the **Gabba** (Brisbane Cricket Ground; Map pp90-1; ☎ 3008 6166; www.thegabba.org.au) in Woolloongabba, south of Kangaroo Point. The cricket season runs from October to March.

During the other half of the year, rugby league is the big spectator sport. The Brisbane Broncos plays home games at **Suncorp Stadium** (Map pp90-1; ☎ 3331 5000; Castlemaine St, Milton).

Once dominated by Victorian teams, the Australian Football League (AFL) has been challenged by the Brisbane Lions, who won the flag in 2001, 2002 and 2003 (and who then lost the final in 2004). You can watch them kick the ball and some southern butt at a home game at the Gabba between March and September.

Australia has the National Basketball League (NBL), which is based on American pro basketball, and the fast-paced NBL games draw large crowds. Brisbane's team,

BRISBANE

the Brisbane Bullets, is based at the **Brisbane Convention and Exhibition Centre** (Map pp80-2; ☎ 3308 3000; www.bcec.com.au; cnr Merivale & Glenelg Sts, South Brisbane).

Queensland also has a side in the National Netball League – the Queensland Firebirds. Their home stadium is the **Chandler Arena** (Old Cleveland & Tiley Rd, Chandler). You can book tickets through Ticketek, or online at http://firebirds.netballq.org.au.

SHOPPING

As a capital city, Brisbane is well stocked with shops and boutiques selling everything from designer fashions to 'I Love Australia' fridge magnets.

Around the intersection of Ann and Brunswick Sts in Fortitude Valley there are numerous trendy fashion boutiques, where budding designers sell their handmade wares. You can also get the latest street and surf wear here.

The Queen St Mall is a playground for shoppers, with several shopping centres, all the big brands and a few boutiques thrown in for good measure.

Aboriginal Art

Queensland Aboriginal Creations (Map pp80-2; ☎ 3224 5730; Little Stanley St, South Bank) This is probably Brisbane's best Indigenous art store, stocking a good range of authentic Aboriginal art, craft and souvenirs, including paintings and prints, didgeridoos, boomerangs, jewellery, clapsticks, bullroarers, woomeras and clothing.

Earth Spirit (150 Queen St Mall) This small but excellent gallery, inside a city tourist store (see Australia the Gift on below), sells beautiful Indigenous pieces.

Fire-Works Aboriginal Gallery (Map pp90-1; ☎ 3216 1250; 11 Stratton St, Newstead) This place is also worth a look for contemporary and often quite political Aboriginal art.

Australiana

The Australian tourism marketing machine goes into overdrive in Queensland, and there are numerous emporiums in the city centre selling such treats as kangaroo and merino sheep skins, boomerangs, 'Kangaroo Crossing' road signs, Akubra hats, 'G'day' T-shirts and machine-made didgeridoos.

Australia the Gift (Map pp80-2; ☎ 3210 6198; 150 Queen St Mall) This is the biggest vendor of this

kind of souvenir in the city. It carries extensive stocks of mass-produced Australiana.

Australian Geographic Wintergarden Centre (Map pp80-2; ☎ 3003 0355; Queen St Mall); Myer Centre (Map pp80-2; ☎ 3220 0341; Queen St Mall) Stocks everything from books and calendars on Australian flora and fauna to glow-in-the-dark dinosaurs.

Clothing

RM Williams (Map pp80-2; ☎ 3229 7724; Level 2, Wintergarden Centre, Queen St Mall) One of the best-known makers of Aussie gear, this store stocks an excellent (and expensive) range of Akubras, boots, oilskins, moleskins, belts, jumpers and flannelette shirts.

Dogstar (Map pp80-2; ☎ 3852 2555; 713 Ann St, Fortitude Valley) The Japanese-born designer of the beautiful pieces in this shop has infused more than a touch of her land of birth into their designs. Beautiful fabrics are used to make pants, skirts and ensembles that will be envied anywhere.

Blonde Venus (Map pp80-2; ☎ 3216 1735; 707 Ann St, Fortitude Valley) Head here to pick up a splash of Zimmerman, Akira or Morrissey. This shop also sells cutting-edge designers on the verge of being discovered.

Maiocchi (Map pp80-2; ☎ 3852 3353; 370 Brunswick St, Fortitude Valley) This is a great little store for individual pieces without the price tag of its glamorous neighbours.

For something a bit more à la mode, there are numerous Australian and international fashion boutiques in the upmarket **Elizabeth Arcade** (Map pp80–2), between Elizabeth and Charlotte Sts, and in the even plusher, split-level **Brisbane Arcade** (Map pp80–2), between the Queen St Mall and Adelaide St.

Markets

Crafts Village markets (Map pp80-2; Stanley St Plaza, South Bank; ☺ 5pm-10.30pm Fri, 10am-6pm Sat, 9am-5pm Sun) These popular markets have a great range of clothing, craft, art, handmade goods and interesting souvenirs. Stalls are set up in rows of colourful tents.

Brunswick St Markets (Brunswick St, Fortitude Valley; ☺ 8am-4pm Sat & Sun) These colourful markets fill the mall in Fortitude Valley with a diverse collection of crafts, clothes, work by budding designers and the inevitable junk.

King George Square Contemporary Craft & Art Market (King George Sq; ☺ 8am-4pm Sun) These markets transform a pocket of the city centre into a bustling arts and crafts fair on the weekends. This is a nice spot to bring the kids.

Farmers Market (Brisbane Powerhouse, 119 Lamington St, New Farm; ☺ from 6am every 2nd & 4th Sat of the month) More than 100 stalls sell fresh produce, much of it organic, at this excellent and deservedly popular farmers market. Here you can buy everything from flowers to yabbies.

Every Sunday the carnival-style **Riverside Centre** and **Eagle St Pier markets** have more than 150 stalls, including glassware, weaving, leatherwork and children's activities.

GETTING THERE & AWAY

The **Roma St Transit Centre** (Map pp80–2), 500m northwest of the city centre, is the main terminus and booking point for all long-distance buses and trains, as well as Citytrain services. Airport buses and trains leave from here. The centre also has shops, food outlets, a post office and the Brisbane Visitors Accommodation Service (p79).

Air

Brisbane's main airport is about 16km northeast of the city centre at Eagle Farm, and has separate international and domestic terminals about 2km apart, linked by the **Airtrain** (☎ 3215 5000; www.airtrain.com.au; tickets $3; ☺ 5am-8pm), which runs every 15 minutes. It's a busy international arrival and departure point with frequent flights to Asia, Europe, Pacific islands, North America, New Zealand and Papua New Guinea. See p452 for details of international airlines that fly into Brisbane.

Only one domestic airline, **Qantas** (Map pp80-2; ☎ 13 13 13; www.qantas.com.au; 247 Adelaide St; ☺ 8.30am-5pm Mon-Fri, 9am-1pm Sat), has an office in Brisbane, although you can book any airline online or by phone.

Several airlines link Brisbane to the rest of the country. Qantas has an extensive network, connecting Brisbane with Sydney ($100, 1½ hours), Melbourne ($150, 2½ hours), Adelaide ($170, 2½ hours), Canberra ($140, two hours), Hobart ($210, four hours), Perth ($300, five hours) and Darwin ($180, four hours).

Virgin Blue (☎ 13 67 89; www.virginblue.com.au) also flies between Brisbane and Sydney ($105), Melbourne ($120), Adelaide ($140), Canberra ($110), Hobart ($150), Perth ($250) and Darwin ($180).

Jetstar (☎ 13 15 38; www.jetstar.com.au) connects Brisbane with Melbourne and Cairns (both $120) and Hobart ($150).

Within Queensland, one-way fares include Proserpine ($110, 1¾ hours), Townsville ($120, two hours), Rockhampton ($80, 1¼ hours), Mackay ($90, 1½ hours) and Cairns ($140, 2½ hours).

Macair (☎ 13 13 13; www.macair.com.au) flies to many destinations in the Queensland outback, including Mt Isa ($380, four hours).

Sunshine Express (☎ 13 13 13; www.sunshineexpress .com.au) connects Brisbane with the Sunshine Coast ($95), Hervey Bay and Maryborough ($165).

See p456 for more details on flying to/from Brisbane and around Queensland.

Bus

Bus companies have booking desks on the 3rd level of the Roma St Transit Centre. **Greyhound Australia** (☎ 13 14 99; www.greyhound .com.au) is the main company on the Sydney–Brisbane run; you can go via the New England Hwy (17 hours) or the Pacific Hwy (16 hours) for $100. **Premier Motor Service** (☎ 13 34 10; www.premierms.com.au) operates the same routes often with slightly cheaper deals.

You can also travel between Brisbane and Melbourne ($164, 24 to 28 hours) or Adelaide ($290, 40 hours), although competitive airfares may enable you to fly for the same price or less.

North to Cairns, Premier Motor Service runs two services daily and Greyhound runs five. The approximate fares and journey times to places along the coast are as follows:

Destination	Duration	One-way fare
Noosa Heads	2½hr	$24
Hervey Bay	5½hr	$50
Rockhampton	11½hr	$70
Mackay	16½hr	$140
Townsville	23hr	$180
Cairns	29hr	$200 (3 free stops)

There are also daily services to the Northern Territory: it's a 46-hour trip to Darwin ($560) via Longreach ($115, 17 hours) and Mt Isa ($155, 26 hours).

AIRPORT TO THE GOLD COAST & BEYOND

Coachtrans (☎ 3238 4700; www.coachtrans.com.au) operates the Airporter direct services from

Brisbane Airport to the Gold Coast ($35). Services meet every flight and will drop you anywhere on the Gold Coast.

AIRPORT TO THE SUNSHINE COAST
Suncoast Pacific (☎ 07-5449 9966; www.suncoast pacific.com.au) is one of several operators with direct services from Brisbane Airport to the Sunshine Coast (see p172).

Car & Motorcycle
There are five major routes, numbered from M1 to M5, into and out of the Brisbane metropolitan area. The major north–south route, the M1, connects the Pacific Hwy to the south with the Bruce Hwy to the north, but things get a bit confusing as you enter the city.

Coming from the Gold Coast, the Pacific Hwy splits into two at Eight Mile Plains. From here, the South East Freeway (M3) runs right into the centre, skirting along the riverfront on the western side of the CBD before emerging on the far side as Gympie Arterial Rd.

If you're just passing through, take the Gateway Motorway (M1) at Eight Mile Plains, which bypasses the city centre to the east and crosses the Brisbane River at the Gateway Bridge ($3 toll). From either direction, the Eagle Farm exit on the northern side of the bridge provides a quick route to the Valley and CBD. Just north is the turn-off to Brisbane Airport. The Gateway Motorway and Gympie Arterial Rd meet in Bald Hills, just south of the Pine River, and merge to form the Bruce Hwy.

Heading inland, the Ipswich Motorway (M2) branches off the M1 south of the centre and crosses the M3 before snaking off southwest to Ipswich and the Darling Downs. For a quick route from the city, pick up Milton Rd at the northwestern tip of the CBD and follow it out to the M5, which runs south to meet the Ipswich Motorway at Wacol (Milton Rd is also the way to get to Mt Coot-tha).

HIRE
All of the major companies, **Hertz** (☎ 13 30 39), **Avis** (☎ 13 63 33), **Budget** (☎ 13 27 27), **Europcar** (☎ 13 13 90) and **Thrifty** (☎ 1300 367 227), have offices at the Brisbane Airport terminals and throughout the city.

There are also several smaller companies in Brisbane that advertise slightly cheaper deals:

Abel Rent A Car (Map pp80-2; ☎ 1800 131 429, 3236 1225; www.abel.com.au; Ground fl, Roma St Transit Centre, Roma St)

Can Do Car Rentals (Map pp80-2; ☎ 3832 3666; www.candorentals.com.au; cnr Wickham & Warren Sts, Fortitude Valley)

Car-azy Rentals (Map pp90-1; ☎ 3257 1104; carazy@bigpond.net.au; 86 Bridge St, Fortitude Valley)

Hawk Rent A Car (Map pp80-2; ☎ 3236 0788; www .hawkrentacar.com; 3rd fl, Roma St Transit Centre, Roma St)

ABC Integra (Map pp90-1; ☎ 1800 067 414; 3620 3200; www.abcintegra.com.au; 398 St Pauls Tce, Fortitude Valley)

Train
Brisbane's main station for long-distance trains is the Roma St Transit Centre. For reservations and information visit the **Queensland Rail Travel Centre** (☎ 13 22 32; www.qr.com.au) Central Station (Map pp80-2; ☎ 3235 1323; Ground fl, Central Station, 305 Edward St; ☯ 7am-5pm Mon-Fri); Roma St (Map pp80-2; ☎ 3235 1331; Roma St Transit Centre, Roma St; ☯ 7am-5pm Mon-Fri). You can also make reservations online or over the phone.

For details of intrastate train services to/from Brisbane, see p464.

GETTING AROUND
To/From the Airport
The easiest way to get to/from the airport is the **Airtrain** (☎ 3215 5000; www.airtrain.com.au; per adult/child $10/5; ☯ 5am-8pm), which runs every 15 minutes between the airport and the Roma St Transit Centre and Central Station. There are also half-hourly services to the airport from Gold Coast Citytrain stops.

Coachtrans (☎ 3238 4700; www.coachtrans.com.au) runs the half-hourly Skytrans shuttle bus between the Roma St Transit Centre and the airport between 5.45am and 10pm. It costs $9 per adult and $6 per child for the trip from the airport to the city, or $11 per adult and $7 per child to be dropped at your city accommodation. A taxi into the centre from the airport will cost around $30.

Bicycle
See p89 for information on cycling in and around Brisbane.

Car & Motorcycle
There is free two-hour parking on many streets in the CBD and in the inner suburbs,

but the major thoroughfares become clearways (ie parking is prohibited) during the morning and afternoon rush hours. If you do park in the street, pay close attention to the times on the parking signs, as Brisbane's parking inspectors take no prisoners. Parking is free in the CBD during the evening.

Less risky but more expensive are the big commercial car parks dotted around the centre, which charge about $7 per hour or $25 per day. Weekend rates are often around $8 per day. **King's Parking** (☎ 3229 4377) operates at least a dozen multistorey car parks in the CBD.

There is off-street parking at most midrange and top-end places to stay, but at few of the hostels. If you stay at the Palace or any of the hostels along Roma St, you'll have to park in the street or pay for a car park.

Queensland's motoring association is the RACQ (p79), which provides insurance, maps and a breakdown service.

See opposite for information about car-hire companies.

Public Transport

Brisbane boasts a world-class public transport network, and information on bus, train and ferry routes and connections can be obtained from the **Trans-Info Service** (☎ 13 12 30; www.transinfo.qld.gov.au; ⓨ 6am-10pm).

Bus and ferry information is also available at the Brisbane Visitor Information Centre (p79), the **bus station information centre** (Map pp80-2; ⓨ 8.30am-5.30pm Mon-Thu, to 8pm Fri, 9am-4pm Sat, 10am-4pm Sun) under the Queen St Mall, and the Queensland Rail Travel Centre (opposite).

Fares on buses, trains and ferries operate on a zone system. There are 23 zones in total, but the city centre and most of the inner-city suburbs fall within Zone 1, which means most fares will be $2/1 per adult/child.

If you're going to be using public transport more than once on any single day, it's worth getting a daily ticket (adult/child Zone 1 $4/2, Zone 2 $4.80/2.40, Zone 3 $5.60/2.80). These allow you unlimited transport on all buses, trains and ferries and are priced according to the number of zones you'll be travelling in. You can also buy off-peak daily tickets (Zone 1 $3/1.50, Zone 2 $3.60/1.80, Zone 3 $4.20/2.10), which allow you to do the same thing between 9am and 3.30pm, and after 7pm from Monday to Friday and all weekend. A ten-trip saver (Zone 1 $16/8, Zone 2 $20/9.60, Zone 3 $23/11.20) gives you 10 trips for the price of eight.

BOAT

Brisbane's nippy blue CityCat catamarans run every 20 to 30 minutes between 5.50am and 10.30pm from the University of Queensland in the west to Bretts Wharf in the east, and back. Stops along the way include North Quay (for the Queen St Mall), South Bank, Riverside (for the CBD) and New Farm Park. CityCats are wheelchair accessible at all stops except for West End, QUT Gardens Point, Riverside, Bulimba and Brett's Wharf.

Also useful are the Inner City Ferries, which zigzag back and forth across the river between North Quay, near the Victoria Bridge, and Mowbray Park. Services start at 6am from Monday to Saturday and from 7am on Sunday, and run until about 9pm from Sunday to Thursday, and until about 11pm on Friday and Saturday. There are also several cross-river ferries; most useful is the Eagle St Pier to Thornton St (Kangaroo Point) service.

Like all public transport, fares are based on zones. Most stops you'll need will be city-based and will therefore cost $2/1 per adult/child for one trip. If you're using the CityCats or ferries for sightseeing, get a daily ticket or off-peak daily, which will give you a day to ride the CityCats to your heart's content.

BUS

The Loop, a free bus that circles the city area, and stops at QUT, the Queen St Mall, City Hall, Central Station and Riverside, runs every 10 minutes on weekdays between 7am and 6pm.

The main stop for local buses is in the basement of the Myer Centre, where there's a small information centre (left). You can also pick up most of the useful buses from the colour-coded stops along Adelaide St, between George and Edward Sts.

Red City Circle bus No 333 does a clockwise loop round the area, stopping at City Plaza, Anzac Sq, Riverside, QUT and the Queen St Mall. Buses run every 10 to 20 minutes Monday to Friday from 5am until about 6pm, and with the same frequency on Saturday morning (starting at 6am). Services are less frequent at other times, and cease at 7pm Sunday and midnight on other days.

Useful buses from the city centre include Nos 190 and 191 to Fortitude Valley and New Farm, which leave from Adelaide St between King George Sq and Edward St. You can pick up Bardon bus No 375 to Paddington from opposite the transit centre or on Adelaide St. In the opposite direction, this bus will take you from the city to the Valley.

TRAIN

The fast Citytrain network has seven lines that run as far as Nambour, Cooroy and Gympie in the north (for the Sunshine Coast), and Nerang and Robina in the south (for the Gold Coast). Other useful routes include Rosewood (for Ipswich) and Cleveland (for the North Stradbroke Island ferry). The lines to Pinkenba, Shorncliffe and Ferny Grove are mainly for suburban commuters.

The Airtrain service (see p112) integrates with the Citytrain network in the CBD and along the Gold Coast line. All trains go through the Roma St Transit Centre and Central Station in the city, and Brunswick St Station in Fortitude Valley.

Trains run from around 4.30am, with the last train on each line leaving Central Station between 11.30pm and midnight. On Sunday the last trains run at around 10pm.

The frequency of trains varies: you can expect a train every 10 minutes on weekdays during the rush hour (from 7am to 9.30am and from 3pm to 6pm); once an hour on weekends, and after 10pm during the week; and half-hourly at other times.

Taxi

There are usually plenty of taxis around the city centre, and there are taxi ranks at the Roma St Transit Centre and at the top end of Edward St, by the junction with Adelaide St.

You can book a taxi by telephone. The major company is **Black & White** (☎ 13 10 08). Rivals include **Yellow Cab Co** (☎ 13 19 24) and **Brisbane Cabs** (☎ 13 22 11). Most cabs have Eftpos facilities.

Around Brisbane

AROUND BRISBANE

CONTENTS

HIGHLIGHTS

- Trekking around **North Stradbroke Island** (p119) and cooling your heels in a freshwater lake
- **Surfing** or **sea-kayaking** (p121) the fine breaks lapping at 'Straddie's' extensive coastline
- Bushwalking on **Moreton Island** (p124) and snorkelling at the dazzling **Tangalooma Wrecks** (p124)
- Dining with the dolphins – heading to **Tangalooma** (p124) and feeding Moreton Island's oceanic residents
- Catching a day cruise from **Manly** (p117) and spotting dugongs, dolphins and whales in beautiful Moreton Bay
- Meandering along the scenic esplanade at **Redcliffe** (p116) and casting a line off the old Hornibrook Hwy
- Bush camping in **Moreton Island National Park** (p124) and waking up to the calls of a bird symphony
- Sharing fish and chips with your best mate while dangling your legs off Redcliffe's lengthy **jetty** (p116)

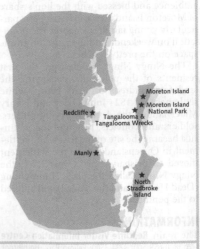

Moreton Island

Moreton Island National Park

Redcliffe ★

Tangalooma & Tangalooma Wrecks

Manly ★

North Stradbroke Island

- www.redcliffe.qld.gov.au
- www.stradbrokeholidays.com.au

The landscape surrounding Brisbane can be explored on some exquisite day trips and longer stays. Beyond the suburban spread, and sitting at the mouth of the Brisbane River, Moreton Bay is reckoned to have some 365 islands, around which whales, dolphins and dugongs frolic. There are a number of unique and accessible islands that lure people with spectacular scenery.

Moreton Island is a mass of rugged wilderness sitting on top of a vast sandy base. Bushwalking and four-wheel driving are highlights here, but a resident pod of dolphins at Tangalooma steals the show. North Stradbroke is the most developed of the islands, with established communities providing low-key infrastructure to holidaying families from Brisbane. It's known for glorious stretches of beach and protected coves, where the surfing, swimming and fishing are excellent. Bushwalking is popular here too, with tracks leading to some gorgeous freshwater lakes. If you want to escape the urban hustle for a day, head to the small and tranquil islands of St Helena, Coochiemudlo and Bribie.

The bayside suburbs around Brisbane provide a slower pace than the city, but they offer plenty to fill a day's itinerary. Redcliffe is an excellent excursion for families, with languid bike rides along the esplanade, sunny breakfasts and fish and chips on a striking jetty. Also here is the interesting Redcliffe Historical Museum with displays of local memorabilia.

REDCLIFFE

On the bay, 35km north of the state capital, the Redcliffe Peninsula is a picturesque jut of land doused in an ambling, happy coastal ambience and blessed with the lion's share of Moreton Island views. Day-trippers, particularly young families, engorge the population on weekends, indulging in the ample space on the pretty beaches.

The Ningy Ningy people were the first residents of the peninsula, occupying the land for hundreds of years before white settlement. In 1824 John Oxley and Henry Miller landed the *Amity,* carrying settlers, soldiers and convicts, here and the peninsula became the site of the first white settlement in Queensland. When the settlement moved to Brisbane only a year later, the Ningy Ningy called the place Humpybong (Dead Houses) and the name is still applied to the peninsula.

INFORMATION

The main **Redcliffe Visitor Information Centre** (☎ 1800 659 500, 3284 3500; Pelican Park, Hornibrook Esplanade, Clontarf; ☺ 7am-4pm) is at the base of the peninsula. There's also another smaller, central **branch** (☎ 1800 659 500; cnr Redcliffe Pde & Irene St; ☺ 9am-4pm) in Redcliffe.

SIGHTS & ACTIVITIES

A pedestrian and cycle path hugs the peninsula's shore from Scarborough in the north to Redcliffe Point in the centre. It's the most scenic way to see the area, and there are frequent stairs to the shops and cafés on the esplanade atop the slight slope. On the way you can stretch your legs on the sizable **Redcliffe Jetty**, which has had several makeovers since its beginnings in 1885. A few hundred metres south of the jetty sits **Settlement Cove Lagoon**, a small lagoon that looks like it migrated from Toyland. It's a veritable Utopia for little ones, who get to scramble over colourful boats and castles and cool off in the various pools. Understandably it's a fantastic spot for families and the BBQs and shady spots facilitate an all-day visit.

At the base of the peninsula, on Clontarf Beach, the Redcliffe Visitor Information Centre feeds the voracious local pelicans every day at 10am. These birds don't mess about and sometimes the whole affair can be over in 10 minutes, but it's good fun.

A few blocks east, the old Hornibrook Hwy used to be the main access point for folk heading onto the peninsula from the south. Having long been replaced by a dirty great concrete slab running parallel to it, the old highway is now a 2.8km jetty and popular fishing spot.

The small but interesting **Redcliffe Historical Museum** (☎ 3883 1898; 75 Anzac Ave; admission free; ☺ 10am-4pm Tue-Sat) details the peninsula's history through information boards, artefacts and a great series of personal accounts from locals. The excellent *Spectravision* wraps Redcliffe's story up in a 15-minute multimedia presentation. Although the museum captures the area's colloquial charm, there seems to be little information about the Ningy Ningy people and their history here.

For a respite other than the beach, head to the **Redcliffe Botanical Gardens** (Victoria Ave; admission free; ☺ 7.30am-3.30pm Mon-Fri, 9am-4pm Sat & Sun). Occupying most of a block several streets from the water, the dense and varied foliage provides plenty of cool, dappled picnic spots.

EATING

There are plenty of cafés and takeaways along the esplanade.

Morgans (☎ 3203 5744; Bird of Passage Pde, Scarborough; mains $17-40; ☺ lunch & dinner) Near the Scarborough jetty, this is an award-winning seafood restaurant. Bugs (the fishy sort), shellfish and fish are sourced locally and cooked to perfection without too many adulterating sauces. There's an equal amount of indoor and outdoor seating, so it's an all-weather splurge.

Oasis Café (☎ 3283 1677; Redcliffe Pde, Redcliffe; meals $6-15; ☺ breakfast & lunch) Blessed with an abundance of outdoor seating, this casual café churns out good focaccias, wedges, the odd inventive salad and scrambled eggs so big they may take a collective effort. It's friendly and popular with visitors of all kinds.

Schooners Bistro (☎ 3284 6247; 41 Redcliffe Pde, Redcliffe; meals $9-17; ☺ breakfast, lunch & dinner) On the ground floor of the Ambassador Hotel, this bistro is a good spot for fresh seafood in pub surrounds. Here you can dig into garlic sizzled Moreton Bay bugs or a bucket of prawns, and Schooners also cooks up a hearty steak.

DETOUR

The easiest way to travel between Brisbane and Redcliffe is by turning right at Anzac Ave off the Bruce Hwy at Mango Hill, but an earlier turn-off will steer you into scenic seaside suburbs and afford ocean views.

Heading north from Brisbane, turn right off the highway onto Telegraph Rd at Bald Hills. The route takes you through to the seaside resorts of **Sandgate** and **Brighton**, where you can pause for a coffee and take in the idyllic views.

Then head north along Beaconsfield Tce, Brighton's esplanade with vast views of the bay off to the east, and hook up with the Houghton Hwy, which travels over the water and into Redcliffe.

GETTING THERE & AROUND

Translink bus Nos 11, 310 and 315 service the Redcliffe area, including Scarborough, from Brisbane ($4, one hour).

Vehicle ferries to Moreton Island leave from Scarborough at the northern tip of the headland.

MANLY

Lying just a few kilometres south of the Brisbane River mouth, Manly has the largest marina (after Fremantle) in the southern hemisphere, and is an attractive hangout for yachties.

INFORMATION

The **tourist information office** (☎ 3348 3524; 43 Cambridge Pde; ☺ 8.30am-5pm Mon-Thu, 9am-4pm Sat & Sun) is very helpful.

SIGHTS & ACTIVITIES

Various sailing companies offer day trips out on Moreton Bay for around $80 per person. **Moreton Bay Escapes** (☎ 1300 559 355; www.moretonbayescapes.com.au; adult/child/family $110/90/335) operates day tours in its racing yacht *Solo*, which has won the Sydney-to-Hobart yacht race. The tours include three hours of sailing and three hours of snorkelling, swimming or just being lazy on Moreton Island, plus lunch.

Bay Dolphin Sailing Tours (☎ 3207 9620; www.baydolphin.com.au; adult/child/family $85/45/210) also

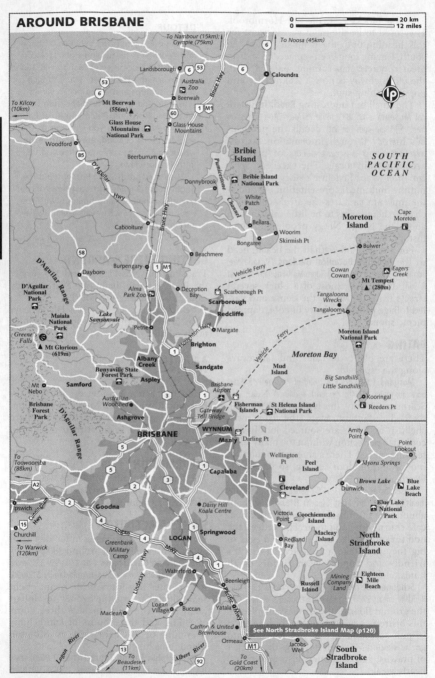

operates day sailing tours around Moreton Bay on large catamarans. **Manly Eco Cruises** (☎ 3396 9400; www.manlyecocruises.com; adult/child $90/40) takes folk out on the MV *Getaway*, with boom nets, for full-day cruises. It also operates a very popular Sunday BBQ breakfast tour (adult/child $30/15), which lasts two hours.

The **Royal Queensland Yacht Squadron** (☎ 3396 8666; 578 Royal Esplanade), south of the centre, has yacht races every Wednesday afternoon, and many of the captains are happy to take visitors on board for the ride. Contact the club secretary for more information. You may also be able to pick up a yacht ride along the coast from here: the club has a notice board where people advertise for crew. Another port of call is the **Wynnum-Manly Yacht Club** (☎ 3393 5708).

SLEEPING & EATING

Almost everything in Manly is on Cambridge Pde, which runs inland from the shorefront Esplanade.

Moreton Bay Backpackers Lodge (☎ 1800 800 157, 3396 3824; www.moretonbaylodge.com.au; 45 Cambridge Pde; dm $22, s $35-50, d $55-75) Upstairs on Manly's main strip, this attractive, terraced guesthouse offers very good rooms and can organise all sorts of activities in the area. Some of the dorms have bathrooms. Also here is the excellent **Bay Window Café** (mains from $12; ⏰ lunch Fri-Sun, dinner Tue-Sun).

Manly Hotel (☎ 3249 5999; Cambridge Pde, Manly; meals from $7-10; ⏰ breakfast, lunch & dinner) Across from the Bay Window, this friendly, unfussy pub has inexpensive bistro meals along the lines of lasagne, fish and chips and good ol' chicken parma.

NORTH STRADBROKE ISLAND

Popularly known as 'Straddie', this lovely sand island is one of the largest in the world and just a 30-minute ferry ride from Cleveland, 30km south of Brisbane. The surf beaches here are excellent and there are some great walking tracks. The wild southeastern coast is a playground for 4WD drivers.

North and South Stradbroke Islands (for information on South Stradbroke, see p130) used to be joined, but a savage storm sev-

ered the sand spit between the two in 1896. Sand mining used to be a major industry here, but these days only the southwest of the island is mined. Elsewhere the vegetation has recovered impressively, creating some beautiful scenery, especially in the middle of the island.

It's a popular escape from Brisbane for families and holidaymakers and there are consequently some great accommodation and dining options. It can get pretty busy during the Christmas and Easter holidays though.

ORIENTATION & INFORMATION

There are three small settlements on the island, Dunwich, Amity Point and Point Lookout, which are all grouped around the northern end of the island. Point Lookout, on the main surf beach, is the nicest place to stay. Apart from the beach, the southern part of the island is closed to visitors because of mining.

The **Stradbroke Island visitor information centre** (☎ 1800 099 049, 3409 9555; www.stradbroke tourism.com; ⏰ 8.30am-5pm) is 200m from the ferry terminal in Dunwich.

There are post offices in Dunwich and Point Lookout that can give cash advances on credit cards, and there are Eftpos facilities at the BP Roadhouse, Point Lookout Bowls Club, Stradbroke Island Hotel bottle shop and Bob's 727 store at the Centre Point shopping centre in Point Lookout.

SIGHTS

There's a good walk around the **North Gorge** (30 minutes) on the headland at Point Lookout, and porpoises, dolphins, manta rays and sometimes whales are spotted from up here.

Dunwich, on the western coast, is where the ferries dock, but there isn't much here apart from a few cafés and the tiny **North Stradbroke Historical Museum** (☎ 3409 8318; adult/child $2.20/0.50; ⏰ Wed & Sat 10am-noon) on Welsby Rd, near the post office.

The eastern beach, known as **Eighteen Mile Beach**, is open to 4WD vehicles and campers, and there are lots of walking tracks and old 4WD roads in the northern half of the island. Just off the road from Dunwich to the beach, **Blue Lake** is reached by a sandy 4WD track. Much more pleasant is the 2.7km walking trail through the forest,

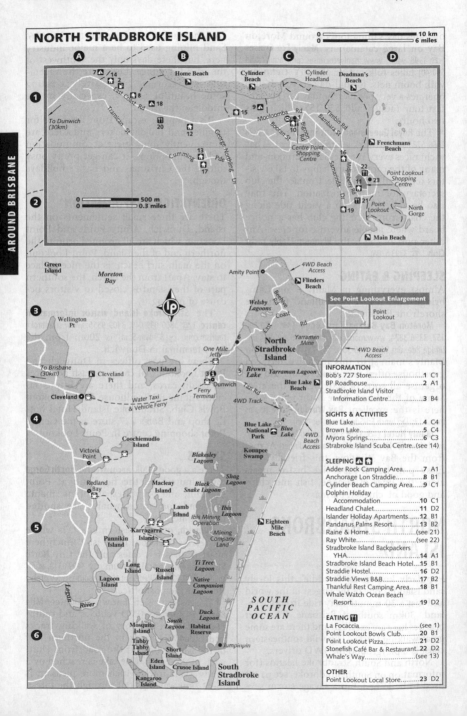

NORTH STRADBROKE ISLAND

AROUND BRISBANE

starting from near the turn-off to the 4WD track. The freshwater lake is a beautiful spot for a swim, if you don't mind the spooky unseen depths. There's also good swimming at **Brown Lake**, about 3km along Tazi Rd from Dunwich.

If you want to hike the 20km across the island from Dunwich to Point Lookout, a number of dirt track loops break the monotony of the bitumen road. A pleasant diversion is a visit to the **Myora Springs**, which are surrounded by lush vegetation and walking tracks, near the coast about 4km north of Dunwich.

Every second Sunday the **Point Lookout Flea & Craft Market** (Point Lookout Hall; 🕒 8am-noon) sets up camp opposite the Point Lookout Bowls Club (p123). Locally made arts and crafts of the usual sort are on sale, but mostly the market is a pleasant way to soak up a bit of Straddie culture.

ACTIVITIES

Straddie's most obvious lure is a string of beautiful **beaches**. At Point Lookout, there's a series of points and bays along the headland, and endless stretches of white sand. Cylinder Beach and Amity Point generally provide calm swimming opportunities, while Main Beach churns some good swells and breaks for **surfing**. There are also unpatrolled and exposed breaks all along Eighteen Mile Beach. The Stradbroke Island Backpackers YHA (right) has surfboards. You can also hire surfboards and bodyboards from various places at Point Lookout; kayak hire is around $20/50 per hour/day, surfboards $15/40 and bodyboards $10/30.

Straddie Adventures (🕿 3409 8414; Point Lookout) offers sea-kayaking trips including snorkelling stops ($35) around Straddie, and sandboarding ($25), which is like snowboarding, except on sand.

Stradbroke Island Scuba Centre (🕿 3409 8888; www.stradbrokeislandscuba.com.au; 1 East Coast Rd), based at Stradbroke Island Backpackers YHA (right), offers snorkelling for $60 inclusive of a two-hour boat trip and all the gear. Open-water courses cost $350, while a trip with two dives for certified divers goes for $170. The centre will also hire gear ($55) if you already know what you're doing. Some of the diving sites are fairly spectacular, with sightings of grey nurse sharks and other marine life common.

The island is also famous for its **fishing**, and the annual Straddie Classic, held in August, is one of Australia's richest and best-known fishing competitions. **Dunwich Sports & Hobbies** (🕿 3409 9252; Bingle Rd; 🕒 7.30am-5pm Mon-Fri, 7.30am-4pm Sat, 7.30am-3pm Sun) hires out fishing gear. See below for fishing tours.

With a 4WD you can drive all the way down the eastern beach to Jumpinpin, the channel that separates North and South Stradbroke, a legendary fishing spot. Access is via George Nothling Dr or Tazi Rd. Permits cost $10.30 for 48 hours, $16 for a week or $21 for a month and are available from the Dunwich visitor information centre, the BP Roadhouse, and Bob's 727 store in Point Lookout. You can also call **Redlands Tourism** (🕿 3821 0057) to purchase one.

TOURS

A number of tour companies offer good 4WD tours of the island. Generally they take in a strip of the eastern beach and visit several freshwater lakes. All tour operators will collect you from either the ferry at Dunwich or your accommodation.

Awesome Wicked Wild (🕿 3409 8045) Offers tours of Amity Point and the lakes in 20ft glass-bottomed canoes (half-/full-day tours $35/50).

Coastal Island Safaris (🕿 5547 4120; www.coastal islandsafaris.com; adult/child $175/125) Offers full-day tours, picking up in either Brisbane or on Straddie. Prices include morning tea, a BBQ lunch, fishing and swimming.

North Stradbroke Island 4WD Tours & Camping Holidays (🕿 3409 8051; straddie@ecn.net.au) Operates tours by negotiation, based on numbers and the time of year. Generally, half-day tours cost $30/15 per adult/child. This outfit also operates half-day fishing tours for the same price.

Point Lookout Fishing Charters (🕿 5538 4300) Organises six-hour fishing trips that cost $130 per person.

Straddie Kingfisher Tours (🕿 3409 9502; www .straddiekingfishertours.com.au; adult/child $70/40) Operates ecotours that last for six hours.

SLEEPING

Almost all of the island's accommodation is in Point Lookout, strung out along 3km of coastline.

Budget

Stradbroke Island Backpackers YHA (🕿 3409 8888; www.stradbrokeislandscuba.com.au; 1 East Coast Rd; dm $22, tw & d $50) This large beachside hostel is clean and well kept, and has excellent facilities, including a dive school right on the doorstep.

OODGEROO NOONUCCAL

North Stradbroke Island's most famous daughter was the poet and Aboriginal activist Oodgeroo Noonuccal. Born Kath Walker in 1920, she belonged to the Noonuccal tribe, which has inhabited the Moreton Bay area for thousands of years.

Oodgeroo attended school on North Stradbroke Island until the age of 13, when she left to become a domestic servant. At the time it was apparent to her that even with an education, Aboriginal people had little hope of working in better jobs.

In 1942 her path shifted again when she volunteered for service in the Australian Women's Army Service. However it was her role as the Queensland State Secretary of the Council for the Advancement of Aboriginal and Torres Strait Islanders (CAATSI) during the 1960s that began an era when her two passions would flourish.

During her 10-year tenure, Oodgeroo travelled throughout Australia and across the globe, campaigning for equality for Indigenous Australians. It was her mission to expose their plight and promote their cultural survival. Her efforts played no small role in the 1967 legislation that gave Indigenous Australians the right to vote for the first time.

This decade also gave birth to Oodgeroo's other great passion and talent, poetry. In 1964 she became the first Aboriginal woman to be published (under the name of Kath Walker), with her collection of verse *We Are Going*. The publication sold out in three days, and during the 1970s and '80s her subsequent work received international acclaim and was acknowledged through several prestigious awards, including the Fellowship of Australia Writers' Award, and several honorary doctorates.

Perhaps the most recognised of her awards was the Member of the Order of the British Empire (MBE) for services to the community, which she received as Kath Walker in 1970. When Oodgeroo accepted her nomination for the award, it was because she felt the honour would increase awareness of Aboriginal culture. Seventeen years later, she felt this vision had not transpired and famously returned her MBE to protest the 1988 Australian bicentenary celebrations.

Oodgeroo spent the later years of her life back on North Stradbroke Island, teaching more than 30,000 children of all races about Aboriginal culture. Her death in 1993 was mourned by people of all skin colour. Throughout her life she used her poetry to voice her desire for greater understanding between white and black Australians. Among her most celebrated collections, which also included short stories, plays, speeches and children's books, are *Dawn at Hand* and *My People*.

Guests can make use of surfboards and bodyboards and rent bikes for $10/15 per half-/full-day. The hostel runs a pick-up bus from opposite the transit centre in Brisbane, but you need to book ahead.

Headland Chalet (☎ 3409 8252; 213 Midjimberry Rd, Point Lookout; d & tw cabins per person Sun-Thu $25, Fri & Sat $30; ⚑) An excellent budget option is this cluster of cabins on the hillside overlooking Main Beach, near the roundabout. The cabins are attractive inside and have good views, and there's a pool, a TV room and a small kitchen.

Straddie Hostel (☎ 3409 8679; straddiehostel@ hotmail.com; 76 Mooloomba Rd; dm/d $20/45) This relaxed and friendly hostel is about halfway between Main and Cylinder Beaches, and has surfboards for hire.

Stradbroke Island Beach Hotel (☎ 3409 8188; straddie@itxpress.com.au; East Coast Rd; s/d Sun-Thu $55/80,

s & d Fri & Sat $100; ⚑) Straddie's only pub sits on a headland above Cylinder Beach and offers comfortable, plain, motel-style rooms.

There are six camping grounds on the island operated by **Stradbroke Camping** (☎ 1300 551 253; unpowered/powered sites per adult $9/12, per child $5.30/4.20, foreshore camping adult/child $5.30/3.20), but the most attractive are the places grouped around Point Lookout. The Adder Rock Camping Area and Thankful Rest Camping Area both overlook lovely Home Beach, while the Cylinder Beach Camping Area sits right on Cylinder Beach, one of the most popular beaches on the island. Sites should be booked well in advance.

Midrange & Top End

There are dozens of holiday apartments and private houses for rent on Straddie. These places can be good value for groups, especially outside the holiday season. Numerous real estate agents, including **Ray White** (☎ 3409 8255; Mintee St), **Dolphin Holiday Accommodation** (☎ 3409 8455; 1 Endeavour St) and **Raine & Horne** (☎ 3409 8213; 4 Kennedy Dr), manage the rentals, which vary from $170 to $500 per night, dropping significantly for multiday stays.

Prices for overnight stays at hotels and resorts on Straddie tend to be quite expensive, but drop by as much as 40% for stays of five or more nights.

Whale Watch Ocean Beach Resort (☎ 1800 450 004, 3409 8555; www.whalewatchresort.com.au; Samarinda Dr; apt per 2/5 nights from $326/720; ☒ ▢ ▣) These sublime and secluded apartments will make you feel like a million bucks. Cavernous interiors are filled with this year's mod cons, polished and pretty bathrooms, stylish furniture and large decks. Outside, classy timber dining furniture facilitates lunch with private views.

Straddie Views B&B (☎ 3409 8875; www.north stradbrokeisland.com/straddiebb; 26 Cumming Pde; r per weeknight/weekend night $100/120) The purpose-built rooms at this friendly B&B are spacious and classy. The hosts make a real effort to provide little comforts and each room comes with a bar fridge, tea and coffee facilities and a spot of port. Brekkie is served with views on the upstairs deck.

Pandanus Palms Resort (☎ 3409 8106; fax 3409 8339; 21 Cumming Pde; apt $200-250; ▣) Perched high above the beach, with a thick tumble of vegetation beneath, this resort has extremely comfortable self-contained units, a tennis court and a pool. The best units are the (pricier) two-bedroom ones with private courtyards, BBQs and outdoor dining settings.

Anchorage on Straddie (☎ 3409 8266; www.north stradbrokeisland.com/anchorage; East Coast Rd; apt $190-$220, per 5 nights $390-460; ▣) This complex looks a little like a brown brick monolith from the outside, and although the rooms have a touch of the hotel lobby bar about them, they're spotless and cool inside. All are self-contained and come with balconies shaded by a canopy of tropical forest.

Islander Holiday Apartments (☎ 3409 8388; islander@itxpress.com.au; East Coast Rd; apt per 2/5 nights from $170/400; ▣) Resembling a Mediterranean villa on steroids, this resort has a range of rooms to suit most folk. The best value rooms are one- and two-bedroom

apartments, which are spacious and slightly more up-to-date than the studios.

EATING

There are a couple of general stores selling groceries at Point Lookout, and most also offer Eftpos facilities, but it will save you quite a bit of dosh to bring your own supplies if you're self-catering. There are plenty of dining choices (the ones here are all in Point Lookout), but few restaurants on the island are open after 8pm.

Whale's Way (☎ 3409 8106; mains $20-30; ☙ dinner Tue-Sat) If you're looking for a special feast, this is the spot to head. This restaurant raises the bar on Straddie, serving delicate concoctions such as Moreton Bay bugs and ocean king prawns layered between filo pastry with a light curry sauce. The elevated views are just as special.

Stonefish Cafe Bar & Restaurant (☎ 3409 8549; cnr Mooloomba Rd & Mintee St; ☙ breakfast & lunch) No boring bacon and eggs to be had at this funky spot – you'll be filling up on vanilla-bean French toast or an Israeli breakfast with coriander toast instead. The eclectic menu represents Middle Eastern, Thai and Aussie flavours, and most of the seating is outdoors, and catches the sea breeze.

La Focaccia (☎ 3409 8778; Meegera Pl; mains $15-22; ☙ dinner) This casual pizzeria cooks up fresh pasta and excellent pizza. There's also a list of more traditional Italian mains such as *saltimbocca* (braised veal rolled in ham and cheese and seasoned with sage) or scaloppine marsala.

Point Lookout Pizza (☎ 3409 8179; Kennedy Dr; pizzas $12-22; ☙ dinner) Don't be fooled by the takeaway façade, the ladies here cook up a mean pizza and they don't hold back on the toppings. The usual suspects are up for grabs or you can delve into a garlic prawn, spicy chicken or smoked salmon pizza.

Point Lookout Bowls Club (☎ 3409 8182; East Coast Rd; mains $7-18; ☙ dinner) The bistro at the bowls club isn't as exciting as the competition outside, but you can fuel up on a roast, steak or chicken parma fairly cheaply.

GETTING THERE & AWAY

The gateway to North Stradbroke Island is the seaside suburb of Cleveland. Regular **Citytrain** (☎ 13 12 30; www.transinfo.qld.gov.au) services run from Central or Roma St to Cleveland station ($4, one hour) and buses to the ferry terminals meet the trains at Cleveland station ($1, 10 minutes).

Several ferry companies head across to Straddie. **Stradbroke Ferries** (☎ 3286 2666) runs a water taxi to Dunwich almost every hour from about 6am to 6pm ($13 return, 30 minutes). It also has a slightly less frequent vehicle ferry (per vehicle including passengers return $95, 45 minutes) from 5.30am to 6.30pm (later at weekends).

The **Stradbroke Flyer** (☎ 3821 3821; www.flyer .com.au) also runs an almost-hourly catamaran service from Cleveland to One Mile Jetty ($13 return, 45 minutes), 1.5km north of central Dunwich.

GETTING AROUND

Local buses (☎ 3409 7151) meet the ferries at Dunwich and One Mile Jetty and run across to Point Lookout ($10.50 return). The last bus to Dunwich leaves Point Lookout at about 6pm. There's also the **Stradbroke Cab Service** (☎ 0408-193 685), which charges $30 from Dunwich to Point Lookout.

MORETON ISLAND

North of Stradbroke, Moreton Island comes a close second to Fraser Island for sand driving and wilderness, and sees far fewer visitors. Apart from a few rocky headlands, it's all sand, with Mt Tempest, the highest coastal sandhill in the world, towering to 280m. The island's birdlife is prolific, and at its northern tip is a lighthouse, built in 1857. Sand-mining leases on the island have been cancelled and 90% of the island is now a national park. Off the western coast are the Tangalooma Wrecks, which provide good snorkelling and diving.

ORIENTATION & INFORMATION

Moreton Island has no paved roads, but 4WD vehicles can travel along the beaches and a few cross-island tracks – seek local advice about tides and creek crossings before venturing out. You can get Queensland Parks & Wildlife Service (QPWS) maps from the vehicle-ferry offices or the **rangers** (☎ 3408 2710) at Tangalooma. Vehicle permits for the island cost $31 and are available through the ferry operators or from the Naturally Queensland office in Brisbane (p79). Note that ferry bookings are *man-*

datory if you want to take a vehicle across; see opposite for operators.

SIGHTS & ACTIVITIES

Tangalooma, halfway down the western side of the island, is a popular tourist resort sited at an old whaling station. The main attraction is the **wild-dolphin feeding** that takes place each evening around sundown. Usually about eight or nine dolphins swim in from the ocean and take fish from the hands of volunteer feeders. You have to be a guest of the resort to participate, but on-lookers are welcome.

The only other settlements, all on the western coast, are **Bulwer**, near the northwestern tip, **Cowan Cowan**, between Bulwer and Tangalooma, and **Kooringal**, near the southern tip.

Without your own vehicle, walking is the only way to get around the island, and you'll need several days to explore it. Fortunately there are loads of good **walking trails** and decommissioned 4WD roads. It's worth making the strenuous trek to the summit of Mt Tempest, 3km inland from Eagers Creek.

About 3km south and inland from Tangalooma is an area of bare sand known as the **Desert**; the **Big Sandhills** and the **Little Sandhills** are towards the narrow southern end of the island. The biggest lakes and some **swamps** are in the northeast, and the western coast from Cowan Cowan past Bulwer is also swampy.

You can hire snorkelling gear from **Get Wet Sports** (☎ 3410 6927; Tangalooma Wild Dolphin Resort; per 4hr $12) and immerse yourself amid the colourful coral and marine life of the Tangalooma Wrecks. This company also offers tours (see below).

TOURS

Get Wet Sports (☎ 3410 6927; Tangalooma Wild Dolphin Resort) Offers 1½-hour snorkelling trips around the Tangalooma Wrecks (adult/child $26/18) and three-hour diving trips for qualified divers ($75). You can also do an open-water PADI dive course here for $400.

Gibren Expeditions (☎ 1300 559 355; www.gibren expeditions.com.au; 2-/3-day tours from $210/320) Offers tours of the island with heaps of activities thrown in, including snorkelling, sandboarding, sea kayaking and scuba diving. The guides are locals and really know the island.

Moreton Bay Escapes (☎ 1300 559 355, 3893 1671; www.moretonbayescapes.com.au; 1-day tours adult/child from $110/90, 2-day camping tours incl meals from $210) Its itineraries are similar to those of Gibren Expeditions.

Sunrover Expeditions (☎ 1800 353 717, 3880 0719; www.sunrover.com.au; adult/child $120/90) A friendly and reliable 4WD tour operator with good day tours, which include lunch. Tours depart the Roma St Transit Centre on Friday, Sunday and Monday. It also operates two-day camping tours (adult/child $195/150) and three-day national-park safaris (camping $300/250, in cabins $400/350). Both of these options include meals.

SLEEPING & EATING

There are a few holiday flats and houses for rent at Kooringal, Cowan Cowan and Bulwer.

Bulwer Cabins (☎ 3203 6399; www.moreton-island.com/accommodation.html; cabins from $90) These accommodating self-contained units, 200m from the beach at Bulwer, sleep up to six.

Tangalooma Wild Dolphin Resort (☎ 1300 652 250, 3410 6000; www.tangalooma.com; 1-night packages $230-330; 🅿 🐾 🅳) This modern resort is the most desirable locale. It has plush rooms, nice beaches and tame dolphins. Rates include transfers, overnight accommodation and dolphin feeding.

There are nine (including four on the beach) national park **camping grounds** (sites per person/family $4/16), all with water, toilets and cold showers. For information and camping permits, contact the Naturally Queensland office in Brisbane (p79) or the **ranger** (☎ 3408 2710). Camping permits are also available from the ferry operators (see below).

The shops at Kooringal and Bulwer are expensive, so bring what you can from the mainland.

GETTING THERE & AROUND

A number of ferries operate from the mainland. The **Tangalooma Flyer** (☎ 3268 6333; www.tangalooma.com/tangalooma/transport; per adult/child return $60/30; 🅿 6am, 10am & 5pm Mon, 8am, 10am & 5pm Tue-Fri, 8am, 10am, noon & 5pm Sat & Sun), a fast catamaran operated by the resort, sails to the resort on Moreton Island daily from a dock at Holt St, off Kingsford Smith Dr (in Eagle Farm). A bus ($5) to the flyer departs the Roma St Transit Centre at 9am. You can use the bus for a day trip (it returns at 9am and 4pm daily as well as at 2pm on Saturday and Sunday) or for camping drop-offs. Bookings are necessary. The trip takes 1¼ hours.

The **Moreton Venture** (☎ 3895 1000; www.moretonventure.com.au; adult/child/vehicle & 2 passengers return $30/20/135; 🅿 8.30am daily, 6.30pm Fri & 2.30pm Sun) is a vehicle ferry that runs from Howard-Smith

Dr, Lyton, at the Port of Brisbane, to Tangalooma. It leaves the island at 3.30pm daily, as well as at 8pm on Friday and 4.30pm on Sunday.

The **Combie Trader** (☎ 3203 6399; www.moreton-island.com/how.html; adult/child/vehicle & 4 passengers return $35/20/150; 🅿 8am & 1pm Mon, 8am Wed & Thu, 8am, 1pm & 7pm Fri, 6am & 11am Sat, 8am, 1pm & 5.30pm Sun) sails between Scarborough and Bulwer and takes about 2½ hours to make the crossing. The Saturday morning crossings are slightly cheaper for pedestrians.

You can hire 4WDs in Bulwer from **Moreton Island 4WD hire** (☎ 3410 1338; www.moretonisland.com.au/4wd_page.htm), which will save you the cost of taking a vehicle over on the ferry. Rates for Suzuki Jimnys start at $145 per day. Toyota Landcruisers are also available for around $175 per day.

ST HELENA ISLAND

Now a national park, little St Helena Island, only 6km from the mouth of the Brisbane River, was a high-security prison until 1932. You can now see the remains of several **prison buildings**, plus the parts of Brisbane's first **tramway**, built in 1884. The old trams were pulled by horses, but these days a tractor pulls the coaches as part of the island tour.

AB Sea Cruises (☎ 3893 1240; www.sthelenaisland.com.au; 🅿 9.15am Mon-Fri, 10am Sat & Sun) runs day trips to St Helena from Manly Harbour, including a tramway ride and a 'dramatised tour' of the prison (adult/child $70/40), complete with floggings if you so desire. Its ghost tour ($80/45) leaves at 7pm.

You can reach Manly from central Brisbane in about 35 minutes by train on the Cleveland line.

COOCHIEMUDLO ISLAND

Tiny Coochiemudlo (or Coochie) Island is a 10-minute ferry ride from Victoria Point on the southern side of Moreton Bay. It's a popular outing from the mainland, with good **beaches**, though it's more built up than most other Moreton Bay islands you can visit.

Coochie Island Resort (☎ 3207 7521; Victoria Pde; apt 2 nights $150-170) is a relaxed family resort with self-contained units and a licensed **restaurant** (mains $10-20; 🅿 lunch & dinner Thu-Sun), which specialises in Mongolian steamboats. Accommodation rates increase significantly in peak seasons.

The **Coochiemudlo Ferry Service** (☎ 3820 7227; adult/child return $5.60/2.80) departs from Victoria Point and travels to Coochiemudlo Island around 40 times daily. Once on the island, the **Coochie Bus Service** (☎ 3820 6993; tickets $6; ☺ hourly from 6.30am-5pm) picks up from the ferry point and spends 45 minutes touring the island with interesting commentary thrown in.

BRIBIE ISLAND

This slender sand island at the northern end of Moreton Bay is joined to the mainland by a bridge at its southern tip, where you'll find the small settlements of Woorim, Bellara and Bongaree. The northwestern coast of the island is protected as **Bribie Island National Park**, and has some beautifully remote **camping areas** (4WD access only, per person/family $4/16). There's a **ranger station** (☎ 3408 8451) at White Patch on the southeastern fringes of the park.

Woorim, on the eastern coast, is an old-fashioned holiday township with good,

sandy ocean beaches and a range of accommodation. As you cross the bridge onto the island, you'll see the **Bribie Island information centre** (☎ 3408 9026; www.bribie.com.au; Benabrow Ave; ☺ 9am-4pm Mon-Fri, 9am-3pm Sat & 9.30am-1pm Sun), in the middle of the median strip.

There are a few places to stay on the island. **Bribie Island Caravan Park** (☎ 1800 649 831; 3408 1134; www.bribieislandcaravanpark.com.au; Jacana Ave; powered sites $20-30, on-site vans from $35, cabins from $55; ☒) is a nice, shady park with spotless facilities. Prices are for two people.

Sylvan Beach Resort (☎ 3408 8300; www.sylvan beachresort.com.au; 19-23 Sylvan Beach Esplanade; apt $90-150; ☒ ☒) is a good midrange resort with comfortable two- and three-bedroom self-contained units. There are also BBQs on site.

Bribie Island SLSC (☎ 3408 4420; Rickman Pde; mains $8-15), at the southern end of the beach, overlooks the ocean and serves up Aussie tucker.

There are frequent Citytrain services between Brisbane and Caboolture. A Trainlink bus runs between the station and Bribie Island. The total fare for both trips is $6/3 per adult/child and the journey takes close to two hours.

Gold Coast

GOLD COAST

HIGHLIGHTS

- Flying on roller coasters, losing yourself in Hollywood and getting wet and wild at the Gold Coast **theme parks** (p135)
- Indulging in extravagance at **Palazzo Versace** (p132) and dining at Main Beach's seaside **eateries** (p132)
- Overdosing on glitz and good times and partying hard in heady **Surfers Paradise** (p133)
- Meeting the furred and feathered locals at the **wildlife sanctuaries** (p142) near Burleigh Heads
- Bunking down for a while to master the killer breaks at Coolangatta's **Kirra Beach** (p144)
- Revelling in the tumbling waterfalls, spectacular views and rich green palette of **Springbrook plateau** (p147)
- Ambling through the **hinterland** (p149) on horseback, and snacking on tea and damper
- Bushwalking through deep gorges and towering rainforests in **Lamington National Park** (p149)

Theme Parks ★

★ Hinterland

★ Main Beach

★ Surfers Paradise

★ Burleigh Heads

Lamington National Park ★

Springbook Plateau ★

Kirra Beach ★

■ www.hellogoldcoast.com.au

■ www.goldcoastguide.com

GOLD COAST

Welcome to Australia's playground, folks – you're in for a ride. Stretching for 35km between Southport and the New South Wales border, the Gold Coast is a tumbling mass of intensive tourist development oozing from its theme parks, airport-sized shopping malls and clusters of ultra-expensive high-rise apartments. You can definitely leave your culture hats in the suitcase.

This grand scale of commercialism doesn't appeal to everyone, but the Gold Coast receives more than two million visitors every year. Most are drawn by the surf, sun and fun, but there is also a spectacular hinterland less than 30km from the beach. Although little-visited, this densely forested region contains two of Queensland's best national parks: Lamington and Springbrook. The Gold Coast also has some excellent surfing breaks, and surfers young and old go giddy over the waves at Burleigh Heads, Kirra and Duranbah.

The undisputed capital is Surfers Paradise, which, depending on your viewpoint, is either the heart of the action or the place you'll most want to avoid. Here the bonanza of eateries, drinking holes and artificial attractions peak. The dizzying fun sucks you into a relentless spin and spits you back out exhausted. For respite, however, you won't need to head far. Mermaid Beach, Broadbeach and Southport are part of the same urban sprawl as Surfers Paradise, but the hype diminishes drastically outside the epicentre.

At the southern end of the Gold Coast, Coolangatta is the quietest (and cheapest) of the resorts. More unexpected peace can be found at the northern end of the strip on South Stradbroke Island, the sandbar that extends north from the Broadwater inlet at the mouth of the Nerang and Coomera rivers.

Dangers & Annoyances
Car theft is a major problem all the way along the Gold Coast; park in well-lit areas and don't leave valuables in your vehicle.

The Gold Coast turns into party central for thousands of school leavers between mid-November and mid-December during an event known locally as schoolie's week. Although it's generally a lot of fun for those celebrating, it can be hell for everyone else.

Getting There & Away
AIR
The Gold Coast airport is based at Coolangatta, about 25km south of Surfers Paradise. **Qantas** (Map p134; ☎ 13 13 13; www.qantas.com; 3047 Gold Coast Hwy, Surfers Paradise) flies direct to Coolangatta airport from Sydney ($110, 1½ hours) and Melbourne ($165, two hours). **Jetstar** (☎ 13 15 38; www.jetstar.com.au) also operates flights between Coolangatta and Sydney ($80) or Melbourne ($120).

See p452 for information about international flights into Coolangatta.

BUS
Long-distance buses stop at the bus transit centres in Southport, Surfers Paradise and Coolangatta. Most companies will let you stop on the Gold Coast if you have a through ticket.

Greyhound Australia (☎ 13 14 99; www.greyhound.com.au) has frequent services between Surfers Paradise and Brisbane ($15, 1½ hours), Byron Bay in northern New South Wales ($25, two hours) and Sydney ($100, 15 hours). **Premier Motor Service** (☎ 13 34 10; www.premierms.com.au) serves the same routes for slightly less. **Kirklands** (☎ 1300 367 077) travels to Surfers Paradise from Byron Bay ($27) and Brisbane ($15), stopping at most Gold Coast settlements along the way.

Coachtrans (☎ 13 12 30, 3238 4700; www.coachtrans.com.au) operates the Airporter direct services from Brisbane airport to the Gold Coast ($35). Services meet every flight and will drop you anywhere on the Gold Coast. Coachtrans also has straightforward services between Brisbane and Surfers ($23, 1½ hours) or Coolangatta/Tweed Heads ($23, two hours) or to the theme parks.

Aerobus (☎ 3238 4700; www.aerobus.net; one-way tickets $25) also operates transfers from Brisbane airport to Gold Coast accommodation and private residences.

TRAIN

Citytrain services link Brisbane to Helensvale station ($7.60, one hour), Nerang station ($8.40, 1¼ hours) and Robina station ($10, 1¼ hours) roughly every half hour.

Surfside Buslines (☎ 13 12 30, 5571 6555; www.trans info.qld.gov.au) runs regular shuttles from the train stations down to Surfers ($3 to $4) and beyond, and to the theme parks.

Getting Around
TO/FROM THE AIRPORT

Coachtrans (☎ 13 12 30, 3238 4700; www.coachtrans .com.au) operates a shuttle between Tweed Heads and Brisbane, with 18 stops along the way, including Dreamworld, Movie World and Wet 'n' Wild. **Gold Coast Tourist Shuttle** (☎ 1300 655 655, 5574 5111; www.gc shuttle.com.au; adult/child/family $15/8/38) meets every flight into Coolangatta Airport and operates door-to-door transfers to most Gold Coast accommodation. It also offers a

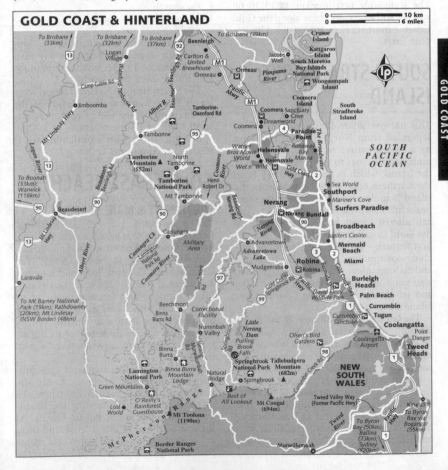

GOLD COAST & HINTERLAND

Freedom Pass, which includes return transfers to your accommodation plus unlimited theme-park transfers and unlimited Surfside Buslines travel from $50/23/115 per adult/child/family for three days.

BUS

Surfside Buslines (☎ 13 12 30, 5571 6555; www .transinfo.qld.gov.au) runs a frequent service up and down the Gold Coast Hwy from Tweed Heads, with services stopping at Dreamworld, Sanctuary Cove and Paradise Point. You can buy individual fares or get an Ezy Pass for a day's unlimited travel ($10), or a weekly pass ($43).

TAXI

The state-wide taxi number ☎ 13 10 08 will get you a taxi anywhere along the Gold Coast – most services are provided by Regent Taxis.

SOUTH STRADBROKE ISLAND

This narrow, 20km-long sand island was separated from North Stradbroke Island by a savage storm in 1896. These days, most people cross to the Southport end of the island, which is just 200m away from the northern end of The Spit. Most of the island is undeveloped, and there are some peaceful camping grounds where you can almost forget how close you are to the Gold Coast. In fact, this is the island's best feature – the main activities here include swimming, surfing, bushwalking and fishing. More adventurous types can also get stuck into canoeing, bike riding and jet-skiing through the Couran Cove Island Resort.

The **Couran Cove Island Resort** (☎ 1800 268 726, 5597 9000; www.couran.com; d from $310; 🖭 🖭) is an exclusive luxury resort with four restaurants, a day spa and a private marina. All rooms have spectacular water views.

For something less extravagant, you can head to the **Couran Point Island Beach Resort** (☎ 5501 3533; www.couranpoint.com.au; d from $130; 🖭), which has colourful and comfortable hotel rooms, and slightly larger units with kitchenettes. All rates include a continental breakfast, but ferry transfers are extra

(adult/child/family return $20/10/50). Nonguests can access the resort as day visitors for $60/24/155 per adult/child/family, which includes a BBQ lunch.

The South Stradbroke Island Resort ferry leaves from Runaway Bay Marina at the northern end of the Gold Coast every day at 10.30am and 4pm, returning at 2.30pm and 5pm. The return adult/child fare is $25/12.50 (20 minutes each way).

GOLD COAST BEACHES

SOUTHPORT & MAIN BEACH

☎ 07 / pop 24,830

Sitting atop Surfers Paradise, and sheltered by the sandbar known as the Spit, Southport is the gateway to the Gold Coast's fun and mayhem. This said, Southport is largely a residential area and the neat grids of suburban housing and low-rise bustle of its heart hums with locals going about their business rather than with tourists. There's not a great deal to do here, but its big attraction is a peaceful night's rest and a great foreshore.

Immediately to the southeast of Southport is Main Beach, where the tourist developments begin in earnest. From here, the Spit runs 3km north, dividing the Broadwater from the South Pacific Ocean. At the southern end of this strip of land there are several malls and the Sea World theme park (see the boxed text on p135). Near the

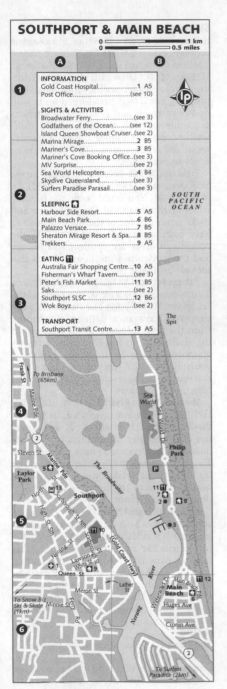

SOUTHPORT & MAIN BEACH

0 ————— 1 km
0 ————— 0.5 miles

INFORMATION
Gold Coast Hospital.....................1 A5
Post Office...............................(see 10)

SIGHTS & ACTIVITIES
Broadwater Ferry.......................(see 3)
Godfathers of the Ocean...........(see 12)
Island Queen Showboat Cruiser..(see 2)
Marina Mirage...........................2 B5
Mariner's Cove...........................3 B5
Mariner's Cove Booking Office...(see 3)
MV Surprise...............................(see 2)
Sea World Helicopters................4 B4
Skydive Queensland..................(see 3)
Surfers Paradise Parasail............(see 3)

SLEEPING 🏠
Harbour Side Resort....................5 A5
Main Beach Park.........................6 B6
Palazzo Versace..........................7 B5
Sheraton Mirage Resort & Spa....8 B5
Trekkers....................................9 A5

EATING 🍴
Australia Fair Shopping Centre...10 A5
Fisherman's Wharf Tavern.........(see 3)
Peter's Fish Market.....................11 B5
Saks..(see 2)
Southport SLSC..........................12 B6
Wok Boyz..................................(see 2)

TRANSPORT
Southport Transit Centre............13 A5

SOUTH PACIFIC OCEAN

The Spit

To Brisbane (65km)

Sea World

Frank St

Marine Pde

Steven St

Marine Pde

Sea World Dr

Philip Park

Laylor Park

Southport

North St

Scarborough St Nth

The Broadwater

High St Sth

Nerang St

Lawson St

Whitte St

Queen St

Lawson St

Meron St

Lather St

To Snow Biz Ski & Skate (1km)

Minnie St

Ferry Rd

Nerang River

Waterways Dr

Main Beach

Main Beach Pde

Huges Ave

Cronin Ave

To Surfers Paradise (2km)

Marina Mirage, an upmarket shopping and dining complex, is Mariner's Cove and the marina, which is the departure point for cruises and other activities. On the ocean side, the beaches and surf are excellent, under-used and backed by a peaceful area of parkland.

Information

There are numerous ATMs dotted along Scarborough St.

Gold Coast Hospital (☎ 5571 8211; 108 Nerang St, Southport)

Post Office (☎ 13 13 18; Shop 301, Australia Fair Shopping Centre, Southport; 🕑 9am-5pm Mon-Wed & Fri, to 6pm Thu, 9am-2pm Sat, 10.30am-2pm Sun)

Sights & Activities

You can indulge in just about any water activity from numerous operators based at Mariner's Cove. The easiest way to sift through them is to book at the **Mariner's Cove Booking Office** (☎ 5591 8883; Mariner's Cove). The following are recommended.

SURFING & KAYAKING

Australian Kayaking Adventures (☎ 0412-940 135; www.australiankayakingadventures.com.au; 3-hr/half-day tours to South Stradbroke Island $45/65) Guided tours to South Stradbroke Island are recommended and they include breakfast.

Godfathers of the Ocean (☎ 5593 5661; www.god fathersoftheocean.com; Southport Surf Life Saving Club; 2-hr lessons from $35) This respected surf school promises to have you standing after one lesson.

Gold Coast Kayaking (☎ 0419-733 202; 3-hr kayak tours adult/family $35/95) Guided tours including breakfast or afternoon tea and snorkelling.

CRUISING & FISHING

Gone Fishing (☎ 5510 9611; www.gonefishing.net.au; 4-/5-hr tours $55/85, full-day tours $135) Game fishing for beginners all the way up to experts.

Tall Ship (☎ 5532 2444; www.tallship.com.au; Mariner's Cove Marina; half-day cruises adult/child/senior/family from $90/60/80/240) Cruises to South Stradbroke Island on yachts dressed up to look like tall ships.

WATER SPORTS

Queensland Scuba Diving Company (☎ 5526 7722; Mariner's Cove Marina; dives from $100) Single dives including fish feeding.

Scream Machine (☎ 5591 5100; Mariner's Cove Marina; tours $60; 🕑 10am, noon, 2pm) Speedboat tours at 50 knots.

GOLD COAST

Seabreeze Sports (☎ 5527 1099; jet-ski & parasailing packages $80, Aquanaut $100) These guys do everything, but best of all is the underwater scuba cruise 'Aquanaut'.

Shane's Watersports World (☎ 5591 5225; shaneswatersports@retnet.net.au) Jet-ski hire from $75 per half-hour. Jet-ski and parasailing packages from $100.

Snorkelling Adventures (☎ 0405-427 174; snorkellingadventures@bigpond.com; 3-hr tours $35) Snorkelling and fish feeding off Wavebreak Island.

OTHER ACTIVITIES
Sea World Helicopters (☎ 5588 2224; Sea World Dr, Main Beach) offers flights starting from $50/40 per adult/child for five minutes up to $150/115 for 30-minute flights. The longer flights take in Burleigh Heads, Coolangatta and the Gold Coast hinterland. Just up the road, **Dreamworld Helicopters** (☎ 5588 1111; www.dreamworld .com.au; Pacific Hwy, Coomera) does the same.

Snow Biz Ski & Skate (☎ 5531 3035; 7 Nerang St, Southport) hires in-line skates with pads and all the gear from $12.50/20 for two hours/ overnight.

Tours

Various cruise operators depart the marina at Mariner's Cove and explore the surrounding canals. Operators change from season to season, but one popular, reliable one is **Island Queen Showboat Cruises** (☎ 5557 8800; www.islandqueen.com.au; Marina Mirage), which offers dinner and cabaret cruises (adult/ child from $55/35), day cruises to South Stradbroke Island (from $75/45), including morning tea, lunch and boom netting, and a 1½-hour morning-tea cruise (adult/ child/family $38/23/100 including theme park transfers) to Sanctuary Cove. Alternatively, **Wyndham Cruises** (☎ 5539 9299; www .wyndhamcruises.com.au; adult/child/family $40/20/95) operates two-hour cruises up to and around the Broadwater with morning or afternoon tea included.

Several companies cruise between Main Beach and Tiki Village Wharf in Surfers Paradise:

Broadwater Ferry (☎ 0412-179 582; tickets $14) Hop-on hop-off cruise between Mariner's Cove and Surfers Paradise.

MV Surprise (☎ 0418-768 801; www.mv-surprise .com; Marina Mirage; 2-hr cruises adult/child/senior/family $37/20/30/100) Heads north from Marina Mirage, touring the Broadwater before cruising south to Surfers Paradise. Includes morning or afternoon tea.

Sleeping

Harbour Side Resort (☎ 5591 6666; www.harbour sideresort.com.au; 132 Marine Pde, Southport; studio & 1-bedroom apt low/high season $80/100, 2-bedroom apt $120/140; 🅿 🌊) Disregard the overwhelming brick façade; within this sprawling property you'll find pastel-hued units with oodles of room and charm. The kitchens are equipped with microwaves and dishwashers and the complex also has a laundry room and tennis courts. High-season rates apply on weekends.

Trekkers (☎ 1800 100 004, 5591 5616; www.trekkers backpackers.com.au; 22 White St, Southport; dm $23, d & tw $60; 🖳 💻) You could bottle the friendly vibes of this beautiful Queenslander and make a mint. Some of the themed doubles have bathrooms and come with TV, the communal areas are spotless and homey and the garden is a mini oasis. Rates also include breakfast.

Palazzo Versace (☎ 1800 098 000, 5509 8000; www .palazzoversace.com; Sea World Dr, Main Beach; d $380-725, apt from $1200; 🅿 🌊) The Palazzo is quite simply extravagance defined. Everything from the pool furniture to the buttons on the staff uniforms has Donatella Versace's glamorous mark on it. If you can draw yourself from the sumptuous rooms, you can venture to the resort's equally indulgent restaurants and bars.

Sheraton Mirage Resort & Spa (☎ 1800 073 525, 5591 1488; www.sheraton.com/goldcoast; Sea World Dr, Main Beach; d from $320, ste $500-650; 🅿 🌊) It may not have designer furnishings, but the exquisitely classy rooms do have stereos, cable TV, views and all the five-star touches. The lagoon-style pool takes you right onto the beach and there are three restaurants and three bars to explore.

Main Beach Tourist Park (☎ 5581 7722; www.gctp .com.au/main; Main Beach Pde, Main Beach; unpowered/ powered sites from $26/27, cabins from $120; 🅿 🌊) Just across the road from the beach, this caravan park is a favourite with families, who fill it to bursting during busy periods. It's a tight fit between sites, but the facilities are good and the colourful cabins are accommodating. Rates are for two people.

Eating

The cheapest place to eat is the food court in the Australia Fair Shopping Centre. Counters here serve up pizza, noodles, roasts, kebabs and more. Small sandwich shops and cafés can be found along Scarborough St.

Saks (☎ 5591 2755; Marina Mirage, 74 Sea World Dr, Main Beach; mains $15-25; ☙ lunch daily, dinner Wed-Sun) This smart, salubrious bar and restaurant lures cultured palettes with a brief but sophisticated menu boasting delights such as roast duck and macadamia nut salad and spectacular gourmet wood-fired pizzas. Tall glass windows offer uninterrupted views of the marina.

Fisherman's Wharf Tavern (☎ 5571 0566; 60-70 Mariner's Cove, Main Beach; mains $14-25; ☙ lunch & dinner) The menu at this styled-up tavern is an impressive combo of fresh fish (prawn rolls with 'really hot chilli' or Atlantic salmon with coconut, chilli and lime butter) and multicultural infusions, including a mean jungle curry. There's an atmospheric deck and it's a social haunt as much as a restaurant.

Peter's Fish Market (☎ 5591 7747; Sea World Dr, Main Beach; meals $10; ☙ lunch & dinner) Park yourself at one of the wooden tables outside and dig into outstanding fresh fish and chips at this no-nonsense eatery. As the name suggests, it's also a fish market with fresh seafood in all shapes and sizes at reasonable prices.

Attached to the Fisherman's Wharf Tavern is **Fisho's** (mains around $12), where you can munch on barramundi and chips in less-fancy surrounds.

Also recommended:

Southport SLSC (☎ 5591 5083; MacArthur Pde; dishes $9-17; ☙ lunch & dinner) Great bistro serving pasta, roasts, sangers and burgers.

Wok Boyz (☎ 5591 6808; Marina Mirage, Main Beach; dishes $12; ☙ lunch & dinner) Towering, tasty bowls of noodles.

Getting There & Away

The Southport Transit Centre is on Scarborough St, between North and Railway Sts. Premier, Coachtrans, Kirklands and Greyhound buses all stop here. Surfside bus Nos 1 and 1A run to Surfers day and night from outside the Australia Fair Shopping Centre on Scarborough St.

SURFERS PARADISE

☎ 07 / pop 24,090

In 1965 local entrepreneur Bernie Elsey had the brainwave of employing meter maids in skimpy gold-lamé bikinis to feed the parking meters on the main strip, and Surfers

Paradise has never looked back. Imagine Daytona Beach or Miami shifted down under, and you'll have some idea of what to expect.

The popularity of Surfers these days rests not so much on the sand and surf (which is better down the coast) but on the shopping, nightlife and its proximity to attractions such as the theme parks.

For visitors it's probably the most partying place in Queensland and hostel staff do their best to ensure it goes off every night of the week. If you love party nights and lazy days, you're almost guaranteed to have a good time. The partying reaches its peak during the IndyCar races in October. If this isn't your thing, there's always the rest of the Gold Coast to choose from.

Orientation

The downtown part of Surfers consists of just two or three main streets. The main thoroughfare, Cavill Ave, runs down to the seafront, ending in a pedestrian mall. Orchid Ave, one block back from the Esplanade, is the nightclub and bar strip. The Gold Coast Hwy runs through Surfers one block back from Orchid Ave. It takes southbound traffic while Ferny Ave, the next road inland, takes northbound traffic.

Information
INTERNET ACCESS

Internet access costs $3 to $4 per hour.

Email Centre (☎ 5538 7500; Orchid Ave; ☙ 9am-11pm)

Mercari Imaging (☎ 5538 4937; 3189 Gold Coast Hwy; ☙ 9am-7.30pm)

Network Zone (☎ 5570 6166; RSL Centre, 9 Beach Rd; ☙ 7am-9pm)

MEDICAL SERVICES

National Medical Clinic (☎ 5592 3999; Centro Surfers Paradise, Cavill Ave Mall; ☙ 8am-5.30pm Mon, Tue & Fri, 8am-5pm Wed, 9am-5.30pm Thu, 9am-noon Sat)

Surfers Paradise Day & Night Surgery (☎ 5592 2299; 3221 Gold Coast Hwy; ☙ 7am-10pm) Pharmacy attached.

MONEY

American Express (Amex; ☎ 1300 139 060; Pacific Fair Shopping Centre, Hooker Blvd, Broadbeach)

Travelex (☎ 5531 7917; Cavill Ave Mall; ☙ 8.30am-9pm Mon-Fri, 9am-9pm Sat & Sun)

GOLD COAST

SURFERS PARADISE

INFORMATION
Australia Post..................................**1** B5
Backpacker Tour Desk................(see 56)
Email Centre.................................(see 45)
Gold Coast Tourism Bureau...........**2** A5
Mercari Imaging.............................**3** A4
National Medical Clinic..................**4** B5
Network Zone.................................**5** A5
Police...**6** B5
Surfers Paradise Day & Night Surgery..**7** A2
Travelex...**8** A5

SIGHTS & ACTIVITIES
Aqua Duck....................................**9** A5
Aquabus......................................(see 9)
Banzai Bungey.............................**10** A2
Flycoaster..................................(see 10)
Go Ride a Wave...........................**11** B5
Infinity..**12** A4
Ripley's Believe It or Not..............**13** B5
Sling Shot..................................(see 10)
Vomatron...................................(see 10)

SLEEPING
Chateau Beachside......................**14** A4
Cheers Backpackers.....................**15** A5
Cosmopolitan Apartments...........(see 17)
Courtyard Marriott.......................**16** A5
Gold Coast Accommodation
    Service..................................**17** A5

EATING
Arirang.......................................**30** A5
Bavarian Haus.............................**31** A5
Chateau Beachside....................(see 14)
Centro Surfers Paradise...............**32** A5
Charlies......................................**33** B5
Chevron Renaissance Shopping
    Centre...................................(see 12)
Costa Dora..................................**34** A5
Go Sushi...................................(see 32)
Grumpy's Wharf..........................**35** A3
La Porchetta...............................**36** A5
Marmalade Cafe.........................(see 12)
Melbas.......................................**37** A5
Tandoori Place............................**38** A3

DRINKING
Gilhooley's..................................**39** A5
Liquid...**40** A5
Melbas......................................(see 37)
O'Malleys...................................**41** B5
Surfers Paradise SLSC..................**42** A4
The Clock Hotel...........................**43** A4

ENTERTAINMENT
Ambassee...................................**44** A5
Cocktails & Dreams......................**45** A5
Howl at the Moon.......................(see 33)
MP's...**46** A4
Shooters...................................(see 45)
Troccadero.................................**47** B3

Gold Coast International Hotel........**18** A2
International Beach Resort............**19** A2
Olympus.....................................**20** A2
Pacific View Holiday Apartments...**21** A2
Quarterdeck Apartments..............**22** A2
Raffles Royale.............................**23** A2
Silver Sands Motel.......................**24** B4
Sleeping Inn Surfers.....................**25** A4
Surf 'n' Sun Backpackers..............**26** A2
Surfers International Apartments....**27** B3
Surfers Paradise Backpackers Resort.**28** B5
Trickett Gardens Holiday Inn.........**29** B3

TRANSPORT
All Age Car rentals.......................**48** B4
Avis..**49** A2
Budget..**50** A2
Bus Stop for Burleigh Heads..........**51** A5
Bus Stop for Southport.................**52** A3
Bus Stop for Southport.................**53** A5
Mopeds City...............................**54** A2
Qantas..**55** A3
Red Back Rentals.......................(see 56)
Red Rocket Rent-A-Car...............(see 45)
Transit Centre.............................**56** A5

SOUTH
PACIFIC
OCEAN

To The Spit; Marina Mirage;
Sea World (4km)
Ocean Ave
To Marriott Resort
(250m); Southport (4km); Brisbane (70km)
Staghorn Ave
Pine Ave
Palm Ave
Cypress Ave
View Ave
Ferny Ave
Thomas Dre
To Gold Coast
Arts Centre (1.4km)
Cavill Ave
Beach Rd   Hanlan St
Trickett St
Laycock St
Clifford St
Hamilton Ave
Gold Coast Hwy
Markwell Ave
Enderley Ave
Vista St
Thornton St
Aubrey St
Frederick St
Fern St
Old Burleigh Rd
Surf Rop
Wharf Rd
Paradise Island
Nerang River
To Nerang (18km)
Remembrance Dr
Watson Esp
Leonard St
Whelan St
Surfers Paradise Beach

See Enlargement

Elkhorn Ave
Esplanade
Orchid Ave
Cavill Ave
Beach Rd   Hanlan St
Ferny Ave
Gold Coast Hwy

0 —— 100 m
0 —— 0.1 mi

To Broadbeach
(3km); Pacific Fair
Shopping Centre (2km);
American Express (2km);
Mermaid Beach (4km);
Mermaid Beach Motel (4km);
Burleigh Heads (11km);
Coolangatta (25km)

- - - - IndyCar Circuit

0 —— 200 m
0 —— 0.1 miles

POST
Post Office (☎ 13 13 18; Shop 165, Centro Surfers Paradise, Cavill Ave Mall; ☼ 9am-5.30pm Mon-Fri, 9am-12.30pm Sat)

TOURIST INFORMATION
There are plenty of free glossy booklets available for visitors, including *Wot's On*,

Destination Surfers Paradise, Today To-night on the Gold Coast and *Point Out*. Some have street plans and a smattering of useful information, but their main purpose would seem to be to rake in advertising dollars.

Backpacker Tour Desk (☎ 1800 359 830, 5592 2911; Surfers Paradise Transit Centre, cnr Beach & Cambridge

Rds) If you're looking for help finding somewhere to stay, try the helpful backpackers' accommodation booking desk. **Gold Coast Tourism Bureau** (☎ 5538 4419; www .goldcoasttourism.com.au; Cavill Ave Mall; ☺ 8.30am-5.30pm Mon-Fri, 8.30am-5pm Sat, 9am-4pm Sun) Information booth with comprehensive information on the Gold Coast.

Sights

Surfers is all about fun and for the most part its attractions are in keeping with its theme-park environment. The emphasis is on entertainment and parting you with your cash. This said, the **Gold Coast Art Gallery** (☎ 5581 6567; www.gcac.com.au; Gold Coast Arts Centre, 135 Bundall Rd; ☺ 10am-5pm Mon-Fri, 11am-5pm Sat & Sun) features two galleries displaying excellent temporary exhibitions. The curatorship is insightful and inventive.

Infinity (☎ 5538 2988; www.infinitygc.com.au; Chevron Renaissance, cnr Gold Coast Hwy & Elkhorn Ave; adult/child/family $20/12/53; ☺ 10am-10pm) promises to 'ignite your imagination' by transporting you into the future. Essentially the future

is a walk-through maze cleverly disguised by an elaborate sound and light show. It's great for families and the squeals of wonder and delight from little tackers indicate it's a winner with the kids.

At **Ripley's Believe It or Not** (☎ 5592 0040; Raptis Plaza, Cavill Ave Mall; adult/child $13.50/8; ☺ 9am-11pm) you can feast your eyes on all manner of freaky sights, including the world's tallest and heaviest humans, 'genuine' shrunken heads, the skeleton of a mermaid and musical instruments that appear to play themselves. Many of the exhibits are in the form of reproductions or photos, however, and chances are you probably will believe it.

Activities
AIRBORNE ACTIVITIES

You can go hot-air ballooning with **Balloon Down Under** (☎ 5593 8400; www.balloondownunder .com; 1-hr flights adult/child $255/210) or **Balloon Aloft** (☎ 5578 2244; www.balloonaloft.net; 1-hr flights adult/child $255/185). Both offer early morning flights over the Gold Coast hinterland,

---

GOLD COAST THEME PARKS

If it weren't for the bush you could be forgiven for thinking you'd landed in Los Angeles. Just northwest of Surfers, four American-style theme parks summon you with thrilling rides and entertaining shows. Discount tickets are sold in most of the tourist offices on the Gold Coast; the 3 Park Super Pass (adult/child $160/100), available at Sea World, Movie World and Wet 'n' Wild, covers entry to all three parks.

　　Dreamworld (☎ 5588 1111; www.dreamworld.com.au; Pacific Hwy, Coomera; adult/child $60/38; ☺ 10am-5pm) On the Pacific Hwy 17km north of Surfers, this is thrill-ride central. Squeals and shrieks are mandatory on such delights as the Tower of Terror, where you accelerate to 161km/h in seven seconds, Wipeout, a twisting, tumbling roller coaster, or The Giant Drop, a terminal-velocity machine, where you free fall from 38 storeys. There are also plenty of attractions to keep the kids entertained, including the Nickelodeon Park and a bunch of wildlife shows, the highlight of which is the interactive tiger show.

　　Sea World (☎ 5588 2222, show times 5588 2205; www.seaworld.com.au; Sea World Dr, Main Beach; adult/child $60/38; ☺ 10am-5.30pm) A huge aquatic theme park, Sea World has loads of animal performances, including twice-daily dolphin and sea-lion shows, and shark feeding. There are also waterslides and roller coasters, and a zoo with two resident celebrity polar bears.

　　Warner Bros Movie World (☎ 5573 8485; www.movieworld.com.au; Pacific Hwy, Oxenford; adult/child $60/38; ☺ 10am-5.30pm) Otherwise known as 'Hollywood on the Gold Coast', Movie World claims to be Australia's number-one tourist attraction. You can mingle with your favourite Loony Tunes characters here, all of whom leap at photo opportunities with the kids. There's a constantly changing 'ride of the moment' as well as stunt shows and movie-themed whizzing rides.

　　Wet 'n' Wild (☎ 5573 2255; www.wetnwild.com.au; Pacific Hwy, Oxenford; adult/child $38/24; ☺ 10am-5pm Feb-Apr & Sep-Dec, 10am-4pm May-Aug, 10am-9pm 27 Dec–26 Jan) If the beach is too sedate, this colossal water-sports park offers plenty of creative ways to get wet – it's loads of fun. You can slide down inventive water slides, dip into huge pools or zoom down the mighty Mammoth Falls, a white-water rapids ride, at 70km/h on a giant rubber ring. If all that sounds too energetic, you can always just float around on a big rubber ring.

including transfers and ending with a hot breakfast.

You can also get high with **Tandem Skydive** (☎ 5599 1920; Hanger 22, Coolangatta Airport) or **Skydive Queensland** (Map p131; ☎ 5544 6323; www.skydiveqld.com.au; Mariner's Cove), both of which offer tandem jumps from 10,000ft to 14,000ft (from $250).

If jumping out of a plane isn't quite your style, **Surfers Paradise Parasail** (Map p131; ☎ 5591 5100; Mariner's Cove; rides $55) gives you a pretty good rush without quite so many zeros from the ground.

BUNGEE JUMPING

Almost a rite of passage in Surfers is betting your life on the strength of a giant rubber band at **Banzai Bungey** (☎ 5526 7611; cnr Cypress & Ferny Aves; jumps from $100). But wait! On the same block there are new and inventive ways to revisit your breakfast. **Flycoaster** (☎ 5539 0474; www.flycoaster.com; rides $39) swings you like a pendulum after you've been released from a hoist 20m up. **Sling Shot** (☎ 5570 2700; rides $30) catapults you into the air at around 160km and **Vomatron** (☎ 5570 200; rides $30) warns you from the get-go and whisks you around in a giant arc at about 120km an hour. The continuous stream of delighted whoops serve as hearty recommendations.

SURFING & KAYAKING

Surfers is a great place to get wet, and behind the seemingly impenetrable wall of high rises, Surfers Paradise Beach has enough swell to give beginners a feel for the craft of surfing. Surf schools are abundant and charge between $40 and $50 for a two-hour lesson. **Brad Holmes Surf Coaching** (☎ 5539 4068, 0418-757 539; www.bradholmessurfcoaching.com) Also caters to disabled travellers.

Cheyne Horan School of Surf (☎ 1800 227 873, 0403-080 484; www.cheynehoran.com.au; 3 lessons $100) World Champion surfer Cheyne Horan offers excellent tuition.

Go Ride a Wave (☎ 1800 787 337, 5526 7077; www.gorideawave.com.au; Cavill Ave Mall; per hr/3hr/day $15/25/40; ⏱ 9am-5pm) Also rents out surfboards.

Splash Safaris Sea Kayaking (☎ 0407-741 748; www.SeaKayakingTours.com; tours $45-65) Kayak tours ranging from introductory courses to five-hour safaris including snorkelling, dolphin searching, bushwalking and lunch.

HORSE RIDING

Numinbah Valley Adventure Trails (☎ 5533 4137; www.numinbahtrails.com) has three-hour horse-riding treks through beautiful rainforest and river scenery in the Numinbah Valley, 30km south of Nerang ($60/50 per adult/child, with pick-ups from the coast $70/60).

Gumnuts Horseriding (p149) operates out of Canungra in the Gold Coast hinterland, with courtesy transfers from the coast.

Tours

Semi-aquatic bus tours are all the rage in Surfers, and several operators offer the curious experience of exploring Surfers by road and river in a boat on wheels. Try **Aquabus** (☎ 5539 0222; 7 Orchid Ave) or **Aqua Duck** (☎ 5538 3825; 7 Orchid Ave). Both charge around $35/26/90 per adult/child/family and it's certainly an unusual way to explore Surfers Paradise.

Several boat companies operate cruises between Main Beach and Surfers Paradise (see p132 for more information).

You can also access the Gold Coast hinterland with a number of tour operators from Surfers Paradise. See p146 for more information.

Festivals & Events

Big Day Out (www.bigdayout.com) Huge international music festival in late January.

Quicksilver Pro-Surfing Competition See some of the world's best surfers out on the waves in mid-March.

Surf Life-Saving Championships Also in mid-March, expect to see some stupidly fit people running about wearing very little.

Gold Coast International Marathon Run in July.

IndyCar October. See the boxed text opposite for more.

Schoolies week Month-long party by school-leavers from mid-November to mid-December. Generally involves lots of alcohol and a few organised events in the first week.

Sleeping

The helpful **Gold Coast Accommodation Service** (☎ 5592 0067; www.goldcoastaccommodationservice.com; Shop 1, 1 Beach Rd) can arrange and book accommodation for you.

BUDGET

Surfers has several decent hostel options, all of which offer vouchers for the nightclubs in town.

Cheers Backpackers (☎ 1800 636 539, 5531 6539; 8 Pine Ave, Surfers Paradise; dm/d $23/60; 🖥 🖳) Amid the friendly blur of theme nights, karaoke, pool comps, pub crawls, happy hours and BBQs here, you'll also find adequate rooms and good facilities. Cheers is undeniably a

INDYCAR

Since 1991 Surfers Paradise has been host to what has been dubbed Queensland's biggest party – the Australian leg of the IndyCar series (the US equivalent of Formula One motor racing). Each October, the main streets of central Surfers are transformed into a temporary race circuit, around which hurtle some of the world's fastest cars, with drivers who push them up to speeds of more than 300km/h. The champ cars are the main attraction, but plenty of folk come to see rivals Ford and Holden battle it out in the V8 Supercars.

Like all good motor festivals, the attractions aren't restricted to four wheels. Devoted rev heads can put themselves as close to the action as possible by shelling out $22 and taking a tour through either the champ car pit lanes or a V8 Supercar pit lane. The noise and heat from the cars in these pits can be deafening – just what the mechanic ordered. Over the entire four days, when the tracks aren't screeching with races or practice sessions, you can catch motorcycle stunt shows and quite spectacular air shows. There are also plenty of opportunities to meet the masters for autograph sessions.

On a good year, around a quarter of a million spectators descend for the festival. Surfers is fairly over the top at the best of times, but IndyCar gives the town a chance to *really* let its hair down. Accommodation is chockers, and bars and restaurants hum with happy race-goers making the most of their visit. It's a great time to be here, or a great time to be anywhere else, depending on how you feel about the place.

General admission to the races ranges from $30 to $75 per day at the gate, but it's cheaper if you book ahead. Four-day grandstand seating costs between $210 and $530. For more information call ☎ 1800 300 055 or check www.indy.com.au.

party hostel, and the fun frequently trickles out to the action of Surfers.

Sleeping Inn Surfers (☎ 1800 817 832, 5592 4455; www.sleepinginn.com.au; 26 Peninsular Dr; dm $21, d with/ without bathroom $65/55; 🖳) A bit flashier than your average hostel, this converted motel has modern facilities and a wide choice of rooms, from basic dorms to classier doubles with TVs. It's also large enough to cater to party punters as well as those in dire need of a quiet sleep.

Surf 'n' Sun Backpackers (☎ 1800 678 194, 5592 2363; www.surfnsun-goldcoast.com; 3323 Gold Coast Hwy, Surfers Paradise; dm/d $23/60; 🖳) Rivalling Cheers as party central, this hostel is the best option for Surfers' beach and bars. Staff are chipper, there's a constant hum of music, surfboards for hire and pool tables, and if the hop to the beach is too strenuous, the pool is a nice, lazy alternative.

Also recommended:

Mermaid Beach Motel (☎ 5575 5688; www.mermaid beachmotel.com.au; 2395 Gold Coast Hwy, Mermaid Beach; r $55-65; 😢 🖳) Small motel with clean, self-contained rooms.

Surfers Paradise Backpackers Resort (☎ 1800 282 800, 5592 4677; www.surfersparadisebackpackers.com .au; Gold Coast Hwy, Surfers Paradise; dm/d/tr $22/55/80; 🖳 🖳) Motel-style hostel with sauna, tennis court, pool room and bar.

MIDRANGE

Surfers is riddled with self-contained units courtesy of its prolific high-rises. These are great value, and it seems almost impossible to find a good-value hotel anymore.

Surfers International Apartments (☎ 1800 891 299, 5579 1299; www.surfers-international.com.au; 7-9 Trickett St; r per 3 nights $420-510; 😢 🖳) This high-rise, just off the beach, has plush apartments bathed in classy blue hues. Each contains a modern kitchen, sizable bedrooms and little extras such as cable TV and modem ports. Balconies with spectacular beach views are standard, and the complex comes with a small gym and poolside BBQ.

Gold Coast International Hotel (☎ 1800 074 020, 5584 1200; www.gci.com.au; cnr Staghorn Ave & Gold Coast Hwy; d $135-235; 😢 🖳) The polished rooms at this hotel have all been recently refurbished and not a penny has been spared on the colour-coordinated linen, décor and furnishings. There's plenty of room to stretch out and all rooms come with a view of either the hinterland or ocean, although the balconies are fairly snug.

Cosmopolitan Apartments (☎ 5570 2311; cnr Gold Coast Hwy & Beach Rd; r from $85; 😢 🖳) Set back from the beach a tad but still very central, this complex contains 55 privately owned, self-contained apartments. Each has been uniquely furnished by the owners, but standards include dishwashers, balconies, laundries and phones. Most also have cable TV. There's also a BBQ area, spa and sauna.

Chateau Beachside (☎ 5538 1022; www.strand .com.au; cnr Elkhorn Ave & The Esplanade; d $100-130, r $110-140, ste $120-150; 🅿 🔌) Right in the heart of Surfers, this seaside complex has comfortable, spacious units. The views are excellent, and if you don't want sand in your bathers you can cool off in the pool or heat up in the spa and sauna. There's also a restaurant attached (see opposite).

Trickett Gardens Holiday Inn (☎ 5539 0988; www.trickettgardens.com.au; 24-30 Trickett St; d/f $85/150; 🅿 🔌) This friendly low-rise block is great for families, with a central location and well-equipped, self-contained units.

Raffles Royale (☎ 5538 0099; www.rafflesroyale.com .au; 69 Ferny Ave; r from $85; 🅿 🔌) This unobtrusive, low-rise block has bright and cheerful self-contained units, which are blessed with a healthy dose of sunlight. It's incredibly secure and a popular choice with families.

Pacific View Holiday Apartments (☎ 5570 3788; www.viewpacific.com; 5 View Ave; r from $80; 🔌) The self-contained units in this wee complex are a little dated and the fixtures slightly weary, but they're spacious and still offer good value. All contain life's necessities (except for air-con!), including washers and dryers, and balconies get glimpses of the beach through the surrounding buildings.

International Beach Resort (☎ 1800 657 471, 5539 0099; www.internationalresort.com.au; 84 The Esplanade, Surfers Paradise; apt $80-105; 🅿) Another seafront high-rise, this place is just across from the beach, and has good studios and one- and two-bedroom units. The more expensive options have sea views.

Olympus (☎ 5538 7288; bookings@olympusapart ments.com.au; 62 The Esplanade, Surfers Paradise; d $130) Just 200m north of Elkhorn Ave and opposite the beach, this high-rise block has well-kept, spacious apartments with one or two bedrooms.

Also recommended:

Quarterdeck Apartments (☎ 1800 635 235, 5592 2200; fax 5538 0282; 3263 Gold Coast Hwy; r $90; 🔌) Comfortable one-bedroom apartments, some with great views.

Silver Sands Motel (☎ 5538 6041; www.silversands motel.com.au; 2985 Gold Coast Hwy; d Mon-Thu $70, Fri-Sun $90; 🅿 🔌) Reasonable motel rooms just out of the centre.

TOP END

Courtyard Marriott (☎ 1800 074 317, 5579 3499; www.marriott.com; cnr Gold Coast Hwy & Hanlan St; d/ste from $155/165; 🅿) Right in the centre of Surfers, this plush top-end hotel is attached to the Paradise Centre Mall and offers all the luxury you would expect in this price range, including sea views, and spa baths in the top-price suites.

Marriott Resort (☎ 5592 9800; fax 5592 9888; 158 Ferny Ave; d/ste from $350/415; 🅿 🔌) Just north of the centre, this resort is ridiculously sumptuous, from the sandstone-floored foyer with punka-style fans to the lagoon-style pool, complete with artificial white sand beaches and waterfall.

Eating

Surfers Paradise has a multicultural palate, and although there are plenty of options for a good feed, haute cuisine is in short supply. Instead the streets are brimming with cafés and offerings of quantity over quality. The exceptions are the diminutive Korean and Japanese eateries, which cook up authentic and tasty dishes in no-nonsense surrounds.

Grumpy's Wharf (☎ 5531 6177; Tiki Village, Cavill Ave; mains $25-35; 🕒 lunch & dinner) Right on the water, Grumpy's is a secluded and tranquil retreat serving fine seafood in a fine atmosphere. There's plenty from the deep on the menu and aside from a few Asian-inspired dressings and risottos, the chefs let the flavour of the seafood work your tastebuds.

Melbas (☎ 5592 6922; 46 Cavill Ave; mains $25-35; 🕒 lunch & dinner) Melbas' menu is revolutionary amid Surfers' churned-out fare; think Thai-baked lamb rack with Tom Yum broth or oven-baked, butter-curried snapper with cashews. Unfortunately vegetarian options are limited. There's a lunch menu (mains $12) and the atmosphere is *Miami Vice* meets the new millennium. It's also a popular drinking hole (see opposite).

Marmalade Cafe (☎ 5504 7353; Shop 36, Chevron Renaissance; mains $10-15; 🕒 lunch & dinner) This little café steps outside the square with a pocket of sheltered seating outside, and long cushioned benches inside. The breakfast menu is downright funky, but if you just want toast, try it with the pineapple and macadamia-nut jam. Lunches include Thai fish cakes and Moroccan spiced lamb salad.

Tandoori Place (☎ 5592 1004; cnr Gold Coast Hwy & Trickett St; mains $15-20; ☒ lunch & dinner) On the extensive menu here you'll find seafood, poultry, lamb, beef and even kangaroo done in subcontinental style. Vegetarians are also spoiled for choice and the *tandoor* (clay-oven) dishes are very good. This place has deservedly won awards, and the service is friendly and efficient.

Bavarian Haus (☎ 5531 7150; 41 Cavill Ave; mains $20-25; ☒ lunch & dinner) In a kitschy alpine ski lodge setting you can dig into authentic German sausages and Aussie lamb courtesy of lovelies wearing plenty of frills and lederhosen. The good selection of German beers is just as enticing.

Costa Dora (☎ 5538 5203; 27 Orchid Ave; dishes $12-22; ☒ lunch & dinner) The Italian village setting painted into the backdrop of this popular restaurant goes nicely with the authentic, if not predictable, pasta, pizza, salads and mains. A splash of shellfish graces the menu as does a kids' selection, and the $10 pasta-and-cappuccino lunch deal is a bargain.

Charlies (☎ 5538 5285; Cavill Ave Mall; meals $10-20; ☒ breakfast, lunch & dinner) With décor devoted to Charlie Chaplin, who undoubtedly never ate here, this sprawling café has a hint of American diner about it and serves hearty hamburgers, pizza, pasta, sandwiches and breakfasts. The outdoor seating is pleasant and it's open 24 hours.

Two kid pleasers serving cheap and tasty pizzas and pasta are **La Porchetta** (Orchid Ave; ☎ 5527 5273; 3 Orchid Ave; Elkhorn Ave; ☎ 5504 5236; Elkhorn Ave; meals $10-15; ☒ breakfast, lunch & dinner) and **Chateau Beachside** (☎ 5526 9994; cnr Elkhorn Ave & The Esplanade; meals $6-10; ☒ breakfast, lunch & dinner), which also dishes up good burgers and an all-you-can-gobble $10 breakfast. Supermarkets can be found in **Centro Surfers Paradise** (Cavill Ave Mall) and **Chevron Renaissance Shopping Centre** (cnr Elkhorn & Gold Coast Hwy).

More cheap eats:

Arirang (☎ 5539 8008; Shop 8, Centre Arcade; mains $8-16; ☒ lunch & dinner) Authentic Korean noodle dishes.

Go Sushi (☎ 5526 8766; Centro Surfers Paradise, Cavill Ave Mall; sushi $2-4; ☒ lunch & dinner)

Drinking

Surfers takes its drinking more seriously than oxygen.

O'Malleys (☎ 5570 4075; Level 1, 1 Cavill Ave) By day this is a quaint respite from the hectic heat of Cavill Ave and the $8 jugs are pure

> **BABYSITTING BLISS**
>
> We know you love the little tackers – bless their cotton socks – but in the event you need an adult-only spell, help is at hand. The **Gold Coast Baby Sitters Service** (☎ 1800 064 192) provides certified baby sitters and nannies, who specialise in hotel babysitting all along the coast. All have a government-issued suitability certificate and a first-aid certificate. They can sit for an hour up to overnight, but you'll need to give 24 hours' notice.

medicine. The network of booths and stools overlooking the ocean fill up at night when the atmosphere is happy and rowdy.

Gilhooley's (☎ 5538 9122; cnr Gold Coast Hwy & Cavill Ave) Another pseudo-Irish pub nestled into a convenient spot on the main drag, Gilhooley's hosts live Irish music and DJs (not at the same time) and big-screen TV sports…or you can just people-watch on the terrace out the front.

Melbas (☎ 5592 6922; 46 Cavill Ave) This excellent restaurant (opposite) hangs on to its glitzy edge once the dinner plates are cleared and satiates a well-heeled crowd with cocktails, dim lighting and pumping music. The recipe is popular and it heaves most nights.

Liquid (☎ 5538 0111; Shop 1, 18 Orchid Ave) Spilling out onto the sidewalk, Liquid's wide-open entrance parades a glossy bar highlighted by electric blue neon. Water cascades down the back walls and the trendy patrons sip cocktails before succumbing to the hip-luring soundtrack. Eventually it all ends up naughty and noisy.

Clock Hotel (☎ 5539 0344; 3282 Gold Coast Hwy) By day this Surfers institution is a favourite with the older crowd, which dominates the bar like characters in an episode of *Cheers*. Each night, however, it's the 20- and 30-somethings who dig the 'Latin Fire' Tuesday, 'Champers' Thursday, karaoke Sunday and big-screen sports.

Surfers Paradise SLSC (☎ 5531 5966; The Esplanade) This sprawling life-saving club is a great place for unpretentious drinking and socialising. Don't expect the Ritz; the unadorned expanse is Surfers' best joint for cheap beer, with workaholics behind the bar and beach views. Start early if you want a table.

GOLD COAST

Entertainment

Orchid Ave is Surfers' main bar and nightclub strip, but venues change hands, names and orientation regularly. Many offer vouchers for backpackers, and Wednesday to Saturday are generally the big party nights. Cover charges are usually between $5 and $10.

NIGHTCLUBS

Ambassee (☎ 5592 0088; 26 Orchid Ave) This chic venue is the closest Surfers has to a serious club. Wear your fancy threads; even the bouncers look polished. Doors don't open until around 10pm and resident DJs spin edgy house, techno and funk from Thursday to Sunday.

Cocktails & Dreams (☎ 5592 1955; Level 1, The Mark, Orchid Ave) Others may come and go but Cocktails & Dreams has been the stomping ground for young party-goers for years. Drink deals, dancing and general debauchery pulls the crowds in and spits them out again in the wee hours after an exhausting good time.

Party (☎ 5538 2848) Linked to Cocktails & Dreams by a stairway, Party offers more of the same with $2 drink deals from Thursday to Sunday nights, theme nights and bubbly prizes.

Shooters (☎ 5592 1144; 15 Orchid Ave) Apparently food is served here, but who could tell with all the alcohol? It's an American-style saloon with pool tables, big-screen videos and occasional live entertainment. On weekends it's packed to almost bursting.

MP's (☎ 5526 2337; Forum Arcade, 26 Orchid Ave) This popular gay club has cheap drinks and drag shows on Tuesday, Thursday and Sunday. On Friday and Saturday it fills with a happy, mixed crowd soaking up a generic nightclub atmosphere.

LIVE MUSIC

Howl at the Moon (☎ 5527 5522; Shop 7, Upper Level, Centro Surfers Paradise) Surfers' 'it' bar of the moment, Howl at the Moon occupies a great possie above Cavill Ave Mall. No-one's looking out though; all eyes are firmly turned towards the talented musos belting out everything from rap to blues on the pianos. Howl-alongs are encouraged. The queues start early.

Basement (☎ 5588 4000; Gold Coast Arts Centre, 135 Bundall Rd) Beneath the Arts Centre (right) this funky bar hosts touring performers who excel in jazz, blues and folk. Regular Sunday sessions specialise in blues, roots and world music courtesy of the resident band. Tickets cost around $16.

Troccadero (☎ 5536 4200; 9 Trickett St) When the big guns are in town they strut their stuff at Troccadero. If it's not high profile Aussie and international acts playing, you'll catch live rock in all its genres.

Gilhooley's (☎ 5538 9122; cnr Gold Coast Hwy & Cavill Ave) It wouldn't be an Irish pub without live music, now would it, and this one accommodates regularly with acoustic rock and folk.

THEATRE

The excellent **Gold Coast Arts Centre** (☎ 5588 4000; www.gcac.com.au; 135 Bundall Rd), located beside the Nerang River, has a 1200-seat theatre, which regularly hosts impressive theatrical productions. Big names in the Australian industry often feature as headliners. The theatre also screens art-house movies (all shows $8 on Tuesday) and there's a restaurant and bar.

Getting There & Away

The transit centre is on the corner of Beach and Cambridge Rds. Surfers is a major stop on the east coast route and all the major bus companies have desks here. For more information on buses and trains, see p128.

Getting Around

CAR & BICYCLE

There are plenty of car-rental firms around with fliers in every hostel, motel and hotel. Local outfits that consistently offer good deals include **All Age Car Rentals** (☎ 1800 671 361; 3024 Gold Coast Hwy; used cars per day from $19), **Red Back Rentals** (☎ 5592 1655; Transit Centre; per day from $25) and **Red Rocket Rent-A-Car** (☎ 1800 673 682, 5538 9074; Shop 9, The Mark, Orchid Ave; per day from $15), which also rents scooters and bicycles. Insurance costs extra.

Sometimes **Budget** (☎ 1300 362 848, 5538 1344; cnr Ferny & Norfolk Aves) and **Avis** (☎ 13 63 33; 5539 9388; cnr Ferny & Cypress Aves) offer unbeatable deals.

Mopeds City (☎ 5592 5878; 102 Ferny Ave) hires out brand new mopeds (per hour/day $35/70) and bicycles (per hour/day $10/20).

BROADBEACH

☎ 07 / pop 5180

A few kilometres south of Surfers Paradise, Broadbeach marks the southern entry (or exit depending on your direction) of the Gold Coast's giddy core. There's a strong community feel here, and for a taste of the beach and sun lifestyle it's exquisite. It's also a good alternative to Surfers if you want a peaceful night's sleep.

Sights & Activities
As far as attractions go, Broadbeach's main claim to fame is the temple to Mammon that is **Conrad Jupiters Casino** (☎ 5592 8100; www.conrad .com.au; Gold Coast Hwy; admission free; ⏰ 24hr). Hundreds of thousands of optimistic gamblers filter through the Conrad every year and leave with their pockets slightly lighter and their addiction briefly sated. This was the first legal casino in Queensland, and it features more than 100 gaming tables, including blackjack, roulette, two-up and craps, and hundreds of bleeping poker machines. Also here is **Jupiters Theatre** (☎ 1800 074 144), with live music and glamorous dinner shows. You have to be over 18 years of age to enter, and the usual dress codes apply – no thongs (flip-flops), vests or ripped clothes. A monorail runs here from the Oasis Shopping Centre.

Sleeping
Mermaid Beach Motel (☎ 5575 5688; www.mermaid beachmotel.com.au; 2395 Gold Coast Hwy; apt Mon-Thu from $60, Fri-Sun from $70; 🖳) This small, personable motel has spotless units that are a mark above the surrounding litter of cheapie options.

Conrad Jupiters (☎ 1800 074 344, 5592 8130; www .conrad.com.au; Gold Coast Hwy; r $280-880, penthouse ste $2100; 🅿 🖳) The penthouse suite at this spectacular hotel is the place to stay if you hit the jackpot at the casino downstairs. The hotel's facilities include six restaurants, four tennis courts, three pools, two spas and a gym.

Eating
Broadbeach's culinary offerings are fewer but finer than Surfers', and there are a number of good options to choose from.

Champagne Brasserie (☎ 5538 3877; 2 Queensland Ave; mains $20-28; ⏰ lunch Tue-Fri, dinner Tue-Sun) This lively, unassuming restaurant could have been plucked from a French village and the food would give Paris' finest a run for their money. Favourites such as beef bourguignon and snails are on the menu, but some fancy infusions such as home-

made ravioli with chicken, goat's cheese, pine nuts and a tomato and basil dressing make the choice difficult.

Sonatas (☎ 5526 9904; cnr Surf Pde & Queensland Ave; mains $15-25; ⏰ breakfast, lunch & dinner) Locals flock to this sunny, cosmopolitan café on weekend mornings to get their fix of latte culture and indulgent breakfasts. Things don't settle down much over lunch and dinner, owing to a crisp, Mod Oz menu boasting goodies such as wok-tossed prawns and Moreton Bay bugs, Cajun barramundi, and brie-and-almond salad. Vegetarians also get their slice of the pie.

Three Beans Espresso (☎ 5538 8744; Phoenician Bldg, 90 Surf Pde; dishes $5-12; ⏰ 24hr) It's all very casual in this groovy little neck of the woods, but Three Beans takes its coffee very seriously and its café meals aren't bad either. Fresh deli ingredients go into an evolving menu of stacks, wraps and melts.

There are plenty of cheap, junk-food options along the Victoria Ave Mall and inside the Oasis Shopping Centre. Pacific Fair Shopping Centre also has a food court.

Entertainment
Mermaid 5 Cinemas (☎ 5575 3355; 2514 Gold Coast Hwy)
Pacific Square 12 Cinemas (☎ 5572 2666; cnr Hooker Bvd & Gold Coast Hwy) Buried in the huge Pacific Fair Shopping Centre.

BURLEIGH HEADS
☎ 07 / pop 8430
Among a certain subset of Australians with surfboards, Burleigh Heads is legendary. In the right weather conditions, the headland here produces a spectacular right-hand point break, famous for its fast, deep barrel rides, but it definitely isn't for beginners. The shore is lined with vicious black rocks and the rip is ferocious.

You don't need Kelly Slater's talents to enjoy this town though. With the vast majority of construction firmly below the tree line, Burleigh Heads is positively chilled and an exquisite reminder of all the reasons you love the beach. It's a perfect, tranquil surfie town that draws wave craftsmen of all generations and a healthy dose of folk just soaking up the atmosphere.

The Burleigh Heads National Park is a small but diverse forest reserve with walking trails around the rocky headland. There

GOLD COAST

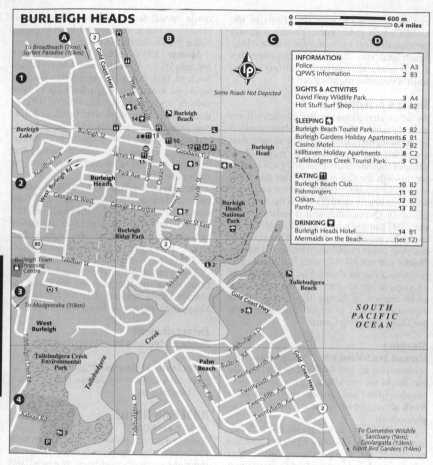

BURLEIGH HEADS

INFORMATION
Police..1 A3
QPWS Information......................2 B3

SIGHTS & ACTIVITIES
David Fleay Wildlife Park.............3 A4
Hot Stuff Surf Shop.....................4 B2

SLEEPING
Burleigh Beach Tourist Park.........5 B2
Burleigh Gardens Holiday Apartments.6 B1
Casino Motel...............................7 B2
Hillhaven Holiday Apartments......8 C2
Tallebudgera Creek Tourist Park...9 C3

EATING
Burleigh Beach Club...................10 B2
Fishmongers..............................11 B2
Oskars.......................................12 B2
Pantry.......................................13 B2

DRINKING
Burleigh Heads Hotel..................14 B1
Mermaids on the Beach.........(see 12)

are also several good commercial wildlife sanctuaries in the area.

Information

You can get more information on the natural environment of the area from the **Queensland Parks & Wildlife Service Information Centre** (QPWS; ☎ 5535 3032; 3032 Gold Coast Hwy; ⏰ 9am-4pm) at the northern end of Tallebudgera Creek.

Sights

WILDLIFE SANCTUARIES

There are three wildlife sanctuaries in the vicinity of Burleigh Heads.

Currumbin Wildlife Sanctuary (☎ 5534 1266; www.currumbin-sanctuary.org.au; Gold Coast Hwy, Currum-

bin; adult/child $22/15; ⏰ 8am-5pm) provides one of your best opportunities (outside of going walkabout) to see Australian native animals in bush and rainforest habitats. Tree kangaroos, koalas, emus, wombats and other cute-and-furries are joined daily by flocks of brilliantly coloured rainbow lorikeets, which take great delight in eating out of your hand. Throughout the day you can catch a number of informative and sometimes interactive shows focussing on a particular species, and there is also an Aboriginal dance show. One of the best ways to see the sanctuary is on a Wildnight Tour (adult/child $38/21), when the native nocturnal animals go about their business. To get here catch Surfside bus Nos 1 or 1A in either direction.

David Fleay Wildlife Park (☎ 5576 2411; West Burleigh Rd; adult/child/senior/family $13/6.50/8.50/33; ☾ 9am-5pm) is run with the help of the QPWS. Nestled in a sheltered pocket of bush, a fine collection of native wildlife is scattered around three dams. With 4km of walking tracks through mangroves and rainforest and plenty of informative shows throughout the day, it's an excellent opportunity to experience Australian fauna. The platypus was first bred in captivity here and the park still runs a research and breeding programme for rare and endangered species. Take the Tallebudgera-Burleigh exit from the Gold Coast Hwy.

Esprit Bird Gardens (☎ 5533 0208; 746 Currumbin Creek Rd; adult/child $2.50/free; ☾ 9.30am-5pm Fri-Sun, daily during school holidays) is an attractive subtropical garden with several aviaries housing exotic and native birds. There are also walking tracks. To get here, turn off the Bruce Hwy south of Currumbin Creek.

Activities
SURFING
The right-hand point break at Burleigh Heads is the best wave here, but it's usually crowded with pro surfers. There are plenty of other waves to practise on along the beach. The **Hot Stuff Surf Shop** (☎ 5535 6899; 1706 Gold Coast Hwy) rents out surfboards for $20/30 a half/full day.

Sleeping
Hillhaven Holiday Apartments (☎ 5535 1055; www.hillhaven.com.au; 2 Goodwin Tce; apt per week from $605; ☒ ☐ ☒) If you want to holiday in style, these opulent apartments perched high on the headland overlooking Burleigh Heads are the go. Neutral tones and snug furnishings fill the bright rooms and the views are easily the best in town. The apartments are fully self-contained with all the mod cons from home. Baby sitting can be arranged if you need to occupy the little tackers. Call to enquire about shorter stays.

Burleigh Gardens Holiday Apartments (☎ 5576 3955; www.Burleighgardens.com; 1849 Gold Coast Hwy; 1-bedroom apt per night/week from $90/460, 2-bedroom apt from $100/550; ☒) These comfortable, self-contained units are solid value and their proximity to the beach and balcony views make them popular. Interiors vary, but they all have plenty of room and all amenities are included.

Burleigh Beach Tourist Park (☎ 5581 7755; www.gctp.com.au/burly; Goodwin Tce; unpowered/powered sites from $21/23, cabins $115; ☒) This council-run park is snug, but it's in a great spot. There are a few shady sights – get in quick to bag one. The good news is that you can stumble to the beach and the barbies are free! Rates are for two people.

Tallebudgera Creek Tourist Park (☎ 5581 7700; www.gctp.com.au/tally; 1544 Gold Coast Hwy; unpowered/powered sites from $24/26, cabins $105-140; ☒) This sprawling park is colossal compared to other council-run versions, but it's well laid out with it's own road system and sits right on the banks of Tallebudgera Creek. Aside from cabins and sites there are also basic rooms with a TV and fridge. Rates are for two people.

Casino Motel (☎ 5535 7133; fax 5576 8099; 1761 Gold Coast Hwy; d $70-85, with kitchenette $75-90) This is the closest motel to Burleigh Heads and it isn't bad value. Rates increase on Friday and Saturday nights and it's worth paying the few bucks more for a room with a kitchenette.

Eating
There are plenty of eatery choices along the seafront. The Burleigh Beach Pavilion on Goodwin Tce is home to a couple of top-notch restaurants.

Oskars (☎ 5576 3722; 43 Goodwin Tce; dishes $19-30; ☾ lunch & dinner) One of the Gold Coast's finest, this elegant restaurant constantly lands a coveted place on best-dining lists from all quarters, and for good reason. Against elevated, sweeping views of the coastline you'll dine on a changing selection of seafood, depending on the day's catch, but expect something along the lines of snapper tempura with starfruit, coriander and red chilli salsa, or twice-baked sand crab soufflé, buttered English spinach, garlic-and-dill cream sauce. Spectacular meat dishes are also available.

Fishmongers (☎ 5535 2927; 9 James St; dishes $7-15; ☾ lunch & dinner) People pile into this fishmonger–fish-and-chip shop–restaurant because its goods from the deep are the business. You can buy your dory fillets, whiting, prawns or calamari untouched or take them away hot and wrapped, but why do either when you can sit down with a glass of vino and have it all grilled for the same price?

Pantry (☎ 5576 2818; 15 Connor St; dishes $7-15; ✆ 6am-5pm) A looong breakfast menu greets the cappuccino set at this cheery café, and if the sun's already too hot to park yourself under the umbrellas outside, the air-conditioning beckons from within. For lunch you can tuck into tasty burgers, wraps, melts and salads. This is a good spot for families.

Burleigh Beach Club (☎ 5520 2972; cnr Goodwin Tce & Gold Coast Hwy; dishes $10-18; ✆ lunch Mon-Sat, dinner Sun-Thu) For pure beach bistro nosh and family-friendly surrounds, this club is hard to beat. The ubiquitous burgers, steak, fish and chicken dishes are on offer, but it's all tasty and the portions are huge.

Drinking

Mermaids on the Beach (☎ 5520 1177; 31 Goodwin Tce) This is the best spot for a drink. Outside of meal hours the bistro environment makes way for a snappy beach bar with trimmings, the best of which are the views stretching from the sand at your feet and ending somewhere past Southport.

Burleigh Heads Hotel (☎ 5535 1000; 12 The Esplanade) Alternatively, this hotel is not bad for a drink, if you don't mind the pokies in the background. There are live bands on Friday and Saturday evenings.

COOLANGATTA & TWEED HEADS
☎ 07 / pop 45,024

The 'twin towns' of Coolangatta and Tweed Heads straddle the border between Queensland and New South Wales, but the border between the two is pretty arbitrary. This friendly little surf resort is probably the most laid-back spot on the Gold Coast and it's a great place to kick back and catch a few waves. There are good views down the coast from Point Danger, the headland at the end of the state line.

Information

Coolangatta visitors centre (☎ 5536 7765; infocoolangatta@gctb.com.au; cnr Griffith & Warner Sts; ✆ 8am-5pm Mon-Fri, 8am-4pm Sat, 9am-1pm Sun)

PB's OZ Internet Cafe (☎ 5599 4536; 152 Griffith St; per 30min $4; ✆ 9am-6pm)

Post Office (☎ 13 13 18) Coolangatta (cnr Griffith St & Marine Pde); Tweed Heads (Tweed Mall)

Showcase Medical Centre (☎ 5536 6771; Shop 41-2 Showcase on the Beach Centre; ✆ 7.30am-noon & 1-5pm Mon, Tue, Thu & Fri, 8am-5pm Wed)

Activities

The most difficult break here is Point Danger, but Kirra Point often goes off and there are gentler breaks at Greenmount Beach and Rainbow Bay. If you're looking for a cheap surfboard there are plenty of op-shops in town. The huge **Kirra Surf** (☎ 5536 3922; 6 Creek St) has a vast range of boards and accessories.

You can rent boards for around $30 per day from **Retro Groove** (☎ 5599 3952; 3 McLean St) or **BKD** (backdoorsurfwear@yahoo.com; Boundary St).

The **Australian Diving Institute** (☎ 1300 662 955, 5524 3683; 33 Machinery Dr, Tweed Heads; dives from $100) offers a range of instructed scuba dives in the Cook Island Marine Sanctuary and surrounding reefs.

Tours

Catch-A-Crab (☎ 5599 9972; www.catchacrab.com.au; adult/child incl lunch $90/54) operates great half-day tours along the Terranora Inlet of the Tweed River. As the name suggests, the cruise involves mud-crab catching (try to say that in a hurry), fishing, pelican feeding and, if the tides permit, yabbie hunting. You get to eat your haul for lunch.

Sleeping
BUDGET

Kirra Beach Tourist Park (☎ 5581 7744; www.gctp .com.au/kirra; Charlotte St, Kirra; unpowered sites $21-24, powered sites $23-26, cabins from $70; ✖ ✆) This large park is spread out and has plenty of grassy sites, modern self-contained cabins and good-value doubles. Facilities include a TV room, BBQs and wheelchair access. Rates are for two people.

Sunset Strip (☎ 5599 5517; www.sunsetstrip.com .au; 199 Boundary St, Coolangatta; dm/s/d $28/39/60, ste per 3 nights $225-330; ✆) This informal resort (with three- to four-bed dorms) caters mainly to surfers and easily offers the best value in town for backpackers. There's a TV lounge and a large, clean kitchen. Guests can rent surfboards and boogie boards for only $5 a day. The self-contained units aren't five star, but they're certainly good value and consequently attract crowds of all ages.

Coolangatta YHA (☎ 5536 7644; booking@coolan gattayha.com; 230 Coolangatta Rd, Bilinga; dm $22-24, s/d $35/50; ✆ ✆) A looooong haul from the bustle, this well-equipped YHA is favoured by surf junkies (of all vintages) who overdose on the excellent breaks across the road. You can also hire boards and bikes,

COOLANGATTA & TWEED HEADS

INFORMATION
Coolangatta Visitors Centre.......**1** A1
PB's OZ Internet Cafe...............**2** B1
Post Office.............................**3** A1
Showcase Medical Centre.....(see **24**)

SIGHTS & ACTIVITIES
BKD.....................................**4** B1
Kirra Surf..............................**5** B4
Retro Groove..........................**6** A1
Tandem Sydvie........................**7** A4

SLEEPING
Aries Holiday Apartments...........**8** A1
Beach House Seaside Resort......**9** A1
Bella Mare...........................**10** D3
Coolangatta YHA....................**11** A3
Kirra Beach Tourist Park...........**12** B4
Kirra Vista Holiday Units..........**13** B4
Shipwreck Motel....................**14** B4
Sunset Strip.........................**15** D3

EATING
Beaches Grill & Coffee Bar...(see **23**)
Coolangatta SLSC..................**16** A1
Farley's...............................**17** A1
Greenmount Beach SLSC.......**18** B1
Jellies...............................(see **1**)
Markwell's Cafe & Bar............**19** A1
Rainbow Bay SLSC.................**20** D3
Tweed Mall.........................**21** D4
Twin Towns Services Club.......**22** D4

DRINKING
Coolangatta Hotel.................**23** A1

ENTERTAINMENT
Coolangatta 6 Cinema Centre.**24** A1

TRANSPORT
Travelscene........................**25** B1

and breakfast is included in the price. Courtesy transfers from Coolangatta and Surfers are available.

MIDRANGE

Bella Mare (☎ 5599 2755; www.bellamare.com.au; 5 Hill St; r per night/week from $80/560, villas per night/week $95/665; ✷ ▨) Adding just a hint of the Mediterranean to Coolangatta, this fancy apartment block has cool, crisp apartments and indulgent villas. Everything inside is glistening, modern and fabulous, and aside from all the mod cons, you get free cable TV as well. There is a minimum two-night stay and the weekly rates are very reasonable.

Aries Holiday Apartments (☎ 5536 2711; 82 Marine Pde; apt per night/week from $130/590; ▨) A hop from

the beach, these sunny, self-contained units are huge. All contain two bedrooms and two bathrooms plus all the facilities you'd need for a long-term stay. The balconies catch the ocean breeze and vista, and they can accommodate a small army. Most visitors stay for at least a week, but outside of peak season, shorter stays should be available.

Kirra Vista Holiday Units (☎ 5536 7375; fax 5536 5640; 12-14 Musgrave St, Kirra; apt $80-100) The friendly owners here offer several well cared-for holiday units that sleep two to four people and have kitchens, TVs and balconies.

Beach House Seaside Resort (☎ 5599 0909; www .classicholidayclub.com.au; 52 Marine Pde, Coolangatta; s/d from $100/130; ▨) Although it belongs to a holiday club, this apartment complex often

GOLD COAST

has rooms available to nonmembers. The décor is fairly generic, but the units are fully self-contained and sleep up to six people. Also within the complex is a gym, spa and sauna.

Shipwreck Motel (☎ 5536 3599; fax 5536 3742; cnr Musgrave & Winston Sts, Kirra; r $55-60, 1-2 bedroom apt $80-120) This tidy motel is just across from the beach and offers self-contained units as well as motel rooms.

Eating

Jellies (☎ 5536 1741; 91 Griffith St; mains $20-30; ⏰ breakfast, lunch & dinner) The Mediterranean meets the Pacific in this sun-flooded restaurant. The menu is the most inventive in town; the fish of the day is topped with a chilli mango, macadamia-nut and coriander salsa. Pizza, snacks and kids' meals are also served.

Markwell's Cafe & Bar (☎ 5536 4544; 64 Griffith St; mains $10-20; ⏰ breakfast & lunch) This licensed café serves a cosmopolitan mix of salads, melts, pasta and sandwiches. There's also a good selection of fresh seafood and some pleasant outdoor seating where you can soak up the sun.

Beaches Grill & Coffee Bar (☎ 5536 9311; Coolangatta Hotel, cnr Marine Pde & Warner St; mains $12-18; ⏰ breakfast, lunch & dinner) This is the best spot in town for hungry, midrange wallets. The menu exceeds any pub-bistro expectations with dishes such as salt-and-pepper seared and curried chicken, and New York sirloin dusted with pepper and rosemary. Then, of course, there's the fish. There's plenty of room and it's kid-friendly.

Farley's (☎ 5536 7615; Beach House Arcade, Coolangatta; mains $10-21; ⏰ breakfast, lunch & dinner Tue-Sun) One of several licensed pavement cafés on the main strip, Farley's serves all-day breakfasts and delicious pasta, such as spaghetti with tiger prawns and tomato pesto, and potato gnocchi with roasted pumpkin and oregano cream. You can also dig into gourmet sandwiches, snacks and grills.

You can fill up on a club meal for $8 to $20 at one of the **surf life-saving clubs** (Coolangatta Beach; ☎ 5536 8474; Marine Pde; Greenmount Beach; ☎ 5536 1506; Marine Pde; Rainbow Bay; ☎ 5536 6736; 2 Snapper Rocks Rd) or the **Twin Towns Services Club** (☎ 5536 2277; Wharf St, Tweed Heads).

There's also an inexpensive food court at the **Tweed Mall** (Wharf St, Tweed Heads), open seven days.

Drinking & Entertainment

Coolangatta Hotel (☎ 5536 9311; cnr Marine Pde & Warner St) The Sunday sessions at this pub on Coolangatta's esplanade are huge – it seems everyone in town is settling into a coldie and getting into the loud, live acoustic gigs. Friday and Saturday nights are also busy, but on weekdays things quieten down to a sunny lull.

Coolangatta 6 Cinema Centre (☎ 5536 8900; Level 2, Showcase on the Beach Centre, Griffith St) This cinema offers six screens of mainstream releases. Tuesday is discount day ($8).

Surfies congregate on the decks of the three surf clubs (Rainbow Bay is the most popular). There are family-oriented shows and regular free movies at the **Twin Towns Services Club** (☎ 5536 1977; Wharf St, Tweed Heads) – call for details.

Getting There & Away

Travelscene (☎ 5536 1700; 29 Bay St, Tweed Heads), southeast of the centre, is the bus terminal for Greyhound, Kirklands and Coachtrans. See p128 for more information.

GOLD COAST HINTERLAND

Inland from Coolangatta, the mountains of the McPherson Range stretch back 60km to the New South Wales border. The settlements that speckle this area are influenced by the cooler air and vast sea of dense forest, and the culture of surf and sun found on the coast feels a million miles away. The national parks here are a paradise for walkers and this unspoiled environment is easily accessible by car or organised tour from the Gold Coast – a perfect antidote to the noise and clamour of the seaside strip. Expect a lot of rain in the mountains from December to March, and in winter the nights can be cold.

Tours

The only way to access the hinterland without your own wheels is on a tour. All the following arrange pick-ups from points along the Gold Coast. **Bushwacker Ecotours** (☎ 5520 7238; www.bushwacker-ecotours.com.au; adult/child from $90/50), an ecofriendly tour group, has quite an extensive array of ecotours to the hinterland, starting with day-long bushwalking tours and topping out at four-night excursions.

4X4 Hinterland Tours (☎ 1800 604 425, 0429-604 425; sales@hinterlandtours.com.au; day tours adult/child $130/80) is another company specialising in small-group 4WD ecotours to either Springbrook or Lamington National Park and Mt Tamborine. **Mountain Trek Adventures** (☎ 5536 1700) offers half-day tours that include Springbrook National Park and Mt Tamborine for $85/50 per adult/child.

Several big guns operate large coach tours out of Surfers Paradise. Generally, morning tea and a spot of bird feeding is included in tours. **Australian Day Tours** (☎ 1300 363 436; www.daytours.com.au; day tours adult/child $70/40, 2-day tours $340/140) travels via Mt Tamborine and Canungra to O'Reilly's Rainforest Guesthouse (p150), where you'll stay if you take the two-day tour.

O'Reilly's (☎ 5524 4249; adult/child/family $45/25/120) operates day tours to O'Reilly's Rainforest Guesthouse in Lamington National Park, via Mt Tamborine, with jump-out stops along the way.

Some companies also offer night tours, but these change regularly – ask at any tourist office for more information. See p96 for hinterland tours from Brisbane.

TAMBORINE MOUNTAIN

Just 45km northwest of the Gold Coast, the 600m-high plateau of Tamborine Mountain is on a northern spur of the McPherson Range. Patches of the area's original forests remain in nine small national parks, offering tumbling cascades and great views of the Gold Coast. The cutesy heritage communities of Mt Tamborine, North Tamborine and Eagle Heights exist to service the Gold Coast tour buses with Devonshire teas, and art and crafts.

Some of the best spots are **Witches Falls National Park**, southwest of North Tamborine, and **Cedar Creek Falls** and **Cameron Falls**, northwest of North Tamborine. **Macrozamia Grove National Park** has some extremely old macrozamia palms.

In the town of North Tamborine, the **visitor information centre** (☎ 5545 3200; Doughty Park; ⌚ 10.30am-3.30pm Sun-Fri, 9.30am-3.30pm Sat) has plenty of brochures, a small display on the area's ecology, and information on the well-established wineries scattered around the mountain.

The fabulous **Tamborine Mountain Distillery** (☎ 5545 3452; 87-91 Beacon Rd, North Tamborine; ⌚ 10am-3pm Wed-Sun) is a boutique distiller that manufactures its own schnapps, liqueurs and other spirits from organically grown fruits.

To get to Tamborine Mountain, turn off the Pacific Hwy at Oxenford or Nerang.

The friendly **Tall Trees Motel** (☎ 5545 1242; www.talltreesmotel.com.au; Eagle Heights Rd, Curtis Falls, North Tamborine; r Mon-Thu $80, Fri & Sun $90, Sat $100) on the edge of the forest is dressed up in a quaint cottage façade. The rooms are tidy and accommodating and the pretty English garden is visited regularly by warbling birds.

In a lovely setting, the **Mt Tamborine Motel** (☎ 5545 0088; www.mttamborinemotel.com.au; 99 Alpine Tce, Mt Tamborine; s/d Sun-Fri $70/85, Sat $95/120; 🖳🖳) has neat and comfy motel units with killer views of stunning Guanaba Gorge from the balconies. The pleasant rooms have tea- and coffee-making facilities and bar fridges, and there are laundry facilities and a tennis court on the property.

St Bernards Hotel (☎ 5545 1177; fax 5545 2733; 101 Alpine Tce, Tamborine; mains $10-18; ⌚ lunch daily, dinner Mon-Sat), next door to the motel, is a rustic old mountain pub (1911) and one of the most atmospheric spots in the hinterland. A large deck out the back captures commanding views of the gorge, and high-backed chairs and lofty ceilings add pedigree to the interior. The nosh is good pub grub.

SPRINGBROOK PLATEAU

The forested, 900m-high Springbrook Plateau, like the rest of the McPherson Range, is a remnant of the huge volcano that used to be centred on Mt Warning in New South Wales. It's an excellent, winding drive up from the Gold Coast via Mudgeeraba, with great views over the surrounding countryside.

Much of the area is protected as **Springbrook National Park**, which has three sections: Springbrook, Mt Cougal and Natural Bridge. The vegetation is temperate rainforest and eucalypt forest, with gorges, cliffs, forests, waterfalls and an extensive network of walking tracks and picnic areas.

Each section is reached by a long access road, and there are no shortcuts between the sections, so make sure you get on the right road. Coming from Nerang, take Springbrook Rd for the Springbrook section and Nerang-Murwillumbah Rd for the Natural

Bridge section. Mt Cougal is reached via Currumbin Creek Rd from Currumbin.

There's a **ranger's office and information centre** (☎ 5533 5147; 2873 Springbrook Rd; ☾ hours vary) at Springbrook where you can pick up a copy of the national park's walking-tracks leaflet for all three sections.

Springbrook

The village of Springbrook is balanced right on the edge of the plateau, with numerous waterfalls that tumble more than 100m down to the coastal plain below. The 'town' is really a series of properties stretched along a winding road, and the dearth of civilisation makes the area pristine and beautiful. Understandably, lookouts are the big attraction here, and there are several places where you can get the giddy thrill of leaning right out over the edge.

At **Gwongorella Picnic Area**, just off Springbrook Rd, the lovely **Purling Brook Falls** drop 109m into the rainforest. There are two easily-accessed lookouts, so views of the falls can be seen from either side. From both you get a full dose of the lush canopy and towering falls tumbling into the pools below. There are coin-operated BBQs at the picnic area, a pleasant camping ground and a number of walking trails, including a 6km-return walk to Waringa Pool, a beautiful swimming hole. Just to the south is the national park information centre and **Canyon Lookout**, which affords jagged views through the valley all the way to the coast, with a domineering sheer rock face jutting into the right-hand side. The starting points for a 4km circuit walk to **Twin Falls** and the 17km **Warrie Circuit** are here.

At the end of Springbrook Rd, the **Goomoolahra Picnic Area** is another pleasant picnic area with BBQs beside a small creek. A little further on, there's a great lookout point beside the falls, with views across the plateau and all the way back to the coast.

True to its name, the **Best of All Lookout**, which is reached via Lyrebird Ridge Rd, offers spectacular views from the southern edge of the plateau to the flats below. There's a 350m trail from the car park to the lookout, and it takes you past a clump of mighty Antarctic beech trees.

Most guesthouses are along or signposted off Springbrook Rd. **Springbrook Mountain Chalets** (☎ 5533 5205; smchalets.com.au; 2058 Springbrook Rd; d $140-170) has *very* stylish wooden chalets

---

---

peppered throughout a thick plot of bush, providing plenty of privacy. All are split-level and capacious. The newer, more expensive chalets are pure style, with walls of glass that flood the interiors with light. Potbelly stoves, spas and views are all standard.

The hidden A-frame red-cedar cottages at **Mouses House** (☎ 5533 5192; www.mouseshouse .com.au; 2807 Springbrook Rd; d 2 nights $300) make for the perfect romantic getaway. The beautifully polished interiors are classy and warm and each has a wood stove, DVD player and private view. There's also a hot tub and plunge pool, which can only be used by one cottage at a time.

English Gardens (☎ 5533 5244; 2832 Springbrook Rd; r $120-$140) has two self-contained cottages set amid a sprawling English-Australian garden. Both are laden with character and contain plump beds, spacious living areas and spas. The smaller one also has antique furnishings and cable TV. The hosts are incredibly friendly and there's also a small **café** (mains $4-11; ☾ breakfast & lunch), which sells cakes, toasted sandwiches and pies.

With Canyon Lookout at your doorstep, **Rosellas at Canyon Lookout** (☎ 5533 5120; 8 Canyon Pde; s/d $85/95) is a lovely place to stay. It's a homely guesthouse and the rooms, which have bathrooms, contain TVs and bar fridges. Also here is a nice **restaurant** (dishes $10-20; ☾ 10am-4pm Wed-Fri, 9am-5pm Sat & Sun, dinner Fri & Sun), which serves up great bangers and mash, homemade soups and steak sangas.

Springbrook Homestead (☎ 5533 5200; 2319 Springbrook Rd; mains $8-18; ☾ lunch) serves ploughman's lunches and steaks. A lively gang of rainbow lorikeets visits regularly and demands much attention.

Right by the car park for Purling Brook Falls, **Kimba's Kitchen** (☎ 5533 5335; 33 Forestry Rd; dishes $4-7; ☯ 10am-4pm) is a simple tearoom offering sandwiches and light meals. The feathered visitors well and truly outnumber the two-legged ones.

The small national park **Purling Brook Falls camping ground** (per person $4) is near Gwongorella picnic ground. It has no showers or bins. You need to book in advance through **QPWS** (☎ 13 13 04; www.smartservice.qld .gov.au/AS).

Natural Bridge

The Natural Bridge section of the park is just a couple of kilometres west of Springbrook as the crow flies, but you'll have to drive back up to Numinbah and then down the Murwillumbah road to get here – a trip of about 35km. A steep 1km walking circuit leads to a rock arch spanning a water-formed cave, which is home to a huge colony of glow-worms, and a small waterfall tumbling into a swimming hole.

Mt Cougal

The Mt Cougal section is also linked to Springbrook, but to get here, you'll have to go all the way back to the Pacific Hwy and pick up Currumbin Creek Rd at Currumbin. On Currumbin Creek there's a walking trail that passes several cascades and swimming holes, and also a restored sawmill from the wasteful days when the rainforest was felled to make packing cases for bananas!

CANUNGRA

This small town is 25km west of Nerang. It's at the junction of the northern approach roads to the Green Mountains and Binna Burra sections of the Lamington National Park. The **tourist information office** (☎ 5543 5156; cnr Kidston St & Lawton Lane; ☯ 9.30am-4pm Sun-Fri, 9.30am-2pm Sat) is in the Canungra Library.

If you're heading up to Green Mountains, **Canungra Valley Vineyards** (☎ 5543 4011; Lamington National Park Rd) is housed in an old homestead and is open daily for tastings and sales.

Gumnuts Horseriding (☎ 5543 0191; Biddaddaba Creek Rd) operates half-day horse rides which include damper and tea and transfers to accommodation throughout the Gold Coast.

Morning rides last for about two hours and cost $55/33 per adult/child. Afternoon rides are slightly longer and cost $60/38.

If you've got the gumption, you should definitely take a gander at the hinterland from above. The **Paragliding Centre** (☎ 5543 4000; Shop3, 40 Christie St) operates tandem paragliding flights (from $165) in the area.

The lovely old **Canungra Hotel** (☎ 5543 5233; 18 Kidston St; mains $10-20; ☯ lunch & dinner) greets you with a long, tiled bar where the cold beer goes down particularly well. The sizable bistro serves mountainous portions of pub grub and you can dine out on the back veranda.

Canungra Motel (☎ 5543 5155; Kidston St; d/t $80/90) is a small brick building with standard motel rooms. This place is an OK choice.

LAMINGTON NATIONAL PARK

West of Springbrook, the 200-sq-km Lamington National Park covers much of the McPherson Range and adjoins the Border Ranges National Park in New South Wales. The park covers most of the spectacular Lamington Plateau, which reaches 1100m in places, as well as the densely forested valleys below. Much of the vegetation is subtropical rainforest and there are beautiful gorges, caves, waterfalls and lots of wildlife. Commonly spotted animals include satin and regent bowerbirds and the curious Lamington spiny crayfish, and you'll almost certainly see pademelons, a type of small wallaby, on the forest verges in the late afternoon.

The two most popular and accessible sections of the park are **Binna Burra** and **Green Mountains**, both of which are reached via Canungra. Binna Burra can also be reached from Nerang. Renowned as a bushwalker's paradise, the park has 160km of walking tracks ranging from a 'senses trail' for the blind at Binna Burra and an excellent tree-top canopy walk along a series of rope-and-plank suspension bridges at Green Mountains, to the 24km **Border Trail**, which links the two sections of the park.

Walking trail guides are available from the **ranger stations** Binna Burra (☎ 5533 3584; Binna Burra; ☯ 1.30-3.30pm Mon-Fri, 9am-3.30pm Sat & Sun); Green Mountains (☎ 5544 0634; Green Mountains; ☯ 9-11am & 1-3.30pm Mon-Fri).

Binna Burra Mountain Lodge (☎ 1800 074 260, 5533 3622; www.binnaburralodge.com.au; Binna Burra Rd, Beechmont; unpowered/powered sites $20/27, on-site safari tents $40, d incl breakfast with/without bathroom

GOLD COAST

$300/240) is an excellent mountain retreat at the hub of the Binna Burra area and is surrounded by forest; it offers rustic log cabins and camp sites (rates are for two people) clustered around a central **restaurant** (mains $13-18; ☺ lunch & dinner) that has good views over the national park. Cabin tariffs include guided bushwalks, spotlighting and abseiling. There is a small shop and a tea house here, but self-caterers are best to bring their supplies up.

The famous **O'Reilly's Rainforest Guesthouse** (☎ 1800 688 722, 5544 0644; www.oreillys.com.au; Lamington National Park Rd; guesthouse s/d $125/200, units s/d $160/330) at Green Mountains is still run by the O'Reilly family and has been very stylishly redeveloped over the years. Tariffs include activities such as bushwalks, spotlighting walks and 4WD-bus trips. There's a plush **restaurant** (mains $25-40), or the more affordable **Gran O'Reilly's Bistro** (snacks $5-15; ☺ 7.30am-4pm), serving light meals.

There's a national-park camping ground close to O'Reilly's, and bush camping is permitted in several areas within the park, but only a limited number of permits (per person $4) are issued. Camping permits must be obtained in advance from the ranger at Green Mountains or by booking online.

The **Binna Burra bus service** (☎ 5533 3622; one way adult/child $22/11) operates a bus for guests, picking up from Coolangatta airport (1.30pm) and Nerang train station (2pm) daily. The trip takes about an hour from Nerang. Departures from Binna Burra are at 11.30am daily.

They also operate an **Adventure Day Tour** (per person $75), which picks up from Surfers Paradise Transit Centre at 8.45am and departs Binna Burra at 3.30pm. The price includes abseiling and guided walks, but if you just want the bus ride without the activities, it's $45 per person. Bookings for all of these services are essential.

Allstate Scenic Tours (☎ 3285 1777; return day-trip adult/child $55/35) runs a bus service between Brisbane and O'Reilly's from Sunday to Friday, leaving the Roma St Transit Centre at 9.30am and arriving back at the transit centre at around 5.45pm.

Mountain Coach Company (☎ 5524 4249; return day-trip adult/child/family $45/24/117) has a daily service from the Gold Coast to O'Reilly's

---

DETOUR

Drive about 1km south of Rathdowney and turn right onto the Boonah-Rathdowney Rd. After about 8km Upper Logan Rd veers off to the left and takes you another 12km or so south into **Mt Barney National Park**. This World Heritage Area is one of Queensland's largest areas of pristine vegetation, making it pure bliss for bushwalkers and climbers. It's fairly rugged, though, so experience is recommended for any significant walks through the park. There's a basic **camping ground** (per person $4) for bushwalkers; you'll need to purchase a permit from the **Boona Rangers Station** (☎ 5463 5041) before you get there.

You can still enjoy the park – without the strenuous exercise – at Yellow Pinch Reserve picnic area, which sits at the base of Mt Barney. Nearby, **Mt Barney Lodge** (☎ 5544 3233; www.mtbarneylodge.com.au; Upper Logan Rd; unpowered sites $16, d cabins with/without bathroom $110/75) has a series of picturesque homesteads and self-contained cabins, which make for a lovely base for incursions into the park. Rates are for two people.

Araucaria Ecotours (p96) runs a three-day tour of the region using Mt Barney Lodge as a base.

---

via Tamborine Mountain (one hour). If you want to use this service to stay overnight at O'Reilly's, the cost is $30 each way.

MT LINDESAY HIGHWAY

This road runs south from Brisbane, across the Great Dividing Range west of Lamington National Park, into New South Wales at Woodenbong. About 20km southwest of Tamborine Mountain, **Beaudesert** is a small cattle centre with a pioneer museum and **tourist information office** (☎ 5541 2740; cnr Brisbane & McKee Sts; ☺ 9am-4pm) and several motels and hotels.

West of Beaudesert is a part of the Great Dividing Range known as the **Scenic Rim**, the gateway to the Darling Downs. Heading south, the **Rathdowney Information Centre & Historical Museum** (☎ 5544 1222; ☺ 10.30am-2pm Tue, noon-5pm Thu, 1-4pm Fri, 9am-4pm Sat & Sun) is on the highway at Rathdowney.

Darling Downs

CONTENTS

DARLING DOWNS

HIGHLIGHTS

- Hunting down your favourite tipple and relaxing in the sun at the Granite Belt wineries around **Stanthorpe** (p157)

- Waking up with the wallabies at **Bunya Mountains National Park** (p168), a great place to camp among friendly, furry and feathered friends

- Bushwalking followed by a picnic among the rugged granite boulders of **Girraween National Park** (p158)

- Getting into the action at one of the many Darling Downs **festivals** (p161)

- Experiencing the old grandeur of the Downs with a stroll through the wonderful gardens of **Jimbour House** (p165) near Dalby

- Staying at a traditional homestead such as **Passchendaele** (p169) and taking part in life on a working property

Passchendaele ★ ★ Bunya Mountains National Park

★ Dalby

Stanthorpe ★
★ Girraween National Park

- www.qldsoutherndowns.org.au

West of the Great Dividing Range stretch the rolling plains and rural townships of the Darling Downs, some of the most fertile and productive agricultural land in Australia. Setting out from Sydney, English botanist Allan Cunningham first explored this region in 1827, describing it as the best piece of country he had ever seen.

Today the attractions are not only the tranquil rural setting and vast horizons of rich pastoral land; this region of Southeast Queensland is awash with hidden gems. You can explore the wonderful Girraween and Sundown National Parks with their dramatic landscape and excellent bushwalking routes or spend the day with a glass in hand at the scenic Granite Belt vineyards, Queensland's most promising wine-growing district.

The Downs was the first part of Queensland to be settled after the establishment of the Moreton Bay penal colony, and towns such as Warwick and Toowoomba are among the state's oldest. Almost every town in the region is full of old buildings and some have changed little since the 1950s. Scattered around Toowoomba are some interesting attractions, including the historic Jondaryan Woolshed Complex, the Dalby Saleyards and the impressive historical village at Miles.

To the north and west of Brisbane is the South Burnett region with the imposing mass of the Bunya Mountains National Park, where you can camp with the wallabies or discover walking trails which take you through rainforest and thick pine woods to breathtaking vistas over the Darling Downs' black soil plains.

Dangers & Annoyances

The roads through the Downs may seem peaceful and uncrowded, but remember that you're sharing the highway with two of Australia's most lethal inhabitants – the road train and the kangaroo. During one morning drive from Texas to Roma, we saw 35 freshly killed kangaroos and wallabies. If you have to drive at night, keep your speed well below 70km/h.

Getting There & Around

AIR

Qantas (☎ 13 13 13; www.qantas.com.au) flies from Brisbane to Roma.

BUS

Greyhound Australia (☎ 13 14 99; www.greyhound .com.au) has two major bus services that pass through the Darling Downs. The Brisbane–Longreach service runs along the Warrego Hwy via Toowoomba ($23, two hours), Dalby ($34, four hours), Miles ($41, 5½ hours) and Roma ($56, eight hours), while

its inland Brisbane to Adelaide and Brisbane to Melbourne services pass through Warwick ($40, four hours) and Stanthorpe ($50, 4½ hours) or Goondiwindi ($55, five hours), depending on the route.

Greyhound also has buses between Toowoomba and the Gold Coast ($33, three hours), and between Brisbane and Rockhampton (13 hours) via Toowoomba (two hours) and Miles (five hours). See p163 for more details of Greyhound services.

Crisps' Coaches (☎ 3236 5266; www.crisps.com.au) is the biggest local operator, with services from Brisbane to Warwick, Toowoomba, Goondiwindi, Stanthorpe and south to Tenterfield in New South Wales (NSW).

Brisbane Bus Lines (☎ 3355 3633; www.brisbane buslines.com.au) has daily services from Brisbane into the South Burnett region.

CAR & MOTORCYCLE

The major route through the Darling Downs is the Warrego Hwy, which runs west from Ipswich to Charleville. There's

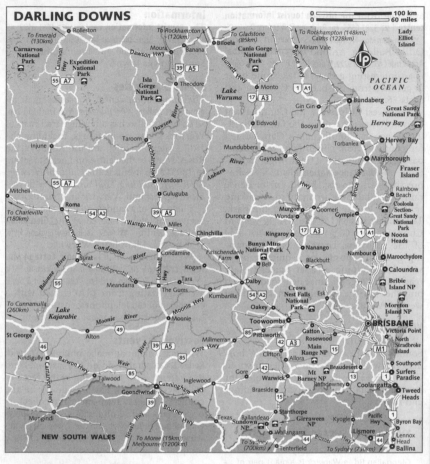

also the Cunningham Hwy, which runs southwest from Ipswich to Warwick and Goondiwindi.

The two main north–south routes in the Downs are the Leichhardt Hwy, which runs north from Goondiwindi to Rockhampton via Miles, and the Carnarvon Hwy, which runs north from Mungindi on the NSW border to Roma. Highway 17 runs inland between Brisbane and Rockhampton, passing through the South Burnett region.

The most scenic drives in this region pass through the Great Dividing Range, particularly around Stanthorpe and the Bunya Mountains. West of the mountains most of the highways are pretty dull.

TRAIN

The air-conditioned *Westlander* runs from Brisbane to Charleville on Tuesday and Thursday, returning on Wednesday and Friday, stopping in Ipswich (45 minutes), Toowoomba (four hours) and Roma (11 hours). The 777km journey from Brisbane to Charleville takes about 16 hours; there are connecting bus services from Charleville to Cunnamulla and Quilpie.

IPSWICH TO WARWICK

Virtually an outer suburb of Brisbane, Ipswich was established in 1827 as a convict settlement and has some fine old houses and public buildings, described in the excellent *Ipswich Heritage Trails* leaflets available from the **Ipswich tourist information centre** (☎ 3281 0555; cnr Brisbane St & D'Arcy Doyle Pl; ☉ 9am-4pm Mon-Fri, 10am-3pm Sat & Sun) in the Post Office Building. Around the corner, **Global Arts Link** (☎ 3813 9222; D'Arcy Doyle Pl; ☉ 10am-5pm) is an interesting gallery. It takes one hour to get here from Brisbane by Citytrain and costs $6.90.

Southwest of Ipswich, the Cunningham Hwy to Warwick crosses the Great Dividing Range at Cunningham's Gap, named for a botanist from London's Kew Gardens, passing through the 1100m-high mountains of **Main Range National Park**. This impressive park covers 184 sq km of dense rainforest and there are numerous walking trails that lead to lookouts over the park. The **rangers station** (☎ 4666 1133) is west of Cunningham's Gap on the southern side of the highway. There's a small camping ground opposite, or a quieter, more secluded camping area at Spicer's Gap, reached via a good, unsealed road, which branches off the Cunningham Hwy 5km west of Aratula.

WARWICK
☎ 07 / pop 12,011

Southwest of Brisbane, near the NSW border, Warwick is the second-oldest town in Queensland after Brisbane and is noted for its roses, dairy produce, historic buildings and rodeo.

THE FASTEST SHEARS IN THE WEST

On the corner of the Cunningham Hwy and Glengallan Rd in Warwick is a giant pair of blade shears atop a block of stone. This monument commemorates Jackie Howe, born on Canning Downs Station near Warwick and acclaimed as the greatest 'gun' (the best in the shed) shearer the country has ever seen. He holds the amazing record of having shorn 321 sheep with a set of hand shears in less than eight hours. Established in 1892, the record still stands today – it wasn't even beaten by shearers using machine-powered shears until 1950.

Jackie had a habit of ripping the sleeves off his shirts when he was working, and to this day the sleeveless blue singlets favoured by many Australian workers are known as 'Jackie Howes'.

Information

The **tourist information centre** (☎ 4661 3122; 49 Albion St; ☉ 9am-5pm Mon-Sat, 10am-3pm Sun) has plenty of material on the neighbouring South Downs towns.

Sights & Activities

The information centre houses a small **regional art gallery** (☉ 10am-4pm Mon-Fri, 10am-2pm Sat & Sun), and also has a heritage trail map of Warwick's historic buildings, including the 1917 Criterion Hotel and the Abbey of the Roses, south of the centre on Lock St, dating to 1893. Also useful is the *Cultural Heritage & Historic Building Trail* brochure, with scenic drives around Warwick and Stanthorpe.

The ruins of a sandstone homestead have been completely restored at the **Glengallan Heritage Centre** (☎ 4667 3866; New England Hwy; ☉ 10am-4pm) 15km from Warwick.

Well worth a visit is **Pringle Cottage Museum** (☎ 4661 2028; 81 Dragon St; adult/child $5/1; ☉ 10am-noon & 2-4pm Wed-Fri, 11am-4pm Sat & Sun), a cottage dating from 1870 stuffed with a collection of old telephones, costumes, photos and assorted historical contraptions.

Festivals & Events

Warwick's major annual event is the **Warwick Rodeo & Campdraft** held on the last weekend in October. Also interesting is the **Facetors' Guild Meeting** every Easter, said to be the country's biggest swap-meet for collectors of precious and semiprecious stones. **Jumpers and Jazz in July**, where the trees on Warwick's main street are knitted up in cosy jumpers, is another big event.

Sleeping

Abbey of the Roses (☎ 4661 9777; www.abbeyoftheroses.com; cnr Locke & Dragon Sts; d midweek/weekend $88/110) This beautiful old abbey is National Trust listed and has been converted into a stylish heritage retreat. The rooms are period furnished and there are lovely rose gardens and cloisters to wander around in, plus a very good restaurant that is open for dinner Thursday to Saturday.

Grafton Rose B&B (☎ 4667 0151; 134 Grafton St; d $120) This elegant old Queenslander has a lovely deck and garden to relax in. It's not terribly exciting, but it's an attractive restoration job and the rooms are pleasant.

Jackie Howe Motel (☎ 4661 2111; www.jackiehowemotel.com.au; cnr Palmerin & Victoria Sts; s/d $65/75)

This budget motel is a family-run business fairly close to the centre, but quiet nonetheless. It has some wheelchair-friendly units.

Eating

Bramble Patch Cafe (☎ 4661 9022; 8 Albion St; ☘ breakfast & lunch) A friendly café housed in a curious, dome-topped building serving good gourmet sandwiches for under $10 as well as a range of delicious preserves from its farm, Bramble Patch Berry Gardens, near Stanthorpe. There's also a pleasant outdoor area and a stack of magazines to flick through.

Mussels (☎ 4661 1525; Palmerin St; mains $13-22; ☘ breakfast, lunch & dinner) Monopolising the main street food options is this insanely popular steak and seafood joint where locals dig into hefty gourmet burgers (from $5.50) and value-pack fry ups.

Il Mulino (☎ 4661 7712; 73a Palmerin St; mains $9-18; ☘ dinner) This Italian restaurant is a decent choice if you want to escape an early roast dinner at the RSL club. All the usual favourites are adequately prepared.

Warwick's clubs are a good bet for lunch or dinner, but they close at 8pm. Try **Warwick RSL Club** (☎ 4661 1229; cnr Albion & King Sts; dishes $6-12) or the **Condamine Sports Club** (☎ 4661 1911; 131-3 Palmerin St) for cheap Aussie tucker.

Getting There & Away

The **Warwick Transit Centre** (☎ 4661 8333; 78 Grafton St) is near the Albion St corner. Warwick lies on the daily **Crisps' Coaches** (☎ 3236 5266; www .crisps.com.au) runs from Brisbane to Goondiwindi or Stanthorpe. Fares from Warwick are $33 to Brisbane (three hours), $16 to Stanthorpe (45 minutes) and $37 to Goondiwindi (2½ hours). There are also buses to Toowoomba ($20, 1½ hours). **Greyhound Australia** (☎ 13 14 99; www.greyhound.com.au) stops here on the inland Brisbane–Melbourne run ($32 from Brisbane, four hours).

QUEEN MARY FALLS NATIONAL PARK

The pretty Queen Mary Falls National Park is 43km southeast of Warwick near the NSW border. The park is centred on Spring Creek, which tumbles 40m into a rainforest gorge with several walking trails.

The privately run **Queen Mary Falls Caravan Park** (☎ 4664 7151; fax 4664 7122; Spring Creek Rd; unpowered/powered sites $16/18) is just across the road from the park. A rough, unsealed road continues north to Boonah, through

the southern reaches of the Main Range National Park.

STANTHORPE & BALLANDEAN

☎ 07 / pop 9600

The attractive highland town of Stanthorpe is most famous for being cold – it sits at an altitude of 915m and is one of the few places in the state that gets snow – and even celebrates its chilly climate with an annual **Brass Monkey Festival** every July.

The four-season climate makes Stanthorpe ideal for growing fruit and vegetables, including wine grapes, which flourish in the Granite Belt region just south of town around the village of Ballandean. There are at least 40 wineries within 20km of

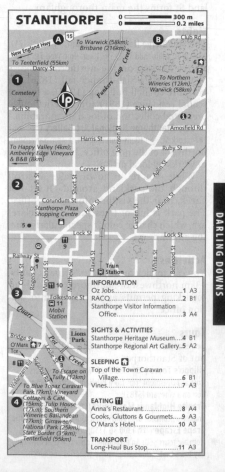

INFORMATION	
Oz Jobs...1 A3	
RACQ..2 B1	
Stanthorpe Visitor Information	
Office...3 A4	

SIGHTS & ACTIVITIES	
Stanthorpe Heritage Museum....4 B1	
Stanthorpe Regional Art Gallery..5 A2	

SLEEPING	
Top of the Town Caravan	
Village...6 B1	
Vines...7 A3	

EATING	
Anna's Restaurant......................8 A4	
Cooks, Gluttons & Gourmets....9 A3	
O'Mara's Hotel..........................10 A3	

TRANSPORT	
Long-Haul Bus Stop.................11 A3	

Stanthorpe – see the boxed text opposite – or pick up a list at the visitor information office.

There is plenty of fruit-picking work here from October to mid-June, if you don't mind the chilly mornings. **Oz Jobs** (☎ 468 13746; cnr Railway & Rogers Sts) can help you find placements on farms and vineyards.

Stanthorpe holds a popular rodeo in March and a huge **Apple & Grape Festival** in late February or early March, with street parades, sheep shearing and grape crushing.

Information & Orientation

Stanthorpe Visitor Information Office (☎ 4681 2057; Leslie St; ☺ 9am-3pm Mon, 8.30am-5pm Tue-Sat, 9am-4pm Sun) is just south of the creek. Maryland St forms the main thoroughfare.

Sights

The **Stanthorpe Heritage Museum** (☎ 4681 1711; 12 High St; adult/child $3/1; ☺ 10am-4pm Wed-Fri, 1-4pm Sat, 9am-1pm Sun), on the northern outskirts of town, has a slab-timber jail (1876), an old shire council building (1914), a former school residence (1891) and a meticulously presented collection of local memorabilia.

The **Stanthorpe Regional Art Gallery** (☎ 4681 1874; Lock St; ☺ 10am-4pm Mon-Fri, 1-4pm Sat & Sun), northwest of the post office, has exhibitions of works by local artists.

While you're in town, take a stroll through the parkland around Quart Pot Creek, near the visitor information office. The park is full of trees such as the claret ash, which change colour spectacularly during autumn.

Activities

You can fossick for topaz at Swiper's Gully, 13km northwest of Stanthorpe – ask about fossicking permits at the visitor information office.

Tours

Several companies run tours of the wineries out of Stanthorpe:

Filippo's Tours (☎ 4683 5126; www.filippostours .com.au) Overnight trips from Brisbane with accommodation on a vineyard ($185).

Granite Highlands Maxi Tours (☎ 4681 3969; www .maxitours.com.au) Offers individual tours out of Stanthorpe.

Grape Escape (☎ 1300 36 1150; www.grapeescape .com.au; tours $60) An established operator that runs full-day tours that include visiting five wineries and lunch.

A great alternative, especially if you have kids to entertain, is the Seed to Salad tour at **Giardino's** (Eagle's Produce; ☎ 4683 3351; www.eagles giardinocafe.com.au; adult/child $11/8) in Amiens, 15km from Stanthorpe. Tours run for about an hour and leave at 9am and 1.30pm. There is also a nice café at the farm.

Sleeping

BUDGET

Top of the Town Caravan Village (☎ 4681 4888; fax 4681 4222; 10 High St; powered sites $18, dm $20, cabins from $72; ☒ ☒) On the northern outskirts, this caravan park has had a recent upgrade but still happily caters to seasonal workers, who camp or stay in the bunkhouse. The owners run an information desk and can help to find work.

Blue Topaz Caravan Park (☎ 4683 5279; New England Hwy, Severnlea; powered sites $15, cabins $50) Pets are welcome at this popular camping spot, and there is a convenience store with fuel on site. Prices are for two people.

MIDRANGE & TOP END

The Stanthorpe Visitor Information Office has an extensive list of midrange and top-end accommodation.

Vineyard Cottages & Café (☎ 4684 1270; www.vine yard-cottages.com.au; New England Hwy; 2-person cottages midweek/weekend from $155/175, 4-person cottages from $225/265) This interesting place on the northern outskirts of Ballandean has four comfortable, attractive, heritage-style brick cottages with spas and private verandas overlooking several acres of English-style gardens. There is also an excellent **restaurant** (☺ lunch Sat & Sun, dinner Fri & Sat) in a converted wooden church that has a fine reputation for its fresh, seasonal menu.

Escape on Tully (☎ 4683 7000; www.escapeontully .com; 934 Mt Tully Rd; d midweek/weekend $90/140) This stylish cottage would make a great weekend retreat for a couple or group of friends. Everyone will enjoy the sunny north-facing deck (complete with bathtub!) and gorgeous views. Despite absolute privacy, it's only 10 minutes into town and the nearby wineries.

Happy Valley (☎ 4681 3250; www.happyvalley retreat.com; Glenlyon Dr; d midweek/weekend $120/150) An impressive resort 4km west of Stanthorpe (signposted off the Texas road), this fine complex offers modern homestead units or more secluded timber cabins, all with their own bathrooms and wood fires.

It stands on a bush property studded with granite outcrops, and has a tennis court, a restaurant and daily winery tours.

Amberley Edge Vineyard B&B (☎ 4683 6203; www .amberleyedge.com.au; 47 Clarke Lane; d midweek/weekend $125/195) If you want to stay at a vineyard, this charming place is a great option tucked into a private wing of the homestead. There are seriously lovely views of the grapes, which are best enjoyed with the Shiraz that the friendly hosts will happily arrange for you.

There are also half a dozen motels in town to choose from, including the **Vines** (☎ 4681 3844; www.thevinesmotel.com.au; 2 Wallan-garra Rd; d midweek/weekend $95/105; 🔀), a four-star choice south of the centre near Quart Pot Creek and next to a lovely park.

Eating

Cooks, Gluttons & Gourmets (☎ 4681 2377; 137a High St; mains $12-24; 🕑 dinner) This understated mod-Oz eatery has a creative menu and a warm, casual vibe, though there's nothing casual about the food preparation. A towering plate of Atlantic salmon and prawns comes served on handmade pappardelle, and the tea-smoked kangaroo fillet is tender and delicious. There's also a tempting dessert menu.

GRANITE BELT WINERIES

Everyone in the Granite Belt has an opinion on the tricky debate whether the area should be considered a cool- or a warm-climate region. However, what they do agree on is that this elevated plateau of the Great Dividing Range, with heights of up to 950m above sea level, has a wonderful climate for viticulture. This burgeoning cluster of vineyards constitutes Queensland's best known wine district, and it's set among some spectacular scenery – there are definitely worse places to sit and sip a glass of vino!

Grapes were first grown in the district in the 19th century, but the wine industry really took off during WWII when Italian immigrants were brought into the countryside to work on farms (at the time, Australia was at war with Italy). These forced emigrees flourished, and in recent years have been joined by professionals leaving the cities and planting acres of vines in their backyards. There are now some 40 wineries dotted around the New England Hwy between Cottonvale and Wallangarra.

Don't expect Hunter Valley–style enterprises though; all the wineries are boutique producers that sell their wines through their cellar doors and mail order. The area doesn't have a particular speciality, but Shiraz and Cabernet Sauvignon are becoming popular regional styles for red varieties, and Semillon, Verdelho and Chardonnay the best white varieties.

The following list includes just a few of the more highly regarded vineyards in the Granite Belt area. Robert Channon Wines has had exceptional success, and a visit to his vineyard is definitely recommended.

Heading south from Stanthorpe:

Kominos Wines (☎ 07-4683 4311; New England Hwy, Severnlea; 🕑 9am-5pm)
Lucas Estate (☎ 07-4683 6365; Donges Rd, Severnlea; 🕑 10am-5pm)
Mountview (☎ 07-4683 4316; Mt Stirling Rd, Glen Aplin; 🕑 9.30am-4.30pm Fri-Sun)
Felsberg Winery (☎ 07-4683 4332; Townsends Rd, Glen Aplin; 🕑 9am-5pm)
Bungawarra (☎ 07-4684 1128; Bents Rd, Ballandean; 🕑 10am-4.30pm)
Ballandean Estate (☎ 07-4684 1226; Sundown Rd, Ballandean; 🕑 9am-5pm)
Granite Ridge Wines (☎ 07-4684 1263; Sundown Rd, Ballandean; 🕑 9am-5pm)
Robinsons Family Vineyards (☎ 07-4684 1216; Curtin Rd, Ballandean; 🕑 10am-5pm)
Symphony Hill Wines (☎ 07-4684 1388; 2017 Eukey Rd, Ballandean; 🕑 10am-5pm)
Pyramids Road Wines (☎ 07-4684 5151; Pyramids Rd, Wyberba; 🕑 10am-4.30pm Sat & Sun)
Bald Mountain Winery (☎ 07-4684 3186; Hickling Lane, Wallangarra; 🕑 10am-5pm)

There are also several wineries north of Stanthorpe:

Robert Channon Wines (☎ 07-4683 3109; Bradley Lane, Stanthorpe; 🕑 10am-5pm Feb-Dec)
Boireann Wines (☎ 07-4683 2194; Donnellys Castle Rd, The Summit; 🕑 10am-4.30pm)
Summit Estate (☎ 07-4683 2011; 291 Granite Belt Dr, Thulimbah; 🕑 9am-5pm)
Heritage Estate (☎ 07-4685 2197; Granite Belt Dr, Cottonvale; 🕑 9am-5pm)

DARLING DOWNS

Anna's Restaurant (☎ 4681 1265; cnr Wallangarra Rd & O'Mara Tce; mains $9-17; ☾ dinner Mon-Sat) A family-run, Italian BYO restaurant set in a cosy Queenslander, Anna's is famous locally for its weekend buffets (adult/child $28/14) where you can gorge yourself on antipasto platters, hearty pasta and a vast array of veal, poultry and seafood dishes. If you forget it's all you can eat, and actually save room for dessert, the tiramisu and crème caramel slide down ever so well.

Tulip House (☎ 4684 1349; Bents Rd, Ballandean; mains $12-18; ☾ lunch Thu-Mon, dinner Fri & Sat) There's no windmill out the back, but this touch of the Netherlands countryside in Ballandean is the place for smooth Dutch coffee and a light meal.

O'Mara's Hotel (☎ 4681 1044; 45 Maryland St; dishes $7.50-16; ☾ lunch & dinner) This friendly little pub has an open fire and good, cheap meals.

Getting There & Around

Greyhound Australia (☎ 13 14 99; www.greyhound .com.au) and **Crisps' Coaches** (☎ 3236 5266; www .crisps.com.au) stop at the Mobil garage on the corner of Folkestone and Maryland Sts. There are buses to Warwick (45 minutes), Toowoomba (2¼ hours), Brisbane (4½ hours) and Tenterfield in NSW (1½ hours), where you can pick up the Kirklands bus to Byron Bay. Brisbane to Stanthorpe costs $39 (4½ hours).

For taxi tours of the Granite Belt wineries, try **Stanthorpe Taxi Service** (☎ 4681 1522).

GIRRAWEEN NATIONAL PARK

Wonderful Girraween National Park adjoins Bald Rock National Park over the border in NSW and features the same towering granite boulders surrounded by pristine forests. Wildlife is everywhere, and there are 17km of walking trails to take you to the top of some of the surreal granite outcrops. Shortest is the 3km walk and scramble up the 1080m Pyramids, while the granddaddy of Girraween walks is the 10.4km trek to the top of Mt Norman (1267m).

There are two good camping grounds in the park, which teem with wildlife and offer facilities such as drinking water, hot showers and BBQs. Access is via a paved road from Ballandean, 17km south of Stanthorpe on the New England Hwy.

The **visitors centre** (☎ 4684 5157; ☾ 1-3.30pm Mon-Fri & 9am-5pm Sat & Sun) accepts camping

---

THE AUTHOR'S CHOICE

An outdoor spa is a treat at the best of times; when you can enjoy the sunset over Girraween National Park and watch wallabies frolicking nearby, it's nothing short of indulgent. But relaxing in the bubbles under the stars is just one of the pleasures at **Girraween Environmental Lodge** (☎ 4684 5138; fax 4684 5148; Pyramids Rd; d $180, each additional person $45), 20 minutes from Stanthorpe. The private two-bedroom, self-contained cabins are ultra-comfy and tastefully decorated. You can cosy up to a DVD, although you will probably be spending more time outdoors, be it barbecueing on your deck or bushwalking in the national park. There's no restaurant at the lodge, but the charming managers have a range of gourmet frozen meals (homemade Thai green curry, lamb shanks) and the breakfast basket filled with fresh juice, eggs and cereals is more than generous. Don't miss the chance to taste at the nearby Granite Belt wineries, and bring a bottle of Robert Channon's rosé back to enjoy in the spa!

---

bookings; usual national park rates apply. Although winter nights here can be cold, it's hot work climbing the boulders, so take plenty of water when you hike.

If you aren't up for camping, there are several good places to stay on the access road from Ballandean. **Wisteria Cottage** (☎ 4684 5121; www.wisteriacottage.com.au; Pyramids Rd; cottages per adult/child $70/30) is a very friendly pottery and chocolate shop with three well appointed wooden cabins (sleeping up to six people) in the field behind, with wide verandas and cosy fireplaces. A huge breakfast is included as well as fresh bread.

Girraween Country Inn (☎ 4683 7109; fax 4683 7203; Eukey Rd; d incl breakfast from $110) is a two-storey, chalet-style guesthouse located on the northern edge of the park, with a restaurant downstairs and a great location. To get here, turn off the New England Hwy at Ballandean and follow Eukey Rd for 9km.

SUNDOWN NATIONAL PARK

On the Queensland–NSW border, about 80km southwest of Stanthorpe, Sundown National Park is dominated by the steep, spectacular gorges of the Severn River. There are several ruined mines in the park, but the rugged wilderness and plentiful wildlife are the main attractions. At the southern end of the park, the Broadwater camping ground can be reached in a conventional vehicle along a 4km gravel road. The northern section is only accessible by 4WD vehicles from Ballandean. For information and to book camping permits, contact the rangers at **Girraween National Park** (☎ 4684 5157).

GOONDIWINDI
☎ 07 / pop 4370
West of Warwick, on the NSW border, Goondiwindi (*gun*-doo-windy) is something of a one-horse town, the horse in question being Gunsynd, a remarkably successful racehorse.

Information & Orientation
The **municipal tourist office** (☎ 4671 2653; 4 McLean St; ⏰ 9am-5pm) is housed in the Goondiwindi–Waggamba Library complex opposite the museum. You can use the Internet here for $5 per hour.

The main thoroughfare, Marshall St, runs parallel to the MacIntyre River.

Sights & Activities
There's a memorial statue of the 'the Goondiwindi Grey', Gunsynd, in MacIntyre St, beside the bridge across the MacIntyre River. There's also a Gunsynd memorial lounge in the **Victoria Hotel** (cnr Marshall & Herbert Sts), a beautiful old country pub with broad verandas and an eccentric tower (ruined only slightly by the beer logo on top!).

The **Customs House Museum** (☎ 4671 3041; 1 MacIntyre St; ⏰ 10am-4pm Wed-Mon), with its gorgeous flower-filled garden, has a collection put together by the local historical society. There are also a couple of other interesting historical buildings in town; around the corner from the Customs House Museum, on Bowen St, the **Holy Trinity Church** has fine stained-glass windows, while 200m east **Martha's Cottage** is a dwelling constructed of bush timber and is more than 100 years old.

If you've been driving all day, the **Botanic Gardens & Western Woodlands** (St George Rd; ⏰ 7am-9.30pm), 3km from town, makes a tranquil spot to stretch your legs.

Goondiwindi means resting place for birds, and it's true, with more than 200 species identified in the area. There are a

number of good **bird-watching** sites in and around town. Pick up a route guide from the tourist office.

Sleeping & Eating
'Gundy' is an important staging post between NSW and Queensland, so there are plenty of motels, caravan parks and pubs with accommodation.

Country Comfort (☎ 4671 1855; 110 Marshall St; s/d $85/89; 🅿 🖭) The top place in town, this modern motel is just east of the junction with McLean St. Always busy, it has an above-average restaurant, the **Town House**, which serves up well-presented, fresh dishes.

Goondiwindi Motel (☎ 4671 1544; Old Cunningham Hwy; s/d $79/89; 🅿 🖭) At the back of town along the old highway, this friendly motel also has a decent restaurant, a real plus when there are so few options in town. However, it's within spitting distance of the trains that might occasionally rumble through on their way out west.

Gundy Backpackers (☎ 4671 0042; greatstay@ goondiwindibackpackers.com.au; 17 Albert St; dm/s/d $20/35/45; 🅿 🖳) Opposite the town swimming pool, this pleasant backpackers is owned and efficiently run by the energetic Peter Matthews, who teams with local farms to find work placements for travellers. There are plenty of jobs during cotton season, which runs from the end of November to February. If you aren't out in the fields, there's a cosy TV lounge with a small collection of books, a well-equipped kitchen and a big backyard.

Goondiwindi Tourist Park (☎ 4671 2566; goondi winditouristpark@bigpond.com; Hungerford St; unpowered/powered sites $17/21, cabins $45-75; 🖭) This spacious caravan park is a nice place to stop over, with incredibly clean facilities and a shady camping ground by the billabong. On Sunday morning everyone gets out of bed for a huge pancake brekkie. Prices are for two people.

Goondiwindi RSL Memorial Club (☎ 4671 1269; dishes from $8) If you're watching the pennies, this club is good for lunch and dinner. On Friday night, get down with the locals and demolish a roast for around $8.

Getting There & Away
Brisbane–Melbourne and Brisbane–Adelaide buses stop at the BP Bridge Garage, 1km east of town on the Cunningham Hwy.

WEST OF GOONDIWINDI

At the junction of the Carnarvon, Moonie and Balonne Hwys, **St George** is 200km west of Goondiwindi. It's at the centre of a major cotton-growing district, and has a petrol station, two motels and a caravan park. From here it's another long and lonely 290km west to Cunnamulla, which is well and truly in the outback (see p433 for details of this area).

TOOWOOMBA

☎ 07 / pop 197,555

On the edge of the Great Dividing Range and the Darling Downs, 138km inland from Brisbane, Toowoomba is the largest town in the region. It has a commanding location perched 700m above sea level on the crest of the Great Dividing Range. There are great views from the parks and gardens that fringe the eastern side of town, earning Toowoomba the nickname 'Garden City'. It's a pleasant place to stop for a few days and the centre is graced by some stately old buildings.

Orientation & Information

The heart of town is loosely centred on Ruthven St (part of the north–south New England Hwy) 1km north of its junction with James St (part of the east–west Warrego Hwy).

American Express (☎ 4632 4522; 172 Margaret St)
City Info (476 Ruthven St; ☺ 10am-4pm Tue-Fri, 10am-2pm Sat)

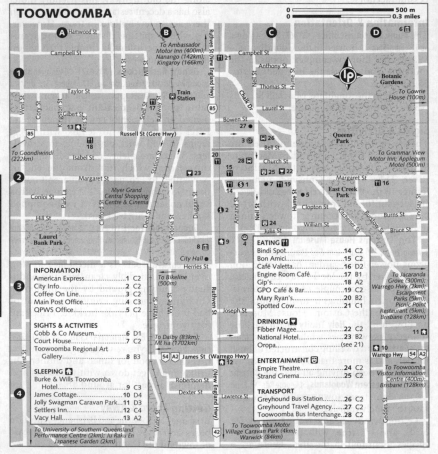

TOOWOOMBA

INFORMATION
American Express................1 C2
City Info............................2 C2
Coffee On Line...................3 C2
Main Post Office.................4 C2
QPWS Office.....................5 C2

SIGHTS & ACTIVITIES
Cobb & Co Museum............6 D1
Court House.......................7 C2
Toowoomba Regional Art
Gallery...........................8 B3

SLEEPING
Burke & Wills Toowoomba
Hotel.............................9 C3
James Cottage...................10 D4
Jolly Swagman Caravan Park...11 D3
Settlers Inn.......................12 C4
Vacy Hall........................13 A2

EATING
Bindi Spot........................14 C2
Bon Amici........................15 C2
Café Valetta.....................16 D2
Engine Room Café.............17 B1
Gip's..............................18 A2
GPO Café & Bar...............19 C2
Mary Ryan's....................20 B2
Spotted Cow....................21 C1

DRINKING
Fibber Magee...................22 C2
National Hotel..................23 B2
Oropa..........................(see 21)

ENTERTAINMENT
Empire Theatre.................24 C2
Strand Cinema.................25 C2

TRANSPORT
Greyhound Bus Station........26 C2
Greyhound Travel Agency....27 C2
Toowoomba Bus Interchange..28 C2

Coffee On Line (☎ 4639 4686; 12 Russell St; per 30 min $6.60; ⏱ 8.30am-8pm Mon-Fri, 8.30am-7pm Sat, 10am-7pm Sun) Lots of terminals and fast connection.

Main Post Office (66 Annand St) One block east of Ruthven St.

QPWS (☎ 4639 4599; 158 Hume St; ⏱ 8.30am-5pm Mon-Fri)

Toowoomba Visitor Information Centre (☎ 4639 3797; www.toowoomba.qld.gov.au; 86 James St; ⏱ 9am-5pm) Located southeast of the centre, at the junction with Kitchener St. The staff are thorough and efficient.

Sights

In spite of creeping development, there are some wonderful old buildings in the centre. The visitor information centre publishes a superb series of *A Walk Through History* brochures, which cover the different estates that grew together to form the town. Two structures that you can't miss are the splendid white sandstone **post office** and **courthouse** on Margaret St, which date from the 1870s.

Toowoomba's **Queens Park Gardens**, in the northeastern corner of Queens Park, are pleasant for a stroll, particularly in autumn, when the changing leaves provide a real contrast to the green eucalypts of the coastal plain. There are lawns, rose gardens and shady avenues of old bunya pines.

Laurel Bank Park (cnr Herries & West Sts) has a scented garden for the visually impaired.

Immediately north of Queens Park Gardens is the ever-expanding **Cobb & Co Museum** (☎ 4639 1971; 27 Lindsay St; adult/child $8/4; ⏱ 10am-4pm) with some evocative displays of life in the horse-drawn age, including carriages and buggies, mail coaches, bullock wagons and sulkies. There's also a café.

The **Toowoomba Regional Art Gallery** (☎ 4688 6652; 531 Ruthven St; admission free; ⏱ 10am-4pm Tue-Sat,

1-4pm Sun) is small but beautifully designed. It houses three permanent micro collections (including examples of colonial Australian painting, European and Asian painting and some porcelain and furniture), plus frequently changing temporary exhibitions.

The **Ju Raku En Japanese Garden** (☎ 4631 2627; West St; ⏱ 7am-dusk) is a beautiful spot for picnicking, with 3km of walking trails around a lake, waterfalls and streams. It's several kilometres south of the centre at the University of Southern Queensland in West St.

Toowoomba's other great parks are the **escarpment parks** strung along the eastern edge of the plateau. The seven separate bushland areas – Jubilee, Redwood, Picnic Point, Table Top, McKnight, Duggan and Glen Lomond – offer great views and a variety of walking trails. Picnic Point, just south of the Warrego Hwy, is the most accessible, while Table Top, reached by a 2km dirt track, offers the best views. The visitor information centre has two free maps, *Toowoomba Pathways* and *Escarpment Bushwalks*.

All the gardens are a long haul from the centre, so a car or bicycle is the best way to go. City bus Nos 2 and 4 pass along MacKenzie St, a few blocks west of the parks.

Festivals & Events

Toowoomba's **Carnival of Flowers** is a colourful celebration of spring held over the last week in September. It includes floral displays, a grand parade and exhibition gardens (call ☎ 4638 7143 for details). More than 30,000 people gather each Easter for the **Australian Gospel Music Festival** (www.agmf.com.au), which runs the gamut from country to heavy metal. In early September, the **Ag Show** is a three-day agricultural and horticultural festival.

TOP FIVE DARLING DOWNS FESTIVALS

Watch the Darling Downs come to life at one of these local festivals:

Australian Gospel Music Festival (Toowoomba; Easter) No drugs, no alcohol, but three days of Christian music to rock to.

B&S Ball (Meandarra, Nindigully & Goondiwindi) Bachelors and spinsters, a marquee in a paddock, and a whole heap of XXXX. Held at various times of the year.

Chinchilla Melon Festival (Chinchilla; February – even years) Melon skiing is not as easy as it looks, nor is growing an 87kg watermelon!

Easter in the Country (Roma; Easter) Goat races, rodeos, country music and sausage sizzles galore, Roma puts on a party that will have those boots stompin' all weekend long.

Kingaroy Peanut Festival (Kingaroy; September) From nummy spitting to the Australian peanut thrasher pull championships, you can go absolutely nuts in Kingaroy.

DARLING DOWNS

Sleeping

Toowoomba's accommodation can fill surprisingly fast and it's best to book ahead, especially during festivals.

BUDGET

Settlers Inn (☎ 4632 3634; cnr James & Ruthven Sts; s/d/tr $30/40/45) At the time of writing this busy motel was beginning to style itself as a backpackers place. The accommodation is plain and the service a touch abrupt, but it's a cheap and clean option.

There are lots of caravan parks here, but none in the city centre.

Jolly Swagman Caravan Park (☎ 4632 8735; 47 Kitchener St; unpowered/powered sites $15/17, on-site vans $35, cabins $57, units $65-70) This place is closest to the centre and offers clean facilities in a quiet location with award-winning gardens and a nice undercover BBQ spot.

Toowoomba Motor Village Caravan Park (☎ 4635 8186; fax 4636 1825; 821 Ruthven St; powered sites $20, on-site vans $32, cabins & units $50-70) This excellent, modern park is further out, but better equipped. It has terrific views.

MIDRANGE & TOP END

Vacy Hall (☎ 4639 2055; www.vaceyhall.com.au; 135 Russell St; d $100-190) Just uphill from the town centre this is a magnificent 1880s mansion that offers heritage-style accommodation of the highest standard – it's like stepping back into another era. All rooms are decorated in period style and the pricier rooms have bathrooms and verandas. The extensive grounds are well worth a stroll.

James Cottage (☎ 4637 8377; www.jamescottage.com;128 James St; s/d $95/135) More like visiting a friends' well restored home than bedding down in a hotel, this elegant B&B features 11ft pressed-metal ceilings and a wonderful leadlight door. The experienced hosts can make dinner on request, or it's only a short walk into town.

Ambassador Motor Inn (☎ 4637 6800; 200 Ruthven St; s/d $100/110) Up a notch from the run of the mill highway motel, this bustling four-star option has successfully transformed its comfortable rooms into well-appointed suites that attract travellers and business people alike.

Jacaranda Grove (☎ 4635 8394; 92 Tourist Rd; s/d $110/190; 🖭) Wonderfully luxurious, though rather twee, this B&B is heavy on home-made goodies, from the natural Darling Downs toiletry products to the chocolate on your pillow. The garden is delightful (game of croquet anyone?).

Burke & Wills Toowoomba Hotel (☎ 4632 2433; fax 4639 2002; 554 Ruthven St; d $99-155; 🖭) Situated in the centre of town, this is a Mercure-owned five-storey hotel with 90 modern rooms. The hotel has several bars and an upmarket conservatory restaurant.

There are two more upmarket options opposite the historic Toowoomba Grammar School on the eastern outskirts of town. **Grammar View Motor Inn** (☎ 4638 3366; 39 Margaret St; s/d $90/100) and **Applegum Motel** (☎ 4632 2088; fax 4639 1334; 41 Margaret St; s/d $90/100) are no-nonsense business motels with a licensed restaurant.

Eating

For budget eating there's a food court on the 1st floor of Myer Grand Central shopping centre at the western end of Margaret St, with the usual fast-food outlets. Otherwise, Margaret St has the greatest concentration of restaurants and cafés.

GPO Café & Bar (☎ 4659 9240; 1/140 Margaret St; mains $12-25; ☙ breakfast & lunch daily, dinner Tue-Sat) Slick and modern with a stainless-steel bar and airy dining room, GPO's surrounds reflect the kind of food served up, big on flavour and very inner city. Corn, crab and chilli chowder comes with a polenta muffin, or try a gourmet burger. A casual coffee in the sun is a nice way to spend a morning in Toowoomba.

Spotted Cow (☎ 4632 4393; cnr Ruthven & Campbell Sts; mains $10-16; ☙ breakfast Sat & Sun, lunch & dinner daily) This Toowoomba institution is the place to come for upmarket pub grub served in the cosy dining room of a nicely restored hotel. Famous for its steaks, we'll be awfully impressed if you get through a 700g Kimberley Red T-bone! There's a fantastic wine list of Aussie labels and warm country service.

Picnic Point Restaurant (☎ 4631 5101; mains $13-27; ☙ lunch Tue-Sun, dinner Tue-Sat) With top-notch cuisine and even better views, this smart place by the Picnic Point lookout is a popular venue for big Toowoomba weddings. The menu walks a well-trodden Euro-Asian path, but does it with quite a bit of style.

Gip's (☎ 4638 3588; 120 Russell St; mains $20-30; ☙ lunch & dinner Mon-Sat) The other top-end choice here is this sophisticated place housed in the billiard room of beautiful old Clifford House, which was owned by a mayor of Toowoomba in the late 19th century (the restaurant is named after his Jack Russell dog!). To match the surroundings, the adventurous menu includes treats such as pasta with Moreton Bay bugs and asparagus.

Bon Amici (☎ 4632 4533; 191 Margaret St; light meals $4-10; ✆ 8am-late) For a stiff drink or a good coffee, join Toowoomba's culture-vultures at this sophisticated, red-walled café for delectable cakes. There's often live music or poetry in the evenings and jazz every Sunday between 2.30pm and 5.30pm.

Bindi Spot (☎ 4638 0044; 164 Margaret St; mains $12.50-18; ✆ lunch & dinner) A popular Indian joint with colourful curries, smiling staff and an array of dependably good dishes as well as some tasty standouts such as salmon steak served with pomegranate chutney and mango salsa. As the staff are prone to saying at this place, get it India.

Also recommended:

Café Valetta (☎ 4632 0332; 96 Margaret St; mains $10-20; ✆ breakfast & lunch daily, dinner Fri & Sat) A gorgeous sunny courtyard, a bubbling fountain and chocolate fondue for two.

Engine Room Café (☎ 4637 8444; 1 Railway St; mains $6-12; ✆ 7am-5pm Tue-Sun) A relaxed, artsy vibe and special homemade ice-cream.

Mary Ryan's (☎ 4632 0800; 400 Ruthven St; ✆ 7.30am-5.30pm Mon-Fri, 8am-4pm Sat, 10am-4pm Sun) It may be a chain, but you can't beat a books, music and coffee combo.

Drinking

Oropa (Spotted Cow; ☎ 4632 4393; cnr Ruthven & Campbell Sts) A European beer café is a rarity in regional Queensland, and to see the locals exchanging XXXX Gold for a Leffe Blond is a rare experience not to be missed. Soak up your favourite brew with a 1kg pot of mussels and a pile of *frites*.

Fibber Magee (☎ 4639 2702; 153 Margaret St) If you fancy a beer without the noise, this agreeable, Irish-themed pub is popular and central, and there's a garden out the back.

National Hotel (☎ 4639 2706; 59 Russell St) This lovely old hotel has been given an Art Deco rehash with slick tiles, chandeliers, mood lighting and couches. An interesting addition is the Manly Sea Eagles rugby league team memorabilia plastered on the walls, no doubt saving the owner, a former league player, space at home!

Entertainment

Toowoomba's *Chronicle* newspaper has an entertainment section on Thursday, or pick up a copy of the *Time Out* brochure from the visitor information centre.

Strand Cinema (☎ 4639 3861; cnr Margaret & Neil Sts) and **Grand Central** (☎ 4638 0879; Myer Centre) screen predictable, mainstream movies.

For something a bit more highbrow, the stylishly restored **Empire Theatre** (☎ 1300 655 299; 56 Neil St) has regular concerts and cabaret.

From theatre to opera, there's generally a colourful programme of events running at the **University of Southern Queensland Performance Centre** (☎ 4631 1111; West St), be it student artists or high-profile national performers.

Getting There & Away

BUS

Greyhound Australia (☎ 13 14 99; www.greyhound .com.au; 28-30 Neil St) has numerous daily services from Toowoomba to Brisbane and the Gold Coast. It also has regular services west along the Warrego Hwy to Dalby (1½ hours), Chinchilla (2½ hours), Roma (3½ hours) and Charleville (11 hours).

Greyhound also acts as the local agent for several other local companies. **Crisps' Coaches** (☎ 07-3236 5266; www.crisps.com.au) runs to Warwick twice daily ($16, 1½ hours, once a day Saturday), with connections on to Stanthorpe, Tenterfield, Goondiwindi and Moree. **Kynoch Coaches** (☎ 4639 1639) runs to St George ($57, five hours, daily except Tuesday and Saturday), Cunnamulla ($85, nine hours, Sunday, Wednesday and Friday) and Lightning Ridge ($85, 8½ hours, Monday and Thursday). **Suncoast Pacific** (☎ 07-5449 9966; www.suncoastpacific.com .au) runs to the Sunshine Coast on Friday and Sunday (about four hours). Tickets for all buses can be bought from the **Greyhound travel agency** (☎ 4690 9888; 1 Russell St).

TRAIN

You can get here on the *Westlander,* which runs between Brisbane and Charleville twice a week. The seat-only fare from Brisbane to Toowoomba is $27.50. The attractive old train station is northeast of the town centre, just off Russell St, and has a **ticket office** (☎ 4631 3381; ✆ 9am-3.45pm Mon-Fri).

Getting Around

Sunbus services depart from the Toowoomba bus interchange on Neil St. There's

---

DETOUR

If you want to get a feel for the rural side of this region, drive south from Toowoomba to the Granite Belt on the New England Hwy and turn right at the Cambooya turnoff. **Cambooya** is real grain and crop country, with giant silos and acres and acres of the Darling Downs' most productive farming land. Head south from Cambooya towards **Nobby**, home of the 100-year-old Rudd's Pub stocked with photos and memorabilia of author Arthur Hoey David, who wrote *On Our Selection* and the Dad and Dave stories under the pen name Steele Rudd. Continue south towards **Clifton** where locals are proud of their graceful old train station, which you may recognise from Australian films such as the *The Thorn Birds*. From Clifton turn east back onto the highway.

---

an information booth in the terminal where you can find out which bus will take you where.

Bikeline (☎ 4638 2242; 13 Railway St; per 8hr $26) hires out bikes with locks and helmets.

TOOWOOMBA TO NANANGO

The route north along the New England Hwy travels the ridges of the Great Dividing Range, passing through a series of small villages.

The pretty little township of **Crow's Nest** is worth a stop for the **Crow's Nest Falls National Park**, an impressive waterfall in an area of eucalypt forest punctuated by craggy, granite outcrops. The park is about 6km east of town and there's a **rangers station** (☎ 4698 1296; ⏱ 3.30-4pm Mon-Fri) at the park entrance. For accommodation there's the **Crows Nest Caravan Park** (☎ 4698 1269; New England Hwy) and **Crows Nest Motel** (☎ 4698 1399; New England Hwy).

Beyond Crow's Nest the road continues 96km north to **Nanango**, entering the region of South Burnett (see p167 for details).

TOOWOOMBA TO MILES
Jondaryan Woolshed Complex
Built in 1859, the huge **Jondaryan Woolshed Complex** (☎ 4692 2229; www.jondaryanwoolshed.com; Evanslea Rd; adult/child self-guided $9/5, guided $13/8; ⏱ 9am-4pm, tours 1pm Wed-Fri, 10.30am & 1pm Sat, Sun & school holidays), 45km northwest of Toowoomba, played a pivotal role in the his-

tory of the Australian Labor Party. It was here in 1890 that the first of the legendary shearers' strikes began. See p22 for more information.

Today the woolshed is the centrepiece of a large tourist complex with an interesting collection of rustic old buildings and blacksmithing and shearing demonstrations on weekends. It also has period displays and antique farm and industrial machinery, including a mighty, steam-driven 'roadburner', which applied the first tarmac to many of Australia's roads.

There are several rustic accommodation choices here, all organised through the Woolshed reception. At the Woolshed complex, the **shearers quarters** (adult/child $12/6) are basic rooms around an open-sided communal cooking and dining shelter with sawdust-covered floors. They score top marks for atmosphere, and there are a few comforts such as hot showers and toilets. You can also **camp** (up to 4 people $10) or stay in one of the **safari tents** ($32). You need to bring your own linen for all these options.

Jondaryan hosts a number of annual events, including an **Australian Heritage Festival** over nine days in late August and early September, a **New Year's Eve bush-dance**, an **Australia Day** celebration, and a **Working Draught Horse Expo** in June.

Dalby
☎ 07 / pop 9731
Dalby is a relaxed rural town in the centre of Queensland's richest grain-growing region. The huge Supastock Feeds factory sets the character for the town, but there are a few tourist sights that the staff at the **tourist office** (☎ 4662 1066; cnr Drayton & Condamine Sts; ⏱ 9am-4.30pm Mon-Sat, 9.30am-2pm Sun) will be glad to tell you about.

Pioneer Park Museum (☎ 4662 4760; 3 Black St; adult/child $5/1; ⏱ 8am-5pm), signposted off the Warrego Hwy west of the centre, has a collection of old buildings and farm machinery. The livestock sales at the **Dalby Saleyards** (☎ 4662 2125; Yumborra Rd) are quite a spectacle, especially the cattle and pig sales on Wednesday from 7.30am. The lamb and sheep sales from 10.30am on Monday are tamer. The **Cactoblastis Cairn**, beside the creek on Marble St, is a monument to the tiny moth that saved the Downs from an infestation of Prickly Pear in the 1920s and '30s.

DARLING DOWNS

About 27km from Dalby is grand **Jimbour House** (www.jimbour.com; Jimbour Station Rd), built in 1875 (the explorer Leichhardt stayed here before setting out on his epic trek) and a superb reminder of the early pastoral industry of the Darling Downs. While it is a private residence, you can stroll through the expansive grounds, which feature a mix of formal rose gardens, tropical plants, citrus orchards and colourful flower beds that bloom all year. The **café** (☎ 4663 6221; ⏰ 10am-4.30pm) is a great spot for a cold drink or some wine tasting, with its lovely views across the black-soil plains. It also does interesting dishes such as toasted olive bread with homemade relish and Kingaroy camembert ($9).

Off the main highway, the modern **Dalby Midtown Motor Inn** (☎ 4662 6400; 60 Condamine St; d from $75; 🖳 🖭) motel has well-appointed rooms and very friendly hosts. The selec-

tion of free DVDs at the front desk is an added bonus.

With lots of shady sites on the banks of Myall Creek, **Myall Creek Caravan Park** (☎ 4662 4793; 32 Myall St; powered sites $18, cabins $50-70) is a short walk from town.

The cheerful Phoenix bistro at **Russell Tavern** (☎ 4662 2122; 1 Cunningham St; mains $10-20; ⏰ lunch daily, dinner Mon-Sat) is a nice place to have an evening meal where Aussie standards such as big steaks and decent seafood are rolled out.

Dalby RSL (☎ 4662 2309; 69 Drayton St; dishes $6-10) is hugely popular for its Sunday night roast, and you can't beat it for a cheap meal with absolutely no atmosphere.

MILES
☎ 07 / pop 1200

This small rural centre at the intersection of the Warrego and Leichhardt Hwys is

---

ANDREW MCGAHAN *David Kramer*

It seems strange recommending the novels of Andrew McGahan in a guidebook, considering this writer, hailed as the 'award-winning purveyor of Australian dirty realism', has such a knack for describing places and characters likely to be avoided by all but the most curious traveller.

All four of his books are predominantly set in his childhood home of Queensland, yet he isn't interested in its glittery façade: the Gold Coast sand and top-end resorts. His third novel, *Last Drinks*, depicts a Brisbane inhabited by dodgy cops and dodgier politicians. A city where the electricity might short because someone has been found wired naked to a power substation panel by his arms and legs.

McGahan's first novel, *Praise*, which won him the prestigious Australian/Vogel award in 1992, is set in a grotty Brisbane boarding house packed to the brim with rowdy, ageing Chinese workers. The house sets the stage for his protagonist's romance with an eczema-riddled, drug-guzzling nymphomaniac.

As far as Queensland's outback and farmland is concerned, to McGahan it is home to gun-collecting hermits who cultivate their own pot and eccentric estate owners who self-publish racially charged manifestos. In *1988*, McGahan's alter ego, Gordon, retreats to an isolated weather station and finds the untouched national park gloomy and maddening, its mangroves teaming with predators and its locals condescending and cold.

But you'd be wrong to think McGahan despises the Sunshine State. The fact that it's the setting for his books is a telling sign of his affection. He may paint a harsh portrait, but it's only to lift the veil, revealing the state's human side. His most recent work, *The White Earth*, explores how a young white boy on the verge of inheriting his uncle's farm in the Darling Downs relates to a region he is so new to, yet feels such a spiritual bond with.

Brisbane has paid tribute to the writer by including him on its Albert St literary trail. 'It was almost midnight and there it was', begins McGahans' plaque, an excerpt from *1988*. 'The glow in the sky. Orange streetlights. Outlying suburbs. It was beautiful. The highway turned onto the six-lane arterial. We came in through Oxley and Annerley, flowing with the traffic. Then the city high rises were in view, alight, multicoloured. Brisbane. It was impossibly beautiful.'

If you like McGahan's work, you'll probably also enjoy young journalist Brendan Shannahan's new book, *The Secret Life of the Gold Coast*, which gives a brutal introduction to schoolies week among other Gold Coast chaos.

DARLING DOWNS

known as 'The Crossroads of the Golden West' and was established by the eccentric Prussian explorer Ludwig Leichhardt on his 31st birthday on 23 October 1844. Disappointingly, the town was named for a local politician, rather than because it was miles from anywhere!

On the main road is **Dogwood Crossing** (☎ 4627 2455; ⏱ 8.30am-5pm Mon-Fri, 9am-4pm Sat & Sun), a $1.6 million community project that combines visual arts, social history and literature into a museum, gallery, library and multimedia resource centre. It's a very slick venture, and certainly worth stopping by for an insight not only into the colourful tales of the Downs, but also to see how a small town was born, grew up and prospered. There's an information centre in the complex with the same opening hours.

At the eastern end of town is the excellent **Miles Historical Village** (☎ 4627 1492; Murilla St; adult/child/family $10/2/20; ⏱ 8am-5pm). This is one of the best historical villages in the state and is well worth a visit. The main building houses a collection of glass cabinets crammed with all sorts of bits and pieces, from rocks and gems to tie stretchers and silk-screen printers. There are also numerous historic shop settings, including a bootmaker, a saddlery, a general store and a bank.

In 1942, the Brisbane Line was a last-ditch line of defence against the advancing Japanese. **Possum Park** (☎ 4627 1651; Leichhardt Hwy; s/d $55/$60), or RAAF Kowguran Central Reserve Explosive Store as it was called during WWII, is a living reminder of Australia's wartime activities in the region and an opportunity to sleep in one of the refurbished underground bunkers that used to house thousands of tonnes of bombs and munitions. There's also accommodation in well-restored train carriages from the 1950s. Possum Park is 20km north of Miles.

There are several caravan parks and motels in town including the well looked-after **Crossroads Caravan Park** (☎ /fax 4627 2165; 82 Murilla St; unpowered/powered sites $14/17, cabins from $50), right opposite the Historical Village, and the **Golden West Motor Inn** (☎ 4627 1688; fax 4627 1407; 50 Murilla St; s/d $65/75), the most central of the motels. Camping prices for Crossroads are for two people.

The Leichhardt Hwy runs north from Miles all the way to Rockhampton. If you're heading this way, see p249.

ROMA
☎ 07 / pop 6440

An early Queensland settlement, and now the centre of a sheep and cattle-raising district, Roma also has some curious small industries. There's enough oil in the area to support a small refinery, which produces just enough petroleum for local use. The gas deposits are larger, and Roma contributes to Brisbane's supply through a 450km pipeline.

Information
The **visitor information centre** (☎ 1800 222 399; Warrego Hwy; ⏱ 9am-5pm) is located in the Big Rig complex.

Sights & Activities
Tourist attention is focused on the **Big Rig complex** (☎ 4622 4355; www.thebigrig.com; Warrego Hwy; adult/child $14/9, combined entry & night show $25/15; ⏱ 9am-5pm, night show 7pm), a museum of oil and gas exploration centred on the old, steam-operated oil rig to the east of town. Unfortunately, it's not as big as most people would expect. As well as displays on the history of oil exploration, there is a nightly sound and light show at 7pm with plenty of gas-powered pyrotechnics.

Roma is a major centre for livestock sales, and if you want to see how up to 12,000 head of cattle are sold in one morning, you can watch the farmers (and animals) in action every week at the **Roma Bungil Saleyards** (☎ 4622 1201; ⏱ from 9am Tue, from 8am Thu), Australia's largest cattle-selling centre.

The **Bottle Tree Bush Tours** (☎ 4622 1525; adult/child $25/14) is a 1½-hour town tour which leaves at 2pm on Monday, Wednesday, Friday and Saturday.

Roma's major festival is **Easter in the Country**, which includes a rodeo, markets, horse races, parades, bush dances and country music held over the Easter weekend.

Sleeping & Eating
Roma has several caravan parks, and a few motels that mainly cater to sales reps.

Overlander Homestead Motel (☎ 4622 3555; fax 4622 2805; Warrego Hwy; d from $80) Easily the best motel is this colonial-style place on the eastern outskirts of town, with comfortable rooms and an above-average, licensed steak restaurant that is openly nightly.

Auburn B&B (☎ 4622 2295; 146a Northern Rd; s/d $80/105) When there are drab motels on every corner, this relaxed guesthouse opposite the park makes a fine change with a friendly host. The hearty home cooking is an added plus; book ahead if you plan to eat in.

Roma Big Rig Van Park (☎ /fax 4622 2538; 4 Mc-Dowall St; unpowered/powered sites $15/18, cabins $45-70) Just down the road from the Big Rig, this is a quiet park facing the river. Prices are for two people.

Bogarts Coffee Shop (☎ 4622 5666; 37 Hawthorne St; mains $6-12; ☯ 9.30am-8.30pm) Tucked away at the back of Cinema Roma, this is an oasis for the caffeine addicted, with cheerful staff who serve unpretentious food on outside tables, or in the denlike lounge.

Golden Dragon Restaurant (☎ 4622 1717; 60 Mc-Dowall St; mains from $8; ☯ lunch Mon-Sat, dinner daily) If you've had your fill of pub grub, try this licensed Chinese restaurant opposite the post office; there are no surprises on the extensive menu.

Bakearoma (☎ 4622 4395; 63 McDowall St; snacks from $4; ☯ from 7am) This popular bakery and café is good for breakfast, with lots of pastries and cakes.

Entertainment
Cinema Roma (☎ 4622 5666; 37 Hawthorne St) This small cinema alternates between several mainstream releases every day. Tickets are $7.70 on budget Wednesday.

Getting There & Away
Qantas has flights between Roma and Brisbane ($192). **Greyhound Australia** (☎ 13 14 99; www.greyhound.com.au) has daily buses through Roma on the Brisbane–Mt Isa run; buses stop at **Kookas Travel** (☎ 4622 1333; Bowen St). The fare from Brisbane is $56 (eight hours).

The *Westlander* train passes through twice weekly on its way from Brisbane to Charleville. From Roma to Brisbane is 11 hours (economy seat/sleeper $65/118).

ROMA TO CHARLEVILLE
About 40km past Roma, **Muckadilla** is just a service station, a train station and the **Muckadilla Hotel-Motel** (☎ 4626 8318; Warrego Hwy; s/d $55/70), where you can get a meal or a room.

On the Maranoa River, about 50km further west, **Mitchell** is a relaxed commercial centre with a huge windmill, an artesian well spa and a couple of pubs and supermarkets. There is a small **tourist information office** (☎ 1800 6482 4355) with brochures on

the local area – it's in the library near the windmill. Mitchell is the southern access point for the Mt Moffat Section of the Carnarvon National Park (p247) but the park is a rough, mostly unsealed 200km from Mitchell. If you want to stop over, there's a council-run caravan park beside the river on the eastern side of town. The **Berkeley Lodge Motel** (☎ 4623 1666; fax 4623 1304; 20 Cambridge St; s/d $60/80) has reasonably priced motel rooms.

Continuing west from Mitchell, it's another 89km to the small highway town of **Morven**, a drivers' watering hole with two pubs serving meals, a café and a general store, plus the **Morven Hotel-Motel** (☎ 4654 8101; Albert St; s/d $45/60) with OK motel units.

The junction of the Warrego and Landsborough Hwys is 3km west of Morven. From here, you can continue west to Charleville (90km; p431) or take the Landsborough Hwy northwest to Augathella (90km; p431).

SOUTH BURNETT REGION

Stretching northwest from Brisbane, the South Burnett region centres on the Burnett River and its various tributaries. Highway 17 starts near Ipswich and runs north for almost 600km to Rockhampton, providing a popular alternative, inland route for those who want to avoid the much more hectic Bruce Hwy. The road meanders through a succession of small rural centres, and it's quite a leisurely drive during the day. At night, the road trains and kangaroos come out in force and wise drivers stay off the roads. There are several natural attractions in the region, including the Bunya Mountains National Park and the Cania Gorge National Park.

Getting There & Away
Brisbane Bus Lines (☎ 07-3355 0034) operates two services daily from Brisbane to Murgon ($38, four hours). The routes cover a wide area. Buses run via Caboolture (one hour) and Kingaroy (3¼ hours) except on Monday morning when the bus travels to Murgon via the Sunshine Coast, returning via the inland road. The afternoon bus to Brisbane on Saturday also travels via the Sunshine Coast. On Tuesday and Thursday buses continue up the Burnett Hwy

to Gayndah (6¼ hours), Mundubbera (6¾ hours), Eidsvold (7¼ hours), Monto (eight hours) and Biloela (nine hours). There are also services from Brisbane to Bundaberg via the Burnett Hwy on Wednesday.

BUNYA MOUNTAINS NATIONAL PARK

If you really want to see wildlife, Bunya Mountains National Park, 56km southwest of Kingaroy, is a pretty safe bet. Wallabies, crimson rosellas and king parrots are almost guaranteed, and there are plenty of less-common beasts in the various environments around the park, which include rainforest, eucalyptus scrub and heath land.

The Bunyas rise abruptly from flat country to over 1000m and have been protected as a national park since 1908, which may explain the confident, friendly wildlife. The park is also extremely popular, attracting large crowds at weekends and on public holidays. An extensive network of walking tracks zig-zags through it, from a gentle 500m discovery walk to the 10km trek to the Big Falls Lookout.

The park is named for the curious bunya pine, which every few years produces a crop of huge edible nuts, each the size of a pineapple. Before European settlers came and started logging these forests in the 1860s, Aboriginal tribes used to gather for feasts and ceremonies whenever the bunya nuts were ripe. Beware of falling bunya nuts during the season, which is late January to April.

The main access route to the park from the south is via Dalby or Jondaryan on the Warrego Hwy.

If you wish to stay in the park, there is a **rangers station** (☎ 4668 3127; www.epa.qld.gov .au; Bunya Ave) in **Dandabah**, near the southern entrance to the park; you can usually catch the rangers between 2pm and 4pm. There are several places to camp including at the lovely, green site adjacent to the station. The Burton Wells and Westcott sites are for tent campers only. It's $4 per person, or $16 for a family of more than four. Also at Dandabah is a general store including an **accommodation booking desk** (☎ /fax 4668 3131), a small museum and a snack bar.

If you don't feel like camping in the park, there are several accommodation options in and around Dandabah.

Away from Dandabah, on the road south to Dalby, we highly recommend the homey

Munro's Camp Cabins (☎ 4668 3150; just off Bunya Ave; d cabins $50, each additional person $10) to anyone looking for peace, solitude and wallabies! The self-contained cabins sleep up to six people.

Tucked away behind the trees, a pretty cottage garden leads to the cosy four-room **Bunya Mountain Lodge** (☎ 4668 3134; MS 501 Bunya Mountains Rd; s/d $165/230 incl breakfast, lunch & dinner; ✗) guesthouse. The room décor is a little quaint, but that's offset by a welcoming lounge, with couches and an open fire, and the hearty country fare cooked up by the hosts.

The friendly **Rice's Log Cabins** (☎ /fax 4668 3133; Bunya Mountains Rd; d cabins $75, each additional person $10) has a number of self-contained log cabins and well-manicured grounds. There's a licensed restaurant that opens for dinner on Saturday nights.

There are great views along with clean amenities and ultra-hot showers at **Bushland Park** (☎ 4663 4717; Soldiers Rd; unpowered/powered sites $12/18, cabins from $50) camping ground, which is 10km south of Dandabah on the road to Dalby. Rates are for two people.

For a good sit-down meal, **Rosella's Rainforest Restaurant & Brasserie** (☎ 4668 3131; Bunya Ave; mains $8-$20; ✆ lunch & dinner) is near the rangers station. The brasserie serves up high quality light lunches. Try the bunya nut cookies and cake.

With a focus on Australian bush ingredients, the peaceful **Bunya Forest Gallery & Tearoom** (☎ 4668 3020; 14 Bunya Ave; mains $6-12; ✆ 10am-5pm Tue-Sun) has a rainforest outlook and serves up delicious treats straight from the oven – the scones are heavenly – as well as a range of teas and coffee.

KINGAROY

☎ 07 / pop 11,140

Kingaroy, at the junction of the Bunya Mountains and D'Aguilar Hwys, is the prosperous little capital of the South Burnett region and the centre of Australia's most important peanut-growing area. In fact, peanuts dominate almost every facet of life in Kingaroy.

Other than peanuts (and the fact that Queensland's notorious ex-premier, Joh Bjelke-Petersen, came from here), Kingaroy's main point of interest is a promising wine industry. South Burnett was the first official wine region in Queensland, but was quickly overshadowed by the Granite Belt. The Verdelho, Chardonnay, Shiraz and

Merlot are the standouts. Some of the more noted wineries are **Barambah Ridge** (☎ 4168 4766; 79 Goschnicks Rd, Redgate via Murgon; ⏱ 10am-5pm), **Clovely Estate** (☎ 3216 1088; Steinhardts Rd, Moffatdale via Murgon; ⏱ 10am-5pm Fri-Sun) and **Stuart Range** (☎ 4162 3711; 67 William St; ⏱ 9am-5pm).

Kingaroy is also the northern access point for the Bunya Mountains National Park.

The **visitor information centre** (☎ 4162 3199; 128 Haly St; ⏱ 9am-5pm), just north of the centre, opposite the white peanut silos, is very helpful.

The town's **Bicentennial Heritage Museum** (☎ 4162 4953; Haly St; adult/child $2.50/1; ⏱ 9am-4pm Mon-Fri, 9am-2pm Sat & Sun) is devoted to the early days of the peanut industry, with plenty of photos and old machinery.

If you want to relive the days of mangled grammar and the gerrymander, tours of **Bethany** (☎ 4162 7046; 218 Petersen Dr; admission $8), the home of the Bjelke-Petersen family, are held every Wednesday and Saturday at 2pm. Try the famous pumpkin scones. Booking at the visitor information centre is essential. If you can't get enough of the Flo and Joh show, you can stay in an attractive self-contained cottage on the property. The small **Bethany Cottages** (☎ 4162 7046; www.bethany.net.au; 218 Peterson Dr; d midweek/weekend $110/120 incl breakfast; ⌨) are on top of a hill, so there's a spectacular view from the veranda.

About 60km from Kingaroy, **Passchendaele** (☎ 4164 8147; www.pfarm.com.au; d $120 or $155 pp incl dinner & breakfast) is a farmstay that gets excellent reports from travellers who have enjoyed the insight into life on a Darling Downs property. It's not just about milking cows and collecting eggs – guests can take part in seasonal mustering and checking stock water and fencing. The less active can picnic by the creek.

Captains Cottage (☎ 4162 4534; 18 Millers Rd; d midweek/weekend $100/130, extra person $10, incl breakfast) is a secluded, architecturally-designed cottage nestled in the Captains Paddock Vineyard about 7km from Kingaroy. Kids will love the Booie Monster sculptured fireplace. The owners' children are both sculptors, so keep a lookout for some other strange creatures lurking near the vines.

The uninspiring but friendly **Pioneer Lodge Motel** (☎ 4162 3999; fax 4162 4813; 100 Kingaroy St; s/d $65/75; ⌨ ⓡ) has tidy rooms and a licensed restaurant.

The neat **Kingaroy Caravan Park & Cabins** (☎ 4162 1808; fax 4162 1808; 48 Walter Rd; unpowered/powered sites $15/17.50), 1.5km out of the town centre just off the Brisbane-Nanango Hwy, has a nice grassy area and lots of shady spots to set up camp. Rates are for two people.

Kingaroy's restaurants are generally on the dull side, but the **Bell Tower** (☎ 4162 7000; Haydens Rd; mains $12-23; ⏱ lunch Sat & Sun, dinner Thu-Sat) at Booie Range Distillers, is a carnivore's paradise, and worth a visit for the regional produce and excellent views.

For all your nutty needs, the **Peanut Van** (☎ 4162 2737; 77 Kingaroy St; ⏱ 8.30am-5pm) has stocks of toffee-coated Vienna peanuts, hickory smoke flavour and bags of good old salt roast in a shell.

KINGAROY TO MONTO
Murgon
☎ 07 / pop 2147

Heading north from Kingaroy the first place you hit is Murgon, a pleasant little cattle centre. There's a **tourist information centre** (☎ 4168 3864; Lamb St; ⏱ 9am-4pm). The interesting **Queensland Dairy Industry Museum** (Gayndah St; ⏱ 9.30am-2.30pm Mon-Fri, 1.30-4pm Sat & Sun) is on the northern outskirts of town.

For accommodation, try the luxury B&B cottage at **Dusty Hill Estate** (☎ 4168 4700; Barambah Rd; d midweek/weekend $220/240), which has lovely views of Lake Barambah.

About 4km from Murgon the Cherbourg Aboriginal community runs the **Barambah Emu Farm** (☎ 4168 2655; Barambah Rd; adult/child $5.50/2.20; ⏱ tours 9.30am, 11am & noon Mon-Fri, 9.30am & 11am Sat), which has a stunning spot on top of a hill with great views of Lake Barambah and vineyards from the Bert Button lookout. It also sells intricately carved emu eggs and emu oil and leather.

Gayndah
☎ 07 / pop 1797

The Burnett Hwy branches north at Goomeri. The next big settlement is Gayndah, which was settled in 1852 and is possibly Queensland's oldest town. It's famous for its oranges and mandarins and the lively **Orange Festival**, held in odd-numbered years on the Queen's Birthday weekend in June. The **Gayndah & District Historical Museum** (☎ 4161 2226; 3 Simon St; ⏱ 9am-4pm) has an interesting local history collection spanning three buildings, including a one-teacher school display, war memorabilia and an 1864 slab-timber hut. For accommodation there's the **River-View**

DARLING DOWNS

Caravan Park (☎ 4161 1280; 3 Barrow St) or the **Colonial Motel** (☎ 4161 1999; 58 Capper St).

Eidsvold

☎ 07 / pop 495

Eidsvold, the next town north, was established as a gold town by two Norwegian brothers and is the centre of an important cattle-rearing area. The **Eidsvold Historical Complex** (☎ 4165 1311; 1 Mount Rose St; ☯ 9am-3pm) comprises seven heritage buildings housing an extensive and quirky range of displays, including a vast collection of old bottles and various fossicked gems and minerals. You can stay, eat and get tourist information at the **Eidsvold Motel & General Store** (☎ 4165 1209; 51 Morton St).

MONTO

☎ 07 / pop 1115

Monto is near the junction of the Burnett River and Three Moon Creek. According to local legend, the creek was named by a swagman who was boiling his billy on the banks of the creek one night when he saw three moons – one in the sky, one reflected in the creek, and another reflected in his billy. The centre of town is just northeast of where the railway line is bridged by the Burnett Hwy. The main drag, Newton St, has three big, old pubs with cheap accommodation and meals.

Just off the highway at the southern end of town, **Colonial Motor Inn & Restaurant**

(☎ 4166 1377; fax 4166 1437; 6 Thomson St; s/d motel units $55/65) is a pleasant place fronted by a 100-year-old timber building, which houses an atmospheric, colonial-style restaurant open for dinner Monday to Saturday.

Campers can set up at the **Monto Caravan Park** (☎ 4166 1492; Flinders St), just west of town on the highway.

CANIA GORGE NATIONAL PARK

About 26km north of Monto, the small Cania Gorge National Park preserves a range of habitats from dry eucalyptus forest and rugged sandstone escarpments to deep gullies filled with mosses and ferns. The scenery is spectacular, wildlife is plentiful and there are numerous walking trails to the most impressive rock formations.

You can't camp at the park itself, but **Cania Gorge Caravan & Tourist Park** (☎ 07-4167 8188; www .caniagorge.com.au; Phil Marshall Dr; unpowered/powered sites $20/23, 9-bed bunkhouses $45, cabins $55-85; ☒) is about 7km beyond the picnic area in the national park. It's well equipped, with a shop and a campers' kitchen. The bunkhouse costs $9/7 extra for each additional adult/child when more than three people are staying. You can hire boats and kayaks here.

MONTO TO ROCKHAMPTON

The Burnett Hwy continues north from Monto to Rockhampton via Biloela and Mt Morgan. See p237 for details of this area.

Sunshine Coast

CONTENTS

HIGHLIGHTS

- Smiling a while with the crocodiles and other critters at the Crocodile Hunter's **Australia Zoo** (p174)
- Driving the scenic route in-between the towering and ethereal **Glass House Mountains** (p173)
- Escaping the crowds and indulging in sun, surf and space at **Coolum** and **Peregian** (p181)
- Wowing the tastebuds with cultivated cuisine at Noosa's renowned **restaurants and cafés** (p186)
- Spotting koalas, tracking the coastline and going bush with a walk through **Noosa National Park** (p182)
- Canoeing or kayaking your way up the Cooloola Section of **Great Sandy National Park** (p190)
- Feeling the fishies, plunging beneath the waves and diving with sharks at Mooloolaba's **Underwater World** (p177)
- Immersing yourself in the local – and foreign – culture, food, clothes and mind-boggling array of wares at the **Eumundi Markets** (p191)

Great Sandy National Park ★
Noosa ★★ Noosa National Park
Eumundi ★
Coolum & Peregian ★
Mooloolaba ★
Australia Zoo ★
Glass House Mountains ★

SUNSHINE COAST

- www.sunshinecoast.org
- www.sunzine.net/suncoast

When visitors who've endured one unforgiving winter too many book a flight to Queensland, it's visions of euphoric families frolicking in the sand, couples engaged in romantic scenarios and singles wallowing in bliss that call to them in the wee hours. As it happens, those well-marketed subliminal messages are more than just advertisements; they're a fairly apt reflection of the kind of holidays to be had in this pocket of Queensland's coast. What the tourist brochures don't tell you is that this string of low-key resort towns has contained the flow of tourism to a manageable trickle. Instead of assemblies of high-rises you'll find only the odd splatter, and rather than mixing with a glut of commercial dollar scoffers you'll be spending your days on miles of free, golden beach with laid-back locals.

The Sunshine Coast stretches from the top of Bribie Island to just north of Noosa. Caloundra, the first place on the strip, is a sleepy beach resort backed by the ethereal Glass House Mountains. Further along the coast is the laconic suburban swell of Maroochy, the most developed quarter in the Sunshine neighbourhood. Home to many permanent residents, its population mushrooms during school holidays when Australian families converge en masse. North of Maroochy, there's a patch of still-unspoilt coastline at Coolum and Peregian. After this you arrive in Noosa, an exclusive, staunchly low-rise and leafy resort that sometimes feels like an antipodean answer to France's Nice.

Filling the space between the beach and the vast emptiness of Queensland's interior is the Sunshine Coast's undulating hinterland, where charming villages linger on the outskirts of national parks.

Getting There & Away

AIR

The Sunshine Coast's airport is on the coast road at Mudjimba, 10km north of Maroochydore and 26km south of Noosa, although it's called Maroochydore Airport. **Sunshine Express** (☎ 13 13 13; www.sunshineexpress.com.au) flies there daily from Brisbane ($95, 30 minutes). **Jetstar** (☎ 13 15 38; www.jetstar.com.au) and **Virgin Blue** (☎ 13 67 89; www.virginblue.com.au) have daily connections to Sydney ($90) and Melbourne ($130). Virgin Blue also flies to the Sunshine Coast from other state capitals.

BUS

Greyhound Australia (☎ 13 14 99; www.greyhound .com.au) and **Premier Motor Service** (☎ 13 34 10; www.premierms.com.au) both stop at Maroochydore and Noosa en route from Brisbane to destinations further north.

Suncoast Pacific (www.suncoastpacific.com.au; Brisbane ☎ 3236 1901; Caloundra ☎ 5491 2555; Maroochydore ☎ 5443 1011) runs between Brisbane's Roma St Transit Centre and airport and the coast.

There are seven services on weekdays and six on Saturday and Sunday. One-way trips from Brisbane include Caloundra ($24, two hours), Maroochydore ($21, two hours) and Noosa ($24, three hours). Suncoast has standby fares to the above for $15.

Getting Around

Several companies offer transfers from Maroochydore Airport and Brisbane to points along the coast. Fares from Brisbane cost $35 to $40 for adults and $20 to $25 for children. From Maroochydore Airport fares are around $15 per adult and $11 per child. The following are recommended:

Col's Airport Shuttle (☎ 5473 9966; www.airshuttle .com.au)

Henry's (☎ 5474 0199)

Noosa Transfers & Charters (☎ 5449 9782; noosatransfers@powerup.com.au)

Sun-Air Bus Service (☎ 1800 804 340, 5478 2811; www.sunair.com.au)

Suncoast Link (☎ 3236 1901; www.suncoastpacific .com.au)

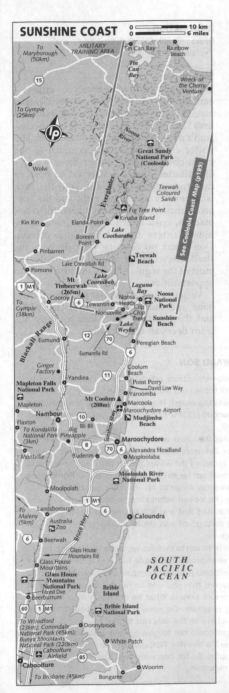

The blue minibuses run by **Sunbus** (☎ 5492 8700) buzz frequently between Caloundra and Noosa, stopping along the way. Sunbus also has regular buses from Noosa across to the train station at Nambour on the Bruce Hwy ($4.40, one hour), via Eumundi and Yandina.

CABOOLTURE
☎ 07/pop 40,400

This rural town, just off the Bruce Hwy 49km north of Brisbane, is worth a stop if you're heading north up the coast. A prosperous dairy centre, Caboolture has several museums including the wonderful **Abbey Museum** (☎ 5495 1652; 1 The Abbey Place; adult/child $8/4.50; ☑ 10am-4pm Mon-Sat). The impressive art and archaeology collection here spans the globe and includes items up to 250,000 years old. Budding anthropologists will go gooey over Egyptian death masks (1000 BC), Grecian sculptures (3000 BC), Flemish oil paintings (15th century) and more. The museum is about 7km east of Caboolture, on the far side of the Bruce Hwy, just off Toorbul Point Rd.

In Caboolture itself, the **Caboolture Historical Village** (☎ 5495 4581; Beerburrum Rd; adult/child $8.80/6.60; ☑ 9.30am-3.30pm) is a re-creation of a historical village. More than 60 structures, including council buildings, a courthouse and general stores, create a vivid effect. Adults might not be fooled, but kids will probably feel like they've walked onto a movie set.

Nearby is the **Caboolture Warplane Museum** (☎ 5499 1144; Hangar 104, Caboolture Airfield, McNaught Rd; adult/child/family $6.50/3.50/16.50; ☑ 10am-4pm), with a collection of restored WWII warplanes, all in flying order.

GLASS HOUSE MOUNTAINS

About 20km north of Caboolture, the Glass House Mountains are 16 ethereally shaped volcanic crags sticking up from the coastal plain. It's well worth diverting off the Bruce Hwy onto the slower Glass House Mountains Rd to snake your way between them. Towering higher than 500m, with sheer, rocky sides, the mountains emerge from the humid green surrounds in sporadic and magnificent style. If it weren't for the odd caravan park and diminutive village, you could easily convince yourself you'd entered Jurassic Park.

SUNSHINE COAST

The Glass House Mountains National Park is broken into several sections and surrounds Mts Tibrogargan, Cooee, Beerwah, Coonowrin, Ngungun, Miketeebumulgrai and Elimbah, with picnic grounds and lookouts but no camping grounds. The peaks are reached by a series of sealed and unsealed roads known as Forest Dr, which heads inland from Glass House Mountains Rd. You need a permit to access Mt Coonowrin, which you can get from the Queensland Parks & Wildlife Office (QPWS), which also has information on the area.

There are challenging walking trails (read: low-grade mountain climbs) on several of the peaks, which offer spectacular views of the region. Tibrogargan is probably the best climb, with a steep, rock-cut trail and several amazing lookouts from the flat summit. Reaching the summit requires a reasonable level of fitness and skill, though, and you should allow three to four hours for the return trip. Mt Beerwah and Mt Ngungun can also be climbed via steep trails.

Information

QPWS (☎ 5494 0150; Bells Creek Rd, Beerwah; ⌚ 7am-3.30pm).

Sights

Located just north of Beerwah is – crikey! – **Australia Zoo** (☎ 5494 1134; www.crocodilehunter .com; Glasshouse Mountains Rd, Beerwah; adult/child/ family $29/19/90; ⌚ 9am-4.30pm), one of Queensland's most popular tourist attractions. The visitor crowds head here as much to see khaki-clad, celebrity owner Steve 'Crocodile Hunter' Irwin as they do to observe the crocs and other wildlife. But the park is impressive in its own right and the gorgeous menagerie includes tigers, tortoises, macaws, crocodiles (of course) and many more critters from home and abroad. Don't bank on catching yer man here; instead marvel at the animals and make the most of the regular shows and ample photo opportunities.

Various companies offer tours from Brisbane and the Sunshine Coast (see p192) and the zoo operates a free courtesy bus from Beerwah train station.

THE WEEPING MOUNTAIN AND HIS WAYWARD SON

According to Aboriginal legend, the Glass House Mountains are a family of mountain spirits, fathered by Tibrogargan (364m), the father of all tribes, and his wife Beerwah (555m). They had several offspring, of whom Coonowrin (377m) was the eldest. His siblings include Tunbubudla – the twins (293m and 312m), Coochin (235m), Ngungun (253m), Tibberoowuccum (220m), Miketeebumulgrai (199m) and Elimbah (129m).

One day Tibrogargan was looking out towards the coast when he noticed the sea level rising. Anticipating a flood, he became fearful for Beerwah, who was close to the water. Having borne many children she would have difficulty escaping the waves on her own. But he was also concerned about his children and realised he would not be able to save them all. So Tibrogargan called out to his eldest and strongest son, Coonowrin, to go to his mother's assistance.

As Tibrogargan gathered his younger children he looked behind him to see if Coonowrin and Beerwah were safe, but to his dismay Coonowrin had fled and left his mother unassisted. In a blinding rage, Tibrogargan picked up his *nulla nulla* (club) and struck his eldest son with such force that the blow dislocated Coonowrin's neck.

Once the waters subsided the family were able to return to their home. Upon seeing his crooked neck, Coonowrin's siblings began to tease him relentlessly. This made him feel ashamed and he went to his father for forgiveness. Tibrogargan wept huge tears of despair and asked his son how he could abandon his mother. Coonowrin answered that she was so much bigger than any of them he thought she should be able to take care of herself. What he did not realise, however, was that Beerwah was not just big, but heavily pregnant. Coonowrin's siblings began to weep too; their tears formed many streams, some reaching all the way out to sea.

According to the law of the tribe, Tibrogargan could not forgive his son who had disgraced him, so he turned his back on Coonowrin forever. To this day Tibrogargan faces out to sea while his son hangs his crooked neck in shame and cries. As for Beerwah, well, she is still pregnant, because it takes many years to give birth to a mountain.

Tours

The easiest way to see the Glass House Mountains from Brisbane is with Rob's Rainforest Tours, which also includes a trip to Kondalilla National Park. See p96 for details.

Sleeping & Eating

Rates for the following parks are for two people.

Glasshouse Mountains Holiday Village (☎ /fax 5496 9338; Glasshouse Mountains Rd, Glasshouse Mountains; unpowered/powered sites $16/19, cabins from $65; ⌘ ⌘) This cutesy park has comfortable, self-contained cabins and pretty sites. Facilities include BBQs, a tennis court and a small takeaway.

Glasshouse Mountains Tourist Park (☎ 5496 0151; www.glasshousetouristpk.com.au; Glasshouse Mountains Rd, Beerburrum; unpowered/powered sites $16/19, cabins from $50; ⌘) Something of a caravan jungle, there's not a great deal of space between sites at this ageing park, but it's a reasonable spot for an overnighter. The mountain views in the background are quite spectacular.

Glasshouse Mountains Tavern (☎ 5493 0933; 10 Reed St, Glasshouse Mountains; mains $12-23; ⌥ lunch & dinner) Part kit home, part old country tavern, this welcoming pub cooks up good steaks, curries and chicken parma in a lovely dark-wood interior. The open fire keeps things cosy during winter and a peppering of outdoor seating is great for a midday middy on sunny days.

CALOUNDRA

☎ 07 / pop 50,150

At the southern end of the Sunshine Coast, Caloundra is a popular family resort with good fishing and pleasant surf beaches. The curvaceous shoreline is interrupted by a small crew of medium-rise condos, but the impact is minimal. The humble spread of weatherboard and brick bungalows, mixed with pockets of pine and scrub, still allow the coastal scenery to prevail.

Information & Orientation

The **Caloundra Visitor Information Centre** (☎ 5491 0202; 7 Caloundra Rd; ⌥ 9am-5.30pm) is out on the roundabout at the entrance to town.

Bulcock St is the main thoroughfare, with a post office, banks, a cinema and a few takeaway cafés.

Sights & Activities

Caloundra's beaches are its major attraction. **Bulcock Beach**, just down from the main street and pinched by the northern tip of Bribie Island, captures a good wind tunnel, making it popular with kite-surfers. For conventional surfing, you're best off heading north to **Moffat Beach** or **Dicky Beach**. **North Caloundra Surf School** (☎ 0411-221 730; 2-hr lessons from $55) is highly regarded. The more people in your party, the lower the rates. You can rent boards from **Beach Beat** (surfboards/body boards per day $35/25; Caloundra ☎ 5491 4711; 119 Bulcock St; ⌥ 9am-5pm; Dicky Beach ☎ 5491 8215; 4-6 Beerburrum St; ⌥ 9am-5pm).

Caloundra is a very popular spot for skydiving and **Sunshine Coast Skydivers** (☎ 5437 0211; Caloundra Aerodrome; dives from $180) will facilitate any urges to jump out of a plane (tandem) and whoop for joy. It's almost as much fun watching from the ground.

The **Queensland Air Museum** (☎ 5492 5930; 7 Pathfinder Dr, Caloundra Aerodrome; adult/child $8/4; ⌥ 10am-4pm), suitably housed in a small hangar, is community-run and best for budding aviators. Plenty of photos, displays and old machinery parts provide a decent insight into Queensland's aviation history.

The **Sunshine Coast Turf Club** (☎ 5491 6788; www.sctc.com.au; Pierce Ave), west of town, has popular race meets every Sunday.

An increasingly popular way to see the water around Caloundra is to cruise Pumicestone Channel, the snake of water separating Bribie Island from the mainland. **Caloundra Cruise** (☎ 5492 8280; www.caloundracruise .com; Majova Ave Jetty; adult/child/concession/family $14.50/5/13.50/35; ⌥ 11am & 1pm) operates great eco-cruises, taking in the channel and coursing around Bribie Island. The tours take about 1½ hours.

Sleeping

Belaire Place (☎ 5491 8688; www.belaireplace.com; 34 Minchinton St; r $105-175; ⌘ ⌘) Overlooking Bulcock Beach, these spacious, sunny apartments are great value. Rates increase as the views improve, but the bright and modern interiors all contain sparkling kitchens, cable TV and balconies big enough to park a truck on.

Dicky Beach Family Holiday Park (☎ /fax 5491 3342; 4 Beerburrum St; unpowered/powered sites from $20/24, cabins from $60; ⌘ ⌘) This well-ordered park right on the beachfront could win a

CALOUNDRA

| | | | 0 —— 1 km |
| | | | 0 —— 0.5 miles |

INFORMATION
Caloundra Visitor Information Centre..1 A3
Police Station....................................2 C3
Post Office.......................................3 C3

SIGHTS & ACTIVITIES
Beach Beat......................................4 C1
Beach Beat......................................5 C1
Caloundra Cruise..............................6 B3
Queensland Air Museum....................7 A3
Sunshine Coast Skydivers.................8 A3

SLEEPING
Anchorage Motor Inn.......................9 B3
Belaire Place..................................10 C3
Dicky Beach Family Holiday Park.....11 C1
Hibiscus Holiday Park.....................12 B3
Tourist Accommodation..................13 B3

EATING
Above Board.................................14 C3
Caloundra RSL..............................15 C3
Caloundra Surf Club.......................16 D3
Dicky Beach Surf Club....................17 C1
Naked Turtle................................18 D3
Ontrato's Cafe.............................19 C3

ENTERTAINMENT
Caloundra Cinemas.......................20 C3

TRANSPORT
Bus Terminal...............................21 C3

tidy suburbs competition; absolutely everything is in its place. Aside from the immaculate cabins, there is plenty of green grass and tree cover for comfortable tent-pitching. Rates are for two people.

Anchorage Motor Inn (☎ 5491 1499; fax 5491 7279; 18 Bowman Rd; s/d $80/85; ⚡ ⚡) This decent motel has simple and clean rooms. There's also a pleasant pool set in a mini oasis à la Las Vegas to offset the concrete, and management is downright friendly.

Also recommended:
Hibiscus Holiday Park (☎ 1800 550 138, 5491 1564; fax 5492 6938; cnr Bowman Rd & Landsborough Park Rd; unpowered sites $18.50-25, powered sites $23-30, units $75-85, vans/cabins $55/60; ⚡) Reasonable sites, good facilities and lovely villas on the water. Rates are for two people.
Tourist Accommodation (☎ 5499 7655, fax 5499 7644; 84 Omrah Ave; dm/tw/d $17/40/48) Hostel-cum-motel with functional, spotless rooms.

Eating

Above Board (☎ 5491 6388; Shop 8, The Esplanade; mains $10-24; ☀ breakfast, lunch & dinner) The dress code may be jeans and a T-shirt, but the menu at this cruisy haunt is a cut above.

Dinner highlights include mahi mahi fillets with macadamia pesto dressing, or pistachio-stuffed pork fillets sitting on wine-glazed mash. Brekkie and lunch are simpler affairs.

Naked Turtle (☎ 5491 7565; Shop 2, Shearwater Resort, The Esplanade, Kings Beach; mains $15-25; ☀ breakfast, lunch & dinner) This spunky eatery serves café fare with flair – lentil samosas, tandoori chicken, spring rolls, tapas and salt and vinegar dory fillets are but a few of the tasty treats on offer. Diners sit in a big glass dome, which provides plenty of people-watching entertainment.

Caloundra RSL (☎ 5491 1544; 19 West Tce; dishes $10-25; ☀ breakfast, lunch & dinner) Some RSLs are small and unassuming affairs – this one isn't. With enough flamboyance to outdo Liberace, Caloundra's award-winning RSL features two huge restaurants plus a café. The glitzy atmosphere can be a little overwhelming, but the food is excellent and everyone is catered for.

Ontrato's Cafe (☎ 5437 0944; cnr Bulcock St & Ontrato Ave; dishes $5-11; ☀ breakfast, lunch & dinner) Sweet and savoury crepes, fancy focaccias and fresh wraps are the go at this cute and breezy café on the main drag. It's also family friendly and a good spot to dig into fat cakes and scrummy breakfasts.

For cheap and tasty pub grub you can't beat the **Caloundra Surf Club** (☎ 5491 8418; fax 5492 5730; Ormonde Tce; mains $12; ⏰ lunch & dinner) and the **Dicky Beach Surf Club** (☎ 5491 6078; Coochin St; mains $12; ⏰ lunch & dinner). Both dish up big portions of steak, fish, lasagne, salad and, of course, chicken parma.

Entertainment

Caloundra Cinemas (☎ 1902 240 508; cnr Knox & Bulcock Sts) Located on the upper floor of an arcade, this multiscreen complex showing latest releases has budget days on Tuesday and Thursday ($7.50).

Getting There & Away

Suncoast Pacific buses stop at the **bus terminal** (☎ 5491 2555; Cooma Tce); see p172 for more information on these services. **Sunbus** (☎ 5492 8700) has frequent services linking Caloundra and Noosa ($5.20, 1½ hours) via Maroochydore ($2.80, 50 minutes).

MAROOCHY

☎ 07 / pop 44,100

Maroochy, a large chunk of the coast encompassing Maroochydore, Cotton Tree, Alexandra Headland and Mooloolaba, is a happily developed suburban spread and home to many a Sunshine Coaster. The surf culture here has been adulterated somewhat by shopping plazas and the shoreline sports vistas of high-rise apartments dressed in glaring colours, but the affable and relaxed ethos of the beach is dominant. In summer the area bursts with families indulging in good fishing and surf beaches, but it quickly reverts back to the tranquil epitome of coastal Oz for the remainder of the year.

Mooloolaba is the most pleasant, and most developed, of the suburbs, with a good beach, good surf and some excellent restaurants and nightspots.

Orientation

The main thoroughfare in Maroochydore is Aerodrome Rd, which becomes Alexandra Pde along the seafront at Alexandra Headland, before becoming Mooloolaba Esplanade at Mooloolaba.

Information

Computer Rescue (☎ 5451 0750; cnr Ocean Ave & Duporth Ave, Maroochydore; per hr $6; ⏰ 8am-5pm Mon-Fri, 8am-noon Sat) Internet access.

Maroochy Tourism Information Booths Mooloolaba (☎ 5478 2233; cnr Brisbane Rd & First Ave, Mooloolaba; ⏰ 9am-5pm) Maroochydore Airport (☎ 5448 9088; Friendship Dr, Marcoola; ⏰ 9.30am-3pm)

Maroochy Visitors Centre (☎ 1800 882 032, 5479 1566; www.maroochytourism.com; cnr Sixth Ave & Melrose St, Maroochydore; ⏰ 9am-5pm Mon-Fri, 9am-4pm Sat & Sun) Main office with plenty of information and helpful staff. Free accommodation booking service.

Maroochydore Library (☎ 5475 8900; Sixth Ave, Cotton Tree; ⏰ 9am-5.30pm Mon, Wed & Fri, 9am-8pm Tue & Thu, 9am-5pm Sat) Free Internet access but bookings essential.

QPWS Office (☎ 5443 8940; 29 The Esplanade, Cotton Tree; ⏰ hours vary)

Sights & Activities

Mooloolaba's **Underwater World** (☎ 5444 8488; The Wharf, Mooloolaba; adult/child/family $23/13/60; ⏰ 9am-6pm) is the largest oceanarium in the southern hemisphere and an utter thrill for nature nuts. Grey nurse sharks, stingrays and what seems like enough fishies to fill the ocean envelop a transparent tunnel with a moving walkway. There are also billabong environments, jellyfish, seal shows and a touch tank. If you've got the gusto you can do a shark dive (ask at reception for details).

There are good surf breaks along the strip – probably the best is **Pin Cushion**, near the mouth of the Maroochy River, which is particularly good in winter thanks to the southerly swells and southwesterly winds. Its lure in summer is fewer numbers; most visitors head to the more easily accessed Maroochy and Memorial Ave. If you want to dance the waves like a pro you'll need lessons. **Robbie Sherwell's XL Surfing Academy** (☎ 5478 1337; 63 Oloway Cres, Alexandra Heads; lessons per person $20; ⏰ 9.30am Mon-Fri, 7.30am Sat) offers good one-hour lessons.

People who already know how to surf can rent boards from **Beach Beat** (☎ 5443 2777; 164 Alexandra Pde, Alexandra Headland; surfboards/body boards per day $35/25; ⏰ 9am-5pm).

Scuba World (☎ 5444 8595; www.scubaworld.com.au; The Wharf, Mooloolaba; shark dives certified/uncertified divers $95/145, coral dives from $55, PADI course $450) arranges shark dives at Underwater World and takes certified divers on coral dives off the coast. Beginners can also do a PADI course.

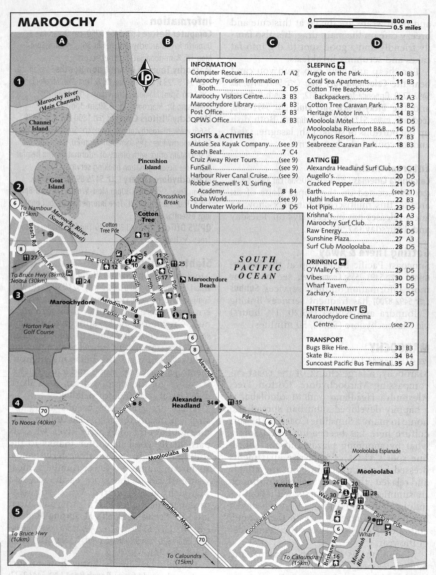

MAROOCHY

INFORMATION
Computer Rescue.....................1 A2
Maroochy Tourism Information
    Booth...............................2 D5
Maroochy Visitors Centre.........3 B3
Maroochydore Library.............4 B3
Post Office...........................5 B3
QPWS Office.........................6 B3

SIGHTS & ACTIVITIES
Aussie Sea Kayak Company.....(see 9)
Beach Beat...........................7 C4
Cruiz Away River Tours...........(see 9)
FunSail................................(see 9)
Harbour River Canal Cruise......(see 9)
Robbie Sherwell's XL Surfing
    Academy...........................8 B4
Scuba World..........................(see 9)
Underwater World..................9 D5

SLEEPING
Argyle on the Park..................10 B3
Coral Sea Apartments..............11 B3
Cotton Tree Beachouse
    Backpackers.....................12 A3
Cotton Tree Caravan Park.......13 B2
Heritage Motor Inn................14 B3
Mooloola Motel....................15 D5
Mooloolaba Riverfront B&B....16 D5
Myconos Resort....................17 B3
Seabreeze Caravan Park.........18 B3

EATING
Alexandra Headland Surf Club..19 C4
Augello's..............................20 D5
Cracked Pepper.....................21 D5
Earth................................(see 21)
Hathi Indian Restaurant..........22 D5
Hot Pipis.............................23 D5
Krishna's.............................24 A3
Maroochy Surf Club...............25 D5
Raw Energy..........................26 D5
Sunshine Plaza......................27 A3
Surf Club Mooloolaba............28 D5

DRINKING
O'Malley's............................29 D5
Vibes.................................30 D5
Wharf Tavern........................31 D5
Zachary's.............................32 D5

ENTERTAINMENT
Maroochydore Cinema
    Centre..........................(see 27)

TRANSPORT
Bugs Bike Hire......................33 B3
Skate Biz.............................34 B4
Suncoast Pacific Bus Terminal..35 A3

FunSail (☎ 5446 6410; www.funsail.com.au; The Wharf, Mooloolaba; per person $99) spends three hours teaching you the finer points of sailing a 37ft yacht.

Tours

Aussie Sea Kayak Company (☎ 5477 5335; www.aus seakayak.com.au; The Wharf, Mooloolaba; 1-/2-day tours

$135/250) offers sea-kayaking adventures on the Sunshine Coast, with tours out to North Stradbroke or Moreton Islands.

Several outfits offer cruises along the Mooloolah River and its canals, departing from the Wharf in Mooloolaba. **Cruiz Away River Tours** (☎ 0419-704 797; www.cruizaway.com; The Wharf, Mooloolaba; eco-tours adult/child $35/25, sunset cruises $25/15) operates great two-hour eco-tours into the Mooloolah River National Park as well as one-hour sunset cruises. Call for departure times. **Harbour River Canal Cruise** (☎ 5444 7477; www.sunshinecoast.au.nu/canalcruise .htm; The Wharf, Mooloolaba; adult/child/concession/ family $13.50/5/12.50/35; ☺ 11am, 1pm & 2pm) operates one-hour cruises with historical commentary aboard the MV *Mudjimba*.

Sleeping

The self-contained unit craze has hit Maroochy and during the week you can stumble across some good standby rates, but most places have a two-night minimum stay. Over school holidays and Christmas, rates for anything other than hostels hit the roof.

BUDGET

Cotton Tree Beachouse Backpackers (☎ 5443 1755; www.cottontreebackpackers.com; 15 The Esplanade, Cotton Tree; dm/d non-YHA $21/46, YHA $19/42; ▣) Virtually on the beach and sheltered by plenty of foliage, this charming timber hostel is friendly and homey, but the spa and good facilities add a touch of class. Best of all, the surfboards, boogie boards and kayaks are all free.

Cotton Tree Caravan Park (☎ 1800 461 253, 5443 1253; www.maroochypark.qld.gov.au; Cotton Tree Pde, Cotton Tree; unpowered/powered sites from $19/22, villas 2 nights from $210; ✖) A merger of two caravan parks, this baby right on the beach is huge. In summer it resembles a teeming suburb, but it's a grassy spot with great facilities and it caters well to disabled travellers. Rates are for two people, and there's a two-night minimum stay in the villas.

Seabreeze Caravan Park (☎ 1800 461 167, 5443 1167; www.maroochypark.qld.gov.au; Melrose Pde, Maroochydore; unpowered/powered sites from $19/27, cabins $120-150) This council-run park has beach frontage and top-notch facilities. Rates are for two people.

MIDRANGE

Coral Sea Apartments (☎ 5479 2999; www.coralsea -apartments.com; 35-7 Sixth Ave, Maroochydore; apt 2 nights from $240; ✖ ▣) These yawning two- and three-bedroom apartments occupy a lovely spot close to Maroochy Surf Club and the beach. Inside you'll find tasteful décor and extra goodies such as dishwashers, wide-screen TVs and videos. The balconies are plenty big.

Argyle on the Park (☎ 5443 3022; www.argyle onthepark.com.au; 31 Cotton Tree Pde, r $125-145, f per 2 nights from $300; ✖ ▣) Within the walls of this medium-rise, bulbous condo complex are classy units swimming in wicker furnishings, pale hues and sunlight. Mod cons are standard and some of the views on the upper levels are fantastic. Several units have bedroom balconies as well as those off the living area.

Heritage Motor Inn (☎ 5443 7355; heritagemotor inn@hotmail.com; 69 Sixth Ave, Mooloolaba; r $85-95; ✖ ▣) Push past the kitsch exterior – as motels go this one's a winner. The spacious rooms are cool, bright and spotless. The hosts are super friendly and if a spot of rain dampens your beach plans there are free in-house movies. It's also wheelchair friendly.

Mooloolaba Riverfront B&B (☎ 5452 5400, 0418-989 099; pm@rpdata.com.au; 7 Bindaree Cres, Mooloolaba; s/d incl breakfast $100/125; ✖) This small riverfront residence is tucked away from the main drag, but is within walking distance of the action. The lovely bedrooms with bathrooms have kitchens and balconies and there's a huge three-bedroom apartment.

Mooloola Motel (☎ 5444 2988; moolmool@bigpond .com; 45-56 Brisbane Rd, Mooloolaba; s $95-105, d$100-110; ▣) The rooms in this decent motel are dressed in tutti-frutti colours and each has a wee veranda overlooking the pool out the back. It's comfy rather than spectacular, but the price is right.

TOP END

Myconos Resort (☎ 1800 041 166, 5451 1711; www .myconosresort.com; 45 Sixth Ave, Maroochydore; apt per 2 nights $265-285, 5 nights from $520; ▣ ✖) From the outside this loud tower looks like every other high-rise, but inside are a multitude of stylish, themed rooms with overtones of Africa, the Middle East and the Mediterranean. Of course all come with spas, kitchens to make you envious, big balconies, cable TV and stereos.

Eating

Maroochy is home to some excellent dining options, most of which are in Mooloolaba.

BUDGET

Raw Energy (☎ 5446 1444; Shop 3, Mooloolaba Esplanade, Mooloolaba; dishes $6-13; ☺ breakfast & lunch) This fresh fuel stop is devoted to health food, but it's not all alfalfa wraps and mung beans. Marinated tofu or macadamia and lentil burgers, savoury tartlets and toppling vegetable stacks are the order of the day, plus a smorgasbord of fresh juices and smoothies.

Krishna's (Shop 2, 7 First Ave, Maroochydore; lunch $7, dinner $8; ⏳ lunch Mon-Fri, dinner Fri & Sun) Krishna's may not have extended their decorating budget too far but the Indian veggie buffet here is excellent value and the food is hot and healthy.

Sunshine Plaza (Horton Pde, Maroochydore; food court meals $5-8) has a whole host of quick-eat options in its large food court as well as supermarkets for self-caterers.

MIDRANGE

Hot Pipis (☎ 5444 4441; Shop 3, 11 Mooloolaba Esplanade, Mooloolaba; dishes $15-24; ⏳ breakfast, lunch & dinner) Amid a sea of pavement eateries, Hot Pipis distinguishes itself with effortless style. The atmosphere is cool but the menu, dominated by seafood, sizzles with items such as red curry of Moreton Bay bugs, blacklip mussels, tiger prawns and barramundi. Leave room for dessert.

Cracked Pepper (☎ 5452 6700; Shop 1, Mooloolaba International, cnr Venning St & The Esplanade, Mooloolaba; mains $10-20; ⏳ breakfast, lunch & dinner) Another good alfresco option, Cracked Pepper has a sophisticated café menu and copious outdoor seating. Tapas, mezzes, fajitas and steak sandwiches are served a tad fancier than usual and the lamb rump Corsica and vegetable baklava speak for themselves.

Maroochy Surf Club (☎ 5443 1298; 34-6 Alexandra Pde, Maroochydore; mains $10-18; ⏳ lunch & dinner) Sure, you can get a decent slab of lasagne here, but who cares if you can eat grilled prawn tails with egg noodles and tomato chilli broth or marmalade pork salad. The wall to wall views are an eye-goggling distraction, but the atmosphere is downright casual.

Augello's (☎ 5478 3199; cnr The Esplanade & Brisbane Rd, Mooloolaba; mains $15-25; ⏳ lunch & dinner) This Mooloolaba institution spoils hungry folk of all ages with outstanding Italian food and a solid reputation. Authentic pizzas, including the hefty Milanese, join nouveau concoctions such as Moroccan chicken with sun-dried tomatoes and lime yoghurt dressing. The mains are a step up again and you also get ocean views if you sit upstairs.

Hathi Indian Restaurant (☎ 5443 5411; 37 Aerodrome Rd, Maroochydore; mains $12-16; ⏳ lunch Thu-Sun, dinner daily) Another authentic option, this cosy Indian restaurant covers a good part of the subcontinent on its menu. The fare is crowd pleasing with plenty of tandoori options plus curries ranging from meek to whoa mamma.

The **Surf Club Mooloolaba** (☎ 5444 1300; Mooloolaba Esplanade, Mooloolaba; mains $10-18; ⏳ lunch & dinner) and **Alexandra Headland Surf Club** (☎ 5443 6677; Alexandra Pde, Alexandra Headland; mains $10-18; ⏳ lunch & dinner) serve up good, reasonably priced meals.

TOP END

Earth (☎ 5477 7100; Level 1, Mooloolaba International, cnr Venning St & The Esplanade, Mooloolaba; mains $26-30; ⏳ lunch & dinner) More like heaven – this chic restaurant with its 90-degree ocean views, flawless service and sublime cuisine offers immaculate ingestion. Expect creations such as blue-swimmer crab risotto or twice-cooked pork curry with Thai basil and chilli. The wine list is suitably divine.

Drinking

Vibes (☎ 5478 3222; Ground fl, Peninsula Bldg, Brisbane Rd, Mooloolaba) It doesn't have beach frontage and the theme is more suburban than sophisticated, but Vibes pulls in a mixed and happy crowd with busy Sunday sessions, cheap cocktails on Tuesday nights and live music most nights of the week.

Zachary's (☎ 5477 6877; 17 Brisbane Rd, Mooloolaba) This sleek bar serves gourmet pizza, but that's just a ruse. Trendy things sporting plenty of hair products and rips in the right places come for the avid socialising amid dim lighting, black leather block couches and wide-screen TVs.

If you're just looking to take the edge off the heat with a cool beer, head to **O'Malley's** (☎ 5452 6344; Ground fl, Mooloolaba International, The Esplanade, Mooloolaba) or the **Wharf Tavern** (☎ 5444 8383; The Wharf, Parkyn Pde, Mooloolaba). Both have live music most nights, sports on the telly, cold beer and no pretensions.

Entertainment

Maroochydore Cinema Centre (☎ 5409 7222; Sunshine Plaza Shopping Centre, Aerodrome Rd, Maroochydore) This modern multiplex cinema screens mainstream movies.

Getting There & Away

Greyhound Australia (☎ 13 14 99; www.greyhound.com.au) and **Premier Motor Service** (☎ 13 34 10;

Surfers at Coolangatta (p144)

JOHN BORTHWICK

JULIET COOMBE

Crafts Village markets (p110), Brisbane

Surfers Paradise (p133)

JOHN BANAGAN

Rainforest on South Stradbroke Island (p130)

RUSSELL MOUNTFORD

Brisbane's riverfront (p84)

The Pyramids, Girraween National Park
(p158)

Bunya Mountains National Park (p168)

Roller coaster at Dreamworld (p135),
Gold Coast

www.premierms.com.au) have two services to Brisbane each day ($19, 1½ hours). Suncoast Pacific does the sme; see p172 for information. Long-distance buses stop at the **Suncoast Pacific bus terminal** (☎ 5443 1011; First Ave, Maroochydore).

Sunbus (☎ 5492 8700) has frequent services between Maroochydore and Noosa ($4.40, one hour).

Getting Around

Bugs Bike Hire (☎ 5443 7555; 42 Aerodrome Rd, Maroochydore; per day $12) hires out good bicycles. **Skate Biz** (☎ 5443 6111; 150 Alexandra Pde, Alexandra Headland; per hr/2hr $8.50/12) hires out in-line skates with all the gear as well as bicycles.

COOLUM & PEREGIAN

If you came to the Sunshine Coast to soak up the sunshine and swim in the tepid waters then you can escape the crowds by heading to the much less crowded beach towns of **Coolum** and **Peregian**. There's a small **tourist information office** (David Low Way; ⏰ 9am-1pm Mon-Sat).

The southern section of the Noosa National Park buffers the beach between Coolum and Peregian with coastal heathland and several walking trails.

In the heart of Coolum and close to the beach, **Coolum Beach Resort** (☎ 5471 7744; www .coolumbeachresort.com; 7-13 Beach Rd, Coolum Beach; r $135-195; ✷ ✸) has a trendy, urban edge but a laid-back atmosphere. The sunny, self-contained units are very comfortable and all come with balconies and cable TV. There's also a spa and sauna onsite to relax sunkissed limbs.

It's only small, but you can't miss the electric blue **Pacific Blue Apartments** (☎ 5448 3611; www.sun.big.net.au/~pacificblue; 236 David Low Way, Peregian Beach; r $80-$85; ✷ ✸). Close to the pub *and* the beach, Pacific Blue has cheerful studios and one-bedroom units, all self contained with a healthy dose of space.

Hidden behind a cool and leafy veranda, this modest row of bungalows at **Villa Coolum** (☎ 5446 1286; www.villacoolum.com; 102 Coolum Tce, Coolum Beach; r $80; ✸) is kitted out with simple gear, but the rooms are spacious and spotless, and you won't need a thing. There's a communal BBQ by the pool and this is a good spot for families.

The wee council-run **Coolum Beach Caravan Park** (☎ 1800 461 474, 5446 1474; www.maroochy park.qld.gov.au; David Low Way, Coolum; unpowered sites $18-26, powered sites $21-30) is rudimentary, but it's nudged onto a grassy plot in front of the beach and just across the road from Coolum's main strip. Prices are for two people.

The convivial **Castro's Bar & Restaurant** (☎ 5471 7555; cnr Frank St & Beach Rd, Coolum; mains $15-25; ⏰ dinner) may not be revolutionary, but there's a definite zeal on the menu. Delicious wood-fired pizzas are the speciality, or you could opt for an Oriental duck wonton salad or sweet corn, smoked chicken and macadamia risotto. Radicals of all ages are welcome.

Also recommended:

Coolum Beach Surf Club (☎ 5446 3694; David Low Way; mains $7-17; ⏰ lunch & dinner) Cheap steaks and seafood.

Hyatt Regency Coolum (☎ 5446 1234; www.coolum .regency.hyatt.com; Warran Rd, Coolum Beach; s & d from $220; ✷ ✸) Five-star golf and spa resort.

There's a bakery and some takeaway shops on David Low Way in Coolum.

NOOSA

☎ 07 / pop 36,400

Gorgeous Noosa, with its tropical vegetation, crystalline beaches and towering gum trees, is where the Sunshine Coast's vogue, vivacious and very dishy have been marinating for more than 40 years. It has an exclusive quality to it, and is very popular with glammed-up fashionistas and wealthy holiday makers. Despite the glut of stylish condominiums and exquisite cuisine, though, the beach and bush are still free, so the well-heeled simply share the beat with thongs, boardshorts and bronzed bikini bodies bearing their bits.

Noosa is undeniably developed, but the trendy café latte landscape has been cultivated without losing sight of simple seaside pleasures. From the eastern 'Paris end' of bustling Hastings St, it's only a short walk to the beachfront Noosa National Park, thick with stunning views, birdlife and native flora. The area north of the Noosa River is preserved as the Cooloola Section of Great Sandy National Park, and offers great opportunities for 4WD driving, hiking and kayaking.

Orientation

Noosa consists of three areas around the mouth of the Noosa River: Noosa Junction,

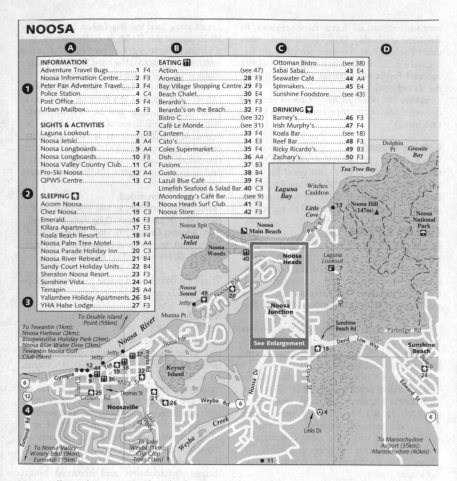

NOOSA

INFORMATION
Adventure Travel Bugs	1 F4
Noosa Information Centre	2 F3
Peter Pan Adventure Travel	3 F4
Police Station	4 C4
Post Office	5 F4
Urban Mailbox	6 F3

SIGHTS & ACTIVITIES
Laguna Lookout	7 D3
Noosa Jetski	8 A4
Noosa Longboards	9 A4
Noosa Longboards	10 A4
Noosa Valley Country Club	11 C4
Pro-Ski Noosa	12 A4
QPWS Centre	13 C2

SLEEPING
Accom Noosa	14 F3
Chez Noosa	15 C3
Emerald	16 F3
Killara Apartments	17 E3
Koala Beach Resort	18 F4
Noosa Palm Tree Motel	19 A4
Noosa Parade Holiday Inn	20 C3
Noosa River Retreat	21 B4
Sandy Court Holiday Units	22 B4
Sheraton Noosa Resort	23 F3
Sunshine Vista	24 D4
Terrapin	25 A4
Yallambee Holiday Apartments	26 B4
YHA Halse Lodge	27 F3

EATING
Action	(see 47)
Aromas	28 F3
Bay Village Shopping Centre	29 F3
Beach Chalet	30 E4
Berardo's	31 F3
Berardo's on the Beach	32 F3
Bistro C	(see 32)
Café Le Monde	(see 31)
Canteen	33 F4
Cato's	34 E3
Coles Supermarket	35 F4
Dish	36 A4
Fusions	37 B3
Gusto	38 B4
Lazuli Blue Café	39 F3
Limefish Seafood & Salad Bar	40 C3
Moondoggy's Café Bar	(see 9)
Noosa Heads Surf Club	41 F3
Noosa Store	42 F3

Ottoman Bistro	(see 38)
Sabai Sabai	43 E4
Seawater Café	44 A4
Spinnakers	45 E4
Sunshine Foodstore	(see 43)

DRINKING
Barney's	46 F3
Irish Murphy's	47 F4
Koala Bar	(see 18)
Reef Bar	48 F3
Ricky Ricardo's	49 B3
Zachary's	50 F3

Noosaville and Noosa Heads. The latter is the fanciest sibling with trendy Hastings St. Heading west along the river, you'll find Tewantin, the departure point for the Noosa River ferry. Around the headland from Noosa Heads on the eastern coast is the peaceful and ambient resort of Sunshine Beach, with some good surf breaks.

Information
There are several ATMs and banks in Noosa Junction.
Adventure Travel Bugs (☎ 1800 666 720, 5474 8530; 9 Sunshine Beach Rd, Noosa Junction; per hr $1; ☙ 8am-8pm Mon-Fri, 9am-7pm Sat & Sun) Internet access.
Noosa information centre (☎ 5447 9088; www .tourismnoosa.com.au; Hastings St; ☙ 9am-5pm)

Extremely helpful and professional setup. Free tour and accommodation booking service.
Peterpan Adventure Travel (☎ 1800 777 115; www.peterpans.com; Shop 3, 75 Noosa Dr, Noosa Junction; per hr $1; ☙ 9am-6.30pm Mon-Sat, 10am-6.30pm Sun) Internet access.
Post Office (☎ 5473 8591; 91 Noosa Dr)
Urban Mailbox (☎ 5473 5151; Shop 3, Ocean Breeze, Noosa Dr, Noosa Heads; per hr $6; ☙ 9am-9pm Mon-Fri, 9am-7pm Sat, 10am-7pm Sun) Expensive but super-fast Internet access.

Sights
One of Noosa's best features, the small but lovely **Noosa National Park** extends 2km southwest from the headland that marks the end of the Sunshine Coast. It has fine walks,

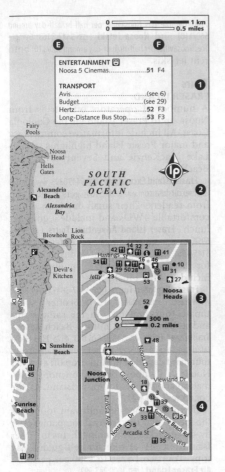

great coastal scenery and a string of bays on the northern side with waves that draw surfers from all over the country. Alexandria Bay on the eastern side has the best beach, and is also an informal nudist beach.

The most scenic way to access the national park is to follow the boardwalk along the coast from town. This continues all the way to the park's main entrance at the end of Park Rd (the eastern continuation of Hastings St). Here you'll find a car park, picnic areas and the **QPWS centre** (☎ 5447 3243; 🕑 9am-3pm), where you can obtain a walking track map.

Sleepy koalas are often spotted in the trees in the afternoon and dolphins are commonly seen from the rocky headlands around Alexandria Bay.

For a panoramic view of the park, you can walk or drive up to the **Laguna Lookout** from Viewland Dr in Noosa Junction. From Sunshine Beach, access to the park is via McAnally Dr or Parkedge Rd.

Activities

CANOEING & KAYAKING

The Noosa River is excellent for canoeing; it's possible to follow it up through Lakes Cooroibah and Cootharaba, and through the Cooloola Section of Great Sandy National Park to just south of Rainbow Beach Rd. The Elanda Point Canoe Company (p190) rents canoes and kayaks from Elanda Point and can collect and return you from the bus stop at Sidoni Street in Tewantin. See p184 for tour options.

Noosa Ocean Kayak Tours (☎ 0418-787 577; 2-hr tours $50, kayak hire per day $40) offers kayaking tours around Noosa National Park and along Noosa River.

ADVENTURE ACTIVITIES

Pedal & Paddle (☎ 5449 2671; www.pedalandpaddle.com.au; tours $70) operates great four-hour hike, bike and kayak tours that combine all three activities and cater to all fitness levels. Prices include morning and afternoon tea and local transfers.

Noosa Bike Hire & Tours (☎ 5474 3322; www.noosabikehire.com; tours $55) offers half-day mountain bike tours down Mt Tinbeerwah, including morning tea and transfers.

GOLF & TENNIS

Golfers should head for **Noosa Valley Country Club** (☎ 5449 1411; Links Dr, Noosa Heads; golf 9/18 holes $20/35, tennis per hr $15), which has an 18-hole championship golf course and tennis courts. **Tewantin Noosa Golf Club** (☎ 5447 1407; Cooroy-Noosa Rd, Tewantin; 9/18 holes $22/35) is a quieter alternative. Bookings are essential for both.

HORSE RIDING & CAMEL SAFARIS

South of Noosa **Clip Clop Treks** (☎ 5449 1254; www.clipcloptreks.com.au; Eumarella Rd, Lake Weyba; 2-hr/day rides $60/145, 4-day pub treks $1320) offers horse rides around Lake Weyba and the surrounding bush. Better yet is the all-inclusive four-day pub trek, which takes you through the northern Sunshine Coast hinterland, staying at historic pubs along the way.

Noosa North Shore Horse Riding, based at Noosa North Shore Retreat (p189), also offers beach rides and bush trail riding. Just as much fun is Camel Safaris (p189).

SURFING

With a string of breaks around an unspoilt national park, Noosa is a fine place to catch a wave. Generally the waves are best in December and January but Sunshine Corner, at the northern end of Sunshine Beach, has an excellent year-round break, although it has a brutal beach dump. The point breaks around the headland only perform during the summer, but when they do, expect wild conditions and good walls at Boiling Point and Tea Tree, on the northern coast of the headland. There are also gentler breaks on Noosa Spit at the far end of Hastings St, where most of the surf schools do their training.

Novices are spoilt for choice and this must be one of the most scenic places you can learn how not to fall off a board.

Recommended companies:

Merrick's Learn to Surf (☎ 0418-787 577; www.learntosurf.com.au; 2-hour/2-lesson/5-day courses $45/85/180)

Noosa Surf Lessons (☎ 0412-330 850; www.noosa surflessons.com.au; 1-/3-/5-day lessons from $45/120/170)

Wavesense (☎ 5474 9076, 1800 249 076; www.wavesense.com.au; 1/3 classes $50/135)

If you just want to rent equipment, **Noosa Longboards** (www.noosalongboards.com; Noosa Heads ☎ 5447 2828; 64 Hastings St; Noosaville ☎ 5474 2722; 187 Gympie Tce; longboards per half-/full day $30/45, surfboards $20/30, body boards $15/20) rents longboards as well as surfboards and body boards.

Surfing masters can try their hands at kite-surfing. For lessons, call **Kitesurf Australia** (☎ 5455 6677; www.kite-surf.com.au; 2-/4-hr lessons $140/260) or **Noosa Adventures & Kite-Surfing** (☎ 0438-788 573; www.noosakitesurfing.com.au; 2-/8-hr lessons $120/$380, equipment rental per hr/day $30/100). Conditions at the river mouth and Lake Weyba are best between October and January, but on windy days the Noosa River is a playground for serious daredevils.

OTHER ACTIVITIES

Both **Noosa Blue Water Dive** (☎ 5447 1300; www .fishingnoosa.com.au/DiveNoosa.htm; Noosa Harbour, Tewantin; per person $399) and **Resort 2 Diving** (☎ 5455 6488; www.resort2diving.com; Noosa Harbour; per person $350) offer PADI dive courses.

With all that water, another popular activity here is jet-skiing. **Pro-Ski Noosa** (☎ 5449 7740; Gympie Tce, Noosaville; per half-hr/half-day around $60/110) and **Noosa Jetski** (☎ 5447 3163; Gympie Tce, Noosaville; per half-hr/half-day around $60/110) both rent jet-skis.

Tours

FRASER ISLAND

A number of operators offer trips from Noosa up to Fraser Island via the Cooloola Coast. All include informative commentary and major Fraser Island highlights such as Lake MacKenzie and Seventy Five Mile Beach.

Fraser Island Excursions (☎ 5449 0393; www.fraser islandexcursions.com.au; tours $160) gets a huge rap from readers. Their small day tours are in comfortable 4WDs and include a gourmet lunch. **Fraser Island Adventure Tours** (☎ 5444 6957; www.fraserislandadventuretours.com.au; adult/child $145/105) has won several industry awards for its day tours in 4WD minibuses that include a BBQ lunch.

Fraser Explorer Tours (☎ 5447 3845, 5449 8647; www.fraser-is.com; adult/child $115/65) offer less intimate tours but take in the same sights and stop for lunch at Eurong Beach Resort. **Trailblazer Tours** (☎ 1800 626 673, 4125 2343; 3-day safaris adult/child $295/225) operates small group tours and can pick up and drop off at either Noosa or Rainbow Beach. For more information about tours to Fraser Island, see the boxed text on p210.

If you're cashed up and want to do this the spectacular way, several companies offer fly-drive packages including flights to Fraser Island and 4WD hire for self-guided day trips. Tours cost $250 to $300 per person:

Air Fraser Island (☎ 1800 247 992; www.airfraserisland.com.au)

Fraser Island Heli-Drive (☎ 1800 063 933, 4125 3933; www.fraserislandco.com.au/helidrive.html)

Sunshine Coast Scenic Flights (☎ 5450 0516; www.noosaaviation.com)

EVERGLADES

Several companies run boats from the Noosa Harbour at Tewantin up the Noosa River into the 'Everglades' area (essentially the passage of the Noosa River that cuts into the Great Sandy National Park).

Companies include:

Beyond Noosa (☎ 1800 657 666, 5449 9177; www.beyondnoosa.com.au; morning tours adult/child $28/15, day tours incl lunch adult/child $70/30) All tours include Noosa transfers.

Everglades Water Bus Co (☎ 1800 688 045, 5447 1838; 4-hr tours adult/child/family $55/40/180, 6-hr tours incl lunch adult/child/family $65/45/210) Tours include Noosa transfers.

MV Noosa Queen (☎ 5455 6661; tours adult/child incl lunch $38/19; ☾ 12.30pm) Lunch cruises up the river.

For the more adventurous, **Peterpan Adventure Travel** (☎ 1800 777 115; www.peterpans.com; Shop 3, 75 Noosa Dr, Noosa Junction; tours $130) offers three-day canoe tours into the park including tents and equipment. Alternatively, the **Elanda Point Canoe Company** (☎ 1800 226 637, 5485 3165; www.elanda.com.au/noosa; Elanda Point; tours adult/child $60/50; ☾ 9.30am) offers three-hour canoe tours including transfers.

Festivals & Events

Noosa Jazz Festival (☎ 5449 9189; www.noosajazz .com.au) Four-day annual jazz festival, attracting artists from around the globe and held in late August and early September.

Noosa Triathlon (☎ 5449 0711; www.usmevents.com .au) Week-long sports festival in early November culminating in the very popular triathlon.

Sleeping

Although Noosa has a reputation as a resort for the rich and fashionable, there are several backpacker hostels and caravan parks in among the resort hotels and apartments. With the exception of backpackers' hostels, accommodation prices can rise by 50% in busy times and 100% in the December to January peak season. All prices quoted below are for the low season.

BUDGET

Bougainvillia Holiday Park (☎ 1800 041 444; 5447 1712; jsjs@optusnet.com.au; 141 Cooroy-Noosa Rd, Tewantin; unpowered/powered sites from $24/26, cabins $55-95; ⊠ ☎) Neat as a pin and meticulously landscaped, this is the best camping option in the area. The facilities are spotless, there's an onsite café and petrol station and disabled travellers are well catered for. Prices are for two people.

Sandy Court Holiday Units (☎ 5449 7225; fax 5473 0397; 30 James St, Noosaville; d $55-70; ☎) Down a quiet residential street, these self-contained units offer unbeatable value. The décor is a wee bit weary and the furnishings and crockery are mix and match, but they're clean, comfortable and well managed. Longer stays attract bargain rates.

YHA Halse Lodge (☎ 1800 242 567, 5447 3377; backpackers@halselodge.com.au; 2 Halse Lane, Noosa Heads; dm/d $27/70, meals $6-11; ☐) Elevated from Hastings St by a steeeep driveway, this splendid timber Queenslander is a legend on the backpacker route for its colonial charm and good looks. The dorms and kitchen are a tad cramped, but the bar is a mix-and-meet bonanza and serves great meals. The hostel offers a discount to YHA members.

Koala Beach Resort (☎ 1800 357 457, 5447 3355; www.koala-backpackers.com; 44 Noosa Dr, Noosa Junction; dm $22, tw & d $55; ☐ ☎) One of the Koala chain, this hostel has the usual trademarks – popular bar, central location and party atmosphere – but there's nothing haphazard about this setup. Your buck also buys huge dorms, good facilities, professional staff and plenty of bench seating and grassy patches outside to rest surf-weary bones.

MIDRANGE

Accommodation on Hastings St can be ridiculously expensive, but there are a few bargains in town. One of the best areas for cheaper accommodation is along Gympie Tce, the riverside main road through Noosaville. **Accom Noosa** (☎ 1800 072 078; www.accomnoosa.com.au; Shop 5, Fairshore Apartments, Hastings St, Noosa Heads) has an extensive list of private holiday rentals which are good for stays of a week or more.

Noosa Parade Holiday Inn (☎ 5447 4177; www .noosaparadeholidayinn.com; 51 Noosa Pde, Noosa Heads; r $110; ⊠ ☎) Not far from Hastings St, these tiled and spotless apartments are reminiscent of an Ikea showroom. The pleasant and cool interiors are clad in bold colours and face away from the street and passing traffic. Longer stays attract good discounts.

Noosa Valley Winery B&B (☎ 5449 1675; fax 5449 1679; 855 Noosa Eumundi Rd, Doonan; r $120; ☎) This pretty B&B is away from the bustle and incorporated into a boutique winery. Surrounded by thin pockets of bush and with just a hint of the Med, the elegant rooms are swimming in sunlight and have private alcoves where breakfast is served. Wheelchair friendly.

Terrapin (☎ 5449 8770; www.terrapin.com.au; 15 The Cockleshell, Noosaville; r per night/week $140/580; ☎) If you're hanging about for a week or so, these two-storey townhouses are a good option. The earthy interiors are lifted by bold furnishings and balconies or gardens. All contain every mod con you need to sustain a serious stay, plus either a video or DVD.

Noosa River Retreat (☎ 5474 2811; pauline@escapes resorts.com.au; cnr Weyba Rd & Reef St, Noosaville; r $75-85; ✗ ⊠) Your buck goes a long way at this orderly complex, which houses spick, span and spacious units. Onsite are a central BBQ and laundry and the corner units are almost entirely protected by small native gardens. It's a popular spot so bookings are advised.

Killara Apartments (☎ 5447 2800; www.killara noosa.com; 42 Grant St, Noosa Junction; r per 3 nights/week from $280/630; ✗ ⊠) These functional and modern units have plenty of space and colour. They're in a picturesque street, close to the river and Hastings St, and some come with private BBQs and courtyards. There's a three-night minimum stay.

Noosa Palm Tree Motel (☎ 5449 7311; fax 5474 3246; 233 Gympie Tce, Noosaville; r $80-95; ✗ ⊠) Close to the water, this solid complex has sound motel rooms with kitchenettes and larger, fully equipped units with cheery furnishings. This is a practical option for beach-addicted kiddies.

Also recommended:

Chez Noosa (☎ 5447 2027; www.cheznoosa.com.au; 263 David Low Way, Sunshine Beach; d $75-85; ✗) Modern, self-contained units low on flair but heavy on value and comfort.

Sunshine Vista (☎ 1300 551 999, 5447 2487; www .sunshinevista.com.au; 45 Duke St, Sunshine Beach; r per 2 nights/week from $260/660; ✗ ⊠) Comfortable units in an excellent location. Generally weekly bookings only.

Yallambee Holiday Apartments (☎ 5449 8632; 29 Weyba Rd, Noosaville; r from $65) An older-style building with individually owned units. Spotless and shady.

TOP END

Sheraton Noosa Resort (☎ 5449 4888; www.starwood hotels.com/sheraton; 14-16 Hastings St, Noosa Heads; r $280-400; ✗ ⊠) This five-star hotel is elegance personified. Tastefully coordinated rooms contain sueded fabrics, fabulous beds, balconies, kitchenettes and spas. The hotel also has four bars, three restaurants and a gym, sauna and spa. There are some great deals if you book online. Wheelchair friendly.

Emerald (☎ 1800 803 899, 5449 6100; www.emerald noosa.com.au; 42 Hastings St, Noosa Heads; r $230-450; ✗ ⊠) The stylish Emerald has indulgent rooms bathed in ethereal white and sunlight. Expect clean, crisp edges and exquisite furnishings. All rooms are self-contained and the mod cons are so lovely you'll miss them when you leave.

Eating

RESTAURANTS

Sabai Sabai (☎ 5473 5177; 46 Duke St; mains $22-28; ⊙ lunch & dinner) Like the chilled village it resides in, inconspicuous Sabai Sabai is class without the brass. The Asian-infused menu shows moments of genius with items such as silken fried tofu with green pawpaw salad and kaffir limes or grilled cuttlefish with cashews, coconut and chilli.

Café Le Monde (☎ 5449 2366; Hastings St; mains $17-28; ⊙ breakfast, lunch & dinner) There's not a fussy palate or dietary need that isn't catered for on Café Le Monde's enormous menu. The large, open-air patio buzzes with diners digging into burgers, seared tuna steaks, curries, pastas, salads and plenty more. Great for families and groups.

Cato's (☎ 5449 4888; 12-14 Hastings St, Noosa Heads; mains $18-26, seafood buffet $60; ⊙ breakfast, lunch & dinner) Cato's voluptuous bar beckons thirsty style cats with a dazzling array of alcoholic wares and an impressive wine list. Once they've soaked up the scene, refined punters savour European-inspired cuisine or hover over the spectacular seafood buffet.

Spinnakers (☎ 5474 5177; Sunshine Beach SLSC, the Esplanade, Sunshine Beach; mains $15-25; ⊙ lunch & dinner) This club bistro treats the tastebuds with dinner dishes such as braised lamb shanks and a *brunoise* of winter veggies and a tomato-celery sauce, or Indian bean and eggplant curry. The T-bones and fish dishes are huge; lunch is a tamer affair.

Seawater Café (☎ 5449 7215; 197 Gympie Tce, Noosaville; meals $8-20; ⊙ breakfast, lunch & dinner) This kitsch and colourful restaurant serves excellent seafood. Mermaids, portholes and sea paraphernalia adorn the walls, and calamari, prawns and plenty of fish fill out the menu. If you prefer something nonfishy, the nightly roast and daily sandwiches are also good.

Bistro C (☎ 5447 2855; On the Beach Arcade, Hastings St; mains $18-26; ⊙ breakfast, lunch & dinner) Famous for its quirky people sculptures, this boisterous bistro is pure yuppie. The egg-fried calamari with chilli lime coriander dip is legendary and you get to wine and dine in a wonderful location overlooking the beach.

Also recommended:

Berardo's on the Beach (☎ 5448 0888; 49 Hastings St, Noosa Heads; dishes $10-26; ⊙ lunch & dinner) Excellent Asian, Italian and Middle Eastern flavours served with stunning beachside views.

Noosa Heads Surf Club (☎ 5474 5688; Hastings St; mains $10-20; ⊙ breakfast Sat & Sun, lunch & dinner daily) Popular surf club serving good club grub.

CAFÉS

Sunshine Foodstore (☎ 5474 5611; 46 Duke St, Sunshine Beach; dishes $6-14; ⊙ breakfast & lunch) Long wooden benches are attended by many a local conquering newspapers and crosswords at this ambient outdoor café. Brekkies include plenty of egg options with fresh pesto, veggies and coffee. For lunch you can savour gargantuan ciabattas, and the cakes are exhausting.

Aromas (☎ 5474 9788; 32 Hastings St, Noosa Heads; mains $16-25; ⊙ breakfast, lunch & dinner) Unashamedly ostentatious, Aromas' Parisienne-style seating deliberately faces outwards for maximum people-watching. The menu is brief but the Victorian lamb with roasted pumpkin, eggplant and hummus or buttermilk panna cotta with strawberry-rhubarb soup distract the happy audience. Most folk come for the coffee and atmosphere.

Fusions (☎ 5474 1699; 271 Gympie Tce, Noosaville; mains $15-20; ⊙ breakfast, lunch & dinner) Catching plenty of beach breeze through the wideopen doorways, families, couples, locals and tourists sit at Fusions' high-backed Balinese chairs inside or the oversized tables outside. Gourmet sandwiches, wood-fired pizzas and spruced-up café fare graces the menu. Ideal breakfast spot.

Beach Chalet (☎ 5447 3944; 3 Tingira Cres, Sunrise Beach; dishes $5-8; ⊙ breakfast & lunch) A sneeze south of Sunshine Beach in Sunrise Beach, this small café is just an extension of a general store. The brekkies, burgers and sandwiches border on legendary, though, as do the views of the breakers.

Lazuli Blue Café (☎ 5448 0055; 9 Sunshine Beach Rd, Noosa Junction; meals $7-12; ⊙ breakfast & lunch) Slow and lazy eating is mandatory at this relaxed café, where colossal fresh juices and smoothies are the speciality. The breakfasts, Turkish toasties, salads and meatier dishes such as Cajun chicken are pretty special too.

Also recommended:

Canteen (☎ 5447 5400; 4-6 Sunshine Beach Rd, Noosa Junction; dishes $7-20; ⊙ breakfast & lunch) Sassy café with hearty fare.

Limefish Seafood & Salad Bar (☎ 5447 4650; Shop 2, 2 Hastings St, Noosa Heads; dishes $6-12; ⊙ lunch & dinner) Fresh and funky eat-in or takeaway fish and chippy.

Moondoggy's Café Bar (☎ 5449 9659; 187 Gympie Tce, Noosaville; meals $5-12; ⊙ breakfast & lunch) Cute café with a gourmet twist.

You can eat well for around $8 at the **Bay Village Shopping Centre** (Hastings St, Noosa Heads)

ABSOLUTELY FABULOUS

Noosa's culinary cultivation is legendary throughout Queensland, and dining out here is an essential cog in your holiday wheel. Several venues have published cookbooks and the competition is fierce, so even the most demanding gourmand should find something here to tease their palate. The following exceptional eateries are recommended:

Gusto (☎ 5449 7144; 257 Gympie Tce, Noosaville; mains $17-30; ⊙ lunch & dinner) This outstanding restaurant must be the very definition of Mod Oz cuisine. Chic and casual surrounds complement flawless mains such as Mooloolaba prawn and garlic ravioli or crisp-fried cuttlefish salad with Persian fetta and olives. The wine list is extensive and the service perfect.

Berardo's (☎ 5447 5666; Hastings St, Noosa Heads; mains $26-33; ⊙ dinner) Beautiful Berardo's serves utopian cuisine in a heavenly venue. Amid a sea of pristine white and perched above the street, delicate dishes such as spiced seafood hotpot with saffron and tomato or grilled chorizo and cuttlefish with lemon couscous are served. Elegant and romantic.

Dish (☎ 5449 0094; Shop 2, 14 Thomas St, Noosaville; mains $16-25; ⊙ dinner Mon-Sat) Tucked into a quiet corner, this diminutive restaurant serves fabulous food on a wee wooden deck. The menu is a work of art – think seared caraway and roasted coffee oil marinated kangaroo with roasted mash. There's also a kids menu and plenty of veggie options.

Ottoman Bistro (☎ 5447 1818; 249 Gympie Tce, Noosaville; mains $18-27; ⊙ lunch & dinner) This fantastic Turkish-bazaar-meets-Noosaville-restaurant gets a big thumbs up for Middle Eastern cred such as Harissa spatchcock, Persian black beans, traditional *labne* (yoghurt spread) or seafood *tagine* (stew). You can recline on the wall couches, sit beneath shady sailcloths or play a round of backgammon while you dine.

food court. Self-caterers can stock up at the **Noosa Store** (33 Hastings St, Noosa Heads), **Action** (Plaza Shopping Centre, Sunshine Beach Rd, Noosa Junction) supermarket or **Coles** (Noosa Fair Shopping Centre, Lanyana Way, Noosa Junction) supermarket.

Drinking

Zachary's (☎ 5447 3211; 30 Hastings St, Noosa Heads) Set back above Hastings St, this slinky bar imbues a splash of urban cool into Noosa's coastal milieu. Dark colours, dim lighting and ambient beats swirl about as trendy young things get down to the business of being cool. Bar snacks are served, but who cares?

Ricky Ricardos (☎ 5447 2455; The Wharf, Quamby Pl, Noosa Heads) This genial bar is a great spot for cocktails, sultry Latin music and partaking in some meet-and-greet action. The snappy bar staff and waterfront location add to the sophisticated air.

Barney's (☎ 5447 4800; Noosa Dr, Noosa Heads) A bit of an all-day drinking bonanza, this outdoor bar plays a relentless soundtrack of loud music to an appreciative crowd. Threads shift from board shorts to strappy heels and shirts as the sun goes down.

Koala Bar (☎ 5447 3355; 44 Noosa Dr, Noosa Junction) Noosa's backpackers and other free spirits start their nightly revelry at this popular hostel bar. Live rock fills every crevice several nights a week. and when it doesn't the place hums to the harmony of beer jugs, beery chatter and beer tunes.

Reef Bar (☎ 5447 4477; 9 Noosa Dr, Noosaville) A little bit country, a little bit coast and a whole lot Oz, Reef Bar is a cruisy watering hole with a strong local feel. You've every chance of grasping the secrets of Aussie Rules football while listening to Australian rock or dancing to doof doof.

Also recommended:

Cato's (p186)

Irish Murphy's (☎ 5455 3344; cnr Sunshine Beach Rd & Noosa Dr; 🕃) Irish theme pub with good ales.

Entertainment

Noosa 5 Cinemas (☎ 1300 366 339; 29 Sunshine Beach Rd, Noosa Junction) is a plush, comfortable cinema that screens the latest blockbusters.

Getting There & Away

Long-distance buses stop at the bus stop near the corner of Noosa Dr and Noosa Pde. All of Noosa's hostels have courtesy buses that will pick up from the bus stop (except Halse Lodge, which is only 100m away!).

Both **Greyhound Australia** (☎ 13 14 99; www.greyhound.com.au) and **Premier Motor Service** (☎ 13 34 10; www.premierms.com.au) have two connections to Brisbane daily ($24, 2½ hours), as well as destinations north including Hervey Bay ($27, 3½ hours). Suncoast Pacific also connects Noosa and Brisbane; see p172 for more information.

Sunbus (☎ 5492 8700) has frequent services between Maroochydore and Noosa ($4.40, one hour) and between Noosa and the Nambour train station ($4.40, one hour).

Getting Around

BICYCLE

Noosa Bike Hire and Tours (☎ 5474 3322; www.noosabikehire.com; per 4hr/day $15/20) hires bicycles out from several locations in Noosa including YHA Halse Lodge (p185). Alternatively, it will deliver and collect the bikes to/from your door for free.

BOAT

Riverlight Ferry (☎ 5449 8442) operates ferries between Noosa Heads and Tewantin (one way adult/child/family $9.50/4/25, all-day pass $13.50/5/35, 30 minutes, six to 10 daily). Tickets include onboard commentary, so the ferry provides a tour as well as being a people-mover.

BUS

During the peak holiday seasons – 26 December to 10 January and over Easter – there are free shuttle buses every 10 to 15 minutes between Weyba Rd, just outside Noosa Junction, travelling all the way to Tewantin, and stopping just about everywhere in-between. Sunbus has local services that link Noosa Heads, Noosaville, Noosa Junction etc.

CAR

The **Other Car Rental Company** (☎ 5447 2831; www.noosacarrental.com; per day from $45) delivers cars and 4WDs to your door. The big guns are also in town and rent cars from around $35 per day. They include **Avis** (☎ 5447 4933; Shop 1, Ocean Breeze Resort, cnr Hastings St & Noosa Dve, Noosa Heads), **Hertz** (☎ 5447 2253; Noosa Blue Resort, 16 Noosa Dve, Noosa Heads) and **Budget** (☎ 5474 2820; Bay Village Mall, Noosa Heads).

COOLOOLA COAST

Stretching for 50km between Noosa and Rainbow Beach, the Cooloola Coast is a remote strip of long sandy beaches backed by the Cooloola Section of Great Sandy National Park. Although it's undeveloped, the Toyota Landcruiser and tin boat set flock here in droves so it's not always as peaceful as you might imagine. If you head off on foot or by canoe along the many inlets and waterways, you'll soon escape the crowds.

From the end of Moorindil St in Tewantin, the **Noosa North Shore Ferry** (☎ 5447 1321; pedestrians/cars one way $1/5; ⏱ 5am-12.30am Fri & Sat, 6am-10.30pm Sun-Thu) shuttles folk across the river to Noosa North Shore. The trip takes a matter of minutes; if you're sporting a caravan on the back of your car it's an extra $5/7 for up to 4.7m/7.7m. A small section of the Great Sandy National Park is here, but most people head here for activities along the Noosa River and on Lake Cooroibah. If you have a 4WD you can drive right up the beach to Rainbow Beach (and on up to Inskip Bay, from where you can take a ferry across to Fraser Island), but check the tide times before setting out.

On the way up the beach you'll pass the **Teewah coloured sand cliffs**, estimated to be about 40,000 years old, and the rusting **Cherry Venture**, a 3000-tonne freighter swept ashore by a cyclone in 1973.

Lake Cooroibah

A couple of kilometres north of Tewantin, the Noosa River widens into Lake Cooroibah. If you take the Noosa North Shore Ferry, you can drive up to the lake in a conventional vehicle and camp along sections of the beach.

For a taste of the exotic, and possibly the most fun you can have traversing up a beach, **Camel Company Australia** (☎ 5442 4402; www.camelcompany.com.au; Beach Rd, Noosa North Shore; 1-hr rides adult/child $40/30, 2-hr rides adult/child $55/45) operates glorious camel treks. Die-hards will also love the six-day Fraser Island safari (per adult/child $1400/850).

Noosa North Shore Horse Riding (☎ 5447 1369; 1-/2-hr rides $40/70), based at Noosa North Shore Retreat, operates great rides along Teewah Beach and through the surrounding bush.

Noosa North Shore Retreat (☎ 5447 1706; www .noosanorthshore.com.au; Beach Rd; unpowered/powered sites from $14/19.50, r from $70, cabins from $90, mains $8-15;

COOLOOLA COAST

0 —— 2 km
0 —— 1 mile

lunch & dinner;) is a sprawling park with camping, cabins, motel rooms, large cottages and a host of options in-between to suit everyone. There's also a pub and small shop here. Activities on offer include bushwalking, canoeing, fishing, tennis and horse riding. Camping prices are for two people.

If you've ever wanted to emulate the bush tucker man, **Gagaju** (☎ 1300 302 271, 5474 3522; www.travoholic.com/gagaju; 118 Johns Dr, Tewantin; unpowered sites/dm $11/17) is a riverside eco-wilderness camp with basic dorms that were constructed entirely from recycled timber. Expect castaway digs rather than the Ritz, but the folk who head here love it. Activities include canoeing, mountain biking and bushwalking. You need to bring your own food and the Gagaju minibus shuttles to and from Noosa three times a day. Camping prices are for two people.

Lake Cootharaba & Boreen Point

Cootharaba is the biggest lake in the Cooloola Section of Great Sandy National Park, measuring about 5km across and 10km in length. On the western shores of the lake and at the southern edge of the national park, Boreen Point is a relaxed little community with several places to stay and eat. The lake is the gateway to the Noosa Everglades, offering bushwalking, canoeing and bush camping.

From Boreen Point, an unsealed road leads another 5km up to **Elanda Point**, where there's a ranger's station (opposite), and the headquarters of the **Elanda Point Canoe Company** (☎ 1800 226 637, 5485 3165; www.elanda.com .au/noosa; Elanda Point; hire per day for 1 or 2 people $25), which rents canoes and kayaks. If you want to do a self-guided safari up the river, this company also rents camping equipment, arranges permits and organises transfers from Noosa. If it's just the transport you're after they'll shuttle you up to Kinaba or Fig Tree Point (one way $25) and Harry's Hut (one way $45) camping grounds. Rates are much cheaper if you rent a canoe. **Everglades Waterfront Holidays** (☎ 5485 3164; Boreen Point Pde, Boreen Point; kayak hire per day $45, extra days $15) also rents out kayaks. See p184 for more information on guided tours to the area.

The two self-contained units at **Lake Cootharaba Gallery Units** (☎ 5485 3153; 64 Laguna St, Boreen Point; r per night/week from $80/400) are homey and practical. The gallery they're

attached to is a tad on the eccentric side, but the hosts are lovely.

On a serene strip by the river, the quiet and simple **Boreen Point Caravan & Camping Area** (☎ 5485 3244; Dun's Beach, Teewah St, Boreen Point; unpowered sites $12) is dominated by large gums and native bush. Take a right turn off Laguna St onto Vista St and bear right at the lake. Rates are for two people.

Apollonian Hotel (☎ 5485 3100; fax 5485 3499; Laguna St, Boreen Point; dm/d with shared bathroom $25/45, mains $12; lunch & dinner) is a gorgeous old pub with sturdy timber walls, shady verandas and a beautifully preserved interior. Rooms are in the Queenslander out the back and the pub grub is tasty and popular.

Cooloola Section – Great Sandy National Park

The Cooloola Section of Great Sandy National Park covers more than 54,000 hectares from Lake Cootharaba north to Rainbow Beach. It's a varied wilderness area with long sandy beaches, mangrove-lined waterways, forest, heath and lakes, all featuring plentiful bird life – including rarities such as the red goshawk and the grass owl – and lots of wildflowers in spring.

The Cooloola Way, which runs from Tewantin all the way up to Rainbow Beach, is open to 4WD vehicles unless there's been heavy rain – check with the rangers before setting out. Most people prefer to bomb up the beach, though you're restricted to a few hours either side of low tide.

Although there are many 4WD tracks running to lookout points and picnic grounds, the best way to see Cooloola is by boat or canoe along the numerous tributaries of the Noosa River. Boats can be hired from Tewantin and Noosa (along Gympie Tce), Boreen Point and Elanda Point on Lake Cootharaba, and from Gagaju (left).

There are some fantastic walking trails starting from Elanda Point on the shore of Lake Cootharaba, including the 46km Cooloola Wilderness Trail to Rainbow Beach and a 7km trail to the **QPWS information centre** (☎ 5449 7364; 7am-4pm) on Kinaba Island.

Before you go, pop into the **QPWS Great Sandy Information Centre** (☎ 5449 7792; 240 Moorindil St, Tewantin; 7am-4pm), which can provide information on park access, tide times and fire bans within the park. The centre issues camping permits for Great Sandy National

Park and car and camping permits for Fraser Island. There is also a **ranger's station** (☎ 5485 3245; ⌚ 7am-4pm) at Elanda.

There are around 15 camping grounds in the park, many of them along the river. The most popular (and best equipped) camping grounds are Fig Tree Point, at the northern end of Lake Cootharaba, Harry's Hut, about 4km upstream, and Freshwater, about 6km south of Double Island Point on the coast. You can also camp on the beach if you're driving up to Rainbow Beach. Standard national park rates (per person/family $4/16) apply and you must purchase permits for all camping grounds along the river at Elanda ranger's station. You can purchase permits for Harry's Hut, Fig Tree Point, Freshwater and all beach camping at the QPWS Great Sandy Information Centre. Apart from Harry's Hut and Freshwater, all sites are accessible by hiking or river only.

EUMUNDI

Sweet little Eumundi has the quaint ambience of a highland village thawed generously by the coast, only a whiff away. There's a pervading New-Age vibe running through the main street, amplified greatly during the famous **Saturday market**, when thousands of visitors descend to potter through the 200-plus stalls. You'll find everything from homemade cheese graters to aromatic sneeze abators, and then there's the clothing, food and music. The market is open from 6.30am to 2pm every Saturday, and a smaller version is held on Wednesdays from 8am to 1.30pm.

Sights & Activities

The town's other claim to fame is Eumundi Lager, originally brewed in the Imperial Hotel. Nowadays it's made down at Yatala on the Gold Coast, but you can still sample it on tap in the **Imperial Hotel**. The former brewing room is now an art gallery with glass-blowing displays.

The **Eumundi Historical Museum** (☎ 5442 8762; Memorial Dr; admission free; ⌚ 9am-4.30pm Wed & Fri, 9am-3pm Sat) offers an insight into the town's history.

About 10km northwest of Eumundi, the little village of **Pomona** sits in the shadow of looming Mt Cooroora (440m) and is home to the wonderful **Majestic Theatre** (☎ 5485 2330; tickets $6) – one of the only places in the world where you can see a silent movie accompanied by the original Wurlitzer organ soundtrack. The Majestic only plays one film, Rudolph Valentino's last screen performance, *The Son of the Sheik*, every Thursday at 8.30pm (in fact, the Majestic has shown *The Son of the Sheik* every Thursday for 13 years!).

Sleeping & Eating

Taylor's Damn Fine B&B (☎ 5442 8685; fax 5442 8168; www.taylorsbandb.com.au; 1502 Eumundi-Noosa Rd; d incl breakfast $120-175) The damn fine rooms in this pleasant B&B are a well-designed combination of antique Oz and contemporary class. All have private balconies and bar fridges, or there are simpler rooms in the converted railcar in the garden. It's about 1km from Eumundi on the Noosa road.

Eumundi Rise B&B (☎ 5442 8855; www.eumundirise bandb.com.au; 37-9 Crescent Rd; s/d from $90/125) Behind a sweeping veranda, this attractive Queenslander is home to pleasant, neat rooms. There are tea- and coffee-making facilities for guests and it's wheelchair friendly.

Eumundi Caravan Park (☎ 5442 8411; fax 5442 7414; 141 Memorial Dr; unpowered/powered sites $16/19; ⛴) About 1km north of the centre of town this pretty caravan park has plenty of flat grass and tree clusters. Outside of school holidays you should get plenty of space to yourself.

Treefellers Café (☎ 5442 7766; 69 Memorial Dr; mains $13-22; ⌚ breakfast & lunch Wed-Sun, dinner Fri & Sat) Eumundi's most cosmopolitan eatery extends itself under a beautiful timber shelter, and treats your palate to global dishes such as Moroccan spiced chicken salad, almond and ricotta gnocchi or grilled Atlantic salmon.

Imperial Hotel (☎ 5442 8303; Memorial Dr; ⌚ breakfast Wed & Sat, lunch Tue-Sun, dinner Tue-Sat) The Queensland drawl is thick behind the bar at this big old timber pub. There's a breezy, shady beer garden where you can dig into hearty pub nosh, with live music or comedy on the weekends.

Getting There & Away

Sunbus (☎ 5492 8700) Nos 631 and 630 ($4, one hour, roughly hourly) head here from Noosa Heads, stopping in the centre of town. Alternatively, both **Storeyline Tours** (☎ 5474 1500; www.sunshinecoastdaytours.com.au) and **Henry's** (☎ 5474 0199) offer door to door transfers from Noosa accommodation (adult/child $15/10, 30 minutes, Wednesday and

Saturday), allowing around two hours at the markets. **Everglades Water Bus Co** (☎ 1800 688 045, 5447 1838; adult/child $65/50) does a Eumundi Markets tour every Saturday, which also includes a cruise on the Everglades.

SUNSHINE COAST HINTERLAND

The Blackall Range rises a short distance inland from the coast, with spectacular countryside, some appealing national parks, and numerous (rather chintzy) rustic villages full of Devonshire tearooms, antiques shops and craft emporiums. There are plenty of tours, but it's worth coming up here with your own transport as the landscape between the villages is the real attraction.

Tours

Plenty of tour companies operate through the hinterland. Most combine a trip through the Blackall Range with other attractions such as the Glass House Mountains, the Big Pineapple, the Ginger Factory or Australia Zoo, and will pick up from anywhere along the Sunshine Coast.

Mystic Mountain Tours (☎ 5445 7874; www.mystic mountaintours.com.au; adult/child $40/30) operates excellent small-group tours. They have set itineraries, but can tailor a trip to your preference. In a similar vein, **Off Beat Rainforest Tours** (☎ 5473 5135; www.offbeattours.com.au; adult/ child $125/80) offers excellent 4WD eco-tours to Conondale National Park, including morning tea, a gourmet lunch and transfers. **Storeyline Tours** (☎ 5474 1500; adult/child $65/30) is another good operator, with small-group tours to Montville and nearby rainforests, as well as winery tours and tours to the Glass House Mountains. **Henry's** (☎ 5474 0199; adult/child $55/20) offers the same.

For more tours to the Sunshine Coast hinterland from Brisbane, see p96.

NAMBOUR & YANDINA

Nambour is the main commercial centre in the hinterland, but there's not much here for travellers.

The famous **Big Pineapple** (☎ 5442 1333; Nambour Connection Rd, Nambour; ⏱ 9am-5pm) is one of Queensland's kitschy 'big things'. You can walk through the 15m-high fibreglass fruit itself for free, but the main attractions lie beyond. A plantation train tour (adult/child $11.50/9.50) takes you through pineapple fields with informative commentary on everything you wanted to know about growing a lot of pineapples. There are also tours through macadamia orchids and rainforests ($9.70/8) and a harvest boat ride ($9.70/8) through hydroponic waterways. If you want to do the lot you can buy a combined ticket (adult/child/family $26/21/75). Don't forget to spend more money at the souvenir shop.

On the Bruce Hwy about 7km north of the Big Pineapple is Yandina, where you'll find the **Ginger Factory** (☎ 5446 7096; 50 Pioneer Rd; admission free; ⏱ 9am-5pm), a tacky souvenir store and tourist attraction. There are train rides, factory and plantation tours and, of course, a huge range of ginger products and souvenirs on sale.

Spirit House Restaurant (☎ 5446 8994, 4 Ninderry Rd, Yandina; mains $23-33; ⏱ lunch daily, dinner Wed-Sat) is legendary on this route. The subtropical surrounds create an authentic Southeast Asian setting, while the kitchen creates Thai-infused innovations such as whole crispy reef fish with tamarind and chilli or salmon spring rolls with sambal dressing.

Nambour is on the main coastal train line, and is well connected to Brisbane by frequent **Citytrain** (☎ 13 12 30; www.transinfo .com.au) services ($11.60, 1¾ hours). **Sunbus** (☎ 5492 8700) runs regular buses from the train station to Noosa ($4.40, one hour), via Eumundi and Yandina.

MALENY

Beautiful Maleny nestles on a rolling patch of hinterland and complements the wealth of greenery surrounding it with a quirky bohemian edge. There's a refreshing lack of tacky heritage developments and ye olde tourist-trap shoppes. Maple St, the main drag, offers pleasant street cafés and craft shops selling work by local artists.

Information

There's a small **information centre** (☎ 5499 9033; www.tourmaleny.com.au; ⏱ 9am-5pm) at the Maleny Community Centre. Maleny has a craft market on Sunday morning.

Sights & Activities

Mary Cairncross Scenic Reserve (☎ 5499 9907; Mountain View Rd; admission free; ⏱ 8am-6pm) is a pristine rainforest shelter spread over 130 acres southeast of town. A plethora of Queensland flora, including spectacular strangler fig trees, inhabits the area, as does a healthy population of birdlife and unbearably cute pademelons. Wheelchair-friendly walking tracks enable visitors to traverse the park without damaging the ecology, and the best time to visit is early morning or late afternoon, when the birds are most active.

Festivals & Events
The famous **Woodford Folk Festival**, which is held on a property near the town of Woodford, runs annually over the five days leading up to New Year's Day. The festival programme features a huge diversity of music including folk, traditional Irish, indigenous and world music, as well as buskers, belly dancers, craft markets, visual arts performances and a visiting squad of Tibetan monks. If you want to settle in for the festival, camping grounds are set up on the property with toilets, showers etc.

Tickets cost around $75 per day including camping ($85 on New Year's Eve) and can be bought at the gate or in advance through the **festival office** (☎ 5496 1600). Check online at www.woodfordfolkfestival .com for a programme of performances.

Sleeping
Maleny Lodge Guest House (☎ 5494 2370; www .malenylodge.com; 58 Maple St; s incl breakfast $95-140, d incl breakfast $130-185; ☒) This rambling B&B boasts a myriad of gorgeous rooms with cushy, four-poster beds and lashings of stained wood and antiques. There's an open fire for cold winter days and an open pool house for warm summer ones.

Maleny Palms Tourist Park (☎ 5494 2933; book ings@malenypalms.com.au; 23 Macadamia Dr; unpowered sites $22, cabins $70-80, villas $95-120; ☒) Northwest of the centre, this tidy park has villas the size of small houses and self-contained cabins. The grounds are landscaped with native flora, but the tent sites (rates are for two people) aren't much to write home about.

Other options:

Maleny Hills Motel (☎ 5494 2551; www.malenyhills .com.au; 932 Montville Rd; s/d from $60/70; ☒) Comfortable and clean motel option.

Maleny Hotel (☎ 5494 2013; fax 5494 3108; 6 Bunya St; s/d $55/70) Basic rooms with shared bath upstairs in this convivial pub.

Eating
Maleny is known for its fine dining, with several very posh restaurants just south of the centre. There are several good cafés along Maple St.

Terrace (☎ 5494 3700; Mary Cairncross Cnr; mains $25-30; ☒ lunch & dinner) One of Queensland's best, this award-winner serves delectable seafood and has spectacular views of the Glass House Mountains. If you're ravenous try the Moreton Bay bugs, king prawns, salmon and mahi mahi served on a sizzling granite tile with vegetable skewers, wild rice and garlic aioli.

Up Front Club (☎ 5494 2592; 31 Maple St; dishes $6-9; ☒ breakfast Mon-Sat, lunch Mon-Fri, dinner daily) This cosy café injects funk by the bucketful into Maleny's main strip, with organic breads and tofu and tempeh salads. Live music takes to the stage Friday to Sunday nights (cover charges $5 to $8) and you'll catch anything from reggae to a bout of folk. Musicians are welcome to the blackboard sessions on Monday evenings. Dinner is snacks only, so don't pack your appetite.

Perry's (☎ 5494 2822; 76 Maple St; mains $14-26; ☒ dinner) The chef at this intimate place fills the menu with goodies such as prawn and calamari curry with lime leaves, and the drunken chocolate sponge with Belgian chocolate sauce and macadamias will indeed leave you with that choco-intoxicated slur. Perry's also does Thai takeaway ($12 to $18).

Monicaz Cafe & Deli (☎ 5494 2670; 11/43 Maple St; mains $7-15; ☒ breakfast & lunch) Snazzy Monicaz dishes up excellent lamb and asparagus stacks, grilled tofu salad, Sicilian risotto balls and spicy Mexican tortillas. There are no packets to be found in this kitchen, and the coffee is excellent.

MONTVILLE
On a ridge midway between Mapleton and Maleny, the historic village of Montville has long since vanished under a mountain of chintzy fudge emporiums, Devonshire tearooms and craft shops shaped like antique German cuckoo clocks. Nearby Flaxton offers more of the same.

More interesting is **Kondalilla National Park**, 3km northwest of Mapleton. Kondalilla Falls drop 80m into a rainforested valley; there's a 4.8km round-trip walk to the bottom.

There's a helpful **information centre** (☎ 5478 5544; 168 Main St; ☒ 10am-4pm) that can help

DETOUR

From Mapleton, instead of heading east and back to the Bruce Hwy, head west onto Obi Obi Rd. A few kilometres out of town is the wee but pretty **Mapleton Falls National Park**, where Pencil Creek plunges 120m down into Obi Obi Valley. There's a lookout point just a couple of hundred metres from the car park and several walking tracks with plenty of colourful birdlife.

If you head further west for around 18km you'll come to Kenilworth, where you should take a break at **Kenilworth Country Foods** (☎ 5446 0144; 45 Charles St; ☯ 9am-4pm Mon-Fri, 10.30am-3.30pm Sat & Sun), which sells wickedly good cheeses and ice creams.

Heading north, Kenilworth–Brooloo Rd snakes its way past the Imbil State Forest on the western side. Traditional old farmhouses dot the scenic route, in-between the occasional mountain and floods of jacarandas.

After 23km turn right (east) onto Tuchekoi Rd, and travel for 5km before reaching a T-junction at Kenilworth-Skyring Creek Rd. Turn left (north) for 6km and you'll be back on the Bruce Hwy.

you find B&Bs in the area, but if you want something truly divine, make a beeline for **Treehouses of Montville** (☎ 1800 444 350; www.treehouses.com.au; Kondalilla Falls Rd; r incl breakfast Mon-Fri $130-260; per 2 nights Sat & Sun $400-660) If the Sultan of Brunei had a tree house, perhaps it would be something like these. All rates are for self-contained cabins, starting with

the 'budget' cottages, which come with log fires, spas, stereos, videos and warm interiors. The best and priciest of the lot are the extravagant Seaview tree houses with their mind-blowing views. You can also rest your head at the low-key **Montville Mountain Inn** (☎ 5442 9499; fax 5442 9303; Main St; r Sun-Thu $85, Fri & Sat $95, B&B packages incl dinner per person Sun-Fri $85, Sat $95), which has a themey Tudor exterior and modern motel rooms.

At the friendly **Pennefathings Inn** (☎ 5442 9489; 96 Main St; mains $15-25; ☯ lunch & dinner daily, breakfast Sun) you can start with an imported or domestic boutique beer and chase it up with vegetarian ratatouille, spicy New England chowder or swordfish curry.

MAPLETON

Mapleton is a laid-back little township 8km north of Montville. It has a couple of craft and pottery galleries and a good pub that has fine views from the veranda.

Those suffering from urban decay are advised to recharge the batteries at **Obilo Lodge** (☎ 5445 7705; www.obilolodge.com.au; Lot 9, Suses Pocket Rd; r incl breakfast $140-160; ☒ ☒). This boutique B&B has posh but unpretentious rooms with little extras such as pampering products in the bathroom and TVs, plus big extras in the way of sublime views. The most expensive room also has a spa.

Just north of Mapleton, **Lilyponds Caravan Park** (☎ 1800 003 764, 5445 7238; www.lilyponds.com.au; 26 Warruga St; unpowered/powered sites from $20/22, cabins $65-85) overlooks the Mapleton Lily Ponds and has self-contained cabins. Quoted camping rates are for two people.

Fraser Coast

CONTENTS

HIGHLIGHTS

- Cruising up the beach 'highway' on **Fraser Island** (p210) and getting an eyeful of the coast from Indian Head
- Slipping into Fraser Island's vivid **lakes** and coursing through the dense **rainforest** (p212)
- Being humbled by the bulk of humpback whales as they show off in **Hervey Bay** (p204)
- Taking time out with a languid stroll through Bundaberg's florid **Botanic Gardens** (p216)
- Tasting history in charming **Maryborough** (p200) and ogling at the town's gracious old timber Queenslanders
- Watching tiny loggerhead turtles hatch and make the first stumble to water at **Mon Repos** (p220)
- Introducing yourself to spectacular marine life on a dive off **Barolin Rocks** (p217) near Bargara
- Soaking up the views of Rainbow Beach's coloured cliffs at the **Carlo Sandblow** (p198)

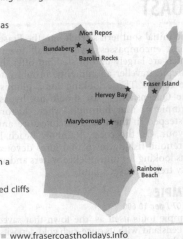

- www.seefraserisland.com
- www.frasercoastholidays.info

The sassy, social bustle of the Sunshine Coast diminishes distinctly as you journey north into the Fraser region. The population density drops and the landscape opens right up, revealing rural flavours and oceans of green space. The interior of this part of Queensland is peppered with towns steeped in history and the coast is thick with national parks.

The jewel that lures people to this patch of coast is of course enigmatic Fraser Island, the world's largest sand island. If you have even the slightest taste for the great outdoors a trip here is mandatory. Essentially one long, forest-backed beach, Fraser Island offers stunning scenery, dense rainforests, luminous lakes, excellent bushwalking and thrilling four-wheel driving along its broad beaches at low tide. You can take the whole lot in, whether you're travelling in five-star luxury or camping out under the stars.

On either side of the island are contrasting gateways. Tiny Rainbow Beach hooks avid fisher-folk with its deserted beaches, but you don't need to cast a line to enjoy the views of the vivid, coloured cliffs. To the north is Hervey Bay, a coastal community with a suburban edge. From July to October whales stream into the bay to chill out before continuing their trek south to Antarctica.

Bundaberg, the largest city in the area, is the home of Queensland's favourite spirit, Bundaberg rum, made from local sugar cane, and there are numerous natural attractions in the area, including the southern Barrier Reef islands and the turtle hatchery at lovely Mon Repos beach. Many backpackers stop here to take advantage of plentiful seasonal fruit- and vegetable-picking work.

SOUTHERN FRASER COAST

The initial southern stretch into the Fraser Coast encompasses several small towns, which are largely untouristed but offer the intrepid traveller an authentic insight into the region. Those looking for a glimpse into Queensland's past should not bypass Gympie or Maryborough, where history is steeped in the towns' architecture and flavour. On the coast, Rainbow Beach is a tranquil fishing town that lures devoted fans looking for untrafficked waters and an easy trek to Fraser Island.

GYMPIE

☎ 07 / pop 10,600

Gympie touts itself as 'the town that saved Queensland' with its once-rich gold deposits, but the congestion and excitement of the rush has long been replaced by an ambling pace. It's a peaceful little town that seems to have settled into some time warp, and it makes for a perfect stopover to stretch the legs and nibble on a snippet of rural Queensland. The town was named Gympie after *gimpi gimpi*, the Aboriginal name for a local tree.

Orientation & Information

The Bruce Hwy forms the western border of town, and changes its name several times to River Rd, Wickham, Rove, Violet and Chatsworth Sts as it heads north, before reverting back to the Bruce Hwy. The town is really a small grid of streets and most activity hums along Mary, Nash and O'Connell Sts, which run more or less parallel to the highway.

There are three offices of the helpful **Cooloola Regional Development Bureau** (www.cooloola .org.au; Matilda ☎ 5483 5554; Matilda Service Centre, Bruce Hwy; 🕑 9am-5pm; Lake Alford ☎ 5483 6411; Bruce Hwy, Gympie; 🕑 8.30am-4pm; Gympie ☎ 5483 6656; 224 Mary St; 🕑 9am-5pm), all of which can provide

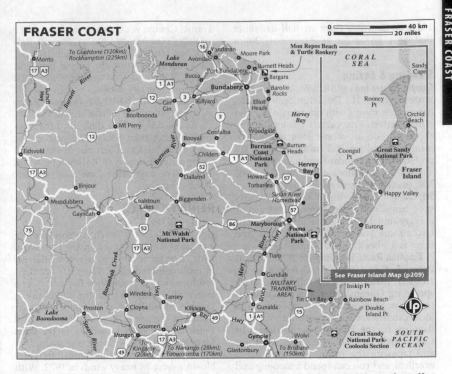

information for the whole of the Fraser Coast. They also stock the (free) *Heritage Walking Tour Map*, which details Gympie's relics of the gold-mining days.

The **Queensland Parks & Wildlife Service office** (QPWS; ☎ 1300 130 372, 5482 4189; O'Connell St; ⏰ 8.15am-5pm Mon-Fri) can provide general information, but no permits for Fraser Island or Great Sandy National Park. For these you'll need to head to the offices at Rainbow Beach (p198) or Tewantin (p190).

Sights & Activities

The **Cooloola Shire Public Gallery** (☎ 5482 0733; 39 Nash St; admission free; ⏰ 10am-4pm Wed-Fri, 11am-4pm Sat & Sun) is set in a big two-storey Queenslander amid the pubs and businesses of Nash St. It displays temporary exhibits of Australian art, with a third of the gallery devoted to local works. There are sporadic talks and lectures by visiting artists.

The **Gympie Gold Mining & Historical Museum** (☎ 5482 3995; 215 Brisbane Rd; adult/child/family $8.80/ 4.40/24; ⏰ 9am-4.30pm), on the southern outskirts of town, has a large and diverse collection of mining equipment and func-

tioning steam-driven engines. It also offers the more traditional exhibits of a historical museum.

The lucrative forestry industry, which has been intrinsic to the region's character, is well depicted at the **Woodworks Forestry & Timber Museum** (☎ 5483 7691; cnr Fraser Rd & Bruce Hwy; adult/student $4/2; ⏰ 9am-4pm Mon-Fri, 1-4pm Sun). Machines, trucks and wagons from all stages of the industry's history are on display with informative documentation. The highlight of the museum (and perhaps the lowlight of the industry) is a cross section of a magnificent kauri pine that lived through the Middle Ages, Columbus' discovery of America and the industrial revolution, only to be felled in the early 20th century.

The **Valley Rattler steam train** (☎ 5482 2750; www.thevalleyrattler.com; half-day tours per adult/child/ senior/family $23.50/12/20/60, day tours $29.50/15/25/75) runs the 40km from the old Gympie train station on Tozer St to the tiny township of Imbil and back, departing Gympie on Wednesday and Sunday morning at 10am. There are stops along the way where you can get your caffeine and souvenir fixes. At

10am on Saturday there are half-day tours that only go as far as Amamoor, 20km away.

Sleeping & Eating

Gympie Muster Inn (☎ 5482 8666; fax 5482 8601; 21 Wickham St; d $100; ⌘) This large, central motel has spotless rooms with summery décor and plump settees. Free cable TV is included in the price and all rooms have telephones, mini-bars and tea and coffee facilities. It's popular for its standard and location.

Great Eastern Motor Inn (☎ 1800 072 093, 5482 7288; gteasternmi@bigpond.com; 27-9 Geordie Rd; d from $95; ⌘ ⌘) Just south of town this pretty spot has slightly bigger rooms than your average motel, and good facilities. For a few bucks more you get an upstairs view, and there is a wheelchair-accessible room.

Kingston House Impressions (☎ 5483 6733; 11 Channon St; mains $16-28; ⌘ lunch & dinner Tue-Sat) Nestled inside a beautifully renovated, sprawling Queenslander, this restaurant is pure class. Seafood dominates the menu and local catches are mixed with international flavours; try the Thai snapper fish-cakes or Cajun mahi mahi. There's also red meat and tapas on the menu. The wine list is excellent and you can spend a loooong and lazy dinner or lunch on the veranda or atop a sueded couch inside.

Imperial Hotel (☎ 5482 1506; 170 Mary St; mains $8-15; ⌘ breakfast, lunch & dinner) The striking Imperial is Gympie's most attractive pub, but the set-up inside is no-nonsense. The bar is made for downing cold beers and the functional bistro serves hot and simple pub grub.

Gympie Caravan Park (☎ 5483 6800; gympark@tpg .com.au; 1 Jane St; powered sites $18.50, cabins $40-55; ⌘ ⌘) Gympie's camping option is central but a little on the cramped side. There are plenty of trees, however, and a good mix of on-site accommodation. The self-contained cabins are good value, but there is only a smattering of actual camp sites. Rates are for two people.

Getting There & Away

Greyhound Australia (☎ 13 14 99; www.greyhound .com.au) services Gympie from Noosa ($15, two hours, three daily) and Hervey Bay ($20, 1½ to two hours, frequently). **Premier Motor Service** (☎ 13 34 10; www.premierms.com.au) operates the same routes (once daily). All long-distance coaches stop at the Gympie Transit Centre, which is also the head office for **Polley's Coaches** (☎ 5482 2700; 28 Duke St). Polley's has buses to Rainbow Beach ($13.50, 1¾ hours), departing the transit centre at 6am, 1.30pm and 3pm weekdays. See p200 for return journey details.

Traveltrain (☎ 1300 131 722; www.traveltrain .au) operates the *Tilt Train* (adult/child $36/18, 2½ hours, one to three daily) and the *Sunlander* (adult/child $36/18, 2½ hours, four weekly), which travel between Brisbane and Gympie, on their way to Rockhampton and Cairns. The **train station** (Tozer St) is 1km east of the centre.

RAINBOW BEACH
☎ 07 / pop 1050

Gorgeous Rainbow Beach is a smidgeon of a town at the base of the Inskip Peninsula, with cheerful locals and a spectacular set of multicoloured cliffs. The cliffs arc their red-hued way around Wide Bay and offer a sweeping panorama from the lighthouse at Double Island Point in the south to Fraser Island in the north. Beyond Double Island Point is the Cooloola Section of the **Great Sandy National Park**, with the rusting hulk of the *Cherry Venture*, a Singaporean freighter blown ashore by heavy winds in 1973. With a 4WD it's possible to drive all the way to Noosa (see p190 for more information).

Information
QPWS Office (☎ 5486 3160; Rainbow Beach Rd; ⌘ 7am-4pm) Car and camping permits for Fraser Island.
Rainbow Beach visitors centre (☎ 5486 3227; 8 Rainbow Beach Rd; ⌘ 7am-6pm) Privately run and moderately helpful.
Rainbow Photographics (☎ 5486 8777; 12 Rainbow Beach Rd; per hr $4; ⌘ 9am-5pm Mon-Fri, 9am-3pm Sat, 9am-noon Sun) Internet access.

Sights & Activities
A 600m track along the cliffs at the southern end of Cooloola Dr takes you to the **Carlo Sandblow**. This 120m-high dune sits atop a hill overlooking town, and reveals views that have been known to make the most cynical sightseer gasp. The **coloured sand cliffs**, after which the town is named, are accessed by a 2km walk along the beach.

There's a good surf break at Double Island Point, but fishing is the most popular activity here. The vast shoreline provides abundant beach fishing and really serious anglers can access Tin Can Bay (p200) inlet from either the Carlo Point or Bullock Point Boat Ramps. Both are just north of town.

Rainbow Paragliding (☎ 5486 3048, 0418-754 157; glides $130) offers tandem glides above the Carlo Sandblow, where the national championships are held every January. If you've got the gumption, this must be one of the most remarkable ways to take in the surrounding views.

The myriad of visitors to Rainbow Beach includes a pod of dolphins, which drops in regularly. **Rainbow Beach Dolphin View Sea Kayaking** (☎ 0408-738 192; 4-hr tours per person $65) operates kayaking safaris and are so confident they guarantee sightings or offer a partial refund. **Carlo Canoes** (☎ 5486 3610; per half-/full day $30/45) hires canoes if you want to do your own exploring.

Teeming with gropers, turtles, manta rays and harmless grey nurse sharks, Wolf Rock, a congregation of four volcanic pinnacles off Double Island Point, is widely regarded as one of Queensland's best scuba-diving sites. The **Wolf Rock Dive Centre** (☎ 5486 8004; wolfrockdive@bigpond.com) offers four-day PADI courses ($360) that include four ocean dives at Wolf Rock.

Tours
Surf & Sand Safaris (☎ 5486 3131; www.surfandsand safaris.com.au) runs half-day 4WD tours south down the beach, taking in the lighthouse at Double Island Point, the *Cherry Venture* wreck and the coloured sands (adult/child $55/28). It also offers half-day tours on an amphibious vehicle (adult/child $65/35).

Sun Safari Tours (☎ 5486 3154) offers day trips to Fraser Island (adult/child $90/50), which take in all the southern highlights and include morning tea and lunch. They also offer two- and three-day tours (from $195/250 per person), which explore the island far more comprehensively and include accommodation at Eurong Beach Resort.

Sleeping & Eating
Rainbow Sands Holiday Units (☎ 5486 3400; fax 5486 3492; 42-6 Rainbow Beach Rd; d $80, 1-bedroom apt $100; ✷ ⊠) This low-rise, palm-fronted complex has neat, appealing motel rooms with poolside glass doors and bar fridges, and self-contained units with full laundries for comfortable, longer stays. The owners are utterly genuine and helpful.

Rainbow Shores Resort (☎ 5486 3999; www.rain bowshores.com.au; 12 Rainbow Shores Dr; r from $115; ✷ ⊠) If you like a little luxury with your beach, you've hit the jackpot with this sprawling resort. Accommodation options include standard holiday units, funky, individual three-bedroom beach houses and polished split-level villas steeped in architectural genius and style. The latter two have two-night minimum stays and rates for everything leap in high season. Onsite is a nine-hole golf course, BBQs, a children's playground, a restaurant and plenty of bush.

Frasers on Rainbow YHA (☎ 1800 100 170, 5486 8885; bookings@frasersonrainbow.com; 18 Spectrum St; dm/d from $20/55; ✷ ⊒) In a nicely converted motel this hostel has roomy dorms with bathrooms and fabulously comfy beds. Locals join guests for a tipple at the sprawling outdoor bar and there are enough nooks and crannies for a quiet night.

Rainbow Beach Hotel (☎ 5486 3125; 1 Rainbow Beach Rd; mains $15-25; ⊗ breakfast Sat & Sun, lunch & dinner daily) The smoky public bar at this pub is a great spot to mingle with the locals, but if you want to stick to yourself, the front beer garden and bistro are quiet and classy. The typical menu offers fresh fish alongside juicy steak, calamari and chicken dishes.

Archie's (☎ 5486 3277; 12 Rainbow Beach Rd; mains $5.50-15; ⊗ breakfast, lunch & dinner) This popular café perfectly encapsulates Rainbow's laid-back surfer chic, serving delicious smoothies, veggie burgers, nachos and more.

Rainbow Beach Holiday Village (☎ 1300 366 596, 5486 3222; www.beach-village.com; unpowered/powered sites from $20/22, cabins from $90; ✷ ⊠) This excellent park has a decent camping ground and a range of self-contained cabins, including villas that were shipped up after housing athletes during the 2000 Sydney Olympics. There's enough foliage to accommodate a small jungle, and its extremely popular rates are for two people.

There's also a supermarket and bakery on Rainbow Beach Rd for quick eats and self-catering.

More accommodation options:
Dingo's Backpacker's Resort (☎ 1800 111 126, 5486 8200; www.dingosatrainbow.com; 3 Spectrum Ave; dm/d $20/50; ✷ ⊒ ⊠) A backpackers menagerie with reasonable dorms and a festive bar.
Rainbow Getaway Holiday Apartments (☎ 5486 3500; www.rainbowgetaway.com.au; cnr Double Island Dr & Rainbow Beach Rd; r per night/week from $95/570;

⊠ ⊠) Slick one-, two- and three-bedroom self-contained units with cable TV and modern fittings.

Getting There & Around
Both **Greyhound Australia** (☎ 13 14 99; www.greyhound.com.au) and **Premier Motor Service** (☎ 13 34 10; www.premierms.com.au) have daily services to Rainbow Beach from Brisbane ($35, 5½ hours, daily), via Noosa ($20, 2½ hours), which continue to Hervey Bay ($19, 1½ hours). **Polley's Coaches** (☎ 5482 2700) has buses from Rainbow Beach to Gympie ($13.50, 1¾ hours), departing at 7.30am and 3.45pm on weekdays only. See p198 for return journey details.

Rainbow Beach is a good spot to hire a 4WD for Fraser Island, and several companies oblige. For more information see the boxed text on p210. **Cooloola Coast & Country Realty** (☎ 5486 3411; Shop 2, 6 Rainbow Beach Rd; per night $90) rents lock-up garages if you need to leave your own car in town. Companies in Rainbow Beach:

Aussie Adventure 4WD Hire (☎ 5486 3599; fax 5486 3388; 2/26 Goondi St)

DETOUR

En route between Rainbow Beach and Maryborough, turn north off Rainbow Beach Rd onto Tin Can Bay Rd and travel for about 10km before reaching the idyllic and quiet settlement of **Tin Can Bay**. Sitting at the southern tip of the Great Sand Strait, it's the perfect way to escape the beaten track.

Mystique, the resident dolphin, makes regular breakfast visits to the Tin Can Bay marina boat ramp and monitored feeding takes place from 8am to 10am.

On the main road into town, the **Sandcastle Motel** (☎ 5486 4555; sandcastle@spiderweb.com.au; Tin Can Bay Rd; d $65; ⊠ ⊠) has large rooms with small kitchenettes, or you could live it up at **Dolphin Waters** (☎ 5486 2600; admin@dolphinwaters.com.au; 40-1 The Esplanade; d per 2-nights/week from $185/470; ⊠ ⊠), which has spotless, self-contained units with balconies.

You can fuel up on pub nosh at the boisterous **Sleepy Lagoon Hotel** (☎ 5486 4124; 18 Bream St; mains $10-20; ⊗ lunch & dinner) or the more sedate **Yacht Club** (☎ 5486 4308; The Esplanade; mains $15-25; ⊗ lunch Sat & Sun, dinner Wed-Sun).

Aussie All Terrain Vehicle Hire (☎ 5486 8000; Shop 1, 54 Rainbow Beach Rd)
Rainbow Beach Adventure Centre 4WD Hire (☎ /fax 5486 3288; 66 Rainbow Beach Rd)
Safari 4WD (☎ 1800 689 819, 5486 8188; 3 Karoonda Ct)

MARYBOROUGH
☎ 07 / pop 21,200
Maryborough is called 'the heritage town'. Beautifully maintained timber Queenslanders line the wide, sweeping streets, vastly outnumbering the functional brick suburban bungalows elsewhere. Many have stood since 1860, when Maryborough came to prominence as the port of entry to Australia for some 21,000 European immigrants. The town also distinguishes itself with possibly the friendliest population in Queensland, and the refreshing quality of not trying to be something it isn't. It's worth visiting on Thursday for the heritage market, held between 8am and 2pm along Adelaide and Elena Sts.

Orientation & Information
Kent St is the main strip, but you'll find most of Maryborough's residents at the modern Railway Sq Shopping Centre, near the intersection of Kent St and the Bruce Hwy (Ferry St).

The excellent **Maryborough Visitor Information Centre** (☎ 4121 4111; City Hall, Kent St; ⊗ 9am-5pm Mon-Fri) is staffed by knowledgeable locals and stocks plenty of leaflets and brochures on the Fraser Coast region.

Sights & Activities
The National Trust–classified **Brennan & Geraghty's Store** (☎ 4121 2250; 64 Lennox St; adult/child/family $5/3.5/12; ⊗ 10am-3pm) is a historical gem and well worth a visit. Having opened in 1871, the store traded for 100 years before becoming a museum, and everything other than the souvenir postcards and tea towels are original contents. Hundreds of tins, bottles and packets are crammed onto the ceiling-high shelves, including early Vegemite jars and curry powder from the 1890s. Correspondence from poverty-stricken customers unable to pay their accounts affords a personal insight into the difficulties of life at the turn of the 20th century.

Housed inside the original Bond Store, dating from 1864, is the **Heritage Gateway and**

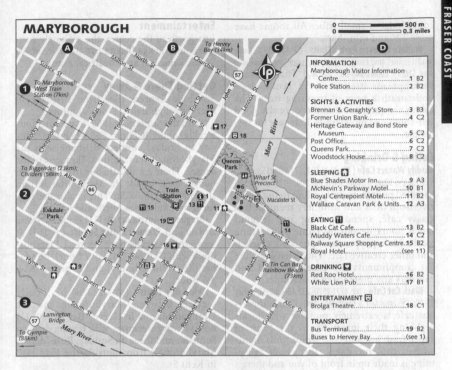

MARYBOROUGH

0   500 m
0   0.3 miles

INFORMATION
Maryborough Visitor Information
   Centre..**1** B2
Police Station...................................**2** B2

SIGHTS & ACTIVITIES
Brennan & Geraghty's Store........**3** B3
Former Union Bank........................**4** C2
Heritage Gateway and Bond Store
   Museum.....................................**5** C2
Post Office.....................................**6** C2
Queens Park...................................**7** C2
Woodstock House..........................**8** C2

SLEEPING 🛏
Blue Shades Motor Inn...................**9** A3
McNevin's Parkway Motel............**10** B1
Royal Centrepoint Motel..............**11** B2
Wallace Caravan Park & Units.....**12** A3

EATING 🍴
Black Cat Cafe...............................**13** B2
Muddy Waters Cafe.......................**14** C2
Railway Square Shopping Centre.**15** B2
Royal Hotel..............................(see 11)

DRINKING 🍷
Red Roo Hotel...............................**16** B2
White Lion Pub..............................**17** B1

ENTERTAINMENT 🎭
Brolga Theatre..............................**18** C1

TRANSPORT
Bus Terminal..................................**19** B2
Buses to Hervey Bay..................(see 1)

Bond Store Museum (☎ 4190 5730; 101 Wharf St; adult/child $3/1; 🕙 10am-4pm Mon-Fri, 10am-1pm Sat & Sun). This complex is like a two-pronged historical journey, with informative and well-assembled displays of Maryborough's immigration, Kanakas and industrial history in the traditional Bond Store Museum, and an interactive wing in the Heritage Gateway.

There are many fine old buildings in the historic port district along Wharf St. The 1866 Italianate **post office**, on the corner of Bazaar and Wharf Sts, is Queensland's oldest. Over on Richmond St is the revival-style **Woodstock House** and the neoclassical **former Union Bank**, where PL Travers, the author of *Mary Poppins*, was born.

Between Lennox St and the Mary River in the north of town is pretty **Queens Park**, which is also heritage listed, with a profusion of glorious and ancient trees, including a Banyan fig that's more than 140 years old. The free **Mary Ann Steam Train** is a miniature railway that runs through the park on the last Sunday of each month and every Thursday.

Sleeping

Royal Centrepoint Motel (☎ 4121 2241; ron_beryl@ bigpond.com; 326 Kent St; s/d $55/60; 🖳) Ambling through the 1920s-influenced corridors of the lovely Centrepoint makes you feel like you've stepped into Fred Astaire's shoes. The style doesn't quite infiltrate the standard, spotless rooms but perks, including video players, street views and friendly hosts, pick up the slack.

McNevin's Parkway Motel (☎ 1800 072 000, 4122 2888; fax 4122 2546; 188 John St; r/ste from $95/130; 🖳) This well-run complex is popular with business folk, but the fresh, light motel rooms are comfortable, regardless of your reason for staying. A step up in style and price are the smart, executive suites, which have separate bedrooms and spas. All rooms come with kitchenette areas but do not have utensils.

Blue Shades Motor Inn (☎ 4122 2777; www.blue shades.au00.com; cnr Ferry & Queen Sts; r/ste from $80/130; 🖳) A close second to the Parkway, this large motel complex has a range of accommodation, from generic and simple motel rooms to modern executive rooms, which could lodge a small tribe. All rooms have cable TV and mini-bars.

Wallace Caravan Park & Units (☎ 4121 3970; www .wallacemotel.4mg.com; 22 Ferry St; unpowered/powered sites $16/19, cabins $40-60; ☒ ☒) This pleasant park spreads itself across a gentle slope underneath a bevy of towering trees. The cabins are quite new and there are also good self-contained motel units. Rates are for two people.

Eating & Drinking

Muddy Waters Cafe (☎ 4121 5011; 71 Wharf St; mains $15-25; ☒ 10am-3.30pm Sun & Tue, 10am-10pm Wed-Sat) Satisfied punters happily relent to the shady riverfront deck and summery menu at this classy café, spending long and languid lunch hours devouring flame-grilled tuna steak, pink peppercorn–poached chicken and other creative fare. The extensive wine list compliments the excellent food and murders any pretence of a schedule.

Black Cat Cafe (☎ 4121 2870; 222 Adelaide St; dishes $5-10; ☒ breakfast & lunch Mon-Sat) This industrious café is extremely popular with locals grabbing their lunch fix in the form of super-fresh hot and cold wraps, rolls, sandwiches, pies and cakes. Just about everything is made up in front of you and there's oodles of seating.

Royal Hotel (☎ 4121 6225; 340 Kent St; mains $16; ☒ lunch & dinner) Beneath the Royal Centrepoint Motel, this affable pub serves an unbeatable $6.99 buffet daily, as well as fancier à la carte pub grub. A section of the bistro has been renovated and dressed up in pretty greenery, providing a very pleasant environment indeed in which to dine.

White Lion Pub (☎ 4121 3374; 37 Walker St) Don't mistake this warm, friendly local for just another generic pub. The threads might not be fancy but a 'g'day' will be directed your way almost as soon as you step inside. This convivial atmosphere is embraced by punters and staff alike, and you're likely to make new mates at the bar.

Red Roo Hotel (☎ 4121 3586; 100 Adelaide St) So Oz it's almost kitsch, this historic old pub has great murals of Australiana on the wall and a gorgeous beer garden nestled under a high tin roof out the back.

The cheapest place to eat is the generic food court at the Railway Sq Shopping Centre, with fish and chips, noodles, kebabs and sandwiches.

Entertainment

Just north of the centre, the strikingly contemporary **Brolga Theatre** (☎ 4122 6060; 5 Walker St) hosts musical and theatrical events.

Getting There & Away

Sunshine Express flies from Brisbane to Maryborough daily ($140, 50 minutes).

Both the *Sunlander* ($55, five hours, four weekly) and *Tilt Train* ($55, 3½ hours, Sunday to Friday) connect Brisbane with the Maryborough West station, 7km west of the centre. There's a shuttle bus from the main bus terminal beside the Maryborough train station on Lennox St. This is also the stop for long-haul buses north and south.

Greyhound Australia (☎ 13 14 99; www.greyhound .com.au) and **Premier Motor Service** (☎ 13 34 10; www.premierms.com.au) both connect Maryborough with Gympie ($15, one hour), Bundaberg ($27, three hours) and Brisbane ($44, 4½ hours).

Wide Bay Transit (☎ 4121 3719) has hourly services between Maryborough and the Urangan Marina in Hervey Bay ($5.90, 1½ hours) every weekday, with five services on Saturday and three on Sunday. Buses depart Maryborough from outside the City Hall in Kent St.

HERVEY BAY

Headlined by a 10km stretch of sand that connects the five suburbs of Point Vernon, Pialba, Scarness, Torquay and Urangan, Hervey Bay is coastal Queensland in a seashell. The pockets of sedate suburbia rubbing shoulders with flawless beach diminish steadily towards the town's outskirts, which dissolve into an industrial jungle. This infrastructure makes Hervey Bay the most popular launching pad to Fraser Island, and its proximity to this marvel is intrinsic to the town's culture. Fortunately, the genuine affability of the locals prevents Hervey Bay from becoming a tacky string of souvenir shops and overpriced motels.

Hervey Bay's second celebrated drawcard is the opportunity to see the whales that churn in and tune out in the town's sheltered waters every spring. This spectacular sight, complimented by sublime swimming, fishing and other water activities, lures Queensland families by the campervan-load.

It seems many have been coming for so long they've not bothered to leave, and the town has a healthy percentage of retirees among its permanent population of 36,100.

INFORMATION

There is only one official tourist office, but numerous booking agents in town also give out tourist information.

Adventure Travel Centre (☎ 1800 554 400, 4125 9288; 410 The Esplanade, Torquay; per hr $4; ⏱ 7am-10pm) Offers Internet access and is a booking agent for tours and activities.

Hervey Bay Tourism & Development Bureau (☎ 1800 811 728; www.herveybaytourism.com.au; cnr Urraween & Maryborough Rds; ⏱ 8.30am-5pm Mon-Fri, 10am-4pm Sat & Sun) Helpful and professional tourist office on the outskirts of town.

Hervey Bay Visitor and Tourist Information Centre (☎ 1800 649 926, 4124 4050; 401 The Esplanade, Torquay; per hr $4; ⏱ 8.30am-8.30pm Mon-Fri, 9am-5pm Sat & Sun) Privately run booking office with Internet access.

Post Office (☎ 4125 1101; 414 The Esplanade, Torquay) There are also branches at Pialba and Urangan.

Whale Watch Tourist Centre (☎ 1800 358 595; Urangan Marina, Urangan; ⏱ 9am-5pm) Privately run, but with good information.

SIGHTS

Activities are the big lure in Hervey Bay, but there is also a handful of attractions.

Reef World (☎ 4128 9828; Pulgul St, Urangan; adult/child $14/8, shark dives $50; ⏱ 9.30am-5pm) is a small aquarium exquisitely stocked with some of the Great Barrier Reef's most colourful characters. You can get nose to nose with the fish and coral through glass, but the resident turtles reputedly love a good pat on the back – there's ample opportunity to test the theory. You can also take a dip with lemon, whaler and other nonpredatory sharks.

Operated by the Korrawinga Aboriginal Community, the **Scrub Hill Community Farm** (☎ 4124 6908; Scrub Hill Rd; tours per adult/child/family $16.50/5.50/33; ⏱ by appointment) is an initiative designed to provide Hervey Bay's indigenous community with training and employment in tourism and related industries. The community produces organic vegetables, tea tree oil and excellent artworks, including didgeridoos. The guided tours (call ahead to arrange) detail how the farm operates, and the slightly more expensive option (adult/child/family $25/10/55) includes bush tucker and a traditional dancing display.

With more than 3000 items on display, the emphasis at the **Hervey Bay Historical Museum** (☎ 4128 1064; 13 Zephyr St, Scarness; adult/child $2.50/0.50; ⏱ 1-5pm Fri-Sun) is on quantity rather than quality, but some of the trips down history's corridors are priceless. Gems include a list of rules for female teachers in 1915 (we liked 'You may not loiter in ice cream parlours' best) and several artefacts from the *Maheno* shipwreck on Fraser Island (p212).

Hervey Bay's pretty **Botanic Gardens** (Elizabeth St, Urangan) are a lush mix of small

---

WHOA MOBY

Every year from August to early November Hervey Bay becomes the languid stomping ground of thousands of humpback whales (*Megaptera novaeangliae*), which hang out in the sheltered waters to escape predators and rest before continuing their arduous migration south to the Antarctic. Having mated and given birth in the warmer waters off northeastern Australia, they arrive in Hervey Bay in groups of about a dozen (known as pulses), before splitting into smaller groups of two or three (pods). The new calves utilise the time to develop the thick layers of blubber necessary for survival in icy southern waters by consuming around 600L of milk a day.

Viewing these majestic creatures in the flesh is simply awe-inspiring, and if you're even remotely in the vicinity you'd be downright silly not exploit the opportunity. Their annual trek has endowed the whales, which can measure up to 15m in length and weigh 40 tonnes, with a surprising tolerance for spectators in the bay and it appears many indulge in extended bouts of showmanship to exact astounded 'ooohs' and 'aahs' from above the water. You may see the same whale cruise around a boat for several hours before breaking into a spontaneous bout of jumping and tail flipping. Young whales often mimic their mothers' antics, producing adorable half-jumps and almost-flips. Whales are also curious creatures and some even roll up beside the numerous whale-watching boats with one eye clear of the water, making those on board wonder who's actually watching whom.

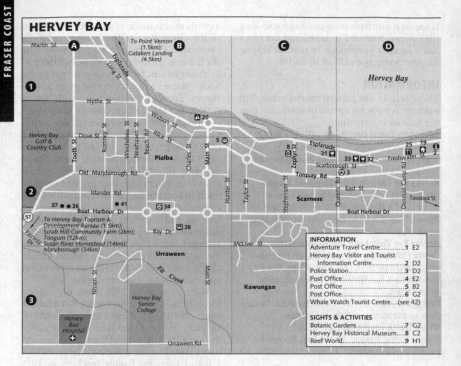

HERVEY BAY

INFORMATION
Adventure Travel Centre............................1 E2
Hervey Bay Visitor and Tourist
    Information Centre..............................2 D2
Police Station...3 D2
Post Office...4 E2
Post Office...5 B2
Post Office...6 G2
Whale Watch Tourist Centre....(see 42)

SIGHTS & ACTIVITIES
Botanic Gardens..7 G2
Hervey Bay Historical Museum....8 C2
Reef World..9 H1

lagoons, dense foliage and walking tracks.
It's a beautiful spot for a picnic and the
scattered water holes attract around 80 bird
species. There's also a small but beautiful
orchid house (adult/child; ☼ 10am-3.45pm Mon-Fri)
and an Aboriginal bush-tucker garden.

ACTIVITIES
Whale-Watching
Whale-watching tours operate out of Hervey
Bay every day, weather permitting, between
mid-July and November. Sightings of the
mighty cetaceans are guaranteed from August to the end of October (you get a free
return trip if the whales don't show). Out of
season many boats offer dolphin-spotting
tours, with the same free-trip guarantee.

The boats cruise from Urangan Harbour
out to Platypus Bay and then zip around
from pod to pod to find the most active
whales. Most vessels offer half-day (four-
hour) tours that cost from $80 to $95 for
adults, and $45 to $65 for children, and
generally include breakfast or lunch. Prices
tend to rise as the maximum number of
passengers decreases. The larger boats run

¾-day trips and the amenities are better,
but they take around two hours to reach
Platypus Bay.

Bookings for boats can be made with
your accommodation or the information
centres. Take a hat, sunglasses and sunscreen and don't forget your camera – the
whales can make spectacular breaches.

Tours available:

MV Tasman Venture (☎ 1800 620 322;
www.tasmanventure.com.au; ☼ 8.30am & 1.30pm)
Maximum of 80 passengers, underwater microphones
and viewing windows.

Spirit of Hervey Bay (☎ 1800 642 544, 4125 5131;
www.spiritofherveybay.com; ☼ 8.30am & 1.30pm)
Large vessel with underwater viewing rooms, carrying up
to 150 passengers.

Tasman Venture II (☎ 1800 099 636; www.tasman
venture.com.au; ☼ 9.30am) One tour a day, lasting five
hours. Maximum of 50 passengers.

Quick Cat II (☎ 1800 671 977, 4128 9611;
www.herveybaywhalewatch.com.au; ☼ 8am & 1pm)
With underwater cameras, a maximum of 80 passengers
and wheelchair access.

Whale Planet (☎ 1800 800 862; ☼ 5.30am, 7.30am
& 10.30am)

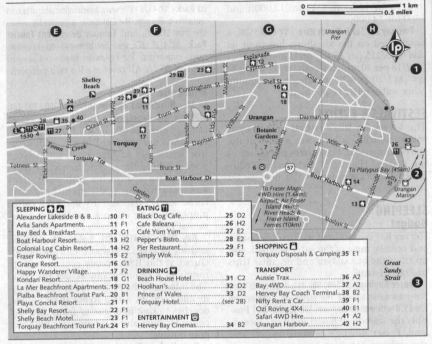

SLEEPING			EATING			
Alexander Lakeside B & B	10	F1	Black Dog Cafe	25	D2	
Arlia Sands Apartments	11	F1	Cafe Baleana	26	H2	
Bay Bed & Breakfast	12	G1	Café Yum Yum	27	E2	
Boat Harbour Resort	13	H2	Pepper's Bistro	28	E2	
Colonial Log Cabin Resort	14	H2	Pier Restaurant	29	F1	
Fraser Roving	15	E2	Simply Wok	30	E2	
Grange Resort	16	G1				
Happy Wanderer Village	17	F2	DRINKING			
Kondari Resort	18	G1	Beach House Hotel	31	C2	
La Mer Beachfront Apartments	19	D2	Hoolihan's	32	D2	
Pialba Beachfront Tourist Park	20	B1	Prince of Wales	33	D2	
Playa Concha Resort	21	F1	Torquay Hotel	(see 28)		
Shelly Bay Resort	22	F1				
Shelly Beach Motel	23	F1	ENTERTAINMENT			
Torquay Beachfront Tourist Park	24	E1	Hervey Bay Cinemas	34	B2	
			SHOPPING			
			Torquay Disposals & Camping	35	E1	
			TRANSPORT			
			Aussie Trax	36	A2	
			Bay 4WD	37	A2	
			Hervey Bay Coach Terminal	38	B2	
			Nifty Rent a Car	39	F1	
			Ozi Roving 4X4	40	E1	
			Safari 4WD Hire	41	A2	
			Urangan Harbour	42	H2	

Whalesong (☎ 1800 689 610, 4125 6222; whalesong@bigpond.com; ⏱ 7.30am & 1pm) Maximum of 70 passengers. Caters to disabled travellers.

Fishing
The fishing in and around Hervey Bay is excellent, and if you're not one of the fanatics who converge by the trailer load with their own gear and boats, numerous vessels operate fishing safaris. **SilverStar Fishing Charters** (☎ 4128 9778; silverstar_fishing@bigpond.com; full-day trips $150), **MV Fighting Whiting** (☎ 4124 6599; adult/child/family $55/30/150) and **MV Princess II** (☎ 4124 0400; trips $90) all offer calm-water fishing trips that run for around eight hours and include lunch. These also leave from Urangan Harbour.

Riding
The **Susan River Homestead** (☎ 4121 6846; www .susanriver.com; Hervey Bay Rd), about halfway between Maryborough and Hervey Bay, gets a huge rap from readers. Horse-riding packages, which include comfortable accommodation, all meals and use of the on-site swimming pool and tennis courts, cost

$155/120 per adult/child. Casual two-hour horse rides through bushland cost $60. You need to book ahead.

Humpback Camel Safaris (☎ 0419-648 629; rides $55) operates very relaxing camel rides through the bush and beach at Toogum, just north of Hervey Bay. The company can arrange courtesy transfers to/from your accommodation.

Scenic Flights
Several operators offer a bird's-eye view of the Fraser Coast. **Air Fraser Island** (☎ 1800 247 992, 4125 3600) operates whale-watching flights ($40) and scenic flights over Fraser Island and the southern fringes of the Great Barrier Reef ($135). **Suncoast Helicopters** (☎ 4125 6799; flights $155-360) operates a range of scenic flights lasting from 25 minutes to one hour.

Other Activities
Skydive Hervey Bay (☎ 4124 9249; www.skydive fraser.com) offers tandem skydives over the beach. Rates start at $180 for 8000ft dives, and increase with the altitude and free fall

to $270 for 10,000ft, $310 for 12,000ft and $360 for 14,000ft.

Torquay Jet Ski & Beach Hire (☎ 4125 5528), a beach shed on the foreshore, hires out jet skis ($35/115 per 15 minutes/hour), canoes ($12/18 per 30 minutes/hour) and windsurfers ($12/20 per 30 minutes/hour) among other water-related equipment.

FESTIVALS & EVENTS

The **Hervey Bay Whale Festival** (www.herveybay whalefestival.com.au) is held over a week at the start of August and celebrates the return of the whales. Highlights include the Teddy Bears' Picnic, blessing of the fleet and a street parade.

SLEEPING
Budget

Hervey Bay is inundated with caravan parks and hostels; most of the latter will pick you up from the bus station and organise trips to Fraser Island.

Fraser Roving (☎ 1800 989 811, 4125 6386; www .fraserroving.com.au; 412 The Esplanade, Torquay; dm $20-25, d with/without bathroom $55/50; ☐ ☎) Possibly the friendliest hostel in all of Queensland, Fraser Roving's genuine owners and atmospheric bar guarantee new mates. If you're desperate for a quiet night, however, there's plenty of space to buffer the noise. The rooms are Spartan but spacious, and there are spotless bathrooms and a decent kitchen. Good wheelchair facilities.

Colonial Log Cabin Resort (☎ 1800 818 280, 4125 1844; www.coloniallogcabins.com; 820 Boat Harbour Dr, Urangan; dm $22, d & tw from $55, cabins from $80; ☒ ☐) Dorms, cabins and villas at this excellent YHA are scattered throughout a tranquil pocket of bush in the 'burbs. Possums and parrots entertain regularly and the facilities are excellent. Some rooms have air-con.

Happy Wanderer Village (☎ 1800 444 040, 4128 9048; hwanderer@hervey.com.au; 105 Truro St, Torquay; unpowered/powered sites from $21/25, cabins from $50, villas from $85; ☒ ☎) The manicured lawns and profuse gum-tree cover at this large park make for great tent sites. The cabins, studios and two-bedroom villas, with videos, verandas and outdoor furniture, are excellent. The spotless facilities include a spa, free BBQs and a laundry, and it's wheelchair accessible. Rates are for two people.

Two appealing council-run caravan parks along the Esplanade are **Pialba Beachfront Tour-**ist Park (☎ 4128 1399; www.beachfronttouristparks.com .au/parks/pialba.php; The Esplanade; unpowered/powered sites from $17/22), and **Torquay Beachfront Tourist Park** (☎ 4125 1578; www.beachfronttouristparks.com.au /parks/torquay.php; The Esplanade; unpowered/powered sites from $17/22). All rates are for two people.

Midrange

La Mer Beachfront Apartments (☎ 1800 100 181, 4128 3494; www.lamer.com.au; 396 The Esplanade, Torquay; r per night/week $120/600; ☒ ☎) Plenty of holiday units use the word luxury with creative license, but La Mer comes up with the goods. Behind the generic façade are fresh and modern apartments with open plans and spanking-new mod-cons including full laundries, DVDs, cable TV and even coffee plungers. There's also a spectacular communal BBQ.

Bay B&B (☎ 4125 6919; baybedandbreakfast@big pond.com; 180 Cypress St, Urangan; s $65, d $95-110; ☎) Guests at this B&B occupy cool and comfy rooms in a secluded annexe out the back. The interior is the perfect blend of modernity and comfort, with a stylish share lounge, couches to sink into, guests' fridge, tea and coffee facilities and a lagoon-style saltwater pool outside.

Boat Harbour Resort (☎ 4125 5079; www.boathar bourresort.com; 650 The Esplanade, Urangan; r $80-95; ☒ ☎) This series of timber studios and two-bedroom villas have mountain-flavoured exteriors, but they're bright and summery inside. The studios have sizable decks out the front and the roomy villas are great for families.

Arlia Sands Apartments (☎ 4125 3778; www.arlia sands.com.au; 13 Ann St, Torquay; r $120; ☒ ☎) This refurbished series of units contains plush furniture, wide-screen TVs, stereos and beautiful kitchens. They're the self-contained unit for the style cat, and each has an ample balcony as well as a personal clothesline.

Alexander Lakeside B&B (☎ 4128 9448; www .herveybaybedandbreakfast.com; 29 Lido Pde, Urangan; d/tr/f $105/120/140; ☒) In a quiet street, this warm and friendly B&B offers secluded indulgence in a lakeside setting. The back of the property is a wall of glass and the purpose-built rooms contain private bathrooms and TVs. Guests also have access to a kitchen and laundry.

Shelly Bay Resort (☎ 4125 4533; www.shellybay resort.com.au; 466 The Esplanade, Torquay; r $95-130; ☒ ☎) The bold, cheerful self-contained units at this complex have slightly dated facilities, but the views are worth a mint and the sun-kissed balconies bless each room with a sea breeze. You're also nice and close to the beach.

Kondari Resort (☎ 1800 072 131, 4128 9702; www .kondari.com.au; 49-63 Elizabeth St, Urangan; r $60-135; 🐕 🖭) Within this sprawling, low-rise resort are two pools, tennis courts, BBQs and a profusion of native bush. Rates start with simple, neat motel rooms, climb to bright studios, and peak at one-bedroom family villas. The style factor of each abode also increases with the tariff.

Also recommended:

Playa Concha Resort (☎ 4125 1544; www.playa concharesort.com; 475 The Esplanade, Torquay; r from $90, ste from $105; 🐕 🖭) Good variety of rooms with 1980s décor – perfect for large and loud families.

Shelly Beach Motel (☎ 4128 9888; www.shelly beachmotel.com.au; 510 The Esplanade, Torquay; d $80; 🐕) Functional and comfortable. Lovely owners.

Top End

Grange Resort (☎ 4125 2002; www.thegrange-hervey bay.com.au; cnr Elizabeth & Shell Sts, Urangan; r $160-185; 🐕 🖭) Reminiscent of a stylish desert resort, this new complex is home to fancy split-level condos filled with life's little luxuries. Glossy kitchens and bathrooms with stainless-steel appliances, plump couches, spacious boudoirs and commodious decks are the norm; bookings are advised.

EATING

Pier Restaurant (☎ 4128 9695; 573 The Esplanade, Urangan; mains $20-40; 🕑 dinner) Arguably Hervey Bay's finest seafood restaurant, the Pier serves exquisite 'marine cuisine', such as mignon scallop kebabs, prawns Provençale and whole baked fish with ginger and peppercorn sauce. There's also a good dose of nonfishy items on the menu and the service and surrounds are first class.

Cafe Balaena (☎ 4125 4799; Shop 7, Terminal Bldg, Buccaneer Ave, Urangan; mains $10-25; 🕑 breakfast, lunch & dinner) This waterfront café provides expensive views, atmosphere with a decidedly laid-back twist and wallet-friendly prices. The menu is hip café fare – mountainous paninis and salads – with a good dose of fresh seafood.

Pepper's Bistro (☎ 4125 2266; 421 The Esplanade, Torquay; mains $10-20; 🕑 lunch & dinner) Perennially popular, Pepper's at the Torquay Hotel dishes out voluminous servings of tasty

pub fare in the way of steak, pasta, salad, seafood and Thai curries. The streetside alfresco dining allows for a dash of people-watching panache and the atmosphere is relaxed and friendly.

Simply Wok (☎ 4125 2077; 417 The Esplanade, Torquay; mains $7-15; 🕑 breakfast, lunch & dinner) Actually there's nothing simple about the variety here, including gourmet sandwiches, divine salads, seafood and inventive Asian cuisine. The food is positively grown-up, but you get to be 10 again with the markers and paper at every table. Honestly, it's hard to resist.

Black Dog Cafe (☎ 4124 3177; 381 The Esplanade, Torquay; mains $10-20; 🕑 lunch & dinner) This funky café oozes groove, starting with the chilled funk on the speakers and ending with the East-meets-West inventions on your fork. Sushi, Japanese soups, fresh burgers, club sambos and seafood salads are on offer, and the service is so friendly you'll want to tip. Good for families.

Self-caterers can stock up at the supermarkets inside the Urangan Central and Bay Central shopping centres. There are also plenty of takeaways and good fish-and-chip shops on the Esplanade in Torquay and Urangan.

Also recommended:

Café Yum Yum (☎ 4125 4107; cnr Bideford & Truro Sts; dishes $5-10; 🕑 breakfast & lunch Mon-Fri) Nooky little café serving excellent curries, moussaka, kofta, *lavash* (flat bread) and wraps.

Gatakers Landing (☎ 4124 2470; The Esplanade, Point Vernon; mains $25-35; 🕑 breakfast Sunday, lunch & dinner daily) Atmospheric restaurant serving spectacular seafood, tapas and Asian infusions.

DRINKING

Beach House Hotel (☎ 4128 1233; 344 The Esplanade, Scarness) Hervey Bay's most relaxed pub is a favourite with local locals. Cable sports and pool tables entertain the stimulus-needy, while ample tables accommodate those just looking to indulge in some amicable conversation. The whole lot is seasoned nicely with sea breezes from the beach across the road.

Torquay Hotel (☎ 4125 2266; 421 The Esplanade, Torquay) This place settles for RSL-flavoured décor, but the vibes are convivial and social. International sports get a workout on the big-screen TV, and once the diners have had their fill the outside tables get back to being a beer garden.

FRASER ISLAND GREAT WALK

Opened in 2004, the Fraser Island Great Walk is a stunning way to see this enigmatic island in all its diverse colours. The trail undulates through the island's interior for almost 87km from Dilli Village to Happy Valley. Broken up into sections of around six to eight kilometres, it follows the pathways of Fraser Island's original inhabitants, the Butchulla people. En route, the walk passes underneath rainforest canopies, circles some of the island's vivid lakes and courses through shifting dunes.

The first leg is 6.2km and connects Dilli Village with Lake Boomanjin. The track cuts inland, affording brilliant views of the island from Wongi Sandblow en route. Lake Boomanjin to Lake Benaroon is the next leg, a total of 7.2km in length. You'll begin to leave the dry scribbly-gum woodlands and forests regenerating from logging and mining behind as you enter the rainforest.

The third section travels for 7.5km and follows the western shore of Lake Benaroon, before zig-zagging to follow Lake Birabeen's southern shore. From Birabeen the trail continues on an old logging road, dwarfed by towering satinay forests and brush box, to land you at Central Station.

Central Station to Lake McKenzie forms the fourth leg, and you have two options here. If you turn west you'll walk via Basin Lake (6.6km), which is a popular haunt for turtles. If you turn east the trail takes a lengthy route through Pile Valley (11.3km).

The fifth section sweeps for 11.9km in a slight arc from Lake McKenzie back towards the island's eastern coast and Lake Wabby. This leg reveals some of the island's most stunning rainforest as well as the east-coast dunes, which buffer Lake Wabby from the coast. The next leg, from Lake Wabby to the Valley of the Giants, is the longest at 16.2km. As the name suggests, it passes beneath some of Fraser's oldest and largest trees.

The seventh leg (13.1km) tags along an old tramline from the Valley of the Giants to Lake Garawongera, uncovering evidence of the earliest logging camps on the island. From Lake Garawongera to Happy Valley it's another 6.6km, mostly downhill through open forests and dunes.

Throughout, the Great Walk's trail is mostly stable sand and not of considerable difficulty, but the island itself has the potential to throw a few whammies your way. Weather conditions, notably heavy rain, can affect the track, although this is mostly a blessing as it firms up the patches of soft sand on the trail. Storms can also fell trees, though, so you'll need to be wary of the occasional hazard crossing your path. Before you go, pick up the *Fraser Island Great Walk* brochure from a QPWS office (or download it from www.epa.qld.gov.au/parks_and_forests/great_walks/fraser_island) and seek updates on the track's conditions.

Two theme pubs that are heavy on the kitsch but equally relaxed and convivial are the **Prince of Wales** (☎ 4124 2466; 383 The Esplanade, Scarness) and **Hoolihan's** (☎ 4194 0099; 382 The Esplanade, Scarness).

ENTERTAINMENT

For movies, check out **Hervey Bay Cinemas** (☎ 4124 8200; 128 Boat Harbour Dr). This big, six-screen cinema shows Hollywood flicks and offers $8 seats all day Tuesday and at all 9.30am sessions.

SHOPPING

If you're lookin' to stock up on camping gear for your trip to Fraser Island, try **Torquay Disposals & Camping** (☎ 4125 6511; 424 The Esplanade, Torquay; ☟ 8.30am-5pm Mon-Fri, 9am-3pm Sat).

GETTING THERE & AWAY
Air

Sunshine Express has a daily service between Brisbane and Hervey Bay ($140, one hour). Hervey Bay airport is off Booral Rd, Urangan, on the way to River Heads.

Boat

Boats to Fraser Island leave from River Heads, about 10km south of town, and Urangan Marina (see p214). Most tours leave from Urangan Harbour.

Bus

Long-distance buses depart **Hervey Bay Coach Terminal** (☎ 4124 4000; Central Ave, Pialba); hostels run minibuses to meet the coaches. **Greyhound Australia** (☎ 13 14 99; www.greyhound.com.au)

and **Premier Motor Service** (☎ 13 34 10; www.pre mierms.com.au) run several times daily between Hervey Bay and Brisbane ($50, 5½ hours), Noosa ($27, 3½ hours), Bundaberg ($17, 1½ hours) and Rockhampton ($55, 5½ hours).

Wide Bay Transit (☎ 4121 3719) has hourly services between Maryborough and Uran- gan Marina every weekday, with five on Saturday and three on Sunday ($5.90, 1½ hours), but they aren't much use for local transport; most places to stay will pick you up from the bus station.

There are Trainlink buses between Mary- borough West train station and Hervey Bay Coach Terminal ($5.50, 45 minutes).

GETTING AROUND
Car & Motorcycle
Nifty Rent a Car (☎ 4125 4833; 463 The Esplanade) has small cars from $29 a day (based on several days' hire).

Plenty of choice makes Hervey Bay the best place to hire a 4WD for Fraser Island:

Air Fraser Island (☎ 1800 247 992, 4125 3600; per person $210) Fly-drive-camp packages, including flights from/to Hervey Bay, 4WD hire and camping gear. Food, petrol and permits are extra.

Aussie Trax (☎ 1800 062 275, 4124 4433; 56 Boat Harbour Dr, Pialba)

Bay 4WD (☎ 1800 687 178, 4128 2981; www.bay4wd.com.au; 52-4 Boat Harbour Dr, Pialba)

Fraser Magic 4WD Hire (☎ 4125 6612; www.fraser -magic-4wdhire.com.au; Lot 11, Kruger Court, Urangan)

Ozi Roving 4X4 (☎ 4125 6355; 10 Fraser St, Torquay)

Safari 4WD Hire (☎ 1800 689 819, 4124 4244; www .safari4wdhire.com.au; 102 Boat Harbour Dr, Pialba)

Bicycle
Bay Bicycle Hire (☎ 0417-644 814; per half-/full day $15/20) rents bicycles from various outlets along the Esplanade, or can deliver bikes to your door.

FRASER ISLAND

It is said that all the sand from the east- ern coast of Australia eventually ends up at Fraser Island, a gigantic sandbar measuring 120km by 15km and created by thousands of years of longshore drift. Seen from the coast this beautiful enigma appears too lush and green to be the world's biggest sand island, but the island's diverse ecology is one of the many wonders of the place. The fringe

of pounding surf belies an interior of dense tropical rainforests, gorges, mineral streams and some 200 vivid freshwater lakes. Dunes, known locally as 'sandblows', tower up to 224m tall, reminding you that the island contains more sand than the Sahara desert (allegedly). Off shore, whales, dolphins, sharks and turtles can often be seen from

FRASER ISLAND
0   15 km
0   8 miles

CORAL SEA

Sandy Cape

Sandy Cape Lighthouse
Panama
Rooney Pt
Lake Marong
Lake Wanhar
Manann Beach

Marloo Bay

The western beach is dangerous for driving due to soft sand and swampy areas

No swimming: sharks & undertow. Also applies to the eastern side of Fraser Island

Lake Carree
Lake Minker

Platypus Bay
Orchid Beach
Waddy Pt
Middle Rocks

Wathumba
Champagne Pools
Indian Head

Triangle Cliff
Great Sandy National Park

Hervey Bay
Yathon Cliffs
Lake Gnarann
Corroboree Beach

Arch Cliff
Lake Bowarrady
Bimjella Hill (174m)
Bowarrady (244m)
Dundubara

Coongul Pt
Lake Allom
Frasers at Cathedral Beach

Moon Pt
The Pinnacles

Hervey Bay
Blackfellow Pt
Lake Garawongera
Yidney Scrub
Maheno
Maheno Beach

Big Woody Island
Happy Valley
Fraser Island Retreat & Sailfish on Fraser
Yidney Rocks

Kingfisher Bay Resort
Leading Hill (184m)
Rainbow Gorge

River Heads
Lake McKenzie
Poyungan Valley

Wanggoolba Creek
Basin Lake
Lake Wabby
Poyungan Rocks
Valley of the Giants

Unnowa
Central Station

Lake Jennings
Lake Birrabeen
Lake Benaroon
Eurong Beach Resort
Eurong

Boomanjin Hill (211m)
Lake Boomanjin
Fraser Island Beachhouses

Maaroom
Yankee Jack Lake
Dilli Village
Dilli Village Recreation Camp

Figtree Lake
SOUTH PACIFIC OCEAN

Tuan

To Maryborough (24km); Gympie (80km)
The Bluff (64m)

Hook Pt

Inskip Pt

Great Sandy Strait

high points; on shore there are some 40 different mammal species and a profusion of birds and reptiles. It's an amazing environment, but as 350,000 people arrive annually to delight in its beauty, Fraser can also feel like a giant sandpit with its own peak hour and congested beach highway.

Fraser was inscribed on the World Heritage List in 1993 and since 1990 the island has been protected as the Great Sandy National Park. For anyone with a yen for camping, fishing, walking, off-road driving or simply the exhilaration of the great outdoors, it's pure Utopia.

There are some essentials about the island that all visitors should know. Four-wheel drives are necessary (see the boxed text below). The lakes are lovely to swim in, but the sea is lethal: undertows and sharks make it a definite no-go. The native dingoes are one of Fraser's highlights, but feeding them has made them increasingly aggressive in recent years (see the boxed text on p213).

Yet none of this detracts from the enjoyment of a location unlike any other on earth. If the dunes, the forests, the lakes and the birds and mammals aren't enough, gaze up at the night sky. With little light behind you, the Milky Way blazes bright.

INFORMATION & ORIENTATION

General supplies and expensive fuel are available from stores at Cathedral Beach, Eurong, Kingfisher Bay, Happy Valley and

---

SAND SAFARIS

There's a sci-fi other-worldliness to Fraser Island, as 4WDs and buses with towering wheel bases and chunky tyres pull in to refuel against an idyllic beach backdrop of white sand and waving palm trees. The surfeit of sand and the lack of paved roads mean that only these 4WD vehicles can negotiate the island. If you're a committed hiker, you can cover some attractions on foot, perhaps with the help of the fairly expensive **Fraser Island Taxi Service** (☎ 4127 9188), but for most travellers transport comes down to the following three options. Please bear in mind that the greater the number of individual vehicles driving on the island, the greater the environmental damage.

Self-Drive Tours

Unbeatable on price, these tours are incredibly popular with backpackers. Nine new friends are assigned to a vehicle to drive their own convoy to the island and camp out, usually for two nights and three days. Some instruction about driving 4WD vehicles is given and drivers are nominated.

Unfortunately, there have been complaints about dodgy vehicle-damage claims upon return, which can be quite costly. Booking through a local hostel reduces the risk. Either way, check your vehicle beforehand.

Advantages: Cheap! You get to choose when and how you see everything and if your group is good, even getting rained on is fun.

Disadvantages: If your group doesn't get along it's a loooong three days. Inexperienced drivers get bogged in sand all the time, although if it doesn't take too long to get moving again, this can be part of the fun.

Rates hover around $140 and exclude food and fuel (usually $30 to $40).

Recommended operators:

Colonial Log Cabin Resort (☎ 1800 818 280, 4125 1844; www.coloniallogcabins.com) Hervey Bay.
Dingo's Backpacker's Resort (☎ 1800 111 126, 5486 8200; www.dingosatrainbow.com) Rainbow Beach.
Fraser Roving (☎ 1800 989 811, 4125 6386; www.fraserroving.com.au) Hervey Bay.
Koala Adventures (☎ 1800 354 535, 4125 3601; www.koala-backpackers.com) Hervey Bay.

Tours

There are plenty of organised tours in anything from private 4WDs to large coaches. Most include accommodation (for two or more days) and all meals, and they typically visit rainforests, Eli Creek, Lakes McKenzie and Wabby, the coloured Pinnacles and the *Maheno* shipwreck.

Orchid Beach. Most stores stock some camping and fishing gear, and those at Kingfisher Bay, Eurong and Happy Valley sell alcohol. There are public telephones at these locations and at most camping grounds.

There are several ranger stations with information, tide times and drinking water:

Central Station (☎ 4127 9191; ☒ 10am-noon)
Dundubara (☎ 4127 9138; ☒ 8-9am)
Eurong (☎ 4127 9128; ☒ 10.30am-3.30pm Mon, 8am-3.30pm Tue-Thu, 8am-1pm Fri)
Waddy Point (☎ 4127 9190; ☒ 7-8am & 4-4.30pm)

There are tow-truck services at **Eurong** (☎ 4127 9188) and **Yidney Rocks** (☎ 4127 9167). See p212 for information on the main settlements on the island.

Maps

When you get your vehicle permit you'll receive an information pack with a basic map and leaflets about camping, natural features and walking trails on the island. The Queensland government publishes the excellent *Sunmap Tourist Fraser Island Map*, and Hema and other companies produce decent, detailed maps at around a 1:130,000 scale (about $8).

Permits

You'll need a permit to take a vehicle onto the island and to camp, and these must be purchased before you arrive. You can do this online at www.epa.qld.gov.au or by calling ☎ 13 13 04. If you're heading

---

Advantages: Tours can generally be booked at the last minute, you don't have to cook, drive or think for yourself and you can jump on at Hervey Bay and return to Rainbow Beach or Noosa, or vice versa. The commentary provides a much greater understanding and appreciation of the island's ecology than you'll get on your own.

Disadvantages: During peak season you could share the experience with 40 others.

Among the many:

Fraser Experience (☎ 1800 689 819, 4124 4244; www.fraserexperience.com; 2-day tours $195) Small groups and more freedom about the itinerary.

Fraser Island Company (☎ 1800 063 933, 4125 3933; day tours adult/child from $105/60, 2-day tours from $195/140) Range of tours available, from small groups to coaches.

Fraser Venture (☎ 1800 249 122, 4125 4444, www.fraser-is.com; day tours adult/child from $105/55, 2-/3-day tours from $215/305) Lively drivers and sizable coaches on strict schedules.

Kingfisher Bay Tours (☎ 1800 072 555, 4120 3353; www.kingfisherbay.com; Fraser Island; day tours adult/child $125/65, 2-/3-day adventure tours from $230/305) Ranger-guided day tours in 4WDs. Multiday tours targeted at 18 to 35 year olds.

Sand Island Safaris (☎ 1800 246 911; 3-day tours from $315) Well-regarded small group tours.

Organised tours also leave from Rainbow Beach (p199) and Noosa (p184).

4WD Hire

The bevy of 4WD hire companies spoil renters for choice in Hervey Bay, but there are also a few in Rainbow Beach, where the ferry is quicker and cheaper (see p214). Rates for multiday rentals start at around $120 per day for a Suzuki Sierra to $180 for a Land Cruiser, and most companies also rent camping gear. For one or two people a Suzuki or single cab Hilux is the way to go. Suzukis don't have the power or clearance (which can be crucial depending on the conditions) of a Hilux, but they're much lighter and tend to skim along the surface of the sand rather than dig in. All companies require a hefty bond, usually in the form of a credit-card imprint, which you *will* lose if you drive in salt water – don't even think about running the waves!

A driving instruction video will usually be shown, but when planning your trip, reckon on covering 20km an hour on the inland tracks and 50km an hour on the eastern beach. Fraser has had some nasty accidents, often due to speeding.

Advantages: Complete freedom to roam the island and escape the crowds.

Disadvantages: You may find you have to tackle beach and track conditions even experienced drivers find challenging.

See p209 for rental companies in Hervey Bay and p200 for companies in Rainbow Beach.

over from Hervey Bay, there's a **QPWS kiosk** (☎ 07-4125 8485; ⏱ 6.15-11.15am & 2-3.30pm) at the River Heads ferry terminal, or you can get your permits from the QPWS office at Rainbow Beach (p198) if you're heading over from there. Vehicle permits cost $33 and camping permits cost $4 per person per night. Permits aren't required for the private camping grounds or resorts.

Other issuing offices:

Bundaberg QPWS Office (p216)
Great Sandy Information Centre (p190)
Naturally Queensland Information Centre (p79)

SIGHTS & ACTIVITIES

Starting at the island's southern tip, where the ferry leaves for Inskip Point on the mainland, a high-tide access track cuts inland, avoiding dangerous Hook Point, and leads you to the entrance of the eastern beach's main thoroughfare. The first settlement you reach is **Dilli Village**, the former sand-mining centre. **Eurong**, with shops, fuel and places to eat, is another 9km further north. From here, an inland track crosses to **Central Station** and **Wanggoolba Creek** (for the ferry to River Heads).

Right in the middle of the island is the ranger centre at Central Station, the starting point for numerous walking trails. From here you can walk or drive to the beautiful **McKenzie**, **Jennings**, **Birrabeen** and **Boomanjin** lakes. Most of Fraser Island's lakes are 'perched' lakes, formed by the accumulation of water on top of a thin, impermeable layer of decaying leaves and other organic material. They're also open-air beauty salons, where you can exfoliate your skin with the mineral sand and soften your hair in the clear water. Lake McKenzie is spectacularly clear and is ringed by sand beaches, making it a great place to swim, but many locals prefer Lake Birrabeen, which sees fewer tour and backpacker groups.

About 4km north of Eurong along the beach is a signposted walking trail, which leads you across sandblows to the beautiful **Lake Wabby**, the most accessible of Fraser's lakes. An easier route is from the lookout on the inland track. Lake Wabby is surrounded on three sides by eucalypt forest, while the fourth side is a massive sandblow that is encroaching on the lake at a rate of about 3m a year. The lake is deceptively shallow and diving is not recommended –

in the past people have been left paralysed after diving into it. There are often turtles and huge catfish in the eastern corner of the lake under the trees.

As you drive up the beach you may have to detour inland to avoid Poyungan and Yidney Rocks during high tide before you reach **Happy Valley**, with more places to stay and a shop and bistro. About 10km north is **Eli Creek**, a fast-moving, crystal-clear waterway that will carry you effortlessly downstream. About 2km from Eli Creek is the rotting hulk of the *Maheno*, a former passenger liner that was blown ashore by a cyclone in 1935 as it was being towed to a Japanese scrap yard.

Roughly 5km north of the *Maheno* you'll find the **Pinnacles**, an eroded section of coloured sand cliffs, and, about 10km beyond, **Dundubara**, with a ranger station and a very good camping ground. Then there's a 20km stretch of beach before you come to the rock outcrop of **Indian Head**, the best vantage point on the island. Sharks, manta rays, dolphins and, during the migration season, whales, can often be seen from the top of the headland.

Between Indian Head and Waddy Point the trail branches inland, passing **Champagne Pools**, which offer the only safe saltwater swimming on the island. There are good camping areas at **Waddy Point** and **Orchid Beach**, the last settlement on the island.

Many tracks north of this are closed for environmental protection. The 30km of beach up to **Sandy Cape**, the northern tip, with its lighthouse, is off limits to hire vehicles. The beach from Sandy Cape to Wathumba is closed to all vehicles, as is the road from Orchid Beach to Platypus Bay.

On the island you can take a scenic flight with **MI Helicopters** (☎ 1800 600 345; 10-/25-/60-minute flights from $70/145/310), based at Fraser Island Retreat (opposite), or with **Air Fraser** (☎ 1800 600 345; 10-minutes flights from $60).

SLEEPING & EATING

If you're camping or self-catering, come well equipped as supplies on the island are limited and costly. Be prepared for mosquitoes and March flies.

Camping

You need a permit to camp in any of the QPWS camping grounds, or in any public area (ie along the beach). The most developed

GREG ELMS

Beachside restaurant, Noosa (p186)

A baby loggerhead turtle (p220), Mon Repos

OLIVER STREWE

CHRIS MELLOR

Mt Ngungun, Glass House
Mountains (p173)

View from Indian Head (p212), Fraser Island

WAYNE WALTON

Flock of Noddies, Heron Island (p232)

MICHAEL AW

Dingo (p213), Fraser Island

MARTIN COHEN

Whitsunday Islands (p265)

RICHARD I'ANSO

Sunset near Airlie Beach (p270)

JOHN BANAGAN

QPWS camping grounds (per person/family $4/16) with coin-operated hot showers, toilets and BBQs are at Waddy Point, Dundubara and Central Station. Campers with vehicles can also use the smaller camping grounds with fewer facilities at Lake Boomanjin and Lake Allom, and Ungowa and Wathumba on the western coast. There is also a camping ground for hikers only at Lake McKenzie. Camping is permitted on designated stretches of the eastern beach, but there are no facilities. Fires are prohibited, except in communal fire rings at Waddy Point and Dundubara, and to utilise these you'll need to bring your own firewood in the form of untreated, milled timber. All rates below are for two people.

Frasers at Cathedral Beach (☎ 4127 9177; www .fraserislandco.com.au; Cathedral Beach; unpowered/powered sites $18/28, cabins from $110) This spacious, privately run park with its abundant flat, grassy sites is a fave with families. The excellent facilities include large, communal BBQ areas and spotless amenities. The quaint, comfortable cabins come with private picnic tables.

Dilli Village Recreation Camp (☎ 4127 9130; Dilli Village; unpowered sites $20, dm $20, cabins $100) Managed by the University of the Sunshine Coast, Dilli Village offers good sites on a softly sloping camping ground. The facilities are neat as a pin and the cabins are ageing but accommodating.

Midrange & Top End

Sailfish on Fraser (☎ 4127 9494; www.sailfishonfraser .com.au; Happy Valley; d/f from $200/220; 🖭) Any notions of rugged wilderness and roughing it will be forgotten quick smart at this plush, indulgent retreat. All 10 of the 4½-star apartments are cavernous and classy, with wall-to-wall glass doors, spas, mod cons, mod furnishings and an alluring pool. Bookings are recommended.

Fraser Island Beachhouses (☎ 1800 626 230, 4127 9205; www.fraserislandbeachhouses.com.au; Eurong Second Valley; d per 2 nights $250-350, f per 2 nights from $400; 🖭) Another luxury option, this complex contains sunny, self-contained units kitted out with polished wood, cable TVs and ocean views. Rates start with studios and climb to $600 (per two nights) for six-bed beachfront houses. There's a two-night minimum stay in the low season, and a five-night minimum in the high season.

Fraser Island Retreat (☎ 4127 9144; www.fraser islandco.com.au; Happy Valley; d & tr $125-160, f $160-200;

mains $10-20; 🕑 breakfast, lunch & dinner; 🖭) Behind the restaurant and shop at this small resort, a series of self-contained, timber lodges cascade down a gentle slop amid plenty of tropical foliage. The lodges have a rustic edge to them and are fairly unobtrusive, but they're a good, comfortable, midrange option.

Kingfisher Bay Resort (☎ 1800 072 555, 4120 3333; www.kingfisherbay.com; Kingfisher Bay; r from $270; 🕱 🖭) This elegant ecoresort has smart hotel rooms with private balconies and sophisticated two- and three-bedroom timber villas (with a three-night minimum stay from $820), which are elevated to limit their environmental impact. The villas are utterly gorgeous and some even have spas on their private decks. There are also restaurants, bars and shops.

Eurong Beach Resort (☎ 4127 9122; www.fraser-is .com; Eurong; r $100-170, mains $15-30; 🕑 breakfast, lunch & dinner; 🕱 🖭) Bright, cheerful Eurong is the main resort on the east coast and the most accessible for all budgets. At the cheaper end of the market are simple motel rooms and units. The comfortable apartments and A-frame chalets are good value

---

DEADLY DINGOES

The decades-old argument over whether dingoes are dangerous to humans was laid tragically to rest on 30 April 2001, when a nine-year-old Brisbane boy was mauled to death, just 75m from his family camping ground at Waddy Point. In response to the attack, around 30 of Fraser Island's estimated 160 dingoes were culled on the orders of the Queensland government, drawing condemnation from Aboriginal and environmental groups. The saddest fact is that this event and the growing aggressiveness of the animals was surely brought about by tourists hand feeding or harassing the dingoes over the years.

Dingoes first came to Australia from Asia around 4000 years ago and are comparatively common on the mainland, but the Fraser population is genetically pure. There is now a minimum fine of $225 (and a maximum one of $3000!) for feeding dingoes or leaving food where it may attract them to camping grounds. The QPWS provides a leaflet on being 'Dingo Smart' in its Fraser Island information pack.

for families. On site is a cavernous restaurant, a lagoon-style pool and the popular Beach Bar.

GETTING THERE & AWAY
Air
Air Fraser Island (☎ 1800 247 992, 4125 3600) charges $60 for a return flight (20 minutes each way) to the island's eastern beach, departing Hervey Bay airport.

Boat
Several large vehicle ferries (known locally as barges) connect Fraser Island to the mainland. Most visitors use the two services that leave from River Heads, about 10km south of Hervey Bay, or from Inskip Point, near Rainbow Beach.

Fraser Venture (☎ 4125 4444; pedestrian/vehicle & 4 passengers return $18/115, additional passengers $6) makes the 30-minute crossing from River Heads to Wanggoolba Creek on the western coast of Fraser Island. It departs daily from River Heads at 9am, 10.15am and 3.30pm, and returns from the island at 9.30am, 2.30pm and 4pm. On Saturday there is also a 7am service from River Heads that returns at 7.30am from the island. This company also operates the Fraser Dawn Vehicular Ferry from the Urangan Marina in Hervey Bay to Moon Point on Fraser Island, but car-hire companies won't allow you to drive their cars here so it's limited to car owners and hikers. Rates are the same as for the River Heads to Wanggoolba Creek service.

Kingfisher Vehicular Ferry (☎ 1800 072 555, 4120 3333; pedestrian/vehicle & 4 passengers return $18/115, additional passengers $6) operates two boats. Its vehicle ferry makes the 45-minute crossing from River Heads to Kingfisher Bay daily, departing at 7.15am, 11am and 2.30pm, and returning at 8.30am, 1.30pm and 4pm. The **Kingfisher Fast Cat Passenger Ferry** (adult/child return $45/22) makes the 30-minute crossing between Urangan Marina and Kingfisher Bay at 8.45am, noon and 4pm daily, returning at 7.40am, 10.30am, 2pm, 5pm and 8pm daily. There are additional services from Thursday to Sunday.

Coming from Rainbow Beach, **Rainbow Venture** (☎ 5486 3227; pedestrian/vehicle & 4 passengers return $10/60) and **Manta Ray** (☎ 0418-872 599; pedestrian/vehicle & 4 passengers return $10/60) both make the 15-minute crossing from Inskip

Point to Hook Point on Fraser Island continuously from about 7am to 5.30pm daily.

GETTING AROUND
See the boxed text on p210 for information on getting around Fraser Island. If you've somehow landed on Fraser without transport, you can hire a 4WD through **Kingfisher Bay 4WD Hire** (☎ 4120 3366), but expect to pay at least $200 per day.

NORTH OF HERVEY BAY

Northeast of Hervey Bay, the tourist frenzy of Fraser Island and Hervey Bay vanishes as the landscape stretches into pretty Burrum Coast National Park. Inland is Childers; an archetypal day-trip town, with rolling orchards and historic buildings.

CHILDERS
☎ 07 / pop 1500
Childers is an attractive strip of a town, littered with heritage buildings that still thrive off the surrounding orchards. It's best known as a sure bet to earn some dosh through fruit-picking work, but the town was marked indelibly by a devastating fire at the Palace Backpackers Hostel in June 2000, in which 15 backpackers died. Childers is blessed with a remarkably tight and supportive community, though, a quality that has been highlighted in abundance since that tragedy. There is now a beautiful, moving memorial at the **Childers Palace Memorial Art Gallery and Information Centre** (☎ 4126 3886; ☯ 9am-5pm Mon-Fri, 9am-noon Sat & Sun), where you'll also find a good gallery and the visitor information centre.

Sights & Activities
Interesting old buildings along Churchill St include the **Federal Hotel**, on the corner of North St, and the historic, wooden **National Bank**, built in 1895 for one of its rivals, the Bank of North Queensland.

The **Isis Historical Complex** (Taylor St; adult/child $2/free; ☯ 9am-noon Mon-Fri, 9am-3pm Sun) is a mock historical town, with cottages, a general store and a post office. There's also a museum here that houses Aboriginal artefacts and photos. It won't take long to explore, but it's worth a visit and there are picnic tables under a glorious jacaranda tree.

Even if you're merely passing through, it's worth stopping at **Mammino** (☎ 4126 2880; 115 Lucketts Rd; ☑ 9am-6pm), whose macadamia-nut and other confectionery will leave you muttering a Homer Simpsonesque 'Mmmm, ice cream'. The company is just outside Childers; as you head along the Bruce Hwy to Bundaberg, turn left towards Woodgate.

In late July, Childers holds a large **Multicultural Festival**, with music and food celebrating the region's diverse cultural mix.

Sleeping

Avocado Motor Inn (☎ 4126 1608; avocadomotorinn@bigpond.com; Bruce Hwy; r $56-65; ☒ ☒) No, it's not another giant fruit, and while the name scores big points for this friendly motel, it's the comfortable and gleaming rooms that earn it the jackpot. Ignore the 1970s décor and grab a room down the back; the views of the valley below are priceless.

Sugarbowl Caravan Park (☎ /fax 4126 1521; 4660 Bruce Hwy; unpowered sites $15, cabins with/without bathroom $60/50; ☒) This gem of a caravan park has plenty of space and a good scattering of foliage between sites. The cabins with their own bathrooms are a cut above and the spectacular views they get of the tumbling valley are free. The owners can help backpackers find work and provide transport to the farms. Rates are for two people.

Also recommended:

Motel Childers (☎ 4126 1177; fax 4126 2266; 136 Churchill St; s/d $65/75; ☒) Standard motel with good facilities.

Palace Backpackers (☎ 4126 2244; www.childers backpackers.com; Churchill St; dm/d $25/60, per week $150/170; ☒) New, modern hostel behind the site of the original.

Eating

Laurel Tree Cottage (☎ 4126 2911; 89 Churchill St; dishes $10-14; ☑ breakfast & lunch) This boutique café has an even balance of frills and funk; the interior is very tea shoppe but the gourmet sandwiches, burgers and breakfasts are definitely from this century. Outside, tourists and Childers' cosmopolitan set sup lattes and savour smoked salmon on the appealing timber deck.

Grand Hotel (☎ 4126 1763; Churchill St; mains $10-16; ☑ lunch & dinner) Once the sun goes down Childers' culinary offerings become drastically limited and the Grand Hotel's pub menu is about as diverse as things

THE AUTHOR'S CHOICE

Three Big Fig Trees B&B (☎ 4126 1838; www.the3bigfigtrees.com.au; 87 Hawes Rd; s/d $70/90) About 3km east of town, this gorgeous B&B occupies a stately position on top of a hill, with commanding 360-degree views of the surrounding valleys. The Swiss master builder–owner has attached four unique rooms, all with private bathrooms and veranda access, in keeping with the house's heritage structure. There's a room here for everyone: the cool and simple 'green' room is a solo affair, but there's also a family room with bunks. The corner windows of the 'Honeymoon Suite' steal the best of the views, although with the large ornate bed and romantic touches you might be looking somewhere else. Breakfast is a cracker!

get. It takes its food seriously, though, so whether you're ordering the crumbed calamari, T-bone steak or Cajun chicken salad, expect quantity and taste.

Tropicana Cafe (☎ 4126 1871; 102 Churchill St; meals $3-7; ☑ breakfast, lunch & dinner) This is probably the best of the takeaways on the main road.

There are good bakeries on Churchill St, where you can pick up fresh meat pies or rolls.

Getting There & Away

Greyhound Australia (☎ 13 14 99; www.greyhound .com.au) and **Premier Motor Service** (☎ 13 34 10; www.premierms.com.au) stop just north of town at the Shell service station and have daily services to/from Brisbane ($60, eight hours), Hervey Bay ($15, one hour) and Bundaberg ($15, 1¾ hours).

BURRUM COAST NATIONAL PARK

The attractive Burrum Coast National Park covers two sections of coastline on either side of the little holiday community of Woodgate, 37km east of Childers. The Woodgate section of the park begins at the southern end of the Esplanade, and has nice beaches, good fishing and a **camping ground** (per person $4) at Burrum Point, reached by a 4WD-only track. Several walking tracks start at the camping ground or at Acacia St in Woodgate. There are more isolated bush-camping areas in the Kinkuna section of the park, a few kilometres north of Woodgate, but you'll need a 4WD to reach them. Contact the **park rangers** (☎ 4126 8810) to book camping permits.

Barkala Caravan Park (☎ 4126 8802; barkala@isisol .com.au; 88 The Esplanade, Woodgate Beach; unpowered sites $15.50, powered sites $18-21, cabins $40-65; ⊠) is a tidy, tranquil park close to the national park, and with spacious sites and a variety of cabins. Rates are for two people. The **Woodgate Beach Hotel-Motel** (☎ 4126 8988; fax 4126 8793; 195 The Esplanade, Woodgate; d Mon-Thu $80, Fri-Sun $90), at the northern end of the Esplanade, has a block of reasonable motel units just across from the beach and dishes up decent pub grub.

BUNDABERG

From 'the hummock', the only hill in this flat landscape, the eye sees fields of waving sugar cane from Bundaberg to the coral-fringed coast. That's the source of the famous Bundy rum, and the income for some, but not all, local 'cockies' (farmers).

Bundaberg may have seen the odd aesthetic alteration over the years, but essentially not much has changed in this typical Australian country town. The main strip, embellished with wide streets and waving palms, is positively gracious and the suburban development that extends outwards is still dominated by stoic old Queenslanders (that's the houses).

'Bundy', as it's popularly known, attracts large numbers of working backpackers, who come here to pick fruit and vegetables on the surrounding farms and orchards. However the town offers distractions for travellers of any ilk in the way of museums, spectacular gardens, scuba diving and the chance to see unbearably sweet turtles make their first stumble down the beach at nearby Mon Repos.

INFORMATION

Bundaberg Email Centre (☎ 4154 3417; 200 Bourbong St; per hr $4; ☯ 9am-10pm Mon-Fri, 10am-7pm Sat, 10am-10pm Sun) Internet access.
Bundaberg visitors centre (☎ 1800 308 888; www .bundabergregion.info) 271 Bourbong St (☎ 1800 308 888, 4153 8888; ☯ 9am-5pm); 186 Bourbong St (☎ 4153 9289; ☯ 9am-5pm Mon-Fri, 9am-noon Sat & Sun)
Cosy Corner Internet Cafe (☎ 4153 5999; Barolin St; per hr $4; ☯ 8am-7pm Mon-Fri, 9am-5pm Sat, 11am-5pm Sun) Internet access.

Post Office (☎ 4151 6708; cnr Bourbong & Barolin Sts)
QPWS (☎ 4131 1600; 46 Quay St) Sells permits for Fraser Island.

SIGHTS

The **Botanic Gardens** (Mt Perry Rd; ☯ 5.30am-6.45pm Sep-Apr, 6am-6.30pm May-Aug), 2km north of the centre, are utterly splendid. Their vast grounds display a network of lakes and small islands populated by colonies of ibises and geese. The foliage is diverse and lush, ranging from colourful tropical shrubs to towering palms and gums, and even rose beds. There are enough picnic possies here to service a small country. Within the reserve are three museums. The **Hinkler House Museum** (☎ 4152 0222; adult/child $5/2.50; ☯ 10am-4pm) is set inside the house of Bundaberg's most famous son, the aviator Bert Hinkler, who made the first solo flight between England and Australia in 1928. The house was painstakingly relocated from Southampton, where he spent the latter part of his life, to Bundaberg in 1983. Inside is a collection of memorabilia (including personal items such as the letters he wrote to his youngest sister), all detailing his life and times.

Nearby, the interesting **Bundaberg & District Historical Museum** (☎ 4152 0101; adult/child $4/2; ☯ 10am-4pm) has plenty of colonial-era antiques to provide visitors with a peek into Bundaberg's history. The collection ranges from the quaint (quilts handmade by locals in the 1920s) to the quirky (a series of albums showcasing every wedding in Bundaberg since 1974).

At the southern end of the park, the **Fairymead House Sugar Museum** (☎ 4153 6786; adult/child $4/2; ☯ 10am-4pm) has good displays about the sugar industry, including some frank displays on the hardships endured by Kanakas in the cane fields.

The **Bundaberg Arts Centre** (☎ 4152 3700; www .bundaberg.qld.gov.au/arts; cnr Barolin & Quay Sts; admission free; ☯ 10am-5pm Tue-Fri, 11am-3pm Sat & Sun) is Bundaberg's premier platform for the visual arts, showing temporary exhibits of Australian art. The works on display are eclectic, often using mixed media and demonstrating considerable thought and talent.

Bundaberg's biggest claim to fame in Australia is the iconic Bundaberg rum – you'll see the Bundy rum polar bear on billboards all over town. Aficionados of the good stuff can see the vats where the sugary gold is

BUNDABERG

INFORMATION
Bundaberg Email Centre.........(see 15)
Bundaberg visitors centre..........1 A4
Bundaberg visitors centre..........2 C3
Cosy Corner Internet Cafe.........3 C3
Police...................................4 A4
Post Office...........................5 C3
QPWS.................................6 C3

SIGHTS & ACTIVITIES
Alexandra Park & Zoo.............7 B3
Botanic Gardens....................8 A1
Bundaberg & District Historical
    Museum...........................9 A2
Bundaberg Aqua Scuba...........10 C3
Bundaberg Arts Centre............11 C3
Bundaberg Ferry Company......12 C3
Fairymead House Sugar
    Museum..........................13 A2

EATING
Grand Central Hotel.......27 C3
IGA Supermarket............28 C3
Indulge.......................29 C3
Les Chefs.....................30 B4

Hinkler House Museum....14 A1
Salty's Dive Centre..........15 C3
School of Arts Building....16 C3
Union Bank Building........17 C3

SLEEPING
Alexandra Park Motor Inn..18 B3
Bundaberg Backpackers &
    Travellers Lodge.........19 C4
Finemore Caravan Park....20 A3
Inglebrae......................21 B4
Lyelta Lodge & Motel......22 C3
Oscar Motel..................23 B4
Quality Hotel.................24 C3
Robbie's Place...............25 A4
Sugar Country Motor Inn.26 B3
The Dive Inn.............(see 38)

Spices Plus................(see 17)
Talking Point Cafe.........31 C3
The Spinnaker Restaurant &
    Bar.......................32 D2

DRINKING
Banjo's Tavern..............33 B3
Club Hotel..................34 C3
Metropolitan Hotel.........35 C3
Queenslander...............36 C3

ENTERTAINMENT
Moncrieff Theatre............37 C3

TRANSPORT
Stewart's Coach Terminal...38 C3
Target bus stop..............39 C3

made at the **Bundaberg Rum Distillery** (4131 2999; www.bundabergrum.com.au; Avenue St; adult/child $9.90/4.40; 1-hr tours 10am-3pm Mon-Fri, 10am-2pm Sat & Sun). Tours follow the rum's production from start to finish, and if you're old enough, you get to sample the final product at the end.

The **Bundaberg Ferry Company** (4152 9188; Quay St; 2½-hr tours per adult/child/family $20/13/60; 9.30am & 1.30pm) operates the *Bundy Belle*, an old-fashioned ferry that chugs pleasantly to the mouth of the Burnett River twice a day. The pace and scenery are lovely, and tours include commentary and morning or afternoon tea.

The small **Alexandra Park & Zoo** (Quay St; admission free; 6.30am-3.30pm) is tucked into

a green corner on the banks of the Burnett River. A handful of animals, including the ubiquitous kangaroo and some vivid and vocal parrots, reside here. It's a pretty spot and the large, grassy park adjoining begs for a picnic.

There are numerous interesting old buildings in town, including the ornate **Union Bank building** (Targo St), and the lovely **School of Arts Building** (Bourbong St). Pick up a copy of *A Walking Tour of the Bundaberg City Centre* from the Bundaberg visitors centre.

ACTIVITIES
Diving
About 16km east of Bundaberg, the small beach hamlet of Bargara entices divers and

FRASER COAST

snorkellers with a dazzling bank of coral near the shore around Barolin Rocks and in the Woongarra Marine Park. This is one of the cheapest places in the southern hemisphere to learn how to dive. **Salty's Dive Centre** (☎ 1800 625 476, 4151 6422; www.saltys .net; 208 Bourbong St) and **Bundaberg Aqua Scuba** (☎ 4153 5761; www.aquascuba.com.au; Shop 1, 66 Targo St) both offer four-day, PADI open-water diving courses for $170, but this only includes shore dives. Advanced open-water dive courses cost from $245.

Salty's also offers an extremely popular three-day, three-night diving package to Lady Musgrave and other islands on the Great Barrier Reef ($500). The price includes all meals and accommodation aboard its boat and up to 10 ocean dives.

TOURS

Lady Musgrave Barrier Reef Cruises (☎ 1800 072 110, 4159 4519; www.lmcruises.com.au; Shop 1, Bundaberg Port Marina, Port Bundaberg; adult/child $140/75) offers day trips to Lady Musgrave Island from Port Bundaberg, 17km northeast of the centre. Cruises leave on Monday, Tuesday, Thursday, Saturday and Sunday at 7.45am, returning to the marina at 6pm. The price includes lunch, snorkelling gear and rides in a semisubmersible, glass-bottomed boat. Scuba dives for certified divers are an extra $60. If you don't have wheels, there's a transfer to/from Bundaberg for an additional $10.

You can also fly to Lady Elliot Island with **Lady Elliot Island Resort** (☎ 1800 072 200, 5536 3644; www.ladyelliot.com.au; adult/child $240/230). The day trip includes at least five hours on the Great Barrier Reef, a glass-bottomed boat or snorkel tour, lunch and use of the resort's facilities.

See p230 for information about longer stays on the islands. All reef trips incur a $5 environmental management charge.

Bundaberg Coach Tours (☎ 1800 815 714, 4153 1037) offers a variety of tours to local sights, including a day trip to Town of 1770, with sand-boarding, lunch and an amphibious vehicle ride (adult/child $75/50).

FESTIVALS & EVENTS

Bundy Easter Roundup (☎ 4152 9370; Easter) Annual country-music talent quest and festival.
Bundaberg Regional Show (☎ 4153 5030; late May) Bundy's annual show has rides and agricultural displays.

SLEEPING
Budget
Bundaberg Backpackers & Travellers Lodge (☎ 4152 2080; fax 4151 3355; cnr Targo & Crofton Sts; dm per night/week $20/110; 🖳 🖳) Behind the bland, brick exterior and practical furnishings of this hostel lies a warm, cheerful buzz, perpetuated by helpful owners and a constant stream of working travellers. Little extras such as dressers in the dorms and oodles of couches create a homely environment.

Lyelta Lodge & Motel (☎ 4151 3344; 8 Maryborough St; s with/without bathroom $50/35, d $55/47) Something of a cross between a hostel and a motel, this basic but clean lodge seems to have changed little since the 1950s. The owners are friendly and accommodating though, it's fairly central and the price is impressive.

Finemore Caravan Park (☎ 4151 3663; www .bundabergcity.qld.gov.au/tourism/finemore; 33 Quay St; unpowered/powered sites from $10/12.50, cabins from $45; 🖳 🖳) This small, tidy park sits on an attractive plot on the banks of the Burnett River. Quite a few long-termers pitch their digs here and it's probably due for a wee makeover, but the facilities include laundries and a BBQ area and the rates are more than fair. Rates are for two people.

Other budget options:
Dive Inn (☎ 4153 5761; diveinn@aquascuba.com.au; 66 Targo St; dm for divers/nondivers $17/15; 🖳 🖳) Simple but friendly hostel.
Midtown Caravan Park (☎ 4152 2768; midtown touristvillag@bigpond.com; 61 Takalvan St; unpowered/ powered sites $13/18, cabins with/without bathroom from $57/40; 🖳 🖳) Reasonable park that's best for caravans. Rates are for two people.

Midrange
Bundaberg has plenty of functional but fairly characterless motels, so you shouldn't have difficulty finding a bed. Most can be found on Takalvan St as you head into town from the south.

Robbie's Place (☎ 4152 7511; www.babs.com .au/robbiesplace; 109 Woongarra St; d incl breakfast $100, f $120; 🖳 🖳) A stylish timber extension to a beautiful old Queenslander accommodates visitors at this excellent B&B. Mock-period bedrooms with plump beds sidle up to a new kitchen, lounge with a stereo and cable TV, and a large balcony with private BBQ. Families and groups can rent the whole lot out (it sleeps up to six) on a room-only basis.

Country Comfort Bundaberg (☎ 4151 2365; www .countrycomforthotels.com; 73 Takalvan St; d $95; ☒ ☒) Bundaberg's most comfortable motel has enough space to make you feel like the only sardine in the tin. The décor is a little dated, but the rooms see plenty of sunlight, the bathrooms positively glisten and mini-bars, cable TV and hairdryers are all standard.

Quality Hotel (☎ 4155 8777; www.flagchoice.com .au; 7 Quay St; s/d $110/140; ☒ ☒) This modern pit stop is popular with conferences and travelling business folk, but the good facilities and décor from the new millennium set it apart from just about every other option in town. The rooms are quite stylish and there's a gym, a sauna, laundry service and disabled facilities. Bookings are recommended.

Oscar Motel (☎ 4152 3666; oscarmotel@hotmail .com; 252 Bourbong St; d $71-85; ☒ ☒) The Oscar offers a range of rooms; smaller digs are functional and warm and the larger rooms can be utterly cavernous, so ask when you check in. All have cable TV and tea and coffee facilities. The proud and professional owners keep the whole place spotless.

Alexandra Park Motor Inn (☎ 1800 803 419, 4152 7255; alex.parkmotorinn@bigpond.com; 66 Quay St; d $85-95; ☒ ☒) A gracious timber exterior, complete with sweeping balcony, greets visitors to this quiet motel off the main road into town. Inside the atmosphere is more 1970s than 1870s, but the downstairs rooms are cosy and the more expensive rooms upstairs are large and contain kitchenettes.

Inglebrae (☎ 4154 4003; www.inglebrae.com; 17 Branyan St; r incl breakfast $90-110) If staying in a glorious old Queenslander appeals, this place is just the ticket. Polished timber and stained glass seep from the entrance into the rooms, which come with high beds and small antiques. Breakfasts are big and hot, and time-wastage on the gorgeous veranda is mandatory.

Also recommended:

Reef Gateway Motor Inn (☎ 4132 6999; www.reefgateway.com.au; 11 Takalvan St; d $85; ☒ ☒) Tidy, large rooms with multiple beds, shielded from the main road. A good option for families.

Sugar Country Motor Inn (☎ 4153 1166; fax 4153 1726; 220 Bourbong St; s/d $85/95; ☒) In a central spot with a licensed restaurant.

EATING

Bundaberg doesn't exactly scale any culinary heights, but there are a few gems amid

the cornucopia of steak, fish and chicken dishes.

Les Chefs (☎ 4153 1770; 238 Bourbong St; mains $20; ☺ lunch Mon-Fri, dinner daily) One for the carnivores, this upmarket, intimate restaurant goes global, treating diners to duck, veal, seafood, chicken and beef dishes à la Nepal, Mexico, France, India and more. It comes highly recommended by locals so dinner bookings are recommended.

Spices Plus (☎ 4154 3320; 1 Targo St; dishes $8-14; ☺ dinner) Bundaberg's spicy little secret debunks the myth that small towns don't have culinary delights. The authentic Indian food served inside the beautiful old Union Bank building will have your tastebuds dancing to the tune of *jalfrezi* (hot curry), marsala, vindaloo and tandoori. There is also a host of vegetarian dishes on the menu.

Spinnaker Restaurant & Bar (☎ 4152 8033; 1A Quay St; dishes $17-30; ☺ lunch Mon-Fri, dinner Mon-Sat) Bundaberg's classiest restaurant woos diners with a picturesque perch above the Burnett River, and fine food. As its name suggests, most of the fare at Spinnakers is seafood, and in addition to perfectly cooked fish you can also savour Moreton Bay bugs and macadamia nut–crumbed calamari. A few upmarket poultry dishes also grace the menu here.

Indulge (☎ 4154 2344; 80 Bourbong St; dishes $8-14; ☺ breakfast & lunch) With its sophisticated ambience and intoxicating pastries, this narrow café is a sliver of Europe. Fancy brekkies and lunches steer well clear of the sambo and lasagne brigade, and the highlight is all things sweet. Eye-boggling, homemade cakes, slices and muffins show off from behind the glass counter and it all goes down well with a fresh coffee.

Talking Point Cafe (☎ 4152 1811; 79 Bourbong St; dishes $5-10; ☺ breakfast & lunch) The cooking smells swimming about this cosy café are mouthwatering and the paninis, focaccias, soups and coffee are just as divine. The couches by the front window can be difficult to climb out of, so you'll just have to stay for cake.

Good pub grub at good prices is up for grabs at the bistros at the **Grand Central Hotel** (☎ 4151 2441; 81 Bourbong St; mains $9-19) and the **Club Hotel** (☎ 4151 3262; cnr Tantitha & Bourbong Sts; mains $8-12; ☺ lunch & dinner). Self-caterers can stock up at the **IGA Supermarket** (Woongarra St).

FRASER COAST

DRINKING

You won't go thirsty in Bundaberg, but the host of pubs with glorious exteriors around town contain functional public bars and gambling outlets. The locals will probably provide all the animation you need.

Metropolitan Hotel (☎ 4151 3154; 166 Bourbong St) The Metro's public bar has had a fancy makeover in recent years, and although the chrome and fire-engine red looks about as comfortable in Bundy's main street as a cowboy at a Barbie convention, the locals flock here, filling the place with genuine, lively chatter and charm.

Club Hotel (☎ 4151 3262; cnr Tantitha & Bourbong Sts) The bar at this big corner pub is friendly enough, but the best spot for a coldie is in the beer garden attached to the bistro. It's a cosy spot, sheltered from the wind and traffic.

Queenslander (☎ 4152 4691; 61 Targo St) This big old corner pub, painted in an animated collage of all things Bundaberg, has sadly suffered from a pokies infestation, but the vacuous tropical beer garden out back remains a great spot for a drink.

Banjo's Tavern (☎ 4151 6010; 221 Bourbong St) This popular tavern underneath a backpackers hostel makes no bones about its main focus: drinking, pool, loud music, and plenty of it. It's a popular backpacker haunt and also draws Bundy's younger drinkers.

ENTERTAINMENT

Queenslander (☎ 4152 4691; 61 Targo St) Live gigs are a constant at this pub, which entertains folk with either rock or DJs every Friday and Saturday night, and on sporadic weeknights. When the weather is fine, the gigs move into the beer garden, which, for Bundy, is positively cosmopolitan!

Moncrieff Theatre (☎ 4153 1985; 177 Bourbong St) Bundaberg's lovely old cinema may not have a huge selection showing at any one time, but there's something special about catching a flick here. You almost expect an intermission but the carte du jour is Hollywood's latests.

Reading Cinema (☎ 4152 1233; Takalvan St) This big, modern complex, on the way to the airport, screens commercial blockbusters.

GETTING THERE & AROUND
Air

Bundaberg's **Hinkler Airport** (Takalvan St) is about 4km southwest of the centre. There are sev-

---

TALKING TURTLE

You almost expect to hear the hushed commentary of wildlife documentary–maker David Attenborough during the egg-laying and hatching at **Mon Repos**, Australia's most accessible turtle rookery. However on this beach 15km northeast of Bundaberg it's no disappointment to be accompanied instead by the knowledgeable staff from the **QPWS visitors centre** (☎ 4159 1652; ⏱ 7.30am-4pm Mon-Fri). From November to late March, loggerhead and other marine turtles drag themselves up the beach to lay their eggs, after which the young emerge. The office organises ranger-guided **tours** (adult/child/family $5.50/3/13; ⏱ 7pm-midnight). Bookings are mandatory and can be made through the **Bundaberg visitors centre** (p216). Alternatively you can take a turtle-watching tour with the highly recommended **Foot Prints Adventures** (☎ 4152 3659; www.footprintsadventures.com.au; adult/ child incl transfers $50/25). Either way, take warm clothing, rain protection and insect repellent.

---

eral flights each day between Bundaberg and Brisbane ($133, one hour) run by **Qantaslink** (☎ 13 13 13; www.qantas.com.au).

Bus

The main bus stop is **Stewart's Coach Terminal** (☎ 4153 2646; 66 Targo St). Both **Greyhound Australia** (☎ 13 14 99; www.greyhound.com.au) and **Premier Motor Service** (☎ 13 34 10; www.premierms .com.au) have daily services connecting Bundaberg with Brisbane ($65, seven hours), Hervey Bay ($25, 1½ hours), Rockhampton ($55, four hours) and Gladstone ($45, 2½ hours).

Local bus services are handled by **Duffy's Coaches** (☎ 4151 4226). It has four services every weekday to Bargara ($5, 35 minutes) and Port Bundaberg ($5, 35 minutes); buses depart from the **Target bus stop** (Woongarra St) in front of the Target superstore.

Train

Both the *Sunlander* ($60, seven hours, four weekly) and the *Tilt Train* ($60, five hours, Sunday to Friday) travel from Brisbane to Bundaberg on their respective routes to Cairns and Rockhampton.

AROUND BUNDABERG

In many people's eyes, the beach hamlets around Bundaberg are more attractive than the town itself. Some 25km north of the centre is **Moore Park**, with wide, flat beaches. Locals and visitors also flock to **Mon Repos** to see baby turtles hatching from November to March (see the boxed text opposite).

Some 16km east of Bundaberg lies the cruisy beach village of **Bargara**. This picturesque little spot is drawing increasing numbers of tourists who come for the seaside golf. Families also find Bargara attractive for both the turtle-shaped playground on its main foreshore and the sheltered swimming areas for kids at Kellys Beach. Local buses run to these places from the Target bus stop in Bundaberg (see opposite).

Bargara Beach Dive (☎ 4159 2663; www.bargara dive.com; Shop 4, 16 See St) operates open-water dive courses with small classes for $300. If you're already an expert, you can hire equipment from them. **Shoreline Apartments** (☎ 4159 1180; www.shorelineapartments.com.au; 104 Miller St, Bargara; d $75-90, 1-/2-bedroom apt $100/140; ⛭ ⛭) has excellent accommodation to suit just about everyone without a tent. The motel rooms are clean and simple, and the bright and breezy apartments are fully self-contained. The whole lot is only 500m or so from the beach.

Turtle Sands (☎ 4159 2340; www.turtlesands.com .au; Mon Repos; sites from $16.50, on-site vans from $27.50, cabins from $45; ⛭) is a pretty caravan park with good facilities and a great location right on the beachfront.

Kacy's Restaurant and Bar (☎ 4130 1100; cnr See & Bauer Sts, Bargara; mains $10-25; ☾ lunch & dinner) at the Bargara Beach Hotel is like a fantastic South Pacific oasis. Relaxing on the capacious deck you can choose from New Orleans gumbo, Thai curry prawns, and bugs done any way you please from the huge menu.

Capricorn Coast

CONTENTS

HIGHLIGHTS

- Exploring the twists and turns, ancient rock art and awesome scenery of **Carnavon Gorge** (p248)
- Diving the exceptionally clear and coral-crammed waters of **Heron Island** (p232)
- Surfing and chilling at Queensland's most northerly surf beach, **Agnes Water**, and town of the moment, **Town of 1770** (p225)
- Fossicking with lady luck for that sapphire from **Sapphire** or ruby from **Rubyvale** (p245) at the Capricorn Gemfields
- Cooling off in a precious rock pool after a hot trek through rugged gorge country in remote **Blackdown Tableland National Park** (p243)
- Riding a bucking bronco, or at least a mechanical bull, at Australia's beef capital, **Rockhampton** (p232)
- Lying back with a good book on a great beach after a big night on **Great Keppel Island** (p240)

- www.capricorncoast.com.au
- www.capricorntourism.com.au

This central coastal area of Queensland takes its name from its position straddling the tropic of Capricorn. Latitude 23.5 South passes through Rockhampton, the area's major hub and Australia's brash beef-farming capital, where oversized bulls greet visitors and raging bulls are ridden by locals. Just north of town, and officially tropical, you can visit a bat cave or discover the charms of popular and accessible Great Keppel Island.

South of Rockhampton is Gladstone, one of Queensland's major industrial and shipping centres. Offshore are the Capricornia Marine Park and the southern reef islands. This southernmost part of the Great Barrier Reef offers some of the best diving and snorkelling on the entire Reef. Lady Elliot and Heron Islands both have resorts geared for underwater activity and are rightly popular with divers. You can also take day trips to and camp on uninhabited Lady Musgrave Island and several others. On the coast south of Gladstone are the laid-back but increasingly popular holiday towns of 1770 and Agnes Water, the focus of a pristine coastline known as the Discovery Coast.

The Capricorn hinterland is one of Queensland's richest natural resources; the fertile soils support grazing and cropping, and the vast coal deposits supply the majority of the state's coal exports. Dominating the scenery, though, are the broad, flattened plateaus of the Great Dividing Range, with several spectacular outcrops of sandstone escarpment, most notably around the Carnarvon and Blackdown Tableland National Parks. Numerous trails in these rugged parks reward bushwalkers with breathtaking scenery, unusual plants and Aboriginal rock art. The hinterland Gemfields region, directly west of Rockhampton, conceals another hard-earned reward; it is the best area in Queensland to go fossicking for gemstones, particularly sapphires.

Getting There & Around

AIR

Rockhampton and Gladstone have major domestic airports, and **Jetstar** (☎ 13 15 38; www.jetstar.com.au) connects Rockhampton with Brisbane and Sydney. **Qantas** (☎ 13 13 13; www.qantas.com.au) connects Rockhampton with Mackay, Gladstone, Brisbane and Sydney, and Gladstone with Brisbane. Through Qantaslink they also connect Emerald with Brisbane. **Virgin Blue** (☎ 13 67 89; www.virginblue.com.au) has a daily flight between Rockhampton and Brisbane.

BUS

Greyhound Australia (☎ 13 20 30; www.greyhound.com.au) and **Premier Motor Service** (☎ 13 34 10; www.premierms.com.au) both have regular coach services along the Bruce Hwy. Greyhound operates regular services to and from Rockhampton, Gladstone and Agnes Water, while

Premier Motor Services runs a Brisbane to Cairns service that stops at Miriam Vale and Rockhampton.

Emerald Coaches (☎ 1800 28737; www.emeraldcoaches.com.au) makes the run from Rockhampton inland to and from Emerald (daily) and Longreach (twice weekly). It also operates a daily service to and from Emerald and Mackay.

CAR & MOTORCYCLE

The Bruce Hwy runs all the way up the Capricorn Coast, although it goes a long way inland and only touches the coast briefly at Clairview. The major inland route is the Capricorn Hwy, which takes you west from Rockhampton through Emerald and the Gemfields. From Gladstone, the Dawson Hwy takes you west towards Carnarvon National Park and the town of Springsure.

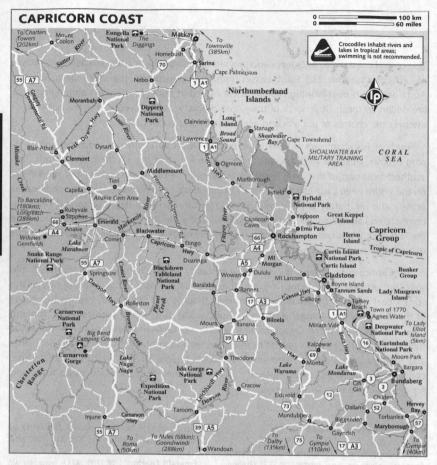

CAPRICORN COAST

0 ——— 100 km
0 ——— 60 miles

Crocodiles inhabit rivers and lakes in tropical areas; swimming is not recommended.

The Burnett Hwy, which starts at Rockhampton and heads south through the old gold-mining town of Mt Morgan, is an interesting and popular alternative route to Brisbane.

TRAIN

Queensland Rail (☎ 13 22 32; www.traveltrain.com.au) operates frequent services between Brisbane, Townsville/Cairns and Longreach. The high-speed *Tilt Train* and the more sedate *Sunlander* operate on the coastal route. The *Spirit of the Outback* leaves Brisbane twice weekly and turns inland from Rockhampton to Longreach. For details, see the Getting There & Away sections of the relevant towns and cities.

GLADSTONE AREA

MIRIAM VALE

Miriam Vale, 70km south of Gladstone, is a tiny cluster of buildings either side of the Bruce Hwy. Nevertheless, it's the administration centre of the surrounding shire, and the main turn-off point for the coastal havens of Agnes Water and Town of 1770.

The town's **Discovery Coast Information Centre** (☎ 4974 5428; Bruce Hwy) has brochures and local tourist information.

Budget accommodation and good pub food is available at the rustic **Miriam Vale Hotel** (☎ 4974 5209; 9 Bloomfield St; s/d $22/30, self-contained cabins d $55). The rooms at **Miriam Vale Motel**

(☎ 4974 5233; fax 4974 5134; Bruce Hwy; s/d $50/60, budget s/d $33/44) are nothing special, but they're clean and good value. A 100m walk away at the roadhouse, the **Big Crab** (☎ 4974 5224; cnr Dougall & Roe Sts; mains $8-15) has roadhouse-quality steak and seafood.

AGNES WATER & TOWN OF 1770
☎ 07 / pop 2000
The twin coastal towns of Agnes Water and Town of 1770 are among the state's most appealing seaside destinations. Although experiencing a boom in popularity, these towns, which are surrounded by national parks, beaches and the ocean, are far enough off the main track to retain their natural charms.

Agnes Water's pretty beach is Queensland's most northerly surf beach and a major drawcard. Town of 1770, 5km further up the track, is a little more laid back than its sibling. Originally gazetted as Round Hill, the Town of 1770, on a narrow and hilly peninsula on the eastern side of the estuary of Round Hill Creek, was renamed in 1936 in honour of Lieutenant Cook's landing here on Bustard Beach on 24 May 1770 – the second place he landed in Australia, and the first in what is now Queensland. Most people come here for fishing, boating or visiting the neighbouring national parks and southern cays of the Great Barrier Reef.

Information
The **Agnes Water Visitor Information Centre** (☎ 4974 7002; Rural Transaction Centre, Round Hill Rd) is opposite Endeavour Plaza, near the intersection of Springs and Round Hill Rds. The **Discovery Centre** (☎ 4974 7002; Shop 12, Endeavour Plaza, cnr Round Hill Rd & Captain Cook Dr, Agnes Water) is a helpful, privately run information service. Both places can help with accommodation, activities and tours.

Queensland Parks & Wildlife Service (QPWS; ☎ 4974 9350; www.epa.qld.gov.au; Captain Cook Dr, Town of 1770) has information and brochures on the Eurimbula and Deepwater National Parks. It sells camping permits and takes bookings three months in advance for the holiday periods. Note that camping permits in these national parks cannot be booked over the Internet.

There's a Westpac bank branch in Endeavour Plaza, and an ATM that takes most cards in the small AUR supermarket at the Agnes Water Shopping Centre.

Agnes Water Library (☎ 4902 1501; Rural Transaction Centre, Round Hill Rd; ☺ 9am-noon, 1-4pm) Internet costs $2.60 for 30 minutes.
Yok Attack Internet (☎ 4974 7454; Shop 22, Endeavour Plaza, cnr Captain Cook Dr & Round Hill Rd, Agnes Water; per hr $4) Internet access.

Sights
The **Miriam Vale Historical Society Museum** (☎ 4974 9511; Springs Rd, Agnes Water; admission $2; ☺ 1-4pm Mon & Wed-Sat & 10am-4pm Sun) displays a small collection of artefacts, rocks and minerals, as well as extracts from Cook's journal.

Activities
Agnes Water is Queensland's northernmost **surf beach**. A surf life-saving club patrols the main beach and there are often good breaks along the coast. Learn to surf on the gentle breaks of the main beach with **Reef 2 Beach Surf School** (☎ 4974 9072; 1/10 Round Hill Rd, Agnes Water). Classes cost $16 per person for four or more students.

Dive 1770 (☎ 4974 9359) offers courses (PADI Open Water $200) and Great Barrier Reef dives aboard the *Spirit of 1770* (see p226). Two dives plus gear costs $65 plus your boat ticket.

Round Hill Creek at the Town of 1770 is a calm anchorage for boats. There's also good **fishing** and **mudcrabbing** upstream, and the southern end of the Great Barrier Reef is easily accessible from here, with Lady Musgrave Island about 1½ hours offshore.

1770 Marine Services (☎ 4974 9227) hires out aluminium dinghies for exploring Round Hill Creek at $80/50 for a day/half-day. There are also **catamarans** (☎ 4974 9539) at $15 for 30 minutes; a **houseboat** (☎ 4974 9643) from $100 per half day; and **canoes** (☎ 4974 9470) at $30 per half day. **Jetski 1770** (☎ 4974 7765) conducts jet-ski tours starting at $60 per half hour.

There are also charter boats available for fishing, surfing, snorkelling and diving trips to the Great Barrier Reef, including the *Fitzroy Reef Jet* and *Spirit of 1770* (see p226). The **MV James Cook** (☎ 1800 1770 11) sleeps up to 10 people for tours of up to seven days duration, and **Sport Fish 1770** (☎ 4974 9686) offers sport-, game-, reef- and fly-fishing tours of the Great Barrier Reef at $380/600 per adult/child.

STINGERS

The potentially deadly Chironex box jelly-fish and Irukandji, also known as sea wasps or 'marine stingers', occur in Queensland's coastal waters north of Agnes Water (occasionally further south) from around October to April, and swimming is not advisable during these times. These potentially lethal jellyfish are usually found close to the coast, especially around river mouths. Fortunately, swimming and snorkelling are usually safe around the reef islands throughout the year; however, the rare and tiny (1cm to 2cm across) Irukandji has been recorded on the outer Reef and islands.

The large (up to 30cm across) Chironex box jellyfish's stinging tentacles spread several metres from its body; by the time victims see the jellyfish, they've already been stung. Treatment is urgent and similar for both species: douse the stings with vinegar (available on many beaches or from nearby houses) and call for an ambulance (if there's a first-aider present, they may have to apply CPR until the ambulance arrives). Do *not* attempt to remove the tentacles.

Some coastal resorts erect 'stinger nets' that provide small areas offering good protection against Chironex, but not necessarily the smaller, rarer Irukandji. Elsewhere, you can wear a stinger suit for protection or simply stay out of the sea when stingers are around.

Tours

From the Town of 1770 marina, **1770 Holidays** (☎ 1800 1770 11, 4974 9422; www.1770holidays .com; 535 Captain Cook Dr) operates the *Fitzroy Reef Jet* (adult/child $130/70), which whisks passengers out to pristine Fitzroy Reef Lagoon on the Great Barrier Reef for a day's snorkelling (diving is a $65 optional extra). The tour departs at 8am and returns around 5pm; lunch and morning and afternoon teas are provided.

1770 Holidays also runs enjoyable full-day tours in its amphibious vehicles, *Sir Joseph Banks* and *Dr DC Solander*. The tours take in Middle Island, Bustard Head and Eurimbula National Park, and operate Monday, Wednesday and Saturday. It costs $95/65 per adult/child, including

lunch. There are also daily one-hour sunset cruises ($22/12).

1770 Great Barrier Reef Cruises (☎ 4974 9077; Captain Cook Dr; adult/child $135/70) has excellent day trips to Lady Musgrave Island aboard the *Spirit of 1770*. It takes 1¼ hours to get there and six hours is spent at the island and its acclaimed lagoon. Lunch, snorkelling and fishing gear are provided on the cruises which depart the Town of 1770 marina on Tuesday, Wednesday, Thursday, Saturday and Sunday – more often during holiday periods. Island camping transfers are also available for $225 per person ($245 in school holidays), which include lunch and reef fishing on the return journey.

Discovery Coast Detours (☎ 4974 9794) has 4WD tours of Deepwater and Eurimbula National Parks featuring seldom-visited coastline and wildlife. The full-/half-day tour costs $51/28 per person. Guided fishing trips are also available.

Extreme Adrenaline Ocean Runners (☎ 1300 66 1770; www.oceanrunners.com.au) zooms adrenaline junkies around Bustard Bay in a fast boat ($75 per person), which can also be chartered for Great Barrier Reef trips.

Sleeping

AGNES WATER

Accommodation ranges from a salubrious B&B to excellent budget backpackers.

Hideaway (☎ /fax 4974 9144; thehideawaybb@big pond.com; 2510 Round Hill Rd; d $130; 🐾) This B&B is an idyllic rural treat in a bush setting just 4km west of Agnes Water. The colonial-style homestead has three luxurious double bedrooms with bathrooms, a lounge room, outdoor dining area and BBQ area. For an extra $35 you can get dinner, and you can stay seven nights for the price of five.

Cool Bananas (☎ 1800 227 660; www.coolbananas .biz.com; 2 Springs Rd; dm $23; 🖳) This purpose-built backpackers has roomy eight-bed dorms, comfortable communal areas, tropical gardens and friendly staff. Phone for pick-ups from Bundaberg.

Mango Tree Motel (☎ /fax 4974 9132; 7 Agnes St; s/d from $80/90; 🐾) Only 100m from the beach, this motel offers large self-contained rooms (sleeping up to six per room) with the option of continental breakfasts. There's also a licensed restaurant.

Backpackers 1770 (☎ /fax 4974 9849; 3 Captain Cook Dr; dm/d $20/40) This backpackers has a large, clean kitchen, good-sized rooms and Internet terminals. The friendly owners do pickups from Miriam Vale.

Agnes Water Caravan Park (☎ 4974 9193; 51 Jeffrey Court; unpowered/powered sites $18/25, cabins $55-80) With absolute beach frontage and a variety of cabins, this park is a great budget choice. Prices are for two people.

TOWN OF 1770
In 1770 you can stay in 'shacks' with a view or camp beside the beach.

Beach Shacks (☎/fax 4974 9463; beachshack@1770 .net; 578 Captain Cook Dr; d from $148) These delightful self-contained 'shacks' are decorated in timber, cane and bamboo. They offer grand views and magnificent private accommodation just a minute's walk from the water.

Sovereign Lodge (☎ 4974 9257; mickeyd73@big pond.com; 1 Elliot St; d from $85-220; 🔀 🖳) As well as a range of immaculate self-contained rooms, some with excellent views, there is a Balinese 'Body Temple' here where, among other offerings, you can be massaged, wrapped in clay, rubbed with hot rocks and scrubbed with salt.

1770 Camping Grounds (☎ 4974 9286; fax 4974 9583; campground1770@bigpond.com; Captain Cook Dr; unpowered/powered sites $18/21) A small, peaceful park with sites right by the beach and plenty of shady trees. Prices are for two people.

Captain Cook Holiday Village (☎ 4974 9219; www .1770holidayvillage.com; 385 Captain Cook Dr; unpowered/ powered sites $16/19, dm bungalows $50, self-contained cabins from $75) This large and well-equipped caravan and camping ground is in a pleasant bush setting and has a good restaurant, Deck. Prices are for two people.

Eating
Saltwater Café 1770 (☎ 4974 9599; Captain Cook Dr, Town of 1770; mains $10-26; ☯ lunch & dinner) This little salt-encrusted waterfront diner has plenty of charm and a bar. Choose between fish and chips or a delicious mud crab. Tuesday is pizza night and on Wednesday it's curry.

Yok Attack (☎ 4974 7454; Shop 22, Endeavour Plaza, cnr Captain Cook Dr & Round Hill Rd, Agnes Water; mains $13-19; ☯ lunch & dinner) This place is run by a Thai family and its authentic home-style dishes come highly recommended. You can also surf the Net over your noodles.

Deck (☎ 4974 9219; Captain Cook Holiday Village, Captain Cook Dr, Town of 1770; mains $15-20; ☯ lunch & dinner) With a pleasant, leafy, outdoor setting

and spectacular views over Bustard Bay, the Deck has tasty menu choices including seafood, pasta and curry.

Aggies Restaurant (☎ 4974 9469; Agnes Water Tavern, 1 Tavern Rd, Agnes Water; mains $22-26; ☯ lunch & dinner) The restaurant offers delicious seafood and excellent steaks and a shaded outdoor dining area, though cheaper pub grub is available in the bar.

Getting There & Away
Only one of several daily **Greyhound Australia** (☎ 13 20 30; www.greyhound.com.au) buses detours off the Bruce Hwy to Agnes Water. Others are met at Fingerboard Rd by a local shuttle service ($17; phone 'Macca' ☎ 4974 7540, who can also book Greyhound tickets). The direct bus leaves Bundaberg at 4.35pm and arrives at Agnes Water (opposite Cool Bananas) at 6pm. In the other direction the bus leaves Agnes Water at 6.45am and arrives in Bundaberg at 8.15am.

EURIMBULA & DEEPWATER NATIONAL PARKS
There are several coastal national parks around Agnes Water and Town of 1770. For information or to book camp sites, contact the **QPWS** (www.epa.qld.gov.au; Bundaberg ☎ 4131 1600; Town of 1770 ☎ 4974 9350). Alternatively, the parks have self-registration stands. Note that you cannot use the website for booking sites at these camping grounds.

The 78-sq-km Eurimbula National Park, on the northern side of Round Hill Creek, has a landscape of dunes, mangroves and eucalypt forest. There are two basic camping grounds, one at Bustard Beach with toilets and (unreliable) rainwater and the other at Middle Creek (no facilities). The main access road to the park is about 10km southwest of Agnes Water.

South of Agnes Water is Deepwater National Park. This park has an unspoiled coastal landscape with long sandy beaches, freshwater creeks, good fishing spots and two camping grounds. It's also a major breeding ground for loggerhead turtles, which dig nests and lay eggs on the beaches between November and February. You can watch the turtles laying and see hatchlings emerging at night between January and April, but you need to observe various precautions outlined in the QPWS park brochure (obtainable at the office in Town of 1770).

CAPRICORN COAST

The northern park entrance is 8km south of Agnes Water and is only accessible by 4WD. It's another 5km to the basic camping ground at Middle Rock (no facilities) and a further 2km to the Wreck Rock camping ground and picnic areas, with rain and bore water and composting toilets. Wreck Point can also be accessed from the south by 2WD vehicles via Baffle Creek.

GLADSTONE
☎ 07 / pop 26,625

About 20km off the Bruce Hwy, Gladstone is one of the busiest ports in Australia, handling agricultural, mineral and coal exports from central Queensland. Gladstone's marina is the main departure point for boats to the coral cay islands of Heron, Masthead and Wilson on the Great Barrier Reef. That Gladstone is an industrial town first and foremost can't be missed. The huge port with coal- and bauxite-loading terminals, oil tanks, the world's largest alumina refinery and a power station represent a few of the town's big industries. But when the working clothes come off, Gladstone is well placed for exploring some beautiful coral cays and lagoons on the southern Great Barrier Reef.

Information

Gladstone City Library (☎ 4976 6400; 39 Goondoon St; ⏲ 9.30am-5.45pm Mon-Fri, 9am-4.30pm Sat) Free Internet access but you must book in advance.

Post Office (☎ 13 13 18; Valley Shopping Centre, Goondoon St)

QPWS (☎ 4971 6500; 3rd fl, 136 Goondoon St; ⏲ 8.30am-5pm Mon-Fri) Provides information on all the southern Great Barrier Reef islands, as well as the area's mainland parks.

Visitor information centre (☎ 4972 9000; Bryan Jordan Dr; ⏲ 8.30am-5pm Mon-Fri, 9am-5pm Sat & Sun) Located at the marina, the departure point for boats to Heron Island.

Sights

The beautiful **Tondoon Botanic Gardens** (☎ 4979 3326; Glenlyon Rd; admission free; ⏲ 9am-6pm Oct-Mar, 8.30am-5.30pm Apr-Sep), about 7km south of the town centre, comprises 83 hectares of rainforest and Australian native plants with walking trails and lakes. There's a visitor centre, botanical displays including an

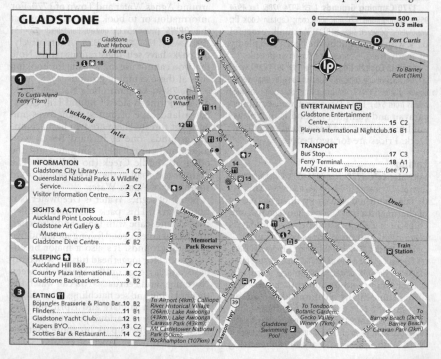

GLADSTONE

0 ————— 500 m
0 ————— 0.3 miles

Port Curtis

To Curtis Island Ferry (1km)

To Barney Point (1km)

Gladstone Boat Harbour & Marina

Macfarlane Rd

O'Connell Wharf

Auckland Inlet

INFORMATION
Gladstone City Library.................1 C2
Queensland National Parks & Wildlife
Service..................................2 C2
Visitor Information Centre.........3 A1

SIGHTS & ACTIVITIES
Auckland Point Lookout............4 B1
Gladstone Art Gallery &
Museum..............................5 C3
Gladstone Dive Centre.............6 B2

SLEEPING
Auckland Hill B&B......................7 C2
Country Plaza International........8 C2
Gladstone Backpackers.............9 B2

EATING
Bojangles Brasserie & Piano Bar.10 B2
Flinders...................................11 B1
Gladstone Yacht Club..............12 B1
Kapers BYO.............................13 C2
Scotties Bar & Restaurant.........14 C2

ENTERTAINMENT
Gladstone Entertainment
Centre.................................15 C2
Players International Nightclub.16 B1

TRANSPORT
Bus Stop................................17 C3
Ferry Terminal........................18 A1
Mobil 24 Hour Roadhouse.....(see 17)

Memorial Park Reserve

To Airport (4km); Calliope River Historical Village (26km); Lake Awoonga (43km); Lake Awoonga Caravan Park (43km); Mt Castletower National Park (50km); Rockhampton (107km)

Gladstone Swimming Pool

To Tondoon Botanic Gardens; Gecko Valley Winery (7km)

Train Station

To Barney Beach (2km); Barney Beach Caravan Park (2km)

Drain

orchid house, and free guided tours (see below). It's a beautiful garden with extensive wheelchair access.

In the old town hall, the **Gladstone Art Gallery & Museum** (☎ 4976 6766; cnr Goondoon & Bramston Sts; admission free; ⏰ 10am-5pm Mon-Fri, 10am-4pm Sat) has a small, permanent collection of contemporary Australian paintings and ceramics, and regularly features visiting theme exhibitions.

The **Auckland Point Lookout** has good views over Gladstone harbour, the port facilities and shipping terminals. A brass tablet on the lookout maps the harbour and its many islands.

Activities

Gladstone Dive Centre (☎ 4972 9366; 16 Goondoon St) offers PADI dive courses ($545) and three-day, two-night trips to the Reef (approximately $500 per person including food, air-fills and all hire gear).

For wine buffs and quaffers, the picturesque **Gecko Valley Winery** (☎ 4979 0400; Bailiff Rd; ⏰ 11am-4pm) welcomes visitors for tastings. Unashamedly pushing the boundaries of viticulture, this surprising vineyard and winery is worth a taste test. It's in a bush setting adjacent to the botanic gardens.

Tours

Gladstone's big-ticket industries, including the alumina refineries, aluminium smelter, power station and port authority, open their doors for free industry tours. The one- or 1½-hour tours start at different times on different days of the week depending on the industry. Book at the visitor information centre.

Tondoon Botanic Gardens runs one-hour guided walks every Tuesday between April and September at 10am. Book at the visitor information centre.

Fishing, diving and sightseeing cruises to the Swains and Bunker Island groups are the speciality of the 20m **MV Mikat** (☎ 4972 3415; www.mikat.com.au). Cruises can be two to 14 days in duration with all meals catered, and there's a licensed bar on board. Trips leave from the marina.

Festivals & Events

The **Gladstone Harbour Festival** is held every year from the Monday before Easter until Easter Monday. It coincides with the **Brisbane to Gladstone yacht race**, and features different activities each day, including street parties, fireworks and an Easter parade.

Sleeping

Auckland Hill B&B (☎ 4972 4907; www.ahbb.com.au; 15 Yarroon St; s/d $99/125; 🅿 🖳) This sprawling, comfortable Queenslander has six spacious rooms with king-sized beds. Each is differently decorated: there is a spa suite and one with wheelchair access. Breakfasts are hearty and the mood is relaxed.

Country Plaza International (☎ 1800 244 904; 100 Goondoon St; d $109-124; 🅿 🖳) The Country Plaza is a 4½-star high-rise containing spacious rooms with balconies and views, a restaurant and a bar. Catering primarily to the business traveller, the rooms are well appointed and substantially discounted on the weekend.

Barney Beach Caravan Park (☎ 4972 1366; fax 4972 7549; Friend St; unpowered/powered sites $18/20, cabins $42-56, self-contained villas $80; 🅿) About 2km east of the city centre and close to the foreshore, this is the most central of the caravan parks. It's large and tidy, with a good camp kitchen and excellent self-contained accommodation, and there's a Saturday night sing-along. There are complimentary transfers to the marina for guests visiting Heron Island and you can leave your vehicle here while you are island-hopping. Prices are for two people.

Gladstone Backpackers (☎ 4972 5744; 12 Rollo St; dm/d $22/48) This fairly central hostel (with three- and four-bed dorms) is friendly if a little scruffy, with good kitchen and bathrooms. There's free use of bicycles and free pick-ups from the marina, bus and train.

Eating

Flinders (☎ 4972 8322; 2 Oaka Lane; mains $30-40; ⏰ lunch & dinner Mon-Sat) This delightful, cosy restaurant specialises in seafood and does it well. Chilli mud crab is just one of the four mouth-watering ways this tasty local crustacean is presented. Although the quality, prices and ambience draw visiting suits and romantic couples most evenings, there is also a good-value lunch menu (eg $11 Barra Burger) and kids' menu ($15), keeping it casual during the day.

Scotties Bar & Restaurant (☎ /fax 4972 9999; 46 Goondoon St; mains $21-27; ⏰ dinner Mon-Sat, lunch Fri only) Thai, Mediterranean, steak, seafood and pasta: this popular restaurant with a decidedly blue theme has an eclectic and always changing menu that includes a couple of vegetarian options.

Bojangles Brasserie & Piano Bar (☎ 4972 2847; 6 Goondoon St; mains $17-20; ☺ dinner Wed-Sat) The piano man pulls out all the Billy and Elton favourites while you choose to sip your cocktail on one of the plentiful, comfy lounges, at a pool table or on one of the outdoor tables. There are also excellent wood-fired pizzas ($10 to $20).

Kapers BYO (☎ 4972 7902; 124b Goondoon St; mains $26-30; ☺ dinner Mon-Sat) A bright, breezy, offbeat place with hand-painted tables, blackboards scrawled with gems on the meaning of life, and an imaginative and varied menu. There's always a friendly reception and several excellent vegetarian dishes available.

Gladstone Yacht Club (Yachties Bistro; ☎ 4972 8611; 1 Goondoon St; mains $10-19; ☺ lunch & dinner) The yacht club is a popular place to wine and dine on a budget, and with good reason. The steak, chicken, pasta and seafood is tasty and generous, there are daily buffet specials ($8) and you can eat on the deck overlooking the water.

Entertainment

Gladstone Entertainment Centre (☎ 4972 2822; 58 Goondoon St; ☺ box office 8.30am-5.30pm Mon-Fri, 9am-12.30pm Sat) Showcases various visiting live acts.

Players International Nightclub (☎ 4972 6333; Flinders Pde; ☺ 10pm-late)

Getting There & Away

AIR
Qantaslink (☎ 13 13 13; www.qantas.com.au) has several daily flights between Brisbane and Gladstone and one flight a day between Rockhampton and Gladstone. The airport is 7km from the centre and about $15 by taxi.

BUS
Greyhound Australia (☎ 13 20 30; www.greyhound .com.au) has several coach services along the Bruce Hwy each day, about half of which stop at Gladstone. The terminal for long-distance buses is at the Mobil 24 Hour Roadhouse, on the Dawson Hwy about 200m southwest of the centre.

TRAIN
Queensland Rail (☎ 13 22 32; www.traveltrain.com .au) has frequent services between Brisbane and Rockhampton, Cairns and Longreach that stop at Gladstone. Choose between the high-speed *Tilt Train* or the more sedate *Sunlander* and *Spirit of the Outback*. Fares and departure times vary greatly, so check the website or a timetable to find the most convenient train. As an example, the *Spirit of the Outback* leaves Brisbane (6.25pm Tuesday and Saturday) and reaches Gladstone at 2.36am the following morning. Fares start at $85. Going to Brisbane, it leaves Gladstone at 10.41pm (on Tuesday and Friday) arriving at 6.55am the following morning.

Getting Around
Buslink Queensland (☎ 4972 1670) runs local bus services on weekdays only, including a service along Goondoon St to Barney Point and the beach, which stops out the front of the caravan park there. To book a taxi, call **Blue & White Taxis** (☎ 4972 1800).

AROUND GLADSTONE
Calliope, on the Calliope River 26km south of Gladstone, has the **Calliope River Historical Village** (☎ 4975 7428; Dawson Hwy; admission $2; ☺ 8am-4pm), with restored heritage buildings including an old pub, church, schoolhouse and a slab hut.

About 7km south of Calliope is an artists' retreat called **Cedar Galleries** (☎ 4975 0444; Lot 100 Bruce Hwy; admission $2; ☺ 9am-4pm Thu-Sun). There are eight slab-hut studios nestled in the gardens here, and visitors can watch the painters and sculptors at work. There is also a café.

Lake Awoonga, created by the construction of the Awoonga Dam in 1984, is a popular recreational area south of Gladstone. Backed by the rugged **Mt Castletower National Park**, the lake, which is stocked with barramundi, has a scenic setting with landscaped picnic areas, a café, BBQs, walking trails, birdlife and the **Lake Awoonga Caravan Park** (☎ 4975 0155; Awoonga Dam Rd; unpowered/powered sites $18/23, cabins from $67). Prices are for two people.

SOUTHERN REEF ISLANDS
The Capricornia section of the Great Barrier Reef, which includes the southern reef islands, begins 80km northeast of Bundaberg around Lady Elliot Island. The coral reefs and cays in this group dot the ocean for about 140km up to Tryon Island, east of Rockhampton.

Several cays in this part of the Reef are excellent for snorkelling, diving and just

DETOUR

Curtis Island, just across the water from Gladstone, can't be confused with a resort island. Apart from swimming, fishing and curling up with a good book, its only real drawcard is the annual appearance of rare flatback turtles on its eastern shores between November and January. With advance notice (contact Capricorn Lodge), you can accompany the volunteer rangers on their nightly patrols. Accommodation is absolutely without frills. There's a free council camping ground and the basic, self-contained units at **Capricorn Lodge** (☎ 4972 0222; d $61). The **Curtis Endeavour Ferry Service** (☎ 4975 6990; return adult/child/family $20/12/50) connects the island with Gladstone on Monday, Wednesday, Friday, Saturday and Sunday.

getting back to nature – though reaching them is generally more expensive than reaching islands nearer the coast. Some of the islands are important breeding grounds for turtles and seabirds, and visitors should be aware of precautions to ensure the wildlife's protection, outlined in the relevant QPWS information sheets.

Camping is allowed on Lady Musgrave, Masthead and North West national park islands, and campers must be totally self-sufficient and abide by certain rules and restrictions. Numbers are limited, so it's advisable to apply well ahead for a camping permit ($4/16 per person/family). You can book up to 11 months ahead for these islands instead of the usual six to 12 weeks for other Queensland national parks. Contact the Gladstone **QPWS** (☎ 4971 6500; www .epa.qld.gov.au).

Access is from Bundaberg, Town of 1770, Gladstone, or Rosslyn Bay near Yeppoon.

Lady Elliot Island

About 80km northeast of Bundaberg, Lady Elliot is a 40-hectare vegetated coral cay at the southern end of the Great Barrier Reef. The island has a resort and its own airstrip. It is popular with divers and snorkellers, and has superb diving straight off the beach, as well as numerous shipwrecks, coral gardens, bommies and blowholes to explore.

Lady Elliot Island is not a national park, and camping is not allowed.

The rates at **Lady Elliot Island Resort** (☎ 1800 072 200; www.ladyelliot.com.au; s/d tents $220/290, s/d rooms from $250/390) include breakfast and dinner, snorkelling gear and some tours. The resort is a no-frills kind of place, with basic tent cabins, simple motel-style units and more expensive self-contained suites with two bedrooms. Most people are here for the spectacular diving, not the resort lifestyle.

Scenic Air (book through the resort) flies guests to the resort from Bundaberg and Hervey Bay for $175/88 per adult/child return. From Bundaberg or Hervey Bay, you can pay $279/139 for a day trip, which includes the flight, lunch and snorkelling gear.

Lady Musgrave Island

Lady Musgrave Island, a 15-hectare cay in the Bunker group, is an uninhabited national park about 100km northeast of Bundaberg. The island sits at the western end of a huge lagoon, which is one of the few places along the Great Barrier Reef where ships can safely enter. Lady Musgrave Island offers some excellent snorkelling and diving opportunities, and the day-trip boats can supply you with gear.

The island has a dense canopy of pisonia forest, which is brimming with terns, shearwaters and white-capped noddies during nesting. The birds nest from October to April, and green turtles nest from November to February.

You can walk around the island in 30 minutes, and there is a trail across the middle to the **national park camping ground** (per person/family $4/16) on the western side. Its only facilities are bush toilets, and campers – a maximum of 40 – must be totally self-sufficient. Bring your own drinking water and a gas or fuel stove – open fires are not permitted and the island's timber and driftwood cannot be burned.

Lady Musgrave Barrier Reef Cruises (☎ 1800 072 110, 4159 4519; www.lmcruises.com.au; adult/child $140/72) operates day trips from Port Bundaberg marina at 8am Monday, Thursday, Saturday and Sunday, returning at 5.45pm. The tour includes lunch, snorkelling gear and a glass-bottomed boat ride. The trip takes 2¼ hours and you have about four hours on the island. You can also use this service for camping drop-offs ($260 return).

There are also day trips from Town of 1770 (see p226).

Heron & Wilson Islands

Only 1km long and 17 hectares in area, Heron Island is 72km east of Gladstone. It's a true coral cay, densely vegetated with pisonia trees and surrounded by 24 sq km of reef. There's a resort and research station on the northeastern third of the island – the remainder is national park.

Heron, famed for superb scuba diving, is a Mecca for divers and there's excellent snorkelling over the shallow reef. The resort's dive boat runs excursions to the numerous diving sites and the dive shop has a full range of diving equipment for hire – dives start from $35 including air, weights and boat trip. Introductory scuba courses cost $150.

Heron Island Resort (☎ 1800 737 678, 4972 9055; www.heronisland.com; s/d from $350/480) has several levels of comfortable accommodation suited to families and couples – the Point Suites have the best views. This is the only place to stay on the island and there are no day trips. All meals are included in the tariff, though guests pay $180/90 per adult/child return transfer from Gladstone. The helicopter option, also from Gladstone, costs $495/248. Standby rates can be as low as $185 per person.

The resort also offers get-away-from-it-all trips to **Wilson Island** (www.wilsonisland.com; 5 nights s/d from $2600/4000), a national park island north of Heron with six permanent tents and solar-heated showers. There are excellent beaches and superb snorkelling. All guests must buy a combined Wilson/Heron package to stay two nights on Heron Island and three on Wilson, with all meals provided.

Other Islands

There are three other islands in this group worth mentioning, all major nesting sites for **loggerhead turtles** and various **seabirds**, notably shearwaters and black noddies. The turtles nest between November and February, the birds between October and April. All three islands allow self-sufficient camping with limited facilities.

Southwest of Heron Island, 45-hectare, uninhabited **Masthead Island** is the second largest of the nine vegetated cays in the Capricorn group. **Camping** is permitted from April to October; there is a limit of 50 campers and bookings (essential) can be made 11 months in advance.

At 106 hectares, **North West Island** is the second-biggest cay on the Reef. Formerly a guano mine and turtle-soup factory, it is now a national park popular with campers. **Camping** is closed from January 26 to Easter, and there's a limit of 150 campers. There are no scheduled services to North West; contact **QPWS** (☎ 4971 6500; www.epa.qld .gov.au) in Gladstone for details on suitable launches and barges to access the island.

Tryon Island is a tiny, beautiful, 11-hectare national park cay north of North West Island. There is a camping ground, but the island is currently closed to visitors to allow for revegetation. Check with the Gladstone **QPWS** (☎ 4971 6500; www.epa.qld.gov.au) for the latest details.

ROCKHAMPTON AREA

ROCKHAMPTON
☎ 07 / pop 59,475
Rockhampton spans the tropic of Capricorn and is the administrative and commercial centre of central Queensland. The town's fortunes are closely linked to the cattle industry, and the city proclaims itself the 'beef capital' of Australia. There are more than two million cattle within a 250km radius of the city, and large statues of Brahman, Braford and Santa Gertrudis bulls mark the northern and southern approaches. Not surprisingly, this is a great place to tuck into a steak.

Queensland's largest river, the Fitzroy, flows through the heart of Rockhampton, which was established as a river trading port in 1853. Its growth was boosted by a minor gold rush at Canoona in 1858, but the real development began with the discovery of rich gold and copper deposits at Mt Morgan in 1882. Rockhampton quickly developed into the major trading centre for the surrounding region, and its early-20th-century prosperity is evident in the many fine Victorian-era buildings around the older parts of the city. Sheep and, later, cattle have gradually replaced mining as the region's major industries.

Rockhampton styles itself as quintessentially Australian, but in reality it's a fascinating amalgam of US-influenced country

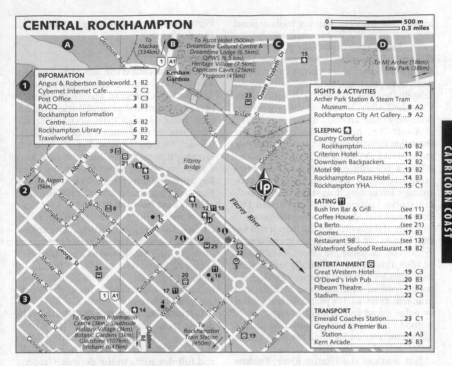

CENTRAL ROCKHAMPTON

INFORMATION
Angus & Robertson Bookworld..1 B2
Cybernet Internet Cafe.............2 C2
Post Office...............................3 C3
RACQ....................................4 B3
Rockhampton Information
Centre..................................5 B2
Rockhampton Library.................6 B3
Travelworld.............................7 B2

SIGHTS & ACTIVITIES
Archer Park Station & Steam Tram
Museum................................8 A2
Rockhampton City Art Gallery....9 A2

SLEEPING
Country Comfort
Rockhampton.......................10 B2
Criterion Hotel........................11 B2
Downtown Backpackers...........12 B2
Motel 98................................13 B2
Rockhampton Plaza Hotel.........14 B3
Rockhampton YHA...................15 C1

EATING
Bush Inn Bar & Grill.............(see 11)
Coffee House..........................16 B3
Da Berto..............................(see 21)
Gnomes................................17 B3
Restaurant 98....................(see 13)
Waterfront Seafood Restaurant..18 B2

ENTERTAINMENT
Great Western Hotel.................19 C3
O'Dowd's Irish Pub..................20 B3
Pilbeam Theatre......................21 B2
Stadium................................22 C3

TRANSPORT
Emerald Coaches Station.........23 C1
Greyhound & Premier Bus
Station.................................24 A3
Kern Arcade..........................25 B3

CAPRICORN COAST

and western music, big white hats and Coke mixed in with Australian V8 utes, pig dogs and Bundaberg Rum.

As well as having several attractions of its own, including an excellent art gallery, an Aboriginal cultural centre and some attractive gardens and parks, Rocky is the gateway to Yeppoon and Great Keppel Island.

Orientation

Rockhampton is about 40km from the coast. The Fitzroy River flows through the heart of the city, with the small commercial centre, the oldest part of Rocky, on the southern bank. The long Fitzroy Bridge connects the city centre with the newer northern suburbs. Coming in from the south, the Bruce Hwy skirts the centre and crosses the river via the Neville Hewitt Bridge.

Information

Angus & Robertson Bookworld (☎ 4922 5541; Fitzroy St) Has a large outlet inside the City Centre Plaza shopping centre. It has a good travel section.

Capricorn Information Centre (☎ 4927 2055; Gladstone Rd; ⏰ 8am-5pm) Helpful centre on the

highway beside the tropic of Capricorn marker, 3km south of the centre.

Cybernet Internet Cafe (☎ 4927 3633; 12 William St; ⏰ 10am-5.30pm; per hr $5) Internet access.

Post Office (☎ 13 13 18; 150 East St; ⏰ 9am-5pm Mon-Fri)

QPWS (☎ 4936 0511; 61 Yeppoon Rd, North Rockhampton) About 7km northwest of central Rockhampton.

Rockhampton Information Centre (☎ /fax 4922 5339; 208 Quay St; ⏰ 8.30am-4.30pm Mon-Fri, 9am-4pm Sat & Sun) Very helpful central office in the beautiful former Customs House.

Rockhampton library (☎ 4936 8265; 69 William St; ⏰ 9.15am-5.30pm Mon, Tues & Fri, 1-8pm Wed, 9.15am-8pm Thu, 9.15am-4.30pm Sat) Free Internet access, but you'll need to book.

Royal Automobile Club of Queensland (RACQ; ☎ 4927 2255; 134 William St)

Travelworld (☎ 4922 6111; cnr Denham & Bolsover Sts) For bus, train and plane tickets.

Sights & Activities

There are many fine old buildings in the town, particularly on **Quay St**, which has grand Victorian-era buildings dating back to the gold-rush days. You can pick up leaflets that map out walking trails around the town from the visitors centres.

The **Rockhampton City Art Gallery** (☎ 4936 8248; 62 Victoria Pde; admission free; ⏰ 10am-4pm Tue-Fri, 11am-4pm Sat & Sun) boasts an impressive collection of Australian paintings, including works by Sir Russell Drysdale, Sir Sidney Nolan, Jeffrey Smart and Albert Namatjira. Visiting exhibitions may incur an entrance fee.

About 7km north of the centre is the **Dreamtime Cultural Centre** (☎ 4936 1655; Bruce Hwy; adult/child $13/6; ⏰ 10am-3.30pm Mon-Fri, tours 10.30am & 1pm), a rewarding Aboriginal and Torres Strait Islander heritage display centre, providing a fascinating insight into the region's indigenous history. The recommended 1½-hour tours include boomerang throwing.

South of the centre are the wonderful **Botanic Gardens** (☎ 4922 1654; Spencer St; admission free; ⏰ 6am-6pm, zoo feeding 2.30-3.30pm). Established in 1869, this oasis is beautifully landscaped and includes a formal Japanese garden, lagoons covered with lilies and birdlife, and immaculate lawns. It's particularly admired by palm, cycad and fern enthusiasts. There is good disabled access, a kiosk, an attractive picnic area and a small **zoo** with koalas and a walk-through aviary.

Just north of the Fitzroy River, **Kershaw Gardens** (☎ 4936 8254; via Charles St; admission free; ⏰ 6am-6pm) is an excellent botanical park devoted to Australian native plants. Its attractions include artificial rapids, a rainforest area, a fragrant garden and heritage architecture.

Mt Archer rises 604m out of the landscape northeast of Rockhampton, offering stunning views of the city and hinterland from the summit, especially at night. It's an environmental park with walking trails weaving through eucalypts and rainforest abundant in wildlife. Rockhampton City Council publishes a brochure to the park, available from the information centres.

Rockhampton's **Heritage Village** (☎ 4936 1026; Bruce Hwy; adult/child/family $6.50/2/15; ⏰ 9am-3pm Mon-Fri, 10am-4pm Sat & Sun) is 10km north of the city centre. This is an active museum of replica historic buildings, and even has townspeople at work in period garb.

The **Archer Park Station & Steam Tram Museum** (☎ 4922 2774; Denison St; adult/child/family $5.50/3.30/13.20; ⏰ 10am-4pm Tue-Sun) is housed in a former train station built in 1899. It tells the station's story, and that of the unique Purrey steam tram, through photographs and displays.

Tours

Beef n Reef Adventures (☎ 1800 753 786; www.beefn reef.com) Promising the real Australia and the unexpected, Capricorn Dave takes punters on a whirlwind tour around Rocky's hidden bush gems. He also visits Koorana Crocodile Farm or Capricorn Caves. The (very) full-day tour costs $85 and includes lunch. Overnight trips can include the tidal bore on the Styx River, a ghost town and Great Keppel Island adventures. Transfers to and from your accommodation are available.

Rocky Road Tours (☎ 4928 6894) Rocky Road offers half- and full-day town tours including the Botanic Gardens, Dreamtime Cultural Centre, Archer Park Station and museum, and the Koorana Crocodile Farm. Half-day tours start at $44/22 per adult/child, and full-day tours are $70/40, lunch included. Tours depart from the Rockhampton Information Centre.

Capricorn Day Explorer (☎ 4934 2883) The people from Capricorn Caves (p236) run several guided tours to sights around Rocky as well as tours to the caves. There are half-and full-day tours to the Botanic Gardens, Dreamtime Cultural Centre, a beef cattle farm and the Koorana Crocodile Farm. Half-day tours cost $40/20 per adult/child and full-day tours are $99/50 including lunch. Transfers can be arranged.

Festivals & Events

Beef Australia (www.beefaustralia.org; 1-7 May 2006) Held every three years this is a huge exposition of everything beefy.

Rocky New Year's Bash & Ball (www.ballevents.org .au; 30 Dec–2 Jan) The theme is outdrink, outlast, outplay; and there are bull rides and a ute show of course.

Sleeping

BUDGET

Criterion Hotel (☎ 4922 1225; fax 4922 1226; 150 Quay St; s $40-45, d $60; 🅿) The Criterion is Rockhampton's grandest old pub with an elegant foyer and function room, a friendly bar and a great bistro (opposite). Its top two storeys have dozens of period rooms, some of which have been lovingly restored. The corner suites overlooking the nearby Fitzroy River are the best. Further restoration works and 4½-star rooms are planned.

Rockhampton YHA (☎ 4927 5288; fax 4922 6040; peter.karen@yhaqld.org; 60 MacFarlane St; dm members/nonmembers $19/23, d $50-59) Near the Greyhound terminal north of the river, the Rocky YHA is well looked after, with spotless six- and nine-bed dorms and amenities. The kitchen is excellent and there's a spacious lounge and dining area. It also has doubles and cabins with bathrooms and does courtesy pick-ups.

Ascot Hotel (☎ 4922 4719; 177 Musgrave St; dm/d $18/36; ✖ ▣) A bit inconvenient as it's about 2km north of the centre, this clean, friendly and comfortable backpackers has a good pub restaurant downstairs and is a base for Beef n Reef Adventures (opposite).

Downtown Backpackers (☎ 4922 1837; fax 4922 1050; Oxford Hotel, 91 East St; dm $19.50) Located upstairs over a boisterous bar, Downtown Backpackers offers basic, clean budget accommodation right in the centre of town.

Southside Holiday Village (☎ 1800 075 911, 4927 3013; fax 4927 7750; Lower Dawson Rd; unpowered/powered sites $15/23, cabins $45-65) This is one of the city's best caravan parks. It has neat, self-contained cabins with elevated decking, large grassed camp sites, a courtesy coach and a camp kitchen with a microwave and fridge. Prices are for two people.

MIDRANGE

Coffee House (☎ 4927 5722; www.coffeehouse.com.au; 51 William St; d from $99; ✖ ▣) Popular with the business traveller, the Coffee House offers beautifully appointed motel rooms, self-contained apartments and spa suites in central Rocky. It also has a restaurant (right) and wine bar and a café with Rocky's best coffee and cakes.

Motel 98 (☎ 4927 5322; www.motel98.com.au; 98 Victoria Pde; d $109; ✖ ▣ ▣) The smart Motel 98 has well-appointed, spacious rooms around the inviting pool. The elegant dining room (right) has a terrace overlooking the river.

Country Comfort Rockhampton (☎ 4927 9933; fax 4927 1615; 86 Victoria Pde; d $105-180; ✖ ▣ ▣) The Country Comfort boasts big rooms with views and excellent service. There are luxurious penthouses and family rooms available and downstairs you'll find a stylish restaurant and bar.

Rockhampton Plaza Hotel (☎ 1800 00 1800, 4927 58555; 161-7 George St; d $99-109; ✖ ▣ ▣) The Plaza has well-appointed, pretty typical four-star hotel rooms that overlook a park.

There's a bar and restaurant and it's located a short stroll southwest of the centre and close to the train station.

Eating

Coffee House (☎ 4927 5722; www.coffeehouse.com.au; 51 William St; mains $20-30; ✖ breakfast, lunch & dinner) A stylish though relaxed café/restaurant/wine bar that is popular throughout the day. The big breakfasts and excellent coffee help kick-start your day, while the extensive wine menu and the main dishes, which showcase local seafood and beef, provide an excellent way to wind down in the evening.

Restaurant 98 (☎ 4927 5322; www.motel98.com.au; 98 Victoria Pde; mains $22-34 ✖ lunch & dinner) This elegant licensed dining room features modern Australian versions of kangaroo, steak, lamb and seafood. Sit inside or out on the terrace overlooking the Fitzroy River.

Bush Inn Bar & Grill (Criterion Hotel; ☎ 4922 1225; 150 Quay St; dishes $10-20; ✖ lunch & dinner) The Bush Inn serves some of the best pub food in town and is very popular. There are huge steaks, slabs of barra, chicken dishes and pizzas on the menu.

Gnomes (☎ 4927 4713; 106 William St; mains $13-19; ✖ lunch & dinner Tue-Sat) If you're looking for excellent seafood and vegetarian dishes in a casual BYO setting where you can dine in a charming courtyard, then look no further.

Waterfront Seafood Restaurant (☎ 4922 0855; 179 Quay St; mains $25-50; ✖ lunch & dinner Mon-Sat, lunch Sun) Despite the name, you'll find more than seafood on the pricey Asian/Mediterranean-influenced menu. The location, in a riverside building with a balcony over the river, is terrific.

Da Berto (☎ 4922 3060; Pilbeam Theatre, Victoria Pde; mains $19-29; ✖ lunch Tue-Fri, dinner Tue-Sun) A cosy Italian restaurant near the foyer to the theatre where you can grab a pre- or post-show pasta, pizza or parmagiana.

Entertainment

Great Western Hotel (☎ 4922 1862; 39 Stanley St; admission $7.70) Looking like a spaghetti western film set, this is Lee Kernaghan's pub and home to Rocky's cowboys and gals. On Friday night there's a DJ and occasional live acts. Out back there's a big bullring where each Wednesday night you can watch brave fools try to ride real bucking bulls and broncos. Great entertainment. Professional rodeos are held throughout the year.

Criterion Hotel (☎ 4922 1225; 150 Quay St) Easily Rockhampton's favourite pub, the Criterion resonates with a good-time feel in its front bar and in the Bush Inn Bar & Grill. There's live music Wednesday to Saturday nights.

Stadium (☎ 4927 9988; 234 Quay St; admission $5 after 10pm; ☺ late Wed-Sun) This is the place most partygoers head after the pubs. It's a large, flashy club with a sporty theme (you dance on a mini basketball court), a central bar and pool tables.

O'Dowd's Irish Pub (☎ 4927 0344; 100 William St) You can get your fix of Irish music (and Guinness) here, with bands providing a lively atmosphere on most Friday and Saturday nights.

Pilbeam Theatre (☎ 4927 4111; Victoria Pde) This plush 967-seat theatre is located in the Rockhampton Performing Arts Complex (Rokpac) and hosts a range of national and international acts.

Getting There & Away

AIR
Jetstar (☎ 13 15 38; www.jetstar.com.au) Connects Rockhampton with Brisbane and Sydney.
Qantas (☎ 13 13 13; www.qantas.com.au) Connects Rockhampton with Mackay, Gladstone, Brisbane and Sydney.
Virgin Blue (☎ 13 67 89; www.virginblue.com.au) Has a daily flight between Rockhampton and Brisbane.

BUS
Greyhound Australia (☎ 13 20 30; www.greyhound .com.au) and **Premier Motor Service** (☎ 13 34 10; www.premierms.com.au) have regular services along the Bruce Hwy, and the Rocky terminus for both carriers is at the **Mobil roadhouse** (91 George St). Greyhound has regular services from Rocky to Mackay ($50, four hours), Brisbane ($85, 11 hours) and Cairns ($130, 16 hours). Premier operates a Brisbane–Cairns service, stopping at Rockhampton.

Emerald Coaches (☎ 1800 28737; www.emerald coaches.com.au) makes the run from Rockhampton (the terminal is just north of the Fitzroy Bridge) inland to/from Emerald (daily) and Longreach (twice weekly). It also has a daily run to/from Emerald to Mackay.

Young's Bus Service (☎ 4922 3813) operates several services to Yeppoon including a loop that includes Rosslyn Bay and Emu Park. Young's also has buses to Mt Morgan, Monday to Friday. Buses depart the Kern Arcade in Bolsover St.

Rothery's Coaches (☎ 4922 4320) does three runs a day from Rockhampton airport (one way/return $15/30), or Rockhampton accommodation ($8.25/16.50) by arrangement to Rosslyn Bay – the ferry terminal for Great Keppel Island.

Yeppoon Backpackers (☎ 4939 4702) runs a free daily bus between Rockhampton and Yeppoon for guests.

TRAIN
Queensland Rail (☎ 13 22 32; www.traveltrain.com .au) has frequent services between Brisbane, Cairns and Longreach that stop at Rockhampton. Choose between the high-speed *Tilt Train* or the slower *Sunlander* and *Spirit of the Outback*. Fares and departure times vary greatly, so check the website or a timetable to find the most convenient train. As an example, the *Sunlander* departs Brisbane (8.55am Sunday, Tuesday, Thursday and Saturday) and reaches Rockhampton at 7.55pm. Fares start at $94. To Brisbane, it departs Rockhampton at 5am (Monday, Tuesday, Thursday and Saturday) arriving at 3.55pm.

The slow *Spirit of the Outback* runs between Brisbane, Rockhampton, Emerald and Longreach twice weekly. Book with the **Queensland Rail Travel Centre** (☎ 4932 0453) at the train station, 1km southeast of the centre.

Getting Around
Rockhampton airport is 5km south of the centre. A taxi – **Rocky Cabs** (☎ 13 10 08) – costs about $12. There's a reasonably comprehensive city bus network operating all day Monday to Friday and Saturday morning. All services terminate in Bolsover St, between William and Denham Sts.

AROUND ROCKHAMPTON
The rugged Berserker Range, which starts 25km north of Rockhampton, is noted for its spectacular limestone caves. About 3.5km from the Caves township, **Capricorn Caves** (☎ 4934 2883; www.capricorncaves.com.au; Caves Rd; adult/child $16/8; ☺ 9am-4pm) is excellent value. Its informative one-hour Cathedral Tour is an easy guided walk leaving on the hour, and its highlight is the stone cathedral, where 'Amazing Grace' is played to demonstrate the incredible acoustics. For the more daring, the three-hour adventure tour ($60) takes you through tight spots with names such as 'Fat Man's Misery'. You

must book in advance and be at least 16 for this tour.

The complex has BBQ areas, a pool and kiosk, and **accommodation** (unpowered/powered sites $16/20, cabins from $60). Prices are for two people.

Each year the caves celebrate the **Summer Solstice Light Spectacular**. From 1 December to 14 January, when the sun is directly overhead at midday, sunlight beams into the caves via fissures in the rock, creating an incredible spectacle. To see the light, take the 11am Cathedral Tour.

Nearby, **Mt Etna National Park** (☎ 4936 0511; adult/child $7.50/3.70; ☺ tours 5.30pm Mon, Wed, Fri & Sat Dec-Feb) is one of only five known maternity sites of the little bent-wing bat. There are no facilities and access is restricted. Rangers run night tours of the bat caves (bookings essential) from the Caves township.

MT MORGAN
☎ 07 / pop 2397

The historic gold- and copper-mining town of Mt Morgan is 38km southwest of Rockhampton on the Burnett Hwy. William Mackinlay, a stockman, discovered gold here in 1880. Two years later the Morgan brothers, Thomas, Frederick and Edwin, arrived and started mining, and within a couple of years had made their fortunes.

Thinking the mine's future prospects were limited, the Morgan brothers sold out to a mining syndicate for £90,000 – a huge sum of money at the time, but nothing compared to what would later come out of the ground. In its first 10 years of operations from 1886, the Mt Morgan Gold Mining Company returned massive dividends on the initial capital, making its major investors some of Australia's richest and most powerful people. Gold yields fell dramatically by 1900, but in 1903 the company began extracting the rich copper deposits deeper in the mine. Open-cut operations continued until 1981.

Mt Morgan has a well-preserved collection of late-19th-century buildings, and is registered as a heritage town. There's an interesting historic museum and you can tour the former mine site.

Information

The **tourist information centre** (☎ 4938 2312; Railway Pde; ☺ 8am-4pm) is located in the old train station. Mt Morgan's **library** (☎ 4938 1169; 31 Morgan St; ☺ 8.45am-4.30pm Tue-Fri) has free Internet access.

Sights & Activities

The **Mt Morgan Historical Museum** (☎ 4938 2122; 87 Morgan St; adult/child $5/1; ☺ 10am-4pm Mon-Sun) is one of the better country museums you'll see. It has an extensive collection of artefacts, including a 1921 black Buick hearse, old mining equipment, photographs tracing the mine's history and even an old fire engine.

Mt Morgan's lovely **train station** (☎ 4938 2312; Railway Pde) is a focal point for the town. It houses the tourist information centre and is the departure point for mine tours and the historic **steam train rides** (adult/child/family $15/12/42) to Cattle Creek and back. A **market** is held here from 8am on the first Saturday of each month.

The **Running the Cutter monument** (cnr Morgan & Central Sts) commemorates the old custom of serving 'cutters' (two-quart billy cans) of beer to the mine workers in Cutter Lane, behind the hotels.

Tours

Mt Morgan Tours (☎ 4938 2312), based in the old train station, runs several value-packed tours that take in the town's sights, opencut mine, and a large cave with dinosaur footprints on the roof. The one-hour tours of the mine and cave depart at 2.30pm and cost $25/20/70 for an adult/child/family. The two-hour town, mine and cave tour departs at 11.30am and costs $35/30/100 including a lunch voucher. All tours depart from the tourist office.

Festivals & Events

The **Golden Mount Festival** is held every May Day weekend. It features a 'Running the Cutter' event.

Sleeping & Eating

Ferns' Miners Rest (☎ 4938 2350; 44 Coronation Dr; cottages $50; ⊠) These small but comfortable self-contained units sleep a family of four and are exceptionally good value. Each has a timber floor, spa, queen-sized bed and kitchenette. Meals can be supplied if required and booking ahead is advised.

Mount Morgan Motel & Van Park (☎ /fax 4938 1952; 2 Showground Rd; unpowered/powered sites $13/15, motel r $50; ⊠ 🔊) Open, grassy and spacious, this is the best option for camping, and the small motel units are good value. Prices are for two people.

Georgies on East (☎ 4938 2929; 113 East St; mains $13-28; ⓥ 10am-late Wed-Sun) An unexpected culinary gem that serves delicious country breakfasts and huge juicy steaks on sizzling hot volcanic rocks.

Getting There & Away

Young's Bus Service (☎ 4922 3813) operates a regular bus from Rockhampton to Mt Morgan and back Monday to Saturday. The one-way fare is $7.50.

Greyhound Australia (☎ 13 20 30; www.greyhound .com.au) also passes through Mt Morgan four times a week on the inland run between Rocky ($11 one way) and Brisbane ($76).

ROCKHAMPTON TO BARALABA

Myella Farm Stay (☎ 4998 1290; www.myella.com; Baralaba Rd) is a 1040-hectare beef property 120km southwest of Rockhampton that's popular among travellers looking to experience life on a working station. You stay in a comfortable, renovated four-bedroom homestead with polished timber floors and a wide veranda. You can stay for one day ($65 per person), two days ($170) or more. Guests can relax, ride a horse or a motorbike and help with the daily chores, then eat a large, home-cooked meal around the campfire. Rates include meals and activities.

If you're driving, take the Leichhardt Hwy and turn off towards Baralaba, between Wowan and Banana. The farm is signposted off the Baralaba Rd, 18km west of the Leichhardt Hwy. If you don't have transport, ring the farm to make arrangements for pick-ups from Rockhampton.

YEPPOON

☎ 07 / pop 10,778

Yeppoon is an attractive little seaside township 43km northeast of Rockhampton. Although Great Keppel Island is the area's main attraction, Yeppoon is a popular holiday town in its own right with attractive beaches and a pleasant hinterland. Boats to Great Keppel leave from Rosslyn Bay, 7km south of town.

Information

The **Capricorn Coast Information Centre** (☎ 1800 675 785, 4939 4888; www.capricorncoast.com.au; Scenic Hwy; ⓥ 9am-5pm), beside the Ross Creek

roundabout at the entrance to the town, has plenty of information on the Capricorn Coast and Great Keppel Island.

Click On Central (☎ 4939 5300; cnr Mary & James Sts) has Internet access for $5 per hour, and the **Yeppoon library** (☎ 4939 3433; 78 John St) has free Internet access.

Sleeping

While Away B&B (☎ 4939 5719; www.whileawaybandb .com.au; 44 Todd Ave; d from $105; ⓧ) With four good-sized rooms and an immaculately clean house with wheelchair access, this B&B is a perfect, quiet getaway – note that there are no facilities for kids. There are complimentary nibbles, tea, coffee, port and sherry as well as generous breakfasts.

Driftwood Motel & Holiday Units (☎ 4939 2446; fax 4939 1231; 7 Todd Ave; s/d $75/85; ⓧ ⓡ) Huge self-contained units at motel prices with absolute beach frontage make driftwood a great bargain. There are good family units with separate bedrooms and there's a children's playground.

Rydges Capricorn Resort (☎ 1800 075 902, 4925 2525; www.capricornresort.com; Farnborough Rd; d $250-320; ⓧ ⓡ) This is a large and lavish golf resort about 8km north of Yeppoon. Its accommodation ranges from standard hotel rooms to plush self-contained apartments, and there's a huge pool, a gym and several bars and restaurants. As usual, package deals are available. The resort's two immaculate golf courses are open to the public at $69 for 18 holes, which includes a motorised buggy. Club hire costs another $30.

Bayview Tower Motel (☎ 4939 4500; www.bay viewtower.com.au; 4 Adelaide St; d $88-105; ⓧ ⓡ) On the beachfront, the eight-storey Bayview Tower looks luxurious, but is reasonably priced and most rooms are fairly standard. The best feature is the balconies with views of the ocean and the Keppel islands. The rates increase the higher up you go.

Yeppoon Backpackers (☎ 1800 636 828, 4939 4702; 30 Queen St; dm/d $20/42; ⓡ) This is a friendly and homey backpackers in a rambling old timber house on the hill overlooking the town and beach. It has a big backyard, clean facilities, OK rooms, and does free pick-ups from Rockhampton twice daily.

Beachside Caravan Park (☎ 4939 3738; Farnborough Rd; unpowered/powered sites $15/18) This basic but neat little camping park north of the town centre boasts an absolute beachfront location. It has good amenities and grassed sites with some shade but no cabins or on-site vans. Rates are for two people.

Eating

Maggy's Café-Bistro (☎ 4939 4566; cnr James & Mary Sts; mains $8-22; ☺ breakfast & lunch daily, dinner Fri & Sat) Maggy's has a cultivated air that suggests a serious gourmet is at work in the kitchen. It's still a casual café by day and a great place for breakfast and lunch. The coconut crumbed fish of the day for $12.50 was excellent. Friday is curry night and on Saturday night there is a small à la carte selection. Maggy's is BYO.

Lure (☎ 4939 4666; 14 Anzac Pde; mains $17-28; ☺ dinner) A modish bar and café with extra-friendly staff who serve up excellent soup, pasta, steak, fish of the day and nightly specials with a minimum of fuss.

Thai Take-Away (☎ 4939 3920; shop 1, 24 Anzac Pde; mains $15-20; ☺ dinner) A deservedly popular Thai BYO restaurant where you can sit outside on the sidewalk, catch a sea breeze, and satisfy those chilli and coconut cravings. There's a large selection of seafood dishes and snappy service.

Dreamers Cafe (☎ 4939 5797; 4 James St; dishes $5-12; ☺ breakfast & lunch) Dreamers is a neat little café selling excellent coffee, as well as 'overstuffed sandwiches', melts, fajitas and salads.

Keppel Bay Sailing Club (☎ 4939 9537; Anzac Pde; mains $8-25 ☺ lunch & dinner) Choose between the beachfront clubhouse and deck with good steak and seafood, such as mouth-watering crumbed coral trout, or cross the road for a cheap buffet meal and the din of countless pokies at Spinnakers.

Entertainment

Strand Hotel (☎ 4939 1301; 2 Normanby St; cnr Anzac Pde) The Strand has plans for major refurbishment, but it's still a good place for a beer and live music. Bands play on Friday, Saturday and Sunday night in the open dining section.

Getting There & Away

If you're heading for Great Keppel or the Reef, some ferry operators will transport you between your accommodation and Rosslyn Bay Harbour. Otherwise, **Young's Bus Service** (☎ 4922 3813) runs buses from Rockhampton to Yeppoon ($7.70 one way, daily). **Rothery's Coaches** (☎ 4922 4320) does

three runs a day from Rockhampton airport ($15/30 one way/return), or Rockhampton accommodation ($8.25/16.50) by arrangement to Rosslyn Bay.

If you're driving to Rosslyn Bay there's a free day car park at the harbour and, associated with the Rosslyn Bay Inn Resort, is the **Great Keppel Island Security Car Park** (☎ 4933 6670; per day $8), which is the closest lock-up car park.

YEPPOON TO BYFIELD

The coastal hinterland north of Yeppoon is largely undeveloped; Byfield State Forest and Byfield National Park border the large Shoalwater Bay military training area. There are several forest picnic and camping grounds, though you can't get to the coast without a 4WD. You can visit galleries near tiny Byfield, 40km from Yeppoon, where there are also a couple of excellent, mid-range bush retreats.

The drive north from Yeppoon takes you through the pine plantations of the Byfield State Forest, with turn-offs along the way to various picnic and camping grounds and the Upper Stoney Dam.

Just south of Byfield, there are turn-offs to the **Nob Creek Pottery** (☎ 4935 1161; 216 Arnolds Rd; admission free; ☺ 9am-5pm), where you can visit the workshop and gallery, and to the **Waterpark Creek Camping Ground** (☎ 13 13 04; sites family/adult $16/4) which must be prebooked. It's 2km east from the main road to the creek crossing, beyond which are an attractive picnic area, with toilets, tables and gas BBQs. From here, a dirt road continues 10km through the pine plantations to **Byfield National Park**, an undeveloped area of mostly low coastal scrub. If you have a 4WD you can continue to Five Rocks and Nine Mile Beach, which are popular with anglers.

Byfield consists of a general store and café, a school, a handful of houses, and a private gallery that was closed at the time of research. There is no bottle shop in Byfield – so come prepared.

Signposted just north of Byfield, **Ferns Hideaway** (☎ /fax 4935 1235; www.fernshideaway .au; 76 Cahills Rd; unpowered sites $24, d $130-150; ☒ ☒) is a beautiful, secluded bush oasis in immaculate gardens that offers canoeing and nature walks. The timber homestead has a quality à la carte **restaurant** (mains $13-25; ☺ lunch & dinner Sat, lunch Sun), while nestled among the trees are the cosy self-contained cabins with wood fires. There are also double rooms with shared facilities; or you can camp, with hot showers included in the tariff. Camping tariff is for two people.

Near Ferns Hideaway is another retreat, **Waterpark Cabins** (☎/fax 4935 1241; Yaxley Rd; d $110-130), which is even more secluded. It has four imaginatively finished log cabins surrounded by bush, offering lovely rustic comfort, along with a log fire, spa and wood-fired BBQ.

YEPPOON TO EMU PARK

There are beaches dotted all along the 19km coastline running south from Yeppoon to Emu Park. Most of the towns along this stretch of coast have caravan parks, motels and holiday flats.

About 7km south of Yeppoon, **Rosslyn Bay Harbour** is the departure point for Great Keppel Island and other Keppel Bay islands. A great place to stay here is the **Rosslyn Bay Inn** (☎ 4933 6333; www.rosslynbayinn.com.au; Vin E Jones Dr; s/d from $79/99; 🛏 🖳), offering comfortable studio rooms and one- and two-bedroom units, as well as a bar and restaurant.

Further on there are three fine headlands with good views – **Double Head**, **Bluff Point** and **Pinnacle Point**. After Pinnacle Point the road crosses **Causeway Lake**, a saltwater inlet, and further south at **Emu Park** there are more good views and the 'Singing Ship' memorial to Captain Cook – drilled tubes and pipes that emit whistling or moaning sounds in the breeze.

The **Koorana Crocodile Farm** (☎ 4934 4749; Coowonga Rd; adult/child $15/7; 🕙 10am-3pm, tours 10.30am & 1pm) is off the Emu Park to Rockhampton road, about 15km from Emu Park. This simple farm has lots of crocs destined to become fashion accessories or the odd restaurant meal.

On the beachfront, **Bell Park Caravan Park** (☎ 4939 6202; Pattinson St, Emu Park; unpowered/powered sites $15/18; cabins $72) has spacious sites, clean amenities and comfortable cabins a stone's throw from the beach.

GREAT KEPPEL ISLAND

Great Keppel is one of the cheapest and easiest Queensland islands to reach, and though it's not on the Great Barrier Reef, its 18km of fine, white beaches make it the equal of most islands up the coast. It's only 13km offshore, and at 14 sq km, 90% of which is natural bushland, it is big enough to take a few days to explore.

The good news about Great Keppel is that there are plenty of good budget and midrange accommodation options. And although the resort area is dominated by a Mercure resort, it's usually pretty quiet on the island.

There's a wide range of activities and entertainment to keep guests busy and the island is also popular with day visitors; the resort has a separate section for day-trippers, with a small pool, bar, outdoor tables and umbrellas, a restaurant and a café, and all sorts of water-sports gear for hire.

Sights

Great Keppel's beaches are among the best of any of the resort islands. Take a short stroll from the busy main resort area and you'll find your own deserted stretch of white, sandy beach lapped by clear, warm water. There is fairly good coral and excellent fish life around, especially between Great Keppel and Humpy Island to the south. A 30-minute walk around the headland south of the resort brings you to **Monkey Beach**, where there's good snorkelling. A walking trail from the southern end of the airfield takes you to **Long Beach**, perhaps best of the island's beaches.

There are several bushwalking tracks from **Fisherman's Beach**, the main beach. The longest, and perhaps most difficult, leads to the 2.5m 'lighthouse' near **Bald Rock Point** on the far side of the island (three hours return).

There's an **underwater observatory** by Middle Island, close to Great Keppel. A confiscated Taiwanese fishing junk was sunk next to the observatory to provide a haven for fish.

Activities

The **Beach Shed** (☎ 925 0624; Putney Beach) and the **Mercure Watersports Hut** (Fisherman's Beach) both hire out sailboards, catamarans, motorboats, fishing tackle and snorkelling gear, and the staff can also take you parasailing or waterskiing. The **Great Keppel Island Dive Centre** (☎ 4939 5022; www.keppeldive.com; Putney Beach) offers introductory dives with all gear supplied for $100, or two qualified boat dives for $130.

Tours

Keppel Tourist Services (☎ 4933 6744; Rosslyn Bay marina) has a 'ferry plus one cruise' deal from

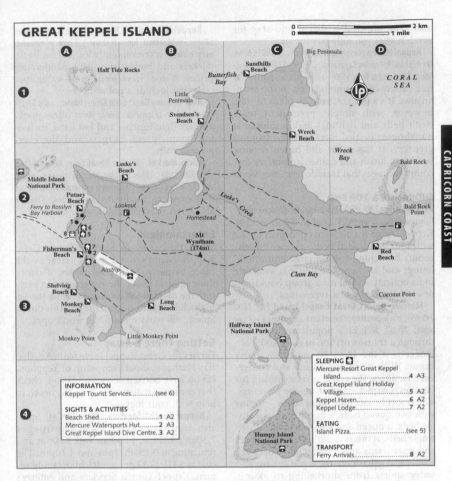

GREAT KEPPEL ISLAND

0 —————— 2 km
0 —————— 1 mile

CORAL SEA

Half Tide Rocks

Butterfish Bay

Sandhills Beach

Big Peninsula

Little Peninsula

Svendsen's Beach

Wreck Beach

Wreck Bay

Bald Rock

Leeke's Beach

Middle Island National Park

Putney Beach

Ferry to Rosslyn Bay Harbour

Lookout

Leeke's Creek

Homestead

Bald Rock Point

Fisherman's Beach

Mt Wyndham (174m)

Red Beach

Airstrip

Shelving Beach

Long Beach

Clam Bay

Coconut Point

Monkey Beach

Monkey Point

Little Monkey Point

Halfway Island National Park

Humpy Island National Park

INFORMATION
Keppel Tourist Services............(see 6)

SIGHTS & ACTIVITIES
Beach Shed...........................**1** A2
Mercure Watersports Hut..........**2** A3
Great Keppel Island Dive Centre.**3** A2

SLEEPING 🏠
Mercure Resort Great Keppel
  Island................................**4** A3
Great Keppel Island Holiday
  Village............................**5** A2
Keppel Haven.........................**6** A2
Keppel Lodge.........................**7** A2

EATING
Island Pizza............................(see 5)

TRANSPORT
Ferry Arrivals.........................**8** A2

CAPRICORN COAST

Rosslyn Bay and Fisherman's Beach. The morning tour includes a commentary cruise of Great Keppel Island, a visit to **Middle Island Underwater Observatory** and coral viewing on a glass-bottomed boat. It departs Rosslyn Bay at 9.15am and Fisherman's Beach at 10am, and costs $52/26 per adult/child. The two-hour afternoon cruise leaves Fisherman's Beach at 2.15pm, and includes boom netting (riding on a net trailed behind a boat) and snorkelling. The full-day cruise incorporates both ($77/44 with lunch).

Freedom Fast Cats (☎ 1800 336 244, 4933 6244; Rosslyn Bay marina) operates a coral cruise to the best location of the day (depending on tides and weather), which includes viewing through a glass-bottomed boat and

fish feeding. The cruise costs $51/28 per adult/child and leaves Rosslyn Bay marina at 9am. Freedom also runs lunch cruises and other options including a 'ferry plus one cruise' deal from Rosslyn Bay.

Sleeping
BUDGET
Great Keppel Island Holiday Village (☎ 4939 8655; www.gkiholidayvillage.com.au; s/d tents $40/60, dm $27, s/d cabins with bathroom $90/100) This YHA-affiliated resort is a collection of various types of good budget accommodation (including four- and six-bed dorms and cabins that sleep four). It's a very friendly, relaxed place with good shared bathroom facilities and a good communal kitchen and BBQ

area. The big deal is that if you stay for seven nights you only pay for six.

Keppel Haven (Keppel Tourist Services; ☎ 4933 6744; fax 4933 6429; Rosslyn Bay marina; s/d tents $28/40, d bunkhouse $80, cabins from $120) This place squeezes in a variety of accommodation in too small an area. It's a pleasant enough place to stay, however, with simple, permanent tents (with beds and lighting) and comfortable bunkhouses nestled in established tropical greenery. It has a bar and bistro serving breakfast, lunch and dinner, and offers discount packages that include ferry transfers.

MIDRANGE & TOP END

Keppel Lodge (☎ 4939 4251; info@keppellodge.com.au; Fisherman's Beach; s/d $90/110, each additional person $40) Keppel Lodge is a pleasant open-plan house with four good-sized bedrooms with bathrooms branching from a large communal lounge and kitchen. The house is available in its entirety – ideal for a group booking – or as individual motel-type suites.

Mercure Resort Great Keppel Island (☎ 1800 245 658; www.greatkeppelresort.com.au; r from $142 per night; ✖ ☐ ☑) This popular resort went through a transformation in early 2005. No longer is it the 18 to 30-something party venue. With a new Kid's Club and conference facilities, the resort is now aiming for families, couples and mature-age travellers. The resort boasts four room styles – rooms with two queen beds, a queen and two single beds, a queen and single bed, and three single beds. It offers facilities including bars and restaurants and a nightclub. There are tennis and squash courts, a golf course and water sports from snorkelling to skiing. More than 40 of the activities are free to guests. The resort offers a range of package deals to make longer stays cheaper, and two meals are included in the tariff.

Eating

If you want to cook, it's best to bring supplies with you, although the kiosks at Keppel Haven and the adjacent Great Keppel Island Holiday Village have a few basics such as soup and noodles.

Island Pizza (☎ 4939 4699; The Esplanade; dishes $6-30; ✖ dinner Tue-Sun, lunch Sat & Sun) This friendly place prides itself on unique, healthy pizzas with plenty of toppings. The pizzas are rather pricey but still tempting. Also available are hot dogs and pasta.

Keppel Haven Bar & Bistro (☎ 4933 6744; dishes $7-25; ✖ breakfast, lunch & dinner) This pleasant, airy eatery is conveniently located for backpackers and budget travellers. Moderately pricey, it does have some good-value specials that include a pot of beer.

Reef (Mercure Resort Great Keppel Island; mains $7-20) In the day-trippers' area, Reef offers pretty average light lunches and hot food, including wraps, pizza, burgers and the ever-present chips.

Micro Market (Mercure Resort Great Keppel Island; ✖ 10am-5pm) Also in the day-trippers' area, the Market offers ordinary espresso coffee as well as snacks and limited groceries. There's also Internet access and newspapers.

Entertainment

Splash, the bar in the Mercure Resort Great Keppel Island's day-trippers' area, is the place to party, with pool tables, a dance floor and live music. Resort guests can party into the night at **Salt** (admission $5; ✖ late Mon-Sat) nightclub. If patronage in the resort is down, Splash will party on and Salt won't open.

Getting There & Away

Ferries for Great Keppel leave from Rosslyn Bay Harbour, about 7km south of Yeppoon. If you have booked accommodation, check that someone will meet you on the beach to help with your luggage.

Keppel Tourist Services (☎ 4933 6744) operates daily ferries to the island, departing at 7.30am, 9.15am, 11.30am and 3.30pm and returning at 8.15am, 2pm and 4.30pm. The cost is $32/16/80 per adult/child/family return. Keppel Tourist Services and **Rothery's Coaches** (☎ 4922 4320) run a daily bus service from Rockhampton to Rosslyn Bay, picking up from the airport ($30 return) and accommodation in Rocky ($16 return).

Freedom Fast Cats (☎ 1800 336 244, 4933 6244) departs the Keppel Bay marina in Rosslyn Bay at 9am, 11.30am and 3pm, and leaves Great Keppel at 10am, 2pm and 4pm. The return fare is $32/16/78 per adult/child/family.

OTHER KEPPEL BAY ISLANDS

Great Keppel is the biggest of 18 continental islands dotted around Keppel Bay, all within 20km of the coast. You can visit **Middle Island**, with its underwater observatory, or **Halfway** and **Humpy** Islands if you're staying on Great Keppel.

Some of the islands are national parks where you can maroon yourself for a few days of self-sufficient camping. Most have clean, white beaches and several, notably Halfway Island, have good fringing coral reefs excellent for snorkelling or diving.

To camp on a national park island, you need to take all your own supplies, including water. Camper numbers on each island are restricted. You can get information and permits from the **QPWS** (www.epa.gov.au; Rockhampton ☎ 07-4936 0511; Rosslyn Bay ☎ 07-4933 6608).

The second-largest of the group and one of the most northerly is **North Keppel Island**. It covers 6 sq km and is a national park. The most popular camping spot is Considine Beach on the northwestern coast, which has toilets and a shower. There are a few small palms and other scattered trees, but shade is limited. Take insect repellent.

Other islands with camping grounds include Humpy, Miall and Middle.

Pumpkin Island (☎ 4939 2431; sites $15, cabins $155) is a tiny, privately owned island, just south of North Keppel. It has camp sites and five simple, cosy cabins. They have water and solar power, and each has a stove, fridge, BBQ and bathroom. All you need to bring is food and linen.

Funtastic Cruises (☎ 0438-909 502) can organise camping drop-offs from Rosslyn Bay to the islands. For Pumpkin Island it costs a minimum of $175 return for one person, and gets cheaper per person for larger groups.

CAPRICORN HINTERLAND

The Capricorn Hwy, or Rte 66, runs inland from Rockhampton, virtually along the tropic and across the central Queensland highlands to Barcaldine.

The area was first opened up by miners chasing gold and copper around Emerald, and sapphires around Anakie, but coal, cattle and grain are its lifeblood today. Carnarvon, south of Emerald, and the Blackdown Tableland, southeast of the coal-mining centre of Blackwater, are spectacular sandstone escarpments and two of Queensland's most spectacular and interesting national parks.

The Gemfields region, around the towns of Sapphire and Rubyvale, is a fascinating

area and you can try your luck fossicking for valuable gemstones.

ROCKHAMPTON TO EMERALD

It's 261km from Rockhampton to Emerald. On the way, you can take an interesting detour to the impressive Blackdown Tableland National Park and rest your head at a popular farmstay at Dingo.

Blackdown Tableland National Park

The Blackdown Tableland is an amazing sandstone plateau that rises out of the flat plains to a height of 600m. It features stunning panoramas, great bushwalks to waterfalls and lookouts, Aboriginal rock art, creeks and eucalypt forests. There's also a good camping ground here.

The turn-off to the park is signposted from the Capricorn Hwy, 11km west of Dingo and 35km east of Blackwater. From here, it's 23km to the top, the last 8km of which are steep, winding and often slippery. Caravans are not recommended.

At the top you come to the breathtaking **Horseshoe Lookout**, with picnic tables, BBQs and toilets. There's a walking trail starting here to **Two Mile Falls** (2km).

South Mimosa Creek camping ground (☎ 4986 1964; per person/family $4/16) is a picturesque self-registration camping area about 6km on from Horseshoe Lookout. It has pit toilets and fireplaces – you'll need to bring drinking water, firewood and/or a fuel stove, and bookings are essential during the Christmas and Easter holidays. Several other walking trails start from the camping ground.

Dingo

Near Dingo, **Namoi Hills Cattle Station** (☎ 7935 9277; namoi_hills@bigpond.com.au; Namoi Hills Rd; per person $45 incl dinner & breakfast) is a popular farmstay catering specifically to backpackers and budget travellers, and has a real focus on fun. It has cheap beds in ranch-style units and a special deal for longer stays. The station offers a three-hour cross-country tour (included in the overnight package), a make-your-own-didgeridoo trip ($150), a helicopter flight ($65) and a bush camp out ($95).

EMERALD

☎ 07 / pop 10,092

At the junction of the Gregory and Capricorn Hwys, Emerald is the gateway to the

Capricorn hinterland region. Established in 1879 as a railway siding, it has grown into a major centre for the surrounding mining and agricultural industries.

Most of the town's older buildings were destroyed in disastrous fires in 1936, 1940, 1954 and 1968. One notable exception is the fine old **Emerald Railway Station**, on Clermont St in the town centre, built in 1900 and restored in 1987.

Information

The **Central Highlands Tourist Information Centre** (☎ 4982 4142; Clermont St; ☒ 9am-5pm Mon-Sat, 10am-2pm Sun) is in Morton Park.

The **library** (☎ 4982 8347; 44 Borilla St; ☒ noon-5.30pm Mon, 10am-5.30pm Tue, Thu & Fri, 10am-8pm Wed, 9am-noon Sat) has free Internet access that must be prebooked in half-hour slots. Alternatively, **Jab Electronics** (cnr Egerton & Ruby Sts; per hr $6) is nearby.

Sights

The **Emerald Pioneer Cottage & Museum** (☎ 4982 1050; 3 Centenary Dr; adult/child $4/1; ☒ 2-4pm Mon-Fri Apr-Oct) has a collection of historic buildings including the town's first church and jail.

Kiely's Farm & Animal Sanctuary (☎ 4987 6700; Weemah Rd; adult/child $7.50/3.50; ☒ 11.30am-5pm) is an interesting little place 7km east of Emerald. It has a menagerie of animals enclosed in fairly spacious enclosures, from dingoes and foxes to rats and camels. There's a good canteen and cotton-farm tours in season.

If you're into art on a grand scale, Morton Park, on Dundas St next to the tourist office, has a 25m-tall easel sporting an enormous replica of **van Gogh's Sunflowers**, a celebration of the region's reputation as a major sunflower producer.

Sleeping

Western Gateway Motel (☎ 4982 3899; fax 4982 3107; cnr Hospital Rd & Theresa St; s/d $110/125; ☒ ☒) The Western Gateway is a large, comfortable motel with a couple of restaurants and a coffee shop. The rooms are big and quiet in typical motel style. Rates include a hot and cold buffet breakfast and there are cheaper Friday night and weekend rates.

Central Inn (☎ 4982 0800; fax 4982 0801; 90 Clermont St; s/d $45/55) Squeezed between the main road and the rail yard this budget motel has double-glazed windows and fire doors to help keep out the noise. Nevertheless,

the rail yard side is much quieter than the road. The rooms are Spartan but spotless with clinically clean shared facilities, and the tariff includes breakfast.

Emerald Cabin & Caravan Village (☎ 4982 1300; fax 4987 5320; 64 Opal St; unpowered/powered sites $18/23, cabins $63; ☒) This large park is only a pitching wedge from the golf course and a short stroll to the public pool. It has rows of neat cabins, immaculate amenities and a shaded camping area with a camp kitchen and BBQ. Prices are for two people.

Getting There & Away

Emerald Coaches (☎ 1800 28737; www.emeraldcoaches .com.au; Old Railway Station, Clermont St) makes the run from Rockhampton inland to/from Emerald ($40, 3½ hours, daily) and Longreach ($55, five hours, twice weekly). It also has a daily run to/from Emerald to Mackay.

You can also get here on the twice-weekly *Spirit of the Outback* train, which runs from Rocky to Longreach (Wednesday and Sunday) and returns Monday and Thursday. **Qantaslink** (☎ 13 13 13; www.qantas .com.au) flies between Brisbane and Emerald several times a day.

AROUND EMERALD

Queensland's second-largest artificial lake, **Lake Maraboon**, is 18km southwest of Emerald. There's a boat ramp, attractive picnic areas and, just 100m from the water, is the pleasant **Lake Maraboon Holiday Village** (☎ 4982 3677; fax 4982 1932; Fairbairn Dam Access Rd; unpowered/powered sites $18/22, cabins $65-80; ☒ ☒). Rates are for two people.

Tiny **Capella** is midway between Emerald and Clermont. It has a small historic village and is the starting point for several interesting self-drive tour options, including Scotts Peak, Mt Roper and Bundoora Dam. The town has a pub with budget accommodation, a caravan park and a motel.

CLERMONT

☎ 07 / pop 2042

Just over 50km northwest of Emerald is Clermont and the huge Blair Athol open-cut coal mine, with the world's largest seam of steaming coal. Clermont is Queensland's oldest tropical inland town, founded on gold, copper, sheep and cattle – influences commemorated in murals on four train carriages in Herchel St.

In December 1916 a flood virtually destroyed the town and claimed 65 lives. After the disaster, Clermont was moved building by building to higher ground, and the beautiful Hoods Lagoon occupies its former site. A concrete tree stump at the lagoon's southern end shows the high-water mark (14ft 6in or 4.35m).

The town has a helpful **information centre** (☎ 4983 3001; 57 Capella St; ⏰ 8.30am-5pm Mon-Fri, 8.30am-noon Sat).

The **Historical Society Museum** (☎ 4983 3311; Peak Downs Hwy; adult/child $6/2; ⏰ hours vary), about 3km north of the centre, has an interesting collection, including a steam traction engine used to relocate the flooded buildings.

Wombat Wanderers (☎ 4983 3292; 6 Kitchener St; ⏰ tours 8.45am Tue & Fri) takes fascinating, free four-hour tours of the **Blair Athol Mine**, departing from the information centre. Ring in advance to book.

Clermont's best motel is the four-star **Peppercorn Motel** (☎ 4983 1033; peppercorn@cqhinet .net.au; 51 Capricorn St; s/d $83/98; ⏰ ⏰), which has spacious rooms and a good **restaurant** (mains $18-25).

Clermont Caravan Park (☎ /fax 4983 1927; 1 Haig St; unpowered/powered sites $13/17, on-site vans from $25, cabins from $45; ⏰ ⏰) This friendly park is well maintained, with plenty of grass and two large, clean amenities blocks. Rates are for two people.

GEMFIELDS
West of Emerald, about 270km inland from Rockhampton, the gemfields around Anakie, Sapphire, Rubyvale and Willows are renowned for sapphires, zircons, rubies, jasper, and even diamonds and gold.

These are among the world's richest sapphire deposits, and it is still possible to find valuable gems in the area. The 2000-carat ($1 million plus) Centenary Sapphire was found in 1979, and in 2000, some Bundaberg tourists stumbled upon the 221-carat Millennium Sapphire, which sold for $87,000.

There are several fossicking parks in the area that sell buckets of dirt that you can wash and sieve by hand – 'doing a bucket' is great fun and a good way to learn to identify raw sapphires. There are also several tourist mines that take underground tours. If you strike it lucky, there are professional cutters who can cut your stones and even arrange to have them set in jewellery.

To go fossicking you need a licence (adult/family $5.55/7.80) from the Emerald Courthouse or one of the gemfields' general stores or post offices. You can obtain bush camping permits from the same places, which allow you to pitch a tent anywhere in the fields. Basic fossicking equipment includes sieves, a pick and shovel, water and a container. You can bring this with you or hire it when you arrive.

The most popular times to visit are the drier, cooler months from April to September – when the population can more than double.

Information
The **Gemfields Information Centre** (☎ 4985 4525; 1 Anakie Rd) has a wealth of information about the area, sells licences and a handy self-drive tour booklet ($2), and hires fossicking equipment combinations such as pick, shovel and sieves for $16.50 for 24 hours. BYO luck.

Rubyvale
☎ 07 / pop 689
Rubyvale is the main centre for the gemfields, but don't expect bright lights or hustle and bustle. It's a small, ramshackle place with a scattered collection of dwellings, a pub, a few gem shops and galleries, a general store and a service station.

Rubyvale is 18km north of Anakie. From here, it's another 62km to Capella. About half of the road is bitumen.

SIGHTS & ACTIVITIES
About 2km north of Rubyvale, **Miners Heritage Walk-in Mine** (☎ 4985 4444; Heritage Rd; adult/ child $9.50/3; ⏰ 9am-5pm) has informative 20-minute underground tours throughout the day in which you descend into a maze of tunnels 18m beneath the surface. There is also an underground gem shop, and you can 'do a bucket' for $7 in the spacious picnic area up above.

Bobby Dazzler Mine (☎ 4985 4170; Main St; adult/ child/family $6/4/20; ⏰ tours 10am, noon & 2pm) offers similar tours that take 30 minutes. Again, you can sort through a bucket of dirt ($8), and there's a little museum here.

Fascination (☎ 4985 4142; adult/child $60/45) conducts day-long, self-drive fossicking tours which include licences, equipment and guiding. BYO transport and food and drink.

SLEEPING & EATING

Rubyvale has a small range of accommodation options.

Rubyvale Holiday Units (☎ /fax 4985 4518; www .rubyvaleholiday.com.au; 35 Heritage Rd; d motel $65, 1-/2-bedroom apt $80/110; ✂ ☒) If you're looking for some luxury after rummaging around in the dirt, these spacious motel and self-contained units, about 1km north of Rubyvale, are just the ticket. The friendly owners are experienced miners and gem cutters. They have a small gem shop and provide a gem-cutting service.

New Royal Hotel (☎ 4985 4754; fax 4985 4463; 2 Keilambete Rd; d $85; mains $9-18; ✂) The attractive New Royal has four cosy, self-contained log cabins in keeping with the theme of the pub. They sleep eight (extra persons $12.50) and all feature open fires while some also have a spa bath. Good counter lunches and dinners are served daily, with the usual fare of steak, chicken and pasta.

Bedford Gardens Caravan Park (☎ 4985 4175; 10 Vane Tempest Rd; unpowered/powered sites $14/18, d cabins $50-70; ✂ ☐ ☒) There are some excellent camp sites (prices are for two people) amid the attractive lawns and gardens here, as well as BBQs and a camp kitchen. There are also cabins with facilities for the disabled.

Sapphire

☎ 07 / pop 690

About 10km north of Anakie, Sapphire has a petrol station, a post office and a few houses scattered around the hillside. It also has a distinctive accommodation option and several fossicking parks.

ACTIVITIES

Pat's Gems (☎ 4985 4544; 1056 Rubyvale Rd; ✆ 8.30am-5pm), 1km north of Sapphire, has buckets of dirt for $7 each or six buckets for $30. It also has fossicking gear available for hire.

SLEEPING & EATING

Sapphire offers interesting rustic cabins and alfresco dining.

Sunrise Cabins (☎ 4985 4281; 57 Sunrise Rd; unpowered/powered sites $13/16, d cabin $35, d self-contained cabins $55) In an attractive bush setting near Sapphire, these cabins are built from 'billy boulders', the smooth, round stones common to the area. They're simple and rustic but comfortable, and you can choose basic doubles or spacious self-contained options.

Camping prices are for two people, and there are good communal amenities, BBQs and a large camp kitchen with fridge and freezer.

Pat's Gems (☎ 4985 4544; 1056 Rubyvale Rd; lunch $4-8; ✆ 8.30am-5pm) This is a pleasant place to regain your strength after a morning's fossicking. It sells sandwiches, burgers, cake and coffee, and you can eat alfresco under shade.

Anakie

About 1km south of the highway, Anakie has a train station, a caravan park and a pub with units and good counter meals. On the second week in August, Anakie hosts the annual **Gemfest Festival of Gems**, featuring exhibitions of gems, jewellery, mining and fossicking equipment, art and craft markets and entertainment.

Ramboda Homestead (☎ 4985 4154; fax 4985 4210; Capricorn Hwy; s/d incl breakfast & dinner $50/100), just east of Anakie, is an attractive old timber homestead on a working cattle property. It has country-style bedrooms with shared bathrooms on the 2nd floor.

The turn-off to **Willows Gemfields** is about 27km west of Anakie, and it's another 11km to the village. There are a couple of caravan parks here.

Getting There & Away

You can get to Anakie on the **Emerald Coaches** (☎ 1800 28737; www.emeraldcoaches.com.au) twice-a-week run from Rockhampton to Longreach. Or take the twice-weekly *Spirit of the Outback* train. **Vaughan's Bus Service** (☎ 4982 1275) has school buses that you can catch from Emerald to Rubyvale on weekdays at 3.10pm, returning from Rubyvale at 7.30am ($7 one way).

SPRINGSURE

☎ 07 / pop 774

Springsure, 66km south of Emerald, has a striking backdrop of granite mountains and surrounding sunflower fields. The **Virgin Rock**, an outcrop of Mt Zamia on the northern outskirts, was named after early settlers claimed to have seen the image of the Virgin Mary in the rock face.

About 10km southwest at Burnside is the **Old Rainworth Fort** (☎ 4984 1674; off Wealwandangie Rd; adult/child $6/1; ✆ 9am-2pm Mon-Wed & Fri, 9am-5pm Sat & Sun), built following the Wills Massacre of 1861 when Aborigines killed 19 whites on Cullin-La-Ringo Station northwest of Springsure.

The **Queen's Arms Hotel** (☎ 4984 1533; fax 4984 1150; 14 Charles St; s/d $55/75; ✷) is on the highway that skirts the town. It's an old pub with modern, comfortable rooms with shared facilities and is good value.

Springsure also has a couple of budget motels and the **Springsure Roadhouse & Caravan Park** (☎ 4984 1418; 86 William St; unpowered/powered sites $12/15). Rates are for two people.

ROLLESTON

Rolleston, on the Dawson Hwy 70km southeast of Springsure, is the northern turn-off for Carnarvon National Park.

For accommodation and RACQ service head to the simple and friendly **Rolleston Caravan Park** (☎ 4984 3145; fax 4984 3003; Comet St; unpowered/powered sites $6/15, on-site vans $35, cabins $55). Prices are for two people. The **Rolleston Hotel** (☎ 4984 3440; Warrijo St; d from $58) has basic motel-style units and counter meals, while **Corrugated Cuisine** (☎ 4984 3399; Warrijo St; mains $5-10), in the old tin picture theatre, offers takeaway or sit-down steaks, chips, burgers and sandwiches.

CARNARVON NATIONAL PARK

Rugged Carnarvon National Park, in the middle of the Great Dividing Range, features dramatic sandstone gorge scenery and numerous Aboriginal rock paintings and carvings. The extensive national park has several sections, but most people visit the impressive Carnarvon Gorge (see the boxed text on p248). The other, less accessible sections are Mt Moffatt, Ka Ka Mundi and Salvator Rosa.

Carnarvon Gorge

About 3km into the Carnarvon Gorge section of the park there's an **information centre** (☎ 4984 4505; ⏰ 8am-10am & 3-5pm) and a scenic picnic and camping ground. The main walking track starts beside the information centre and follows Carnarvon Creek through the gorge. Detours lead to various points of interest, such as the **Moss Garden** (3.6km from the picnic ground), **Ward's Canyon** (4.8km), the **Art Gallery** (5.6km) and **Cathedral Cave** (9.3km). Allow *at least* a whole day for a visit. Basic groceries and ice are available at Takarakka Bush Resort (see right).

Mt Moffatt

The more westerly, rugged Mt Moffatt section of the park has some beautiful scenery and diverse vegetation and fauna, and **Kenniff Cave**, which is an important Aboriginal archaeological site with stencil paintings on the rock walls. It's believed Aborigines lived here as many as 19,000 years ago.

Tours

Australian Nature Guides (☎ 4984 4535) runs guided tours, including day ($40) and nightlife tours ($18), and free information sessions from Takarakka Bush Resort.

Sunrover Expeditions (☎ 1800 353 717, ☎ /fax 3203 4241; www.sunrover.com.au) runs a six-day camping safari into Carnarvon Gorge. The cost per person is $940, including transport, meals and camping equipment. Or you can choose to stay at Takarakka ($1270) or the Wilderness Lodge ($1600).

CQ Travel Link (Emerald Coaches; ☎ 4982 1399; Old Railway Station, Clermont St, Emerald), offers day trips to Carnarvon Gorge, including lunch, for $192 per person.

Sleeping & Eating

Carnarvon Gorge Wilderness Lodge (☎ 1800 644 150, 4984 4503; www.carnarvon-gorge.com.au; Wyseby Rd; d $390; ✷) This upmarket safari-style accommodation option is located near the park entrance, offering attractive cabins nestled in the bush. There's a restaurant and a bar and the rates, which include breakfast, lunch, dinner and a guided tour, drop considerably for longer stays and between November and April.

Takarakka Bush Resort (☎ /fax 4984 4535; www .takarakka.com.au; Wyseby Rd; unpowered/powered sites $18/24, cabins $70) About 5km from the picnic ground, Takarakka is a picturesque bush oasis with a big open camping area and a ring of simply furnished, elevated canvas cabins (BYO linen) with private verandas. There's a large camp kitchen and dining area, and hot showers. The reception/store sells drinks, groceries, ice and gas.

Carnarvon Gorge Visitor Area & Big Bend Camping Ground (☎ 13 13 04, 4984 4505; www.epa.qld.gov .au; sites per adult/family $4/16) The visitor area around the information centre is open to camping only during the Easter, June–July and September–October school holidays and bookings are essential. The isolated Big Bend camping ground is a 10km walk up

CAPRICORN COAST

CARNARVON GORGE'S ANCIENT WONDERLAND

Carnarvon Gorge is simply stunning. Massive, crumbling, yellow-white sandstone cliffs, up to 200m high, conceal a 'lost world' of giant cycads, cool moss gardens, king ferns and rare palms. Over millions of years Carnarvon Creek and its tributaries have carved 30km of twisting gorges and waterfalls through the soft sedimentary rock. The ruggedness of the terrain proved too much for would-be farmers; the pastoral lease was forfeited to the government in 1931, and in 1932 the national park was declared. Now, 21km of well-maintained walking trails bring you to the best that the park has to offer – majestic scenery, rare plants, wildlife and poignant Aboriginal art. All in all it's well worth exploring over several days.

The 2km **nature trail** circuit is an easy stroll starting at the information centre, best done in the early morning when platypuses can be seen where the trail crosses Carnarvon Creek. For a more energetic start to the day, head up to **Boolimba Bluff** (6.5km return) for a magnificent view of the cream-coloured cliffs being warmed by the rising sun. Longer walks up the gorge are even more rewarding. Start early and be aware of the hot midafternoon temperatures and the possibility of violent afternoon storms in summer. The many side trails to narrow tributary gorges, waterfalls and art sites should not be missed. If you have the gear, camp at Big Bend camping ground so you can spend more time exploring.

Nourished by the permanent creek that carved this refuge from the surrounding dry plains, wildlife is abundant. The platypuses, eastern grey kangaroos and smaller macropods, and the numerous and colourful bird species, seem oblivious to the many visitors this park attracts and so quickly impresses. Look for bright red-and-green king parrots in the river oaks and flashy red-backed fairywrens among the tall grasses. If one plant epitomises the 'lost world' feeling that Carnarvon evokes it is the zamia cycad, *Macrozamia moorei*. This ancient-looking plant is the largest of its type and individuals may be more than 400 years old. At about 50 years of age they start to produce cones. These large 'fruits' are extremely toxic, yet the local Aboriginal people found a way to neutralise the toxins and the cycads became an important part of their diet.

Vivid reminders of the rich indigenous culture of the gorge can be found under several rocky overhangs. This art can be viewed at three main sites – the Art Gallery, Cathedral Cave and Balloon Cave – where there are also descriptions and interpretive material. The freehand drawings and mouth-sprayed stencils in ochre and the unique rock engravings reveal similarities and differences to the culture of the present-day Bidjarra people of the Carnarvon area. The **Art Gallery** features more than 2000 stencils, paintings and engravings along 62m of rock wall. It is one of the finest examples of stencil art in Australia, with boomerangs, axes, arms and hands. The **Cathedral Cave**, near Big Bend camping ground, is an enormous rock shelter with numerous stencils and an intriguing figure painting. Smaller **Balloon Cave**, reached from a car park east of the visitors centre, again features stencilling, and there is information on traditional Aboriginal culture.

---

the gorge, about 500m upstream from Cathedral Cave. It is open all year and campers require permits and bookings. There are toilets here, but no showers, and fires are not permitted so you will need a fuel stove.

Mt Moffatt Camping Ground (☎ 4626 3581; www .epa.qld.gov.au; sites per adult/family $4/16) In the Mt Moffatt section, camping with a permit is allowed at four sites, but you need to be completely self-sufficient and a 4WD and extra fuel are advisable. Bookings are essential and can be made online.

Getting There & Away

CQ Travel Link (Emerald Coaches; ☎ 4982 1399; Old Railway Station, Clermont St, Emerald) provides transfers to/from the park and Emerald for $110 one way.

From Rolleston to Carnarvon Gorge the road is bitumen for 70km and unsealed for 25km. From Roma via Injune and Wyseby, the road is good bitumen for about 215km then unsealed and fairly rough for the last 30km. After heavy rain, both these roads can become impassable.

To get into the Mt Moffatt section of the park there are two roads from Injune – one through Womblebank Station (mostly unsealed), the other via Westgrove Station (all unsealed). There are no through roads from Mt Moffatt to Carnarvon Gorge or the park's other remote sections.

INJUNE

☎ 07 / pop 391

Injune is the southern gateway to the Carnarvon National Park. **Carnarvon Gateway Service Station** (☎ 4626 1279) is the local RACQ depot. You can continue along the Carnarvon Developmental Rd to the turn-off to the gorge section of the park 110km north at Wyseby, or turn off here and take the unsealed road that leads 140km northwest into the Mt Moffat section of the park.

The **Injune Motel** (☎ 4626 1328; fax 4626 1168; 60 Hutton Ave; s/d from $60/75) offers typical motel accommodation, while at the basic **Injune Caravan Park** (☎ 4626 1053; cnr Station St & Third Ave; sites $10) your second and third nights are free. There's also a pub with budget rooms and meals in town.

ROLLESTON TO BANANA – THE DAWSON HIGHWAY

Planet Downs Station (☎ 3265 5022; www.bloxsom .aust.com; Dawson Hwy; tw per person per night $695) is a cut above your average farmstay, with luxury accommodation (including pot-belly stoves and gold-plated fittings in the bathrooms), and a tariff that includes all meals and activities. There is a minimum three-night stay.

Another more affordable farmstay option is **Cooper Downs Cattle Station** (☎ 4996 5276; fax 4996 5259; Leichhardt Hwy), a working cattle property 37km northeast of Banana.

Banana has a caravan park and two service stations. The town is named after Banana Gully, which in turn is named after a bullock buried there.

BANANA TO MILES – THE LEICHHARDT HIGHWAY

It's an uneventful 280km south along the Leichhardt Hwy from Banana to Miles. After about 100km is **Isla Gorge National Park**. A 1.5km gravel road leads off the highway to the **lookout**, where there is a small self-registration camping ground and picnic area. The lookout has views over a landscape of eroded gorges and escarpments.

From here you move on to the small towns of **Taroom** (55km south), which has a tree initialled by Ludwig Leichhardt, and **Wandoan** (59km north of Miles), both of which have caravan parks, pubs and motels.

Possum Park (☎ /fax 4627 1651; Leichhardt Hwy; unpowered/powered sites $12/16, apt $60), 50km south of Wandoan, has old RAAF bunkers

and troop train carriages that have been converted into simple self-contained guest units. This unique and peaceful accommodation complex, in about 3 sq km of bush, also has camping facilities.

See p165 for information about Miles and surrounds.

BILOELA

☎ 07 / pop 5485

At the junction of the Dawson and Burnett Hwys, Biloela is a modern commercial centre servicing the surrounding agricultural, pastoral and coal-mining industries.

The town's small **tourist information centre** (☎ 4992 2405; Callide St; ☺ 9am-5pm Mon-Fri, 9am-noon Sat) is near the junction of the Dawson and Leichhardt Hwys.

Biloela isn't exactly a tourist Mecca, but there are some notable diversions here, including the **Silo** (☎ 4992 2400; Exhibition Ave; adult/child/family $5.50/4.50/15; ☺ 9am-4pm), an interesting interactive museum dedicated to the area's primary industries.

Greycliffe Homestead (☎ 4992 3959; Gladstone Rd; admission by donation; ☺ by appointment) is a National Trust–listed slab-timber home, built in the 1870s.

In contrast, **Callide B Power Station** (☎ 4992 9202; Callide Mine Rd; admission free; ☺ museum 6am-6pm Mon-Fri, tours 1.30pm Tue-Fri), east of town, was built more than 100 years later and is a major supplier of electricity to Queensland. There are tours of the plant and a museum.

Biloela's best motel is the **Silo Motor Inn** (☎ 1800 992 555, 4992 5555; fax 4992 2627; 75 Dawson Hwy; s/d $85/95; ☒ ☒). The best place to grab a meal is the **Settlers Inn Restaurant** (mains $15-25; ☺ lunch & dinner), which specialises in steaks.

Less expensive alternatives include:
Boomerang Caravan Park (☎ 4992 1815; fax 4992 6304; 10 Dunn St; unpowered/powered sites $14/18; cabins $55) The more central of the two options. Prices are for two people.
Sun Valley Motel (☎ 4992 1281; fax 4992 3295; 57-9 Dawson Hwy; s/d $55/65; ☒ ☒)

AROUND BILOELA

Thirty-five kilometres from Biloela, **Kroombit Lochenbar Station** (☎ 4992 2186; www.kroombit .au; 2-night packages $220; ☒ ☒) is a highly recommended cattle station that offers several farmstay packages: horse riding, cattle mustering, camp fires and bush walking. Rates include meals and pick-up from Biloela.

Whitsunday Coast

CONTENTS

HIGHLIGHTS

- Strolling and swimming along the brilliant white arc of **Whitehaven Beach** (p283) on Whitsunday Island

- Snorkelling over the magnificent outer **Great Barrier Reef** (p268) from a moored pontoon

- Taking the helm and sailing a course through the magnificent **Whitsunday Islands** (p266) – the ultimate sailing venue

- Gliding your kayak over coral gardens fringing idyllic **Hook Island** (p278)

- Spotting playful platypuses and trekking under a misty rainforest canopy at **Eungella National Park** (p262)

- Swimming up to the bar as you unwind in luxury at **Daydream Island** (p279) or another island resort of your choice

- Detouring back to nature for much-needed rejuvenation at serene **Cape Hillsborough National Park** (p264)

- Getting burnt, getting wet, getting dr...getting some fun at **Airlie Beach** (p270) – sunburn, wet T-shirts, bed bugs and beer

- www.queenslandholidays.com.au/whitsundays/index.cfm
- www.whitsunday.com

The backdrop is cloudless skies and calm blue seas, the lighting is provided by the tropical sun and the stars of the show are the Whitsunday Islands – numerous, diverse and, for the most part, completely natural. The Whitsundays justifiably enjoy star billing as Australia's holiday hotspot. This half-drowned mountain range plays host to coral gardens, sea turtles and myriad fishes. Much of the archipelago and the surrounding turquoise water belong to the Great Barrier Reef Marine Park, ensuring that this huge adventure playground stays as pristine as possible and that its delights are accessible to all budgets. For once the reality lives up to the dream; whether that dream is a wilderness getaway or five-star indulgence.

The Whitsunday Islands steal the show, yet there is plenty more to see up and down the coast, from platypus havens to backpacker foam parties – yes, the sublime to the ridiculous. Party central is Airlie Beach: gateway to the Whitsundays and home to budget accommodation, restaurants, bars and clubs. Wildlife certainly isn't restricted to the Whitsundays, with more and more people learning about the great walks and bush camping found along this coast and in the rainforest-clad mountains beyond the sugar-cane plains. Guaranteed sightings of wild platypuses, another show stealer, and superb rainforest walks are featured at Eungella National Park in the Mackay hinterland. And don't be surprised if you meet kangaroos while beachcombing at Cape Hillsborough National Park, north of Mackay.

This chapter covers the coastal strip from Sarina to Bowen and the corresponding hinterland, and is split into two sections: Mackay is the region's major town and base for Eungella National Park and several islands, including Brampton; the other section covers the main event for travellers – the Whitsundays, and the area centred around Airlie Beach.

Getting There & Around

AIR

Mackay airport is a major domestic hub, and **Jetstar** (☎ 13 15 38; www.jetstar.com.au), **Qantas** (☎ 13 13 13; www.qantas.com.au) and **Virgin Blue** (☎ 13 67 89; www.virginblue.com.au) all have regular flights to/from the major centres. Brampton Island also has its own airport, which is serviced by Macair (Qantas) from Mackay.

If you're heading for the Whitsundays, Jetstar and Qantas have frequent flights to Hamilton Island, from where there are boat/air transfers to all the other islands. All three companies fly into Proserpine (aka Whitsunday Coast) on the mainland. From there you can take a charter flight to the islands or a bus to Airlie Beach or nearby Shute Harbour.

There's also the Whitsunday airport, a small airfield near Airlie Beach, with regular services to the islands. Lindeman Island has its own airstrip.

BOAT

Airlie Beach and Shute Harbour are the main launching pads for boat trips to the Whitsundays – see p270 for details.

BUS

Greyhound Australia (☎ 13 20 30; www.greyhound.com.au) and **Premier Motor Service** (☎ 13 34 10; www.premierms.com.au) operate regular coach services along the Bruce Hwy with stops at all the major towns. They also detour off the highway from Proserpine to Airlie Beach.

TRAIN

Queensland Rail (☎ 13 22 32, 1300 13 17 22; www.traveltrain.com.au) has frequent services between Brisbane and Townsville/Cairns passing through the region. Choose between the high-speed *Tilt Train* or the more sedate *Sunlander*. For details see the Getting There & Away sections of the relevant towns and cities.

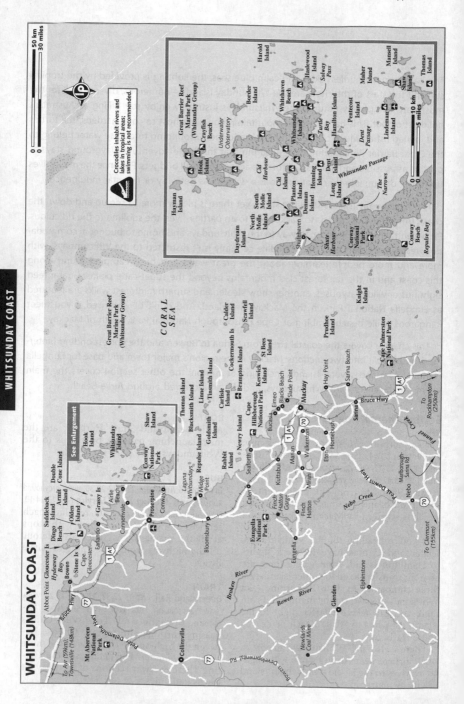

WHITSUNDAY COAST

Crocodiles inhabit rivers and lakes in tropical areas; swimming is not recommended.

MACKAY AREA

SARINA

☎ 07 / pop 3200

Sarina, 38km south of Mackay in the foothills of the Connors Range, is a service centre for the surrounding sugar-cane farms and home to CSR's Plane Creek sugar mill and ethanol distillery. Ethyl alcohol from Sarina may end up in fuel, Philippine gin or Japanese sake. The **Sarina Tourist Art & Craft Centre** (☎ 4956 2251; Railway Sq, Bruce Hwy; ✆ 9am-5pm) showcases locally made handicrafts and assists with regional information.

On the highway north of the centre, the friendly **Tramway Motel** (☎ 4956 2244; fax 4943 1262; 110 Broad St (Bruce Hwy); s/d $65/75; ✖ ✆) has clean, bright units, family rooms ($130) and even a separate cottage that sleeps eight.

The **Diner** (☎ 4956 1990; 11 Central St; mains $4-6; ✆ 4am-6pm Mon-Fri, 4-10am Sat) is a rustic roadside shack that has served tucker to truckies and cane farmers for decades. Hearty breakfasts top the inexpensive menu and there can't be too many places with $4 spaghetti bolognaise. To find it, take the turnoff to Clermont in the centre of town and look for the humble building on your left, just before the railway crossing.

The town centre straddles the Bruce Hwy and boasts a couple of pubs and cafés, a bakery, and a fruit and vegetable shop.

AROUND SARINA

There are a number of low-key beachside settlements a short drive east of Sarina, where the clean, uncrowded beaches and mangrove-lined inlets provide excellent opportunities for exploring, fishing, beachcombing and spotting wildlife such as sea eagles and nesting marine turtles. Nature takes a back seat at Hay Point, which is dominated by the largest coal-exporting facility in the southern hemisphere.

Sarina Beach

Set on the shores of Sarina Inlet, this laidback coastal village boasts a long beach, a general store–service station, a surf lifesaving club on the beachfront, and a boat ramp at the inlet.

Fernandos Hideaway (☎ 4956 6299; www.sarina beachbb.com; 26 Captain Blackwood Dr; B&B d $90-110; ✖ ✆) is a Spanish hacienda perched on a rugged headland offering magnificent coastal views. Choose between the panoramic double with a spa in the bathroom, and a double or family room that share a bathroom. The friendly owners can provide

---

DETOUR

It's 36km from Sarina to Mackay via the Bruce Hwy, but a longer alternative route takes you deep into the cane fields and past several points of interest. Take the turn-off to Homebush, 2km north of Sarina on the Bruce Hwy. The road is narrow and is regularly crossed by cane-train tracks, so drive carefully, particularly during harvest (July to November).

After about 24km you'll see the signpost to two of the area's main attractions, located side by side about 800m off the main road. **Orchidways** (☎ 4959 7298; fax 4959 7344; Masotti's Rd; adult/child $9.90/3.30; ✆ 9am-4pm Mon, Wed, Fri & Sun Apr-Jan) is a landscaped orchid garden with waterfalls and moats. Admission includes a free cuppa and there is a kiosk serving Devonshire teas and snacks. There are also BBQ facilities and a short bushwalking trail. On the same farm is **Polston Sugar Cane Farm** (☎ 4959 7298; fax 4959 7344; Masotti's Rd; adult/child/family $14.30/6.60/35.20; ✆ tours 1.30pm Mon, Wed & Fri Jun-Oct), where you can take a two-hour tour in a covered wagon to be shown how sugar cane is grown and harvested and sugar is produced.

Further on is **Homebush Pottery** (☎ 4959 7339; ✆ 9am-4pm Fri-Tue), a craft and pottery gallery displaying the work of local artists. If you need a drink after all this activity, call in at the **General Gordon Hotel** (☎ 4959 7324), an old country pub in a sea of sugar cane. Shortly after the pub take the turn-off to the left, cutting north to the Peak Downs Hwy and Walkerston. When you reach the highway you'll have to backtrack a few kilometres to reach historic **Greenmount Homestead** (☎ 4959 2250; adult/child/concession $5.50/1.50/4.40; ✆ 9.30am-12.30pm Sun-Fri), a classic Queenslander built by the Cook family in 1915 on the property where Mackay's founder, John Mackay, first settled in 1862. To head back to Mackay, return to Walkerston and keep going until you reach the Bruce Hwy.

meals other than breakfast and the large house offers both privacy and spacious communal areas.

Located at the northern end of the Esplanade, most rooms at the **Sarina Beach Motel** (☎ 4956 6266; fax 4956 6197; The Esplanade; d $75, apt $64-94; ☒ ☒) have beach frontage. In addition to the pool, there's a children's playground and tennis courts, and the beach is a stone's throw away. There are also BBQ areas, a bar and **Palms Restaurant** (mains $16-29, ☺ dinner).

Boasting a veranda overlooking the beach, the boisterous **Sarina SLSC** (☎ 4956 6490; The Esplanade; mains $10-15; ☺ 3pm-late Mon-Thu, 11am-late Fri-Sun) is a good place for a cheap meal and a drink. Dinner is served Wednesday to Sunday and there's usually an inexpensive roast and dessert on Sunday.

Armstrong Beach

Only a few kilometres southeast of Sarina, **Armstrong Beach Caravan Park** (☎ 4956 2425; 66 Melba St; unpowered/powered sites $18/20) is the closest coastal van park to Sarina. Prices are for two people.

MACKAY
☎ 07 / pop 74,000

Agriculture, mining and tourism power this vibrant regional city where one-third of Australia's sugar crop is processed and loaded onto carriers at one of the world's biggest sugar-loading terminals. The colourful marina precinct is rapidly gaining its own personality with residential, tourism and dining developments. The city's surrounding coastal plains and hinterland are carpeted in sugar cane, and there are good beaches a short bus ride away. Mackay is an excellent base for visiting Eungella National Park and its famous platypuses, and for exploring the wilds of Finch Hatton Gorge and the attractive Pioneer Valley. Mackay is also the access point for ruggedly beautiful Cape Hillsborough National Park to the north, and several tropical islands including the popular resort at Brampton Island.

Orientation

Mackay's inviting, compact town centre, with its historic buildings, modern art centre and palm-shaded streets, sits on the southern bank of the broad Pioneer River. The main thoroughfare of Victoria St is lined with cafés, pubs, restaurants and shops.

Long-distance buses stop at the Mackay Bus Terminal, located in Macalistar St adjacent to Travelworld. The train station, airport, Botanic Gardens and visitor information centre are all about 3km south of the city centre.

Sydney St crosses the Pioneer River over the Forgan Bridge to North Mackay, Mackay Harbour, Mackay Marina and the northern beaches. Mackay Harbour, 6km north of the centre, is dominated by the massive sugar terminal, while the adjacent marina has a select offering of waterfront restaurants.

Information

Chatline Internet (Map p256; cnr Victoria & Wood Sts; per hr $6) One of several places in the CBD offering Internet access; this one is in an ice cream shop.
Mackay Library (Map p256; ☎ 4957 1787; Gordon St; per 30min $2.50; ☺ 9am-5pm Mon & Wed, 10am-6pm Tue, 10am-8pm Thu, 9am-3pm Fri,10am-3pm Sat) Internet access.
Mackay Visitor Information Centre (Map p255; ☎ 4952 2677; www.mackayregion.com; 320 Nebo Rd; ☺ 8.30am-5pm Mon-Fri, 9am-4pm Sat & Sun) About 3km south of the centre.
Post Office (Map p256; ☎ 13 13 18; Sydney St) Near the corner of Gordon St.
Queensland Parks and Wildlife Service (QPWS; Map p256; ☎ 4944 7800; fax 4944 7811; cnr Wood & River Sts)
Royal Automobile Club of Queensland (RACQ; Map p256; ☎ 4957 2918; 214 Victoria St; ☺ 8.30am-5pm Mon, Tue, Thu & Fri, 9am-5pm Wed, 8.30am-noon Sat)
Town Hall Visitor Information Centre (Map p256; ☎ 4951 4803; Sydney St; ☺ 9am-5pm Mon-Fri, 9am-2pm Sat & Sun)

Sights & Activities

Artspace Mackay (Map p256; ☎ 4957 1775; www.art spacemackay.com.au; Gordon St; admission free; ☺ 10am-5pm Tue-Sun) is a regional museum and venue for local and visiting art and artists. Enquire about current events and activities, delve deeper by consulting the extensive collection of art books or browse the art before grazing at **foodspace** (☺ 10am-4pm Tue-Fri, 9am-4pm Sat & Sun), the in-house licensed café. Inspiration abounds in Mackay and its surrounds, and the *Mackay Self-Drive Art Gallery, Pottery & Craft Tour* brochure, available at the visitor centres, details several private galleries, exhibition spaces and art cafés.

Mackay Regional Botanic Gardens (Map p255; ☎ 4952 7300; Lagoon St; admission free) is an impressive 'work in progress' located 3km south of the city centre. The 33-hectare site

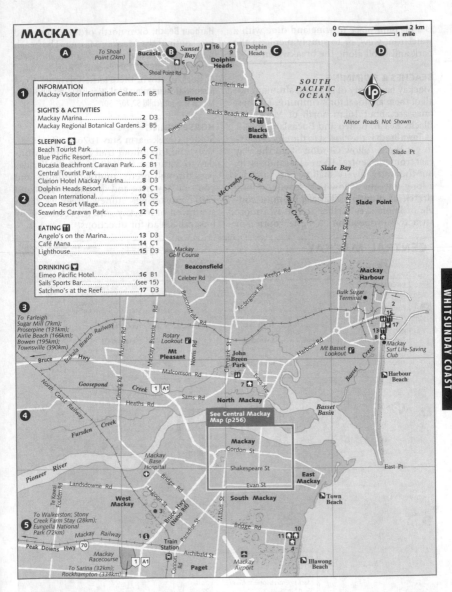

MACKAY

WHITSUNDAY COAST

includes several themed gardens, a **Tropical Shade Garden** (8.45am-4.45pm) and **Lagoons Café** (10am-4pm).

Mackay's lovely collection of **Art Deco buildings** owe much to a powerful cyclone in 1918 which flattened many of the town's earlier buildings. Enthusiasts should pick up a copy of *Art Deco Mackay* from the

Town Hall Visitor Information Centre. History buffs should also grab the brochure *A Heritage Walk in Mackay*, which guides you around 22 of the town's historic sites.

There are good views over the harbour from **Mt Basset Lookout** (Map p255), and at **Rotary Lookout** (Map p255) on Mt Oscar in North Mackay. **Mackay Marina** (Map p255)

is a pleasant place to wine and dine with a waterfront view, or to simply picnic in the park and stroll along the breakwater.

BEACHES & SWIMMING

Mackay has plenty of beaches, although not all of them are ideal for swimming. The best ones are about 16km north of Mackay at Blacks Beach, Eimeo and Bucasia (p260).

Town Beach is the closest to the city centre – to get there, follow Gordon St all the way east from the centre. There is a sandy strip, but the water is very shallow and subsides a long way out at low tide, leaving a long stretch of mudflats. **Illawong Beach**, a couple of kilometres further south, is a more attractive proposition. A better option is

Harbour Beach, 6km north of the centre and just south of the Mackay Marina. The beach here is patrolled and there's a foreshore reserve with picnic tables and BBQs.

Back in town, there's the Olympic-sized **Memorial Swimming Pool** (Map p256; ☎ 4968 4533; Milton St; adult/child $2.70/1.50).

HORSE RIDING

Stoney Creek Farm Stay (p261) offers 1½-, two-, and three-hour trail rides from Monday to Saturday for $40/50/60. Trail rides pass through pretty, undulating bush, and you can stay here and do longer rides and cattle mustering. Stoney Creek is 28km southwest of Mackay, and it's accessible by bus; call ahead for directions.

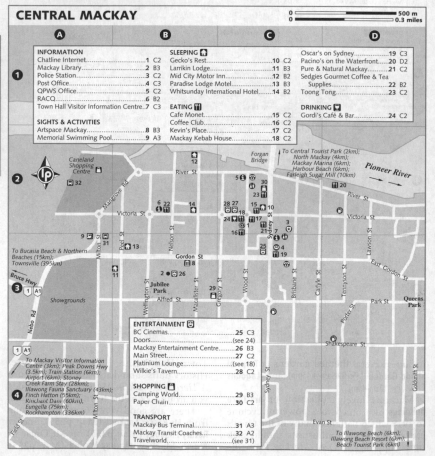

WHITSUNDAY COAST

Tours

Aviation Training & Transport (☎ 4951 4300; Casey Ave) Offers scenic flights from $50 (30 mins) to $210 per person. Flights leave from the airport, 3km south of town.

Farleigh Sugar Mill (☎ 4963 2700; admin@skillsstm .com.au; adult/child/family $17/10/40; 2hr tours 1pm Mon-Fri Jun-Nov) In the cane-crushing season you can see how the sweet crystals are made. Learn all about the history, production and technology, but dress prepared for a working mill, which means long sleeves, long pants and enclosed shoes. The mill is 10km northwest of Mackay.

Jungle Johno Tours (☎ 4951 3728; larrikin@mackay .net.au) Offers day trips to Eungella National Park for $75/40/68 an adult/child/YHA member. These Platypus Safaris, which include Finch Hatton Gorge and the Broken River platypuses, operate out of Larrikin Lodge, and are a good way to see the best bits of Eungella and surrounds in one day. The tour includes pick-up, morning tea and lunch. Overnight camping is also available.

Mackay Water Taxi & Adventures (☎ 4942 7372, 0417-073969; tjpic@mcs.net.au) Offers fishing charters (from $165 per person), day trips to Keswick and St Bee's Islands (from $135) and snorkelling and diving trips to the Great Barrier Reef and the Whitsunday and Cumberland Island groups. Trips leave from the marina, and there are free transfers from Mackay accommodation.

Reeforest Adventure Tours (☎ 1800 500 353; www .reeforest.com) The day-long Platypus & Rainforest Eco safari (adult/child/family $75/64/225) explores Finch Hatton Gorge and visits the platypuses of Broken River. It includes lunch at a secluded bush retreat near the gorge. Another option is a day tour to Cape Hillsborough ($90/64/265), which features Aboriginal middens, stone fish-traps and a bush-tucker trail.

Festivals & Events

Each year around May the **Wintermoon Folk Festival** (☎ 4958 8390; www.wintermoonfestival.com; day tickets adult/child/family $80/30/10) is held at Cameron's Pocket, 70km north of Mackay. This is a great opportunity to hear local and interstate musicians fiddle, strum and sing their stuff. Most people make a weekend of it and camp near the festival grounds (additional cost). Discounted prepaid tickets can be bought from the **Mackay Entertainment Centre** (☎ 4957 1777), or you can buy tickets at the festival. **Wintermoon Springfest** (day tickets adult/child/family $20/5/50) is a similar event held at the same location around October.

Sleeping

BUDGET

There are oodles of budget and midrange motels strung along busy Nebo Rd south of the centre. The budget options (around $50 for a double) post their prices out the front but there's little to recommend them as the rooms vibrate with road noise.

Larrikin Lodge (Map p256; ☎ 4951 3728; fax 4957 2978; 32 Peel St; dm/tw/f $19/44/69; ⏰ 7am-2pm & 5-8.30pm) This is a small YHA-associated hostel in an airy, high-ceiling timber house. It's clean, quiet and friendly. The owners also operate Jungle Johno Tours (left) and will pick you up from the bus terminal if you ring during office hours.

Gecko's Rest (Map p256; ☎ 4944 1230; info@geckos rest.com.au; 34 Sydney St; dm/s/d $20/30/46; 🍴 🖳) This centrally located backpackers has comfortable, well-presented quads and triples, though some lack windows. There's a large kitchen, comfortable lounge and games area, and there should be a roof deck for alfresco lounging by the time you read this.

Paradise Lodge Motel (Map p256; ☎ 4951 3644; fax 4953 1341; 19 Peel St; s/d $62/72; 🍴) Neat and tidy and nothing too special, the friendly Paradise is a good budget motel in the heart of town.

Central Tourist Park (Map p255; ☎ 4957 6141; Malcomson St, North Mackay; unpowered/powered sites $13/18, cabins $28-40; 🖳) Row after row of cabins (many with bathrooms) make this park, about 2km north of the centre, rather boring, but it's an inexpensive option relatively close to the city and accessible by bus Nos 5 and 6. Prices are for two adults.

Beach Tourist Park (Map p255; ☎ 4957 4021; www .beachtouristpark.com.au; 8 Petrie St, Illawong Beach; unpowered/powered sites $18/24, cabins $48-98; 🍴 🖳) About 3km south of the centre, this large, modern beachfront caravan park has a shop, gym, campers kitchen and BBQ area. Prices are for doubles and there are five configurations of cabins.

MIDRANGE

Ocean International (Map p255; ☎ 1800 635 104, 4957 2044; www.ocean-international.com.au; 1 Bridge Rd, Illawong Beach; d $130-219; 🍴 🖳 🍴) On the beach, close to the airport and only 3km south of the centre, this four-star, four-storey complex overlooks Sandringham Bay and the Coral Sea. There's an excellent restaurant and cocktail bar, a spa and sauna, business centre, and harbour/airport transfer service.

Mid City Motor Inn (Map p256; ☎ 4951 1666; fax 4951 1968; 2 Macalister St; s/d $70/75; 🍴 🖳) On the banks of the river in a quiet locale, yet

WHITSUNDAY COAST

handy to the city centre, this spic 'n' span motel has the best of both worlds.

Ocean Resort Village (Map p255; ☎ 1800 075 144, 4951 3200; www.oceanresortvillage.com.au; 5 Bridge Rd, Illawong Beach; apt $79-125; ⚡ ⚡) This is a good-value beachside resort comprising 34 self-contained apartments (studio, and one- and two-bedroom) in a cool, shady setting with two pools, BBQ areas and half-court tennis.

Illawong Beach Resort (Map p255; ☎ 4957 8427; fax 4957 8460; 73 Illawong Dr, Illawong Beach; 2-person apt $120-140, extra person $15.50; ⚡ ⚡) This manicured beachside resort has 37 two-bedroom, fully self-contained villas ideal for families. As well as the pool there's a tennis court, a children's games room and a small lake for fishing.

Whitsunday International Hotel (Map p256; ☎ 4957 2811; fax 4951 1785; 176 Victoria St; d $66-99; ⚡) This large centrally located hotel has well-maintained motel-style and self-contained rooms. There are a couple of bars, a restaurant and a nightclub on the ground floor, but there's very little noise disturbance in the rooms.

TOP END

Clarion Hotel Mackay Marina (Map p255; ☎ 1800 386 386, 4955 9400; www.mackaymarinahotel.com; Mulherin Dr, Mackay Harbour; d $165-275; ⚡ ⚡ ⚡) Part of the rapidly developing Marina precinct, the Clarion was just about ready for business when we visited. Every room boasts ocean views and there's the option of standard or deluxe studios as well as spa or family suites. There's a bar and restaurant, while beaches, parks and waterfront restaurants are all just a short stroll away.

Eating
RESTAURANTS
Angelo's on the Marina (Map p255; ☎ 4955 5600; Mulherin Dr, Mackay Marina; mains $15-33; ⚡ 8am-late) A large, lively restaurant in a delightful marina setting, with an extensive range of pasta and a mouth-watering Mediterranean menu. It's fully licensed and there's a free courtesy bus for parties of six or more people, so join a group and enjoy. *Alla tua salute!* (Cheers!)

Kevin's Place (Map p256; ☎ 4953 5835; cnr Victoria & Wood Sts; mains $18-25; ⚡ lunch & dinner) Sizzling, spicy Singaporean dishes and efficient, revved-up staff combine with the building's

colonial ambience and the tropical climate to create a Raffles-esque experience.

Pacino's on the Waterfront (Map p256; ☎ 4957 8131; 8 River St; mains $15-35; ⚡ lunch & dinner) Set among the warehouses, Pacino's is a romantic Mediterranean restaurant and bar with a breezy alfresco deck overlooking the water. The speciality is seafood, though there's pasta and pizza as well.

Lighthouse (Map p255; ☎ 4955 5022, takeaway ☎ 4955 5699; Mulherin Dr, Mackay Harbour; mains $22-29; ⚡ 6am-late) A very popular seafood restaurant in a nautical setting that doubles as a takeaway. Its forte is fresh seafood, but the specials board usually has steak, chicken and lamb options.

Toong Tong (Map p256; ☎ 4957 8051; 10 Sydney St; mains $12-20; ⚡ lunch & dinner) This cosy Thai restaurant capably serves up all the usual Thai dishes plus a few chef's specials you may not have seen before. It's BYO, and there's a busy takeaway service.

CAFÉS & QUICK EATS
Sedgies Gourmet Coffee & Tea Supplies (Map p256; ☎ 4957 4845; cnr Nelson & Victoria Sts; breakfast & lunch dishes $5-11; ⚡ 8am-3pm Mon-Fri, 8am-noon Sat) A deservedly popular place to breakfast, sip a coffee or grab a sandwich and read the newspapers. Sedgies offers a huge range of teas and coffees. Breakfast is served from 8am to 10.30am and the lunchtime sandwiches and salads are excellent.

Oscar's on Sydney (Map p256; ☎ 4944 0173; cnr Sydney & Gordon Sts; mains $10-23; ⚡ 7am-10pm Tue-Sat, 7am-9.30pm Sun & Mon) Pancakes for breakfast, pizza and grills for lunch, more-sophisticated mains in the evening – there's something for all tastes at this licensed café. Try the delicious *poffertjes*, authentic Dutch pancakes with traditional toppings ($5). Yum!

Coffee Club (Map p256; ☎ 4957 8294; 48 Wood St; breakfast $6-14, mains $11-22; ⚡ breakfast, lunch & dinner) This big, relaxed meeting place offers a range of meals and a licensed bar, in addition to the excellent espresso and cakes. Try the tapas before heading around the corner to see a movie.

Pure & Natural Mackay (Map p256; ☎ 4957 6136; NAB Plaza, Sydney St; mains $5-10; ⚡ 7am-4.30pm Mon-Fri, 7am-3pm Sat) Specialising in anything low-fat, this café offers a range of healthy meals, from quiches and baguettes to salads and juices. Apparently it gets very busy in the new year.

Mackay Kebab House (Map p256; ☎ 4944 0393; cnr Victoria & Wood Sts; kebabs $5-7; ☯ lunch & dinner) Head to Kebab House for cheap takeaway with Middle Eastern flavours, such as the $5.50 falafel roll.

Drinking

Sails Sports Bar (Map p255; ☎ 4955 5022; Mulherin Dr, Mackay Harbour) This outdoors bar, adjacent to Lighthouse restaurant, usually hums with a good crowd on the weekends.

Gordi's Café & Bar (Map p256; ☎ 4951 2611; 85 Victoria St; mains $14-20) Cruisey café by day with lunchtime specials, such as noodles and curries for $6-8, and a good bar atmosphere in the evening.

Satchmo's at the Reef (Map p255; ☎ 4955 6055; Mulherin Dr, Mackay Harbour) A classy wine-and-tapas bar full of boaties and featuring live music on Sunday afternoon.

Entertainment

NIGHTCLUBS & LIVE MUSIC

Karaoke seems to be taking over many of the pub venues, but **Wilkie's Tavern** (Map p256; ☎ 4957 2241; cnr Victoria & Gregory Sts) usually has someone strumming a guitar on Thursday, Friday and Saturday nights.

Platinum Lounge (Map p256; ☎ 4957 2220; 83 Victoria St; ☯ Wed-Sun) On the 1st floor above the corner of Victoria and Wood Sts, the Platinum Lounge is a good place to unwind and converse without shouting. Be forewarned or forearmed: Wednesday and Thursday nights are karaoke nights.

Also recommended:

Doors (Map p256; ☎ 4951 2611; 85 Victoria St; admission $5; ☯ Tue-Sun) Techno and dance nightclub above Gordi's Cafe & Bar.

Main Street (Map p256; ☎ 4957 7737; 148 Victoria St; admission $5; ☯ Thu-Sun) Retro and techno situated above Molloy's Irish Bar.

THEATRE & CINEMA

BC Cinemas (Map p256; ☎ 4957 3515; 30 Gordon St; adult/child $13.50/9.50) This complex screens all the latest flicks.

Mackay Entertainment Centre (Map p256; ☎ 4957 2255; Gordon St) The city's main venue for live performances; phone the box office to find out what's on.

Shopping

Camping World (Map p256; ☎ 4957 6658; cnr Gregory & Alfred Sts) Happy campers, look no further – this shop has everything you'll need for that national-park getaway.

Paper Chain (Map p256; ☎ 4953 1331; 8a Sydney St; ☯ 8.45am-5pm Mon-Fri, 9am-12.30pm Sat & Sun) Large secondhand bookshop and exchange.

Getting There & Away

Located at the long-distance bus station, **Travelworld** (Map p256; ☎ 4944 2144; roseh@mkytworld .com.au; cnr Victoria & Macalister Sts; ☯ 7am-6pm Mon-Fri, 7am-4pm Sat) handles air, bus and train tickets, and can help with transport connections. On Sunday, bus tickets can be purchased at the nearby café.

AIR

The airport is about 3km south of the centre. **Jetstar** (☎ 13 15 38; www.jetstar.com.au) offers flights to/from Brisbane (from $89 one way) and Sydney (from $189). **Qantas** (☎ 13 13 13; www.qantas .com.au) has direct flights most days between Mackay and Brisbane (from $110), Sydney ($467), Rockhampton ($89) and Townsville ($88). **Virgin Blue** (☎ 13 67 89; www.virginblue.com.au) operates two flights a day to/from Brisbane (from $125 one way), which connect with services to several major centres.

BUS

Buses stop and tickets can be booked at the **Mackay Bus Terminal** (Map p256; ☎ 4944 2144; cnr Victoria & Macalister Sts; ☯ 7am-6pm Mon-Fri, 7am-4pm Sat). **Con-X-ion**; (☎ 1300 308718; www.con-x-ion .com) connects Mackay airport and Mackay Bus Terminal with Airlie Beach twice a day. Adult/child one-way fares are $44/22. **Greyhound Australia** (☎ 13 20 30; www.greyhound.com .au) travels up and down the coast between Brisbane and Cairns, stopping in Mackay. Sample one-way adult fares and journey times from Mackay are: Airlie Beach ($26, two hours), Townsville ($64, six hours), Cairns ($110, 12 hours), Rockhampton ($47, four hours), Hervey Bay ($101, 11 hours) and Brisbane ($130, 15 hours). **Premier Motor Service** (☎ 13 34 10; www.premierms.com.au) is cheaper than Greyhound, but does not have as many services. Sample fares from Mackay are: Airlie Beach ($20), Townsville ($62), Cairns ($98), Rockhampton ($35), Hervey Bay ($81) and Brisbane ($114).

TRAIN

Queensland Rail (☎ 13 22 32, 1300 13 17 22; www .traveltrain.com.au) has several services stopping at Mackay on their way between Brisbane and Townsville/Cairns. The speedy *Tilt*

Train departs at 7.25am on Monday, Wednesday and Friday, heading to Cairns ($162, 12 hours) via Townsville ($92, 5½ hours), and 8.20pm on Sunday, Wednesday and Friday heading to Brisbane ($207, 13 hours). Fares shown are adult business class.

The *Sunlander* departs at 1.55am heading to Townsville on Tuesday and Saturday, and to Cairns on Sunday and Thursday. Brisbane-bound, it departs Mackay at 10.44pm on Monday, Tuesday, Thursday and Saturday. There are several classes: sitting, economy berth, 1st-class berth and the luxurious Queenslander class. Adult fares between Mackay and Brisbane (17 hours) are $138/190/571 in sitting/economy berth/Queenslander, Townsville (6½ hours) $62/114/443, and Cairns (12½ hours) $108/161/528.

The train station is at Paget, about 3km south of the centre. Bookings can be made at any travel agency.

Getting Around
Avis (☎ 4951 1266), **Budget** (☎ 4951 1400) and **Hertz** (☎ 4951 3334) have counters at the airport. **Mackay Transit Coaches** (Map p256; ☎ 4957 3330) has several services around the city, and also connecting the city with the harbour and the northern beaches – pick up a timetable from one of the visitor-information centres. Routes begin from Canelands Shopping Centre and there are many signposted bus stops, but you can hail a bus anywhere along the route as long as there is room for it to pull over. For a taxi, call **Mackay Taxis** (☎ 13 13 08). Count on about $15 for a taxi from either the train station or the airport to the city centre.

AROUND MACKAY
Mackay's Northern Beaches
The coastline north of Mackay is made up of a series of headlands and bays. The small residential communities strung along here are virtually outer suburbs of Mackay. There are some reasonably good beaches for swimming and fishing along here and the prevailing winds keep the kite-surfers happy.

At **Blacks Beach** the beach stretches for 6km, so stretch those legs and claim a piece of Coral Sea coast for a day. There are several accommodation options, but if you are just passing through, you can grab breakfast, lunch or a coffee at **Café Mana** (Map p255; ☎ 4954 9480; Turtle Shores Shopping Centre, Blacks Beach; ☺ 6am-4pm Tue-Fri, 8am-5pm Sat & Sun) and enjoy the local art on display. For accommodation try **Blue Pacific Resort** (Map p255; ☎ 1800 808 386, 4954 9090; www.bluepacificresort.com.au; 26 Bourke St, Blacks Beach; d $92-145; ✖ ☒) where all the units are fully self-contained and set in an immaculate garden. A good budget option is the beachfront **Seawinds Caravan Park** (Map p255; ☎ 4954 9334; 16 Bourke St, Blacks Beach; unpowered/powered sites $18/19, caravans $32, cabins $44; ☒), which has lots of shade for camping, although the cabins are pretty average. Prices are for two people.

At the northern end of Blacks Beach is **Dolphin Heads** (named for it's distinctive headland), where you can stay at the four-star **Dolphin Heads Resort** (Map p255; ☎ 1800 075 088, 4954 9666; www.dolphinheadsresort.com.au; Beach Rd, Dolphin Heads; d $110-160; ✖ ☒). The 80 comfortable motel-style units overlook an attractive (but rocky) bay.

North of Dolphin Heads is **Eimeo**, where the **Eimeo Pacific Hotel** (Map p255; ☎ 4954 6105; Mango Ave, Eimeo; mains $13-21) crowns a headland commanding magnificent Coral Sea views. It's open every day, and is a great place for a drink. The food is ordinary pub fare, but the $8 lunch specials aren't bad value.

Bucasia and **Shoal Point** are across Sunset Bay from Eimeo and Dolphin Heads. The beachfront parks of these holiday towns offer shady BBQ and picnic areas, and Bucasia beach has a safe swimming enclosure. **Bucasia Beachfront Caravan Resort** (Map p255; ☎ 4954 6375; fax 4954 6952; bucasia@bigpond.com; 2 The Esplanade; unpowered/powered sites $15/20, cabins $43-70; ☒) has cabins with bathrooms right on the beach. Prices are for two people.

Pioneer Valley
West of Mackay, the Pioneer River wends its way through the verdant **Pioneer Valley.** The first sugar cane was planted here in 1867, and today almost the entire valley floor is planted with the stuff. The route to Eungella National Park (p262), the Mackay-Eungella Rd, branches off the Peak Downs Hwy about 10km west of Mackay and follows the river through vast fields of cane to link up with the occasional small town or steam-belching sugar mill and the odd local attraction.

Marian is dominated by an enormous sugar mill that crushes much of the valley's cane. **Melba House**, where Dame Nellie Melba and her husband (manager of the mill) lived, is on the right as you approach

Marian from Mackay. It operates as a **tourist information centre** (☎ 4954 4299; ⏰ 10am-3pm Mon-Sun), gallery and home to Melba memorabilia. At Marion there's a turn-off to **Kinchant Dam** (10km) and the fishing fraternity's **Kinchant Waters Leisure Resort** (☎ 4954 1453; Kinchant Dam Rd; unpowered/powered sites $10/24, cabins $75). Prices are for two people.

The next town is **Mirani**, where there's a **local history museum** (☎ 4959 1100; Victoria St; adult/child $4/1.50; ⏰ 9.30am-2.30pm Sun-Fri) behind the library and the **Illawong Fauna Sanctuary** (☎ 4959 1777; fax 4959 1888; Eungella Rd; adult/child $12/6; ⏰ 9am-6.30pm). The sanctuary lies in a patch of bushland just past Mirani and the admission cost is for the entire day, allowing you to come and go as you like. Crocodile feeding (not to be missed) is at 2.30pm, and koalas are fed at 5.15pm. There's also the option of dinner, bed and breakfast at the sanctuary's **homestay** (per peson $50; ☒).

About 27km west of Mirani is the turn-off for Finch Hatton Gorge (see p262), part of Eungella National Park. About 1.5km past the turn-off is the pretty township of **Finch Hatton**. The historic **railway station** (⏰ 10am-3pm) doesn't see trains anymore, but it has an interesting collection of photos, brochures on local history, walks and bike rides, and Internet access ($2 per 30 minutes). **Finch Hatton Caravan Park** (☎ 4958 3222; Zahmel St; unpowered/powered sites $14/17, on-site vans from $30) has plenty of shade and is a good option for Eungella National Park visitors towing a large caravan (the road up to Eungella may not be suitable for towing). Prices are for two people. The friendly **Criterion Hotel** (☎ 4958 3252; 9 Eungella Rd; s/d $15/30; mains $5-16) has spotless hotel rooms atop a spiral staircase and good, inexpensive counter meals.

From Finch Hatton it's another 18km to Eungella, a quaint mountain village overlooking the valley, and the gateway to the Broken River section of Eungella National Park (see p262). The last section of this road climbs suddenly and steeply, with several incredibly sharp corners – towing a large caravan up here is not recommended.

Eungella

Perched at the head of the Pioneer Valley is the lovely village of Eungella (*young*-gulla, meaning 'land of clouds'). There's a **General Store** (☎ 4958 4520) with snacks, groceries and

fuel, and a couple of accommodation and eating options.

Eungella Chalet (☎ 4958 4509; fax 4958 4503; s without bathroom $38, d with/without bathroom $72/50, 1-/2-bedroom cabins $88/109, mains $5-25; ☒) is an old-fashioned guesthouse perched on the mountain edge, commanding magnificent views and attracting the occasional hang-glider or paraglider, who can launch from the backyard. Its once-grand atmosphere is friendly but slightly musty. Upstairs rooms are clean and simple, and there's a lovely but sparse guests' lounge with arresting views. Behind the chalet are modern timber cabins. There's a small bar downstairs, and the dining room serves breakfast ($7 to $9), lunch ($5 to $13) and dinner ($16 to $25). The pub-type fare includes steak, chicken, seafood and pasta.

Eungella Holiday Park (☎ 4958 4590; unpowered/powered sites $16/20, cabins $75-110) is a small, friendly park located just north of the township, right on the edge of the escarpment. Prices are for two people. The owner is happy to shuttle guests to bushwalks in the national park and there's a kiosk with groceries, snacks and an ATM.

The charming Suzanne welcomes visitors to her balconied café-gallery, **Hideaway Cafe** (☎ 4958 4533; Broken River Rd; light meals $4-8; ⏰ 9am-4pm Mon-Sun), which overlooks the township. Be tempted by wonderful (and great-value) home-cooked pasties, apple strudel and more, including several excellent vegetarian options from the European menu. Afterwards take a stroll around Suzanne's whimsical garden or check out some of the local art and crafts in her gallery.

Stoney Creek

Just south of the town of **Eton**, on the Peak Downs Hwy about 28km southwest of Mackay, is a popular farm stay and horse-riding centre. **Stoney Creek Farm Stay** (☎ 4954 1177; Peak Downs Hwy; camp sites/dm/d $20/20/120) is a working cattle station that offers the chance to hop on a horse and muster cattle, or mosey on down to a secluded swimming hole. You can park your campervan, pitch a tent, or spend the night in the budget cabin with shared facilities or in the quaint, hand-hewn cottage for two. The half-day cattle ride costs $65 per person, and there are also shorter ride options available. There's a $240 three-day package that's designed for backpackers and includes the budget accommodation, meals and activities. It's possible to get to Stoney Creek by bus; ring ahead for directions.

EUNGELLA NATIONAL PARK

Eungella National Park is 84km west of Mackay, and covers nearly 500 sq km of the Clarke Range, climbing to 1280m at Mt Dalrymple. The mountainous park is largely inaccessible, except for the walking tracks around Broken River and Finch Hatton Gorge. The large tracts of tropical and subtropical vegetation have been isolated from other rainforest areas for thousands of years and now boast several unique species. The Eungella honeyeater is a bit of a Holy Grail for birders, while spotting the Eungella gastric brooding frog, which incubates its eggs in its stomach and then gives birth by spitting out the tadpoles, would be a rare treat. However it's the platypuses that steal the show.

Most days of the year you can be pretty sure of seeing a platypus or two in Broken River. The best times to see the creatures are the hours immediately after dawn and before dark; you must remain patiently silent and still. Platypus activity is at its peak from May to August, when the females are fattening themselves up in preparation for gestating their young. Other river life you're sure to see are the large northern snapping turtles and, flitting above the feeding platypuses, brilliant azure kingfishers.

There are no buses to Eungella or Finch Hatton, but Reeforest Adventure Tours and Jungle Johno (see p257) both run day trips from Mackay and will drop off and pick up those who want to linger.

Broken River

There's a **QPWS information office** (☎ 4958 4552; ☯ 8am-4pm), picnic area and **kiosk** (☯ 10am-5pm) near the bridge over Broken River, 5km south of Eungella. A **platypus-viewing platform** has been built near the bridge, and birdlife is prolific. There are some excellent walking trails between the Broken River picnic ground and Eungella; maps are available from the information office, which is (unfortunately) rarely staffed.

For accommodation, you have the choice of camping or cabins. **Fern Flat Camping Ground** (☎ 4958 4552; fax 4958 4501; per person/family $4/16) is a lovely place to camp, with the shady sites

adjacent to the river where the platypuses play. Inquisitive brush turkeys and rufous bettongs watch your every move, and there's the most amazing bird chorus in the morning. The camping ground is about 500m past the information centre and kiosk, and the amenity block can probably claim to have the coldest showers in Queensland. To claim a site you need to self-register, so it's best to arrive in the morning.

If you forgot the tent, **Broken River Mountain Retreat** (☎ 4958 4528; fax 4958 4564; d $80-125; ✷ ✷) is a very comfortable alternative. Accommodation comprises cedar cabins ranging from small motel-style units to large self-contained units sleeping up to six. There's a large guests' lounge with an open fire and the friendly **Platypus Lodge Restaurant & Bar** (mains $18-25) with a good selection of steak, seafood and chicken dishes, and a moderately priced wine list. The retreat organises several (mostly free) activities for its guests including spotlighting, canoeing and guided walks.

Finch Hatton Gorge

About 27km west of Mirani, just before the town of Finch Hatton, is the turn-off for the Finch Hatton Gorge. The last couple of kilometres of the 10km drive from the main road are on unsealed roads with several creek crossings that can become impassable after heavy rain. At the car park, there's a good picnic area with BBQs, and a couple of small swimming holes where the creek tumbles over huge boulders. A 1.6km walking trail leads from the picnic area to **Araluen Falls**, with its spectacular waterfalls and swimming holes. A further 1km takes you to the **Wheel of Fire Falls**, another tumbling cascade and excellent swimming hole.

A fun and informative way to explore the rainforest is to go **Forest Flying** (☎ 4958 3359; www.forestflying.com; rides $45). Get harnessed to a 350m cable suspended up to 25m above the ground and glide through the rainforest canopy to get a whole new angle on forest life. There's a seasonal fruit-bat colony (August to May) to see, and plenty of information and guidance is provided. Bookings are essential.

The following accommodation places are signposted on the road to the gorge. **Platypus Bushcamp** (☎ 4958 3204; www.bushcamp.net; Finch Hatton Gorge; sites $16, dm/d $20/60) is a true bush retreat. The back-to-nature camp is nestled in a beautiful forest setting just a couple of kilometres from Finch Hatton Gorge. A creek with platypuses and great swimming holes runs next to the camp, and accommodation is in slab-timber huts – basically roofed-over sleeping platforms. The communal kitchen–eating area is the heart of the place. There are wonderful hot showers with a forest view and a cosy stone hot tub. Bring your own food and linen. Camping prices are for two people. Booking ahead is strongly advised and transport to/from Mackay can be arranged by the owner.

The comfortable self-contained cabins at **Finch Hatton Gorge Cabins** (☎ 4958 3281; sites $16, dm/d $15/77, extra person $5.50; ⛺) sleep up to five, which is perfect if you're travelling with young kids. Linen is provided in the cabins and the bunkhouse, and there's a well-equipped camp kitchen. There's a large grassed area and the creek runs close by. Camping prices are for two people.

The friendly **Gorge Kiosk** (☎ 4958 3321) serves up excellent ice creams (delicious mango plus other flavours), pies and lemonade – all homemade. Picnic and BBQ packs are available to take up the road to the national-park picnic ground.

BRAMPTON ISLAND

Brampton Island, about 32km northeast of Mackay, has a midrange resort that's popular with couples, honeymooners and those wanting a relaxed island experience; it's not a party island, and kids are not catered for. This mountainous island is a national park and wildlife sanctuary with lush forests surrounded by coral reefs. There are stunning beaches and a couple of good walking trails, as well as all the frills associated with a big resort.

In the 19th century, the island was used by the Queensland government as a nursery for palm trees, of which there are still plenty. The Bussutin family, who moved to the island in 1916 to raise goats and horses, established the first resort here in 1932. Brampton is connected to nearby Carlisle Island (p264), which has a couple of national-park camp sites, by a sand bar that you can sometimes walk across at low tide.

Activities

The resort has two swimming pools, one salt, one fresh. There are tennis courts and

a small chip-and-putt golf course, as well as complimentary snorkelling gear, catamarans, windsurfers and surf skis. Other water sports cost extra, including: fishing trips ($50 per two hours), and water skiing ($50 per 30 minutes) and tube rides ($15). For the not-so-active, a sunset champagne cruise is $55.

The main beach at Sandy Point is very pleasant, but there are half a dozen other beaches for the more adventurous. There's good snorkelling over the coral in the channel between Brampton and Carlisle Islands.

There are two excellent walking trails on the island. The 7km walk circumnavigates the central section of the island, and side tracks lead down to Dinghy and Oak Bays. The 2km steady climb to the top of 219m Brampton Peak takes about two hours, and is rewarded with fine views along the way.

Sleeping & Eating

Brampton Island Resort (☎ 1300 134 044, 4951 4499; www.brampton-island.com; s $345-485, d including meals $460-740; ⛺ 🖳 🐕) There are four grades of room depending on the view and facilities. All meals are served in the Blue Water Restaurant; breakfast and lunch are buffet style, while dinner is a more formal affair. Occasionally there are seafood and Asian buffets or beach BBQs. As with many resorts, discounted stand-by rates and packages are often available, so it's worth checking.

Getting There & Away

Organise your transfers with the resort when booking accommodation.

AIR

Australian Helicopters (☎ 4951 0888) depart daily from Mackay Airport (15 minutes). The fare for adults and children alike is $99/198 per one-way/return flight.

BOAT

The resort has its own launch that leaves Mackay Marina daily at 11.30am. The trip takes about 1¼ hours. The return voyage to Mackay departs at 1.15pm. There's a courtesy bus connecting passengers to/from the airport. A one-way/return ticket for an adult is $50/100, for a child it is $25/50.

CUMBERLAND ISLANDS

There are about 70 islands in the Cumberland group, which includes Brampton Island

and is sometimes referred to as the southern Whitsundays. The islands are all designated national parks except for Keswick, St Bees and part of tiny Farrier Island.

Carlisle Island is connected to Brampton by a narrow sand bar, and at some low tides it's possible to walk or wade from one island to the other. Carlisle is uninhabited and covered in dense eucalypt forests, and there are no walking trails. However, there are national-park camping grounds at Southern Bay, which is directly across from the Brampton Island Resort, and another site further north at Maryport Bay. Southern Bay has a gas BBQ, rainwater tank and shelter; there are no facilities at Maryport Bay.

If you fancy a spot of Robinson Crusoeing and own a boat, or have chartered a boat or seaplane, most other islands in the Cumberland group and the Sir James Smith group to the north are also national parks. **Scawfell Island**, 12km east of Brampton, is the largest island in the group. Refuge Bay, on its northern side, has a safe anchorage, a beach, a camping ground with water (but always bring your own supply), BBQs and toilets. In the Sir James Smith Island Group, just northwest of Brampton, **Goldsmith Island** has a safe anchorage on its northwestern side, good beaches and a camping ground with toilets, tables and fireplaces.

Camp site (per person/family $4/16) bookings and permits for Carlisle, Scawfell and Goldsmith Islands, and the more remote islands mentioned in the following sections, can be made at www.epa.qld.gov.au or at the Mackay QPWS (p254).

Keswick Island is a quiet, inhabited island, part national park and part freehold. There are grand plans for future development of this idyllic island, but for now you are unlikely to bump into many people other than the few who already live here, and those also staying at the guesthouse. **Keswick Island Guest House** (☎ 4965 8001; www.keswickislandguesthouse.com.au; 26 Coral Passage Dr; full-board d $273-460) offers three comfortable double rooms with ocean views and three home-cooked meals a day. It's a place to relax and perhaps hit the water for a leisurely swim or snorkel. In addition there's kayaking, fishing or exploring the island's bush tracks and sandy beaches.

Carlisle Island can be reached from Brampton Island via the sand spit at low tide, or by chartering a boat at Brampton

resort. Scawfell and Goldsmith Islands are reached by charter boat, which can be organised through the Mackay Visitor Information Centre (p254). Transfers out to these islands depend on the weather, how many people are travelling, and so forth. Keswick Island transfers can be arranged for you by the guesthouse.

CAPE HILLSBOROUGH NATIONAL PARK

This small coastal park, 54km north of Mackay, takes in the rocky, 300m-high Cape Hillsborough, and Andrews Point and Wedge Island, which are joined by a causeway at low tide. The park features rugged cliffs, a broad beach, rocky headlands, sand dunes, mangroves, hoop pines and rainforest. Kangaroos, wallabies, sugar gliders and turtles are quite common in the park; the roos are likely to be seen on the beach in the evening and early morning. There are also the remains of Aboriginal middens and stone fish-traps, which can be accessed by good walking tracks. On the approach to the foreshore area there's also an interesting boardwalk leading out through a tidal mangrove forest.

Cape Hillsborough Nature Resort (☎ 4959 0152; www.capehillsboroughresort.com.au; MS 895 Mackay; unpowered/powered sites $13/18, d $39-74; 🖳 🖳) offers quite a range of cabin and motel accommodation. It's an idyllic, low-key resort. Campsites are nicely terraced into the forest and wildlife abounds. Facilities include a bar and **restaurant** (mains $12-19). Camping prices are for two people.

Smalleys Beach Campground (per person/family $4/16) is a small, pretty, grassed camping ground hugging the foreshore and jumping with kangaroos. Self-register or pay at the camping ground.

NEWRY ISLAND GROUP

The Newry Island Group is a cluster of small islands just off the coast from Seaforth, about 50km northwest of Mackay. They are rocky, wild-looking continental islands with grassy, open forests and small patches of rainforest. Five of the islands are national parks and you may spot a dugong along this part of the coast, as it's a dugong-protection area where net fishing is banned. From November to January green turtles nest on the beaches.

The largest of the Newry Island Group is **Rabbit Island**. Its camping ground has toilets and a rainwater tank (which can be empty in dry times). It also has the only sandy beaches in the group, although because of its proximity to the mainland, box jellyfish may be present in summer. **Newry Island** and **Outer Newry Island** each have a camping ground with shelter, water (seasonal) and toilets.

Most of the visitors to these islands are local anglers (with their own boat transport). Camping permits can be obtained online at www.epa.qld.gov.au or at the **Mackay QPWS** (☎ 4944 7800; cnr River & Wood Sts).

WHITSUNDAYS AREA

The 74 islands that comprise the Whitsunday archipelago are probably the best known of Queensland's islands. Protected by the Great Barrier Reef and offering countless secluded anchorages, these jewels of the Coral Sea have attracted sailors since the time of Cook, and would-be yachties can easily get a taste of the action. With several island resorts, from backpackers to five star, and Airlie Beach from which to base yourself, the turquoise waters, palm-fringed beaches and coral gardens beckon from your doorstep.

The Whitsundays is a drowned landscape – these continental islands are the tips of mountains fringed with coral. The passage weaving between the islands and the mainland was named Whitsunday Passage by Lieutenant Cook, who sailed through here on 3 July 1770. The islands themselves Cook called the Cumberlands, but this grouping was later subdivided and the 22 islands scattered around the Whitsunday Passage became the Whitsunday Islands. All are within 50km of Shute Harbour. The Great Barrier Reef proper is at least 60km out from Shute Harbour; Hook Reef is the nearest part of it.

The islands and the waters between them are natural treasures, and while seven are developed with tourist resorts, most are uninhabited and several offer the chance of back-to-nature beach camping and bushwalking. All but four islands – Dent, Hamilton, Daydream and Hayman – are predominantly or completely national park and the surrounding waters fall into the Great Barrier Reef Marine Park.

Orientation & Information

Airlie Beach is the mainland centre for the Whitsundays, with plenty of accommodation options, travel agents and tour operators. Shute Harbour, about 10km east of Airlie, is the port for most day-trip cruises and island ferries, while most of the yachts berth at Abel Point Marina at Airlie Beach.

The Whitsunday district office of the QPWS (p272) is 3km past Airlie Beach on the road to Shute Harbour. This office deals with camping permits for the islands, and its staff are very helpful and a good source of information on a wide range of topics. This should be your first place to visit if you are interested in exploring the islands independently.

The main **Tourism Whitsundays Information Centre** (☎ 1800 801 252, 4945 3711; www.whitsunday tourism.com) is on the Bruce Hwy on the southern entry to Proserpine.

BOOKS & MAPS

David Colfelt's *100 Magic Miles of the Great Barrier Reef – The Whitsunday Islands* is sometimes referred to as the bible to the Whitsundays and is widely available in the area. It contains great colour photos, articles on the islands and resorts, features on diving, sailing, fishing, camping and natural history, and an exhaustive collection of charts with descriptions of all boat anchorages around the islands.

Other than nautical charts of the coast and islands, the best map to this area is Hema's *Mackay & Whitsundays* map.

ZONING

The Great Barrier Reef Marine Park Authority's zoning system divides the waters around the Whitsundays into five zones, each with certain restrictions on what you can and can't do.

Briefly, most of the waters around the Whitsundays are zoned General Use A and B and Marine National Park (MNP) A, with some important exceptions where MNP B zoning applies. For the visitor, the main consideration is that all these zones permit boating and diving, while MNP A permits limited fishing and MNP B excludes fishing.

Activities

Most activities that take place around the islands, either in, under or on top of the water, attract a Great Barrier Reef Marine Park levy of $4.50 to $6 per person per day. Check to see if it is included in quoted prices.

SAILING

What could be better than sailing from one island paradise to another? Don't answer just yet. Read the boxed text below before checking out what the following companies have on offer.

There are a number of bareboat charter companies around Airlie Beach:

Charter Yachts Australia (☎ 1800 639 520; www.cya.com.au; Abel Point Marina)

Cumberland Charter Yachts (☎ 1800 075 101; www.ccy.com.au; Abel Point Marina)

SAILING THE WHITSUNDAYS

Sailing is the number-one activity in the Whitsundays. Catamarans, superseded racing maxis and antique tall ships all vie for a clear passage to the tourist dollar, and it doesn't matter if you can't remember the last time you spliced a mainbrace, or you have sailed into too many ports to recall, there'll be a boat to suit.

Sailing through the Whitsunday Passage in 1770, Cook wrote that 'the whole passage is one continued safe harbour'. In fact, stiff breezes and fast-flowing tides can produce some tricky conditions for small craft, yet, with a little care, the Whitsundays offer superb sailing, and bareboat charters have become enormously popular. 'Bareboat' doesn't refer to what you wear on board – it simply means you rent the boat without skipper, crew or provisions.

While you don't require formal qualifications to hire a yacht, you will need to prove to the company that at least one person in your group is fully competent in operating the vessel. On the first day you should receive around four hours of briefing and familiarisation with the yacht, during which time your abilities will be assessed. If necessary you may be required to pay for additional tutoring for around $200 per day, or it may be necessary for you to hire a skipper for an hourly rate. If you lack experience, it's a good idea to hire an experienced skipper at least for the first day, although even then it's difficult to absorb the amount of instruction you are given in such a short time.

The operators usually require a booking deposit of between $500 and $750, and a security bond of between $1000 and $2000 (depending on the kind of boat), payable on arrival and refunded after the boat is returned undamaged. Bedding is usually supplied and provisions can also be included if you wish. Most companies have a minimum hire period of five days.

Most of the charter companies have a wide range of yachts and cruisers available. You'll pay $500 to $800 a day in the high season (September, October, December and January) for a yacht that will comfortably sleep four to six passengers. The larger the boat, the higher the price. Remember that the maximum passenger capacity is always more than what is reasonably comfortable: for example, a 10m yacht may hold six but any more than four adults is uncomfortable. It's worth asking if the company you choose belongs to the Whitsunday Bareboat Operators Association, a self-regulatory body that guarantees certain standards. Check that the latest edition of David Colfelt's *100 Magic Miles* is stowed on board, and pick up a copy of the *Public Moorings and Anchoring* leaflet from QPWS.

There's a bamboozling array of sailing tours that supply professional crew and catering, on offer in Airlie Beach. It can be hard work sorting through the glossy brochures, the stand-by rates and the word of mouth. Price can be a very good indication; we get stacks of letters complaining about the cheaper companies: everything from lengthy delays, boats breaking down, unsanitary conditions and even serious safety concerns. Look out for the tick of approval from the Whitsunday Charter Boat Industry Association (WCBIA) on the brochure. The usual package is three days and two nights, but longer cruises are possible, as are day tours, sailing courses and ocean racing.

A third option is to crew a private vessel by responding to 'Crew Wanted' notices pasted up in backpackers or at the marina and yacht club. Just like hitching a ride in a car, the experience could be life affirming or life threatening. Think about yourself stuck with someone you don't know on 10m of boat, several kilometres from shore, before you actually find yourself there. Be sure to let others know where you are going, with whom, and when you expect to return.

Queensland Yacht Charters (☎ 1800 075 013; www.yachtcharters.com.au; Abel Point Marina)
Sail Whitsunday (☎ 1800 075 045; www.sailwhitsunday.com.au; Abel Point Marina)
Whitsunday Escape (☎ 1800 075 145, 4946 5222; www.whitsundayescape.com.au; Abel Point Marina)
Whitsunday Rent A Yacht (☎ 1800 075 111; www.rentayacht.com.au; Trinity Jetty, Shute Harbour)

The following are some of the numerous sailing tour companies/vessels that have been recommended by readers:
Aussie Adventure Sailing (☎ 1800 359 554; www.aussiesailing.com.au; Shute Harbour Rd, Airlie Beach) This company has a range of vessels on its books including three tall ships, four racers and four sail-and-dive boats. There's also a sailing school if you catch the bug. Three-day, two-night packages start from $420 per person.
Maxi Action Ragamuffin (☎ 1800 454 777; www.maxiaction.com.au) *Ragamuffin* has two day trips: on Monday, Wednesday and Saturday she visits Hayman Island's beautiful Blue Pearl Bay for snorkelling; on Tuesday, Thursday and Sunday she heads for Whitehaven Beach. Cruises depart Shute Harbour at 8.45am and return about 4.30pm (adult/child/concession/family $99/50/89/248). There is also a Two Cruise Special for two separate days.
Prosail (☎ 1800 810 116; www.prosail.com.au; cnr Waterson Rd & Begley St, Airlie Beach) Prosail runs a range of vessels including racing yachts and a traditionally rigged schooner. There's also a sailing school and cruises geared for diving enthusiasts. Three-day, two-night packages start at $430 per person. The popular America's Cup challenge is a hands-on, three-hour challenge (two races) on board either *Australia* or *Steak'n Kidney*, 12m America's cup contenders (adult/child $79/59).
Southern Cross Sailing Adventures (☎ 1800 675 790; www.soxsail.com.au; 4 The Esplanade, Airlie Beach) Southern Cross runs adventure sailing cruises on racing yachts such as *Siska* and *Southern Cross*, as well as more-sedate cruises aboard the magnificent tall ship *Solway Lass*. You can also combine the racing yacht and tall ship experience. Three-day, two-night packages start from $409 per person.

The Whitsundays is also one of the best and most popular places to learn how to sail. Should you choose this activity, there are numerous courses on offer. The following are a selection of Airlie Beach sailing schools, each with several courses:
Prosail (☎ 1800 810 116; www.prosail.com.au; cnr Waterson Rd & Begley St, Airlie Beach)
Whitsunday Marine Academy (☎ 4948 2350; www.whitsundaysailtraining.com; 277 Shute Harbour Rd) Run by Aussie Adventure Sailing.
Whitsunday Sailing Club (☎ 4946 6138; Airlie Point)

DIVING

The ultimate diving experience to be had here is on the actual Great Barrier Reef, at places such as Black, Knuckle and Elizabeth Reefs. Dive boats should leave in the evening so that you wake up at your dive site. The dive companies listed below also offer a good range of diving trips for certified divers (from day trips to overnighters) that combine the Reef with the islands.

The Whitsundays is a great place to learn to dive, and the dive-specific outfits offering certificated courses are listed here. Many of the day trips and overnight sailing cruises offer dive instruction or 'introductory dives'. Be sure about what you are paying for. Costs for open-water courses with several ocean dives start at around $500, and note that any cheaper courses you may dig up will probably have you spending most of your 'dives' in a pool. It's worth paying more to get to enjoy what you've learned and, more importantly, build up invaluable open-water experience. Generally, courses involve two or three days' tuition on the mainland with the rest of the time diving on the Great Barrier Reef – meals and accommodation are usually included in the price. Check that the Great Barrier Reef Marine Park levy and any other additional costs are included in the price.
Oceania Dive (☎ 1800 075 035, 4946 6032; www.oceaniadive.com; 257 Shute Harbour Rd, Airlie Beach)
Pro Dive (☎ 1800 075 035, 4948 1888; www.prodivewhitsundays.com.au; 344 Shute Harbour Rd, Airlie Beach)
Reef Dive & Sail (☎ 1800 075 120, 4946 6508; www.reefdive.com.au; 16 Commerce Close, Cannonvale)

Apart from these companies, most of the island resorts also have their own dive schools and free snorkelling gear.

SEA KAYAKING

Paddling serenely in search of an island with dolphins and turtles as company would have to be one of the best ways to experience the Whitsundays. **Salty Dog Sea Kayaking** (☎ 4946 1388; www.saltydog.com.au) offers guided tours and kayak rental. Half-/full-day tours from Shute Harbour cost $50/90, and extended island camping trips can be arranged. Tours can be fully catered or BYO, and if you want to discover it all by yourself, the guides will freely offer advice. All safety gear is included, and camping and snorkelling gear is available for hire.

WHITSUNDAY COAST

FISHING

Charter-boat operators provide all-inclusive day trips to the outer Whitsundays. The **MV Jillian** (☎ 4948 1301) departs Abel Point Marina, Airlie Beach, and the **MV Moruya** (☎ 4946 6665) departs from Shute Harbour. Both charge $120/75 per adult/child. Hiring your own boat is also an option and not all boats require a boating licence. **Harbour Side Boat Hire** (☎ 4946 9330; Ferry Terminal, Shute Harbour) have various runabouts from $80 to $250 per day.

Tours

There are several ways to tour the islands and the Great Barrier Reef. For information about overnight sailing packages see p266. If sailing isn't your cup of tea but you want to visit the islands and beaches, do a bit of snorkelling, or even try out some of the resorts, then it's just a matter of hunting down the tour that will suit you.

Most day trips include activities such as snorkelling or boom netting, with scuba diving as an optional extra. Children generally pay half fare. Following are some (by no means all) of the day trips on offer and bookings can be made at any of the tour agents in Airlie Beach:

Cruise Whitsundays (☎ 4946 4662; www.cruisewhit sundays.com; Shingley Dr, Abel Point Marina, Airlie Beach) A huge wave-piercing catamaran speeds out to a pontoon moored at Knuckle Reef Lagoon on the Great Barrier Reef for spectacular snorkelling. There's an underwater observatory, waterslide and children's swimming enclosure, and optional extras such as diving and sea walking. Lunch is included in the price (adult/child/family $166/90/405) and there's an expensive but thrilling option of flying in or out by helicopter.

Fantasea/Blue Ferries (☎ 4946 5111; www.fantasea .com.au; 11 Shute Harbour Rd, Jubilee Pocket) The largest tour operator in Airlie Beach, and the operator of the island ferries, offers a number of options. A high-speed catamaran cruises to Hardy Reef on the Great Barrier Reef, where you transfer to a large pontoon for snorkelling, lunch and coral viewing in a semisubmersible (adult/child/family $152/81/355). An overnight 'Reefsleep' costs from $325. The Yellow Sub tour includes Whitehaven Beach, snorkelling and semisubmersible coral viewing on Bali Hai Island (adult/child/family $99/59/257). There are several options for spending a day at one of the island resorts utilising Blue Ferries, as well as a Three Island Discover Cruise that visits Long, Daydream and Hamilton (adult/child/family $59/40/158).

Mantaray Charters (☎ 1800 816 365; www.mantaray charters.com; adult/child/family $99/55/295) This tour allows you to spend the most time on Whitehaven Beach, followed by a visit to Mantaray Bay; includes snorkelling and lunch.

Voyager 3 Island Cruise (☎ 4946 5255; adult/child $74/37) A good-value day cruise that includes snorkelling at Hook Island, beachcombing and swimming at Whitehaven Beach, and checking out Club Croc on Long Island. On-board lunch (adult/child $11/6) and introductory scuba dives ($60) are optional extras.

Most of the cruise operators that operate from Shute Harbour do coach pick-ups from Airlie Beach and Cannonvale. You can take a bus to Shute Harbour, or you can leave your car in the Shute Harbour carpark ($8 per 24 hours); **Shute Harbour Secured Parking** (☎ 4946 9666) costs $6/11 per day/overnight.

SCENIC FLIGHTS

Air Whitsunday Seaplanes (☎ 4946 9111) Flying is the only way to do day trips to exclusive Hayman Island (adult/child $175/155). Other tours include a three-hour Reef Adventure ($265/165) and a four-hour Panorama ($295/195).

Island Air/Helireef (☎ 4946 9102) This company has a range of seaplane and helicopter tours including a Whitehaven Beach Picnic ($289) and a 10-minute Whitsunday Highlight trip ($79). There is also a Hayman Island day trip ($379).

Sleeping

CAMPING

QPWS (www.epa.qld.gov.au) manages national-park camping grounds on several islands for both independent and commercial campers (tour companies). There's also a privately run camping ground at Hook Island – see p278 for details.

You must be self-sufficient to camp in the national-park sites. You're advised to take 5L of water per person per day, plus three days' extra supply in case you get stranded. You should also have a fuel stove – wood fires are banned on all islands.

The national-parks leaflet, *Island Camping in the Whitsundays*, describes the various sites and provides detailed information on what to take and do. Camping permits are available online and from the Whitsunday QPWS office (see p272) and cost $4 per person ($16 per family) per night. If you book online, don't forget to pick up your permit/tag from the office.

Get to your island by **Blue Ferries** (☎ 4946 5111; www.fantasea.com.au; 11 Shute Harbour Rd, Jubilee Pocket) or a day-cruise boat; the booking agencies in Airlie Beach will be able to

WHITSUNDAY ISLANDS CAMPING GROUNDS

Island	Camping ground	Maximum number of permits issued	Toilet facilities	Commercial camping
Armit	southwestern side	12	pit	all year
Cid	Homestead Bay	12	bush	all year
Denman		4	bush	none
Gloucester	Bona Bay	36	pit	all year
	East Side Bay	8	bush	none
Henning	Northern Spit	24	pit	all year
	Geographers Bay	12	bush	all year
Hook	Maureens Cove	36	pit	all year
	Steen's Beach	12	bush	all year
	Bloodhorn Beach	12	bush	all year
	Crayfish Beach	12	bush	all year
	Curlew Beach	12	bush	all year
Lindeman	Boat Port	12	pit	all year
Long	Sandy Bay	12	pit	all year
North Molle	Cockatoo Beach	48	pit	all year
Olden		12	bush	all year
Planton		4	bush	none
Saddleback	western side	12	bush	all year
Shaw	Neck Bay	12	bush	all year
	Burning Point	12	bush	all year
South Molle	Paddle Bay	12	pit	peak season
	Sandy Bay	36	pit	all year
South Repulse	western side	12	bush	all year
Tancred	northern end	12	bush	all year
Thomas	Naked Lady Beach	12	bush	all year
Whitsunday	Dugong Beach	36	pit	off peak
	Sawmill Beach	24	pit	off peak
	Joe's Beach	12	pit	off peak
	Whitehaven Beach	12	pit	all year
	Turtle Bay	12	bush	all year
	Chance Bay	12	bush	all year
	Peter Bay	12	bush	all year
	Nari's Beach	6	pit	none

assist. You can also use an island camping specialist such as **Island Camping Connections** (☎ 4946 5255), which can drop you at North or South Molle, Planton or Denman Islands ($45 return, minimum of two people); Whitsunday Island or Henning Island ($109); and Hook Island ($150). **Camping Whitsunday Islands** (☎ 4946 9330) has similar prices and both operations can help with provisions and snorkelling gear.

The possibilities for camping in national parks in the Whitsundays are summarised in the table. Note that some sites are subject to seasonal closures because of bird nesting.

Northern islands such as Armit, Gloucester, Olden and Saddleback are harder to reach since the water taxi and cruises from Shute Harbour don't usually go there. Gloucester and Saddleback are best reached from Dingo Beach or Bowen.

Independent campers can stay on the islands at all times of the year, provided they have a permit.

RESORTS
There are resorts on seven of the Whitsunday Islands. Each resort is quite different from the next, ranging from Hayman's

five-star luxury to the basic cabins on Hook, and from the high-rise development of Hamilton to the beachfront huts of eco-friendly South Long Island Nature Lodge.

The rates quoted in this chapter are the standard rates, but hardly anyone pays these. Most travel agents can put together a range of discounted package deals that combine air fares, transfers, accommodation and meals.

It's also worth noting that, unless they're full, almost all resorts offer heavily discounted stand-by rates. The limiting factor is that you usually have to book less than five days in advance. All the agents in Airlie Beach can provide information on the resorts.

Getting There & Around
AIR
The two main airports for the Whitsundays are Hamilton Island and Proserpine (Whitsunday Coast). Qantas flies to both these places. See p281 and right for details.

The Whitsunday airport also has regular flights from the mainland to the islands – light planes, seaplanes and helicopters. See p276 for details. Lindeman Island also has its own airstrip.

BOAT
The services to the islands all operate out of Shute Harbour or Abel Point Marina near Airlie Beach. **Blue Ferries** (☎ 4946 5111; www.fantasea.com.au; 11 Shute Harbour Rd, Jubilee Pocket) provides ferry transfers to the islands – see the individual islands for details.

The Whitsunday Sailing Club is at the end of Airlie Beach Esplanade; check the noticeboards here and at the Abel Point Marina for possible rides or crewing opportunities on passing yachts.

BUS
Greyhound (☎ 13 20 30; www.greyhound.com.au) and **Premier Motor Service** (☎ 13 34 10; www.premierms .com.au) buses detour off the Bruce Hwy to Airlie Beach. **Whitsunday Transit** (☎ 4946 1800) connects Proserpine, Cannonvale, Abel Point, Airlie Beach and Shute Harbour. Get a schedule from any travel agency.

MIDGE POINT
Two-thirds of the way from Mackay to Proserpine are Midge Point and Laguna Quays, an elaborate and upmarket tourism resort

and residential development centred on a marina and the **Turtle Point golf course**. This testing course is open to the general public: 18 holes costs $66 midweek and $77 on weekends including golf cart (club hire $33).

Laguna Whitsundays (☎ 4947 7777; fax 4947 7770; www.lagunawhitsundays.com.au; Kunapipi Springs Rd; golf & B&B from $191; 🅿 🕭) offers restaurants, bars, tennis and pools, but above all golf. Everywhere are people armed with clubs; guests practise their action in the lobby and the place hums with the shared anticipation of chasing the little white ball. The resort often hosts the **Australian Skins** tournament in January or February. Frankly, you would have to be a golf nut to stay here – and if you are, this is probably heaven.

Right on the beach, **Travellers Rest Caravan & Camping Park** (☎ 4947 6120; fax 4947 6111; 29 Jackson St; unpowered/powered sites $15/20, cabins from $45; 🕭) is a very friendly, very leafy budget option with manicured grounds and well-spaced sites (and no golfers).

PROSERPINE
The turn-off point for Airlie Beach and the Whitsundays, Proserpine is a busy sugar-mill town, and an industrial centre for the region. Although it can't be mistaken for a tourist town, it is the home of the **Whitsunday Information Centre** (☎ 1800 801 252; www .whitsundaytourism.com.au; ⏱ 10am-6pm), the main source of information about the Whitsundays and surrounding region, on the Bruce Hwy south of town.

Proserpine Airport is 14km south of town and is serviced from Brisbane as well as some other capitals by **Jetstar** (☎ 13 15 38; www.jetstar .com.au), **Qantas** (☎ 13 13 13; www.qantas.com.au) and **Virgin Blue** (☎ 13 67 89; www.virginblue.com.au).

In addition to meeting all planes and trains, **Whitsunday Transit** (☎ 4946 1800) has six scheduled bus services daily from Proserpine to Airlie Beach; tickets from the airport/train station cost $16/8.

AIRLIE BEACH
☎ 07 / pop 4000
Airlie Beach is the gateway to the Whitsunday Islands. The whole town revolves around tourism and pleasure boating, and it attracts a diverse bunch of boaties, backpackers, holidaymakers and divers, all here for a good time. Airlie has a wide range of accommodation, good cafés and restaurants, lively

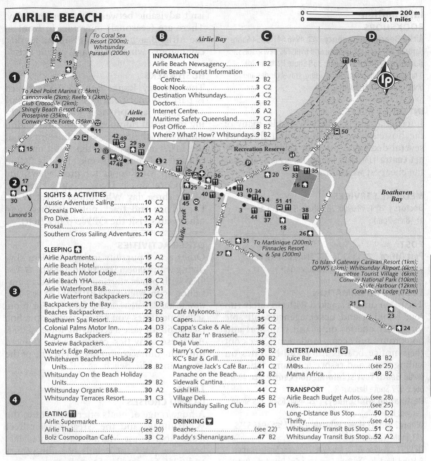

AIRLIE BEACH

0 _____ 200 m
0 _____ 0.1 miles

To Coral Sea
Resort (200m);
Whitsunday
Parasail (200m)

Airlie Bay

Airlie Lagoon

To Abel Point Marina (1.5km);
Cannonvale (2km); Reefo's (2km);
Club Crocodile (2km);
Shingly Beach Resort (2km);
Proserpine (35km);
Conway State Forest (35km)

Recreation Reserve

The Esplanade

Boathaven Bay

To Colden Orchid Dr

To Martinique (200m);
Pinnacles Resort
& Spa (200m)

To Island Gateway Caravan Resort (1km);
QPWS (3km); Whitsunday Airport (6km);
Flametree Tourist Village (6km);
Conway National Park (10km);
Shute Harbour (12km);
Coral Point Lodge (12km)

Hermitage Dr

WHITSUNDAY COAST

INFORMATION
Airlie Beach Newsagency.............1 B2
Airlie Beach Tourist Information
  Centre.............................2 B2
Book Nook..............................3 B2
Destination Whitsundays.............4 C2
Doctors...................................5 B2
Internet Centre.........................6 A2
Maritime Safety Queensland.......7 C2
Post Office...............................8 B2
Where? What? How? Whitsundays.9 B2

SIGHTS & ACTIVITIES
Aussie Adventure Sailing.............10 C2
Oceania Dive............................11 A2
Pro Dive..................................12 A2
Prosail....................................13 A2
Southern Cross Sailing Adventures..14 C2

SLEEPING
Airlie Apartments.......................15 A2
Airlie Beach Hotel......................16 C2
Airlie Beach Motor Lodge............17 A2
Airlie Beach YHA........................18 C2
Airlie Waterfront B&B.................19 A1
Airlie Waterfront Backpackers.......20 D3
Backpackers by the Bay...............21 D3
Beaches Backpackers...................22 B2
Boathaven Spa Resort.................23 D3
Colonial Palms Motor Inn.............24 D3
Magnums Backpackers.................25 B2
Seaview Backpackers...................26 C2
Water's Edge Resort...................27 C3
Whitehaven Beachfront Holiday
  Units....................................28 B2
Whitsunday On the Beach Holiday
  Units....................................29 B2
Whitsunday Organic B&B.............30 A2
Whitsunday Terraces Resort..........31 C3

EATING
Airlie Supermarket......................32 B2
Airlie Thai...........................(see 20)
Bolz Cosmopoiltan Café..............33 C2

Café Mykonos..........................34 C2
Capers....................................35 C2
Cappa's Cake & Ale...................36 C2
Chatz Bar 'n' Brasserie...............37 C2
Deja Vue.................................38 C2
Harry's Corner..........................39 B2
KC's Bar & Grill........................40 B2
Mangrove Jack's Café Bar............41 B2
Panache on the Beach.................42 B2
Sidewalk Cantina.......................43 C2
Sushi Hi!.................................44 C2
Village Deli..............................45 B2
Whitsunday Sailing Club...............46 D1

DRINKING
Beaches.............................(see 22)
Paddy's Shenanigans..................47 B2

ENTERTAINMENT
Juice Bar................................48 B2
M@ss................................(see 25)
Mama Africa............................49 B2

TRANSPORT
Airlie Beach Budget Autos......(see 28)
Avis.................................(see 25)
Long-Distance Bus Stop..............50 D2
Thrifty...............................(see 44)
Whitsunday Transit Bus Stop...51 C2
Whitsunday Transit Bus Stop...52 A2

nightlife and a lovely manmade lagoon –
a year-round safe swimming area on the
foreshore.

Airlie is a great base for sampling the
island resorts and all the sun-soaked possibilities that the Whitsundays have to
offer. The town has a reputation as a centre
for sailing and scuba diving, with beginners' courses and countless tours available.
There's also whale-watching between July
and September, and horse riding and hiking in the hinterland. Airlie is also a great
place to stop travelling and start partying.

Orientation
Nearly everything lies along Shute Harbour Rd, a short, busy strip packed with

tour agents, cafés, restaurants and backpackers. The town faces Airlie Bay with a
couple of small beaches, east and west of
Airlie Creek, but the manmade lagoon is
the best place to swim, particularly at night
under lights. The hills rise steeply behind
the town and numerous top-end resorts
boasting picture-perfect views cling to
their sides. The large recreation reserve
between the shore and the Esplanade at the
east end of town hosts a Saturday morning market and a dusty car park where
the long-distance buses pull in. Shute Harbour, where the island ferries depart, is
about 10km east, and Abel Point Marina,
home to many of the cruising yachts, is
about 1km west.

Information

BOOKSHOPS

Airlie Beach Newsagency (☎ 4946 6410; 354 Shute Harbour Rd) Stocks interstate and overseas newspapers.
Book Nook (☎ 4946 6410; 388 Shute Harbour Rd) A large selection of holiday reading, travel guides and books on the Whitsundays.

INTERNET ACCESS

Internet access is widely available; many of the hostels have terminals, and there are several dedicated Internet cafés. The **Internet Centre** (346 Shute Harbour Rd; per hr $2.50) was the cheapest we found.

MEDICAL SERVICES

Doctors (☎ 4948 0900; 283 Shute Harbour Rd; ⏱ 8am-7pm)

POST

Post Office (☎ 13 13 18; 372 Shute Harbour Rd; ⏱ 9am-5pm Mon-Fri, 9am-12.30pm Sat)

TOURIST INFORMATION

The main drag is stacked with privately run tour-booking and ticket agencies, all able to answer queries on island transport and book tours and accommodation. Check out their notice boards for stand-by rates on sailing tours and resort accommodation.
Airlie Beach Tourist Information Centre (☎ 4946 6665; 277 Shute Harbour Rd)
Destination Whitsundays (☎ 4946 6846; 295 Shute Harbour Rd)
Where? What? How? Whitsundays (☎ 4946 5255; 283 Shute Harbour Rd)
QPWS (☎ 4946 7022; fax 4946 7023; cnr Shute Harbour & Mandalay Rds; ⏱ 9am-5pm Mon-Fri) Past Airlie Beach, 3km towards Shute Harbour. It should be your first port of call if you need information and permits for camping in the Conway and the Whitsunday Islands national parks. The staff here are very helpful and can advise you on which islands to camp on, how to get there, what to take etc.

Activities

For details on sailing, diving and kayaking around the islands, see p265.

SWIMMING & WATER SPORTS

The pretty lagoon on Airlie's foreshore provides year-round safe swimming and is an attractive, popular public space. The beaches at Airlie Beach and Cannonvale are OK for swimming, but the presence of marine stingers means swimming in the sea

isn't advisable between October and May. There are (seasonal) operators in front of the Airlie Beach Hotel that hire out jet skis, catamarans, windsurfers and paddle skis.

BUSHWALKS

The Conway Range behind Airlie Beach is part national park (see p277) and part state forest, and provides some great walking in coastal rainforest. With information supplied at the tracks, you can learn about the forest ecology and the traditional life of local indigenous people. Try the 2.4km climb up Mt Rooper for great views, the short Coral Beach Track at Shute Harbour, or the three-day Whitsunday Great Walk. For advice and track notes on these and other walks visit the QPWS office (left).

OTHER ACTIVITIES

Other active pursuits include tandem skydiving with **Tandem Skydive Airlie Beach** (☎ 4946 9115) with prices starting at $249, and parasailing with **Whitsunday Parasail** (☎ 4948 0000; www.whitsundayparasail.com.au) for $55. For more sedate pastimes you can always drop a line (see p268) or take a scenic flight (see p268). All these activities can easily be booked through your accommodation or one of the agents in Airlie Beach.

Tours

ISLAND CRUISES

A huge range of boats offer trips out to the Whitsundays and the Great Barrier Reef from Abel Point Marina and Shute Harbour. See p266 for details of sailing tours and p268 for details of tour boats.

RAINFOREST/NATIONAL PARK TOURS

Fawlty's 4WD Tropical Tours (☎ 4946 6665) departs daily at 10.30am, and returns at 4pm. This tour is a great way to see the beautiful Cedar Creek Falls (when they're running that is) and some rainforest close up. Lunch and pick-ups are included in the price (adult/child $49/35).

Festivals & Events

Airlie Beach is the centre of activities during the annual **Whitsunday Fun Race Festival** (www.whitsundaysailingclub.com.au) each September. Apart from the yacht races, the Miss Figurehead and Mr Six-pack competitions set the tone for the festivities.

Sleeping
BUDGET
Hostels

Backpackers are spoiled for choice in Airlie, with countless budget alternatives. Some are so popular and well used that upkeep of rooms can seem long overdue. If you are unsure about the odour of your room, ask to look at another.

Backpackers by the Bay (☎ 1800 646 994, ☎ /fax 4946 7267; www.backpackersbythebay.com; 12 Hermitage Dr; dm $22, d $52; 🅿 🖳 🚱) Smaller and quieter than some of the other hostels, this relaxed place is a 5- to 10-minute walk from the centre of town. The atmosphere is friendly, the dorms have just four beds and the double rooms are some of the best around (air-conditioning costs an extra $0.50 per person).

Airlie Beach YHA (☎ 1800 247 251, 4946 6312; airliebeach@yhaqld.org; 394 Shute Harbour Rd; dm $25, d from $59; 🅿 🖳 🚱) This friendly hostel is located in a converted motel at the end of the main drag. The rooms are spotless and most of them have bathrooms. Although it was once a motel, parking is now severely limited.

Reefo's (Reef Oceania Village; ☎ 1800 800 795, 4946 6137; www.reeforesort.com; 147 Shute Harbour Rd, Cannonvale; dm $12-18, d $55; 🅿 🖳 🚱) This big, comfortable backpackers resort with a bar, restaurant, and huge pool, is about 3km west of Airlie, but there's a regular courtesy bus to/from town. The spacious doubles and family rooms here are particularly good value and there are discounts for three-, five- and seven-night bookings. The 24-hour reception and tour desk can organise all your tour needs.

Magnums Backpackers (☎ 4946 6266; www.magnums.com.au; 366 Shute Harbour Rd; sites $15-18, dm $14-17, d $44; 🅿 🖳) Magnums is a budget resort with plenty of nightlife right in the heart of Airlie; its location, prices and package deals keep it popular. Dorms sleep eight and the double and twin rooms with shared bathrooms are surrounded by gardens. There's also room to hook up a campervan or pitch a tent; site prices are for two people. The bar and nightclub at the front of the complex are very popular, and there's live music most evenings.

Seaview Backpackers (☎ 4946 6911; seaview@mackay.net.au; 404 Shute Harbour Rd; dm $18, d $48; 🅿 🚱) A centrally located backpackers with bright and airy six-bed dorms that boast great views over Boathaven Bay.

Beaches Backpackers (☎ 1800 636 630; 4946 6244; www.beaches.com.au; 356 Shute Harbour Rd; dm $23, d $60; 🅿 🖳 🚱) This big, converted motel with a party attitude has an unmissable streetfront bar and restaurant – it's always buzzing with travellers and locals alike. All rooms (of varying sizes) share bathrooms, and the communal kitchen is well set-up. There's entertainment in the bar and plenty of partying – even in the corridors.

Airlie Waterfront Backpackers (☎ 1800 089 000, 4948 1300; www.airliebackpackers.com.au; 6 The Esplanade; dm $18-22, d $60) Up a couple of flights of stairs and tucked under a big A-frame roofline, the rooms can feel a bit closed in. Thank goodness for the great balconies, clean kitchen and lounge.

Camping & Van Parks

There are no caravan parks in Airlie Beach itself, but in Cannonvale and on the road between Airlie and Shute Harbour there are several parks to choose from.

Island Gateway Caravan Resort (☎ 4946 6228; www.islandgateway.com.au; Shute Harbour Rd, Jubilee Pocket; unpowered/powered sites $19/25, cabins $50-95; 🅿 🚱) This is a big park about 1.5km east of Airlie Beach, making it the closest camping ground to the town centre. The sites are shady and the facilities are excellent and include a camp kitchen, a shop, half-court tennis and mini-golf. Prices are for two people.

Flametree Tourist Village (☎ 4946 9388; www.flametreevillage.com.au; Shute Harbour Rd; unpowered/powered sites $17/21, cabins from $62; 🅿 🚱) Not as glitzy as the other big parks, but the spacious sites are scattered through lovely, bird-filled gardens and there's a good camp kitchen and BBQ area. The park is 6km west of Airlie, about midway to Shute Harbour. Prices are for two people.

MIDRANGE
B&Bs

Whitsunday Organic B&B (☎ 4946 7151; www.whitsundaybb.com.au; 8 Lamond St; s/d $90/120) This is a very stylish ecofriendly B&B, with well-appointed rooms and wholesome organic breakfasts. Dinners are also available, as are help with tours and wonderfully relaxing massages. There are discounts for longer stays.

Hotels & Motels

The following hotel and motel options are all good and most offer discounted stand-by rates.

Airlie Beach Hotel (☎ 1800 466 233, 4964 1999; www.airliebeachhotel.com.au; cnr The Esplanade & Coconut Grove; s from $89-159, d $99-169; ⊠ ⛭) With one of the best locations downtown, this slick hotel is hard to beat. There are comfortable motel-style rooms surrounding the pool and spacious hotel rooms and suites with great views in the modern high-rise. There are also facilities for disabled guests and a couple of excellent restaurants at street level.

Airlie Beach Motor Lodge (☎ 1800 810 925, 4946 6418; www.airliebeachmotorlodge.com.au; 6 Lamond St; d from $105; ⊠ ⛭) Tucked away in a residential area of Airlie, this quiet motel is just a short walk from the Shute Harbour Rd action and the lagoon. As well as neat motel rooms there are self-contained units and a purpose-built facility for disabled guests.

Colonial Palms Motor Inn (☎ 4946 9500; fax 4946 9469; cnr Shute Harbour Rd & Hermitage Dr; d from $105; ⊠ ⛭) This motel is in a great location – central but quiet – and has spacious rooms, some self-contained, and a large restaurant. Plus there's a 10% discount if you belong to a motoring club.

Coral Point Lodge (☎ 4946 9500; fax 4946 9469; 54 Harbour Ave, Shute Harbour; d from $88; ⊠ ⛭) This is the place if you want to be out of the hubbub of Airlie. Clinging to the ridge overlooking Shute Harbour, the views are superb. Some rooms are self-contained, and there's a café, which is also open to nonguests, and serves meals and snacks.

Resorts & Holiday Apartments

There are quite a few blocks of older-style holiday apartments as well as more-modern resorts in and around Airlie Beach, and they can be good value, especially for a group of friends or a family. Many have discounts for stays of three days or more and some have minimum stays of two nights.

Airlie Apartments (☎ 4946 6222; www.airlieapartments.com; 22-4 Airlie Cres; apt $84-116; ⊠ ⛭) Airlie Apartments is a good-value option that's ideal for families. The one-, two-, and three-bedroom apartments are fully self-contained, there are views over Abel Point and the action on Shute Harbour Rd is not far away.

Shingly Beach Resort (☎ 4948 8300; www.shingley beachresort.com; 1 Shingley Dr; apt $115-220; ⊠ ⛭)

These midrange, self-contained holiday apartments are close to Abel Point Marina and feature good views. There's four different room configurations, a bar and restaurant, a massage and yoga studio, and a seriously deep pool.

Whitehaven Beachfront Holiday Units (☎ 4946 5710; fax 4946 5711; 285 Shute Harbour Rd; s/d $85/95; ⊠) Smack bang in the centre of Airlie Beach, these six older-style, though well-presented studio apartments have balconies overlooking the foreshore park. As they're set back from the main road, noise is not a problem.

Whitsunday on the Beach Holiday Units (☎ 4946 6359, fax 4946 7995; 269 Shute Harbour Rd; apt $95-100 ⊠) In the centre of Airlie, with the magnificent lagoon at your doorstep, this block of airy, spacious, self-contained units is convenient to everything.

Whitsunday Terraces Resort (☎ 1800 075 062, 4946 6788; www.whitsundayterraces.com.au; Golden Orchid Dr; apt $135-150; ⊠ ⛭) Overlooking Airlie Beach, these studios and one- and two-bedroom apartments all share stunning views and a convenient location.

Boathaven Spa Resort (☎ 1800 985 856, 4946 4948; www.boathavenresort.com; 440 Shute Harbour Rd; apt $150-180; ⊠ ⛭) The very comfortable self-contained rooms here all boast private balconies with spas and great views over Boathaven Bay.

Club Crocodile (☎ 1800 075 151, 4946 7155; www.clubcroc.com.au; Shute Harbour Rd, Cannonvale; d incl breakfast from $98; ⊠ ⛭) Club Crocodile is a popular, midrange resort 1.5km west of Airlie Beach. Motel-style units are built around an attractive central courtyard featuring fountains, a tennis court, restaurants and a bar.

TOP END
B&Bs

Airlie Waterfront B&B (☎ 4946 7631; www.airliewaterfrontbnb.com.au; cnr Broadwater Av & Mazlin St; d from $169; ⊠) Beautifully presented and sumptuously furnished with antiques, this is a lovely, relaxing option that is still convenient to the action. Two double rooms have their own private spa.

Resorts

Most of the resorts here have package deals and stand-by rates that are much cheaper than their regular ones.

Coral Sea Resort (☎ 1800 075 061, 4946 6458; www.coralsearesort.com; 25 Ocean View Ave; d $195-335,

1-/2-bedroom apt $285/295; 🛏 🍽) At the end of a low headland overlooking the water, Coral Sea Resort has one of the best positions around. There's a huge range of well-appointed rooms that are motel style and self-contained, many with stunning views. The excellent swimming pool is large and flanked by ocean on one side and a bar-restaurant on the other. Parasailing and ocean-rafting launch from the resort's private jetty.

Water's Edge Resort (☎ 4948 2655; fax 4948 2755; www.watersedgewhitsundays.com.au; 4 Golden Orchid Dr; apt $190-230; 🛏 🍽) The Southeast Asian theme, cool stone architecture, wet-edge pools and attentive service all convey an initial impression of luxury, and the rooms don't disappoint. One-, two-, or three-bedroom apartments boast large lounges. They're fully self-contained and some have spas. The views are superb, the resort offers a poolside restaurant and gym, and it's only a short stroll to the shops and the lagoon.

High above Airlie Beach, top-end resorts stretch up to grab more of the exquisite Coral Sea views. The luxury and the views can't be questioned, but it's a steep walk home should you find yourself without a car.

Martinique (☎ 4948 0401; fax 4948 0402; www.martiniquewhitsunday.com.au; 18 Golden Orchid Dr; apt $180; 🛏 🍽) French Caribbean is the theme. Luxurious wet-edge pool, glorious views and one-, two-, and three-bedroom apartments.

Pinnacles Resort & Spa (☎ 4948 4800; fax 4948 4901; www.pinnaclesresort.com; 16 Golden Orchid Dr; d from $380; 🛏 🍽) Five-star luxury throughout. All spacious, self-contained rooms enjoy a spa, a terrace and magnificent views.

Eating
RESTAURANTS
Shute Harbour Rd abounds with restaurants, though also consider some of the resorts if you are after a quiet restaurant with a view.

Bolz Cosmopolitan Café (☎ 4946 7755; 7 Beach Plaza, The Esplanade; mains $10-25; 🕐 breakfast, lunch & dinner) Sit in zebra-skin booths, or out on the terrace at this classy little restaurant. There's pasta, pizza and more. The service can be a little erratic, but the mango and prawn pizza was a delightful surprise.

Panache on the Beach (☎ 4946 5541; Mango Tce, 263 Shute Harbour Rd; mains $19-27; 🕐 lunch & dinner) With a lovely position opening out onto the lagoon and foreshore, Panache offers

Mediterranean cuisine, with brasserie-style meals (until 6pm) and a more formal menu reflecting the chef's French origins.

Mangrove Jack's Café Bar (☎ 4964 1888; 297 Shute Harbour Rd; mains $19-26; 🕐 lunch & dinner) A breezy, open-air, streetfront restaurant that offers Asian and continental mains; but it's the imaginative and individual wood-fired pizzas that keep people coming back.

KC's Bar & Grill (☎ 4946 6320; 282 Shute Harbour Rd; mains $16-33; 🕐 3pm-3am) KC's happy hour(s) are followed by dinner, between 6pm and 9pm, and then there's usually live music. It's lively and licensed, and the menu has croc and roo grills, as well as steak and seafood.

Chatz Bar 'n' Brasserie (☎ 4946 7223; 390 Shute Harbour Rd; mains $16-26; 🕐 breakfast, lunch & dinner) There's a popular front bar, while the cosy restaurant section up the back offers seafood and Italian main courses. There are always a few inexpensive specials on the blackboard and you can get a decent breakfast or lunch here for under $10.

Airlie Thai (☎ /fax 4946 4683; 1st fl, Beach Plaza, The Esplanade; mains $16-26; 🕐 lunch & dinner) This pleasant, licensed restaurant is upstairs in the Beach Plaza complex; sit out on the veranda and tuck into the delicious pad thai, among other traditional dishes.

Capers (☎ 4946 1777; The Esplanade; mains $17-29; 🕐 7am-late Mon-Sun) On the ground floor of the Airlie Hotel complex, this is a big restaurant-bar offering the usual breakfasts and slightly more-imaginative lunches and

---

THE AUTHOR'S CHOICE

Deja Vue (☎ 4946 5700; 301 Shute Harbour Rd; mains $21-30; 🕐 dinner Tue-Sat) Tucked away in a small courtyard at the eastern end of the main drag is an unpretentious BYO restaurant that consistently delivers high-quality meals with a minimum of fuss. The menu promises modern interpretations of Thai, Mediterranean, Indian and others, and the execution and presentation is faultless. We had the chef's favourite – warm Indian lamb rubbed in dry spices and accompanied by grilled vegetables and raita – sensational and righteously healthy. Luckily the decadent chocolate soufflé balanced the meal. The ambience is relaxed – elegant but still Airlie.

dinners; you can escape the game machines by sitting out on the pleasant patio.

Whitsunday Sailing Club (☎ 4946 7894; Airlie Point; mains $14-32; ☺ lunch & dinner) The sailing-club terrace is a great place for a meal and a drink. Choose from the usual steak and schnitzel culprits, off the inexpensive bistro blackboard, or select from the more upmarket Commodore's Table menu.

Sushi Hi! (☎ 4948 0400; 390 Shute Harbour Rd; light meals $13-25; ☺ 10am-9pm) Sushi, sashimi and other Japanese delicacies are complemented by fresh fruit salads and juices.

CAFES & QUICK EATS

If you're looking for a quick coffee, breakfast or light lunch, Airlie has plenty of places to go.

Village Deli (☎ 4964 1121; 351 Shute Harbour Rd; mains $10-15; ☺ 8am-5.30pm) This casual, funky café-deli serves tasty light meals – and the staff know how to make coffee. The mixed salad plate is great value, and big, healthy breakfasts, gelati and juices are on the go all day. Takeaway provisions and picnic boxes are a speciality.

Harry's Corner (☎ 4946 7459; 273 Shute Harbour Rd; mains $8-12; ☺ 7am-4pm) This small, popular café cooks up huge, tasty breakfasts, and delivers coffee, cakes and snacks until closing. A great meeting place.

Cappa's Cake & Ale (☎ 4946 5033; Pavilion Arcade, Shute Harbour Rd; mains $6-15; ☺ 8am-8pm) In a small arcade off the main drag, this busy café serves up breakfasts, burgers, pizza and more. If it can be wrapped, sandwiched, toasted or grilled you'll find it here, with good coffee, smoothies and juices to wash it down.

Sidewalk Cantina (☎ 4946 6425; The Esplanade; dishes $10-25; ☺ 7am-2pm Mon-Sun, 6pm-late Thu-Mon) The daytime café and takeaway serves breakfasts and light lunches such as pancakes and focaccias. At night the cantina transforms into a Mexican restaurant.

Café Mykonos (☎ 4946 5888; Shop 9, Shute Harbour Rd; mains $6-10; ☺ 11am-9pm) Yiros, souvlaki, moussaka, falafel rolls and more. Fast and delicious.

SELF-CATERING

If you're preparing your own food, there's the small **Airlie Supermarket** (277 Shute Harbour Rd), which is open daily and in the centre of town, and a larger one in Cannonvale.

Drinking & Entertainment

Airlie Beach has a reputation for partying hard. The bars at **Magnums** (☎ 4946 6266; 366 Shute Harbour Rd) and **Beaches** (☎ 4946 6244; 356 Shute Harbour Rd), the two big backpackers, are usually crowded, and are good places to meet travellers. Drinks tend to be cheap here and there's usually live music or some other entertainment at night.

M@ss (☎ 4946 6266; 366 Shute Harbour Rd; ☺ 10pm-5am) The Gothic-inspired nightclub at Magnums plays crowd favourites and hosts foam parties.

Mama Africa (☎ 4948 0438; 263 Shute Harbour Rd; ☺ 10pm-5am) Tribal cool and dance favourites keep this place rockin' all night.

Juice Bar (☎ 4946 6465; 354 Shute Harbour Rd; ☺ 10pm-5am) Upstairs from the Irish bar Paddy Shenanigans, the bare Juice Bar pounds to dance and techno, but just about anything else is likely to pop up.

Paddy's Shenanigans (☎ 4946 5055; 352 Shute Harbour Rd; ☺ 5pm-late) A friendly bar, Paddy's occasionally has live fiddles but always has Guinness on tap.

Getting There & Away

AIR

The closest major airports are Hamilton Island and Proserpine (Whitsunday Coast). See p281 and p270 for details. **Whitsunday airport** (☎ 4946 9933), a small airfield 6km east of Airlie Beach, is midway between Airlie Beach and Shute Harbour. Half a dozen different operators are based here, and you can take a helicopter, light plane or seaplane out to the islands or the Reef.

Island Air Taxis (☎ 4946 9933) flies to Hamilton and Lindeman for $60. **Air Whitsunday Seaplanes** (☎ 4946 9111) flies to Hayman, Daydream, Long, and South Molle for $450 per flight, carrying a maximum of six passengers. **Helireef** (☎ 4946 9102), Air Whitsunday Seaplanes, and Island Air Taxis all offer joy flights out over the Reef.

BOAT

Transfers between Shute Harbour and the islands are provided by **Blue Ferries** (☎ 4946 5111; www.fantasea.com.au; 11 Shute Harbour Rd, Jubilee Pocket) – see the Getting There & Away sections for the individual islands for details. There are notice boards at the Whitsunday Sailing Club and Abel Point Marina showing when rides or crewing are available.

WHITSUNDAY COAST

BUS

Greyhound (☎ 13 20 30; www.greyhound.com.au) and **Premier Motor Service** (☎ 13 34 10; www.premierms .com.au) buses detour off the Bruce Hwy to Airlie Beach. There are buses between Airlie Beach and all the major centres along the coast, including Brisbane ($148, 18 hours), Mackay ($26, 2½ hours), Townsville ($46, four hours) and Cairns ($92, 11 hours).

Long-distance buses stop on the Esplanade, between the sailing club and the Airlie Beach Hotel. Any of the booking agencies along Shute Harbour Rd can make reservations and sell bus tickets.

Con-X-ion (☎ 1300 308718; www.con-x-ion.com) connects Mackay airport and Mackay bus terminal with Airlie Beach twice a day. Adult/child one-way fares are $44/22.

Whitsunday Transit (☎ 4946 1800) connects Proserpine (Proserpine Airport), Cannonvale, Abel Point, Airlie Beach and Shute Harbour. Buses operate from 6am to 10.30pm daily and stop outside Mangrove Jack's and just up from Pro Dive. Schedules are readily available from any tour agency.

Getting Around

Airlie Beach is small enough to cover by foot, and all the cruise boats have courtesy buses that will pick you up from wherever you're staying and take you to either Shute Harbour or the Abel Point Marina. To book a taxi, call **Whitsunday Taxis** (☎ 13 10 08); there's a taxi rank on Shute Harbour Rd, opposite Magnums.

There are several car-rental agencies:
Airlie Beach Budget Autos (☎ 4948 0300; 285 Shute Harbour Rd) In the courtyard of Whitehaven Holiday Units.
Avis (☎ 4946 6318; 366 Shute Harbour Rd) Next to Magnums.
Thrifty (☎ 4946 7727; 390 Shute Harbour Rd) Next to Sushi Hi!

CONWAY NATIONAL PARK

The mountains of this national park and the Whitsunday Islands were once part of the same coastal mountain range, but rising sea levels after the last Ice Age flooded the lower valleys and cut off the coastal peaks from the mainland.

Most of the park is composed of rugged ranges and valleys covered in rainforest, although there are also areas of mangroves and open forest. Only a small area of the park is accessible by road.

The road from Airlie Beach to Shute Harbour passes through the northern section of the park. Several **walking trails** start from near the picnic and day-use area, including a 1km circuit track to a mangrove creek. About 1km past the day-use area and on the northern side of the road, there's a 2.4km walk up to the **Mt Rooper lookout**, which provides good views of the Whitsunday Passage and Islands. Further along the main road, and up the hill towards Coral Point (before Shute Harbour), there's a pleasant 1km track leading down to Coral Beach and the **Beak lookout**. This track was created with the assistance of the Giru Dala, the traditional custodians of the Whitsunday area; a brochure available at the start of the trail explains how the local Aborigines used plants growing in the area.

There's bush **camping** (per person/family $4/16) on the coast at Swamp Bay; access is only by foot.

Cedar Creek Falls & Conway Beach

To reach the beautiful Cedar Creek Falls, turn off the Proserpine–Airlie Beach road on to Conway Rd, 8km north of Proserpine. It's then about 15km to the falls – the roads are well signposted. This is a popular picnic and swimming spot – when there's enough water, that is!

At the end of Conway Rd, 20km from the turn-off, is **Conway Beach**. A small coastal community on the shores of Repulse Bay and at the southern end of the Conway National Park, it consists of a few old houses, pleasant picnic areas along the foreshore and the **Conway Beach Whitsunday Caravan Park** (☎ 4947 3147; 10 Daniels St, Conway Beach; unpowered/powered sites $14/16, cabins $40; ⌨), a friendly, basic van park with a kiosk. Prices are for two people.

LONG ISLAND

The closest of the resort islands to the coast, Long Island is mostly national park, with three resorts on offer. The island is about 11km long but not much more than 1.5km wide, and a channel only 500m wide separates it from the mainland. There are 13km of walking tracks and some fine lookouts, and day-trippers to the island can use the facilities at Club Crocodile or Peppers Palm Bay resorts. Peppers uses its own launch from Shute Harbour and charges $85 per person including transfers, lunch and activities.

Activities

The **beaches** on Long Island are quite attractive and some of the best in the Whitsundays. The two northern resorts have a range of water-sports equipment. Club Crocodile has a wider selection, hiring out dinghies ($99 per day) and jet skis ($55 per 20 minutes) and offering water-skiing ($30 per 10 minutes). Day-trippers and guests at Palm Bay can also use these facilities. **Long Island Dive & Snorkel** (☎ 0417-161 998) has a range of courses, gear for hire and trips for certified divers.

Sea kayaking is a featured activity at the South Long Island Nature Lodge on the southern side of the island (guests only).

Sleeping & Eating

Long Island has one large mainstream resort, two smaller, quieter resorts and camping.

Peppers Palm Bay (☎ 1800 095 025, 4946 9233; www.peppers.com.au/palmbay; d $380-680; 🞅 🞷) Peppers is a boutique resort that stands out for the fact that it's peaceful – there are no telephones or TVs in the 21 cabins that house a maximum of 42 guests in comfort. The cabins, complete with swinging double hammock, sit around the pretty, sandy sweep of Palm Bay. At the heart of the resort is a pool and a large, comfortable building that serves as the main dining area, bar and lounge.

South Long Island Nature Lodge (☎ 3839 7799; www.southlongisland.com; 5-night packages per person $2990) This secluded lodge on Paradise Bay consists of spacious, waterfront cabins; there's no phone, no TV and no air-con, but the cabins are positioned to make the most of the sea breezes. The lodge is staffed by a friendly crew of just three – informality is the name of the game – and the maximum number of guests is just 12. All meals are included in the tariff and served buffet style. There's a five-night minimum stay, no day visitors or children, and no motorised water sports, so you're guaranteed peace and tranquillity. The tariff is inclusive of helicopter transfer from Hamilton Island, a helicopter tour to a snorkelling site, sailing tours and use of water-sports equipment.

Club Crocodile (☎ 1800 075 125, 4946 9400; www .clubcroc.com.au; d incl all meals $240-368; 🞅 🞷) Sitting on Happy Bay in the north of the island, Club Croc is a midrange, well-used resort with three levels of accommodation. It's popular with families and couples, and there are plenty of activities to keep all age

groups busy. The lodge units are small and austere, and bathroom facilities are shared; for the price, you're better off spending the extra to stay in the beachfront or garden rooms. Always check the Internet or the agents in Airlie Beach for stand-by rates.

The pleasant, motel-style beachfront units overlook Happy Bay; while the similar-standard garden rooms are, obviously, in the garden! The resort has two swimming pools, tennis courts, a gym and mini-golf; guests also have free use of all the nonpowered water-sports gear. Kids from four to 14 years can be kept busy in the free kids club. All meals are included in the tariff, and breakfast, lunch and dinner are served in the Palms, a big and rather stylish restaurant.

Cafe Paradiso (🕒 8am-10pm) is more casual, serving up coffee, snacks and light meals that can be purchased throughout the day.

There's a secluded national park **camping ground** (per person/family $4/16) at Sandy Bay, midway along the western side of the island. For details, see the boxed text on p269.

Getting There & Away

Blue Ferries (☎ 4946 5111; www.fantasea.com.au; 11 Shute Harbour Rd, Jubilee Pocket) connects Long Island (Club Crocodile) to Shute Harbour by frequent daily services. The direct trip takes about 15 minutes, and costs $18/12 per adult/child. Return fares are $36/24.

It's 2km between the Club Croc and Peppers Palm Bay resorts and you can walk between them in about 25 minutes.

HOOK ISLAND

The second largest of the Whitsundays, the 53-sq-km Hook Island is predominantly national park and rises to 450m at Hook Peak. There are a number of good beaches dotted around the island, and Hook boasts some of the best diving and snorkelling locations in the Whitsundays.

The southern end of the island is indented by two very long fjord-like bays. Beautiful **Nara Inlet** is a popular deep-water anchorage for yachts, and Aboriginal rock paintings have been found there. Hook has an old underwater observatory, a small, low-key resort and several camping grounds.

While it's basic, **Hook Island Wilderness Resort** (☎ 4946 9380; www.hookislandresort.com; sites $50, dm $20-35, d with/without bathroom $130/90; 🞅 🞷) is also the cheapest resort in the Whitsundays, and its other advantage is that there's great snorkelling just off shore. The simple, adjoining units each sleep up to six or eight people; the bathrooms are *tiny*, and rates include linen but not towels. Tea and coffee facilities are supplied in each room, and there's a camp kitchen strictly for the use of campers only, plus a couple of BBQs. Camping prices are for two people.

Food is not a priority at the resort. The licensed **restaurant** (mains $14-18) serves seafood, steak and pasta, and there's usually a vegetarian option at night; snacks are available the rest of the day and there's also a small bar.

There are some wonderful camping opportunities in basic national-park **camping grounds** (per person/family $4/16) at Maureen Cove, Steen's Beach, Bloodhorn Beach, Curlew Beach and Crayfish Beach. For details see the boxed text on p269.

Transfers to the resort are arranged when you book your accommodation. Return transfers are by regular tour boat. The **Voyager** (☎ 4946 5255) does a daily three-island cruise (Hook Island, Whitehaven Beach and South Molle Island, see p268) as well as return transfer to Hook (adult/child $40/20). Transfers to other islands can be arranged. **Island Camping Connections** (☎ 4946 5255) or **Camping Whitsunday Islands** (☎ 4946 9330) can organise drop offs to the camping grounds for around $150.

DAYDREAM ISLAND

Daydream, the closest of the resort islands to Shute Harbour, is just over 1km long and only a couple of hundred metres across at its widest point. It's a popular day-trip destination, with a wide range of watersports gear available for hire (free for resort guests); water-skiing is also big here.

A steep, rocky path, taking about 20 minutes to walk, links the southern and northern ends of the island. There's another short walk to the tiny but lovely Sunlovers Beach, and a concreted path leads around the eastern side of the island. And once you've done these walks, you've just about covered Daydream from head to foot.

In addition to catamarans, kayaks and windsurfers, Daydream offers a variety of motorised water sports for guests, including parasailing ($65), jet-skiing ($69 per 30 minutes), and water-skiing ($35 per 15 minutes).

Surrounded by beautifully landscaped tropical gardens, and with a stingray-, shark- and fish-filled lagoon running through it, the large (296 rooms) **Daydream Island Resort & Spa** (☎ 1800 075 040, 4948 8488; www.daydream .net.au; 6-night packages $670; ⚄ ⚄) has tennis courts, a gym, catamarans, windsurfers and three swimming pools – all of which are included in the tariff. There are five grades of accommodation and most, but not all, package deals include a buffet breakfast. There's a club with constant activities to keep children occupied. This is a large resort on a small island, so it's not the place to head if you're seeking isolation.

Breakfast is served buffet style at the Waterfall Restaurant, which stays open all day, serving snacks, lunch and dinner (buffet $39, vegetarian $29). More formal is **Mermaids** (mains $24-35), which is on the beachfront and does a sumptuous seafood platter for two ($120), or there's the Boathouse bakery, which provides coffee, sandwiches and other lunchtime snacks. The casual **Fishbowl Tavern** (mains $15-30; ☯ Mon, Wed & Fri) provides meals and refreshments on the nights that the outdoor cinema is showing movies.

In addition, the resort's three bars, Splashes Pool, Gilligans and Lagoon, offer nightly entertainment.

Blue Ferries (☎ 4946 5111; www.fantasea.com.au; 11 Shute Harbour Rd, Jubilee Pocket) connects Daydream Island to Shute Harbour by frequent daily services (one-way adult/child $18/12, return $36/24). Daydream can be visited as part of a three-island day-trip package (adult/child $59/40) by **Fantasea/Blue Ferries** (☎ 4946 5111; www.fantasea.com.au; 11 Shute Harbour Rd, Jubilee Pocket).

SOUTH MOLLE ISLAND

Largest of the Molle group of islands at 4 sq km, South Molle is virtually joined to Mid Molle and North Molle Islands – indeed you can walk across a causeway to Mid Molle. Apart from the resort area and golf course at Bauer Bay in the north, the island is all national park. There is some forest cover around the resort, and the trees are gradually reclaiming the once overgrazed pastures. The island is criss-crossed by 15km of walking tracks, and has some superb lookout points. The highest point is Mt Jeffreys (198m), but the climb up Spion Kop is also worthwhile.

The island is known for its prolific birdlife. The most noticeable birds are the dozens of tame, colourful lorikeets and black currawongs. The endangered stone curlews are also common and rather intimidating. The beaches are reasonably good at high tide, but severe tidal shifts mean some time will be spent at the pool. The resort, which is decidedly nonglitzy, also has a nine-hole golf course, a gym, and tennis and squash courts. There is also a wide range of watersports gear available for day-trippers to hire (nonmotorised water-sports equipment is free for resort guests).

Full-board tariffs at **South Molle Island Resort** (☎ 1800 075 080, 4946 9433; www.southmolleisland .com.au; d from $240, full-board d from $350; ✷ ⌘) include three buffet meals a day, and all tariffs include use of the golf course, tennis courts, nonmotorised water-sports equipment and nightly entertainment. South Molle is a popular resort with families as children are well catered for, and at high tide the jetty is one of the prettiest around.

Breakfast and lunch buffets are served in the main **Island Restaurant** (mains $20-30); bistro-style dinners (steak, chicken and seafood dishes) are also served here. On Wednesday and Saturday nights there is the alternative of a BBQ beside the pool, and Friday is Polynesian Feast Night, with an extensive spread and live entertainment. The Discover Bar has nightly entertainment and there's a coffee shop for drinks and snacks.

There are national park **camping grounds** (per person/family $4/16) located at Sandy Bay in the south and at Paddle Bay near the resort. For more information see the boxed text on p269.

Blue Ferries (☎ 4946 5111; www.fantasea.com.au; 11 Shute Harbour Rd, Jubilee Pocket) frequently stops off en route between Hamilton, Daydream and Long Islands and Shute Harbour. In addition, there are direct connections with Shute Harbour (adult/child $18/12, return $36/24). South Molle can also be visited as part of a three-island day-trip package (adult/child $59/40) with **Fantasea/Blue Ferries** (☎ 4946 5111; www.fantasea.com.au; 11 Shute Harbour Rd, Jubilee Pocket).

HAMILTON ISLAND

The most heavily developed island in the Whitsundays, Hamilton is more like a town than a resort. Such development isn't every-

one's cup of tea, but in addition to its own airport and huge marina there's an extensive range of accommodation, restaurants, bars and shops to cater for more than 2000 guests.

Sights & Activities

The sheer size of this resort means there are plenty of entertainment possibilities, which makes Hamilton an interesting day trip from Shute Harbour as you can use some the resort facilities. The resort has tennis courts, squash courts, a gym, a golf driving range and a mini-golf course. From **Catseye Beach**, in front of the resort, you can hire windsurfers, catamarans, jet skis and other equipment, and go parasailing or water-skiing. Among the other options are helicopter joy rides, game fishing and even paintball skirmish.

A dive shop by the harbour organises dives and certificate courses; you can take a variety of cruises to other islands and the outer reef. Half-day fishing trips cost $90 per person, with fishing gear supplied.

There are a few **walking trails** on the island, the best being from Catseye Bay up to Passage Peak (230m) on the northeastern corner of the island. Hamilton also has daycare and a free Clownfish Club. Kids aged from zero to 14 years stay and play free of charge.

Sleeping

Hamilton Island Resort (☎ reservations 1800 075 110, 4946 9999; www.hamiltonisland.com.au; ✷ ⌘ ⌘) has options ranging from hotel rooms to self-contained apartments to penthouses. Rates listed are for one night, twin-share accommodation only; meals are not included. All bookings need to be made through the central reservations number.

Beach Club (d $550) Flanking the main resort complex with its reception area, restaurants, bars, shops and pools, these 55 five-star rooms all enjoy absolute beachfront positions.

Palm Bungalows (d $310) These attractive, individual units behind the resort complex are closely packed but buffeted by lush gardens. Each has a double and single bed, and a small patio.

Palm Terraces (d $250) These rooms are in low-rise complexes with big balconies overlooking the garden.

Reef View Hotel (d from $340) The large 20-storey, four-star hotel has 386 spacious rooms, mostly balconied; some have Coral Sea views, others garden views.

Self-Catering Accommodation (d $470-1500) There are several types of fully self-contained units, from standard to luxury.

Whitsunday Holiday Apartments (d $260) These serviced one- to four-bedroom apartments are on the resort side of the island.

Eating

RESORTSIDE

The following restaurants are to be found within the main resort complex. Alternatively, you can head down to the harbour where there are several other options to choose from.

Beach House (☎ 4946 8580; mains $22-42; ☺ lunch & dinner) Modern Australian cuisine forms the basis of the menu at Beach House, Hamilton's signature restaurant. Dishes include tuna, eye fillet and spatchcock.

Toucan Tango Cafe & Bar (☎ 4946 8562; mains $14-26; ☺ breakfast, lunch & dinner) This large, casual eatery has a large à la carte menu except on Friday and Saturday nights, when there's a seafood buffet.

Outrigger Restaurant (☎ 4946 8582; mains $35-50) In a Polynesian long house, Outrigger's modern menu includes pork, kangaroo, lamb and salmon.

HARBOURSIDE

These restaurants, all along the waterfront in what is known as Marina Village (or simply Harbourside), are independently run, though you can charge all bills to your room and pay for the lot on departure. There's also a supermarket–general store for those in apartments preparing their own meals.

Mariners Seafood Restaurant (☎ 4946 8628; fax 4946 8886; mains $26-38; ☺ dinner Mon-Sat) In a big, enclosed veranda overlooking the harbour, Mariners is both licensed and BYO. While the emphasis is on seafood, grills are also available; it's a stylish restaurant with a menu to match.

Spinnakers Bar & Grill (☎ 4946 8019; mains $25-33; ☺ dinner Thu-Tue) Located upstairs, Spinnakers boasts great views over the marina. On the beefy menu is grain-fed rib fillet, eye fillet, T-Bone, rump, sirloin and veal rib fillet – if it moos, they cook it. Other mains include lighter meals such as warm chicken salad or bug tails.

Romano's (☎ 4946 8212; mains $30-37; ☺ dinner Thu-Tue) This is a relaxed Italian restaurant with a large enclosed deck built right out over the water. The Italian menu includes pasta entrees and wicked desserts, and kids are well catered for (kids meals $13).

Manta Ray Cafe (☎ 4946 8213; mains $15-28; ☺ breakfast, lunch & dinner) If you come to Hamilton on a day trip that includes lunch, this café is one of the choices you have. Late breakfasts are popular here and so is the gourmet pizza.

Hamilton Island Bakery (☎ 4946 8281; ☺ 7am-4pm) The bakery has cabinets and fridges filled with fresh bread, sandwiches, great-looking pastries and delicious punnets of fresh fruit salad.

Ice Cream Parlour (☎ 4946 8620; ice creams $3-5; ☺ 8am-5pm) This is a busy kiosk opposite the ferry terminal and serves iced coffee, espresso and frozen yogurt, in addition to numerous flavours of ice cream.

Entertainment

The bars in the resort and harbourside offer nightly entertainment. The Toucan Tango has a pianist or other live entertainment most nights, or you can head to the harbourside **Boheme's NightClub** (☺ 9pm-late).

Getting There & Away

AIR

The Hamilton Island airport is the main arrival centre for the Whitsundays and receives domestic and international charter flights. **Jetstar** (☎ 13 15 38; www.jetstar.com.au) has flights to/from Brisbane, Sydney and Melbourne. **QantasLink** (☎ 13 13 13; www.qantas .com.au) has flights to/from Townsville and Cairns, and **Island Air Taxis** (☎ 4946 9933) and **Hamilton Island Aviation** (☎ 4946 8249) connect Hamilton with Mackay (one way $135), Airlie Beach ($60) and Lindeman Island ($60). Helicopter transfers from Hamilton are available to several of the other resort islands and Airlue Beach ($210).

BOAT

Blue Ferries (☎ 4946 5111; www.fantasea.com.au; 11 Shute Harbour Rd, Jubilee Pocket) connects Hamilton Island to Shute Harbour by frequent daily services (adult/child $24/12, return $48/24, 30 minutes). Hamilton can be visited as part of a three-island day-trip package (adult/child $59/40) with **Fantasea/Blue Ferries** (☎ 4946 5111; www.fantasea.com.au; 11 Shute Harbour Rd, Jubilee Pocket).

With regular daily flights to/from the major capital cities, Hamilton is also the main arrival point for Long, South Molle, Daydream, Hayman and Lindeman Islands.

WHITSUNDAY COAST

Blue Ferries meets all incoming and outgoing flights, and connects Hamilton to the other islands. Blue Ferries transfers to South Molle and Long Islands (adult/child $18/12, return $36/24). Transfers to Lindeman Island are usually included in accommodation packages.

Getting Around

On arrival and departure there's a free bus service for guests between the airport or marina and the resort.

Hamilton is a large island, and there are a few alternatives to walking. One is the island shuttle between the airport, harbour and resort, which costs $2.50 per trip, but is complimentary between 5pm and 10pm, and is usually included in guest transfers. You can also scuttle around like Mr McGoo in a golf buggy ($35/60 per hour/day), available from the office near reception or from the Charter Base near the ferry terminal.

HAYMAN ISLAND

The most northern of the Whitsunday group, Hayman is just 4 sq km in area and rises to 250m above sea level. It has forested hills, valleys and beaches. It also has one of the most luxurious resorts on the Great Barrier Reef. The resort is fronted by a wide, shallow reef that emerges from the water at low tide.

Hayman is closer to the outer reef than the other islands, and there is good diving around its northern end and at nearby Hook Island. There are several small, uninhabited islands close to Hayman, and you can walk out to Arkhurst Island at low tide. Langford Island, a couple of kilometres southwest, has some good coral around it, as do Black and Bird Islands nearby.

Activities

Resort guests have free use of catamarans, windsurfers and paddle skis, but there are charges for just about everything else, including tennis and squash. There's also a driving range for golf, a putting green and a well-equipped gym.

Hayman has a free kids club and creche that keeps children entertained. The resort has a dive shop and marine centre, and offers a range of diving and snorkelling trips to the Great Barrier Reef. Dinghies can be hired with fishing and snorkelling gear.

Bushwalks include an 8km island circuit, a 4.5km walk to Dolphin Point at the northern tip of the island, and a 1.5km climb up to the Whitsunday Passage lookout.

Tours

Coral Air Whitsunday (☎ 4946 9111) offers several options for seaplane tours for resort guests. Destinations include a 2½-hour stop at Whitehaven Beach ($195) and a 2¾-hour snorkelling trip to Blue Lagoon on Hardy Reef ($295).

Sleeping

The private **Hayman Great Barrier Reef** (☎ 1800 075 175, 4940 1234; www.hayman.com.au; d $620-4,400; ⊠ ▣ ▨) is a member of the exclusive 'Leading Hotels of the World' group, and is the most luxurious resort on the Great Barrier Reef. If you're looking for five-star comfort dripping with style and sophistication, look no further.

An avenue of stately 9m-high date palms leads to the main entrance, and with its 244 rooms, five restaurants, four bars, a hectare of swimming pools, landscaped gardens and grounds, an impressive collection of antiques and arts, and exclusive boutiques, Hayman is certainly impressive. The rooms and suites have all the usual five-star facilities. There are also 11 individually styled penthouses for big spenders.

If you don't have to plan ahead, remember to keep an eye out for stand-by rates – check the newspapers in Airlie Beach and Mackay.

Eating & Drinking

Breakfast is served buffet-style in Azure, a relaxed indoor-outdoor restaurant with a great outlook over the beach.

Other restaurants include the casual open-air **Beach Pavilion** (mains $20-30), where there's a choice of lunch-time grills, salads, sandwiches and desserts; La Fontaine, the most formal of the restaurants, with a Louis XIV–style dining room and classic French cuisine (mains $30-45; ☾ dinner); the **Oriental** (mains $30-40), in a beautiful Japanese garden; and **La Trattoria** (mains around $25-32), a casual Mediterranean café with live music.

The Hayman wine cellar numbers more than 20,000 bottles of Australian and European wine, and La Fontaine has an additional 400 vintages.

Getting There & Away

Guests flying in to Hamilton Island are met by Hayman staff and escorted to one of the resort's fleet of luxury cruisers (adult/child one way $205/103) for a pampered transfer to the resort. **Air Whitsunday Seaplanes** (☎ 4946 9111) provide a seaplane service from Hamilton ($675 per plane).

Flying is the only way to do day trips to Hayman. Check out **Air Whitsunday Seaplanes** (☎ 4946 9111; adult/child $175/155) and **Island Air/ Helireef** (☎ 4946 9102; $379 per person).

LINDEMAN ISLAND

One of the most southerly of the Whitsundays, Lindeman covers 8 sq km, most of which is national park. In 1992, Lindeman Island became the site of Australia's first Club Med resort. The island has 20km of walking trails and the highest point is Mt Oldfield (210m). With plenty of little beaches and secluded bays, it's no hassle at all to find one to yourself. There are also a lot of small islands dotted around, some of which are easy to get to.

Activities

The resort's daily activities sheet lists an array of things to do, although nothing is compulsory or too regimented. There's a good golf course as well as tennis courts, an archery range, a gym, beach volleyball, bingo etc. You can even take lessons on the resort's impressive flying trapeze set-up or bounce on a bungee.

The usual range of water-sports equipment is available, and a diving school offers various dive courses and snorkelling trips. Children are also kept busy with all sorts of organised activities.

Sleeping

Club Med Resort (☎ 1800 258 2633, 4946 9333; www .clubmed.com; packages per person per night $215-310; ⊠ ▣) The famous Club Med style is evident here, with plenty of activities, nightly entertainment and young, friendly staff to help you get the most out of your stay. The main resort complex, with its pool, dining and entertainment areas, is flanked by three-storey accommodation blocks looking out over the water; all the motel-style rooms have their own balconies.

Rates include all meals and most activities. There are also five-night packages that are available from major cities and include airfares and transfers, and special deals from Mackay and Airlie Beach. Contact the resort for details.

There is a national-park **camping ground** (per person/family $4/16) at Boat Port, in the north of the island. For details, see the boxed text on p269.

Eating

All meals and beer, wine and juices are included in the tariff. The Main Restaurant serves buffet-style breakfasts, lunches and dinners; the casual Top Restaurant, by the pool and tennis courts, has barbecued steaks and chicken, salads and fruit; and Nicholson's, a smaller à la carte restaurant, opens nightly for dinner.

Entertainment

Every night there's a live show in the main theatre, and you're likely to find yourself up on stage at some time. Later in the evening Silhouettes nightclub opens.

Getting There & Away

Island Air Taxis (☎ 4946 9933) has flights to Lindeman from Airlie Beach (one way/return $60/120) and Mackay ($135/270). Club Med has its own launch that connects with flights from the airport on Hamilton Island.

WHITSUNDAY ISLAND

The largest of the Whitsunday group, this island covers 109 sq km and rises to 438m at Whitsunday Peak. There's no resort, but it has some fine bushwalking. The 6km-long **Whitehaven Beach**, on the southeastern coast, is the longest and best beach in the group (some say in the country), with good snorkelling off its southern end. Many of the day-trip boats visit Whitehaven. The pure-white silicon sand can be dazzling on a sunny day, so make sure you have sunglasses!

There are national-park **camping grounds** (per person/family $4/16) at Dugong, Sawmill, Nari's and Joe's Beaches in the west, and at Turtle Bay and Chance Bay in the south; at the southern end of Whitehaven Beach; and Peter Bay in the north. For details see the boxed text on p269.

OTHER WHITSUNDAY ISLANDS

The northern islands of the Whitsundays group are undeveloped and seldom visited

WHITSUNDAY COAST

by cruise boats or water taxis. Several of them (Gloucester, Saddleback, Olden and Armit Islands) have national-park **camping grounds** (per person/family $4/16). See the boxed text on p269 for details. The QPWS office (p272), 3km south of Airlie Beach, can issue camping permits and advise you on which islands to visit and how to get there. The northern islands are best reached from Dingo Beach or Bowen.

There's also camping on **North Molle Island** at Cockatoo Beach, on the island's southern end, with tables, toilets and water. **Henning Island**, just off the western side of Whitsunday Island, also has camping grounds at Northern Spit and Geographers Bay.

Between Cid and Whitsunday Islands, **Cid Harbour** was the anchorage for part of the US Navy before the Battle of the Coral Sea, the turning point in the Pacific theatre of WWII. Today, visiting cruise liners anchor here, and there is a camping ground at Homestead Bay on Cid Island.

DINGO BEACH, HYDEAWAY BAY & CAPE GLOUCESTER

Back on the mainland, north of Airlie Beach, there's a lonely road leading to some lovely coastal retreats, where peace and tranquility (and fish) are virtually guaranteed. **Dingo Beach** is a quiet little place with an evocative name, set on a long sandy bay backed by low, forested mountains. True, nothing much happens here outside the odd 'one that got away' yarn, but it's a popular spot with families and the fishing fraternity. There's a pleasant, shady foreshore with picnic tables and BBQs, and a couple of interesting places to stay in the vicinity.

The only facilities are on the foreshore at the **Dingo Beach General Store**, which sells fuel, booze, takeaway meals, a small range of groceries and bait. Next door is the **Dingo Beach Hotel & Units** (☎ 4945 7153; 1 Deicke Cres; d $80), a modest block of spacious two-bedroom, self-contained units with a very casual **dining area** (mains $13-16) replete with pool table and photos of fish.

There are two islands a little way off either end of the bay. **Gloucester Island** is to the north-west and **Saddleback Island** sits to the north-east. Both have small national-park **camping grounds** (per person/family $4/16). See the boxed text on p269 for details. **Dingo Beach Escape** (☎ /fax 4945 7215) offers day trips from Airlie Beach

to Dingo Beach ($80), which includes lunch and water sports. They also provide transfers to Saddleback ($30 return) and Gloucester Islands ($40), and rent out dinghies for $15/75 per hour/day (including fuel).

At secluded **Hydeaway Bay**, there's the friendly **Hydeaway Bay Caravan Park** (☎ 4945 7170; www.hydeawaybaycaravanpark.com.au; 414 Hydeaway Bay Dr; unpowered/powered sites $15/18, on-site vans $40) where shade is at a premium, but there's plenty of fishy conversations in the shop-kiosk. Further down the track are a couple of real surprises. **Cape Gloucester Eco-Resort** (☎ 4945 7242; www.capegloucester.com; d $120-150) is a very modern, very well-executed resort with spacious self-contained units and motel-style rooms facing the sandy beach. A 25m pool fronts the comfortable bar and restaurant, the **Oar** (mains $21-24; ☾ breakfast, lunch & dinner), where visiting yachties (moorings per night/week $10/50) enjoy excellent seafood, pasta and Thai dishes. There are kayaks and catamarans, and the resort owners' large cat is available for sunset sailing. Bookings are recommended, and pick-ups from Proserpine (Whitsunday Coast) airport can be arranged.

Also along the rough dirt track out to Cape Gloucester is an older, more under-stated (but no less enjoyable) resort. **Montes Reef Resort** (☎ 4945 7177; d $120-130) is the sort of place where outback graziers have been bringing the family for their annual seaside holiday for eons. Montes has discovered that the secret to achieving eco-style is to keep things simple and let a couple of decades of modern trends pass by. The spacious bungalows are designed to catch the breeze and are literally a few steps from the beach. The licensed **restaurant** (mains $14-18) is almost austere; but simplicity is the name of the game here.

BOWEN

Bowen, founded in 1861, was the first coastal settlement to be established north of Rockhampton. Although soon overshadowed by Mackay to the south and Townsville to the north, Bowen survived, and today it's a thriving fruit- and vegetable-growing centre that attracts hundreds of people for seasonal picking work between April and November. Bowen is spread out, with beaches, resorts and some lovely bays to the northeast of the town centre.

Information

Bowen Visitor Information Centre (☎ /fax 4786 4222; www.bowentourism.com.au; ⏰ 8.30am-5pm) About 7km south of Bowen on the Bruce Hwy. Look for the big mango.

Brazil's Auto Service (☎ 4786 1412, 0408-180 941; 28 Don St) The local RACQ depot is here.

Post office (cnr Powell & Herbert Sts)

Sights & Activities

For a spectacular view of the Coral Sea and the Whitsunday Islands, head up to **Flagstaff Hill**, overlooking Kings Beach and to the east of the town centre. Several walls and buildings around the centre of town are decorated with terrific **murals** depicting the town's history. Painted by Queensland artists, there are currently 24 mural sites, most within the block made by Gregory, Powell, Herbert and George Sts. The town's early history is displayed at the **Bowen Historical Museum** (☎ 4786 2035; 22 Gordon St; adult/child $4/2; ⏰ 9.30am-3.30pm Mon-Fri, 10.30am-noon Sun).

A couple of kilometres north of the town centre are Bowen's **beaches**. At Queens Beach you can catch a movie at the 1948 **Bowen Summer Garden Cinemas** (☎ 4785 1241; Murroona Rd, Queens Beach), where you'll sit in the original canvas seats. Driving east around the sandy sweep of Queens Bay you come across a series of secluded coves and bays, including the picturesque **Horseshoe Bay**. There's an impressive **coastal walking track** linking Horseshoe and Rose Bays.

Sleeping

BUDGET

Bowen's hostels specialise in finding seasonal fruit- and vegetable-picking work for travellers. In season, budget accommodation can be full of pickers and any available cheap beds are far from salubrious.

Coral Coast Caravan Park (☎ 4785 1262; fax 4785 1428; Soldiers Rd; unpowered/powered sites $20/22, on-site vans $44, cabins $88; 🅿 🖳 🖲) A delightfully attractive beachfront park with excellent amenities.

Harbour Lights Caravan Park (☎ 4786 1565; fax 4786 1770; 40 Santa Barbara Pde; powered sites $20, cabins from $60; 🅿 🖲) Opposite the harbour, this friendly caravan park is a few minutes' walk to the centre of town. Prices are for two people.

Bowen Backpackers (☎ 4786 3433; fax 4786 1073; cnr Herbet & Dalrymple Sts; dm from $21, d $50; 🅿)

Offers beds in four- and six-bed dorms, some air-conditioned, and with cheaper weekly rates available.

MIDRANGE

Bowen's midrange resorts are tucked into the beautiful bays that line the coastline to the northeast and stretch to Cape Edgecumbe. Cheaper weekly rates are available and there's usually a two-night minimum stay.

Murrays Bay Resort (☎ 4786 2402; fax 4786 3388; Murray Bay; d $77; 🖲) With its own palm-fringed sandy beach, this small complex of 11 old-fashioned but very spacious and comfortable self-contained units offers the perfect get-away-from-it-all holiday. There's an excellent palm-shaded, grassed foreshore leading down to the private beach with first-rate swimming and snorkelling.

Horseshoe Bay Resort (☎ 4786 2564; fax 4786 3460; Horseshoe Bay; powered sites $20-23, d cabins $50, self-contained units $65-100; 🖲) This resort is right on Horseshoe Bay, nestled among the granite boulders and with only a short walk to beaches, viewpoints and great fishing spots. It has good facilities, including a camp kitchen, and is convenient to the excellent Horseshoe Bay Cafe.

Rose Bay Resort (☎ 4786 1064; fax 4786 5740; Pandanus Pde, Rose Bay; d $125-220; 🖳 🖳 🖲) Four-storey blocks of very comfortable, modern self-contained units front the beach at Rose Bay, and every unit here boasts sea and island views from its own private balcony.

Whitsunday Sands Resort (☎ 4786 3333; fax 4786 3388; Horseshoe Bay; d $66-90; 🖳 🖲) Out on the headland of Cape Edgecumbe, this resort is in a pleasant setting, with access to several coves and beaches. The complex has motel-style rooms, self-contained units, a bar, a kiosk and a restaurant.

Eating

Horseshoe Bay Cafe (☎ 4786 3280; Horseshoe Bay; mains $18-29; ⏰ 10am-10pm) Tucked into a palm grotto on the foreshore at Horseshoe Bay, this unassuming café serves up huge breakfasts and great coffee for sleepy holidaymakers, and is the perfect lunch and dinner venue. There's a wide menu to choose from, or you could just sip coffee and sample cake at an outdoor table and admire the pretty beach.

360 on the Hill (☎ 4786 6360; Flagstaff Hill; mains $10-27; ⏰ 8am-4.30pm Sun-Mon, 9.30am-9pm, Wed-Sat) This licensed restaurant and café is perched on the top of Flagstaff Hill. It's a spectacular setting for sunset drinks and an evening meal of sumptuous seafood.

Yacht Club Restaurant (☎ 4786 3490; Starboard Dr; mains $7-20; ⏰ lunch & dinner) This waterfront restaurant has steaks and seafood, and popular Hawaiian-style buffet on Sunday.

Bowen's pubs tend to cater to the fruit-pickers, offering very ordinary blackboard dishes for under $10. Other places to try:

Fellows Fish Bar (☎ 4786 2462; 19 Gregory St; ⏰ 10am-2pm & 4.30-8pm) Fellows is a popular little takeaway fish-and-chip place.

Hot Wok (☎ 4786 3404; 23a Gregory St; ⏰ 11am-2pm & 5-9pm Mon-Sat, 5-8.30pm Sun) A busy Chinese take-away with the usual extensive range of dishes.

Getting There & Away
BUS
Long-distance buses stop outside **Bowen Travel** (☎ 4786 2835; 40 Williams St), where you

can book and purchase bus tickets. **Greyhound Australia** (☎ 13 20 30; www.greyhound.com .au) and **Premier Motor Service** (☎ 13 34 10; www .premierms.com.au) have frequent bus services to/from Rockhampton ($94, eight hours), Airlie Beach ($26, 1½ hours) and Townsville ($42, three hours).

TRAIN
Queensland Rail (☎ 13 22 32, 1300 13 17 22; www .traveltrain.com.au) runs the *Sunlander* and *Tilt Train*, which stop at Bootooloo Siding, 3km south of the centre, *not* at the Bowen train station. An economy sleeper/seat on the *Sunlander* from Brisbane costs $250/150.

Getting Around
Bowen Bus Service (☎ 4786 4414) runs local buses to Queens Beach, Rose Bay and Horseshoe Bay, Monday to Friday and Saturday morning, from near the post office.

Townsville & North Coast

CONTENTS

HIGHLIGHTS

- Hiring a pushbike and cycling from end to end of rugged (and hilly) **Magnetic Island** (p300)
- Mooching about in perky **Townsville** (p289)
- Looking for a cassowary in the rainforests behind **Mission Beach** (p318)
- Snorkelling over a bommie while you inspect the **Great Barrier Reef** (p320)
- Waiting for a cane train to cross the road in the main street of small-town **Ingham** (p311)
- Stopping by **Dunk Island** (p323) – a resort island that's part national park and entirely gorgeous
- Being one of the lucky few who explore the natural surrounds on Hinchinbrook's **Thorsborne Trail** (p315)

- www.townsville.qld.gov.au
- www.gbrmpa.gov.au

Though it's the largest city in northern Queensland, cheerful Townsville presents a fresh, neighbourly face. Locals pass greetings back and forth in the street and along the Strand, and endless blue skies coax people out of doors to gather around café tables or huff up Castle Hill. Not only does Townsville have a beach within walking distance of the city centre, it also has an island just off shore. Virtually a suburb of Townsville, Magnetic Island has substantial bush tracks, a military history and beautiful sandy bays.

The waters around Magnetic Island and Townsville are home to hundreds of varieties of fish and coral that form part of the Great Barrier Reef. The eerie wreck of the *Yongala*, which has attracted its fair share of marine life and divers, lies on the ocean floor out from Townsville.

Little islands line the entire stretch of coast like crumbs from the mainland. Some are uninhabited, some sacred, while others – such as Bedarra – are privately owned and visited exclusively by high-paying guests. Many are at least partly national park, and available to everyone. The stunning Hinchinbrook Island is entirely protected park, with a boot-busting 32km walking trail on its east coast.

Running parallel to the coast are the mountains of the Great Diving Range; cloaked in heavy rainforest, they form part of the precious Wet Tropics World Heritage Area.

If you fossick around just inland, you'll strike the former gold-mining towns of Ravenswood and Charters Towers. They provide a taste of the outback – where it seems the sun evaporated everything, leaving sparse, open country fit only for cattle and prospectors.

Dangers & Annoyances

Dangerous marine stingers are present in coastal waters in the summer months (November to May; see the boxed text on p226 for more information). Saltwater crocodiles inhabit the mangroves, estuaries and open water north from around Lucinda. Warning signs are posted around waterways where crocs may be present.

Getting There & Away

AIR

Townsville is the major airport servicing the north coast, with domestic flights to/from all major centres and capital cities.

Dunk Island has its own airport, with regular flights to/from Townsville and Cairns.

BOAT

The major ferry services along this coast are from Townsville to Magnetic Island, from Cardwell to Hinchinbrook Island and from Mission Beach to Dunk Island.

BUS

Bus services follow the Bruce Hwy on the main Brisbane–Cairns run, with detours to Mission Beach. Brisbane to Townsville takes 22 hours, Townsville to Cairns around six.

Inland services operate from Townsville to Mt Isa via Charters Towers, continuing on to the Northern Territory.

CAR & MOTORCYCLE

The Bruce Hwy is the major route up the coast, while the Flinders Hwy from Townsville is the major inland route.

The Gregory Developmental Rd runs parallel to the coast, on the inland side of the Great Dividing Range, passing through Charters Towers and on to Lynd Junction. From here, the Kennedy Hwy continues north to the Atherton Tableland.

TRAIN

The train line from Brisbane to Cairns runs parrallel to the Bruce Hwy, with stops at

TOWNSVILLE & NORTH COAST

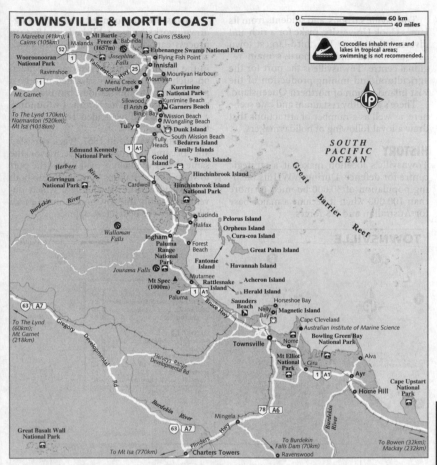

Crocodiles inhabit rivers and lakes in tropical areas; swimming is not recommended.

SOUTH PACIFIC OCEAN

Great Barrier Reef

Ingham, Cardwell and Tully. The Brisbane to Townsville trip takes around 24 hours. The trip from Townsville to Cairns is just under eight hours.

The *Inlander* (p464) runs between Townsville and Mt Isa twice a week (Sunday and Wednesday); the trip from Townsville to Charters Towers takes three hours.

TOWNSVILLE

☎ 07 / pop 150,000

Townsville's sweeping waterfront esplanade, city mall (where ibis, rather than seagulls, forage) and faultless blue skies bring about a wholesale sunny demeanour. The residents

of Townsville are proud of their home, keeping it and themselves shipshape. There's a seemingly endless trail of people power-walking along the pristine Strand, or heading up Castle Hill, from whose peak there are stellar views over this neat city. Most glide through the day seemingly unaware of Townsville's substantial military presence. No-one looks up from their latte when faux explosions erupt from the beautiful Deco building that was Townsville's hospital, and camouflage-clad soldiers scuttle along its balcony. And no-one is perturbed when a truck moves slowly across the sky – carried by an enormous chopper. Behind Townsville's genial, evenly paced goings-on there's a hive of secret military activity.

Townsville's troops, and students from its James Cook University, make for a rich and diverse population. The third-largest town in Queensland and the north's main regional centre, Townsville is the port for the agricultural and mining production of the vast inland region of northern Queensland.

There's a healthy restaurant and café scene here, as well as a number of attractions that draw a loyal following of holidaymakers.

HISTORY

Townsville's location makes it a strategic centre for defence. During WWII its bustling population of 30,000 boomed to more than 100,000 when it became a major base for Australian and US forces.

Townsville was founded when a boiling-down works was established in 1864 to process carcasses on the coast. John Black and Robert Towns owned pastoral leases in the highlands and their farms depended on such a facility. Towns wanted it to be a private depot for his stations, but Black saw the chance to make his fortune by founding a settlement, and persuaded Towns to fund the project.

Despite a cyclone in 1867, Black persisted and became Townsville's first mayor the same year. Eventually a road linked the port town to Towns' stations, contributing to both their survival and Townsville's, which developed mainly due to Chinese and Kanaka labour (see the boxed text opposite).

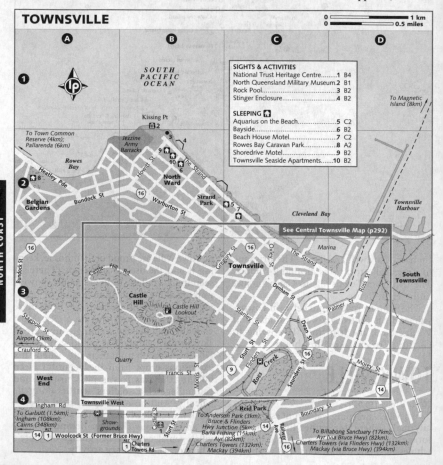

TOWNSVILLE

SIGHTS & ACTIVITIES	
National Trust Heritage Centre........1	B4
North Queensland Military Museum..2	B1
Rock Pool.....................................3	B2
Stinger Enclosure...........................4	B2

SLEEPING	
Aquarius on the Beach..................5	C2
Bayside...6	B2
Beach House Motel........................7	C2
Rowes Bay Caravan Park...............8	A2
Shoredrive Motel...........................9	B2
Townsville Seaside Apartments......10	B2

SLAVERY OF SORTS

Queensland's sugar industry boomed between 1863 and 1891. It was during this time that the government brought 46,387 South Pacific Islanders to Australia to work primarily in the cane fields as cheap labour. Known as Kanakas, the men worked 10-hour days for four pence per day, under three-year contracts. There are many stories of men going without pay and working in terrible conditions. Mortality figures of the time reinforce this: for non–Pacific Islanders the mortality rate was 13.03 per 1000, for Pacific Islanders it was 62.89.

Australia introduced its White Australia Policy in 1901 when there were around 9000 Kanakas still working in Queensland's cane fields. By 1914 more than 7000 Islanders had been repatriated.

ORIENTATION

Imposing Castle Hill (300m) presides over Townsville. Ross Creek winds about the city centre, which is on the west side of the creek. Townsville's centre is relatively compact and easy to get about on foot. Over the Dean St Bridge or pedestrian-only Victoria Bridge is what is known as South Townsville, where there's the secondary tourist-oriented hub of Palmer St.

The Strand is the centrepiece of Townsville, and there are several accommodation options, pubs and restaurants stretching the length of its coveted waterfront location. Townsville's shopping precinct stretches south along the Flinders St Mall, which runs from the Dean St Bridge down towards the train station. Flinders St E is lined with many of the town's oldest buildings, many of which have been repurposed to house a number of eateries, pubs and clubs. The Sunferries terminal for Magnetic Island is also located along here, with a second terminal on Sir Leslie Thiess Dr on the breakwater.

The arrival and departure point for long-distance buses is the Townsville Transit Centre on the corner of Palmer and Plume Sts – just south of Ross Creek. This is not to be confused with the Transit Mall on Stokes St (between Sturt St and Flinders St Mall), which is the departure point for local buses and taxis.

INFORMATION

Bookshops

Ancient Wisdom Bookshop (Map p292; ☎ 4721 2434; Shaw's Arcade) New Age titles; off Flinders St Mall.

Bumble Bee Bookshop & Music (Map p292; ☎ 4771 6091; 305 Flinders St Mall) Mainstream titles, with a large travel section.

Jim's Book Exchange (Map p292; ☎ 4771 6020; Shaw's Arcade) Wide range of secondhand books; off Flinders St Mall.

Mary Who Bookshop (Map p292; ☎ 4771 3824; 414 Flinders St) Small but bountiful range of books and music.

Internet Access

Internet Den (Map p292; ☎ 4721 4500; 265 Flinders St Mall; per hr $5; ☺ 9am-9pm Mon-Fri, 10am-8pm Sat & Sun) Also has chessboards.

Townsville City Library (Map p292; ☎ 4727 9666; 272-8 Flinders St Mall; ☺ 9.30am-5pm Mon-Fri, 9am-noon Sat & Sun) Free Internet access.

Medical Services

Townsville Hospital (☎ 4796 1111; 100 Angus Smith Dr, Douglas)

Post

Main post office (Map p292; Post Office Plaza, Shop 1, Sturt St) Enter via Sturt St; the poste restante section is a small window around the back.

Tourist Information

Flinders Mall visitors centre (Map p292; ☎ 4721 3660; www.townsvilleonline.com.au; Flinders St Mall, btwn Stokes & Denham Sts; ☺ 9am-5pm Mon-Fri, 9am-12.30pm Sat & Sun) Two desks: one has general information, the other specialises in diving and reef tours (www.divecruisetravel.com).

Great Barrier Reef Marine Park Authority (Map p292; ☎ 4750 0700; www.gbrmpa.gov.au; Reef HQ, 2-68 Flinders St E; ☺ 9am-5pm) Detailed and technical information on the Reef.

Queensland Parks & Wildlife Service Northern Region Office (QPWS; ☎ 4722 5211; Marlow St, Townsville)

Townsville Enterprises main visitors centre (Map p292; ☎ 4726 2700; www.townsvilleonline.com.au; 6 The Strand; ☺ 9am-5pm Mon-Fri) HQ for the booth in Flinders St Mall.

SIGHTS

Townsville has a range of attractions, some formal and purpose-built, others simply characteristic of a city with a glorious waterfront aspect.

CENTRAL TOWNSVILLE

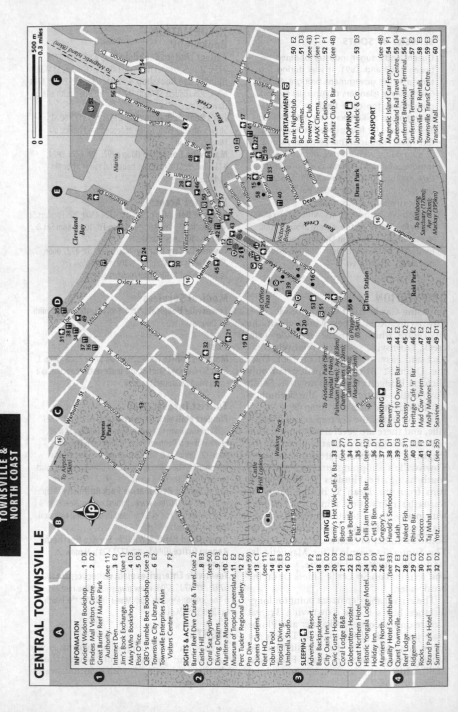

Strand

Townsville's vibrant waterfront promenade flaunts a number of parks, pools, cafés and playgrounds. The promenade is busy with perky locals walking from end to end, talking over the swish of sports shorts and the rhythmic pad of sneakers on concrete. The long stretch of beach is patrolled and protected by two **stinger enclosures** (Map p290) in the danger months (November to May).

At the northeast tip is the **rock pool** (Map p290; admission free; 🕑 24hr), an enormous artificial swimming pool surrounded by lawns and sandy beaches; a huge filtration system keeps it clean and stinger-free. If you want to be 100% sure, head to the safety of the chlorine at the **Tobruk Pool** (Map p292; ☎ 4772 6550; The Strand; adult/child $2.50/1.50; 🕑 5.30am-7pm Mon-Fri, 7am-6pm Sat & Sun), an Olympic-sized swimming pool with an endearingly lame Hall of Fame.

Castle Hill

A scramble to the top of **Castle Hill** (Map p290; 300m) marks the start or finish of the day for many Townsville townsfolk. More than a mound, but not quite a mountain, walking or running to the top of the hill is great exercise. You'll be rewarded with stellar views over Townsville from the peak. Access the 'goat track' (2km, 30 minutes) from Hillside Cres; or you can drive up via Gregory St.

Reef HQ

This excellent **aquarium** (Map p292; ☎ 4750 0800; www.reefhq.com.au; Flinders St E; adult/child/concession $19.50/9.50/15; 🕑 9am-5pm) houses many of the creatures and corals that live on the Great Barrier Reef. The complex delivers facts and figures through interpretive displays and touch-tanks, and allows you to experience a living coral reef with cruising sharks from behind a comforting thick wall of glass. Also in the huge main tank is an eerie replica of the *Yongala* wreck – the passenger ship that went down off the coast of Townsville in 1911, taking all 125 people with it. Sawfish and shovel-nosed rays show off their namesake facial features, and there are daily talks and tours that highlight particular aspects of the Reef. To maintain the natural conditions essential for the survival of this complex ecosystem, a wave machine simulates the ebb and flow of the ocean, circular currents keep the water in motion and marine algae are used in the purification system.

You can continue to experience life underwater without getting wet at the **IMAX cinema** (Map p292; ☎ 4721 1481; Flinders St E; adult/child/concession $14/8/12; 🕑 10.30am-4.30pm) next door. Its 18m-high screen and surround sound is enough to turn a person into a plankton.

Museum of Tropical Queensland

Instead of fusty old relics labelled behind glass, the **Museum of Tropical Queensland** (Map p292; ☎ 4726 0606; www.mtq.qld.gov.au; 70-102 Flinders St E; adult/child/student $9/5/6.50; 🕑 9.30am-5pm) attempts to reconstruct scenes by using detailed models with interactive displays. The wreck of the *Pandora* is showcased at the museum, including a replica of the ship with a giant topless Pandora straddling the bow. Other galleries include the kid-friendly science centre, displays on natural history and an exhibition of Aboriginal and Torres Strait Islander artefacts and culture.

Perc Tucker Regional Gallery

This **contemporary art gallery** (Map p292; ☎ 4727 9011; ptrg@townsville.qld.gov.au; cnr Denham St & Flinders St Mall; admission free; 🕑 10am-5pm Mon-Fri, 10am-2pm Sat & Sun), in a heritage corner building, has a packed schedule of exhibitions each year. Shows feature work by artists from overseas and interstate, though the focus is on north Queensland artists. On the annual calendar you might find a touring exhibition examining the continuing influence of the Pop Art movement, or a show of graduate works from James Cook Uni's visual art and photography departments.

Other Museums & Galleries

Pick up the free *Galleries & Museums Directory* brochure from the visitors centre, which lists venues, provides maps and gives a précis of the town's cultural collections. You might consider stopping at one of the following.

Answering all those burning questions, such as how they get those model ships inside bottles, and how to tie a reef knot, the **Townsville Maritime Museum** (Map p292; ☎ 4721 5251; www.townsvillemaritimemuseum.org.au; 42-68 Palmer St; adult/child/concession $5/2/4; 🕑 10am-4pm Mon-Fri, noon-4pm Sat & Sun) will entertain more than just your naval buffs. They'll be satisfied, too, with historical exhibits on northern Queensland's maritime and naval industries. And everyone loves a shipwreck story; there's a gallery dedicated to the wreck of the *Yongala*, which went down in a cyclone in 1911 with 125 passengers and wasn't located until 1958.

Umbrella Studio (Map p292; ☎ 4772 7817; www.umbrella.org.au; 482 Flinders St; admission free; ☟ 9am-5pm Mon-Fri, 9am-1pm Sun) has a dynamic calendar of shows that aim to make contemporary visual art accessible and engaging. Drop in to the studio, which also runs industry seminars, guest lectures and performance art with a range of practitioners; past participants include Tracey Moffat and Mike Parr.

You'll need photo ID to access the **North Queensland Military Museum** (Map p290; ☎ 4771 1043; Jezzine Army Barracks, Kissing Point; admission by donation; ☟ 9am-12.30pm Mon, Wed & Fri, 10am-2pm Sun) as it's in the grounds of the Jezzine Army Barracks. Apart from the military paraphernalia that's displayed in the old gun stores, there is a fabulous spot to perch, with picnic facilities and views over the water.

Three historic houses make up the **National Trust Heritage Centre** (Map p290; ☎ 4771 5873; 5-7 Castling St, West End; adult/child/concession $5/1.50/3; ☟ 10am-2pm Wed, 1-4pm Sat & Sun). The houses provide an insight into life in Townsville in the 19th and early 20th centuries. Castling St is 2km from the city centre along Ingham Rd. A block east is West End Cemetery, with graves dating from the 1880s.

Botanical Gardens

Townsville's Botanical Gardens are spread across three locations: each has its own character, but all have tropical plants and are abundantly green. They're open seven days from sunrise to sunset.

The **Queens Gardens** (Map p292; cnr Gregory & Paxton Sts) is 1km northwest of the town centre. These are the town's original gardens, which were first planted in 1870 with trial plants (including mango and coffee) to potentially boost the economy. They've since been thoroughly redesigned, after 100,000 US soldiers squatted on them during WWII. They're now formal, ornamental gardens at the base of Castle Hill, with a children's playground and herb garden.

Anderson Park (Gulliver St, Mundingburra), established in 1932, is 6km southwest of the centre. The large gardens cover a 20-hectare site and were originally planted in taxonomic lots. They feature plants and palms from northern Queensland and Cape York Peninsula, lotus ponds and a tropical-fruit

orchard. Don't be tempted to eat the fruits of the garden – no matter how enticing that Miracle Fruit sounds.

The **Palmetum** (University Rd), about 15km southwest of the centre, is a 17-hectare garden devoted to just one plant family – the humble palm. More than 300 species are represented here, including around 60 that are native to Australia.

ACTIVITIES

Apart from the strolls and swimming along the Strand, which are incidental to any visit to Townsville, there are a few formal guided activities to enrich your experience of the area.

City slickers looking for a quintessential country experience must join the cattle muster at **Woodstock Trail Rides** (☎ 4778 8888; Flinders Hwy; rides $120). For one day you can help move 'em in and brand their hides raw, eat a camp-cooked lunch and down a cold beer at day's end; the price includes transfers to and from Townsville. Trail rides and an overnight bush camp are also possible.

Coral Sea Skydivers (Map p292; ☎ 4772 4889; www.coralseaskydivers.com.au; 181 Flinders St E; tandem from $290) will assist you to throw yourself from a plane. The tandem jump requires no prior knowledge; just a lot of guts (but not too much: there's a weight limit of 95kg).

Talk about shooting fish in a barrel; at **Barra Fishing** (☎ 0419-739 442; www.barrafishing.net; Allambie Lane, Kelso; tickets $35) you can throw a line in at the fish farm. Rod hire is $3, and if you want to keep your catch, it costs extra.

Dive Courses

Two operators based in Townsville offer PADI-certified courses, where you'll learn to dive with two days' training in the pool, plus three days and three nights living aboard the boat. Dive sites include a number of reefs, as well as the SS *Yongala* wreck. (In addition to the operator costs you'll need to obtain a dive medical and passport photos.) Try **Pro Dive** (Map p292; ☎ 4721 1760; www.prodivetownsville.com.au; 14 Plume St, South Townsville; courses from $645) or **Diving Dreams** (Map p292; ☎ 4721 2500; www.divingdreams.com; 252 Walker St; courses from $595), which has a choice of sites.

TOURS

Take a slow coach tour with **Day Tours** (☎ 4728 5311), which goes to Hinchinbrook Island

($125), the rainforest and waterfalls of Mt Spec National Park ($85) and the historic mining town of Charters Towers ($85). **Tropical Tours** (☎ 4721 6489; www.townsvilletropicaltours .com.au) covers the region with day tours including the option of a waterfall-shower at Paluma Range National Park ($120) and ye olde Charters Towers ($130).

Great Barrier Reef

The **Barrier Reef Dive Cruise & Travel** (Map p292; ☎ 4772 5800; www.divecruisetravel.com) booking agent is part of the Flinders St Mall visitors centre; it has a comprehensive list of operators and offers. Most trips travel to the Reef as well as the famous *Yongala* wreck – the sunken passenger ship that has created an artificial reef.

The following operators run trips to the Great Barrier Reef; trips include lunch and snorkelling. If you do want to just snorkel, take a day trip that just goes to the Reef; the *Yongala* is for diving only. Multiday liveaboards are the best option for divers, with some operators offering advanced courses.

Adrenalin Dive (☎ 4724 0600; www.adrenalindive .com.au; 121 Flinders St E) *Yongala* day trips including two dives (from $180); also offers advanced diving certification courses.

Coral Princess (☎ 4721 1673; www.coralprincess .com.au; per person from $1270; ⏰ 12.30pm Tue) Offers a four-day cruise between Townsville and Cairns, via Hinchinbrook and Dunk Islands.

Diving Dreams (☎ 4721 2500; www.divingdreams .com) Day trip to the *Yongala* (from $175) as well as advanced dive courses.

Remote Area Dive (☎ 4775 4000; www.remotearea dive.com; 229 Charters Towers Rd) Dive trips to Orpheus and Pelorus Islands, overnighting on the islands in safari-style tents (from $425 including meals and transfers).

Sunferries (☎ 1800 447 333; www.sunferries.com.au; Sir Leslie Thiess Dr) Day trips to the Reef (from $140); add $70 to include a certified or introductory dive.

Tropical Diving (Map p292; ☎ 1800 776 150; www .tropicaldiving.com.au; 14 Palmer St) Day trips to the Reef (from $130), certified dives $60, introductory dives $60.

SLEEPING
Budget

Quite a few caravan parks are strung along the Bruce Hwy to the north and south of Townsville. There are three hostels on Palmer St, along the southern side of Ross Creek, close to the transit centre, restaurants and cafés; it's a short walk across the

river to the city centre. Townsville's other hostels are on the northern side of Ross Creek, in and around the city centre.

Great Northern Hotel (Map p292; ☎ 4771 6191; fax 4771 6190; 496 Flinders St; s/d $35/45; ☒) The rickety air-con and daggy '70s décor are to be adored at this charismatic hotel. The faded vinyl floor tiles and heavy bedhead-cum-storage units fixed to the wall imbue a holiday-house frivolity to the place. All rooms have bathrooms; ask for a room that opens out to the broad encircling veranda. Downstairs in the pub there are nightly bistro specials ($6). Come for the Aussie pub culture, not just because it's cheap.

Civic Guest House (Map p292; ☎ 1800 646 619, 4771 5381; www.backpackersinn.com.au; 262 Walker St; dm $20, s $39-43, d & tw $42-48, with bathroom $60; ☒ ☒) Behind the palms and bushes bursting out of the cyclone-wire fence is this converted home. Easy-going and sedate, this hostel hosts a free BBQ for guests on Friday night and offers deals with the dive school next door. The pricier rooms have air-con, and dorms sleep four to six.

Coral Lodge B&B (Map p292; ☎ 1800 614 613, 4771 5512; www.corallodge.com.au; 32 Hale St; s/d $60/70; ☒) This quaint old Queenslander has two self-contained units upstairs (single/double $65/75) and eight guest rooms downstairs that share a bathroom and nifty communal kitchen. It's a good-value, quiet place with lots of ornate character, such as lace and floral flourishes. There's a garden area framed by ferns and vines, and a continental breakfast is included in the tariff.

Globetrotters Hostel (Map p292; ☎ 1800 008 533, 4771 3242; globetrotters@austranet.com.au; 45 Palmer St; dm $20-21, r with/without bathroom $60/50; ☒ ☐ ☒) This comfortable hostel offers rooms in an old house, as well as in a newer building behind. You'll share the outdoor pool area with tropical palms and flowering creepers. Rooms are functional, with coin-operated air-con, and the dorms sleep six. This is a good choice if you're travelling on a budget but that doesn't necessarily entail full-moon parties and big boozy nights; Globetrotters is a quieter option.

Reef Lodge (Map p292; ☎ 4721 1112; www.reef lodge.com.au; 4-6 Wickham St; dm $17-19, r $42, motel r $58; ☒ ☐) The idea here is that you'll be out at the town's pubs just on the Lodge's doorstep, so the small rooms don't matter. Ramshackle rooms are clustered around a concrete courtyard, and you can pull up a seat streetside at the Lodge's attached Internet café.

Base Backpackers (Map p292; ☎ 1800 628 836, 4721 2322; www.basebackpackers.com; 21 Plume St; dm/d $21/60; 🛇 🖳) Base has fairly basic rooms and facilities, but includes that all-important one – the inhouse bar. After sipping on a bright, alcoholic fizzy drink, you could get lost in the maze of corridors here. Base is above the transit centre and convenient to the bus and ferry terminals.

Adventurers Resort (Map p292; ☎ 4721 1522; www.adventurersresort.com; 79 Palmer St; dm/s $20/32, d $42-48; 🛇 🖳 🖭) The multilevel Adventurers has better-than-average facilities, with bike hire (per day $8), a big industrial kitchen and a small shop to sate those sudden urges for chocolate. Lazing around the rooftop pool will make you feel like a celebrity, though the windowless rooms may have you clambering for air throughout the night.

Rowes Bay Caravan Park (Map p290; ☎ 4771 3576; fax 4724 2017; Heatley Pde, Rowes Bay; unpowered/powered sites $12.50/23, cabins $55-76; 🖭) The leafy grounds, with a pool and shop, are opposite the grass flats of Soroptimist's Park and the beautiful Rowes Bay foreshore, about 3km north of the city centre. This place is often full during peak holiday periods, particularly the cabin accommodation.

Midrange

Rocks (Map p292; ☎ 4771 5700; www.therocksguesthouse.com; 20 Cleveland Tce; s/d $100/120; 🛇 🖳) This boutique B&B beautifully balances personal service and professionalism, with a daub of theatrics. Antique furnishings and period pieces set the stage in the drawing room – where you can take your six o'clock sherry as though it really were the 1930s. This historic home features lavish furnishings, an outdoor spa and a huge balcony from which you gaze out to Magnetic Island. There is wheelchair access, and breakfast is included.

Beach House Motel (Map p290; ☎ 4721 1333; www.beachhousemotel.com.au; 66 The Strand; s/d $86/96; 🛇 🖭) Louvred windows usher in the sea breeze from Cleveland Bay, which is just out the front of these modern motel rooms. Big bathrooms, spacious sleeping quarters and cheerful décor are a feature here. Rooms are well equipped with all the modern conveniences, such as a bar fridge,

phone and TV, as well as a few more traditional ones, such as a bedside Bible.

Shoredrive Motel (Map p290; ☎ 4771 6851; fax 4772 6311; 117 The Strand; s/d $72/82; 🛇 🖭) The 30 units here are dispersed across a two-storey building with a coveted Strand address. The functional rooms include a kettle and TV, and there's a restaurant and laundry on the premises. Shoredrive is good for families, with the protected rock pool a beach ball's bounce away.

Historic Yongala Lodge Motel (Map p292; ☎ 4772 4633; www.historicyongala.com.au; 11 Fryer St; motel r $100-110, units from $115; 🛇 🖭) When they decided to use 'historic' in this motel's name, they probably weren't referring to the '80s décor. Still, it was a comfortable decade, and so are these rooms; most of which have heritage-style fittings. Self-contained units are also available, and there's a restaurant on the premises that's licensed and open for breakfast and dinner.

Townsville Seaside Apartments (Map p290; ☎ 4721 3155; www.townsvilleseaside.com.au; 105 The Strand; studios $75, 1-/2-bed units $85/120; 🛇 🖭) In a strip of renovated 1960s apartments, these dowdy units won't win any interior-design prizes, but they're comfortable and fully equipped with kitchens. Prices vary according to the season and the number of people, and there's a two-night minimum stay.

Holiday Inn (Map p292; ☎ 4772 2477; www.townsville.holiday-inn.com; 334 Flinders St Mall; r $116-128; 🛇 🖭) There's usually little to distinguish these international hotels, but you can't miss this one. The 'sugar shaker' is a prominent fixture of Townsville's skyline – a 20-storey circular building in the city's mall housing 197 rooms. Guests have free use of a gym, can order room service and wake up to a free newspaper slipped under the door. You can also pay a premium for a room with a view.

Strand Park Hotel (Map p292; ☎ 4750 7888; www.strandparkhotel.com.au; 59-60 The Strand; r $115-145; 🛇 🖭) This waterfront complex houses 30 self-contained units. Your standard room is situated on the ground floor, moving up, literally, to the superior and deluxe rooms with ocean views, balconies and perhaps a spa. The Strand Hotel is at the end of the Strand, and has a decent restaurant, Naked Fish (opposite).

Quest Townsville (Map p292; ☎ 4772 6477; www.questapartments.com.au; 30-4 Palmer St; apt from $130; 🛇 🖭) This high-rise apartment complex houses hundreds of happy holidaymakers in its studio apartments. Rooms are serviced daily and are fully self-contained. Families are also catered for with one- and two-bedroom apartments and a babysitting service.

Quality Hotel Southbank (Map p292; ☎ 4726 5265; www.southbankhotel.com.au; 23 Palmer St; r from $105; ✕ ☐ ☒) The handsome rooms at this hotel cater mostly to business travellers, with practical, unfussy interiors; there are also separate meeting rooms available. Those here on holiday will also appreciate the hotel's facilities, and whatever your reason for visiting, you'll love the opulent executive rooms with lounge rooms and ocean views.

Bayside (Map p290; ☎ 4721 1688; fax 4724 1231; 102 The Strand; r $105; ✕ ☒) The '70s brick exterior of this apartment complex belies the relative comfort of the one- and two-bedroom units inside. Bayside's position opposite the beach makes it good value.

Up the hill overlooking town are two sister motel complexes, **Summit** (Map p292; ☎ 4721 2122; www.summitmotel.com.au; 6-8 Victoria St; r $95; ✕) and **Ridgemont** (Map p292; ☎ 4771 2164; www.ridgemont.com.au; 15-19 Victoria St; r $105; ✕).

Top End
Mariners North (Map p292; ☎ 4722 0777; www.marinersnorth.com.au; 7 Mariners Dr; apt from $165; ✕ ☒) In the breakwater of the marina, this soaring apartment complex provides spectacular views of the traffic out in Cleveland Bay. The two-bedroom, two-bathroom apartments sleep up to four adults and two children, and have fully equipped kitchens and laundries. Guests have free reign over the complex's tennis court and BBQ facilities.

City Oasis Inn (Map p292; ☎ 1800 809 515, 4771 6048; www.cityoasis.com.au; 143 Wills St; r $170-200; ✕ ☒) There are so many sparkling white surfaces that you'll have to allow time for your eyes to adjust upon entering. The fabulous loft apartments here have an upstairs bedroom separate from the downstairs kitchen, or you can opt for even more space between you and the kids by going for the two-bedroom apartments. There's a restaurant, children's playground and laundry facilities on the premises.

Aquarius on the Beach (Map p290; ☎ 1800 622 474, 4772 4255; www.aquariusonthebeach.com.au; 75 The Strand; r $150-175; ✕ ☒) If size matters, then the Aquarius will impress: the tallest build-

ing on the Strand has more than 130 self-contained units, all with great views, mod cons and kitchenettes. All rooms are serviced daily, and staff are smilingly obliging.

EATING
For an honest meal in casual surrounds head to one of Townsville's pubs (see p298). Wherever you go, the seafood is usually sublime.

Restaurants
C Bar (Map p292; ☎ 4724 0333; Gregory St Headland; meals $12-16; ✆ breakfast, lunch & dinner) Everything tastes better with views like this. From the broad outdoor deck on the waterfront, an ordinary pannini takes on extraordinary qualities, and sausages and mash become 'gourmet sausages and mash'. Drag yourself inside to order and pay at the counter at this good-looking licensed restaurant.

Naked Fish (Map p292; ☎ 4724 4623; 60 The Strand; mains $18-24; ✆ dinner Mon-Sat) The ocean inspiration in the menu at Naked Fish spills over into the décor, with cool green-blue walls and a starry ceiling. Apart from seafood, the extensive menu includes Cajun and Moroccan dishes, tempura and risotto. Naked Fish has some outdoor seating beneath the giant strangled fig, and is licensed.

Benny's Hot Wok Café & Bar (Map p292; ☎ 4724 3243; 17-21 Palmer St; mains $15-20; ✆ lunch Thu, Fri & Sun, dinner Tue-Sun) Take a streetside seat amid the concrete Buddha statue and palms, or glide across the shiny floor to find a seat inside. Benny's exudes funky Asian ambience and offers a fusion of Japanese, Thai and Chinese cuisine. You might try the sizzling honey-pepper steak or the salt-and-pepper calamari. Benny's is licensed with a good range of wines and beers.

Bistro 1 (Map p292; ☎ 4771 6333; 30-4 Palmer St; mains $19-24; ✆ breakfast, lunch & dinner) While there is outdoor seating at Bistro 1, the big bifold doors on either wall bring the outside in. This licensed casual place offers café fare, with a kids menu and wood-fired pizza: try the pumpkin with pine nuts and three cheeses. Mains include Thai fish curry and baked chicken breast on garlic mash.

Scirocco (Map p292; ☎ 4724 4508; 61 Palmer St; mains $16-21; ✆ breakfast, lunch & dinner Tue-Sat, breakfast & lunch Sun) For something a little more refined, try Scirocco. Its high ceilings and motif-painted walls present an understated sophistication that's also present in the service and food. You might try the pickled beetroot and goat's cheese risotto, and for dessert, a lime and pineapple tart with coconut ice cream. A good selection of wines is available by the glass.

Yotz (Map p292; ☎ 4724 5488; Gregory St Headland, The Strand; mains $23-26; ☙ lunch & dinner) Linen-covered tables and walls painted in Gauguin-inspired colours create a frisky ambience at this bar and grill. There's an outside area where you can smoke Cuban cigars ($5 to $25), or just look at the panoramic views of the harbour and Magnetic Island. The menu includes double-baked sandcrab soufflé and mushroom angel-hair noodles, as well as a range of Australian wines.

Rhino Bar (Map p292; ☎ 4771 6322; 3 Palmer St; mains $15-29; ☙ dinner) This slick loungy place has a long bar along one wall, where you can turn your back on the diners and focus on your vodkatini. Food is limited to breads and tapas, as well as steak. Good-looking staff and clean-cut décor make it hard to ignore this newcomer to the Palmer St scene.

Taj Mahal (Map p292; ☎ 4772 3422; 235 Flinders St E; mains around $15; ☙ lunch & dinner) This BYO Indian-Persian restaurant has loads of vegetarian options, as well as a range of meat dishes. The speciality is the chicken tandoori, which is so potent it'll stain your lips orange. Cool things down with a sticky rose-flavoured dessert. The décor is lovely and rich, with rugs and hookahs. Takeaway is also available.

Cafés & Quick Eats

Ladah (Map p292; ☎ 4724 0402; cnr Sturt & Stanley Sts; lunch $7-10; ☙ breakfast & lunch Mon-Fri & Sun) This is a fabulous casual city café. Seating is on chocolate- and cream-coloured cubes scattered on the polished-wood floors. Come for breakfast: perhaps rice porridge, granola or raisin toast with smashed banana and brown sugar. The coffee is good, and there's a range of sweet and savoury muffins, cakes and tarts ($3.50 to $4).

C'est Si Bon (Map p292; ☎ 4772 5828; 48 Gregory St; meals $8-15; ☙ breakfast & lunch) Order your quiche, bagel or breakfast at the counter, then find a seat along the communal table that runs the length of this large café. Polished concrete floors, brushed steel and wood furnishings provide a pared-back ambience that's warmed slightly by the jazzy

tunes that drift out of the speakers. C'est Si Bon is licensed, but has good nonalcoholic drinks too, such as San Pelegrino and Tiro.

Harold's Seafood (Map p292; ☎ 4724 1322; cnr The Strand & Gregory St; fish boxes $6.50; ☙ lunch & dinner) Frying up all your favourites, this is a superb fish-and-chip joint. It has a window full of prawns that are ready to go: wait for a side of chips then scurry over to the waterfront to tear off their heads and legs…mmmm.

Gregory's (Map p292; ☎ 4772 0553; 48 Gregory St; dishes $5-9; ☙ breakfast & lunch) This bright little café has fresh juices, Lavazza coffee, eggs any way, and banana-and-date loaf for breakfast. It's solid, healthy fare, and there's outdoor seating. After you've ordered at the counter, find a seat and the friendly staff will find you; it's hard to miss you sitting there with a pineapple on a stick – which is what you're given instead of a number; that or an apple, an eggplant, kiwi fruit…

Blue Bottle Cafe (Map p292; ☎ 4771 2121; cnr Gregory St & The Strand; mains $22-26; ☙ brunch & lunch Mon-Sat, dinner Tue-Sat) Almost on the waterfront, but well within the path of sea breezes and the Strand foot traffic, Blue Bottle was born into a good area. Its large homely interior is the setting for comfort food: go for the specials such as stuffed chicken breast or confit of duck. Lunch is mostly wraps and rolls, and there's a brunch menu starring the humble egg. Blue Bottle is licensed.

Chilli Jam Noodle Bar (Map p292; ☎ 4721 5199; 211 Flinders St E; meals $9-11; ☙ dinner) This peppy place does noodles (udon, egg and rice) in soup or fried, served hot and cold. There are a few outdoor tables or you can sit in the brightly lit interior. It's relaxed and licensed, and does takeaway too.

DRINKING

Many of Townsville's multitalented pubs and bars also serve decent food. Most of the action is along Flinders St and winds down between 1am and 3am.

Brewery (Map p292; ☎ 4724 9999; 242 Flinders St E; meals $11-15; ☙ lunch & dinner) This crowd-pleasing place in the gorgeous old post-office building is an all-in-one venue that contains a sports bar, nightclub, bistro and brewery. An after-work crew crowd the outdoor deck, with hearty bistro meals available between drinks. You might try one of the Brewery's own: Ned's Red Ale or Lager Lout, as well as seasonal brews such as chilli beer, apple-wheat beer and the winning Belgian blonde. The sports bar down the back caters to arm-chair sportspeople, with 17 TVs and an assortment of sporting paraphernalia.

Embassy (Map p292; ☎ 4724 5000; 13 Sturt St; mains $24-27) This sophisticated bunker in the business district of town is velvety smooth. Dress smart and come for the tantalising meals on offer, or stride in later for the DJ who spins funk and house vinyl. Embassy's downstairs location, split-level interior, subdued lighting and effortless chic imbue it with an in-the-know ambience.

Molly Malones (Map p292; ☎ 4771 3428; 87 Flinders St E; meals $7-10; ☺ lunch Mon-Fri, dinner nightly) This good-looking Irish pub serves wrist-snapping plates of food, such as rissoles and mash, and Irish stew. Or consume the equivalent of a week's worth of required iron in the steak accompanied by a Guinness. Molly's has a discreet gaming area, stages live music most nights and has a nightclub out the back called Mantaz.

Heritage Café 'n' Bar (Map p292; ☎ 4771 2799; 137 Flinders St; meals $28-24; ☺ lunch & dinner) The Heritage is reminiscent of a wine bar, with a sedate ambience. The seafood-heavy menu is displayed along one wall; the prices are a bit heavy too. There's a large outdoor seating pen that holds an after-work crowd, which lingers on well into the night.

Cloud 10 Oxygen Bar (Map p292; ☎ 4724 0202; Shop C, 194 Flinders St E; 5min & 3 flavours $7.50) 'Death by chocolate', 'sex on the beach' and 'fuzzy navel' are all oxygen 'cocktails'. While it's not strictly drinking, people hit this oxygen bar before they hit the other bars – testing the promise that inhaling pure oxygen will offset a pending hangover.

Seaview (Map p292; ☎ 4771 5005; cnr The Strand & Gregory Sts) It seems the entire population jams into the huge concrete courtyard at the Seaview on a Sunday, when there's live music and entertainment.

Mad Cow Tavern (Map p292; ☎ 4771 5727; 129 Flinders St E) Although it seems there are more bouncers than patrons at the Mad Cow, it does have its supporters – mostly heralding from the military.

ENTERTAINMENT

If you fancy a flick, **BC Cinemas** (Map p292; ☎ 4771 4101; cnr Sturt & Blackwood Sts) screens mainstream films.

For a flutter head to **Jupiters Casino** (Map p292; ☎ 4722 2333; Sir Leslie Thiess Dr), which signals for attention with its neon faux fireworks.

Nightclubs
Licensed until 5am, Townsville's clubs pick up from where the bars leave off.

Bank Niteclub (Map p292; ☎ 4771 6148; 169 Flinders St E; admission $5; ☺ closed Sun) House and dance beats; slinky surrounds.

Brewery Club (Map p292; ☎ 4724 2999; 242 Flinders St E; Fri & Sat) Resident DJ spins dance and progressive house, as well as beats and breaks.

Mantaz Club & Bar (Map p292; ☎ 4771 3428; 87 Flinders St; ☺ Fri & Sat) Behind Molly Malones.

Playpen (☎ 4721 5555; cnr Flinders St W & Knapp St; admission $6 after 10pm) Multilevel place with dance downstairs, and pool tables.

SHOPPING

Cotters Market (Flinders St Mall; ☺ 8.30am-1pm Sun) has about 200 craft and food stalls, as well as live entertainment; it's wheelchair accessible. There's also a night market along the Strand on the first Friday of the month from May to December.

John Melick & Co (Map p292; ☎ 4771 2292; 481 Flinders St) is the place to go for a good range of camping and bushwalking gear, Driza-a-Bone oilskins, Akubra hats, boots and workwear.

GETTING THERE & AWAY
Air
Virgin Blue (☎ 13 67 89; www.virginblue.com.au) and **Qantas** (☎ 13 13 13; www.qantas.com.au) – and its subsidiaries – fly from Townsville to all the major cities, at least daily. Following are ballpark fares for flights from Townsville to: Brisbane ($130, 1¾ hours), Sydney (via Brisbane $170, three hours), Melbourne ($240, 3¾ hours), Perth ($290, 11 hours), Adelaide ($260, 4½ hours), Canberra (via Brisbane $250, 2¾ hours) and Hobart (via Brisbane $250, 4¾ hours).

Bus
The long-distance bus station is at **Townsville Transit Centre** (Map p292; ☎ 4721 3082; transit tsv@bigpond.com.au; cnr Palmer & Plume Sts). You'll find agents for the major companies, including **Transit Centre Backpackers** (☎ 4721 2322), who are agents for Premier Motor Service.

Also in the transit centre is **Greyhound Australia** (☎ 13 20 30, 4772 5100; www.greyhound.com.au;

Townsville Transit Centre, cnr Palmer & Plume Sts), with services at least daily to Brisbane ($175, 23 hours), Rockhampton ($100, 11 hours), Airlie Beach ($55, four hours), Mission Beach ($50, four hours) and Cairns ($55, six hours). There's also a daily service to Charters Towers ($30, one hour 40 minutes) continuing to the Northern Territory.

Car

The larger car-rental agencies are all represented in Townsville:

Avis (☎ 1300 137 498, 4721 2688; www.avis.com.au; 81 Flinders St) Also has an airport counter.

Europcar (☎ 1300 131 390, 4762 7050; www.delta europcar.com.au; 305 Ingham Rd, Garbutt) Also has an airport counter and rents 4WDs.

Hertz (☎ 13 30 30, 4775 5950; www.hertz.com; Stinson Ave, Garbutt)

Thrifty (☎ 4725 4600; www.thrifty.com.au; 289 Ingham Rd, Garbutt)

Train

The train station and **Queensland Rail Travel Centre** (☎ 4772 8358; www.traveltrain.qr.com.au; 502 Flinders St; ☺ 9am-5pm Mon-Fri, 1-4.30pm Sat, 8.30am-4.15pm Sun, closed for lunch) are about 1km south of the centre.

The Brisbane to Cairns *Sunlander* travels through Townsville four times a week. Prices quoted here are for one-way adult fares. From Brisbane to Townsville takes 24 hours (economy seat/sleeper $165/215, 1st-class sleeper $340). Proserpine is four hours from Townsville (economy seat $58), Rockhampton is 11 hours (economy seat $110) and Cairns is 7½ hours (economy seat $60). The more luxurious Queenslander class, which includes a sleeper and meals, is available on two services per week.

The *Inlander* heads from Townsville to Mt Isa on Wednesday and Sunday (economy seat/sleeper $110/165, 1st-class sleeper $255, 20 hours) via Charters Towers (economy seat $23, three hours).

GETTING AROUND
To/From the Airport

Townsville airport is 5km northwest of the city centre at Garbutt. A taxi to the centre costs about $20. **Abacus Tours** (☎ 4775 5544) operates a shuttle servicing all Qantas and Virgin arrivals and departures; if you arrive after 11pm you'll need to book. The one-way/return fare is $8/14, and it will drop off/pick up anywhere within the central business district.

Bus

Sunbus (☎ 4725 8482; www.sunbus.com.au) runs local bus services around Townsville. Route maps and timetables are available at the visitors centre in Flinders St Mall and at the newsagent in the Transit Mall (Map p292).

Car

Townsville Car Rentals (Map p292; ☎ 4772 1093; 12 Palmer St, South Townsville) hires small cars, bikes and scooters.

Taxis congregate outside the Transit Mall, or call **Townsville Taxis** (☎ 13 10 08, 4778 9555).

MAGNETIC ISLAND

☎ 07 / pop 2500

Not long after stepping ashore at lovely Magnetic Island, you'll slip into its easy-going attitude and lazier pace of life. The four tiny beach villages here offer few distractions, but there are some excellent bushwalks, and with a little effort you can have a tropical beach all to yourself.

Even at its busiest Magnetic is relatively quiet, with holidaymakers dispersed over a dozen bays, and sailing boats stopping in occasionally as they travel up and down the coast on the Trade Winds. 'Maggie' is almost a suburb of Townsville; it has a suburban atmosphere but with a pretty spectacular backyard. The island is steadily and gradually being developed – with construction of a shopping complex and marina underway at Nelly Bay and a waterfront facelift at Picnic Bay (the bandages have probably not long been lifted by the time you read this), but Magnetic remains unpretentious. Families splash about in the bays, and it's OK to wear a terry-towelling hat and flip-flops to dinner.

Magnetic's natural environment is certainly attractive. Giant granite boulders, hoop pines and eucalypts cover the island, which is half national park and a haven for rock wallabies, bats and brushtail possums. Birdlife bursts out of the bush, with curlew darting about the streets like mini roadrunners, and brush turkeys foraging in any leaf litter. The surrounding waters are also part of the precious Great Barrier Reef World Heritage Area. Captain Cook named Mag-

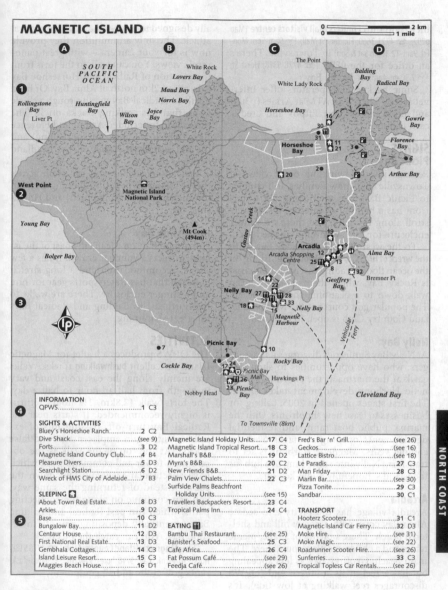

MAGNETIC ISLAND

0 ————— 2 km
0 ————— 1 mile

SOUTH PACIFIC OCEAN

White Rock
Lovers Bay
Maud Bay
Norris Bay

The Point
White Lady Rock

Balding Bay
Radical Bay

Rollingstone Bay
Liver Pt
Huntingfield Bay
Wilson Bay
Joyce Bay

Horseshoe Bay

Gowrie Bay

Horseshoe Bay

Florence Bay

Arthur Bay

West Point

Magnetic Island National Park

Young Bay

Bolger Bay

Mt Cook (494m)

Gustav Creek

Arcadia
Arcadia Shopping Centre

Alma Bay

Bremner Pt

Geoffrey Bay

Nelly Bay

Nelly Bay

Magnetic Harbour

Vehicular Ferry

Picnic Bay

Cockle Bay

Rocky Bay

Picnic Bay Mall

Hawkings Pt

Nobby Head

Picnic Bay

Cleveland Bay

To Townsville (8km)

TOWNSVILLE & NORTH COAST

netic Island in 1770, when his ship's compass went peculiar as he sailed by; if only he had known what he was missing.

ORIENTATION & INFORMATION

Magnetic Island is easy and cheap to get to, being only 8km from Townsville. It's roughly triangular in shape. A sealed road follows the east coast for 10km from Picnic Bay, on the island's southern point, to Horseshoe Bay in the north. A local bus ploughs the route regularly. There's a rough 8km track along the west coast leading from Picnic Bay to a secluded beach at West Point.

All passenger ferries dock at Nelly Bay, where a visitors centre is planned; until then, pop into **Flinders Mall visitors centre** (Map p292; ☎ 4721 3660; Flinders St Mall; ☺ 9am-5pm Mon-Fri, 9am-12.30pm Sat & Sun) in Townsville. There's an office for the **QPWS** (☎ 4778 5378; Hurst St; ☺ 7.30am-4pm) at Picnic Bay.

Some backpacker operators offer Internet access. There's an ATM at Arkies (p304) and most places have Eftpos and credit-card facilities.

SIGHTS
Picnic Bay
Perhaps it's the twinkling night views of Townsville that draw families and couples to Picnic Bay. The mall along the waterfront has a handful of eateries, it's a lovely stroll along the jetty, and there's a stinger enclosure for safe swimming on the beach.

To the west of town is Cockle Bay, with the **wreck of HMS City of Adelaide** languishing on the ocean floor. Heading east round the coast is Rocky Bay, where there's a short, steep walk down to a beautiful, sheltered beach. The popular golf course at the Magnetic Island Country Club is open to the public.

Nelly Bay
At Nelly Bay Sunferries disgorges its passengers, who have opportunities to shop and gawk at the marina as the enormous Magnetic Harbour development takes shape. The first stages opened in 2005, calling for businesses to lease new shopfronts, with the marina, public boat ramp and residential developments opening in stages over the coming years. Magnetic Harbour is set to transform Nelly into something of a hub for the island – hopefully a low-key one.

Arcadia
Arcadia village has the pretty and sedate Alma Bay cove, with a grassy hill and sheltered beach. There's plenty of shade, picnic tables and a children's playground here. The main beach, Geoffrey Bay, is less appealing but has a reef at its southern end (QPWS discourages reef walking at low tide). It's also the access point for the car ferry, but this may change as Nelly Bay develops. There are a number of places to stay in Arcadia as well as a few shops and eateries.

Radical Bay & The Forts
Townsville was a supply base for the Pacific during WWII, and the **forts** were strategic-ally designed to protect the town from naval attack. The only ammunition they provide now is for your camera – with great panoramic views. You can walk to the forts from the junction of Radical and Horseshoe Bay Rds, about 2km north of Alma Bay. Or head north to Radical Bay via the rough vehicle track that has walking tracks off it. The tracks lead to secluded Arthur and Florence Bays (which are great for snorkelling) and the old **searchlight station** on the headland between the two.

From Radical Bay you can walk across the headland to beautiful Balding Bay (an unofficial nude-bathing beach) and Horseshoe Bay.

Horseshoe Bay
Horseshoe Bay, on the north coast of the island, attracts a younger crowd. It has a few shops, accommodation and a long stretch of beach that has water-sports gear for hire and a stinger enclosure. There are walks to the northeast to Balding and Radical Bays for great swimming.

ACTIVITIES
The QPWS produces a leaflet for Magnetic Island's excellent **bushwalking** tracks. Walks are mainly along the east coast and vary in length from half an hour to half a day. The forts walk (2.8km, 1½ hours return) is highly recommended. It starts near the Radical Bay turn-off, passing lots of ex-military sites, gun emplacements and false 'rocks'. At the top of the walk is the observation tower and command post, which have spectacular views up and down the coast. Instead of returning the same way, you can continue on along the connecting paths, which run past Radical and Balding Bays, eventually depositing you at Horseshoe Bay. You can catch the bus back.

The **Magnetic Island Country Club** (☎ 4778 5188; Hurst St, Picnic Bay; 9/18 holes $14/20; ☺ dawn-dusk) rents golf clubs and all equipment.

Diving
Learn to dive with **Pleasure Divers** (☎ 4778 5788; www.magnetic-island.com.au/plsr-divers; 10 Marine Pde, Arcadia; 3-/4-day PADI open-water courses from $220/340) or **Dive Shack** (☎ 4778 5690; www.diveshack.com.au; Shop 2, Marine Pde, Arcadia; PADI open-water courses from $250), which also runs advanced courses and dive trips to the *Yongala*.

Sunferries (Map p292; ☎ 1800 447 333; www.sunferries.com.au; Sir Leslie Thiess Dr, Townsville) and **Tropical Diving** (Map p292; ☎ 1800 776 150; www.tropicaldiving.com.au; 14 Palmer St, Townsville) run day trips (around $200 including snorkelling and one dive) from Townsville that pick up at Magnetic on their way out to the Reef.

TOURS

See opposite for dive operators that run trips to the outer reef.

Barnacle Bill (☎ 4758 1237; tours per person $50) Bill knows the sea like the bristles on his beard; all gear is included on this two-hour fishing tour out of Horseshoe Bay.

Bluey's Horseshoe Ranch (☎ 4778 5109; 38 Gifford St, Horseshoe Bay; rides per person $70) Offers two-hour rides taking you through bush to the beach, where you can swim your horse.

Jazza Sailing Tours (☎ 4758 1887; www.jazza.com.au; day trips $95) For snorkelling trips; offers a day trip on a 42ft yacht that includes boom netting and seafood lunch.

Magnetic Island Sea Kayaks (☎ 4778 5424; www.seakayak.com.au; 93 Horseshoe Bay Rd; tours from $60) Has four-hour tours departing Horseshoe Bay and paddling to Balding Bay and back; includes brekky.

Reef EcoTours (☎ 0419-712 579; www.reefecotours.com; tours adult/child $60/50) For a 1½-hour guided snorkel that's suitable for families.

Tropicana Tours (☎ 4758 1800; www.tropicanatours.com.au; full-day tours $135) If you're time poor, this full-day tour with well-informed guides takes in the island's best spots in its stretch 4WD. Enjoy close encounters with wildlife, nibbles and wine at sunset on West Point and chummy karaoke on the way home.

SLEEPING

Rates for a bed on Magnetic change with the seasons. You're likely to find cheaper rates outside the high season, on standby or with a multinight stay. Choose from backpackers, budget resorts or B&Bs.

If you're planning on staying more than a few days, **First National Real Estate** (☎ 4778 5077; www.magneticislandfn.com.au; 21 Marine Pde, Arcadia) manages some great places, as does **About Town Real Estate** (☎ 4778 5570; www.magneticislandrealestate.com; Shop 4, 5 Bright Ave, Arcadia). Rates range from $80 to $200 per night, and accommodation ranges from apartments to homes that sleep up to seven.

Picnic Bay

Magnetic Island Holiday Units (☎ 4778 5246; 16 Yule St; d $94; ✷ ▣ ▣) These self-contained units are homely – in the nicest possible way.

The units are tightly spaced, set amid a leafy garden and manicured lawn. Apart from the one-bedroom units, two-bedders are also available for $110; any more than two people costs $10 per night per person.

Travellers Backpackers Resort (☎ 1800 000 290, 4778 5166; travellers@getonit.net.au; 1 The Esplanade; dm $12-20, r with/without bathroom $55/46; ✷ ▣ ▣) We hope that you can find your way out of this enormous complex with rooms across several buildings. It's basic, but at least you know there'll always be a bed; dorms sleep from four to six. There's a pub and bistro that are part of the complex, as well as a concrete outdoor courtyard and crocodile…uh huh!

Tropical Palms Inn (☎ 1800 777 076, 4778 5076; tropicalpalmsinn@hotmail.com; 34 Picnic St; s/d $85/92; ✷ ▣) These bright rooms could be described as motel-style, without the drive-to-your-door facility. But few people have cars on Magnetic, so that shouldn't be a problem. And if you did want a car, you can hire one here. All rooms have a sink, microwave and TV to keep you semi-self-contained.

Nelly Bay

Gembhala Cottages (☎ 4778 5435; 28 Mango Parkway; d from $90; ✷ ▣) The pathway to these Balinese-inspired cottages passes through a flourishing lantern-lit tropical garden that's trafficked by butterflies. Inside, louvre windows filter the light, and bright bed linen, carved wood features and open-air bathrooms complete the unique design. A little pocket of the garden is set aside for lazing outdoors, and the bus pulls up at the doorstep. Thumbs up.

Base (☎ 1800 242 273, 4778 5777; www.basebackpackers.com; 1 Nelly Bay Rd; unpowered sites $20, dm/d $20/70; ▣ ▣) Even if you're not into full-moon parties and boozy nights around the pool, you should consider staying at this backpackers. Ask for a beachfront A-frame, where the Coral Sea laps just below. The large decking and dining area is also absolutely beachfront and absolutely gorgeous. Base will pick up from Nelly Bay ferry terminal and there is a dive school on site. Camping prices are for two people.

Magnetic Island Tropical Resort (☎ 1800 069 122, 4778 5955; www.magnetictropicalresort.com; 56 Yates St; d $130; ✷ ▣) A-frame cabins with bathrooms encircle large bird-filled gardens here. This secluded resort often plays host to wedding parties, so if this is the first place you visit, don't think taffeta and tuxes are Magnetic Island's dress code. The resort features lawn tennis courts and an alluring restaurant, Lattice Bistro.

Island Leisure Resort (☎ 4778 5000; www.island leisure.com.au; 4 Kelly St; d $145, extra person $10; ⊠ ⚊) A block back from the bay, and with palms leaping from every patch of surrounding dirt, Island Leisure Resort is well situated. The self-contained rooms are spacious and suitable for families – though there may be fights over the TV remote. There is a communal laundry, tennis court and games room on the premises.

Palm View Chalets (☎ 4778 5596; 114 Sooning St; d $90; ⊠ ⚊) Crunch your way up the gravel driveway to these self-contained A-frames. The wooden exteriors, pine-panelled interior and rambling gardens might lead you to think that all the families staying here are Swiss Robinsons. Cheaper rates are readily available in the low season, and cabins sleep up to six.

Surfside Palms Beachfront Holiday Units (☎ 4778 5855; surfside.palm@bigpond.com; 15 The Esplanade; d $90, extra person $10; ⊠ ⚊) These older-style rooms are uncomplicated yet functional, and decked out in sensible '70s décor. Each of the three rooms is self-contained and spacious. The waterfront location is prime real estate, which hasn't gone unnoticed by the developers just across the water at Magnetic Harbour. Surfside remains a low-key option in the eye of the development storm.

Arcadia

Centaur House (☎ 1800 655 680, 4778 5668; www.bpf .com.au; 27 Marine Pde; dm/s/d $18/35/42) The beds here are romantically strung with mosquito netting, which hangs from the high painted ceilings. Add to that the gentle whir of an overhead fan and a beachfront location, and you'll be swooning. This little hostel's rooms are all upstairs, with a shambolic shared undercroft area downstairs.

Arkies (☎ 1800 663 666, 4778 5177; www.arkieson magnetic.com; 7 Marine Pde; dm $15-20, d $50; ⊠ ⚊ ⚊) Arkies is a large backpackers complex that's short on charm but big on the hands-in-the-air party vibe. The complex has a bistro and bar with loads of entertainment, including toad racing and trivia nights. The big daggy rooms were set to be refurbished during 2005.

Marshall's B&B (☎ 4778 5112; 3-5 Endeavour Rd; s/d $50/70) Marshall's friendly hosts have four basic rooms in their humble home. You're welcome to use the lounge room and pleasant bird-filled garden with outdoor seating.

Horseshoe Bay

New Friends B&B (☎ 4758 1220; 48b Horseshoe Bay Rd; s/d $70/90; ⚊) Lovely modern rooms with their own bathrooms are nestled in the main house, which makes for some friendly, communal living. There's a fabulous garden inlaid with a swimming pool and backed by jungle palms. In the morning a large breakfast spread welcomes you from the dining area, with windows crowded by flowering plants.

Myra's B&B (☎ 4758 1277; 101 Swenson St; s/d $50/70; ⊠) Like your privacy, but don't mind a bit of wildlife? You'll love this little cabin at the back of the property, set in rambling bush you'll share with possums and birds. The cabin has its own bathroom, and there's a room in the main house with a shared bathroom. Myra's is a bit out of the way, but great value; there's free use of bikes and the owners will shuttle you to/from the ferry.

Bungalow Bay (☎ 1800 285 577, 4778 5577; www .bungalowbay.com.au; 40 Horseshoe Bay Rd; unpowered/ powered sites $20/50, dm $22, d $57; ⚊ ⚊) Cedar A-frames are propped on expansive natural land here. It's the sort of place you'd expect to find a tree frog in the toilet and, if it's your first night here, be spooked into thinking that the ghosts of children haunt the grounds (you'll get it when you hear the nocturnal bushstone-curlew call). The good facilities here will comfort you though: an excellent pool, low-key bar and restaurant, as well as a good communal kitchen and bike hire. The eight-bed dorm cabins have their own bathroom, while the four-bed dorms don't. Camping prices are for two people.

Maggies Beach House (☎ 4778 5144; www.mag giesbeachhouse.com.au; Pacific Dr; dm $21-26, d $52-75; ⊠ ⚊ ⚊) Maggies has the best location, right on the beachfront, and some dorms have balconies with views. The concrete-floored functional rooms are colourfully painted; prices increase according to whether you have a bathroom and/or view. Also on the premises is a bar and Geckos restaurant.

EATING

Each of Magnetic's villages has its dining hub: of them, Horseshoe Bay is the most fruitful and diverse.

Picnic Bay

Fred's Bar 'n' Grill (☎ 4778 5911; Picnic Bay Mall; mains $15-20; ☯ lunch & dinner Tue-Sat) A big corner location overlooking Picnic Bay, with seats inside and out, makes Fred's a top spot to eat and drink. This unpretentious place offers bistro favourites, such as steak and pasta, that are well prepared, as well as daily specials.

Café Africa (☎ 4758 1119; Picnic Bay Mall; dishes $5-9; ☯ breakfast & lunch) Linger over a coffee, smoothie or juice among plush animal-print décor or propped at one of the quaint outdoor tables overlooking the bay. Café Africa specialises in all-day breakfast, and sweet and savoury crepes.

Feedja Café (☎ 4778 5833; Picnic Bay Mall; dishes $6-10; ☯ breakfast & lunch) This neo-hippy café serves dishes prepared from locally grown produce in bright, whimsical surrounds. There are soy products aplenty, plus juices and wraps.

Nelly Bay

Le Paradis (☎ 4778 5044; cnr Mandalay & Sooning Sts; mains $14-20; ☯ breakfast Sun, lunch & dinner Tue-Sun) This polished BYO restaurant offers a range of Mediterranean-inspired dishes on its extensive menu. The mostly outdoor seating is sheltered by large, angular sails and the tables are smartly dressed in linen.

Lattice Bistro (☎ 4778 5955; 56 Yates St; dishes $15-25; ☯ dinner Thu-Tue) The Tropical Resort's restaurant is open to nonguests who fancy a hearty steak or seafood meal. You might try barramundi, scallops or chicken, and there is usually a veggie option and kid-friendly meal or two. The open-sided restaurant is licensed and you may be serenaded with live music Thursday and Friday nights in season.

Man Friday (☎ 4778 5658; 37 Warboy St; mains $15-20; ☯ dinner Wed-Mon) This laid-back Mexican place is so relaxed you'll adopt the *mañana* mantra. In the front garden of a house, Man Friday serves up familiar dishes such as enchiladas and burritos. Bring a bottle and settle in; takeaway is also available.

Fat Possum Café (☎ 4778 5409; 55 Spooning St; dishes $5-10; ☯ breakfast, lunch & dinner) This no-fuss café cheerily dishes up just-assembled sandwiches, gourmet pies and sushi from its daytime menu. Coffee is a popular adjunct, with a shady roadside courtyard from which to drink it. Night-time is BYO and bowls of noodles.

If you feel like pizza tonight, **Pizza Tonite** (☎ 4758 1400; 53 Spooning St; dishes $10-12; ☯ dinner) has the standard range, with outdoor tables or delivery to your accommodation.

Arcadia

Bambu Thai Restaurant (☎ 4778 5645; Bright Ave; mains $16-20; ☯ dinner Thu-Tue) This intimate little restaurant serves boutique Thai in its back courtyard. It's BYO, and takeaway is also available. The **gallery** (☯ 10.30am-5.30pm Wed-Sun) is open for coffee and cake.

For finger-lickin' fish and chips, **Banister's Seafood** (☎ 4778 5700; 22 McCabe Cres; mains $5-22; ☯ lunch & dinner) is a good takeaway, with an open-air BYO dining area out the front.

Horseshoe Bay

In addition to those listed here, Horseshoe Bay's waterfront Pacific Dr is a bustling little strip with a number of takeaway places and shops.

Sandbar (☎ 4778 5477; Pacific Dr; mains $15-20; ☯ breakfast & lunch daily, dinner May-Dec) This licensed café-restaurant is all class – excepting the snowboard wall piece. A confident menu presents a range of interesting dishes comprised of fresh ingredients and sassy flavours. The lunch and dinner menu favour seafood, and breakfasts are big plates of all your favourites. There are a few outdoor tables just big enough to hold plates that are sized to receive satellite frequencies.

Marlin Bar (☎ 4758 1588; 3 Pacific Dr; mains $10-20; ☯ lunch daily, dinner Tue-Sat) The Marlin Bar is a lively waterfront pub that does decent veggie dishes and pasta (we dare you to overdose on dairy with the four-cheeses pasta in cream sauce). The range of mains takes in the entire farm, with veal, chicken, beef and pork dishes. Salads are obviously hard to come by, with a basic Greek salad costing as much as a steak ($20). Order and pay at the counter, grab a number and a window seat, and your food will find you when it's ready.

Geckos (☎ 4778 5144; Pacific Dr; mains $10-18; ☯ breakfast, lunch & dinner) The restaurant at Maggie's Beach House is open to nonguests, and serves bistro-style meals all day. It's a super-relaxed, order-at-the-bar type of affair, with outdoor seating at white plastic settings. The bar here occasionally stages live music.

GETTING THERE & AWAY

Sunferries (☎ 4771 3855; www.sunferries.com.au; ⏰ 6.45am-7pm Mon-Fri, 7am-5.30pm Sat & Sun) operates a frequent passenger ferry between Townsville and Magnetic Island (return $20), which takes about 20 minutes. Ferries depart from the terminal on Flinders St E in Townsville (Map p292), and also stop at the breakwater terminal on Sir Leslie Thiess Dr (Map p292). There is car parking here ($4 per day).

The **Magnetic Island Car Ferry** (Map p292; ☎ 4772 5422; Ross St, South Townsville; ⏰ 7.15am-5.30pm, to 3.45pm Sat) does the crossing six times daily from the south side of Ross Creek. It costs $127 (return) for a car and three passengers, and $17 (return) for a passenger only. The ferry currently docks at Arcadia, with murmurs of it moving to Magnetic Harbour; check when you book.

GETTING AROUND
Bicycle

Magnetic Island is ideal for cycling. Most places to stay rent bikes for around $15 a day; if where you're staying doesn't, call **Adventure Bike Hire** (☎ 0425-244 193), which has a free delivery service.

Bus

The **Magnetic Island Bus Service** (☎ 4778 5130; fares $2-4.50) ploughs between Picnic Bay and Horseshoe Bay at least 14 times a day, meeting all ferries and stopping at all major accommodation places. To book a wheelchair-accessible bus, call during office hours (8am to 4.30pm Monday to Friday, 8am to noon Saturday and Sunday).

Moke & Scooter

Expect to pay around $45 per day (plus extras such as petrol and a per-kilometre fee) for a nifty little Moke. You'll need to be over 21 and carrying a current international (or Australian) drivers license. It's a good idea to have your credit card too, so you don't have to carry the wads of cash required for the deposit. Scooter hire starts at around $30 per day.

Hooterz Scooterz (☎ 4778 5317; 3/11 Pacific Dr; Horseshoe Bay)
Moke Hire (☎ 4778 5491; 13 Pacific Dr, Horseshoe Bay)

Moke Magnetic (☎ 4778 5377; www.mokemagnetic .com; Nelly Bay)
Roadrunner Scooter Hire (☎ 4778 5222; Picnic Bay Mall, Picnic Bay)
Tropical Topless Car Rentals (☎ 4758 1111; Picnic Bay)

AYR TO TOWNSVILLE

Ayr, 90km southeast of Townsville, is on the delta of the Burdekin, one of the biggest rivers in Queensland, and is the major commercial centre for the rich farmlands of the Burdekin Valley. The towns and territory are devoted to the production and harvesting of sugar cane, melons and mangoes.

The **Burdekin visitors centre** (☎ 4783 5988; www .burdekintourism.com.au; Bruce Hwy) is in Plantation Park on the southern side of town.

If you're interested in marine biology, you can visit the **Australian Institute of Marine Science** (AIMS; ☎ 4753 4444; www.aims.gov.au; ⏰ 8am-3pm), a marine research facility at Cape Ferguson. Free two-hour tours are conducted every Friday at 10am (March to November) covering the institute's research (such as coral bleaching and management of the Great Barrier Reef) and how it relates to the community; advance bookings required. The turn-off to AIMS is on the Bruce Hwy about 53km northwest of Ayr, or 35km southeast of Townsville.

The unique wetlands of **Bowling Green Bay National Park** foster an assortment of wildlife in their mudflats, mangroves and salt marshes. Various species of birds wade through the waters, and the seagrass beds in the bay are home to turtles and dugongs. The turn-off from the Bruce Hwy to the park is at **Alligator Creek**, 28km south of Townsville. Alligator Creek tumbles down between two rugged ranges that rise steeply from the coastal plains. The taller range peaks with Mt Elliot (1234m), whose higher slopes harbour some of Queensland's most southerly tropical rainforest. A sealed road heads 6km inland from the highway to the park entrance, from where a good gravel road leads to pleasant picnic areas. Further on there's a camping ground with toilets, showers and BBQs; the 23 self-registration sites suitable for camping and caravans can be booked with **QPWS** (☎ 4796 7777; www.epa.qld .gov.au; per person $4). Alligator Creek has some superb **swimming holes**, and there are two

walking trails: one to Hidden Valley and Alligator Falls (17km, five hours return), the other following Cockatoo Creek (3km, one hour return).

The **Billabong Sanctuary** (☎ 4778 8344; www.billabongsanctuary.com.au; Bruce Hwy; adult/child $24/13; ☺ 8am-5pm), 17km south of Townsville, is a 10-hectare wildlife park of Australian native animals and birds. There are BBQ areas, a swimming pool and a kiosk in the park, and various shows (eg hold-a-koala/wombat/python) throughout the day.

TOWNSVILLE TO CHARTERS TOWERS

The North Coast's sparse, open hinterland is in stark contrast to the verdant rainforests present along the coast. This is the outback, where you can almost always see a horizon cutting across a giant sky.

The Flinders Hwy heads inland from Townsville and runs virtually due west for its entire length – almost 800km from Townsville to Cloncurry. The first section of the highway takes you 135km southwest from Townsville to the gold-mining town of Charters Towers, with a turn-off at the halfway mark to Ravenswood, another gold-mining centre. Both are easily accessible on a day trip from Townsville.

RAVENSWOOD
☎ 07 / pop 350
At Mingela, 88km from Townsville, a road leads 40km south to Ravenswood. It's a tiny mining town, among scattered red-earth hills, that dates back to gold-rush days. There is little to see, but that's the point. You come here to experience the solitude of mining life. A few historic buildings are preserved as testament to the town's former gold-mining glory.

Gold was unwittingly discovered here in 1868 by a pastoralist who, while on a cattle muster, dipped his pannikin into the river and found more than he bargained for in his drinking water. And so the rush was on. Ravenswood experienced a number of booms and subsequent busts, reaching its climax between 1900 and 1912, when it brought in 12,500kg of gold and supported a population of around 4000.

More recently, mining operations have again moved in to Ravenswood, which keeps the ghosts away from this intermittent ghost town. Hop on a stool at the ornate pubs and chat over a beer; most miners are happy to welcome a fresh face. You could also visit the old **post office** and **mining & historical museum** (☎ 4770 2047; adult/child $2.20/1.10; ☺ 10am-3pm Wed-Mon) housed in the restored courthouse, police station and lock-up and hosted by the gregarious Woody.

The grandiose, two-storey **Imperial Hotel** (☎ 4770 2131; Macrossan St; s/d $50/60) has character for mortar. Its solid red-brick façade and iron lace–trimmed veranda are features of the architectural style known as 'goldfields brash'. The timber-lined bedrooms upstairs, some with old brass beds and opening out onto the veranda, are clean and well presented. Basic meals are available from the magnificent red cedar bar.

An imposing, solid, red-brick pub, the **Railway Hotel** (☎ 4770 2144; Barton St; s/d $30/45) was built in 1871. A great ancient staircase leads up to basic bedrooms, mostly opening onto the big front veranda. Evening meals are available here, though the focus is firmly on the beer.

The council **camping ground** (unpowered sites $6) is more like a sunbaked sports oval, with some old shady trees around the periphery.

CHARTERS TOWERS
☎ 07 / pop 9,400
The gold rush is over, but the locals don't seem to know it. Charters Towers thrives in isolation 135km inland from Townsville. Its main industries are cattle and mining, with a gold revival in place since the 1980s, with modern processes enabling companies to rework old deposits. These most recent gold ventures are unlikely to cause the boon of 1900 that funded the construction of the magnificent homes and public buildings – a remarkable number of which remain preciously intact.

According to legend, a team of prospectors and an indigenous boy they called Jupiter went looking for horses that had bolted during a thunderstorm in 1871. Jupiter saw the gleam of gold in the local creek when he leant in to drink. Within a few years, the surrounding area had a number of diggings and a large town had grown. In its heyday, around the end of the 19th century,

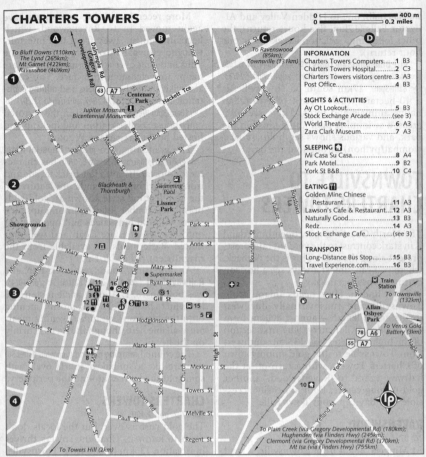

CHARTERS TOWERS

Charters Towers was referred to as 'the World' because of its wealth and diversity. It had almost 100 mines, a population of 30,000, a stock exchange and 25 pubs.

Orientation & Information

Gill St, which runs from the train station to Mosman St, is Charters Towers' main street. Towers Hill stands over the town to the south. Lissner Park, a couple of blocks north of the centre, is the town's best park and the swimming pool is at its northern end.

You'll find all services along Gill St, including **Charters Towers Computers** (☎ 4787 2988; 59 Gill St; 9am-5pm Mon-Fri, 9am-noon Sat) for Internet access, ATMs for a number of major banks, the post office and the **Charters Towers**

visitors centre (☎ 4752 0314; www.charterstowers.qld .gov.au; 74 Mosman St; 9am-5pm) at the top of the street. The centre displays interpretive panels and a video, and runs a number of tours. **Charters Towers Health Centre** (☎ 4787 0333; 237-9 Gill St) provides medical services.

Sights & Activities

A walk down Gill and Mosman Sts will present many of Charters Towers' historically significant buildings. Almost on the corner is the picturesque **Stock Exchange Arcade** built in 1887 and now lined with shops; the free 'Calling of the Card' audio presentation runs four times a day.

A wonderful place to escape in time is the **Zara Clark Museum** (☎ 4787 4661; 36 Mosman St;

adult/child $4.50/2.20; ⊙ 10am-3pm). The clutter of memorabilia, from old photos and farming equipment to period costumes and military items, is fascinating.

The original Australia Bank of Commerce building, built in 1891, now houses the **World Theatre** (82 Mosman St). It comprises a theatre, cinema, gift shop and restaurant.

You'll need the free cuppa to recover from the caretaker's ghost stories at **Ay Ot Lookout** (☎ 4787 2799; cnr High & Hodgkinson Sts; admission $5; ⊙ 8am-3pm). The timber building is one of many around town built using a method known as 'balloon framing', where the walls lack external cladding, and so do not have a cavity that can lead to vermin problems. It's said to be haunted by its former owner and a mysterious young woman.

The **Venus Gold Battery** (☎ 4752 0314; Millchester Rd; admission $6; ⊙ 9.30am-4.30pm Mon-Fri), where gold-bearing ore was crushed and processed from 1872 until as recently as 1973, is the largest preserved battery in Australia. An imaginative presentation tells the story of this huge relic.

Towers Hill Lookout, the site where gold was first discovered, has inspiring views over the plain. There are interpretive panels, as well as an open-air theatre screening the *Ghosts of Gold* each evening at around 7pm ($6, 20 minutes).

Tours

The **visitors centre** (☎ 4752 0314; 74 Mosman St; ⊙ 9am-5pm) runs guided walks through the centre providing an overview of the town's sights, including its impressive civic buildings, such as the Stock Exchange Building, the *Ghosts of Gold* film at Towers Hill, and the Venus Gold Battery.

Gold City Bush Safaris (☎ 4787 2118; ⊙ 8am-4pm) is run by a fourth-generation Charters Towers local. Geoff Phillips has more than 100 years of stories to tell on his $20, two-hour orientation tour or Venus Battery tour (adult/child $11/5). Transfers are included in the price.

Festivals & Events

Ten Days in the Towers (www.charterstowerscountry music.com) in April/May is 10 days of country music (the largest amateur gathering in the country), line dancing, bush poetry and busking. In late January, around a hundred amateur cricket teams descend on Charters

Towers to play for the **Goldfield Ashes**, which runs for three days over the Australia Day long weekend.

Sleeping

York St B&B (☎ 4787 1028; 58 York St; dm/s/d $17/65/90; ⊠ ⊛) The lofty brass beds in the heritage-themed rooms may inspire you to don a bonnet and nightshirt. These rooms – located in the main house, which was built in the 1880s – are busy with lace and floral patterns, and each has a bathroom. The dorm rooms are in a separate, less glorious wing. There's a good communal country-style kitchen and wheelchair access.

Park Motel (☎ 4787 1022; www.parkmotel.citysearch .com.au; cnr Mosman & Deane Sts; s $66-70, d $76-80; ⊠ ⊛) The guest rooms upstairs at this historic building have loads of character, high ceilings and a resident ghost (supposedly). Downstairs is a cosy, deep-pink bar and quaint bistro restaurant, **Lissners** (mains $8-15; ⊙ dinner). There is also a row of motel rooms out the back.

Mi Casa Su Casa (☎ 4787 2146; casamiassu@hotmail .com; 21 Mill Lane; d $80; ⊠ ⊛) The outdoor swimming pool and garden here are an oasis from the dusty surrounds. Four rooms are available in the house, which you'll share with three friendly dogs. You won't have to share your breakfast (which is included in the tariff) with anyone though.

If you want to glimpse the tough outback life, stay at a cattle station. **Bluff Downs** (☎ 4770 4084; www.bluffdowns.com.au; dm/d $25/150; ⊠), 110km northwest of Charters Towers, has a range of accommodation packages. **Plain Creek** (☎ 4983 5228; reid.robyn@bigpond.com; Clermont Rd; d from $100) is about two hours' drive from town, between Clermont and Charters Towers. There's always plenty of activity such as cattle branding and ear marking, but you'll spend more time watching than participating. (Credit-card payment facilities are not available.)

Eating

Naturally Good (☎ 4787 4211; 58 Gill St; dishes $5-8; ⊙ breakfast & lunch Mon-Sat) Freshly made sandwiches and homemade cakes and pastries are the go at this super-friendly lunchtime spot. Dine in at one of the heavy wooden tables, or take away.

Stock Exchange Cafe (☎ 4787 7954; Mosman St; mains $7-10; ⊙ lunch Mon-Sat May-Jan) Try not to slurp when you get to the bottom of your iced coffee – there's an echo in the charmingly restored arcade that houses this café. Stop in for a pleasant lunch of a baked potato with lashings of sour cream or lasagne.

Lawson's Cafe & Restaurant (☎ 4787 4333; 82 Mosman St; mains $17-23; ☺ breakfast, lunch & dinner) There is something for everyone here, at any meal time. In the evening the tables are candlelit and topped with tasty dishes such as chicken burgers, vegetable stacks or goat curry.

Redz (☎ 4787 8044; 32 Gill St; dishes $4-6; ☺ breakfast & lunch) It's always a treat to sit down to coffee with a book; at Redz stacks of brand new ones'll surround you. This hip bookshop and café serves cakes, smoothies and juices, as well as a few light savouries.

Golden Mine Chinese Restaurant (☎ 4787 7609; 64 Mosman St; mains $9-12; ☺ lunch & dinner) The all-you-can-eat smorgasbord at the licensed Golden Mine is still the best deal in town. There's lots of fried food, meats in sweet sauces and noodles, served in a large dining room.

Getting There & Away

Greyhound Australia (☎ 13 20 30; www.greyhound .com.au) has daily services from Townsville to Charters Towers ($30, one hour 40 minutes) continuing to the Northern Territory. The long-distance bus stop is outside the Catholic church on Gill St.

The train station is on Enterprise Rd, 1.5km east of the centre. The twice-weekly *Inlander* runs from Townsville to Charters Towers on Sunday and Wednesday (economy seat $23, economy/1st class sleeper $76/115, three hours).

In town **Travel Experience.com** (☎ 4787 2622; 13 Gill St) is a travel agent that handles travel tickets.

TOWNSVILLE TO INNISFAIL

Much of the action between Townsville and Innisfail is focussed on the beaches and offshore islands; in parts, though, the rainforest comes down to meet the coast, so you can walk in the morning and flake out on a beach in the afternoon.

The national parks stretching inland contain special pockets of rainforest, waterfalls and walks.

PALUMA RANGE NATIONAL PARK

Part of the Wet Tropics World Heritage Area, Paluma Range National Park and the teeny village of Paluma provide a secluded respite from the drone of the Bruce Hwy.

Mt Spec Section

It's not uncommon for the lofty rainforest in this section of the park to be shrouded in mist or capped by cloud. Straddling the summit and escarpment of the Paluma Range, the Mt Spec Section stands over the Big Crystal Creek flood plain below. As you head up, the landscape changes from eucalypt stands to the closed canopy of the rainforest, containing a range of habitats to support the diverse bird species that live here.

There are two roads into this section of the park, both leading off a bypassed section of the Bruce Hwy: either 60km north of Townsville or 40km south of Ingham.

Take the northern access route to **Big Crystal Creek** where goannas scamper away from your approaching footsteps as you walk the few hundred metres from the picnic area to the popular Paradise Waterhole. There's a self-registration **QPWS camping ground** (☎ 13 13 04; www.epa.qld.gov.au; per person $4) that's well equipped with toilets, gas BBQs and drinking water. Access to Big Crystal Creek is via the 4km road, 2km north of Mt Spec Rd.

The southern access route, Mt Spec Rd, was built by relief labour during the 1930s Depression. It's a dramatic, narrow road (with lose-your-lunch twists) that weaves its way up the mountains to the village of Paluma. After 7km you come to **Little Crystal Creek**, where a pretty stone bridge (built in 1932) arches across the creek. This is a great swimming spot, with waterfalls and a couple of deep rock pools, and there's a small picnic area opposite the car park. From here it's another steep 11km up to Paluma village.

PALUMA VILLAGE

The sleepy mountain-top village of Paluma was founded in 1875 when tin was discovered in the area. A smattering of places to stay protrude from the rainforest surrounds, and there is little activity to disturb the cool, clear mountain air.

A number of walks lead through the rainforest surrounding the village. If not cushioned in cloud, **McClelland's Lookout**, 100m before Paluma village, provides humbling views out to Halifax Bay and the Palm Islands. (This was also the site of a US Army radar station during WWII.) From the car park here a trail leads to **Witts Lookouts** (1.5km, 45 minutes return) and the steep **Cloudy Creek Falls** (3.5km, two hours return). Otherwise take the **H Track** (1.3km, 45 minutes) circuit walk, which leads from the rear of Lennox Cres along a former logging road containing evidence of the tin-mining industry.

The peace of Paluma may inspire you to stay a night or two. Unless you plan to subsist on scones and tea, bring supplies. If you *do* fancy Devonshire tea, stop by **Ivy Cottage** (☎ 4770 8533; Devonshire teas $6; ⏰ 9am-4pm).

The candy-pink self-contained units at **Misthaven** (☎ 4771 5964; d $60) are fabulously kitsch. Each of the one-bedroom units is large and fully fitted, with cutlery, a fridge and microwave. They're set on a neat patch of grass and have flowering pot plants around the entrance. (No credit-card payment facilities are available.) Otherwise **Paluma Rainforest Cottages** (☎ 4770 8520; www .palumarainforest.com.au; d $75-90) manages several self-contained properties in the area that sleep up to five people and include all linen and laundry facilities.

Approximately 11km beyond Paluma is **Lake Paluma**, a drinking-water storage dam, with a dedicated foreshore area for swimming and picnicking. You can camp with permission from **NQ Water** (☎ 4770 8526; www.nqwater .com.au) or stay in out-of-the-way log cabins at **Hidden Valley Cabins** (☎ 4770 8088; www.hiddenval leycabins.com.au; s/d $55/75), which also has motel-style backpacker rooms (single/double $30/40) and a licensed restaurant.

Jourama Falls Section

Jourama Falls and a series of cascades and rapids tumble along Waterview Creek, which is enclosed by palms and umbrella trees. It's a small area that's well developed, with a few lookouts, picnic areas and a **QPWS camping ground** (☎ 13 13 04; www.epa.qld.gov.au; per person $4) with drinking water, toilets and showers.

Access to this part of the park is via a 6km dirt road, 90km north of Townsville and 25km south of Ingham. Access may be restricted during the wet season.

Back on the Bruce Hwy, at Mutarnee, is **Frosty Mango** (☎ 4770 8184; www.frostymango.com .au; Bruce Hwy; light meals $5-10; ⏰ 9am-5pm). It's a roadside restaurant serving everything and anything to do with mangoes – try the mango slushie.

INGHAM
☎ 07 / pop 4673

The clock stopped around 1950 in beautiful Ingham. Some of the main street's untenanted buildings are fading with neglect, which doesn't detract from the town's overall wholesome gleam. Located 110km north of Townsville and about 200km south

---

PUB WITHOUT BEER

Probably Ingham's best-known local is Dan Sheahan (1882–1977): a cane cutter, horseman and poet. Dan's poems carried on the Australian literary tradition, started by Banjo Paterson and Henry Lawson, of investigating Australian bush identity through verse. Sheahan's focus, though, was on examining the Australian identity during WWII. The **Ingham Library** (☎ 4776 4683; 25 Lannercost St; ⏰ 9.30am-5pm Mon, 8.30am-5pm Tue-Fri, 9am-noon Sat) stocks a few titles of his collected works. Though Sheahan enjoyed mild success from his poetry, one of his poems was to become wildly popular as a song. Sheahan penned 'Pub Without Beer' (over a glass of wine) at Ingham's Day Dawn Hotel, after arriving to find that US troops had just been through his local and drained it dry of beer. (The Day Dawn was demolished in 1960; Lees Hotel now stands in its place.) The weekly *North Queensland Register* published the poem in 1944.

It wasn't until 1956 that Gordon Parsons used Sheahan's poem as inspiration to compose the song 'Pub with No Beer' (over whisky) at a pub in Taylors Arms, New South Wales. The song was then immortalised by the late Australian country-music icon Slim Dusty, who went on to record 'Duncan' ('…love to have a beer with…') in 1980, and whose album *Beer Drinking Songs* (1986) went gold within three weeks of its release.

Which all goes a fair way to proving that the humble beer is an integral part of the Australian identity.

of Cairns, Ingham services the surrounding sugar-cane district. It has banks, supermarkets and civic service outlets along Lannercost St. Still, it's lucky that no-one in Ingham is in a hurry, as cane trains frequently lumber across the main road stopping traffic. The first sugar-cane farms were established in this area in the 1880s, and from early in its history the region attracted a large number of Italian immigrants. For three days each May the **Australian-Italian Festival** (www.acecomp.com.au/Italian) gets pasta flying with cooking displays, street markets, children's rides, fireworks and a troubadour competition.

Information & Orientation
Ingham has a super-helpful, well-stocked **visitors centre** (☎ 4776 5211; www.hinchinbrooknq .com.au; 21 Lannercost St; �) 8.45am-5pm Mon-Fri, 9am-2pm Sat & Sun), and a **QPWS office** (☎ 4776 1700; www.epa.qld.gov.au; 49 Cassady St; � 9am-5pm Mon-Fri) that can handle permits for camping in the area.

Sights & Activities
The Ingham **cemetery**, about 3km out of town via Forrest Beach Rd, is unique for its sprawl of ornate Italianate mausoleums. In death as in life, these dwellings are adorned with flamboyant statuary and tiles and shuttered with Venetian blinds.

Under an hour's drive west from Ingham (about 50km) are the dazzling heights of **Wallaman Falls** – the longest single-drop waterfall in Australia. The falls plunge around 300m off Seaview Range in the Girringun National Park, and have much more oomph in the wet season, after rains. There's a walking track to the base of the falls (4km, two hours return) or a shorter track to rock pools (1.2km, 30 minutes return) that leaves from the camping ground. You can swim both at the base of the falls and in the rock pools, if the water level is not too high.

Further in to Girringun National Park is the dormant volcanic peak of **Mt Fox**, with its well-formed crater. A short scramble will allow you to peer over the edge; the 160m-long path is neither marked nor maintained, and so is reserved only for fit and experienced walkers (allow an hour). Access is via unsealed roads and a 4WD is recommended in the wet season.

THE AUTHOR'S CHOICE
Station Hotel (☎ 4776 2076; 91 Cartwright St; s/d $20/40) This is the kind of place where you can still leave your wallet on the bar without fear of anybody snatching it, and where you can have a room key if you want, but it's not necessary. Its bar is where you'll be privy to such local wisdom as the steel bar-fridge doors frosting over signalling that it's going to rain.

Dulcie and Keith run and maintain the Station Hotel – keeping it in the same mint condition it was in when Dulcie's mum, Gladys Harvey, bought it in 1952. It's full of fabulous '50s furniture and has an encircling veranda and general rosy demeanour. Gladys was hotelier at the Day Dawn Hotel during WWII, and used to ride horses with Dan Sheahan (see the boxed text on p311); in 2004 she celebrated her 101st birthday at the Station Hotel where she lived.

Sleeping & Eating
Herbert Valley Motel (☎ 4776 1777; fax 4776 3646; 37 Townsville Rd; s/d $55/70; ☒ ☒) There are 30 identical motel rooms set back from the main approach into Ingham. The forgettable rooms all have bathrooms, kettles and what you've really come for, a comfy bed.

Lees Hotel (☎ 4776 1577; leeshotel@ozemail.com.au; 58 Lannercost St; s/d $50/60; ☒) The moulded horseman on the roof and talking dog out the front make it hard to miss Lees. On the same site as the Day Dawn Hotel, of 'Pub Without Beer' fame (see the boxed text on p311), Lees has decent rooms upstairs (rates include breakfast). Lunch and dinner are available in the downstairs bistro (Monday to Saturday).

Elda's (☎ 4776 2039; 78 Lannercost St; sandwiches $4-5; �)) breakfast & lunch Mon-Fri, to noon Sat, to 11am Sun) What looks like a humble fruit shop and deli is also the provider of truly spectacular sandwiches. Past the Italian imported dry goods and fresh fruit and veg is where John deftly assembles ingredients from the deli, including those he has lovingly marinated – think aniseed and sweet chilli.

Victory Café (☎ 4776 2108; 92 Cartwright St; meals $5-12; ☒ lunch & dinner Tue-Sun) You won't need to wear your good shirt to dinner here, but this BYO diner-style café has a varied menu with hearty helpings of food. You might try a pizza, steak or burger, but the home-made lasagne comes highly recommended. Takeaway also available.

Olive Tree Coffee Lounge (☎ 4776 5166; 45 Lannercost St; mains $8-12; ✆ lunch & dinner) Robust pastas and mains and industrial-strength coffee are why we love Italian food, and that's precisely why we love Olive Tree.

Getting There & Away

Greyhound Australia (☎ 13 14 99; www.greyhound .com.au) buses run between Townsville and Ingham ($27, 1¼ hours), and stop in the centre of town on Townsville Rd, close to the corner of Lannercost St (and the information centre). Ingham is also on the **Queensland Rail** (☎ 1300 131 722; www.traveltrain .com.au; ✆ 6am-9pm) Brisbane–Cairns train line, which also stops in Townsville.

LUCINDA

☎ 07 / pop 783

Most people come to the small seaside town of Lucinda to fish or gawk at its 6km-long jetty. The world's longest bulk sugar-loading jetty, it allows enormous carrier ships to dock. About 25km northeast of Ingham, Lucinda sits at the southern end of the Hinchinbrook Channel – a protected waterway that contains interconnecting streams supporting mangroves, barramundi and crocs. Lucinda is also the closest mainland connection to the stunning Hinchinbrook Island.

Hinchinbrook Wilderness Safaris (☎ 4777 8307; www.hinchinbrookwildernesssafaris.com.au; 12 Bruce Pde) runs fishing tours ($150, four hours) between March and November, tours along the channel ($30 per person, 2½ hours) and transfers to Hinchinbrook from $46.

If the fish are biting, think about staying at **Wanderer's Holiday Village** (☎ 4777 8213; www .wanderers-lucinda.com.au; Bruce Pde; unpowered/powered sites $16/20, d $70; ✆ ✆). It's extremely well equipped, with BBQs, a children's play area, a laundry and an activities room; the cabins are self-contained (linen hire $6 per bed, includes towels). **Lucinda Point Hotel-Motel** (☎ 4777 8103; cmusso@bigpond .com.au; cnr Halifax & Dungeness Rds; r $75-95; ✆ ✆) has self-contained rooms, and you'll have to contain yourself in the plush executive rooms that include bath robes, biscuits and Egyptian cotton towels. You can tell the story of the one that got away over a bistro meal (lunch and dinner) and a beer in the main hotel.

ORPHEUS ISLAND

The secluded Orpheus Island lies about 25km off the coast of Ingham. It's mostly national park, protecting macaranga trees with huge heart-shaped leaves, and eucalypts standing on a foundation of volcanic rocks. However it's the magnificent fringing reef that is the main attraction here.

Large coral bommies may be found in Little Pioneer Bay, Cattle Bay and around the Yank's Jetty area. The snorkelling is best around the island's northeast tip. The beaches at Mangrove Bay, Yanks Bay and Pioneer Bay are simply beautiful, but shallow at low tide.

Apart from national park, with three camping grounds, the island has two leases: one an exclusive resort, the other a marine research station.

During the 1800s goats were released on the island as part of a madcap scheme to provide food for possible shipwreck survivors. The goats thrived to the extent that at one stage they numbered over 4000. A national parks 'control programme' significantly reduced numbers.

Only 11km long and about 1km wide, Orpheus is the second largest of the Palm Islands Group. There are 10 other islands in the group; apart from Orpheus and nearby council-run Pelorus, all of the islands are Aboriginal communities with restricted access.

Established in the 1940s, the luxurious **Orpheus Island Resort** (☎ 1800 077 167, 4777 7377; www.orpheus.com.au; d from $1450; ✆ ✆) trades on its isolation from the outside world: no interlopers, and no phones or TVs in the rooms. Everything is included: meals, snacks, snorkelling and tennis. The resort also runs diving trips and courses for guests; children under 15 years of age aren't welcome.

There are bush camping sites at Yank's Jetty, South Beach and Pioneer Bay. There are toilets at Yanks Jetty and Pioneer Bay, and picnic tables at all sites, but you'll need to bring drinking water and a fuel stove. Permits can be obtained from **QPWS** (☎ 13 13 04; www.epa.qld.gov.au; per person $4), which has offices in Cardwell and Ingham.

The resort has a seaplane that handles transfers from Townsville ($450 return, 30 minutes) and Cairns ($780, 60 minutes) to Orpheus.

There are no public ferry services to Orpheus; access is by private charter. **Lucinda Reef & Island Charters** (☎ 4777 8220; per person $120) taxis to Orpheus on demand, as does **Orpheus Island Diving** (☎ 0407-378 968, 4777 9062; www .orpheusislanddiving.com.au; per person $130), which provides water and a mobile phone.

CARDWELL & AROUND
☎ 07 / pop 1420

The idling seaside holiday town of Cardwell (120km north of Townsville) is one of north Queensland's oldest towns (established in 1864), which might explain its general torpor. Cardwell is a conduit for the wealth of sights that surround it: Hinchinbrook Island and a number of smaller islands lie just off shore, and forests and falls beckon those with their own wheels to explore Cardwell's fringes. Its coastal waters and inland waterways are also popular spots to angle for a red emperor, mangrove jack or barramundi.

Information & Orientation

The **QPWS Reef & Rainforest Centre** (☎ 4066 8601; www.epa.qld.gov.au; ⏰ 8am-4.30pm), next to the main jetty, has a rainforest interactive display and information about Hinchinbrook Island and the nearby state and national parks.

Port Hinchinbrook Marina, 2km south of town, is where boats depart for Hinchinbrook Island. It's an ongoing development comprising residential properties and resort accommodation that it is hoped will enliven the town without affecting the surrounding natural resources.

Sights & Activities

The **Cardwell Forest Drive** starts from the centre of town and is a scenic 26km round trip, with excellent lookouts, walking tracks and picnic areas signposted along the way. There are super swimming opportunities at Attie and Dead Horse Creek, as well as Spa Pool.

The **Murray Falls State Forest** has pretty falls that tumble into fine rock pools suitable for swimming; take care as the rocks are slippery. There's a boardwalk viewing platform (that's wheelchair accessible) and a rainforest walk (1.8km return, one hour), as well as a BBQ and camping area. Murray Falls are 22km west of the highway, signposted about 27km north of Cardwell.

Just off the Bruce Hwy, about 7km south of Cardwell, the **Five Mile Swimming Hole** is another good swimming spot with picnic facilities that are wheelchair accessible.

The **Dalrymple Gap Walking Track** was originally an Aboriginal foot track made into a road by George Dalrymple in the 1860s as a stock route. The track is 8km long (eight hours return) and passes through Girringun National Park and an old stone bridge that is registered by the National Trust. The turn-off to the track is off the highway, 15km south of Cardwell.

Tours

Hinchinbrook Explorer (☎ 4088 6154; www.hexplorer .com.au; per person $130) offers fishing tours in the Hinchinbrook Channel, and Girringun and Edmund Kennedy National Parks. Take a scenic flight with **Cardwell Air Charter** (☎ 4066 846; www.oz-e.com.au/cardair) around the local attractions ($50, 20 minutes) or the grand tour ($180, 1¼ hours) over the Reef and islands, inland falls and Hinchinbrook Channel.

Sleeping & Eating

Mudbrick Manor (☎ 4066 2299; www.mudbrickmanor .com.au; Lot 13 Stony Creek Rd; d $100-125; 🅿 🅶) This hand-built mud-brick home is outstanding. You'll spend lazy days on the veranda overlooking the sprawling courtyard, soaking up the casual country finesse. The huge indoor lounge area has activities aplenty, or you can occupy yourself poking around all the decorative pieces. Breakfast is included, but ask about the three-course dinners; they may entice you to stay another night.

Kookaburra Holiday Park (☎ 4066 8648; www .kookaburraholidaypark.com.au; 175 Bruce Hwy; unpowered/ powered sites $18/20, d $35-90; 🅿 🅶) This enormous holiday village almost outsizes Cardwell itself. Set in attractive tropical grounds, there's an accommodation option to suit all tastes and budgets: from on-site vans to two-bedroom villas. Out the back is the **Hinchinbrook YHA** (unpowered sites s/d $11/18, dm/s/d $18/35/40), a bright backpackers with access to all of the park's fabulous facilities.

Island Lure (☎ 4066 8787; 17 Victoria St; d $48; 🅿 🅶) Lure's large, old-fashioned, self-contained units were built back in the days when we had bigger families. Each of the comfy functional units has three bunks, plus a bed and sitting area, with a gorgeous pool on the doorstep.

Beachcomber (☎ 4066 8550; beachcombercardwell@ bigpond.com; 43 Marine Pde; unpowered/powered sites

$15/20, d $35-85; 🅧 🅡) Choose from grassy camping sites or on-site vans and cabins. Among Beachcomber's facilities, such as a communal laundry and communal BBQ area, is the **Bar & Grill** (mains $15-18; 🅨 breakfast & dinner daily, lunch Thu-Sun) serving familiar fare such as steak and pizza.

Port Hinchinbrook Resort Hotel (☎ 4066 2000; www.porthinchinbrook.com.au; Bruce Hwy; d from $155; 🅧 🅡) The comfortable, modern cabins here are compact, yet well equipped. As a resort, the complex has big plans but a long way to go, and generally lacks ambience. Its **Portside Café** (mains around $20; 🅨 breakfast, lunch & dinner), open to nonguests, offers a slightly upmarket pub menu serving reef 'n' beef, parmigiana and pastas.

The string of takeaway joints along the main drag is interrupted by **Latitudz** (☎ 4066 8907; Victoria St; mains $17-20; 🅨 lunch & dinner Wed-Mon), a smart-looking café serving barramundi, oysters and other seafood. Otherwise, basic pub grub is available in the concrete court-yard of the **Marine Hotel** (☎ 4066 8662; 59 Victoria St; mains around $14; 🅨 lunch & dinner).

Getting There & Away

Greyhound Australia (☎ 13 20 30; www.greyhound.com.au) buses stop at Cardwell: from Towns-ville they cost $32 (two hours), from Cairns $31 (three hours).

Cardwell is also on the Brisbane-to-Cairns train line; contact **Queensland Rail** (☎ 1300 131 722; www.traveltrain.qr.com.au) for details.

HINCHINBROOK ISLAND

Hope that you're one of the fortunate 40 who are allowed to traverse the Thorsborne Trail at any one time. If not, there's a range of other ways to explore this stunning and unspoilt wilderness. Hinchinbrook's granite mountains rise dramatically from the sea. The mainland side is dense with lush tropi-cal vegetation, while long sandy beaches and tangles of mangrove curve around the east-ern shore. All 399 sq km of the island is na-tional park, and rugged Mt Bowen (1121m) is its highest peak. There's plenty of wild-life, including the pretty-faced wallaby and iridescent blue Ulysses butterfly. There are also bush rats, crocodiles and sandflies.

Hinchinbrook is well known to bushwalk-ers and naturalists. Walking opportunities here are excellent, even though some trails may close between November and March due to adverse weather. The highlight is the **Thorsborne Trail** (also known as the East Coast Trail), a 32km coastal track from Ramsay Bay to Zoe Bay (with its beautiful waterfall) and on to George Point at the southern tip. It's recommended that you take three nights to complete the trail, al-lowing for swimming stops and quiet time. Return walks of individual sections are also possible if you're time poor. This is the real bush experience; you'll need to wear a layer of insect repellent, protect your food from ravenous rats, draw water from creeks as you go (water is reliably available at Nina, Little Ramsay and Zoe Bays), and be alert to the possibility of crocs being present around the mangroves. The trail is ungraded and at times rough, including challenging creek crossings; you should carry a map, drinking water, a fuel stove and a trowel.

Apart from the Thorsborne Trail, camp-ing and short walks are available at **Macushla Bay** (5km to 8km, 1½ to two hours), and the **Haven circuit** (1km, 15 minutes) at Scraggy Point.

In general, beach fishing is allowed, but be mindful of marine stingers that are present in the sea and waterways from Oc-tober to April.

Bookings for the Thorsborne Trail need to be made in advance: for a place during the high season, **QPWS** (☎ 13 13 04; www.epa.qld.gov.au; per person $4) recommends booking a year ahead and six months ahead for other dates. Its Reef & Rainforest Centre (op-posite) in Cardwell stocks the imperative *Thorsborne Trail* brochure and screens the 15-minute *Without a Trace* video, which walkers are required to view. Cancellations for places on the trail are not unheard of, so it's worth asking about the possibility of a place, if you've arrived without a booking.

Hinchinbrook Island Ferries runs **day tours** (per person $85) to Hinchinbrook Island, de-parting from Cardwell's Port Hinchinbrook Marina. The tour includes exploration of the mangroves, visiting the long stretch of beach at Ramsay Bay and the option of walking through the rainforest at Macushla Bay.

Built into the steep hillside behind Or-chid Beach, in the island's north, are the elevated tree houses with floor-to-ceiling windows, a balcony, kitchenette and bath-room at **Hinchinbrook Island Wilderness Lodge & Resort** (☎ 4066 8270; www.hinchinbrookresort.com.au;

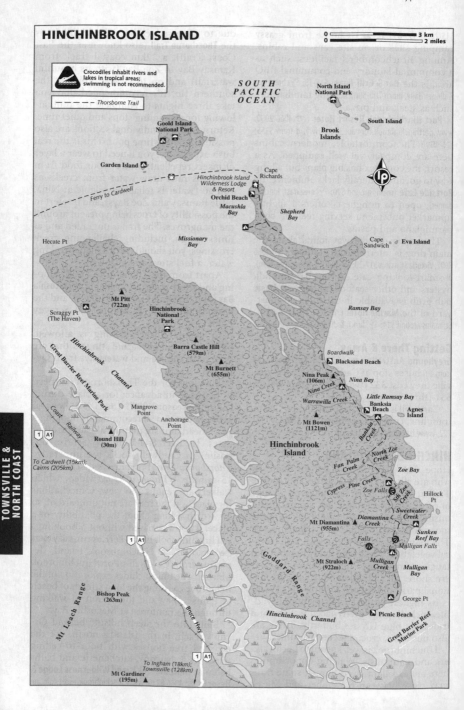

HINCHINBROOK ISLAND

0   3 km
0   2 miles

Crocodiles inhabit rivers and
lakes in tropical areas;
swimming is not recommended.

– – – Thorsborne Trail

*SOUTH
PACIFIC
OCEAN*

North Island
National Park

South Island

Brook
Islands

Goold Island
National Park

Garden Island

Ferry to Cardwell

Hinchinbrook Island
Wilderness Lodge
& Resort

Cape
Richards

Orchid Beach

*Macushla
Bay*

*Shepherd
Bay*

*Missionary
Bay*

Cape
Sandwich   Eva Island

Hecate Pt

Mt Pitt
(722m)

Scraggy Pt
(The Haven)

Hinchinbrook
National
Park

Ramsay Bay

Hinchinbrook Channel

Great Barrier Reef Marine Park

Barra Castle Hill
(579m)

Mt Burnett
(655m)

Boardwalk
Blacksand Beach

Nina Peak
(106m)   *Nina Creek*   *Nina Bay*

Warrawilla Creek

Little Ramsay Bay
Banksia
Beach

Agnes
Island

Coast Railway

Mangrove
Point

Anchorage
Point

Round Hill
(30m)

Mt Bowen
(1121m)

**Hinchinbrook
Island**

Banksia Creek

To Cardwell (15km);
Cairns (205km)

Fan Palm
Creek

*North Zoe
Creek*

Zoe Bay

Cypress Pine Creek

Zoe Falls

*Sth Zoe
Creek*

Hillock
Pt

Sweetwater
Creek

Mt Diamantina
(955m)

*Diamantina
Creek*

Sunken
Reef Bay

Falls

Mulligan Falls

Bishop Peak
(263m)

Mt Straloch
(922m)

*Mulligan
Creek*

*Mulligan
Bay*

Goddard Range

George Pt

Bruce Hwy

Picnic Beach

Hinchinbrook Channel

*Great Barrier Reef
Marine Park*

Mt Leach Range

To Ingham (18km);
Townsville (128km)

Mt Gardiner
(195m)

beach cabins $165, tree houses $300; ⊛). The beach-front cabins are self-contained and the price is for up to four people. Guests are free to use the resort's canoes, surf-skis and snorkelling gear, or just laze in the hammocks strung along the beach. All meals are available from the licensed restaurant and are not included in the accommodation rates, although full-board packages are also available. Transfers also cost extra.

There are six **QPWS camping grounds** (☎ 13 13 40; www.epa.qld.gov.au; per person $4) along the Thorsborne Trail, plus the two at Macushla Bay and the Haven in the north.

Hinchinbrook Island Ferries (☎ 4066 8270; www .hinchinbrookferries.com.au) operates daily services from May to October and three services a week from November to March; services are suspended in February during the wet season. Boats depart from Cardwell's Port Hinchinbrook Marina and dock at the Hinchinbrook Resort. The journey takes about 50 minutes and costs from $100 return. If you're walking the Thorsborne Trail, a one-way transfer costs $60. Walkers usually pick up the **Hinchinbrook Wilderness Safaris** (☎ 4777 8307; www.hinchinbrookwilderness safaris.com.au; one way/return $47/57) service at the southern end of the trail.

GOOLD & GARDEN ISLANDS

These uninhabited islands provide the perfect setting for you to play castaway. Both are national parks and off the every-day tourist radar, so you could find you have the islands to yourself. **Goold Island**, just 17km northeast of Cardwell, supports open forest, mangroves and a sandy beach on both the west and south sides. There's a **QPWS camping site** (☎ 13 13 04; www.epa.qld.gov .au; per person $4) on the island's west, with toilets, picnic tables and a gas BBQ. Bring drinking water, a book and frayed-legged pants.

Just south of Goold Island is tiny **Garden Island**, with a recreation reserve controlled by the local council. Permits to camp are required and available from the **Cardwell Newsagency** (☎ 4066 8622; 83 Victoria St; per person $3.85). The island has a good sandy beach but no fresh water; no people under six years are permitted.

Hinchinbrook Island Ferries (☎ 4066 8270; www .hinchinbrookferries.com.au; return transfers $85) can ferry campers on request.

TULLY

☎ 07 / pop 2700

The tiny town of Tully is an inland sugar town whose giant mill chimney pushes puffs of sweet-smelling smoke into the cool, damp air. Tully carries the reputation as the wettest place in Australia. It holds the record for the highest annual rainfall in a populated area of Australia – which it 'won' in 1950 when it received 7.9m. (It's no coincidence that the giant gumboot at the entrance to town is also 7.9m tall.) The banana plantations around Tully provide seasonal employment that attracts droves of young backpackers on working holidays, and the rapids in the nearby rivers provide hours of frothy excitement for white-water rafters. Commercial rafting trips on the Tully River are timed to coincide with the hydro-electricity company opening the floodgates.

The **Tully visitors centre** (☎ 4068 2288; info@ tropicalaustralia.com.au; Bruce Hwy; ☯ 8.30am-4.45pm Mon-Fri, 9am-2.30pm Sat & Sun) is on the highway just south of the Tully turn-off. Book here for **Tully Sugar Mill Tours** (adult/child $10/6.50; ☯ 10am, 11am & 1.30pm Mon-Fri, 11am Sat & Sun Jun-Nov). During the crushing season the mill operates 24/7 and processes around two million tonnes of cane. The mill generates its own power by burning fibre residue. The 1½-hour tours must be booked at least half an hour before departure (as minimum numbers are required); wear closed shoes and a shirt with sleeves.

There are good walking opportunities in the **Tully State forests**, located 40km from Tully along Cardstone Rd. There are picnic facilities, as well as river access for swimming at **Tully Gorge**: though you may be converged upon by pumped and paddle-wheeling kayakers, and the gentle burble of the Tully River can turn suddenly into a rapid when the hydro-electricity company opens its floodgates. A number of disused logging roads in the area have been revitalised into walking trails; the visitors centre in Tully has a map, as does www.misty mountains.com.au.

Day trips with **Raging Thunder Adventures** (☎ 4030 7990; www.ragingthunder.com.au/rafting.asp) or **R'n'R White Water Rafting** (☎ 4051 7777; www .raft.com.au) cost about $150 and include a BBQ lunch and transfers from Mission Beach, Cairns or Port Douglas.

IMPERIAL ISLANDS OF THE PIED-IMPERIAL PIGEON

The dense vine forests of the Brook Islands are the imperial lands of the pied-imperial pigeon. These plump birds arrive in their thousands every September, each one laying a single white egg in a scraggly nest.

The four islands in the Brook Islands Group lie about 8km northeast of Cape Richards, to the north of Hinchinbrook Island. The islands support a colony of around 40,000 pigeons, which arrives each September and departs with its offspring in February. Visiting the islands is prohibited during nesting time.

North Island has a sandy beach that you're able to visit from March to September (providing you have a boat). Although it was used for mustard-gas experiments in 1944, the Environment Protection Agency reports 'virtually no trace of this remains'. North, Middle and Tween Islands have superb fringing corals that are popular with recreational snorkellers, and South Island has a Commonwealth lighthouse. However it's the trees that the pigeons come for.

The pigeons migrate from New Guinea every summer to breed in Australia. Known by various names, including nutmeg pigeon, Torresian imperial-pigeon and pied-imperial pigeon, they are large, striking birds – pure white with black tail and wing tips. They fly to the mainland each day to feed on fruit trees, before returning to the islands each afternoon. Farmers on the mainland used to consider the birds pests, and regularly shot them in their thousands on the islands. However thanks to the efforts of Margaret and Arthur Thorsborne (after whom Hinchinbrook's trail is named) in the 1960s and '70s, the birds are now protected and numbers have increased.

The Brook Islands are also a breeding place over summer for a variety of terns, as well as the vulnerable beach-stone curlew, which is believed to lay its eggs directly onto the beaches of North Brook Island.

Sleeping & Eating

Tully Motel (☎ 4068 2233; tullymotel@bigpond.com; Bruce Hwy; s/d $65/75) Persevere past the terse reception you may receive to the pleasant motel rooms here. You can also buy dinner at the motel's Plantation Restaurant.

Tully's limited accommodation is geared towards fruit pickers. There's the high-density **Banana Barracks** (☎ 4068 0455; www.bananabarracks.com; 50 Butler St; dm $18; ⚼) with a busy after-work bar and budget bistro meals, as well as the more homely **Savoy** (☎ 4068 2400; 4 Plumb St; dm $18) with mainly three to a room. Both hostels can assist travellers to find work year-round.

The **Green Way Caravan Park** (☎ 4068 2055; fax 4068 0681; Murray St; unpowered/powered sites $14/16.50, cabins $50), near the centre of town, is a good option if you're towing a 'van; the cabins and campsites are often full of long-termers.

Getting There & Away

Greyhound Australia (☎ 13 14 99; www.greyhound .com.au) has services from Townsville to Tully ($36, 3¼ hours). Tully is also on the Brisbane–Cairns train line; contact **Queensland Rail** (☎ 1300 131 722; www.traveltrain.qr.com.au) for details.

MISSION BEACH

☎ 07 / pop 1090

Mission Beach is a collection of small settlements that exist entirely to serve you. A range of accommodation, eateries and tour operators comprise the five contented settlements: Wongaling Beach and South Mission Beach are to the south, Mission Beach is in the middle, and Bingil Bay and beautiful Garners Beach are in the north. Sophisticated restaurants and boutique B&Bs mix in with modest cafés and casual backpackers, united in their endeavours to facilitate your enjoyment of the 14km stretch of palm-fringed beach. And when you tire of long languorous days on the sand, there's a boat operator poised to ferry you across to the tropical-island playground of Dunk Island or out to the stunning Great Barrier Reef. The Mission Beach coastline reaches back, touching World Heritage rainforest just inland, with a range of easily accessible walks. There's also a range of 'woo-hoo'-inducing activities such as white-water rafting or skydiving.

History

Mission Beach's calm repose contrasts with its troubled past.

In 1848 early European explorers floundered in the area on an ill-fated search for a path north to Cape York. Assisted by an indigenous man named Jackey Jackey, Edmund Kennedy led 13 men, 28 horses and a flock of sheep north from Tam O'Shanter Point. Before long most of the horses had to be destroyed or died from exhaustion, one man was taken ill and another accidentally shot himself. Only Jackey Jackey made it to the ship waiting at Cape York, and guided officials on a number of searches to locate the other members of the expedition. Kennedy had been speared by an Aborigine, seven men had starved to death, and the other three were never found. There's a memorial to the expedition at Tam O'Shanter Point.

An Aboriginal mission, set up by the Queensland government at present-day South Mission Beach, had existed for only four years when it was destroyed by one of the state's worst cyclones in 1918. Every building was ruined by the 150km/h winds, giant waves and flooding, and it's estimated that at least 40 people lost their lives.

Information

Mission Beach village has comprehensive services: Internet access is available at a number of places on the main strip; ATMs are located in the newsagent and supermarket; and you'll find the post office in the main group of shops.

The Mission Beach **visitors centre** (☎ 4068 7099; www.missionbeachtourism.com; Porters Promenade; ⏱ 9am-5pm) has a wall of pamphlets (in a number of languages). It shares the premises with the **Wet Tropics Environment Centre** (☎ 4068 7179; www.wettropics.gov.au) with rainforest and cassowary conservation displays. It's staffed by volunteers from the **Community for Cassowary & Coastal Conservation** (C4; www.cassowary conservation.asn.au). Proceeds from purchases of some items available at the centre go towards buying cassowary habitat, which is being depleted by development and threatens the survival of the species (see the boxed text on p383).

Sights & Activities

Dunk Island (p323) is a popular day trip from Mission Beach. The Great Barrier Reef is around an hour away, and rainforest walks can get exciting if you come across a cassowary.

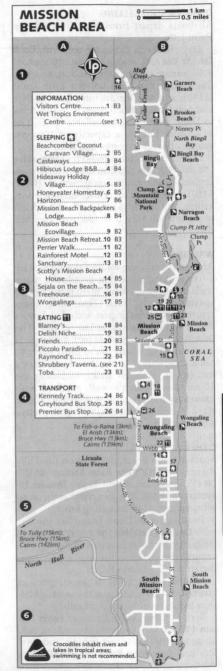

MISSION BEACH AREA

0   1 km
0   0.5 miles

INFORMATION
Visitors Centre............1 B3
Wet Tropics Environment
  Centre...................(see 1)

SLEEPING
Beachcomber Coconut
  Caravan Village.......2 B5
Castaways.................3 B4
Hibiscus Lodge B&B....4 B4
Hideaway Holiday
  Village....................5 B3
Honeyeater Homestay.6 B5
Horizon....................7 B6
Mission Beach Backpackers
  Lodge....................8 B4
Mission Beach
  Ecovillage...............9 B4
Mission Beach Retreat.10 B3
Perrier Walk.............11 B2
Rainforest Motel........12 B3
Sanctuary................13 B1
Scotty's Mission Beach
  House....................14 B5
Sejala on the Beach...15 B4
Treehouse................16 B1
Wongalinga...............17 B5

EATING
Blarney's.................18 B4
Delish Niche.............19 B3
Friends...................20 B3
Piccolo Paradiso.........21 B3
Raymond's...............22 B4
Shrubbery Taverna..(see 21)
Toba.......................23 B3

TRANSPORT
Kennedy Track..........24 B6
Greyhound Bus Stop..25 B3
Premier Bus Stop......26 B4

To Fish-o-Rama (3km);
El Arish (13km);
Bruce Hwy (13km);
Cairns (139km)

To Tully (15km);
Bruce Hwy (15km);
Cairns (142km)

Muff Creek

Garners Beach

Brookes Beach

Ninney Pt

North Bingil Bay

Bingil Bay Beach

Bingil Bay

Clump Mountain National Park

Narragon Beach

Clump Pt Jetty

Clump Pt

Mission Beach

Mission Beach

Seaview St

CORAL SEA

Wongaling Beach

Wongaling Beach

Webb St

Licuala State Forest

Reid Rd

South Mission Beach Rd

North Hull River

South Mission Beach

South Mission Beach

Kennedy St

Cassowary Dr

Bingil Bay Rd

Cedar Creek

Alexander Dr

Porters Promenade

Crocodiles inhabit rivers and lakes in tropical areas; swimming is not recommended.

TOWNSVILLE & NORTH COAST

DIVING & SNORKELLING

All boats depart from busy little Clump Point jetty.

Day cruises to the outer reef with **Quick Cat** (☎ 4068 7289; www.quickcatscuba.com) include a 45-minute stop at Dunk Island, snorkelling, lunch and glass-bottom boat jaunt ($140); add $80 for an introductory dive and $60 for a certified dive. A return ferry to Dunk Island is also available ($34). The MV *Quick Cat* has a capacity of 100 passengers, though averages half that.

Experienced divers should try **Calypso Dive** (☎ 4068 8432; www.calypsodive.com), which runs cruises to the *Lady Bowen* wreck (from $160) on Friday. Day cruises include snorkelling and lunch ($100), with the option of an introductory dive ($60) or certified dive ($40).

WALKING

At the visitors centre walkers should pick up a free walking guide that details the many trails in the area. Among them is the superb coastal Kennedy Track (7km, three hours return), which leads past secluded Lovers Beach and the lookout at Lugger Bay. The inland walks through state park are tropical rainforest, and where you're most likely to see a cassowary. Licuala State Forest has a number of rainforest walks, including the 10-minute children's walk marked with cassowary footprints, and the Lacey Creek track (1.2km, 45 minutes) with interpretive signage and a cassowary display.

OTHER ACTIVITIES

From Mission Beach, day trips on the Tully River with **R'n'R White Water Rafting** (☎ 1800 079 039; www.raft.com.au) and **Raging Thunder Adventures** (☎ 4030 7990; www.ragingthunder.com.au/rafting.asp) cost $140, including lunch.

Paddle over to Dunk Island for the day with **Coral Sea Kayaking** (☎ 4068 9154; www.coralseakayaking.com; half-/full-day tours $60/95) or bob around the coastline for half a day; trips depart South Mission Beach.

Jump the Beach (☎ 4031 1822; www.jumpthebeach.com; tandem dives from $295) uses the sand of Mission Beach to cushion your landing.

Serious fishers should contact **Fishin' Mission** (☎ 4088 6121; fishinmission@bigpond.com; half-/full-day tours $95/140) for reef fishing, and novices could try **Fish-o-Rama** (☎ 4068 5350; www.fish-o-rama.com.au; per hr $20; ⏰ 10am-5pm), a fish-

ery that allows you to fish in its 'lakes'; or you can visit the display tanks and feed really big barras (adult/child $5/3).

Tours

Aussie Farm Entertainment (☎ 4065 3310; adult/child $11/5.50) Will turn out a bit of bush poetry, and show you the farm animals on request – advance bookings required.

Clump Mountain (☎ 4068 7408; clumpmountain@dodo.com.au; half-day tours $40) A guided walk through the Clump Mountain rainforest with a real local, learning about bush tucker, bush medicine and the Dreamtime.

Henry's Tours (☎ 4064 2255) To the cheese factory and dairy in Millaa Millaa (full-day tours adult/child $80/50). Foodies could consider taking one of these on Sunday, or the Wine Culture & Cuisine tour ($60), with a tipple at a few wineries and dinner.

Hinchinbrook Explorer (☎ 4088 6154; www.hexplorer.com.au; adult/child $50/25) Similarly informed four-hour wildlife tours of the Hull River.

River Rat Eco Cruises (☎ 4068 8018; www.riverratcruises.com; adult/child $50/25) Informed wildlife-spotting tours along the Hull River that last for around four hours and include a light meal.

Sellars Banana Farm Tours (☎ 4068 7099; 1½-hr tours adult/child $15/10; ⏰ 1.30pm Tue & Thu) Visit a plantation.

Sleeping

Mission Beach is generally less affected than areas like Cairns and Port Douglas, and so prices remain pretty stable year-round; there might be a slight dip during the Wet. Most of the action is clustered around Mission Beach, and to a lesser extent around Wongaling.

SOUTH MISSION BEACH

Horizon (☎ 4068 8154; www.thehorizon.com.au; Explorer Dr; r $220-420; ❌ 🐕) Mission Beach's secluded resort, Horizon is tucked away in the rainforest, pertinently positioned above Luggers Beach, with views out to Dunk Island and beyond. If you go for the best they've got, you could appreciate that view from your king-sized bed. There's a tour-booking desk and a restaurant, which is open to nonguests.

Beachcomber Coconut Caravan Village (☎ 1800 008 129, 4068 8129; big4bccv@bigpond.com.au; Kennedy St; unpowered/powered sites $24/28, d cabins $55-80, 2-bedroom villas $110; ❌ 🐕) A superb family option, the Beachcomber is often booked up during school holidays, when there's a bright holiday commune feel to the place – the kids can muck around in the pool or playground with the kids next door, and leave you with the place to yourself. Accommodation prices are for two adults; add $8 for each kid and $8 for linen hire. Cabin prices vary according to their position (beachfront or behind the loos).

WONGALING BEACH

Hibiscus Lodge B&B (☎ 4068 9096; hibiscuslodge@ bigpond.com; 5 Kurrajong Close; s/d $75/120; ☒ ☒) Make sure you eat that little chocolate on your pillow before you bed down for the night, or things could get messy. Which is very uncharacteristic of this tidy B&B, propped on a manicured lawn. Three rooms in this capacious modern home have been set aside for guests – all with their own bathrooms. Rates include a cooked breakfast, and the beautifully shaded pool makes the property unsuitable for littlies.

Wongalinga (☎ 4068 8221; www.wongalinga.com .au; 64 Reid Rd; 1-/2-/3-bedroom apt $180/210/250; ☒ ☒) If you've always wanted your own beachfront holiday apartment, stay here. Grab a friend or two and live very comfortably for the duration of your stay in Mission Beach. Prices for these fully self-contained contemporary pads are for two people in the one-bedroom, four people in the two-bedroom and six for the three-bedder. Each apartment has an outdoor and indoor entertainment area.

Scotty's Mission Beach House (☎ 1800 665 567, 4068 8676; scottysbeachhouse@bigpond.com; 167 Reid Rd; dm $19-23, d $55; ☒ ☐ ☒) Behind the white picket fence of Scotty's Bar & Grill is a secluded pocket of accommodation with beautiful grounds and stellar facilities. The bright dorm rooms, sleeping four to 12, are a beachy shade of blue, and the sassy doubles have their own bathroom. Friendly staff will welcome you to the fold.

Honeyeater Homestay (☎ 4068 8741; www.honey eater.com.au; 53 Reid Rd; s/d $85/100; ☒) Huge floor cushions and low-slung heavy wooden furniture distinguish this stylish B&B. Its open-plan, open-ended living area leads to a tropical garden, where your fittingly tropical breakfast is served. Louvred rooms continue the Balinese theme with batik bed linen.

Mission Beach Backpackers Lodge (☎ 4068 8317; www.missionbeachbackpacker.com; 28 Wongaling Beach Rd; dm $18, d $40-44; ☐ ☒) Check out

the pool area festooned with hammocks as you approach the main building here. This building houses the dorm rooms and a few doubles (ask for one with a balcony), while the front single-story building near the car park has four doubles that share facilities between them.

MISSION BEACH

Mission Beach Ecovillage (☎ 4068 7534; www.eco village.com.au; Clump Point Rd; d $141-155; ☒ ☒) A palm-lined path meanders through the property, which has 17 units tucked away off the main pathway. Each unassuming unit has a kitchen and dining area, big beds and – if you go for the deluxe room – a spa. The free-form pool is a stunner, and you can see the beach from the bar area.

Rainforest Motel (☎ 4068 7556; www.mission beachrainforestmotel.com; 9 Endeavour Ave; d $80; ☒ ☒) A few tidy rooms enclose the rainforest re-enactment in the courtyard, which is something like Mission Beach's version of a gnome garden: here there's a big stone cassowary, a snake and a lizard. Each of the good-sized rooms has a little fridge, a kettle, a microwave and its own bathroom. A path leads out the back of the motel through to the shops on the main street.

Sejala on the Beach (☎ 4088 6699; http://mission beachholidays.com.au/sejala; 1 Pacific St; d $175-195; ☒ ☒) These first-class beach huts are screened to allow sea breezes through. The open-plan interior, with kitchen and bathroom, makes a comfortable retreat for couples. There are three huts of varying sizes: each painted a saucy solid colour.

Hideaway Holiday Village (☎ 1800 687 104, 4068 7104; hideaway@austarnet.com.au; 58-60 Porter Promenade; unpowered/powered sites $23/27, d $58-75; ☐ ☒) This centrally located caravan park provides cool, shady sites for you to pitch or park. Cabins with/without a private bathroom are also available for couples. And families could check out the larger villas that sleep up to five.

Castaways (☎ 1800 079 002, 4068 7444; www .castaways.com.au; Pacific Pde; r $85-180; ☒ ☒) This extensive multilevel resort offers a range of rooms starting with your standard non-balcony configuration and moving up to a self-contained suite with a balcony. If you like your accommodation innocuous and impersonal, try Castaways, which also has a restaurant and bar.

Mission Beach Retreat (☎ 1800 001 056, 4088 6229; www.missionbeachretreat.com.au; 49 Porter Promenade; dm/d $21/44; ✷ ▢ ▨) This budget hostel, located on the main street, feels a bit like being in a bunker, with its low ceilings and concrete bricks. So stock up on tinned food; there's a good communal kitchen, as well as useful facilities such as bike hire and Internet access.

BINGIL BAY

Sanctuary (☎ 4088 6067, 1800 777 012; www.sanctuaryatmission.com; Holt Rd; dm $33, s/d huts $60/61, s/d cabins $130/150; ▢ ▨) A rainforest boardwalk connects these minimalist huts designed to make you feel at one with the surrounding nature. And the peaceful communal lounge area makes the most of natural light and breezes. The Om ambience is not so hardline as to disallow a few indulgences, however: the restaurant serves such treats as vodka-and-lime chicken, and perhaps *affogato* for dessert. Deluxe cabins are also available, with private bathrooms and handcrafted natural wood furnishings. Sanctuary hosts regular yoga retreats and classes, and is unsuitable for anyone under 11 years.

Treehouse (☎ 4068 7137; www.yha.com.au; Bingil Bay Rd; unpowered sites $12, dm/d $20/50; ▨) You'll be impressed by the large timber building here that merges effortlessly with the surrounding rainforest. The generous balcony space is dotted with heavy wooden tables that are strewn with board games, international newspapers and books. It all makes for a remarkably restful and affable stay. Treehouse is a YHA-affiliated hostel.

Eating

Mission Beach is seasoned with a medley of places to eat: from main-street cafés, with familiar menus of sandwiches and light lunches, to stylish restaurants with attentive service.

Friends (☎ 4068 7107; Porter Promenade, Mission Beach; mains $17-25; ☾ dinner Tue-Sun) Palms wave behind the lattice walls and candlelight flickers at this cosy licensed and BYO restaurant. Dutiful staff cruise around the low-key surrounds with plates of steaming seafood laksa, or familiar favourites such as roast chicken held high. There's a small selection of specials, and an especially good wine list.

Blarney's (☎ 4068 8472; 10 Wongaling Beach Rd, Wongaling; mains $24; ☾ dinner Tue-Sat, lunch Sun)

Blarney's is blessed with a big backyard in which to serve its hearty dishes. Its bamboo-thatched ceilings and lattice screens contribute to the casual space. The professional service delivers mostly meat dishes, such as beef Wellington and steak-and-kidney pie, from the à la carte menu.

Toba (☎ 4068 7852; 37 Porter Promenade, Mission Beach; mains $21-25; ☾ dinner Wed-Sun) Toba dishes up polite portions of Asian-inspired meals, such as salmon with Chinese black vinegar and Thai green curry. The courtyard is the main attraction, though, especially the platform hut with cushioned seating. Well-spaced tables, sultry lighting and formal service make Toba's popular with small groups and couples.

Raymond's (☎ 4068 8177; cnr Banfield & Webb Sts, Wongaling; mains $22-26; ☾ lunch & dinner Tue-Sun) Being on the beachfront makes the Thai prawns and coral trout with *chermoula* (Moroccan marinade) that extra little bit tastier. Or if you think their friends might be watching from the shallows, you can dine inside.

Shrubbery Taverna (☎ 4068 7803; David St; mains $17-20; ☾ lunch Sat & Sun, dinner daily) Locals like the laid-back service and courtyard dining here at the Shrubbery. Balmy nights and the sound of waves washing the beach do wonders for the Mediterranean-Greek menu. And there's a happy hour-and-a-half between 4.30pm and 6pm.

Delish Niche (☎ 4088 6004; Porter Promenade; dishes $6-10; ☾ breakfast & lunch) This home-style café can whip up fine cooked breakfasts and light lunches such as quiche or a sandwich. Sit inside, among the curious collection of crafty gift items, or preferably under a big umbrella on the street.

Piccolo Paradiso (☎ 4068 7008; David St, Mission Beach; ☺ breakfast, lunch & dinner) This casual place is always busy, which may account for the sometimes perfunctory service, resulting in your order never finding the kitchen. Still, we all have bad days. The dinner menu is predominantly pizza and pasta, with a selection of specials such as barramundi. By day it's also an Internet café, serving breakfast 'til 10.30am.

There are supermarkets for self-caterers at Mission Beach and Wongalinga.

Getting There & Around

Greyhound Australia (☎ 13 20 30; www.greyhound .com.au) makes the detour from the Bruce Hwy stopping on Porters Promenade in the village of Mission Beach. **Premier** (☎ 13 34 10; www.premierms.com.au) buses stop in Wongaling Beach. The average bus fare from Cairns is $25 (two hours) and from Townsville $45 (3¾ hours).

The **Trans North** (☎ 4068 7400; tickets from $3; ☺ Mon-Sat) local bus runs almost every hour between Bingil Bay and South Mission Beach; the visitors centre has timetables.

DUNK ISLAND

You almost expect a greeting from Mr Roarke and Tattoo as you step off the long jetty onto the resort island of Dunk. Instead, staff sing out salutations from passing golf buggies, and holidaymakers splash about in hyper-blue water and disappear into the folds of the interior's rainforest.

Part national park, part resort, Dunk Island (one of the Family Islands Group) is about 4km (20 minutes) off the coast and an easy day trip from Mission Beach. Once there you can take a walk in the park, swim, snorkel or partake in the range of water sports on offer.

The island's abundant species of birds (more than 100), butterflies, coral gardens and marine life were the inspiration for the transcendentalist EJ Banfield, who wrote four novels while living on the island between 1897 and 1923. Of them, *The Confessions of a Beachcomber* is probably the most well known. **Banfield's grave** is a short walk

from the jetty towards Muggy Muggy. Visual artists also use the island as inspiration, staying at the artists' colony established in 1974 by Bruce Arthur – known for his tapestries. At the south end of Pallon Beach you can visit **Bruce Arthur's Gallery** (admission $4; ☺ 10am-1pm Mon & Thu), which exhibits pottery, jewellery and paintings by resident artists.

You can almost circumnavigate the island using the park's well-marked **walking trails** (9km, three hours). Otherwise, a walk to the top of Mt Kootaloo (271m, 5.6km, 1½ hours return) allows you to look back to the mainland and see Hinchinbrook Channel fanning out before you. There's good **snorkelling** over bommies at Muggy Muggy and great swimming at Coconut Beach.

Otherwise daytrippers can utilise a limited number of the resort's facilities by purchasing a Resort Experience Pass (adult/child $40/20) available from the Watersports Centre just south of the jetty. This entitles you to lunch at one of the resort's cafés and an hour's use of a paddle ski.

Sleeping & Eating

Options here are limited to the resort's offerings or camping.

Dunk Island Resort (☎ 4068 8199, reservations 1800 737 678; www.dunk-island.com; s $365-520, d $500-800; ☒ ☒) Rates include breakfast and dinner, plus unlimited use of nonmotorised water-sports equipment. The rooms are pretty nice too, and become pretty superb if you choose to stay in a beachfront suite. Think split-level accommodation, a huge bed, personal access to the beach and views over Brammo Bay.

The **QPWS camping ground** (☎ 4068 8199; www .epa.qld.gov.au; per person $4) has nine sites on a gravel patch just back from the jetty; there are toilets and showers.

Daytrippers can buy basic food and beverages from the licensed café just south of the jetty.

Getting There & Away

Macair (☎ 13 13 13; www.macair.com.au) has regular flights to/from Cairns for around $190 (40 minutes).

Combination bus-and-boat transfers to Dunk with **Mission Beach Dunk Island Connections** (☎ 4059 2709; www.missionbeachdunkconnections .com.au) cost $50 from Cairns (2½ hours) and $75 from Port Douglas (3¾ hours).

Return ferry trips (including snorkelling) to Dunk Island from Mission Beach cost about $22, with **Dunk Island Express Water Taxi** (☎ 4068 8310; Banfield Pde, Wongaling) and **Dunk Island Ferry & Cruises** (☎ 4068 7211; www.dunkferry.com.au; Clump Point), which also does a cruise to Bedarra Island.

Quick Cat (see p320) also offers transfers, or you can paddle over with Coral Sea Kayaking (see p320).

BEDARRA ISLAND

The privately owned Bedarra Island is famed for its exclusive resort. Part of the Family Islands Group, Bedarra is cloaked in rainforest and fringed with sandy beaches. It was first purchased from Queensland Lands for £20 in 1913 by a European, inspired by Banfield's writings. It was subdivided in the 1930s and it seems properties were subsequently passed between artists' hands every five years or so. There are eight private homes in Doorila Bay, and then there's the resort.

What began as a small tourist resort in 1979 blossomed into the exclusive Bedarra Resort, variously owned and renovated by Qantas, P&O and most recently Voyager.

So what does two grand a night buy you these days? Seclusion mostly. With only 16 beachfront villas, **Bedarra Island Resort** (☎ 4068 8233; www.bedarraisland.com; s $1240-1850, d $1980-3200; ✷ ▢ ▨) boasts that there are often more beaches than guests. Each stunning split-level villa has its own private plunge pool and outdoor area with a day bed – where a bucket of ice and plate

---

DETOUR

Continuing the Family Islands theme of tropical-island seclusion, **Wheeler** and **Coombe Islands** are little-visited destinations that are known for their beauty and position. Unlike their other well-known Family members, however, these two are short of a luxury resort. The only facilities on these islands are picnic tables, and there's a toilet on Wheeler Island at the **QPWS camping sites** (☎ 4068 8199; www.epa.qld.gov.au; per person $4), which can be booked from the visitors centre in Mission Beach. You'll need to be entirely self-sufficient and charter a boat to get there; ask at the visitors centre.

---

of canapés is delivered daily. There's a bar open 24/7 and all meals are included whenever you're peckish; choose from the daily menu. Be sure to order a gourmet picnic hamper before you shoot off in the dinghy to explore other parts of the island.

MISSION BEACH TO INNISFAIL

The road north from Mission Beach rejoins the Bruce Hwy at El Arish. From here you can take the more direct route north by continuing straight along the Bruce Hwy, or you can detour west and take the Old Bruce Hwy.

The Bruce Hwy passes through Mourilyan, about 7km south of Innisfail. Mourilyan is home to the **Australian Sugar Industry Museum** (☎ 4063 2306; www.sugarmuseum.org.au; Bruce Hwy; adult/child $8/6; ☾ 9am-5pm Mon-Sat, 9am-3pm Sun May-Oct & 9am-5pm Mon-Fri, 9am-3pm Sat, 9am-noon Sun Nov-Apr), which focuses on the significant influence on Queensland culture that the industry has wielded. In a refurbished old cinema, the museum houses a collection of photographs, artefacts and oral histories, as well as contemporary visual exhibitions.

The Old Bruce Hwy (Japoonvale Rd) is generally the more scenic route north. It runs along banana and sugar-cane plantations, with cane trains intermittently cutting across the road during harvest (June to December). Among all this agricultural activity are the enchanting ruins of a once-grand castle at **Paronella Park** (☎ 4065 3225; www.paronellapark.com.au; Japoonvale Rd; adult/child $20/10; ☾ 9am-9.30pm), just south of Mena Creek. It reveals an intriguing history of a couple's quest to bring a whimsical entertainment centre to the area's hard-working folk. Built in the 1930s, the rambling mossy Spanish ruins have an almost medieval feel, and a number of walking trails lead through the stunning gardens past a waterfall and swimming hole. Take the tour that's included in your ticket price to hear the full, fascinating story.

INNISFAIL & AROUND

☎ 07 / pop 8530

Innisfail's beautiful buildings may incite wolf whistles from passing motorists with an appreciation for Art Deco. Essentially a service centre for the area's agricultural industries, Innisfail (80km south of Cairns) gracefully goes about its business unper-

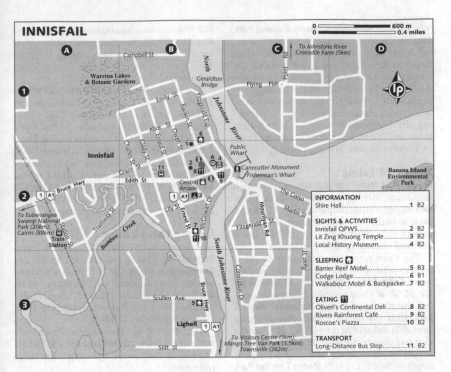

INNISFAIL

INFORMATION	
Shire Hall	1 B2

SIGHTS & ACTIVITIES	
Innisfail QPWS	2 B2
Lit Zing Khuong Temple	3 B2
Local History Museum	4 B2

SLEEPING ⌂	
Barrier Reef Motel	5 B3
Codge Lodge	6 B1
Walkabout Motel & Backpacker	7 B2

EATING ⑪	
Oliveri's Continental Deli	8 B2
Rivers Rainforest Café	9 B2
Roscoe's Piazza	10 B2

TRANSPORT	
Long-Distance Bus Stop	11 B2

TOWNSVILLE & NORTH COAST

turbed by the tourist commotion on either side of it. At the confluence of the North and South Johnstone Rivers, a stroll along Fitzgerald Esplanade's waterfront reveals a line of stocky fishing boats to one side and the tops of grand buildings to the other.

Innisfail's cosmopolitan past credits Chinese settlers with establishing the area's banana plantations. Italians also influenced the area; arriving in the early 20th century to work the cane fields, a local branch of the Mafia known as the Black Hand oversaw certain operations. Founded on sugar around 1880, Innisfail was called Geraldton until 1910 after a ship bound for Western Australia's Geraldton mistakenly arrived here.

The prosperous sugar city suffered a devastating cyclone in 1918, but its reconstruction came at the height of the sleek 1920s and '30s Art Deco movement.

Information & Orientation

The **visitors centre** (☎ 4061 7422; Bruce Hwy; ☼ 9am-5pm Mon-Fri, 10am-3pm Sat & Sun), about 3km south of town, has a town walk brochure. There's also a **QPWS office** (☎ 4061 5900; Flying Fish Point Rd; 8.30am-4.30pm) in Innisfail. Otherwise you can take a guided **Art Deco Tour** (☎ 4061 9008; artdecotour@bigpond.com; adult/child $15/7; ☼ 7.30-9am & 10.30am-noon) departing from the stunning Shire Hall in the town's elegant Rankin St (advance bookings required).

Sights & Activities

The **Local History Museum** (☎ 4061 2731; 11 Edith St; admission $3; ☼ 10am-noon & 1-3pm Mon-Fri) is in the old School of Arts building, and displays various items evidencing Innisfail's history. Further evidence lies in the red façade of **Lit Zing Khuong** (Temple of the Universal God; Owen St; admission by donation); its puffs of incense a gentle reminder of the area's Chinese heritage.

Head east over Geraldton Bridge to the **Johnstone River Crocodile Farm** (☎ 4061 1121; www.crocfarm.com; Flying Fish Point Rd; adult/child $16/8; ☼ 8.30am-4.30pm, feeding times 11am & 3pm) where crocs are bred for handbags and steak. Tours run frequently (from 9.30am) where you can watch one of the guides sit on one-tonne Gregory – the farm's fattest reptile.

About 20km north of Innisfail on the Bruce Hwy is the turn-off to the bird-rich

wetlands of **Eubenangee Swamp National Park**.
During the Wet the water level of the Russell River rises such that it causes the Alice
River to flow backwards, which floods the
swamp. A 1km walking trail follows the
Alice River (a waterway with a healthy croc
population) through the mangroves and
leads to an elevated grassy knoll overlooking the lily-studded wetlands. From here
there are also views over to Mt Bartle Frere
in Wooroonooran National Park (p345).

Sleeping & Eating

Barrier Reef Motel (☎ 4061 4988; www.barrierreef
motel.com.au; Bruce Hwy; s/d $75/85; ✷ ⬛ ☎) This
two-storey motel complex houses 41 rooms:
each a bathroom and enough TV channels to wear out the remote. There's also a
licensed restaurant on the premises.

The town's hostels cater to the banana-
pickers who work the surrounding plantations. **Codge Lodge** (☎ 4061 8055; 63 Rankin St; dm
$20; ✷ ⬛ ☎) is in a superb home overlook-
ing the river. Or there's **Walkabout Motel &
Backpacker** (☎ 4061 2311; motelwalkabout@bigpond
.com; 20-24 McGowan Dr; dm/d $20/60; ✷), which
also has dowdy motel-style rooms.

Just off the Bruce Hwy, about 3.5km
south of town, the tidy **Mango Tree Van Park**
(☎ 4061 1656; mangotreepark@bigpond.com; unpowered
sites $15, d $70; ✷) has two great cottage-style
cabins and camping sites among tropical-
fruit gardens on the banks of the South
Johnstone River.

For lunch, **Oliveri's Continental Deli** (☎ 4061
3354; 41 Edith St; sandwiches $6; ✷ 8.30am-5.30pm Mon-
Fri, 8.30am-1pm Sat) is an authentic Italian deli-
catessen with loads of goodies to build you
a delicious pannini. The more formal **Rivers
Rainforest Cafe** (☎ 4061 9490; 2 Edith St; meals $10-13;
✷ breakfast & lunch Mon-Sat) is a licensed place
with outdoor seating and a varied menu,
and the homely **Roscoe's Piazza** (☎ 4061 6888, 3b
Ernest St; mains $10-14; ✷ lunch & dinner) is a popu-
lar local serving pizza and pasta.

Getting There & Away

Bus services operate at least daily with
Premier (☎ 13 34 10; www.premierms.com.au) and
Greyhound Australia (☎ 13 14 99; www.greyhound
.com.au) from Innisfail to Townsville ($46,
4½ hours) and Cairns ($22, 1½ hours), de-
parting from the bus stop opposite King
George Square on Edith St.

Innisfail is on the Cairns–Townsville
train line; contact **Queensland Rail** (☎ 1300 131
722; www.traveltrain.com.au; ✷ 6am-9pm) for more
information.

Cairns, Islands & Highlands

CONTENTS

HIGHLIGHTS

- Hoping that a ripple on the river is a platypus surfacing in picturesque **Yungaburra** (p362)
- Counting turtles in beautiful **Lake Eacham** (p364), picnicking lakeside and sunbathing on its green sloping bank
- Making like a castaway (who was fortuitously stranded with snorkel gear) on the secluded **Frankland Islands** (p352) off Cairns
- Appreciating the idyllic **waterfalls** (p361) of the lofty Tableland
- Being a guest of the many fish, turtles and anemones that live in the colourful corals of the **Great Barrier Reef** (p335)
- Taking a breather from busy Cairns in the **Botanic Gardens & Tank Arts Centre** (p333)
- Blessing the sun god from your prostrate position on one of **Cairns' Northern Beaches** (p346)

Cairns' Northern Beaches ★
Great Barrier Reef
Cairns ★
Yungaburra ★ ★ Lake Eacham
★ Frankland Islands
★ Waterfalls

- www.tropicalaustralia.com.au
- www.athertontableland.com

Cairns and its neighbouring beaches, islands and rainforest areas comprise one of the most favoured holiday destinations in the world. Most visitors come to pull on a skin-tight rubber suit and dive the magnificent Great Barrier Reef, while on land groups of sightseers in bright tropical shirts are shepherded from one photo opportunity to the next. This region is like a 'best of' northern Queensland, where all the essential ingredients have been appropriated and made readily accessible. Animal sanctuaries abound, so visitors are assured of wildlife encounters; boardwalks lead through carefully selected tracts of rainforest, and you don't even have to leave the car to see some of the area's abundance of waterfalls.

The Cairns region contains diverse pockets of reef, rainforest, coast and rural land that can be appreciated in numerous ways. You can dive, snorkel, cruise, kayak, skydive, fish, bird-watch, hot-air balloon, golf or take a scenic flight. Cairns is also the hub for tours to areas further afield. Or you can sloth on a palm-fringed beach where turning the page of a novel is the most you'll exert yourself.

The highland region of the Atherton Tableland forms a leafy backdrop to the coast. Its lush folds of rainforest conceal volcanic crater lakes, waterfalls, natural swimming holes and giant strangled fig trees. Further inland, rural patches provide the ingredients for the area's developing boutique food industry, including coffee, dairy and tropical-fruit products. And the supporting towns and villages always have a pub or three where you'll find an honest meal and an empty stubby-holder with your name on it.

Getting There & Away

Cairns is the main link for transport services to far north Queensland.

AIR

The major international airport servicing north Queensland is in Cairns, with flights from Asia and New Zealand stopping here. There are also frequent domestic flights to/from all Australian capital cities.

BOAT

There are daily ferry services between Cairns and Port Douglas.

BUS

Cairns is the end of the line for bus services travelling the Bruce Hwy from Brisbane. It is also the starting point for services north to Port Douglas, Mossman, Cape Tribulation and Cooktown.

CAR & MOTORCYCLE

The Bruce Hwy is the major coastal route from the south, and the Captain Cook Hwy extends north from Cairns to Port Douglas. Most people heading north do so by car or 4WD. Drivers can also reach Ravenshoe and the Atherton Tableland via the inland Kennedy Highway from Charters Towers.

TRAIN

There are at least four services a week from Brisbane to Cairns on Queensland Rail's *Sunlander* (p465).

CAIRNS

☎ 07 / pop 98,981

The majority of people who come to Cairns can't wait to get out – to the Great Barrier Reef off shore. Many of the 1.4 million dives made on the Reef each year set out from Cairns, making it one of the most popular diving destinations in the world; a staggering number of operators vie for your business. This purpose-built tourist centre can cater to all your holiday needs – even those you didn't know you had. Have a sudden urge to bungee between breakfast and souvenir-shopping? No problem.

Cairns' popularity is global: its international airport services four Japanese cities weekly, street signs are written in two or three languages and the city's restaurants represent a huge range of world cuisines. Extensive planning and over $45 million have gone into ensuring Cairns is well liked, which has resulted in a contrived, theme-park ambience. An artificial beach was constructed over the natural mudflats and mangroves to comply with visitors' expectations of tropical Queensland – there's a slither of sand (dredged off shore) and the sea has been replicated in the Esplanade's saltwater swimming lagoon. You'll find a simulated rainforest habitat at the casino, replete with the 4m crocodile, Goliath, and you can even buy professionally-taken photos that attest to the beauty of the region – even if that's not how you experienced it.

Anything is possible here. It's a city built for leisure, designed to please and available in a variety of styles: from easy-listening to raucous. There are always busloads of other travellers here, and the plethora of tours and transport options make it an exceptionally convenient place to start a trip.

ORIENTATION

Cairns' business district runs from the Esplanade on the waterfront back to Sheridan St, and is bordered by Wharf and Aplin Sts.

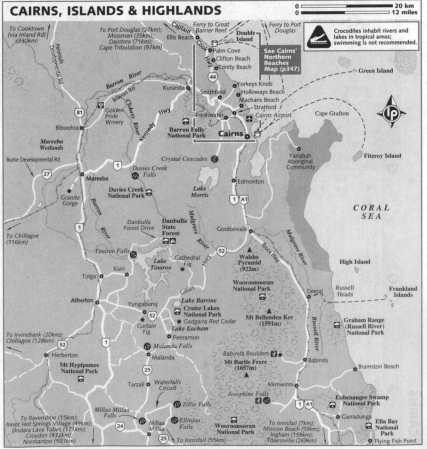

CAIRNS, ISLANDS & HIGHLANDS

CAIRNS

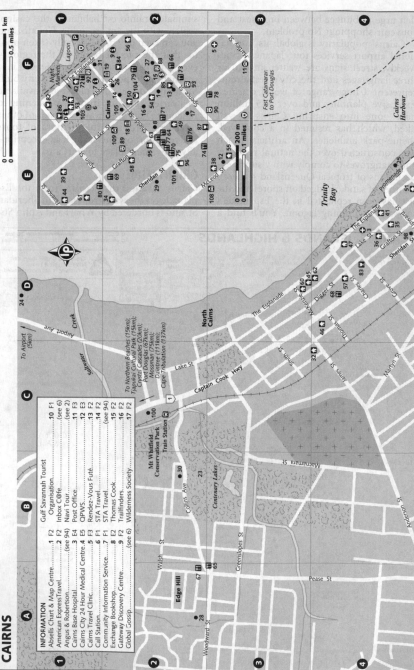

INFORMATION

Absells Chart & Map Centre......................1	F2
American Express Travel..........................2	F2
Angus & Robertson...............................(see 2)	
Cairns Base Hospital...............................3	E4
Cairns City 24 Hour Medical Centre...4	E5
Cairns Travel Clinic..............................5	F3
Call Station..6	F1
Community Information Service...........7	F1
Exchange Bookshop................................8	E2
Gateway Discovery Centre....................9	F2
Global Gossip.......................................(see 6)	
Gulf Savannah Tourist	
Organisation.....................................10	F1
Inbox C@fe..(see 2)	
Navi Tour...11	F3
Post Office...12	E3
QPWS...13	F2
Rendez-Vous Futé...............................14	F2
STA Travel...15	F2
STA Travel..(see 94)	
Thomas Cook.......................................16	F2
Trailfinders...17	F2
Wilderness Society...........................(see 6)	

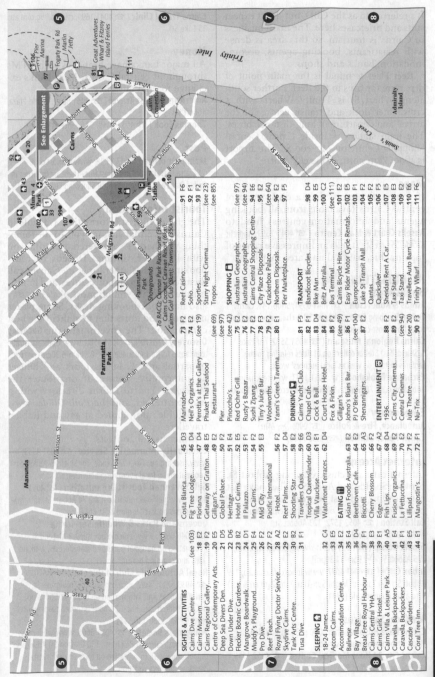

SIGHTS & ACTIVITIES
Cairns Dive Centre	(see 103)	
Cairns Museum	18	F2
Cairns Regional Gallery	19	F2
Centre of Contemporary Arts	20	E5
Deep Sea Divers Den	21	D5
Down Under Dive	22	D6
Flecker Botanic Gardens	23	B2
Mangrove Boardwalk	24	D1
Muddy's Playground	25	E4
Pro Dive	26	E4
Reef Teach	27	F2
Royal Flying Doctor Service	28	A2
Skydive Cairns	29	E2
Tank Arts Centre	30	B2
Tusa Dive	31	F1

SLEEPING
18-24 James	32	C4
Accom Cairns	33	E5
Accommodation Centre	34	E2
Balinese	35	E4
Bay Village	36	D4
Break Free Royal Harbour	37	F1
Cairns Central YHA	38	E3
Cairns Girls Hostel	39	E1
Cairns Villa & Leisure Park	40	A5
Caravella Backpackers	41	E4
Caravella Backpackers	42	F1
Cascade Gardens	43	E5
Coral Tree Inn	44	E1

Costa Blanca	45	D3
Fig Tree Lodge	46	D4
Floriana	47	D4
Getaway on Grafton	48	E5
Gilligan's	49	E2
Global Palace	50	F2
Heritage	51	E4
Hotel Cairns	52	E5
Il Palazzo	53	E4
Inn Cairns	54	F2
Mid City	55	E3
Pacific International Hotel	56	F2
Reef Palms	57	D4
Shooting Star	58	E2
Travellers Oasis	59	E6
Tropical Queenslander	60	D3
Villa Vaucluse	61	E1
Waterfront Terraces	62	D4

EATING
Asian Foods Australia	63	E2
Beethoven Cafe	64	E2
Biscotti	65	A3
Cherry Blossom	66	F2
Edge	67	A2
Fish Lips	68	D4
Fusion Organics	69	E2
La Fettuccina	70	E2
Lillipad	71	F2
Mangostin's	72	F1

Marinades	73	F2
Neil's Organics	74	E2
Perotta's at the Gallery	(see 19)	
Phuket Thai Seafood Restaurant	(see 69)	
Pier	(see 97)	
Pinocchio's	75	E2
Red Ochre Grill	76	E2
Rusty's Bazaar	77	E2
Sushi Zipang	78	F3
Tiny's Juice Bar	79	F2
Woolworths	80	E1
Yanni's Greek Taverna		

DRINKING
Cairns Yacht Club	81	F5
Chapel Cafe	82	F1
Cock & Bull	83	D4
Court House Hotel	84	F2
Fox & Firkin	85	F2
Gilligan's	(see 49)	
Johno's Blues Bar	86	F1
PJ O'Briens	(see 104)	
Shenannigans	87	E2

ENTERTAINMENT
1936	88	F2
Cairns City Cinemas	89	E2
Central Cinemas	(see 94)	
Jute Theatre	90	E2
Nu-Trix	91	F3

Reef Casino	91	F6
Soho	92	F1
Sporties	93	D4
Starry Night Cinema	(see 23)	
Tropos	(see 85)	

SHOPPING
Australian Geographic	(see 97)	
Australian Geographic	(see 94)	
Cairns Central Shopping Centre	94	E6
City Place Disposals	95	E2
Crackerbox Palace	(see 64)	
Northern Disposals	96	E2
Pier Marketplace	97	F5

TRANSPORT
Bandicoot Bicycles	98	D4
Bike Man	99	E5
Britz Australia	100	C2
Bus Terminal	(see 111)	
Cairns Bicycle Hire	101	E2
Easy Rider Motor Cycle Rentals	102	E5
Europcar	103	F1
Lake St Transit Mall	104	F2
Qantas	105	E2
Quicksilver	106	F5
Sheridan Rent A Car	107	E5
Taxi Stand	108	E3
Taxi Stand	109	E2
Travellers Auto Barn	110	E6
Trinity Wharf	111	F6

It's referred to as the CBD, but don't expect suits and briefcases here. The main business in Cairns is tourism, so this area is dense with restaurants, booking agents, accommodation, banks and shops.

Reef Fleet terminal is the main point of departure for trips to the Reef. Further south along Wharf St is Trinity Wharf, with a cruise-liner dock and transit centre for the arrival and departure of long-distance buses. The train station is inside Cairns Central Shopping Centre on McLeod St. The airport is about 7km north of the city centre.

Maps
If you're after more than a dinky map of central Cairns (available from all booking agents and information centres) head to **Absells Chart & Map Centre** (☎ 4041 2699; Andrejic Arcade, 55 Lake St). It sells an impressive range of topographic, nautical and area maps.

INFORMATION
Bookshops
Angus & Robertson (☎ 4041 0591; Shop 141, Cairns Central Shopping Centre, McLeod St) A chain store carrying titles from most categories.
Cairns Regional Museum (☎ 4051 5582; cnr Lake & Shields Sts) Stellar collection of titles relating to the region's history, as well as local authors' works.
Exchange Bookshop (☎ 4051 1443; www.exchange bookshop.com; 78 Grafton St) New and secondhand books.

Emergency
Ambulance, Fire & Police (☎ 000; ☯ 24hr)
Cairns Police Station (☎ 4030 7000)

Internet Access
Internet cafés are clustered along Abbott St, between Shields and Aplin Sts. They have fast connections, and cost between $2 and $5 per hour. You could try one of the following:
Call Station (☎ 4052 1572; 123 Abbott St; ☯ 8.30am-11.30pm)
Global Gossip (☎ 4031 6411; www.globalgossip.com; 125 Abbott St; ☯ 9am-11.30pm)
Inbox C@fe (☎ 4041 4677; www.inboxcafe.com.au; 119 Abbott St; ☯ 7am-midnight Sun-Thu, 7am-2am Fri & Sat) Also a hip licensed café (p341).

Medical Services
Cairns Base Hospital (☎ 4050 6333; The Esplanade) Has a 24-hour emergency service.
Cairns City 24 Hour Medical Centre (☎ 4052 1119; cnr Florence & Grafton Sts)

Cairns Travel Clinic (☎ 4041 1699; ctlmed@iig.com.au; 15 Lake St)

Money
All major banks have branches with ATMs throughout central Cairns. Most banks exchange foreign currency.
American Express Travel (☎ 4051 8811; Orchid Plaza, Abbott St)
Thomas Cook (☎ 4031 3040; 13 Spence St)

Post
Main post office (☎ 13 13 18; www.auspost.com; 13 Grafton St) Handles poste restante. There are branches in Orchid Plaza and in Cairns Central Shopping Centre.

Tourist Information
The glut of tourist information available in Cairns can either inspire you to do something you hadn't considered, or baffle you with its sheer volume. Dozens of tour-booking agents operating in Cairns call themselves 'information centres' and brandish the blue 'i' symbol; most places to stay also have tour-booking desks. Some places may push the tours that give them the best commission. The government-run **Gateway Discovery Centre** (☎ 4051 3588; www.tropicalaustralia .com.au; 51 The Esplanade; ☯ 8.30am-6.30pm) offers impartial advice, books tours and houses an interpretive centre. It distributes the *Welcomes You to Cairns* directory with a map centrefold, and the *Pink Guide* (www .pinkguide.info), aimed at gay and lesbian travellers.

Other useful contacts:
Community Information Service (☎ 4051 4953; www.cisci.org.au; Tropical Arcade, cnr Shield & Abbott Sts) Information on local events and activities.
Gulf Savannah Tourist Organisation (☎ 4051 4658; www.gulf-savannah.com.au; 74 Abbott St) Information on this outback region west of Cairns.
Queensland Parks & Wildlife Service (QPWS; ☎ 4046 6602; www.epa.qld.gov.au; 2-4 McLeod St) Information on national parks and state forests, walking trails and camping permits.
Royal Automobile Club of Queensland (RACQ; ☎ 4033 6711; www.racq.com.au; 520 Mulgrave St, Earlville) Maps and information on road conditions up to Cape York. It also has a 24-hour recorded road-report service (☎ 1300 130 595).
Wilderness Society (☎ 4051 6666; www.wilderness .org.au/local/cairns/index.html; 130 Grafton St) Advocacy organisation with information on local environmental issues; volunteers welcome.

Travel Agencies

Navi Tour (☎ 4031 6776; www.navitour.com.au in Japanese; Shop 38, 1st fl, Orchid Plaza, 58 Lake St) Caters to Japanese travellers.

Rendez-Vous Futé (☎ 4031 3533; www.australie -voyages.com in French; 28 Spence St) French-speaking agency.

STA Travel (www.statravel.com.au) CBD (☎ 4031 4199; 9 Shields St) Cairns Central Shopping Centre (☎ 4031 8398; Shop 39, McLeod St)

Trailfinders (☎ 4041 1199; www.trailfinders.com.au; Hides Corner, Lake St) Worldwide travel agency.

DANGERS & ANNOYANCES

Dangerous stingers are found in the waters close to shore along this stretch of coast between October and April (see the boxed text on p226). Swimming off the coast is not advised during this time, except at beaches fitted with stinger nets, or unless you're wearing protective clothing. It's generally safe to swim out on the Great Barrier Reef.

SIGHTS

Cairns' snazzy foreshore is the city's main attraction. It features a pedestrian **promenade**, which is favoured by walkers and joggers and stretches for almost 3km, and a 4800-sq-metre saltwater swimming **lagoon**, which caused a splash upon opening, attracting topless bathers – unofficially, it's OK as long as you're lying down. Locals and travellers spill out of the Esplanade's restaurants, bars and hotels to claim a patch of grass or bench seat and soak up the waterfront views.

Flecker Botanic Gardens & Tank Arts Centre

These tropical **gardens** (☎ 4044 3398; www.cairns .qld.gov.au; Collins Ave, Edge Hill; ☺ 7.30am-5.30pm Mon-Fri, 8.30am-5.30pm Sat & Sun) are an explosion of green. The main section of the gardens is a riot of rainforest plants. Other sections include an area for bush-tucker plants and the Gondwanan Evolutionary Trail, which traces the 415-million-year heritage of tropical plants. Hour-long **guided walks** (adult/child under 14 $10/free; ☺ 1pm Mon-Fri) through the gardens are available. There are also a few self-guided walks nearby (see p334).

Tank Arts Centre (☎ 4032 2349; 46 Collins Ave, Edge Hill; ☺ gallery 11am-4pm Mon-Fri), just north of the Botanic Gardens, is Cairns' community arts centre. Giant ex-WWII fuel-storage tanks have been transformed into a gallery for local artists' work and a superb performing-arts space.

Cairns Regional Gallery

The **gallery** (☎ 4031 6865; www.cairnsregionalgallery .com.au; cnr Abbott & Shields Sts; adult/child under 10 $4/free; ☺ 10am-5pm Mon-Sat, 1-5pm Sun), located in a handsome heritage building, is worth a wander. Exhibitions reflect the consciousness of the region, with an emphasis on indigenous works. The gallery shop stocks crafty items including jewellery, ceramics and glassware.

Tjapukai Cultural Park

Tjapukai (☎ 4042 9999; www.tjapukai.com.au; Kamerunga Rd, Carevonica; adult/child $29/14.50, incl transfers from Cairns & Palm Cove $48.50/24.25; ☺ 9am-5pm) is an extravaganza, combining interesting aspects of indigenous culture with show biz. It includes the Creation Theatre, which tells the story of creation using giant holograms and actors; there's also a Dance Theatre, as well as boomerang- and spear-throwing demonstrations.

By Night (adult/child $84/42, incl transfers $99/49.50; ☺ 7.30pm) is a dinner-and-show deal; you're allowed to laugh when the performers hop out of their canoe and break into the Broadway-esque 'No Food Blues'.

The park is sites just off the Captain Cook Hwy, about 15km north of the centre.

Centre of Contemporary Arts

CoCA (☎ 4050 9401; www.coca.org.au; 96 Abbott St; ☺ 11am-5pm Tue-Sun) houses the KickArts galleries of contemporary visual art. You might see exhibitions such as 'FNQ Souvenir' in which locals sharing their perspectives of their hometown with up to 55,000 visitors per day. Works might include a giant boomerang-shaped installation of Australiana figurines all 'Made in China'. The attached KickArts shop sells locally made art and design products.

Cairns Museum

The **museum** (☎ 4051 5582; www.cairnsmuseum.org .au; cnr Lake & Shields Sts; adult/child $5/2; ☺ 10am-4pm Mon-Sat) is housed in the former School of Arts building. State of the art it aint, but you'll see displays on the various stages of development that have influenced Cairns and its surrounds. Exhibits include the construction of the Cairns-to-Kuranda railway, the contents of a Chinese temple and information on the Palmer River and Hodgkinson River goldfields.

Royal Flying Doctor Service

The **RFDS** (☎ 4053 5687; www.flyingdoctorqueensland .net; 1 Junction St; adult/child $5.50/2.75; ☺ 9am-4.30pm Mon-Sat) attends to remote medical emergencies and health clinics. The Cairns base services an outback region the size of England. At the visitors centre you'll learn about the service's origins and workings since it began operating in 1928.

ACTIVITIES
Dive Courses

Cairns is the scuba-diving capital of the Barrier Reef and a popular place to attain PADI open-water certification. There's a plethora of courses on offer, from budget four-day courses that combine pool training and reef dives (at around $320), to four-day open-water courses ($480). Five-day courses ($540 to $650) include two days' pool theory and three days' living aboard a boat. These live-aboard courses are generally more rewarding as you'll dive parts of the Reef that are less frequented.

Dive school standards are first-rate, and there is little differentiation between them. Find out whether prices include a medical check (around $50), daily reef tax ($5) and passport photos (around $8). Many operators also offer advanced courses for certified divers. See opposite for more operators offering snorkelling and dive trips.

Following is a selection of reputable dive schools (in alphabetical order):

Cairns Dive Centre (☎ 4051 0294; www.cairnsdive .com.au; 121 Abbott St; ☺ 8am-7pm) Live-aboard tours (three days $460) and day tours ($130) are offered.

Deep Sea Divers Den (☎ 4046 7333; www.diversden .com.au; 319 Draper St; ☺ 6am-6pm) Multiday live-aboard courses and trips offered, as well as day trips ($180).

Down Under Dive (☎ 4052 8300; www.downunder dive.com.au; 287 Draper St; ☺ 7am-7pm) Multilingual instructors. Also offers day cruises ($80) and live-aboard trips on a sailboat – with a spa (two days $320).

Pro Dive (☎ 4031 5255; www.prodive-cairns.com.au; cnr Abbot & Shields Sts; ☺ 9am-9pm) Offers instruction in English, German and Japanese. Other dive options include day trips (from $180) and three-day live-aboard trips ($560).

Tusa Dive (☎ 4031 1248; www.tusadive.com; cnr Shields St & The Esplanade; ☺ 8am-6pm) German course available, as well as day trips (from $180).

Take your knowledge of the Reef to greater depths at **Reef Teach** (☎ 4031 7794; www.reefteach .com.au; 14 Spence St; admission $13; ☺ 10am-9pm Mon-Sat, lecture 6.15-8.30pm Mon-Sat). The madcap lecturer *talksveryfast*, and will explain how to identify specific types of coral and fish, and how to treat the Reef with respect.

Walking

The **Rainforest Boardwalk** leads from the Botanic Gardens through lowland swamp forest to the Centenary Lakes. The area covers 38 hectares and includes a freshwater lake and, leading off from Saltwater Creek, a saltwater lake. There are BBQs, picnic areas and children's play areas at both lakes.

Just behind the Botanic Gardens is the **Mt Whitfield Conservation Park**. Its two walking tracks lead through rainforest with patches of eucalyptus and grasslands; there's the Red Arrow circuit (1.3km, one hour) and Blue Arrow circuit (5.4km, three hours).

Halfway along the airport road (Airport Ave) is the **Mangrove Boardwalk**. It's an easy 2km circuit walk, which is also wheelchair accessible and includes a viewing tower and observation platforms along the mangroves.

Just beyond the terminus of the Skyrail Rainforest Cableway (see p355) is the turn-off south along Redlynch Intake Rd to **Crystal Cascades**. About 20km from Cairns, this series of waterfalls and pools is popular in summer – when the stingers arrive at the beaches. The area is accessed by a 1.2km (30 minutes) pathway (suitable for wheelchairs).

White-Water Rafting

There's white-water rafting down the Barron, Tully, Russell and North Johnstone Rivers. The excitement level is hitched to the season: obviously the wetter the weather, the whiter your water. Trips on the Tully River are timed to coincide with when the nearby hydroelectric power company opens its floodgates, so there are rapids year-round.

Tours are graded according to the degree of difficulty, from armchair rafting (Grade 1) to white-knuckle (Grade 5). For tours leaving Cairns, expect to pay about $150 for a full day to Tully, $85 for a half-day to the Barron River, $650 for a two-day North Johnstone River trip (and $1500 for four days) and $130 for a full-day trip to the Russell River; check whether wetsuit hire (around $10) and national-park fees ($6) are included.

Major rafting companies in Cairns:
Foaming Fury (☎ 4031 3460; www.foamingfury.com.au)
Raging Thunder Adventures (☎ 4030 7990; www.ragingthunder.com.au)
R'n'R White Water Rafting (☎ 4051 4055; www.raft.com.au)

Other Activities
AJ Hackett Bungee & Minjin (☎ 4057 7188; www .ajhackett.com.au; bungee jumps $110-140, s/tw/tr minjin swing per person $80/59/39, bungee & minjin swing combo $140; ✆ 10am-5pm) Swing from the trees on the minjin (a harness swing). Transfers available.
Cairns Golf Club (☎ 4054 1208; www.cairnsgolfclub .com.au; Southern Access Rd, Woree; per person 9/18 holes $25/37) Hires equipment.
Fishing Cairns (☎ 4038 1144; www.fishingcairns .au) Can arrange river fishing (half-day $75) and reef fishing (day trip $145). Minimum numbers apply.
Hot Air Cairns (☎ 4039 2900; www.hotair.com.au; rides adult/child $180/124) Hot-air ballooning. Set your alarm for the 5am start. Includes breakfast; transfers available.
Skydive Cairns (☎ 4031 5466; www.skydivecairns .au; 59 Sheridan St; tandem jumps from 8000ft $250) The higher you go (up to 14,000ft) the higher the price; it's a free-fall thing.
Springmount Station Horse Riding (☎ 4093 4493; www.springmountstation.com; half-/full-day rides $90/110) Go bush on horseback (based near Mareeba; pick up from Cairns).

CAIRNS FOR KIDS
Muddy's playground (The Esplanade, btwn Minnie & Upward Sts) is suitable for all ages, with climbing nets, water-play and story-telling areas, as well as classic slides and swings. Also on the Esplanade, the **lagoon** is popular with kids and is patrolled all day (6am to 10pm October to March, 7am to 9pm April to September). **Cairns Regional Gallery** (p333) runs theme-based workshops for children aged between six and 12 during school holidays.

Central childcare facilities that offer day care:
Child's Play (☎ 4031 1095; Anderson St; over/under 3 per day $40/45)
Juniors Child Care Centre (☎ 4032 1390; 160-2 Hoare St; over/under 2 per day $40/42)

QUIRKY CAIRNS
Imagine wearing a cross between a snow dome and a space helmet on your head, so you can walk on a submerged platform and, *voilà*, you have helmet diving. Hoses attached to the helmet deliver air so you can breath normally. Because you're 'walking', helmet diving is recommended for nonswimmers – and those who don't like to get their hair wet. A number of the dive boats offer this kooky activity, including (but not exclusive to): **Sunlover Cruises** (☎ 4050 1313; www.sunlover.com.au; dives $130) and **Quicksilver** (☎ 4087 2100; www.quicksilver-cruises.com; dives $130).

TOURS
More than 600 tours bus, boat, fly and drive out of Cairns each day.

Great Barrier Reef
Most of the innumerable operators working on the Reef include transport, lunch and snorkelling gear in their tour prices. When choosing a tour, consider the vessel (catamaran or sailing ship), its capacity (ranging from six to 300 people), what extras are offered and the destination. Generally, the outer reefs are more pristine; the inner reef areas can be patchy – showing signs of damage from humans, coral bleaching and crown-of-thorns starfish. Some operators provide you with the option of a trip in a glass-bottomed boat or semisubmersible; they may also offer guided snorkel swims.

The majority of cruise boats depart from the Pier Marina and Reef Fleet Terminal at about 8am, returning around 6pm. As well as the popular day trips, a number of operators also offer multiday live-aboard trips, which include specialised dive opportunities such as night diving and shark-feeding. Companies that run dive courses (see opposite) also offer tours. For trips to the islands surrounding Cairns, see p350.

Following is a list (in alphabetical order) of operators you might consider. All prices include reef tax; if you're just snorkelling, take about $100 off the quoted price.
Coral Princess (☎ 4040 9999; www.coralprincess.com .au; ✆ 11am Sat) *Coral Princess* does four-day cruises ($1270) between Cairns and Townsville, as well as a range of other cruises; meals are extra.
Coral Sea Diving Company (☎ 4041 2024; www.coralseadiving.com.au) This company offers a four-day live-aboard trip (from $1000) to Holmes Reef, as well as specialised trips to feed fish kebabs to sharks.
Explorer Ventures (☎ 4031 5566; www.explorerventures.com) This live-aboard trip ($1600) dives the Ribbon Reef and the Cod Hole for five days ending at Cooktown, where you'll be flown back to Cairns. Longer trips also available.

> **QUEASY?**
>
> If you're prone to motion sickness, it's worth noting that boat trips to the outer reef take around two hours. Consider taking ginger root or whatever other remedy works for you before your departure.

Great Adventures (☎ 1800 079 080, 4044 9944; www.greatadventures.com.au; adult/child from $165/85) This company has a range of combination day cruises on its fast catamaran. There's a day trip to its floating pontoon, with the option of a stopover on Green Island, as well as semisubmersibles and a glass-bottomed boat. Maximum 350 passengers.

Mike Ball Dive Expeditions (☎ 4031 5484; www.mikeball.com) These three-day live-aboard expeditions (from $1110) head to the Cod Hole; a longer seven-day option is also available.

Spirit of Freedom (☎ 4040 6450; www.spiritof freedom.com.au; 3-/7-day tours from $1130/2310) This three-deck vessel runs live-aboard dive trips to the Cod Hole and Ribbon Reefs; includes night dives.

Sunlover (☎ 1800 810 512, 4050 1333; www.sunlover .com.au; adult/child $150/75) Sunlover's fast catamaran takes day cruises to Arlington Reef, as well as to the outer Moore Reef via Fitzroy Island (adult/child $185/95). Options include semisubmersible and glass-bottomed boat trips. Maximum of 250 passengers.

Taka (☎ 4051 8722; www.takadive.com.au; 131 Lake St; 4-/5-day tours from $1010/1150) Dives the Cod Hole and the Coral Sea.

Vagabond (☎ 4031 4361; www.vagabond-dive.com; 2-/3-day tours from $280/400) This luxury yacht has a maximum of 10 guests.

SCENIC FLIGHTS

Cairns Heliscenic (☎ 4031 5999; www.cairns -heliscenic.com.au; Pier Marketplace; per person $330) Thirty-minute helicopter rides over Green Island.

Cairns Seaplanes (☎ 4031 4307; www.cairnssea planes.com; Cairns Airport; per person $260) Scenic seaplane flights running for 40 minutes; transfers available.

Atherton Tableland

Tours to the Kuranda Scenic Railway and Skyrail are deservedly popular (see p355). Most operators offer transfers from Cairns accommodation.

Bandicoot Bicycle Tours (☎ 4055 0155; 59 Sheridan St; full-day tours $100; ✆ Mon, Wed & Fri) Offers bike tours of the Atherton Tableland.

Food Trail Tours (☎ 4041 1522; www.foodtrailtours .com.au; adult/child incl lunch $125/90; ✆ 8am-5pm

Mon-Sat) Graze on macadamias, tropical-fruit wine, ice cream and coffee.

On the Wallaby (☎ 4050 0650; www.onthewallaby .com; day/overnight tours $85/155) Activity-based tours including cycling, hiking and canoeing.

Tropical Horizons Day Tours (☎ 4058 1244; www.tropicalhorizonstours.com.au; adult/child $125/85; ✆ 8.30am-5.15pm) A full day including the Kuranda Scenic Railway, Skyrail and Kuranda.

Uncle Brian's Tours (☎ 4050 0615; www.unclebrian .com.au; adult/child $85/55; ✆ 8am-8.30pm Mon-Wed, Fri & Sat) Popular tours covering Babinda, Josephine Falls and Lake Eacham.

Cape Tribulation & the Daintree

After the Great Barrier Reef, Cape Trib is the next most popular day trip – taking in the Daintree River. It's accessed via a well signposted, sealed road, so don't discount hiring your own vehicle for the trip, especially if you want to take your time.

Adventure Tours (☎ 4032 5600; www.adventuretours .com.au; day tours $130; ✆ 7.30am-5pm) Includes lunch and a cruise on the Daintree River.

Australian Wild Escapes (☎ 1300 792 213; www.australianwildescapes.com; adult/child $165/115; ✆ daily) Personalised tours (maximum six people), including lunch, 4WD vehicle and river cruise.

Billy Tea Bush Safaris (☎ 4032 0077; www.billytea .com.au; day trips adult/child $130/90; ✆ 7.10am-6.45pm) Ecotours.

Cape Trib Connections (☎ 4041 7447; www.capetrib connections.com; day trips $110; ✆ 8am-6pm) Includes Mossman Gorge, Cape Tribulation Beach and Port Douglas.

Trek North Safaris (☎ 4051 4328; www.treknorth .com.au; Cape Tribulation tours adult/child $140/95, Daintree Village tours $115/70; ✆ daily) Lunch, including tropical fruit, is provided on both tours.

Cooktown & Cape York

Daintree Air Services (☎ 1800 246 206, 4034 9300; www.daintreeair.com.au; day tours $880; ✆ Wed Apr-Oct) This trip to the Tip includes flights, a 4WD tour and lunch.

Wilderness Challenge (☎ 4055 4488; www.wilder ness-challenge.com.au; 2-day tours from $360; ✆ Mon, Wed & Fri) This 4WD tour goes to Cooktown via the inland road and returns via the Bloomfield Track (coastal route).

Undara Lava Tubes

For an inland adventure, **Undara Experience** (☎ 4097 1411; www.undara.com.au; 2-day tours adult/child $422/210; ✆ daily May-Oct, Tue & Fri Apr-Nov) runs coach trips to the Undara Lava Tubes – part of the longest lava flow from a single volcanic crater (see p408). Shorter trips are also available.

Other Tours

Cairns Discovery Tours (☎ 4053 5259; cairns discovery@austarnet.com.au; adult/child $56/28; ☺ 12.45-5.45pm) Run by horticulturists and includes Palm Cove in its itinerary.

My Town (☎ 4033 2095; www.mytown.net.au; 2½-hr tours $30; ☺ 10am & 2pm) Runs city tours that include a trip to the Botanic Gardens and the Royal Flying Doctor Service.

FESTIVALS & EVENTS

The **Cairns Festival** (www.festivalcairns.com.au) is held annually for three weeks in September. This regional festival features a stellar programme of performing arts, music, visual arts and family events such as sand sculpting.

SLEEPING

There's an excellent range of accommodation in Cairns, from backpackers to private apartments. Prices peak from 1 June to 31 October with the tourist high season; prices quoted here are high-season rates. Even during this time, you may find heavily reduced walk-in or stand-by rates for midrange and top-end places. In the shoulder and low seasons (1 November to 31 May) prices drop dramatically. Lower weekly rates are par for the course.

Accommodation agencies have up-to-date listings and can assist in locating suitable places to stay. The **Accommodation Centre** (☎ 1800 807 730, 4051 4066; www.cairnsaccommodation .com.au; 36 Aplin St) has wheelchair access and tourist information; it's also a contact point for working holidays in Japan. **Accom Cairns** (☎ 4051 3200; www.accomcairns.com.au; 127 Sheridan St) gives advice on midrange and top-end options, as well as short-term rental studio apartments.

Budget

Floriana (☎ 4051 7886; flori@cairnsinfo.com; 183 The Esplanade; s $40, d & tw $65; ⛒ ⛘) Oozing charm, the charismatic Floriana guesthouse boasts personalised rooms, with polished boards and original Art Deco fittings. Right on the Esplanade, some rooms have balconies and are almost self-contained, with a sink, microwave and little telly. The communal kitchen area out the back is poolside. Floriana is a 15-minute walk from the centre of town.

Global Palace (☎ 4031 7921; www.globalpalace.com .au; City Place, cnr Lake & Shields Sts; dm/tw/d $23/50/52; ⛒ ⛘ ⛙) This stylish, well-groomed backpackers in a refurbished cinema building is a fine choice. There are no bunks in the dorm rooms (which have three to five beds), there's a small rooftop pool and a classic double veranda overlooking the street. Open and spacious communal areas, including lofty two-storey thoroughfares, are a welcome contrast to the rooms.

Gilligan's (☎ 4041 6566; www.gilligansbackpackers .com.au; 57-89 Grafton St; dm $24-28, r $80; ⛒ ⛘ ⛙) Gilligan's brings the enormous resort-complex experience to the budget traveller. It offers basic dorm accommodation (four to six bunk beds) and hotel-style rooms, with a fridge and TV. Its Internet café doubles as a pizzeria, the 1000-capacity beer hall offers meals (breakfast, lunch and dinner), and the gaming room and swimming pool are also licensed.

Cairns Girls Hostel (☎ 4051 2767; cairnsgirlshostel@ bigpond.com; 147 Lake St; dm/tw $16/36) Sorry fellas, this female-only hostel is one of the cheapest and cleanest in town. The ladies enjoy two large refurbished communal kitchen and lounge areas, which are handy as sleeping quarters are cramped. The service is nurturing and personalised – you'll be a name to staff rather than just a room number.

Cairns Central YHA (☎ 4051 0772; www.yha.com.au; 20-6 McLeod St; dm $25.50-28.50, r $61-71; ⛒ ⛘ ⛙) This cheery hostel's dorm accommodation (four to 10 share) and room rates vary according to whether the bathroom is shared or private. It's spic-and-span, and caters to all travellers, including families (rooms from $80). It's not the best value for money, though if you're a YHA member you'll pay $3.50 less.

Caravella Backpackers (☎ 4031 5680 (No 149), 4051 2159 (No 77); www.caravella.com.au; 149 & 77 The Esplanade; dm $18-20, d $45-48; ⛒ ⛘ ⛙) In two locations along the Esplanade, Caravella offers a range of accommodation options so you can prioritise your purse or your comfort level. Dorms have four to eight bunk beds, and some rooms have their own bathrooms. No 77 is smaller and more central than No 149, though it has all the ambience of an undercroft car park.

Costa Blanca (☎ 4051 3114; canislupus@bigpond .com.au; 239-41 The Esplanade; apt from $80; ⛒ ⛘) This low-rise family-run apartment complex has a coveted location on the Esplanade. It's a little scruffy, but suitably priced. All apartments are self-contained, and the higher off the ground you are, the higher the price – 2nd-storey apartments have mountain or waterfront views.

Travellers Oasis (☎ 4052 1377; www.travoasis.com .au; 8 Scott St; dm/s/d $20/30/44; ✱ ☐ ☎) This boutique backpackers eschews the party vibe, keeping things low-key and limited with a maximum of 50 guests. All rooms have a ceiling fan, and you'll pay a little extra for air-con. It has all the usual facilities (kitchen and laundry) painted primary cartoon colours.

Campers and travellers towing caravans might try:

Cairns Coconut Caravan Resort (☎ 4054 6644; www.coconut.com.au; cnr Bruce Hwy & Anderson Rd; unpowered/powered sites $31/34, cabins from $65; ℗ ☐)

Cairns Villa & Leisure Park (☎ 4053 7133; www .cairnsvilla.com.au; 28 Pease St; unpowered/powered sites $20/25, cabins from $50; ℗ ☐ ☎)

Midrange

Shooting Star (☎ 4047 7200; www.shootingstarapart ments.com.au; 117 Grafton St; apt $90; ℗ ✱ ☐ ☎) These studio-style apartments, with kitchens, living and sleeping all in the one area, are a great deal. The blue-and-white complex resembles a cluster of oversized beach boxes, and houses a large number of neat, tiled rooms. The complex is suitable for couples and families. There are also specially fitted wheelchair-accessible rooms.

Balinese (☎ 4051 9922; www.balinese.com.au; 215 Lake St; s $85, d & tw $95; ℗ ✱ ☐ ☎) When you wake up and see the authentic wood furnishings and ceramic pieces here at the Balinese, you may be taken with the sudden urge to have your hair beaded. This small-scale, low-rise resort brings a smidgen of Bali to Cairns. The room rates include a basic cold breakfast, as well as access to the communal kitchen should you fancy a fry-up.

Cascade Gardens (☎ 1800 817 902, 4047 6300; cas cadegardens@harveyworld.com.au; 175 Lake St; apt $120-140; ℗ ✱ ☎) The rooms here aren't about to win any design awards (think cane furniture and floral drapes), but they're spacious, well equipped and super comfy. Each contains a self-contained kitchen, lounge area, balcony and bathroom, and some have their own washing machine and dryer. Apartments are spread over three levels – mobility

impaired visitors (and slackers) will note that there is no lift.

Inn Cairns (☎ 4041 2350; www.inncairns.com.au; 71 Lake St; apt $160; ✱ ☎) Live in an inner-city apartment while you're on holiday, making a habit of catching the lift to the rooftop each day to watch the champagne level and sun go down simultaneously. These elegant self-contained apartments feature modern furnishings and fittings. There is also a licensed bistro on the premises.

Mid City (☎ 4051 5050; www.midcity.com.au; 6 McLeod St; 1-bed apt $150; ℗ ✱ ☐ ☎) You just might forget you're not at home after a night here. Each apartment is fitted with a superb kitchen, washing machine and dryer. The functional rooms, with wrought-iron furnishings and terracotta tiled floors, are serviced daily. That means fresh towels and new soap. Each room also has its own balcony, but some of the views are inglorious – unless you enjoy gazing out to department stores.

Villa Vaucluse (☎ 1800 623 263, 4051 8566; www .villavaucluse.com.au; 141-3 Grafton St; 1-bed apt $140; ℗ ✱ ☎) These sturdy modern pads are private and sumptuously fitted. The Vaucluse has only been open for a few years, so the apartments are still fresh and trim. The separate kitchen is fully equipped and the bathroom has a bath. There's a dash of Mediterranean in the décor, a tropical central atrium and a secluded swimming pool.

Heritage (☎ 4051 1211; www.heritagecairns.com.au; 8 Minnie St; r $100-150; ℗ ✱ ☎) It's appropriate that this compact hotel is located on Minnie St. Rooms are your stock-standard hotel style, with everything you could need crammed in. A space-saving altarlike shelving unit holds your TV, bar fridge and kettle. Premium rooms are larger, with a kitchen, lounge and separate bedroom. Heritage is a tidy, unassuming hotel.

Bay Village (☎ 4051 4622; www.bayvillage.com.au; cnr Lake & Gatton Sts; r $135-165; ℗ ✱ ☐ ☎) This sprawling resort is smart and handsome. Bay Village is on the package-tour itinerary, favoured by more mature folks: if you peek in the rooms' mini-fridges, you're more likely to find milk (for the tea- and coffee-making facilities) than a six-pack or sports drink. The pricier rooms are self-contained, with kitchen and loungeroom, and there's an on-site restaurant and tour desk.

Hotel Cairns (☎ 4051 6188; cnr Abbott & Florence Sts; r $135-155; ℗ ✱ ☎) The sprawling Hotel

Cairns is a striking presence, with its corner location and bright white façade. Crunch over the gravel driveway to your downstairs 'courtyard' room, or muse in your ivory 'tower' room (which is more costly). The tariff includes breakfast in the adjoining restaurant, or you can opt to forego breakfast and pay $20 less.

Coral Tree Inn (☎ 4031 3744; www.coraltreeinn.com .au; 166-72 Grafton St; r $115, 1-bedroom ste $140; P ⌘ ⌚) The rooms here are spacious and have their own private balcony. There's a fully equipped communal kitchen for those who want to make more than tea and coffee. If you prefer to have your own kitchen, go for one of the self-contained apartments on offer. Rooms have a touch of retro (without an iota of irony): think plush emerald-green bed quilts and matching easy chairs, with not-so-easy on the eye contrasting velvet and floral fabrics. Wheelchair-accessible rooms are available.

Fig Tree Lodge (☎ 4041 0000; www.figtreelodge .com.au; 253 Sheridan St; r $105, apt $115; P ⌘ ⌚ ⌚) This resort-style accommodation offers hotel rooms with a beachy blue-and-white theme, and self-contained apartments with full kitchens. If you want a holiday away from the kitchen, Fig Tree has an Irish-themed restaurant and bar; better still, order room service while you're soaking in the tub. Wheelchair-friendly rooms are available.

Reef Palms (☎ 1800 815 421, 4051 2599; www.reef palms.com.au; 41-7 Digger St; apt $85-125; P ⌘ ⌚) The crisp white interiors of Reef Palms' apartments will have you wearing your sunglasses inside. All rooms have cooking facilities, and increase in price commensurate with size – the larger ones include a lounge area and a spa. If you don't mind sharing there's a communal outdoor spa and a mini-waterfall at the edge of the pool.

Tropical Queenslander (☎ 4031 1666; www.queens landerhotels.com.au; 287 Lake St; apt from $100; P ⌘ ⌚ ⌚) You can double dip here in the Tropical Queenslander resort's two pools. Apartments typically feature a kitchenette, bathroom and balcony. Larger apartments with a separate bedroom are available, and are suitable for families. The Queenslander is one of a chain of resorts; it's polite and professional.

18-24 James (☎ 1800 621 824, 4051 4644; www.18 -24james.com.au; 18-24 James St; s $110, d & tw $140; P ⌘ ⌚ ⌚) This gay accommodation is mostly for male guests. The pool area is clothing-optional and the resort's gym is apparently clothing-minimal. The handsome rooms, inclusive of airport transfers and breakfast, could represent a pot of gold at the end of that big rainbow.

Getaway on Grafton (☎ 4052 1200; 157 Grafton St; apt from $115; P ⌘ ⌚ ⌚) These schmick one- and two-bedroom apartments all come with their own kitchens and are furnished with Indonesian-style pieces. There's plenty of space to swing a cow, or two children and two adults, which is how many the larger apartments sleep.

Top End

Il Palazzo (☎ 4041 2155; www.ilpalazzo.com.au; 62 Abbott St; r from $180; P ⌘ ⌚) This charming boutique high-rise hotel is quietly stylish: in a soft-focus, terracotta-urns and water-feature kind of way. The welcome and service are remarkable; you can flit between the attached beauty parlour and your opulent apartment. It features a balcony, laundry and full kitchen – although room service is always an option – and is right in the centre of town.

Waterfront Terraces (☎ 4031 8333; www.cairns luxury.com; 233 The Esplanade; 1-/2-bedroom apt $170/205; P ⌘ ⌚) This low-rise Queenslander-style building is set in neat and trim tropical grounds, just across the road from the waterfront. Handsomely furnished apartments have a separate tiled lounge and kitchen area, with one or two bedrooms.

Pacific International Hotel (☎ 4051 7888; www .pacifichotelcairns.com; 43 The Esplanade; r $240; P ⌘ ⌚) This is one of Cairns' original hotels. It has more of a boutique ambience, with all the good things you'd expect from an international hotel, such as three restaurants and a grand entrance foyer replete with a huge chandelier.

Break Free Royal Harbour (☎ 4080 8888; www .breakfree.com.au; 73-5 The Esplanade; r from $176; ⌘ ⌚) This hotel is in a great position overlooking the Esplanade – above the night markets. All rooms have ocean views, spa bath, TV, video and stereo.

EATING

Cairns' status as an international city is reflected in its food offerings. You'll find a huge range of national cuisines, from Indian to Italian, and a combination of styles and ingredients, such as kangaroo *tsukudani* (roo in sweet soy sauce served cold). Restaurants and cafés are spread throughout town, though many cluster together along the Esplanade to take advantage of the waterfront (you may pay extra for the privilege).

Generally, competition keeps standards pretty high; be it boisterous barnlike eateries or sedate specialist restaurants, they do what they do well.

Restaurants

Pier (☎ 4031 4677; Pier Complex, Pier Point Rd; mains around $18; ✆ lunch & dinner Mon-Sun) For instant popularity, just add water. On the marina and waterfront, it's all hands on the broad outdoor deck area of this fledgling place. Punters love to watch their boutique beer moving through the Perspex pipe overhead. There's a handful of mains, such as salmon on papaya salad, a few pastas, starters and nibbles. Wood-fired pizzas are available until late, as is dessert: hazelnut-chocolate spread, marshmallows and coffee ice cream anyone?

Cherry Blossom (☎ 4052 1050; cnr Spence & Lake Sts; mains $14-24; ✆ lunch Wed-Fri, dinner Mon-Sat) This upstairs Japanese restaurant is reminiscent of an *Iron Chef* cook-off, with two chefs working at opposite ends of the restaurant floor. A lobster head provides the finishing touch to the sushi chef's inspired dish, answered by the conjured steam cloud and hiss from the teppanyaki chef across the floor. A range of Japanese beers is available, and in among the authentic dishes, such as tempura and yakitori, you'll find item No 17: 'Aussie Animals – crocodile, kangaroo and emu in a cheese basket'.

Phuket Thai Seafood Restaurant (☎ 4031 0777; 3/135 Grafton St; dishes $13-17; ✆ lunch Mon-Fri, dinner nightly) We're all familiar with Thai food: the creeping chilli kick partnered with ginger and basil, perhaps tempered by coconut milk; well this is a cut above and may surpass your expectations. Phuket Thai is licensed, with a modest, clean-cut interior and courtyard dining – and nary a gilt Buddha in sight.

Mangostin's (☎ 4031 9888; 65 The Esplanade; mains around $25; ✆ lunch & dinner) This formal two-storey restaurant sits proudly in its prime location on the Esplanade. There are separate lunch and dinner menus, both leaning towards the Mod Oz category, and relying on rich meats (veal, roo and duck), as well as seafood. You might try steamed North Queensland mudcrab with a chilli and kaffir-lime sauce. Mangostin's has a can't-go-wrong wine list (they're all good), with stellar Australian wines, as well as champagne (French of course).

Red Ochre Grill (☎ 4051 0100; 43 Shields St; mains $26-30; ✆ lunch Mon-Fri, dinner nightly) Red Ochre's inventive menu utilises native Australian ingredients and locally produced products, artfully prepared to pioneer its own culinary genre. There are the animals (croc, roo and emu), but Aussie flora also appears on the menu. You might want to try the wattleseed pavlova with plum sorbet and macadamia toast. A good selection of wine and beer is also on offer in slick, sophisticated surrounds.

Marinades (☎ 4041 1422; 43 Spence St; mains around $16; ✆ lunch Tue-Fri, dinner Tue-Sun) The Indian food at Marinades is so authentic you'll want to throw away your fork and get stuck into it with your hands. You might try the veggie and cheese dumplings in mild curry, or cardamom spiced lamb curry. Polite service and a refined, unfussy interior make Marinades a good choice.

La Fettuccina (☎ 4031 5959; 43 Shields St; mains $20-24; ✆ dinner) Be prepared to stain the white linen tablecloths as you slurp saucy homemade pastas. This small, atmospheric Italian restaurant offers the gamut of pastas and sauces. It's licensed and BYO, with a suave décor that'll transport you to Rome – especially after a few grappas.

Fish Lips (☎ 4041 1700; 228 Sheridan St; mains $24-27; ✆ lunch & dinner) Serving seafood done every which way but always good, Fish Lips is a convivial restaurant with professional service. You might order the barramundi served with eggplant pickle and rocket pesto, charred zucchini, onion and polenta. And for the anti-quarians, there are a few meat options, as well as a vegetarian dish. Be sure to book during the high season.

Yanni's Greek Taverna (☎ 4041 1500; cnr Aplin & Grafton Sts; mains $21-28; ✆ dinner) At Yanni's Friday and Saturday are belly-dancing nights, which means occasional participation from diners. So make sure you've finished your char-grilled lamb, calamari, Greek salad and seafood by 9pm – when all the hip-shaking action begins. Yanni's is licensed and offers courtyard dining replete with grape vines.

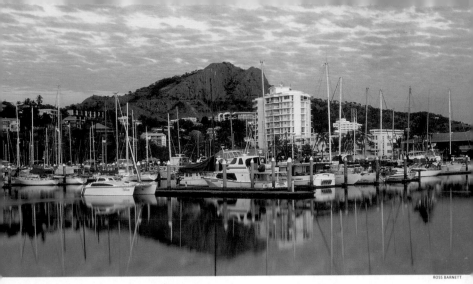

ROSS BARNETT

The Breakwater Marina with Castle Hill in the background, Townsville (p289)

Trekking the Thorsborne Trail (p315), Hinchinbrook Island

WILL SALTER

Southern cassowary, Mission Beach (p318)

MARTIN COHEN

Dunk Island Resort (p323), Dunk Island

JOHN BANAGAN

Buying ice creams, Port Douglas (p367)

Millaa Millaa Falls (p361), Atherton Tableland

LAWRIE WILLIAMS

Hinchinbrook Island (p315)

MARK ANDREW KIRBY

Swimming lagoon on the Esplanade (p333), Cairns

PAUL DYMOND

Cafés & Quick Eats

Perrotta's at the Gallery (☎ 4031 5899; 38 Abbott St; mains around $25; ⏰ breakfast, lunch & dinner) The long-black-aproned staff swish about the deck delivering a superb range of food and beverages. Come for the coffee alone (excellent), or break the fast with ricotta hotcakes basking in honeycomb butter and banana. The dinner menu has more than a hint of a Mediterranean influence, and the choice wine list favours boutique producers.

Beethoven Cafe (☎ 4051 0292; 105 Grafton St; dishes $5-7; ⏰ breakfast Mon-Sat, lunch Mon-Fri) Become an Augustus Gloop sympathiser: just try to save some room for later after a big, beautiful roll or sandwich. Choose from the combinations suggested – like *Buendnerfleisch* (air-dried beef, Swiss cheese and gherkin) – or get creative and invent your own. And this is what you're saving room for: slabs of poppy-seed cake and cheesecake.

Biscotti (☎ 4032 0222; 3/139 Collins Ave, Edge Hill; dishes $5-9; ⏰ breakfast & lunch) Join the ladies who lunch at this sleek café with a hard-edged interior softened by warm service and comfort food. Black banquette seating faces glass-fronted cabinets: one keeps a selection of savoury quiches, filo pastries and gourmet rolls made off the premises. A second cabinet displays handmade chocolates and other little sweet things, such as fig shortbread biscuits.

Lillipad (☎ 4051 9565; 72 Grafton St; dishes $5-7; ⏰ breakfast & lunch Mon-Sat) Walk down the long, narrow seating area of Lillipad, and meet the maker of your fabulously big breakfast – who toils in the kitchen just behind the service counter. There's love in your Full Monty fry-up, your pannini and your salad. Vegetarians are spoilt for choice here, and there's a range of cakes available until 4pm.

Edge (☎ 4053 2966; 1/138 Collins Ave, Edge Hill; dishes $5-8; ⏰ breakfast & lunch) Street eating at its best: a capacious corner location right in the centre of the boutique shopping strip of Edge Hill – up the road from the Botanic Gardens. Edge is a fruit and veggie grocer, as well as a perky café serving dishes such as pasta bake and frittata. It also stocks a range of locally produced sauces, jams and chocolate.

Inbox C@fe (☎ 4041 4677; 119 Abbott St; meals $9-15; ⏰ breakfast, lunch & dinner) It's a café; it's an Internet point; it's a bar; no…it's a 'travellers lounge'. This multipurpose place effortlessly blends its services, making it a cushy

spot to stop. Its menu dutifully offers up the standards: hot breakfasts starring the egg, filled and topped doughy things for lunch, as well as a few dinner options, including Cajun chicken, rump steak or spinach and ricotta lasagne.

Tiny's Juice Bar (☎ 4031 4331; 45 Grafton St; meals $5-8; ⏰ breakfast & lunch Mon-Fri) No vegetables were harmed to make your scrumptious rolls and wraps. This teeny café cheerily serves up veggie-focussed fare such as tofu burgers charged with a spicy peanut sauce. You could also bump up the wattage of your aura with a vitamin-packed juice or smoothie.

Pinocchio's (☎ 4051 9029; 79 The Esplanade; pizza $8-15; ⏰ 24hr) This long-serving pizzeria isn't flash, but then you probably aren't either when you arrive at 3am for an alcohol-neutralising pizza. Churning them out around the clock, its Esplanade position puts Pinocchio's in the 'legendary' category – much like its Forester (artichoke) pizza. Pinocchio's pizzas come in four sizes: small, medium and large – plus mini, for Jimminy-sized diners. Cash only.

Sushi Zipang (☎ 4051 3328; 39 Shields St; sushi $2-5, meals $8-16; ⏰ lunch & dinner Mon-Sat) The novelty of a conveyor belt wending its way around the bar carrying your sushi just never wears off, does it? Zipang also serves traditional noodle and rice dishes in large double-fronted premises, with street seating.

Self-Catering

There's a **Woolworths** (Lake St) the size of a small city in town stocking everything you can

---

THE AUTHOR'S CHOICE

Fusion Organics (☎ 4051 1388; cnr Grafton & Aplin Sts; dishes $5-10; ⏰ breakfast & lunch Mon-Sat) Pluck a word for the day from the bowl next to the cash register where you order and pay: 'enthusiasm', 'patience'? Fusion is inspiring to the core. Its sublime Genovese coffee (all the way from way down south – Melbourne) and juice brews will rouse even the weariest of bodies, and its stellar quiches, frittata and filled breads stir the senses. The decorous interior features local art; settle in the spacious undercover courtyard (with students from the upstairs Longevity Foundation sneaking a ciggy after class).

think of, and you'll find at least two super-markets in Cairns Central Shopping Centre. However if you prefer a little ambience with your shopping, head to **Rusty's Bazaar** (Grafton St, btwn Sheilds & Spence Sts; ⓨ Fri & Sat); it has fresh fruit and veg, herbs and honey.

Niche self-catering options:

Asian Foods Australia (☎ 4052 1510; 101-5 Grafton St) Asian goods.

Neil's Organics (☎ 4051 5688; 21 Sheridan St) Organic fruit, veg and other produce.

DRINKING

The number of places to drink in Cairns is intoxicating. Most places are multipurpose, offering food, alcohol and some form of entertainment – be it a giant TV or a guitar duo. Bars and pubs are generally licensed until 1am. Local street rag *Barfly* (www.the fly.com.au) publishes listings and reviews of music gigs, pubs and clubs; pick it up in cafés and venues.

Court House Hotel (☎ 4031 4166; 38 Abbott St; meals $6-19) You should stay for at least one drink to do this old courthouse justice. A spacious courtyard encircles the main room, with a well-stocked bar at its centre. A mixed crew – generally suave and clean cut – gathers at the Court House, which also serves Mediterranean fare.

Gilligan's (☎ 4041 6566; 57-89 Grafton St) You're guaranteed a crowd here, as the 400-odd backpackers staying in this resort complex (p337) work up a thirst; it's also popular with locals. Gilligan's is a respectable venue that features regular club nights, as well as special live-music events – no naff cover bands here.

Shenannigans (☎ 4051 2490; 48 Spence St; meals $8-15) This Irish-themed pub has a public bar decked out in dark timber. There's also a huge beer garden and outdoor bistro. From Thursday to Saturday night, a band plays before a DJ moves in for the night shift. There's also a gaming lounge and kara-oke Monday nights.

PJ O'Briens (☎ 4031 5333; 87 Lake St) This is a popular pub with an Irish theme; there are 'Thank Guinness It's Friday' nights (when the dark ale's cheap), and Wednesday's en-tertainment is dancing girls: not that there's anything particularly Irish about girls in bikinis dancing on the bar.

Cairns Yacht Club (☎ 4031 2750; 4 Wharf St; meals $10-18) Patrons here tend to sport a leathery

tan and a nautical appearance – think boat shoes without socks. Drinks are extremely well priced, and big meals are turned out of the bistro-style kitchen.

Chapel Cafe (☎ 4041 4222; Level 1, 91 The Espla-nade; meals $18-26) Large groups drink and dine in the stylish surrounds of green booths lit by low-slung, low-wattage bulbs. There's a large balcony overlooking the Esplanade, which makes a stellar place for a drink. Acoustic music plays live most nights.

Fox & Firkin (☎ 4031 5305; cnr Spence & Lake Sts; meals $15-20) 'For a firkin good time' is the not-so-subtle slogan of the Fox. This fine drink-ing establishment's wide veranda groans under the weight of animated backpackers comparing reef trips. Live music plays from Tuesday through to Sunday.

You might also try the following:

Cock & Bull (☎ 4031 1160; 6 Grove St; dishes $8-12) English-style tavern.

Johnos Blues Bar (☎ 4031 5008; cnr Abbott & Aplin Sts) Live music every night.

Woolshed Chargrill & Saloon (☎ 4031 6304; 24 Shields St; meals $12-16) A barely-legal crowd that drinks to get drunk.

ENTERTAINMENT

Starry Night Cinema (Flecker Botanic Gardens, Col-lins Ave, Edge Hill; admission $10; ⓨ May-Nov) Every third Wednesday of the month, classic films screen in the tropical outdoors of the Bo-tanic Gardens. Tickets are available from the gate on the evening; gates open at 6.30pm, shorts start at 7.30pm.

Cairns City Cinemas (☎ 4031 1077; 108 Grafton St) and **Central Cinemas** (☎ 4052 1166; Cairns Cen-tral Shopping Centre) screen mainstream new-release flicks.

Jute Theatre (☎ 4050 9444; www.jute.com.au; CoCA, 96 Abbott St; admission $22-30) Staging a variety of contemporary Australian works, check out what's currently playing at the Just Us Theatre Ensemble's sexy new venue in the Centre of Contemporary Arts.

Reef Casino (☎ 4030 8888; www.reefcasino.com.au; 35-41 Wharf St; ⓨ to 4am Mon-Thu, 24hr Fri-Sun) Gam-ble on table games such as blackjack and roulette, or feed your coins into one of the 500 electronic machines.

Nightclubs

If you want to move things up a gear, head to one of Cairns' innumerable clubs. Most open around 10pm and close between 5am and 6am. That said, entry is generally refused after 3am, so get to where you're going by then. Cover charges are from $5 to $10.

1936 (28 Spence St; ☺ Wed-Sun) At its new two-level premises, 1936 is a thumping-hard venue featuring respected local and touring DJs. A second room plays funk and hip-hop. Freakquency on Friday is always popular.

Soho (☎ 4051 2666; cnr The Esplanade & Shields St; ☺ Wed-Sun) The funky spot features resident DJs, as well as touring local and national turntableists. Fall into the leather lounge, or prop up one of the bars.

Tropos (☎ 4031 2530; cnr Spence & Lake Sts; ☺ from 8pm) Wear something short, tight and white. This young, high-energy crowd drinks cocktails with names such as 'attitude improvement' on the enormous balcony furnished with pool tables.

Nu-Trix (☎ 4051 8223; 53 Spence St; ☺ Wed-Sun) Drag shows are a feature at this gay venue. The shiny metal-clad exterior acts as armour against the morning sun, keeping things dark and doofing until late.

Sporties (☎ 4041 2533; 33 Spence St; ☺ from 6pm) Sporties hosts its own brand of sporting events, such as body-painting, and the Saints and Sinners Ball. Choose to spectate from the bar, or get amongst it on the dance floor.

SHOPPING

Cairns offers the gamut of shopping opportunities, from exclusive boutiques such as Louis Vuitton to garishly kitsch souvenir barns, and everything in-between. You'll have no trouble finding a box of macadamia nuts, some emu or crocodile jerky, and tropical-fish fridge magnets.

Head to the **Night Markets** (The Esplanade; ☺ 4.30pm-midnight) and **Mud Markets** (Pier Marketplace; ☺ Sat morning) if your supply of 'Cairns Australia' T-shirts is running low, or you need your name on a grain of rice.

Cairns has two multilevel shopping centres, where you can peruse a vast array of shops in a climate-controlled bubble: **Pier Marketplace** (www.piershopping.com.au; Pierpoint Rd) and **Cairns Central Shopping Centre** (www.cairns central.com.au; McLeod St). For food-related shopping, see p341.

Australian Geographic Cairns Central Shopping Centre (☎ 4051 4947; Shop 146, cnr McLeod & Spence Sts); Pier Marketplace (☎ 4041 6211; Ground level, Shop F3) This is the retail arm of the Australian Geographic Society, which publishes a glossy quarterly journal (of the same name) and is dedicated to the promotion of Australia's unique environment. These excellent stores sell ace science-type toys for kids, as well as calendars, specialist titles and other fun things for adults.

Crackerbox Palace (☎ 4031 1216; 97 Grafton St) If you like your retro, you'll like Crackerbox. You may not fit the fabulous '50s furniture in your backpack, but a *Viva Tijuana!* record makes for easy carry-on luggage. Polyester and paisley hang from the clothes racks, and preloved books and titbits cram the shelves.

City Place Disposals (☎ 4051 6040; cnr Grafton & Shields Sts) and **Northern Disposals** (☎ 4051 7099; 47-9 Sheridan St) stock camping and outdoor gear, including hats, footwear, goggles and gloves.

GETTING THERE & AWAY
Air

Departures for international cities leave Cairns frequently, with **Australian Airlines** (www .australianairlines.com.au) heading to four Japanese cities, Hong Kong and Singapore; **Cathay Pacific** (www.cathaypacific.com) flying to Hong Kong; and **Air New Zealand** (www.airnewzealand .com) heading to Auckland.

For domestic connections between Cairns and Brisbane ($140, two hours), Sydney ($190, four hours) and Melbourne ($210, 5½ hours) try **Virgin Blue** (☎ 13 67 89; www.virginblue .com.au), **Qantas** (☎ 13 13 13, 4050 4000; www.qantas .com.au; cnr Shields & Lake Sts) or its subsidiary **Jetstar** (☎ 13 15 38; www.jetstar.com.au), with around four departures daily. Qantas and Virgin also fly at least daily to other capital cities including Darwin via Alice Springs ($250, seven hours), Hobart ($250, 6½ hours), Perth ($300, 9½ hours) and Adelaide ($280, 9½ hours).

Macair (☎ 13 13 13; www.macair.com.au) flies to Lizard Island ($300, one hour) and Dunk Island ($180, 45 minutes). Rates can drop by as much as 20% if you purchase your ticket three days in advance.

Skytrans (☎ 1800 818 405, 4046 2462; www.sky trans.com.au) flies twice a day between Cairns and Cooktown (adult/child $107/54, 45 minutes).

Boat

Quicksilver (☎ 4031 4299; www.quicksilver-cruises .com; one way/return $26/39) departs from the Pier

Marina in Cairns at 8am for Port Douglas, and returns at 5.15pm; the journey takes 1½ hours.

Bus

Greyhound Australia (☎ 13 14 99; www.greyhound .com.au) has daily services, departing Cairns' bus terminal at Trinity Wharf, for Brisbane ($200, 28½ hours), Rockhampton ($140, 17 hours) and Townsville ($53, six hours). You can stop over at any point along the way as long as you hop back on within six days.

Premier (☎ 13 34 10; www.premierms.com.au) runs a daily service from Cairns to Innisfail ($15, 1½ hours), Mission Beach ($15, two hours), Tully ($22, 2½ hours), Cardwell ($26, three hours), Ingham ($29, 3¼ hours) and Townsville ($48, 5½ hours).

Sun Palm Express (☎ 4032 4999; www.sunpalm transport.com) runs a daily service from Cairns (Trinity Wharf) to Port Douglas ($25, 1½ hours), Mossman ($31, 1¾ hours) and Cape Tribulation ($45, 3¼ hours). It travels to Cooktown ($70) on the inland route (5¼ hours) Wednesday, Friday and Sunday, and via the coast road (7½ hours) Tuesday, Thursday and Saturday.

Coral Reef Coaches (☎ 4098 2600; www.coralreef coaches.com.au) also runs a daily service from Cairns to Cape Tribulation ($40, four hours) stopping in Port Douglas ($20, 1¼ hours), Mossman ($25, two hours) and Cow Bay ($37, 2½ hours).

John's Kuranda Bus (☎ 0418-772 953; tickets $2) operates a service between Cairns and Kuranda at least twice a day, and up to seven times Wednesday to Friday. Buses depart from the **Lake St Transit Mall**. **Kuranda Shuttle** (☎ 0402-032 085; tickets $2) departs Cairns' Lake St Transit Mall every two hours between 9am and 3pm, and Kuranda (Therwine St) at 10am, 12.15pm and 2pm. **Whitecar Coaches** (☎ 4091 1855; tickets $4) has five departures from 46 Spence St, outside Shenannigans. The trip takes around half an hour.

Car & Motorcycle

Hiring a car or motorcycle is a good way to travel from Cairns to Far North Queensland. Most rental companies restrict the driving of conventional vehicles to sealed roads; if you want to travel to Cooktown via the unsealed Bloomfield Track (or the coastal route), hire a 4WD. A number of rental companies are located on Lake St,

between Aplin and Florence Sts. Try one of the following:

Britz Australia (☎ 4032 2611; www.britz.com.au; 411 Sheridan St) Campervans.

Easy Rider Motor Cycle Rentals (☎ 4052 1188; www.easyridermotorcyclehire.com.au; 144 Sheridan St)

Europcar (☎ 4051 4600; www.deltaeuropcar.com.au; 135 Abbott St) With an airport desk.

Sheridan Rent a Car (☎ 4051 3942; owers@top.net .au; 36 Water St)

Thrifty (☎ 1300 367 277; www.thrifty.com.au; Cairns International Airport)

Travellers Auto Barn (☎ 4041 3722; www.travellers -autobarn.com.au; 123 Bunda St) Campervans.

If you're in for the long haul, consider buying a vehicle; **Cairns Cars Online** (www.cairnscars .com) sells mostly budget-priced cars.

Train

Queensland Rail (☎ 1300 131 722; www.traveltrain .com.au; Cairns Central Shopping Centre, McLeod St) has at least four trains per week between Cairns and Brisbane (from $190). It also operates the Scenic Railway to Kuranda (see p355).

GETTING AROUND
To/From the Airport

The airport is about 7km from central Cairns. **Australia Coach** (☎ 4048 8355; adult/child $8/4) meets all incoming flights and runs a shuttle bus to the CBD. **Black & White Taxis** (☎ 4048 8444) charges around $15.

Bicycle

You can hire bikes from the following:

Bandicoot Bicycles (☎ 4055 0155; 153 Sheridan St; per day $18)

Bike Man (☎ 4041 5566; www.bikeman.com.au; 30 Florence St; per week $40)

Cairns Bicycle Hire (☎ 4031 3444; 47 Shields St; per day/week $10/40) Groovy bikes and scooters.

Bus

Sunbus (☎ 4057 7411; www.sunbus.com.au) runs regular services, in and around Cairns, that leave from the Lake St Transit Centre, where schedules for most routes are posted. Buses run from early morning to late evening. Useful destinations include: Edge Hill (Nos 6, 6a and 7), Flecker Botanic Gardens (No 7), Machans Beach (No 7), Holloways Beach (Nos 1c, 1d and 1h), Yorkeys Knob (Nos 1c, 1d and 1h), Trinity Beach (Nos 1, 1a and 2x), Clifton Beach (Nos 1 and 1b) and Palm

Cove (Nos 1, 1b and 2x). All are served by the (almost) 24-hour night service (N) on Friday and Saturday. Heading south, bus No 1 goes as far as Gordonvale.

Taxi
Black & White Taxis (☎ 4048 8333) has a rank near the corner of Lake and Shields Sts, and one on McLeod St, outside Cairns Central Shopping Centre.

SOUTH OF CAIRNS

Just south of the boundary of Cairns lies a lush pocket of rainforest that makes a rewarding visit for walkers and wildlife watchers. The surrounding towns and settlements provide fascinating windows into the area's heritage.

WOOROONOORAN NATIONAL PARK
Part of the Wet Tropics World Heritage Area, Wooroonooran National Park is a veritable who's-who of natural spectacles: it has the state's highest peak, dramatic falls and everything in-between.

Palmerston Section
More than 500 types of trees, waterfalls and walks are good reasons to visit the Palmerston Section of Wooroonooran National Park, home to some of the oldest continually surviving rainforest in Australia. The high rainfall of the area and rich soils make it a particularly biologically diverse park.

Leaving the Bruce Hwy 4km northwest of Innisfail, the Palmerston Hwy follows the original route taken in 1882 by the bushman, gold prospector and explorer Christie Palmerston. Assisted by Aboriginal guides, the group made the passage in a mere 12 days.

While traversing one of the park's numerous trails, you may cross paths with a few creatures, including Boyd's forest dragons or the double-eyed fig-parrot. There are a number of marked platypus-viewing areas, with first or last light of day the best viewing times.

At the southeast corner of the park, **Crawford's Lookout** has views of the white water of the North Johnstone River, but it's worth the walk down to view it at a closer distance. Among the walks in the park is the lovely **Nandroya Falls Circuit** (7.2km, three to

four hours), which crosses a swimming hole (look out for leeches). There are shorter walks too, starting at half an hour.

There are also picnic areas throughout the park, and at **Henrietta Creek**, just off the highway, is a superb self-registration **QPWS camping ground** (☎ 13 13 04; www.epa.qld.gov.au; per person $4) with composting toilets and coin-operated BBQs. Water is available from the creek (which should be boiled for five minutes before drinking).

The Palmerston Hwy continues west to Millaa Millaa, passing the entrance to the Waterfalls Circuit just before the town (see the boxed text on p361).

Josephine Falls
The rugged tropical rainforest in this section of the park covers the foothills and creeps to the peak of Queensland's highest mountain, Mt Bartle Frere (1657m). It provides a shielded and exclusive environment for a number of plant and animal species. This section's namesake, the Josephine Falls, are an 800m walk from the car park along a mossy creek. You can swim in a circle of natural, clear pools fringed by the massive roots of towering trees. The smooth rocks connecting the pools are slippery and can be treacherous, and the flow can be powerful after rain, so be extremely careful. The car park to the falls is signposted from the Bruce Hwy, about 20km north of Innisfail.

The falls are at the foot of the Bellenden Ker Range, which includes the mighty Mt Bartle Frere. The **Mt Bartle Frere Summit Track** (15km, two days return) leads from the Josephine Falls car park to the summit. Don't underestimate this walk: the ascent is for fit, experienced and well-equipped walkers only; rain and cloud can close in suddenly. There's also an alternative 10km (eight hours) return walk to Broken Nose. It's best that you don't walk alone, and let someone know where you're heading before you go. Pick up a trail guide from the nearest visitors centre or contact the **QPWS** (☎ 13 13 04; www.epa.qld.gov.au). Camping is permitted along the trail (per person $4); there are self-registration boxes at both ends of the trail.

BABINDA
☎ 07 / pop 1175
Tucked behind an enormous sugar mill fronting the Bruce Hwy, Babinda is a small

town with a big history and a mythical rainforest. The town consists of veranda-fronted buildings and old timber pubs, shadowed by the Bellenden Ker Range. The Yidinyji tribe occupied the land before white settlement, and the town's name is said to come from the Aboriginal *bunna binda*, loosely meaning 'water fall'.

The **Babinda visitors centre** (☎ 4067 1008; cnr Munro St & Bruce Hwy; ☺ 9am-4pm) is wallpapered with flyers containing information on the area.

Try to see a film at the timeless **Munro Theatre** (☎ 4067 1032; Munro St; ☺ 7.30pm Fri & Sat), which dates back to the 1950s. Recline in a hessian-slung seat and enjoy the acoustics of its canvas-covered ceiling with the regulars who travel some distance to attend. The **Babinda State Hotel** (☎ 4067 1202; 73 Munro St) was built in 1917 by the government – Queensland's only state-owned pub. It controlled the sale of alcohol, which was otherwise prohibited within the Babinda Sugar Works Area. Not surprisingly, it was regularly flooded with cane cutters at the end of a shift.

Seven kilometres inland from Babinda, the **Boulders** is an enchanting spot where a fast-running creek rushes between 4m-high granite rocks. Since 1959, 15 people (mostly young men) have drowned here – held under by the strong current. According to Aboriginal legend, the boulders were formed when a tremendous upheaval shook the local tribe. A young couple, whose love was forbidden, were discovered and forcibly separated at this spot. Rather than go back to her tribe without her lover, the young woman threw herself into the creek. The moment she did so, calling for her lover, rushing water flooded the area and the land shuddered, throwing up the giant boulders. It is said that her spirit still guards the rocks, and that her cries can sometimes be heard, luring young men into the dangerous waters.

Walking trails lead to **Devil's Pool Lookout** (470m) and the **Boulders Gorge Lookout** (600m), and a suspension bridge takes you across the river to an 850m circuit through the rainforest.

GORDONVALE & YARRABAH
☎ 07 / pop 5670
Gordonvale is a delightfully old-fashioned town just south of Cairns. It features a disproportionate number of timber pubs set around a central park, plus an enormous sugar mill – all backed by the looming presence of Walshs Pyramid. Gordonvale also has the dubious honour of being the first place where cane toads were released in 1935 (see the boxed text on p42).

Between Gordonvale and Edmonton is a turn-off to the Yarrabah Aboriginal community. It's a scenic 37km drive through cane fields and mountains to Yarrabah, set on Mission Bay, a pretty cove backed by palm trees. You can visit the **Yarrabah Menmuny Museum** (☎ 4056 9154; http://cwpp.slq.qld.gov .au/Yarrabah; Back Beach Rd; adult/child $6/4; ☺ 8am-4pm Mon-Fri), which has a collection of Aboriginal artefacts and cultural exhibits. The museum also has spear-throwing demonstrations and a guided boardwalk tour (adult/child $14/10, including museum admission). To reach the museum, turn right at the police station. It's down the road and opposite the high school.

CAIRNS' NORTHERN BEACHES

A string of communities cling to their own patches of beach on the 26km stretch of coast north of Cairns. Each of Cairns' northern beaches has its own signposted turn-off leading from the Captain Cook Hwy. In places where the water is too shallow to swim, residential neighbourhoods enjoy the quiet life from the city's hem. Where the beach is suitable for swimming, you'll find resorts and restaurants bunched along the waterfront esplanade. Stinger nets are set up at such beaches during summer, and there's a distinctive beach-holiday repose. Within 30 minutes' drive from Cairns, you can almost pass the suntan lotion between the beaches and the city.

The first suburb north of Cairns is **Machans Beach**; its shallow sandflats have kept it free from tourist developments. Locals enjoy fishing at the mouth of the Barron River (a block back from the Esplanade), and keep their houses front-fence free and open to the waterfront.

HOLLOWAYS BEACH
The Coral Sea meets a rough ribbon of sand at a suitable depth for swimming at

CAIRNS' NORTHERN BEACHES

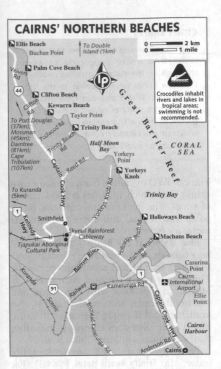

Holloways Beach. It's a mostly residential area, with beachside homes making way for a few tourist developments.

Pacific Sands (☎ 4055 0277; www.pacificsands cairns.com; 1-19 Poinciana St; apt $110; ✼ ⌘) has 38 two-bedroom apartments in a complex that stretches out one block back from the beach. Each apartment is fully self-contained; you can DIY in the modern kitchen or use the communal BBQ on the grounds.

The sprite two-bedroom apartments at **Cairns Beach Resort** (☎ 4037 0400; www.cairnsbeach resort.com.au; 129 Oleander St; apt $135; ✼ ⌘) are located on the beachfront. Each has all the modern timesaving appliances such as a microwave, washing machine and dryer, so you can focus on spending time at the beach, reading, contemplating your navel…

Strait on the Beach (☎ 4055 9616; 100 Oleandar St; meals $6-16; ✼ breakfast & lunch) is more than just a café with an exceptional setting just back from the sand; it's also a small shop where you can stock up on the basics. The café carries the beach theme through to its driftwood-inspired seating; it's best for Sunday breakfast.

Next door, **Coolum's on the Beach** (☎ 4055 9200; cnr Hibiscus & Oleandar Sts; mains $15-27; ✼ break-fast & lunch Sun, dinner daily) is renowned for its Sunday afternoon jazz sessions. The beachfront location and licensed Mod Oz menu might inspire you to linger for three courses, which might begin with stuffed mushrooms, followed by steak or seafood and a homemade dessert.

YORKEYS KNOB

Yorkeys is a sprawling, low-key settlement located on a windswept, white-sand beach. Nestled within the crescent-shaped Half Moon Bay is the marina: supporting 200 bobbing boats. 'Yorkey' was the nickname of a fisherman who originally hailed from Yorkshire and worked here in the 1880s. He was apparently known for his gump-tion and dogged nature: he attempted to grow pumpkins on the top of the knob and established a bêche-de-mer curing station over on Green Island. Yorkeys Knob is the rocky headland that cradles the bay to the north, allowing the wind to whip the water south. This wind is fuel for the many kite-surfers and windsurfers; **Kite Rite** (☎ 4055 7918; 471 Varley St; per hr $75) offers instruction, including gear hire.

It doesn't get much more convenient for families than **Beach Place** (☎ 4055 7139; thebeachplace79@hotmail.com; 79 Sims Esplanade; apt $205; ✼ ⌘). Large, two-bedroom, two-bath-room apartments front the beach; on the ground floor there's a newsagency and take-away café: pick up the day's paper and a cof-fee each morning before hitting the beach. There's a three-night minimum stay in the high season.

The self-contained **Yorkeys Beach Bunga-lows** (☎ 4055 7755; www.yorkeysbeachbungalows.com; 23 Sims Esplanade; d $80; ⌘) are set close to each other in leafy rainforest surrounds. Halfway up the wall, the timber turns to a sturdy mesh wire, which keeps the mozzies out and lets the breeze in. The interior is sparsely furnished, lending the accommo-dation a rustic feel.

York Beachfront Apartments (☎ 4055 8733; www.yorkapartments.com.au; 61-3 Sims Esplanade; apt $120; ✼ ⌘) is a midsized complex offering apartments with fully equipped kitchens and laundries, and separate bedrooms. Throw open those sliding doors to your own balcony, from where you can see the sea.

For camping, head to the compact **Yorkeys Knob Beachfront Van Park** (☎ 4055 7201; 69-73 Sims Esplanade; unpowered/powered sites $18/22, cabins $70).

Yorkeys Knob Boating Club (☎ 4055 7711; 25 Buckley St; mains $12-18; ☺ lunch & dinner daily, breakfast Sun) serves grills, pastas and burgers, and has sea views. You can also stop in for a quiet brew: quiet if you position yourself away from the pokies.

TRINITY BEACH

Take the Trinity Beach Rd turn-off to thriving Trinity Beach, a long stretch of sheltered white sand. High-rise developments detract from the castaway ambience, but holidaymakers love it – turning their backs to the buildings and focusing on what is one of Cairns' prettiest beaches.

Around the next bay is **Kewarra Beach**, a residential area with a large resort.

From its lofty position atop the headland, **Amaroo** (☎ 4055 6066; www.amarooresort.com; 92 Moore St; apt $170; ☒ ☎) has commanding views of the beach below, which makes it feel like a castle – though way more welcoming and less formal. It has its own steps leading down to the beach, a tennis court and tasteful self-contained apartments.

Roydon (☎ 4057 6512; www.roydon.com.au; 83-7 Vasey Esplanade; apt $120-150; ☒ ☎) offers one- or two-bedroom apartments that are just back from the beach and good value. Each has its own spacious balcony, living area and full kitchen. The snazzy white décor is fresh and modern.

There's something slightly incongruous about families wearing swimwear sitting around faux igloos in sweltering heat. Nevertheless, the self-contained concrete domes at **Casablanca Domes** (☎ 4055 6339; www.casablanca domes.com; 47 Vasey Esplanade; s/d $80/85; ☒ ☎) are popular and reasonably priced.

The exclusive **Sea Change** (☎ 4057 5822; www .seachange-beachfront-apartments.com; 31-5 Vasey Esplanade; apt from $280; ☒ ☐ ☎) apartments keep the riff-raff out with high walls and security intercom. The Balinese landscaping contrasts with the handsome, formal interiors. The apartments have two to four bedrooms and each has a kitchen with stainless-steel appliances and a laundry.

L'unico Trattoria (☎ 4057 8855; 75 Vasey Esplanade; mains $18-23; ☺ breakfast, lunch & dinner) is a stylish Italian restaurant with professional service and a stellar corner beachfront location.

CIGGY LIMITS

In 2005, a law was introduced that made it illegal to smoke a cigarette between the flags on the state's patrolled beaches. (The law brings new meaning to the official slogan: 'Where else but Queensland'.) It's one of a number of antismoking laws proposed by the Queensland government, which aims to extend smoking bans to pubs and clubs by mid-2006.

You can BYO or choose from L'unico's own drinks list, which includes a solid choice of wines. The menu features risotto, pizza, pasta and mains, and there's a separate menu for *bambinis*.

Blue Waters at the Beach (☎ 4055 6194; 77 Vasey Esplanade; mains around $17; ☺ breakfast, lunch & dinner) is an informal restaurant-cum-café. The dinner menu features such dishes as Moroccan meatballs with cous-cous and a seafood platter; homemade pasta is also available. And if you're eating on the run, Blue Waters also does takeaway, including that Australian icon, the Chiko Roll.

Perched high on a hill overlooking the water, the **Trinity Beach Hotel** (☎ 4055 6106; Moore St; dishes $6.50-15; ☺ lunch & dinner) is a popular watering hole. It has a beer garden with a small bistro and incredible views.

CLIFTON BEACH

Local and leisurely, Clifton Beach has a good balance of residential and resort accommodation and services. It's popular with groups and families during the high season.

The freestanding single-storey apartments at **Clifton Palms** (☎ 4055 3839; www.clifton palms.com.au; 35-41 Upolu Esplanade; cabins/units $70/110; ☒ ☎) are backed by a curtain of green hills. There's a huge range of accommodation options to suit any budget, and stand-by and low-season rates are jaw-droppingly good. The huge poolside BBQ area will win you over.

Clifton Sands Holiday Units (☎ 4055 3355; 81-7 Guide St; apt $75; ☒ ☎) are fully self-contained apartments that are excellent value. Apartments are in an older motel-style block and sleep a maximum of four people. The décor is a bit frumpy, but they're functional and clean. It's a short walk to the beach, and there's a small pool.

There are 45 self-contained apartments within the four-storey complex at **Agincourt** (☎ 4055 3500; 69-73 Arlington Esplanade; apt from $125; ✿ ▣ ▣). Low-key fittings and décor make for functional and comfortable surrounds. It's located on the waterfront and set on big grassy grounds.

What it may lack in beach frontage, **Paradise Gardens Caravan Resort** (☎ 4055 3712; cnr Captain Cook Hwy & Clifton Rd; unpowered/powered sites $15/22.50, cabins $52-77; ▣) makes up for with well-tended grassy grounds. The same grey nomads flock here each year before heading north for the winter.

Clifton Capers Bar & Grill (☎ 4055 3355; 14 Clifton Rd; mains around $18; ☾ dinner Tue-Sun) is a licensed restaurant that offers diners a range of international dishes and pizza, and has a selection of nightly specials. Casual service befits the pleasant, relaxed setting.

PALM COVE

Time to adopt the mantra 'I don't get out of bed for anything less than a 27°C day spent on an uninterrupted stretch of white-sand beach'. Palm Cove encourages idleness and indulgence, with an idyllic tropical beach backed by sprawling international resorts offering everything from massage to marriage. And if you've already tied the knot, join countless other couples honeymooning in Palm Cove.

Information & Orientation

From the Captain Cook Hwy, turn off at Veivers Rd and follow it to Williams Esplanade, which extends the length of the beach as far as the jetty (Quicksilver and Sunlover pick up here for reef trips; see p370). At **Paradise Village Shopping Centre** (113 Williams Esplanade) there's a post office, a newsagent, a moneychanger and Internet access.

Sights & Activities

Beach strolls and leisurely swims will be your chief activities here, but if you need more stimuli head to **Cairns Tropical Zoo** (☎ 4055 3669; www.wildworld.com.au; Captain Cook Hwy; adult/child $25/12.50; ☾ 8.30am-5pm). It has crocodile shows (11.30am and 3pm) and koala photo sessions at 2pm; you can even wed at the Wildlife Wedding Chapel, which dispatches two newlywed couples a day at peak times.

Privately owned **Double Island** (☎ 1300 301 992; www.doubleisland.com.au) is visible from the beach. It's available to rent on a whole-island basis, sleeping from one privacy-savouring guest to a wedding or conference party of 50.

Sleeping

Angsana Resort & Spa (☎ 4055 3000; www.angsana .com; 1 Veivers Rd; r from $455; ✿ ▣ ▣ ▣) This resort, though extensive (with 67 suites), is personal and oh-so chic. Folding louvered doors open out to your own balcony, and design touches such as contrasting fabrics and feature walls make for a stylish décor. Resort facilities include three swimming pools, a chapel wedding service, spa treatments (with practitioners trained in Thailand), plus two bars and a fine restaurant.

Outrigger (☎ 4059 9200; www.outrigger.com; 123-7 Williams Esplanade; r from $295; ✿ ▣) Outrigger outdoes many of Palm Cove's international resorts: both in size and opulence. It starts with the bathrobes in your room, continues to the swimming pools – one with waterfall, one with sand edges – and doesn't end at the optional spa treatments, such as the 45-minute 'rainbar', which alternates warm and cold jets directed at your exfoliated body. Did we mention the resort's two *Gourmet Traveller*–listed restaurants: Nu Nu and Tamara?

Silvester Palms (☎ 4055 3831; www.silvesterpalms .com; 32 Veivers Rd; d from $100; ✿ ▣) These self-contained apartments, in a small block, are a refreshing alternative to the area's city-sized resorts. The communal BBQ area and fenced swimming pool make Silvester a great option for families.

Palm Cove Accommodation (☎ 4055 3797; 19 Veivers Rd; s/d $65/80) This is the only budget option in Palm Cove. Next door to the beautician, this small complex offers a limited number of rooms, which are all bright and airy.

Melaleuca Resort (☎ 4055 3222; www.melaleuca resort.com.au; 85-93 Williams Esplanade; apt $180; ✿ ▣) Named after the melaleuca trees that line Palm Cove's esplanade, this is a boutique resort with 24 self-contained apartments. Each has its own kitchen, balcony and laundry facilities. The resort is on the waterfront behind a thatch of shady trees.

Villa Paradiso (☎ 1800 683 773, 4055 3533; www.villa paradiso.com.au; 111-13 Williams Esplanade; 1-bedroom apt $280; ✿ ▣) These apartments, with polished timber floors and Mediterranean flourishes, come with a fully equipped kitchen. A range of options is on offer: from one-bedroom apartments through to the penthouse (sleeping six).

Coral Horizons (☎ 4059 1565; www.coralhorizons.com.au; 137 Williams Esplanade; apt $245; ☒ ☒) There are seven two-bedroom apartments in this block, each overlooking the beachfront. Smaller one-bedders are located at the back of the building. As you'd expect, apartments are fitted with their own kitchen and laundry.

Sebel Reef House (☎ 4055 3633; www.reefhouse.com.au; 99 Williams Esplanade; r from $360; ☒ ☒) 'Discretion' is the Sebel's motto, so pretend you didn't notice return visitors Bill and Hillary at the next table. The Sebel offers ultimate luxury: its rooms feature white wicker furniture and big beds romantically draped in muslin (which are turned down each evening). Equally refined is the Reef House Restaurant.

Palm Cove Camping Ground (☎ 4055 3824; 149 Williams Esplanade; unpowered/powered sites $13/17) Just south of the jetty (and ever so close to the road) you can wave to the fisherfolk from your tent of a morning. This is a small beachfront camping ground run by the local council.

Eating

Far Horizons (☎ 4055 3000; www.angsana.com; 1 Veivers Rd; mains $17-24; ☺ breakfast, lunch & dinner) This fine restaurant can be found at the chic Angsana Resort & Spa.

Reef House Restaurant (☎ 4055 3633; www.reefhouse.com.au; 99 Williams Esplanade; mains around $30; ☺ lunch & dinner) As refined as the discrete Sebel Reef House, where it's located; you might try the ginger and pumpkin soup with passionfruit cream for starters and follow up with grilled tuna with wasabe cake, bok choy and lime *ponzu* (citrus and soy sauce dressing).

Blue (☎ 4055 3999; cnr Williams Esplanade & Veivers Rd; mains around $30; ☺ lunch & dinner) This is a hotel restaurant that does delicate dishes (such as steamed salmon with black mussels and caviar in a champagne sauce) with pizzazz. If that doesn't dazzle you, the wood-fired pizza might. Service is attentive and the décor is sparse and modern.

Cocky's at the Cove (☎ 4059 1691; Veivers Rd; dishes $5-10; ☺ breakfast & lunch) For casual all-day breakfasts or an honest sandwich for lunch, Cocky's is a solid choice.

Cairns SLSC (☎ 4059 1244; Veivers Rd; meals $10-20; ☺ lunch & dinner) This locals' haunt serves decent pub grub in its fabulous garden bar. Cairns SLSC has a strict dress code: 'thongs or shoes must be worn at all times'.

Il Fornio Pizzeria (☎ 4059 1666; Paradise Village; pizza $15-17; ☺ dinner) This small, stylish pizzeria bakes thin-crust pizzas; bring your own bottle.

Apres Beach Bar & Grill (☎ 4055 3300; 119-21 Williams Esplanade; dishes $8-28; ☺ breakfast, lunch & dinner) The large outdoor seating area is often full of people either having a drink or partaking in the food menu. There's something for everyone, with veggie dishes, steak dishes, seafood, pasta and servings for children.

Palm Cove Tavern (☎ 4059 1339; Veivers Rd; mains $13-22; ☺ lunch & dinner) serves basic bistro meals and is a lively spot for a drink on Sunday.

ELLIS BEACH

The last beach before Port Douglas, Ellis is a stunner, with a long sheltered bay.

Ellis Beach Oceanfront Bungalows (☎ 1800 637 036, 4055 3538; www.ellisbeachbungalows.com; Captain Cook Hwy; unpowered sites $26, powered sites $28-32, cabins $75, bungalows $140-175) is a tidy beachfront park, with both camping and cabins. If you're planning to stay during the high season it's best to book the bungalows and cabins in advance.

Across the road, **Ellis Beach Bar 'n' Grill** (☎ 4055 3534; Captain Cook Hwy; meals $8-22; ☺ lunch & dinner) turns out burgers and fried food; it has live music every Sunday. For a quiet ale, try the **SLSC** (☎ 4055 3695; Captain Cook Hwy) a few doors down.

Just past Ellis Beach is **Hartley's Creek Crocodile Farm** (☎ 4055 3576; www.crocodileadventures.com; adult/child $25/12.50; ☺ 8.30am-5pm). Free tours of the farm run at 10am and there are crocodile-feeding demonstrations at 11am and 3pm. You can have your photo taken with a koala at 3.45pm (for an additional cost).

ISLANDS OFF CAIRNS

Green Island and Fitzroy Island are popular day trips from Cairns; each has a resort, so you can play castaway for a few days. The picturesque Frankland Islands Group is also a popular day trip. All the islands are good for snorkelling and lolling on a beach.

GREEN ISLAND

Green Island's long, doglegged jetty receives boatloads of daytrippers. This small

---

TOURISTS TAKEN IN BY CROCS

In 1991 Charlie was awarded the title of 'Queenslander of the Year' for his outstanding contribution to tourism. Charlie was a crocodile who for 65 years entertained thousands of tourists to Hartley's Creek by snapping for dangling chickens and performing the occasional death roll. Even at their least hospitable – these giant beady-eyed predators will attack humans – it seems, there's a morbid fascination with crocodiles. Especially if there's a tough, Aussie human element to the story, such as in the late-2004 reports of the grandmother who threw herself on the back of a 4.2m croc that was dragging a fellow camper down the beach.

'Salties' are often-aggressive saltwater crocodiles that can grow to 7m (though most are under 5m). They inhabit coastal waters and are mostly seen in the tidal reaches of rivers, though on occasion they're spotted on beaches and in freshwater lagoons. Throughout north Queensland signs placed at access points to waterways and beaches alert people to the potential presence of estuarine crocs. Use common sense in these areas. If in doubt, seek advice from a local – they generally know where crocs live. Obviously, don't swim in these areas, don't clean fish or prepare food near the water's edge, and camp at least 50m away from waterways. Crocodiles are particularly mobile, and potentially dangerous, around breeding season (October to March).

Crocodiles have been a protected species in Queensland since 1974. Since it became illegal to harm or kill a wild crocodile, the once dwindling population has recovered greatly. Some argue that numbers are too high; whenever there's a crocodile encounter in a built-up area, there are cries for controlled culling. Problem, or rogue, crocs – those deemed a threat to landowners – are ideally captured and relocated to commercial crocodile farms.

Crocodile farms, where khaki-clad tough guys who enter the croc's pen take on the risks, while tourists are safely entertained from the bleachers, are extremely popular places to see crocs. A number of crocodile farms, with live animals as a spectacle, also operate as closed-cycle breeding establishments. This is where animals are farmed for use in restaurant dishes or as a handbag, wallet or pair of shoes; they also end up as taxidermied trophies, known as 'stuffies'. Souvenir shops in Cairns sell stuffed crocodile feet fixed to a stick as backscratchers.

It's a fine line between fascination and fetishism.

---

island, just 45 minutes from Cairns, has a rainforest interior with interpretive walks and is hemmed by stunning beach, with snorkelling just off shore. The island's sole resort is partly open to daytrippers, offering a number of eateries and water sports.

Before Green Island was named after the astronomer on Cook's *Endeavour*, the Gunganyi people used it as a retreat to perform initiation ceremonies for the young men of their group. Commercial activity began around 1857 when the waters around Green Island were heavily fished for bêche-de-mer (see the boxed text on p352). The animals were cured here before export, and many of the island's trees were logged in the process. The resultant traffic around the island and reports of people going missing inspired the government to plant coconut palms on the island – thinking that shipwreck survivors could live on coconut meat and milk until they were found.

Today the island and its surrounding waters are protected by their national-

and marine-park status. Activities involve swimming, snorkelling and gentle walks through the leafy interior, or you can walk around the island in about 30 minutes.

Marineland Melanesia (☎ 4051 4032; adult/child $10/5) has an aquarium with fish, turtles, stingrays and crocodiles, as well as a collection of Melanesian artefacts.

The luxurious **Green Island Resort** (☎ 4031 3300; www.greenislandresort.com.au; r $480-570; ☒ ☒) has stylish split-level rooms, each with its own private balcony. Two styles of room are available: the larger ones sleep up to four, or you can have them all to yourself and shuffle around in your complimentary slippers and bathrobe.

Great Adventures (☎ 4051 0455; www.greatadventures.com.au; 1 Wharf St, Cairns) has Green Island transfers by fast catamaran ($56), departing Cairns' Reef Fleet terminal at 8.30am, 10.30am and 1pm and returning at noon, 2.30pm and 4.30pm. Snorkelling gear and use of the resort's swimming pool are included in the price.

Big Cat (☎ 4051 0444; www.bigcat-cruises.com.au; tours from $58) also runs half- and full-day tours departing Cairns' Reef Fleet terminal at 9am and 1.15pm. Prices include use of snorkelling gear.

You can sail to the island with **Ocean Free** (☎ 4041 1118; www.oceanfree.com.au; from $90), which spends most of the day offshore at Pinnacle Reef, with a short stop on the island. It departs Cairns' Marlin Wharf at 8.30am, returning around 6pm, and includes snorkelling equipment, snorkel tour and lunch.

FITZROY ISLAND

A steep mountain-top peeping from the sea, Fitzroy Island has coral-strewn beaches, woodlands and walking tracks, as well as a budget resort.

Fitzroy Island is also known as Gabarra to the indigenous Gungandji people, who have hunted and fished from the island for centuries. Captain Cook named the island Fitzroy after the prime minister of the day when the *Endeavour* left for its Pacific journey. In 1877 the island was used to quarantine Chinese immigrants bound for the goldfields.

BÊCHE-DE-MER

Those black sluglike creatures languishing on the ocean floor are variously known as bêche-de-mer, sea cucumbers, and *hai shen* to the Chinese, who consider them a delicacy.

Hai shen (which roughly translates as 'sea ginseng') is dried and subsequently used in soup. *Hai shen* soup is up there with shark's fin and bird's nest in the delicacy stakes, and considered a longevity tonic and disease preventative. And, of course, there are the aphrodisiacal claims. Far from experiencing sudden amorous bursts as soon as you put down the spoon, it is believed that bêche-de-mer can aid impotence caused by kidney problems.

There are hundreds of species of bêche-de-mer. What they all have in common, however, are extraordinary physiological characteristics, which enable them to breathe through their anuses and purge their innards. If sufficiently irritated, the bêche-de-mer's defence is to eject most of its internal organs, which it quickly regenerates.

Thousands were compulsorily detained for 16 days and observed for signs of smallpox. Squalid conditions contributed to the deaths of hundreds of Chinese, and a number of unmarked graves remain from that period. The island also supported a bêche-de-mer business, as well as an Aboriginal mission.

Today the island is national park, with the resort occupying a small portion. Daytrippers can use the resort's facilities, and hire water-sports equipment; it also runs dive courses and sea-kayak tours. There are a number of places to snorkel; the most popular spot is around the rocks at **Nudey Beach** (1.2km from the resort).

There are two walking tracks on the island where you might spot some of the island's resident birds and butterflies. The 20-minute **Secret Garden Walk** is a leisurely stroll through rainforest that returns along the same path. The hour-long **Lighthouse & Summit Trail** leaves from the northern end of Welcome Bay and heads steeply up to the lighthouse, which was the last staffed lighthouse in Australia. From here there are views to Little Fitzroy Island below.

Fitzroy Island Resort (☎ 4051 9588; www.fitzroy island.com.au; dm/d $31/58, cabin $220; ▨ ⌨) has all rooms, except the beachfront cabins, with shared bathroom, laundry and kitchen facilities. The resort has a kiosk serving snack food such as burgers and wedges, as well as a **restaurant** (meals $12-20; ☺ breakfast, lunch & dinner) and bar: you might try the reef 'n' beef or seafood nachos between drinks. Saturday night is Party Night, when the resort shuttles revellers over from Cairns ($15, leaving Cairns at 4pm and 7pm).

Fitzroy Island Ferries (☎ 4030 7907; Reef Fleet terminal, Cairns) runs return transfers to the island (adult/child $38/18) departing Cairns at 8.30am, 10.30am and 4pm. Departures from Fitzroy Island are at 9.30am, 3pm and 5pm. The trip takes 45 minutes each way. Full- and half-day tours, including lunch and transfers, are also available.

Sunlover Cruises (☎ 1800 810 512; www.sunlover .com.au; adult/child $40/20; Reef Fleet terminal, Cairns) runs to the island once a day, leaving Cairns at 10am and arriving back around 5.30pm. The trip each way takes around an hour.

FRANKLAND ISLANDS

Five uninhabited coral-fringed islands with excellent snorkelling and stunning white sandy beaches make up the Frankland Group National Park. These continental islands consist of High Island to the north and four smaller islands to the south: Normanby, Mabel, Round and Russell.

Campers can be dropped at High or Russell Islands: both feature rainforest areas. Permits must be obtained from the Cairns **QPWS** (☎ 4046 6602; www.epa.qld.gov.au; 2-4 McLeod St). You must be fully self-sufficient as there is no water on the islands, and you'd be wise to book in advance during the high season. There's a four-night maximum stay at this time – in case you were getting any ideas about dropping out of life for a while.

Frankland Islands Cruise & Dive (☎ 4031 6300; www.franklandislands.com.au; adult/child $150/70) runs excellent day tours, which include a cruise down the Mulgrave River, and transfers for campers ($145 return).

ATHERTON TABLELAND

Inland from the coast between Innisfail and Cairns, the Atherton Tableland is a diverse region of rural hubs at the centre of vast cultivated fields, as well as beautiful natural areas sporting lakes, waterfalls and Queensland's highest mountains: Bartle Frere (1657m) and Bellenden Ker (1591m) (see p345).

Non-Indigenous Australians and other migrants first came to the Tableland in the 1870s in search of gold. Mining spurred the development of roads and railways, though farming soon became the chief commercial activity. European occupation of the country severely impacted on the original inhabitants (from the Djirbal language group), who were displaced from their lands, trade routes and ceremonial areas. Today, efforts are being made to protect areas of cultural significance through education and site management.

You could easily spend a few days exploring the tableland. The region is well stocked with accommodation, and known for its luxurious B&Bs. Three major roads lead in from the coast: the Palmerston Hwy from Innisfail, Gillies Hwy from Gordonvale and Kennedy Hwy. The text in this section follows the Kennedy Hwy from Cairns and heads south before looping up along the Gillies Hwy back to Cairns.

Getting There & Around

To get to/from the many sights between the major towns, you'll need your own car; see p344 for hire-car operators.

There are bus services to the main towns from Cairns, but not to all the interesting areas *around* the towns, so hire car is the best way to get around.

Whitecar Coaches (☎ 4091 1855) has regular bus services connecting Cairns with the tableland, departing from 46 Spence St. There are roughly three services a day to Mareeba ($13.50, one hour), Atherton ($17.60, 1¾ hours), Herberton ($22.60, two hours) and Ravenshoe ($25.10, 2½ hours). Five daily services leave for Kuranda ($4, 30 minutes).

KURANDA

Between 10am and 4pm Kuranda is a flurry with daytrippers. Tours, purpose-built attractions and B-grade merchandise make Kuranda akin to a theme park. It does have another side, however, when the tourists go home. It's then that the town knocks off, revealing a mellow community living in beautiful rainforest surrounds – the characteristics that made it so popular with tourists in the first place. It's during the town's tourist shift that you might see the wizard. Believing the town's magic is being drained by all the activity and development, the wizard walks about blessing the place. Ironically, when the shire heard of this, they offered to employ him – thinking he would make an entertaining spectacle for tourists. The wizard scrupulously declined.

In the 1960s and 1970s affordable land prices and the area's stunning beauty made Kuranda a haven for alternative lifestylers. Its original markets (selling handcrafted goods), boutique atmosphere and lush setting are responsible for Kuranda's fame.

Information & Orientation

The **Kuranda visitor centre** (☎ 4093 9311; www.kuranda.org; ☒ 10am-5pm) is located in Centenary Park.

Sights & Activities

It's about the journey as much as the destination with Kuranda. The Skyrail and Scenic Railway, which travel between Kuranda and Cairns, are themselves major attractions (see p355). Consider travelling to and fro on different modes of transport.

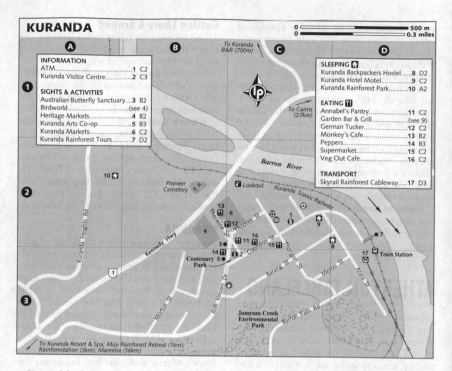

KURANDA

0 —————— 500 m
0 —————— 0.3 miles

INFORMATION
ATM..1 C2
Kuranda Visitor Centre.................2 C3

SIGHTS & ACTIVITIES
Australian Butterfly Sanctuary...3 B2
Birdworld.......................................(see 4)
Heritage Markets............................4 B2
Kuranda Arts Co-op........................5 B3
Kuranda Markets.............................6 C2
Kuranda Rainforest Tours............7 D2

SLEEPING
Kuranda Backpackers Hostel......8 D2
Kuranda Hotel Motel.....................9 C2
Kuranda Rainforest Park.............10 A2

EATING
Annabel's Pantry..........................11 C2
Garden Bar & Grill.....................(see 9)
German Tucker.............................12 C2
Monkey's Cafe..............................13 B2
Peppers...14 B3
Supermarket..................................15 C2
Veg Out Cafe...............................16 C2

TRANSPORT
Skyrail Rainforest Cableway.....17 D3

To Kuranda
B&B (700m)

To Cairns
(27km)

Barron River

Pioneer
Cemetery

Lookout   Kuranda Scenic Railway

Kuranda Heights Rd

Kennedy Hwy

Therwine St

Thooree St

Coondoo St

Thongon St

Barang St

Rob Veivers Dr

Morton St

Meroo St

Arara St

Centenary
Park

Train Station

Jumrum Creek
Environmental
Park

Barron Falls Rd

To Kuranda Resort & Spa; Miju Rainforest Retreat (1km);
Rainforestation (3km); Mareeba (36km)

Kuranda's famous markets remain ever popular. The original **Kuranda Markets** (☎ 4093 8772; 7 Therwine St; ☺ 9am-3pm Wed-Fri & Sun), once famous for genuine art and craft products, are supplemented by the **Heritage Markets** (☎ 4093 8060; www.kurandaline.com.au; Rob Veivers Dr; ☺ 9am-3pm). Between them you'll find souvenirs such as ceramics, emu oil, jewellery, food and figurines made from pistachio nuts. For genuine crafts produced by professional artists, try the **Kuranda Arts Co-op** (☎ 4093 9026; www.artskuranda.asn.au; Kuranda Settlement Village, 12 Rob Veivers Dr; ☺ 10am-4pm).

There are a number of **walking trails** (www .wettropics.gov.au) in and around Kuranda. Many are the traditional pathways of the indigenous Djabagny; some paths later became pack routes linking the goldfields with the coast. Across the train line by the station a path leads down to the Barron River. Follow the path downstream to the railway bridge (1km, 30 minutes). This bridge marks the start of the Jungle Walk section (0.8km, 15 minutes), which is a paved track that runs between Barron Gorge Rd meeting the Jumrum Creek Walk (0.8km, 15

minutes). You can walk the 2.6km loop or take one section as a short return walk.

Also behind the train station, over the footbridge, **Kuranda Rainforest Tours** (☎ 4093 7476; adult/child $12/6; ☺ hourly 10.30am-2.30pm) runs sedate 45-minute cruises along the Barron River. Check opening times during the Wet (October to March).

There's loads of wildlife in Kuranda – albeit in zoos. **Rainforestation** (☎ 4085 5008; www.rainforest.com.au; Kennedy Hwy; adult/child $34/17; ☺ 8.30am-4pm) is an enormous tourist park with a wildlife section, river cruises and an Aboriginal show. The **Australian Butterfly Sanctuary** (☎ 4093 7575; www.australianbutterflies .com; 8 Rob Veivers Dr; adult/child $12/5; ☺ 10am-4pm Mon-Fri) is a butterfly aviary, and is next door to **Birdworld** (☎ 4093 9188; www.birdworldkuranda .com; Heritage Markets; adult/child $12/5; ☺ 9am-4pm), displaying both native and exotic birds.

Sleeping

Kuranda Rainforest Park (☎ 4093 7316; www.kuranda rainforestpark.com.au; Kuranda Heights Rd; unpowered/ powered sites $17/20, s/d $30/50, units from $100; ☒) Located on a large rainforest block, you'll wake in the morning to birds trilling. A range of accommodation is available suitable for families, solo travellers and couples. Budget rooms share a kitchen and bathroom, while units are self-contained with poolside or garden views. The park is a 10-minute walk from town.

Kuranda B&B (☎ 4093 7151; http://users.tpg.com .au/users/ausavsup/; 28 Black Mountain Rd; s/d $80/130; 🐾) This excellent B&B is 20 minutes' walk from town, on Ripple Creek. There are two large rooms, each with its own bathroom and veranda overlooking the lovingly tended garden. There's a communal kitchen available, and breakfast is part of the package.

Kuranda Backpackers Hostel (☎ 4093 7355; www .kurandabackpackershostel.com; cnr Arara & Barang Sts; dm/ d $18/42; 🖳) This agreeably rambling doublestorey home is surrounded by a large garden. There are lots of communal spaces over two levels to hang about in, which promotes a low-key chummy environment. You can show off in the large kitchen, or retreat to the reading room.

Kuranda Resort & Spa (☎ 4093 7556; www.liberty resort.com.au; 3 Green Hills Rd; dm $35, r from $180; 🐾 🖳) You'll feel as though you've stepped inside a magazine spread when you enter the stylish apartments on offer here. There's a range of accommodation options to suit any budget. Facilities include a gym and bar-restaurant.

Kuranda Hotel Motel (☎ 4093 7206; cnr Coondoo & Arara Sts; s/d $45/60; 🖳) Out the back of the hotel, which serves as Kuranda's local, 12 basic motel-style rooms are available. The sparse, tidy rooms provide a perfectly good place to rest your head for a night.

Miju Rainforest Retreat (☎ 4093 9304; www.miju rainforestretreat.com; 47 Bangalow Place; r $120; 🖳) Emerge from your cosy room to be greeted by a continental breakfast. Each of the two rooms has its own kitchen and shares a laundry. Free pick-up is available from Cairns airport.

Eating

Annabel's Pantry (☎ 4093 7605; Therwine St; pies $4-6; 🕒 breakfast & lunch) Offering more varieties of pie than there are letters in the alphabet, Annabel's has some creative fillings, such as the Matilda (roo filled). A few flimsy outdoor settings are available to sit at.

Monkey's Cafe (☎ 4093 7451; 1 Therwine St; mains $12-16; 🕒 lunch) The fabulous garden at Monkey's might inspire you to swing from the trees. Specialising in big gourmet sandwiches, this licensed café is a welcome place to retreat and linger.

German Tucker (☎ 4057 9688; Therwine St; dishes $6-9; 🕒 lunch) Fat kransky sausages with sauerkraut or kangaroo sausage with potato salad? German Tucker serves extreme Australiana and traditional German fare, and stocks German beer. Sandwiches and a range of salads are also available.

Veg Out Cafe (☎ 4093 8483; Shop 5, 24 Coondoo St; meals $5-10; 🕒 lunch) You'll be lulled by Hare Krishna chanting as you tuck into your wholesome vegetarian dish here. Wheat- and sugar-free meals are also on offer; Veg Out is located in the Red House mall.

Peppers (☎ 4093 8733; Kuranda Settlement Village, 12 Rob Veivers Dr; meals around $15; 🕒 lunch & dinner Wed-Sun) Fresh food focussing on homemade and organic produce is on offer at Peppers. The breads are baked daily on the premises, and there are daily specials that might include curries, pasta or tofu with wild rice. Peppers also makes gourmet pizza; try the Greek – caramelised onion, feta, blue cheese and oregano. Bring your own bottle and dine in or take away.

Garden Bar & Grill (☎ 4093 7206; cnr Coondoo & Arara Sts; dishes $9-13; 🕒 lunch daily, dinner Mon-Sat) In the Kuranda Hotel Motel's backyard, this is a pleasant spot. It serves up counter lunches of the steak and sanger variety.

There's a small supermarket on Coondoo St for self-caterers.

Getting There & Away

Kuranda Scenic Railway (☎ 4036 9288; www.travel train.com.au; Cairns train station, Bunda St; adult/concession/ child $35/27/17.50) winds 34km from Cairns to Kuranda through picturesque mountains and no less than 15 tunnels. The line took five years to build, and was opened in 1891. The trip takes 1¾ hours and trains depart Cairns at 8.30am and 9.30am Sunday to Friday (8.30am Saturday), returning from pretty Kuranda station (known for its floral displays) at 2pm and 3.30pm Sunday to Friday (3.30pm Saturday).

Skyrail Rainforest Cableway (☎ 4038 1555; www .skyrail.com.au; adult/child $35/17.50; 🕒 8.15am-5.15pm) is one of the world's longest gondola cableways at 7.5km. The Skyrail runs from the corner of Kemerunga Rd and the Cook Hwy in Smithfield, a northern suburb of Cairns, to Kuranda (Arara St), taking 90 minutes. It includes two stops along the way and features boardwalks with interpretive panels passing the burly Barron Falls (reduced to a drip in the dry season). The last departure from Cairns and Kuranda is at 3.30pm; transfers to/from the terminal (15 minutes' drive north of Cairns) and combination (Scenic Railway and Skyrail) deals are also available. As space is limited, only daypacks are allowed on board Skyrail.

John's Kuranda Bus (☎ 0418-772 953; tickets $2) runs a service between Cairns and Kuranda at least twice a day and up to seven times between Wednesday to Friday. Buses depart from Cairns' Lake St Transit Centre. **Kuranda Shuttle** (☎ 0402-032 085; tickets $2) departs Cairns' Transit Mall every two hours between 9am and 3pm, and Kuranda (Therwine St) at 10am, 12.15pm and 2pm. **Whitecar Coaches** (☎ 4091 1855; tickets $4) has five departures from 46 Spence St, Cairns.

MAREEBA

Functional Mareeba is at the centre of industrious cattle, coffee and sugar enterprises. The area was once a major producer of tobacco, but that has been gradually phased out. Mareeba's main street boasts some quaint old façades, such as that of the defunct tobacco marketing board. A number of Mareeba's food producers have opened their doors for tours, and you can appreciate the region's natural beauty in its accessible parklands.

Continue through town to the Cooktown Developmental Rd, known as the inland route to Cooktown.

Sights & Activities

Mareeba Heritage Museum & Tourist Information Centre (☎ 4092 5674; www.mareebaheritagecentre .com.au; Centenary Park, 345 Byrnes St; museum adult/child $5/2.50; ☯ 8am-4pm) has displays on the area's past and present commercial industries, as well as its natural surrounds.

Mareeba Wetlands (☎ 4093 2514; www.mareeba wetlands.com; adult/child $8/5; ☯ 8.30am-4pm Wed-Sun Apr-Dec) is a 20-sq-km reserve featuring wood- and grasslands, lagoons and swamps. A huge range of bird species flock here, and you might see other animals such as kangaroos and freshwater crocs (not the big salties). The Wetlands' visitors centre has information on self-guided walks around the reserve. From

here you can join a guided boat or walking tour; you can also hire a canoe ($11 per hour). To reach the wetlands, take the Pickford Rd turn-off from Biboohra, 7km north of Mareeba.

Granite Gorge (admission $2) is known for its resident population of rock wallabies. There are walking tracks, waterfalls tumbling into a swimming hole and huge granite boulders. Granite Gorge is 12km southwest of Mareeba. Follow Chewco Rd out of Mareeba for 7km; there's a turn-off to your right from there. It's an unsealed road, but suitable for conventional vehicles.

To sample some of the region's speciality produce, head to **Coffee Works** (☎ 4092 4101; www.arabicas.com.au; 136 Mason St; tours $5; ☯ 9am-4pm), a roaster that has daily tasting tours at 10am, noon and 2pm; or **Bruno's** (☎ 4093 2269; Dimbulah Rd; admission free; ☯ 8am-5pm), which takes you through the growing, harvesting and roasting process on the family's plantation. For the harder stuff, **Golden Pride Winery** (☎ 4093 2750; www.goldendrop.com.au; Bilwon Rd, Bilwon; ☯ 8am-5pm) offers tastings of its sweet mango wine, and **Mt Uncle Distillery** (☎ 4086 8008; www .mtuncle.com; 1819 Chewko Rd, Walkamin; ☯ 10am-5pm) proffers its seasonal liqueurs including banana, coffee, mulberry and lemon.

Aviation and military buffs should check out the **Beck Museum** (☎ 4092 3979; Kennedy Hwy; adult/child $13/7; ☯ 10am-4pm). It's the biggest collection in Queensland, including P39 American fighter planes used over the Coral Sea during WWII.

Festivals & Events

The **cattle saleyards**, just north of town on the road to Mt Molloy, provide a genuine taste of country Australia; there are sales every Tuesday morning at the crack of dawn.

Mareeba's **Rodeo**, held annually in July, is one of Australia's biggest. There's bull and bronco riding, and 'cowboy protection' provided by clowns.

Sleeping & Eating

Jackaroo Motel (☎ 4092 2677; www.jackaroomotel.com; 340 Byrnes St; r $77; ☒ ☒) This modern motel has a great range of facilities, including a saltwater swimming pool, BBQ and laundry. Rooms are comfortable and tidy; some have wheelchair access.

Arriga Park (☎ 4093 2114; www.bnbnq.com.au/arriga; 1720 Dimbulah Rd; r $65) Three rooms are available in this homestead set on a sugar-cane farm and fruit orchard. You can soak in the outdoor spa and order home-cooked meals prepared from organic produce grown on the property. Full board is also available.

Mareeba Motor Inn (☎ 4092 2451; Kennedy Hwy; s/d $72/77; ✵ ✷) These basic, functional rooms are supplemented by a communal laundry, room service and wheelchair access. The complex stretches along a grassy plain and caters mostly to itinerant workers.

Riverside Caravan Park (☎ 4092 2309; 13 Egan St; unpowered/powered sites $11/14, on-site vans $25-35) On the Barron River, you'll be lulled to sleep by the sound of running water. This is a shady ground, with wheelchair-accessible facilities.

Nastasi's (☎ 4092 2321; 10 Byrnes St; meals $4-7; ✵ breakfast, lunch & dinner; ▣) If it's fried, they've got it: dim sims, fish and chips, eggs and bacon, and burgers sizzle out the door. Nastasi's also does good honest sandwiches and pizza. You can eat in (BYO) or take away.

ATHERTON

'Capital' of the tableland, Atherton is a commercial hub and a pleasant place to regroup. It takes its name from the first white settler to find tin, and farm in the region, John Atherton.

The **Atherton Tableland Information Centre** (☎ 4091 4222; www.athertonsc.qld.gov.au; cnr Robert & Herberton Sts; ✵ 9am-5pm) has loads of useful information on the region, including brochures outlining the network of heritage trails. **Washouse** (☎ 4091 2619; 1 Robert St; per hr $5; ✵ 9am-5pm Mon-Fri, 9am-noon Sat) doubles as an Internet café and laundry.

Hallorans Hill is a panoramic lookout, from where the surrounding farmland looks like an earthy-coloured patchwork quilt. The hill features an outdoor sculpture park and is adjacent to an interpretive rainforest trail. To get there, head up Robert St from the information centre and follow the easily visible signs.

The **Hou Wang Temple** (☎ 4091 6945; 86 Herberton Rd; adult/concession/child $7/5.50/2; ✵ 10am-4pm) is testament to the Chinese migrants who flooded the area to search for gold in the late 1800s. It occupies the site of historical Atherton's Chinatown. Inside are displays of objects, photographs and interpretive panels.

To see geodes and thunder eggs, head to **Crystal Caves** (☎ 4091 2365; www.crystalcaves.com.au;

DETOUR

Chillagoe, 140km west from Mareeba, lives up to any romantic notion you may have of the outback. This charismatic former mining town presents a genuine getaway with a raw, unhurried quality. It's at the centre of an area imbued with impressive limestone caves, indigenous rock-art sites, and ruins of an early-20th-century smelting plant.

From Mareeba, take the Burke Developmental Rd west. After passing through Dimbulah, a regional centre that developed in the 1930s around tobacco, you cross Eureka Creek. It's here that the terrain becomes characteristic of the outback, with rugged rusty plains supporting spindly vegetation, termite hills and hump-backed Brahman cattle. Twenty-five kilometres past Petford – population 10 – is Almaden. It's no surprise that the residents of Almaden wander freely about town, except that the town has more cows than people, hence the nickname 'Cow Town'. Soon you'll start to see the limestone bluffs for which Chillagoe is known, and the giant marble pits that are dotted around the region.

The **Hub** (☎ 4094 7111; Queen St; ✵ 8.30am-5pm Mon-Fri, 8am-3pm Sat & Sun) is the visitors centre and where you book tours of the surrounding caves ($11 to $14). There are rock-art sites at Balancing Rock and Mungana (15km northwest).

While accessible on a day trip, it's worth staying over to get the most out of your visit. Try the fabulous self-contained cabins at **Chillagoe Cabins** (☎ 4094 7206; www.chillagoe.com; Queen St; s/d $80/100; ✷), or the equally excellent options at **Chillagoe Bush Camp & Eco Lodge** (☎ 4094 7155; Hospital Ave; s/tw $30/52, d $55-70).

69 Main St; adult/child $12.50/6; ✵ 8.30am-5pm Mon-Fri, 8.30am-4pm Sat, 10am-4pm Sun). This mineralogical museum is in an artificial cave setting and winds underground for a block. You must wear a hard hat, and the last 'miners' need to be there one hour before closing. There is wheelchair access.

Section cars are set to start running again along the historic train line between Atherton and Herberton. The scenic ride negotiates steep gradients, and goes through tunnels and past waterfalls. Phone **Railco**

(☎ 4097 7402, 4096 2124) to see if the service is running.

Tolga Woodworks (☎ 4095 4488; www.tolga woodworks.com.au; Kennedy Hwy, Tolga; ☾ 9am-5pm), 5km north of Atherton, has stunning wood pieces for sale or to just stare at. Typically, the **café** (dishes $5-7; ☾ lunch) area features wooden furniture and panelling; you might stop in for a slice of hummingbird cake or a bowl of celery soup.

The two beautiful, self-contained apartments (named after the owner's grandmothers, Hazel and Frances) at **Pteropus House** (☎ 4091 2683; www.athertontablelands.com/bats; 134 Carrington Rd; s/d from $80/90) are superb value. Tolga's bat-rescue operation, which was set up to save flying foxes threatened by ticks and loss of habitat, is coordinated from here. Tours to a local colony are also run from here. Bookings are essential.

Atherton Motel (☎ 4091 1500; Maunds Rd; r $85; ✘ ✜) has comfortable, well-equipped rooms housed in a long strip 2km from town. The room service is pretty special here: dial '9' for chicken breast with tomato and olive sauce ($16.50) or eye fillet steak ($21.50). The motel is also licensed, with a limited range of wine available.

The rooms upstairs at the pink Art Deco **Atherton Hotel** (☎ 4091 7611; thestump@austarnet.com .au; 90 Main St; r $75-95; ✘) are priced according to whether they have a window and/or a spa. Lovely big meals are available at the hotel's restaurant, the **Stump** (meals $13-18; ☾ breakfast, lunch & dinner). You might try Spanish mackerel or steak with potatoes and salad, pumpkin risotto or spaghetti bolognaise.

Atherton Blue Gum B&B (☎ 4091 5149; www .athertonbluegum.com; 36 Twelfth Ave; r from $95) is in a double-storey home with great views from its 2nd-storey veranda – a good place for breakfast. Rooms are functional, with pine panelling and big windows.

Atherton Woodlands (☎ 4091 1407; www.wood landscp.com.au; 141 Herberton Rd; unpowered/powered sites $16/22, d cabins $55-65; ✜) caravan and camping park, 1.5km south of town, has a range of accommodation options, including cabins. Facilities are excellent; its camp kitchen is fitted with a gas BBQ, and the bathrooms are large and light-filled.

The commanding corner **Grand Hotel** (☎ 4091 4899; cnr Main & Vernon Sts; dm/s/d $28.50/ 38.50/46.50) has reasonable rooms upstairs, with a communal kitchen and sitting area.

The downstairs **bistro** (mains $15-20; ☾ lunch & dinner) does decent food and has a good range of wine available.

LAKE TINAROO

Picturesque Lake Tinaroo is a great spot for families and fisherfolk. The enormous artificial lake and dam were originally created for the Barron River hydroelectric power scheme. Tinaroo's foreshore enjoyed a million-dollar makeover in 2004 and now features BBQ facilities, a children's playground and landscaped walkways.

Barramundi fishing is legendary here, with the biggest fish caught on the lake weighing over 38kg. Barra fishing is permitted year-round. To obtain a compulsory permit (per week $7), which are readily available from tourist-oriented businesses around the tableland, contact **Queensland's Department of Primary Industries** (☎ 13 13 04; www.dpi.qld.gov.au/fishweb), which has a list of outlets. The **Barra Bash** fishing competition is held annually at the end of October; think

---

TIDY TOWNS

Something akin to a beauty contest for towns, the Tidy Town awards are a national competition established in 1971. In the early days, keeping clean and litter free was the main criterion. Lately, there's been provision to consider a town's environmental awareness. In 2004 Atherton took out the award for Queensland's Tidiest Town. Factors that made it a winner included bright and creative signage, as well as an accredited visitors centre (whose uniform could also be described as bright and creative). The state prize puts Atherton in the running to snaffle the title of Australian Tidy Town 2005.

The title is open to all Australian states and territories, and comprises part of the government's Keep Australia Beautiful programme. The national awards' judge, Dick Olesinski, inspects the seven finalist towns. Feted by each town's counsellors and volunteers, you can bet that in his 11 years as judge, Mr Olesinski has consumed more tea and lamingtons than any man. The winner of the national comp receives the perpetual trophy, which resembles a bowing robotic kangaroo.

twice about coming at this time if you're after a quiet escape.

Danbulla Forest Drive leaves from the dam. It's 28km of unsealed road through rainforest and softwood plantations. A number of attractions are signposted along the way, including **Lake Euramoo** and the **Cathedral Fig** – a gigantic strangler fig tree shouldering epiphytes nesting in its branches. The road emerges at the Gillies Hwy 4km northeast of Lake Barrine (see p363).

The options at **Lake Tinaroo Terraces** (☎ 4095 8555; www.laketinarooterraces.com.au; cnr Church & Russel Sts; r $80-150; ⚟) are great value, ranging from a room with a bathroom to two-bedroom, self-contained two-storey terraces. Located on the lakefront, it also has a swimming pool, laundry and BBQ area.

Tinaroo Tropical Houseboats (☎ 4095 8322; www .laketinaroo.com; 2 nights from $550) are fabulously kitsch caravan-style houseboats, and a great option. They sleep up to four and have a kitchen and shower, as well as their own private deck. Two-storey, luxury boats that sleep up to six are also available. There's a complex pricing structure, and petrol and insurance cost extra.

Forget renting a room, at **Tinaroo Haven Holiday Lodge** (☎ 4095 8686; www.fire-break.com; Lot 42, Wavell Dr, Tinaroo Waters; d $145) you get the whole house – a comfy, timber pole-house. There's wheelchair access, and features include a potbelly stove, board games and gas BBQ.

Lake Tinaroo Holiday Park (☎ 4095 8232; www .ppawd.com/tinaroo; Dam Rd; unpowered/powered sites $15/20, cabins from $50) is a pleasantly shady camping ground by the lake.

The relaxed, lakeside **Pensini's Café & Restaurant** (☎ 4095 8242; 12 Church St; mains $17-20; ⚟ lunch daily, dinner Sat) has a range of dishes that utilise local tableland produce (including barramundi of course). There's also a pretty hefty wine list.

There are five **QPWS campsites** (☎ 13 13 04; www.epa.qld.gov.au) in the Danbulla State Forest. They have water, BBQs and toilets. You'll need to book for School Point, Downfall Creek and Kauri Creek. Platypus and Fong-On Bay don't require bookings and are self-registration sites.

HERBERTON

Peaceful Herberton is nestled in the crease of one of the area's rolling hills. It was founded on the Wild River after the discovery of a tin lode in 1880. Dozens of mines opened in the area, and by the early 1900s Herberton had rapidly developed, producing two newspapers and sporting 17 pubs. The establishment of the town decimated the indigenous Bar Barrum community – members of the now extinct Mbabaram language group. More recently the shire reinstated Native Title to Herberton and acknowledged the cultural significance of certain areas to the Bar Barrum.

The **visitors centre** (☎ 4096 2244; Great Northern Mining Centre, Jack's Rd) on the site of an old mine, stocks brochures outlining walks in and around town. Or you can let someone else do most of the work and let a donkey carry your gear on a trek with **Wilderness Expeditions** (☎ 4096 2266; www.wildex.com.au; day treks adult/child $125/95); longer treks are also available.

You can also ride the historic railway between Herberton and Atherton if it's operational (see p357).

Ye Olde Camera & Photography Museum (☎ 4096 2092; 49 Grace St; admission $3; ⚟ 10am-5pm) is reputedly operated by an ex–secret agent; some of the cameras in this vast collection may have seen some undercover action.

Heritage-style rooms at **Herberton Heritage Cottage B&B** (☎ 4096 2032; www.herbertoncottage.com; 2 Perkins St; s/d $120/130; ⚟) are the best option in town. Expect lots of polished wood surfaces, potbelly heating and high, comfy beds.

The historic **Australian Hotel** (☎ 4096 2263; 44 Grace St; s/d $25/50; mains $12-16; ⚟ lunch & dinner) is located in the centre of town and has basic motel-style rooms. You can also stop by for a counter lunch or dinner.

Wild River Caravan Park (☎ 4096 2121; 23 Holdcroft Dr; unpowered/powered sites $9/17, caravans $30, cabins $40) is on the edge of town, with an attractive aspect; the cabins here are self-contained.

MT HYPIPAMEE NATIONAL PARK

Between Atherton and Ravenshoe, the Kennedy Hwy passes the eerie Mt Hypipamee **crater**. It is anomalous due to the granite rock it's cut from, which is not associated with volcanic activity. It's over 120m deep, which makes for one giant wishing well. It's an easy 800m (return) walk from the car park to the crater. A separate path forks off the train taking you past **Dinner Falls** (which ultimately becomes the Barron River) to a rock pool and swimming hole.

DETOUR

This inland detour chases the warm waters that spring up from the ground and those that fall spectacularly down. Take the Kennedy Hwy (part of Australia's Hwy 1 at this point) from Ravenshoe, which continues southwest for 114km, where it forks. The road south goes to Charters Towers and is sealed all the way; to the west is the Gulf Developmental Rd to Croydon and Normanton via the Undara lava tubes.

About 32km west of Ravenshoe is the small township of **Innot Hot Springs**, where a hot spring measuring 73°C heats up the cool waters of the town's Nettle Creek. The spring water is said to be therapeutic, and after a steaming soak you might agree. You can 'take the waters' at **Innot Hot Springs Village** (☎ 4097 0136; unpowered/powered sites $17/19, budget s/d $35/45, s/d cabins $67/77; ☒). Visitors have free use of the park's seven **thermal pools** (nonguests adult/child $6/4; h8am-6pm) of varying temperatures.

Continuing 15km to the tidy little mining town of **Mt Garnet**, the landscape starts to thin out, punctuated by multicoloured termite mounds: from red to yellow and brown. Just north of town is the Wurruma Swamp, a wetlands area that attracts a huge range of birdlife.

Spectacular **Blencoe Falls**, the setting for the second US *Survivor* series, is 84km southeast of Mt Garnet on the unsealed Gunnawarra Rd. The first waterfall drop is a massive 91m. It's an excellent spot to retire from life for a while and do some bush camping.

About 60km past Mt Garnet, the Kennedy Hwy passes through **Forty Mile Scrub National Park**. There are toilets and picnic facilities, but watch your crumbs – the leaf litter is home to the giant cockroach. There's a short circuit walk (300m, 10 minutes) that's boarded and wheelchair-friendly. Just past the park is the turn-off to the Undara Laval Tubes (see p408) and the Gulf Savannah.

RAVENSHOE

Ravenshoe was founded on the timber industry, though today it's known for providing more sustainable resources – with its hill-top wind farm. At an altitude of 930m, Ravenshoe is the highest town in Queensland, and well positioned to catch the prevailing winds.

The **Ravenshoe Visitor Centre** (☎ 4097 7700; www .ravenshoevisitorcentre.com.au; 24 Moore St; h 9am-4pm) supplies local maps and houses the **Ngayaji Interpretive Centre**, which explains the Jirrbal people's traditional lifestyle.

WindyHill wind farm is Australia's largest, with 20 turbines producing a clean, green energy supply. These modern windmills share the undulating hills with grazing cattle. The public can view the turbines 24 hours a day. You can reach WindyHill via the Kennedy Hwy from Ravenshoe, or along the scenic Old Palmerston Hwy from Millaa Millaa.

There are a number of **waterfalls** nearby. Little Millstream Falls are 2km south of Ravenshoe on the Tully Gorge Rd, and Tully Falls are 24km south. About 6km past Ravenshoe and 1km off the road are the 13m-high Millstream Falls; in flood they're said to be the widest in Australia.

Train enthusiasts can take a ride on the **Railco Scenic Heritage Steam Railway** (☎ 4097 6005;

adult/child $15/7.50; h departs 2.30pm Sat & Sun), a historic steam train that runs 7km north to Tumoulin, returning to Ravenshoe at 4pm. The railway closes from February to March.

There are a number of boutique B&B-type options in the vicinity; the visitors centre has a full list.

Central to town, the **Old Convent** (☎ 4097 6454; www.bnbnq.com.au/oldconvent; 23 Moore St; s/d $65/75) has rooms with high ceilings, polished floors and period furniture. The Old Convent building moved here in 1950 – not that old?

Turn off the Kennedy Hwy, down a 4.5km unsealed road, and you'll find two cottages clinging to the fringe of World Heritage–listed rainforest. **Possum Valley Rainforest Cottages** (☎ 4097 8177; www.bnbnq.com .au/possumvalley; Evelyn Central, via Ravenshoe; s/d $60/75, plus $5 per person) are fully self-contained and very green in both senses of the word: they are surrounded by rainforest and use solar and hydroelectricity, and tank water.

Millstream Retreat (☎ 4097 6785; www.mill streamretreat.com.au; 12028 Kennedy Hwy; d $110) is about 12km from Ravenshoe, with comfy, self-contained cottages overlooking the Millstream River, which you can paddle along in the property's canoe. Cottages come with laundry, kitchen and wood-fired heater.

MILLAA MILLAA

On the spectacular Waterfalls Circuit, Millaa Millaa is a tiny, respectable village originally established to support the thriving local dairy industry. The workers – black-and-white Friesian cows – still dot the surrounding green pastures.

At **Mungalli Creek Dairy** (☎ 4097 2232; www.millaa.com/Mungalli/mungalli.htm; 254 Brooks Rd; ⏱ 10am-4pm) you can sample boutique bio-dynamic dairy products, including yoghurt, cheese and sinfully rich cheesecake.

Mungalli Falls Rainforest Village (☎ 4097 2358; www.mungallifalls.com; Junction Rd; dm $25, cabins $55-85), 5km off the Palmerston Hwy, caters to groups and has beds for up to 600 people. There's a kiosk (meals from $10 to $25), and horse-riding ($65 for 3½ hours) is available.

Millaa Millaa Tourist Park (☎ 4097 2290; www.millaapark.com; cnr Malanda Rd & Lodge Ave; unpowered/powered sites $15/18, dm $15, s $30, d $45-85), 1.5km from Millaa Millaa Falls, has a range of accommodation options set on large grounds.

About 7km north of Millaa Millaa, rooms at **Iskanda Park Farmstay** (☎ 4097 2401; www.iskanda.com; Nash Rd; r $110-125) are in the farm's homestead. There are views over the rolling hills, and opportunities to lend a hand around the farm.

WATERFALLS CIRCUIT

The circuit passes some of the most picturesque waterfalls on the tableland. Enter the circuit by taking Theresa Creek Rd, 1km east of Millaa Millaa on the Palmerston Hwy. **Millaa Millaa Falls**, the first you reach, are the most spectacular; surrounded by tree ferns and flowers, the waterfall forms a perfect white foam of water falling from a drop of about 12m. These falls have the best swimming hole and a grassy area for picnickers.

Continuing around the circuit, you reach **Zillie Falls**, where a short walking trail leads to a lookout beside the falls. Further on you come to **Ellinjaa Falls**, with a 200m walking trail down to a swimming hole at the base of the falls, before returning to the Palmerston Hwy just 2.5km out of Millaa Millaa. A further 5.5km down the Palmerston Hwy there's a turn-off to **Mungalli Falls**.

Lunch at the **Falls Teahouse** (☎ 4097 2237; www.fallsteahouse.com.au; Palmerston Hwy; s $65-95, d $95-140, meals $8-14; ⏱ 10am-5pm), overlooking the rolling tableland hills, is a treat. You might try laksa, curry or sandwiches made from home-baked bread. Rooms are individually furnished with period fixtures and fittings. It's just out of the township, on the turn-off to Millaa Millaa Falls.

MALANDA

Malanda has long been synonymous with milk – ever since 500 bedraggled cattle made the arduous overland journey from New South Wales (taking 16 months) in 1908. About 15km south of Lake Eacham, compact Malanda sports some quaint historic buildings. The **Malanda Falls Visitors Centre** (☎ 4096 6957; Atherton Rd; ⏱ 9am-4.30pm) has thoughtful displays on the area's human and geological history, and runs guided rainforest walks ($10, by appointment) led by members of the Ngadjonji community.

On the Atherton Rd on the outskirts of town are the **Malanda Falls**. They don't 'fall' so spectacularly, but the resulting pool, surrounded by lawns and forest, makes a popular swimming spot; a 1km walking trail passes through the forest nearby.

If you're staying in the town, try to catch a double feature at the **Majestic Theatre** (☎ 4096 5726; www.majestictheatre.com.au; Eacham Place). Built in 1927, with traditional oak-framed, lay-back canvas bleachers, it screens mainstream movies on Friday and Saturday nights.

A couple of kilometres west of Malanda is **Bromfield Swamp**, an important waterbird sanctuary best visited late in the afternoon. A viewing area beside the road overlooks an eroded volcanic crater.

There is plenty of B&B accommodation tucked away in the forests and farms around Malanda.

A pristine patch of old-growth rainforest is the stunning setting for the group of all-timber pole houses at **Fur 'n' Feathers** (☎ 4096 5364; www.rainforesttreehouses.com.au; Hogan Rd, Tarzali via Malanda; d $195-480). The riverfront treehouses are self-contained, private and perfect for spotting wildlife (including the resident cassowary). Boutique B&B accommodation doesn't get much better.

Lumholtz Lodge (☎ 4095 0292; www.users.bigpond.com/lumholtzlodge; Upper Barron Rd; B&B d $140, full-board d $260; 🖳) is a B&B where, enveloped in foliage, you'll be well placed to watch the surrounding wildlife. Guests have free reign of the lodge, which includes shelves stocked with books about nature and a spa.

At **Hattons Hideaway** (☎ 4096 5239; www.hat tonshideaway.com.au; 37 Whiteing Close; d $195; ⌨) the froufrou rooms feature layers of lace and display colours that lean towards soft pastels. Meals are also available for an extra fee, and Hattons caters to couples and groups, with the option of having a fully hosted dinner party.

The double spa, big bed and cosy fire at **Foxwell Park** (☎ 4096 6183; www.foxwellpark.com.au; Foxwell Rd; d from $125; ⌨) are aimed at attracting couples – to Foxwell and to each other. The tariff includes breakfast, and there's a separate **restaurant** (⌚ lunch Sun, dinner Wed-Sun) on the premises.

Set amid rolling pastures just 3km south of Malanda, **Fairdale Farmstay** (☎ 4096 6599; www.bnbnq.com.au/fairdale; Hillcrest Rd; s/d $65/95, cottages $110-165) offers visitors accommodation in the family homestead or in separate, self-contained cottages. The cottages are great for families: they sleep up to six people, and the little 'uns can participate in farm activities.

Malanda Lodge Motel (☎ 4096 5555; www.malanda lodgemotel.com.au; Millaa Millaa Rd; s/d $80/90; ⌨ ⌨) has a good range of facilities including a restaurant and laundry. If it feels as though those solid brick walls of your room are closing in, escape to the beautiful gardens or swimming pool.

Wow: if the fluffy booties and bathrobes don't get you, the sliding glass wall in the bathroom will. **Rivers Edge Rainforest Retreat** (☎ 4096 2255; www.riversedgeretreat.com.au; d $255; ⌨ ⌨) is a staggeringly beautiful retreat on the Johnstone River that's surrounded by trees. It's self-contained, with lavish touches such as big, soft chairs to fall into while you read from the library, huge beds, a wood heater and veranda with a BBQ. There's a minimum two-night stay.

Located right next to Malanda Falls, you'll probably see more wildlife in the spacious grounds of **Malanda Falls Caravan Park** (☎ 4096 5314; 38 Park Ave; unpowered/powered sites $15/18, dm $35, cabins $50-70) than you will at any purpose-built sanctuary.

Next door to the visitors centre is the **Tree Kangaroo Cafe** (☎ 4096 6658; meals $4-10; ⌚ breakfast & lunch) with diner-style stopgap food.

YUNGABURRA

Yungaburra's chocolate-box prettiness has made it a popular retreat for Cairns' wage slaves. Its streets are lined with quaint timber buildings, many of which are historically significant. The **Yungaburra Folk Festival** (www.yungaburrafolkfestival.org) is a fabulous community event held annually over a late October weekend; it features music, workshops, poetry readings and kids activities.

Information & Orientation

The **visitors centre** (☎ 4095 2416; www.yungaburra .com; Cedar St; ⌚ 9am-6pm) is located in the corrugated-iron faux shed. At the end of this street turn left, which leads to the river and platypus-spotting platform; before breakfast is best.

Sights & Activities

The **Yungaburra Markets** (☎ 4095 2111; Gillies Hwy; ⌚ 7am-noon) are held in town on the fourth Saturday of every month; at this time the village is besieged by people mooching among craft and food products.

The magnificent **Curtain Fig** is a must-see. Looking a prop from *The Lord of the Rings*, this 500-year-old tree has aerial roots that hang down to create a feathery curtain. A wheelchair-accessible viewing platform snakes around the tree, and bush turkeys forage in the leaf litter below.

Sleeping

Gables B&B (☎ 4095 2373; 5 Eacham Rd; r $65-75) The room downstairs at this historic Queenslander is without its own bathroom and attracts a cheaper rate. The two upstairs rooms are self-contained, one endowed with a spa, the other with lots of space. All rates include a big breakfast of bread and fruit.

Lake Eacham Hotel (☎ 4095 3515; fax 4095 3202; Gillies Hwy; s/d $50/65) The downstairs dining room and swirling wooden staircase of this grand old hotel are inspirational. The upstairs rooms are less exciting but perfectly functional, and have their own bathroom.

Kookaburra Lodge (☎ 4095 3222; www.kooka burra-lodge.com; cnr Oak St & Eacham Rd; d $75; ⌨ ⌨) These stylish rooms fan out around the pale-blue pool. Behind a high fence and amid a tropical garden, Kookaburra is an intimate option. There are big soft couches to sink into in the communal lounge. Kookaburra is not suitable for small children.

On the Wallaby (☎ 4095 2031; www.onthewallaby .com; 34 Eacham Rd; unpowered sites $10, dm/d $20/50) The timber interiors and attentive greeting are welcome and warming at this backpackers lodge. Nature-based tours run from here daily and packages that include transfers from Cairns and trips to the falls are offered. Camping is in the backyard.

Gumtree Getaway (☎ 4095 3105; www.gumtree getaway.com.au; Gillies Hwy; d $110; 🖳) Individually themed cabins skirt the globe, with Australian-, African- and Egyptian-inspired fittings. A few things they all have in common: open fireplaces, big beds and breakfast included. This is a luxurious and stylish option; you hearing this honeymooners?

Eden House (☎ 4095 3355; www.edenhouse.com .au; 20 Gillies Hwy; d $165-185; 🖭 🖳) There are six Heritage-themed cottages here at Eden House. The pricier rooms are fitted with a big spa, and the bed commands over the space from its raised platform. You need never leave the room as room service is available – and breakfast is included.

Mt Quincan Crater Retreat (🕥 4095 2255; www .mtquincan.com.au; Peeramon Rd; d from $250; 🖭) Double spas, king-sized beds, open fireplaces, an isolated location in the forest – you get the picture. These luxurious, self-contained cabins have been built by cupid for couples; occasionally he organises some rolling mist for added effect. Follow the road between Yungaburra and Peeramon to the signposted turn-off.

THE AUTHOR'S CHOICE

Curtain Fig Motel (☎ 4095 3168; www.curtain fig.com; 16 Gillies Hwy; r $95; 🖭 🖳 🖳) The comfortable rooms here look like ordinary motel accommodation, but if you peer a little closer you'll discover special touches such as a DVD player with 60-odd films to borrow free of charge, 'real' local coffee and a plunger, and scented roses on each balcony. You're free to use the industrial laundry on the premises, and walk-in rates are sometimes available. The same people manage the smart **Allumbah Pocket Cottages** (☎ 4095 3023; www.allumbahpocket cottages.com.au; 24-6 Gillies Hwy; cottages incl breakfast $165; 🖭 🖳 🖳) – a cluster of spiffy self-contained cottages next door. Breakfast includes home-baked bread.

Eating

Flynn's (☎ 4095 2235; 17 Eacham Rd; mains $17-22; 🕥 lunch Thu-Mon, dinner Thu-Sun) Plunge your fork into some authentic French- and Italian-style dishes at Flynn's. You can dine street-side or on the terrace out the back. Flynn's is BYO and cash only.

Eden House (☎ 4095 3355; 20 Gillies Hwy; mains around $28; 🕥 dinner Fri-Wed) There's a story behind each dish: the rib-eye is slow-cooked for four hours, and the fish is line-caught on the Barrier Reef. This well-respected place has a limited and specialised menu, and a comprehensive wine list. And you can dine in the garden at Eden, set beneath a giant tree.

Burra Inn (☎ 4095 3657; 1 Cedar St; mains around $22; 🕥 dinner Wed-Mon) This charming little BYO restaurant opposite the pub serves Mod Oz cuisine, which might be veggie terrine with satay sauce or seafood lasagne. The early-bird special promises free dessert if you order before 6pm.

Nick's Swiss-Italian Restaurant & Yodeller's Bar (☎ 4095 3330; Gillies Hwy; mains $23-30; 🕥 lunch Fri-Sun, dinner Tue-Sun) This restaurant sports an extensive menu and chalet-style interior filled with knick-knacks and lace. It's licensed with friendly service, which sometimes includes a piano-accordion serenade. Your spinach-and-ricotta ravioli or crocodile fillets may be as tasteless as the décor.

Keddie's (☎ 4095 3265; Gillies Hwy; dishes $6-12; 🕥 breakfast, lunch & dinner) The broad, open deck is a great place to watch the comings and goings of the main street. Keddie's makes sandwiches and cooks up eggs and bacon, as well as falafel rolls and pizza.

CRATER LAKES NATIONAL PARK

Part of the Wet Tropics World Heritage Area, the two mirrorlike crater lakes of Lake Eacham and Lake Barrine are pleasant, forested areas. Walking tracks fringe both lakes: 6km around Lake Barrine and 3km around Lake Eacham. Access to the lakes is by sealed roads off the Gillies Hwy; camping is not permitted.

Accessible from either lake and 12km from Yungaburra is the native **Gadgarra Red Cedar**. The 500-year-old tree is a 600m walk from the car park.

Lake Barrine

Reeds protrude through the surface of Lake Barrine, making swimming less viable here. The **Lake Barrine Rainforest Cruise & Tea House** (☎ 4095 3847; Gillies Hwy; ☺ breakfast & lunch) dominates the lakefront. Upstairs at the tea house you can take Devonshire tea or sandwiches. Downstairs is a small shop and booking desk for a 40-minute **lake cruise** (adult/child $12/6; ☺ 10.15am, 11.30am, 1.30pm, 2.30pm & 3.30pm).

A short hop from the tea house are twin, neck-tilting, 1000-year-old **Kauri pines**.

Lake Eacham

The crystal-clear waters of Lake Eacham are great for swimming and spotting turtles; there are sheltered lakeside picnic areas as well as a boat ramp. Stop in to the rangers' station for information on the area or to gawk at the native Australian python.

Crater Lakes Rainforest Cottages (☎ 4095 2322; www.craterlakes.com.au; Eacham Close, off Lakes Dr; d incl breakfast $190-290; ☒) are individually themed, with wood-burner heating, spa baths, fully fitted kitchens and a breakfast hamper for

your first morning. Cabins are well spaced so you can enjoy your own patch of rainforest.

Embedded in the national park, the self-contained cabins at **Chambers Wildlife Rainforest Lodge** (☎ 4095 3754; http://rainforest-australia.com; Eacham Close; r $120; ☒) cater to bird-watchers and nature groups. There are landing platforms about the place for visiting birds – all of which enjoy celebrity status.

Treehouses have grown into luxurious self-contained pads at **Rose Gums** (☎ 4096 8360; www.rosegums.com.au; Land Rd, Butcher's Creek; d from $190), with spas, wood-burning heaters and king-sized beds. Great for couples and families, these beautiful pole homes are private and can sleep up to six.

Less than 2km down the Malanda road from Lake Eacham, **Lake Eacham Van Park** (☎ 4095 3730; www.lakeeachamtouristpark.com; 71 Lakes Dr; unpowered/powered sites $13/19, cabins $65) is a pretty camping ground with decent self-contained cabins.

Far North Queensland

HIGHLIGHTS

- Snorkelling or diving on the stunning **Great Barrier Reef** (p370)
- Swimming in crisp, clear water amid the ancient boulders of **Mossman Gorge** (p375), which forms the beginning of Daintree National Park
- Sitting in a vehicle and experiencing inertia as the **Daintree River ferry** (p378) leaves the south bank for the wilderness of the north
- Dodging the shade of palm trees silhouetted against the fine sand of stunning **Myall Beach** (p381)
- Trudging joyously upward on the **Mt Sorrow Ridge Walk** (p381), which leads to humbling views over Cape Tribulation
- Exploring the relatively untapped beauty of **Cooktown** (p387)
- Knowing that you can be a castaway on an island for a week or so, or even better, actually doing it; try the **Hope Islands** (p390)
- Eating a bucket of prawns with abandon at one of the exquisite eateries at **Port Douglas** (p372)

Cooktown ★

Hope Islands ★

Great Barrier Reef

Mt Sorrow Ridge Walk ★

★ Myall Beach

Daintree River Ferry ★

Mossman ★ Gorge

★ Port Douglas

- www.dctta.asn.au
- www.cook.qld.gov.au

The geographically small region of Far North Queensland (FNQ) is bursting with diverse natural environments, such that it contains the richest pockets of biodiversity in Australia, if not the world. Its rich rainforest crowds around rivers and tumbles out onto beautiful beaches – where the magnificent Great Barrier Reef lies a short distance offshore.

The world recognised the area's significance by adding it to the cradle of the World Heritage list as part of the Wet Tropics World Heritage Area. This confirmed what the locals had always known; the environment has imbued them with a rare and reverent respect, where human impact is closely checked.

Tourist services are contained to a few small settlements. Port Douglas is the hub – a sleek resort town from where visitors can duck out to significant sites led by an armada of operators, and where a stellar range of restaurants and accommodation attracts leisure seekers from around the globe. Cape Tribulation is Port Douglas' rugged sibling – where development is limited so as to give way to the surrounding environment. Most accommodation is set amid the rainforest, with just a wire screen between you and the forest critters. (You'll be happy to know the rainforest-cloaked mountains of the Cape Tribulation section of Daintree National Park may contain unidentified species of spiders and bugs.) Further north is the frontier town of Cooktown. Its relative isolation has preserved its unique character and produced a population of distinctive characters.

FNQ is home to two significant Aboriginal communities, with substantial tracts of land shared between the traditional custodians and nonindigenous settlers. A number of tours, run by members of these communities, explain the significance of the landscape from an Aboriginal perspective.

Climate
FNQ has two distinct seasons: the Wet (roughly from January to March) and the Dry, which lingers on for the rest of the year. The Wet is characterised by high temperatures and humidity. Tropical downpours are a regular feature and rain can set in for days on end. The effect is so dramatic that services in the Daintree usually cease come February, and the Bloomfield Track often becomes impassable. Cooktown's tourist services virtually shut down between November and March.

Dangers & Annoyances
From October to May swimming in coastal waters is inadvisable due to the presence of box jellyfish, Irukandji and other marine stingers (see the boxed text on p226).

Saltwater crocodiles inhabit the mangroves, estuaries and open water of FNQ, so avoid swimming or wading in these places. Warning signs are posted around waterways where crocs may be present.

National Parks
The far north's main attraction is undoubtedly the Daintree National Park. Its lush rainforest areas have been the subject of conservation debates nationwide. You can access the southern section of the park at Mossman (p375) or, most popularly, north of the croc-laden Daintree River.

A number of the north's islands are also protected as national parks. Lizard Island (p392) and the Hope Islands (p390) are well known for their relative pristine natural environments.

Getting There & Around
Cairns is the main link for air, bus and train services to FNQ (see p343). Adventurers

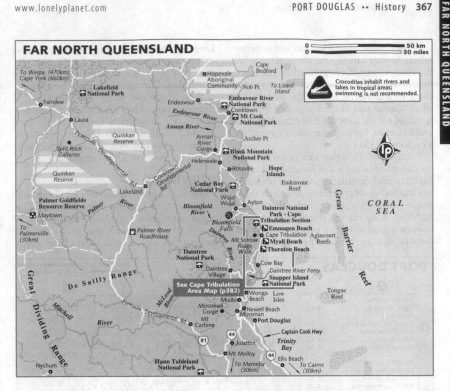

FAR NORTH QUEENSLAND

Crocodiles inhabit rivers and lakes in tropical areas; swimming is not recommended.

See Cape Tribulation Area Map (p382)

should hire a 4WD in Cairns, Port Douglas or Cooktown.

PORT DOUGLAS

☎ 07 / pop 5867

While those boutique clothing stores, innumerable studio-apartment rentals and swish restaurants soften the edges of the far north frontier image, Port Douglas retains an endearing character. It's a low-rise settlement with a range of quality services and facilities, and a place where everybody is on holiday, which means most people in the Port are pretty happy.

And no wonder: Port has all the comforts of a big city condensed into a small town, with an uninterrupted stretch of palm-fringed white-sand beach. It's also within air-conditioned reach of the far north's more rugged regions. Families and empty nesters enjoy the convenience of a resort or self-contained apartment and the range of boutique eateries specialising in everything from seafood to ice cream. It's also

the destination of choice for a number of celebrities, and restaurants brandish photos of famous diners; look out for Bill and Hilary, Kiefer and Kylie.

HISTORY

Port Douglas has a history of infamy, influence and affluence. It was largely developed by Christopher Skase, the archetype of the flashy 1980s. Among other ventures, his company backed what was to be the genesis of Port Douglas: its first luxury resort, the Mirage. Within a few years, the Port attracted a great deal of investment, which resulted in multimillion-dollar resorts, a golf course and heliport, a marina and shopping complex, and an avenue of palms lining the road from the highway to Port Douglas. In 1991, Skase's company filed for bankruptcy and he fled to Europe, eventually settling in Majorca. This was to be the beginning of a decade-long battle with the Australian government, which attempted to bring Skase back to Australia to repay a reputed $172 million in debts. Skase died in 2001 without ever returning to Australia.

Before Skase, Port Douglas was a sleepy village founded in 1877 as the port town for the Hodgkinson River goldfields. The town flourished at the outset, but its prosperity came to a grinding halt in the mid-1880s, when Cairns was chosen ahead of it as the terminal for the new rail line from Kuranda and Mareeba. Port was largely destroyed by a cyclone in 1911.

Today Port Douglas exacts its revenge on Cairns by being a less-bloated and more sophisticated destination. Careful planning has limited development to less than three stories, and it's rare to find an unkempt building. A significant chunk of the town's houses are investment properties, whose owners live in Melbourne or Sydney –

keeping the population down. The few permanent residents come for the lifestyle: there are very few suits in Port Douglas wardrobes. The casual existence here means that most people wear white linen and a bronzed tan. And while there is money here – one beachfront home recently sold for $4.5 million – Port Douglas' wealth is discreetly tucked behind long driveways, tinted windows or Dior sunglasses.

ORIENTATION

From the Captain Cook Hwy it's 6km along a low spit of land to Port Douglas. The main entry road, Davidson St, ends in a T-intersection with Macrossan St. To the left is the town centre with most of the shops

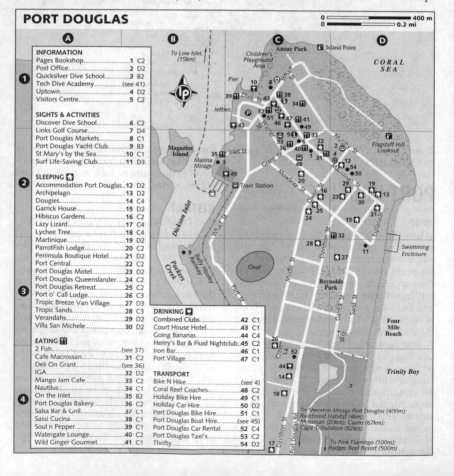

PORT DOUGLAS

0   400 m
0   0.2 mi

INFORMATION
Pages Bookshop..................1 C2
Post Office..........................2 D2
Quicksilver Dive School.....3 B2
Tech Dive Academy........(see 41)
Uptown.............................4 D2
Visitors Centre..................5 C2

SIGHTS & ACTIVITIES
Discover Dive School........6 C2
Links Golf Course..............7 D4
Port Douglas Markets.......8 C1
Port Douglas Yacht Club...9 B3
St Mary's by the Sea........10 C1
Surf Life-Saving Club.......11 D3

SLEEPING
Accommodation Port Douglas..12 D2
Archipelago.....................13 D2
Dougies...........................14 C4
Garrick House..................15 D2
Hibiscus Gardens.............16 C2
Lazy Lizard......................17 C4
Lychee Tree.....................18 C4
Martinique.......................19 D2
ParrotFish Lodge..............20 C2
Peninsula Boutique Hotel...21 D2
Port Central.....................22 C2
Port Douglas Motel...........23 D2
Port Douglas Queenslander...24 C2
Port Douglas Retreat........25 C2
Port o' Call Lodge............26 C3
Tropic Breeze Van Village...27 D3
Tropic Sands....................28 C2
Verandahs.......................29 D2
Villa San Michele.............30 D2

EATING
2 Fish...........................(see 37)
Cafe Macrossan...............31 C2
Deli On Grant...............(see 36)
IGA.................................32 C2
Mango Jam Cafe..............33 C2
Nautilus..........................34 C1
On the Inlet.....................35 B2
Port Douglas Bakery.........36 C2
Salsa Bar & Grill..............37 C1
Sassi Cucina....................38 C1
Soul n Pepper..................39 C1
Watergate Lounge............40 C1
Wild Ginger Gourmet.......41 C1

DRINKING
Combined Clubs...............42 C1
Court House Hotel............43 C1
Going Bananas.................44 C4
Henry's Bar & Fluid Nightclub..45 C2
Iron Bar..........................46 C1
Port Village.....................47 C1

TRANSPORT
Bike N Hike..................(see 4)
Coral Reef Coaches..........48 C2
Holiday Bike Hire.............49 C1
Holiday Car Hire..............50 D2
Port Douglas Bike Hire......51 C1
Port Douglas Boat Hire...(see 45)
Port Douglas Car Rental....52 C2
Port Douglas Taxi's..........53 C2
Thrifty............................54 D2

To Low Isles (15km)

Children's Playground Area

Anzac Park

Island Point

CORAL SEA

Pier

Dixie St

Jetties

Magazine Island

Marina Mirage

Inlet St

Grant St

Wharf St

Warner St

Flagstaff Hill Lookout

Murphy St

Macrossan St

Owen St

Mowbray St

Train Station

Dickson Inlet

Wharf St

Bally Hooley Railway

Packers Creek

Port St

Oval

Reynolds Park

Mudlo St

Garrick St

Sand St

Tide St

Warner St

Esplanade

Swimming Enclosure

Four Mile Beach

Trinity Bay

Crane La

Davidson St

Davidson Rd

Port Douglas Rd

To Sheraton Mirage Port Douglas (400m); Rainforest Habitat (4km); Mossman (20km); Cairns (67km); Cape Tribulation (82km)

To Pink Flamingo (100m); Rydges Reef Resort (500m)

and restaurants; the beach is to the right. Marina Mirage is the departure point for most of the reef trips.

INFORMATION

All the major banks have branches with ATMs along Macrossan St. The main post office is on Owen St.

Pages Bookshop (☎ 4099 5094; Shop 3, 35 Macrossan St; ⏰ 9am-6pm) Has a range of fiction and nonfiction titles.

Port Douglas visitors centre (☎ 4099 5599; 23 Macrossan St; ⏰ 8am-6.30pm) Has maps and can provide full accommodation lists and general information, as well as book tours.

Uptown (☎ 4099 5568; www.uptown.com.au; 48 Macrossan St; per 30min $5) Net access.

SIGHTS

You're likely to put in at least a few hours or days on gorgeous **Four Mile Beach**: a band of white-sand beach backed by palms that goes as far as your squinting eyes can see. At the northern end is a **surf life-saving club**, in front of which is a swimming enclosure patrolled and protected with a stinger net during summer. Water-based activities are offered from a hut on the beachfront (right), or you could just lie there for hours – the Munch buggy plies the length of the beach selling ice creams and snacks.

The excellent tourist park **Rainforest Habitat** (☎ 4099 3235; www.rainforesthabitat.com.au; Port Douglas Rd; adult/child $28/14; ⏰ 8am-5.30pm) is suitable for ages one to 100. It's a wildlife sanctuary that endeavours to keep and showcase native animals in enclosures that closely mimic their natural environment. As well as koalas, kangaroos, crocs and tree kangaroos, Rainforest Habitat is home to parrots, wading birds and the prehistoric-looking cassowary. Come early for **Breakfast with the Birds** (incl admission $39/19.50; ⏰ 8-10.30am) or visit the **Habitat After Dark** (adult/child $85/35; ⏰ 5-9.30pm), which includes a steak-and-salad dinner and a twilight tour.

The **Port Douglas Markets** (Anzac Park, bottom of Macrossan St; ⏰ 8.30am-1.30pm Sun) make for a leisurely Sunday morning wander along the grassy foreshore of Anzac Park. Bring a bag and an appetite for arts and crafts, and local food products such as tropical fruits, ice creams and coconut milk.

St Mary's by the Sea is a teeny nondenominational white timber church that regularly dispatches newlyweds and their entourages to the surrounding lawns with sea views. Built in 1911, the chapel was restored and relocated to its present site in 1989.

ACTIVITIES

On Four Mile Beach, you can go parasailing and jet-skiing from a **waterfront shack** (☎ 4099 3175; xtraactionwater@optusnet.com.au; tandem parasail/jet-ski $60/100).

Glide between holes in your electric buggy at the esteemed **Links Golfclub** (☎ 4099 5888; www.thelinks.com.au; 18 holes $105), part of the Mirage resort; it also has practice fairways, and putting and pitching greens. The **Port Douglas Yacht Club** (☎ 4099 4386; www.users.big pond.com/pdy; Wharf St) offers free sailing every Wednesday from 4pm. You can also get on the water with **Port Douglas Boat Hire** (☎ 4099 6277; boathire@internetnorth.com.au; Marina Mirage; ⏰ 8am-8pm), which hires a range of boats including some suitable for children.

Dive Courses

Several companies offer courses for PADI open-water certification as well as advanced dive certificates.

Discover Dive School (☎ 4099 6800; www.discover diveschool.com; Shop 6, Grant St, 4-day courses $580) and **Tech Dive Academy** (☎ 4099 6880; www.tech-dive -academy.com; 1/18 Macrossan St; 4-day courses $575) provide instruction with limited numbers per class (four to six). **Quicksilver Dive School** (☎ 4099 5050; www.quicksilverdive.com; Marina Mirage; 4-day courses $550) holds two days of its training course in Palm Cove; transfers from Port Douglas are included.

TOURS

Port Douglas is a hub for tours. The number-one destination is the Reef, with the rugged rainforests of Cape Tribulation the next most-popular stop on the tour circuit. Many of the Cairns operators pick up passengers at Port Douglas on their way up the Daintree, Cape Trib and Cooktown (see p336).

Fishing

Reef, river and land-based fishing charters operate regularly out of Port Douglas. Prices range from $80 for a half-day group tour on the Daintree River to anywhere between $2500 and $7000 per day to charter a large boat for up to 11 people. **Fishing Port Douglas** (☎ 4098 5354; www.fishingportdouglas.com .au) has details.

Great Barrier Reef

As with Cairns, the unrelenting surge of visitors to the Reef off Port Douglas has had an impact on its general condition. You'll still see colourful corals and marine life, but it is patchy in parts. Access to the majority of spots that operators visit is around an hour from Port Douglas. Operators usually make two to three stops per day on the outer reefs, including St Crispins, Agincourt, Chinaman and Tongue Reefs. A few tours visit the Low Isles: an idyllic little island with a lighthouse and fringing coral just 15km offshore.

Tour prices include reef tax, snorkelling, transfers from your accommodation, lunch and refreshments. To include an introductory dive add around $200 and for up to two certified dives add around $180.

Aristocat (☎ 4099 4727; www.aristocat.com.au; adult/child $150/105) Maximum 45 passengers.

Calypso (☎ 4099 3377; www.calypsocharters.com.au; adult/child $145/105) Maximum 50 passengers.

Haba (☎ 4099 5254; www.habadive.com.au; adult/child $140/90) Maximum 40 passengers.

Poseidon (☎ 4099 4772; www.poseidon-cruises.com.au; adult/child $150/115) Maximum 48 passengers.

Quicksilver (☎ 4087 2100; www.quicksilver-cruises.com) This major operator has two boats that visit the outer reef: the *Quicksmart* (adult/child $145/110) with around 80 passengers and giant *Wavepiercer* (adult/child $185/100) that can take over 400. It also runs family-oriented sailing trips to the Low Isles on the *Wavedancer* (adult/child from $77/42).

Sailaway (☎ 4099 4772; www.sailawayportdouglas.com; adult/child $125/75) This sailing and snorkelling trip (maximum 27 passengers) to the Low Isles is great for families.

Shaolin (☎ 4099 1231; http://home.austarnet.com.au /shaolin; adult/child $135/65) A refitted Chinese junk, the *Shaolin* has snorkelling cruises (maximum 24 passengers) to the Low Isles – a good option for families.

Synergy 2 (☎ 4050 0675; www.synergyreef.com.au; adult/child $230/160) With a capacity of 12 passengers, the *Synergy* sails to the outer reefs and land transfers are by limo.

Tallarook (☎ 4099 4990; www.tallarooksail.com; adult/child $145/105) *Tallarook* sails to Tongue Reef in just under two hours (maximum 25 passengers).

Wavelength (☎ 4099 5031; www.wavelength.com.au; adult/child $155/105) This is a snorkelling cruise only (maximum 30 passengers).

Other Tours

There are numerous operators offering day trips to Cape Tribulation, some via Mossman Gorge. Many of the tours out of Cairns also do pick-ups from Port Douglas.

Bike N Hike (☎ 4099 4000; www.bikenhike.com.au; half-day hike, bike or kayak tours $88-98) Caters to beginners through to experienced adventurers; sights along the way include waterfalls and river crossings.

BTS Tours (☎ 4099 5665; return adult/child $16/8) Leaves Port Douglas for Mossman Gorge twice daily.

De Luxe Safaris (☎ 4099 6406; www.deluxesafaris .com.au; adult/child $140/115) Takes in Cape Trib and Mossman Gorge.

Fine Feather Tours (☎ 4094 1199; www.finefeather tours.com.au; half-/full-day tours $145/205) Serious ornithologists and amateurs will be all aflutter with the number of bird varieties that are regularly sighted on these tours.

Lady Douglas (☎ 4099 1603; ladydouglas@bigpond .com; 1½-hr cruises adult/child $25/12) A paddlewheeler that runs croc-spotting cruises down the Dixon Inlet; price includes refreshments.

R 'n' R (☎ 4051 7777; www.raft.com.au; day tour $160) White-water rafting on the Tully River.

Reef and Rainforest Connections (☎ 4099 5333; www.reefandrainforest.com.au) This operator runs a range of day-long ecotours that combine a number of attractions. There's a Cape Trib and Bloomfield Falls 4WD safari (adult/ child $165/125), a trip to Kuranda including the Skyrail and the Scenic Railway (adult/child $104/52), as well as a 30-minute hot-air balloon flight over the Tableland that includes entry to one of Kuranda's tourist parks, plus the Skyrail cableway (adult/child $300/195).

Skysafari (☎ 4099 4915; www.skysafari.com.au; 2-person 30-min flights $245) Scenic helicopter flights.

Wonga Beach Equestrian Centre (☎ 4098 7583; adult/child $100/90) Offers half-day rides twice a day along Wonga Beach, with pick-ups from Port Douglas at 7.45am (returning at noon) and 2.05pm (returning at 6.30pm).

SLEEPING

Port Douglas has a lot of accommodation, but it's limited in variety to self-contained apartments or resort rooms. There isn't a huge range of budget options in this well-heeled town, and price brackets move up a notch. Much of the mid- to upper-range accommodation is geared to longer-term stays; there are cheaper weekly rates and minimum-stay requirements. Discounts are often available online and prices drop during the low season, outside school-holiday periods.

Accommodation Port Douglas (☎ 4099 5355; www.accomportdouglas.com.au; 1/48 Macrossan St; ⏰ 9am-5pm Mon-Sat) is an agent for many holiday rentals.

Budget

ParrotFish Lodge (☎ 4099 5011; www.parrotfishlodge .com; 37-39 Warner St; dm $23-26, d $75-85; ☒ ▢ ☒)

You'll wake up happy at this central, cheerful place, decorated with local mural-sized contemporary art. Dorm rooms sleep four to six in beds that used to furnish the Sydney Olympic Village. The décor is extreme beach, with bright yellow walls and iridescent blue swirling floors. All rooms have lockers and there are laundry facilities on each floor.

Dougies (☎ 4099 6200; www.dougies.com.au; 111 Davidson St; dm $25, d & tw $68; ✕ ☐ ☒) Set in spacious grounds, Dougies is a backpacker resort where you're encouraged to hang about the grounds in a hammock by day, and move to the bar at night. Included in your lodging fee is a steam train ride into town (there's a station just through the trees). Free transfers are available from Cairns on Monday, Wednesday and Saturday.

Port o' Call Lodge (☎ 4099 5422; www.portocall.com.au; cnr Port St & Craven Close; dm $23-28, d $60-110; ✕ ☐ ☒) This is a large YHA-associated hostel with a range of rooms and facilities. What it lacks in spirit it makes up for in services: there's a bar, bistro, communal kitchen and laundry, plus individual lockers. The bunkhouse here sleeps 18, with a premium charged for four-bed dorms. If you stay no less than two nights then you're eligible for the free bus service to/from Cairns (Monday to Saturday).

Port Central (☎ 4051 6722; www.portcentral.com.au; 36 Macrossan St; s/d from $65/76; ✕) Central – and how! In the middle of the main street, access to the upstairs rooms is through an unassuming doorway. The manager is off-site here, so there's no reception, just a phone link-up where the nifty code-for-the-keypad exchange takes place. As there is no on-site manager, everything is bolted down in your tidy little room – except the remote control for the TV.

Port Douglas Motel (☎ 4099 5248; www.portdouglasmotel.com; 9 Davidson St; d $100-115; ✕ ☒) The motel's functional rooms are often full, but when they're not, walk-in rates are available. Larger rooms have a basic kitchen with a fridge, sink and microwave. It's well situated: near both the beach and main street, but rooms are crammed together – definitely without views.

Tropic Breeze Van Village (☎/fax 4099 5299; 24 Davidson St; unpowered/powered sites $20/24, on-site cabins from $80) Next door to the IGA supermarket, this park is a short walk from the beach and has shady tent sites.

Midrange

Archipelago (☎ 4099 5387; www.archipelago.com.au; 72 Macrossan St; d from $130; ✕ ☒) This complex is very near the beach, with 12 self-contained rooms spread over three levels. The upper rooms have 'filtered' views through trees and other properties to the beach. Rooms are neat and functional, with a writing desk, a balcony and cane furniture.

Tropic Sands (☎ 4099 4533; www.tropicsands.com.au; 21 Davidson St; r $160; ✕ ☐ ☒) The handsome open-plan rooms are in a beautiful white colonial-style building. From your private balcony you can catch a whiff of the sea or whatever's cooking in your fully equipped kitchen. There's a saltwater pool, guest laundry service, in-room TV and safe.

Hibiscus Gardens (☎ 4099 5315; www.hibiscusportdouglas.com.au; cnr Mowbray & Owen Sts; r from $165; ✕ ☐ ☒) This stylish resort features Balinese influences with its teak furnishing and fixtures, such as bifold doors and plantation shutters, as well as the occasional Buddha. The on-site spa specialises in indigenous healing techniques and products. The Paudi head massage with a quandong hair wrap should stimulate your senses.

Lychee Tree (☎ 4099 5811; www.lychee-tree.com.au; 95 Davidson St; apt $115-140; ✕ ☒) The single-storey self-contained apartments here are available with one or two bedrooms. They're all well equipped with a bathroom, washing machine and dryer, a TV and a DVD. The spacious rooms are suitable for families, as well as mobility-impaired guests.

Garrick House (☎ 4099 5322; www.garrickhouse.com.au; 11-13 Garrick St; apt $140-220; ✕ ☒) Garrick is a deceptively large house containing 18 apartments – all with fully equipped kitchens, bathrooms and balconies. Accommodation ranges from studio apartments downstairs, through one- and two-bedroom apartments to a penthouse with two bedrooms and two bathrooms. There is a two-night minimum stay.

Port Douglas Retreat (☎ 4099 5053; www.portdouglasretreat.com.au; 31-33 Mowbray St; apt $150; ✕ ☒) Recline on the sun lounge and relax on the wide wooden decking that surrounds the swimming pool beset with palms. A total of 36 self-contained apartments sprawl over two levels in this traditional Queenslander-style complex.

Port Douglas Queenslander (☎ 4099 5199; www.queenslander.com.au; 8-10 Mudlo St; r $145; ✕ ☒)

This midsized complex with self-contained units is good for families. Units are available in studio, and one- and two-bedroom configurations. Each has its own balcony, washing machine and dryer. There's a board displaying tour information, and you can book from the in-room phones.

Lazy Lizard (☎ 4099 5900; www.lazylizardinn.com .au; 121 Davidson St; r from $135-165; ✷ ▣ ▣) Pricier units at this large family-oriented place comprise two bedrooms: one for the grown-ups and one for the young 'uns. All rooms are serviced daily, and the bathrooms have a bath and shower. Some rooms have wheelchair access.

Martinique (☎ 4099 6222; www.martinique.com.au; 66 Macrossan St; r $140; ✷ ▣) This terracotta-coloured block contains 19 one-bedroom apartments; each with decked-out kitchen and private balcony. The Martinique is close to the beach on the main street; it has laundry facilities and landscaped gardens. Apartments are large, with some fitted for wheelchair access.

Villa San Michele (☎ 4099 4088; www.villasan michele.com.au; 39-41 Macrossan St; apt from $175; ✷ ▣) These luxurious one- and two-bedroom self-contained apartments are barely visible above street level. Set around a courtyard swimming pool each apartment has a large balcony and sports Mediterranean-influenced décor – think terracotta tiled floors and wrought-iron furnishings.

Pink Flamingo (☎ 4099 6622; www.pinkflamingo .com.au; 115 Davidson St; r $125-185; ✷ ▣ ▣) The pink flamingo statue at the entrance to your room holds your 'Do Not Disturb' sign at this gay-friendly resort. You might find the bright primary-coloured interiors disturbing; not so the giant beds and oversized spas. The resort has fitness facilities and outdoor movie nights.

Top End

Verandahs (☎ 4099 6650; www.verandahsportdouglas .com.au; 7 Davidson St; r $275; ✷ ▣) These stylish two-bedroom, two-bathroom apartments come with stainless-steel kitchens, polished floorboards and modern furnishings, serviced daily. The namesake verandas have BBQs and are great for entertaining. Go the whole hog and have a masseuse sent to your room. Walk-in rates may be available.

Peninsula Boutique Hotel (☎ 4099 9100; www .peninsulahotel.com.au; 9-13 Esplanade; s/d $300/340;

✷ ▣ ▣) This modern building full of smart self-contained apartments stands right across from Four Mile Beach. Private and luxurious, it's geared towards couples and newlyweds, with special honeymoon deals available. Children under 15 are not catered for.

Sheraton Mirage Port Douglas (☎ 4099 5888; www.sheraton.com/mirageportdouglas; Davidson St; r from $480; ✷ ▣ ▣) Port Douglas' original luxury resort, Sheraton Mirage is surrounded by five acres of swimmable lagoons, has five eating establishments (open to nonguests), a golf course, childcare facilities and a florist. The resort has its own beachfront, shuttle service into town, tennis courts and gym.

Rydges Reef Resort (☎ 4099 5577; www.rydges .com; 87-109 Port Douglas Rd; r $180-500; ✷ ▣) This link in the Rydges chain boasts a slew of facilities including a kids club, five pools and a range of restaurants and bars. Accommodation options start with your basic hotel-style room, moving up to deluxe three-bedroom, three-bathroom villas.

EATING

You need not go without in Port Douglas: your espresso cravings, seafood fancies and cosmopolitan palette are well catered for. You can eat a downright honest meal in one of the town's lively pubs (p374) or frock up for some fine dining in one of Port Douglas' special-occasion establishments. The choices are abundant, the ingredients the freshest, and the experience unforgettable. Eat out often.

Restaurants

Sassi Cucina (☎ 4099 6100; cnr Wharf & Macrossan Sts; mains $28-38; ❤ breakfast, lunch & dinner) Faux wicker chairs brand many tanned thighs with hatch marks – the sign of a long and fulfilling meal at Sassi. This Italian eatery serves genuine fare, where the pastas and risottos are pared back to just a few perfectly balanced ingredients. Of course the coffee is deftly prepared, and there's a range of inspired desserts. Italian Sassi goes Japanese, with a fine sushi bar next door.

2 Fish (☎ 4099 6350; 7/20 Wharf St; mains $25-36; ❤ lunch & dinner) Fish and chips just got a whole lot classier. Have your favourite fish, perhaps coral trout or red emperor, prepared any one of six ways. Think pan-seared with a light curry, crispy seaweed and watermelon salsa; or baked and crusted with coconut,

PETER PTSCHELINZEW

Rainforest canopy, Daintree National Park (p377)

MICHAEL AW

Freckled Hawkfish, Great Barrier Reef (p57)

PAUL DYMOND

Novel beach advertising, Port Douglas (p367)

Cooktown (p387)

OLIVER STREWE

Passengers aboard an interisland ferry, Torres Strait (p404)

OLIVER STREWE

Australian Stockman's Hall of Fame & Outback
Heritage Centre (p426), Longreach

ROSS BARNETT

DAVE LEVITT

Quinkan rock art (p400), Laura

Tip of Australia (p404), Cape York Peninsula

OLIVER STREW

mint and candlenut – served with spinach and potato. A selection of meat dishes is also available in this family-friendly restaurant in semiformal surrounds.

Salsa Bar & Grill (☎ 4099 4922; 26 Wharf St; mains $25-32; ☯ lunch & dinner) Set in a Queenslander across from Dickson's Inlet, Salsa Bar & Grill offers a considered range of Mediterranean-inspired dishes. You might try the drunken chicken breast with sweet potato and calamari *ceviche* (marinated raw calamari), while working on your own creation – the drunken patron, seduced by that fabulous cocktail list. There's a large courtyard for those who prefer to eat outside.

Nautilus (☎ 4099 5330; 17 Murphy St; mains $38-40; ☯ dinner) Nautilus has been a dining institution in Port Douglas for more than 50 years. Its tables are set amid two lush outdoor settings, and stiffly dressed in white linen. You may not want to disturb the plate when it arrives, with Peking duck artfully arranged around the sweet-potato mash, shitake mushrooms and bok choy. A vegetarian option is available each night. And you'll *need* a drink after perusing the extensive wine list. Children under eight are not welcome.

THE AUTHOR'S CHOICE

On the Inlet (☎ 4099 5255; 3 Inlet St; mains around $25; ☯ lunch & dinner) The service is unmatched at this excellent seafood restaurant, where the waiters know exactly what you want a nanosecond before you do. They're still smiling too, even after the hundredth recitation about the movements of the 6ft groper who visits most days at 5.30pm. Located on Dicksons Inlet, tables are spread along a sprawling deck where you can wave to the passing boats, with some set aside in the 'child-free' area. Laid-back lounge music merges with the general hubbub. Your waiter will happily recommend a wine to match your main, which may be yellowfin tuna crusted in vermicelli with a light soy and ginger sauce, or salmon stacked with prawn and avocado. Make the most of the early-dinner deal here – between 3.30pm and 5.30pm $16.50 gets you a bucket of prawns and a drink. Did we mention the bread-and-butter pudding made from chocolate croissants?

Mango Jam Cafe (☎ 4099 4611; 24 Macrossan St; mains $17-20; ☯ lunch & dinner) This large licensed family restaurant has a separate kids menu. The grown-up's menu has all your casual favourites, such as roast chicken, leg of lamb, crumbed calamari and lasagne. Mango's speciality is gourmet, wood-fired pizza, which it'll also deliver to your accommodation. Service is efficient and friendly, regardless of how busy the place is.

Watergate Lounge (☎ 4099 6665; www.watergate lounge.com.au; Shop 5, 31 Macrossan St; mains $18-26; ☯ lunch & dinner) This '70s retro bar-restaurant is the sequel to the popular Brisbane Watergate. Opened in late 2004, it's yet to be seen whether there are enough wannabe young blondes in Port Douglas to support this establishment's preferred clientele; but it's highly likely.

Cafés & Quick Eats

Soul 'n' Pepper (☎ 4099 4499; 2 Dixie St; meals $9-18; ☯ breakfast & dinner daily, lunch Mon-Sat) This laid-back outdoor café, opposite the pier, is welcoming – excitable young children excepted. Soul 'n' Pepper promotes an easy pace, with soul music and casual service and surrounds. You can also hire bait and tackle supplies from the shop next door.

Cafe Macrossan (☎ 4099 4372; Shop 1, 42 Macrossan St; mains $13-20; ☯ breakfast, lunch & dinner) This reliable licensed café opens out to the street and is often full – despite the sometimes-prickly service. Breakfast might include muesli with tropical fruits and minted honey yoghurt. You can also have eggs (any way) and there's decent coffee.

Deli On Grant (☎ 4099 5852; 11 Grant St; meals $8-12; ☯ lunch) A range of boutique produce and home-cooked meals to take away are on offer here. The Deli also does picnic hampers. Give it three hours' notice and it'll assemble a cane hamper with enough sandwiches, cheeses, salads and breads to sustain even the most insatiable couple.

Port Douglas Bakery (3 Grant St; pastries & sandwiches $4-9; ☯ breakfast & lunch) Bless the Bakery: because even in swanky Port Douglas there'll come a time when you just want a pie with sauce, or an egg sandwich followed by a lamington or doughnut. It has a few outside tables, and of course it sells fresh baked loaves and rolls.

Wild Ginger Gourmet (☎ 4099 5972; 22 Macrossan St; dishes $4-9; ☯ lunch Wed-Sun) Bursting with gourmet goodies, the sandwiches and wraps on offer here are so healthy that eating one will absolve you of a week's worth of junk food. Especially if you team it with a perky juice or smoothie.

Self-Catering

You'll find a large well-stocked supermarket in **Port Village** (Macrossan St), and an **IGA** (Davidson St) at the other end of town; both are open seven days.

DRINKING

Iron Bar (☎ 4099 4776; 5 Macrossan St; mains $18-27; ☺ lunch & dinner) The meaty meals on offer at Port Douglas' favourite pub must be good, as nobody seems to notice the fridge suspended from the ceiling and nobody minds that the place is made up to look like a country woolshed. After polishing off your T-bone or reef 'n' beef, you can have a flutter on the cane-toad races, which feature every Tuesday, Thursday and Sunday night.

Court House Hotel (☎ 4099 5181; cnr Macrossan & Wharf Sts; meals $15-21; ☺ lunch & dinner) Commanding a corner location, there's often a queue of dads (waiting to order bistro meals) here that snakes its way through the pleasant open-air courtyard. After the families have eaten, the low-key drinkers move in – entertained by cover bands (on weekends) and pokies in the gaming room, and joined by their friends.

Combined Clubs (☎ 4099 5553; Ashford St; mains $13-19; ☺ lunch & dinner) Mature gentlemen and their lady friends politely elbow other couples for space on the prime outdoor deck area. Between drinks, you might order grilled sausages and bacon served with onion gravy and veggies or tropical-style chicken breast with banana and pineapple. There's also a children's menu and computer games to keep the kids occupied.

Henry's Bar & Fluid Nightclub (☎ 4099 5200; Shop 54, Marina Mirage; ☺ 9pm-5am) What begins downstairs at Henry's moves upstairs later into the night to Fluid. Open until 5am every night, Fluid reiterates the notion that punters in Port Douglas are not operating within a nine-to-five schedule. Tuesday night is backpacker night, and there are occasional touring bands and DJs.

Going Bananas (☎ 4099 5400; 87 Davidson St; mains $24-30; ☺ dinner Mon-Sat) The zany interior and retro kitsch here is unabashedly displayed –

and equally lapped up. Who needs live music and formal entertainment when you have this place?

Daintree Lounge (☎ 4099 5888; Davidson St; ☺ 3pm-midnight) In the lobby of the opulent Sheraton Mirage, you don't have to be a guest to appreciate the resort's ambience – for a few hours at least.

GETTING THERE & AWAY

For information on getting to Cairns, see p343.

Sun Palm (☎ 4084 2626; www.sunpalmtransport.com) runs daily (except Monday) services from Port Douglas to Cairns ($25, 1½ hours), Mossman ($8, 20 minutes), Mossman Gorge ($12, 30 minutes), Cape Tribulation ($45, three hours) and Cooktown ($69, six hours). Its return fares are better value.

Coral Reef Coaches (☎ 4098 2600; www.coralreefcoaches.com.au) runs from Port Douglas to Mossman ($5, 20 minutes), Cow Bay ($22, two hours), Daintree Village (on request, two hours) and Cape Trib ($30, 2½ hours). It also connects with Cairns ($20, 1¼ hours).

Quicksilver (☎ 4031 4299; www.quicksilver-cruises.com; one way/return $26/39) has a fast catamaran service that departs from Marina Mirage, Port Douglas at 5.15pm, arriving in Cairns at around 6.45pm.

GETTING AROUND
To/From the Airport

Airport Connections (☎ 4099 5950; www.tnqshuttle.com; one way $23; ☺ 3.30am-4.30pm) runs an hourly shuttle-bus service to/from Cairns airport, as does **Sun Palm** (☎ 4084 2626; www.sunpalmtransport.com; adult $25), though less frequently.

Bicycle

Cycling around Port Douglas is a sensible method of transport. All of the following hire mountain bikes:

Bike N Hike (☎ 4099 4000; www.bikenhike.com.au; 62 Davidson St; per day $15-18; ☺ 9am-5pm) Also hires baby seats and tandem bikes.

Holiday Bike Hire (☎ 4099 6144; Macrossan St; per day $17-21; ☺ 9am-5pm)

Port Douglas Bike Hire (☎ 4099 5799; 40 cnr Wharf & Warner Sts; per day from $15; ☺ 9am-5pm)

Bus

Sun Palm (☎ 4084 2626; www.sunpalmtransport.com; tickets $1.50-4; ☺ 7am-midnight) runs in a continuous loop every half-hour from the Rainforest Habitat (near the Captain Cook Hwy turn-off) to the Marina, stopping regularly. Flag the driver down at the marked bus stops.

Car
If you're planning to continue north up the Bloomfield Track to Cooktown, Port Douglas is the last place you can hire a 4WD vehicle for the job.
Holiday Car Hire (☎ 4099 4999; 54 Macrossan St; ⏱ 8am-5.30pm Mon-Fri, 8am-noon Sat & Sun)
Port Douglas Car Rental (☎ 4099 4988; www.portcarrental.com.au; 81 Davidson St; ⏱ 6.30am-8.30pm Mon-Fri, 6.30am-1.30pm Sat & Sun)
Thrifty (☎ 4099 5555; www.thrifty.com; 50 Macrossan St; ⏱ 9am-4pm Mon-Fri, 9am-noon Sat & Sun)

Taxi
Port Douglas Taxis (☎ 4099 5345; 45 Warner St) offers 24-hour service.

AROUND PORT DOUGLAS

MOSSMAN
☎ 07 / pop 1941
Pleasant, unpretentious Mossman is the eye of the surrounding tourist storm. Of the millions of holidaymakers staying in Port Douglas and Cairns, who hurry through Mossman on their way north to Cape Tribulation, few slow down long enough to notice the fine-looking old architecture found here, especially in the back streets, and many only stop if they're held-up by a cane train, where the tracks cut across the main road. Just over the tracks, marking the northern fringe of town, is a stand of 80-year-old rain trees that are native to Southeast Asia.

Information
Mossman's **Queensland Parks & Wildlife Service** (QPWS; ☎ 4098 2188; www.epa.qld.gov.au; Demi View Plaza, 1 Front St; ⏱ 10am-4pm Mon-Fri) has information on the Daintree National Park up to and beyond Cape Tribulation.

Sights & Activities
Stunning **Mossman Gorge**, 5km west of Mossman town, is in the southeast corner of Daintree National Park and forms part of the traditional lands of the Kuku Yalanji indigenous people. Carved by the Mossman River, the gorge is a boulder-strewn valley

where sparkling water washes over ancient rocks. Take a memorable dip with the jungle perch (identified by two black spots on their tails), but take care particularly after downpours as swift currents will result. Beyond the swimming hole, a suspension bridge takes you across the river to a 2.7km circuit trail through the lowland rainforest. The easy walk passes interpretive signs and trees dripping with jungle vines.

The tropical setting of **Mossman Golf Club** (☎ 4098 1570; www.mossmangolf.com.au; 18 holes $28) may have you seeing both a golfing birdie and native birdies such as kookaburras and kingfishers.

Tours
Excellent 1½-hour guided walks are run by **Kuku-Yalanji Dreamtime Walks** (☎ 4098 2595; www.yalanji.com.au; Mossman Gorge; adult/child $17/8.50; ⏱ 10am, noon & 2pm Mon-Fri), located 1km before the gorge car park. Indigenous guides lead you through the rainforest pointing out and explaining the significance of rock-art sites, plants and natural features. The tour includes billy tea and damper.

Discover the process of turning giant tropical grass into sugar at **Mossman Mill Tours** (☎ 4030 4190; Mill St; adult/child $20/10; ⏱ 2pm Mon, 10am & 2pm Tue-Fri Jun-Nov); wear closed shoes.

Sleeping & Eating
Mossman Gorge B&B (☎ 4098 2497; www.bnbnq.com.au/mossgorge; Lot 15, Gorge View Cres; s $65-75, d $85-95; ✕ ⌘) Escape the tourist jungle for the real thing – or at least views of it. This timber B&B has lavishly large verandas from which to view the dense trees of the national park. Rates include a breakfast including muffins, croissants and fruit.

White Cockatoo (☎ 4098 2222; www.thewhitecockatoo.com; 9 Alchera Dr; s & d cabins $80-120; ✕ ⌘) About 1km south of town, White Cockatoo has spacious self-contained timber cabins that can sleep up to five. Part of the property operates as a nudist resort from 1 October to 1 May; it's the section of the resort with the pool. The pool is open to all guests, but between October and May being naked is a prerequisite. Nude tours of the Reef and Daintree can also be arranged.

Silky Oaks Lodge (☎ 4098 1666; www.silkyoakslodge.com.au; Finleyvale Rd; treehouses per person s/d $500/350, riverhouses per person s/d $590/400; ✕ ⌘) Spend languorous afternoons in the hammock strung on the veranda of your designer cabin. Or keep busy with the spa treatments on offer. This international resort targets honeymooners and stressed-out execs looking for a retreat. As the name suggests, the riverhouse rooms overlook the Mossman River; all rooms feature huge beds that are turned down each evening – nice touch. The resort's stunning **Treehouse Restaurant** (mains $26-32; ☉ breakfast, lunch & dinner) is open to interlopers.

Demi View Motel (☎ 4098 1277; fax 4098 2102; 41 Front St; s/d $60/66; ☒ ☒) Drive up to the door of one of the 24 traditional ground-floor motel-style rooms on offer here. Rooms are behind the motel's restaurant, **Mojo's** (mains $17-23; ☉ lunch & dinner Tue-Sun), where you might try a tofu curry or oysters.

For fresh juices, wraps and sandwiches try **Tropical Boost** (☎ 4098 1089; 10 Front St; dishes $7-9; ☉ breakfast & lunch Mon-Sat), or **Goodies Cafe** (☎ 4098 1118; 33 Front St; mains around $10; ☉ lunch) for healthy meals homemade from organic produce.

Getting There & Away
Coral Reef Coaches (☎ 4098 2800; www.coralreef coaches.com.au) stops in Mossman from Cairns ($25, two hours) and Port Douglas ($5, 20 minutes).

Sun Palm (☎ 4084 2626; www.sunpalmtransport.com) runs regular bus services between Mossman and Cairns ($31, two hours) and Port Douglas ($8, 20 minutes).

MOSSMAN TO DAINTREE
Travelling north from Mossman, it's 36km through cane fields and farmland before you reach Daintree Village. En route are the turn-offs to Newell and Wonga Beach – two long stretches of uninterrupted beach with little to do, which is precisely their appeal.

Five kilometres from Mossman you'll come to the palm-fringed stretch of **Newell Beach**. It's a lazy 2.5km long, and you can fish off the beach or use the boat ramp (at the northern end). You could drop out of life for a while and stay at the **Newell Beach Caravan Park** (☎ 4098 1331; www.newellbeachcaravan park.com.au; unpowered/powered sites $18/20, d $70-80; ☒ ☒) located right on the water, with shady sites and self-contained cabins.

At Miallo, about 8km northwest of Mossman, is the **Karnak Playhouse & Rainforest Sanctuary** (☎ 4098 8144; www.karnakplayhouse .com.au; Whyanbeel Rd, via Miallo; adult $45; ☉ May-Nov).

This amphitheatre has a magical setting – the seats look down onto a timber stage set beside a small lake, and a backdrop of rainforest-covered hills surrounds the whole set-up. It stages a limited number of performances each year – all by highly acclaimed performers. Past performances include music by the My Friend the Chocolate Cake and cabaret by the Kransky Sisters.

The turn-off to **Wonga Beach** is 22km north of Mossman. It's a peaceful 7km beach – made more so by the absence of sandflies – with three maintained graves of well-known mariners. There are a number of accommodation options here. **Pinnacle Village Holiday Park** (☎ 4098 7566; www.pinnaclevillage .com; Vixies Rd; unpowered/powered sites $18/20, cabins $55-77; ☒ ☒) has beach frontage and grassy surrounds. **Daintree Palms** (☎ 4098 7871; www .daintreepalms.com; 17 Oasis Dr; dm/r $20/70; ☒ ☒ ☒) is a budget-style resort with a shop, a bottle shop and tennis courts. If you've got a van in tow, head for the waterfront **Wonga Beach Caravan Park** (☎ 4098 7514; fax 4098 7704; unpowered/ powered sites $14/16). **Wonga Beach Equestrian Centre** (☎ 4098 7583; adult/child $100/90) offers half-day rides twice a day along the beach.

The road north continues past ponds for barramundi farming and paddocks for cattle grazing. The turn-off to Cape Tribulation and the Daintree River crossing is to the right (24km from Mossman). Continue straight ahead to reach Daintree Village.

DAINTREE

Daintree is a loose term encompassing the coastal lowland area between the Daintree and Bloomfield Rivers – also known as the Daintree Coast. There is also the Daintree National Park (which stretches inland from Mossman Gorge to the Bloomfield River) and Daintree Village, about 12km upstream from the ferry crossing.

DAINTREE VILLAGE
☎ 07 / pop 200

The tiny settlement at Daintree Village was originally established as a logging town in the 1870s. Loggers sought the area's red cedars for their strength, versatility and beauty, and the logs were floated down the Daintree River for further transportation. The river is now more commonly used for cruises, with frequent crocodile sightings the main selling point. While neither Daintree Village nor the surrounding countryside are part of the Wet Tropics World Heritage Area, there are still pockets of untouched rainforest.

Daintree Village is a low-key tourist hub, with plenty of accommodation, eating and tour options. The tidy little settlement's main street is Stewart St, just back from the river, at the end of which is a public-access wharf – the departure point for a number of small tour operators. Loads of tour operators have their own departure points along Daintree Rd between the Daintree River ferry crossing and the village.

Tours

All tours focus on the Daintree River and the resident wildlife, including birds and butterflies, but particularly crocs. Bookings are advised for all tours.

Bruce Belcher's Daintree River Cruises (☎ 4098 7717; www.daintreerivercruise.com; adult/child $20/18; ⏰ 8.15am, 9.30am, 11am, noon, 1.30pm, 2.30pm, 3.30pm & 4pm Mar-Jan) One-hour cruises on a covered boat.

Chris Dahlberg's Specialised River Tours (☎ 4098 7997; www.daintreerivertours.info; Daintree Village; 2-hr

tours $45; ☎ 6.30am Apr-Oct, 6am Nov-Jan) Specialises in bird-watching.

Crocodile Express (☎ 4098 6120; Daintree Village; 1½-hr cruises adult/child $22/10; ⏰ hourly 9.30am-3.30pm & 4pm) Also has one-hour cruises departing 11 times per day from the ferry crossing (adult/child $18/8).

Electric Boat Cruises (☎ 1800 686 103; 1-hr cruises adult/child $18/9; ⏰ hourly 10.30am-2.30pm, 4pm & 5pm Mar-Jan) Also offers a 1½-hour tour at 8am including muffins and coffee (adult/child $31/15).

Solar Whisper (☎ 4098 7131; www.solarwhisper.com; 1¼-hr cruises adult/child $20/10; ⏰ 9.30am, 11am, 12.30pm & 3.30pm) Electric boat fitted with croc-cam.

Sleeping

There are several excellent B&Bs in the village and the surrounding farmland.

Red Mill House (☎ 4098 6233; www.redmillhouse.com.au; Stewart St; d $105; ✷ ▯ ▨) Don't mind those other guests with their heads in the pot plants – they'll be looking for tree frogs. This excellent B&B plays host to more than just paying guests, with several types of birds and frogs regularly stopping by. Rooms are well appointed (with bathrooms), and there's a large communal lounge area stacked with nature books.

Kenadon Homestead Cabins (☎ 4098 6142; www.daintreecabins.com; Dagmar St; s/d $80/100; ✷ ▨) These self-contained cabins are good for families as they sleep up to five. Set on the fringe of a 400-acre cattle farm, this property has been in the same family for more than 100 years. The cabins are clustered together near the pool and face out to the vast pastures; rates include breakfast.

River Home Cottages (☎ 4098 6225; www.riverhomecottages.com.au; Upper Daintree Rd; d incl breakfast $150; ✷) Drive 5km down an unsealed road, ignoring the curious cattle who live on this property, and you'll come to these secluded self-contained cottages. Each is perched on a rise overlooking lush pasture filtered by the surrounding trees. Barney, the owner, can show you to a secluded waterfall and swimming hole at the back of the property, or you can use the spa fitted in each cabin.

Daintree Valley Haven (☎ 4098 6206; www.daintreevalleyhaven.com.au; Stewart Creek Rd; s/d incl breakfast $110/130; ✷) Most self-contained accommodation trumpets the inclusion of a TV in your room – not here. No mobile-phone coverage and no children under 12 make for a peaceful getaway. Cabins are well spaced from one another and overlook a dam.

Daintree Eco Lodge & Spa (☎ 4098 6100; www.daintree-ecolodge.com.au; 20 Daintree Rd; s/d from $440/480; ☒ ☐ ☒) Just 15 boutique villas prop on stilts in the rainforest canopy. Each has its own spa, or there's the solar-heated swimming pool and the spa treatments. This retreat has received world attention for its luxurious offerings and unique setting. Transfers from Port Douglas and Cairns are available.

Eating
Papaya (☎ 4098 6173; Stewart St; mains $12-18; ☾ lunch & dinner Wed-Sun) This snappy bar and bistro serves a range of standard favourites, such as fish and chips, and beef pies, as well as tourist-teasers such as crocodile wontons.

Blingkumu Restaurant (☎ 4098 6100; 20 Daintree Rd; mains $18-23; ☾ breakfast, lunch & dinner) Part of the Daintree Eco Lodge & Spa, you can expect fine things to come from the kitchen here. Dishes are prepared using local produce, incorporating indigenous berries, nuts, leaves and flowers – gourmet bush tucker.

Jacanas Restaurant (☎ 4098 6125; Stewart St; mains $10-16; ☾ breakfast, lunch & dinner) This is a casual licensed café and takeaway with an outdoor section. You might try a steak or eggplant parmigiana.

Daintree Tea House Restaurant (☎ 4098 6161; Daintree Rd; meals from $13; ☾ lunch) About 3km south of Daintree Village, by Barratt Creek, the Tea House specialises in wild barramundi and light meals.

Big Barra (☎ 4098 6186; 12 Stewart St; mains $9-12; ☾ lunch) Proving that even tiny rainforest towns aren't immune to the Australian propensity for building really big things, the giant fish atop Big Barra makes this barbecue-café hard to miss. As well as the obvious, it also serves croc and 'roo burgers.

Getting There & Away
Public transport is limited to **Coral Reef Coaches** (☎ 4098 2800; www.coralreefcoaches.com.au), which runs daily from Cairns and Port Douglas to Cape Tribulation, and will stop in Daintree Village on request; from Cairns it's $37 (2½ hours).

DAINTREE RIVER TO CAPE TRIBULATION
About 10km before Daintree Village is the turn-off to the Daintree River ferry that takes you into the Cape Tribulation area. Though short-lived and inglorious (you

stay in the car), there's a real feeling that you're about to arrive somewhere special; there's also an incredible inertia – you're not sure whether the car or the ferry is moving. After crossing the river it's another 34km by sealed road to Cape Tribulation village. The indigenous Kuku Yalanji people called the area Kulki; the name Cape Tribulation was given by Captain Cook after his ship ran aground on an outlying reef (see p20).

Part of the Wet Tropics World Heritage Area, the region from the Daintree River north to Cape Tribulation is extraordinarily beautiful and famed for its ancient rainforest, sandy beaches and rugged mountains: Thornton's Peak (1375m) and Mt Sorrow (770m). Of the tropical lowland rainforest that existed presettlement, 96% has been cleared for cane, cattle and residences. Only north of the Daintree River does the forest remain relatively intact. It's one of the few places in the world where the tropical rainforest meets the sea.

In recognition of this unique environment, much of the area is protected as the Daintree National Park – declared in 1981. This section of the park, the Cape Tribulation section, stretches from the Daintree River to the Bloomfield River, with the mountains of the McDowell Range providing the western boundary. The Cow Bay area is largely privately owned and excluded from the national park, but development is restricted (see the boxed text on p380).

Cow Bay and Cape Tribulation are loosely termed villages, with general stores selling fuel, but the length of Cape Tribulation Rd is scattered with places to stay and eat. Electricity is powered by generators in this section; few places have air-con and not everywhere has 24-hour power. Cape Trib is one of the most popular trips from Port Douglas and Cairns, and accommodation is booked solid in peak periods.

Fuel and limited supplies are available at **Cow Bay Service Station & General Store** (☎ 4098 9127; Buchanan Creek Rd). If you plan on self-catering, stock up in Mossman, which also has the closest banks. Most places to stay and eat and the general stores have Eftpos and credit-card facilities. There's a post box at the ferry crossing, on the north bank of the Daintree River.

Daintree River ferry (car/motorcycle/bicycle & pedestrian $16/8/3; ☾ 6am-midnight), a cable ferry, runs every 15 minutes or so, and the crossing takes about four minutes.

Sun Palm (☎ 4084 2626; www.sunpalmtransport .com) runs a daily (except Monday) service from Cape Tribulation to Cairns ($45, three hours). It also travels up the coastal road to Cooktown every second day. **Coral Reef Coaches** (☎ 4098 2800; www.coralreefcoaches.com.au) runs a daily bus service from Cape Tribulation to Cairns ($40, four hours).

Cape Kimberley Beach

Cape Kimberley Rd, 3km beyond the Daintree River crossing, leads to Cape Kimberley Beach, a beautiful quiet beach with **Snapper Island** just off shore. The island is national park, with a fringing reef. Access to the island is by private boat; Crocodylus Village (right) takes a sea-kayaking tour there.

At the beach is **Daintree Koala Beach Resort** (☎ 4090 7500; www.koala-backpackers.com; Cape Kimberley; unpowered/powered sites $10/13, dm $18-25, d $50-85; 🐾 🚍). This huge family-friendly camping ground has secluded sites, small cabins with bunk beds, and a welcoming bar and restaurant. Activities include fishing and the occasional fire twirling.

You'll need to obtain a permit for the **QPWS camping ground** (☎ 4098 2188; www.epa.qld .gov.au; per person $4) on the southwest side of Snapper Island, where there's a toilet and picnic tables. Take a fuel stove, as fires are not permitted.

Cow Bay

Cow Bay is simply beautiful. Trees provide beach shade, and you can fish or just lie there – it doesn't get much more relaxing or picturesque. Before the turn-off to the Jindalba Boardwalk is the **Walu Wugirriga (Alexandra Range) lookout**, with an information board and superb views over the Range.

The **Daintree Discovery Centre** (☎ 4098 9171; www.daintree-rec.com.au; cnr Cape Tribulation & Tulip Oak Rds; adult/child $20/7.50; 🕑 8.30am-5pm) is a rainforest interpretive centre. Its aerial walkway takes you over the forest floor to a 23m tower. There are a few short walks with interpretive panels and a small theatre running films on cassowaries, crocodiles and conservation. You can hire an audio guide ($5), and included in your admission fee is an interpretive booklet, which will help you identify, among other things, a viscious-hairy-mary.

Jindalba Boardwalk is a 700m circuit that snakes through the rainforest behind the centre.

Epiphyte B&B (☎ 4098 9039; www.rainforestbb .com; 22 Silkwood Rd; s/d/tr $45/65/80) is a spectacularly laid-back B&B with rooms that are individually styled – some bigger than others. The encircling veranda is festooned with hammocks, from where you'll catch views of imposing Thornton's Peak. If you arrive unannounced, a blackboard indicates whether there's a vacancy. Let yourself in and head to the beach, which is where you'll probably find the manager.

The beds are as comfy as clouds in the modern rooms at **Daintree Rainforest Retreat** (☎ 4098 9101; www.daintreeretreat.com.au; 336 Cape Tribulation Rd; r $100-120; 🚍). All rooms have their own bathroom, TV and kettle. Rates include breakfast at whatever time you nominate, and the quiet setting is ruffled only when someone is splashing about in the pool.

A number of green canvas safari-style huts merge with the surrounding trees at the YHA-associated **Crocodylus Village** (☎ 4098 9166; www.crocodyluscapetrib.com; Buchanan Creek Rd; dm/d $20/75; 🖥 🚍). Dorm rooms contain 16 to 20 beds and have all the ambience of school camp. There's a restaurant and bar, as well as a range of activities. Crocodylus runs excellent two-day sea-kayaking tours to Snapper Island ($180) that leave early in the morning, so you'll need to overnight in Cow Bay. Guided walks ($20, three hours) are also available in the morning and afternoon.

Daintree Wilderness Lodge (☎ 4098 9105; www .daintreewildernesslodge.com.au; 83 Cape Tribulation Rd; r $250; 🚍) has seven timber cabins separated by lush rainforest and connected by a series of boardwalks. Each cabin has a ceiling window to watch the rainforest canopy. If there's not enough action for you, watch a DVD that's also in your room. Rates include breakfast; there's a restaurant and 'jungle Jacuzzi'.

About 5km north of Cow Bay, **Lync Haven** (☎ 4098 9155; www.lynchaven.com.au; Cape Tribulation Rd; unpowered/powered sites $19/24, d $140-165), set on a 16-hectare property, has basic cabins (some with bathrooms) and self-contained bungalows that sleep up to six. The property contains its own walking trails, a hand-reared pen of kangaroos and a licensed café.

This open-air licensed **Fan Palm Boardwalk Cafe** (☎ 4098 9119; Cape Tribulation Rd, Cow Bay; mains $8-16; 🕑 breakfast, lunch & dinner) serves perky wraps and sandwiches, as well as more substantial fare, such as fish and chips, and rib-eye steak. There's a wheelchair-accessible deck leading through giant palms (nonguests $2).

Daintree Ice Cream Company (☎ 4098 9114; Cape Tribulation Rd; ice cream $4; ✆ noon-5pm) doesn't serve your average ice cream: here you'll lick your way through four delectable scoops, selecting from a range of seasonal and exotic flavours such as wattleseed, macadamia, mango and durian.

The boutique **Le Bistrot** (☎ 4098 9016; Cape Tribulation Rd; mains 19-30; ✆ lunch) serves formal savoury and sweet dishes in thatched huts dotted around the grounds. Also on the premises is the tiny Floravilla gallery displaying the owners' photographs and plants.

If you have a hankering for a basic pub counter meal and a pot of beer, the **Cow Bay**

Hotel (☎ 4098 9011; Cape Tribulation Rd; mains $10-16; ✆ dinner) is where you should stop.

Cooper Creek

There's a smattering of sights and accommodation options nestled in Cooper Creek at the base of dramatic Thornton's Peak.

Daintree Entomological Museum (☎ 4098 9045; www.daintreemuseum.com.au; Turpentine Rd; adult/child $12/6; ✆ 10.30am-4pm) displays a large private collection of local or exotic bugs, butterflies and spiders. As well as the delicately pinned specimens, there are also live exhibits of giant cockroaches.

Book ahead for your place on one of the **Cooper Creek Wilderness** (☎ 4098 9126; www.ccwild .com; Cape Tribulation Rd; adult $30) guided walks. Bring your swimming costume for the day walks (departing 9am and 2pm), which take you through Daintree rainforest and

---

DAINTREE: LOVING IT TO DEATH?

People have been fighting over the Daintree for decades. The traditional opponents, conservationists and those with commercial interests such as loggers and farmers, joined forces in the 1980s to curb a new and encroaching force that threatened both groups' interests: mass tourism.

Far North Queensland's Wet Tropics World Heritage Area contains amazing pockets of biodiversity. The area covers only 0.01% of Australia's surface area, but has 36% of the continent's mammal species, 50% of its bird species, around 60% of its butterfly species and 65% of its fern species. The Daintree is a small part of the World Heritage–listed area that stretches from Townsville to Cooktown, and covers 8944 sq km of coast and hinterland. Within the area's 3000km boundary are diverse habitats of swamp and mangrove forests, eucalypt woodlands and tropical rainforest.

The Daintree was brought to the international stage when in 1983 the controversial Bloomfield Track was bulldozed through sensitive coastal lowland rainforest from Cape Tribulation to the Bloomfield River. The publicity generated by protests indirectly led to the federal government's moves in 1987 to nominate Queensland's wet tropical rainforests for World Heritage listing. Despite resistance by the Queensland timber industry and state government, the area was inscribed on the World Heritage list in 1988 and one of the key outcomes was a total ban on commercial logging in the area.

Today, the Daintree area remains controversial. The Daintree rainforest reaches as far as the Bloomfield River and much of it is upland rainforest on steep slopes protected as part of Daintree National Park. However, the Cow Bay area that many travellers visit, an area of unique and threatened plant species, is a subdivision on freehold private land – look around and you'll see 'for sale' signs aplenty. In an effort to curb development and limit human impact on the area, the state and federal governments have spent $23 million on buying back jungle properties and adding them to the Daintree National Park. A submission by 26 leading international scientists stating that any further development would have an impact on the entire ecosystem contributed to a moratorium on building – affecting 400 absentee landowners. In retaliation, the Forest Creek Ratepayers Association recently wrote to the UN requesting that the Daintree rainforest be removed from the World Heritage list, arguing that the subdivided area forms only a tiny percentage of the Daintree rainforest.

Presently it looks as though the adage of *Paradise Lost* is being stalled by local efforts, and the Daintree just could be Paradise Found…and preserved.

include a dip in Cooper Creek. Night walks (departing at 8pm) focus on spotting nocturnal wildlife.

Heritage Lodge (☎ 4098 9138; www.heritagelodge .net.au; Turpentine Rd; r from $205; ☒) is a secluded resort consisting of 20 rooms, and makes a great retreat for couples. Spa treatments are available, and there's a pool and a nearby natural swimming hole. Breakfast is included in the rate, and the resort's **restaurant-bar** (mains $26-30; ☺ lunch & dinner) has a small but varied menu, including such dishes as char-grilled vegetable stack and smoked salmon fettuccine.

There are few better settings to practise, or learn, meditation and yoga than the ancient rainforest of the Daintree. **Prema Shanti** (☎ 4098 9006; www.premashanti.com; Turpentine Rd; 2-day retreat $110) yoga retreats include two hours of daily instruction in Iyengar, as well as breakfast and dinner. Accommodation is shared with one other person.

Three ground-level self-contained units provide comfortable lodgings in a rainforest setting at **Daintree Deep Forest Lodge** (☎ 4098 9162; www.daintreedeepforestlodge.com.au; Cape Tribulation Rd; r $100-150). There are two studio units and a one-bedroom unit that sleeps up to five people. Each has a veranda with a BBQ for alfresco cooking.

The little timber cabins at **Daintree Drifters** (☎ 4098 9192; www.daintreedrifters.com.au; Lot 15, Cape Tribulation Rd; d $100) are propped amid an exotic garden with beautiful flowering plants. Cabins have screened open sides, and the water to the communal bathroom is pumped from a nearby stream. Breakfast is included and served in the open-plan main house.

Thornton Beach
A slither of vegetation separates Cape Tribulation Rd from magnificent Thornton Beach. A towel-length from the beach is **Cafe on Sea** (☎ 4098 9718; Thornton Beach; mains $10-15; ☺ breakfast & lunch), with excellent meals such as Thai fish burgers and decent espresso.

Noah Beach
Marrdja Botanical Walk is a beautiful 540m (30-minute) interpretive boardwalk that follows the creek through the rainforest and mangroves to a lookout over Noah Creek.

Noah Beach camping area (☎ 4098 0052; www .epa.qld.gov.au; Cape Tribulation Rd; per person $4) is a QPWS self-registration camping site set

100m back from the beach. Big red-trunked trees provide shade for the 16 sites. There are toilets, and drinking water is available. Bookings and permits are required. Note that the ground may be closed after heavy rain and during the wet season.

CAPE TRIBULATION
The village of Cape Tribulation marks the end of the road, literally, and the beginning of the 4WD-only coastal route along the Bloomfield Track. Despite its popularity with day-trippers, it retains a frontier quality – where road signs alert drivers to cassowary crossings and crocodile warnings make beach strolls that little bit less relaxing.

Limited supplies and tourist information are available at **Mason's Store** (☎ 4098 0070; Cape Tribulation Rd; ☺ 7am-7pm), about 1.5km south of the cape, and there's an IGA supermarket and pharmacy next to PK's Jungle Village. Most places to stay can provide information on the area.

Sights & Activities
There are a few windows for visitors to peer into the shielded wilderness of Cape Trib.

Bat House (☎ 4098 0063; Cape Tribulation Rd; www .austrop.org.au; admission $2; ☺ 10.30am-3.30pm Tue-Sun) is an information and education centre run by volunteers from Austrop, a local conservation organisation. As the name suggests, it's also a nursery for fruit bats, and there's always one hanging around (sorry) for you to meet.

You can appreciate the rainforest and the beach simultaneously, just by turning your head. Prop on the stunning swathes of **Cape Tribulation Beach** or **Myall Beach**, where lush green vegetation abruptly gives way to fine sand and the shallows of the Coral Sea. The **Dubuji Boardwalk** is a 1.8km circuit walk down to Myall Beach through rainforest and mangroves.

Serious walkers should lace-up early for the strenuous **Mt Sorrow Ridge Walk** (7km, six hours return). The start of the trail is about 150m north of the Kulki picnic area car park, on your left. The steep climb takes you to a lookout, with awesome views across windswept vegetation over the cape.

Organised activities include horse riding with **Cape Tribulation Horse Rides** (☎ 4098 0030; per person $95; ☺ 8am & 1.30pm), where you'll be collected from your accommodation; yoga

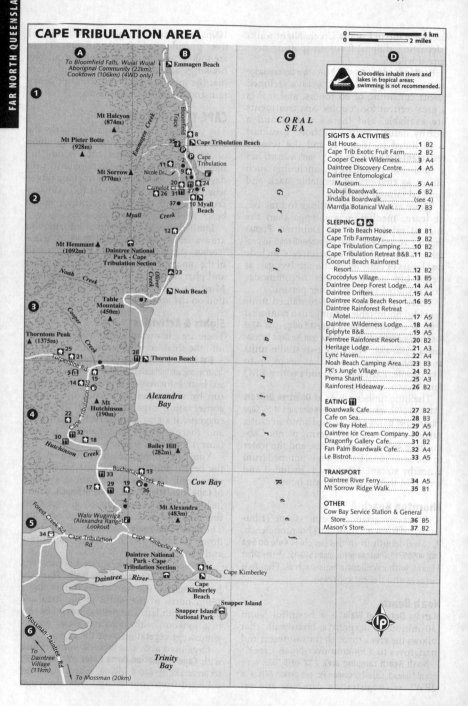

CAPE TRIBULATION AREA

0 ——————— 4 km
0 ——————— 2 miles

To Bloomfield Falls, Wujal Wujal
Aboriginal Community (22km);
Cooktown (106km) (4WD only)

Emmagen Beach

**CORAL
SEA**

Crocodiles inhabit rivers and
lakes in tropical areas;
swimming is not recommended.

Mt Halcyon
(874m)

Mt Pieter Botte
(928m)

Cape Tribulation Beach

Cape
Tribulation

Mt Sorrow
(770m)

Nicole Dr

Camelot Cl

Myall   Creek

Myall
Beach

Mt Hemmant
(1092m)

Daintree National
Park - Cape
Tribulation Section

Noah Creek

Oliver Creek

Noah Beach

Table
Mountain
(450m)

Thorntons Peak
(1375m)

Turpentine Rd

Cooper Creek

Cape Tribulation Rd

Thornton Beach

Alexandra
Bay

Mt
Hutchinson
(190m)

Hutchinson   Creek

Bailey Hill
(282m)

Buchanan Creek Rd

Cow Bay

Walu Wugirriga
(Alexandra Range)
Lookout

Mt Alexandra
(483m)

Forest Creek Rd

Cape Tribulation
Rd

Cape Kimberley Rd

Daintree National
Park - Cape
Tribulation Section

Daintree   River

Cape
Kimberley
Beach

Cape Kimberley

Mossman–Daintree Rd

Snapper Island

Snapper Island
National Park

To
Daintree
Village
(11km)

Trinity
Bay

To Mossman (20km)

Great   Barrier   Reef

SIGHTS & ACTIVITIES
Bat House	1 B2
Cape Trib Exotic Fruit Farm	2 B2
Cooper Creek Wilderness	3 A4
Daintree Discovery Centre	4 A5
Daintree Entomological Museum	5 A4
Dubuji Boardwalk	6 B2
Jindalba Boardwalk	(see 4)
Marrdja Botanical Walk	7 B3

SLEEPING
Cape Trib Beach House	8 B1
Cape Trib Farmstay	9 B2
Cape Tribulation Camping	10 B2
Cape Tribulation Retreat B&B	11 B2
Coconut Beach Rainforest Resort	12 B2
Crocodylus Village	13 B5
Daintree Deep Forest Lodge	14 A4
Daintree Drifters	15 A4
Daintree Koala Beach Resort	16 B5
Daintree Rainforest Retreat Motel	17 A5
Daintree Wilderness Lodge	18 A4
Epiphyte B&B	19 A3
Ferntree Rainforest Resort	20 B2
Heritage Lodge	21 A3
Lync Haven	22 A4
Noah Beach Camping Area	23 B3
PK's Jungle Village	24 B2
Prema Shanti	25 A3
Rainforest Hideaway	26 B2

EATING
Boardwalk Cafe	27 B2
Cafe on Sea	28 B3
Cow Bay Hotel	29 A5
Daintree Ice Cream Company	30 A4
Dragonfly Gallery Cafe	31 B2
Fan Palm Boardwalk Cafe	32 A4
Le Bistrot	33 A5

TRANSPORT
Daintree River Ferry	34 A5
Mt Sorrow Ridge Walk	35 B1

OTHER
Cow Bay Service Station & General Store	36 B5
Mason's Store	37 B2

FAR NORTH QUEENSLAND

classes on Cape Trib beach (out the front of Cape Trib Beach House) with **Prema Shanti** (☎ 4098 9006; www.premashanti.com; 1-hr class $20); and sea kayaking with **Paddle Trek** (☎ 4098 0040; www.daintreecoast.com/paddletrek; morning 3½-hr tours $45, afternoon 2½-hr tours $38) and **Tropical Paradise** (☎ 4098 0077; www.tropicalparadise.com.au; 3½-hr tours; $45). Both sea-kayaking companies will collect you from your accommodation.

Tours

The Great Barrier Reef is just 45 minutes to an hour off shore. Two operators run trips that include snorkelling, and offer certified and introductory diving opportunities. The sailing catamaran **Rum Runner** (☎ 1300 556 332; www.rumrunner.com.au; tours $116; ⏱ Apr-Feb) is a local outfit, with a maximum of 40 passengers. **Odyssey H2O** (☎ 1300 134 044; www.voyages.com.au; tours $136), operated by the Voyages resort company, uses a motorised boat. Tours leave from Cape Tribulation, and both companies will collect you from your accommodation.

Jungle Adventures (☎ 4098 0090; www.junglesurfingcanopytours.com; tours $25-28) runs zany guided night and day walks that explain the significance of the flora and fauna encountered along the way. **Mason's Store** (☎ 4098 0070; www.masonstours.com.au, Cape Tribulation Rd) also offers interpretive walks lasting two hours (adult/child $30/23) or a half-day (adult/child $36/28), as well as extended 4WD tours.

Cape Trib Exotic Fruit Farm (☎ 4098 0057; www.capetrib.com.au; tastings $15; ⏱ 4pm) runs tours of the orchards; bookings essential.

Sleeping & Eating

Rainforest Hideaway (☎ 4098 0108; www.rainforesthideaway.com; 19 Camelot Close; r $85-115) This beautifully rambling accommodation is in a homemade home – single-handedly built by the owner. Walk through the dense forest backyard to the self-contained rustic haven with an outdoor shower. It's extremely private, if you don't count the cassowary that occasionally has a look-in. There's a small cabin at the front of the house, plus a two-level room inside suitable for families.

Cape Trib Beach House (☎ 4098 0030; www.capetribbeach.com.au; dm $25-32, r $70-135; ✕ 🖳 🕭) Park your car at reception and hike down the pedestrian-only path to these A-frame rainforest huts. Most of the rooms (including dorms) have air-con, and the complex includes a small communal kitchen and **restaurant-bar** (mains $15-20; ⏱ breakfast, lunch & dinner) with a pool table, games and trashy magazines. You can access the beach down some stairs leading from the restaurant.

PK's Jungle Village (☎ 4098 0197; www.pksjunglevillage.com; unpowered sites $30, dm $25, d $88-110; ✕ 🖳 🕭) Close to the excellent Myall Beach, PK's has the works: from postal facilities through to volleyball and salsa dance classes from its vibrant bar area. Dorms

---

THE CASSOWARY'S PRECIOUS POO

The flightless cassowary is as tall as a grown man, has three toes, a blue-and-purple head, red wattles (the fleshy lobes hanging from its neck), a helmetlike horn and unusual black feathers – that look more like ratty hair. Traditional gender roles are reversed, with the male bird incubating the egg and rearing the chicks on his own. The Australian cassowary is also known as the Southern cassowary, though it's only found in the north of Queensland. This begins to make sense when you realise that other species are found in Papua New Guinea, which lise to the north of Australia.

The cassowary is considered an important link in the rainforest ecosystem. It is the only animal capable of dispersing the seeds of more than 70 species of trees whose fruit is too large for other rainforest animals to digest and pass. Cassowaries swallow fruit whole and excrete the fruit's seed intact in large piles of dung, which acts as fertiliser encouraging growth of the seed. Without them, the rainforest as we know it would look very different.

The cassowary is an endangered species; its biggest threat is loss of habitat, and eggs and chicks are vulnerable to dogs and wild pigs. A number of birds are also hit by cars: heed road signs warning drivers to be casso-wary. You're most likely to see cassowaries around Mission Beach and the Cape Tribulation section of the Daintree National Park. They can be aggressive, particularly if they have chicks. If you feel threatened, do not run; give the bird right-of-way and try to keep something solid between you and it – preferably a tree.

have eight beds, and air-conditioned rooms with bathrooms are available. Camping prices are for two people. There's also a **restaurant** (mains $15-20; ☺ breakfast, lunch & dinner) and communal kitchen.

Cape Tribulation Retreat B&B (☎ 4098 0028; www.capetribretreat.com.au; 19 Nicole Dr; d $150) At the end of Nicole Drive, past the boot fence – a curious stretch of wire fencing laden with retired shoes, flippers and slippers – is this gorgeous B&B. A creek runs alongside this high-ceiling, modern timber home, with rainforest in the backyard. All rooms have bathrooms and rates include breakfast. The unfenced creek makes Cape Tribulation Retreat unsuitable for small children.

Cape Trib Farmstay (☎ 4098 0042; www.capetrib farmstay.com; Cape Tribulation Rd; d $100) This fruit orchard has neat and private timber cottages with joyous views of Mt Sorrow. One of the eight cabins – all with bathrooms – has wheelchair access. There's a common kitchen and open grass areas between fruit trees.

Coconut Beach Rainforest Resort (☎ 4098 0033; www.voyages.com; Cape Tribulation Rd; r $370; ☒ ☒) This luxurious resort has stunning designer rooms with polished boards and trendy décor. All bathrooms have a bath and an essential-oil burner for ambience. There are two pools, a natural swimming hole nearby and beach access. Services include babysitting and tour bookings. The beachside **Cape Tribulation Restaurant & Bar** (mains $30-40; ☺ lunch & dinner) offers sumptuous dining overlooking the turtle pond and pool.

Ferntree Rainforest Resort (☎ 4098 0000; www .voyages.com; Camelot Close, Cape Tribulation; d from $240-305; ☒ ☒) The large Rainforest Resort has eight poolside rooms with private balconies, plus 46 standard rooms. Facilities include two pools, a babysitting service and the **Cassowary Rest** (mains $20-30; ☺ breakfast, lunch & dinner), also open to nonguests.

Cape Tribulation Camping (☎ 4098 0077; www .capetribcamping.com.au; unpowered/powered sites $22/28, d $50) has beach frontage and a good range of facilities, including beach showers and a camp kitchen with BBQs. Linen for the cabin accommodation costs an extra $5.

Dragonfly Gallery Cafe (☎ 4098 0121; Lot 9, Camelot Close; mains $15-20; ☺ lunch & dinner) is a licensed café in a timber pole-house with beautiful garden views. Internet access is available upstairs in the loft, and you can peruse local art displayed around the interior.

Boardwalk Cafe (dishes $6-10; ☺ breakfast, lunch & early dinner) is a takeaway that serves burgers, sandwiches and the only pizza on the Cape.

Getting There & Around
See above for details of buses between Cape Tribulation, Cairns and Cooktown.

NORTH TO COOKTOWN

There are two routes to Cooktown from the south: the coastal route from Cape Tribulation via the 4WD Bloomfield Track, and the inland route via the Peninsula and Cooktown Development Rds, which are accessible to conventional vehicles.

Most visitors use both, travelling north up the inland route and returning via the coastal route.

INLAND ROUTE
The inland route stoically retains its arid, outback character whatever the season. It's 332km (about 4½ hours' drive) from Cairns to Cooktown. Access the Peninsula Development Rd from Mareeba, or via the turn-off just before Mossman. The road travels past rugged ironbarks and cattle-trodden land before joining the Cooktown Development Rd at Lakeland. From here it's another 80km to Cooktown, with just 30km left to seal – due for completion by the end of 2005.

Mt Molloy to Palmer River
The historical township of **Mt Molloy** marks the start of the Peninsula Development Rd (about 40km north of Mareeba). Since its heady gold- and copper-mining days, the town has shrivelled to comprise a pub, bakery, post office and café. James Venture Mulligan is buried in the cemetery just south of town. He was the prospector credited with first finding gold in the Palmer and Hodgkinson Rivers, which dominoed into the establishment of Cairns and Port Douglas. He mined copper around Mt Molloy in the 1890s, and bought the town pub where he sustained injuries while breaking up a brawl that eventually killed him.

You might see small teams of people with binoculars and cameras on their way to or from **Abattoir Swamp Environment Park**. Just out of town, this wetlands area, blanketed in lotus flowers, is popular with bird-watchers.

The **National Hotel** (☎ 4094 1133; Main St; s/d $25/50, mains $10-17; ⏰ lunch & dinner) is a welcoming local, where you can wear your work boots to lunch, and with lovely rooms upstairs that even the pickiest mother would approve of. Rates include cereal and toast in the morning, which you can eat with a view from the encircling veranda. For beautiful burgers that'll rate a mention on your next postcard, head to **Mt Molloy Cafe & Takeaway** (☎ 4094 1187; Main St; dishes $5-15; ⏰ breakfast, lunch & dinner). Otherwise known as Lobo Loco, this licensed café also has homemade burritos and enchiladas, and garden seating.

Mt Carbine, 30km northwest of Mt Molloy, is a one-pub town – literally, that's about all there is. The pub was established for wolframite (a mineral used for tungsten) miners in the area, and well known for the bull that used to drink there. The mine closed in 1986 and the abandoned Brooklyn mining village has been transformed into the **Mt Carbine Village & Caravan Park** (☎ /fax 4094 3160; unpowered/ powered sites $14/16, d $55). Located south of the pub, the park has good facilities, with self-contained cabins and a laundry. The grounds are visited by birds and other wildlife, and retain evidence of the village's former life with a disused Olympic-sized pool, a playground and a recreation hall.

After crossing the McLeod River, 15km west of Mt Carbine, the road climbs through the De Sailly Range, where there are panoramic views over the savannah. The road continues north reaching the **Palmer River**, a further 60km from Mt Carbine. You'll find food and fuel at the **Palmer River Roadhouse** (☎ 4060 2020; unpowered & powered sites $12.50, s/d $25/35, mains $12-17 ⏰ breakfast, lunch & dinner). You can also pitch a tent, park your van or stay in the roadhouse's bivouac.

Lakeland to Cooktown

From the Palmer River it's another 15km to **Lakeland**, a hamlet at the junction of the Peninsula Development Rd and the Cooktown Development Rd. Lakeland is in the fertile basin of the Laura Valley, producing cereal grains, sugar and coffee (almost the full complement for the breakfast table). Head west and you're on your way to Laura and Cape York; continue straight northeast and you've got another 80km to Cooktown.

Should you require fuel, a feed or a sleep, Lakeland can oblige. **Lakeland Coffee House** (☎ 4060 2040; www.users.bigpond.com/coffeehouse; Sesame St; ⏰ 6.30am-6.30pm) has petrol, basic supplies and an ATM; it also sells sandwiches and locally grown coffee. **Lakeland Downs Hotel-Motel** (☎ 4060 2142; simmonskelli@bigpond .com.au; Peninsula Development Rd; s $35-50, d $60-70; ✕) has comfortable motel-style rooms, as well as budget dongas (single occupancy accommodation with a shared bathroom). Its **pub** (mains $10-18; ⏰ breakfast, lunch & dinner) serves hearty, familiar food, such as steak. The **Lakeland Caravan Park** (☎ 4060 2008; fax 4060 2179; Peninsula Development Rd; unpowered/ powered sites $15.50/17.50, d $55) is a lovely spot,

---

DETOUR

The Palmer River's alluvial gold deposits spurred a mighty gold rush, which created thriving, if transitory, townships. The remains of two major townships from the Palmer River rush (1873 to 1883) lie inland from the Palmer River Roadhouse. There's an unmarked turn-off from the Peninsula Development Rd, which runs west for 35km to the ghost town of **Maytown**, and **Palmerville** 30km further on. This is rugged 4WD-only territory where the only passing traffic you might see is the odd cow from the neighbouring cattle station. The turn-off is about 17km south of the Palmer River Roadhouse, just before the White's Creek crossing.

The Palmer goldfields are legendary not only for the 46°C days and lack of comforts that prospectors endured but also for the thousands who walked overland to get here. Maytown was the second settlement to be established, after Palmerville, and it became the major centre in 1875.

All that remains of Maytown's 12 hotels, three bakeries, butcher and lemonade factory are a few stumps, some plaques and slate roads that the earth is gradually reclaiming. The population of 252 Europeans and 422 Chinese had largely abandoned Maytown by 1945, when the gold dried up. There's a camping spot just beneath the site of Maytown, before you cross the river. Contact **QPWS** (Mossman ☎ 4098 2188, Cooktown ☎ 4069 5777) for a permit and an update on the current condition of the track. You'll need to backtrack the same way you came in.

with accommodation available in on-site vans.

About 50km past Lakeland is the **Annan River Gorge**, which has a natural swimming hole and picnic area. Downstream the river has carved an impressive gorge through solid rock; the water pools briefly before cascading into impressive falls.

A little further down the road is the turn-off to Helenvale and the coastal route.

Continuing to Cooktown, the road soon passes the staggering **Black Mountain National Park**, with its thousands of stacked, square, black granite boulders that look unnervingly precarious, as though they might tumble down with the slightest movement. The mountain is home to unique species of frogs, skinks and geckoes. It was formed 260 million years ago by a magma intrusion below the surface, which then solidified and was gradually exposed by erosion. Black Mountain marks the northern end of the Wet Tropics World Heritage Area. From here, it's another 30km to Cooktown.

COASTAL ROUTE

From Cape Trib to the Bloomfield River, the 4WD-only Bloomfield Track traverses creek crossings, steep climbs and patchy surfaces that can be boggy or bald. This infamous stretch of road can be impassable for weeks during the Wet; ask locally at **Mason's Store** (☎ 4098 0070; Cape Tribulation Rd; ⏱ 7am-7pm) about current conditions. The Bloomfield Track runs for about 80km before linking up with the Cooktown Development Rd 30km south of Cooktown.

The track was built in 1983 despite vociferous opposition from locals. The official justification for the track was to open up the region to tourism and to halt the illegal trade in drugs, wildlife and plants. Local views, supported by scientific reports, expressed concern over the environmental impact of the track on the surrounding rainforest and reef. Cape Trib became the scene of a classic greenies-versus-bulldozers blockade, yet after several months and numerous arrests, it took just three weeks to cut the track through the forest. The debate over the Bloomfield Track continues today, with the majority of locals seeking its staged closure over the next 10 to 15 years.

Cape Tribulation to the Bloomfield River

It's 5km from Cape Trib to Emmagen Creek, which is the official start of the Bloomfield Track. Just before you reach Emmagen Creek, you'll see a huge strangler fig. From beside the tree, a walking path leads down to the pretty crescent-shaped **Emmagen Beach**.

A little way beyond the Emmagen Creek crossing, the road climbs and dips steeply and turns sharp corners over fine, slippery bull dust. This is the most challenging section of the drive, especially after rain. The road then follows the broad Bloomfield River before crossing it 30km north of Cape Trib. The Bloomfield River is a tidal crossing, so you'll need to check with locals about the best times to cross.

Turn left immediately after the bridge to see the **Bloomfield Falls**. The falls are for looking only: crocs inhabit the river and the site is significant to the indigenous Wujal Wujal community located just north of the river. Residents of Wujal Wujal, the **Walker Family** (☎ 4060 8069; ffw@bigpond.com) runs recommended tours of the falls ($15, 30 minutes), departing daily from the car park, and of the nearby rainforest ($55, two hours), departing daily from Thompson Creek Landing. Bookings are essential.

From Wujal Wujal to Cooktown the road is unsealed, but possible to traverse (slowly) with a conventional vehicle.

About 10km beyond Wujal Wujal is the small hamlet of **Ayton** where the Bloomfield River empties out to the Coral Sea. You can tour the river with **Hire a Boat** (☎ 4060 8252; cnr West & First Sts; tours adult/child $25/15, boat hire per hr $25; ⏱ 7am-6pm) or do it yourself in a tinnie. And there are a few out-of-the-way places to stay.

Bloomfield Camping & Cabins (☎ 4060 8207; www.bloomfieldcabins.com; 20 Bloomfield Rd, Ayton; unpowered sites $14, d $60) is just north of Ayton and has a great setting, with tall, shady gum trees. A path from the property leads to Weary Bay where you can walk for 9km (and appreciate its name). There's a bar and casual restaurant, but you'll need to book in advance, as it opens on demand.

Peppers Bloomfield Lodge (☎ 4035 9166; www.bloomfieldlodge.com.au; Weary Bay; 4-night minimum d $1345-1955; ✷) is only accessible from the sea, and the tariff includes transfers from Cairns (which involves a 30-minute flight, a boat trip and a 4WD journey). The cabins at this luxury resort are spaced well apart, with verandas overlooking the rainforest and/or sea (sea views will cost you). All meals are included in the rate, and optional extras, such as spa treatments and excursions, are also available. It's favoured by honeymooners, and children over 12 are welcome.

Bloomfield River to Cooktown

North of Bloomfield, the road passes through the **Cedar Bay (Mangkal-Mangkalba) National Park**. Access to the park is either by boat, which is difficult in most conditions, or by a walking trail (17km, seven hours). There's a self-registration camp site at Cedar Bay, and you can obtain a permit from **QPWS** (www.epa.qld.gov.au; Mossman ☎ 4098 2188; Cooktown ☎ 4069 5777; per person $4). This and other walks begin from **Home Rule Rainforest Lodge** (☎ 4060 3925; fax 4060 3902; Rossville; unpowered sites $16, dm/d $18/40), at the end of a bumpy 3km driveway. The lodge caters to groups, and the grounds and facilities are spotless. There is a communal kitchen and Elsie will cook on request (order in advance: breakfast $6 to $8, dinner $12). The turn-off to this lodge is signposted from Rossville, 33km north of the Bloomfield River crossing.

The **Lion's Den Hotel** (☎ 4060 3911; www.lions denhotel.com.au; Helensvale; unpowered sites $7.50, dm/d $25/50; 🍺), 9km further north, attracts a steady stream of travellers and local characters. This well-known watering hole dates back to 1875, and sports genuine corrugated, graffiti-covered décor. Pitch a tent by the river or bed down in safari-style cabins; linen hire is extra. Its **restaurant** (mains around $12; 🕒 breakfast, lunch & dinner) serves up excellent pub grub, including pizza and lasagne.

Mungumby Lodge (☎ 4060 3158; www.mungumby .com; Helensvale; d $200; 🍺) is a verdant little oasis of lawns and mango trees, with timber cabins scattered around. The communal lounge area overlooks the pool. The straightforward yet comfortable cabins all have bathrooms. Meals and tours are also available.

About 4km north, the Bloomfield Track meets the Cooktown Development Rd.

COOKTOWN

☎ 07 / pop 1638

Peak hour in Cooktown is early evening, when the fish are biting and the beer is flowing. About a dozen 4WDs gather at either end of town: half park at the wharf, the other half outside the pub. Years of isolation and hard living have imbued the locals with a matter-of-fact, laconic character and a great sense of humour. They're not afraid of hard work, and equally not shy of a smoko – say from October to June…

The Wet has traditionally cut Cooktown off from the south to all but those with 4WDs. Both access roads became impassable, and Cooktown received few, if any, visitors during this time. Its isolation has kept it shielded from the burgeoning tourist industry that is creeping north, with an anticipated boon in tourism once the Cooktown Development Rd is completely sealed in 2005, providing easy access to conventional vehicles.

As such, unlike its southern siblings, Cooktown exists despite tourism. It remains unadorned and unfussed by the attention it receives. Traditionally it has been Cooktown's history of European contact that draws travellers, but there's increasing recognition for the area's indigenous community and unspoilt natural environment. It has diverse habitats of wetlands, mangroves, rainforest and long, lonely beaches.

History

On 17 June 1770 Cooktown became the site of Australia's first nonindigenous settlement, however transient, when Captain James Cook beached his barque, the *Endeavour*, on the banks of its river. The *Endeavour* had earlier struck a reef offshore from Cape Tribulation, and Cook and his crew spent 48 days here while they repaired the damage. During this time, Joseph Banks, the chief naturalist, and botanist Daniel Solander kept busy studying the plants and animals along the banks of the Endeavour River, while the artist Sydney Parkinson illustrated their finds. Banks collected 186 plant species and 'observed, described, sketched, shot, ate and named the kangaroo'.

In 1874 Cooktown became a large and unruly port town at the centre of the Palmer River gold rush. At its peak there were no less than 94 pubs and the population was more than 30,000. A large percentage of this population was Chinese, and their industrious presence led to some wild race-related riots. And here, as elsewhere in the country, the indigenous population was overrun and outcast, with much blood shed.

Cooktown's glory was short-lived, and as the gold ran out, the population dwindled. Two cyclones and an evacuation in WWII didn't do much to lift Cooktown's profile. By 1970, just a few hundred people turned up to see Queen Elizabeth II open the James Cook Historical Museum…and a rock. The rock sits just out in the water from Bicentennial Park and marks the spot where Cook ran aground; the Queen's Steps were constructed so Her Majesty could reach it.

Orientation & Information

Cooktown is on the inland side of a headland sheltering the mouth of the Endeavour River. The main street is Charlotte St, which runs south from the wharf. Over-

looking the town from the northern end of the headland is Grassy Hill, and east of the town centre are Cherry Tree Bay and Finch Bay, the Botanic Gardens and Mt Cook National Park.

Cooktown hibernates during the Wet (known to locals as the 'dead season') and reduced hours or closure applies to the town's museums and cruises.

Information services available:

Cooktown Library (☎ 4069 5009; Helen St) Internet access.

Cooktown QPWS (☎ 4069 5777; Webber Esplanade; ☺ 8am-3pm Mon-Fri) Closes for lunch.

Cooktown Travel Centre (☎ 4069 5446; cooktown travel@bigpond.com; Charlotte St; ☺ 8.30am-5pm Mon-Fri, 8.30-noon Sat) Tourist information.

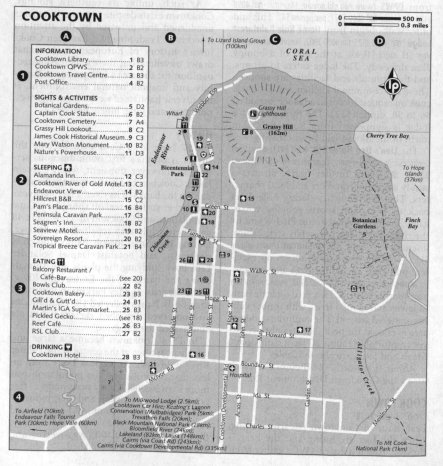

COOKTOWN

INFORMATION		
Cooktown Library	1	B3
Cooktown QPWS	2	B2
Cooktown Travel Centre	3	B3
Post Office	4	B2

SIGHTS & ACTIVITIES		
Botanical Gardens	5	D2
Captain Cook Statue	6	B2
Cooktown Cemetery	7	A4
Grassy Hill Lookout	8	C2
James Cook Historical Museum	9	C3
Mary Watson Monument	10	B2
Nature's Powerhouse	11	D3

SLEEPING		
Alamanda Inn	12	C3
Cooktown River of Gold Motel	13	C3
Endeavour View	14	B2
Hillcrest B&B	15	C2
Pam's Place	16	B4
Peninsula Caravan Park	17	C3
Seagren's Inn	18	B2
Seaview Motel	19	B2
Sovereign Resort	20	B2
Tropical Breeze Caravan Park	21	B4

EATING		
Balcony Restaurant / Café-Bar	(see 20)	
Bowls Club	22	B2
Cooktown Bakery	23	B3
Gill'd & Gutt'd	24	B1
Martin's IGA Supermarket	25	B3
Pickled Gecko	(see 18)	
Reef Café	26	B3
RSL Club	27	B2

DRINKING		
Cooktown Hotel	28	B3

To Lizard Island Group
(100km)

CORAL SEA

To Hope Islands
(37km)

Cherry Tree Bay

Grassy Hill Lighthouse

Grassy Hill
(162m)

Wharf

Endeavour River

Bicentennial Park

Chinaman Creek

Green St

Furneaux St

Walker St

Botanical Gardens

Finch Bay

Hogg St

Adelaide St

Charlotte St

Helen St

Hope St

John St

May St

Howard St

Garden St

Alligator Creek

McIvor Rd

Cooktown Developmental Rd

Hospital

Boundary St

Amos St

Ida St

Charles St

Melaleuca St

To Airfield (10km);
Endeavour Falls Tourist
Park (30km); Hope Vale (60km)

To Milkwood Lodge (2.5km);
Cooktown Car Hire; Keating's Lagoon
Conservation (Wulbabidgee) Park (5km);
Trevathen Falls (20km);
Black Mountain National Park (28km);
Bloomfield River (74km);
Lakeland (82km); Laura (148km);
Cairns (via Coast Rd) (243km);
Cairns (via Cooktown Developmental Rd) (335km)

To Mt Cook
National Park (1km)

0   500 m
0   0.3 miles

Nature's Powerhouse (☎ 4069 6004; www.natures
powerhouse.info; Walker St; ☺ 9am-5pm) Information
centre.

Sights & Activities

There are a few formal attractions in Cooktown, plus a number of natural settings that
are well worth the legwork or 4WD trip
involved to reach them.

Nature's Powerhouse (☎ 4069 6004; www.natures
powerhouse.info; Walker St; both galleries adult/child $2/free;
☺ 9am-5pm) is an environment interpretive
and information centre at the edge of Cooktown's public **Botanic Gardens**. The Powerhouse has an information stand, a bookstore
and a café, plus two excellent galleries. The
Charlie Tanner Gallery is dedicated to Cooktown's 'snake man' – Charlie's backyard pets
included venomous snakes that he milked to
make anti-venins, and crocodiles. The gallery displays pickled and preserved exhibits
of only-on-the-Cape wildlife (such as the
nightmare-inducing bare-backed fruit bat)
and inspirational stories from Taipan-bite
survivors. The **Vera Scarth-Johnson Gallery** is a
collection of intricate and beautiful botanical
illustrations of the region's native plants. Nature's Powerhouse hands out the *Cooktown
Heritage & Scenic Rim* flyer, which details the
gamut of the town's excellent **walking trails**.

Cooktown's major formal attraction is
the **James Cook Historical Museum** (☎ 4069 5386;
cnr Helen & Furneaux Sts; adult/child $7/2.50; ☺ 9.30am-
4pm). Built as a convent in 1889, the mu-
seum displays relics from Cook's time in
the town, including journal entries, and
the cannon and anchor from the *Endeavour*. Photographs, artefacts and interpretive
panels explain other topics that are influ-
ential to the shaping of Cooktown, such as
indigenous Guugu Yimithirr Bama culture,
the gold rush and Chinese presence.

The **Grassy Hill Lookout** has sensational 360-
degree views of the town, river and ocean.
Captain Cook climbed this hill looking for
a passage out through the reefs. At the top
sits a compact, corrugated, 19th-century
iron lighthouse. A 1½km walking trail (45
minutes) leads from the summit down to
the beach at Cherry Tree Bay.

The **Cooktown Cemetery** on McIvor Rd has
a walking trail leading to the Jewish and
Chinese sections, giving an indication of the
earlier multicultural nature of the town. A
tall palm tree marks the site of Mary Watson's

grave (see the boxed text on p392); there's
also a **monument** in Bicentennial Park.

Charlotte St and Bicentennial Park have a
number of interesting monuments, including the much-photographed bronze **Captain
Cook statue**. There's also the rock (marking
the spot where the *Endeavour* careened) and
Queen's Steps. Next to this, the **Milbi Wall
(Story Wall)** tells the story of European contact
from the local Gungarde indigenous community's perspective. The 12m-long mosaic
begins with creation stories and moves to
European contact up to WWII through to
recent attempts at reconciliation. Captain
Cook's 1770 landing is re-enacted here every
June over the Queen's Birthday weekend.

Off Cooktown Development Rd, 5km
from Cooktown, is **Keatings Lagoon Conservation (Mulbabidgee) Park**, a woodland with
melaleuca swamps frequented by birds,
particularly in the dry season; there's a bird
hide and 1½km (30 minutes) walking trail.

Shhhh: 4WDers listen-up; **Trevathen Falls**
is a hidden treasure, with a safe, secluded
swimming hole under the forest canopy.
From Cooktown, head south, turning left
at Mt Amos Rd. After about 9km you'll see
a track to your right; take it for about 1km
until you reach a fork. Take the right-hand
path for about 2km until you reach a gate.
Don't go through the gate, turn left, which
will lead you to the falls. Take a picnic and
your swimming costume. It's divine.

Tours

Limited tours operate from November to
at least April. All water-based tours depart
from the wharf; pick-ups can be arranged
for other tours unless stated otherwise.

Barts Bush Adventures (☎ 4069 6229; bartbush@
tpg.com.au; tours adult/child $165/85) Runs a variety of
tours, including the Bush & Beach, which goes to Coloured
Sands and Elim Beach, and the Miner's Adventure with
accredited savannah guides.

Catch-a-Crab (☎ 4069 5381; cathyadams@fni.aunz
.com; per person from $95) Assumes a minimum of two.
Catch mud crabs while touring the Endeavour and Annan
Rivers; great for kids.

Cooktown Cruises (☎ 4069 5712; 2-hr cruises adult/
child $25/13) Scenic cruises up the Endeavour River; also
hires boats by the hour (from $23).

Cooktown Tours (☎ 4069 5125; www.cooktowntours
.com) Offers 1½-hour town tours (adult/child $20/12) and
half-day trips to Black Mountain and the Lion's Den Hotel
(adult/child $55/23); both depart daily at 9am.

GETTING AWAY FROM IT ALL

Visiting the **Hope Islands** means that there's just you and nature (and the odd passing boat). **East Hope** and **West Hope Islands** are sand cays 37km southeast of Cooktown. Both are national parks, which protects the hardy mangroves and shrub vegetation. West Hope is an important nesting site for pied-imperial pigeons: access is not permitted from 1 September to 31 March. Snorkelling is possible around both islands, but best on the leeward margin of the East Hope Island reef; beware of strong currents. East Hope Island has four camp sites, toilets, tables and fire places. Permits are required and there's a time limit on your stay; contact **Cooktown QPWS** (☎ 4069 5777; www.epa.qld.gov.au; Webber Esplanade; per person $4). Take drinking water, food and a fuel stove.

To get there you'll need to charter a boat; ask at **Cooktown Travel Centre** (☎ 4069 5446; cooktowntravel@bigpond.com; Charlotte St; ⏰ 8.30am-5pm Mon-Fri, 8.30-noon Sat) for details of charters operating at the time of your visit.

Gone Fishing (☎ 4069 5980; www.fishingcooktown .com; 4-hr tours from $75) River fishing tours; price is per person, with a minimum of two people. Private charters are also available; the larger the group the cheaper the cost per person.

Guurrbi Tours (☎ 4069 5166; williegordon@fni.aunz .com; 2-/4-hr tours $80/105, self-drive $55/70) Willie, a Nugal-warra elder, runs a unique tour that uses the physical landscape to describe the emotional landscape. The tour includes drinking water and perhaps a snack of green ants, and takes you to a number of rock-art sites. Book at Pam's Place, from where tours depart.

Marine Air Seaplanes (☎ 4069 5915; www.marine air.com.au) Offers scenic reef flights ($125 to $175) and an extraordinary Lizard Island tour ($330), which lands in Watson's Bay by seaplane. Tours depart from the airstrip.

Paradise Blue (☎ 0408-183 261; www.paradise-blue .com; snorkelling tours $110) Don't expect to battle other tour boats on the Great Barrier Reef from here. Sailing tours to the Reef or river, including fishing.

Festivals & Events

The **Cooktown Endeavour Festival** is held over the Queen's Birthday Weekend (early June) to commemorate Captain Cook's landing in 1770.

Sleeping

There's an even spread of accommodation catering to all budgets.

BUDGET

Pam's Place (☎ 4069 5166; www.cooktownhostel.com; cnr Charlotte & Boundary Sts; dm/s/d $20/40/50; 🖥 💻) This comfortable YHA-associated hostel has a leafy garden and an assortment of neurotic parrots. There are also four new self-contained units (two people $80). All facilities are top-notch, and management can provide loads of useful information about the area.

Alamanda Inn (☎ 4069 5203; phscott@tpg.com.au; cnr Hope & Howard Sts; guesthouse s/d $40/50, motel s/d $50/60, unit s/d $65/75; 🖥 💻) There's a range of functional accommodation on offer at the Alamanda. Rooms in the guesthouse share a bathroom and kitchen, while the motel rooms have bathrooms and the units have both bathrooms and kitchenettes.

Peninsula Caravan Park (☎ 4069 5107; fax 4069 5255; 64 Howard St; unpowered sites $18, s/d cabins $60/65) On the outskirts of the town at the eastern end of Howard St, this place has a lovely bush setting with stands of big, old paperbark and gum trees. The cabins are self-contained.

Tropical Breeze Caravan Park (☎ 4069 5417; fax 4069 5740; cnr Charlotte St & McIvor Rd; unpowered sites $16, d $55-80; 💻) The basic cabins here vary in price according to whether they have bathrooms; all have kitchens. The facilities include a small shop and two swimming pools.

Out of town, 30km northwest, the **Endeavour Falls Tourist Park** (☎ 4069 5431; Endeavour Valley Rd; unpowered/powered sites $18/20, s/d $60/75; 🖥) has a natural swimming hole and waterfalls at the rear of the property – nice. The grounds are well cushioned with grass, and self-contained cabins are fully equipped; there is a laundry and general store with fuel.

MIDRANGE & TOP END

Hillcrest B&B (☎ 4069 5305; www.hillcrestb-b.com; 130 Hope St; guesthouse s/d/tr $40/50/70, unit s/d $60/70; 🖥 💻) Backed by a secret garden concealed beneath large greenhouse awnings, this charming old-style guesthouse has basic rooms with a shared bathroom, and units with air-con and private bathrooms. Breakfast is an extra $5, and there's a beautiful outdoor area in which to eat it.

Seaview Motel (☎ 4069 5377; seaviewm@tpg
.com.au; Webber Esplanade; s/d from $75/85; ☒ ☒)
A low-rise motel stretching along prime
water frontage, the rooms here are tidy and
homely. There's an informal grassed area
in front of the rooms that makes a pleasant
gathering place around the pool.

Milkwood Lodge (☎ 4069 5007; www.milkwood
lodge.com; Annan Rd; s/d $90/110; ☒) Located about
2.5km south of town, these six breezy self-
contained timber-pole cabins have bushland oozing up between them, and there are
views from each private balcony. Cabins are
spacious and split-level.

Endeavour View (☎ 4069 5676; 168 Webber Esplanade; d $90; ☒) These safari-style cabins, each
with its own bathroom and front deck area,
are cheek by jowl. There's a large outdoor
spa to close your eyes and relax in – imagine that you're not sandwiched between
the cabins and main house. Breakfast is
optional, and $8 for two.

Seagren's Inn (☎ 4069 5357; Charlotte St; s/d $75/85)
Upstairs in a heritage home (that's home
to the Pickled Gecko restaurant), the rooms
here have spunk. Each is individually styled,
with lots of wood and high puffy beds. From
the open second-level veranda you can see
the Endeavour River's mouth open wide.

Cooktown River of Gold Motel (☎ 4069 5222; cnr
Hope & Walker Sts; r $80; ☒ ☒) You may exper-
ience *déjà vu* in these rooms, which are
straight out of the motel manual: inoffensive
décor, a bed, a bathroom – you know the
deal. There are laundry facilities, as well as
a room that's wheelchair-friendly. The big
home-cooked meals, available for lunch and
dinner, lift this place out of the ordinary.

Sovereign Resort (☎ 4069 5400; www.sovereign
-resort.com.au; cnr Charlotte & Green Sts; r $155-185;
☒ ☒) This swish resort is well equipped:
you could sleep, eat and drink there without
experiencing a smidge of Cooktown. Room
prices vary according to size, ranging from
a standard studio-style room up to a two-
bedroom apartment. The complex also contains the Balcony Restaurant & Café-Bar.

Eating & Drinking

Drinking is one of Cooktown's more popular pastimes, and there is a good number of
clubs and hotels that keep the amber fluid
flowing and the hot plate on high.

Gill'd & Gutt'd (☎ 4069 5863; Fisherman's Wharf,
Webber Esplanade; meals $8-17; ☒ lunch & dinner)
Drive up to the takeaway window of this
mighty fine fish and chippery and take
your hot paper parcel to the pier. These
are fancy fish and chips, with your choice
of barramundi or Spanish mackerel. Alternatively you can walk around to the riverside and dine in. The restaurant is licensed,
with waterfront tables highly sought after
(though the ambience is flat).

Bowls Club (☎ 4069 6173; Charlotte St; mains $12-20;
☒ dinner) Sign yourself in at the door, and
join the club for the night. Apart from
enormous, wholesome mains (such as fish
or steak) you're able to visit the salad bar as
often as you like, though you'd struggle to
go for seconds. The club fills up on weekends, when you might just win yourself a
meat tray in the raffle.

RSL Club (☎ 4069 5780; Charlotte St; mains $10-16;
☒ dinner) The word on Charlotte St is that
compared with the Bowls Club, the RSL meals
are not quite as good, though they're cheaper.
Try for yourself: you might be bowled over
by the bistro-style meals on offer here.

Pickled Gecko (☎ 4069 5357; Charlotte St; mains
$16-28; ☒ lunch & dinner Apr-Sep) This licensed
café offers Mod Oz cuisine in smart surrounds, downstairs from the Seagren's Inn.
Thankfully the café's namesake appears
only on the walls, not on the menu.

Balcony Restaurant & Café-Bar (☎ 4069 5400; cnr
Charlotte & Green Sts; mains $10-28; ☒ breakfast, lunch &
dinner) The Sovereign Resort has the formal
dining option of the Balcony Restaurant,
serving breakfast and dinner, as well as the
casual Café-Bar, which serves light meals
and coffee. Both are licensed, and the Balcony's balcony has views over the river.

Reef Café (☎ 4069 5361; Charlotte St; dishes $5-10;
☒ breakfast, lunch & dinner) If you're in a hurry
you can take away that hamburger or hot
dog, or you can eat it on the covered balcony around the side. Reef Café also fries
up fish and chips and bakes pizza; it has a
giant fridge full of ice-cold fizzy drinks and
a glass counter with mixed lollies.

Cooktown Hotel (☎ 4069 5308; Charlotte St; mains
$10-15; lunch & dinner) Known as the Top Pub,
this large hotel has character on tap and
makes a pleasant place to prop for a while.
There are pool tables and basic counter
meals are also available.

Don't miss having a sandwich made of
home-baked bread and stuffed full of fresh
ingredients from **Cooktown Bakery** (☎ 4069 5612;

cnr Hogg & Charlotte Sts; ✆ 8am-4pm); it also makes delicious cakes. Stock up on supplies at **Martin's IGA supermarket** (☎ 4069 5633; cnr Helen & Hogg Sts; ✆ 8am-6pm Mon-Sat, 10am-3pm Sun).

Getting There & Around

If you don't have your own vehicle, consider coming to Cooktown on a tour from Cairns (see p336).

Sun Palm (☎ 4084 2626; www.sunpalmtransport .com) travels up and down both the coastal and inland routes to Cairns ($70, Tuesday to Sunday). It's possible to hop on and off along the way – stopping in Port Douglas and Mossman.

Cooktown's airfield is 10km west of town along McIvor Rd. **Skytrans** (☎ 1800 818 405, 4046 2462; www.skytrans.com.au) flies twice a day between Cooktown and Cairns (adult/child $107/54, 45 minutes).

To get to sights outside town, **Cooktown Car Hire** (☎ 4069 5007; www.cooktown-car-hire.com; Milkwood Rainforest Lodge) rents 4WDs from $100 to $150 per day, with a $2200 bond.

For a taxi call ☎ 4069 5387.

LIZARD ISLAND GROUP

The islands of the Lizard Island Group are clustered just 27km off the coast about 100km from Cooktown. **Lizard Island** is a continental island with a dry, rocky and mountainous terrain. It has about 20 superb beaches for swimming and relatively untouched fringing reef for snorkelling and diving. Bushwalking is another possibility, with great views from Cook's Look (360m), the highest point on the island. Apart from the ground where the luxury resort stands, the entire island is national park, which means it's open to anyone who makes the effort to get here.

There are four other smaller islands in the Lizard group. **Osprey Island**, with its nesting birds, is right in front of the resort and can be waded to. Around the edge of Blue Lagoon, south of the main island, are **Palfrey Island**, with an automatic lighthouse, and **South Island** – both have beaches accessible by dinghy. **Seabird Islet**, further south, is a popular nesting site for terns, and visitors should keep their distance.

History

The traditional custodians, the Dingaal people, know Lizard Island as Jiigurru. In the Dingaal creation story, the island group is associated with the stingray – with Jiigurru forming the head and the other islands snaking south forming the tail. Historically, the Dingaal used the islands as a place for important meetings and initiation ceremonies; they were also used as a base for collecting shellfish, fish, turtles and dugongs.

Captain Cook and his crew were the first nonindigenous people to visit Lizard Island. Having successfully patched up the *Endeavour* in Cooktown, they sailed north and stopped on Lizard Island, where Cook and the botanist Joseph Banks climbed to the top of what's now known as Cook's Look, to search for a way through the Barrier Reef maze and out to the open sea. Banks named the island after its large lizards, known as

---

WORLDS COLLIDE

For 3000 years the Dingaal people have viewed Jiigurru (Lizard Island) as a sacred place. Shell middens found on the island date back that far, and later records from Cook note the presence of aboriginal huts. The island group is also a spiritual place, with its own creation story and symbology.

In 1881 Robert and Mary Watson settled on the island to collect bêche-de-mer, a noted Chinese delicacy. They built a small, granite cottage overlooking the southern end of what is now Watson's Bay. In September of that year, Robert Watson left the island to search for new fishing grounds, leaving Mary Watson with their baby, Ferrier, and two Chinese workers, Ah Sam and Ah Leong. In October a group of Dingaal people arrived on the island and attacked the group, killing Ah Leong and wounding Ah Sam. The following day Mary Watson fled the island and, with a few supplies, the baby and Ah Sam, paddled away in a bêche-de-mer boiling tank.

For 10 days they drifted from coral cay to island to reef to mangrove swamp, signalling unsuccessfully to passing steamers, all the while suffering from dehydration. Their bodies were found on No 5 Howick Island, east of Cape Flattery, in January 1882. During this ordeal Mary kept a diary (now held at the Queensland Museum in Brisbane), which reveals a brave and surprisingly calm reaction to her situation. The ruined walls of the stone cottage can still be seen on the island.

Gould's monitors, which are from the same family as Indonesia's Komodo dragons.

Sights & Activities

Lizard Island's **beaches** are nothing short of sensational, and range from long stretches of white sand to idyllic little rocky bays. The water is crystal clear and magnificent coral surrounds the island – snorkelling here is superb.

Immediately south of the resort are three postcard beaches – Sunset, Pebbly and Hibiscus Beaches. Watson's Bay to the north of the resort is a wonderful stretch of sand with great snorkelling at both ends and with a giant-clam garden in-between. There are also plenty of other choices right around the island.

The island is noted for its **diving**. There are good dives right off the island, and the outer Barrier Reef is less than 20km away, including two of Australia's best known dive sites; **Cod Hole** and **Pixie Bommie**. The resort offers a full range of diving facilities to its guests, and some live-aboard tours from Cairns dive the Cod Hole.

The climb to the top of **Cook's Look** is a great walk (three hours return). Near the top there are traces of stones marking an Aboriginal ceremonial area. The trail, which starts from the northern end of Watson's Bay near the camp site, is clearly signposted and, although it can be steep and a bit of a clamber at times, it's easy to follow. The views from the top are sensational, and on a clear day you can see the opening in the Reef where Cook made his exit.

The **Lizard Island Research Station** (☎ 4060 3977; www.lizardisland.net.au) is a permanent research facility that has examined topics as diverse as marine organisms for cancer research, the deaths of giant clams, coral reproductive processes, sea-bird ecology, and life patterns of reef fish during their larval stage. The station runs a one-hour tour on Monday at 11am for the island's visitors. It also runs week-long volunteer programmes – contact the station for details.

Lizard Island has plenty of **wildlife**. There are 11 different species of lizards, including Gould's monitors, which can be up to 1m long. More than 40 species of birds have also been recorded on the island and a dozen or so actually nest there, including the beautiful little sunbirds with their long, hanging nests. Bar-shouldered doves, crested terns, Caspian terns and a variety of other terns, oystercatchers and large sea eagles are other resident species.

Sleeping & Eating

Accommodation is only available on Lizard Island, and the choice is extreme – camping or five-star luxury.

Lizard Island Resort (☎ 1800 737 678, 4060 3999; www.lizardisland.com.au; Anchor Bay; s/d from $1025/1530; ✕ ▣) You don't have to be a rock star to stay here, but judging by recent guests – Tiger Woods and Al Gore – an uncanny ability for sport or politics would help. With a maximum of 80 guests in 40 villas, a menu that changes daily, and spa treatments that are inspired from the sea, this is a genuine island retreat. Rooms have designer décor, a private deck, books for all those hours on the beach, and bathrobes. Rates include all meals and a range of activities.

The **camping ground** is at the northern end of Watson's Bay; contact **QPWS** (☎ 4069 5777; www.epa.qld.gov.au; per person $4) in Cooktown or go online to obtain a permit. There are toilets, gas BBQs, tables and benches, and fresh water is available from a pump about 250m from the site. Campers should bring all supplies with them as there are no shops on the island.

Getting There & Away

Macair (☎ 13 15 28; www.macair.com.au) flies to Lizard Island from Cairns ($260, one hour), and from Cooktown **Marine Air Seaplanes** (☎ 4069 5915; Charlotte St) has day tours to Lizard Island ($330), flying into Watson's Bay and walking to the top of Cook's Look. The tour includes lunch and snorkelling gear; camping drop-off can also be arranged.

The fishing and boat-hire places in Cooktown also offer personalised charters and may be able to take you over. Ask at the **Travel Centre** (☎ 4069 5446; Charlotte St).

Cape York Peninsula & Gulf Savannah

CAPE YORK PENINSULA & GULF SAVANNAH

HIGHLIGHTS

- Exploring the remote and wild **Lakefield National Park** (p399), wetland home to estuarine crocodiles and a multitude of water birds
- Marvelling at the Aboriginal rock art at **Split Rock and Guguyalangi galleries** (p400), near Laura, Cape York
- Celebrating the end of the epic journey to reach the **Tip of Australia** (p404)
- Paddling the clean spring waters under the 60m sandstone walls of Lawn Hill Gorge in **Boodjamulla (Lawn Hill) National Park** (p414)
- Riding the quaint and anachronistic **Gulflander** (p408) train between Normanton and Croydon
- Probing the depths of the fascinating lava tubes at **Undara Volcanic National Park** (p408)
- Watching serene tropical sunsets and 'morning glory' roll clouds in the colourful Gulf port of **Karumba** (p411)

★ Tip of Australia
★ Lakefield National Park
★ Split Rock and Guguyalangi Galleries
★ Karumba
★ Croydon
★ Undara Volcanic National Park
★ Boodjamulla (Lawn Hill) National Park

- www.cypda.com.au
- www.gulf-savannah.com.au

The Cape and Gulf country are true frontiers, beckoning the adventurous traveller. Mainly undeveloped, this is a landscape of climatic extremes, challenging and beautiful scenery and inimitable characters. While many of the region's sights can be accessed by conventional vehicle or a regional flight, a well-equipped 4WD throws open the door to adventure.

The overland pilgrimage to the Tip of Australia is one of the greatest 4WD routes on the continent. The Cape boasts big crocs, vehicle- and character-testing roads, tropical rainforests and wetlands that rival Kakadu with their rich birdlife. Only well-prepared expeditions make a success of it. Yet it's not about making a dash to the Tip and back; many of the highlights of this journey are found on the detours, planned and unexpected, and simply by experiencing the isolation and wilderness.

Running west from the Cape across to the Northern Territory border, the Gulf Savannah is a vast, flat and empty landscape of tropical grasslands, shimmering horizons, saltpans and impenetrable mangroves. Connecting the scattering of historic mines, gem-fossicking centres, geological wonders and colourful fishing towns are the vital but tenuous Gulf roads. Dusty, corrugated, narrow and arrow straight, these infamous thoroughfares are monstered by 60m road trains and crossed by jaywalking cattle; they frequently become an impassable quagmire or are cut by flood waters in the wet season.

Climate

Though most of the rain in northern Queensland falls in the period from January to March, vehicle movement will intermittently be restricted on Cape York and in parts of the Gulf Savannah during the whole wet season, roughly from November to May. The best time to tackle a Cape trip is early in the dry season, generally from the beginning of June. The country is still green, there are fewer travellers and the roads are less chopped up than later in the season. The peak travel period is June to September, with the last travellers generally out of the Cape by mid-November.

Likewise, travel is not recommended in the Gulf Savannah between the beginning of December and the end of March. Extreme heat and humidity make conditions uncomfortable and potentially dangerous, and heavy rain can close roads for lengthy periods. The best time to visit the Gulf is also during the winter months, when you will encounter cool mornings and warm days.

If you plan to visit early or late in the season, it pays to check what the roads are like. Calling local police, national park rangers or roadhouses is recommended. You should also make use of the recorded **RACQ Road Reports** (☎ 1300 130 595; www.racq.com.au).

CAPE YORK PENINSULA

Bordered to the east by the Coral Sea and to the west by the Gulf of Carpentaria, Cape York covers around 207,000 sq km but has only around 16,000 people – it's a true frontier. Most of the peninsula is a low-lying patchwork of tropical savannah overlaid by wild, snaking rivers and streams, while along its eastern flank is the elevated northern section of the Great Dividing Range, whose northernmost tip ends in Dauan, a remote outer island of Torres Strait.

The largest towns in the region are Cooktown to the southeast, Weipa, a large mining community on the central-western coast, Bamaga near the tip, and Thursday Island in Torres Strait. A handful of smaller towns and cattle stations make up the remainder of the communities throughout the Cape.

Information

The foremost consideration of a Cape trip is good preparation. Before heading off

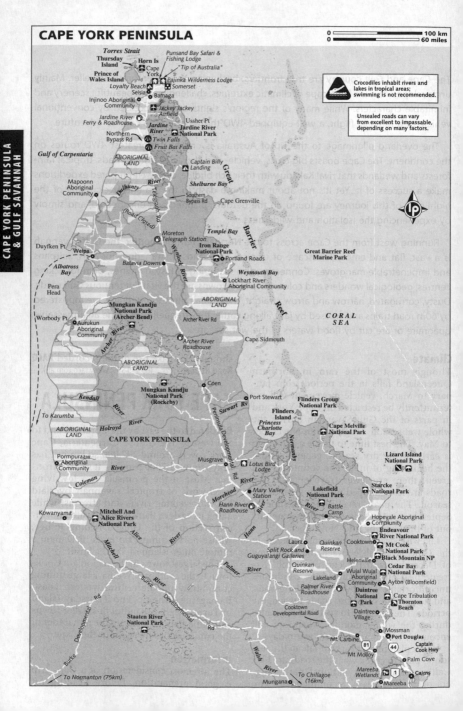

CAPE YORK PENINSULA

0 ————————— 100 km
0 ————————— 60 miles

Crocodiles inhabit rivers and lakes in tropical areas; swimming is not recommended.

Unsealed roads can vary from excellent to impassable, depending on many factors.

Torres Strait
Thursday Island
Horn Is
Cape York
Prince of Wales Island
Punsand Bay Safari & Fishing Lodge
"Tip of Australia"
Pajinka Wilderness Lodge
Loyalty Beach
Somerset
Seisia
Bamaga
Injinoo Aboriginal Community
Jackey Jackey Airfield
Jardine River Ferry & Roadhouse
Jardine River
Ussher Pt
Jardine River National Park
Northern Bypass Rd
Twin Falls
Fruit Bat Falls
Gulf of Carpentaria
Captain Billy Landing
Great Barrier Reef
ABORIGINAL LAND
Delhunty River
Shelburne Bay
Mapoonn Aboriginal Community
Southern Bypass Rd
Cape Grenville
Telegraph Rd
(Road Closed)
Moreton Telegraph Station
Temple Bay
Iron Range National Park
Duyfken Pt
Welpa
Wenlock River
Portland Roads
Great Barrier Reef Marine Park
Batavia Downs
Weymouth Bay
Lockhart River Aboriginal Community
Albatross Bay
Pera Head
ABORIGINAL LAND
Reef
CORAL SEA
Worbody Pt
Aurukun Aboriginal Community
Mungkan Kandju National Park (Archer Bend)
Archer River
Archer River Rd
Cape Sidmouth
ABORIGINAL LAND
Archer River Roadhouse
Kendall River
Coen
Flinders Group National Park
Mungkan Kandju National Park (Rockehy)
Port Stewart
Flinders Island
Cape Melville National Park
Holroyd River
Stewart Rv
Princess Charlotte Bay
Normanby
ABORIGINAL LAND
CAPE YORK PENINSULA
Lizard Island National Park
Pormpuraaw Aboriginal Community
Peninsula Developmental Rd
Musgrave
Lotus Bird Lodge
River
Coleman River
Starcke National Park
To Karumba
Morehead River
Lakefield National Park
Kowanyama
Mitchell And Alice Rivers National Park
Mary Valley Station
Hann River Roadhouse
Hann River
Battle Camp
Hopevale Aboriginal Community
Endeavour River National Park
Alice River
Laura
Quinkan Reserve
Cooktown
Mt Cook National Park
Mitchell River
Split Rock and Guguyalangi Galleries
Black Mountain NP
Helenvale
Cedar Bay National Park
Burke Developmental Rd
Palmer River
Quinkan Reserve
Lakeland
Wujal Wujal Aboriginal Community
Ayton (Bloomfield)
Palmer River Roadhouse
Daintree National Park
Cape Tribulation
Thornton Beach
Staaten River National Park
Cooktown Developmental Road
Daintree Village
Mossman
Port Douglas
Mt Carbine
81
Captain Cook Hwy
44
To Normanton (75km)
Walsh River
Mt Molloy
Palm Cove
To Chillagoe (16km)
Mungana
Mareeba Wetlands
1
Cairns
Mareeba

CAPE YORK PENINSULA & GULF SAVANNAH

to each new destination on the peninsula, seek expert advice on routes from police, national-park rangers, locals or other travellers, and make sure you're carrying at least one of the recommended maps.

You need all the usual gear for travelling in a remote area, including a first-aid kit, and you *must* carry food and water. Although you will cross a number of rivers south of the Archer River, water can be scarce along the main track, especially late in the dry season, and you can only pick up basic food provisions along the way.

It's also vital that you make sure your vehicle is in good condition for the trip, and carry spares, tools and equipment and recovery gear. If you do break down or get stuck, it's a long way between mechanics, and repair work will be costly.

EMERGENCY

As well as emergency assistance, the following police stations can provide up-to-date information to travellers on road conditions:

Bamaga (☎ 4069 3156)
Coen (☎ 4060 1150)
Cooktown (☎ 4069 5320)
Hopevale Aboriginal (☎ 4060 9224)
Laura (☎ 4060 3244)
Lockhart River Aboriginal Community (☎ 4060 7120)
Weipa (☎ 4069 9119)

MAPS & BOOKS

The Hema maps *Cape York & Lakefield National Park* and the RACQ maps *Cairns/Townsville* and *Cape York Peninsula* are the best. Ron and Viv Moon's *Cape York – an Adventurer's Guide* is the most comprehensive guide for 4WD and camping enthusiasts. Lonely Planet's *Outback Australia* also has extensive coverage of this region.

MEDICAL SERVICES

Hospitals and medical clinics on Cape York Peninsula include:

Bamaga (☎ 4069 3166) Hospital.
Coen (☎ 4060 1166) Clinic.
Cooktown (☎ 4069 5433) Hospital.
Laura (☎ 4060 3320) Clinic.
Weipa (☎ 4069 9155) Hospital.

MONEY

Banking facilities are very limited on Cape York, and full banking facilities are only available at Cooktown, Weipa and Thursday Island. Credit cards including MasterCard and Visa are widely accepted, although cash advances may be difficult. Eftpos is readily available in roadhouses and general stores and at some accommodation.

PERMITS

Once you are north of the Dulhunty River you will need a permit to camp on Aboriginal land, which in effect is nearly all the land north of the river. The Injinoo people are the traditional custodians of much of this land and the Injinoo Aboriginal Community who run the ferry across the Jardine River include a camping permit in the ferry fee.

Travelling across Aboriginal land elsewhere on the Cape may require an additional permit which you can obtain by contacting the relevant community council. The **Balkanu Cape York Development Corporation** (www.balkanu.com.au) website lists contact details for all the Cape York Aboriginal communities.

TOURIST INFORMATION

In Cairns, **Tourism Tropical North Queensland** (☎ 4031 7676; www.tnq.org.au; 51 The Esplanade, Cairns; 🕑 8.30am-6.30pm) can provide tour and travel information before you head off. There are no official tourist information centres along the route to the tip of Cape York, although you'll find information readily available in the roadhouses, towns and camping grounds along the way.

You should also visit the **Queensland Parks and Wildlife Service** (QPWS; www.epa.qld.gov.au) in Cairns (p332) and Cooktown (p388) when planning your trip.

Dangers & Annoyances

You are entering crocodile country, so while there are plenty of safe places to swim, be aware that many stretches of water can hold a big hungry saltie. If in doubt, don't swim.

The most common accidents on the Cape are head-on collisions in the heath country south of the Jardine River. The track is narrow here with many blind corners and people often travel too fast. Keep in mind that there's a lot of traffic on these roads during the dry season.

Tours

There's a host of tour operators who can organise your trip to the Cape. Four-wheel drive tours are the most popular and generally range from six to 16 days, travelling with five to 12 passengers, and taking in Cooktown, Laura, the Split Rock and Guguyalangi Galleries, Lakefield National Park, Coen, Weipa, the Elliot River (including Twin Falls), Bamaga, Somerset and Cape York itself. Many 4WD trips also visit Thursday Island (often an optional extra).

Most companies kick their tour off from Cairns (but also see Cooktown-based tours on p389), and offer a range of transport options, such as flying or sailing one way and travelling overland the other. Most also offer the choice of camping or motel accommodation. Prices are inclusive of all meals, accommodation and fares from Cairns:

Billy Tea Bush Safaris (☎ 4032 0077; www.billytea .com.au; 9-day fly/drive tours $2100, 13-day cruise/drive tours $2200, 14-day overland tours $2200) An experienced operator, Billy Tea offers many tours and options including a luxurious 'Seafari'.

Cape York Air (☎ 4035 9399; www.capeyorkair.com .au) Operates the Peninsula Mail Run, the world's longest mail run, to remote Cape York communities.

Daintree Air Services (☎ 1800 246 206, 4034 9300; www.daintreeair.com.au; day tours $800) Do the Tip in a day from Cairns. Airfare, lunch, 4WD and guide are included. See p336.

Exploring Oz (☎ 1300 888 112, 4093 8347; www .exploring-oz.com.au; 6-day overland tours $800-1000) The six-day trip takes in Musgrave Station, Coen, Wenlock River, Loyalty Beach, the Tip and Twin Falls.

Guides to Adventure (☎ 4091 1978; www.guides toadventure.com.au; 12-/16-/22-day Cape York tours $1125/1500/2055) These are 4WD tag-along safaris, which means you need to bring your own 4WD vehicle and tent. The company supplies guides, catering, permits etc.

Heritage Tours (☎ 4038 2628; www.heritagetours .com.au; 6-day fly/drive tours from $1580; 9-day cruise/ drive tours from $1850) Numerous tours and accommodation options are offered.

Oz Tours Safaris (☎ 1800 079 006, 4055 9535; www .oztours.com.au; 7-day fly/drive tours $1750, 12-day overland tours $2300) Numerous tours, air/sea/overland options, and camping or motel options.

Wilderness Challenge (☎ 4035 4488; www.wilder ness-challenge.com.au; 7-day camping tours $1695, 7-day fly/drive tours $2600) Huge range of camping and accommodation options.

Getting There & Around
AIR
QantasLink (☎ 13 13 13; www.qantas.com.au) flies daily from Cairns to Horn Island ($436) and

Weipa ($230). **Skytrans** (☎ 1800 818 405; www .skytrans.com.au), based in Cairns, has flights from Cairns to Coen and Yorke Island, and various flights around the Cape, as well as a charter service.

BOAT
MV Trinity Bay (☎ 4035 1234; www.seaswift.com.au) runs a weekly cargo ferry to Thursday Island and Bamaga, which takes up to 38 passengers. It departs Cairns every Friday and reaches Thursday Island on Sunday. The five-day return trip costs from $840 per person twin share and includes meals.

CAR & MOTORCYCLE
From Cairns to the top of Cape York is 952km via the shortest and most challenging route. However, there are a host of worthy diversions on this route, including Lakefield and Iron Range National Parks, and these will add considerably to the total distance covered.

The first 175km of the Peninsula Developmental Rd from Mareeba is sealed. The journey from Lakeland to Weipa is nearly 600km of well-formed, unsealed road. You can either travel straight up the heart of the Cape or go via Cooktown and through Lakefield National Park to Laura or Musgrave. Initially, the corrugated Peninsula Developmental Rd cuts its way right through the middle of the Cape, turning west to get to the mining town of Weipa. As you head further north of the Weipa turn-off, the real adventure begins along the Telegraph Rd (also known as the Overland Telegraph Track) to Cape York. The creek crossings become more numerous and more challenging, and this is pure 4WD territory. Further north you have the choice of continuing on Telegraph Rd or taking the bypass roads. The bypass roads are better maintained and usually in better condition than Telegraph Rd, but always check road conditions with locals and other travellers.

LAKELAND TO MUSGRAVE
Lakeland to Laura
The Peninsula Developmental Rd turns off the Cairns-to-Cooktown Developmental Rd at Lakeland. From there you're on your way to Laura and Cape York on a formed dirt road with sections of sealed

DETOUR

The 275km route from Cooktown to Musgrave via Lakefield National Park is a great alternative to the main road north. This route, however, is very isolated, without any facilities or fuel stops along the way, and you must carry enough water to get between the permanent water points.

Leaving Cooktown on the McIvor Rd, **Endeavour Falls** is reached after just 33km. Here there's a good, year-round swimming hole and a tourist park with a grocery store and fuel. At the 36km mark is the turn-off for Battle Camp and Lakefield.

Continue straight on (north) to get to the **Hopevale Aboriginal Community** (☎ 4060 9133; cwpp.slq.qld.gov.au/hopevale). Alternatively, turn northwest to continue to **Battle Camp**. About 5km further on there is a stony river crossing and magical **Isabella Falls** – well worth a stop and a cooling swim.

Keep left at the next junction 2.5km up the road. From here the road begins to climb through patches of rainforest. The Normanby River is crossed 66km from Cooktown. Early in the dry season this river may still be flowing. Keep on the main track heading west, and 18km from the river crossing you pass the turn-off to **Battle Camp Homestead**. Battle Camp was the site of a major battle in 1873 during the Palmer River gold rush. A large group of Aborigines attacked a party of diggers and police, but were overpowered by gunfire.

Less than 3km further on you enter **Lakefield National Park**. Lakefield is the second-largest national park in Queensland and covers more than 537,000 hectares. It encompasses a wide variety of country around the flood plains of the Normanby, Kennedy, Bizant, Morehead and Hann Rivers. During the wet season these rivers flood the plains, at times forming a small inland sea. As the dry season begins, the rivers retreat to form a chain of deep waterholes and billabongs where birds and other wildlife congregate.

The Laura River is crossed 25km from the park boundary (112km from Cooktown). The **Old Laura Homestead** is on the far bank. Just past the homestead, and within 1km of the river crossing, you reach a T-junction. Turning left here will take you south to Laura (see p400), 28km away, the nearest place for fuel and supplies.

To continue to Musgrave and deeper into the Lakefield National Park, turn right at the T-junction. The **QPWS ranger station** (☎ 4060 3260) at New Laura Homestead is 25km north of the junction. After another 33km, you pass another ranger station at **Lakefield Homestead** (☎ 4060 3271). About 3km before the ranger station is a turn-off for Kalpowar Crossing, an excellent camping ground with facilities and lots of birdlife.

The first turn-off to Bizant, another **QPWS ranger station** (☎ 4060 3258), is 15km past the Lakefield Ranger Station. About 10km further on is the Hann Crossing of the North Kennedy River. Downstream from the crossing are waterfalls dropping into a large pool. The river is tidal to the base of the falls and swimming here is not advised!

The turn-off to **Low Lake**, a spectacular bird habitat, is found 28km on from the crossing. Continue straight ahead and in less than 2km you'll reach **Saltwater Creek Crossing**. The road then swings southwest as it begins to head towards Musgrave. Stay left at the next few track junctions, as the tracks on the right lead to Marina Plains Station. You leave the national park 16km west of Saltwater Creek, and 34km later you will hit the Peninsula Developmental Rd, opposite Musgrave.

Twenty-six kilometres before Musgrave, **Lotus Bird Lodge** (☎ 1800 674 974, 4060 3295; www.cairns .aust.com/lotusbird; r $195) has accommodation in comfortable, timber cabins, an in-house naturalist, guided walks and a four-star chef. There are fly-in packages available from Cairns and room rates include meals and tours. The lodge operates only in the dry season.

road, and this is about as good as the run north gets.

Just after the Kennedy River crossing, the **Ang-Gnarra Festival Ground** (☎ 4060 3200; unpowered sites $10) has self-registration camping with hot showers and a camp kitchen. The place is overflowing during the biennial **Laura Aboriginal Dance and Cultural Festival**.

About 50km north of Lakeland is the turn-off to the **Split Rock and Guguyalangi Galleries**, magnificent Aboriginal rock art sites (see the boxed text on p400).

Laura

About 12km on from the Split Rock galleries is Laura, a good place to sink in a beer at the pub, have a chat with the locals and explore the surrounding area. From here you can easily visit Lakefield National Park and the Split Rock galleries.

The **Laura Store & Post Office** (☎ 4060 3238), next to the pub, sells a range of groceries, including fruit and veggies, ice, gas and fuel. The historic, corrugated-iron **Quinkan Hotel** (☎ /fax 4060 3255; unpowered/powered sites $12/20, dm $15, s $40) is jammed with character, and has clean, simple rooms and good-value meals. The camping ground is next to the pub and prices are for two people.

Located 42km west of Laura by 4WD, **Jowalbinna Bush Camp** (☎ 4060 3236; Maytown Track) offers camping and accommodation and excellent guided day walks to rock-art sites.

Laura to Musgrave

North from Laura, most of the creek crossings will be dry, but early in the season some may still have water in them. Some of these crossings, such as the Little Laura and Kennedy Rivers, are great places to camp.

On the banks of the Hann River, 76km north of Laura, the **Hann River Roadhouse** (☎ 4060 3242; Peninsula Developmental Rd; powered sites $14, r $25, mains $10-15) sells fuel, groceries and takeaways, does minor vehicle repairs and has a licensed restaurant.

Twenty kilometres from the roadhouse, there's a turn-off east for **Mary Valley Station** (☎ 4060 3254; unpowered sites $12, s/d $30/45), a cattle property offering camp sites, homestead rooms and meals. The station, 6km off the main road, has one of the largest colonies of little red flying foxes in the world – an amazing sight when they take flight in the late evening.

From here to Musgrave it's 61km (one hour). A few bad creek crossings and nasty dips will keep your speed down.

Musgrave

There is only one main building in Musgrave: the historic **Musgrave Telegraph Station** (☎ /fax 4060 3229; unpowered sites $12, s/d $40/50).

QUINKAN ART

Quinkan is one of the great art styles of northern Australia. Vastly different to the X-ray art of Arnhem Land in the Northern Territory, or the Wandjina art of the Kimberley in Western Australia, Quinkan art is named after human-shaped spirit figures with unusually shaped heads.

More than 1200 galleries have been discovered in the escarpment country south of Laura. The rock art is difficult to date, although Aboriginal people have been living in the Laura area for at least 33,000 years. Most of the existing paintings are comparatively younger; in a couple of galleries, images of horses echo the European invasion. The Quinkan artists were killed by settlers or disease during the 1873 Palmer River gold rush, and much mystery still surrounds this art.

Only the Split Rock and Guguyalangi (the Northern Art sites) galleries are open to the public. There are a number of overhangs in the Split Rock group of galleries, and while Split Rock itself is the most visually stunning, there are smaller galleries containing flying foxes, tall Quinkans and hand stencils. The Guguyalangi group of galleries consists of more than a dozen overhangs adorned with a vast array of figures, animals and implements.

A walking trail leads from the car park at Split Rock, past the galleries in this group and then up onto the plateau to a lookout at Turtle Rock. The view from here is stunning. From this point the trail wanders through the open forest of the plateau for 1km to the Guguyalangi group. If you're going to do this walk, save it for the late afternoon or early morning – the plateau bakes in the midday sun – and take water and food.

Percy Trezise, a pilot, artist, historian and amateur archaeologist, opened the sites to the world in the 1960s. Trezise established the wilderness reserve, Jowalbinna Bush Camp, which specialises in guided walking trips to the Quinkan galleries.

For more information on Quinkan art, visit the **Ang-Gnarra Visitor Centre** (☎ 4090 3200) in Laura.

There is a fee of $5 to visit Split Rock, and $10 to do the entire loop (there's a box by the rangers station). No videos or cameras are allowed in the galleries, and you should not touch the painted and engraved surfaces.

Built in 1887, it's now a licensed café and roadhouse selling fuel, basic groceries and takeaway food. Its rooms are simple and its camp sites have showers.

From near here, tracks run east to the Lakefield National Park or west to Edward River and the Pormpuraaw Aboriginal Community.

MUSGRAVE TO ARCHER RIVER

About 95km north of Musgrave you come to a road junction. The better, newer road leads left to Coen, while the older, rougher road swings right, crossing the **Stewart River** twice before reaching Coen. With little traffic, the first crossing of the Stewart River makes a fine camp site. The old road also gives access to **Port Stewart** on the eastern coast of the Cape, with reasonable bush camping and good fishing.

Coen is the 'capital' of the Cape, and unless you take the turn-off into Weipa, it is the biggest town you'll see north of Cooktown. There's a pub, two general stores, a hospital, police station and a couple of accommodation options. **Homestead Guest House** (☎ 4060 1157; s/tw $40/60) has clean, comfortable rooms with ceiling fans and shared bathrooms. The **Exchange Hotel** (☎ 4060 1133; fax 4060 1180; s/d from $40/60; 🌊) has pub rooms with shared bathrooms or motel rooms with their own. **Coen Camping Ground** (☎ 4060 1134; unpowered/powered sites $12/14) has hot showers and toilets; prices are for two people.

For the first 23km north of Coen the road is well maintained, but once you pass the Coen airfield it deteriorates. About 2km past the airfield you reach the main access track to **Mungkan Kandju National Park**. This park straddles much of the Archer River and its tributaries. The **ranger station** (☎ 4060 3256) at Rokeby Homestead is about 70km west from the Peninsula Developmental Rd, or you can visit the district ranger in Coen for more information.

Archer River

Archer River Roadhouse (☎ /fax 4060 3266; unpowered sites $12, s/d $45/60; ⏰ 7am-10pm) is a great place to stop and enjoy a cold beer and the famous Archer Burger. Just down the hill from the roadhouse is the magnificent Archer River. During the dry season this river is a pleasant stream, and its wide, tree-lined sandy bed an ideal spot to camp, al-

---

DETOUR

About 20km north of the Archer River Roadhouse, Archer River Rd turns off east for Iron Range National Park. It's another 110km to the **ranger station** (☎ 4060 7170) at King Park Homestead.

The **Iron Range National Park** is of world significance and conserves the largest area of lowland tropical rainforest in Australia. Birdlife in the area is rich and includes the southern cassowary – this is one of the only habitats where the bird isn't endangered. Also look out for the spotted and the grey cuscus – a monkey-like marsupial with a prehensile tail. Some 10% of Australia's butterfly species also reside in this park; of these, 25 species are found no further south and the park is their stronghold.

There are only a couple of places to camp in the park. Near the East Claudie River and Gordon Creek is the Rainforest camping ground. The other is at the northern end of Chilli Beach. This is where most travellers set up camp. While it's a nice spot, it would be even better if the southeast trade winds would stop blowing! Register with the ranger at King Park Homestead.

---

though at times space is at a premium. The banks are lined with tall paperbark trees (melaleucas), offering shade and attracting hordes of birds and fruit bats that love the sweet-smelling nectar.

The Archer River crossing with its concrete causeway is quite easy; however, any heavy rain in the catchment will quickly cut access to Weipa and places further north.

ARCHER RIVER TO WEIPA

The 145km well-maintained road to Weipa leaves Telegraph Rd 48km north of Archer River. At **Sudley Homestead**, at the 74km mark, a track which leaves Telegraph Rd at Batavia Downs, south of the Wenlock River, joins up with the Peninsula Developmental Rd. This track, often chopped up with a couple of creek crossings, gives people another option to leave or join the route to the Tip.

Weipa

☎ 07 / pop 2502

Weipa is a bauxite-mining town of red dirt, coconut palms and intermittent danger signs. The mine here works the world's largest deposits of bauxite (the ore from which aluminium is processed).

In the suburb of Nanum there's a credit union and ATM, post office and supermarket. At Rocky Point you'll find the police and a hospital. **Weipa Camping & Caravan Park** (☎ 4069 7871; www.fishingcairns.com.au/page13 -7c.html; unpowered/powered sites $18/20, cabins from $60; 🖳) operates as the town's informal tourist office, and can book mine and fishing tours. This relaxed camping ground, by the waterfront and close to the shops, also has facilities for the disabled; prices are for two people. It can also provide permits for nearby camping grounds.

Also by the waterfront, the **Albatross Hotel Resort** (☎ 4090 7314; albatrosshotel@bigpond.com; Duyfken Cres; s/d bungalows $60/70, motel s/d $110/125; 🍴 🖳) has good rooms for most budgets and a pleasant beer garden and restaurant. Also providing motel-style accommodation is the four-star **Heritage Resort** (☎ 4069 8000; www.fishingcairns.com.au/page13-7b.html; Nanum; s/d $130/140; 🍴 🖳), with modern comfortable rooms and a **restaurant** (mains $17-30) serving local delicacies such as mud crab.

ARCHER RIVER TO WENLOCK RIVER

After the turn-off to Weipa, which is 48km north of the Archer River, the road heading north deteriorates. On the left of the road is **Batavia Downs Homestead**, which also marks another turn-off to Weipa. The final 22km to the Wenlock River is along a road that is sandy and very rough in places.

The Wenlock River was once a major challenge on the way north to the Cape, but it is now bridged. The sturdy concrete bridge is raised about 6m above the river, though it still floods in the wet season (when the waters might reach 14m).

On the northern bank of the Wenlock, the **Moreton Telegraph Station** (☎ 4060 3360; unpowered sites $12, r $25) provides homestead accommodation, camping (with hot showers) and very limited stores. Prices are for two people.

WENLOCK RIVER TO JARDINE RIVER
Telegraph Road

The 155km from the Wenlock River to the Jardine River is the best part of the trip, with some great creek crossings and excellent camp sites. Take your time and enjoy all the delights the Cape has to offer.

The challenge of following the rough track along the historic Overland Telegraph Line means that the trip will take at least a very long day, even if all goes well. A newer and easier route, known as the Southern and Northern Bypass Rds, avoids much of Telegraph Rd and bypasses most of the creeks and rivers between the Wenlock and Jardine Rivers. This route is covered on opposite.

Most of the major creek crossings on Telegraph Rd have water in them; however, it's not the water that is the problem but the banks on each side. Take care. The turn-off for **Bramwell Homestead** (☎ 4060 3237) is 26km north of the Wenlock River. The homestead offers very pleasant and reasonably priced accommodation and camping, and meals are available.

The first of the major bypass roads, Southern Bypass Rd, turns off Telegraph Rd 40km north of the Wenlock. Staying on Telegraph Rd there are several challenging creek crossings before you reach the **Dulhunty River**, 70km north of the Wenlock. This is a popular spot to camp. There are also some lovely places to swim, and the falls beside the road make a pleasant natural spa.

After crossing another major stream, a road leaves Telegraph Rd 2km north of the Dulhunty and heads for **Heathlands Ranger Station** (☎ 4060 3241), the base for the Jardine River National Park ranger. This road bypasses the difficult Gunshot Creek crossing.

After Gunshot Creek the track is sandy until you come to the **Cockatoo Creek crossing**, 94km north of the Wenlock River. Once again the steep banks can pose a problem. The Injinoo people have a permanent camp set up at Cockatoo Creek. For the next 24km the road improves slightly. A couple more creek crossings follow, and 14km past Cockatoo Creek, Southern Bypass Rd joins up with Telegraph Rd.

Just 9km further north on Telegraph Rd, the second major bypass, Northern Bypass Rd, heads west to the Jardine River ferry crossing. If you continue on Telegraph Rd, the turn-off to **Twin Falls** is 6.5km north of the turn-off to Fruit Bat Falls (no camping). The Twin Falls track leads less than 2km to an excellent camping ground. This is the most popular camping spot on the trip north, and although it gets crowded, it's still very enjoyable and well worth spending a day or two lazing away at the falls.

There are several challenging creeks to cross over the next 23km to the Jardine River. There are also tracks heading west to Northern Bypass Rd, should any of the crossings prove too challenging.

Bypass Roads

As an alternative to sticking to the old Telegraph Rd, Southern and Northern Bypass Rds avoid most of the creeks and rivers between the Wenlock and Jardine Rivers. Both sections of this road are corrugated and people travel too fast on them. Each year a number of head-on accidents occur in the first two months of the Dry, most on Southern Bypass Rd – be careful!

Southern Bypass Rd leaves Telegraph Rd 40km north of the Wenlock River crossing and heads east and then north. The turn-off east to Shelburne Homestead is 24km north of the junction, while another 35km will find you at the junction to Heathlands Ranger Station, 14km to the west.

When you reach a large patch of rainforest, 11km north of the Heathlands turn-off, the bypass road swings northwest, while a track to **Captain Billy Landing**, on the eastern coast, continues straight ahead. Keep on the bypass road for the next 45km to rejoin Telegraph Rd 14km north of Cockatoo Creek.

Northern Bypass Rd leaves Telegraph Rd 9km north of where Southern Bypass Rd rejoins Telegraph Rd. This route heads west away from Telegraph Rd and for 50km winds through tropical savannah woodland to the Jardine River ferry.

Jardine River

On the southern bank of the river is the **Jardine River Ferry & Roadhouse** (☎ 4069 1369; ⏰ 8am-5pm). The ferry crossing is run by the Injinoo Community Council and operates only during the dry season ($88 return, plus $11 for trailers). The fee includes a permit that allows you to bush camp in the area north of the Jardine River, including Mutee Heads, Somerset, and the mouth of the Jardine. The roadhouse sells fuel and cold drinks and has a camping ground with toilets and hot showers.

The Department of Environment and the Injinoo community ask that all travellers use the ferry crossing at Jardine River and avoid driving across the river at the vehicle ford. The Jardine River has some magical camping grounds along its southern bank,

west of the old treacherous vehicle ford. There are no facilities here, and a camping permit is required from the ranger at Heathlands Station.

Remember, estuarine crocodiles inhabit the Jardine River, and although you might not be able to see them they are definitely there.

JARDINE RIVER TO CAPE YORK

From the ferry crossing to the Tip it is less than 70km and for most of the way the track is in good condition. Once you have crossed the Jardine, the track swings to the east, joining up with the old Telegraph Rd, before heading north to the Tip.

A number of minor tracks in this area lead back down to the river and some reasonable camping grounds. The best is on the northern bank where the telegraph line crosses the river; an old linesman's hut marks the spot. Keeping on the main road will bring you to Bamaga, the first and largest settlement north of the Jardine.

Bamaga

In 1947, Chief Bamaga Ginau decided to move his community to the mainland from Saibai Island, just 8km from Papua New Guinea, to escape flooding and a lack of fresh water. Bamaga is the largest Torres Straight Islander community on Cape York Peninsula. The town has all the facilities most travellers need. There is a hospital, police station, supermarket, bakery, newsagency and service station and a comfortable place to stay.

Resort Bamaga (☎ 4069 3050; www.resortbamaga .com.au; r $180-225; ✖ ⓐ) overlooks Mosby Creek, by the main thoroughfare into town, and is a four-star resort with very good rooms and facilities. The **restaurant** (mains $20-30) is open for breakfast, lunch and dinner, and 4WD hire is available. A few blocks from the resort, **Bakehaus** (☎ 4069 3168; ⏰ 7am-2pm Mon-Sat) bakes rye, wholemeal and grain bread, croissants, pizza and delicious cakes.

Seisia

Five kilometres northwest of Bamaga, the Torres Strait Islander town of Seisia was established at Red Island Point around the same time as fellow Saibai Islanders set up at Bamaga. It's an idyllic spot for the weary traveller to relax at after the long journey to the Tip. The town has fuel, mechanics, takeaways and several places to stay.

Seisia Resort & Campground (☎ 1800 653 243, 4069 3243; www.fishingcairns.com.au/page13-7d.html; unpowered sites $22, s/d $90/115) overlooks the islands of Torres Strait. This pleasant and popular camping ground with good facilities and comfortable self-contained units is the ideal base from which to explore the Tip. It is also the booking agent for all tours, which include guided fishing trips, pearl-farm tours, croc spotting, 4WD tours of the Tip and scenic flights.

Peddells (☎ 4069 1551; www.peddellsferry.com.au) runs regular ferries between Seisia and Thursday Island – see opposite for details.

Bamaga to Cape York

From Bamaga, turn north towards the Tip along a well-formed dirt road. The ruins of Jardine's outstation, **Lockerbie**, are 16km north. Just north of Lockerbie a track heads west to **Punsand Bay**, about 11 bumpy, sandy kilometres away. A few kilometres later the main track north begins to pass through an area of rainforest called the **Lockerbie Scrub**. This small patch of rainforest, only 25km long and between 1km and 5km wide, is the northernmost rainforest in Australia.

About 7km from Lockerbie a Y-junction in the middle of the jungle gives you a choice of veering right for **Somerset** or left for the top of Australia. There's not much left at the former British outpost of Somerset, save for the graves of Frank and Sana Jardine on the pretty foreshore. Back at the junction, the left fork will lead for about 10km to the **Pajinka Wilderness Lodge** (www.pajinka.com.au), which was closed at the time of research, and a camping ground. A walking track leads through the forest bordering the camping ground at Pajinka to the beach near the boat ramp. From the beach you can head overland on the marked trail, or when the tide is low you can head around the coast to the northernmost **Tip of Australia**. Both routes are relatively easy walks of an hour or so.

One of the best, friendliest and most scenic spots on the Cape is **Punsand Bay Safari & Fishing Lodge** (☎ 4069 1722; fax 4069 1403; unpowered sites $22, safari tents $120, cabins $170; ☒) situated on a north-facing beach just a few kilometres west from the Tip. This place is well set up with a licensed restaurant open

for breakfast, lunch and dinner, and it runs 4WD tours to the Tip. Prices are for two people.

THURSDAY ISLAND & TORRES STRAIT

There are a number of islands scattered across the reef-strewn waters of Torres Strait, running like stepping stones from the top of Cape York to the southern coast of Papua New Guinea, about 150km north of the Australian mainland.

The 70-odd islands of the Torres Strait include the rocky, northern extensions of the Great Dividing Range including Thursday Island; a central group of islands east of the Great Barrier Reef, which are little more than coral cays; and the picturesque Murray Islands in the far east of the strait.

While Thursday Island (or 'TI' as it's casually known) is the 'capital' of Torres Strait, there are 17 inhabited islands, the northernmost being Saibai and Boigu Islands, just kilometres from the Papuan coast.

Thursday Island

☎ 07 / pop 2693

No visit to the top of the Cape would be complete without a trip to fascinating, multicultural Thursday Island. The view sailing into the island is unlike anything you'll see elsewhere in Queensland. The timber spires of the 19th-century Sacred Heart Mission Church, and the corrugated roof of the old Federal Hotel mark the skyline, as do the huge wind turbines making good use of the trade winds.

ORIENTATION & INFORMATION

The island is little more than 3 sq km in area, with the town of Thursday Island on its southern shore. There are a few shops, including a general store, fruit barn, chemist, post office and bank (with an ATM).

Hospital (☎ 4069 1109)
Peddells' Ferry Island Tourist Bureau (☎ 4069 1551; Engineers Wharf) For tourist information.
Police station (☎ 4069 1520)

SIGHTS

There are some fascinating reminders of Thursday Island's rich history around town. The **All Souls Quetta Memorial Church** was built in 1893, in memory of the shipwreck of the *Quetta*, which struck an unchartered reef in the Adolphus Channel in 1890, with 133 lives lost. Today its walls are adorned with curious memorabilia, including a porthole recovered from the *Quetta* in 1906.

The Japanese section of the town's cemetery is crowded with hundreds of kanji-inscribed graves of pearl divers who died from decompression sickness. The **Japanese Pearl Memorial** is dedicated to them. **Green Hill Fort**, on the western side of town, was built in 1893 in response to fears of a Russian invasion. The small **Torres Strait Museum** is also here.

TOURS
Peddells (☎ 4069 1551; www.peddellsferry.com.au) offers bus tours of Thursday Island (adult/child $23/11.50), taking in the major tourist sites including All Souls Quetta Memorial Church and Green Hill Fort and museum. You can also do a two-island tour, which includes Horn Island. You can also take these tours from Seisia.

SLEEPING & EATING
Jardine Motel (☎ 4069 1555; www.jardinemotel.com .au; cnr Normanby St & Victoria Pde; s/d $135/155; ☒ ▣ ☒) The comfortable motel rooms here are well appointed, some with disabled access. The motel's Somerset Restaurant (mains $20 to $40) has a seafood menu, including local barramundi and reef fish.

Jardine Lodge (s with/without bathroom $95/75, d $115/95) The budget rooms in this place associated with the Jardine Motel have full use of the motel facilities.

Grand Hotel (☎ 4069 1557; fax 4069 1327; Upper Victoria Pde; s/d from $110/150) Located on a hill behind the wharf, the Grand Hotel was rebuilt after it burned down in 1997. It has comfortable, modern rooms with ocean and mountain views, and there are facilities for disabled guests. The hotel's Malu Paru restaurant (mains $17 to $40) has a balcony with sweeping views and excellent seafood.

Federal Hotel (☎ 4069 1569; Victoria Pde; s with bathroom $95, d with/without bathroom $135/60; ☒) The Federal's motel-style rooms with harbour views are spacious and comfortable. There's also a restaurant serving lunch and dinner.

Rainbow Motel (☎ 4069 2460; fax 4069 2714; Douglas St; s/d $70/100; ☒) This motel has basic rooms and the good Burger Bar takeaway restaurant.

Horn Island
During WWII, Horn Island became a battle zone, suffering eight Japanese air raids. Among the 5000 troops once stationed on the island was the 830-strong Torres Strait Light Infantry Battalion. Today Horn Island, and its small town of Wasaga, is very quiet and undeveloped.

Gateway Torres Strait Resort (☎ 4069 2222; fax 4069 2211; gtsr@bigpond.com; 24 Outie St; s/d $110/140) has basic self-contained units with a fan and TV. There's also a restaurant serving buffet dinners and lunch during the dry season. There's a **museum** and **art gallery** here, and tours of the island's WWII historic sites are available.

Other Torres Strait Islands
The inhabited outer islands are not too difficult to visit, but you must plan well in advance. The islands have very small populations and virtually no tourist infrastructure. To visit any island other than Thursday or Horn, you usually need permission from the island's council; contact the **Torres Strait Regional Authority** (☎ 4069 1247; www.tsra.gov.au; Torres Strait Haus, Victoria Pde, Thursday Is).

Most inhabited islands have an airstrip and quite a few airlines operate light aircraft in the strait. Although it's only a few kilometres away, you cannot travel to Papua New Guinea from the northern islands of the Torres Strait. Under the Torres Strait Treaty between Australia and Papua New Guinea, only traditional inhabitants are permitted to cross the border here.

Getting There & Around
AIR
QantasLink (☎ 13 13 13; www.qantas.com.au) flies daily from Cairns to Thursday Island ($875 return), although the airport is actually on Horn Island. On Thursday Island, **Torres Strait Travel** (☎ 4069 1264; cnr Victoria Pde & Blackall St) is where you can book flights and complete check-in for outgoing flights. The air fare includes a shuttle across the harbour between Horn and Thursday Islands.

BOAT
There are regular ferry services between Seisia, on the mainland, and Thursday Island run by **Peddells'** (☎ 4069 1551; www.peddellsferry .com.au; Engineers Jetty, Thursday Is). From June to October it has two daily services from

Monday to Saturday (one way/return $43/ 85), and from November to May it operates only on Monday, Wednesday and Friday. In the dry season it also has a service between Punsand Bay and Thursday Island for the same fare. These are basically day trips, leaving in the morning and returning from Thursday Island in the evening.

Horn Island Ferry Service (☎ 4069 1011) operates between Thursday Island and Horn Island. The ferries run roughly hourly between 6am and 6pm ($6 one way, 15 minutes).

GULF SAVANNAH

The Gulf Savannah is an immense, flat and empty landscape of sweeping grass plains, scrubby forest and mangrove engraved by an intricate network of seasonal rivers and tidal creeks that drain into the Gulf of Carpentaria. It's remote, hot and sparsely populated, with excellent fishing, extraordinary characters and a large crocodile population.

The Gulf's major attractions are separated by vast distances with only a scattering of cattle stations, roadhouses and historic towns between them. The spectacular Undara lava tubes, an ancient geological wonderland, are near the eastern end of the Savannah Way. Boodjamulla (Lawn Hill) National Park, a stunning river gorge harbouring remnant rainforest, is an oasis in the midst of the arid far northwest. And strung along the steamy, indistinct coastline, the Gulf's main towns of Burketown, Normanton and Karumba retain a pioneer edge and independent colour.

Information

Gulf Savannah Development (☎ 4031 1631; www .gulf-savannah.com.au; 74 Abbott St, Cairns; ⏰ 9am-5pm Mon-Fri) Provides information on all aspects of travel, tourism and business in the Gulf Savannah region.
Tourism Tropical North Queensland (☎ 4031 7676; www.tnq.org.au; 51 The Esplanade, Cairns; ⏰ 8.30am-6.30pm) Can also provide comprehensive tour and travel information on this region.

MAPS
Although a little out of date, the best road guide to use is Sunmap's *Gulf Savannah Tourist Map* (1:750,000), available from most newsagencies and tourist information centres.

Tours
Several operators run guided tours of the Gulf Savannah out of Cairns. Their itineraries are pretty similar:
Billy Tea Bush Safaris (☎ 4032 0077; www.billytea .com.au; 5-day overland tours $1495) The 4WD Gulf experience includes the Chillagoe Caves, Undara, Cobold Gorge and Innot Hot Springs.
Heritage Tours (☎ 4038 2628; www.heritagetours .com.au; 9-day camping tours $1795; 9-day accommodated tours $2295) Visits Undara, Boodjamulla (Lawn Hill, Riversliegh), Karumba, Normanton and more.
Oz Tours Safaris (☎ 1800 079 006, 4055 9535; www.oztours.com.au; 6-/7-/9-day accommodated tours $1695/1855/2350) Includes Chillagoe Caves, Undara, Boodjamulla, Karumba and more.
Wilderness Challenge (☎ 4035 4488; www.wilder ness-challenge.com.au; 9-day accommodated tours $2395) The Gulf Savannah Wanderer visits Undara, Dorunda Station, Boodjamulla, Karumba, Normanton and more.

Getting There & Around
AIR
Macair (☎ 13 13 13; www.macair.com.au) flies a few times a week between Cairns and Normanton (from $190), Burketown ($250) and Mornington Island ($246); and between Mt Isa and Normanton ($200) and Burketown ($180).

BUS
Country Road Coachlines (☎ 4045 2794; countryroad coachlines@msn.com) has a service on Monday and Thursday from Cairns (Trinity Wharf) to Karumba ($125, 12 hours) via Undara ($55, 4½ hours), Georgetown ($70), Croydon ($90) and Normanton ($118). The return service runs Tuesday and Friday.

AICCC runs a bus from Normanton to Mt Isa on Monday, returning on Tuesday. The adult/child one-way fare is $110/85. The Normanton terminal and booking agent is **Gulfland Souvenirs** (☎ 4745 1307; Normanton train station) and the Mt Isa terminal and booking agent is **Campbell's Tours & Travel** (☎ 4743 2006; Outback at Isa, 19 Marion St, Mt Isa).

CAR & MOTORCYCLE
This part of the chapter is divided into sections that follow the routes of the major roads through the Gulf.

From Queensland's eastern coast, the Gulf Developmental Rd takes you from the Kennedy Hwy, south of the Atherton Tableland, across to Normanton and Karumba.

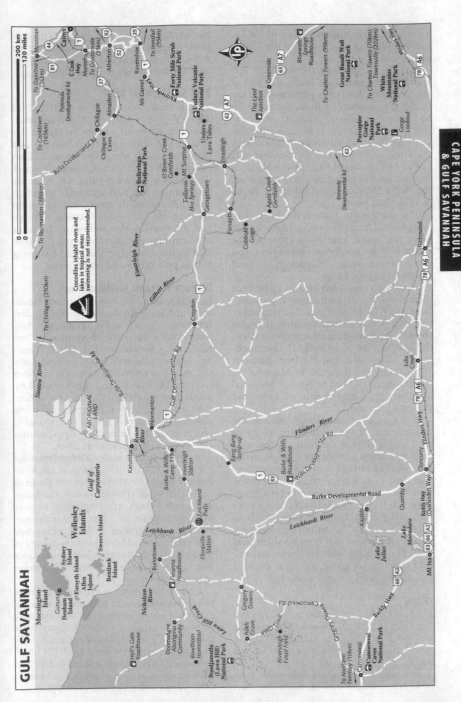

GULF SAVANNAH

Crocodiles inhabit rivers and lakes in tropical areas; swimming is not recommended.

This is the main eastern section of the Savannah Way, an epic route linking Cairns to Broome.

If you're coming from the Northern Territory, the unsealed Gulf Track, also part of the Savannah Way, takes you across the top of the Gulf country to Burketown and on to Normanton. From Burketown you have two options if you're heading south: you can take the unsealed road to Camooweal, via Gregory Downs and the Boodjamulla (Lawn Hill) National Park; or the Nardoo-Burketown Rd, which cuts across to meet the Burke Developmental Rd at the Burke & Wills Roadhouse.

The other major route is the Burke Developmental Rd, a good sealed highway that takes you south from Normanton to the Burke & Wills Roadhouse. From here, you can continue south to Cloncurry or head southeast to Julia Creek.

There aren't too many options apart from these major routes, particularly if you don't have a 4WD. Even if you do, remember that this is very remote country. If you're thinking of attempting other routes, such as the continuation of the Burke Developmental Rd, which takes you east from between Normanton and Karumba to Mareeba via Chillagoe, you'll need to be well prepared and carry good maps, plenty of water and preferably a radio.

And a note on cattle, kangaroos and the monsters called road trains (trucks up to 60m long). Most of the roads in this area are very narrow – more like a single lane – dirt roads at various stages of corrugation. You need to slow down and move over the shoulder of the road as oncoming traffic approaches. If there's a road train coming your way, just pull right over and wait for it to pass by. Cattle and kangaroos can suddenly appear on the road as if from nowhere, and hitting one will probably kill the animal and ruin your car for good; driving at twilight and night should always be avoided.

TRAIN

The historic *Savannahlander* conducts four-day **tours** (☎ 1800 620 324; www.traveltrain.com.au; tours from $590) along its traditional route from Cairns to Forsayth. It's a must for rail buffs.

The quaint, snub-nosed *Gulflander* runs just once weekly in each direction between Normanton and Croydon, alongside the Gulf Developmental Rd. There are connecting bus services from Cairns and Mt Isa to Croydon and Normanton. See p410 for details.

THE SAVANNAH WAY

The Savannah Way links Cairns to Broome across the top of Australia. The Gulf Developmental Rd forms a major section of this passage and is the main route into the Gulf from the east. It leaves the Kennedy Hwy 66km south of Mt Garnet, passing through Georgetown and Croydon en route to Normanton. The first section of the highway is in reasonably good condition. After Georgetown the sealed surface narrows and deteriorates; this section of the route is sometimes impassable during the Wet. The region crossed by this road has many ruined gold mines and settlements.

Undara Volcanic National Park

Just 17km from the start of the Gulf Developmental Rd is the turn-off to the Undara lava tubes, one of inland Queensland's most fascinating attractions. These massive lava tubes were formed around 190,000 years ago following the eruption of a single shield volcano. The eruption continued for three months. The massive lava flows drained towards the sea, following the routes of ancient river beds, and while the surface of the lava cooled and hardened, hot lava continued to race through the centre of the flows, eventually leaving enormous basalt tubes.

A large tourist complex, **Undara Experience** (☎ 1800 990 992, 4097 1411; www.undara.com.au; unpowered & powered sites $12, permanent tents $36, dm s/d $25, s/d $100/150;) provides accommodation and guided tours. It's important to note that you can't see the tubes or tour the surrounding countryside without taking one of these tours, and because of the timing of the tours, the most convenient place to stay is at Undara Experience, which has a range of accommodation.

Undara Experience is a member of **Savannah Guides** (www.savannah-guides.com.au), an association of expert interpreters of Australia's tropical savannahs. It offers full-day tours (adult/child $97/$48) including lunch; half-day ($65/32) and two-hour ($35/17) tours. Other activities include guided sunset and wildlife walks, and an outdoor bush breakfast. All tours depart from the lodge.

Undara Experience has plenty of camp sites scattered throughout the bush. The sites and facilities for campers, which include BBQs, hot showers and laundries, are excellent. The permanent tents, complete with beds and lights, can get uncomfortably warm; a better choice is the Wilderness Lodge, offering share accommodation in four-bed dorms. Top of the range are the beautifully restored old railway carriages; rooms are small but quaint and comfortable, with shared bathroom facilities.

The lodge has a gift shop, a bar and a restaurant that serves breakfast, lunch and dinner, and is open to everyone. There's limited food supplies (frozen BBQ packs) available at the gift shop, but if you're self-catering, you should stock up before you come.

The lodge and lava tubes are along 15km of well-maintained dirt road off the main highway. **Country Road Coachlines** (☎ 4045 2794) can drop you at the turn-off on its run from Cairns to Karumba on Monday and Thursday, and someone from the lodge will collect you from there. The one-way fare is $55. See p406 for details of tours to Undara.

Mt Surprise

Back on the Gulf Developmental Rd, 39km past the Undara turn-off, you'll find the small township of Mt Surprise. Several gem shops line the highway and they can provide tips, tools and licences so you can do a bit of fossicking for yourself: **O'Brien's Creek Gemfields**, 42km northwest of town, is one of Australia's best topaz fields. The **Old Post Office Museum** (☎ 4062 3126; adult/child $2/0.50; ⏱ 7am-6pm) has a small and quirky display of local history items. The **Mobil Service Station & General Store** (☎ 4062 3115) is the local RACQ depot.

Mt Surprise Tourist Van Park & Motel (☎ 4062 3153; fax 4062 3162; 7 Garland St; unpowered/powered sites $12/18, cabins $45, d $85; ✷ ⌨) is set amid lush, shady gardens. Prices are for two people. There's an extensive gem and mineral display, a café and a service station attached.

Bedrock Village (☎ 4062 3193; fax 4062 3166; Garnet St; unpowered/powered sites $14/19, cabins from $32/52) is another good park, away from the main road. Prices are for two people. Tours of Undara and Cobbold Gorge can be organised. **Mt Surprise Hotel** (☎ 4062 3118; Garland St; s/d $30/50, mains $13-15) has basic pub rooms and simple pub meals.

Country Road Coachlines (☎ 4045 2794) stops at Mt Surprise en route between Karumba ($82) and Cairns twice a week ($60; see p412).

Einasleigh & Forsayth

About 32km west of Mt Surprise you can take a slow detour off the highway through the old mining townships of Einasleigh and Forsayth. You can also visit them on the *Savannahlander* (see opposite).

The road is mostly unsealed and fairly rough in sections, but is passable for 2WD vehicles during the dry season. **Einasleigh**, a former copper-mining centre and railway siding, is set in a rugged landscape of low, flat-topped hills. There's hardly anything to it today, but for a few houses, a pub and the beautiful black basalt **Copperfield Gorge**. An early morning or evening stroll around the gorge will reveal a wealth of wildlife including freshwater crocs, turtles, fish, birds and roos. The **Einasleigh Pub** (☎ 4062 5222; Daintree St; s/d $33/44) is a character-filled corrugated-iron pub. Its upstairs accommodation has been tastefully renovated, with rooms opening onto the east-facing veranda and sunrise views of the gorge. The bar downstairs is as casual as they come with snacks or home-cooked meals, and the publican has a fascinating collection of handmade miniatures – ask for a look.

Forsayth is 67km further west. It boasts a train station, a post office and a couple of places to stay. The **Goldfields Tavern** (☎ 4062 5374; First St; s/d $35/60) has basic dongas (prefabricated transportable cabins) with shared bathrooms. Meals, fuel and groceries are available. If you're camping or towing a van, try **Prospector Caravan Park** (☎ 4062 5324; First St; unpowered/powered sites $11/14, s/d cabins $35/45), which has a good camp kitchen and amenities.

Cobbold Gorge

This scenic oasis, with swimming holes, rugged cliffs and an abundance of wildlife, is 45km south of Forsayth. Access to the gorge is by guided tour only. **Cobbold Gorge Tours** (☎ 1800 669 922, 4062 5470; www.cobboldgorge.com .au; unpowered/powered sites $11/22, s/d cabins $50/80; ✷ ⌨) provides tours and accommodation at Cobbold Village. A full-day tour (adult/ child $110/55) includes a boat cruise, agate fossicking, lunch and swimming. A half-day cruise and walk costs $69/34. Other tours and helicopter flights are available.

Mt Surprise to Georgetown

Back on the Gulf Developmental Rd, 40km west of Mt Surprise, is the turn-off to the **Tallaroo Hot Springs** (☎ /fax 4062 1221; adult/child $9/6; 🕑 8am-5pm Easter-Sep), where you can soak in a pool fed from five naturally terraced hot springs. If you want to stay overnight here, there are camp sites ($11 for two adults) by the river.

Georgetown

During the days of the Etheridge River gold rush, Georgetown was a bustling commercial centre, but these days things are very quiet. The big surprise in this little town is the **Terrestrial Centre** (☎ 4062 1485; 🕑 9am-5pm Apr-Sep, 8.30am-4.30pm Mon-Fri Oct-May), home to the outstanding **Ted Elliot Mineral Collection** (admission $10), the town library, the information centre and an Internet café ($2 per 30 minutes). Georgetown has fuel, a post office, a good bakery, a pub (of course) and a tyre-repair outfit.

On the highway (North St), 1km west of Georgetown, **Latara Resort Motel** (☎ 4062 1190; s/d $60/80; 🌣 🖭) is the best place to stay, with modern motel units and meals available. Also on the highway, the **Midway Caravan Park & Service Station** (☎ 4062 1219; unpowered/powered sites $13/16, s/d cabins $45/55; 🌣 🖭) has good cabins, shady sites and a café. **Country Road Coachlines** (☎ 4045 2794) stops at Georgetown en route between Cairns and Karumba (see p412). The one-way adult fare from Cairns is $70.

Croydon

☎ 07 / pop 224

Connected to Normanton by the *Gulflander*, this old gold-mining town was once the biggest in the Gulf. Gold was discovered here in 1885, and within a couple of years there were 8000 diggers living here. It's reckoned there were once 5000 gold mines in the area, reminders of which are scattered all around the countryside. Such was the prosperity of the town that it had its own aerated water factory, a foundry and coach-builders, gas street lamps and more than 30 pubs. The boom years were during the 1890s, but by the end of WWI the gold had run out and Croydon became little more than a ghost town.

Croydon's **information centre** (☎ 4745 6125; cnr Samwell & Aldridge Sts; 🕑 8am-5pm Mon-Fri Nov-Mar), museum, craft shop and Internet café ($2.50 per 30 minutes) are housed in the historic police station alongside several other restored buildings. The centre conducts daily one-hour **walking tours** (☎ 4745 6125; adult/child $5.50/free; 🕑 8am, 10am, 2pm & 4pm) of the town's historic precinct. The **Croydon General Store** (☎ 4745 6163; Sircom St) sells fuel (and just about everything else), does most repairs and is the local RACQ depot. Next door is a small **museum** with a collection of photos, tools, rocks and records, all fairly well hidden under a blanket of dust. **Lake Belmore**, 4km from the town centre and stocked with barramundi, is a popular fishing spot. On the way out to the lake are the Chinese Temple and cemetery ruins.

For accommodation, try the **Club Hotel** (☎ 4745 6184; cnr Brown & Sircom Sts; s $40, d $50-75; 🌣 🖭) with basic pub rooms, dongas and self-contained units; or the very basic **Croydon Caravan Park** (☎ 4745 6238; cnr Brown & Alldridge Sts; unpowered/powered sites $12/15, cabins $40).

Country Road Coachlines (☎ 4045 2794) stop at Croydon en route between Cairns and Karumba (see p412). The one-way adult fare from Cairns is $90.

The *Gulflander*

The Normanton to Croydon railway line was completed in 1891 with the aim of linking the booming gold-mining centre with the port at Normanton.

The *Gulflander* travels the 153km from Normanton to Croydon and back once a week, leaving Normanton on Wednesday at 8.30am and returning from Croydon on Thursday at 8.30am. It's one of the Gulf's most popular attractions – if you have the time, don't miss it. The trip takes a leisurely four hours, with a couple of stops at points of interest along the way; most people stay overnight in Croydon at the Club Hotel, returning to Normanton the next day. The one-way adult fare to Blackbull Siding/ Croydon is $35/48. For bookings, phone the **Normanton train station** (☎ 4745 1391).

Normanton

☎ 07 / pop 1447

Established on the banks of the Norman River back in 1868, Normanton's boom years were during the 1890s, when it acted as the port for the Croydon gold rush. Since those heady days, the town has existed as a major supply point for the surrounding cattle stations, and it is now the Gulf's major town. **Jack's Carlec & Fuels** (☎ 4745 1221; 110 Landsborough St) sells fuel, is the local RACQ depot and does repairs, welding and 24-hour towing.

The historic Burns Philp & Co Ltd store houses the **visitor information centre** and **library** (☎ 4745 1065; cnr Caroline & Landsborough Sts; ⌚ 10am-6pm Mon-Fri, to 8pm Tue, 9am-2pm Sat) with Internet access ($2 per 30 minutes). The **train station** is a lovely old Victorian-era building with a souvenir shop and **museum**. When it's not running, the *Gulflander* rests under the station's arched roof.

Norman River Fishing & Cruises (☎ 4745 1347; www.normanriverfishing.com.au) offers sunset cruises (adult/child $20/5) and fishing trips ($75 per person) aboard the *Savannah Queen*. The 1½-hour sunset tour is probably the best bet if you want to spot a croc. As a base for fishing, Normanton is hard to beat, with the Norman River producing some magic-sized barramundi; each Easter weekend the Barramundi Classic draws a big crowd. The **Normanton Rodeo & Gymkhana** and the **Normanton Races** are both held in June and dominate the social calendar.

For accommodation you won't be disappointed with the **Normanton Caravan Park** (☎ 4745 1121; Brown St; unpowered/powered sites $16/20, dm $25, cabins $65; ⌘ ▣), a very pleasant park with excellent cabins that have bathrooms, and a huge 25m shaded swimming pool with an artesian spa. And you can't miss the **Purple Pub & Brolga Palms Motel** (☎ 4745 1324; fax 4745 1675; cnr Landsborough & Brown Sts; s/d $70/80) offering comfortable motel rooms (there's no pub accommodation) and counter meals. Other options include:

Albion Hotel (☎ 4745 1218; Haig St; s/d $55/60; ⌘) Motel-style rooms out the back. Counter meals.

Central Hotel (☎ 4745 1215; cnr Haig & Landsborough Sts; s/d $55/60, s/d dongas $25/30) Known as the 'barracks', the budget rooms have shared bathrooms.

Gulfland Motel & Caravan Park (☎ 4745 1290; 11 Landsborough St; unpowered/powered sites $16/20, s/d $80/90; ⌘ ▣) Has a licensed restaurant.

Macair (☎ 13 13 13; www.macair.com.au) has regular flights from Mt Isa to Normanton ($200), and from Cairns to Normanton ($190).

Country Road Coachlines (☎ 4045 2794) stops at Normanton on its journey between Cairns and Karumba. The one-way adult fare from Cairns is $118. AICCC runs a coach

to/from Mt Isa. Departing Normanton railway station on Monday at 8am, it arrives at Outback at Isa at 2.15pm. The return journey leaves Mt Isa on Tuesday at 9am and arrives at Normanton at 3.15pm. The adult/child one-way fare is $110/85. All enquiries about this service must be directed to **Gulfland Souvenirs** (☎ 4745 1307; Normanton train station) or to **Cambell's Coaches** (☎ 4743 2006; Outback at Isa, 19 Marion St, Mt Isa). The AICCC bus will continue on to Karumba ($40/30 adult/child).

Karumba
☎ 07 / pop 1346

Karumba, located 70km north of Normanton, lies at the point where the Norman River meets the Gulf of Carpentaria. The town of Karumba itself is on the banks of the Norman River, while Karumba Point, which is a tavern and a collection of holiday units, is several kilometres north on the shores of the Gulf.

Established as a telegraph station in the 1870s, Karumba became a stopover for the flying boats of the Empire Mail Service in the 1930s. The discovery of prawns in the Gulf in the 1960s brought Karumba alive, and today prawning, barramundi fishing and, increasingly, tourism keep the town humming. More and more travellers are enjoying Karumba Point sunsets, local seafood, and the meteorological wonder of the 'morning glory' roll cloud. This tubular cloud, or series of clouds, rolls across the sky with a following wind in the early morning. This phenomena only happens from September to November.

Karumba has a supermarket, banks, a couple of pubs, caravan parks and holiday units, all of which mainly cater for those going fishing. If you have ever wanted to know all the ins and outs of the great barramundi, or just want to see some big fish up close, head to the **Barramundi Discovery Centre** (☎ /fax 4745 9359; 148 Yappar St; adult/child $7.50/2; ⌚ 1-4.30pm).

Ferryman Cruises (☎ /fax 4745 9155) offers a two-hour River & Gulf Sunset cruise (adult/child $24/12). Other tours include birdwatching and croc spotting. **Sky Safari** (☎ 4745 9066) tours the Gulf Savannah, including a tour of Burketown and lunch at Sweers Island ($400 per person). A Karumba joy flight costs $60 per person.

SLEEPING & EATING

Pelicans Inn (☎ 4745 9555; www.pelicanskarumba
.com.au; 2 Gilbert St, Karumba; dm $25, d $85-130; ☐ ☎)
This modern, corrugated-iron building
houses an interesting mix of accommodation: dorms, self-contained units, luxury
rooms with bathrooms with river views and
disabled-friendly rooms. It was still in the
last stages of construction when we visited
and looked destined to be the pace-setter
for accommodation in Karumba.

Ash's Holiday Units & Takeaway (☎ 4745 9132;
cnr Palmer & Ward Sts, Karumba Point; s/d $67/73; ☒ ☎)
Very clean self-contained units and the best
inexpensive barra and chips in town.

Savannah Shores (☎ 4745 9126; www.savannah
shores.com.au; The Esplanade, Karumba Point; s/d $65/71;
☒ ☎) These comfortable self-contained
cabins are right on the foreshore, though
they lack views. Meals are also available.

Gulf Country Van Park (☎ /fax 4745 9148; cnr Yappar
St & Massey Dr, Karumba; unpowered/powered sites $19/22,
s/d cabins $40/60; ☎) This shady caravan park,
with good amenities, is a block back from the
pub and the boat ramp. The old cabins have
a kitchen but the bathrooms are shared.

Sunset Tavern (☎ 4745 9183; The Esplanade,
Karumba Point; mains $11-25; ☺ 10am-midnight) This
barnlike pub, with plenty of outdoor tables,
has a fantastic location on the point. Just
grab a drink and a meal, and watch dancing
jabiru and the glorious sunset.

Karumba Seafoods (☎ 4745 9192; Massey Dr,
Karumba; mains $10-29; ☺ 9-11am & 5-10pm) This
pleasant BYO does excellent seafood dinners – try the prawn and crab platter – and is
also open for scrumptious cakes and coffee
in the morning.

Other options:

Karumba Lodge Hotel (☎ 4745 9143; Gilbert St; s/d
$72/83) This two-storey row of rather plain motel-style
units is on the Norman River. There's a restaurant and a
couple of bars.

Matilda's End Holiday Units (☎ 4745 6500; www
.matildasend.com.au; 62 Yappar St, Karumba; s/d $65/75;
☒ ☎) A row of clean and neat, older style one-, two-
and three-bedroom self-contained units.

GETTING THERE & AWAY

Country Road Coachlines (☎ 4045 2794) connects
Cairns (Trinity Wharf) and Karumba twice
a week. The one-way adult fare from Cairns
is $125 and the bus departs Karumba on
Monday and Thursday, and Cairns on Tuesday and Friday. There's a coach from Mt Isa

to Normanton with an optional connection
to Karumba; see p411 for details.

NORTHERN TERRITORY BORDER TO BURKETOWN

This 228km section of the Savannah Way includes part of the historic Gulf Track, which
stretches from Roper Bar in the Northern
Territory's Top End to Normanton. The entire route is along unsealed roads, although
a 4WD vehicle isn't required during the dry
season. Travel isn't recommended during
the wet season (between the beginning of
December and March), when extreme heat
and humidity make conditions difficult and
heavy rains can close the roads for lengthy
periods.

About 52km east of the border you arrive
at Hell's Gate Roadhouse (☎ 4745 8258; unpowered/
powered sites $15/20, s/d from $50/80; ☒) set among
low outcrops of grey conglomerate rising
from the surrounding sparse bush. The
roadhouse has a licensed restaurant that
serves breakfast, lunch and dinner.

There are a couple of other places to stay
in this remote area, though bookings are
essential. Between Hell's Gate and Doomadgee there's a signposted turn-off to
Kingfisher Camp (☎ 4745 8212; day pass $3, sites per
person/family $7/20, s $20), a camping ground beside a 5km-long water hole on the Nicholson River. Facilities include hot showers,
toilets and laundry. Boats can be hired and
there's a small kiosk selling basic supplies.
About 30km south of Kingfisher Camp,
Bowthorn Homestead (☎ 4745 8132; www.bowthorn
.bigpondhosting.com; r $75) offers a great oppor-
tunity to stay on a working cattle station.
Room rates include dinner and breakfast.
Bowthorn is operated by the same family
that runs Kingfisher Camp. From here you
can head east 72km and join up with the
Gulf Track east of the Nicholson River, or
head south 100km or so to Boodjamulla
(Lawn Hill) National Park.

There is little to break the monotony of
paperbark scrub for the 80km between Hell's
Gate and the turn-off to **Doomadgee Aboriginal
Community** (☎ 47458188). While you are welcome to buy fuel and shop at the store here,
camping and village access is subject to permission being obtained from the council.

About 4km past Doomadgee you arrive at
the **Nicholson River** crossing. The river is about
600m across, and in the dry season its bed

of solid rock presents a desolate picture. In remarkable contrast, the **Gregory River**, 53km further on, presents a lush picture of running water crowded by tropical vegetation. On the other side is the deserted **Tirranna Roadhouse**, and 8km later there's a major road junction – turn right for the Gregory Downs Hotel (90km) and left for Burketown.

Burketown

☎ 07 / pop 221

Burketown is 30km from the waters of the Gulf of Carpentaria. Even so, it sits just a few metres above the high-tide mark, such is the pancake-flat nature of the Gulf shoreline. Founded in 1865, Burketown almost came to a premature end a year later when a fever wiped out most of the residents. In 1887 a huge tidal surge almost carried the town away and, while nothing so dramatic has occurred since, the township is often cut off from the rest of Australia by floodwaters.

Besides the excellent fishing, Burketown also offers the chance to witness the 'morning glory' phenomenon – tubular clouds that roll out of the Gulf in the early morning, often in lines of three or four. This only happens between September and November.

The Burketown and Gulf **Regional Tourist Information Centre** (☎ 4745 5111; Musgrave St; ⏱ 8.30am-4.30pm) can supply information and make arrangements for local tours. The **Burketown Rodeo**, held in the second weekend of July, guarantees a good crowd, and there's a **barramundi fishing competition** each Easter. The **Burketown Show** takes place on the second weekend of September.

The **Burketown Pub** (☎ 4745 5104; fax 4745 5146; Beames St; s/d $44, units $72/92; ⌘) is the heart and soul of Burketown. Originally built as the local customs house, it's the oldest building in town – all its contemporaries have been blown or washed away! It's a friendly, well-run outback pub, the motel units are far enough away from the pub to be quiet, and there's a lovely beer garden and good meals. The basic **Burketown Caravan Park** (☎ 4745 5118; Sloman St; unpowered/powered sites $16/20, s cabins $44, d cabins $55-100; ⌘) offers a little shade and a range of cabin accommodation. The Burketown General Store includes a supermarket, licensed restaurant and takeaway food.

Macair (☎ 13 13 13; www.macair.com.au) has regular flights to Burketown from Mt Isa (from $180) and Cairns ($250).

BURKETOWN TO NORMANTON

From Burketown the Gulf Track/Savannah Way sweeps across the flat plains of the Gulf to Normanton. The road, which follows the original coach route between Darwin and Port Douglas, was once also known as the Great Top Rd. This 233km route is open to conventional vehicles throughout the dry season, though the higher clearance of a 4WD will certainly make for an easier trip.

After 73km the turn-off to Floraville Station and a 'Historic Site' sign indicates the 1.3km diversion to **Walker's Monument**. Frederick Walker died here in 1866. He had been sent out to find Burke and Wills. Although he didn't find them, he did discover Camp 119 (see the boxed text on p414), from which they made their final push to the Gulf.

Just 1km after the turn-off to Floraville, the road drops down the bank of the Leichhardt River and winds its way across the rock bar that makes up the wide bed of the river here. A narrow, short bridge crosses the stream in one spot. The best place to pull over and camp, on the run between Burketown and Normanton, is at the small, sandy, tree-covered island about halfway across the river's rocky bed, just past the narrow bridge. From here it is only a short walk downstream to the spectacular **Leichhardt Falls**. There are pools of water to cool off in (don't swim in the big stretch of water above the road crossing – there are crocs), the trees offer shade and the birdlife is rich and varied.

Only 2km from the Leichhardt River you reach a road junction where you need to turn left for Normanton. Heading right (south) will take you to the Burke & Wills Roadhouse, 146km away on the Wills Developmental Rd.

After 113km and several river crossings, and just as you top the far bank of the Little Bynoe River, there's a signposted turn-off leading right to **Burke and Wills' Camp 119**. Camp 119 is 2km down this track and marked by a ring of trees surrounding a tree blazed by Burke and Wills. This is a good spot to have a brew, and if you want to camp, a track leads a short distance back to the edge of the Little Bynoe. Continuing eastwards you reach the bitumen at a road junction 32km east of the turn-off to Camp 119. Turn left here and 5km later you'll be in Normanton.

CAMP 119

Camp 119 was the northernmost camp of the Burke and Wills expedition. Leaving their companions, Gray and King, to mind the camels and their equipment at Cooper Creek (near present-day Innamincka in South Australia), Burke and Wills pushed north across the wet, flooded country to try to reach the waters of the Gulf. While the water was salty and they observed a rise and fall in the tide, they were disappointed that the barrier of mangroves and mud kept them from seeing the coast. They turned back around 9 February 1861.

Returning to Camp 119, the explorers planned their dash back to Cooper Creek. No longer was it an exploratory expedition with mapping and observing a prime consideration, but a dash south for survival. In the end, only King made it back to Cooper Creek alive.

BURKETOWN TO CAMOOWEAL

The 334km road from Burketown to Camooweal via Gregory Downs is the most direct way for people heading to the Boodjamulla (Lawn Hill) National Park, although for 2WD vehicles the longer route via the Burke & Wills Roadhouse provides much easier access.

From Burketown it's 117km south to **Gregory Downs**, near the banks of the beautiful Gregory River. For accommodation try the **Gregory Downs Hotel** (☎ 4748 5566; s/d $65/75, dongas $30; 🖭). You can also camp behind the pub on the riverbank. **Billy Hangers General Store** (☎ 4748 5540; 🕑 8am-6pm) is jam-packed with just about everything you might need. You can fix your tyres, rent canoes ($8/35 per hour/day) or take a guided canoe tour.

Travelling from Gregory Downs, it's another 217km to Camooweal. About 40km south the road turns from dirt to gravel as you start to move into a series of low hills. About 126km south of Gregory Downs the road forks. The left-hand branch heads south for another 58km, before meeting the Barkly Hwy, and this is the route you'll take if you're heading for Mt Isa. The right-hand branch continues southwest for another 91km, meeting the Barkly Hwy 2km west of Camooweal.

BOODJAMULLA (LAWN HILL) NATIONAL PARK

Stuck between a rock (the Constance Range) and a hard place (the Gulf Savannah) is a beautiful, unexpected oasis. A series of deep flame-red sandstone gorges, fed by spring water and lined with palms, provides a haven for wildlife and one of the top natural attractions in the arid northwest of the state – Lawn Hill Gorge. Aboriginal people have enjoyed this oasis for perhaps 30,000 years. Their paintings and old camp sites abound. Two rock-art sites have been made accessible to visitors.

In the southern part of the park is the World Heritage–listed **Riversleigh fossil field**. The fossils include everything from giant snakes to carnivorous kangaroos. The Riversleigh Fossils Centre, part of Outback at Isa in Mt Isa (p421), has fossils and information about the diggings on display.

There are 20km of walking tracks and a national-park **camping ground** (☎ 4748 5572; sites per person/family $4/16) with showers and toilets near the gorge; it's very popular and sites must be booked in advance. Canoes can be hired, and paddling up the emerald green river with the red cliffs towering above is an experience not to be missed; swimming up near the waterfalls is also a real treat.

Adels Grove (☎ /fax 4748 5502; www.adelsgrove.com.au; sites per adult/child/family $8/4/22, s/d $85/140), 10km east of the park entrance, is a pleasant camping ground set amid trees close to the Lawn Hill Creek. In addition to camp sites, there are several permanently set-up tents with beds and linen. Rates for these include dinner and breakfast. Fuel and basic groceries are also available.

There are a couple of different ways of getting here; it's 100km west of Gregory Downs, though the easiest route for 2WD vehicles is to come via the Burke & Wills Roadhouse. If you're coming from Mt Isa, the last 230km after you leave the Barkley Hwy are unsealed and often impassable after rain, and a 4WD vehicle is recommended.

Campbell's Tours & Travel (☎ 4743 2006; www.campbellstravel.com.au) in Mt Isa offer a three-day safari (adult/child $660/330) out to Lawn Hill and Riversleigh on Tuesday and Friday, with accommodation and meals provided at Adels Grove.

CLONCURRY TO NORMANTON

The major road into the Gulf Savannah from the south is the Burke Developmental Rd, which runs 375km from Cloncurry to Normanton. This is the last section of the route known as the Matilda Hwy, which starts way down south at Cunnamulla near the Queensland–New South Wales border. The highway is sealed all the way.

Quamby, 43km north of Cloncurry, was once a Cobb & Co coach stop and a centre for gold mining, but now there's just the friendly **Quamby Hotel** (☎ 4742 5952; s/d $10/15) offering very basic accommodation. Continuing north across the rolling hills you reach the turn-off to **Kajabbi**, 29km north of Quamby. Kajabbi's focal point is the **Kalkadoon Hotel** (☎ /fax 4742 5979; s/d $30/50), while Battle Mountain, about 30km south, is the site of the last stand of the Kalkadoon people, who actively resisted the white invasion during the 1880s.

Just before you get to the Burke & Wills Roadhouse, 180km north of Cloncurry, the Wills Developmental Rd from Julia Creek intersects with the Burke Developmental Rd. Nearly everyone stops at **Burke & Wills Roadhouse** (☎ 4742 5909; unpowered/powered sites $10/18, s/d $39/50; ⏰ 7am-10pm; ✷), where there's a little shade, meals, ice and fuel.

From the roadhouse you can strike northwest along the Wills Developmental Rd to Gregory Downs (see opposite). For those travelling on to Normanton, the route continues north over reasonably flat country. However once you get to **Bang Bang Jump-up**, 80km north of the roadhouse, and descend about 40m to the Gulf plains proper, you really learn what 'flat' means. From this point the road stretches across vast, billiard table–flat plains covered in deep grass, which in the Dry is the colour of gold.

WELLESLEY ISLANDS

There are numerous islands scattered in the Gulf of Carpentaria north of Burketown, most of which are Aboriginal communities and are not open to visitors. There are, however, a couple of places set up specifically to cater to people wanting to fish the abundant waters of the Gulf. Contact the resorts for information on charter flights to/from the islands.

The largest of the Gulf islands, **Mornington Island**, has an Aboriginal community administered from Gununa, on the southwestern coast. **Birri Fishing Paradise** (☎ 4745 7277; www.birri.com.au; 7-night all-inclusive packages $3080) is a remote fishing lodge on the northwestern coast of the island.

The smaller **Sweers Island**, midway between Burketown and Mornington Island, also has its own fishing resort. **Sweers Island Resort** (☎ 4748 5544; www.sweers.com.au) caters for families and the cabins have shared bathroom facilities. The tariff ($240 per person) includes all meals, boat hire, fuel, bait and hand lines.

Outback Queensland

HIGHLIGHTS

- Descending into the **Hard Times Mine** (p421) and drilling a rock face at Mt Isa
- Capturing an outback sunset complete with silhouetted windmill and coolabah tree along the **Matilda Hwy** (p424)
- Discovering the contributions and hardships of outback pioneers at Longreach's **Stockman's Hall of Fame** (p426)
- Staring at the multitude of stars above **Nardoo Station** (p432) while soaking in a warm artesian spa with a cold beer in hand
- Reliving the glory days, listening to a yarn and propping up the bar at Charleville's grand **Hotel Corones** (p432)
- Celebrating the sacrifices and courage of Australia's workers at the **Australian Workers Heritage Centre** (p429) in Barcaldine
- Joining in the festivities and revelry at the absurdly popular **Birdsville Races** (p434)

- www.outbackholidays.info/
- www.queenslandholidays.com.au/outback/index.cfm

Stretching west beyond the Great Dividing Range, the legendary outback is truly reminiscent of Dorothea Mackellar's 'sunburnt country'.

The immeasurable area 'out back' is a semi-arid region of vast grasslands and low scrub drained by coolabah-lined rivers with evocative names such as the Barcoo, the Warrego and Cooper Creek. Beneath it all lies the Great Artesian Basin, an enormous underground reservoir whose steaming, pungent waters provide life-support to the extensive sheep and cattle stations and far-flung towns. There are some outstanding attractions out here that showcase the pioneering spirit of the outback, including the Australian Workers Heritage Centre in Barcaldine, the Stockman's Hall of Fame & Outback Heritage Centre in Longreach, and the Birdsville Working Museum. Yet for many, it is the wide, shimmering horizons, the sunsets, the starry nights and the outback characters that stick in the mind long after the red dust and over-intimate flies have been wiped from the body.

This chapter is divided into three sections: the two major routes along which most towns and attractions are strung – the east–west Overlander's Way and the north–south Matilda Hwy – and the remote Channel Country in the state's southwest corner.

Climate

The best time to travel in the outback is during the cooler months between April and October. Days are mildly warm, with maximum temperatures seldom topping 30°C, and nights are cool to cold – temperatures below freezing are not uncommon. Summer isn't a good time to visit. Average maximum temperatures are over 35°C and frequently soar over 40°C, and travelling in such heat can be hazardous. Summer is also the time of the Wet, when monsoonal rains far away in the north can fill the region's hundreds of rivers and creeks, sometimes flooding vast areas of the Channel Country and cutting off roads. Rain itself is a rare occurrence in the outback, with the southern areas averaging around 150mm a year.

Getting There & Away

AIR

Qantas and **Qantaslink** (☎ 13 13 13; www.qantas .com.au) fly from Brisbane to Barcaldine, Blackall, Charleville and Longreach, with daily flights between Brisbane and Mt Isa.

Macair (☎ 13 13 23; www.macair.com.au) flies between Brisbane and Birdsville via Charleville, Quilpie and Windorah; from Birdsville to Mt Isa with stops at Bedourie and Boulia; from Brisbane to Thargomindah via

Cunnamulla; from Townsville to Mt Isa direct and via Hughenden, Richmond, Julia Creek and Cloncurry; and from Townsville to Longreach via Winton. Macair also services the northwestern corner of the state, connecting Mt Isa to Cairns, Doomadgee, Burketown, and Normanton.

Airlines of South Australia (☎ 1800 018 234; www.airlinesofsa.com.au) does a weekly mail run (reputedly the world's longest) from Port Augusta in South Australia to Bedourie and Boulia on Saturday, and back via Birdsville on Sunday. An all-inclusive tour costs $950, while the airfare only costs $660.

BUS

Greyhound Australia (☎ 13 14 99; www.greyhound .com.au) has a regular coach service from Townsville to Mt Isa via Hughenden, and from Brisbane to Mt Isa via Roma. From Mt Isa buses continue to Three Ways in the Northern Territory; from there you can head north to Darwin or south to Tennant Creek and Alice Springs.

Emerald Coaches (☎ 1800 428 737; www.emerald coaches.com.au) makes the run from Rockhampton to Longreach (twice weekly) via Emerald. There is also a private bus from Normanton to Mt Isa on Monday, returning on Tuesday.

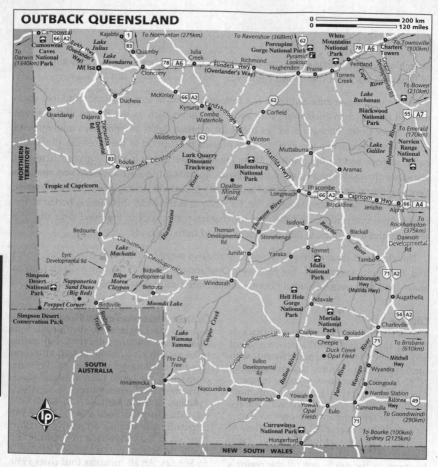

OUTBACK QUEENSLAND

CAR & MOTORCYCLE

The outback, although sparsely settled, is well serviced by major roads – the Flinders and Barkly Hwys, which together are the Overlander's Way, connect northern Queensland with the Northern Territory; the Capricorn Hwy runs along the tropic of Capricorn from Rockhampton to Longreach; and the Landsborough and Mitchell Hwys, which together are the Matilda Hwy, run from the New South Wales border south of Cunnamulla up to Cloncurry, Mt Isa and beyond. The **Department of Natural Resources and Mines** (www.nrm.qld.gov.au) has produced an excellent map called *Outback Queensland*; it can be purchased from Sunmap agencies, service stations and bookshops.

Although access has vastly improved from the time of the early explorers, remember that this is harsh, unforgiving country. No matter how safe you feel sitting in your air-con car, always prepare for unexpected delays, extreme temperatures, scarcity of water and isolation. Away from the major highways, roads deteriorate rapidly; services are extremely limited and you must carry spare parts, fuel and water.

TRAIN

Queensland Rail (☎ 13 22 32, 1300 13 17 22; www.travel train.com.au) has three trains servicing the outback, and all run twice weekly. The *Spirit of the Outback* runs from Brisbane to Longreach via Rockhampton, with connecting bus services to Winton; the *Westlander* runs from Brisbane to Charleville, with connecting bus services to Cunnamulla and Quilpie; and the *Inlander* runs from Townsville to Mt Isa.

CHARTERS TOWERS TO CAMOOWEAL – THE OVERLANDER'S WAY

The Flinders Hwy, which stretches 775km from Townsville to Cloncurry, is the major route across the north of the outback. From Cloncurry, the Barkly Hwy picks up where the Flinders Hwy leaves off and takes you on to Mt Isa and Camooweal and into the Northern Territory. Together they are referred to as the Overlander's Way.

The Charters-Towers-to-Torrens-Creek section passes through the Great Dividing Range, and apart from that the terrain is relentlessly flat – a seemingly endless landscape of Mitchell grass plains. There is little visual relief until you pass Cloncurry and reach the low, red hills that surround Mt Isa. The two highways are sealed all the way and are generally in good condition, although northwest of Mt Isa the road deteriorates in sections to a narrow, single lane of bitumen.

CHARTERS TOWERS TO CLONCURRY

The 246km route from Charters Towers to Hughenden is a former Cobb & Co coach run, and is dotted along the way with tiny townships that were established as stopovers for the coaches.

It's 105km to the small settlement of **Pentland**, and another 94km to the aptly-named town of **Prairie**, which consists of a small cluster of houses, a railway station and the quiet little **Prairie Hotel** (☎ /fax 4741 5121; Flinders Hwy; s/d from $33/44; ✗). First licensed in 1884, this historic pub was originally a Cobb & Co coach stop. It's filled with atmosphere and memorabilia, and even has a resident ghost.

Hughenden

Hughenden is on the banks of the Flinders River, in the same spot where explorer William Landsborough camped in 1862 during his fruitless search for survivors from the Burke and Wills expedition. Today Hughenden is a busy commercial centre servicing the surrounding cattle, wool and grain industries.

Inside the **Flinders Discovery Centre** (☎ 4741 1021; 37 Gray St; adult/child $2/free; ✆ 9am-5pm) is a 7m replica skeleton of *Muttaburrasaurus*, one of the largest and most complete dinosaur skeletons ever found in Australia. The centre has other museum displays and doubles as a visitor information centre.

The **Royal Hotel Resort** (☎ 4741 1183; 21 Moran St; s/d $60/71; ✗) offers spotless motel units, while the venerable **Grand Hotel** (☎ /fax 4741 1588; 25 Gray St; s/d $25/$35; ✗) has classic well-worn pub rooms and good counter meals. The **Allan Terry Caravan Park** (☎ /fax 4741 1190; 2 Resolution St; unpowered/powered sites $14/16, cabins from $45), opposite the train station and next to the pool, has some shady sites. Prices are for two people.

Porcupine Gorge National Park

Porcupine Gorge National Park is an oasis in the dry country north of Hughenden, and off the mostly unpaved Kennedy Developmental Rd. The best spot is **Pyramid Lookout**, about 70km north of Hughenden. You can **camp** (per person/family $4/16) at self-registration sites here, and it's an easy 30-minute walk into the gorge, with some fine rock formations and a permanently running creek.

Richmond

Richmond is halfway between Townsville and Mt Isa, on the Flinders River, and in a fossil-rich region that was once an immense inland sea. The area around Richmond is abundant in sandalwood, and a factory in the town processes the wood for export to Asia, where it is used for incense.

Kronosaurus Korner Information Centre (☎ 4741 3429; 91 Goldring St; ✆ 8.30am-4.45pm) has a huge model of a crocodile-like prehistoric reptile, an advertisement for the impressive **Fossil Centre** (adult/child $10/5) inside, which includes an almost-complete 4.25m pliosaur skeleton – one of Australia's best fossils.

Ammonite Inn (☎ 4741 3932; fax 4741 3934; 88 Goldring St; s/d $78/89; ✗) has the best rooms in Richmond as well as a good restaurant and bar. You'll also find pub accommodation and meals, and a caravan park.

Julia Creek

It's another flat and featureless 144km from Richmond to Julia Creek, a small pastoral centre. About 4km west of town, the sealed Wills Developmental Rd heads north to the Burke & Wills Roadhouse (235km). From the roadhouse you can continue north to Burketown, Normanton and Karumba. The town's limited accommodation options include a motel, hotel and caravan park.

CLONCURRY

Cloncurry's major claim to fame is as the birthplace of the Royal Flying Doctor Service. A more dubious honour is that it had Australia's hottest recorded temperature, a not-so-cool 53.1°C in January 1889. The 'Curry' was the centre of a copper boom in the 19th century, and was once the largest copper producer in the British Empire. Today it's a busy pastoral centre with a recently reinvigorated mining industry. The Burke Developmental Rd, which heads north from Cloncurry, is sealed all the way to Normanton and Karumba, on the Gulf of Carpentaria.

The **Mary Kathleen Park & Museum** (☎ 4742 1361; McIlwraith St; adult/child $7/3; ❂ 8am-4.30pm Mon-Fri, 9am-3pm Sat & Sun) on the eastern side of town is the tourist information centre. Relics of the Burke and Wills expedition, and displays of local rocks and minerals are housed in buildings transported from the former uranium mine of Mary Kathleen. You can also make arrangements here to tour the **Ernest Henry copper and gold mine** (adult/child $15/5).

John Flynn Place (☎ 4742 1251; Daintree & King Sts; adult/child $8.50/4; ❂ 8am-4.30pm Mon-Fri, 9am-3pm Sat & Sun Apr-Oct) commemorates Flynn's work in setting up the invaluable Royal Flying Doctor Service (RFDS). The building incorporates an art gallery, a cultural centre and a theatre.

The historic **Wagon Wheel Motel** (☎ 4742 1866; fax 4742 1819; 54 Ramsay St; s/d from $54/65; ❄ ❑) is a friendly place with clean, comfortable rooms. Its excellent **Prince of Wales Restaurant** (mains $10-30) serves pasta and pizza (from Wednesday to Sunday only) and superb à la carte meals (daily). The attractive **Gidgee Inn** (☎ 4742 1599; gidgeeinn@bigpond.com.au; Matilda Hwy; s/d $98/104) is built from rammed red earth and trimmed with corrugated iron. The rooms are modern and spotless, and there is an excellent **restaurant** (mains $10-25). The **Gilbert Park Tourist Park** (☎ 4742

2300; gilpark@bigpond.com.au; Matilda Hwy; unpowered/powered sites $16/19, cabins from $70) is the best of the van parks. Prices are for two people.

CLONCURRY TO MT ISA

This 117km stretch of the Barkly Hwy has a few interesting stops and detours. Beside the **Corella River**, 44km west of Cloncurry, there's a memorial cairn to the Burke and Wills expedition, which passed here in 1861. Another 1km down the road is the **Kalkadoon & Mitakoodi Memorial**, which marks an Aboriginal tribal boundary.

Another 9km on, you pass the (unmarked) site of **Mary Kathleen**, which was a uranium mining town from the 1950s to 1982, but is now completely demolished. The turn-off to **Lake Julius**, Mt Isa's reserve water supply, is 36km past Mary Kathleen. The lake is on the Leichhardt River, 90km of unsealed road from the highway. It is a popular spot for fishing and water-skiing, and has a low-key camping resort. Nearby is **Battle Mountain**, the scene of the last stand of the Kalkadoon people in 1884.

MT ISA

Mt Isa owes its existence to immensely rich lead, zinc, silver and copper ore bodies beneath the red ridges west of the city. The sandy Leichhardt River divides 'townside' from 'mineside', home from work. 'The Isa', as it is known locally, is inland Queensland's major town.

Prospector John Campbell Miles discovered the first deposits here in 1923. He was recovering his wayward horse 'Hard Times' when he stumbled upon the heavy ore outcrop, or so the story goes. Since the ore deposits were large and of variable grade, working them profitably required the sort of investment only a company could afford. Mt Isa Mines (MIM) was founded in 1924. It was during and after WWII that Mt Isa really took off. Job opportunities attracted people of more than 50 different nationalities – mostly males – to this isolated corner. Today the mine is part of a global mining empire and is among the world's top producers of silver, copper and zinc; and the town is thriving.

Information
Book Country (☎ 4749 0400; 27 Simpson St, Isa Sq) Excellent bookshop with a good travel section.

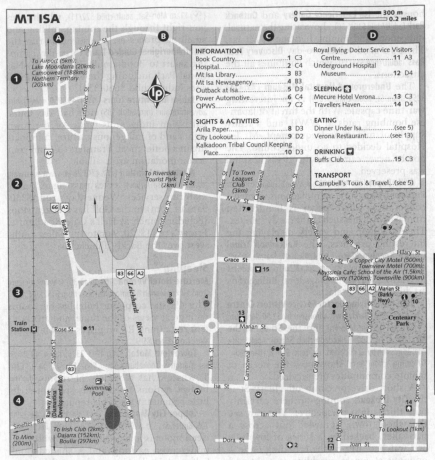

MT ISA

0 ——————— 300 m
0 ——————— 0.2 miles

OUTBACK QUEENSLAND

Mt Isa Base Hospital (☎ 4744 4444; 30 Camooweal St)
Mt Isa Library (☎ 4744 4266; 23 West St; per hr $3)
Internet access.
Mt Isa Newsagency (☎ 4743 9105; 25b Miles St;
per hr $5.50) Internet access.
Outback at Isa (☎ 1300 659 660, 4749 1555; www
.outbackatisa.com.au; 19 Marian St; ☒ 8.30am-5pm)
The number-one tourist attraction also houses a very
helpful information centre, an office and the long-distance
bus terminal.
Power Automotive (☎ 4743 2542; 13 Simpson St)
The RACQ agent.
Queensland Parks & Wildlife Service (QPWS;
☎ 4744 7888; cnr Mary & Camooweal Sts) Provides
information on the national parks in the area, including
Boodjamulla (Lawn Hill) National Park and Camooweal
Caves National Park.

Sights & Activities

The town's major attraction is **Outback at Isa**
(☎ 1300 659 660, 4749 1555; www.outbackatisa.com.au;
19 Marian St; ☒ 8.30am-5pm). It features the underground **Hard Times Mine** (adult/child $45/26), where
you get kitted out in fair-dinkum mining at-
tire and head lamps, and descend a purpose-
built mine complete with fuming, roaring
and rattling machinery. The emphasis is
on creating a real mining experience and
your entertaining guide will most likely be
a miner. It's hands-on, noisy, damp, dark
and highly recommended. Also here is the
fascinating **Riversleigh Fossil Centre** (adult/child
$10/6.50), where you get to see a recreation
of Australia's prehistoric fauna, actual fossils, and a working fossil lab. The centre also

houses the **Isa Experience Gallery** and **Outback Park** (adult/child $10/6.50), showcasing the natural, indigenous and mining heritage of Mt Isa. There's a good-value, two-day **Discovery Tour Pass** (adult/child $55/33), which combines all the attractions.

The **Underground Hospital Museum** (☎ 4743 3853; Joan St; adult/child $10/4) is an interesting war-time capsule. With the threat of Japanese bombing raids in WWII, and a ready supply of miners and equipment, Mt Isa Hospital decided to go underground. The bombs never came and the 1940s hospital was preserved.

Arilla Paper (☎ 4743 0084; www.arillapaper.com; cnr Shackleton & Marian Sts) is an indigenous women's cooperative, where paper is handcrafted from native plants such as the hardy spinifex. There's a shop and gallery displaying the interesting products. The **Kalkadoon Tribal Council Keeping Place** (☎ 4749 1001; Marion St; admission by $2 donation; ☒ 9am-5pm Mon-Fri), adjacent to Outback at Isa, displays local indigenous art, history and artefacts.

The **Royal Flying Doctor Service Visitors Centre** (☎ 4743 2800; Barkly Hwy; admission by $2.50 donation; ☒ 9.30am-4.30pm Mon-Fri) and the **School of the Air** (☎ 4744 9100; Kalkadoon High School, Abel Smith Pde; admission by $2 donation; ☒ tours 9am & 10am Mon-Fri during school term) show how the needs of remote communities are serviced.

A short drive or climb off Hilary St is the **City Lookout**; coming up here certainly puts things into perspective. You can see the whole town, sprawled out across a flat valley, backed by a series of low hills and watched over by the brooding mine – ominous at sunset, sparkling at night and almost attractive at sunrise.

Lake Moondarra, 16km north of town, is a popular spot for swimming, boating, water-skiing, fishing and bird-watching. Mt Isa is also home to Australia's largest **Rodeo** (www.isarodeo.com.au), held over the second weekend in August, following a fortnight of festivities.

Tours

There's a large range of tours and activities that can be booked through the information desk at Outback at Isa.

Campbell's Tours & Travel (☎ 4743 2006; www.campbellstravel.com.au; 19 Marion St), inside the Outback at Isa complex, runs the interesting two-hour **Mt Isa Mines Surface Tour**

(☒ 11am Mon-Sat; adult/child $22/11), which takes you right through the mining, milling and smelting processes. It also helps run the **Yididi Aboriginal Guided Tours** three-day camping safari to Boodjamulla (Lawn Hill) National Park including the Riversleigh fossil sites (adult/child $660/330).

Jabiru Adventure Tours (☎ 4749 5950; www.jabiru adventuretours.com; adult $85) runs half-day tours, led by an indigenous guide, of the town sights and of indigenous culture, culminating in a buffet meal. Transfers to/from your accommodation are available.

Westwing Aviation (☎ 4743 2844; www.westwing .com.au; Mt Isa Airport) takes passengers on its mail run services. Wednesday's run ($330, 9am to 5pm) to the Gulf has a dozen stops including lunch at Hell's Gate Roadhouse. Friday's run ($220, 9am to 1pm) flies southwest over the Barkly Tablelands.

Sleeping

Mercure Hotel Verona (☎ 4743 3024; www.mercure .com.au; cnr Marian & Camooweal Sts; r from $152; ☒ ☒) This 4½-star corporate hotel has big rooms with great views of the mine, and an excellent restaurant. Room prices tumble on the weekend to $99.

Townview Motel (☎ 4743 3328; fax 4749 0409; cnr Marion & Kookaburra Sts; r $65-150; ☒ ☒) The Townview has a variety of rooms, from budget options to spacious spa suites. Its little restaurant has a big reputation.

Copper City Motel (☎ 4743 3904; fax 4743 2290; 105 Butler St; s/d $70/80; ☒ ☒) This friendly, clean motel is in a quiet location with good undercover parking and a shaded pool. Self-contained units are also available.

Travellers Haven (☎ 4743 0313; www.users.bigpond .net.au/travellershaven; 75 Spence St; dm/s/d $20/32/46; ☒ ☒ ☒) The Travellers Haven is the main budget option for backpackers and is generally quiet. The rooms and facilities are adequate. A free pick-up service is offered, though the hostel is not far from the bus terminal.

Riverside Tourist Park (☎ 4743 3904; fax 4743 9417; 195 West St; unpowered/powered sites $16/20, cabins $67; ☒ ☒) This large, palm-lined park is about 2km north of the centre. It's well set out, with a row of neat cabins at the front, clean amenities, camp kitchen (with fridge), gem store, huge pool and pleasant, shaded lawn sites. Prices are for two people.

Eating & Drinking

Mt Isa Irish Club (☎ 4743 2577; Nineteenth Ave) With three bars, a coffee shop, a restaurant and a nightclub, the Irish Club has a venue for any occasion. Keane's Bar & Grill (mains $14 to $22) serves excellent bistro-style meals including aged beef and fresh seafood. Wednesday night is Mexican night, and there's live entertainment most nights. The Blarney Bar (mains $10) has a buffet, and the Tram Stop (mains $6 to $9) is in an old Melbourne tram with coffee, cakes and snacks.

Verona Restaurant (Mercure Hotel Verona; ☎ 4743 3024; cnr Marian & Camooweal Sts; mains $23-28) Located in Mt Isa's top corporate hotel, the elegant Verona has an imaginative menu featuring seafood and Italian cuisine.

Abyssinia Cafe (Townview Motel; ☎ 4743 3328; cnr Marion & Kookaburra Sts; mains $16-25; ☘ dinner Mon-Sat) This cosmopolitan café serves up Ethiopian, Indian, Mexican and other dishes, and is highly regarded for good-value, authentic meals.

Dinner Under Isa (☎ 1300 659 660; 19 Marian St; 3-course meal $69; ☘ 5-8.30pm Mon, Wed, Fri & Sat) Don a hard hat, safety specs and head lamp and enjoy a three-course dinner in the crib room of the Hard Times mine. A mine tour and tall stories are included. The mine is licensed.

Buffs Club (☎ 4743 2365; cnr Grace & Camooweal Sts; mains $19-23) Buffs is a busy bar with a relaxing deck, pokie lounge, somewhere safe to stash the kiddies, courtesy bus, live entertainment, and the Frog & Toad Bar & Grill, which offers steak, chicken and seafood – all with chips.

Town Leagues Club (☎ 4749 5455; Ryan Rd; mains $10-20) Townies has snacks and coffee, and good-value bistro meals. The beer is cheap and all the sporting action you need is covered by the big-screen TVs.

Entertainment

Mt Isa Irish Club (☎ 4743 2577; Nineteenth Ave) The bountiful Irish Club offers a variety of good entertainment. Live bands often play in Keane's Bar & Grill, while downstairs there's the popular nightclub, the Rish (admission $5), and a karaoke bar.

Getting There & Around

AIR

Mt Isa Airport (☎ 4743 4598; Barkly Hwy) is 5km north of town. A taxi to town costs about $12. **Qantas** (☎ 13 13 13; www.qantas.com.au) flies daily between Brisbane and Mt Isa (from $220). **Macair** (☎ 13 13 23; www.macair.com.au), flies to Birdsville, Townsville, Normanton and Cairns from Mt Isa. See p417 for details of stops on each of these routes.

BUS

Campbell's Tours & Travel (☎ 4743 2006; www.camp bellstravel.com.au; 19 Marion St) is the long-distance bus terminal. **Greyhound Australia** (☎ 13 14 99; www.greyhound.com.au) has a regular service to Townsville ($119, 11½ hours) via Hughenden, and to Brisbane ($152, 25 hours) via Longreach and Roma. Services also run west to Three Ways in the Northern Territory, from where you can head north to Darwin ($277) or south to Alice Springs ($227). To reach Rockhampton, you must connect at Longreach with the twice-weekly **Emerald Coaches** (☎ 1800 28737; www.emeraldcoaches.com.au) service via Emerald.

AICCC runs a bus from Normanton to Mt Isa on Monday, returning on Tuesday (adult/child one way $110/85). In Mt Isa the bus leaves from the Campbell's terminal and you can book through Campbell's Tours & Travel.

There are no local bus services.

CAR

If you want a taxi, call ☎ 4743 2333. There are several car-hire firms, all with desks at the airport, including **Avis** (☎ 4743 3733), **Hertz** (☎ 4743 4142) and **Thrifty** (☎ 4743 2911).

TRAIN

Queensland Rail (☎ 13 22 32, 1300 13 17 22; www .traveltrain.com.au) operates the *Inlander* train twice a week between Townsville and Mt Isa, via Charters Towers, Hughenden and Cloncurry. The full journey takes about 20 hours and costs $110/165/255 per economy seat/economy sleeper/1st-class sleeper.

MT ISA TO CAMOOWEAL

Camooweal, 13km east of the Northern Territory border, was founded in 1884 as a service centre for the cattle stations of the Barkly Tableland, and is the turn-off for Camooweal Caves National Park. You can also turn off here for Boodjamulla (Lawn Hill) National Park, Gregory Downs and Burketown.

Once you have seen the **Shire Hall** (1922) and checked out **Freckleton's General Store**, you've pretty much covered the sights. The **Camooweal Roadhouse** (☎ 4748 2155; Barkly Hwy; unpowered/powered sites $11/16, s/d from $30/44) is the local RACQ agent, and has motel rooms and a caravan park. For a home away from home, try the **Rainbow Oasis Backpackers** (☎ 4748 2011; Barkly Hwy; s/d $25/45), with comfortable, private bedrooms.

About 8km south of town, along a rough road, is the entrance to **Camooweal Caves National Park**. This network of unusual caves with sinkhole openings, which floods during the wet season, is for experienced cavers only. There's a self-registration camping ground with toilets, and information is available from **QPWS Mt Isa** (☎ 4744 7888).

There's nothing much for the whole 460km from Camooweal to the Threeways junction in the Northern Territory. There's a petrol station 260km from Camooweal and you can stay nearby at **Barkly Homestead** (☎ 08-8964 4549; fax 08-8964 4543; Barkly Hwy; unpowered/powered sites $14/22, s/d $80/90).

CLONCURRY TO CUNNAMULLA – THE MATILDA HIGHWAY

The Matilda Hwy is the major north–south route through outback Queensland. This bitumen highway runs north from the Queensland–New South Wales border for more than 1700km to Karumba on the Gulf. The highway takes you through most of the outback's major towns and attractions, including the Australian Workers Heritage Centre in Barcaldine and the Stockman's Hall of Fame in Longreach.

The Matilda Hwy comprises sections of the Mitchell Hwy, the Landsborough Hwy and the Burke Developmental Rd. The section from Cloncurry to Cunnamulla is covered in this chapter. See p415 for details of the northern section of the route.

CLONCURRY TO WINTON

About 14km east of Cloncurry, the narrow Landsborough Hwy turns off the Flinders Hwy and heads southeast to Winton via the one-pub towns of McKinlay and Kynuna. The first section of this 341km route, from Cloncurry to McKinlay, passes through a rug-

ged and rocky landscape of low, craggy hills; these gradually give way to the flat, grassy plains that typify most of the outback.

McKinlay is a tiny settlement that would probably have been doomed to eternal insignificance had it not been used as a location in the amazingly successful movie *Crocodile Dundee*. The **Walkabout Creek Hotel** (☎ 4746 8424; fax 4746 8768; Landsborough Hwy; unpowered/ powered sites $18/20, s/d $45/55; ⌨) has movie memorabilia and all the charm of a movie set. There are small, basic motel units a block west of the pub, or there's a camping ground out the back.

Kynuna, another 74km southeast, isn't much bigger than McKinlay. It's home to **Magoffin's Matilda Expo** (☎ 4746 8401; Landsborough Hwy; adult/child $9/5), a gaudy, ramshackle 'museum' owned by Richard Magoffin, a real outback character. The Matilda Expo promises to reveal the true story behind Australia's unofficial anthem, 'Waltzing Matilda'. Told in curling photographs and documents pinned to the walls, the *pièce de résistance* is the original handwritten composition penned by Christina McPherson with 'Banjo' Paterson's words in 1895. You only get a glimpse and, whether you believe it or not, it's well worth a visit and is a stark contrast to the flashy Waltzing Matilda Centre at Winton. Richard Magoffin does live musical renditions of the song and two-hour shows at 7pm from April to October.

You'll find a lot to like about the historic little **Blue Heeler Hotel** (☎ 4746 8650; fax 4746 8643; blueheelerpub@bigpond.com; Landsborough Hwy; unpowered/powered sites $6/10, r $50, d $70; ⌨), from its walls covered with scrawled messages and signatures to its unquestionably essential surf life-saving club. It's a friendly place with good meals, pub rooms, spotless air-con motel units, and camp sites (prices are for two people) in the adjacent Jolly Swag-van Park. The nearest beach may be almost 1000km away, but each April the Blue Heeler hosts a surf life-saving carnival complete with surfboard relays, a tug of war and an evening beach party.

The signposted turn-off for the **Combo Waterhole**, which 'Banjo' Paterson is said to have visited in 1895 before he wrote 'Waltzing Matilda', is off the highway about 12km east of Kynuna. The waterhole is on Dagworth Station.

WINTON

☎ 07 / pop 1321

Winton is a cattle- and sheep-raising centre, and also the railhead from which the beasts are transported after being brought from the Channel Country by road train. The town has two major claims to fame: the founding of Qantas airlines in 1920, and the regionally inspired verse of one of Australia's most famous poets, 'Banjo' Paterson. Both are commemorated inside the impressive Waltzing Matilda Centre on the main street.

Information

Central Motors (☎ 4657 1256; 81 Eldersley St) The local RACQ agent.

Winton library (☎ 4657 0393; 76 Eldersley St) Internet access.

Sights & Activities

Winton's biggest attraction is the **Waltzing Matilda Centre** (☎ 4657 1466; www.matildacentre .com.au; 50 Elderslie St; adult/child $14/12; ☯ 8.30am-5pm), which doubles as the visitor information centre. For a museum devoted to a

song, there's a surprising amount here, including an indoor billabong, complete with a squatter, troopers and a jolly swagman, a hologram display oozing nationalism, and the **Jolly Swagman** statue – a tribute to the unknown swagmen who lie in unmarked graves in the area. The centre also houses a gallery and the **Qantilda Pioneer Place**, which has a huge collection of fascinating artefacts as well as displays on the founding of Qantas.

The **Corfield & Fitzmaurice Building** (☎ 4657 1486; 63 Elderslie St; adult/child $3/1; ☯ 9am-5pm Mon-Fri, 9am-1pm Sat) is a National Trust–classified former general store. It houses a craft cooperative with a gem and mineral collection, and a life-sized re-creation of a dinosaur stampede that occurred at what is now Lark Quarry, southwest of Winton (see p426).

The **Royal Theatre** (☎ 4657 1296; 73 Elderslie St; adult/child $6/4; ☯ 8pm Wed Apr-Sep), at the rear of Wookatook Gift & Gem, is a wonderful open-air theatre with canvas-slung chairs, corrugated tin walls and a star-studded ceiling. It has a small museum in the projection

---

ONCE A JOLLY SWAGMAN

Written in 1895 by 'Banjo' Paterson (1864–1941), 'Waltzing Matilda' is widely regarded as Australia's unofficial national anthem. While not many can sing the official anthem, 'Advance Australia Fair', without a lyric sheet, just about every Aussie knows the words to the strange ditty about a jolly swagman who jumped into a billabong and drowned himself rather than be arrested for stealing a jumbuck (sheep). But what the hell does it mean?

The Waltzing Matilda Centenary festival, held in Winton in April 1995, created controversy among local historians over the origins and meaning of the famous tune; and the continuing Winton and Kynuna rivalry keeps it simmering along.

To understand the song's origins, it has to be seen in the political context of its time. The 1890s were a period of political change in Queensland. Along with nationalistic calls for federation, economic crisis, mass unemployment and severe droughts dominated the decade. An ongoing battle between pastoralists and shearers led to a series of strikes that divided the state and led to the formation of the Australian Labor Party to represent workers' interests.

In 1895 Paterson visited his fiancée in Winton, and together they travelled to Dagworth Station south of Kynuna, where they met Christina McPherson. During their stay they went on a picnic to the Combo Waterhole, a series of billabongs on the Diamantina River, where Paterson heard stories about the violent 1894 shearers' strike on Dagworth Station. During the strike rebel shearers had burned seven woolsheds to the ground, leading the police to declare martial law and place a reward of £1000 on the head of their leader, Samuel Hofmeister. Rather than be captured, Hofmeister killed himself near the Combo Waterhole.

Paterson later wrote the words to 'Waltzing Matilda' to accompany a tune played by Christina McPherson on a zither. While there is no direct proof he was writing allegorically about Hofmeister and the shearers' strikes, a number of prominent historians have supported the theory and claimed the song was a political statement. Others maintain it is just an innocent but catchy tune about a hungry vagrant, but the song's undeniable anti-authoritarianism, and the fact that it was adopted as an anthem by the rebel shearers, weigh heavily in favour of the historians argument.

room (admission $2) and screens old favourites such as Laurel and Hardy.

Arno's Wall (Vindex St) is Winton's quirkiest attraction: a 70m-long work-in-progress featuring a huge range of industrial and household items, from TVs to motorbikes, ensnared in the mortar. Find it behind the North Gregory Hotel.

Winton's major festival is the five-day **Outback Festival** held every odd year in the September school holidays. The annual **Bush Poetry Festival**, in July, attracts entrants from all over Australia.

Sleeping & Eating

North Gregory Hotel (☎ 1800 801 611, 4657 1375; fax 4657 0106; 67 Elderslie St; dm $18, s with/without bathroom $55/33, d $65/44; 🔀) The epitome of the big, friendly country pub, the North Gregory holds its place in history as the venue where 'Waltzing Matilda' reportedly was first performed on 6 April 1895, although the original building burnt down in 1900. There are dozens of comfortable rooms upstairs and the rates include a continental breakfast. There's also a backpackers at the rear of the hotel and free van parking. The **restaurant** (mains $10-20) serves excellent bistro meals in the bar or the dining room.

Boulder Opal Motor Inn (☎ 4657 1211; fax 4657 1331; Elderslie St; s/d $88/95; 🔀 🔊) The Boulder Opal offers large, modern rooms with all the appointments. Its **Matrix Bar & Restaurant** (mains $23-32), has big juicy country steaks and imaginative chicken and seafood dishes.

Matilda Country Tourist Park (☎ /fax 4657 1607; tmatpark@tpg.com.au; 43 Chirnside St; d unpowered/powered sites $18/20, cabins $70) This good camping ground at the northern end of town puts on regular campfire meals, complete with bush poetry and yarns. Prices are for two people.

Tattersalls Hotel (☎ 4657 1309; 78 Elderslie St; mains $10-18) You can eat good pub food in the corrugated iron–decorated dining room, or alfresco on the footpath.

Getting There & Away

Wookatook Gift & Gem (☎ 4657 1296; 73 Elderslie St) operates as a travel agency for air, bus and train tickets. **Macair** (☎ 13 13 23; www.macair .com.au) flies to Townsville and Longreach. **Greyhound Australia** (☎ 13 14 99; www.greyhound .com.au) operates services from Brisbane to Winton ($129) and Winton to Mt Isa ($71). There are also connecting bus services be-

tween Winton and Longreach that meet up with the twice-weekly *Spirit of the Outback* train.

AROUND WINTON

It's a bit out of the way, but the **Lark Quarry Dinosaur Trackways** (www.dinosaurtrackways.com.au), where hundreds of dinosaur footprints are preserved in the rock, is worth the trip. Once a prehistoric lake, the area was the scene of a stampede of small dinosaurs startled by a large predator. It is now protected by a sheltered walkway, although there are no facilities here, other than a toilet and a rainwater tank. The park is well signposted 110km southwest of Winton, and it takes about 90 minutes to drive there, but the mostly dirt road is impassable in wet weather. Contact the Waltzing Matilda Centre at Winton (p425) or the Visitors Information Centre in Longreach (below) for information on tours (April to September).

The **Opalton Mining Field**, 112km south of Winton, is a remote gemfield where boulder opals can be found. There are few facilities here, and the road is unsealed and slow going.

LONGREACH

☎ 07 / pop 3673

Longreach was the home of Qantas early last century, but these days it's equally renowned for the Australian Stockman's Hall of Fame & Outback Heritage Centre, one of outback Queensland's biggest attractions, and as the centre of a prosperous wool- and beef-producing region.

Information

Longreach Library (☎ 4658 4104; 96a Eagle St; 🕘 9.30am-1pm Tue & Thu, 12.30-4.30pm Wed & Fri, 9am-noon Sat) Has free Internet access.
Visitors Information Centre (☎ 4658 3555; 99 Eagle St; 🕘 9am-5pm Mon-Fri, 9am-1pm Sat & Sun) Opposite the library.

Sights & Activities

The **Australian Stockman's Hall of Fame & Outback Heritage Centre** (☎ 4658 2166; www.outbackheritage .com.au; Landsborough Hwy; adult/child/family $20/10/45; 🕘 9am-5pm) is housed in a beautifully conceived building, 2km east of town towards Barcaldine. The centre was built as a tribute to the early explorers and stockmen,

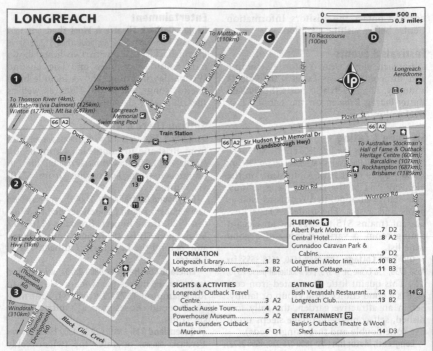

LONGREACH

INFORMATION
Longreach Library.....................1 B2
Visitors Information Centre......2 B2

SIGHTS & ACTIVITIES
Longreach Outback Travel
   Centre..................................3 A2
Outback Aussie Tours..............4 A2
Powerhouse Museum..............5 A2
Qantas Founders Outback
   Museum...............................6 D1

SLEEPING
Albert Park Motor Inn..............7 D2
Central Hotel...........................8 A2
Gunnadoo Caravan Park &
   Cabins.................................9 D2
Longreach Motor Inn..............10 D2
Old Time Cottage...................11 B3

EATING
Bush Verandah Restaurant......12 B2
Longreach Club......................13 B2

ENTERTAINMENT
Banjo's Outback Theatre & Wool
   Shed...................................14 D3

OUTBACK QUEENSLAND

but has gradually developed to encompass much more. There are several themed galleries covering Aboriginal culture, European exploration, pioneering settlers and, of course, stockmen, drovers and droving. There are dozens of static exhibits featuring stories of the outback's characters and some audiovisual displays, such as the Talking Drover, to liven things up. There is the inevitable souvenir shop, a good bookshop, and a café. The admission ticket is valid for two days, so you can move through the centre at your own pace.

The interesting **Qantas Founders Outback Museum** (4658 3737; www.qfom.com.au; Landsborough Hwy; adult/child/family $16/8/38; 9am-5pm) houses a life-sized replica of an Avro 504K, the first aircraft owned by the fledgling airline. Interactive multimedia and working displays tell the history of Qantas. Next door, in the original 1921 Qantas hangar where six DH-50 biplanes were assembled in 1926, is a mint-condition DH-61. Towering over everything is a bright and shiny **747-200B Jumbo** (adult/child/family $12/6/25) which can be toured at additional cost.

The **Powerhouse Museum** (4658 3933; 12 Swan St; adult/child/family $5/3/13; 2-5pm Apr-Oct, hours vary Nov-Mar), in Longreach's former powerhouse, displays the huge old diesel and gas-vacuum engines that were used until 1985, as well as local history relics.

Tours
Longreach Outback Travel Centre (4658 1776; 115a Eagle St) offers a Longreach Lookabout tour (adult/child $174/148) that takes in the town's sites and ends with a dinner cruise on the Thomson River; the Sunset & Stars dinner cruise ($44/30); and a tour to Oakley station ($40/25), a working cattle and sheep property.

Outback Aussie Tours (1300 787 890; 18 Swan St) offers several day and half-day tours including a Dinosaur Matilda tour that includes Carisbrooke Station, Lark Quarry and the Waltzing Matilda Centre in Winton, as well as lunch and morning tea (adult/child $149/80).

You can also privately visit one or more of the area's **sheep and cattle stations**, such as Toobrack, 68km south, and Oakley, 15km north. Contact the Visitors Information Centre before visiting a station.

Festivals & Events

Longreach, along with Winton, Barcaldine and Ilfracombe, hosts **Easter in the Outback** annually. Longreach also hosts the **Outback Muster Drovers Reunion** on the Labour Day weekend in May.

Sleeping & Eating

Albert Park Motor Inn (☎ 1800 812 811, 4658 2411; fax 4658 3181; Sir Hudson Fysh Memorial Dr; s/d $95/105; 🅿 🖳) The Albert Park Motor Inn, on the highway east of the centre, has spacious, four-star, well-appointed rooms as well as pools and a spa. The motel's Oasis Restaurant (mains $15 to $30) has an elegant dining room, a varied menu and a good wine list.

Old Time Cottage (☎ 4658 1550, 4658 3555; fax 4658 3733; 158 Crane St; d $75, per additional person $10; 🅿) This quaint little corrugated-iron cottage is a good choice for a group or family. Set in an attractive garden, the fully furnished, self-contained cottage sleeps up to five (one double and three single beds).

Longreach Motor Inn (☎ 1800 076 020, 4658 2322; fax 4658 1828; 84 Galah St; s/d $88/99; 🅿 🖳) Fairly centrally located and set among shady gardens, this 3½-star motel is a good choice. The licensed Outback Restaurant (mains $14-28) offers pasta, seafood and grills, including some vegetarian dishes.

Bush Verandah Restaurant (☎ 4658 2448; 120 Galah St; mains $14-20; 🕒 dinner Tue-Sat) This is a small, licensed eatery with rustic décor and a country-style à la carte menu featuring beef, poultry and seafood.

Longreach Club (☎ 4658 1016; 31 Duck St; mains $10-15; 🕒 lunch & dinner) The relaxed Longreach Club's restaurant is recommended for its range of inexpensive specials, including smorgasbords and a roast of the day. It also has an à la carte menu.

Other accommodation options include:

Central Hotel (☎ 4658 2263; 126 Eagle St; s/d $25/40) There's nothing too flash about these rooms, but they are clean and good value. There are shared toilets and showers.

Gunnadoo Caravan Park & Cabins (☎ 4658 1781; fax 4658 0034; 12 Thrush Rd; unpowered/powered sites $18/20, cabins $40; 🅿 🖳) This neat, well-grassed and shady park is near the Hall of Fame, just off the Landsborough Hwy. Prices are for two people.

Entertainment

Banjo's Outback Theatre & Wool Shed (☎ 1800 641 661; 4658 2360; Stork Rd; adult/child $12.50/8) is a ramshackle place with two-hour shows most Saturday evenings, and Tuesday and Wednesday morning. Shows include bush poems, songs, yarns and skits, as well as shearing, wool classing and spinning.

Getting There & Away

Qantaslink (☎ 13 13 13; www.qantas.com.au) flies from Brisbane to Longreach (from $330). **Macair** (☎ 13 13 23; www.macair.com.au) flies to Longreach from Townsville (from $210) via Winton.

Greyhound Australia (☎ 13 14 99; www.greyhound .com.au) has a regular coach service to Winton ($28, three hours), Brisbane ($107, 17 hours) and Mt Isa ($77, eight hours). Buses stop behind the Longreach Outback Travel Centre.

Emerald Coaches (☎ 1800 28737; www.emerald coaches.com.au) makes the twice-weekly run to Rockhampton ($72, 9½ hours), returning via Emerald. Buses stop at Outback Aussie Tours.

Queensland Rail (☎ 13 22 32, 1300 13 17 22; www .traveltrain.com.au) operates the twice-weekly *Spirit of the Outback* train service between Longreach and Brisbane (economy sleeper/1st-class sleeper $216/340, 24 hours) via Rockhampton; there are connecting bus services between Longreach and Winton.

LONGREACH TO BARCALDINE

The tiny township of **Ifracombe**, 28km east of Longreach, modestly calls itself 'the Hub of the West' and boasts the **Ilfracombe Machinery & Heritage Museum** (Landsborough Hwy), a brightly painted collection of old tractors and farm machinery and several historic buildings on the side of the highway. The charming **Wellshot Hotel** (☎ 4658 2106; Landsborough Hwy; s/d $20/40) has an eclectic collection of memorabilia and a wall covered with a long poem, *The Wellshot & The Bush Pub's Hall of Fame*, by Robert Raftery. The pub has clean budget rooms with shared facilities and good pub tucker.

BARCALDINE

☎ 07 / pop 1496

Barcaldine (bar-*call*-din) lies at the junction of the Landsborough and Capricorn Hwys, 108km east of Longreach and 575km west of Rockhampton. It's known as the 'Garden City of the West', with good supplies of artesian water nourishing orchards of citrus fruits.

Established in 1886 when the railway arrived, Barcaldine gained a place in Australian history in 1891, when it became the headquarters of the historic shearers' strike, during which more than 1000 men camped in and around the town. That confrontation led to the formation of the Australian Workers' Party, the forerunner of today's Australian Labor Party. The **Tree of Knowledge**, a ghost gum near the train station, was the organisers' meeting place, and still stands as a monument to workers and their rights.

Information
Barcaldine Video Hire (☎ 4651 1611; 111 Oak St) Offers Internet access for $6 an hour.
Library (☎ 4651 1170; 71 Ash St) Also has Internet access.
Visitor Information Centre (☎ 4651 1724; Oak St; ⏰ 8.15am-4.30pm) Next to the train station.

Sights
Built to commemorate the role played by workers in the formation of Australian social, political and industrial movements, the **Australian Workers Heritage Centre** (☎ 4651 2422; www.australianworkersheritagecentre.com.au; Ash St; adult/child $12/7.50; ⏰ 9am-5pm Mon-Sat, 10am-5pm Sun) was opened during the centenary celebrations of the Labor Party in Barcaldine in 1991. Set in landscaped grounds around a central billabong, the centre includes the Australian Bicentennial Theatre with displays tracing the history of the shearers' strike. Other displays include a schoolhouse, a hospital, a powerhouse and a replica of Queensland's Legislative Assembly. The Workers Wall displays a photographic montage of prominent Labor Party members and the newest exhibition celebrates the contribution of working women. The entrance is at the western end of the complex and the admission ticket is valid for seven days.

The **Barcaldine Historical Museum** (☎ 4651 1310; cnr Beech & Gidyea Sts; admission $3; ⏰ 7am-5pm) is in the town's former National Bank and is crammed with a fascinating collection of memorabilia. It offers mini–steam train rides once a month.

Mad Mick's (☎ 4651 1172; 84 Pine St; adult/child $10/6) is a ramshackle, cluttered farmlet with a collection of old buildings and a fauna park. It offers billy tea and damper and is open most mornings between April and September – check with the information centre.

Sleeping & Eating
Ironbark Inn (☎ 4651 2311; fax 4651 2314; 115 Oak St; s/d $63/73; ▨ ▩) This motel south of town has clean, comfortable rooms set in native gardens. Its best feature, though, is the 3Ls Bar & Bistro (mains $14 to $20), a rustic open shed with wooden bench tables and stockmen's ropes and branding irons on the walls. It serves country-style fare, including large steaks, pork chops and barramundi.

Landsborough Lodge Motel (☎ 4651 1100; fax 4651 1744; 47 Box St; s/d $70/80, budget s/d units $50/60) South of the centre, Landsborough Lodge is a large, modern motel with spacious self-contained rooms and a good licensed restaurant. It also has a row of small 'budget' units at the rear.

Blacksmith's Cottage (☎ 4651 1724; fax 4651 2243; 7 Elm St; d $60) This quaint, turn-of-the-19th-century B&B features period furniture and a modern kitchen for the self-serve breakfast.

Homestead Caravan Park (☎ 4651 1308; fax 4651 6308; 24 Box St; unpowered/powered sites from $13/17, cabins $45-65) This neat, friendly park puts on free billy tea and damper for guests in the late afternoons. It has plenty of shady sites for campers, good amenities blocks and excellent cabins.

Shakespeare Hotel (☎ 4651 1610; fax 4651 1331; 95 Oak St; s with/without bathrooms $30/20, d $40/30) With tidy rooms and friendly hosts, this is the best pub accommodation.

Barcaldine's iconic, iron-roofed pubs with their wooden verandas lined up along Oak St make a great display. The beer is cold and the food is filling, if not gourmet. The quintessential Artesian Hotel has the pick of patio tables in its **Drovers Inn Restaurant** (☎ 4651 1691; 85 Oak St; mains $6-15), but the Union Hotel's **Witch's Kitchen** (☎ 4651 2269; 61 Oak St; mains $14-20) delivers the best range of bistro grills, pizza and vegetarian dishes.

Entertainment
Radio Theatre (☎ 4651 2488; 4 Beech St; adult/child $9/7; ⏰ Thu-Sun) A lovely building that offers an old-fashioned movie-going experience, complete with canvas seats, though it shows recent releases.

OUTBACK QUEENSLAND

Getting There & Away

Qantaslink (☎ 13 13 13; www.qantas.com.au) flies from Brisbane to Barcaldine (from $335). **Macair** (☎ 13 13 23; www.macair.com.au) flies to Barcaldine from Townsville (from $210) via Winton.

Greyhound Australia (☎ 13 14 99; www.greyhound.com.au) has a regular coach service to Brisbane ($100, 16 hours), Longreach ($16, one hour) and Mt Isa ($98, 9½ hours). **Emerald Coaches** (☎ 1800 28737; www.emeraldcoaches.com.au) makes the twice-weekly run to Rockhampton ($65) returning via Emerald. Buses stop at the BP roadhouse at the intersection of the Landsborough and Capricorn Hwys.

Queensland Rail (www.traveltrain.com.au) operates the twice-weekly *Spirit of the Outback* train between Longreach and Brisbane. The adult one-way economy seat/economy sleeper/1st-class sleeper fare from Barcaldine to Brisbane costs $165/220/350, and the trip takes 24 hours.

BLACKALL

☎ 07 / pop 1404

Blackall claims to be the site of the mythical black stump – according to outback mythology, anywhere west of Blackall was considered to be 'beyond the black stump'.

Blackall also prides itself on the fact that it was near here, at Alice Downs station, that shearer Jackie Howe set his world record of shearing 321 sheep in less than eight hours with a set of hand shears (see the boxed text on p154).

Blackall is also famous as the site of the first artesian well to be drilled in Queensland, although the well didn't strike water at first, and when it did the product was undrinkable. You'll probably agree with most travellers and say it stinks a little. Locals say it's got 'body', but there's no doubting its refreshing qualities as an essential ingredient in Blackall's delicious soft drinks and invigorating aquatic centre.

Information

Blackall Visitor Information Centre (☎ 4657 4637; www.blackall.qld.gov.au; Shamrock St; ⏱ 9am-5pm) Has information on regional sights, local services and transport.
Central Star Service Station (☎ 4657 4249; 64 Shamrock St) Local RACQ depot.
Library (☎ 4657 4764; 108 Shamrock St) Internet access.

Sights & Activities

The **Blackall Woolscour** (☎ 4657 6042; Evora Rd; adult/child $9.90/5.50; ⏱ 8am-4pm), the only working steam-driven scour (wool-cleaner) left in Queensland, is 4km northeast of Blackall. Built in 1908, it operated commercially until 1978. The complex incorporates a shearing shed, a wool-washing plant and a pond fed by an artesian bore, and tours operate every hour on the hour.

The bronze **Jackie Howe Memorial Statue** has pride of place in the town centre on the corner of Short and Shamrock Sts. When Jackie retired in 1900, he bought Blackall's Universal Hotel. The original pub was demolished in the 1950s, but the façade of the **New Universal Garden Centre & Gallery** (☎ 4657 4344; 53 Shamrock St; admission free; ⏱ 8.30am-5pm), built on the original site, reflects the old pub's design. The gallery houses a display of Jackie Howe memorabilia and souvenirs.

For a dip with a difference, try the **Blackall Aquatic Centre** (☎ 4657 4975; Salvia St; adult/child $1.50/1; ⏱ 6-10am & 2.30-6pm Mon-Fri, 11am-7pm Sat & Sun). The pool and spa are filled with artesian water, which, despite the accompanying aroma, is clean and, some say, therapeutic.

The black stump display, explaining how the mythology came about, is on Thistle St.

Sleeping & Eating

Acacia Motor Inn (☎ 4657 6022; fax 4657 6077; 110 Shamrock St; s/d $75/89; 🅿 🍴) The immaculate Acacia is right in the centre of town, near the Jackie Howe statue, and is a quality four-star motel with a licensed bistro (mains $16 to $25).

Blackall Caravan Park (☎ 4657 4816; fax 4657 4327; 53 Garden St; unpowered/powered sites $13/17, cabins from $52) This orderly little park is tucked into a quiet corner off the main street, not far from the aquatic centre. It's a pleasant place to stay, with shady camp sites, friendly owners and clean amenities blocks.

Blackall's pubs offer very basic accommodation, while the **Barcoo Hotel** (☎ 4657 4197; Shamrock St) has a good bistro featuring Friday and Saturday night BBQs.

Getting There & Away

Qantaslink (☎ 13 13 13; www.qantas.com.au) flies from Brisbane to Blackall (from $315). **Greyhound Australia** (☎ 13 14 99; www.greyhound.com.au) has a regular coach service to Brisbane ($98, 15 hours), Barcaldine ($14, one hour) and Mt Isa ($102, 11 hours). Buses stop at **Blackall Travel** (☎ 4657 4422; 8-10 Shamrock St) in the BP service station. At Barcaldine you can catch an Emerald Coaches bus to Rockhampton and the *Spirit of the Outback* train to Rockhampton and Brisbane.

BLACKALL TO CHARLEVILLE

Continuing southeast, the Landsborough Hwy crosses the **Barcoo River** 42km from Blackall, and east of the road there is an excellent spot to stop, brew a cuppa or camp. The Barcoo is one of western Queensland's great rivers and must be the only river in the world that becomes a creek in its lower reaches. It flows northwest past Blackall, then swings southwest through Isisford and into the Channel Country of southwestern Queensland, where it becomes Cooper Creek, probably the most famous of Australia's inland waterways.

Both 'Banjo' Paterson and Henry Lawson mention the Barcoo in their writings. The name has also entered the Australian idiom, appearing in the Macquarie Dictionary as the 'Barcoo salute' (waving to brush flies from the face).

On the banks of the Barcoo, **Tambo** is surrounded by perhaps the best grazing land in western Queensland, and has some of the region's earliest historic buildings. The old post office (1876) is now the **Old Telegraph Museum** (☎ 4654 6133; 12 Arthur St; admission by donation; 10am-5pm Mon-Fri, 10am-2pm Sat) and doubles as the visitor information centre. Tambo also has a flourishing teddy-bear industry in **Tambo Teddies** (☎ 4654 6233; 17 Arthur St), and road signs warn motorists of crossing bears.

Tambo Mill Motel & Caravan Park (☎ 4654 6466; fax 6454 6497; 34 Arthur St; unpowered/powered sites $15/20, s/d $79/92) is an attractive and beautifully maintained modern motel with shady sites, spacious rooms and an excellent **restaurant** (mains $15-20). Prices are for two people. Both the pubs in the main street have budget rooms and ordinary pub meals.

Augathella, 116km south of Tambo, is 5km north of the junction of the Mitchell Hwy and the southeastern route to Brisbane via Morven. The town has a pub and the well-maintained **Augathella Motel & Caravan Park** (☎ 4654 5177; fax 4654 5353; Matilda Hwy; powered sites $18, s/d $79/88).

CHARLEVILLE

☎ 07 / pop 3519

One of outback Queensland's largest towns, Charleville is situated on the Warrego River, 760km west of Brisbane. Edmund Kennedy passed this way in 1847 and the town was gazetted in 1868, six years after the first settlers had arrived. Cobb & Co built coaches here between 1893 and 1920, and Charleville is also linked to the origins of Qantas. The airline's first regular flight was between Charleville and Cloncurry. By the turn of the 19th century the town was an important centre for the outlying sheep stations.

Information

Library (☎ 4654 1296; 69 Edward St; 8.30am-4pm Mon-Fri, 9am-noon Sat) Internet access.

South West Ford (☎ 4654 1477; 50-6 Alfred St) The local RACQ depot.

Visitor Information Centre (☎ 4654 3057; Sturt St; 9am-5pm Apr-Sep, 9am-5pm Mon-Fri Oct-Mar) In the Graham Andrews Parklands on the southern side of Charleville.

Sights & Activities

The **Cosmos Centre** (☎ 4654 7771; www.cosmoscentre.com; adult/child/family $17/11/39; 10am-6pm, night observatory times vary) is 2km south of the centre, off Airport Dr. Here you can tour the night sky through high-powered telescopes with an expert guide. The 90-minute sessions start soon after sunset. There is also a theatre, interactive displays and a café.

At the **Hotel Corones** (33 Wills St) history buffs can enjoy a **Scones & Stories Tour** (tickets $10; 2pm), and relive the glorious past of this grand old country pub.

The **QPWS office** (☎ 4654 1255; 1 Park St; 8.30am-4.30pm Mon-Fri), just off the Warrego Hwy and across the railway line, runs a captive breeding programme for endangered native species. You can see yellow-footed rock wallabies here, but the enigmatic bilbies have their own show. The **Bilby Show** (Racecourse Complex, Partridge St; admission $5; 6-7pm Mon, Wed, Fri & Sun Apr-Sep) provides a fascinating insight into this rare nocturnal marsupial.

The **Historic House Museum** (☎ 4654 1170; 91-3 Alfred St; adult/child $4/0.50; 9am-5pm) houses an impressive collection of memorabilia and old machinery. In the Bicentennial Park in Sturt St you can see remains of the **Stiger Vortex Rainmaker Guns** used in a bizarre and futile drought-breaking attempt in 1902.

You can visit the vital facilities at the **Royal Flying Doctor Service Visitor Centre** (☎ 4654 1233; Old Cunnamulla Rd; admission $2.50; ⏰ 9am-5pm) and take a guided tour of the **School of Distance Education** (☎ 4654 1341; Parry St; admission $2; ⏰ 9.15am Mon-Fri).

Sleeping & Eating

Mulga Country Motor Inn (☎ 4654 3255; fax 4654 3381; Cunnamulla Rd; s/d $82/93; ✖ ⌘) Charleville's top-of-the-range, four-star motel is on the highway south of the centre adjacent to the airport. It has queen-sized rooms, some with spas and disabled facilities, a good restaurant (mains $15 to $26) and a bar.

Hotel Corones (☎ 4654 1022; fax 4654 1756; 33 Wills St; s with/without bathroom $45/25, tw $55/35, d $75; motel s/d $59/69; ✖) Dominating one of Charleville's main intersections, Corones is one of Queensland's grand old country pubs. Its magnificently preserved interior includes a huge public bar, leadlight windows, open fires and timber floors, and upstairs there are dozens of good rooms, only the cheapest of which have no air-con. The motel rooms are rather characterless and out of keeping with the rest of the hotel. For lunch or dinner you can try the elegant dining room (mains $15 to $20) or have a good-value counter meal in the bar (mains $7).

Bailey Bar Caravan Park (☎ 1800 065 311, 4654 1744; fax 4654 3740; 196 King St; unpowered/powered sites $15/18, cabins from $57) Bailey Bar is the best of the town's caravan parks, with plenty of grass and shady eucalypts, immaculate facilities and a regular bush poet who does evening recitals during winter. Prices are for two people.

Heinemann's Bakery & Coffee@84 (☎ 4654 3991; 84 Alfred St; ⏰ 8.30am-5pm) For pies, sandwiches, cakes, excellent espresso, smoothies and milkshakes, this place is cool, inviting and good value.

Other accommodation options:
Charleville Motel (☎ 4654 1566; fax 4654 2370; 148 King St; s/d $72/82; ✖) A comfortable motel with a good restaurant.
Waltzing Matilda Motor Inn (☎ 4654 1720; fax 4654 3049; 125 Alfred St; s/d from $48/59; ✖ ⌘) A good-value motel with small units arranged around a central courtyard.

Getting There & Away

Western Travel Service (☎ 4654 1260; 94 Alfred St) can handle all bus, train and plane reservations and ticket sales.

THE AUTHOR'S CHOICE

Nardoo Station (☎ 4655 4833; fax 4655 4835; Mitchell Hwy; unpowered/powered sites $13/17, dm $25, cabins from $60; ✖), right beside the highway, only 38km north of Cunnamulla, is a friendly, family-run sheep and cattle station, offering the chance to join in station activities or go bird-watching, walking or fishing. It can be as relaxing or as active as you want, and to warm down after a day's work or play you can hop into the imaginative and therapeutic artesian spas or the invigorating drench. Most people end up staying longer than they planned. The shearers' quarters and jackeroos' cabins are spotless, there is a good grassed camping area with a camp kitchen, and homestead meals are also available. Camping and cabin prices are for two people. Ring for pick-up from Cunnamulla and BYO booze.

Qantaslink (☎ 13 13 13; www.qantas.com.au) flies from Brisbane to Charleville (from $270). **Macair** (☎ 13 13 23, www.macair.com.au) also flies from Brisbane to Charleville (from $230) twice a week, on its Brisbane–Birdsville–Mt Isa route.

Greyhound Australia (☎ 13 14 99; www.greyhound.com.au) buses run daily between Brisbane and Charleville ($68, 11½ hours). Buses leave from the Blue Dolphin Café on the corner of Wills and Watson Sts. To get further north by bus you must catch the daily Brisbane-to-Mt-Isa service from either Morven or Augathella, but at the time of writing there were no connecting services from Charleville.

Queensland Rail (☎ 13 22 32, 1300 13 17 22; www.traveltrain.com.au) operates the twice-weekly *Westlander* from Brisbane to Charleville (economy /1st-class sleeper $143/221, 16½ hours). There is a connecting bus service to Cunnamulla and Quilpie.

CHARLEVILLE TO CUNNAMULLA

This 194km section of the Mitchell Hwy parallels the coolabah-lined Warrego River and the old railway line, and passes through flat grasslands and scattered mulga trees. About 104km south of Charleville is the lonely community of **Wyandra**; further on, about 38km north of Cunnamulla, is the exceptional farm stay at Nardoo Station.

CUNNAMULLA

☎ 07 / pop 1357

The southernmost town in western Queensland, Cunnamulla is on the Warrego River 120km north of the Queensland–New South Wales border. In the 1880s an influx of farmers opened up the country to sheep farming and today millions of sheep graze the open plains around Cunnamulla. The railway arrived in 1898, and since then Cunnamulla has been a major service centre for the district; in good years it is Queensland's biggest wool-loading rail yard.

Cunnamulla's **Visitor Information Centre** (☎ 4655 2481; www.paroo.info; Jane St; ⏱ 9am-4.30pm Mon-Fri year-round, 10am-2pm Sat & Sun Apr-Nov) is next to the Shire Hall in Centenary Park, and you can access the Internet at the town **library** (☎ 4655 2052; 16 John St; ⏱ 9am-5pm Mon-Fri).

The **Bicentennial Historical Museum** (☎ 4655 2052; 16 John St; admission $1; ⏱ 9am-5pm) has an eclectic mix of memorabilia, and the **Robber's Tree**, at the southern end of Stockyard St, is a living reminder of a bungled 1880s robbery.

The **Country Way Motor Inn** (☎ 4655 0555; fax 4655 0455; 17 Emma St; s/d $65/75; 🅿) has cosy, well-equipped, queen-sized rooms with verandas in tidy surrounds.

The pub and motel rooms at **Warrego Hotel-Motel** (☎ 4655 1737; fax 4655 2015; 9 Louise St; hotel s/d $28/38, motel $59/69, cabins $75/85; 🅿) are well maintained and comfortable, and the cabins are self-contained. The pub also boasts a good **restaurant** (mains $10-18; ⏱ lunch & dinner).

Jack Tonkin Caravan Park (☎ /fax 4655 1421; Watson St; unpowered/powered sites $13/16, cabins from $30; 🅿) This large, informal park has some pleasant, grassy camp sites and makes up for its distance from the town centre with a handy milk bar across the road.

There are bus services connecting Cunnamulla with the twice-weekly *Westlander* train service between Charleville and Brisbane (opposite). Make bookings through **Travel West** (☎ 4655 2222; 50 Stockyard St).

THE CHANNEL COUNTRY

The remote and sparsely populated southwestern corner of Queensland, bordering the Northern Territory, South Australia and New South Wales, takes its name from the myriad channels that crisscross the area. In this inhospitable region it hardly ever rains, but water from the summer monsoons further north pours into the Channel Country along the Georgina, Hamilton and Diamantina Rivers and Cooper Creek. Flooding towards the great depression of Lake Eyre in South Australia, the mass of water arrives on this huge plain, eventually drying up in water holes or salt pans.

Only on rare occasions has the vast amount of water actually reached Lake Eyre and filled it. For a short period after each wet season, however, the Channel Country becomes fertile and cattle are grazed here.

Getting There & Around

Some roads from the east and north to the fringes of the Channel Country are paved, but during the October-to-May wet season even these can be cut – and the dirt roads become quagmires. In addition, the summer heat is unbearable, so a visit is best made in the cooler months, from May to September. Visiting this area requires a sturdy vehicle and experience of outback driving. Always carry plenty of fuel and drinking water and notify the police if you are heading off the main roads.

The main road through the Channel Country is the Diamantina Developmental Rd that runs south from Mt Isa through Boulia to Bedourie, and then turns east through Windorah and Quilpie to Charleville. In all it's a long and lonely 1340km, about two-thirds of which is sealed. The paved Kennedy Developmental Rd runs 360km from Winton to Boulia and has a fuel and accommodation stop along the way.

MT ISA TO BIRDSVILLE

The 300km northern section of the Diamantina Developmental Rd from Mt Isa to Boulia is a narrow bitumen road. The only facilities along the 677km route are at **Dajarra**, a small railway siding with a pub and roadhouse, 140km south of Mt Isa.

Boulia

Boulia is the 'capital' of the Channel Country, and home to a supernatural phenomenon known as the Min Min Light. Said to resemble a car's headlights, this 'earthbound UFO' has been terrifying locals for years, hovering a metre or so above the ground before vanishing and reappearing elsewhere.

The **Min Min Encounter** (☎ 4746 3386; Herbert St; adult/child $11/7.70; ☺ 8.30am-5pm Mon-Fri, 9am-noon Sat & Sun) features sophisticated gadgetry, imaginative sets and eerie lighting in its hourly show, which attempts to convert the nonbelievers. The centre is well worth a visit, and it doubles as the town's tourist information centre. Boulia also lays claim to Australia's premier **camel racing** event, held in mid-July.

For accommodation, try the pleasant **Desert Sands Motel** (☎ 4746 3000; fax 4746 3040; Herbert St; s/d $80/90; ✖) with spacious, cool rooms and a handy location near the public swimming pool, or the **Australian Hotel** (☎ 4746 3144; fax 4746 3191; Herbert St; s/d $35/40, motel units $60/70; ✖) with decent pub rooms, motel units and a good bistro.

Bedourie

Almost 200km south of Boulia is Bedourie. First settled in 1880 as a Cobb & Co depot, Bedourie is now the administrative centre for the huge Diamantina Shire. You can get tourist information from the **council offices** (☎ 4746 1202; Herbert St; ☺ 9.30am-4.30pm), where there's a good rest stop with a shaded picnic and BBQ area, and toilets.

There's a caravan park and comfortable motel units at the **Simpson Desert Oasis** (☎ 4746 1291; fax 4746 1208; Herbert St; unpowered/powered sites $10/16, d $95; ✖), which incorporates a fuel stop, supermarket and restaurant. The **Royal Hotel** (☎ 4746 1201; fax 4746 1101; Herbert St; s/d $55/65; ✖), a charming adobe brick building built in 1880, has two motel units out the back.

BIRDSVILLE

The most remote place in Queensland, tiny Birdsville possesses one of Australia's most famous pubs, the Birdsville Hotel, the most infamous horse races, and the hottest water supply.

Birdsville, only 12km from the South Australian border, is at the northern end of the 517km Birdsville Track, which leads to Marree in South Australia. In the late 19th century Birdsville was quite a busy place, as it was here a customs charge was made on each head of cattle being driven to South Australia from Queensland. With Federation, the charge was abolished and Birdsville almost became a ghost town. In recent times, the cattle industry and tourism have revitalised the town.

Information

Birdsville Fuel Service (☎ 4656 3236; Adelaide St; ☺ 7am-6pm) Has banking and postal facilities; opposite the pub.

Wirrarri Centre (☎ 4656 3300; Billabong Blvd; ☺ 8.30am-6pm Mon-Fri, 9.30am-5.30pm Sat & Sun) For tourist information and Internet access.

Sights & Activities

One of Birdsville's highlights is the **Birdsville Working Museum** (☎ 4656 3259; Macdonald St; adult/child $7/5; ☺ 8am-5pm Apr-Oct, tours 9am, 11am & 3pm). Inside this big tin shed is an impressive private collection with items ranging from old tobacco tins and road signs through to shearing equipment, wool presses and mule-driven rounding yards. Another highlight is the **Blue Poles Gallery & Caravanserai Cafe** (☎ 4656 3099; www.birdsvillestudio.com.au; Graham St; mains $17; ☺ 9am-6pm Sun-Thu, 9am-10pm Fri, Sat & school holidays Apr-Nov) where you can inspect and buy outback art by exceptional local artist Wolfgang John and enjoy coffee, cakes, pasta, curries and more.

The town's big moment is the annual **Birdsville Races** (www.birdsvilleraces.com) on the first weekend in September, when up to 6000 racing and boozing enthusiasts converge on the town.

Sleeping & Eating

Birdsville Hotel (☎ 4656 3244; www.theoutback.com .au; Adelaide St; s/d $80/100; ✖) The Birdsville Hotel stands at the western edge of town, facing the Simpson Desert like some final sentinel of civilisation. Built from sandstone in 1884, the pub is the town's icon, full of outback characters and attracting tourists from far and wide. Its colourful history includes fire and cyclone, and nowadays it is tastefully renovated with modern motel units. Breakfast, lunch and dinner are served in the restaurant (mains $15 to $18) or there are cheaper meals in the main and lizard bars. Culinary treats include a coat of arms double: kangaroo fillet or emu fan fillet.

Birdsville Caravan Park (☎ 4656 3214; fax 4656 3214; Florence St; unpowered/powered sites $12/18, s/d cabins from $44/75; ✖) This caravan park has several units overlooking the nearby Diamantina River. Some are basic twins; others are fully self-contained with a kitchen and TV. For campers, the park doesn't have much grass or shade, but there's a big, clean amenities block and BBQs.

OUTBACK QUEENSLAND

Getting There & Away

Macair (☎ 13 13 23; www.macair.com.au) flies between Brisbane and Birdsville via Charleville, Quilpie and Windorah, and from Birdsville to Mt Isa with stops at Bedourie and Boulia.

There are two roads into Birdsville from Queensland: the north–south Eyre Developmental Rd from Bedourie and Boulia, and the east–west Birdsville Developmental Rd from Windorah and Betoota. Both are mostly rough and unsealed and, while a conventional vehicle will do, you're better off in a 4WD. The surfaces vary from gravel and dirt to soft red sand with frequent cattle grids and potentially perilous dry creek beds. Another hazard is the sharp rocks; it's advisable to carry at least two spare tyres and plenty of drinking water and spare parts.

BIRDSVILLE TRACK

The 517km Birdsville Track stretches south of Birdsville to Maree in South Australia, taking a desolate course between the Simpson Desert to the west and Sturt Stony Desert to the east. The first stretch from Birdsville has two alternative routes, but only the longer, more easterly Outside Track is open these days. Before tackling the track, it's a good idea to keep friends or relatives informed of your movements so they can notify the authorities should you fail to report in on time. Contact the **Wirrarri Centre** (☎ 4656 3300) for road conditions.

SIMPSON DESERT NATIONAL PARK

The waterless Simpson Desert occupies a massive 200,000 sq km of central Australia and stretches across the Queensland, Northern Territory and South Australian borders. The Queensland section, in the state's far southwestern corner, is protected as the 10,000-sq-km Simpson Desert National Park, and is a remote, arid landscape of high red sand dunes, spinifex and cane grass.

While conventional cars can tackle the Birdsville Track, the Simpson crossing requires a 4WD and far more preparation. Crossings should only be undertaken by parties of at least two 4WD vehicles equipped with suitable communications to call for help if necessary. Alternatively, you can hire a satellite phone ($23 per day) from **Birdsville police** (☎ 4656 3220) and return it to **Maree police** (☎ 08-8675 8346) in South Australia.

Permits are required and are available from the **QPWS** (☎ 4652 7333) in Birdsville or Longreach, and Birdsville's service stations. You also need a separate permit to travel into the South Australian parks, and these are available through the **South Australian National Parks & Wildlife Service** (☎ 1800 816 078).

BIRDSVILLE TO CHARLEVILLE

The Birdsville Developmental Rd heads east from Birdsville, meeting the Diamantina Developmental Rd after 277km of rough gravel and sand. The old pub that constituted the 'township' of **Betoota** between Birdsville and Windorah closed its doors in 1997, meaning motorists must carry enough fuel and water to cover the 395km distance.

Windorah has a pub, a general store and a basic caravan park. The **Western Star Hotel** (☎ 4656 3166; 15 Albert St; pub s/d $30/44, motel s/d $75/85; ✷) has good pub rooms and motel units, while north of the centre **Cooper Cabins** (☎ 4656 3101; 11 Edward St; s/d $60/66; ✷) has self-contained units.

Quilpie is an opal-mining town and the railhead from which cattle are sent to the coast. The name Quilpie comes from an Aboriginal word for stone curlew, and all but two of the town's streets are named after birds. The **Quilpie Museum & Visitors Centre** (☎ 4656 2166; 51 Brolga St; 8am-5pm Mon-Fri year-round, 10am-4.30pm Sat & Sun Apr-Nov) can provide you with tourist information, and there are regular opal-cutting demonstrations here. The best place to stay is the **Quilpie Motor Inn** (☎ 4656 1277; fax 4656 1231; 80 Brolga St; s/d $60/70; ✷), which has a licensed dining room. The **Channel Country Caravan Park** (☎ 4656 2087; fax 4656 1585; Chipu St; unpowered/powered sites $14/17, cabins from $57; ✷) is a well-maintained park on the town's western edge that also runs tag-along tours to the opal fields.

Macair (☎ 13 13 23; www.macair.com.au) flies to Quilpie from Brisbane and Birdsville. A bus service connects Quilpie with the twice-weekly *Westlander* train service from Charleville to Brisbane (economy seat/economy sleeper/1st class sleeper $115/170/255, 22 hours). Along the 210km section of the Diamantina Developmental Rd from Quilpie to Charleville are a couple of lonely townships: Cheepie, 76km east of Quilpie, and Cooladdi, 45km further east, which has a motel and a general store.

CUNNAMULLA TO INNAMINCKA – THE ADVENTURE WAY

From Cunnamulla, the Adventure Way heads west for 640km to reach Innamincka in South Australia. The first stage, the all-bitumen Bulloo Developmental Rd, takes you through the small settlements of Eulo and Thargomindah to Noccundra. You can take a northern detour to the Yowah Opal Fields and, if you have a 4WD, you can continue west from Noccundra to Innamincka via the famous Dig Tree.

Eulo, 68km west of Cunnamulla, is on the Paroo River close to the Yowah Opal Fields. In late August/early September the town co-hosts the **World Lizard Racing Championships** with Cunnamulla. Eulo boasts an interesting date farm and winery, a pub, a general store with fuel, and a caravan park.

Yowah, a tiny opal-mining settlement about 40km northwest of Eulo, is a popular fossicking field where the unique Yowah opal nut (ironstone matrix opal) is found.

Yowah has a caravan park, a free camping ground, a general store and a motel.

Thargomindah, 130km west of Eulo on the banks of the Bulloo River, was an important stop for camel trains carting Queensland wool to the steamers on the Darling River at Bourke in New South Wales. The town has a couple of motels and a caravan park.

Noccundra, 145km further west on the Wilson River, was once a busy little community. It now has just one hotel supplying basic accommodation, meals and fuel. Continuing on from Noccundra, head 20km north back to the Bulloo Developmental Rd, which continues west for another 75km through the Jackson Oil Field to the Naccowlah Oil Field. The sealed road ends here, but you can continue across to Innamincka on the Strzelecki Track in South Australia via the site of the **Dig Tree**, of Burke and Wills fame. This route is particularly rough and stony with frequent creek crossings, and is only recommended for 4WD vehicles.

Directory

CONTENTS

ACCOMMODATION

Queensland is very well equipped with a wide range of accommodation options, with everything from the tent-pegged confines of camping grounds and the communal space of hostels to gourmet breakfasts in guesthouses and at-your-fingertips resorts, plus the gamut of hotel and motel lodgings.

The listings in the accommodation sections of this guidebook are in order of author preference. In larger towns and cities, the listings are arranged in budget, midrange and top-end categories. We generally treat any place that charges up to $40 per single or $80 per double as budget accommodation. Midrange facilities usually range from $80 to $150 per double, while the top-

end tag is applied to places charging more than $150 per double.

In most areas you'll find seasonal price variations. Over summer (December to February) and at other peak times, particularly school and public holidays, prices are usually at their highest, whereas outside these times useful discounts and lower walk-in rates can be found.

The weekend escape is a notion that figures prominently in the Australian psyche, meaning accommodation from Friday night through Sunday can be in greater demand (and pricier) in major holiday areas. For more information on climatic seasons and holiday periods, see p9.

Useful websites for last-minute or discounted accommodation:

Lastminute.com (www.au.lastminute.com)
Quickbeds.com (www.quickbeds.com.au)
Wotif.com (www.wotif.com.au)

B&Bs

The local bed-and-breakfast (B&B) population is climbing rapidly and options include restored miners' cottages, converted barns, rambling old houses, upmarket country manors, beachside bungalows and simple bedrooms in family homes. Tariffs are typically in the $70 to $150 (per double) bracket, but can be much higher. Some places provide dinner as well as breakfast, and are called DBBs.

Local tourist offices can usually give you a list of options. For online information, try the following:

babs.com.au (www.babs.com.au/qld.htm)

Bed & Breakfast and Farmstay Association of Far North Queensland (www.bnbnq.com.au)

OZBedandBreakfast.com (www.ozbedandbreakfast.com)

Camping

Camping in the bush is for many people one of the highlights of a visit to Australia. The magnificent camping grounds in the state and national parks are a credit to the nation, and nocturnal visits from wildlife add to the bush experience. Permits are mandatory and can be purchased from **Queensland Parks & Wildlife Service** (QPWS; ☎ 13 13 04; www.epa.qld.gov.au). You can book camp sites at some parks online, otherwise you'll need to telephone QPWS. The cost is $4 per person per night, or $16 per family. Some camping grounds fill up at holiday times, so you may need to book well ahead.

You can also pitch your tent in one of the hundreds of caravan parks that are scattered across Queensland; most have pools, toilets, laundry facilities, BBQs and camp kitchens. When it comes to urban camping, remember that most city camping grounds are miles away from the centre of town.

Unpowered sites for two people generally cost between $14 and $22, and powered sites cost $16 to $25. Many caravan parks also have on-site vans that you can rent for the night for around $40, and self-contained cabins, which range from $60 to $110, depending on how motel-like the facilities are.

Farm & Station Stays

Australia is a land of farms (known as 'stations' in the outback), and one of the best ways to come to grips with Australian life is to spend a few days on one. Many farms offer accommodation where you can just sit back and watch how it's done, while others like you to get more actively involved in the day-to-day activities.

Most accommodation is very comfortable – in the main homestead (B&B-style, many providing dinner on request) or in self-contained cottages on the property. Other farms provide budget options in outbuildings or former shearers' quarters.

Several farm stays are included in this guidebook. **Queensland Farm & Country Tourism** (QFACT; ☎ 0500 808 555; www.farmholidays.com.au) produces a brochure called *Farm & Country Holidays*, which lists many of the places with accommodation – it's available from regional information offices.

Hostels

Queensland has a staggering number of backpackers hostels, with standards ranging from the magnificent to the awful, depending on how they are run. Many are small, family-run places in converted wooden Queenslander houses. At the other end of the spectrum are the huge, custom-built places with hundreds of beds, extensive facilities and a party attitude.

Dorm beds typically cost $18 to $26, with singles hovering around $40 and doubles costing $60 to $80.

Useful organisations:

Nomads Backpackers (☎ 1800 819 883, 02-9264 5533; www.nomadsworld.com) Membership ($39 for 12 months) entitles you to numerous discounts.

VIP Backpacker Resorts (☎ 07-3395 6052; www.backpackers.com) Membership ($41 for 12 months) entitles you to a $1 discount on accommodation and a 5% to 15% discount on other products such as air and bus transport, tours and activities.

YHA (☎ 07-3236 1680; www.yha.com.au) Membership ($39 for 12 months) entitles you to discounts at YHA and many independent hostels.

A warning for Australian and Kiwi travellers: some hostels will only admit overseas backpackers, mainly because they've had problems with locals sleeping over and bothering the backpackers. Fortunately it's only a rowdy minority that makes trouble, and often hostels will only ask for identification in order to deter potential troublemakers. Also watch out for hostels that cater expressly to working backpackers, and where facilities are minimal but rent is high.

Hotels & Motels

The top end of the hotel spectrum is well represented – in Brisbane, on the Gold Coast and in Cairns, at least. There are many excellent four- and five-star hotels and quite a few lesser places. They tend to have a pool, restaurant/café, room service and various other facilities. We quote 'rack rates' (official advertised rates) throughout this book, but often hotels/motels will offer regular discounts and special deals.

For comfortable midrange accommodation that's available all over the state, motels (or motor inns) are the places to stay. Prices vary and there's rarely a cheaper rate for single rooms, so motels are better choices for couples or groups of three. You'll mostly pay between $60 and $120 for a room.

Rental Accommodation

Holiday flats are extremely popular and prevalent in Queensland. Essentially apartments, they come with one or two bedrooms, kitchens, bathrooms and sometimes laundries. They're often rented on a weekly basis – higher prices are often reserved for shorter stays. For a one-bedroom flat, expect to pay anywhere from $80 to $110 per night. The other alternative in major cities is to rent a serviced apartment.

If you're interested in a shared flat or house for a long-term stay, delve into the classified advertisements sections of the daily newspapers; Wednesday and Saturday are usually the best days. Notice boards in universities, hostels, bookshops and cafés are also good to check out.

ACTIVITIES

See p46 for information on activities for visitors in Queensland.

BUSINESS HOURS

Business hours are from 9am to 5pm, Monday to Friday. Most shops in Queensland are open on weekdays from around 8.30am or 9am until 5pm and on Saturday till noon or 5pm. Sunday trading is also becoming increasingly popular in the cities. Most of the larger towns and cities will have at least one night a week when the shops stay open until 9pm – usually Thursday or Friday. Supermarkets are generally open till 8pm and sometimes 24 hours. Local stores and convenience stores are also often open till late.

Banks open at 9.30am Monday to Friday and close at 4pm, except Friday, when they close at 5pm. Some large city branches are open from 8am till 6pm weekdays, and a few also open to 9pm on Friday. Post offices are generally open 9am to 5pm weekdays, and some open Saturday morning.

Restaurants typically open at noon for lunch and between 6pm and 7pm for dinner; most dinner bookings are made for 7.30pm or 8pm. Restaurants stay open until at least 9pm, but tend to serve food until later in the evening on Friday and Saturday. That said, the main restaurant strips in large cities keep longer hours throughout the week. Cafés tend to be all-day affairs, opening at 7am and closing around 5pm, unless they simply continue their business into the night. Pubs usually serve food from noon to 2pm and from 6pm to 8pm. Pubs and bars often open at lunchtime and continue well into the evening, particularly from Thursday to Saturday. For more dining information, see p71.

Keep in mind that nearly all attractions and shops are closed on Christmas Day and all attractions closed on Easter Sunday.

CHILDREN

All cities and most major towns have centrally located public rooms where mothers (and sometimes fathers) can go to nurse their baby or change its nappy; check with the local tourist office or city council for details. While many Australians have a relaxed attitude about breast-feeding or nappy changing in public, others frown on it.

Many motels and the better-equipped caravan parks have playgrounds and swimming pools, and can supply cots and baby baths – motels may also have in-house children's videos and childminding services. Top-end hotels and many (but not all) midrange hotels are well versed in the needs of guests who have children. B&Bs, on the other hand, often market themselves as sanctuaries from all things child-related. Some cafés and restaurants make it difficult to dine with small children, lacking a specialised children's menu, but many others do have kids' meals, or will provide small serves from the main menu. Some also supply highchairs.

If you want to leave Junior behind for a few hours, some of Australia's numerous licensed child-care agencies have places set aside for casual care. To find them, check under Baby Sitters and Child Care Centres in the *Yellow Pages* telephone book, or phone the local council for a list. See p94 for some useful websites. Licensed centres are subject to government regulation and usually adhere to high standards; to be on the safe side, avoid unlicensed ones.

Child concessions (and family rates) often apply for such things as accommodation, tours, admission fees and air, bus and train

DIRECTORY

transport, with some discounts as high as 50% off the adult rate. However, the definition of 'child' can vary from under 12 to under 16 years. Accommodation concessions generally apply to children under 12 years sharing the same room as adults. On the major airlines, infants travel free provided they don't occupy a seat – child fares usually apply between the ages of two and 11 years.

Medical services and facilities in Queensland are of a high standard, and items such as baby-food, formula and disposable nappies are widely available in urban centres. Major hire-car companies will supply and fit booster seats for you, for which you'll be charged around $16 for up to three days' use, with an additional daily fee for longer periods.

Lonely Planet's *Travel with Children* contains plenty of useful information.

CLIMATE CHARTS

Australian seasons are the opposite of those in Europe and North America; January is the height of summer and July the depth of winter.

The Queensland seasons are more a case of hotter and wetter, or cooler and drier, than of summer or winter. The tropic of Capricorn crosses Queensland a third of the way up, running through the city of Rockhampton and the outback town of Longreach. The state's northern two-thirds are within the tropics, but only the extreme north lies within the monsoon belt. Although the annual rainfall there looks adequate on paper, it comes in more or less one short, sharp burst.

November/December to April/May is the wetter, hotter half of the year, while the real Wet, particularly affecting northern coastal areas, is January to March. Cairns usually gets about 1300mm of rain in these three months; Tully, 100km south of Cairns, is the wettest place in Australia, receiving up to 4400mm of rain each year!

Summer is also the season for cyclones, and if one hits, the main road north (the Bruce Hwy) can be blocked by the ensuing floods.

By comparison, the southeastern and inland areas have relatively little rain – though they still have a wet season. Brisbane and Rockhampton both get about 450mm of rain from January to March. Further

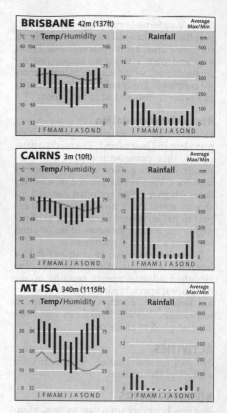

north, Mackay receives about 1250mm in these months, Townsville 850mm, Innisfail 1800mm and Weipa, on Cape York Peninsula, 1300mm. Just halfway across the southern part of the state, Cunnamulla receives only 400mm in the whole year, while Birdsville, in the southwestern corner, receives the least rain, with only 150mm a year.

From about May to September (technically winter) it rarely gets anything like cold, except inland or upland at night. Temperatures in Brisbane peak somewhere in the 20°C-to-29°C range just about every day of the year. In Cairns the daily maximum is usually between 25°C and 32°C, whereas around the Gulf, few days in the year fail to break the 30°C mark. Over at Birdsville you can expect 33°C or more every day from November to March, but rarely more than 20°C from June to August.

See p9 for more information on when to visit.

CUSTOMS

For comprehensive information on customs regulations, contact the **Australian Customs Service** (☎ 1300 363 263, 02-6275 6666; www .customs.gov.au).

When entering Australia you can bring most articles in free of duty provided that customs is satisfied they are for personal use and you'll be taking them with you when you leave. There's a duty-free quota of 2.25L of alcohol, 250 cigarettes and dutiable goods up to the value of $900 per person.

When it comes to prohibited goods, there are a few things you should be particularly conscientious about. The first is drugs, which customs authorities are adept at sniffing out – unless you want to make a first-hand investigation of conditions in Australian jails, don't bring illegal drugs in with you. And note that all medicines must be declared.

The second is all food, plant material and animal products. You will be asked to declare on arrival all goods of animal or plant origin (wooden spoons, straw hats, the lot) and show them to a quarantine officer. The authorities are naturally keen to protect Australia's unique environment and important agricultural industries by preventing weeds, pests or diseases getting into the country – Australia has so far managed to escape many of the pests and diseases prevalent elsewhere in the world.

Weapons and firearms are either prohibited or require a permit and safety testing. Other restricted goods include products made from protected wildlife species (such as animal skins, coral or ivory), unapproved telecommunications devices and live animals.

Australia takes quarantine very seriously. All luggage is screened or X-rayed and it's also likely to get a going over by sniffer dogs. If you fail to declare quarantine items on arrival and are caught, you risk an on-the-spot fine of $220, or prosecution, which may result in fines of more than $60,000, as well as up to 10 years' imprisonment. For more information on quarantine regulations contact the **Australian Quarantine and Inspection Service** (AQIS; www.aqis.gov.au).

DANGERS & ANNOYANCES
Bushfires

Bushfires happen every year in Queensland. Don't be the mug who starts one. In hot, dry, windy weather, be extremely careful

---

CRIKEY – QUARANTINE MATTERS!
Steve Irwin (Crocodile Hunter)

Lucky for us, our remoteness and quarantine keeps pests and diseases out of Australia. But if you're not careful, they can sneak in, hiding in things brought in from overseas. That's why you must declare all food, plant and animal material and have it checked by quarantine. If you don't, and you're caught – and you will be – you could be whacked with a whopping big fine. So if you travel to Australia, remember: quarantine matters. Don't muck with it!

---

with any naked flame, and don't throw live cigarette butts out of car windows. On a day of total fire ban (listen to the radio, watch the billboards on country roads or front pages of daily newspapers) it is forbidden even to use a camping stove in the open. The locals will not be amused if they catch you breaking this particular law, and the legal penalties are severe.

If you're unfortunate enough to find yourself driving through a bushfire, stay inside your car and try to park off the road in an open space, away from trees, until the danger has passed. Lie on the floor under the dashboard, covering yourself with a wool blanket or protective clothing; this is important as it has been proved that heat radiation is the big killer in bushfire situations. The front of the fire should pass quickly, and you will be much safer than if you are out in the open. Bushwalkers should take local advice before setting out. On a day of total fire ban, don't go – delay your trip until the weather has changed. Chances are that it will be so unpleasantly hot and windy, you'll be better off in an air-conditioned pub sipping a cool beer.

If you're out in the bush and you see smoke, even at a great distance, take it seriously. Go to the nearest open space, downhill if possible. A forested ridge is the most dangerous place to be. Bushfires move very quickly and change direction with the wind.

Critters That Bite & Sting

See p470 for information about bed bugs, ticks, leeches, mosquitos, marine creatures, snakes and spiders, as well as some methods for avoiding them.

Swimming

Aside from the obvious – ie don't swim after drinking alcohol – there are a few special conditions in Australia to watch out for. See p469 for information about coral cuts, crocodiles, jellyfish, sharks and a few other marine nasties…and don't be alarmed; that list may sound scary, but only the most foolish of travellers would go all the way to Queensland then stay out of the sea!

Theft

Queensland is a relatively safe place to visit, but it's better to play it safe and take reasonable precautions.

The Gold Coast is notorious for car crime, and more than a few travellers have lost all their belongings from locked vehicles in public car parks. The golden rule is never leave valuables in your car. A steering-wheel lock is also a worthwhile investment.

SWIM BETWEEN THE FLAGS

Drownings and swimming-related accidents have been hugely reduced by Queensland's beach patrol programme (see the bloke on this book's cover). Patrolled beaches are indicated by a red and yellow flag, one at each end of the patrolled area. Swimming conditions are indicated by single flags:

- green flag: safe to swim
- yellow flag: dangerous conditions
- red flag: beach closed, do not enter the water

Swimming and surfing outside of patrolled areas is at your own risk. Blue signs around a swimming beach indicate that surfers are using the water beyond the red and yellow flags. In addition, there's a sound you should listen out for, though it almost never sounds – the siren for a shark in the water.

If you get into trouble in the water, raise one arm above your head to catch the attention of the life-savers.

If you happen to get caught in a rip (strong current) and are being taken out to sea, the first (and hardest) thing to do is not panic. Raise your arm until you have been spotted, and then swim parallel to the shore – *don't* try to swim back against the rip, you'll only tire yourself.

Most accommodation places have somewhere they can store your valuables, and you won't regret taking advantage of this service. It should go without saying, but don't leave hotel rooms unlocked.

If you are unlucky enough to have something stolen, immediately report all details to the nearest police station. If your credit cards, cash card or travellers cheques have been taken, notify your bank or the relevant company immediately.

DISABLED TRAVELLERS

Disability awareness in Australia is pretty high and getting higher. Legislation requires that new accommodation meet accessibility standards, and discrimination by tourism operators is illegal. Many of Australia's key attractions provide access for those with limited mobility, and a number of sites have also begun addressing the needs of visitors with visual or aural impairments; contact attractions in advance to confirm the facilities available for disabled people. Tour operators with accessible vehicles operate from most capital cities. Disabled travellers with some form of identification are often eligible for concession prices.

There are a number of organisations that can supply information for disabled travellers visiting Queensland:

Accessible Tourism Website (www.tq.webcentral.com.au/accessqld) Queensland Tourism website.

ACROD (☎ 07-3366 4366; 240 Waterworks Rd, Ashgrove) Provides information on access issues, accommodation, sporting and recreational activities, transport and specialist tour operators.

Disability Information Awareness Line (DIAL; ☎ 1800 177 120, 07-3224 8444, TTY 07-3224 8021; www.disability.qld.gov.au/dial.cfm) Provides information on disability services and support throughout Queensland.

Disability Services Queensland (☎ 1800 177 120, 07-3224 8031; www.disability.qld.gov.au) In Brisbane; offers telephone information and referral services.

Paraplegic and Quadriplegic Association (☎ 07-3391 2044; 109 Logan Rd, Woolloongabba) In Brisbane; another useful resource.

See p78 for more information.

DISCOUNT CARDS
Seniors Cards

Queensland is a popular retirement destination for Australian seniors, and things are generally well set up for senior travellers.

Australian senior travellers with some form of identification are often eligible for concession prices. Overseas pensioners are entitled to discounts of at least 10% on most express bus fares and bus passes with Greyhound.

Student & Youth Cards

The **International Student Travel Confederation** (ISTC; www.istc.org) is an international collective of specialist student travel organisations. It's also the body behind the internationally recognised International Student Identity Card (ISIC), which is only issued to full-time students aged 12 years and over, and gives the bearer discounts on accommodation, transport and admission to various attractions. The ISTC also produces the International Youth Travel Card (IYTC or Go25), which is issued to people who are between 12 and 26 years of age and not full-time students, and has benefits equivalent to the ISIC. A similar ISTC brainchild is the International Teacher Identity Card (ITIC), available to teaching professionals.

EMBASSIES & CONSULATES
Australian Embassies & Consulates

The website of the **Department of Foreign Affairs & Trade** (www.dfat.gov.au) provides a full listing of all Australian diplomatic missions overseas.

Canada (☎ 613-236 0841; www.ahc-ottawa.org; 7th fl, Ste 710, 50 O'Connor St, Ottawa, Ontario K1P 6L2) Also in Vancouver and Toronto.

France (☎ 01 40 59 33 00; www.france.embassy.gov.au; 4 Rue Jean Rey, 75724 Paris Cedex 15)

Germany (☎ 030-880 08 80; www.australian-embassy.de; Wallstrasse 76-79, Berlin 10179) Also in Frankfurt.

Ireland (☎ 01-664 5300; www.australianembassy.ie; 7th fl, Fitzwilton House, Wilton Terrace, Dublin 2)

Japan (☎ 0352 324 111; www.australia.or.jp; 2-1-14 Mita, Minato-Ku, Tokyo 108-8361) Also in Osaka, Nagoya and Fukuoka City.

Netherlands (☎ 0703 10 82 00; www.australian-embassy.nl; Carnegielaan 4, The Hague 2517 KH)

New Zealand Wellington (☎ 04-473 6411; www.australia.org.nz; 72-76 Hobson St, Thorndon); Auckland (☎ 09-921 8800; Level 7, Price Waterhouse Coopers Bldg, 186-194 Quay St)

Singapore (☎ 6836 4100; www.singapore.embassy.gov.au; 25 Napier Rd, Singapore 258507)

South Africa (☎ 27 12 342 3781; www.australia.co.za; 292 Orient St, Arcadia, Pretoria 0083)

UK (☎ 020-7379 4334; www.australia.org.uk; Australia House, The Strand, London WC2B 4LA) Also in Edinburgh and Manchester.

USA (☎ 202-797 3000; www.austemb.org; 1601 Massachusetts Ave NW, Washington DC 20036) Also in Los Angeles, New York and other major cities.

Consulates in Queensland

Canberra is home to most foreign embassies, but many countries maintain consulates in Brisbane as well. If you need to apply for a visa for other countries, you will need to send your passport to Canberra by recorded delivery. Diplomatic missions in Brisbane:

France (Map pp80-2; ☎ 07-3229 8201; Level 10, AXA Building, 144 Edward St)

Germany (Map pp80-2; ☎ 07-3221 7819; 10 Eagle St)

Japan (Map pp80-2; ☎ 07-3221 5188; Level 17, Comalco Pl, 12 Creek St)

Netherlands (Map pp80-2; ☎ 07-3839 9644; Ground fl, 25 Mary St)

UK (Map pp80-2; ☎ 07-3223 3200; Level 26, 1 Eagle St)

It's important to realise what your own embassy – the embassy of the country of which you are a citizen – can and can't do to help you, if you get into trouble. Generally speaking, it won't be much help in emergencies if the trouble you're in is even remotely your own fault. Remember that while in Australia you are bound by Australian laws. Your embassy will not be sympathetic if you end up in jail after committing a crime locally, even if your actions are legal in your own country.

FESTIVALS & EVENTS

Almost every community in Queensland has at least one annual festival of its own, and these are often unique and quirky celebrations. You might find anything from rodeos and bush race meetings to cooee championships and cockroach races – and these festivals are a great way to meet the locals. Some of Queensland's major annual festivals and events include the following:

January/February

Australia Day The nation celebrates the arrival of the First Fleet in 1788 on 26 January.

Australian Skins (p270) This big-money golf tournament is played over two days at Laguna Quays Resort on the Whitsunday Coast in February.

Big Day Out (p136) This huge open-air music concert tours Australia, stopping over for one day at the Gold Coast. It attracts big-name international acts and dozens of attention-seeking local bands and DJs.

DIRECTORY

International Cricket One-day internationals, Test matches and Sheffield Shield games are played at the Gabba in Brisbane.

March/April

Anzac Day The nation commemorates the landing of the Australian and New Zealand Army Corp (Anzac) troops at Gallipoli in 1915 on 25 April. Veterans of both World Wars and the Korean and Vietnam Wars hold marches.

Brisbane to Gladstone Yacht Race Queensland's version of the Sydney to Hobart, held over Easter.

Easter in the Country (p166) Roma in the Darling Downs gears up for goat races, rodeos, country music and sausage sizzles galore. One big party!

Surf Life-Saving Championships (p136) Life-saving championships are held on the Gold Coast, including the classic Ironman and Ironwoman events.

May/June

Beef Australia (p234) Held every three years in Rockhampton, over several days in May, this is a huge exposition of everything beefy.

Brisbane Pride Festival (p97) Brisbane's fabulously flamboyant gay and lesbian celebration, held in June.

Cooktown Endeavour Festival (p390) A festival commemorating Captain Cook's landing in 1770 is held over the Queen's Birthday weekend.

Outback Muster Drovers Reunion (p428) This major festival is held in Longreach on the Labour Day weekend.

Sorry Day (www.journeyofhealing.com) Each year on 26 May, the anniversary of the tabling in 1997 of the *Bringing Them Home* report, concerned Australians acknowledge the continuing pain and suffering of indigenous people affected by Australia's one-time child-removal practices and policies. Events are held in most cities countrywide.

Ten Days in the Towers (p309) Charters Towers' major country-music festival, held over 10 days in May.

Wintermoon Folk Festival (p257) Several days of world music are enjoyed in Mackay.

July

Gold Coast International Marathon (p136) Queensland's biggest event for distance runners; also includes some less-superhuman events.

National Aboriginal & Islander Day Observance Committee (Naidoc) week Indigenous art exhibitions and performances take place throughout Queensland during Naidoc week.

Queensland Music Festival (p97) This biennial (every odd-numbered year) festival features everything from jazz to indigenous music, from Australia and all over the world.

August

Brisbane International Film Festival (p97) The festival features films from Australia and the Asia-Pacific region.

Hervey Bay Whale Festival (p206) Held over a fortnight, it celebrates the annual migration of these magnificent creatures.

'Ekka' Royal National Agricultural Show (p97) Held at the RNA Showgrounds in Brisbane, this is Queensland's largest agricultural show.

Mt Isa Rodeo (p422) This is one of the country's richest rodeos.

September

Birdsville Races (p434) The country's premier outback horse-racing event is held on the first weekend in September.

Brisbane Riverfestival (p97) Brisbane's annual arts festival is held over two weeks in early September.

Cairns Festival (p337) Annual three-week festival celebrating regional culture.

Carnival of Flowers (p161) Toowoomba's gardens are on display for eight days, with a flower show, a parade and a Mardi Gras.

October

IndyCar (p137) A four-day festival centred on the IndyCar Grand Prix car race around the barricaded streets of Surfers Paradise.

Livid (p97) Annual one-day alternative rock festival held in Brisbane.

Oktoberfests Traditional beer-fests (with food, plenty of beer and live entertainment) for all ages are held in several towns in Queensland.

November

Melbourne Cup Australia's premier horse race is run in Melbourne, Victoria, on the first Tuesday in November. The whole country shuts down for three minutes while the race is run.

December

Woodford Folk Festival (p193) Formerly the Maleny Folk Festival, this huge folk festival is held over five days between 28 December and New Year's Day.

FOOD

The innovative food offered in top-quality Australian eateries doesn't necessarily cost a fortune. Best value are the cafés, where a good meal in casual surroundings costs less than $20 and a full cooked breakfast around $10. Some pubs offer upmarket restaurant-style fare, but most pubs serve standard (often large-portion) bistro meals, usually in the $10 to $19 range. Bar (or counter) meals, which are eaten in the public bar, usually cost between $6 and $10. For general opening hours, consider that breakfast is normally served between 6am and 11am, lunch starts around noon and runs until about 3pm and dinner usually starts after 6pm.

See p69 for more information about Queensland cuisine.

GAY & LESBIAN TRAVELLERS

Historically, Queensland has a poor reputation when it comes to acceptance of gays and lesbians. Homosexuality was only decriminalised in Queensland in 1991, after the fall of the right-wing National Party government.

Brisbane has an increasingly lively gay and lesbian scene centred on the inner-city suburbs of Spring Hill and Fortitude Valley, with quite a few nightclubs and pubs and a couple of guesthouses. See the boxed text on p98 for more information on gay and lesbian culture in Brisbane. There are also gay- and lesbian-only accommodation places in some of the more popular tourist centres, including Brisbane and Cairns. Elsewhere in Queensland, however, there's still a strong streak of homophobia, and violence against homosexuals is a risk, particularly in rural communities.

The website of **Gay & Lesbian Tourism Australia** (GALTA; www.galta.com.au) is a good place to look for general information, though you need to become a member to receive the full benefits. **Gay Australia** (www.gayaustralia.com.au) is another helpful website.

HOLIDAYS
Public Holidays

New Year's Day 1 January
Australia Day 26 January
Labour Day 1 March
Easter (Good Friday to Easter Monday inclusive) March/April
Anzac Day 25 April
Queen's Birthday 2nd Monday in June
Royal National Show Day mid-August, Brisbane only
Christmas Day 25 December
Boxing Day 26 December

School Holidays

The Christmas holiday season (from mid-December to late January) is part of the long summer school vacation in Australia, and the time you are most likely to find accommodation booked out and long queues at attractions. Easter is also a busy holiday time. There are three shorter school-holiday periods during the year that alternate slightly from year to year. Generally, they

fall in mid-April, late June to mid-July, and late September to mid-October.

INSURANCE

Don't underestimate the importance of a good travel-insurance policy that covers theft, loss and medical problems – nothing will ruin your holiday plans quicker than an accident, or having that brand new digital camera stolen. There is a wide variety of policies available, so compare the small print.

Some policies specifically exclude designated 'dangerous activities' such as scuba diving, parasailing, bungee jumping, motorcycling, skiing and even bushwalking. If you plan on doing any of these things, make sure the policy you choose fully covers you for your activity of choice.

You may prefer a policy that pays doctors or hospitals directly rather than you having to pay on the spot and claim later. If you have to claim later, make sure you keep all documentation. Some policies ask you to call back (reverse charges or collect) to a centre in your home country, where an immediate assessment of your problem is made. Check that the policy covers ambulances and emergency medical evacuations by air.

See p466 for information on health insurance. For information on insurance matters relating to cars that are bought or rented, see p460.

INTERNET ACCESS

Email and Internet access is relatively easy in Queensland. Typical costs for casual use are $4 to $6 per hour. If you're staying in a hostel, chances are that Internet access is provided on site, though you may have to wait in line to get online! Hostels, B&Bs and hotels offering guest terminals with Internet access are identified in this book with an Internet symbol (🖳).

Most public libraries have Internet access, but generally there are a limited number of terminals and you need to book in advance. You'll find Internet cafés in cities, sizable towns and pretty much anywhere that travellers congregate.

Most travellers make constant use of Internet cafés and free Web-based email such as Yahoo (www.yahoo.com) or Hotmail (www.hotmail.com).

If you're bringing your own palmtop or notebook computer, check with your

Internet Service Provider (ISP) to find out if there are access numbers you can dial into. Be aware that your modem may not work once you leave your home country. The safest option is to buy a reputable 'global' modem before you leave home, or buy a local PC-card modem, if you're spending an extended time in any one country. For more information on travelling with a portable computer, see www.teleadapt.com.

Australia primarily uses the RJ-45 telephone plugs, although you may see Telstra EXI-160 four-pin plugs; electronics shops such as Tandy and Dick Smith should be able to help. Most motel and hotel rooms have phone/modem sockets.

LEGAL MATTERS

Most travellers will have no contact with the police or any other part of the legal system. Those who do are likely to do so while driving. There is a significant police presence on the roads, with the power to stop you and ask to see your licence (you're required to carry it), check your vehicle for roadworthiness, and to ask you to take a breath test for alcohol – needless to say, drink driving offences are taken very seriously here.

First offenders caught with small amounts of illegal drugs are likely to receive a fine rather than go to jail, but the recording of a conviction against you may affect your visa status. Speaking of which, if you remain in Australia beyond the life of your visa, you will officially be an 'overstayer' and could face detention and expulsion, and then be prevented from returning to Australia for up to three years.

MAPS

The Royal Automobile Club of Queensland (RACQ) publishes a good series of regional

---

LEGAL AGE

For the record:

- You can drive when you're 17, and generally must be 21 to hire a car.
- The legal age for voting is 18.
- The age of consent for heterosexual intercourse is 16. For gay sex, it's 18.
- The legal drinking age is 18.

---

road maps that show almost every drivable road in the state – these are free to RACQ members and to members of affiliated motoring organisations. There are also plenty of road maps published by the various oil companies. These are available from service stations.

Queensland's Department of Natural Resources and Mines produces the Sunmap series, which, together with commercial maps by companies including Hema, Gregory's and UBD, are available from most newsagents and many bookshops in Queensland. **World Wide Maps & Guides** (☎ 07-3221 4330; Shop 30, Anzac Sq, 267 Edward St, Brisbane) has one of the best selections of maps in the state.

For bushwalking and other activities that require large-scale maps, the topographic sheets put out by **Geoscience Australia** (☎ 1800 800 173; www.ga.gov.au) are the ones to get.

MONEY

In this book, unless otherwise stated, all prices given in dollars refer to Australian dollars. Exchange rates are listed on the inside front cover. For an idea of the cost of travelling in Queensland, see p10.

ATMs

ATMs are prominent throughout Queensland and are linked to international networks. They are an excellent way to procure local currency and avoid the hassle of carrying travellers cheques or large sums of cash.

Cash

Australia's currency is the Australian dollar, made up of 100 cents. There are 5c, 10c, 20c, 50c, $1 and $2 coins, and $5, $10, $20, $50 and $100 notes. Although the smallest coin in circulation is 5c, prices are often still marked in single cents and then rounded to the nearest 5c when you come to pay.

Credit Cards

MasterCard and Visa are widely accepted. American Express is limited more to major towns and destinations.

The most flexible option is to carry both a credit and an ATM or debit card; some banking institutions link the two to one card. You can use your debit card at most retail outlets and supermarkets, which carry Eftpos (Electronic Funds Transfer at Point of Sale) facilities.

TAX REFUNDS

If you purchase new or secondhand goods with a total minimum value of $300 from any one supplier no more than 30 days before you leave Australia, you are entitled under the Tourist Refund Scheme (TRS) to a refund of any GST paid. The scheme only applies to goods you take with you as hand luggage or wear onto the plane or ship. Also note that the refund is valid for goods bought from more than one supplier, but only if at least $300 is spent at each. For more information, contact the **Australian Customs Service** (☎ 1300 363 263, 02-6275 6666; www.customs.gov.au).

Moneychangers

Changing foreign currency or travellers cheques is usually no problem at banks throughout Queensland, or at foreign exchange counters such as Travelex or Amex, which you'll find in the major cities.

Tipping

See the boxed text on p74 for information on tipping etiquette in Queensland.

Travellers Cheques

American Express, Thomas Cook and other well-known international brands of travellers cheques are all widely used in Australia. A passport will usually be adequate for identification; it would be sensible to also carry a driver's licence, credit cards or a plane ticket in case of problems.

Buying travellers cheques in Australian dollars is another option. These can be exchanged immediately at banks without being converted from a foreign currency or incurring commissions, fees and exchange-rate fluctuations.

Still, increasingly, international travellers simply withdraw cash from ATMs, enjoying the convenience and the usually good exchange rates.

PHOTOGRAPHY & VIDEO

There are plenty of camera shops in all the big cities and standards of camera service are high. Australian film prices are not too far out of line with those of the rest of the Western world. A 36-exposure Kodak or Fuji film costs around $9 for 100 ASA

and $10 for 400 ASA. Slide film is widely available in larger towns, but is rare in the outback; stock up before you head inland. Remember that slide film is particularly vulnerable to heat damage. Kodak Elite II is the most widely available film and costs around $12 for a 36-exposure, 100-ASA roll. Developing standards are also high, with many places offering one-hour developing of print film; prices range from $10 to $13.

Video cassettes are widely available at camera and electronics stores.

For the best results, try to take most of your photos early in the morning and late in the afternoon, when the light is softer. A polarising filter will help eliminate the glare if you're taking shots of the Great Barrier Reef or other water locations. Remember that heat, dust and humidity can all damage film; keep film dry and cool and process films promptly to guarantee results. For more information, see Lonely Planet's *Travel Photography: A Guide To Taking Better Pictures*.

Cheap disposable underwater cameras are widely available at most beach towns and resorts. These are OK for snapshots when snorkelling or shallow diving and can produce reasonable results in good conditions, but without a flash the colours will be washed out. These cameras won't work below about 5m because of the water pressure. If you're serious about underwater photography, good underwater cameras with flash units can be hired from many of the dive shops along the coast.

As in any country, politeness goes a long way when taking photographs; ask before taking pictures of people. Aborigines generally do not like to have their photographs taken, even from a distance.

POST

Australia's postal services are efficient and reasonably cheap. Posting standard letters or postcards within the country cost 50c. **Australia Post** (www.auspost.com.au) has divided international destinations into two regions: Asia-Pacific and Rest of the World. Airmail letters up to 50g cost $1.10 and $1.65, respectively. Postcards (up to 20g) cost $1 and an aerogram to any country is 85c. There are five international parcel zones and rates vary by distance and class of service.

All post offices will hold mail for visitors, and some city GPOs (main or general post offices) have very busy poste-restante sections. You need to provide some form of identification (such as a passport) to collect mail. See p439 for post office opening times.

SOLO TRAVELLERS

People travelling alone in Queensland face the unpredictability that is an inherent part of making contact with entire communities of strangers: sometimes you'll be completely ignored, and other times you'll be greeted with such enthusiasm it's as if you've been spontaneously adopted. Suffice to say that the latter moments will likely become highlights of your trip.

People travelling solo are a common sight throughout Australia and there is certainly no stigma attached to lone visitors. However in some places there can be an expectation that the visitor should engage in some way with the locals, particularly in rural pubs where keeping to yourself can prove harder than it sounds. Women travelling on their own should exercise caution when in less-populated areas, and will find that men can get annoyingly attentive in drinking establishments (with mining-town pubs arguably the nadir); see also p451.

TELEPHONE

There are a number of providers offering various services. The three main players are the mostly government-owned **Telstra** (www.telstra.com.au) and the fully private **Optus** (www.optus.com.au) and **Primus Telecom** (www.primus.com.au). These are also major players in the mobile (cell) market, along with **Vodafone** (www.vodafone.com.au) – other mobile operators include **AAPT** (www.aapt.com.au), **Orange** (www.orange.net.au) and **3** (www.three.com.au).

Numbers starting with ☎ 190 are usually recorded-information services, charged at anything from 35c to $5 or more per minute (more from mobiles and payphones). To make a reverse-charge (collect) call from any public or private phone, simply dial ☎ 1800-REVERSE (1880 738 3773) or ☎ 12 550.

Toll-free numbers (prefix ☎ 1800) can be called free of charge from anywhere in the country, though they may not be accessible from certain areas or from mobile phones. Calls to numbers beginning with ☎ 13 or ☎ 1300 are charged at the rate of a local call – the numbers can usually be dialled Australia-wide, but may be applicable only to a specific state or STD district. Telephone numbers beginning with ☎ 1800, ☎ 13 or ☎ 1300 cannot be dialled from outside Australia.

Most payphones allow ISD (International Subscriber Dialling) calls, the cost and international dialling code of which will vary depending on which provider you're using. International calls from Australia are very cheap and subject to specials that reduce the rates even more, so it's worth shopping around – look in the *Yellow Pages* for a list of providers.

Mobile Phones

Local numbers with the prefixes ☎ 04xx or ☎ 04xxx belong to mobile phones. Australia's two mobile networks – digital GSM and digital CDMA – service more than 90% of the population but leave vast tracts of the country uncovered, including much of the Queensland outback. Brisbane and the towns lining the coast get good reception, but outside these centres it's haphazard or nonexistent.

Australia's digital network is compatible with GSM 900 and 1800 (used in Europe), but generally not with the systems used in the USA or Japan. It's easy and cheap enough to get connected short-term, though, as the main service providers (Telstra, Optus and Vodafone) all have prepaid mobile systems. Just buy a starter kit, which may include a phone or, if you have your own phone, a SIM card (around $30) and a prepaid charge card. The calls tend to be a bit more expensive than with standard contracts, but there are no connection fees or line-rental charges and you can buy the recharge cards at convenience stores and newsagents. Don't forget to shop around between the three carriers as their products differ.

Phone Codes

When calling overseas you need to dial the international access code from Australia (☎ 0011 or ☎ 0018), the country code and the area code (without the initial 0). So for a London number you'd dial ☎ 0011-44-171, then the number. Also, certain operators will have you dial a special code to access their service.

EMERGENCY

If you need the police, an ambulance or the fire department in an emergency, dial ☎ 000, ask the operator for the service you need and wait to be connected. This is a 24-hour service; your call is free and can be traced. To contact these services for non-emergencies, check regional phone books for local numbers.

If dialling Queensland from overseas, the country code is ☎ 61 and you need to drop the 0 (zero) in the ☎ 07 area code.

Calls from private phones cost from 15c to 25c, while local calls from public phones cost 40c; both involve unlimited talk time. Calls to mobile phones attract higher rates and are timed. Blue phones or gold phones, which you sometimes find in hotel lobbies or other businesses, usually cost a minimum of 50c for a local call.

Although the whole of Queensland shares a single area code (☎ 07), once you call outside of the immediate area or town you are in, it is likely you are making a long-distance (STD) call. STD calls can be made from virtually any public phone and are cheaper during off-peak hours, which are generally between 7pm and 7am. There's a handful of main area codes for Australia:

State/Territory	Area Code
ACT	☎ 02
NSW	☎ 02
NT	☎ 08
QLD	☎ 07
SA	☎ 08
TAS	☎ 03
VIC	☎ 03
WA	☎ 08

Phonecards

There's a wide range of phonecards, which can be bought at newsagents and post offices for a fixed dollar value (usually $10, $20, $30 etc) and can be used with any public or private phone by dialling a toll-free access number and then the PIN on the card. Call rates vary, so shop around. Some public phones also accept credit cards.

TIME

Australia is divided into three time zones. Queensland is on Eastern Standard Time (as are New South Wales, Victoria and Tasmania), which is 10 hours ahead of UTC (Greenwich Mean Time).

The other time zones in Australia are Central Standard Time (Northern Territory, South Australia), which is half an hour behind Eastern Standard Time; and Western Standard Time (Western Australia), which is two hours behind Eastern Standard Time.

When it is noon in Queensland it is 2am in London, 2pm in Auckland, 6pm the previous day in Los Angeles and 9pm the previous day in New York.

Lamentably, Queensland is on Eastern Standard Time all year, while most of the rest of Australia sensibly switches to daylight saving time over the summer months. From roughly October through March, Queensland is one hour behind New South Wales, Victoria and Tasmania. (But at least its curtains don't fade.)

TOURIST INFORMATION

There are a large number of information sources available to visitors to Queensland, and you could easily drown yourself in brochures and booklets, maps and leaflets. Having said that, it's worth noting that most of the tourist information places are also booking agents, and will steer you towards the tour that will pay them the best commission.

There are official tourist offices in just about every city and town in Queensland, staffed largely by friendly and knowledgeable volunteers.

The **Australian Tourist Commission** (ATC; ☎ 1300 361 650, 02-9360 1111; www.australia.com; Level 4, 80 William St, Woolloomooloo, 2011) is the national government body charged with improving foreign tourist relations. A good place to start some pre-trip research is the commission's website, which has information in nine languages (including French, German, Japanese and Spanish), quite of bit of it covering Queensland.

Tourism Queensland (☎ 13 88 33; www.queensland holidays.com.au) is the government-run body responsible for promoting Queensland interstate and overseas. Its Queensland Travel offices act primarily as promotional and booking offices, not information centres, but are worth contacting when you're planning a trip to Queensland.

Australian Capital Territory (☎ 02-6229 8999; 25 Garema Place, Canberra 2601)

New South Wales Sydney (☎ 02-8270 3444; 323 George St, Sydney 2000); Chatswood (☎ 02-9406 0000; Lower Level, Chatswood Chase, 345 Victoria Ave, Chatswood 2067); Parramatta (☎ 02-9633 6444; Shop 2158, Westfield Shoppingtown, Parramatta 2150); Miranda (☎ 02-8536 5555; Shop 1110, Kingsway, Miranda 2228)

Queensland (☎ 07-535 5044; 30 Markerston St, Brisbane 4000)

South Australia (☎ 08-8211 8841; 74 Gawler Pl, Adelaide 5000)

Victoria (☎ 03-8636 4555; 405 Bourke St, Melbourne 3000)

Western Australia (☎ 08-9321 1429; 760 Hay St, Perth 6000)

The Queensland Parks and Wildlife Service provides information on conservation areas throughout the state, including national parks, and is another useful body for travellers heading to Queensland. See the boxed text on p41 for contact details.

Interstate tourist authorities:

New South Wales (www.visitnsw.com.au)
South Australia (www.tourism.sa.gov.au)
Victoria (www.visitvictoria.com)
Western Australia (www.westernaustralia.com)

TOURS

There are all sorts of tours around Queensland, although few that cover much of the state. Most are connected with a particular activity (eg bushwalking or horse riding) or area (eg 4WD tours to Cape York). There are also thousands of flyers in hostels and tourist-information offices.

Up in Far North Queensland, there are plenty of operators offering 4WD tours of Cape York Peninsula, often with the option of driving one way and flying or boating the other. See p397 for details.

There are all sorts of trips from the mainland out to the Great Barrier Reef (see p62). You can fly in a seaplane out to a deserted coral cay; take a fast catamaran to the outer reef and spend the day snorkelling; join a dive boat and scuba dive in a coral garden; or take a day trip to one of the many islands.

There are hundreds of tours operating out of Cairns (p335) and Port Douglas (p370). As well as trips to the Reef and islands, you can take the Kuranda Scenic Railway up to the Kuranda markets; tour the Ather-

ton Tablelands; visit Cape Tribulation on a 4WD tour; cruise along the Daintree River; go white-water rafting; and visit Aboriginal rock-art galleries in Cape York.

Tours of Fraser Island from Noosa (p184) and Hervey Bay (see the boxed text on p210) are a convenient way of seeing one of Queensland's natural wonders for those who don't have their own 4WD.

Dozens of operators in the Whitsundays (p268) offer cruises around the islands, and if you want to do your own thing, you can get a group together and charter a yacht.

From the Gold Coast (p146) there are tours to Lamington and Springbrook National Parks, and numerous tours run out of Brisbane to the Sunshine and Gold Coasts, and the lovely sand islands of Moreton Bay.

VISAS

All visitors to Australia need a visa. Only New Zealand nationals are exempt; they receive a 'special category' visa on arrival.

Visa application forms are available from Australian diplomatic missions overseas, travel agents and the website of the **Department of Immigration and Multicultural and Indigenous Affairs** (DIMIA; Map pp80-2; ☎ 13 18 81; www.immi.gov.au). There are several types of visa.

Electronic Travel Authority

Many visitors can get an Electronic Travel Authority (ETA) through any travel agent or overseas airline registered by the International Air Transport Association (IATA). They make the application direct when you buy a ticket and issue the ETA, which replaces the usual visa stamped in your passport – it's common practice for travel agents to charge a fee for issuing an ETA (usually US$15). This system is available to passport holders of some 33 countries, including the UK, the USA and Canada, most European and Scandinavian countries, Malaysia, Singapore, Japan and Korea. You can also make an online ETA application at www.eta.immi.gov.au, where no fees apply.

Tourist Visas

Short-term tourist visas have largely been replaced by the free ETA. However, if you are from a country not covered by the ETA, or you want to stay longer than three months, you'll need to apply for a visa. Standard visas (which cost $65) allow one (or in some cases multiple) entry and stays of up to three months, and are valid for use within 12 months of issue. A long-stay tourist visa (also $65) can allow a visit of up to a year.

Visa Extensions

Visitors are allowed a maximum stay of 12 months, including extensions. Visa extensions are made through the Department of Immigration and Multicultural and Indigenous Affairs and it's best to apply at least two or three weeks before your visa expires. The application fee is $160 – it's nonrefundable, even if your application is rejected.

Working Holiday Maker Visas

Young, single visitors from Canada, Cyprus, Denmark, Finland, Germany, Hong Kong, Ireland, Japan, Korea, Malta, the Netherlands, Norway, Sweden and the UK are eligible for a Working Holiday Maker (WHM) visa, which allows you to visit for up to 12 months and gain casual employment. From November 2005 WHM visa–holders can apply for a second 12-month WHM visa if they have done at least three months seasonal harvest work in regional Australia. 'Young' is defined as between 18 and 30 years of age and visa holders are only supposed to work for any one employer for a maximum of three months. There is an application fee of $160, and visas must be applied for only at Australian diplomatic missions abroad. For more information on the WHM, see www.immi.gov.au/e_visa/visit.htm.

WOMEN TRAVELLERS

Queensland is generally a safe place for women travellers, although it's probably best to avoid walking alone late at night in any of the major cities. Sexual harassment is rare, although the Aussie male culture does have its sexist elements. Don't tolerate any harassment or discrimination. Some women have reported problems at party hostels on the Gold Coast. With intoxicated men stumbling up from the bar, rural pub rooms are probably best avoided. If you're out on the town, always keep enough money aside for a taxi back to your accommodation. The same applies to outback and rural towns where there are often a lot of unlit, semi-deserted streets between you and your temporary home. When the pubs and bars close and there are inebriated people roaming

around, it's not a great time to be out and about. Lone women should also be wary of staying in basic pub accommodation unless it looks safe and well managed.

Sexual harassment is an ongoing problem, be it via an aggressive cosmopolitan male or a rural bloke living a less-than-enlightened bush existence. Stereotypically, the further you get from 'civilisation' (ie the big cities), the less aware your average Aussie male is probably going to be about women's issues. Having said that, many women travellers say that they have met the friendliest, most down-to-earth blokes in outback pubs and remote roadhouse stops. And cities still have to put up with their unfortunate share of ocker males who regard a bit of sexual harassment as a right, and chauvinism as a desirable trait.

Lone female hitchers are tempting fate – hitching with a male companion is safer.

WORK

Several of the backpackers hostels in Brisbane have job boards with notices of available employment, while many of the bigger hostels have job clubs that aim to find work for guests. Telemarketing, door-to-door sales and table waiting are the most common jobs. The Palace Backpackers (p98) in Brisbane probably has the biggest job club.

If you're in Brisbane and happy with bar work or waiting on tables, the best advice may be to go knocking on doors in Fortitude Valley or New Farm. Many places want staff for longer than three months, though, so it may take a bit of footwork to find a willing employer. The *Courier-Mail* has a daily Situations Vacant listing – Wednesday and Saturday are the best days to look.

Harvest work is popular elsewhere in Queensland. The main hotspots are Bundaberg, Childers, Stanthorpe and Bowen, where everything from avocados to zucchini are harvested almost all year round, and hostels specialise in finding travellers work. The **National Harvest Labour Information Service** (☎ 1800 062 332; www.jobsearch.gov.au/harvest trail) is a good source of information on where to pick up seasonal work.

Other useful websites:
Australian Job Search (www.jobsearch.gov.au)
Career One (www.careerone.com.au)
Seek (www.seek.com.au)

Transport

CONTENTS

GETTING THERE & AWAY

Australia is a *long* way from Europe or America, and even a long-haul flight away from Asia, so be prepared for plenty of in-flight movies. All flights from Europe make a stop in Asia, usually in Bangkok, Hong Kong, Singapore or Kuala Lumpur; flying from the USA usually involves a stop on one of the Pacific islands. Flights into Australia are heavily booked during the European and US summer holidays and at Christmas time.

ENTERING THE COUNTRY

Disembarkation in Australia is generally a straightforward affair, with only the usual customs declarations (p441) and the fight to be first at the luggage carousel to endure. If you're flying in with Qantas, Air New Zealand, British Airways, Cathay Pacific, Japan Airlines or Singapore Airlines, ask the carrier about the 'express' passenger card, which will speed your way through customs.

Recent global instability has resulted in conspicuously increased security in Australian airports, in both domestic and international terminals, and you may find that customs procedures are now more time-consuming.

AIR
International

Many international flights head to Sydney or Melbourne before they fly to Queens-

land, but Brisbane and Cairns receive direct international flights, and a few flights from New Zealand land at Coolangatta airport on the Gold Coast.

Because of Australia's size and diverse climate, any time of the year can prove busy for inbound tourists – if you plan to fly during a particularly popular period (Christmas is notoriously popular), or on a particularly popular route (such as via Hong Kong, Bangkok or Singapore), make your arrangements well in advance.

AIRLINES

Air Canada (☎ 1300 655 767; www.aircanada.ca) Flies to Sydney.

Air New Zealand (☎ 13 24 76; www.airnz.com.au) Flies to Brisbane, Cairns, Sydney and Melbourne.

Air Paradise International (☎ 1300 799 066; www.airparadise.co.id) Flies to Brisbane, Sydney, Melbourne, Adelaide and Perth.

American Airlines (☎ 1300 650 747; www.aa.com) Flies to Brisbane, Cairns, Sydney, Melbourne, Adelaide and Perth.

Australian Airlines (☎ 1300 799 798; http://australian airlines.com.au) Flies to Coolangatta and Cairns, Sydney, Melbourne, Perth and Darwin.

THINGS CHANGE

The information in this chapter is particularly vulnerable to change: prices for international travel are volatile, routes are introduced and cancelled, schedules change, special deals come and go, and rules and visa requirements are amended.

Airlines and governments seem to take a perverse pleasure in making price structures and regulations as complicated as possible. Check directly with the airline or a travel agent to make sure you understand how a fare (and ticket you may buy) works. In addition, the travel industry is highly competitive and there are many lurks and perks.

The upshot of this is that you should get opinions, quotes and advice from as many airlines and travel agents as possible before you part with your hard-earned cash. The details given in this chapter should be regarded as pointers and are not a substitute for your own careful, up-to-date research.

Austrian Airlines (☎ 1800 642 438, 02-9251 6155; www.aua.com/au/eng) Flies to Sydney and Melbourne.
British Airways (☎ 1300 767 177; www.britishairways .com.au) Flies to all major Australian cities, including Brisbane and Cairns.
Cathay Pacific (☎ 13 17 47; www.cathaypacific.com) Flies to Brisbane, Cairns, Sydney, Melbourne, Adelaide and Perth.
Emirates (☎ 1300 303 777; www.emirates.com) Flies to Brisbane, Sydney, Melbourne and Perth.
Freedom Air (☎ 1800 122 000; www.freedomair.com) Flies to Brisbane, Coolangatta, Sydney and Melbourne.
Garuda Indonesia (☎ 1300 365 330; www.garuda -indonesia.com) Flies to Brisbane, Sydney, Melbourne, Perth, Adelaide and Darwin.
Gulf Air (☎ 02-9244 2199; www.gulfairco.com) Flies to Sydney.
KLM (☎ 07-3407 7282; www.klm.com.au) Flies to Brisbane, Sydney, Melbourne, Adelaide and Perth.
Malaysian Airlines (☎ 13 26 27; www.malaysia airlines.com.au) Flies to Brisbane, Sydney, Melbourne, Adelaide and Perth.
Qantas (☎ 13 13 13; www.qantas.com.au) Flies to all major Australian cities, including Brisbane and Cairns.
Royal Brunei Airlines (☎ 1300 721 271; www.royal bruneiairlines.com.au) Flies to Brisbane, Sydney and Perth.
Singapore Airlines (☎ 13 10 11; www.singaporeair .com.au) Flies to Brisbane, Sydney, Melbourne, Adelaide and Perth.
South African Airways (☎ 1800 221 699; ww2.flysaa.com) Flies to Perth and Sydney.
Thai Airways International (☎ 1300 651 960; www.thaiairways.com.au) Flies to Brisbane, Sydney, Melbourne and Perth.
United Airlines (☎ 13 17 77; www.unitedairlines .au) Flies to Sydney and Melbourne.

TICKETS

Be sure you research the options carefully to make sure you get the best deal. The Internet is an increasingly useful resource for checking airline prices.

Automated online ticket sales work well if you're doing a simple one-way or return trip on specified dates, but are no substitute for a travel agent with the low-down on special deals, strategies for avoiding stopovers and other useful advice.

Paying by credit card offers some protection if you unwittingly end up dealing with a rogue fly-by-night agency in your search for the cheapest fare. Most card issuers provide refunds if you can prove you didn't get what you paid for. Alternatively, buy a ticket from a bonded agent, such as one

---

> **DEPARTURE TAX**
>
> There is a $38 departure tax when leaving Australia, but this is incorporated into the price of your air ticket and is not paid as a separate tax.

covered by the **Air Travel Organiser's Licence** (ATOL; www.atol.org.uk) scheme in the UK. If you have doubts about the service provider, at the very least call the airline and confirm that your booking has been made.

Round-the-world tickets can be a good option for getting to Australia.

For online bookings, start with a recommended website:

Airbrokers (www.airbrokers.com) US company specialising in cheap tickets.
Cheap Flights (www.cheapflights.com) Informative site with specials, airline information and flight searches from the USA and other regions.
Cheapest Flights (www.cheapestflights.co.uk) Cheap worldwide flights from the UK; get in early for bargains.
Expedia (www.expedia.msn.com) Mainly US-related travel site.
Flight Centre International (www.flightcentre.com) Respected operator handling direct flights, with sites for Australia, New Zealand, the UK, the USA and Canada.
Opodo (www.opodo.com) Reliable company with UK, German and French sites.
Orbitz (www.orbitz.com) Excellent site for web-only fares for US airlines.
STA (www.statravel.com) Prominent in international student travel, but you don't have to be a student; site linked to worldwide STA sites.
Travel Online (www.travelonline.co.nz) Good place to check worldwide flights from New Zealand.
Travel.com.au (www.travel.com.au) Good Australian site; look up fares and flights into and out of the country.
Travelocity (www.travelocity.com) US site that allows you to search fares (in US dollars) to/from practically anywhere.
Roundtheworld.com (www.roundtheworldflights.com) This excellent site allows you to build your own trips from the UK with up to six stops.
Zuji (www.zuji.com.au) Good Asia Pacific–based site.

FROM ASIA

Most Asian countries offer fairly competitive air-fare deals, with Bangkok, Singapore and Hong Kong being the best places to shop for discount tickets.

Flights between Hong Kong and Australia are notoriously heavily booked. Flights to/ from Bangkok and Singapore are often part of the longer Europe-to-Australia route so they are also sometimes full. The motto of the story is to plan your preferred itinerary well in advance.

Typical return fares to Brisbane from Bangkok, Singapore, Kuala Lumpur and Hong Kong in high season are (in Australian dollars) $1200 to $1600, and in low season $1000 to $1200.

There are several good local agents in Asia:

Hong Kong Student Travel Bureau (☎ 2730 3269) In Hong Kong.

Phoenix Services (☎ 2722 7378) In Hong Kong.

STA Travel Bangkok (☎ 0 2236 0262; www.statravel .co.th); Singapore (☎ 6737 7188; www.statravel.com.sg); Tokyo (☎ 03 5391 3205; www.statravel.co.jp)

FROM CANADA

The air routes from Canada are similar to those from mainland USA, with most Toronto and Vancouver flights stopping in one US city such as Los Angeles or Honolulu before heading on to Australia. Air Canada flies from Vancouver to Sydney via Honolulu and from Toronto to Melbourne via Honolulu.

Canadian discount air-ticket sellers are known as consolidators and their fares tend to be about 10% higher than those sold in the USA. **Travel Cuts** (☎ 1866 246 9762; www .travelcuts.com) is Canada's national student travel agency with offices in major cities.

Fares out of Vancouver to Sydney or Melbourne cost (in Australian dollars) from $1800/2300 in the low/high season via the US west coast. From Toronto, fares cost from around $1950/2400.

FROM CONTINENTAL EUROPE

From the major destinations in Europe, most flights travel via one of the Asian capitals. Some flights are also routed through London before arriving in Australia via Singapore, Bangkok, Hong Kong or Kuala Lumpur.

Fares from Paris in the low/high season coast around €1000/1200.

Some agents in Paris:

Nouvelles Frontiéres (☎ 08 25 00 07 47; www.nouvelles-frontieres.fr in French) Also has branches outside of Paris.

OTU Voyages (☎ 01 40 29 12 12; www.otu.fr in French) Student/youth oriented, with offices in many cities.

Usit Connect Voyages (☎ 01 43 29 69 50; www .usitconnections.fr in French) Student/youth specialists, with offices in many cities.

Voyageurs du Monde (☎ 01 42 86 16 00; www.vdm .com/vdm in French) Has branches throughout France.

A good option in the Dutch travel industry is **Holland International** (☎ 0703 07 63 07; www .hollandinternational.nl in Dutch). From Amsterdam, return fares start at around €1500.

In Germany, good travel agencies include the Berlin branch of **STA Travel** (☎ 030 311 09 50; www.statravel.de). Fares start at around €900/1000 in the low/high season.

FROM NEW ZEALAND

Air New Zealand and Qantas operate a network of flights linking Auckland, Wellington and Christchurch in New Zealand with Brisbane and other Australian cities. Fares from New Zealand to Brisbane (in Australian dollars) start at around $300/600 one way/ return. Also look for foreign carriers such as Emirates, which offers reasonable fares.

Other trans-Tasman options:

Flight Centre (☎ 0800 243 544; www.flightcentre .co.nz) Has a large central office in Auckland and many branches throughout the country.

Freedom Air (☎ 0800 600 500; www.freedomair.com) An Air New Zealand subsidiary that operates direct flights and offers excellent rates year-round.

STA Travel (☎ 0508 782 872, 09-366 6673; www.statravel.co.nz) Has offices in various cities.

FROM SOUTH AFRICA

South African Airways and Qantas both fly from Johannesburg to Perth and Sydney, with connections to Brisbane. One-way/ return fares from Johannesburg to Australia cost around $1400/2100. Some good South African–based travel agents:

Flight Centre (☎ 0860 400 727; www.flightcentre .co.za) South African wing of this international company, with offices throughout the country.

Rennies Travel (www.renniestravel.co.za) Reliable South African–based travel agent.

FROM THE UK & IRELAND

There are two routes from the UK: the western route via the USA and the Pacific, and the eastern route via the Middle East and Asia. Flights are usually cheaper and more frequent on the latter. Some of the best deals around are with Emirates, Gulf Air, Malaysia Airlines, Japan Airlines and Thai Airways International. Unless there are special deals on offer, British Airways, Singapore Airlines and Qantas generally have higher fares but may offer more direct routes.

Discount air travel is big business in London. Advertisements for many travel agencies appear in the travel pages of the weekend broadsheet newspapers, in *Time Out*, the *Evening Standard* and in the free magazine *TNT*. Good agencies in the UK:

Flight Centre (☎ 0870 499 0040; www.flightcentre.co.uk)
Omega Travel (☎ 0870 770 6869; www.omegatravel .ltd.uk)
STA Travel (☎ 0870 160 0599; www.statravel.co.uk)
Trailfinders (☎ 0845 058 5858; www.trailfinders.co.uk)

Typical direct fares from London to Brisbane are £420/640 one way/return during the low season (March to June). In September and mid-December fares go up by as much as 30%, while the rest of the year they're somewhere in-between.

From Australia you can expect to pay around $900/1650 one way/return in the low season to London and other European capitals (with stops in Asia on the way), and $1100/2050 in the high season.

FROM THE USA

Airlines linking Australia nonstop with Los Angeles or San Francisco include Qantas, Air New Zealand and United Airlines. Numerous airlines offer flights via Asia, with stopover possibilities including Tokyo, Kuala Lumpur, Bangkok, Hong Kong and Singapore; and via the Pacific with stopover possibilities like Nadi (Fiji), Rarotonga (Cook Islands), Tahiti (French Polynesia) and Auckland (New Zealand).

As in Canada, discount travel agents in the USA are known as consolidators. San Francisco is the ticket-consolidator capital of America, although some good deals can be found in Los Angeles, New York and other big cities.

Some companies arranging travel from the USA to Australia:

STA Travel (☎ 800 777 0112; www.statravel.com) America's largest student travel organisation.
Travel Australia and New Zealand (☎ 888 333 6607; www.aussie-experience.com)

Return tickets from the US west coast to Melbourne, Sydney or Brisbane cost around US$1300/1700 in the low/high season; flights from the US east coast cost from US$1600/1900.

Domestic

The domestic airline industry has undergone some major upheavals in recent years, with airlines going into receivership, but also a coinciding fare war, which has all boded pretty well for consumers. At the end of a tumultuous period, it turns out there is now more choice and far more accessible pricing in the domestic market. Few people pay full fare as the airlines continue to offer a wide range of discounts. These come and go and there are regular special fares, so keep your eyes open.

The following carriers fly to Queensland from other Australian states:

Jetstar (☎ 13 15 38; www.jetstar.com.au) Flies to Brisbane, Cairns, the Gold Coast, Mackay, Rockhampton, the Sunshine Coast and the Whitsunday Coast from several major cities on the east coast, as well as Adelaide. Most flights involve a stopover.
Qantas (☎ 13 13 13; www.qantas.com.au) Flies to Brisbane, Cairns, the Gold Coast, Mackay, Rockhampton and Mt Isa from all capital cities and most of the smaller ones. Some flights involve a stop.
QantasLink (☎ 13 13 13; www.qantas.com.au) Flies from Sydney to Brisbane and Townsville.
Sunshine Express (☎ 13 13 13; www.sunshineexpress .com.au) Flies from Brisbane to Armidale, Coffs Harbour and Tamworth in New South Wales.
Virgin Blue (☎ 13 67 89; www.virginblue.com.au) Flies to Brisbane, Cairns, the Gold Coast, Mackay, Rockhampton, the Sunshine Coast, Townsville and the Whitsunday Coast from most capital cities.

There are also special deals available only to foreign visitors (in possession of an outbound ticket). If booked in Australia, these fares offer a 40% discount off a full-fare economy ticket. They can also be booked from overseas (which usually works out a bit cheaper). All airports and domestic flights are nonsmoking.

LAND
Border Crossings

Travelling overland to Queensland from elsewhere in Australia will really give you an impression of just how big this country is. The journey from Brisbane to the nearest state capital, Sydney, is a tortuous 1030km, and the journey from Brisbane to Cairns, the next biggest city in Queensland, covers 1700km! To give you a sense of scale, Melbourne is 1735km away from Brisbane, Adelaide is 2130km distant, Perth is a mere

TRANSPORT

4390km away, and the shortest route to Darwin covers 3495km.

The Pacific Hwy is the main access point into Queensland from the south, crossing the border at Tweed Heads and Coolangatta (p144). It runs along the coast between Sydney and Brisbane and passes through a number of popular tourist spots and some great scenery. A lesser-used route from the south is the New England Hwy, which crosses the border at Tenterfield. It's a quieter, longer inland route from Sydney, and the road is the undisputed territory of road trains (a string of trailers pulled by a semitrailer), and kangaroos at night.

The Newell Hwy is the most direct route to Brisbane from Melbourne or Adelaide. It's a good road through the heart of rural New South Wales (NSW), crossing the border at Goondiwindi (p159), before becoming the Leichhardt and Gore Hwys.

The other major route into southern Queensland is the Mitchell Hwy. It crosses the border at Barringun and links Bourke in outback NSW with Charleville (p431) in outback Queensland. In the state's far west, the Birdsville Track crosses the South Australian–Queensland border at Birdsville (p434). This road is in various stages of being paved but a 4WD is still recommended. For those wanting to travel further into the outback, have a look at Lonely Planet's *Outback Australia*.

The main road from the west is the Barkly Hwy, which crosses the Northern Territory–Queensland border around 15km west of Camooweal and cuts across to Mt Isa. From Mt Isa, you can continue eastward along the Flinders Hwy to Townsville on the coast, or head southeast along the Landsborough (Matilda) Hwy towards Brisbane.

See p459 for information on road rules, driving conditions and buying and renting vehicles.

GETTING AROUND

AIR
The state is well serviced by airlines, many of which are subsidiaries of Qantas. The following regional carriers access these locations from within Queensland:

Australian Airlines (☎ 13 13 13; www.australian airlines.com.au) Flies between Cairns and the Gold Coast.

Jetstar (☎ 13 15 38; www.jetstar.com.au) Flies between Brisbane and Hamilton Island.

Macair (☎ 13 13 13; www.macair.com.au) Flies to Birdsville, Cairns, Charleville, Dunk Island, Longreach, Mt Isa, Normanton, Toowoomba and Townsville, and many more outback locations and several locations in the Gulf Savannah.

Qantas (☎ 13 13 13; www.qantas.com.au) Flies to Brisbane, Cairns, Townsville and Mt Isa.

QantasLink (☎ 13 13 13; www.qantas.com.au) Flies to Horn Island, Weipa, Cairns, Townsville, Mackay, Rockhampton, the Whitsunday Coast, Gladstone, Brisbane, Emerald, Longreach, Charleville and Roma.

Skytrans (☎ 1800 818 405, 07-4046 2462; www .skytrans.com.au) Flies between Cairns and Cooktown.

Sunshine Express (☎ 13 13 13; www.sunshine express.com.au) Flies from Brisbane to the Sunshine Coast, Maryborough, Hervey Bay and Biloela.

Virgin Blue (☎ 13 67 89; www.virginblue.com.au) Flies between Cairns, Townsville, the Whitsunday Coast, Mackay, Rockhampton, Hervey Bay, the Sunshine Coast, Brisbane and the Gold Coast.

BICYCLE
Queensland can be a good place for cycling, although you need to choose your areas. There are bike tracks in most cities, but in the country they're variable. Roads such as the Bruce Hwy, from Brisbane to Cairns, can be long, hot and not particularly safe, as there are limited verges and heavy traffic. The humid weather can be draining too. The best areas for touring are probably the Gold Coast hinterland, the Sunshine Coast secondary roads and the area north of Cairns.

Bicycle helmets are compulsory, as are front and rear lights for night riding; you can receive an on-the-spot fine if you ignore these regulations.

Cycling has always been popular in Australia, and not only as a sport: some shearers would ride for huge distances between jobs rather than use less-reliable horses. It's rare to find a reasonably sized town that doesn't have a shop stocking at least basic bike parts.

If you're coming specifically to cycle, it makes sense to bring your own bike. Check with your airline for costs and the degree of dismantling/packing required. Within Australia you can load your bike onto a bus or train to skip the boring bits of road. Note that bus companies require you to dismantle your bike, and some don't guarantee that it will travel on the same bus as you.

Trains are easier, but you should supervise the loading and, if possible, tie your bike upright, otherwise you may find that the guard has stacked crates of Holden spares on your fragile alloy wheels.

Many towns in the east were established as staging posts, a day's horse ride apart, which is pretty convenient if you want a pub meal and a bed at the end of a day's riding. Camping is another option, and it's usually warm enough that you won't need a bulky sleeping bag. You can get by with standard road maps, but as you'll probably want to avoid both the highways and the low-grade, unsealed roads, the government map series is best.

Remember that you need to maintain your body as well as your bike. Exercise is an appetite suppressant, so stock up on carbohydrates at regular intervals, even if you don't feel that hungry. Drink plenty of water: dehydration is no joke and can be life-threatening. Summer in Queensland isn't a great time for cycling. It can get very hot and incredibly humid, and it's no fun at all trying to ride through the torrential downpours that are commonplace during the Wet.

Of course, you don't have to follow the larger roads and visit towns. It's possible to fill your mountain bike's panniers with muesli, head out into the mulga and not see anyone for weeks (or ever again – outback travel is very risky if not properly planned). Water is the main problem, and you can't rely on it being available where there aren't settlements, whatever your map may say.

Always check with locals if you're heading into remote areas, and notify the police if you're about to do something particularly adventurous. That said, you can't rely too much on local knowledge of road conditions – most people have no idea about what a heavily loaded touring bike is like to ride. What they think of as a great road may be pedal-deep in sand or bull dust, and cyclists have happily ridden along roads that were officially flooded out.

Bicycle Queensland (☎ 07-3844 1144; www.bq.org .au) is worth contacting for more information on cycling in Queensland. Additionally, the Queensland Department of Transport has an informative website, including road rules, maps and other resources. Click onto www.transport.qld.gov.au/cycling.

Some of the better bike shops can also be good sources of information on routes, suggested rides, tours and cycling events. For more information on seeing Australia from two wheels, check out Lonely Planet's *Cycling Australia*.

See p47 for more information about cycling in Queensland.

Hire

It is possible to hire touring bikes and equipment from a few of the commercial touring organisations. You can also rent mountain bikes from bike shops in many cities, although these are usually for short-term hire (around $20 a day).

Purchase

If you want to buy a good steel-framed mountain bike that will be able to endure touring, you'll need to spend from $500 up to $1000. You'll also need to add equipment, including panniers, and a bike helmet, which can increase your expenditure to around $1500.

Secondhand bikes are worth checking out in the cities, as are the post-Christmas sales and midyear stocktakes, when newish cycles can be heavily discounted.

Your best bet for reselling your bike is the **Trading Post** (☎ 1300 138 016; www.tradingpost .com.au), which is distributed in newspaper form in urban centres around Australia, and which also has a busy online trading site.

BUS

Queensland's bus network is a relatively cheap and reliable way to get around, though it requires planning if you intend to diverge too far from the coast. Most buses are equipped with air-con, toilets and videos, and all are smoke-free zones. The smallest towns eschew formal bus terminals for a single drop-off/pick-up point, usually outside a post office, a newsagent or a shop.

Greyhound Australia (☎ 13 14 99; www.greyhound .com.au) has the most extensive network in the state, servicing the coast from Coolangatta to Cairns, as well as heading inland to Toowoomba. The company also links up with interstate services to the Northern Territory and New South Wales.

There are also numerous smaller bus companies with more specialised local services, including **Premier Motor Service** (☎ 13 34 10; www .premierms.com.au). Premier is the main competitor to Greyhound on the Brisbane-to-Cairns route along the coast, but it has fewer services per day and costs a few dollars less on most routes. Other operators:

Brisbane Bus Lines (☎ 07-3355 3633; www.brisbane buslines.com.au) Services the Darling Downs area from Brisbane.

Coachtrans (☎ 07-3238 4700; www.coachtrans .com.au) Runs between Brisbane and Surfers Paradise or Coolangatta/Tweed Heads on the Gold Coast.

Con-X-ion (☎ 1300 308 718; www.con-x-ion.com) Runs between Mackay and Airlie Beach.

Coral Reef Coaches (☎ 07-4098 2600; www.coralreef coaches.com.au) Runs from Cairns to popular destinations on the way north to Cape Tribulation.

Crisps Coaches (☎ 07-3236 5266; www.crisps.com.au) Has extensive services throughout the Darling Downs area, with services from Brisbane to Warwick, Toowoomba, Goondiwindi, Stanthorpe and south to Tenterfield in New South Wales.

Emerald Coaches (☎ 1800 428 737; www.emerald coaches.com.au) Runs from Rockhampton to Emerald and Longreach, and between Emerald and Mackay.

Kynoch Coaches (☎ 07-4639 1639; www.kynoch.com .au) Runs from Toowoomba to St George, Cunnamulla and Lightning Ridge.

Sun Palm Express (☎ 07-4032 4999; www.sunpalm transport.com) Operates services between Cairns, Port Douglas, Mossman, Cape Tribulation and Cooktown.

Suncoast Pacific (☎ 07-5449 9966; www.suncoast pacific.com.au) Runs between Brisbane and points along the Sunshine Coast.

See the Getting There & Away and Getting Around sections in the destination chapters for fare information.

Backpacker Buses

If you're backpacking, several party tour buses operate up and down the coast, stopping at sights and pubs along the way and checking into big party hostels each night. These trips are economically priced and will get you from A to B, and can be more fun than conventional buses – the buses are usually smaller and you'll meet other travellers – but you may not see much of Australia except through the bottom of a glass. Travellers have complained of poor service, missed pick-ups and poor accommodation. **Oz Experience** (☎ 1300 300 028; www .ozexperience.com) is the main player.

Bus Passes

Greyhound offers passes that can save you a significant amount of money if bus travel is going to be your main mode of transport over a decent chunk of time (ie four or more weeks). Most involve interstate travel and attract a 10% discount for members of YHA, VIP, Nomads and other approved organisations, as well as card-carrying seniors/ pensioners. The Kilometre Pass gives you go-anywhere flexibility, including the choice to backtrack if you want. Other useful passes for Queensland include the 'Mini Travellers Pass', which gives you 30 days to travel from Sydney to Cairns ($240). The 'Sunseeker Ex Sydney' enables you to do the same thing in 183 days ($385), and the 'Sunseeker Ex Brisbane' allows you to travel between Brisbane and Cairns within 183 days ($325). There are also several passes that include outback destinations en route to the Northern Territory. Check its website for more details.

The Aussie Explorer Pass gives you from one to 12 months to cover a set route. It's the simplest pass, and gives you a specified amount of travel, starting at 2000km ($330) and going up in increments of 1000km to a maximum of 20,000km ($2300). The pass is valid for 12 months and you can travel where and in what direction you like, and stop as many times as you like.

Premier Motor Service also offers bus passes along the eastern coast, between Sydney and Cairns, which are slightly less expensive than Greyhound's.

Costs

Following are the average, nondiscounted, one-way bus fares on some well-travelled routes through Queensland.

Route	Adult/Child/ Concession Fare
Brisbane–Cairns	$201/160/180
Brisbane–Hervey Bay	$50/40/45
Hervey Bay–Rockhampton	$65/55/60
Rockhampton–Mackay	$50/40/45
Mackay–Airlie Beach	$30/21/25
Airlie Beach–Townsville	$50/40/45
Townsville–Cairns	$55/45/50
Cairns–Mt Isa	$175/140/160

Reservations

Over summer, school holidays and public holidays, you should book well ahead on the more popular routes, including intercity and coastal services. At other times you should have few problems getting a seat on your preferred service. However if your long-term travel plans rely on catching a particular bus, book at least a day or two ahead just to be safe.

You should make a reservation at least a day in advance if you're using a Greyhound pass.

CAR & MOTORCYCLE

Queensland is a big, sprawling state and among the locals, the car is the accepted means of getting from A to B. More and more travellers are also finding it the best way to see the country. With three or four of you the costs are reasonable and the benefits many, provided, of course, you don't have a major mechanical problem.

In fact, if you want to get off the beaten track – and in parts of Queensland the track is *very* beaten – then having your own transport is the only way to go, as many of the destinations covered in this book aren't accessible by public transport.

Motorcycles are another popular way of getting around. Between April and Novem-

ber the climate is just about ideal for biking around Queensland and you can bush camp just about anywhere. Bringing your own motorcycle into Australia will entail an expensive shipping exercise, valid registration in the country of origin and a *Carnet De Passages en Douanes*. This is an internationally recognised customs document that allows the holder to import their vehicle without paying customs duty or taxes. To get one, apply to a motoring organisation/ association in your home country. You'll also need a rider's licence and a helmet. The long, open roads are really made for large-capacity machines above 750cc, which Australians prefer once they outgrow their 250cc learner restrictions.

Queensland Transport (☎ 13 23 80; www.trans port.qld.gov.au) is the Queensland government body in charge of roads. It provides a wealth of information on road rules and conditions. It has downloadable brochures summarising Australian road rules for foreigners.

The Queensland government also publishes the extremely useful, free *Guide to Queensland Roads* brochure, which includes

ROAD DISTANCES (km)

	Airlie Beach	Brisbane	Bundaberg	Cairns	Cape York	Hervey Bay	Mackay	Mission Beach	Mt Isa	Noosa Heads	Rockhampton	Surfers Paradise	Townsville
Airlie Beach	---												
Brisbane	1128	---											
Bundaberg	810	347	---										
Cairns	637	1710	1392	---									
Cape York	1677	2750	2432	1040	---								
Hervey Bay	889	276	114	1471	2511	---							
Mackay	150	978	660	732	1772	739	---						
Mission Beach	517	1599	1281	140	1154	1351	621	---					
Mt Isa	1190	1823	1635	1255	2295	1714	1294	1135	---				
Noosa Heads	1022	140	251	1607	2647	183	872	1484	1847	---			
Rockhampton	498	630	312	1080	2120	391	336	960	1323	524	---		
Surfers Paradise	1198	70	417	1780	2820	346	1048	1669	1893	210	700	---	
Townsville	286	1368	1050	351	1391	1120	390	231	904	1253	729	1438	---

road maps, distance charts and other helpful information.

Driving Licence

You can use your own foreign driving licence in Australia, as long as it is in English (if it's not, a translation must be carried). As an International Licence cannot be used alone and must be supported by your home licence, there seems little point in getting one.

Hire

Competition between car-hire firms can be pretty fierce, so rates are flexible and special deals pop up all the time. However you travel on the long stretches, it can be very useful to have a car for local travel.

You must be at least 21 years old to hire from most firms because car-hire companies cannot obtain insurance for people younger than this. If you are 20 years or under, however, and you want to rent a car, certain companies will oblige, but you will need to obtain an original Insurance Certificate of Currency from an insurance company, which will indemnify the car-rental company in the event of an accident. Regardless of your age, you will also require a credit card in order to leave a bond for the car. You may be able to get around this with some rental agencies by leaving a wad of cash with them, but you're looking at a security deposit of several hundred dollars and upwards.

A small car costs between $30 and $40 per day to hire, depending on the length of your rental. A sedan that will seat a family of four comfortably generally costs between $40 and $50 per day. Rates become cheaper if you take a car for more than a week.

Major companies have offices throughout Queensland:

Avis (☎ 13 63 33; www.avis.com)
Budget (☎ 13 27 27; www.budget.com.au)
Europcar (☎ 13 13 90; www.deltaeuropcar.com.au)
Hertz (☎ 13 30 39; www.hertz.com.au)
Thrifty (☎ 1300 367 227; www.thrifty.com.au)

There are plenty of smaller operators that often have cheaper rates – typically $30 per day, based on several days' hire – but they rarely offer one-way trips and may not come down as low as the big players on long-term rentals. Two smaller operators:
Abel Rent A Car (☎ 1800 131 429, 07-3236 1225; www.abel.com.au) Based in Brisbane.

Integra Network Car & Truck Rentals (☎ 1800 067 414, 07-3620 3200; www.abcintegra.com.au) Based in Brisbane, Cairns and Airlie Beach.

See below for important information regarding insurance.

4WD VEHICLES

Having a 4WD enables you to get right off the beaten track and out to some of the natural wonders in the wilderness and the outback that most travellers don't see.

Renting a 4WD vehicle is within the scope of a reasonable budget if a few people share the cost. Something small like a Suzuki costs around $120 per day; for a Toyota Land Cruiser you're looking at around $170, which should include insurance and some free kilometres (typically 100km per day). Check the insurance conditions, especially the excesses, as they can be onerous – in Queensland $4000 is typical, although this can often be reduced to around $1000 on payment of an additional daily charge (around $25). Even for 4WDs most insurance does not cover damage caused when travelling 'off-road'.

Hertz and Avis have 4WD rentals, with one-way rentals possible between the eastern states and the Northern Territory. Budget also rents 4WDs from Darwin and Alice Springs.

CAMPERVANS

Campervan hire is extremely popular with backpackers and several companies oblige. Most have branches in Cairns, Brisbane and other major cities around Australia, and offer one-way hire between certain destinations for a surcharge of around $200. Reliable companies:
Backpacker Campervan Rentals (☎ 1800 670 232; www.backpackercampervans.com)
Britz Australia (☎ 1800 331 454; www.britz.com)
Travellers Auto Barn (☎ 1800 674 374, 02-9360 1500; www.travellers-autobarn.com) One way on coast only.
Wicked Campervans (☎ 1800 246 869; www.wickedcampers.com.au)

Insurance

In Queensland, third-party personal injury insurance is always included in the cost of vehicle registration. This ensures that every registered vehicle carries at least the minimum insurance. You'd be wise to extend that minimum to include third-party property insurance as well – minor collisions with other vehicles can be amazingly expensive.

When it comes to hire cars, know exactly what your liability is in the event of an accident. Rather than risk paying out thousands of dollars if you do have an accident, you can take out your own comprehensive insurance on the car, or (the usual option) pay an additional daily amount to the rental company for an 'insurance excess reduction' policy. This brings the amount of excess you must pay in the event of an accident down from between $2000 and $5000 to a few hundred dollars.

Be aware that if you're travelling on dirt roads you will not be covered by insurance even if you have a 4WD – in other words, if you have an accident you'll be liable for all the costs involved. Also, most companies' insurance won't cover the cost of damage to glass (including the windscreen) or tyres. Always read the small print.

Purchase

Australian cars are not cheap (a result of the small population) but secondhand prices can be quite acceptable, particularly if split between several travellers. If you're buying a secondhand vehicle, reliability is all important. Breakdowns way out in the outback can be inconvenient, expensive and downright dangerous – the nearest mechanic could be a hell of a long way down the road.

What is rather more certain is that the further you get from civilisation, the better it is to be in a locally manufactured vehicle, such as a Holden Commodore or Ford Fal-

con, or one of the mainstream VW, Toyota, Mitsubishi or Nissan campervans. Life gets much simpler if you can get spare parts anywhere from Cairns to Cunnamulla.

When buying or selling a car in Queensland, the vehicle needs to be re-registered locally (ie with Queensland Transport) at the time of sale, for which the buyer and seller must complete a Vehicle Registration Transfer Application form, available from Queensland Transport or the RACQ (see the boxed text below). The seller will usually add the cost of any outstanding registration to the overall price of the vehicle. Before the vehicle can be offered for sale, the seller must also obtain a Safety Certificate (replacing the old Roadworthy Certificate) from a Queensland Transport–approved vehicle inspection station. Stamp duty has to be paid when you buy a car and, as this is based on the purchase price ($2 per $100), it's not unknown for buyer and seller to agree privately to understate the price. It's much easier to sell a car in the state in which it's registered, otherwise the buyer will eventually have to re-register it in the new state. See opposite for information on vehicle insurance.

Shopping around for a used car involves the same rules as anywhere in the Western world. Used-car dealers in Australia are of the same mercenary breed they are everywhere else. You'll probably get a car cheaper by buying through the newspaper classifieds rather than through a dealer. Among other things, dealers are not required to give you any warranty when you buy a car in Queensland, regardless of cost.

RACQ

It's well worth joining the **Royal Automobile Club of Queensland** (RACQ; ☎ 13 19 05; www.racq.com .au); it offers emergency breakdown cover for $95 per year, which will get you prompt roadside assistance and organise a tow to a reputable garage if the problem can't be fixed on the spot. Membership of the RACQ gives reciprocal cover with the automobile associations in other states, and with similar organisations overseas, for example the AAA in the USA or the RAC or AA in the UK. Bring proof of membership with you.

The RACQ also produces a particularly useful set of regional maps of Queensland, which are free to members. Its offices sell a wide range of travel and driving products, including good maps and travel guidebooks; book tours and accommodation; and provide advice on weather and road conditions. It can arrange additional insurance on top of your compulsory third-party personal liability cover, and give general guidelines about buying a car. Most importantly, for a fee (around $115) it will check over a used car and report on its condition before you agree to purchase it.

There are offices all around the state and almost every town has a garage affiliated with the RACQ – see the information sections of the individual destinations for details.

Campervans are a great way to get around Queensland. They'll cut down the cost of accommodation and let you see what you want to see *when* you want to see it. **Travellers Autobarn** (☎ 1800 674 374; www.travellers-autobarn .com.au) sells campervans and has offices in Brisbane and Cairns.

BUY-BACK DEALS

One way of getting around the hassles of buying and selling a vehicle privately is to enter into a buy-back arrangement with a car or motorcycle dealer. However, many dealers will find ways of knocking down the price when you return the vehicle – even if a price has been agreed in writing – often by pointing out spurious repairs that allegedly will be required to gain the dreaded Safety Certificate. The cars on offer have often been driven around Australia a number of times, often with haphazard or minimal servicing, and are generally pretty tired. The main advantage of these schemes is that you don't have to worry about being able to sell the vehicle quickly at the end of your trip.

Road Conditions

Australia doesn't have the traffic volume to justify multilane highways, so most of the country relies on single-lane roads, which can be pretty frustrating if you're stuck behind a slow-moving caravan. Passing areas are usually only found on uphill sections or steep descents, so you may have to wait a long time for an opportunity to pass.

There are a few sections of divided road, most notably on the Surfers Paradise–Brisbane road. Main roads are well surfaced (though a long way from the billiard-table surfaces the Poms are used to driving on) and have regular resting places and petrol stations.

You don't have to get very far off the beaten track to find yourself on dirt roads, though most are quite well maintained. A few useful spare parts are worth carrying – a broken fan belt can be a damn nuisance if the next service station is 200km away. Also look out for the hybrid dirt road: a single, bidirectional strip of tarmac with dirt verges; it's okay to drive down the central strip but be ready to pull into the verges to pass oncoming traffic.

Between cities, signposting on the main highways is generally OK, but once you hit the back roads you'll need a good map – see p446 for suggestions.

Cows, sheep and kangaroos are common hazards on country roads, and a collision is likely to kill the animal and seriously damage your vehicle.

Flooding can occur with little warning, especially in outback areas and the tropical north. Roads can be cut off for days during floods, and floodwaters sometimes wash away whole sections of road.

Road Hazards

The roadkill that you unfortunately see a lot of in the outback is mostly the result of cars and trucks hitting animals during the night. Many Australians avoid travelling altogether once the sun drops because of the risks posed by animals on the roads.

Kangaroos are common hazards on country roads, as are cows and sheep in the unfenced outback – hitting an animal of this size can make a real mess of your car and result in human casualties, depending on the speed at which you're travelling. Kangaroos are most active around dawn and dusk. They often travel in groups, so if you see one hopping across the road in front of you, slow right down, as its friends may be just behind it.

If you're travelling at night and an animal appears in front of you, hit the brakes, dip your lights (so you don't dazzle and confuse it) and only swerve if it's safe to do so – numerous travellers have been killed in accidents caused by swerving to miss animals.

A not-so-obvious hazard is driver fatigue. Driving long distances (particularly in hot weather) can be so tiring that you might fall asleep at the wheel – it's not uncommon and the consequences can be unthinkable. So on a long haul, stop and rest every two hours or so – do some exercise, change drivers or have a coffee.

Motorcyclists need to beware of dehydration in the dry, hot air. Force yourself to drink plenty of water, even if you don't feel thirsty, and *never* ride at night: a road train can hit a kangaroo without stopping, but a motorcycle has no chance. Make sure you carry water – at least 2L on major roads in central Australia, more off the beaten track. And finally, if something does go hopelessly wrong in the back of beyond, park your bike where it's clearly visible and observe the cardinal rule – *don't leave your vehicle.*

Road Rules

Australians drive on the left-hand side of the road just like in the UK, Japan and most countries in South and East Asia and the Pacific.

There are a few variations to the rules of the road as applied elsewhere. The main one is the 'give way to the right' rule. This means that if you approach an unmarked intersection, traffic on your right has right of way. Most places do have marked intersections; Mt Isa doesn't!

The speed limit in towns and built-up areas is 50km/h or 60km/h, sometimes rising to 80km/h on the outskirts and dropping to 40km/h in residential areas and around schools. On the highway it's usually 100km/h or 110km/h, depending on the area.

The police have radar speed traps and speed cameras and are fond of using them. When you're far from the cities and traffic is light, you'll see many vehicles moving a lot faster than 100km/h. Oncoming drivers who flash their lights at you may be giving you a friendly indication of a speed trap ahead (it's illegal to do so, by the way).

Wearing seat belts is compulsory, and small children must be restrained in an approved safety seat. Drink-driving is a real problem, especially in country areas. Serious attempts to reduce the resulting road toll are ongoing and random breath-tests are not uncommon in built-up areas. If you're caught with a blood-alcohol level of more than 0.05%, be prepared for a hefty fine and the loss of your licence.

Night driving is a bad idea anywhere in the state. Drink-driving is common in the country, and at night the roads become the undisputed territory of tired road-train drivers and kangaroos – see opposite.

Outback Travel

If you really want to see outback Queensland, there are lots of roads where the official recommendation is that you report to the police before you leave one end, and again when you arrive at the other. That way if you fail to turn up at your destination, the police can send out search parties.

Many of these roads can be attempted confidently in a conventional car, but you do need to be carefully prepared and to carry important spare parts. Backtracking 500km to pick up a replacement for some minor malfunctioning component or, much worse, to arrange a tow, is unlikely to be easy or cheap.

When travelling to really remote areas it's advisable to travel with a high-frequency outpost radio transmitter that is equipped to pick up the Royal Flying Doctor Service bases in the area.

You will, of course, need to carry a fair amount of water in case of disaster (around 20L a person is sensible) stored in more than one container. Food is less important – the space might be better allocated to an extra spare tyre or spare fuel.

The RACQ can advise on preparation and supply maps and track notes. See p10 for recommended literature that covers outback travel.

Most tracks have an ideal time of year – in Queensland's southwest, it's not wise to attempt the tough tracks during the heat of summer (November to March), when the dust can be severe, the chances of mechanical trouble much greater and water scarce. Similarly, in the north travelling in the wet season may be impossible because of flooding and mud. You should always seek advice on road conditions when you're travelling into unfamiliar territory. The local police will be able to advise you whether roads are open and whether your vehicle is suitable for a particular track.

The RACQ has a 24-hour telephone service with a prerecorded report on road conditions throughout the state – dial ☎ 1300 130 595. For more specific local information, you can call into the nearest RACQ office; these are listed in the information sections throughout this book.

If you do run into trouble in the back of beyond, *stay with your car*. It's easier to spot a car than a human being from the air and plenty of travellers have wandered off into the wilderness and died of thirst long after their abandoned car was found!

LOCAL TRANSPORT
Bus & Train

Brisbane has a comprehensive public transport system with buses, trains and river ferries. The **Trans-Info Service** (☎ 13 12 30; www .transinfo.qld.gov.au; ⏱ 6am-10pm) provides schedule information for Brisbane, the Sunshine and Gold Coasts and for parts of the Darling Downs.

Larger cities such as Surfers Paradise, Toowoomba, Mt Isa, Bundaberg, Rockhampton, Mackay, Townsville and Cairns all have local bus services. There are also local services throughout the Gold and Sunshine Coasts.

At the major tourist centres, most of the backpackers hostels and some resorts and hotels have courtesy coaches that will pick you up from train or bus stations or the airport. Most tour operators include in their prices courtesy coach transport to/from your accommodation. Elsewhere, all of the larger towns and cities have at least one taxi service.

Taxi

Brisbane has plenty of taxis, and it's not hard to hail a cab in Cairns, but outside of these two cities their numbers are far fewer. That doesn't mean they aren't there – even small towns often have at least one taxi. An almost nationwide contact number is ☎ 13 10 08; alternatively you can find numbers for taxis in a local phone book or at the tourist office. Taxi fares vary throughout the state, but shouldn't differ much from those in Brisbane.

TRAIN

Queensland has a good rail network that services the coast between Brisbane and Cairns, with several routes heading inland to Mt Isa, Longreach and Charleville. There are seven services in total, including the Kuranda Scenic Railway, which is primarily a tourist route in northern Queensland. All services are operated by Travel Train, a wing of **Queensland Rail** (QR; ☎ 13 22 32, 1300 13 17 22; www.qr.com.au).

New South Wales' **CountryLink** (☎ 13 22 32; www.countrylink.nsw.gov.au) has a daily XPT (express passenger train) service between Brisbane and Sydney. The northbound service runs overnight, and the southbound service runs during the day (economy seat/1st-class seat/sleeper $115/165/245, 15 hours).

Classes & Costs

Travelling by rail within Queensland is generally slower and more expensive than bus travel, although some of the economy fares are comparable to bus fares. The trains are almost all air-con and you can get sleeping berths on most trains for around $50 extra a night in economy, and $160 to $170 in

1st class. The *Sunlander*, which runs from Brisbane to Cairns, also has the exclusive 'Queenslander Class', which includes comfortable berths, meals in the swanky restaurant car and historical commentary along the way.

You can break your journey on the *Tilt Train* service between Brisbane and Cairns by utilising a stopover fare, whereby you pay slightly extra for up to four stops within a period of 28 days.

Half-price concession fares are available to kids under 16 years of age and students with an International Student Identity Card (ISIC). There are also discounts for seniors and pensioners.

Reservations

There are Queensland Rail Travel Centres throughout the state – these are basically booking offices that can advise you on all rail travel, sell you tickets and put together rail holiday packages that include transport and accommodation:

Brisbane Central Station (☎ 07-3235 1323; Ground fl, Central Station, 305 Edward St); Roma St Transit Centre (☎ 07-3235 1331; Roma St)
Cairns (☎ 1800 620 324, 07-4036 9249; Cairns train station, Bunda St)
Rockhampton (☎ 07-4932 0453; Rockhampton train station, Murray St)
Townsville (☎ 07-4772 8358; Townsville train station, Flinders St)

You can also purchase train tickets through travel agencies. Telephone reservations can be made through one of the Queensland Rail Travel Centres or through Queensland Rail's centralised booking service from anywhere in Australia. For more information visit the QR website.

Train Services
GULFLANDER
The *Gulflander* is a strange, snub-nosed little train that travels once a week between the remote Gulf towns of Normanton and Croydon – it's a unique and memorable journey. See p410 for details.

INLANDER
The *Inlander* does what its name suggests, covering the route from Townsville to Mt Isa twice weekly, leaving Townsville on Sunday and Wednesday afternoons and

Mt Isa on Monday and Friday afternoons (economy seat/economy sleeper/1st-class sleeper $110/165/255, 20 hours).

KURANDA SCENIC RAILWAY

One of the most popular tourist trips out of Cairns is the Kuranda Scenic Railway – a spectacular 1½-hour trip on a historic steam train through the rainforests west of Cairns. See p355 for details.

SPIRIT OF THE OUTBACK

The *Spirit of the Outback* travels the 1326km between Brisbane and Longreach (economy seat/economy sleeper/1st-class sleeper $165/220/350, 24 hours) via Rockhampton ($95/150/230, 10½ hours) twice a week, leaving Brisbane on Tuesday and Saturday evenings and returning from Longreach on Monday and Thursday mornings. A connecting bus service operates between Longreach and Winton.

SUNLANDER

The *Sunlander* travels between Brisbane and Cairns four times a week, leaving Brisbane on Tuesday, Thursday, Saturday and Sunday mornings and leaving Cairns on Monday, Tuesday, Thursday and Saturday mornings (economy seat/economy sleeper/1st-class sleeper/Queenslander-class $190/240/380/690, 30 hours).

TILT TRAIN

The *Tilt Train*, a high-speed economy and business train, makes the trip from Brisbane to Rockhampton (economy/business seat $95/140) in just over seven hours, leaving Brisbane at 11am from Sunday to Friday. There is also an evening train at 5pm on Friday and Sunday (from Monday to Thursday the 5pm train only runs as far as Bundaberg). In economy/business the one-way fare is $60/90 to Bundaberg. Trains return from Rockhampton at 7.25am daily, and additional services leave from Bundaberg at 6.15am Monday to Friday.

The *Tilt Train* also operates a service between Brisbane and Cairns (business seat $280, 25 hours) leaving Brisbane at 6.25pm on Monday, Wednesday and Friday, and Cairns at 8.15am on Sunday, Wednesday and Friday. Economy seats are only available from Brisbane to Rockhampton ($95, eight hours).

WESTLANDER

The *Westlander* heads inland from Brisbane to Charleville every Tuesday and Saturday evening, returning from Charleville to Brisbane on Wednesday and Friday evenings (economy seat/economy sleeper/1st-class sleeper $90/145/225, 16 hours). Once in Charleville there are connecting bus services to Cunnamulla and Quilpie.

Health
Dr David Millar

Australia is a remarkably healthy country in which to travel, considering that such a large portion of it lies in the tropics. Tropical diseases such as malaria and yellow fever are unknown, diseases of insanitation, such as cholera and typhoid, are unheard of, and, thanks to Australia's isolation and quarantine standards, even some animal diseases such as rabies and foot-and-mouth disease have yet to be recorded.

Few travellers to Queensland should experience anything worse than an upset stomach or a bad hangover, and if you do fall ill, the standard of hospitals and health care is high.

BEFORE YOU GO

Since most vaccines don't produce immunity until at least two weeks after they're given, you should visit a physician four to eight weeks before your departure. Ask your doctor for an International Certificate of Vaccination (otherwise known as the yellow booklet), which will list all the vaccinations you've received. This certificate is mandatory for countries that require proof of yellow-fever vaccination upon entry (and is sometimes required in Australia, see right), but it's a good idea to carry it wherever you travel.

Bring medications in their original, clearly labelled containers. A signed and dated letter from your physician describing your medical conditions and medications, including generic names, is also a good idea. If carrying syringes or needles, be sure to have a physician's letter documenting their medical necessity.

INSURANCE

Health insurance is essential for all travellers. While health care in Queensland is of a high standard and not overly expensive by international standards, considerable costs can build up if you require medical care, and repatriation is extremely expensive. If your health insurance doesn't cover you for medical expenses abroad, consider purchasing some extra insurance; check www.lonelyplanet.com for more information. Find out in advance if your insurance plan will make payments directly to providers or reimburse you later for overseas health expenditures. See opposite for details of health care in Queensland.

RECOMMENDED VACCINATIONS

Proof of yellow-fever vaccination is required only from travellers entering Australia within six days of having stayed overnight or longer in a yellow fever–infected country. For a full list of these countries, visit the website of the **World Health Organization** (WHO; www.who.int/wer/) or that of the **Centers for Disease Control and Prevention** (www.cdc.gov/travel/blusheet.htm).

If you're really worried about your health when travelling, there are a few vaccinations you could consider organising for your trip to Australia. The WHO recommends that all travellers should be covered for diphtheria, tetanus, measles, mumps, rubella, chickenpox and polio, as well as hepatitis B, regardless of their destination. Planning a trip is a great time to ensure that all of your routine vaccination cover is complete and up to date. The consequences of these diseases can be severe and while Australia has high levels of childhood vaccination coverage, outbreaks of these diseases do occur.

MEDICAL CHECKLIST

For those who are *really* paranoid about health while travelling...

- antibiotics
- antidiarrhoeal drugs (eg loperamide)
- acetaminophen/paracetamol or aspirin
- anti-inflammatory drugs (eg ibuprofen)
- antihistamines (for hay fever and allergic reactions)
- antibacterial ointment to apply to cuts and abrasions
- steroid cream or cortisone (for poison ivy and other allergic rashes)
- bandages, gauze, gauze rolls
- adhesive or paper tape
- scissors, safety pins, tweezers
- thermometer
- pocketknife
- DEET-containing insect repellent for the skin
- permethrin-containing insect spray for clothing, tents and bed nets
- sun block
- oral rehydration salts
- iodine tablets or water filter (for water purification)

INTERNET RESOURCES

There is a wealth of travel health advice on the Internet. For further information, **Lonely Planet** (www.lonelyplanet.com) is a good place to start. The **WHO** (www.who.int/ith/) publishes a superb book called *International Travel & Health*, which is revised annually and is available online at no cost. Another website of general interest is **MD Travel Health** (www.mdtravelhealth.com), which provides complete travel health recommendations for every country and is updated daily.

FURTHER READING

Lonely Planet's *Healthy Travel Australia, New Zealand & the Pacific* is a handy, pocket-sized guide packed with useful

information including pretrip planning, emergency first aid, immunisation and disease information and what to do if you get sick on the road. *Travel with Children*, from Lonely Planet, also includes advice on travel health for younger children.

IN TRANSIT

DEEP VEIN THROMBOSIS (DVT)

Blood clots may form in the legs (deep vein thrombosis) during plane flights, chiefly because of prolonged immobility. The longer the flight, the greater the risk. Though most blood clots are reabsorbed uneventfully, some may break off and travel through the blood vessels to the lungs, where they could cause life-threatening complications.

The chief symptom of deep vein thrombosis is swelling or pain of the foot, ankle or calf, usually – but not always – on just one leg. When a blood clot travels to the lungs, it may cause chest pain and breathing difficulties. Travellers with any of these symptoms should immediately seek medical attention.

To prevent the development of deep vein thrombosis on long flights, walk around the cabin, perform isometric compressions of the leg muscles (ie flex the leg muscles while sitting), drink plenty of fluids and avoid alcohol and tobacco.

JET LAG & MOTION SICKNESS

Jet lag is common when crossing more than five time zones, and results in insomnia, fatigue, malaise or nausea. To avoid jet lag, try drinking plenty of (nonalcoholic) fluids and eating light meals. Upon arrival, get exposure to natural sunlight and readjust your schedule (for meals, sleep etc) as soon as possible. Antihistamines such as dimenhydrinate and meclizine are usually the first choice for treating motion sickness. Their main side-effect is drowsiness. A herbal alternative is ginger, which works like a charm for some people.

IN QUEENSLAND

AVAILABILITY & COST OF HEALTH CARE

Australia has an excellent health care system, with a mixture of privately-run medical clinics and hospitals, and a system of public

HEALTH

hospitals funded by the government. Medicare covers Australian residents for some health-care costs. Visitors from countries with which Australia has a reciprocal health-care agreement (New Zealand, the UK, the Netherlands, Sweden, Finland, Italy, Malta and Ireland) are eligible for benefits to the extent specified under the Medicare programme. If you are from one of these countries, check the details before departure. In general, the agreements provide for any episode of ill-health that requires prompt medical attention. For further details visit www.health .gov.au/pubs/mbs/mbs3/medicare.htm.

There are excellent, specialised public health facilities for women and children in Brisbane. If you have an immediate and serious health problem, phone or visit the casualty department of the nearest public hospital.

Over-the-counter medications are available at chemists (pharmacies) throughout Queensland. These include painkillers, antihistamines for allergies, and skin-care products. You may find that medications readily available over the counter in some countries are only available in Australia by prescription. These include the oral contraceptive pill, some medications for asthma and all antibiotics. If you take medication on a regular basis, bring an adequate supply and ensure you have details of the generic name as brand names may differ between countries.

In remote locations there may be significant delays in emergency services reaching you in the event of serious accident or illness – do not underestimate the vastness between most major outback towns. An increased level of self-reliance and preparation is essential; consider taking a wilderness first-aid course, such as those offered at the **Wilderness Medicine Institute** (www.wmi.net .au); take a comprehensive first-aid kit that's appropriate for the activities planned; and ensure that you have adequate means of communication. Queensland has extensive mobile-phone coverage, but radio communications are important for remote areas. The Royal Flying Doctor Service provides a back-up for remote communities.

INFECTIOUS DISEASES
Meningococcal Disease
Meningitis occurs worldwide and is a risk with prolonged, dormitory-style accommo-

dation. A vaccine exists for some types of this disease, namely meningococcal A, C, Y and W. No vaccine is presently available for the viral type of meningitis.

Dengue Fever
Dengue fever can occur in northern Queensland, particularly during the wet season (November to April). Also known as 'breakbone fever', because of the severe muscular pains that accompany it, this viral disease is spread by a species of mosquito that feeds primarily during the day. Most people recover in a few days, but more severe forms of the disease can occur, particularly in residents who are exposed to another strain of the virus (there are four types) in a subsequent season.

Ross River Fever
The Ross River virus is spread by mosquitoes living in marshy areas and is widespread throughout Australia. In addition to fever, the disease causes headache, joint and muscular pains and a rash, before resolving after five to seven days.

Tick Typhus
Tick typhus cases have been reported throughout Australia, but are predominantly found in Queensland and New South Wales. A week or so after being bitten a dark area forms around the bite, followed by a rash and possible fever, headache and inflamed lymph nodes. The disease is treatable with antibiotics (doxycycline) so see a doctor if you suspect you have been bitten.

Viral Encephalitis
Also known as Murray River encephalitis, this virus is spread by mosquitoes. Although the risk to most travellers is low, it is a potentially serious disease normally accompanied by headache, muscle pains and light insensitivity. Residual neurological damage can occur and no treatment is available.

Sexually Transmitted Diseases (STDs)
STDs occur at rates similar to almost all other Western countries. The most common symptoms are pain while passing urine and a discharge. Infection can be present without symptoms, so seek medical screening after any unprotected sex

with a new partner. Throughout the country, you'll find sexual health clinics in all of the major hospitals. Always use a condom with any new sexual partner. Condoms are readily available in chemists and through vending machines in many public places, including toilets.

Giardiasis

Drinking untreated water from streams and lakes is not recommended due to the widespread presence of giardiasis in the waterways around Australia. Water filters, and boiling or treating water with iodine, are effective in preventing the disease. Symptoms consist of intermittent bad-smelling diarrhoea, abdominal bloating and wind. Effective treatment is available (tinidazole or metronidazole).

ENVIRONMENTAL HAZARDS
Coral Cuts

Coral can be extremely sharp; you can cut yourself by merely brushing against the stuff. Even a small cut can be very painful, and coral cuts are notoriously slow to heal. If a cut is not adequately cleaned, small pieces of coral can become embedded in the wound, resulting in serious infections. Wash any coral cuts thoroughly and douse them with a good antiseptic. The best solution is not to get cut in the first place – avoid touching coral! It causes serious environmental damage anyway.

Heat Sickness

Very hot weather is experienced year-round in some parts of Queensland. When arriving from a temperate or cold climate, remember that it takes two weeks for acclimatisation to occur. Before the body is acclimatised, an excessive amount of salt is lost by perspiring, so increasing the salt in your diet is essential.

Heat exhaustion occurs when fluid intake does not keep up with fluid loss. Symptoms include dizziness, fainting, fatigue, nausea or vomiting. On observation the skin is usually pale, cool and clammy. Treatment consists of rest in a cool, shady place and fluid replacement with water or diluted sports drinks.

Heatstroke is a severe form of heat illness that occurs after fluid depletion or extreme heat challenge from heavy exercise. This is a true medical emergency with heating of the brain leading to disorientation, hallucinations and seizures. Prevention is by maintaining an adequate fluid intake to ensure the continued passage of clear and copious urine, especially during physical exertion.

A number of unprepared travellers die from dehydration each year in outback Australia. This can be prevented by following these simple rules:

- Carry sufficient water for any trip, including extra in case of breakdown. Always let someone, such as the local police, know where you are going and when you expect to arrive.
- Carry communications equipment of some form.
- In nearly all cases it is better to stay with the vehicle rather than walking for help.

Insect-Borne Illness

Various insects can be a source of irritation. Queensland's most significant insect-borne diseases are Ross River fever and viral encephalitis. Outbreaks are most likely to occur in January and February, but the chances of infection are slight. See p470 for tips on avoiding mozzie bites.

Surf Beaches & Drowning

There are some exceptional surf beaches in the state's south. Beaches vary enormously in the slope of the underlying bottom, resulting in varying power of the surf. Check with the local surf life-saving organisation before entering the water, and be aware of your own limitations and expertise.

Sunburn & Skin Cancer

Australia has one of the highest rates of skin cancer in the world. Monitor exposure to direct sunlight closely. Ultraviolet (UV) exposure is greatest between 10am and 4pm, so avoid skin exposure during these times. Wear a wide-brimmed hat, long-sleeved shirt with a collar and always use 30+ sunscreen, applied 30 minutes before exposure, and repeated regularly to minimise sun damage. At the beach or in the outback protect your eyes with good quality sunglasses.

Water-Borne Illness

Tap water is universally safe in Queensland. Increasing numbers of streams, rivers and lakes, however, are being contaminated by bugs that cause diarrhoea, making water purification essential if you take water directly from these sources. The simplest way of purifying water is to boil it thoroughly. Consider purchasing a water filter. It's very important when buying a filter to read the specifications indicating exactly what it removes from the water and what it doesn't. Simple filtering will not remove all dangerous organisms, so if you cannot boil water it should be treated chemically. Chlorine tablets will kill many pathogens, but not some parasites such as giardia and amoebic cysts. Iodine is more effective in purifying water and is available in tablet form. Follow the directions carefully and remember that too much iodine can be harmful.

CUTS, BITES & STINGS

Calamine lotion or Stingose spray will give some relief for minor bites and stings, and ice packs will reduce the pain and swelling. Wash well and treat any cut with an antiseptic. Where possible avoid bandages and Band-Aids, which can keep wounds moist.

Bed Bugs

Bed bugs are, at varying times, a real problem at hostels along the coast of Queensland. Most hostels ban you from using your own sleeping bag in order to minimise their spread, but it only takes one guest to carry them from hostel to hostel. If you find that you've picked some up in your luggage or clothes, stick the lot in a clothes dryer for an hour; the heat will kill them.

Marine Animals

Marine spikes, such as those found on sea urchins, catfish and stingrays, can cause severe local pain. If this occurs, immediately immerse the affected area in hot water (as hot as can be tolerated). Keep topping up with hot water until the pain subsides and medical care can be reached.

Butterfly cod, scorpion fish and stonefish all have a series of poisonous spines down their back. These can inflict a serious wound and cause incredible pain. Blue-ringed octopuses and Barrier Reef cone shells can also be fatal, so don't pick them up. If someone is stung, apply a pressure bandage, monitor breathing carefully and conduct mouth-to-mouth resuscitation if breathing stops.

Marine stings from jellyfish, such as box jellyfish and Irukandji, also occur in Australia's tropical waters. The box jellyfish has an incredibly potent sting and has been known, very rarely, to cause fatalities. Warning signs exist at any affected beaches (so pay attention and you'll be okay) and stinger nets are in place at the more popular beaches. If you're north of Rockhampton between November and April, it's best to check with locals before diving in, unless there's a stinger net. 'Stinger suits' (full-body Lycra swimsuits) prevent stinging, as do wetsuits. If you are stung, first aid consists of washing the skin with vinegar to prevent further discharge of remaining stinging cells, followed by rapid transfer to a hospital; antivenin is widely available. For more information see the boxed text on p226.

Also watch out for stingrays, which can inflict a nasty wound with their barbed tails, and sea snakes, which are potentially deadly, although they are more often curious than aggressive. Basic reef safety rules are:

- Avoid touching all marine life.
- Wear shoes with strong soles while walking near reefs.
- Don't eat fish you don't know about or can't identify.
- Don't swim in murky water; try to swim in bright sunlight.

Mosquitoes

Mozzies can be a problem, especially in the warmer tropical and subtropical areas. Fortunately, malaria is not present in Australia, although its counterpart, dengue fever, is a significant danger in the tropics (see p468). Protection from mosquitoes, sandflies and ticks can be achieved by a combination of the following strategies:

- Wearing loose, long-sleeved clothing.
- Application of 30% DEET on all exposed skin, repeating application every three to four hours (Rid is effective).
- Impregnation of clothing with permethrin (an insecticide that kills insects but is safe for humans).
- Consider investing in a mosquito net, stocked by most camping shops.
- Mosquito coils are another solution, but the smoke they produce is fairly noxious.
- You'll rarely be bitten if you sleep under a ceiling fan set to a high speed.
- The default technique is to share a room with someone who is tastier to mozzies than you are!

Sharks & Crocodiles

Despite extensive media coverage, the risk of shark attack in Australian waters is no greater than in other countries with extensive coastlines. The risk of an attack from sharks on scuba divers in Queensland is extremely low, as sharks tend to favour the southern states (perhaps southerners taste better?). If you're worried, check with local life-saving groups about local risks.

The risk of crocodile attack in tropical Far North Queensland, on the other hand, is real, but it is predictable and entirely avoidable with some common sense. If you're away from popular beaches anywhere north of Mackay, it would be worth discussing the risk with locals (or the police or tourist agencies in the area) before swimming in rivers, waterholes and in the sea near river outlets.

Snakes

Australian snakes have a fearful reputation that is justified in terms of the potency of their venom, but unjustified in terms of the actual risk to travellers and locals. Snakes are usually quite timid in nature and in most instances will move away if disturbed. They are endowed with only small fangs, making it easy to prevent bites to the lower limbs (where 80% of bites occur) by wearing protective clothing (such as gaiters) around the ankles when bushwalking. The bite marks are small, and preventing the spread of toxic venom can be achieved by applying pressure to the wound and immobilizing the area with a splint or sling before seeking medical attention. Application of an elastic bandage (you can improvise with a T-shirt) wrapped firmly – but not tight enough to cut off the circulation – around the entire limb, along with immobilisation, is a life-saving first-aid measure. Don't use a tourniquet, and *don't* (despite what you might have seen on *Tarzan*) try to suck out the poison!

Spiders

Australia has a number of poisonous spiders, although the only one to have caused a single death in the last 50 years (the Sydney funnel-web) isn't found in Queensland. Redback spider bites cause increasing pain at the site followed by profuse sweating. First aid includes application of ice or cold packs to the bite and transfer to hospital. Some paranoia revolves around the bite of the whitetail (brown recluse) spider, which has been blamed (perhaps unfairly) for causing slow-healing ulcers; if you are bitten, clean the wound thoroughly and seek medical assistance.

The spider you are most likely to encounter in Queensland is the huntsman, a large, tarantula-like spider that can administer a painful but harmless bite. Also common in the Daintree area is the harmless golden orb spider, with its distinctive plum-coloured abdomen.

Ticks & Leeches

The common bush tick (found in the forest and scrub country all along the eastern coast of Australia) can be dangerous if left lodged in the skin because the toxin the tick excretes can cause partial paralysis and, in theory, even death. Check your body for lumps every night if you're walking in tick-infested areas. The tick should be removed by dousing it with methylated spirits or kerosene and levering it out, but make sure you remove it intact. Remember to check children and dogs for ticks after a walk in the bush.

Leeches are common, and while they will suck your blood they are not dangerous and are easily removed by the application of salt or heat. You'll usually find yourself carrying a few 'passengers' at the end of any walk in the Daintree.

Glossary

Australian English

Following are some of the terms and phrases commonly uttered by those strange folk who speak Australian (that's 'Strine', mate), as well as some words derived from Aboriginal languages. See also p74 for food and drink–related terminology.

4WD – four-wheel drive vehicle

Akubra – a brand of hat favoured by farmers, politicians and Channel Nine presenters on rural assignments
arvo – afternoon
Aussie Rules – Australian Football League (AFL), mostly played by *Mexicans*

back o' Bourke – back of beyond, middle of nowhere
banana bender – resident of Queensland
bastard – general form of address between mates that can mean many things, from high praise or respect ('He's the bravest bastard I know') to dire insult ('You bastard!')
B&B – bed-and-breakfast accommodation
BBQ – barbecue
beaut, beauty, bewdie – great, fantastic
bevan – *bogan* in Queensland
block, do your – lose your temper
bloke – man
blowies, blow flies – large flies
blow-in – stranger
bludger – lazy person, one who refuses to work
blue – to have an argument or fight (eg 'have a blue')
bogan – young, unsophisticated person
bommie – large underwater pinnacle surrounded by coral
bonzer – great
boomerang – a curved, flat wooden instrument used by Aboriginal people for hunting
Buckley's – no chance at all
bullroarer – secret instrument used by Aborigines that comprises a long piece of wood swung around the head on a string, creating an eerie roar; often used in men's initiation ceremonies
burl – have a try (eg 'give it a burl'); also a ride in a car
BYO – bring your own (usually applies to alcohol at a restaurant or café)

cane toad – a feral pest; also a nickname for a Queenslander
cark it – to die
cask – wine box (a great Australian invention); also known as 'chateau cardboard'

chocka/chockers – completely full, from 'chock-a-block'
chuck a U-ey – do a U-turn, turn a car around within a road
clobber – to hit; clothes
cocky – small-scale farmer
corroboree – Aboriginal festival or gathering for ceremonial or spiritual reasons; from the Dharug word 'garaabara' (a style of dancing)
crack a mental/the shits – lose your temper
crickey – exclamation of mild surprise as in 'crikey... these khaki pants are way too tight!'

dag – dirty lump of wool at back end of a sheep; also an affectionate or mildly abusive term for a socially inept person
daks – trousers
dead horse – tomato sauce
dead set – true, dinkum
didgeridoo – cylindrical wooden musical instrument traditionally played by Aboriginal men
digger – originally used as a reference to Australian and New Zealand WWI and WWII soldiers; also used to describe miners; see *mate*
dill – idiot
dinky-di – the real thing
donga – small, transportable building widely used in the *outback*
Dreaming/Dreamtime – complex concept that forms the basis of Aboriginal spirituality, incorporating the creation of the world and the spiritual energies operating around us; 'Dreaming' is often the preferred term as it avoids the association with time
dropbear – imaginary Australian bush creature, similar in faunal fiction status to the 'womby-dog' (which has clockwise and anticlockwise breeds)
dunny – outdoor lavatory

fair dinkum – honest, genuine
flat out – very busy or fast
FNQ – Far North Queensland
footy – probably rugby league but (if you're talking to a *Mexican*) might refer to *Aussie Rules*
freshie – freshwater crocodile (the harmless one, unless provoked); new *tinny* of beer

g'day – good day; traditional Australian greeting
grog – general term for alcoholic drinks
grouse – very good
GST - Goods and Services Tax, a 10% tax added to most goods and services purchased in Australia

hicksville – derogatory term usually employed by urbanites to describe a country town
hoon – idiot, hooligan, yahoo

iffy – dodgy, questionable
indie – independent music bands

jackaroo – male trainee on an *outback station*
jillaroo – female trainee on an *outback station*
jocks – men's underpants

Kanaka – person of Pacific Islands heritage brought to Australia as a labourer in the 19th and early 20th centuries
Kiwi – New Zealander
knackered – broken, tired

larrikin – hooligan, mischievous youth
lay-by – to put a deposit on an article so the shop will hold it for you
lemon – faulty product, a dud
little ripper – extremely good thing
loo – toilet

mate – general term of familiarity, whether you know the person or not
Mexican – anyone from south of the border (usually New South Wales or Victoria)
milk bar – small shop selling milk and other basic provisions
mobile phone – cell phone

never-never – remote country in the *outback*
no worries – no problems, that's OK

ocker – an uncultivated or boorish Australian; a knocker or derider
outback – remote part of inland Australia, *back o' Bourke*

piker – someone who doesn't pull their weight, or chickens out
piss – beer
piss weak – no good, gutless
pissed – drunk
pissed off – annoyed
plonk – cheap wine
pokies – poker machines
Pom – English person

Queenslander – high-set weatherboard house noted for its wide veranda and sometimes ornate lattice-work; also a resident of Queensland

rapt – delighted, enraptured
ratbag – friendly term of abuse

ratshit/RS – lousy
rellie – (family) relative
roo – kangaroo
root – have sexual intercourse
rooted – tired, broken
ropable – very bad-tempered or angry
RSL – Returned & Services League; RSL clubs often offer inexpensive food, gambling and entertainment

saltie – saltwater crocodile (the dangerous one)
schoolies – month-long holiday for school leavers on the Gold Coast
sheila – woman
shonky – unreliable
slab – two dozen stubbies or tinnies
SLSC – Surf Life-Saving Club
station – large farm
stolen generations – Indigenous Australian children forcibly removed from their families during the government's policy of assimilation
stroppy – bad-tempered
Stubbies – popular brand of men's work shorts

take the piss – deliberately telling someone a mistruth, often as social sport
tall poppies – achievers (knockers like to cut them down)
tea – evening meal
thongs – flip-flops; an *ocker's* idea of formal footwear
tinny – can of beer; also a small aluminium boat
togs – swimming costume
trucky – truck driver
tucker – food
two-pot screamer – person unable to hold their alcohol
two-up – traditional gambling game using two coins

ute – short for utility; a pick-up truck

van – caravan

walkabout – lengthy walk away from it all
whinge – complain, moan
whoop-whoop – *outback*, miles from anywhere
wobbly – disturbing, unpredictable behaviour (eg 'throw a wobbly')
woomera – stick used by Aboriginal people for throwing spears

XXXX – a brand of beer; Queensland's unofficial state drink

yobbo – uncouth, aggressive person
yonks – ages, a long time
youse – plural of you, pronounced 'yooze'

Behind the Scenes

THIS BOOK

This is the 4th edition of Lonely Planet's *Queensland* guide. The 1st edition was researched and written as an impressive solo effort by Mark Armstrong, the 2nd edition was written by Hugh Finlay and Andrew Humphries, and the 3rd by Joe Bindloss, Kate Daly, Matthew Lane and Sarah Mathers.

Justine Vaisutis wore the coordinator's trilby this edition; see The Authors (p17) to find out who wrote which chapters.

Thanks to Verity Campbell, whose work was used as a starting point for The Culture chapter, and to foodie supremo Matthew Evans, who kick-started our Food & Drink chapter for this guidebook.

THANKS from the Authors

Justine Vaisutis Special thanks to Alan for his unremitting support and to my sister Aidy for keeping me sane while on the road – a tall order even when I'm off it. A huge thanks to Lindsay, Simone and Miriam for all their excellent work and support, and from the in-house team a big thank you to Errol and Corie.

While researching this guidebook I was lucky enough to encounter plenty of friendly and helpful Queenslanders, particularly in tourist offices throughout the state. Their assistance was invaluable, as were the countless tips, laughs, pointers and entertaining conversations I enjoyed from the squillions of travellers I met along the way.

Lindsay Brown Thanks to all the warm-hearted characters of the outback and the Gulf Savannah

who made up for all those lonely miles. A special thanks to the friendly folks in the information centres and travel agencies, coastal and inland, who were, without exception, generous with their knowledge and assistance. Also a huge thanks to the Prado that only had one hiccup – a flat tyre – in 12,000km, and even then it waited until I was parked outside a pub. Thanks to Justine and Errol for coordinating my wayward ways and, finally, thanks to Jenny, Patrick and Sinead for their patience, support and love.

Simone Egger Thanks to Justine Vaisutis, Errol Hunt, Marg Toohey and Paul Piaia from Lonely Planet, and all those vigilant readers who actually get around to writing in. Warren Egger: there's always a place for you...in the boot; kidding – thanks and love. Leahey: know anyone in Bullamakanka I can call in on? As always, I am ever indebted to Simon King, Ruthie Davis and mum.

Miriam Raphael Thanks to my mum Deborah – the Aussie road-trip queen who never forgets her licence, her glasses or the map, and who can make even the most depressing RSL meal a laugh. Cheers to the helpful folk at the visitors centres, particularly in Toowoomba. Thanks also to Justine, Marg, Corie and Errol at Lonely Planet for all their hard work.

CREDITS

The 4th edition of *Queensland & the Great Barrier Reef* was commissioned and developed in Lonely Planet's Melbourne office.

THE LONELY PLANET STORY

The story begins with a classic travel adventure: Tony and Maureen Wheeler's 1972 journey across Europe and Asia to Australia. There was no useful information about the overland trail then, so Tony and Maureen published the first Lonely Planet guidebook to meet a growing need.

From a kitchen table, Lonely Planet has grown to become the largest independent travel publisher in the world, with offices in Melbourne (Australia), Oakland (USA) and London (UK). Today Lonely Planet guidebooks cover the globe. There is an ever-growing list of books and information in a variety of media. Some things haven't changed. The main aim is still to make it possible for adventurous travellers to get out there – to explore and better understand the world.

At Lonely Planet we believe travellers can make a positive contribution to the countries they visit – if they respect their host communities and spend their money wisely. Every year 5% of company profit is donated to charities around the world.

Commissioning Editor Errol Hunt
Coordinating Editor Charlotte Harrison
Coordinating Cartographer Csanad Csutoros
Coordinating Layout Designer Kaitlin Beckett
Managing Cartographers Anthony Phelan, Corie Waddell
Assisting Editors Justin Flynn, Victoria Harrison, Brooke Lyons
Assisting Cartographers Clare Capell, David Connolly, Hunor Csutoros, Owen Eszeki, Daniel Fennessey, Josh Geoghegan, Valentina Kremenchutskaya, Emma McNicol, Malisa Plesa, Bonnie Wintle
Cover Designer Kristin Guthrie
Project Managers Chris Love, Charles Rawlings-Way, Celia Wood

Thanks to Anna Bolger, Stefanie Di Trocchio, Jennifer Garrett, Robin Goldberg, Martin Heng, Darren 'Dazza' O'Connell, Karen Parker, Virginia Maxwell, Louise McGregor, Jennifer Mundy-Nordin, Fiona Siseman, Marg Toohey, Meg Worby, Lachlan Ross and Chris Lee Ack. Thanks to Peter Beattie for all the free publicity last edition.

THANKS from Lonely Planet

Many thanks to the following travellers who used the last edition and wrote to us with helpful hints, useful advice and interesting anecdotes.

A Joel Abbey, Brett Adamel, Elizabeth Adams, John Adams, Cindy Albracht, GW Albury, John J Alderson, Peter Algate, Noel Allen, Oliver Alves, Christian Amon, Rasmus & Signe Andersen, Fiona Anderson, Michael Anderson, Rick & Sandi Anderson, Wayne Antony, Lesley Applebee, Andy Arkway, Ian Arnold, Uwe Artmann, Jennifer Atkins **B** Geoff Bagnall, Chris Bain, John Baisden, Nikki Baker, Peter Baldacchino, Emma Baldock, Caroline Bales, Paul Bancks, Mike Banning, Uri Bar-Joseph, Robert & Emma Barker, Annette Barlow, Cynthia Barnes, Martin & Vivien Barnett, Silke Baron, Greg Barrie, Ann-Marie Barry, Alicea Bayliss, Lars Behnke, Andrew Beitz, Katie Bell, Sara Bendure, Maria & Tony Benfield, Chelsea Benson, Erik Berge, Thomas Berger, Adva Berkovitch, Iris Bernstein, Tom Berry, Ivan Bevan, Kate Bevins, Seweryn Bialasiewicz, Charmaine Bianchi, Ruud Biemans, Heather Bingham, Dean & Kate Biskupovich, Lene & Jan Bjerregaard Pedersen, Mascha Blaaser, Tamsyn Blackman, Rick Blade, Ann Blask, Rafi Bojmel, Gillian Boll, John & Karen Bolton, Oliver Bolz, Kathy Booth, Jenny Bopp, Luca Borra, Christina Borschel, Norbert Bosman, Therese Bourke, Marlene Bowden, Robert Braam, Audrey & Roy Bradford, Paula Brand, Roderick Brazier, Benjamin Brechter, Nadja Bregulla, Nicole Brenner, Samantha Briggs, Nicky Brine, Andrew Brooker, David C Brooks-Wilson, Patrick Broome, Arnold Brouwer, Laura Brown, Trudie & Steve Brown, Claire Brutails, Douglas Buchanan, Lydia Buchholz, Howard Buck, Kara S Buckley, Regula Buehlmann, Margherita Buoso, Kat Burns, Jeff Burridge, Stacey Butterfield, Dawn Byrne, Liz Byrne **C** Mairead Cadden, Lorraine & Rob Callery, Andrew Cameron, Cindy Campbell, Bill & Norma Canfield, Sarah Cantwell, John Capes, Fiona Carmichael-Jones, Mary Carroll, Paul Carter, Julie Cass, Frank Cetrola, Auore Chatelain, Michelle Chavangthrup, Fen Cheah, Ariel Chen, Ivar Christensen, Lennert Christensen, Mireille Cijs, Michael Clark, Tori Clark, Helen Clegg, Amanda Clifford, Jacqui Coals, Linda Cobham, Elroy Cocheret, Christine Cochet, Louise Cock, Maurice Coffey, Nikki Coleman, Dina Coll, Bjorn Collier, Anna Collings, Michael Collins, Sharon Collins, Suzanne Comelli, Ben Cooksey, Russell Cooper, Sharon Cooper, Sue Cope, A Corben, Mark Courtney, Garry K Cowling, Jessica Cox, Hamish Craig, Denise Cronin, Joseph Cullen, Rachel Curley, Marie Curnow, Sarah Curtis-Fawley, Hannah Czeschinski **D** Kacey Dalzell, Joan Darcy, Nadege Daudry, John Davis, Sarah Jane Davis, Chris & Leonie Dawson, Jodie Day, Scott de Bruyne, Leanne de Long, Wilmar de Munnik, Rick de Vries, Pete de Wolff, Alex Deane, Ari den Boer, Walter Denzel, Isabelle Deven, Angela di Virgilio, Ester Dick, Francis Dillon, Armin Dirks, Robert Dixon, Alastair Dobbin, Ed Dobosz, Eddie Dolan, Lyndsey Donald, Philippe Doppler, Greg Dorahy, Joyce Doran, Kathy Douglas, Chris Doyle, Andy Duckworth, Till Dudda, Amber Dunlop, Debbie Dutton, Judith Dwyer, Andrew Dye **E** Annette Eakes, Sandra Eastern, Michael Eckert, Vanessa Eden Evans, liana Edson, Donna Edwards, Neil 'Ned' Edwards, Dominique Ehrmann, Helene Eichholz, Sonia Einersen, Eric Ekert, Frans Eklund, Maxine Eldret, Jen Eldridge, Michael Elliott, Matt & Eileen Erskine, Zef Even **F** Sally Fankhauser, Sascha Farnell, Christina Fevre, Paul Ffrench, Yusuf Fidan, Aletta Filippidou, Berit Fischer, Hannes Fischer, Nick Fisher, Scott Fitzjohn, Inga Fixson, Catherine Fleming, Pam Foster, Moyr Fowler, K Fraser, Natalie Frazer, Claudia Froeb, Ralf Fröhlich **G** Sonia Gagnon, Renata Galimberti, Jeffrey Ganson, Allison Garrett, Gemma Gawthorn, Rinske Geerlings, Paula Gerber, Diego Ghirardi, Dave Gibbon, Michael Gillespie, Julie Gilmore, Iain Gilmour, Anne Glazier, Brad Gledhill, Florian Goessmann, Lisa Goff, Les Goldsmith, Emma Goldsworthy, Shirley Gorring, Georgina Gower, Bill Grable, Darryl Grant, John Gread, Kate Green, Ronalie Green, Natalie Greenway, Simon Greenway, Alice Greer, Asser Gregersen, Monique Gregory, Simi Grewal, Patrick Griessen, Erin Griffin, John Griffith, Victoria Grimshaw, Frank Grinlinton, Aysun Gundogan, Juergen Gutman, Nathan Gutsell **H** Christiane Haase, Lisa Anna Haeger, Denise Haelzle, Felix Halbach, Tim Haldenby, Beverley Halfhide, Stuart Hall, Emanuel Hallgren, Christine & John Hamilton, Nick Hammink, Meg Hammond, Jo Hancock, Kevin Hanson, Christine Harris, Stacey Harrison, Sabine Haschke, PC Hasselgreen, Marie Hatjoullis, Dirk Hauber, Nine Haubirk, Pamela Hayse, Derek Haywood, Alberta Heagney, Katja Hefter, Heidrun Helgert, Jasmin Hellmund, Fay Helwig, David Henderson, Ann & Axel Henning-Ponnet, Jennifer & Louis Hernandez, Claire Hickey, Marese Hickey, PK & LJ Hill, Suzanne Hill, Eva Himmelberg, Margret Hjalmarson, Phillip Hobbs, Raphael Hofstetter, Wolfgang Holzhauer, Alice Hoogland, Penny Hopkins, Nessa Horewitch, Yaron Horing, Karen Louise Hovmand, Maren Hubbard, Adrienne Hughes, David Humphreys, Heidi & Phil Hunt, Gaston & Nynke Hupkens, Mike Hurrell, Leeroy Hutton **I** Craig Illingworth, Julian Ireland, Stephen Ireland, Ilan Ivory **J** Becks Jackson, Ian Jackson, Anette Faye Jacobsen, Helle Jacobsen, Ingrid Janssen, Paul & Brigitte Janssen, Neil Jenkinson, Berit Jensen, Sabine Johnen, Berit

BEHIND THE SCENES

Johns, Hide Johnson, Jill Johnson, Natalie Johnston, Andrea Jones, KT Jones, Ole Jonsson, Ilma Joukes **K** Ralf Kaecks, Ryan Kane, Zena Kane, Stan Kapuchinski, Annemieke Karel, Judith Karena, Pius Karena, Raymond Kawakami, Kaori Kawamura, Adeline Kee, Daniel Keenan, Brinna Keilty, Meaghan Kelly, Noel MJ Kelly, Peter Kelly, Sinead Kelly, Ben Kent, Dave Kerley, Lance Kerr, Mark Kieferle, Robert Kiely, Kenneth Kierath, Daniel Kiernan, Dave Kilmartin, Carol King, Maria King, Lesley Anne Kinnon, Lee Kitson, Lyndall Klein, Silke Kluge, Ken Klunder, Chad Klyne, Kerry Ann Kneale, Steffi Knedlhans, Christina Knoche, Michael Knoll, Liz Knowles, Deborah Koch, Shauna Kocman, Sandra Koegel, Heike Kool, Peter Kootsookos, Barry Kowal, Yvonne Kower, Hannes Krall, Tatiana Krause, Jan Krauss, Daniel Kusterer **L** Terri Lake, Malcolm Lambert, Karen Lander, Chloe Larcombe, Leonna Larder, Ben E Latham, Jacob Lauwring, Jenna Lawless, Elsa le Fevre, Zoe le Grand, Diederik le Grange, Kitty Lee, Mary Lee, Richard Lee, Susie Leeves, Christian Lehmann, Karin Lenk, Katie Lester, Kate Lewis, Peter Lewis, Pam & David Liell, H Lim, Udi Lineal, Gary Liniker, Bron Littlewood, Susan & Toc Lloyd, Pete Long, Christian Lott, Nina Lovell, CJ & JM Lowrey, Sally Loyall, Alexius Ludeman, Robyn Ludwig, Artur Lueders, Ingrid K Lund, Tim Luxford, Rob Lyon **M** Allison Mackie, Andy Mackintosh, Ian & Olivia MacLean, Emma Magson, Deirdre Maguire, Eva Maisel, Dave Malleson, Laura Manley, Regine Marek, Heather Markel, Emilie Martinet, Dan Massey, Muriel Mathers, AW Matthews, Steven Matthews, Claire May, Bill Maynard, Richard Mayo, Kerry McArthur, Craig McBain, Melissa McDevitt, Grace McDonnell, Gill & Neil McKay, Jason McKeen, Bruce McLachlan, Kat McLean, Saul McLeod, Breid McLoone, Adam McMillan, Deirdre McNally, Rachel Meadows, Diane Meige, Lisa Meingassner, Steve Melhuish, Robbie A Meriales, Helene & Laurent Meric, Julie Meston, Alexandra & Beverly Meyer, Denise Michaud, Juan Mier, Marilyn Miller, Martin Mitchell, Johan Mollmyr, Sarah Moore, Scott Moore, Victoria Moore, Diane Morden, Quentin Morley, Caroline Morris, John Morrow, Maya Bar Moshe, Ofrit Moshe, Barbara Mueller, Beat Mueller, Estibaliz Mugeta, Rebecca Muir, Lynneke Mulholland, Laura Mullane, Peter Munday, Adrian Mundow, Frances Murphy, Lauren Mustill **N** Elad Nachman, Lucy Nairn, Natalia Naomi, Lukas Nardella, Rachel Natoff, Emer Naughton, Lorenz & Petra Nef, Roderick Neilsen, Amy Nell, Barnaby Newman, Grant Newman, Terry Newman, Amy Newton, Kerryn Newton, Paul Nicholson, Joe Nicolost, Henrik Skov Nielsen, Carine Nieman, Catriona Nisbet, Adam Nock, Siobhan Noel, Dave Nonen, Collette Noon, Lindsey Noone, Jari Noponen, Matthew Norbury, JM Norfolk, Olly Norton, Andreas Nyenhuis **O** Tracey Oates, Laura O'Donavan, Chris O'Halloran, Marcel Oosting, Catriona O'Reilly, Mary Osborn, Inka Osterman, Patrick O'Sullivan **P** Joanne Page-Chatton, Benjamin Pagel, Matthew Paget, John Parfitt, Park Kyung-Jin, Mike Parrish, Jo Patel, Neil Pattemore, Stephanie Payne, EA Payton, Lucy Peile, Elisabeth Peischl, Joanne Pellow, Patrick Pender, Stacey Perkins, Karen Petley, Steve & Leslie Petri, Karen Phelan, Hilda Phillip, Anna Pickering, Marjaana Pihlajamäki, Ramon Pils, Alexandra Pitman, Erik Polderdijk, Vivien Pollock, Nina Pool, Elizabeth Pope, Michelle Pratley, John Prytherch, Nigel Pugh, Vanessa Purser **R** Adrian Rampoldi, David Rand, Tammie Rasumssen, Kerry & Peter Rauber,

Helen & Nigel Read, T Reddacliff, Sarah Redman, Linsey Reeves, Steven Reeves, Ali Reid, Philip Reiler, Abe Remmo, Margaret & Peter Richards, Kim Richardson, Christopher Richer, Melanie Riemer, Eva Riquelme, Jenny Roberts, Tony Roberts, Jennifer Robertson, Rick Robins, Paul Robinson, Daniel Robson, Keith Rodger, Paul Rogers, Wladyslaw Romanowicz, Alexandra Römer, Elisabeth Ronning, Louise Rose, Erik Rosness, Gail Ross, John Ross, Sian Rosser, Anne Rota, Josef Rottenaicher, Damian Rowsell, Peter Roy, Howard Rundle, Tom Rundle, James Ruse, Kerry Ruse, Cian Rutzinsky, Gregg Ryan, Hannah Ryan, Susan Ryan **S** Charlotte Sadd, Nancy Sader, Matthew Salisbury, Patricia Sanz-Munoz, Sarah, Evan Sarinas, Luke Saunders, J Saxby, Roel Schellens, Ceceile Schent, Philipp Schleenvoigt, Peter Schlesinger, Ditte Schlüntz, Bernd Schmidt, Ulrike Schmidt, Brigitte Schnell, Saskia Schot, Anna Marijke Schriemer, Rolf Schroeder, Karin Schweiger, Kylie Scobie, Evelyn Seale, Andrea Sforazzini, Louise Shepherd, Daniel Sheppard, Ira Sherak, Kristin Sherwood, Joanna Shirley, Barry Short, Kristin Jo Siess, Michael Silber, Martin Silvester, Lorna Simpson, Heather Sinclair, Clare Singleton, Aaron Skogand, Simon Slemint, Tara Smale, Jessica Smith, Margot Smith, Marion Smith, Sean Smith, Thomas Smith, Kuan Sng, Scott Snowball, Ulrika Soderlund, Graeme Sparkes, Andy Sparrow, Diana Spehn, Craig Squire, Martin Staael, Michael Stallard, Mark & Pamela Starnes, Ariane Stevenson, John Stevenson, Des Stewart, Katie Stewart, Tish Stone, Caroline Stout, Robert Strachan, Edwina Strachen, Grant Straw, Heidi Strober, Helene Stromme, John & Finbar Stuart, Phil Stubbs, Kelly Stubson, Aruna Subramanian, Daphne & John

SEND US YOUR FEEDBACK

We love to hear from travellers – your comments keep us on our toes and help make our books better. Our well-travelled team reads every word on what you loved or loathed about this book. Although we cannot reply individually to postal submissions, we always guarantee that your feedback goes straight to the appropriate authors, in time for the next edition. Each person who sends us information is thanked in the next edition – and the most useful submissions are rewarded with a free book.

To send us your updates – and find out about Lonely Planet events, newsletters and travel news – visit our award-winning website: **www.lonelyplanet.com/feedback**.

Note: We may edit, reproduce and incorporate your comments in Lonely Planet products such as guidebooks, websites and digital products, so let us know if you don't want your comments reproduced or your name acknowledged. For a copy of our privacy policy visit www.lonelyplanet.com /privacy.